Fodor's Road Guide USA

Arizona
Colorado
New Mexico

First Edition

Fodor's Travel Publications
New York Toronto London Sydney Auckland
www.fodors.com

Fodor's Road Guide USA: Arizona, Colorado, New Mexico
President: Bonnie Ammer
Publisher: Kris Kliemann
Executive Managing Editor: Denise DeGennaro
Editorial Director: Karen Cure
Director of Marketing Development: Jeanne Kramer
Associate Managing Editor: Linda Schmidt
Senior Editor: Constance Jones
Director of Production and Manufacturing: Chuck Bloodgood
Creative Director: Fabrizio La Rocca

Contributors
Editor: Douglas Stallings
Editorial Production: Tom Holton
Additional Editing: Ensley Eikenburg
Writing: Jim Crutchfield (Colorado and New Mexico) and Kim Westerman (Arizona), with
Christina Paulette Colón, Lori Cumpston, Hannah Fons, Satu Hummasti, Victor Ledezma,
Sidharth Murdeshwar, Sharon Niederman, Eric Peterson, Frances Schamberg, and Marija
Vader.
Research: Helen Kasimis and Alexei Manheimer-Taylor.
Black-and-white Maps: Rebecca Baer, Robert Blake, David Lindroth, Todd Pasini
Production/Manufacturing: Robert B. Shields
Cover: Michael Evans/The Image Finders (background photo), Bart Nagel (photo,
illustration)
Interior Photos: Photodisc (Arizona), Siobhan O'Hare (Colorado), Artville (New Mexico)

First Edition
ISBN 0-679-00493-9
ISSN 1528-1426

Special Sales
Fodor's Travel Publications are available at special discounts for bulk purchases for sales promotions
or premiums. Special editions, including personalized covers, excerpts of existing guides, and corporate
imprints, can be created in large quantities for special needs. For more information, contact your
local bookseller or write to Special Markets, Fodor's Travel Publications, 280 Park Ave., New York,
NY 10017. Inquiries from Canada should be directed to your local Canadian bookseller or sent to
Random House of Canada, Ltd., Marketing Department, 2775 Matheson Boulevard East, Mississauga,
Ontario L4W 4P7. Inquiries from the United Kingdom should be sent to Fodor's Travel Publications,
20 Vauxhall Bridge Road, London SW1V 2SA, England.

PRINTED IN THE UNITED STATES OF AMERICA
10 9 8 7 6 5 4 3 2 1

CONTENTS

Great Road Trips

Of all the things that went wrong with Clark Griswold's vacation, one stands out: The theme park he had driven across the country to visit was closed when he got there. Clark, the suburban bumbler played by Chevy Chase in 1983's hilarious *National Lampoon's Vacation,* is fictional, of course. But his story is poignantly true. Although most Americans get only two precious weeks of vacation a year, many set off on their journeys with surprisingly little guidance. Many travelers find out about their destination from friends and family or wait to get travel information until they arrive in their hotel, where racks of brochures dispense the "facts," along with free city magazines. But it's hard to distinguish the truth from hype in these sources. And it makes no sense to spend priceless vacation time in a hotel room reading about a place when you could be out seeing it up close and personal.

Congratulate yourself on picking up this guide. Studying it—before you leave home—is the best possible first step toward making sure your vacation fulfills your every dream.

Inside you'll find all the tools you need to plan a perfect road trip. In the hundreds of towns we describe, you'll find thousands of places to explore. So you'll always know what's around the next bend. And with the practical information we provide, you can easily call to confirm the details that matter and study up on what you'll want to see and do, before you leave home.

By all means, when you plan your trip, allow yourself time to make a few detours. Because as wonderful as it is to visit sights you've read about, it's the serendipitous experiences that often prove the most memorable: the hole-in-the-wall diner that serves a transcendent tomato soup, the historical society gallery stuffed with dusty local curiosities of days gone by. As you whiz down the highway, use the book to find out more about the towns announced by roadside signs. Consider turning off at the next exit. And always remember: In this great country of ours, there's an adventure around every corner.

HOW TO USE THIS BOOK

Alphabetical organization should make it a snap to navigate through this book. Still, in putting it together, we've made certain decisions and used certain terms you need to know about.

LOCATIONS AND CATEGORIZATIONS

Color map coordinates are given for every town in the guide.

Attractions, restaurants, and lodging places are listed under the nearest town covered in the guide.

Parks and forests are sometimes listed under the main access point.

Exact street addresses are provided whenever possible; when they were not available or applicable, directions and/or cross-streets are indicated.

CITIES

For state capitals and larger cities, attractions are alphabetized by category. Shopping sections focus on good shopping areas where you'll find a concentration of interesting shops. We include malls only if they're unusual in some way and individual stores only when they're community institutions. Restaurants and hotels are grouped by price category then arranged alphabetically.

RESTAURANTS

All are air-conditioned unless otherwise noted, and all permit smoking unless they're identified as "no-smoking."

Dress: Assume that no jackets or ties are required for men unless otherwise noted.

Family-style service: Restaurants characterized this way serve food communally, out of serving dishes as you might at home.

Meals and hours: Assume that restaurants are open for lunch and dinner unless otherwise noted. We always specify days closed and meals not available.

Prices: The price ranges listed are for dinner entrées (or lunch entrées if no dinner is served).

Reservations: They are always a good idea. We don't mention them unless they're essential or are not accepted.

Fodor's Choice: Stars denote restaurants that are Fodor's Choices—our editors' picks of the state's very best in a given price category.

LODGINGS

All are air-conditioned unless otherwise noted, and all permit smoking unless they're identified as "no-smoking."

AP: This designation means that a hostelry operates on the American Plan (AP)—-that is, rates include all meals. AP may be an option or it may be the only meal plan available; be sure to find out.

Baths: You'll find private bathrooms with bathtubs unless noted otherwise.

Business services: If we tell you they're there, you can expect a variety on the premises.

Exercising: We note if there's "exercise equipment" even when there's no designated area; if you want a dedicated facility, look for "gym."

Facilities: We list what's available but don't note charges to use them. When pricing accommodations, always ask what's included.

Hot tub: This term denotes hot tubs, Jacuzzis, and whirlpools.

MAP: Rates at these properties include two meals.

No smoking: Properties with this designation prohibit smoking.

Opening and closing: Assume that hostelries are open year-round unless otherwise noted.

Pets: We note whether or not they're welcome and whether there's a charge.

Pools: Assume they're outdoors with fresh water; indoor pools are noted.

Prices: The price ranges listed are for a high-season double room for two, excluding tax and service charge.

Telephone and TV: Assume that you'll find them unless otherwise noted.

Fodor's Choice: Stars denote hostelries that are Fodor's Choices—our editors' picks of the state's very best in a given price category.

NATIONAL PARKS

National parks protect and preserve the treasures of America's heritage, and they're always worth visiting whenever you're in the area. Many are worth a long detour. If you will travel to many national parks, consider purchasing the National Parks Pass ($50), which gets you and your companions free admission to all parks for one year. (Camping and parking are extra.) A percentage of the proceeds from sales of the pass helps to fund important projects in the parks. Both the Golden Age Passport ($10), for those 62 and older, and the Golden Access Passport (free), for travelers with disabilities, entitle holders to free entry to all national parks, plus 50% off fees for the use of many park facilities and services. You must show proof of age and of U.S. citizenship or permanent residency (such as a U.S. passport, driver's license, or birth certificate) and, if requesting Golden Access, proof of your disability. You must get your Golden Access or Golden Age passport in person; the former is available at all federal recreation areas, the latter at federal recreation areas that charge fees. You may purchase the National Parks Pass by mail or through the Internet. For information, contact the National Park Service (Department of the Interior, 1849 C St. NW, Washington, DC 20240-0001, 202/208—4747, *www.nps.gov*). To buy the National Parks Pass, write to 27540 Ave. Mentry, Valencia, CA 91355, call 888/GO—PARKS, or visit www.national-parks.org.

IMPORTANT TIP

Although all prices, opening times, and other details in this book are based on information supplied to us at press time, changes occur all the time in the travel world, and Fodor's cannot accept responsibility for facts that become outdated or for inadvertent errors or omissions. So **always confirm information when it matters,** especially if you're making a detour to visit a specific place.

Let Us Hear from You

Keeping a travel guide fresh and up-to-date is a big job, and we welcome any and all comments. We'd love to have your thoughts on places we've listed, and we're interested in hearing about your own special finds, even the ones in your own back yard. Our guides are thoroughly updated for each new edition, and we're always adding new information, so your feedback is vital. Contact us via e-mail in care of roadnotes@fodors.com (specifying the name of the book on the subject line) or via snail mail in care of Road Guides at Fodor's, 280 Park Avenue, New York, NY 10017. We look forward to hearing from you. And in the meantime, have a wonderful road trip.

THE EDITORS

Important Numbers and On-Line Info

LODGINGS

Adam's Mark	800/444—2326	www.adamsmark.com
Baymont Inns	800/428—3438	www.baymontinns.com
Best Western	800/528—1234	www.bestwestern.com
	TDD 800/528—2222	
Budget Host	800/283—4678	www.budgethost.com
Clarion	800/252—7466	www.clarioninn.com
Comfort	800/228—5150	www.comfortinn.com
Courtyard by Marriott	800/321—2211	www.courtyard.com
Days Inn	800/325—2525	www.daysinn.com
Doubletree	800/222—8733	www.doubletreehotels.com
Drury Inns	800/325—8300	www.druryinn.com
Econo Lodge	800/555—2666	www.hotelchoice.com
Embassy Suites	800/362—2779	www.embassysuites.com
Exel Inns of America	800/356—8013	www.exelinns.com
Fairfield Inn by Marriott	800/228—2800	www.fairfieldinn.com
Fairmont Hotels	800/527—4727	www.fairmont.com
Forte	800/225—5843	www.forte-hotels.com
Four Seasons	800/332—3442	www.fourseasons.com
Friendship Inns	800/453—4511	www.hotelchoice.com
Hampton Inn	800/426—7866	www.hampton-inn.com
Hilton	800/445—8667	www.hilton.com
	TDD 800/368—1133	
Holiday Inn	800/465—4329	www.holiday-inn.com
	TDD 800/238—5544	
Howard Johnson	800/446—4656	www.hojo.com
	TDD 800/654—8442	
Hyatt & Resorts	800/233—1234	www.hyatt.com
Inns of America	800/826—0778	www.innsofamerica.com
Inter-Continental	800/327—0200	www.interconti.com
La Quinta	800/531—5900	www.laquinta.com
	TDD 800/426—3101	
Loews	800/235—6397	www.loewshotels.com
Marriott	800/228—9290	www.marriott.com
Master Hosts Inns	800/251—1962	www.reservahost.com
Le Meridien	800/225—5843	www.lemeridien.com
Motel 6	800/466—8356	www.motel6.com
Omni	800/843—6664	www.omnihotels.com
Quality Inn	800/228—5151	www.qualityinn.com
Radisson	800/333—3333	www.radisson.com
Ramada	800/228—2828	www.ramada.com
	TDD 800/533—6634	
Red Carpet/Scottish Inns	800/251—1962	www.reservahost.com
Red Lion	800/547—8010	www.redlion.com
Red Roof Inn	800/843—7663	www.redroof.com
Renaissance	800/468—3571	www.renaissancehotels.com
Residence Inn by Marriott	800/331—3131	www.residenceinn.com
Ritz-Carlton	800/241—3333	www.ritzcarlton.com
Rodeway	800/228—2000	www.rodeway.com

Sheraton	800/325—3535	www.sheraton.com
Shilo Inn	800/222—2244	www.shiloinns.com
Signature Inns	800/822—5252	www.signature-inns.com
Sleep Inn	800/221—2222	www.sleepinn.com
Super 8	800/848—8888	www.super8.com
Susse Chalet	800/258—1980	www.sussechalet.com
Travelodge/Viscount	800/255—3050	www.travelodge.com
Vagabond	800/522—1555	www.vagabondinns.com
Westin Hotels & Resorts	800/937—8461	www.westin.com
Wyndham Hotels & Resorts	800/996—3426	www.wyndham.com

AIRLINES

Air Canada	888/247—2262	www.aircanada.ca
Alaska	800/426—0333	www.alaska-air.com
American	800/433—7300	www.aa.com
America West	800/235—9292	www.americawest.com
British Airways	800/247—9297	www.british-airways.com
Canadian	800/426—7000	www.cdnair.ca
Continental Airlines	800/525—0280	www.continental.com
Delta	800/221—1212	www.delta.com
Midway Airlines	800/446—4392	www.midwayair.com
Northwest	800/225—2525	www.nwa.com
SkyWest	800/453—9417	www.delta.com
Southwest	800/435—9792	www.southwest.com
TWA	800/221—2000	www.twa.com
United	800/241—6522	www.ual.com
USAir	800/428—4322	www.usair.com

BUSES AND TRAINS

Amtrak	800/872—7245	www.amtrak.com
Greyhound	800/231—2222	www.greyhound.com
Trailways	800/343—9999	www.trailways.com

CAR RENTALS

Advantage	800/777—5500	www.arac.com
Alamo	800/327—9633	www.goalamo.com
Allstate	800/634—6186	www.bnm.com/as.htm
Avis	800/331—1212	www.avis.com
Budget	800/527—0700	www.budget.com
Dollar	800/800—4000	www.dollar.com
Enterprise	800/325—8007	www.pickenterprise.com
Hertz	800/654—3131	www.hertz.com
National	800/328—4567	www.nationalcar.com
Payless	800/237—2804	www.paylesscarrental.com
Rent-A-Wreck	800/535—1391	www.rent-a-wreck.com
Thrifty	800/367—2277	www.thrifty.com

Note: Area codes are changing all over the United States as this book goes to press. For the latest updates, check www.areacode-info.com.

Fodor's Road Guide USA

Arizona
Colorado
New Mexico

Arizona

Arizona is deceptively diverse. From the air it appears to be desolately stark and earth-toned, but if you travel the state by car, say, from north to south, you'll encounter vast mountain ranges, white-water rapids, Native American tribal lands, and the Sonoran Desert. And, of course, the Grand Canyon—earth's most beautiful scar and one of the Seven Natural Wonders of the World—which covers 277 square mi of the state. Nature has worked on this mile-deep canyon for 2 billion years. In an era of increasing urbanization, more and more travelers make the pilgrimage each year to savor its majestic views, making it by far the state's most popular attraction.

The South Rim of the Grand Canyon is heavily trafficked by tourists, while the North Rim is less visited. If you have an extra few hours, the drive to the North Rim (210 mi from the South Rim) will reward you with unimpeded views of the Painted Desert, Echo Cliffs, and Marble Canyon, sights only about 10% of visitors to Grand Canyon National Park ever see.

Arizona is the southwest pillar of the Four Corners states, which also include Utah, Colorado, and New Mexico. It also shares a border with Mexico, so expect to hear a lot of Spanish spoken wherever you go. You may want to become familiar with names of Mexican foods you might want to sample (*see the box* "A Glossary of Sonoran Mexican Food"). Specialties include *tortas* (Mexican sandwiches filled with various meats) and *menudo* (tripe soup, reputed to cure hangovers).

Six Indian reservations punctuate Arizona's rugged territory. Respectful tourists are welcome to explore the rich and diverse cultures of these self-governed areas. The Hopi, in particular, invite visitors to select ceremonies and ritual dances, and most tribes sell handcrafts, such as silver jewelry, woven baskets, and wool rugs, in all price ranges. The reservations vary in their embrace of modern conveniences. The Tohono O'odham

CAPITAL: PHOENIX	POPULATION: 4,764,025	AREA: 113,909 SQUARE MI
BORDERS: CA, Mexico, NV, NM, UT	TIME ZONE: MOUNTAIN	POSTAL ABBREVIATION: AZ
WEB SITE: WWW.ARIZONAGUIDE.COM		

(who have the second-largest reservation in the United States) run a huge gaming business, while mail is delivered by mule on the Havasupai Reservation.

Phoenix and Tucson are Arizona's principal cities, both desert metropolises. The former is the seat of government, the latter home to the University of Arizona, a major research institution. Both epitomize the state's tri-cultural influence, with Anglos, Native Americans, and Hispanics converging to make for zesty food, cultural events, and politics. Recent decades have seen a boom in their populations, which has been true all over the Southwest.

Arizona has wildly varying climatic regions—from the northern plateaus to the central mountains to the southern deserts, with a vast range of conditions across the state. At almost any time of year, you can find towns in Arizona with high temperatures measuring about 65°F, perfect vacation weather. For example, even when the temperatures are topping 100°F in Phoenix, places such as Flagstaff will be a little chilly at night. The favorable climate has also made Arizona a favorite retirement destination. Famous as a desert state, a great deal of Arizona is also covered with forests, which stretch from north to south.

The cactus wren is the state bird, and you can find it nesting in ancient saguaro cacti, which grow nowhere else on earth than in the Sonoran Basin. Southeastern Arizona is one of the world's most popular bird-watching destinations, with more than 500 species of birds living in or just visiting its desert washes, riparian woodlands, and pine-studded mountains. Spring and summer bring migrant hummingbirds from Mexico, some so small that, in flight, they look like honeybees flitting among wildflowers.

History

Before Arizona became the 48th U.S. state, on Valentine's Day 1912, it was Native American land, then part of New Spain, and later, of Mexico. Its first settlers (as far back as 10,000 BC) were the Paleo-Indians, some of the first inhabitants of North America—hunters and gatherers who stalked big-game beasts such as mammoth, bison, and bear. Slowly, the environment changed and the Archaic people, known for their resourcefulness in the new arid climate, replaced the Paleo-Indians. Agriculture did not appear in the region until 300 BC with the arrival of Mexican peoples like the Hohokam and the Anasazi.

Magnificent adobe cities, crouched beneath shear rock faces, are the remnants of the Anasazi culture, which began building these communal cities around AD 1000. The peak of Anasazi culture lasted two centuries, between 1100 and 1300, when trade with other communities was strong and architectural innovation flourished. The Hohokam, another tribe that settled in the Arizona region at the dawn of agriculture, came to its peak around AD 1000. In contrast to those of the Anasazi, few Hohokam ruins exist today; only one, the four-story Casa Grande, or Big House, just outside Coolidge, stands testament to their architectural prowess. By the 13th century, archaeologists estimate that there may have been as many as 50,000 Hohokam people living in the area that would become Phoenix. Following this peak, the Anasazi and Hohokam, like all

AZ Timeline

10,000 BC	AD 650	900–1100	1100
Paleo-Indians occupy much of the region.	The Sinagua cultivate the land to the northeast of present-day Flagstaff.	Anasazi culture flourishes.	Hohokam Indians build more than 200 mi of canals.

INTRODUCTION
HISTORY
REGIONS
WHEN TO VISIT
STATE'S GREATS
RULES OF THE ROAD
DRIVING TOURS

native groups of the area, suffered an as yet unknown calamity—disease, drought, and war have all been proposed as causes. This enigma is one of the most persistent mysteries of Arizona history.

The first Europeans to arrive—the Spanish in 1540—came seeking fabled riches: the Seven Cities of Cibola. Among the early settlers was Father Eusebio Kino, a Jesuit priest who introduced Christianity to the Tohono O'odham in the early 18th century, founding many missions in southern Arizona. During this period bloody conflicts often erupted between the native peoples and the white invaders.

In 1810 when Mexico seceded from Spain, Arizona flew the Mexican flag. Not until the Texas Revolution and the Mexican War in the years 1836–48 did most of Arizona, along with New Mexico, California, Texas, and Utah, come under United States hegemony. Still, in the mid-19th century Arizonans looked to Mexico for culture and trade. The railway opened the state to the east and west, allowing entrepreneurs like Sam Hughes, Charles Debrille Poston, and Federico Ronstadt to build up the economy and culture of Tucson and neighboring cities. At this same time (1871–86), conflicts with the Apache culminated in what is known as the Apache Wars, punctuated by numerous massacres on both sides. The last of the 23 independent Apache tribes, the one led by Geronimo, held out in the southeastern Arizona mountains until 1886 when it surrendered to General George Crook.

Settlers in the last part of the 19th and first part of the 20th century concentrated their energies into three arenas: cattle ranching, agriculture, and mining. The cattlemen who began raising herds in the 1870s had, by the early 1890s, let the land be overgrazed, leaving it exposed to erosion. This proved to be the end of ranching in Arizona. Mormons, traveling from Utah, were more adept at sustaining themselves in the arid climate and settled agricultural communities along the Colorado River and in the desert south, including what is now Arizona's third-largest city, Mesa. Mining in the state began with a brief gold rush, soon followed by a short-lived silver boom. It wasn't until copper began to be mined that Arizona found its mineralogical niche. Copper mining was primarily financed by deep pockets in the eastern U.S., which led, inevitably, to the out-of-state control of much of Arizona's natural resources, a situation that exists to this day.

The Native Americans who first came to these lands continue to inhabit areas rich with their own history. Navajos, the most populous tribe in the United States, occupy a large reservation which crosses into Utah and New Mexico, encompassing many ancient Anasazi sites. The Apache, related distantly to the Navajos, were some of the fiercest warriors of the Old West, resisting white expansion with numerous raids and guerrilla tactics. The contemporary pottery and katsina dolls of the Hopis, a Pueblo people who inhabit a reservation completely surrounded by the Navajo nation, are justly famous for their refined style and execution.

Since 1950, Arizona has seen more and more business relocate to the state, as well as massive growth in its population, particularly in the Phoenix area. Air-conditioning has made the expansion possible. Once science found a way to get around the searing heat of Arizona's long summers, both businesses and retirees flocked here, primar-

1300	1540	1680	1696	1700
The Anasazi abandon cliff dwellings in Canyon de Chelly and Tsegi Canyon.	Coronado leads expedition to Arizona in search of gold.	Hopi and Pueblo Indians of Arizona revolt against Spanish rule in unison.	San Jose de Tumacacori Mission founded.	San Xavier del Bac mission founded.

ily for the dry climate and moderate winters. Tourism, too, has played a major role in the state's more recent development. From resort towns like Scottsdale and Sedona, to natural wonders like the Grand Canyon and Petrified Forest, to Native American sites like Canyon de Chelly and Monument Valley Tribal Park, tourism helps fuel the state's economy.

Regions

1. NORTHWEST ARIZONA

This is canyon country, with altitudes ranging from 3,000 to 12,000 ft. Grand Canyon National Park is the centerpiece, but Oak Creek Canyon to the south and Marble Canyon to the east are spectacular in their own right. Flagstaff and Sedona sit below the San Francisco Peaks, the state's highest mountains, in this region's southern quarter, and are a mecca for sports and outdoors enthusiasts. Because the summer months, between May and August, see the greatest number of tourists in this region, traveling in the spring (March, April) or in the fall (September, October) will allow you to see the same great sites without the throngs of people.

Towns listed: Flagstaff, Fredonia, Grand Canyon National Park, Marble Canyon, Sedona, Williams.

2. NORTHEAST ARIZONA

Dominated by the 25,000-square-mi Navajo Nation, the largest reservation in the United States, this region encompasses such scenic wonders as Monument Valley to the north, Marble Canyon and Lake Powell to the west, the Hopi mesas of the region's center, as well as petrified forests in the south. Although larger than many eastern states, the Navajo Nation is sparsely populated—only 175,000 residents call it home.

Towns listed: Chinle, Ganado, Holbrook, Kayenta, Page, Tuba City, Window Rock, Winslow.

3. CENTRAL ARIZONA

Bounded by the Verde River to the north, the Verde Valley, McDowell and Superstition mountains to the east, and the Sierra Mountains to the west, this region includes the state capital, Phoenix, with all its culture, as well as the lush valleys and their quaint ghost towns. Jerome, famous for being the largest of America's ghost towns, now is the permanent residence of many artists. Southwest of Jerome, Prescott sits at the edge of a national forest, encircled by pine-capped mountains and cattle-filled grasslands.

Towns listed: Camp Verde, Carefree/Cave Creek, Casa Grande, Chandler, Clarkdale, Coolidge, Cottonwood, Florence, Glendale, Jerome, Litchfield Park, Mesa, Payson, Phoenix, Prescott, Scottsdale, Seligman, Tempe, Wickenburg.

1804–06	1821	1850	1853	1860
Navajo Indians massacred by Spanish in Canyon de Chelly.	Arizona becomes a province of Mexico; Sante Fe Trail trade route opens.	Steamboating commerce begins on the Colorado River.	The Gadsden Purchase is made: the United States obtains the region south of Gila to the present border of Mexico.	First book printed in Arizona.

INTRODUCTION
HISTORY
REGIONS
WHEN TO VISIT
STATE'S GREATS
RULES OF THE ROAD
DRIVING TOURS

4. EAST CENTRAL

Sandwiched between the deserts to the north and south, the high plateaus and mountains of this region offer abundant verdure. Rising to a height of 6,000 ft, the Apache Sitgreaves National Forest attracts tourists to its summer retreats for hiking, boating, and sightseeing—the forest contains many communities settled by Mormons in the 19th century. The eastern edge of this region is dominated by snowcapped Escudilla Mountain which rises 11,000 ft above sea level. Occupying the center of this region are the twin Indian reservations of Fort Apache and San Carlos. Along the southern border of the Fort Apache Reservation extends the Salt River Canyon; majestic buttes and fields of desert shrub color the landscape as the highway descends to Globe and the sun-soaked deserts beyond.

Towns listed: Alpine, Globe, Greer, McNary, Pinetop/Lakeside, San Carlos, Show Low, Springerville/Eagar.

5. FAR WEST

The Colorado River, exiting the Grand Canyon, empties into Lake Mead, just east of Las Vegas, in Arizona's northwestern corner, before turning south and passing Hoover Dam. The bulk of this region's population inhabit this western strip where dams form many lakes. Water-based recreation draws many to towns like Lake Havasu City in the center of this region and Yuma at the southern extreme. Just north of Yuma two riparian wildlife refuges provide sanctuary to fox, coyote, bobcat, and a plethora of birds, tempting tourists with opportunities to sail, fish, and hunt.

Towns listed: Bullhead City, Kingman, Lake Havasu City, Parker, Yuma.

6. SOUTHERN ARIZONA

Traveling west across southern Arizona you will traverse a wide variety of landscapes, beginning with pine-laden mountains like Mount Graham, then the green San Pedro Valley near Benson, onto the cacti-filled deserts of the Saguaro National Forest surrounding Tucson. Old West landmarks like Tombstone and Bisbee dot the southeastern corner near the border with Mexico and offer an interesting counterpoint to this region's single metropolis: Tucson.

Towns listed: Ajo, Benson, Bisbee, Clifton, Douglas, Gila Bend, Nogales, Patagonia, Safford, Sells, Sierra Vista, Tombstone, Tubac, Tucson, Willcox.

When to Visit

Your choice of landscape, mountains or desert, will determine the best times to visit Arizona. If you're looking for outdoor adventures, spring and fall are generally the best seasons to tour all areas (except the ski slopes, of course), when temperatures are mildest and there are fewer tourists to compete with.

Winter temperatures rarely drop much below freezing in the deserts, and summer highs in the mountains are typically in the 70s and 80s. The state's record-high temper-

1863	1868	1873	1883	1886
Arizona becomes a U.S. territory.	Navajo Indian Reservation established in northeast Arizona.	First mining operation started in Globe.	Sante Fe Railroad constructed across northern Arizona.	Geronimo surrenders to the U.S. Army.

ature came in 1990, when Phoenix hit 122°F. The low was -40°F in 1971. So, if your trip is scheduled in summer or winter months, seek out regions that best suit your plans. Don't plan a hiking trip to Tucson and Phoenix environs in July or August.

The monsoon season in the desert is usually in July and/or August, bringing in dramatic storms for 20 or 30 minutes most afternoons. The Phoenix area gets only 35 days of rain a year on average, and most of them come at this time. Flagstaff, on the other hand, sees about 75 days of rain a year. May and June are the driest months.

CLIMATE CHART

Average High/Low Temperatures (°F) and Monthly Precipitation (in inches)

	JAN.	FEB.	MAR.	APR.	MAY	JUNE
FLAGSTAFF	41/14	44/17	48/23	57/28	66/33	77/41
	2.04	2.09	2.55	1.48	.72	.4
	JULY	AUG.	SEPT.	OCT.	NOV.	DEC.
	80/50	78/48	71/41	62/30	51/21	42/15
	2.78	2.75	2.03	1.61	1.95	2.4
	JAN.	FEB.	MAR.	APR.	MAY	JUNE
TUCSON	64/37	68/39	73/44	82/51	89/57	98/66
	.87	.70	.72	.30	.18	.20
	JULY	AUG.	SEPT.	OCT.	NOV.	DEC.
	101/73	96/71	96/68	84/57	73/44	66/39
	2.37	2.19	1.67	1.06	.67	1.07

FESTIVALS AND SEASONAL EVENTS

WINTER

Jan.: **Fiesta Bowl in Tempe.** This nationally televised football classic pits the nation's top two teams against each other at Sun Devil Stadium. | 480/350–0900 or 800/635–5748.

Feb.: **La Fiesta de los Vaqueros in Tucson.** The world's longest non-motorized parade and five-day rodeo. | 520/741–2233.

SPRING

Mar.: **Heard Museum Guild Indian Fair and Market.** A juried show of Native American arts and crafts in Phoenix. | 602/252–8848.

Apr.: **Yaqui Easter.** In Tucson, traditional Yaqui dances and ceremonies are held on the Saturday nights preceding Palm Sunday and Easter Sunday. | 520/791–4609.

1889	**1902**	**1907**	**1912**	**1919**
Territorial capital moves from Prescott to Phoenix.	Senatorial committee proposes combining New Mexico and Arizona as a single state.	Anti-gambling law passes in Arizona.	Arizona becomes the 48th state.	Grand Canyon National Park established.

INTRODUCTION
HISTORY
REGIONS
WHEN TO VISIT
STATE'S GREATS
RULES OF THE ROAD
DRIVING TOURS

SUMMER

June–July: **Prescott Frontier Days and Rodeo.** Started in 1888, this is billed as the world's oldest rodeo. | 520/445–2000 or 800/266–7534.

Aug.: **World's Oldest Continuous PRCA Rodeo.** In Payson, billed as the world's oldest *continuous* rodeo. | 520/474–4515 or 800/672–9766.

Southwest Wings Birding Festival. Lectures by Audubon authorities, field trips. In Sierra Vista. | 520/378–0233.

Summerfest in Flagstaff. A gathering of artists and musicians from around the United States at the Fort Tuthill County Fairgrounds. | 520/774–9541.

AUTUMN

Sept.: **Sedona Jazz on the Rocks.** Live ensembles perform in the red-rock setting at the New Sedona Cultural Park. | 520/282–1985.

Navajo Nation Annual Tribal Fair. The world's largest Native American fair, held in Window Rock. | 520/871–6478.

Oct.: **La Fiesta de los Chiles in Tucson.** Food, music, and educational programs. Chile plants are for sale. | 520/326–9686.

State's Greats

Besides being home to the Seventh Natural Wonder of the World—the Grand Canyon—Arizona is astonishingly varied, both culturally and geographically. In many towns, you can still get the sense of the west as a frontier, in which locals must contend with harsh nature in order to grow food, and provincialism reigns in small-town life. But Arizona also contains within its borders two large (and still growing) cities, Phoenix and Tucson, whose world-class art, sophisticated food, and magnificent vistas draw visitors.

Recreation enthusiasts will find something to their liking in any corner of the state. Arizona has a surprising amount of water, in the form of rivers that fill smooth canyon walls and lakes jumping with fish and water-skiers. It's also possible in some areas (Tucson to Mount Lemmon, for example) to drive from the deepest desert to a high, pine-topped mountain in about an hour.

Forests and Parks

You're never very far from a national park or a national forest in Arizona. Altogether, there are 25 federally managed sites and regions throughout the state, and they offer everything from educational to recreational opportunities. Some concentrate on Native American history, such as **Navajo National Monument** and **Canyon de Chelly**

1921	1930	1936	1948	1962
Economic depression due to copper mining slump.	The planet Pluto discovered at Lowell Observatory in Flagstaff.	Hoover Dam completed.	Arizona Indians receive the right to vote.	Kitt Peak Observatory, the world's largest solar telescope, dedicated.

National Monument, both in the northeast. Others offer simple, scenic beauty and unparalleled hiking, such as **Coronado National Forest,** near Tucson, and **Coconino National Forest,** near Flagstaff.

Culture, History, and the Arts

By and large, the most interesting historical sites are in rural areas, while the best art is found near the cities and on Indian reservations. Old West history is evident in **Tombstone** and **Chiricahua National Monument** (near Willcox). You can visit the sites of great battles throughout the state, learn about the evolution of Arizona from territory status to statehood (in Prescott, most notably), and discover Indian arts and crafts, not only on the reservations, but at the impressive **Heard Museum** in Phoenix. Spanish and Mexican influences are best observed in and around Tucson, at such sites as **Tumacacori National Historic Park.** You'll find musical performances and theater at **Grady Gammage Memorial Auditorium** on the Arizona State University campus in Tempe and at **Centennial Hall** on Tucson's University of Arizona campus.

Sports

Some of the best hiking trails in the world are in **Grand Canyon National Park.** Bright Angel and Kaibab are the two most popular trails, but rangers can help you design a trip that best suits your abilities. There are countless camping spots throughout Arizona, many concentrated around the national parks. **Apache-Sitgreaves National Forest** has particularly impressive facilities for campers.

Lake Powell is great for angling and water sports including waterskiing and sailing.

In winter, lifts haul skiers uphill at the **Flagstaff Arizona Snowbowl** near Flagstaff. The **Mormon Lake Ski Center** is a haven for those who prefer cross-country to downhill.

Golf is popular in the desert. The Phoenix area has perhaps the greatest concentration of good courses, in particular the south course at the **Boulders Resort and Club** and, if you're near Tucson, the **Omni Tucson National Golf Resort and Spa** is the place to go.

Rules of the Road

License requirements: To drive in Arizona you must be at least 16 years old and have a valid driver's license.

Right turn on red: You may make a right turn on red after a full stop unless there is a sign prohibiting it.

Seat belt and helmet laws: If you are sitting in the front seat of any vehicle, the law requires you to wear your seat belt. Kids weighing between 4 and 40 pounds must

1964	**1969**	**1975**	**1996**
Glen Canyon Dam completed.	Navajo Community College built, first ever on a reservation.	Raul Castro becomes the first Hispanic governor of Arizona.	Arizona belatedly recognizes the Martin Luther King, Jr., holiday.

be strapped into an approved safety seat. Anyone under the age of 18 is required to wear a helmet while riding on a motorcycle. For more information call 602/223–2000.

Speed limits: Speed limits in Arizona go as high as 75 mph, but remain at 55 mph in heavily traveled areas. Be sure to check speed limit signs carefully and often.

For more information: Call the **Department of Public Safety** at 602/223–2000.

INTRODUCTION
HISTORY
REGIONS
WHEN TO VISIT
STATE'S GREATS
RULES OF THE ROAD
DRIVING TOURS

The Painted Desert and Indian Country Driving Tour

FROM CAMERON TO THE THIRD MESA

Distance: 430 mi   Time: 3 days
Breaks: Kayenta, Canyon de Chelly (Chinle)

This tour begins in the Painted Desert and runs through both the Navajo and Hopi Indian reservations. Summer is the most popular time along this route, so spring or fall (when the weather is cooler) are ideal touring times. Highlights are the vistas afforded by the Painted Desert and the subcultures of the Navajo and Hopi reservations.

❶ The **Cameron Trading Post** in Cameron is a good place to get your bearings and pick up maps before you begin your journey. There's a large arts-and-crafts store, where you'll find a wide range of Navajo and Hopi pottery, jewelry, baskets, and rugs. The restaurant at the trading post serves wonderful fry bread, tacos, and homemade green chile stew.

When you're ready, take U.S. 89 north from Cameron. You'll drive through the west end of the Painted Desert. Continue for approximately 15 to 20 mi along this brilliant and serene landscape of pink-hued vistas, surreal in its strangeness, until you reach U.S. 160 which will take you to Tuba City. If you're interested, you could take a short detour off U.S. 89 at milepost 316, to visit Dinosaur Tracks, the preserved footprints of what is thought to have been a Dilophosaurus.

❷ Back on U.S. 160, you'll come to **Tuba City.** The landscape around the town includes sediments deposited 20 million years ago. There's a small trading post on Main Street, and it's a good place to stop for gas before heading on. Tuba City is also the home of the administrative center for the **Navajo Indian Reservation.**

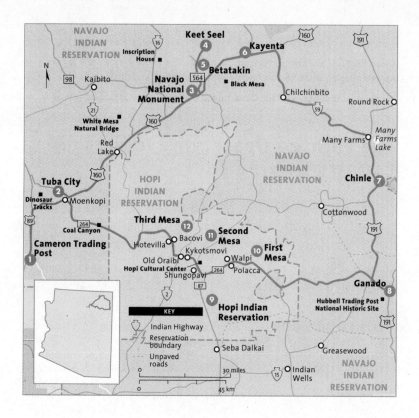

❸ From Tuba City, continue east on U.S.160 to Route 564 and head north for approximately 10 mi to **Navajo National Monument.** Here, in two strikingly spare and beautiful canyons, you'll find two of the largest and best-preserved cliff dwellings in all of the Southwest, Keet Seel and Betatakin, home to the Anasazi between AD 1250 and 1300.

❹ Navajo for "broken pottery," **Keet Seel** is a well-preserved 160-room ruin. It's at an elevation of 7,000 ft, and only 20 visitors are allowed per day (between Memorial Day and Labor Day, when a ranger is on duty). The hike to the actual ruins is a hefty 17 mi round-trip, but it's possible to obtain a permit to camp overnight if you call ahead.

❺ A shorter hike to **Betatakin** (Navajo for "ledge house") is possible, but it, too, is strenuous. Most visitors simply walk the ½-mi trail from the visitor center for a good view of the ruins. Those who hike to the site itself will find a 135-room ruin that seems to hang in midair before a sandstone wall. It was discovered in 1907 by a rancher passing through.

INTRODUCTION
HISTORY
REGIONS
WHEN TO VISIT
STATE'S GREATS
RULES OF THE ROAD
DRIVING TOURS

Even if you don't have the time or energy to hike to the ruins, the visitor center is worth a look. It houses a museum of prehistoric pottery and a lovely arts-and-crafts shop. Picnic facilities are provided, but there are no gas, food, or lodging facilities at the monument.

⑥ Kayenta, about 30 mi to the northeast of Navajo National Monument (just north of U.S. 160 on U.S. 163) is a good place to spend the night. There's not a whole lot to do or see in Kayenta, but it's a good base for touring the monument and the area.

The next morning, head back to U.S. 160 and proceed for approximately 10 mi to Route 59. Take Route 59 southeast for approximately 40 mi to the tiny town of Many Farms. From Many Farms, head south on U.S. 191 to Chinle, a good base for exploring Canyon de Chelly (pronounced d'shay).

⑦ Canyon de Chelly is 3 mi east of **Chinle** on Route 7. It is a magnificent 84,000-acre park, whose two main gorges have dramatic, eroded sandstone walls up to 1,000 ft high. Ancient pictographs adorn many of the cliffs, and the canyon is home to more than 7,000 archaeological sites, some dating back 4,500 years. The bottom of the canyon is lush pasture; you'll see streams, peach orchards, and occupied hogans (Navajo dwellings).

The canyon's first inhabitants were the Anasazi, primarily basket makers. They were followed by the Pueblo people, who built stone cliff dwellings. Descended from the Pueblos were the Hopis, who settled here around AD 780. The Navajo arrived later, around 1300.

Take the **South Rim Drive,** Route 7 from the visitor center, a 36-mi round-trip that takes you through Spider Rock, Tsegi, and Junction overlooks to White House Overlook, where you'll find the trailhead of the only hike to the bottom of the canyon that visitors are permitted to take without a guide. You can hike down this steep but short (1¼ mi) path in just less than an hour (leave a little more time for the uphill return).

Chinle is an ideal place to spend the night after a day of exploring the canyon and environs.

⑧ Day 3 begins on U.S. 191 south out of Chinle. Drive for about 30 mi to Route 264 and then head east for a few miles toward **Ganado** and the **Hubbell Trading Post National Historic Site.** In 1878, a 24-year-old by the name of John Lorenzo Hubbell purchased this establishment, where the Navajo and Hopi traded wool and blankets for brass and tin tokens (called "pesh tai") redeemable for goods at the market. You, too, can purchase goods here, but they'll cost you greenbacks rather than tokens. Hubbell was an advocate for native peoples, translating their letters, settling family disputes, and caring for the sick. You can take an interesting tour of the Hubbell house, viewing his extensive collection of paintings, rugs, and baskets.

⑨ Continue west on Route 264 for approximately 60 mi to the **Hopi Indian Reservation.** The Hopi, a Pueblo people, can trace their presence in the region back more than 1,000 years. They live in villages grouped around three plateaus, designated First Mesa, Second Mesa, and Third Mesa, connected with each other by a 37-mi strip of Route 284.

⑩ The **First Mesa** contains the villages of Walpi, Sichomovi, and Hano, but you must first stop at the **visitor center** to obtain permission to tour the area. To get there, follow the signs to First Mesa villages; you'll see the visitor center at the top of the mesa. Request a guide to help you tour Walpi, a tiny community that houses fewer than 10 families, all without electricity or running water.

⑪ Continue west on Route 264 for approximately 6 mi to the **Second Mesa,** the center of which is the **Hopi Cultural Center.** Here you'll find a compelling museum that traces the Hopi people's turbulent history. There's also a restaurant on the premises that serves traditional Hopi dishes like *nok qui vi* (a lamb hominy and green chile stew), blue corn pancakes, and fry bread.

⑫ At the **Third Mesa,** the **Office of Public Relations** has a wealth of information on local ceremonies and dances held year-round throughout the Hopi Reservation, which you should make every effort to see if the timing is right.

To return to Cameron, continue west on Route 264; at the junction with U.S. 160, make a left. Continue for about 5 mi until you reach U.S. 89 south, which will take you back to Cameron in less than an hour.

Borderlands Driving Tour
FROM TUCSON TO NOGALES

Distance: 475 mi   Time: 3 days
Breaks: Willcox, Bisbee

This tour leads you through Arizona's southern heartland, the territory on which Spanish conquistadores waged bloody wars for rights to this land. The drive will also give you a sense of how much the state's economy is historically tied to the mining industry.

❶ Begin your tour in **Tucson.** You may want to spend some time exploring the city, before you begin the rest of your drive.

❷ Leaving Tucson, head east for approximately 25 mi on Interstate 10 to **Colossal Cave** (take exit 279 at Vail, then follow the signs), a dry limestone cavern that's among the largest in the United States. Its labyrinth of connecting rooms holds evidence of prehistoric Indian occupation. A guided walking tour leads you through stalactites and stalagmites.

❸ Return to Interstate 10 and head east for 39 mi until you get to **Dragoon,** exit 318, where you'll find the **Amerind Museum,** one of the world's most extensive collections of prehistoric artifacts, housed in a Spanish Colonial building.

❹ Continue on Interstate 10 east to **Willcox.** The town is famous for its apples, which can be savored in local restaurants, and it's a good place to spend the night.

❺ Begin the next morning exploring the **Chiricahua National Monument** (about 30 mi southeast of Willcox on Route 18) where fields of desert grass suddenly become dense forests, high mountains, and haunting rock formations. This 12,000-acre monument, dubbed "The Land of the Standing-Up Rocks" by the Chiricahua Apache, is a radically diverse landscape, unusually wet in summer.

INTRODUCTION
HISTORY
REGIONS
WHEN TO VISIT
STATE'S GREATS
RULES OF THE ROAD
DRIVING TOURS

❻ Head west out of the monument on Route 181 until you come to U.S. 191 (about 5 mi). Then proceed south on U.S. 191 to the town of **Douglas,** which is on the Mexican border. Peek into the historic **Gadsden Hotel,** certainly the fanciest spot in town.

❼ A short 16 mi north of Douglas on Route 80 is **Slaughter Ranch/San Bernardino National Historic Landmark,** the former home of cattleman John Slaughter, a Texas ranger who was also a Cochise County Sheriff. The ranch has been impressively restored, and it's easy here to get a sense of what rural life was like in the 19th century.

❽ Backtrack to Douglas on Route 80 (about 15 mi) and continue west for approximately 20 mi into Bisbee. **Bisbee** is an old mining town, blessed with one of the richest copper sources ever found in the United States. It's now a thriving, if sleepy, artist's community, whose chief attractions are its Victorian architecture and mine tours. It's a good place to spend the night.

❾ Approximately 27 mi northwest of Bisbee on Route 80 is the ghost town of **Tombstone,** pretty much a tourist trap these days, but worth a brief stop to see the OK Corral, the infamous site of the 1881 shoot-out. Nearby is **Tombstone Courthouse State Historic Park,** a good place to get an understanding of local mining history.

❿ Leaving Tombstone, take Route 80 to Route 82 (just northwest of Tombstone), and head south for the border. The road ends in **Nogales,** a lively Mexican border town, where you can have lunch and spend the afternoon. It's easiest to park your car on the U.S. side and simply walk across into Mexico (U.S. citizens need only a driver's license or

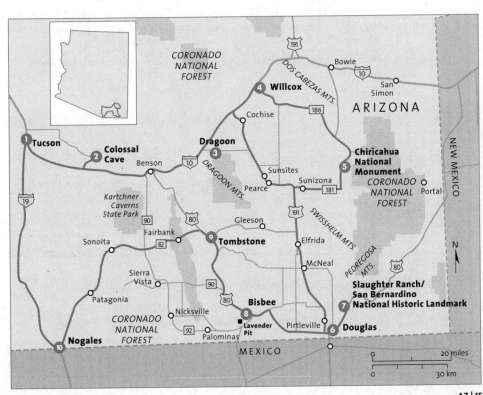

other valid identification). The streets are lined with vendors selling everything from blankets to tequila and handblown glass.

Return to Tucson via Interstate 19 north (about 60 mi from Nogales).

AJO

MAP 3, D9

(Nearby towns also listed: Casa Grande, Sells)

Although *ajo* means "garlic" in Spanish, this town in southwestern Arizona was more likely named for the Tohono O'odham word that means "place of colored clay." After the Calumet & Arizona Mining Company arrived in 1911, Ajo was a thriving copper mining company town, especially after Calumet and Phelps Dodge merged in 1935 and opened the huge New Cornelia pit mine nearby. When the mine was closed in 1985, the town almost followed, but it's been saved by retirees, who came for affordable housing and a temperate climate. The population is now close to 3,000.

The town's central plaza, built in 1917, was designed by Isabella Greenway, the wife of the original Calumet mine manger John Greenway, and evokes the Spanish Colonial architecture of Mexico. It's lined with shops and restaurants, but nothing terribly upscale—just what you might expect in a sleepy desert town. Most travelers use Ajo as a base for exploring Organ Pipe National Monument.

Information: Ajo Chamber of Commerce | 400 Taladro St., Ajo, 85321 | 520/387–7742 | www.ajoinaz.com.

Attractions

Ajo Historical Museum. Historical photographs and artifacts from Ajo's past are on display in this museum in the former St. Catherine's Indian Mission. | 161 Mission St. | 520/387–7105 | Free | Nov.–Apr., daily 1–4; May–Oct. by appointment only.

Cabeza Prieta National Wildlife Refuge. This 860,000-acre preserve was established in 1939 to protect endangered bighorn sheep and other desert wildlife. You need a permit to enter

© Corbis

DID YOU KNOW?

Before Arizona became a territory in 1863, it was part of the New Mexico Territory.

The Gadsden Purchase in 1854 brought southern Arizona into the United Sates.

Father Eusebio Kino, a Jesuit missionary, is credited with introducing cattle to Arizona.

Chinese immigrants provided most of the labor for southern Arizona's first railroad.

The first Indian Reservation in Arizona was the Gila Reservation, home to the Pima Indians.

Tucson is affectionately known as "The Old Pueblo."

Seven Arizona-born crew members perished on the USS *Arizona*.

The Apaches are known as the "Cowboy Indians" for their style of warfare.

Ira Hayes, of the Pima tribe, is the most famous Native American hero of World War II. He appears in the photograph of Iwo Jima.

"Buffalo Soldiers" was the name given to the U.S. Cavalry's black soldiers.

the refuge, and you'll also need a four-wheel-drive vehicle to deal with the rough terrain. Permits are available in the Refuge office. | Refuge office: 1611 N. 2nd Ave., | 520/387–6483 | southwest.fws.gov/refuges/arizona/cabeza.html | Free | Office hrs: weekdays, 7:30–4:30.

Organ Pipe Cactus National Monument. Some 32 mi south of Ajo is where you'll find the largest concentration of organ pipe cacti north of the Mexican border. These multiarmed cousins of the saguaro usually grow only on south-facing slopes, but a drive along one of two scenic loops—Ajo Mountain Drive (21 mi) and Puerto Blanco Drive (53 mi)—will reveal their splendor. Both these are winding, graded dirt roads. | 520/387–6849 or 520/387–7742 | www.nps.gov/orpi | $4 per vehicle | Visitor center daily 8–5.

ON THE CALENDAR

MAR.: *O'odham Festival.* Held at Organ Pipe Cactus National Monument, this one-day festival celebrates the culture of the O'odham, who originally settled the land around Ajo. Demonstrations include basket weaving, clay working, and native dancing. | 520/ 387–6849.

Dining
Copper Kettle. American. In the heart of the Sonoran Desert, this restaurant is known for its succulent steaks and roasted chicken. There are also hot and cold buffets for those who want to try a little of everything. | 23 N. Plaza St. | 520/387–7222 | Breakfast also available; closed Sun. | $6–$10 | AE, D, DC, MC, V.

Señor Sancho. Mexican. Generous portions and reasonable prices are found in this unpretentious roadhouse on the north side of town. Try traditional Sonoran dishes, such as chiles rellenos, flautas, and mole. | 663 N. 2nd Ave. | 520/387–6226 | $6–$10 | No credit cards.

Lodging
Guest House Inn. This inn 25 mi north of Organ Pipe Cactus National Monument was built in 1925 to house VIPs visiting the nearby Phelps-Dodge copper mines. You can enjoy eating breakfast at the stately, handcrafted dining table and later watch Sonoran Desert birds from the patio. Complimentary breakfast. No room phones, no TV. No smoking. | 700 Guest House Rd. | 520/387–6133 | www.wgn.net/~morris/ajo | 4 rooms | $79 | DC, MC, V.

Marine Resort Motel. This small family-owned motel offers very basic rooms 23 mi from Organ Pipe Cactus National Monument. Picnic area. Cable TV. Pets allowed. | 1966 N. 2nd Ave. | 520/387–7626 | fax 520/387–3835 | 22 rooms | $65 | AE, D, DC, MC, V.

ALPINE
MAP 3, I6

(Nearby towns also listed: Clifton, McNary, Show Low, Springerville/Eagar)

On the banks of the San Francisco River, purportedly the route taken by Francisco Vásquez de Coronado more than 400 years ago, Alpine is known as the "Alps of Arizona." This small village offers a variety of winter sports, but when it's all lush and green in the warmer months, it is centrally located for hiking, mountain biking, and fishing.

Information: **Alpine Area Chamber of Commerce** | Box 410, Alpine, 85920 | 520/339–4330.

Attractions
Escudilla National Recreation Trail. This picturesque 3-mi trail wends through the Escudilla Wilderness to the summit of towering 10,912-ft Escudilla Mountain. It's more of a stroll than a strenuous climb. From Alpine, take U.S. 191 north and follow the signs to Hulsey Lake (about 5 mi); turn right on Forest Road 56. | Forest Rd. 56 | 520/339–4384 | Free | Daily | www.fs.fed.us/r3/asnf.

ON THE CALENDAR
MAY: *Dog Trials.* For two days, working dogs compete against each other at Judd's Ranch (at the intersection of Highway 180 and U.S. 191) as they herd sheep over bridges and through various obstacles. | 520/339–4330.

Dining
Bear Wallow Café. American. In the Apache-Sitgreaves Forest, this café serves both American and Mexican cuisine, with everything from chicken-fried steaks to green chile. Outdoor dining on the patio is also available. Closing time is 8 PM from Labor Day to Memorial Day. | 42650 U.S. 180 | 520/339–4310 | $7–$9 | AE, D, MC, V.

Lodging
Hannagan Meadow Lodge. About 22 mi south of Alpine on U.S. 191, this casual, antiques-filled lodge, built in 1926 as a traveler's rest stop for the old Coronado Trail scenic route, has ornate brass beds in each lodge room. The log cabins are more rustic, but some have fireplaces and kitchenettes. Restaurant, bar, complimentary breakfast. No room phones, no TV. Hiking, horseback riding, fishing, bicycles. Cross-country skiing, snowmobiling. | U.S. 191, Hannagan Meadow | 520/339–4370 | fax 520/339–4370 | www.hannaganmeadow.com | 8 rooms, 8 cabins | $60–$115 rooms, $80–$115 cabins | AE, D, MC, V.

Tal-Wi-Wi Lodge. Facing a lush meadow 4 mi north of Alpine on U.S. 191, this lodge's setting is unparalleled. Rooms are simple and clean; three have wood-burning stoves. The lodge saloon draws many locals on weekends and for sporting events shown on the big-screen satellite TV. The lodge restaurant is generally open from May to September. Restaurant, bar. No room phones, no TV. Outdoor hot tub. Pets allowed. | 40 County Rd. 2220, | 520/339–4319 | fax 520/339–1962 | www.talwiwilodge.com | 20 rooms | $65–$95 | AE, MC, V.

BENSON

MAP 3, G9

(Nearby towns also listed: Bisbee, Sierra Vista, Willcox)

In the heart of the San Pedro River valley, Benson was a railroad town on the Southern Pacific line in the 1880s. Today it is home to Kartchner Caverns, a spectacular geological discovery, which is now open to the public. You can tour working cattle ranches and ride the popular San Pedro and Southwestern Railroad excursion train into the San Pedro Riparian National Conservation Area.

Information: **Benson Visitor's Center** | 249 E. 4th St., Benson, 85602 | 520/586–4293 | www.cityofbenson.com.

Attractions
Kartchner Caverns State Park. These caverns 9 mi south of Benson were discovered in 1974, and the state of Arizona worked for over 10 years to prepare them for public viewing. The park opened in fall 1999. You can visit the visitor center, or by reservation, you can take a one-hour tour of two 1,200-ft cave rooms connected by 2¾ mi of tunnel. The cave is one of the most exciting in southern Arizona. | Rte. 90 | www.pr.state.az.us/parkhtml/kartchner.html | 520/586–2283 | $10 per vehicle, cave tours $14 per person | Daily 7:30–6.

ON THE CALENDAR
APR.: *Balloon Rally.* Balloon rides and special children's events are held at this annual event. | 520/586–2842.
MAY: *Mexican Independence Celebration.* An outdoor fair celebrates Mexican Independence with food booths and crafts in City Park. | 520/586–2842.

Dining

Horseshoe Steakhouse and Cantina. Southwestern. Good green chile and chimichangas are served in this café in the glow of a neon horseshoe on the ceiling. Try the chicken-fried steak. Salad bar. Kids' menu. | 154 E. 4th St. | 520/586–3303 | $6–$15 | AE, MC, V.

Ruiz Restaurant. Mexican. On Benson's main street, this restaurant (pronounced "Reese") draws many customers who stop on their way to Tucson for tacos, enchiladas, and the soup of the day. They are also known for their delicious margaritas. | 687 W. 4th St. | 520/586–2707 | $4–$7 | D, MC, V.

Lodging

Best Western Quail Hollow. This modern motel offers spacious and comfortable rooms just off Interstate 10 at exit 304. There are restaurants within walking distance but none on-premises. In-room data ports, some refrigerators, cable TV, some in-room VCRs. Pool. Hot tub. Laundry service. Some pets allowed. | 699 N. Octillo St. | 520/586–3646 | fax 520/586–7035 | www.bestwestern.com | 89 rooms | $60 | AE, D, DC, MC, V.

Days Inn Benson. This two-story motel was built in 1997. The Kartchner Caverns are less than 10 mi away and there are a number of restaurants within walking distance. Complimentary Continental breakfast. In-room data ports, some microwaves, some refrigerators, cable TV. Pool. Outdoor hot tub. | 621 Commerce Dr., | 520/586–3000 or 800/544–8313 | fax 520/586–3000 | www.daysinn.com | 52 rooms, 9 suites | $80–$85, $90–$95 suites | AE, D, DC, MC, V.

Skywatcher's Inn. This B&B two mi south of Benson is on the premises of the privately owned Vega-Bray Observatory. Eight powerful telescopes are available for guests' use, though you don't have to be an astronomer to stay here. Take exit 306 from Interstate 10. Complimentary breakfast. Ponds. | 1311 Astronomer's Rd. | 520/745–2390 | www.communiverse.com/skywatcher | 4 rooms | $74–$125 | MC, V.

BISBEE

MAP 3, H10

(Nearby towns also listed: Benson, Douglas, Sierra Vista)

A registered National Historic Landmark founded in 1880, Bisbee (population 6,500) has several historic sites and museums dedicated to depicting and preserving the town's copper mining history, including the Copper Queen Mine (which, in 1997, became part of the Smithsonian's Hall of Geology) and Lavender Pit, a mine that flourished until 1974. Bisbee is gaining an international reputation as a fine-arts colony with more than 20 galleries showing works in all media. In the southeast corner of the state at an elevation of 5,000 ft, it's also the seat of government for Cochise County. There are plans afoot to reopen the area's old copper mines, so changes are undoubtedly in store for future years.

Information: Greater Bisbee Chamber of Commerce | Box BA, 31 Subway St., Bisbee, 85603 | 520/432–5421.

Attractions

Bisbee Mining and Historical Museum. This award-winning museum illuminates Bisbee's colorful past. You'll find old photographs and artifacts from the mining era, the best of which is a photo-mural, made in 1908, that depicts a crowd of locals celebrating the arrival of the trolley. | 5 Copper Queen Plaza | 520/432–7071 | $4 | Daily 10–4.

Lavender Pit. During its lifespan, 380 million tons of ore were removed from the mine 1 mi south of the Bisbee historical district on Route 80, and the deserted aftermath is eerie. You can park and look into this gaping hole through a chain-link fence. | Rte. 80 | 520/432–5421 | Free | Daily.

Muheim Heritage House Museum. Built in 1898, this museum served as a family residence until 1975. Inside, you can tour the restored interior with its period furnishings. | 207 Youngblood Hill | 520/432–7071 | $2 (suggested) | Mon.–Thurs. 10–5 or by appointment.

Queen Mine Tours. Visitors take real mine cars deep into this former copper mine off Route 80 where temperatures are 47°F year-round. Tours are narrated by former miners who worked the Queen Mine. | 478 N. Dart Rd. | 520/432–2071 | $8 | Daily 8:30–5.

ON THE CALENDAR

MAR.: *Artist's Studio Tour.* A walking tour of local artists' studios is given every year. | 520/432–5421.

MAY: *Bisbee Spring Arts Celebration.* Activities include a paint-a-thon, artist demonstrations, and wine tasting, all in historic downtown Bisbee. | 520/432–5421.

OCT.: *Fiber and Fine Arts Festival.* This festival showcases the work of regional artists. | 520/432–5421.

Dining

Café Roka. Italian. By far the best restaurant in Bisbee, Café Roka offers an inventive northern Italian menu, with such dishes as basil-and-ricotta cannelloni with chicken, and sea scallops with spinach pasta. | 35 Main St. | 520/432–5153 | Closed Sun.–Tues. No lunch | $11–$23 | AE, MC, V.

El Cobre Restaurant. Mexican. At this pleasant restaurant frequented by families, the Mexican plate consisting of tacos, enchiladas, and a beef tamale is very popular. Kids' menu. | 1002 Naco Hwy. | 520/432–7703 | $7–$12 | AE, MC, V.

High Desert Inn Restaurant. French. This restaurant in the High Desert Inn, which was formerly the Cochise County Jail, offers a menu of French dishes, such as medallions of Black Angus beef or an herb-crusted chicken breast served Provençal style, on a bed of chopped tomatoes, olives, garlic, and mushrooms. | 8 Naco Rd. | 520/432–1442 | Closed Sun.–Wed. No lunch | $18–$25 | D, MC, V.

Mike's Steakhouse & Cocktail. Steak. Just off Route 80, this classy spot also has a popular bar. The best-selling dishes include the steaks and shrimp. | 5872 W. Double Adobe Rd. | 520/432–4671 | No lunch | $8–$20 | MC, V.

Lodging

Bisbee Inn. The Bisbee Inn (sometimes called by its original name, Hotel La More) is a restored 1917 hotel in the Bisbee historic district. Regular rooms are basic, but furnished with period antiques, including the original oak dressers from the hotel. Suites are modern apartments with full kitchens and many extra amenities. Complimentary breakfast. In-room data ports, some kitchenettes, some refrigerators, some room phones, some in-room VCRs, no TV in some rooms, TV in common area. Laundry facilities. No smoking. | Box 1855, 45 Oak St. | 520/432–5131 or 888/432–5131 | fax 520/432–5343 | www.bisbeeinn.com | 20 rooms (4 with shared bath), 3 suites | $50–$80, $120–$165 suites | D, MC, V.

Calumet and Arizona Guest House. Most large rooms in this fully restored 1906 Mission-style home are furnished with antiques. It was originally a guest house for visiting mining executives. Complimentary breakfast. No room phones. No kids. No smoking. | 608 Powell St. | 520/432–4815 | 6 rooms (4 with shared bath) | $60–$70 | MC, V.

Copper Queen. This vintage hotel has been operating in Bisbee since 1902. It's as charming as can be, though some rooms are small or oddly laid out, and walls are thin. There's entertainment Friday and Saturday nights. Restaurant, bar. Cable TV. Pool. Business services. | 11 Howell Ave. | 520/432–2216 or 800/247–5829 | fax 520/432–4298 | www.copperqueen.com | 45 rooms | $105–$136 | AE, D, DC, MC, V.

El Rancho Motel. This small chain motel offers basic amenities. There's also an RV park. Picnic area. Some kitchenettes, some microwaves, some refrigerators, cable TV. Laundry facilities. | 1104 Hwy. 92, | 520/432–2293 | fax 520/432–7738 | elranchomotelaz@aol.com | 39 rooms | $49 | AE, D, DC, MC, V.

High Desert Inn. This inn was once the old Cochise County Jail, which was built in 1901, but there are few reminders of the old days. Doric columns adorn the front entrance while the rooms include French wrought-iron beds and tables. It's a sophisticated but friendly place. The restaurant is open for dinner Thursday–Sunday. Restaurant, bar. Cable TV. | 8 Naco Rd. | 520/432–1442 or 800/281–0510 | fax 520/432–1410 | www.highdesertinn.com | 5 rooms | $70–$95 | D, MC, V.

Jonquil Motel. A short walk from historic old Bisbee, the Jonquil is a remodeled old-time motor court that prides itself on its clean and comfortable rooms. Cable TV. No smoking. | 317 Tombstone Canyon | 520/432–7371 | fax 520/432–6915. | www.jonquilmotel.com | 7 rooms | $50–$65 | D, DC, MC, V.

Park Place Bed & Breakfast. This Mediterranean-style home built in 1910 has terraces overlooking Vista Park. The traditional decor includes antiques. Complimentary breakfast. No room phones, no TV in some rooms, TV in common area. Airport shuttle. No smoking. | 200 E. Vista St. | www.theriver.com/parkplace | 520/432–3054 or 800/388–4388 | fax 520/459–7603 | 4 rooms (2 with shared bath), 2 suites | $50–$70 | MC, V.

San Jose Lodge. Only a couple of miles from the Mexican border, this one-level motel is also very close to downtown Bisbee. The local golf course is less than a mile away. There are also a number of full-service RV hookups. Restaurant, bar. Some kitchenettes, refrigerators, cable TV. Pool. Business services. | 1002 Naco Hwy. | 520/432–5761 | fax 520/432–4302 | www.sanjoselodge.com | 43 rooms | $65–$85 | AE, D, DC, MC, V.

★ **School House Inn.** Originally a brick schoolhouse, this building, one block off Highway 80, is perched on the side of a hill. The inn's outdoor patio is shaded by an old oak tree. Each room has a school theme (history, music, geography, etc.). Complimentary breakfast. No air-conditioning, no room phones. No kids under 14. No smoking. | 818 Tombstone Canyon Rd., | 520/432–2996 or 800/537–4333 | 6 rooms, 3 suites | $40–$90 | AE, D, DC, MC, V.

BULLHEAD CITY

MAP 3, B4

(Nearby towns also listed: Kingman, Lake Havasu City)

Bullhead City (population 37,000), on the Nevada border just a few miles from Laughlin, is an economic and shopping center for the western half of Mohave County in Arizona and southeastern Clark County in Nevada. It's a good base from which to explore Arizona's river country. A popular water-sports destination, you'll find waterskiing, jet skiing, and sailing opportunities here. It's also a stone's throw from Las Vegas.

Information: **Bullhead Area Chamber of Commerce** | 1251 Hwy. 95, Bullhead City, 86429 | 520/754–4121 | www.bullheadcityaz.com/chamber.

Attractions
Colorado River Museum. The displays at this small museum ½ mi north of the Laughlin Bridge document the history of the area and include Native American artifacts and photographs. | 2201 Hwy. 68 | 520/754–3399 | $1 | Sept.–June, Tues.–Sun. 10–4; closed Mon. all year.

Davis Dam and Power Plant. Visitors are allowed to go to the spillway gates and view the outside of the power plant here 4 mi north of Bullhead City; however, there are no longer tours inside the plant. Behind the dam is Lake Mohave. | Hwy. 68 | 520/754–3628 | www.lc.usbr.gov/~pao/davis.html | Free | Weekdays 7:30–3:30.

JAN.: *Turquoise Circuit Finals Rodeo.* This event brings together competitors from Arizona and New Mexico. Events include bull riding, calf roping, and barrel steering. | 520/754–4121.

Dining

Darunnes Thai & Chinese Restaurant. Chinese. Traditional decor and friendly service draw customers to this restaurant. Enjoy the sweet-and-sour pork or chicken, and then wash it down with some delicious Thai iced tea (sweetened and mixed with condensed milk). | 1852 Hwy. 95 | 520/763–6961 | $5–$8 | D, DC, MC, V.

El Encanto. Mexican. El Encanto is known for Sonoran standards such as burritos and chimichangas. The decor is decidedly Mexican. Open-air dining on a patio. Kids' menu. | 125 Long Ave. | 520/754–5100 | $5–$9 | AE, MC, V.

Nikki's Too. American. This eatery does not offer much in terms of decor, but customers keep coming back for the standard American fare. The meat loaf and fried chicken are popular with the locals. Make sure to try one of their wonderful salads. | 865 Hancock Rd. | 520/763–4466 | Closed weekends | $8–$14 | D, DC, MC, V.

Lodging

Best Western Bullhead City Inn. This well-maintained, two-story chain motel was built in 1992. Complimentary Continental breakfast. In-room safes, some microwaves, refrigerators, cable TV. Pool. Hot tub. Business services. Pets allowed (fee). | 2360 4th St., | 520/754–3000 or 800/634–4463 | fax 520/754–5234 | www.bestwestern.com | 88 rooms | $45–$75 | AE, D, DC, MC, V.

Bullhead City Super 8. This two-story chain motel offers basic rooms. Room service. Cable TV. Pool. Pets allowed. | 1616 Hwy. 95 | 520/763–1002 | fax 520/763–2984 | www.super8.com | 62 rooms | $40–$55 | AE, DC, MC, V.

Colorado River Resort. This two-story extended stay (by the week or month) resort still offers daily rates when rooms are available. It's right across the street from the Colorado River. The nearest restaurants are about 5 mi away. Kitchenettes, cable TV. Pool. Laundry facilities. Some pets allowed. | 434 River Glen Dr., | 520/754–4101 | fax 520/754–1033 | 32 rooms | $40–$60 | MC, V.

Lake Mohave Resort and Marina. Some rooms have lake views at this resort on spacious grounds about 10 mi north of Bullhead City off Highway 95. Restaurant, bar. Some kitchenettes. Water sports, boating, fishing. Business services. Some pets allowed (fee). | Katherine's Landing | 520/754–3245 or 800/752–9669 | fax 520/754–1125 | www.sevencrown.com | 50 rooms | $70–$100 | D, MC, V.

Lodge on the River. This motel is on the Colorado River. Rooms are clean and basic. Some microwaves, some refrigerators, cable TV. Pool. | 1717 Hwy. 95 | 520/758–8080 | fax 520/758–8283 | 51 rooms, 13 suites | $35–$41, $54–$64 suites | AE, D, DC, MC, V.

Shangri-La Suites. Right on the Colorado River, this motel is a convenient place to stop for the night if you are passing through. A shopping center and restaurants are very close by. Cable TV. No pets. | 1767 Georgia La. | 520/758–1117 | fax 520/758–5975 | 29 rooms | $40–$71 | D, DC, MC, V.

CAMP VERDE

(Nearby towns also listed: Cottonwood, Flagstaff, Payson, Sedona)

A small town of 8,400 on the Verde River, Camp Verde was originally a military outpost known as Fort Verde. Set up in 1871 to protect the area's white settlers and wealth seekers from the region's natives, particularly Apache and Yavapai uprisings, the town later boomed with the region's silver- and gold-mining successes. The main economic base of the town today is agriculture, but tourism is a lure, particularly for visitors drawn to nearby Montezuma's Castle.

Information: **Chamber of Commerce** | 385 S. Main St., Camp Verde, 86322 | 520/567–9294 | www.insightable.com/cvcc.

Attractions

Fort Verde State Historic Park. You can take a self-guided tour of the original fort, a 10-acre spread that preserves three furnished officers' quarters, an administration building, and many ruins to get a sense of the day-to-day living conditions in the late 1800s. There are also photographic displays of soldiers and their families that further document military life in Arizona in that era. | 125 E. Hollamon St. | www.pr.state.az.us | 520/567–3275 | $2 | Daily 8–4:30.

Montezuma Castle National Monument. This striking five-story, 20-room cliff dwelling was originally named by early European explorers who thought it had been erected by the Aztecs. Southern Sinagua Indians actually built the structure, one of the best-preserved prehistoric ruins in North America. From Camp Verde, go 4 mi north of Interstate 17, then 3 mi via Montezuma Castle Highway (exit 289). | Montezuma Castle Hwy. | 520/567–3322 | www.nps.gov/moca | $2 | Memorial Day–Labor Day, daily 8–7; Labor Day–Memorial Day, daily 8–5.

Montezuma Well. A limestone sinkhole is all that remains of an ancient subterranean cavern 11 mi from Montezuma's Castle National Monument but also protected within the national monument. Underground springs filled the sinkhole, which the Hohokam and Sinagua used to irrigate crops. There are also ruins here of Sinagua and Hohokam homes. Take Interstate 17, exit 293, then drive 4 mi. | Off I–17 | 520/567–3322 | www.nps.gov/moca | Free | Memorial Day–Labor Day, daily 8–7; Labor Day–Memorial Day, daily 8–5.

ON THE CALENDAR

OCT.: *Fort Verde Days.* This event celebrates the colorful history of Camp Verde with Old West re-creations, food, and music. | 520/634–7593.

Dining

Gabriela's Mexican Food. Mexican. You'll find traditional Mexican food in this tiny house off the main drag in Camp Verde. Try the *carne asada* tacos (made of marinated beef) or chicken burritos. | 154 Holloman St. | 520/567–4484 | Closed Sun. | $5–$9 | No credit cards.

Lodging

Comfort Inn of Camp Verde. This two-story motel is just off Interstate 17 at exit 287, 2 mi from Montezuma's Castle and 3 mi from the Cliff Castle Casino. Complimentary Continental breakfast. In-room data ports, cable TV. Pool. Hot tub. Pets allowed (fee). | 340 N. Industrial Dr. | 520/567–9000 | fax 520/567–1828 | www.comfortinn.com | 85 | $75–$84 | AE, D, DC, MC, V.

Lodge at Cliff Castle. The two-story Cliff Castle Casino is located on a hill just behind this hotel, and its conference center was once part of the original casino. If you're feeling tired, there is a free shuttle to the casino just two blocks away. Restaurant. Some microwaves, some refrigerators, cable TV. Pool. Outdoor hot tub. Business services. Pets allowed (fee). |

333 Middle Verde Rd. | 520/567–6611 or 800/524–6343 | fax 520/567–9455 | www.cliffcas-tle.com | 76 rooms, 6 suites | $64–$79, $89–$119 suites | AE, D, MC, V.

CANYON DE CHELLY NATIONAL MONUMENT

(see Chinle)

CAREFREE/CAVE CREEK

MAP 3, E6

(Nearby towns also listed: Glendale, Mesa, Phoenix, Scottsdale, Tempe)

These are neighboring communities whose histories overlap. Cave Creek was settled in the 1870s by miners and ranchers looking for seclusion in this rural setting near Black Mountain. Carefree was founded in the 1950s and is one of the earliest planned communities in Arizona. You'll find the largest sundial in the Western Hemisphere here, as well as unique rock outcroppings and boulders visible for miles. (The renowned Mary Elaine's restaurant in Scottsdale serves snails from Cave Creek.) Together the two communities have a population of just over 6,000.

Information: Carefree/Cave Creek Chamber of Commerce | 6710 E. Cave Creek Rd., Cave Creek, 85331 | 480/488–3381 | www.inficad.com/~cfccchamber.

Attractions

Cave Creek Museum. Displays of Native American artifacts and western memorabilia, and photographs provide an introduction to the colorful history of the area. | 6140 E. Skyline Dr., Cave Creek | 480/488–2764 | Free | Oct.–May, Wed.–Sun. 1–4:30.

Sundial. This is the third-largest sundial in the western hemisphere. Take Wampum Road east to Easy Street; the sundial is at the end of the road. | East St., Carefree | 480/488–3381 | Free | Daily.

SIGHTSEEING TOURS/TOUR COMPANIES

Rawhide Land and Cattle Company. This outfitter provides half-day and overnight off-road Jeep tours with certified guides. | 23733 Scottsdale Rd., Rawhide | www.rawhide-jeepadventures.com | 480/488–0023 or 800/294–5337 | $65 | Daily 8 AM–9 PM.

ON THE CALENDAR

APR.: *Fiesta Days.* There's a parade downtown and rodeo shows at Memorial Arena. | 480/488–3381 or 480/488–9118.
JULY: *Annual Fireworks Extravaganza.* Independence Day fireworks light the sky at dusk in Cave Creek. | 480/488–3381 or 480/488–9118.
DEC.: *Live Nativity Pageant.* Luminarias (candles lit inside waxed paper bags) line Cave Creek Road during this annual pageant. | 480/488–3381.

Dining

Cantina del Pedregal. Mexican. At this bright and cheerful spot try Mexican Gulf shrimp or chicken Yucatan. Open-air dining on a second-floor patio. Kids' menu. | 34505 N. Scotts-dale Rd. | 480/488–0715 | $10–$19 | AE, DC, MC, V.

The Latilla. American. In the Boulders Resort and Club, the glass walls of this attractive dining room provide gorgeous panoramic views of the desert. The menu features roast rack of lamb, Angus beef tenderloin, and muscovy duck breast. Sunday brunch. Kids' menu. | 34631 N. Tom Darlington Dr. | 480/488–9009 | Breakfast also available | $24–$34 | AE, D, DC, MC, V.

Le Sans Souci Restaurant. French. At this upscale bistro popular dishes include coq au vin, frog legs, and lamb. | 7030 E. Bella Vista Dr., Cave Creek | 480/488–2856 | Reservations essential for dinner | Closed Mon. | $16–$30 | AE, D, DC, MC, V.

Lodging
Andora Crossing Bed & Breakfast. Out in the desert, this small B&B, which has been decorated by the artist-owner, is a great place to escape the city. Enjoy the wilderness and listen to the sounds of coyotes and quails. Complimentary breakfast. No phones in some rooms, no TVs. No pets. | 6434 Military Rd., Cave Creek | 480/488–3747 | www.cavecreekonline.com/ andoracrossing | 3 rooms, 1 guest house | $100–$150 | No credit cards.

★ **Boulders Resort and Club.** Nestled among ancient boulders, this serene, secluded luxury resort is just outside Phoenix. The architecture is dramatic, with pueblo-style casitas built among the rocks. Each casita has a fireplace, patio, and huge bathroom. 5 restaurants, bar, room service. In-room data ports, refrigerators, cable TV, in-room VCRs. 2 pools. Hot tub, massage. Driving range, 2 18-hole golf courses, putting green, 6 tennis courts. Gym. Business services, airport shuttle. Some pets allowed (fee). | 34631 N. Tom Darlington Dr., Carefree | 480/488–9009 or 800/553–1717 | fax 480/488–4118 | www.grandbay.com | 160 casitas | $545–$700 | AE, DC, MC, V.

Carefree Conference Resort. Accommodations here are in luxury rooms and casitas, each with either a balcony or patio and a view of the Continental Mountains or the main pool. Restaurant, 2 bars. Cable TV. Pool. Beauty salon, spa. Tennis. Bicycles. Pets allowed. | 37220 Mule Train Rd., Carefree | 480/488–5300 or 800/227–7066 | fax 480/595–3795 | www.conferenceresorts.com/carefree | 216 rooms, 26 casitas, 4 suites | $290, $370 casitas, $450 suites | AE, D, DC, MC, V.

Gotland's Inn–Cave Creek. Located on 4 private acres, this small bed-and-breakfast has beautiful desert mountain views. Picnic area, complimentary Continental breakfast. In-room data ports, kitchenettes, microwaves, refrigerators, cable TV, in-room VCRs (and movies). Driving range, putting green. Business services. No smoking. | 38555 N. School House Rd., Cave Creek | 480/488–9636 | fax 480/488–9636 | gotlands@inficad.com | 4 rooms | $110–$199 | Closed mid-June–Aug. | AE, D, MC, V.

CASA GRANDE

MAP 3, E8

(Nearby towns also listed: Coolidge, Florence, Gila Bend)

Casa Grande, a small town of some 22,000 south of Phoenix, was once a stop on the Southern Pacific Rail Line. Its present economic base is agriculture and ranching, but it's also a good base for exploring the ruins at Casa Grande Ruins National Monument, near Coolidge to the northeast.

Information: Greater Casa Grande Chamber of Commerce | 575 N. Marshall St., Casa Grande, 85222 | 520/836–2125 or 800/916–1515 | www.casagrandechamber.org.

Attractions
Casa Grande Valley Historical Society and Museum. Artifacts and photographs document local history. Exhibits cover such topics as the Gila Indians, who originally settled the area, including examples of their handcrafted baskets. | 110 W. Florence Blvd. | 520/836–2223 | $2 | Sept.–May, Tues.–Sun. 10–4. Closed June–Aug.

Dave White Regional Park. This public park has a golf course, racquetball courts, and volleyball courts. | 2121 N. Thornton Ave. | 520/836–9216 | Free | Daily.

Picacho Peak State Park. Arizona's largest Civil War battle took place around this peak 24 mi southeast of Casa Grande, which is actually a 3,382-ft outcrop of solidified lava. It's a great place to hike through wildflower fields in spring. | Off I–10, exit 219, Picacho | 520/466–3183 | www.pr.state.az.us/parksites.html | $5 per vehicle | Daily sunrise–sunset.

Tanger Factory Outlet Center. Brand names sold at this large factory outlet mall include Bass, Big Dog, Guess, Izod, and many others. | 2300 E. Tanger Dr. | 520/836–9663 or 800/405–5016 | www.tangeroutlet.com | Mon.–Sat. 9–8, Sun. 10–6.

ON THE CALENDAR

FEB.: *O'odham Tash–Casa Grande's Indian Days.* An annual event with a rodeo, carnival, arts and crafts, dances, music, and more. | 520/836–4723.

JULY: *Fourth of July Day in the Park.* Bring the entire family for a day of food, games, and a traditional Fourth of July celebration in Carr McNatt Park. | 520/421–8677.

Dining

Barney's Steaks & Seafood. American. Known for chicken-fried steaks and prime rib, this restaurant can seat over 200. A buffet and kids' menu is also offered. | 665 N. Pinal Ave. | 520/426–1377 | $6–$13 | AE, D, DC, MC, V.

Lodging

Best Western Casa Grande Suites. All rooms at this motel are suites. Restaurant. In-room data ports, microwaves, refrigerators, cable TV. Pool. Hot tub. Laundry service. | 665 Via Del Cielo | 520/836–1600 | fax 520/836–7242 | www.bestwestern.com | 81 suites | $64–$105 | AE, D, DC, MC, V.

Francisco Grande Resort and Golf Club. Just 4 mi west of Casa Grande, this resort was the former spring training headquarters for the San Francisco Giants. The pool is shaped like a baseball bat, and the wading pool is shaped like a baseball. The golf course is, at almost 7,600 yards, Arizona's longest. Restaurant, bar, room service. Some microwaves, cable TV. Pool, wading pool. Driving range, 18-hole golf course, putting green. Gym. Business services. | 26000 W. Gila Bend Hwy. (Rte. 84) | 520/836–6444, 800/237–4238 in AZ | fax 520/836–5855 | www.franciscogrande.com | 92 rooms, 20 suites | $99–$119, $189–$300 suites | AE, DC, MC, V.

CHANDLER

MAP 3, E7

(Nearby towns also listed: Glendale, Mesa, Phoenix, Scottsdale, Tempe)

Chandler is a suburb of Phoenix, just south of Tempe, with a population of 180,000. It's fast becoming a high-tech industrial base, but it's also a haven for golfers. The Chandler Center for the Arts offers performances by national and local performing artists.

Information: Chamber of Commerce | 218 N. Arizona Ave., Chandler, 85225 | 480/963–4571 or 800/963–4571 | www.chandlerchamber.com.

Attractions

Chandler Center for the Arts. Performances by local and national artists, musicians, and theater troupes are presented here year-round. | 250 N. Arizona Ave. | 480/782–2680 | www.chandleraz.org | Admission price varies by performance | Box office, Tues.–Fri. 10–3.

Gila River Arts and Crafts Center. This small museum on the Gila River Indian Reservation, 15 mi south of Chandler, has a display of rare Gila baskets. Local pottery, jewelry, and rugs are offered for sale. Take I–10 to exit 175. | Casablanca Rd. | 480/963–3981 | Free | Daily 8–5.

MAR.: *Chandler Ostrich Festival.* Ostrich racing is the centerpiece of this event the second weekend in March. | 602/963–4571 or 800/963–4571.

OCT.: *Cotton Festival.* A celebration of Chandler's history; highlights include a parade, a petting zoo, extreme sports competition, and an all-cotton fashion show. | 480/782–3045.

Dining

C-Fu Gourmet. Chinese. The specialty here is fish. Make your choice from one of the tanks. Try shrimp, steamed and bathed in a potent garlic sauce, or clams in black bean sauce. There's also dim sum during lunch. | 2051 W. Warner Rd. | 480/899–3888 | $7–$20 | AE, D, DC, MC, V.

Citrus Cafe. French. This is one of the best French restaurants in the area. The daily menu is determined by what is freshest in the market. Main dishes are pure French comfort food: veal kidneys, leg of lamb, and occasionally even rabbit. *Vacherin,* a baked meringue, is the signature dessert. | 2330 N. Alma Rd. | 480/899–0502 | Closed Sun., Mon. No lunch Sat. | $15–$23 | AE, D, DC, MC, V.

Lodging

Best Western Inn & Suites of Chandler. This motor hotel is 15 mi from Sky Harbor International Airport. Restaurant, complimentary Continental breakfast. In-room data ports, some microwaves, some refrigerators, cable TV. Pool. Spa. Laundry service. Business services. | 950 N. Arizona Ave. | 480/814–8600 | fax 480/814–1198 | www.bestwestern.com | 48 rooms | $115–$149 | AE, D, DC, MC, V.

Chandler Super 8. This two-story budget-priced motel is 10 mi from Sky Harbor International Airport. Cable TV. Pool. Pets allowed. | 7171 Chandler Blvd. | 480/961–3888 | fax 480/961–3888 ext. 400 | www.super8.com | 75 rooms | $60–$79 | AE, D, DC, V.

Fairfield Inn by Marriott Phoenix-South/Chandler. This three-story, standard chain hotel is 10 mi from Phoenix's Sky Harbor International Airport. Complimentary Continental breakfast. Some microwaves, some refrigerators, cable TV. Pool. Hot tub. Laundry facilities, laundry service. Business services. | 7425 W. Chandler Blvd. | 480/940–0099 or 800/228–2800 | fax 480/940–7336 | www.fairfieldinn.com | 48 rooms, 18 suites | $95, $105 suites | AE, D, DC, MC, V.

Sheraton San Marcos Golf Resort and Conference Center. This contemporary resort has a particularly large, landscaped pool area. Most rooms have views of the golf course, which is one of Arizona's oldest. 2 restaurants, 2 bars, room service. Cable TV. Pool, wading pool. Barbershop, beauty salon, hot tub, massage. Driving range, 18-hole golf course, putting green, 2 tennis courts. Gym. Volleyball, bicycles. Shops. Business services. Pets allowed (fee). | 1 San Marcos Pl. | 480/963–6655 or 800/528–8071 | fax 480/963–6777 | www.sheraton.com | 287 rooms, 8 suites | $149–$179 | AE, D, DC, MC, V.

Windmill Inn of Chandler. An all-suite chain hotel with immaculate rooms. Complimentary Continental breakfast. In-room data ports, minibars, microwaves, refrigerators, cable TV. Pool. Hot tub. Gym. Bicycles. Library. Laundry facilities. | 3535 W. Chandler Blvd. | 480/812–9600 or 800/547–4747 | fax 480/812–8911 | www.windmillinns.com | 123 suites | $109–$139 | AE, D, DC, MC, V.

Wyndham Garden Hotel. This four-story hotel is one of the more aesthetically pleasing chain options in Chandler. It's 10 mi from both the Sky Harbor International Airport and Arizona State University in Tempe. Restaurant, bar, room service. In-room data ports, some microwaves, cable TV. Pool. Hot tub. Gym. Laundry facilities. Business services, airport shuttle. | 7475 W. Chandler Blvd. | 480/961–4444 | fax 480/940–0269 | www.wyndham.com | 140 rooms, 19 suites | $159, $169–$199 suites | AE, D, DC, MC, V.

CHINLE

MAP 3, H3

(Nearby towns also listed: Ganado, Window Rock)

Chinle, a sleepy town of about 5,000, is almost at the geographical center of the Navajo Indian Reservation and right at the mouth of Canyon de Chelly. It's a comfortable base for exploring the area. In late August each year there is a Central Navajo Fair, a public celebration that includes a rodeo, carnival, and traditional dance.

Information: **Navajoland Tourism Dept.** | Box 663, Window Rock, 86515 | 520/871–6436 or 520/871–7371.

Attractions

Canyon de Chelly National Monument. In the northeast corner of the state, Canyon de Chelly (pronounced *d'shay*) is a spectacular place. Its two main gorges—the 26-mi-long Canyon de Chelly and 35-mi-long Canyon del Muerto—have sandstone walls, some as high as 1,000 ft, though they are only 30 ft at the canyon's entrance. Ancient pictographs adorn the cliffs, and there are more than 7,000 archaeological sites, some dating back 4,500 years. Gigantic stone formations tower above streams, hogans, tilled fields, peach orchards, and grazing pastures. The Anasazi were the canyon's first inhabitants. They disappeared around AD 750, replaced by the Pueblo people. The Hopi settled here in AD 780, followed by the Navajo around 1300. Today, visitors can drive around the rim of the canyon (about two hours), hike a well-marked trail to the White House Ruin, or take guided tours of the canyon floors. Contemporary Navajo people still live and farm here. The canyon mouth is

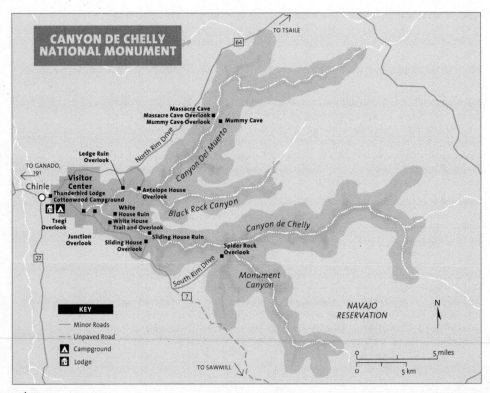

3 mi east of Chinle. | Navajo Rte. 7 | 520/674–5500 | www.nps.gov/cach | Free | Visitor center: May–Sept., daily 8–6; Oct.–Apr., daily 8–5.

South Rim Drive. This 36-mi round-trip around the rim of Canyon de Chelly includes seven overlooks, from which you will be able to see different cliff dwellings and geological formations, including the White House and Spider Rock. Including time to stop and admire the views, allow at least two hours for this drive. | Canyon de Chelly | Visitor center: 520/674–5500 | www.nps.gov/cach | Free | May–Sept., daily 8–6; Oct.–Apr., daily 8–5.

North Rim Drive. This 34-mi round-trip along the rim of Canyon del Muerto leads to four overlooks, including Antelope House, where you can also see the third canyon in the national monument, Black Rock Canyon. Another stop is Massacre Cave Overlook, where over 100 people were killed by Spanish soldiers in 1805. This drive turns into Highway 64. | Canyon de Chelly | Visitor center: 520/674–5500 | www.nps.gov/cach | Free | May–Sept., daily 8–6; Oct.–Apr., daily 8–5.

White House. Construction of the best known of the canyon's cliff dwellings was probably begun around 1060. It derives its name from a wall in the upper part of the dwelling that is covered in white plaster. Nearby, you'll see some of the unique foot-size steps the Anasazi chipped into canyon walls across the Southwest. The dwelling is reached by a 2½-mi round-trip trail, and it's the only part of the canyon that can be visited unescorted. | Canyon de Chelly | Visitor center: 520/674–5500 | www.nps.gov/cach | Free | May–Sept., daily 8–6; Oct.–Apr., daily 8–5.

SIGHTSEEING TOURS/TOUR COMPANIES

Thunderbird Lodge Canyon Tours. Half- and full-day guided Jeep tours of the canyon are available through this tour operator. | Navajo Rte. 7 | www.tbirdlodge.com | 520/674–5841 or 800/679–2473 | fax 520/674–5844 | $37–$60 | Daily.

ON THE CALENDAR

AUG.: *Central Navajo Fair.* Artisans display and sell their wares, and you can munch local specialties at a number of food booths. | 520/674–5500.

Dining

Garcia's Restaurant. American. In the Holiday Inn Canyon de Chelly in Chinle, this is one of the few full-service restaurants in the area. The menu includes standard burgers, chicken, steaks, and pasta. Kids' menu. | Navajo Rte. 7 | 520/674–5000 | $9–$17 | AE, D, DC, MC, V.

Junction Restaurant. Native American. Both Navajo and American cuisine is served in three dining areas. Try the Navajo beef or ham or Navajo burger. | Navajo Rte. 7/U.S. 191 | 520/674–8443 | Breakfast also available | $8–$21 | AE, D, DC, MC, V.

Pizza Edge. Pizza. If you are in the mood for pizza or just something quick, this is the best place to go in Chinle. The menu also includes sandwiches and hot wings. | Basha's Shopping Center, U.S. 191 | 520/674–3366 | Closed Sun. | $3–$11 | AE, D, DC, MC, V.

Lodging

Best Western Canyon de Chelly Inn. Navajo motifs in this standard, two-story motel remind you that you're not in Kansas anymore. It's in Chinle, 3 mi west of Canyon de Chelly. Restaurant. Cable TV. Pool. | 100 Main St. (Navajo Rte. 7) | 520/674–5874 | fax 520/674–3715 | www.bestwestern.com | 102 rooms, 3 suites | $112 | AE, D, DC, MC, V.

Coyote Pass Hospitality. About 30 mi northeast of Chinle, this B&B is run by the Coyote Pass clan of the Navajo Nation. Guests sleep on bedding on the dirt floor of a hogan, use an outhouse, and eat a Navajo-style breakfast that is prepared on a wood-burning stove. It's a unique experience, but definitely not for everyone. Will Tsosie can also put together an individually crafted tour for you. Complimentary breakfast. | Box 91-B, Tsaile | 520/724–3383 | www.navajocentral.org/cppage.htm | Hogan can accommodate up to 15 people | $85 per person | No credit cards.

Holiday Inn Canyon de Chelly. This motel, which was built in 1992, is 1/2 mi from the entrance to Canyon de Chelly. It incorporates part of a historic trading post. Restaurant, room service. Cable TV. Pool. Business services. | Navajo Rte. 7 | 520/674–5000 | fax 520/674–8264 | www.holiday-inn.com | 108 rooms | $95–$115 | AE, D, DC, MC, V.

Thunderbird Lodge. A pink adobe structure right at the mouth of Canyon de Chelly in a grove of cottonwoods, this popular stone-and-adobe lodge has motel-style rooms and is as close as you can get to the canyon. A guide service offering Jeep tours of the canyon operates out of the lodge. Restaurant. Cable TV. Business services, airport shuttle. | Navajo Rte. 7 | 520/674–5841 or 800/679–2473 | fax 520/674–5844 | www.tbirdlodge.com | 72 rooms | $96–$138 | AE, D, DC, MC, V.

CLARKDALE

MAP 3, E5

(Nearby towns also listed: Cottonwood, Jerome, Sedona)

Said to have risen out of a colony of prostitutes and gamblers who were forced out of a mining camp around 1912, Clarkdale mellowed considerably as a copper-mining company town. It's still a two-horse town with little to be seen, though it now has a population of 3,500. But it's also the depot for the Verde Canyon Railroad, which winds through the Verde Valley.

Information: Clarkdale Chamber of Commerce | 1010 S. Main St., Cottonwood, 86326 | 520/634–7593 | www.verdevalley.com.

Attractions

Tuzigoot National Monument. Tuzigoot is a complex of stone ruins left by the Sinagua people, who inhabited the area from about AD 1000 to AD 1400. A small museum displays Native American artifacts and photographs. There are also hiking trails at the site. | Off Rte. 89A | 520/634–5564 | www.nps.gov/tuzi | $2 | May–Sept., daily 8–7; Sept.–May, daily 8–5.

Verde Canyon Railroad. A four-hour, 40-mi train ride takes you through the Sycamore Wilderness Area and North Verde River Canyon, an area not often seen by visitors. The knowledgable announcers will entertain you with colorful stories of the region's history and point out interesting spots along the way. | 300 N. Broadway | www.verdecanyonrr.com | 520/639–0010 or 800/293–7245 | $36–$55 | Mar.–May and Oct., Mon., Wed.–Fri., Sun. at 1, Sat. at 9 and 2:30; June–Sept. and Nov.–Feb., Wed.–Fri. at 1.

ON THE CALENDAR

DEC.: *Made in Clarkdale.* This festival showcases the work of local artists. | 520/634–2913.

Dining

Su Casa. Mexican. Serving some of the best authentic Mexican cuisine in the Verde Valley, this restaurant is a favorite among the locals. The vegetarian menu is very popular, and the chiles rellenos are especially good. | 1000 Main St. | 520/634–2771 | $5–$9 | MC, V.

CLIFTON

MAP 3, H8

(Nearby towns also listed: Alpine, Safford)

Named for Henry Clifton, an early prospector, the place is now a sleepy mining town of about 3,500, known primarily as the beginning of the Coronado Trail (U.S. 191). Clifton is also a good base for exploring the Apache-Sitgreaves National Forest.

Information: **Clifton Chamber of Commerce** | 100 N. Coronado Blvd., Clifton, 85533 | 520/865–3313.

Attractions
Coronado Trail. Originally U.S. Route 666, the Coronado Trail is named for the Spanish explorer who came to Arizona in the 1540s searching for gold. It's a winding, little-traveled 123-mi section of U.S. 191 from Clifton north to Springerville, through the "Alps of Arizona," where you'll find hiking trails, campsites, and lakes. Because of the twists and turns in the road, allow no less than four hours for the drive. | U.S. 191 | 520/865–4146 | Free | Year-round.

Morenci Open Pit Copper Mine. You can take a guided tour, either by van or bus, of this open-pit copper mine. Children under nine not permitted. It's 5 mi northwest of Clifton via U.S. 191, near Morenci. | 4521 U.S. 191 | 520/865–4521 or 800/882–1291 | Free | Tours Mon.– Sat. at 9 AM and 1 PM.

Old Jail and Locomotive. The jail was built into the side of the mountain in 1881. The narrow gauge engine brought ore down the mountain to meet the train from El Paso. | N. Coronado Blvd. | 520/865–4146 | Free | Year-round.

ON THE CALENDAR
DEC.: *Festival of Lights.* This brilliant Christmastime display of lights downtown brings out the whole town. | 520/865–4146.

Dining
Maud's. Mexican. The green chile meat burritos and enchiladas are among the more popular dishes at this drive-in. Patrons can get their food and head over to one of the parks just down the street. | 331 S. Coronado Blvd. | 520/865–5551 | Closed Sun. | $3–$8 | No credit cards.

Lodging
Rode Inn Motel. Close to the Historical Society of Chase Creek, this motel attracts guests who want to bask in the clear country air. For those who enjoy fishing, the San Francisco River is directly across the street. Cable TV. Laundry facilities. Pets allowed (fee). | 186 S. Coronado Blvd. | 520/865–4536 | fax 520/865–2654 | 33 rooms | $54 | D, DC, MC, V.

COOLIDGE

MAP 3, F8

(Nearby towns also listed: Casa Grande, Florence)

An 1800s Apache graveyard here was forever flooded in 1930 by the creation of the Coolidge Dam. This is a good base for exploring the Casa Grande Ruins, which is just outside town. A small farming community of 7,000, Coolidge celebrates its cotton crop each year with its Cotton Days Festival.

Information: **Coolidge Chamber of Commerce** | 320 W. Central Ave., Coolidge, 85228 | 520/723–3009.

Attractions
Casa Grande Ruins National Monument. Casa Grande Ruins National Monument provides an interesting look at a well-preserved structure encountered by European explorers in the 17th century. You can see the remains of a 600-year-old building, the tallest (four-story) Hohokam structure known. There's also a small museum where you can hear talks on Hohokam culture and life. The Hohokam Indians lived in the area until AD 1450, when they mysteriously vanished. It's just north of Coolidge Street on Route 87. | 1100 Ruins Dr. | www.nps.gov/cagr | 520/723–3172 | $4 per vehicle | Daily 8–5.

Coolidge Historical Society. You can view a collection of historical artifacts from Coolidge and the surrounding area. | 161 W. Harding | 520/723–3588 | Free | By appointment only.

ON THE CALENDAR
MAR.: *Coolidge Cotton Days.* A celebration of the cotton crop, this festival includes a street dance, craft demonstrations, a parade, and a cotton ball rolling contest in San Carlos Park. | 520/723–3009.

Dining
Tag's Restaurant. Mexican. Classic pottery surrounds the outside of this restaurant, which serves a wide selection of both Mexican and American dishes. The egg and chorizo burrito is definitely the most popular dish. | 156 N. Arizona Blvd. | 520/723–1013 | Breakfast also available | $3–$9 | AE, D, DC, MC, V.

Lodging
Moonlite Motel. In the middle of town, this tiny motel is only ½ mi from the Casa Grande National Monument. Pets allowed. | 1087 N. Arizona Blvd. | 520/723–3475 | fax 520/723–3745 | 12 rooms | $45 | AE, D, DC, MC, V.

COTTONWOOD

MAP 3, E5

(Nearby towns also listed: Camp Verde, Clarkdale, Jerome, Prescott, Sedona)

Cottonwood, named for the trees that line the washes here, began as a trading community for miners. Today, it's primarily a retirement village of 8,500. Between Sedona and Prescott, it is a good base for exploring Dead Horse Ranch State Park, a 325-acre preserve which offers both high desert and wetlands habitats.

Information: **Cottonwood/Verde Valley Chamber of Commerce** | 1010 S. Main St., Cottonwood, 86326 | 520/634–7593 | www.verdevalley.com.

Attractions
Clemenceau Heritage Museum. You see what classrooms, kitchens, and furniture looked like in the early days of the 20th century. There's also a model train based on the mining trains of the early 1920s. | 1 N. Willard St. | 520/634–2868 | Free (donations accepted) | Wed. 9–12, Fri.–Sun. 11–3.

Dead Horse Ranch State Park. Combining both desert highland and wetland habitats, this state park encompasses 325 acres. Bird-watchers might spot more than 100 different species, depending on the season (bald eagles arrive in winter). Fishing, camping, hiking, and picnic facilities are also available. | 675 Dead Horse Ranch Rd. | www.pr.state.az.us | 520/634–5283 | $4 per vehicle | Daily 8–7.

ON THE CALENDAR
MAY: *Verde Valley Fair.* A carnival offers rides, games, and livestock exhibitions. There are also special children's activities, all at the Cottonwood Fairgrounds. | 520/634–3290.
MAY: *Auto, Airplane and Cycle Show.* This family-oriented event brings the whole town together to view vintage planes and classic cars at the Cottonwood Airport. | 520/634–7593.

Dining
Manzanita Restaurant. Continental. Surprisingly innovative, French-influenced fare is found at this casual restaurant 6 mi west of Cottonwood. Try the wonderful mushroom

soup, duck with orange sauce, or rack of lamb. Extensive wine list. | 11425 Cornville Rd., Cornville | 520/634–8851 | Closed Mon., Tues. | $10–$31 | MC, V.

Ming's House. Chinese. This restaurant, popular with families, is known for its orange chicken and Mongolian beef. There is also an all-day buffet. | 888 S. Main St. | 520/639–2885 | $5–$11 | AE, D, DC, MC, V.

Outsider. American/Casual. Gourmet salads and sandwiches here are made from scratch; the chicken and pastrami are very popular. Outdoor dining under a covered patio is available for patrons. | 901 N. Main St. | 520/634–3829 | Closed weekends. No dinner | $5–$6 | No credit cards.

Lodging

Best Western Cottonwood Inn. This older chain motel is well maintained and clean. Restaurant, room service. Some refrigerators, cable TV. Pool. Hot tub. Laundry facilities. Business services. | 993 S. Main St. | 520/634–5575 or 800/350–0025 | fax 520/634–5576 | www.bestwestern.com | 77 rooms | $69–$129 | AE, D, DC, MC, V.

Cottonwood Super 8 Motel. This standard chain motel is close to local attractions, including Tuzigoot National Monument. Complimentary Continental breakfast. Some refrigerators, cable TV. Pool. Spa. | 800 S. Main St. (U.S. Hwy. 89A & Skyline Dr.) | 520/639–1888 | fax 520/639–2285 | www.super8.com | 52 rooms | $62–$68 | AE, D, DC, MC, V.

Little Daisy Motel. A friendly staff and clean, comfortable rooms await guests at this locally owned motel. Some kitchenettes, cable TV. Pets allowed. | 34 S. Main St. | 520/634–7865 | fax 520/639–3447 | www.littledaisy.com | 23 rooms | $45 | AE, D, DC, MC, V.

Quality Inn. This chain motel is 4 mi from Tuzigoot National Monument. Restaurant, bar, complimentary Continental breakfast. Cable TV. Pool. Hot tub. Business services. | 301 W. Hwy. 89A | 520/634–4207 or 800/228–5151 | fax 520/634–5764 | www.qualityinn.com | 51 rooms | $78 | AE, D, DC, MC, V.

DOUGLAS

MAP 3, H10

(Nearby towns also listed: Bisbee, Sierra Vista)

Twenty-three miles southeast of Bisbee, this Mexican border town of some 15,000 was founded in 1901 by James Douglas to serve as the copper-smelting center for Bisbee mines. Douglas is famous for its ranching and mining history, but with the closing of the Phelps-Dodge mines in the 1980s, it has suffered economically. The international port-of-entry allows easy access to Agua Prieta, Sonora, and all of Mexico. There's a wonderful Mexican restaurant downtown, the Grand Café, that has been featured in *Gourmet* magazine.

Information: **Douglas Chamber of Commerce** | 1125 Pan American Ave., Douglas, 85607 | 520/364–2477 | www.discoverdouglas.com/.

Attractions

Gadsden Hotel. Built in 1907, this turn-of-the-20th-century grand hotel is worth looking at even if you don't stay here. The white marble lobby features a Tiffany mural in stained glass. | 1046 G Ave. | 520/364–4481 | Free | Daily.

Slaughter Ranch/San Bernardino Land Grant National Historic Landmark. Named for John Slaughter, a former Texas ranger and county sheriff, the 300-acre site 17 mi east of Douglas is both a tribute to turn-of-the-20th-century ranching life and a pristine place for bird-watching and visiting the natural springs. You can see the remains of a military outpost established here in 1911. Go east on 15th Street, which turns into Geronimo Trail and leads to the ranch. | 6153 Geronimo Trail, Douglas | 520/558–2474 | www.vtc.net/~sranch | $3 | Wed.– Sun. 10–3.

ON THE CALENDAR

APR.–SEPT.: *Horse Races.* Thoroughbreds race in this popular annual event at the Cochise County Fairgrounds. | 520/364–2477.

MAY: *Cinco de Mayo.* Mexican Independence Day is celebrated each year in Douglas. | 520/364–2477.

SEPT.: *Douglas Fiestas.* Weekly events during the month toast the town's history at Veteran's Memorial Park. | 520/364–2477.

SEPT.: *Cochise County Fair and College Rodeo.* This is an old-fashioned fair with rides, games, livestock exhibits, and special activities for children at the Cochise County Fairgrounds. | 520/364–2477.

Dining

El Conquistador Dining Room. Mexican. Located in the Gadsen Hotel, this spot offers fairly consistent American standards, as well as good burritos and enchiladas. Known for chile. Open-air dining on balcony. | 1046 G Ave. | 520/364–4481 | $7–$14 | AE, D, DC, MC, V.

Grand Café. Mexican. A lively restaurant in a historic building, this place is known for its delicious, homemade Mexican offerings, including cheese-and-potato soup and chiles rellenos. Be sure to see the Marilyn Monroe tribute wall. | 1119 G Ave. | 520/364–2344 | $5–$12 | MC, V.

© Corbis

A GLOSSARY OF SONORAN MEXICAN FOOD

You'll find the largest concentration of good Mexican restaurants in South Tucson, along South 4th and South 6th avenues, and their side streets. Some menus are in Spanish only, so it's helpful to know the key words:

aguas frescas—fresh-fruit drink, sort of a smoothie

albondigas—meatball soup

almendrado—an almond dessert, often the colors of the Mexican flag

birria—traditionally stewed goat, but often made with beef

caldo de queso—cheese-and-potato soup

carne asada—grilled marinated beef

carne seca—sun-dried, marinated beef

carnitas—stewed pork

cazuela—machaca soup

chorizo—spicy pork or pork-and-beef sausage

flautas—rolled, deep-fried tacos

horchata—rice milk and cinnamon drink

machaca—dried beef cooked with tomatoes, onions, chiles, and often egg

menudo—hominy and tripe stew

posole—hominy and pork stew

tortas—sandwich on a white bun

tripitas de leche—tripe (the stomach) of a cow

Las Nubes Steakhouse. Mexican. Bring a healthy appetite when you stop by this restaurant and be sure to try the *parrilladas* (a wide sampling of various meats and appetizers). | 515 Pan American Ave. | 520/364–4936 | $9–$21. | AE, MC, V.

Lodging
Douglas Thriftlodge. This two-story motel is only 1 mi from the Mexican border. Pool. Laundry service. Business services. No pets. | 1030 19th St. | 520/364–8434 | fax 520/364–5687 | 29 rooms | $45 | AE, D, DC, MC, V.

Gadsden Hotel. Built in 1907, this structure has been called "the last of the grand hotels." The white marble staircase in the lobby is particularly grand. The rooms don't live up to the lobby, but it's still a comfortable hotel. Some antiques remain in the rooms as well as in the main lobby. Restaurant. Cable TV. Beauty salon. Laundry facilities. | 1046 G Ave. | www.theriver.com | 520/364–4481 | fax 520/364–4005 | 151 rooms, 9 suites | $40–$85 | AE, D, DC, MC, V.

FLAGSTAFF

MAP 3, E4

FLAGSTAFF

INTRO
ATTRACTIONS
DINING
LODGING

(Nearby towns also listed: Sedona, Williams)

Founded in 1876, Flagstaff is named after a pine tree that was a trail marker for travelers making their way to California. In 1891, it was declared the county seat of Coconino County.

This sleepy college town of almost 60,000, home to Northern Arizona University, is a growing destination for skiers and hikers alike. It's always been a popular stopping point for those traveling along Interstate 40, as the large array of lodging attests. But much of Flagstaff's popularity as an overnight spot stems from a nearby neighbor. Only about 90 mi from the South Rim of the Grand Canyon, Flagstaff has always been a good base for exploring the canyon and surrounding area. But others have discovered that Flagstaff itself is worth a second look. Even with more than 200 restaurants and dozens of hotels and motels, Flagstaff retains its small-town charm. There's a fascinating arboretum, an observatory, and a good symphony.

This region of northern Arizona is geographically diverse, with both desert and rugged woodlands. The surrounding Coconino National Forest has the world's largest contiguous ponderosa pine forest and is home to a variety of wildlife including the American bald eagle and the black bear. The forests, with elevations ranging from 2,600 to 12,633 ft, house plant life from desert cactus to endangered alpine tundra groundsel.

Sunset Crater and Wupatki National Monument are interesting side trips. The former, a volcano that erupted more than 900 years ago, is 15 mi north of Flagstaff. The latter is situated in the rain shadow of the San Francisco Peaks, once home to traders and farmers of the Anasazi and Sinagua people, or Hisatsinom, as their contemporary Hopi descendants call them.

Information: **Flagstaff Chamber of Commerce** | 101 W. Rte. 66, Flagstaff, 86001 | 520/774–4505 | www.flagstaff.az.us.

Flagstaff Visitor Center | 1 E. Rte. 66, Flagstaff, 86001-5588 | 520/774–9541 or 800/842–7293.

Attractions
Arizona Historical Society Pioneer Museum. In a building constructed in 1908 and made of volcanic rock, this museum northwest of Flagstaff was once a hospital for the poor. There are some medical displays (such as an old iron lung), but most of the exhibits involve topics of local history. | 2340 N. Fort Valley Rd. (U.S. 180) | 520/774–6272 | Free | Mon.–Sat. 9–5.

Arizona Snowbowl and Summer Resort. This popular downhill ski resort is 14 mi northwest of Flagstaff. One of Flagstaff's most popular winter attractions, the Snowbowl has 30 runs, four chairlifts, and a vertical drop of 2,300 ft. Though almost a fifth of the runs are classified for advanced skiers, the skiing here is more suited to beginners and intermediates. The summer Sky Ride climbs to 11,500 ft in 25 minutes, affording spectacular views of Coconino National Forest; in summer you can also hike and picnic. | Snowbowl Rd. | 520/779–1951 | www.arizonasnowbowl.com | Mid-Dec.–mid-Apr., daily 9–4.

Flagstaff Nordic Center. More than 25 mi of groomed trails await you at this popular cross-country ski center owned by the Arizona Snowbowl. There are a ski school and equipment rentals on-site. It's 8 mi north of Snowbowl Road on U.S. 180, just beyond Highway 232. | U.S. 180 | 520/779–1951 ext. 195 | www.arizonasnowbowl.com | $10 | Mid-Dec.–mid.-Apr., daily 9–4.

MacDonalds Ranch Trail Rides. In summer, this Scottsdale-based riding stable sets up at Fort Valley Barn, offering trail rides in the Coconino National Forest. Or join an organized hayride and cookout. | U.S. 180 and Snowbowl Rd. | 520/774–4481 | www.arizonasnowbowl.com | Trail rides $24–$36; hayrides $10 per person | Memorial Day–Labor Day, daily 9–5 (last ride leaves at 5).

Scenic Skyride. All summer and into the fall, you can ride this tram up to 11,500 ft in about 25 minutes for fabulous views of Coconino National Forest. From the top, you can see all the way to the Grand Canyon 90 mi away. Fourteen miles north of Flagstaff, take U.S. 180 north to Snowbowl Road, about 7 mi. The skyride is at Agassiz Lodge. | Snowbowl Rd. | 520/779–1951 | www.arizonasnowbowl.com | $9 | Memorial Day–Labor Day, daily 10–4; Labor Day–mid-Oct., Fri.–Sun. 10–4.

Coconino National Forest. Encompassing 1.8 million acres, Coconino National Forest rises on all sides at the outskirts of Sedona and Flagstaff. Its rugged alpine terrain is cool in summer and very cold in winter. There are extensive hiking trails as well as picnic facilities. | Supervisor's Office, 2323 E. Greenlaw La. | www.fs.fed.us/r3/coconino | 520/527–3600 | Free | Office weekdays 7:30–4:30; forest daily.

Peaks Ranger Station. This district office north of Flagstaff has useful hiking and recreational guides to the Coconino National Forest. | 5075 N. U.S. 89 | 520/526–0866 | fax 520/527–8288 | www.fs.fed.us/r3/coconino | Free | Office weekdays 7:30–4:30; forest daily.

Historic Downtown District. Some excellent examples of Victorian, Tudor Revival, and early Art Deco architecture in this district in downtown Flagstaff give a feel for life in this former logging and railroad town. | Between Beaver and San Francisco Sts. | 520/774–4505 | Free | Daily.

Babbitt Brothers Building. This was originally a building-supply store, constructed in 1888, but was later turned into a department store by David Babbitt, a member of one of Flagstaff's wealthiest founding families. | 12 E. Aspen St. | Free | Daily.

Hotel Monte Vista. This hotel was built in 1926 via public subscription when the community raised $200,000 in 60 days. Over the years it has played host to Hollywood stars and presidents. | 100 N. San Francisco St. | 520/779–6971 | www.hotelmontevista.com | Free | Daily.

Santa Fe Depot. This Tudor Revival–style structure was constructed in the early 1900s. Today, it houses the historic district's visitor center, where a walking-tour map of the area is available. It's still a working Amtrak station. | 1 E. Rte. 66 | 520/774–4505 | Free | Daily.

Vail Building. Built in 1888, this brick Art Deco–influenced structure was covered with stucco in 1939. It now houses Sweet Life, an ice-cream parlor. | 1 N. San Francisco St. | Free | Daily.

Lowell Observatory. At this historic 1894 observatory 1 mi west of Flagstaff, Clyde Tombaugh discovered Pluto; other work here led to the theory of an expanding universe. At the Steele Visitor Center, you can view astronomy exhibits, hear lectures, and look at the sun through a solar telescope. Throughout the year, the observatory is open for night viewing and special presentations, but the days and hours vary monthly. Take Interstate 17 to Milton Street. | 1400 W. Mars Hill Rd. | www.lowell.edu | 520/774–2096 | $4, with separate admission for night viewing | Apr.–Oct., daily 9–5; Nov.–Mar., daily noon–5; night viewing varies monthly.

Mormon Lake Ski Center. A cross-country ski center 25 mi southeast of Flagstaff and 1.3 mi south of Mormon Lake with 16 mi of groomed trails and a restaurant on the premises. | Mormon Lake Rd. | 520/354–2240 | $5 and up | Nov.–Mar., daily 9–5.

Museum Club. For real Route 66 color, don't miss this local institution, fondly known as the Zoo because the building housed an extensive taxidermy collection in the late 1930s. This gigantic log cabin is constructed around five trees and now functions as a popular country-and-western club. | 3404 E. Rte. 66 | 520/526–9434 | www.museumclub.com | Free | Sun.–Thurs. 11–1 AM, Fri.–Sat. 11–3 AM.

Museum of Northern Arizona. This museum 3 mi north of Flagstaff is highly regarded for its research in the natural and cultural history of the Colorado Plateau. Artifacts tell the story of life here from 15,000 BC to the present. There is an actual Hopi kiva ceremonial room (not a replica) as well as katsinas and other Native American arts and crafts. Even the building itself, built of native stone in a tree-shaded glen in 1928, is worth seeing. | 3101 N. Fort Valley Rd. (U.S. 180) | 520/774–5211 | www.musnaz.org | $5 | Daily 9–5.

Northern Arizona University. This university was founded in 1899 and is at the base of the San Francisco Peaks. Annual enrollment is close to 20,000. NAU offers degrees in more that 84 majors; nationally recognized programs include environmental science and engineering. | Milton Rd. and University Dr. | 520/523–2491 or 888/667–3628 | www.nau.edu | Free | Daily.

Northern Arizona University Observatory. This observatory was built by Dr. Arthur Adel formerly of the Lowell Observatory, in 1952. It's just north of the Walkup Skydome. Visitors are free to peer through the 24-inch telescope. | NAU campus, Bldg. 47, S. San Francisco St. | 520/523–8121 | Free | Fri. 7:30 PM–10 PM.

Riordan Mansion State Historic Park. This park is a testament to Flagstaff's logging days. Its central attraction is a 13,000-square-ft, 40-room Arts and Crafts mansion built in 1904 for timber moguls Michael and Timothy Riordan. It was designed by Charles Whittlesley, who also built the El Tovar Hotel at the Grand Canyon. Everything on display—family photos, furniture, and the like—is original to the house; much of the furniture is by Gustav Stickley. Guided tours available on the hour. Take Interstate 40 (exit 190) or Interstate 17 (exit Milton Road). | 409 Riordan Rd. | www.pr.state.az.us | 520/779–4395 | $4 | May–Oct., daily 8:30–5; Nov.–Apr., daily 10:30–5.

Sunset Crater Volcano National Monument. This 1,000-ft cinder cone 17 mi north of Flagstaff was an active volcano 900 years ago. Its final eruption contained iron and sulfur, which lends the rim a glow reminiscent of a sunset, hence the crater's name. You can hike around, but not into, the crater. Take U.S. 89 north for 12 mi; turn right onto the road marked "Sunset Crater," and go another 2 mi to the visitor center. | Sunset Crater-Wupatki Loop Rd. | www.nps.gov/sucr | 520/526–0502 | $3 (includes admission to Wupatki National Monument) | May–Sept., daily 8–6; Sept.–May, daily 9–5.

Walnut Canyon National Monument. More than 300 dwellings here were built by the Sinagua about 700 years ago but then were abandoned around 1300. But the cliff dwellings weren't discovered by Europeans until 1883. If you take the 1-mi Island Trail from the visitor center, you can descend 185 ft and actually walk inside some of the dwellings, getting a good sense of what life might have been like back then. Guides conduct tours on Wednesday, Saturday, and Sunday from Memorial Day through Labor Day. Go 7 mi east of Flagstaff on Interstate 40 to exit 204, then 3 mi south. | Walnut Canyon Rd. | www.nps.gov/waca | 520/526–3367 or 520/556–7152 | $3 | July–Aug., daily 8–6; Mar.–Apr. and Sept.–Nov., daily 8–5; Dec.–Feb., daily 9–5.

Wupatki National Monument. This site 30 mi north of Flagstaff via U.S. 89 was once home to a group of Sinagua, established when nearby Sunset Crater erupted some 900 years ago. The immediate area was settled around 1100 but was abandoned by 1250. Wupatki means "tall house" in the Hopi language—the largest dwelling here was three stories high. Three other ruins can be visited, but others are closed to the public. Go north on U.S. 89 for 12 mi; turn right onto the road marked "Sunset Crater" and go 20 mi beyond the Sunset Crater Visitor Center. | Sunset Crater-Wupatki Loop Rd. | www.nps.gov/wupa | 520/774-9541 or 800/842-7293 | $3 (includes admission to Sunset Crater) | May–Sept., daily 8–6; Sept.–May, daily 9–5.

ON THE CALENDAR

FEB.: *Winterfest.* Winterfest showcases Flagstaff's winter landscape and has more than 100 events, including sled-dog races, nordic and alpine skiing competitions, stargazing, special children's activities, sleigh rides, cultural events, and historic walking tours. | 520/774-4505 or 800/842-7293.

MAY–SEPT.: *A Celebration of Native American Art.* Zuni, Hopi, and Navajo art are displayed at the Museum of Northern Arizona. | 520/774-5213.

AUG.: *Summerfest in Flagstaff.* Summerfest is a gathering of artists and musicians from around the United States at the Fort Tuthill Fairgrounds. | 520/774-9541.

SEPT.: *Coconino County Fair.* Rides, games, livestock exhibits, and special children's activities are the draw at this large, old-fashioned Labor Day weekend fair at the Coconino County Fairgrounds. | 520/774-5139.

NOV.–DEC.: *Annual Holiday Lights Festival.* More than 2 million lights are ablaze at this annual festival at the Little America Hotel. | 520/779-7979 or 800/435-2493.

Dining

Beaver Street Brewery. American/Casual. This large space is both a restaurant and microbrewery, known for burgers and wood-fired, California-style pizzas. Try the Enchanted Forest, with Brie, artichoke pesto, Portobello mushrooms, roasted red pepper, and spinach, or perhaps the great chocolate bread pudding. The raspberry ale is a local favorite. | 11 S. Beaver St. | 520/779-0079 | $10–$14 | AE, D, MC, V.

Black Bart's Steakhouse Saloon & Old West Theater. American. Part of an RV park and antiques store, it's a bustling place where you drink from mason jars and are served by Northern Arizona University students, who entertain while they wait on tables. Known for steaks, cowboy beans, salads, and sourdough biscuits. | 2760 E. Butler Ave. | 520/779-3142 | No lunch | $12–$25 | AE, D, MC, V.

Buster's Restaurant. American. Near Northern Arizona University, Buster's offers casual dining. Known for fresh fish, giant burgers, and mesquite-grilled steak. Try the *lahvosh* appetizer, a crispy flat bread heaped with everything from smoked salmon to mushrooms. Raw bar. Kids' menu, early-bird dinners. | 1800 S. Milton Rd. | 520/774-5155 | $9–$19 | AE, D, DC, MC, V.

Café Espress. American/Casual. This lively natural-foods restaurant offers a predominately vegetarian menu. Known for tempeh burgers, pita pizzas, and salads. But there are usually also daily chicken and fish specials. | 16 N. San Francisco St. | 520/774-0541 | Breakfast also available | $6–$9 | AE, MC, V.

Café Olé. Mexican. The kitschy decor, including chile-pepper strings, a neon cactus, and a pastel mural, makes for an upbeat atmosphere at this family-run restaurant. Vegetarian green-chile-and-cheese tamales and the best guacamole in town are among the specialties. | 119 San Francisco St. | 520/774-8272 | Closed Sat.–Mon. | $6–$9 | No credit cards.

Chez Marc Bistro. French. This upscale bistro is somewhat rustic but also decidedly upscale. Try the sautéed veal loin, Australian rack of lamb, or sterling salmon. Open-air dining with view of the nearby mountain peaks. There's also an on-premises cigar club. | 503 Humphreys St. | 520/774-1343 | No lunch Mon.–Wed. | $22–$36 | AE, D, DC, MC, V.

Cottage Place. Continental. This small and intimate restaurant, in a 1901 cottage, is known for traditional dishes, such as chateaubriand, charbroiled lamb chops, and rack of lamb. Its wine list is award-winning. Kids' menu. | 126 W. Cottage Ave. | 520/774–8431 | Closed Mon. No lunch | $21–$40 | AE, MC, V.

Dara Thai. Thai. Many of the dishes at this wonderful Thai eatery in the Western Hills Motel are prepared with tofu instead of meat or poultry. Don't pass up the homemade coconut ice cream served with chopped peanuts. | 14 S. San Francisco St. | 520/774–0047 | Closed Sun. | $7–$12 | MC, V.

Down Under New Zealand Restaurant. New Zealand. This downtown restaurant's cozy dining room is filled with businesspeople for lunch and, when the lights are turned down, couples for dinner. The menu offers traditional New Zealand dishes and ingredients, including lamb stew, pine nut–crusted chicken breast, and stuffed pork loin. There's an outdoor terrace on historic Heritage Square. | 6 E. Aspen Ave. | 520/774–6677 | Closed Sun. No lunch Sat. | $14–$24 | AE, MC, V.

Fiddler's. American. This rustic, casual, western-style restaurant is popular with locals for hearty fare like steaks and barbecue. Kids' menu. | 702 Milton Rd. | 520/774–6689 | Breakfast also available | $8–$19 | AE, MC, V.

Hunan West Restaurant. Chinese. With an imposing dragon decorating the back wall and white cloths dressing the tables, this restaurant on the west side of Flagstaff has more atmosphere than you might expect from its strip-mall setting. The hot-and-sour soup is super, as is the "eight-treasure" shrimp and chicken. | University Plaza Shopping Center, 1302 S. Plaza Way | 520/779–2229 | Closed Mon. | $7–$14 | AE, D, DC, MC, V.

Kachina Downtown. Mexican. A colorful cantina known for typical Mexican fare like enchiladas, tacos, and tostadas. | 522 E. Rte. 66 | 520/779–1944 | $8–$17 | AE, D, DC, MC, V.

Macy's European Coffeehouse and Bakery. Café. You'll find the best coffee in town in this small spot in historic downtown Flagstaff, along with inexpensive pastas, salads, and sandwiches. | 14 S. Beaver St. | 520/774–2243 | $7–$11 | No credit cards.

Mamma Luisa Italian. Italian. A small, casual spot, where you can order great veal *saltimbocca*, chicken marsala, or veal parmigiana. Kids' menu. | 2710 N. Steves Blvd. | 520/526–6809 | No lunch | $8–$17 | AE, D, MC, V.

Marc's Café. French. This contemporary and casual brasserie is known for its rotisserie duckling, jambalaya, and pork tenderloin crêpes. You can dine outdoors on a patio in front of the restaurant. Kids' menu. | 801 S. Milton Rd. | 520/556–0093 | $15–$24 | AE, D, DC, MC, V.

Pasto. Italian. Come to this casual downtown spot for good, reasonably priced southern Italian food, including pasta, chicken marsala, and artichoke orzo. The courtyard in the back has a romantic, urban feel. | 19 E. Aspen Ave. | 520/779–1937 | No lunch | $9–$23 | MC, V.

Sakura Restaurant. Japanese. The fish here is flown in several times a week from the West Coast, but if sushi isn't your thing, you can have food cooked on the teppanyaki grill, with chefs chopping and sautéing on the table in front of you. Kids' menu. | 1175 W. Rte. 66 | 520/773–9118 | No lunch Sun. | $15–$34 | AE, D, DC, MC, V.

Salsa Brava. Mexican. This cheerful spot favors lighter grilled dishes that are popular in Guadalajara. They have the only salsa bar in town. Try the fish tacos, or on weekends the huevos rancheros. Open-air dining on side patio. Kids' menu. | 1800 S. Milton Rd. | 520/774–1083 | Breakfast also available weekends | $8–$15 | AE, MC, V.

Lodging

Amerisuites. This all-suite chain hotel is less than a mile from the intersection of Interstate 17 and Interstate 40, ¼ mi from Northern Arizona University on the south side of Flagstaff. Off Interstate 17 North, exit 341. Complimentary Continental breakfast. In-room data ports, kitchenettes, microwaves, refrigerators, cable TV, in-room VCRs. Gym. Pool. Hot tub. Laundry facilities. Business services, airport shuttle. Some pets allowed. | 2455 S. Beulah Blvd. | 520/774–8042 or 800/833–1516 | fax 520/774–5524 | www.amerisuites.com | 117 suites | $119–$159 | AE, D, DC, MC, V.

Arizona Mountain Inn. This Tudor-style inn borders the Coconino National Forest, 2 mi southeast of Flagstaff. Suites are in the main building, but most accommodations are in cabins (all with full kitchens and fireplaces) scattered around the 13-acre property. Off Interstate 17 North, exit 339 (Lake Mary Road), then 1 mi east. Picnic areas. No air-conditioning, full kitchens (in cabins), no room phones. Hiking, bicycles. Playground. Laundry facilities. Business services. Some pets allowed (fee). | 4200 Lake Mary Rd. | 520/774–8959 or 800/239–5236 | fax 520/774–8837 | www.arizonamountaininn.com | 3 suites, 17 cabins | $90–$110 suites, $110 cabins | D, MC, V.

Best Western Kings House Motel. Rooms at this two-story motel on the east side of Flagstaff are spacious and tidy. It's located on historic Route 66. Restaurant, bar, complimentary Continental breakfast. Cable TV. Pool. Some pets allowed. | 1560 E. Rte. 66 | 520/774–7186 | fax 520/774–7188 | www.bestwestern.com | 57 rooms | $69–$89 | AE, D, DC, MC, V.

Best Western Pony Soldier Motel. This chain motel is on old Route 66, east of historic downtown Flagstaff. Restaurant, bar, complimentary Continental breakfast, room service. Cable TV. Pool. Barbershop, beauty salon, hot tub. Business services. | 3030 E. Rte. 66 | 520/526–2388 or 800/356–4143 | fax 520/527–8329 | www.bestwestern.com | 90 rooms | $69–$89 | AE, D, DC, MC, V.

Birch Tree Inn. This historic home in a tree-filled neighborhood near downtown is nicely appointed with antiques. Complimentary breakfast. TV in common area. Outdoor hot tub. No pets. No kids under 10. No smoking. | 824 W. Birch Ave. | 520/774–1042 or 888/774–1042 | info@birchtreeinn.com | www.birchtreeinn.com | 5 rooms (2 with shared bath) | $69–$109 | AE, D, MC, V.

Comfi Cottages of Flagstaff. These 1920s cottages in a residential neighborhood less than ½ mi from downtown Flagstaff offer more personal accommodations than a motel but with more privacy than a traditional B&B. They come well stocked with breakfast fixings that you prepare yourself, as well as barbecue grills and bicycles. You rent an entire cottage, which ranges in size from one to four bedrooms. Picnic area, complimentary breakfast. Cable TV, TV and VCR in common area. Bicycles. Laundry facilities. | 1612 N. Aztec St. | 520/774–0731 or 888/774–0731 | fax 520/773–7286 | www.comficottages.com | 14 rooms in 6 cottages | $105–$250 | D, MC, V.

Comfort Inn. This two-story motel is a mile north of Interstate 40 and just a few blocks from the University of Northern Arizona. Complimentary Continental breakfast. Cable TV. Pool. Some pets allowed. | 914 S. Milton Rd. | 520/774–7326 or 800/228–5150 | fax 520/774–7328 | www.comfortinn.com | 67 rooms | $69–$95 | AE, D, DC, MC, V.

Days Inn–East. This comfortable chain accommodation is popular with families. Complimentary Continental breakfast. Some refrigerators, cable TV. Pool. Hot tub. Laundry facilities. Business services. Free parking. | 3601 E. Lockett Rd. | www.daysinn.com | 520/527–1477 or 800/435–6343 | fax 520/527–0228 | 52 rooms, 2 suites | $49–$129, $69–$179 suites | AE, D, DC, MC, V.

Days Inn–Route 66. This large chain motel is 1 mi west of historic downtown, on old Route 66. Restaurant, bar, complimentary Continental breakfast. Cable TV. Pool. Laundry facilities. Business services. Some pets allowed. | 1000 W. Rte. 66 | 520/774–5221 or 800/422–4470 | fax 520/774–4977 | www.daysinn.com | 157 rooms | $45–$120 | AE, D, DC, MC, V.

Embassy Suites. This upscale, all-suite hotel is on the south side of Flagstaff, 1 mi north of Interstate 40, exit 195B, and less than 1 mi from Northern Arizona University. Each room has a private bedroom and two televisions. Picnic area, complimentary breakfast. In-room data ports, microwaves, refrigerators, cable TV. Pool. Hot tub. Gym. Business services. Some pets allowed. | 706 S. Milton Rd. | 520/774–4333 | fax 520/774–0216 | www.embassyflagstaff.com | 119 suites | $109–$164 suites | AE, D, DC, MC, V.

Fairfield Inn by Marriott. This three-story chain motor hotel is on the south side of Flagstaff, north of Interstate 40 and 1 mi from Northern Arizona University. Complimentary Continental breakfast. In-room data ports, cable TV. Pool. Laundry service. Business services. | 2005 S. Milton Rd. | 520/773–1300 or 800/228–2800 | fax 520/773–1462 | www.fairfieldinn.com | 135 rooms | $65–$99 | AE, D, DC, MC, V.

Flagstaff University/Grand Canyon Travelodge. This two-story motel is on the southwest side of Flagstaff, two blocks from Northern Arizona University and within walking distance of restaurants. Complimentary Continental breakfast. Cable TV. Hot tub, sauna. Business services. Some pets allowed. | 801 W. Rte. 66 | 520/774–3381 | fax 520/774–1648 | www.travelodge.com | 49 rooms | $89–$109 | AE, D, DC, MC, V.

Hampton Inn. This chain hotel is on the eastern edge of Flagstaff, off historic Route 66. Off Interstate 40, exit 201; hotel is ½ mi up Fanning, on Lockett. Complimentary Continental breakfast. Cable TV. Pool. Hot tub. Laundry service. Business services. | 3501 E. Lockett Rd. | 520/526–1885 or 800/426–7866 | fax 520/526–9885 | www.hamptoninn.com | 48 rooms, 2 suites | $69–$119, $139 suites | AE, D, DC, MC, V.

Holiday Inn. This hotel is on the east side of Flagstaff, just off Interstate 40, exit 198. Restaurant, bar, room service. In-room data ports, cable TV. Pool. Hot tub. Gym. Laundry facilities. Airport shuttle. Pets allowed. | 2320 Lucky La. | 520/526–1150 or 800/533–2754 | fax 520/779–2610 | www.holiday-inn.com | 156 rooms, 1 suite | $59–$119, $150 suite | AE, D, DC, MC, V.

Hanford Hotel. This hotel is just 1½ mi from Northern Arizona State University, exit 198 off Interstate 40. Some of the rooms have views of the San Francisco Peak and there is an elegant two-story fireplace room which is ideal for spending a relaxing evening. Restaurant, bar, room service. Some refrigerators, cable TV. Pool. Hot tub, sauna. Video games. Business services, airport shuttle. Pets allowed (fee). | 2200 E. Butler Ave. | 520/779–6944 | fax 520/774–3990 | 83 rooms, 18 suites | $79, $99–$119 suites | AE, D, DC, MC, V.

Hotel Monte Vista. Over the years many Hollywood stars have stayed at this downtown hotel built in 1926. The lobby is appealing, but rooms and hallways are somewhat dark. Bar. Cable TV. Pets allowed (fee). | 100 N. San Francisco St. | 520/779–6971 or 800/545–3068 | fax 520/779–2904 | www.hotelmontevista.com/home.html | 48 rooms | $65–$125 | AE, D, DC, MC, V.

Inn at 410. Built in 1894, this craftsman-style home is within walking distance of historic downtown Flagstaff, in a quiet but convenient area. It's an inviting, upscale alternative to the usual Flagstaff chain motels. Picnic area, complimentary breakfast. Refrigerators, some in-room hot tubs, no room phones, no TV. No smoking. | 410 N. Leroux St. | 520/774–0088 or 800/774–2008 | fax 520/774–6354 | www.inn410.com | 6 rooms, 3 suites | $125–$145, $160–$175 suites | MC, V.

Jeanette's. If you prefer the clean lines of 1920s design to Victorian froufrou, consider this Art Deco B&B. One room has a private porch, another a fireplace. Complimentary breakfast. No room phones, no TV. No pets. No kids under 10. No smoking. | 3380 E. Lockett Rd. | 520/527–1912 or 800/752–1912. | www.jeanettesbb.com | 4 rooms | $99 | D, MC, V.

Little America Hotel of Flagstaff. The biggest hotel in Flagstaff is surrounded by a 500-acre evergreen forest on the east side of town; it's also one of the most popular places in town. Rooms are plush, with extras like bathroom phones. Just off Interstate 40, exit 198. 2 restaurants, bar, room service. Refrigerators, cable TV. Pool. Hot tub. Gym, hiking, volleyball. Playground. Laundry facilities, laundry service. Business services, airport shuttle. | 2515 E. Butler Ave. | 520/779–2741 or 800/352–4386 | fax 520/779–7983 | www.flagstaff.littleamerica.com | 241 rooms, 7 suites | $119–$129, $150–$225 suites | AE, D, DC, MC, V.

Quality Inn. This two-story chain motel is in a quiet area on south side of Flagstaff, less than 1 mi from Northern Arizona University. Just off Interstate 40, exit 195B. Restaurant, bar. Some in-room data ports, cable TV. Pool. Laundry service. Business services. | 2000 S. Milton Rd. | 520/774–8771 | fax 520/773–9382 | www.qualityinn.com | 96 rooms | $79–$129 | AE, D, DC, MC, V.

Radisson Woodlands Hotel Flagstaff. This upscale chain hotel stands west of downtown Flagstaff on historic Route 66. 2 restaurants (*see* Sakura Restaurant, *above*), bar, room service. Some microwaves, some refrigerators, cable TV. Pool. Hot tub, sauna, steam room. Gym. Laundry facilities. Business services. | 1175 W. Rte. 66 | 520/773–8888 or 800/333–3333 | fax 520/773–0597 | www.radisson.com | 168 rooms, 15 suites | $109–$119, $129–$139 suites | AE, D, DC, MC, V.

Ramada Limited West. This chain hotel is off Interstate 40, exit 195B, on the southwest side of Flagstaff. Its location less than a mile from Northern Arizona University makes it popular with NAU parents. Complimentary Continental breakfast. Microwaves, refrigerators, cable TV. Pool. Hot tub. Gym. Laundry facilities. Business services. Pets allowed (fee). | 2755 Woodland Village Blvd. | 520/773–1111 | fax 520/774–1449 | www.ramada.com | 87 suites | $59–$99 | AE, D, DC, MC, V.

Super 8. This two-story chain motel is on the east side of Flagstaff, off Interstate 40, exit 201. Cable TV. Business services. Pets allowed. | 3725 N. Kasper | 520/526–0818 or 888/324–9131 | fax 520/526–8786 | www.super8.com | 90 rooms | $59–$69 | AE, D, DC, MC, V.

FLORENCE

MAP 3, F8

(Nearby towns also listed: Casa Grande, Coolidge, Superior)

An original Arizona territorial town (founded in 1866), Florence, with a population of a little over 7,500, is a good base for exploring the ancient Hohokam Indian Ruins at Casa Grande National Monument, which are just outside nearby Coolidge. Walking around the town's historic district is a good way to learn about territorial architecture. Buildings, like the Conrad Brunenkant City Bakery (built in 1889), are well preserved. It's still a quiet town, with deep agricultural and mining roots, though like many Arizona towns, it offers itself as a place to retire.

Information: Florence Chamber of Commerce | Box 929, 291 N. Bailey St., Florence, 85232 | 520/868–9433 or 800/437–9433 | www.florenceaz.org.

Pinal County Visitor's Center. The folks here will answer your questions and give you brochures about attractions in the area. | 330 E. Butte St., 85232 | 520/868–4331 or 800/469–0175 | Free | Mon., Fri. 8–4; Tues.–Thurs., Sat. 9–3; Sun. 11–4.

Attractions

McFarland State Historic Park. The museum here houses memorabilia of former Governor and U.S. Senator Ernest W. McFarland. It's housed in the former Pinal County Courthouse, built in 1878. | Ruggles Ave. and Main St. | 520/868–5216 | www.pr.state.az.us | $2 | Thurs.–Mon. 8–5.

Pinal County Historical Society Museum. Here you'll find exhibits of early 20th-century furniture, Native American tools and handcrafts, and early 20th-century photographs. | 715 S. Main St. | 520/868–4382 | Free | Sept.–mid-July, Wed.–Sat. 11–4, Sun. noon–4.

ON THE CALENDAR

FEB.: *Florence Home Tour.* Florence's residents open their historic homes during this annual home tour. | 520/868–9433 or 800/437–9433.
MAY: *Cinco De Mayo.* This celebration of Florence's ties to Mexico includes a parade, mariachi bands, and homemade Mexican foods. | 520/868–9433 or 800/437–9433.
NOV.: *Junior Parada.* This Thanksgiving Day weekend event is the nation's oldest sanctioned junior rodeo. There's also a parade. | 520/868–9433 or 800/437–9433.

Dining

Old Pueblo Restaurant. Mexican. Down-home Mexican food is found at this local favorite. Known for burritos, chimichangas, and a Friday-night shrimp-and-catfish dinner. Kids' menu. | 505 S. Main St. | 520/868–4784 | Breakfast also available; closed Sat. | $8–$17 | AE, D, DC MC, V.

Lodging

Rancho Sonora Inn and RV Park. In this 1930s adobe the rooms open onto a walled courtyard, where the pool is. Picnic area, complimentary Continental breakfast. Some kitchenettes, some microwaves, some refrigerators, some room phones. Pool. Hot tub. Laundry facilities. Business services. Some pets allowed. No smoking. | 9198 N. Hwy. 79 | 520/868–8000 or 800/205–6817 | fax 520/868–8000 | florenceaz.org/ranchosonora | 9 rooms, 4 suites | $74, $75–$135 suites | AE, MC, V.

Taylor's Bed and Breakfast. Built in 1872, this historic inn has a Spanish-style patio surrounded by flowers and native plants where guests can rest and relax. Complimentary Continental breakfast. Cable TV. Laundry facilities. No smoking. | 321 N. Bailey | 520/868–3497 | florenceaz.org | 3 rooms | $45–$65 | D, MC.

FREDONIA

MAP 3, D1

(Nearby town also listed: Grand Canyon National Park)

Fredonia is a small community of 1,200 about 76 mi from the North Rim of the Grand Canyon. It's often referred to as the gateway to the North Rim, but it's also relatively close to Zion and Bryce Canyon national parks.

Information: **Fredonia Town Office** | 130 N. Main St., Fredonia, 86022 | 520/643–7241.

Attractions

Pipe Spring National Monument. Ninety miles from the Grand Canyon's North Rim and 14 mi from Fredonia, this park contains Winsor Castle, a restored rock fort that was the first telegraph station in Arizona territory when it was built in 1871. There are the remains of a cattle ranch run by Mormon settlers, and exhibits of southwestern frontier life. In summer there are interesting living-history demonstrations, along with hiking and camping. | Hwy. 389, | www.nps.gov/pisp | 520/643–7105 | $2 | Oct.–May, daily 8–4:30; June–Sept. daily 7:30–5:30. Winsor Castle tours are on the hr and half hr when the monument is open.

ON THE CALENDAR

SEPT.: *Northern Arizona Fair.* A variety of agricultural displays, a talent show, and a beauty contest are among the highlights of this fair. | 520/643–7241.

Dining

Crazy Jug Restaurant. American. Log-cabin decor and a friendly staff await patrons. Be sure to try the mushroom hamburger and baby-back ribs. | 465 S. Main St. | 520/643–7712 | Breakfast also available | $8–$16 | AE, DC, MC, V.

Nedra's Cafe. Mexican. Native American dreamcatchers and other artwork decorate this casual spot that has been serving up delicious Mexican and southwestern cuisine since 1957. The chimichangas and fajitas are popular, and the homemade hot sauce is renowned. In winter months hours vary depending on weather conditions, daylight, and such. Kids' menu. | 165 N. Main St. | 520/643–7591 | Breakfast also available; closed Mar.–Oct. (Nov.–Feb. call for hrs) | $4–$11 | AE, MC, V.

Lodging

Crazy Jug Motel. All the rooms at this basic motel are furnished with rustic log furniture and decorated in southwestern colors. Restaurant. Cable TV. Pets allowed. | 465 S. Main St. | 520/643–7752 | fax 520/643–7759 | www.xpressweb.com/crazyjug | 14 rooms | $35–$45 | AE, DC, MC, V.

GANADO

MAP 3, H3

(Nearby towns also listed: Chinle, Window Rock)

This tiny town is best known as the home of the Hubbell Trading Post National Historic Site, which hasn't changed much in the last 50 years. It's still an active trading post, with bulk foods lining the shelves. Ganado makes an alternative base for exploring Canyon de Chelly, which is 32 mi north (*see* Chinle).

Information: Hubbell Trading Post | Box 150, Ganado, 86505 | 520/755–3475.

Attractions

Hubbell Trading Post National Historic Site. This trading post 1 mi west of Ganado was established in 1878 by John Lorenzo Hubbell, a merchant and friend of the Navajo people. During an 1886 smallpox epidemic, he turned his home into a hospital to care for the sick and dying. Tours of the Hubbell home are available to visitors. The trading post itself still operates. | Rte. 264 | 520/755–3475 | www.nps.gov/hutr | $2 | Daily 8–5.

ON THE CALENDAR

APR., AUG.: *Native American Art Auction.* Held semiannually, this auction at the Hubbell Trading Post showcases the artwork of the Navajo and Hopi nations. Items on display include rugs, baskets, pottery, jewelry, and paintings. | 520/755–3475.

Dining

Ramon's Restaurant. Native American. While the main focus of the menu is on Native American food, this small restaurant also serves Mexican and American specialties. The Navajo burger and mutton soup are very popular. It's next to the Ganado Post Office. | Hwy. 264 | 520/755–3404 | Closed Sun. No dinner Sat. | $5–$9 | No credit cards.

GILA BEND

MAP 3, D8

(Nearby towns also listed: Ajo, Casa Grande)

This town of 1,700 takes its name from its location on the precise spot where the Gila River changes its southern direction and turns westward. The area was first visited by Europeans when Father Eusebio Kino came to the site, then a Hohokam Village, in 1699. Near Oatman, Gila Bend's Painted Rock petroglyphs draw visitors year-round. There are lots of hiking trails and camping facilities nearby.

Information: Gila Bend Chamber of Commerce | Box CC, 644 W. Pima St., Gila Bend | 520/683–2002.

Attractions

Painted Rocks Petroglyphs Site. These petroglyphs, created by prehistoric peoples centuries ago, line a winding trail through a beautiful rock park 25 mi northwest of Gila Bend. There are also campsites and picnic tables. Go west from Gila Bend on Interstate 8 to exit 102,

then north on Painted Rocks Dam Road. | Rocky Point Rd. | 602/780–8090 |
phoenix.az.blm.gov/paint.htm | Free | Daily.

ON THE CALENDAR
APR.: *Butterfield Stage Days.* Bring the entire family to watch a ranch rodeo that
includes wild cow milking and wild horse racing, and a parade. | 520/683–2002.

Dining
Exit West. Mexican. Housed in a former gas station, this eatery is decorated with gas
pumps and pictures of the old station. Most people like to create their own platter, with
the Mexican pizza and enchiladas among the more popular selections. | 2891 Butterfield
Trail | 520/683–6458 | Breakfast also available | $5–$11 | AE, D, DC, MC, V.

Lodging
Best Western Space Age Lodge. An unusual-looking, single-level chain motel with an
aeronautical theme. Photos of space travel decorate the basic rooms. Restaurant. Some
refrigerators, cable TV. Pool. Hot tub. Pets allowed. | 401 E. Pima St. | 520/683–2273 | fax 520/
683–2273 | www.bestwestern.com | 41 rooms | $65–$85 | AE, D, DC, MC, V.

Gila Bend Super 8 Motel. This standard chain motel is 1 mi east of Highway 89 at Inter-
state 8, exit 119, overlooking the desert. Restaurant. Cable TV. Pool. Business services. | 2888
Butterfield Trail | 520/683–6311 | fax 520/683–2120. | www.super8.com | 63 rooms | $45–$56
| AE, D, DC, MC, V.

GLENDALE

MAP 3, E7

(Nearby towns also listed: Chandler, Mesa, Phoenix, Scottsdale, Tempe)

Established in 1892 as a cotton-farming center, Glendale is now best known for its antiques
shops. With a population of 211,000, it's Arizona's fourth-largest city and is a major suburb
on the northwest side of Phoenix. Glendale was settled more than a century ago when
W. J. Murphy's dam and canal brought water to the barren desert area, allowing many
immigrants to settle here and farm the rich soil. Railroad service and an ice plant made
this agricultural center Arizona's largest shipping center as well. During World War II,
pilots from across the nation and foreign countries converged on what was then a quiet
farm town, training at Luke and Thunderbird fields. After the war, thousands of returning airmen made Glendale their home. Its present-day economic base is tourism and
agriculture, and many residents commute to nearby Phoenix.

Information: Glendale Chamber of Commerce | 7105 N. 59th Ave., Glendale, 85301 | 623/
937–4754 or 800/437–8669 | www.glendaleazchamber.org.

Attractions
Sahuaro Ranch. Listed on the National Register of Historic Places, this turn-of-the-20th-
century Glendale homestead has been converted into an 80-acre historical park. A free
trolley takes visitors through downtown Glendale, including Old Towne and Caitlin Court,
the main shopping district. | 59th Ave. and Mountain View Rd. | 623/939–5782 | Free |
Grounds: daily 6 AM–7 PM; exhibits: Sept.–May., Wed.–Fri. 10–2, Sat. 10–4, Sun. noon–4, or
by appointment.

ON THE CALENDAR
MAR.: *WorldPort.* This cultural and ethnic festival includes live music, traditional
dance, ethnic food, and a bazaar of international merchandise on the Thunderbird
Graduate School campus. | 623/930–2299.

NOV.: *Sahuaro Ranch Days.* Glendale's farming roots are the focus of this annual celebration that includes a parade, music, food, and farm history exhibits at Sahuaro Ranch. | 623/939–5782.

Dining

Cougan's. American/Casual. This microbrewery is noisy, but the eclectic menu makes up for the hubbub with such favorites as New Zealand lamb chops, grilled ahi tuna, and fish-and-chips. Open-air dining on patio with an outdoor fireplace. Entertainment Wednesday. Kids' menu. No smoking. | 7640 W. Bell Rd. | 623/878–8822 | $10–$17 | AE, D, DC, MC, V.

Haus Murphy's. German. Neat, tidy, and friendly, this German restaurant is full of charm. Schnitzel is a specialty, especially the wonderful paprika version, teamed with crispy chunks of fried potatoes and green beans. | 5819 W. Glendale Ave. | 623/939–2480 | Reservations essential | No lunch Sun. Closed Mon. | $7–$14 | AE, D, DC, MC, V.

Lily's Cafe. Mexican. A jukebox with south-of-the-border hits and reasonably priced Mexican fare have kept customers coming here since 1949. The chimichangas and fragrant tamales are excellent. Kids' menu. | 6706 N. 58th Dr. | 623/937–7757 | Closed Mon.–Tues. and Aug. | $5–$8 | No credit cards.

Lodging

Best Western Phoenix Glendale. This affordable chain motel is 1 mi from the Glendale antiques district and 5 mi from the Sun City retirement community. Complimentary Continental breakfast. Refrigerators, cable TV. 2 pools. Laundry facilities. Business services. | 5940 N.W. Grand Ave. | 623/939–9431 or 800/333–7172 | fax 623/937–3137 | www.bestwestern.com | 85 rooms | $59–$85 | AE, D, DC, MC, V.

Holiday Inn Express. This chain hotel is at the Arrowhead Towne Center Mall. Complimentary Continental breakfast. Some microwaves, some refrigerators, cable TV. Pool. Hot tub. Gym. Laundry facilities. Business services. | 7885 W. Arrowhead Towne Center Dr. | 623/412–2000 | fax 623/412–5522 | www.hiexpress.com | 60 rooms | $134–$139 | AE, D, DC, MC, V.

Rock Haven Motel. This basic motel is on Glendale's main thoroughfare, about a mile from the antiques district. Some kitchenettes, cable TV. Pets allowed. | 5120 N.W. Grand Ave. | 623/937–0071 | 44 rooms | $42 | AE, D, DC, MC, V.

Springhill Suites Phoenix/Glendale/Peoria. This four-story, all-suite hotel has especially large rooms, all with a pull-out sofa. It's a block from the Arrowhead Towne Center Mall and 6 mi from both the Sundome and Waterworld. Complimentary Continental breakfast. In-room data ports, kitchenettes, microwaves, refrigerators, cable TV. Pool. Hot tub. Laundry facilities, laundry service. Business services. | 7810 W. Bell Rd. | 623/878–6666 | fax 623/878–6611 | www.springhillsuites.com | 89 rooms | $59 | AE, D, DC, MC, V.

Windmill Inn–Sun City West. This all-suite chain hotel with lovely grounds is 7 mi east of Glendale. Each room has a sleeper sofa. Complimentary Continental breakfast. Microwaves, refrigerators, cable TV. Pool. Hot tub. Gym. Bicycles. Library. Laundry facilities. Business services. Pets allowed. | 12545 W. Bell Rd., Surprise | 623/583–0133 or 800/547–4747 | fax 623/583–8366 | www.windmillinns.com | 127 suites | $116–$145 | AE, D, DC, MC, V.

GLOBE

MAP 3, G7

(Nearby towns also listed: San Carlos, Superior)

On the southern end of Tonto National Forest, the town of Globe, with a population of around 8,000, was a mining center at the turn of the 19th century. It got its name when gold and silver prospectors supposedly found a large, circular silver boulder with lines that reminded them of continents, though now the area is better known as one of North America's richest copper deposits. Historic Broad Street is lined with interesting shops and an artist's cooperative.

Information: **Greater Globe–Miami Chamber of Commerce** | 1360 N. Broad St., Globe, 85502 | 520/425–4495 or 800/804–5623.

Attractions

Apache Gold Casino. Run by the San Carlos Apache Tribe, this casino 5 mi east of Globe on Highway 70 has more than 500 slot machines plus Keno and live and video poker. Bands provide live musical entertainment weekends. | Hwy. 70 | 520/425–7800 or 800/272–2437 | www.apachegoldcasino.com | Free | 24 hrs.

Besh-Ba-Gowah Indian Ruins. Visitors can take self-guided tours of this 800-year-old pueblo, entering the ruins of more than 200 rooms that were once occupied by the Salado during the 13th and 14th centuries. Besh Ba Gowah means "metal camp"—the site was so dubbed by the Apaches, who found it in the 17th century and moved in. Advanced notification is required for guided tours. The ruins are 1½ mi southeast of Broad Street. | Jesse Hayes Rd. | 520/425–0320 | $3 | Daily 9–5.

Cobre Valley Center for the Arts. This arts center in the former Gila County Courthouse showcases works by local artists. A wide variety of paintings and wood and stone sculptures are on display. | 101 N. Broad St. | 520/425–0884 | Donations accepted | Mon.–Sat. 10–4:45, Sun. noon–5.

Gila County Historical Museum. This small museum is devoted mostly to the area's mining days, with rock specimens, photographs, and also some Native American baskets and pottery on display. | 1330 N. Broad St. | 520/425–7385 | Free | Weekdays 10–4.

ON THE CALENDAR

APR.: *Mining Country Boomtown Spree.* A celebration of the region's mining history in Miami; highlights of this event include a car show and parade. | 520/425–4495.
SEPT.: *Gila County Fair.* This four-day fair offers rides, contests, live music, games, livestock exhibits, and fun stuff for kids to do, all at the county fairgrounds. | 520/425–4495 or 800/804–5623.
OCT.: *Apache Days.* Museum exhibits, special lectures, and Native American entertainment honor the area's Native American history. | 520/425–4495 or 800/804–5623.

Dining

Chalo's. Mexican. This casual roadside spot offers some of the best Mexican food north of the border. Try an order of their savory stuffed sopaipillas, filled with beef, beans, and chiles. | 902 E. Ash St. | 520/425–0515 | $6–$9 | MC, V.

Libby's El Rey. Mexican. A family-style café in downtown Globe. The chimichangas are some of the best you'll find anywhere. | 999 N. Broad St. | 520/425–2054 | $4–$6 | MC, V.

Lodging

Globe Days Inn. This two-story chain motel is at the intersection of U.S. 60 and U.S. 70, about 4 mi from Broad Street. Complimentary Continental breakfast. In-room data ports, cable TV. Pool. Spa. Business services. No pets. | 1630 E. Ash St. | 520/425–5500 | fax 520/425–4146 | www.daysinn.com | 42 rooms | $59–$69 | AE, D, DC, V.

Noftsger Hill Inn. Built in 1907, this inn was originally the North Globe Schoolhouse. The original 800-square-ft classrooms with 15-ft ceilings have been converted into guest rooms; their coatrooms are now the private baths. The rooms are furnished with mining-era antiques and offer fantastic views of the Pinal Mountains. Complimentary breakfast. No air-conditioning, no room phones, no TV. No pets. No smoking. | 425 North St. | 520/425–2260 | fax 520/402–8235 | www.clariontek.com/noftsgerhillinn/index.htm | 5 rooms | $75–$125 | Closed July | MC, V.

Ramada Limited. This chain hotel is at the intersection of U.S. 60 and U.S. 70. It's 4 mi from Broad Street and a five-minute drive from the Apache Gold Casino. Picnic area, complimentary Continental breakfast. Refrigerators, cable TV. Pool. Hot tub. Laundry service. Business services. Some pets allowed. | 1699 E. Ash St. | 520/425–5741 or 800/256–8399 | fax 520/402–8466 | www.ramada.com | 77 rooms, 3 suites | $89–$99 | AE, DC, MC, V.

GRAND CANYON NATIONAL PARK

MAP 3, E2

(Nearby towns also listed: Flagstaff, Fredonia, Marble Canyon, Page, Tuba City, Williams)

The Grand Canyon is a sight no visitor to Arizona should pass by, and given that over 5 million people stop by the canyon each year, it would seem that most folks share that opinion. Its grandeur is unparalleled in the southwestern United States.

After the Colorado Plateau, a vast tableland of sandstone across what is now northern Arizona, was created through a long series of geological upheavals more than 65 million years ago, the Colorado River began to cut through the softer rock on its southward route, eroding the main canyon. Side canyons were cut by melting snow and fierce rainstorms that swelled the smaller tributaries of the main river. The harder formations were left over, and those are what you see today, standing in myriad hues

© Corbis

RED ROCK COUNTRY

In north-central Arizona, Sedona makes a good base for exploring red-rock country and the Verde Valley that surrounds it. Sedona, the site of countless Hollywood westerns, is now a chic town of B&Bs, resorts, and good shopping.

Sedona draws in all kinds of vacationers, from low-budget campers who set up along Oak Creek to those with unlimited bankrolls who sign up for a week's worth of massages and facials at one of the spa resorts. New Agers come from all over the world to experience the mysterious energies that supposedly emanate from the vortices around town.

Red Rock State Park and Slide Rock State Park are popular daytime destinations for hikers, as is Tlaquepaque, a shopping complex designed to look like its Mexican namesake.

Good day trips take you to Jerome, a former mining town that's now an artists' colony. Perched high on a hill 25 mi from from Sedona, Jerome offers panoramic views of the Verde Valley. Prescott, the former territorial capital of the state, is another option 67 mi southwest. Some of the best antiques shops in the state are just off Prescott's main square.

Flagstaff is a half-hour north, about 24 mi, reached via a beautiful section of Highway 89A in Oak Creek Canyon. Home to Northern Arizona University, Flagstaff has a diverse population and absorbing museums.

ranging from deep purples to fiery reds and vibrant yellows, depending on how the sun strikes them.

For at least 8,000 to 10,000 years, humans have inhabited the canyon, sometimes building dwellings in the highest, most inaccessible canyon walls. Some of these pueblos were active until about AD 1350, when it is believed periods of harsh and sustained drought drove the pueblo-dwellers away. The first Europeans saw the canyon in 1540, when a band of Spanish soldiers under the command of Captain García de Cárdenas discovered the area on their search for the fabled golden cities of Cibola. Although the Franciscan missionary Francisco Tomás Garcés visited a Havasupai village in the canyon in 1776, the U.S. government didn't begin exploring the area until the army sent Lieutenant Joseph Ives with an expedition in 1857–58; he reported that the region was so inhospitable that the Colorado River would "be forever unvisited and undisturbed." After John Wesley Powell explored the canyon floor by boat in 1869, others quickly arrived to prove Ives wrong, though most of the interest in the region initially came from mining companies. To preserve the area's great beauty, the Grand Canyon was declared a national park in 1919, the year of Theodore Roosevelt's death.

The South Rim is where most visitors enter Grand Canyon National Park, so it's wise to plan your trip carefully. Summer months are the most popular. If you can visit in early spring (before April) or late fall (after October), you'll have a less-obstructed view of the canyon and an easier time securing lodgings.

The North Rim is closed from late October to mid-May, but during the season the 200-mi drive is well worth the effort if you have the time. Along the road to the North Rim, you'll pass through Kaibab National Forest, which offers hiking trails, backcountry camping, and views of the canyon. You'll also pass the Vermilion Cliffs, a spectacular range of brilliantly colored, water-worn stone. Look for the dark silhouettes of large soaring birds— the endangered California condor was recently introduced to the area.

Admission to the Grand Canyon costs $20 per vehicle for seven days and includes both rims. Thereafter, virtually all park attractions are free unless you take a guided tour of some kind. Since the canyon is such a popular destination, reservations for lodging are absolutely essential far in advance most of the year.

Information: **Grand Canyon National Park** | Box 129, Grand Canyon, 86023 | 520/638–7888 | www.nps.gov/grca.

AMFAC Parks and Resorts. | 14001 E. Iliff Ave., Suite 600, Aurora, CO 80014 | 303/297–2757 or 520/638–7888 | www.amfac.com.

GRAND CANYON
NATIONAL PARK

INTRO
ATTRACTIONS
DINING
LODGING

Attractions

Bright Angel Lodge. Mary Jane Cotler designed this 1935 log-and-stone structure that sits within a few yards of the canyon's South Rim. The history room displays memorabilia from the South Rim's early years. | West Rim Dr., Grand Canyon Village | 303/297–2757 | www.grand-canyonlodges.com | Free | Daily.

Bright Angel Point. The trail to this awe-inspiring North Rim overlook starts on the grounds of the Grand Canyon Lodge and proceeds along the crest of a point of rocks that juts into the canyon for several hundred yards. | North Rim | 520/638–7888 | www.nps.gov/grca | Free | Daily.

Bright Angel Trail. This 8-mi trail descends 5,510 ft to the canyon floor. It was originally a bighorn sheep path that was later used by the Havasupai Indians, and it soon became a mule and foot trail. You must get a backcountry permit to camp in the canyon unless you are staying at Phantom Ranch. | South Rim, near Grand Canyon Village | 520/638–7888 | www.nps.gov/grca | Free | Daily.

Cape Royal. This viewpoint 23 mi from Grand Canyon Lodge is the southernmost viewpoint on the North Rim. In addition to a large chunk of the canyon, Angel's Window, a giant

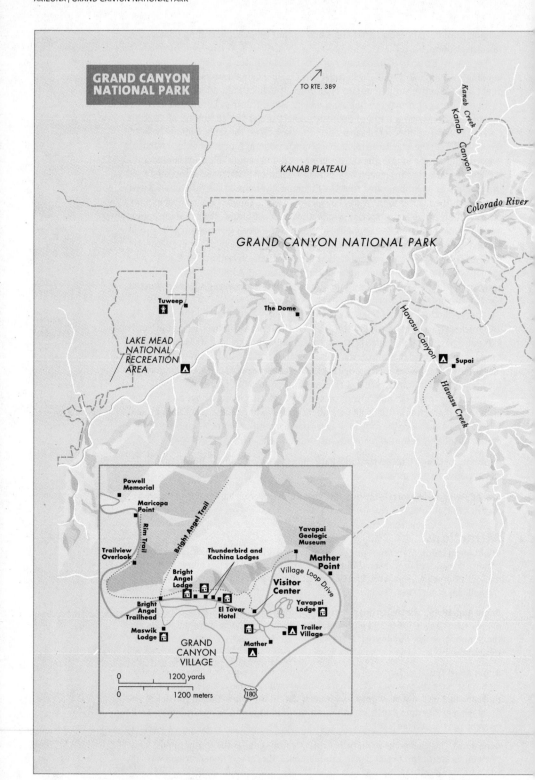

GRAND CANYON
NATIONAL PARK

TO RTE. 389

Kanab Creek
Kanab Canyon

KANAB PLATEAU

Colorado River

GRAND CANYON NATIONAL PARK

Tuweep

The Dome

Havasu Canyon

Supai

LAKE MEAD
NATIONAL
RECREATION
AREA

Havasu Creek

Powell
Memorial

Maricopa
Point

Rim Trail

Bright Angel Trail

Trailview
Overlook

Yavapai
Geologic
Museum

Thunderbird and
Kachina Lodges

Mather
Point

Bright
Angel
Lodge

Village Loop Drive

Visitor
Center

Bright
Angel
Trailhead

El Tovar
Hotel

Yavapai
Lodge

Maswik
Lodge

Trailer
Village

GRAND
CANYON
VILLAGE

Mather

0   1200 yards

0   1200 meters

180

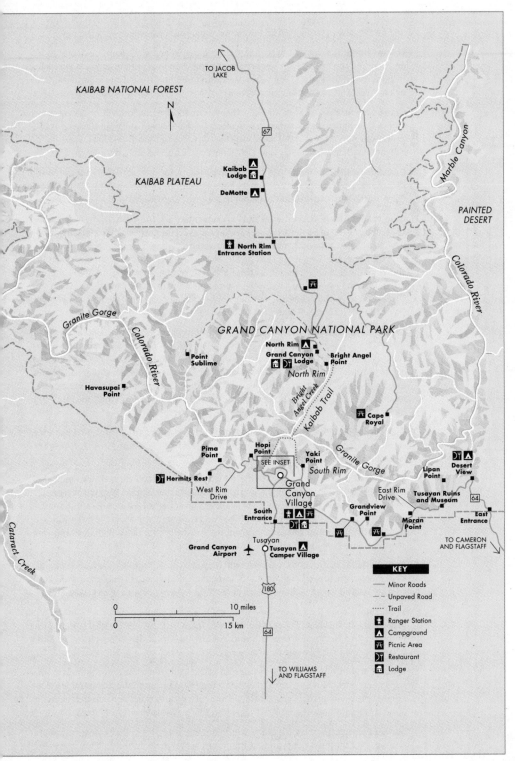

KAIBAB NATIONAL FOREST

N

TO JACOB LAKE

67

KAIBAB PLATEAU

Kaibab Lodge

DeMotte

PAINTED DESERT

Marble Canyon

Colorado River

North Rim Entrance Station

Granite Gorge

Colorado River

GRAND CANYON NATIONAL PARK

Point Sublime

North Rim
Grand Canyon Lodge
Bright Angel Point

North Rim

Havasupai Point

Bright Angel Creek

Kaibab Trail

Cape Royal

Pima Point

Hopi Point

SEE INSET

Yaki Point

South Rim

Granite Gorge

Lipan Point

Desert View

Hermits Rest

West Rim Drive

Grand Canyon Village

East Rim Drive

Tusayan Ruins and Museum

64

East Entrance

South Entrance

Grandview Point

Moran Point

TO CAMERON AND FLAGSTAFF

Cataract Creek

Grand Canyon Airport

Tusayan
Tusayan Camper Village

180

0   10 miles
0   15 km

64

TO WILLIAMS AND FLAGSTAFF

KEY

—— Minor Roads
--- Unpaved Road
···· Trail
Ranger Station
Campground
Picnic Area
Restaurant
Lodge

erosion-formed hole, can be seen through the projecting ridge of Cape Royal. | North Rim, on Cape Royal Rd. | 520/638–7888 | www.nps.gov/grca | Free | Daily.

El Tovar Hotel. This South Rim structure was named in honor of Spanish explorer Pedro de Tovar and constructed out of native stone and Oregon pine to resemble a European hunting lodge. The rustic lobby is decorated with numerous stuffed and mounted animal heads. | West Rim Dr., Grand Canyon Village | 520/638–2631 | www.nps.gov/grca | Free | Daily.

Grand Canyon IMAX Theater. This IMAX theater 1 mi south of the South Rim park entrance, with a 70-ft-high screen, offers hourly screenings, which begin at half-past the hour, of a 34-minute film on the Grand Canyon. | Hwy. 64/U.S. 180 | 520/638–2203 | www.grand-canyonimaxtheater.com | $9 | Mar.–Oct., daily 8:30–8:30; Nov.–Feb., daily 10:30–6:30.

★ **Grand Canyon Lodge.** Built in 1928 by the Union Pacific Railroad at the very edge of North Rim, the massive stone structure is on the National Register of Historic Places. | Bright Angel Point, North Rim | 520/638–2611 | www.nps.gov/grca | Free | Daily.

Grand Canyon Main Visitor Center and Park Headquarters. The main visitor center on the South Rim, operated by the National Park Service, is on the east side of Grand Canyon Village, just west of Yavapai Point. The visitor center is where you can find park rangers who'll answer questions about the canyon and the surrounding area. Short films and slide shows on the canyon are presented throughout the day. A separate exhibit area profiles artifacts of the earliest canyon dwellers, probably nomadic Paleo-Indians. | Village Loop Dr., Grand Canyon Village | 520/638–7888 | www.nps.gov/grca | Free | Memorial Day–Labor Day, daily 8–6; Labor Day–Memorial Day, daily 8–5.

Grand Canyon Valle Airport Museum. This museum, 25 mi south of the Grand Canyon at the junction of Highway 64 and U.S. 180, is a pioneer of the "flying museum" concept: that the very best way to display historic aircraft is in their natural element, the sky. About 30 of the museum's aircraft are flyable, and more restoration projects are planned. Planes are flown at the discretion of the museum, so call for current information. You can see, among others, a Japanese suicide aircraft called the *Yokosuka Ohka*, which means cherry blossom. | Hwy. 64 at U.S. 180 | 520/635–1000 | $5 | Daily 9–6.

Grandview Point. This fine viewpoint on the South Rim at an altitude of 7,496 ft has large stands of ponderosa pine, oak, and juniper trees. | East Rim Dr., South Rim | 520/638–7888 | www.nps.gov/grca | Free | Daily.

Kaibab Trail. The more popular southern leg of this steep trail starts at Yaki Point, 4 mi east of Grand Canyon Village on the South Rim. It goes to the Colorado River where it crosses a suspension bridge and continues on to Phantom Ranch. Beyond Phantom Ranch, the northern stretch of the trail climbs past Roaring Springs to a point 2 mi from the North Rim Visitor Center. You need a backcountry permit to camp below the canyon rim unless you are staying at Phantom Ranch. | Hwy. 64 | www.thecanyon.com/nps | Free | Daily.

Kolb Studio. This South Rim studio was built in 1904 by the Kolb brothers as a photographic workshop, where they showed films and held dances throughout the early half of the 20th century. | Grand Canyon Village | 520/638–7888 | www.nps.gov/grca | Free | Daily.

Lipan Point. This is the canyon's widest point. From this point on the South Rim you can view every eroded layer of the canyon and see Unkar Delta, where a wide creek joins the Colorado River to form powerful rapids. | East Rim Dr., South Rim | 520/638–7888 | www.nps.gov/grca | Free | Daily.

Lookout Studio. Just a half dozen yards east of the Kolb Studio, Lookout was built in 1914 to compete with the Kolbs' studio. It was designed by Mary Jane Cotler to resemble a Hopi pueblo and it contains a collection of fossils and geological samples from around the world. | Grand Canyon Village, South Rim | 520/638–7888 | www.nps.gov/grca | Free | Daily.

Mather Point. Just 4 mi north of the South Rim entrance, this overlook yields extraordinary views of the Inner Gorge and the numerous buttes that rise from it. It is named after the National Park Service's first director, Stephen Mather. | Off the Village Loop Dr., South Rim | 520/638–7888 | www.nps.gov/grca | Free | Daily.

Moran Point. Named after American landscape artist Thomas Moran, who painted Grand Canyon scenes from many points on the rim but was especially fond of this spot. To this day Moran Point is very popular with photographers and painters. | East Rim Dr., South Rim | 520/638–7888 | www.nps.gov/grca | Free | Daily.

Point Imperial. This viewpoint on the North Rim gives you an excellent view of the canyon, not to mention thousands of square miles of the surrounding countryside. At 8,083 ft, this is the highest vista on either rim. | Cape Royal Rd. | Park information 520/638–7888 | www.nps.gov/grca | Free | Mid-May–late Oct., daily.

★ **Point Sublime.** Only those visitors who are driving vehicles with high-road clearance (pickups and four-wheel-drive vehicles) should journey out to Point Sublime. The panorama along the dirt road leading out to the point is one of the most awesome views you'll ever witness from the comfort of your car. To camp out at this overlook you need a permit from the Backcountry Office at the park ranger station. | North Rim | 520/638–7888 | www.nps.gov/grca | Free | Daily.

Rim Trail. This 10-mi walking path runs along the edge of the canyon from Yavapai Museum in Grand Canyon Village west to Hermits Rest. It's paved to Maricopa Point and gives visitors access to a number of historical landmarks. | South Rim | 520/638–7888 | Free | Daily.

Tusayan Ruins and Museum. The ruins here on the South Rim, 3 mi east of Moran Point and 20 mi east of Grand Canyon Village, are evidence of early inhabitants of the canyon. "Tusayan" comes from a Hopi phrase meaning "country of isolated buttes." A museum displays models of the original dwellings as well as exhibits on modern tribes of the region. Several free, one-hour guided tours are given daily. | East Rim Dr. | 520/638–2305 | Free | Daily 9–5.

Watchtower. This 70-ft stone-and-mortar watchtower was built in 1932 in the style of Native American structures. From the top you can see the hues of the distant Painted Desert to the east and the Vermilion Cliffs near the Utah border. | South Rim | 520/638–2736 | 25¢ | May–Sept., daily 8–8; Oct.–Apr. daily 9–5.

Yaki Point. Yaki Point, on the South Rim 4 mi east of Grand Canyon Village, affords spectacular views of Wotan's Throne, a majestic butte named by Francois Matthes, the U.S. Geological Survey scientist who developed the first topographical map of the region. This is also where the popular Kaibab Trail into the canyon begins. | Hwy. 64 | Free | Daily.

West Rim Drive. In order to cut down on congestion, you must travel this route by a free park shuttle from Memorial Day to October; you can't drive your own vehicle. Attractions along this 8-mi route include the Trailview Overlook, the Abyss, and Hermits Rest. | South Rim | 520/638–7888 | Free | Daily.

SIGHTSEEING TOURS/TOUR COMPANIES

Fred Harvey Transportation Company. This company operates daily motorcoach sightseeing trips along the South Rim and to destinations as far away as Lees Ferry and Flagstaff | Village Loop Dr., Grand Canyon Village | 520/638–2822 or 520/638–2631 | $8–$208 | Daily; tour times vary.

Grand Canyon Field Institute. Classes at the institute explore the natural and cultural history of the Grand Canyon region with walks, day hikes, backpacking and river trips, and classroom instruction. Specialized classes in archaeology, backcountry medicine, and photography are also offered. Courses and trips originate throughout the year in various places on the South Rim; advance reservations are necessary. | Box 399, Grand Canyon 86023 | 520/638–2485 | fax 520/638–2484 | www.grandcanyon.org/fieldinstitute | $95–$995 | Office Apr.–Oct., weekdays 9–5.

GRAND CANYON
NATIONAL PARK

INTRO
ATTRACTIONS
DINING
LODGING

Horseback and Mule Rides. Long and short rides are a Grand Canyon tradition and are always popular. Places must be reserved long in advance for the longer trips, but if you don't have time to make the advance reservations, you can rent a mule or horse by the hour or half-day and ride around the rim. **Amfac Parks and Resorts,** the company that operates Grand Canyon's lodges and restaurants, also offers mule rides into the canyon from the South Rim. You descend on the Kaibab Trail and have lunch on the canyon floor if you are doing a one-day trip, or stay overnight at Phantom Ranch if you are doing an overnight trip. You must make reservations 9 to 11 months in advance. Leave from Bright Angel Lodge in Grand Canyon Village. | 14001 E. Iliff Ave., Suite 600, Aurora, CO 80014 | 303/297–2757 or 520/638–7888 | fax 303/297–3175 | www.grandcanyonlodges.com | 1-day $112.94, 2-day $325.94 | Daily trips (reservations required). **Apache Stables.** You can rent gentle horses at this stable at the Moqui Lodge in Tusayan, 2 mi south of the South Rim park entrance. The stables also offers guided rides. | Moqui Lodge, Hwy. 64, Tusayan | 520/638–2891 | www.apachestables.com | $22–$57.50 | Apr.–Nov., daily 7–7. **Canyon Trail Rides.** This outfitter offers full- and half-day mule and horse trips from the North Rim into the canyon. The pick-up location is the Grand Canyon Lodge. | www.onpages.com/canyonrides | 435/679–8665 | $40–$95 | May 15–Oct. 15, daily.

Rafting Trips. There are many companies that offer Colorado River trips. Trips vary in length of time and level of difficulty. It is always advisable to call ahead for details. Rafting trips through the canyon begin in Lees Ferry, near Marble Canyon. Some of these trips, particularly the shorter ones, end at Phantom Ranch, from which you hike to the top of the canyon on the Bright Angel Trail. Below are a couple of tour companies operating in the area. *See also* Fred Harvey Transportation Company and Grand Canyon Field Institute (both *above*), which also offer river-rafting trips. **Canyon Explorations.** This outfit offers 6- to 18-day river trips into the canyon. | Box 310, Flagstaff | www.canyonx.com | 520/774–4655 or 800/654–0723 | $1,260–$3,350 | Apr.–Oct. **Wilderness River Adventures.** These white-water rafting trips last from 3½ to 14 days. Shorter trips begin or end at Phantom Ranch on the canyon floor. | Box 717, Page | 520/645–3296 or 800/992–8022 | fax 520/645–6113 | www.river-adventures.com | $850–$2,873 | Apr.–Oct.

Scenic Flights over Grand Canyon. A number of tours by airplane or helicopter operate out of both Grand Canyon Airport and Tusayan. The following are reliable companies: **Air Grand Canyon.** You may choose from a number of tours in a helicopter or high-wing Cessna at this family-owned and -operated company, including a Monument Tour and a Canyon Tour. There is also a "River Rafting Tour," whereby you will fly over the main gorge of the Grand Canyon and eventually land in Page, where you can raft the Colorado River. | Grand Canyon Airport, South Rim | 520/638–2686 or 800/247–4726 | www.airgrandcanyon.com | $74–$260 | Year-round. **AirStar Helicopters.** This company offers a number of trips that center around different regions of the canyon. The eastern canyon route covers the Little Colorado River and the stone monuments. Trip times range from 30 minutes to 1 hour. | Grand Canyon Airport, South Rim | 520/638–2622 or 800/962–3869 | www.airstar.com | $65–$155 | Year-round. **Grand Canyon Airlines.** Descriptions of the geology and history of the canyon are carried over the headphones of the two-engine Vistaliner aircraft. The route covers more than 100 mi in the heart of the Grand Canyon. | Grand Canyon Airport, South Rim | 520/638–2407 or 800/528–2413 | www.grandcanyonairlines.com | $75 | Year-round. **Kenai Helicopters.** Routes focus on the central corridor of the canyon and provide excellent views of the temples, buttes, and the magnificent Colorado River. | Grand Canyon Airport, South Rim | 520/638–2412 or 800/541–4537 | www.flykenai.com | $99–$155 | Year-round. **Papillon Helicopters.** Both tours offered by this company cover the distance from the North Rim to the South Rim, but the more extensive one also highlights the eastern portion of the canyon, where the Painted Desert can be seen. Papillon also offers exclusive day and overnight trips to the Havasupai Indian Village at the bottom of the Grand Canyon. | Grand Canyon Airport, South Rim | 520/638–2419 or 800/528–2418 | www.papillon.com | $99–$159; $461–$503 Havasupai Excursion | Year-round.

SEPT.: *Grand Canyon Chili Cook-off.* The contest is at the Moqui Cookout Site, just south of the park entrance. Prizes are awarded for the best overall chile, howling hot chile, and best corn bread. | 520/638–2901.

SEPT.: *Grand Canyon Music Festival.* Chamber music in the Shrine of the Ages Auditorium at the South Rim. | 520/638–9215 or 800/997–8285.

Dining

Arizona Steak House. American. This casual steak house in Bright Angel Lodge on the South Rim has Native American–inspired prints and superb canyon views. For dinner, there's good prime rib, rack of lamb, and blackened swordfish. | Bright Angel Lodge, West Rim Dr. | 520/638–2631 | www.grandcanyonlodges.com | Reservations not accepted | Closed Jan.–Feb. No lunch | $13–$24 | AE, D, DC, MC, V.

Bright Angel Restaurant. American. Just a few feet away from the South Rim of the Grand Canyon, the more casual restaurant in Bright Angel Lodge serves standard American fare and is great for family dining. | Bright Angel Lodge, West Rim Dr. | 520/638–2631 | www.grandcanyonlodges.com | Breakfast also available | $10–$18 | AE, D, DC, MC, V.

El Tovar Dining Room. Southwestern. For decades, the El Tovar Hotel's restaurant has enjoyed a reputation for fine food served in a classic 19th-century dining room. Known for dishes featuring local game. Kids' menu. No smoking. It's on the South Rim, 4 mi west of the park entrance. | El Tovar Hotel, Grand Canyon Village | 520/638–2631 | www.grandcanyonlodges.com | Reservations essential | Breakfast also available | $20–$42 | AE, D, DC, MC, V.

Grand Canyon Lodge Dining Room. American. The dining room in this historic 1920s lodge on the North Rim is huge and has a high ceiling; views are spectacular. On the menu: pork kebabs, grilled swordfish, and linguine with cilantro. | Bright Angel Point, North Rim | 520/638–2611 | www.grandcanyonlodges.com | Reservations essential | Breakfast also available | mid-Oct.–mid-May | $15–$27 | AE, D, DC, MC, V.

Grand Canyon Lodge Snackbar. American/Casual. This is where to get a meal tailored to a budget when you're on the North Rim. The selections—hot dogs, burgers, sandwiches, yogurt—are standard but sufficient. | Grand Canyon Lodge, Bright Angel Point | 520/638–2611 | Closed mid-Oct.–mid-May | Breakfast also available | $4–$8 | AE, D, DC, MC, V.

Maswik Cafeteria. American/Casual. This South Rim cafeteria opens every day at 6 AM, making it ideal for those who want to get an early start. In addition to traditional American fare like hamburgers and fried chicken, there are also Mexican items on the menu and a hot and cold sandwich station. | Maswik Lodge, Grand Canyon Village | 520/638–2631 | www.grandcanyonlodges.com | Breakfast also available | $5–$8 | AE, D, DC, MC, V.

Moqui Lodge Restaurant. Mexican. A good option for an informal meal, this rustic restaurant in Moqui Lodge, about ¼ mi south of the South Rim entrance, serves tasty Mexican food, including great fajitas. Combination plates, burgers, and sandwiches are also available. | Moqui Lodge, U.S. 180 | 520/638–2892 | www.grandcanyonlodges.com | No lunch | $8–$15 | D, DC, MC, V.

Steakhouse at Grand Canyon. American. Choice Colorado beef is cooked on an open oakwood fire in this western-style restaurant 9 mi south of the South Rim entrance. Known for steaks, ribs, and chicken. Kids' menu. | Rte. 64 at U.S. 180 | 520/638–2780 | $11–$23 | MC, V.

We Cook Pizza & Pasta. Italian. This family-oriented restaurant 2 mi south of the South Rim park entrance is well known for its delicious pizza. If you like pasta, try the Cajun chicken fettuccine or the penne. | Hwy. 64, Tusayan | 520/638–2278 | $8–$13. | No credit cards.

Yavapai Cafeteria. American/Casual. The cafeteria in Yavapai Lodge serves up an array of typically wide-ranging American fare, including pizza, burgers, fried chicken, and pasta. | Yavapai Lodge, Grand Canyon Village | 520/638–2631 | www.grandcanyonlodges.com | Breakfast also available; closed late Jan.–Mar. | $4–$18 | AE, D, DC, MC, V.

GRAND CANYON
NATIONAL PARK

INTRO
ATTRACTIONS
DINING
LODGING

Lodging

Best Western Grand Canyon Squire Inn. There is a cowboy museum in this full-scale resort 7 mi south of the South Rim park entrance. 2 restaurants, bar. Cable TV. Pool. Beauty salon, hot tub, massage. Bowling, gym. Laundry facilities. Business services. | Hwy. 64 | 520/638–2681 or 800/622–6966 | fax 520/638–2782 | www.bestwestern.com | 250 rooms | $150–$175 | AE, D, DC, MC, V.

Bright Angel Lodge. This historic building 4 mi west of the South Rim park entrance in Grand Canyon Village has a large stone fireplace in its lobby, and some of the cabins contain fireplaces. About half the rooms in the lodge have canyon views. Restaurant, bar. No air-conditioning, no TV in some rooms. | West Rim Dr., Grand Canyon Village | 520/638–2631, 303/297–2757 reservations | fax 520/638–9247 | www.grandcanyonlodges.com | 39 rooms (24 with shared bath), 50 cabins | $46–$63, $73–$234 cabins | AE, D, DC, MC, V.

El Tovar. This hotel, built in 1905 of native stone and pine logs on the South Rim, is considered one of the finest national park lodges. Some rooms are small, but a number have canyon views; if you want to splurge, try for a suite with a canyon view. Restaurant, bar. Cable TV. | Box 699, South Rim | 520/638–2631, 520/638–2401 reservations | fax 520/638–9247 | www.grandcanyonlodges.com | 70 rooms, 8 suites | $116–$174, $199–$284 suites | AE, D, DC, MC, V.

★ **Grand Canyon Lodge.** A great canyon view from the huge sunroom of this North Rim lodge is the draw at this National Historic Landmark. Accommodations are in cabins and motel-style rooms. Restaurant, bar. No air-conditioning. Business services. | Bright Angel Point, North Rim | 520/638–2611, 303/297–2757 reservations | www.amfac.com | 40 rooms, 168 cabins | $78, $108 cabins | Closed mid-Oct.–mid-May | AE, D, DC, MC, V.

The Grand Hotel. This modern three-story hotel is 8 mi from the South Rim park entrance. Restaurant. In-room data ports, cable TV. Pool. Hot tub. | Hwy. 64, Tusayan | 520/638–3333 | fax 520/638–3131 | www.gcanyon.com/grand.htm | 120 rooms | $138 | AE, D, MC, V.

Holiday Inn Express Grand Canyon Suites. This standard chain hotel 1 mi from the South Rim entrance offers basic amenities. Complimentary Continental breakfast. Cable TV. Business services. | Hwy. 64, Tusayan | 520/638–3000 or 888/473–2269 | fax 520/638–0123 | www.hiexpress.com | 165 rooms, 32 suites | $129 | AE, D, DC, MC, V.

Kachina Lodge. The amenities are basic at this modern South Rim lodge, but half face the canyon. Register at the El Tovar Hotel, which is the next hotel east of this lodge. | West Rim Dr., Grand Canyon Village. Cable TV. | 520/638–2631, 303/297–2757 reservations | fax 520/638–9247 | www.grandcanyonlodges.com | 49 rooms | $107–$117 | AE, D, MC, V.

Kaibab Lodge. In a wooded setting 5 mi from the North Rim entrance, this 1920s property offers rustic cabins with simple furnishings. You can rest and relax around a stone fireplace. Restaurant. | Hwy. 67, North Rim | 520/638–2389 | www.canyoneers.com | 29 cabins | $79 | Closed Oct. 15–May 15 | D, MC, V.

Maswik Lodge. This modern motel-style lodge ¼ mi from the South Rim has large, spacious rooms. There are also cabins. | Grand Canyon Village. Restaurant, bar. No air-conditioning in some rooms, cable TV. Business services. No pets. | 520/638–2631, 520/638–2401 reservations | fax 520/638–9247 | www.grandcanyonlodges.com | 278 rooms, 25 cabins | $73–$107, $65 cabins | AE, D, DC, MC, V.

Moqui Lodge. Clean and comfortable rooms are available in this rustic motel just outside the South Rim park entrance. Restaurant, complimentary Continental breakfast. Cable TV. | Hwy. 64/U.S. 180 | 520/638–2424 | www.grandcanyonlodges.com | 136 rooms | $94 | Closed mid Oct.–Apr. | D, DC, MC, V.

Phantom Ranch. Mule riders and hikers can stay at this no-frills lodging at the bottom of the Grand Canyon. Cabins are available only to those on canyon mule trips, but hikers can stay in two dormitory-style, sex-segregated rooms. Reservations are required. Restaurant.

| Grand Canyon, South Rim | 520/638–2631 | www.grandcanyonlodges.com | 40 beds in 2 dorm rooms | $23 per person | AE, D, DC, MC, V.

Quality Inn and Suites Grand Canyon. This large motel is directly behind the Grand Canyon IMAX Theatre, 1 mi south of the South Rim park entrance. Restaurant. Some in-room data ports, some minibars, cable TV. Pool. Hot tub. | Hwy. 64, Tusayan | 520/638–2673 | fax 520/638–9537 | www.qualityinn.com | 232 rooms | $118–$178 | AE, D, DC, MC, V.

Rodeway Inn–Red Feather Lodge. This large, three-story motel was built in 1995. It's 1½ mi south of the South Rim park entrance. Restaurant. Cable TV. Gym. Business services. Pets allowed (fee). | Hwy. 64, Tusayan | www.redfeatherlodge.com | 520/638–2414 or 800/538–2345 | fax 520/638–9216 | 232 rooms | $100–$175 | AE, DC, MC, V.

Thunderbird Lodge. This large, motel-style lodge is 4 mi west of the South Rim park entrance in Grand Canyon Village. Register at the Bright Angel Lodge, the next hotel to the west. Cable TV. | West Rim Dr., Grand Canyon Village | 520/638–2631, 303/297–2757 reservations | fax 520/638–9247 | 55 rooms | $114–$124 | AE, D, DC, MC, V.

Yavapai Lodge. An affordable, motel-style lodge ½ mi from the South Rim in Grand Canyon Village that provides basic amenities. It's the largest lodging facility in the park. Restaurant. No air-conditioning, cable TV. | 520/638–2631, 303/297–2757 reservations | fax 520/638–9247 | 358 rooms | $88–$102 | AE, D, DC, MC, V.

GREER

MAP 3, H6

(Nearby towns also listed: Alpine, McNary, Show Low, Springerville/Eagar)

Tiny Greer, with a population of just 150, is named for Ellen Greer, matriarch of a cattle-ranching pioneer family who lived here in the late 1800s. On the banks of the Little Colorado River, this quaint town sits among pine, spruce, and aspen trees. The horizon is dominated by 11,590-ft Mt. Baldy. Much of the area is governed by the Apache Nation. Greer's Main Street is, oddly, a dead end; locals have dubbed it "the road to nowhere." Since the late 19th century, Greer has been a rest stop for travelers passing through the Lee Valley. Now it's a charming place to stay if you are visiting the White Mountains to hike or fish in summer, or to ski in winter.

Information: **Round Valley Chamber of Commerce** | Box 31, 318 E. Main St., Springerville, 85938 | 520/333–2123 | www.az-tourist.com.

Attractions

Bunch Reservoir. Camping, hiking, and fishing are popular activities here. The reservoir, 1 mi north of Greer, is well stocked with rainbow and brown trout. | U.S. 260 | 520/333–2123 | Free | Daily.

Little House Museum. Antiques and artifacts from the Old West fill up historic cabins and barns dating back to the early 1900s. The collection of automatic musical instruments is one-of-a-kind, and the sounds will leave you mesmerized. It's 5 mi east of Greer. | Off Hwy. 260 | 520/333–2286 | www.xdiamondranch.com | $5 | Tours Thurs.–Sat. 11, 1:30.

Mt. Baldy Trail. Southwest of Greer on Highway 273, this 8-mi trail climbs the northern flank of 11,590-ft Mt. Baldy. Hikers will be rewarded with wonderful views of the Salt River Canyon and Mogolloin Rim. Note that the very summit of the mountain is on White Mountain Apache Reservation land and is off-limits to non-Apaches. | Hwy. 273 | No phone | Free | Daily.

Sunrise Park Resort. In the heart of Arizona's White Mountains this year-round resort 18 mi west of Greer offers a wide range of activities. In winter you can go skiing and snowmobiling. When there's no snow, fishing, hiking, and mountain biking are popular. | U.S. 260 | 520/735–7335 | www.sunriseskipark.com | Ski season: late-Nov.–Apr., daily 8–4; summer season: May–mid-Nov., daily 7 AM–5:30.

ON THE CALENDAR

JUNE: *Greer Day & Chile Cook-off.* This renowned chile cook-off and an arts-and-crafts fair takes place in downtown Greer. | 520/333–2123.

Dining

Greer Mountain Resort Restaurant. American/Casual. Grab a seat by the fireplace and sample the homemade ranch beans, a signature grilled-cheese sandwich with green chiles and tomato, and a slice of fresh-baked cobbler. It's 1½ mi south of Highway 260. | Hwy. 373 | 520/735–7560 | Breakfast also available; no dinner | $4–$8 | MC, V.

Molly Butler Lodge. American. The window-lined dining room in the Molly Butler Lodge is a reliable place to eat in Greer. Known for hand-cut, aged steaks, chicken, and prime rib. | 109 Main St. | 520/735–7226 | Reservations essential | No lunch Nov.–Apr. | $11–$20 | MC, V.

Rendezvous Diner. American. This classic diner offers friendly and prompt service. The chicken-fried steak and mesquite cheeseburger are highly recommended, and if you are there on a Friday try the fish fry. | 117 Main St. | 520/735–7483 | Breakfast also available weekends; closed Nov.–Mar. | $6–$9 | No credit cards.

Lodging

Greer Lodge. You'll find a fireplace and a piano in the common room of this log lodge set on 9 acres with a view of the Little Colorado River. Rooms are simple and fairly large. Restaurant, bar, picnic area. No air-conditioning, some kitchenettes, no room phones, TV in common area. Fishing. Ice-skating, cross-country skiing, sleigh rides. | 44 Main St. | 520/735–7216 | fax 520/735–7720 | www.greerlodge.com | 8 rooms, 3 cabins | $95–$120, $95–$280 cabins | AE, D, MC, V.

Greer Mountain Resort. Nestled in a ponderosa pine forest 1½ mi south of Highway 260, these comfy cabin units appeal to budget travelers and families. Most of the cabins sleep up to six people, but one-bedroom pine studios are available for those seeking more intimate quarters. All have fully equipped kitchens and gas fireplaces, and a log cabin café on the premises serves hearty home-cooked breakfast and lunch dishes. Restaurant, picnic area. Kitchenettes, refrigerators, no room phones, no TVs. Hiking, horseback riding, fishing. Pets allowed (fee). | Hwy. 353 | 520/735–7560 | www.wmonline.com/greermountain | 4 cabins | $65–$90 | MC, V.

Molly Butler Lodge. One of Arizona's oldest guest lodges, which has been around since the turn of the 20th century, this is an inviting place, with simple accommodations and a well-regarded restaurant. Rooms are bright and carefully decorated with handmade quilts and wood furniture; many have views of the Little Colorado River and Greer Meadow. Fishing, hiking, and horseback riding can be arranged with local outfitters. Restaurant, bar. No room phones, no TV in rooms, TV in common area. Pets allowed. | 109 Main St. | 520/735–7226 | www.mollybutlerlodge.com | 11 rooms | $38–$65 | MC, V.

The Peaks at Greer. This is the only hotel-style accommodation in town. In summer months, the deck and patio are lovely spots to enjoy a bite from the restaurant or to relax with a good book. Cabins have full kitchens. Restaurant, bar, complimentary Continental breakfast. No room phones, no TV in rooms, TV in common area. Hot tub. No smoking. | 1 Main St. | 520/735–7777 | fax 520/735–7204 | www.peaksresort.com | 15 rooms, 3 suites, 2 cabins | $109 rooms, $149–$159 suites, $119 cabins | AE, D, MC, V.

Red Setter Inn. This log inn sits on wooded acres along the Little Colorado River. Some rooms contain fireplaces. If you stay for two or more nights, you'll get a free sack lunch. Complimentary breakfast. Some in-room hot tubs, some in-room VCRs (and movies), some in-room

TVs. TV in common area. Fishing. Cross-country skiing. Business services. No kids under 16. No smoking. | 8 Main St. | 520/735–7441 or 888/994–7337 | fax 520/735–7425 | www.red-setterinn.com | 10 rooms, 2 suites in 2 buildings | $130–$195, $195–$220 suites | AE, MC, V.

White Mountain Lodge. Built in 1892, the lodge is the oldest building in Greer. Rooms are all uniquely decorated with mostly southwestern and Mission-style furnishings. Separate cabins have wood-burning or gas-log fireplaces and full kitchens; many of them have whirl-pool tubs. Complimentary breakfast. Some in-room VCRs, no room phones, no TV in some rooms, TV in common area. Hot tub. Some pets allowed (fee). No smoking. | 140 Main St. | 520/735–7568 or 888/493–7568 | fax 520/735–7498 | www.wmlodge.com | 7 rooms, 6 cabins | $85–$105, $85–$195 cabins | D, DC, MC, V.

HOLBROOK

MAP 3, G5

(Nearby towns also listed: Show Low, Winslow)

In 1881, when the railroad reached this area, Holbrook became part of the Aztec Land and Cattle Company. Situated on Historic Route 66, the town of 5,500 is a good base for exploring the sites of northeastern Arizona, including Canyon de Chelly, the Hopi Mesas, and Petrified Forest National Park, which is nearby. But it's ranching that keeps the town going today.

Information: **Holbrook Chamber of Commerce** | 100 E. Arizona St., Holbrook, 86025 | www.ci.holbrook.az.us | 520/524–6558 or 800/524–2449.

Attractions

Bucket of Blood Saloon. Come have a look at this classic western saloon that has remained virtually untouched since it was built in the 1800s. Although not open for inside tours, you can get a good view of the old saloon from the street. | S.E. Central St. | 520/524–6558 | Free | Daily.

McGee's Gallery. This Native American crafts shop has reasonable prices; you'll find pottery, weaving, and jewelry, among other handcrafts here. | 2114 N. Navajo Blvd. | 520/524–1977 | Free | Weekdays 9–5:30, Sat. 9–4.

Petrified Forest National Park. In 1984, archaeologists here discovered the fossil remains of one of the oldest dinosaurs ever unearthed, from the Triassic period of the Mesozoic era, 225 million years ago. More than 500 other sites in this preserve have offered up remnants of ancient humans and their artifacts. The area is covered with petrified tree trunks whose wood was fossilized over centuries, turning it into colorful mineral deposits. Because looters had carried off so many pieces of petrified wood, President Theodore Roosevelt declared the area a national park in 1906. There are two entrances to the park: the north entrance is 26 mi east of Holbrook off Interstate 40, while the south entrance is 19 mi southeast of Holbrook off U.S. 180. A 27-mi marked scenic drive connects the two entrances. | North Entrance: I–40, exit 311; South Entrance: U.S. 180 | www.nps.gov/pefo | 520/524–6228 | $10 per vehicle | Daily 8–5.

ON THE CALENDAR

JUNE: *Old West Celebration.* This event has Old West reenactments, music, food, and children's activities at the historic Holbrook Old West Courthouse. | 520/524–6558 or 800/524–2449.
JUNE–AUG.: *Navajo Indian Dances.* More than two dozen young people perform traditional Navajo dances at this summer event at the Old West Courthouse. | 520/524–6558 or 800/524–2449.
JULY: *Gathering of Eagles.* A free art show displays pottery, rugs, jewelry, baskets, sculpture, and paintings at the Old West Courthouse. | 520/524–6558 or 800/524–2449.

SEPT.: *Navajo County Fair and Rodeo.* An old-fashioned county fair with 4-H contests, and gardening and kitchen shows. The rodeo is the climax of this five-day event at the Navajo County Fairgrounds. | 520/524–6558 or 800/524–2449.

DEC.: *Parade of Lights.* This nighttime Christmas parade down Hopi Boulevard usually brings out the whole town. | 520/524–6558.

Dining

Joe and Aggies Café. Mexican. Customers keep coming back to this café, which is the oldest in town. The chiles rellenos and *chistas* (a fried flour tortilla smothered in cheese and chile) are delicious. | 120 W. Hopi Dr. | 520/524–6540 | Breakfast also available; closed Sun. | $6–$11 | AE, D, MC, V.

Mesa Italiana. Italian. Quaint and casual spot for the basics. Try the New Zealand baby rack of lamb, *osso buco,* or the linguine pescatore, or stop by for lunch and try one of their famous minilunches. | 2318 N. Navajo Blvd. | 520/524–6696 | Closed Mon. | $7–$20 | AE, D, MC, V.

Plainsman Restaurant. American. With two separate dining areas, the Plainsman is perfect for a family dinner or a romantic evening. The BBQ ribs, filet mignon, and frog's legs are all popular. Full bar. | 1001 W. Hopi Dr. | 520/524–3345 | Breakfast also available; closed Dec.–Feb. | $6–$27 | AE, MC, V.

Romo's Cafe. Mexican. This casual restaurant serves up both Mexican and American fare. Try the fajitas or taco dinner. | 121 W. Hopi Dr. | 520/524–2153 | Breakfast also available | $6–$12 | AE, D, MC, V.

Lodging

Best Western Arizonian Inn. The rooms in this chain motel are large and handsome. An all-night diner is just steps from the parking lot. Restaurant. Some microwaves, some refrigerators, cable TV. Pool. Some pets allowed. | 2508 E. Navajo Blvd. | 520/524–2611 or 877/280–7300 | fax 520/524–2611 | www.bestwestern.com | 70 rooms | $58–$72 | AE, D, DC, MC, V.

Comfort Inn. This chain motel is across the road from the Holbrook airport and 18 mi east of Petrified Forest National Park. Restaurant, complimentary Continental breakfast. Some microwaves, some refrigerators, cable TV. Pool. Laundry facilities. Business services. Some pets allowed. | 2602 E. Navajo Blvd. | 520/524–6131 or 800/228–5150 | fax 520/524–2281 | www.comfortinn.com | 60 rooms | $65 | AE, D, DC, MC, V.

Econo Lodge. This chain motel is ½ mi from Interstate 40 on the east side of Holbrook, next to the Comfort Inn. Restaurant, picnic area, complimentary Continental breakfast. Some refrigerators, cable TV. Pool. Laundry facilities. Pets allowed. | 2596 E. Navajo Blvd. | 520/524–1448 | fax 520/524–2281 | www.econolodge.com | 63 rooms | $50 | AE, D, DC, MC, V.

Holiday Inn Express. This chain hotel is at the intersection of Interstate 40 and Highway 60. Complimentary Continental breakfast. Some microwaves, some refrigerators, cable TV. Pool. Hot tub. Laundry service. Business services. Pets allowed. | 1308 E. Navajo Blvd. | 520/524–1466 | fax 520/524–1788 | www.hiexpress.com | 55 rooms, 4 suites | $89–$99, $109–$119 suites | AE, D, DC, MC, V.

Motel 6. This budget motel is on the east side of town at Interstate 40, exit 289. Cable TV. Pool. Laundry facilities. Some pets allowed. | 2514 Navajo Blvd. | 520/524–6101 | fax 520/524–1806 | www.motel6.com | 124 rooms | $35 | AE, D, DC, MC, V.

Ramada Limited. This standard chain motel is ½ mi off Interstate 40 on the east side of Holbrook. Restaurant. Cable TV. Some pets. | 2608 E. Navajo Blvd. | 520/524–2566 | fax 520/524–6427 | www.ramada.com | 41 rooms | $55–$65 | AE, D, DC, MC, V.

Wigwam Motel. This motel consists of concrete "teepees" built in the 1940s. There's a small museum of Native American artifacts and local history lore. Cable TV, no room phones. Pets allowed. | 811 W. Hopi Dr. | 520/524–3048 | www.nephi.com | 15 rooms | $33–$38 | MC, V.

JEROME

(Nearby towns also listed: Clarkdale, Cottonwood, Prescott, Sedona)

Eugene Jerome, a frontier financier, agreed to fund a speculative mining venture here, with the condition that the town be named after him. Jerome was once known as the Billion Dollar Copper Camp, and in 1903 a New York reporter called Jerome "the wickedest town in America" because of its disproportionate number of saloons. After the last mines closed in 1953, the population shrank to 50, making it a true ghost town. Now there are about 500 inhabitants, but you'll find about 50 retail establishments, which makes one for every 10 residents. It is somewhat ramshackle, but still charming because it has held off such invasions as convenience stores. The whole town is almost a mile above sea level, but within Jerome, buildings vary as much as 1,500 ft in elevation, as the town is stacked against Cleopatra Hill.

Information: Jerome Chamber of Commerce | 50 Main Ave., Jerome, 86331 | 520/634–2900 | www.jeromechamber.com.

Attractions

Gold King Mine and Ghost Town. Remnants of the mining operation 1 mi north of Jerome include an old shaft, a miner's hut, a worker's baseball field, and a boardinghouse, though it's sometimes hard to sort out the history from the junk. | Perkinsville Rd. | 520/634–0053 | www.jeromechamber.com/gold_king_mine.htm | $4 | Daily 9–5.

GHOST TOWNS

Jerome is Arizona's largest and most famous ghost town, with a current population of about 500, which makes it hardly a ghost town. Its population during the mining boom of the 1800s reached 15,000 but dwindled to a determined 50 souls after the last mine closed in 1953. It's hard to believe that this tiny, dusty town once had the state's largest JCPenney department store and one of the state's first Safeway supermarkets. Such are the vagaries of economies based on a single industry. Jerome's history is worth investigating. Blasting at the nearby mine caused several buildings to slide down Cleopatra Hill, the largest in town. To reach Jerome, take Interstate 17 north from Phoenix to Cordes Junction. Then take Highway 69 into Prescott. From Prescott, take Highway 89A to Jerome.

If you're going from Kingman to Lake Havasu in northwest Arizona, it's worth stopping by the ghost town of **Oatman,** reached via old Route 66. Oatman's main street is right out of the Old West, and scenes from several westerns, including *How the West Was Won,* were shot here. Burros roam the streets and attract tourists.

The unusually well-preserved **Dos Cabezas** Pioneer's Cemetery is the main attraction here. Mining in the area began in 1878, and the 1880 Census lists 126 residents. The town had an operating post office until 1960. Today, a few people live in the town, among the crumbling adobe ruins. From Phoenix, take Interstate 10 east, past Tucson to Willcox. Then take Route 186 south to Dos Cabezas. You'll come to the cemetery first, followed by the town.

© Corbis

Jerome State Historic Park. This park has a museum with displays on mining and minerals and the history of Jerome, all housed in the home of James S. Douglas, the owner of the Little Daisy Copper Mine. Of the three mining museums in town, this is the most comprehensive. There are also picnic facilities. | Douglas Rd. | 520/634–5381 | www.pr.state.az.us/parkhtml/jerome.html | $2.50 | Daily 8–5.

Mine Museum. This small museum houses a collection of mining stock certificates and is staffed by the Jerome Historical Society. | 200 Main St. | 520/634–5477 | $1 | Daily 9–4:30.

ON THE CALENDAR

MAY: *Paseo de Casas.* The buildings on this home tour once served as housing for miners and mining executives. | 520/634–2900.

Dining

Flatiron Cafe. American/Casual. Drop by this small, eclectic eatery with 1950s-style diner tables, old advertising memorabilia, and Mexican folk art for an afternoon snack, a strong cup of joe, or healthy sandwiches like black-bean hummus with feta cheese. An outdoor patio across the street offers views of the valley and canyons below. | 416 Main St. | 520/634–2733 | Breakfast also available; no dinner | $5–$10 | No credit cards.

Jerome Brewery. American/Casual. Housed in the old fire station, this restaurant is casual and attractive, serving good beer, sandwiches, burgers, pastas, and espresso. | 111 Main St. | 520/639–8477 | $5–$10 | MC, V.

Jerome Palace. American/Casual. After climbing up the stairs from Main Street to this former boardinghouse, you'll be ready for the hearty burgers, cheese steaks, and ribs that dominate the menu. Outdoor dining is available on a deck that overlooks the Verde Valley. | 410 Clark St. | 520/634–0554 | $7–$15 | MC, V.

Lodging

Ghost City Inn. All of the Victorian/Early American–style rooms at this 1898 B&B have access to a huge outdoor veranda that overlooks the Verde Valley and, in the far distance, Sedona. Afternoon tea and magnificent sunrises and starscapes are added pluses. Complimentary breakfast. Cable TV, in-room VCRs. Hot tub. No pets. No smoking. | 541 Main St. | 520/634–4678 | www.ghostcityinn.com | 6 rooms (4 with shared bath) | $85–$100 | AE, D, DC, MC, V.

Jerome Grand Hotel. The conversion of this former hospital into a full-service hotel began in 1994 and it is still underway. The hotel is on Cleopatra Hill, so many of the rooms offer a splendid view of the Verde Valley. Restaurant, complimentary Continental breakfast. Cable TV. | 200 Hill St. | 520/634–8200 or 888/817–6788 | fax 520/639–0299 | www.jeromegrandhotel.net | 22 rooms, 1 suite | $70–$120 | AE, D, MC, V.

Surgeon's House Bed & Breakfast. Gorgeously restored and decorated with plants and handmade quilts, this Mediterranean-style home with hardwood floors and skylights offers knockout views, friendly service, and plenty of sun-filled nooks and crannies. A multicourse gourmet breakfast is prepared by innkeeper Andrea Prince from her own published cookbook. Complimentary breakfast. No room phones, no TVs. Some pets allowed (fee). | 101 Hill St. | 520/639–1452 | www.surgeonshouse.com | 3 suites | $100–$150 | MC, V.

KAYENTA

MAP 3, G2

(Nearby town also listed: Tuba City)

Kayenta, a small town with a small shopping center and some fast-food restaurants, is a good base for exploring Navajo Tribal Park and Navajo National Monument. Route

163 runs through Kayenta and was recently designated a scenic highway by the Arizona Department of Transportation.

Information: **Kayenta Visitor's Center** | Box 545, Kayenta, 86033 | 520/697–3572.

Attractions

Kayenta Visitor's Center. Housed in a circular stone structure reminiscent of Navajo hogans, the center houses a small museum of Navajo artifacts, plus a gift shop stocked with Navajo crafts. Native dancing and performances sometimes take place. | U.S. 160, ½ mi west of U.S. 163 | 520/697–3572 | Free | Daily 9 AM–6 PM.

Monument Valley Navajo Tribal Park. The attraction here is all of Monument Valley, a sprawling, arid, 30,000-acre expanse once home to the Anasazi, now populated by Navajo farming families. You'll see staunch red buttes, smoothly eroded mesas, deep canyons, and strange sculpted rock formations. The park has a 17-mi self-guided driving tour. It's possible to get out of your car for hikes; the walk (about 15 minutes round-trip) from North Window around the end of Cly Butte is worth it for the views. There's a campground and a visitor center 24 mi northeast of Kayenta on U.S. 163, where you can generally find Navajo guides to show you around. | Visitor center: off U.S. 163 | 435/727–3287 or 435/727–3353 | $2.50 | Daily sunrise–sunset.

Navajo Code Talkers Exhibit. Located in Kayenta's Burger King restaurant is an exhibit of World War II memorabilia that honors the Navajo code talkers of the Pacific campaign. These Navajo Marines sent and received military orders and dispatches in the Navajo language, a code the Japanese could not break. | U.S. 160, ½ mi west of U.S. 163 | 520/697–3170 | Free | Daily 7 AM–10 PM.

Navajo National Monument. At Navajo National Monument, two unoccupied 13th-century cliff pueblos, Keet Seel and Betatakin, stand under orange and ocher cliffs. The largest ancient dwellings in Arizona, these stone and mortar dwellings were built by the Anasazi. At the visitors center there's also a small museum, exhibits of prehistoric pottery, and a crafts shop (9 mi north of U.S. 160, about 20 mi southeast of Kayenta.) | Hwy. 564 | www.nps.gov/nava | 520/672–2366 | Free | Daily 8–5.

ON THE CALENDAR

JULY: *Kayenta 4th of July Celebration.* This two-day celebration includes a full rodeo, country-western dancing, and an elaborate fireworks display at the Kayenta Rodeo Grounds. | 520/697–5520.

Dining

Anasazi Inn Restaurant. Native American. In the middle of nowhere, 10 mi west of Kayenta, this is a good place to go for a quiet, peaceful meal. The Navajo fry-bread sandwiches and tacos are especially tasty. | U.S. 160 | 520/697–3793 | Breakfast also available | $8–$15 | AE, D, DC, MC, V.

Golden Sands Restaurant. American. In this ultracasual place next door to the Best Western Wetherill you can get Navajo tacos and hamburgers. It's nothing special, but it's one of the few places to get a bite to eat here. | U.S. 163 | 520/697–3684 | $8–$13 | No credit cards.

Lodging

Best Western Wetherill Inn. Named for John Wetherill, a frontiersman who discovered prehistoric Native American ruins in Arizona, this clean two-story motel on the north side of Kayenta has southwestern decor. Cable TV. Pool. Business services. | Hwy. 163 | 520/697–3231 or 800/780–7234 | fax 520/697–3233 | www.bestwestern.com | 54 rooms | $88–$98 | AE, D, DC, MC, V.

Goulding's Monument Valley Trading Post & Lodge. This historic trading post about 20 mi northeast of Kayenta in Utah and 1 mi from Monument Valley Navajo Tribal Park once served as a set for John Wayne films such as *Stagecoach* and *Fort Apache*. The original trading post houses a museum with movie memorabilia and a mutimedia show on Monument Valley. The two-story motel offers basic, comfortable rooms with spectacular views of Monument Valley. Guided tours of the valley leave from here. Goulding's also runs a campground, a grocery store, and a convenience store. Restaurant, cafe. Refrigerators, in-room VCRs (and movies). Pool. Laundry facilities. Pets allowed. | Indian Hwy. 42 | 435/727–3231 or 800/874–0902 | fax 435/727–3344 | www.gouldings.com | 19 rooms in lodge, 41 rooms motel rooms, 2 cabins | $138 rooms, $150 cabins | AE, D, DC, MC, V.

Hampton Inn Navajo Nation. The newest of Kayenta's lodgings, this 3-story chain property with immaculate rooms and a friendly staff is close to all the local attractions. Room service is available, local phone calls are free, and there are coffee makers and irons in the rooms. The gift shop sells some Navajo crafts. Restaurant, complimentary Continental breakfast. In-room data ports. Cable TV. Pool. | U.S. 160 | 520/697–3170 or 800/426–7866 | fax 520/697–3189 | www.hamptoninn.com | 73 rooms | $99–$102 | AE, D, DC, MC, V.

Holiday Inn Kayenta. This comfortable chain motel is at the junction of U.S. 160 and U.S. 163 in Kayenta, about 25 mi south of Monument Valley. Restaurant, room service. Cable TV. Pool, wading pool. Laundry facilities. Business services. | U.S. 160 at U.S. 163 | 520/697–3221 | fax 520/697–3349 | www.holiday-inn.com | 155 rooms, 8 suites | $109–$129, $149–$169 suites | AE, D, DC, MC, V.

KINGMAN

MAP 3, B4

(Nearby town also listed: Bullhead City)

This mining and ranching area was settled in the late 1800s when the Atlantic and Pacific Railroad made its way here. Historic Route 66 cuts through the town of Kingman (population 20,000), which is surrounded on three sides by rugged hills. The neon-lit roadway here is named for native son Andy Devine, the gravelly voiced actor who played sidekick in innumerable westerns. Because of the junctions of so many highways here (U.S. 93, Interstate 40, Highway 68, and Route 88 all converge here), it's a convenient base for exploring northwestern Arizona, Hoover Dam, and Laughlin, Nevada.

Information: **Kingman Area Chamber of Commerce** | 120 W. Andy Devine Ave., Kingman, 86401 | 520/753–6106 | www.kingmanchamber.com.

Attractions

Bonelli House. This house is an example of Anglo-Territorial architecture that was popular in the 1900s. It's one of 62 buildings in the Kingman business district on the National Register of Historic Places. | 430 E. Spring St. | 520/753–3195 | Free | Thurs.–Mon. 1–4.

Chloride. About 12 mi north of Kingman is a turnoff for this almost–ghost town (there are still 260 residents), which takes its name from a type of silver ore mined in the area. Some historic buildings still remain, including the old bank vault, now a museum; the 1890 Jim Fritz house; and the Tennessee Saloon, now a general store. Take a look at the huge murals painted on the rocks at the outskirts of town by western artist Roy Purcell. | Off U.S. 93 | No phone | www.chloridearizona.com | Free | Daily.

Hoover Dam. In the Lake Mead National Recreation Area 75 mi north of town over the Nevada border, the impressive Hoover Dam is 727 ft high and 660 ft wide. Tours inside are available. | U.S. 93 | 702/294–3523 | www.hooverdam.com | $8 | Daily 8–5:45.

Hualapai Mountain Park. Take a 15-mi drive south of Kingman to this area of more than 2,200 wooded acres at elevations ranging from 6,000 to 8,400 ft. There are 6 mi of hiking trails as well as picnic areas, rustic cabins, and campsites. | Hualapai Mountain Park

Rd. | 520/757–3859 | www.hualapaimountainpark.com | Free; $8–$15 camping, $25–$65 cabins | Daily.

Mohave Country Museum of History and Arts. This museum includes a room of memorabilia devoted to Andy Devine, the famous comic sidekick for Roy Rogers and other cowboys in Hollywood westerns and, later, a TV star. The museum also traces the area's Hualapai Indian history and the construction of Hoover Dam. | 400 W. Beale St. | 520/753–3195 | $3 | Weekdays 9–5, weekends 1–5.

Oatman. A number of westerns were filmed in this ghost town 28 mi southwest of Kingman, including *How the West Was Won* (1963), starring Jimmy Stewart and Henry Fonda. It's really a living museum, as it has changed little since its Hollywood heyday. You can wander into one of the three saloons or visit the Oatman Hotel, where Clark Cable and Carole Lombard had their honeymoon in 1939. | Rte. 66 | 520/768–7400 | Free | Daily sunrise–sunset.

ON THE CALENDAR

SEPT.: *Mohave County Fair.* Music, food booths, an arcade, and children's activities are featured at this popular fair at the Fairgrounds in Kingman. | 2600 Fairgrounds Blvd. | 520/753–6106.
OCT.: *Andy Devine Days and PRCA Rodeo.* This festival honors Andy Devine, the old-time Hollywood actor and TV star, with a rodeo, sports tournaments, and a parade at the local fairgrounds. | 520/753–6106.
OCT.: *Kingman Auto and Air Show.* Aerial performances, glider shows, and an extensive display of vintage and new planes are among the highlights of this show at the Kingman Airport. | 520/692–9599.

Dining

Golden Corral Family Steak House. American. This family-oriented restaurant is known for its extensive hot and cold buffet, which includes a salad, taco, and pizza bar, and five meat selections. If you aren't in the mood for a buffet, try the grilled shrimp or chopped steak. | 3157 Stockton Hill Rd. | 520/753–1505 | $5–$10 | MC, V.

House of Chan. Chinese. Cantonese favorites fill the menu in this casual place. You can request food without MSG, and if you feel like something less Chinese, you can always order the prime rib. | 960 W. Beale St. | 520/753–3232 | $8–$15 | AE, MC, V.

Mi Sarita. Mexican. This small restaurant serves authentic Mexican cuisine and prides itself on the freshness of all the ingredients. Try the gorditas and chiles rellenos. | 3051 Armour Ave. | 520/692–0465 | Closed Sun. | $4–$7 | No credit cards.

Lodging

Best Western—A Wayfarer's Inn. This chain motel is on the motel strip in Kingman. It's a tad more upscale than many of the other motels in town. Microwaves, refrigerators, cable TV. Pool. Hot tub. Laundry facilities. Pets allowed. | 2815 E. Andy Devine Ave. | 520/753–6271 or 800/548–5695 | fax 520/753–9608 | www.bestwestern.com | 98 rooms, 3 suites | $67–$80, $90 suites | AE, D, DC, MC, V.

Brunswick Hotel. Antiques fill the rooms of this downtown hotel, which is a cut above the chains that line this strip. As you step into the lobby, the furnishings and decor will transport you back to the early 1900s. Restaurant, bar, complimentary Continental breakfast. Cable TV. Some kitchenettes. Laundry facilities. Pets allowed. | 315 E. Andy Devine Ave. | 520/718–1800. | fax 520/718–1801 | www.hotel-brunswick.com | 24 rooms | $65–$95 | AE, D, DC, MC, V.

Days Inn. This two-story budget motel is on the main strip in Kingman. Complimentary Continental breakfast. Kitchenettes, microwaves, refrigerators, cable TV. Pool. Hot tub. Laundry facilities. Business services. Pets allowed (fee). | 3023 E. Andy Devine Ave. | 520/753–7500 | fax 520/753–4686 | www.daysinn.com | 60 rooms | $55–$75 | AE, D, DC, MC, V.

Hill Top. An inexpensive independent motel with basic amenities. Some refrigerators, cable TV. Pool. Laundry facilities. Business services. Some pets allowed. | 1901 E. Andy Devine Ave. | 520/753–2198 | fax 520/753–5985 | 29 rooms | $32–$44 | D, MC, V.

Kingman Super 8 Motel. This two-story chain motel is at the northern end of the motel strip in Kingman. In-room data ports, cable TV. Pool. Hot tub. Pets allowed (fee). | 3401 E. Andy Devine Ave. | 520/757–4808 | fax 520/757–4808 | www.super8.com | 61 rooms | $45–$56 | AE, D, DC, MC, V.

Quality Inn. This chain motel has comfortable rooms and a spiffy coffee shop stocked with Route 66 memorabilia. Complimentary Continental breakfast. Some kitchenettes, some refrigerators. Cable TV. Pool. Hot tub, sauna. Gym. Business services, airport shuttle. Pets allowed. | 1400 E. Andy Devine Ave. | 520/753–4747 | fax 520/753–4747 | www.qualityinn.com | 98 rooms | $54–$69 | AE, D, DC, MC, V.

LAKE HAVASU CITY

MAP 3, B5

(Nearby towns also listed: Bullhead City, Parker)

Lake Havasu City was the brainchild of chainsaw magnate Robert P. McCulloch, who offered jobs and cheap housing to workers willing to relocate here on the shores of Lake Havasu, which was formed by the construction of the Parker Dam in 1938. Today, it's a tourist destination, with a permanent population of 46,000, and the home of the transplanted London Bridge, which spans a narrow arm of Lake Havasu. This is an entire theme town, and the Olde English theme is played to the hilt in the Tudor-style village with pubs, red London telephone booths, and all manner of details that will please Anglophiles. But recreational opportunities abound, too, in the form of sailing, waterskiing, and swimming.

Information: **Lake Havasu Tourism Bureau** | 314 London Bridge Rd., Lake Havasu City, 86403 | 520/453–3444 or 800/242–8278 | www.havasutourism.com.

Attractions

Lake Havasu State Park. This 6,200-acre park encompasses several miles of shoreline, including Cattail Cove, where there is access to 140 boat-in campsites that aren't reachable by road. You'll enjoy all kinds of water sports, plus hiking, fishing, and camping. | London Bridge Rd. | www.pr.state.az.us/parkhtml/havasu.html | 520/855–2784 | Free | Daily 8–5.

London Bridge English Village. The heart of Lake Havasu City is its bridge, erected in 1971 after it was imported, piece by piece, from London. A kitschy, faux Tudor community has grown up all around it—a strange sight in the Southwest. This is the main shopping district in town. | London Bridge Rd. | 520/855–0888 | Free | Daily.

Topock Gorge. Accessible only by boat, Topock Gorge consists of steep volcanic banks along the Colorado River. Migratory birds, such as herons, cormorants, and egrets, nest here in the spring. The gorge is 10 mi north of downtown Lake Havasu City, south boundary of Havasu National Wildlife Refuge. | 520/453–3444 or 800/242–8278 | Free | Year-round.

SIGHTSEEING TOURS/TOUR COMPANIES

Outback Off-Road Adventures. This outfitter offers full- and half-day Jeep tours to the Mohave Mountains. | www.outbackadventures.com | 520/680–6151 | $65 and up | Tours daily (reservations required).

MAR.: *County Fair.* Games, rides, food, and children's activities are available at this fair in Lake Havasu City. | 520/855–6246.

MAY: *Cinco de Mayo Regatta.* This sailboat race celebrates Mexican Independence Day at the Lake Havasu Yacht Club. | 520/453–4043.

SEPT.–MAY: *Swap Meet.* At this large gathering of craftspeople and discounters at the London Bridge Shopping Center, you can buy everything from jewelry to blue jeans. | 520/680–5685.

OCT.: *IJSBA Skate-Trac World Finals.* This prestigious, international Jet Ski competition draws over 750 competitors from more than 35 countries to Windsor Beach. | 520/453–3444.

Dining

Angelina's Italian Kitchen. Italian. This dining spot serves up genuine Italian cuisine. The stuffed shrimp and lasagna are recommended, though all the dishes are quite good. Sauces are made from scratch, and the rosemary bread is a specialty. | 2137 Acoma Blvd. W | 520/680–3868 | Closed Sun. No lunch | $8–$13 | MC, V.

Chico's Tacos. Mexican. At this unpretentious, family-oriented fast-food joint, you can sample a fresh salsa bar, homemade tostados, quesadillas, and chiles rellenos, or try the create-your-own-taco platter. Margaritas and imported beers are also available. | 1641 McCulloch Blvd. | 520/680–7010 | $2–$7 | D, DC, MC, V.

Señor Murphies. Mexican. The walls at this casual dining spot are covered with paintings of traditional Mexican villages. The enchiladas and numerous fish dishes are highly recommended. | 1841 Kiowa Blvd. N, #103 | 520/680–0201 | Breakfast also available | $8–$10 | AE, D, DC, MC, V.

Shugrue's. American. By far the best restaurant in the area, with a view of the town's famous bridge, a nautical theme, and a menu of seafood, steak, and chicken. Kids' menu. | 1425 McCulloch Blvd. | 520/453–1400 | $17–$27 | AE, MC, V.

Lodging

Best Western Lake Place Inn. This hotel offers a beautiful lake view and secured boat parking. It's a few minutes from the center of the city, so it's a good place if you want to avoid the crowds and noise. Restaurant, bar. Cable TV. Business services. | 31 Wings Loop | 520/855–2146 | fax 520–855–3148 | www.bestwestern.com | 40 rooms | $59–$89 | AE, D, DC, MC, V.

Bridgeview Motel. Most of the southwestern-style rooms at this modern motel afford views of London Bridge and Lake Havasu. Accomodations are clean and simple, and the property is within walking distance of area restaurants and shops. Satellite TV. Pool. Some pets allowed. | 101 London Bridge Rd. | 520/855–5559 | fax 520/855–5564 | 37 rooms | $59–$145 | MC, V.

El Aztec All Suites Inn. All 16 suites in this small hotel have a living room and full kitchen, making them ideal for families. You'll enjoy great views of the lake and can take advantage of the boating services which are located nearby. Cable TV. Pool. Laundry facilities. | 2078 Swanson Ave. | 520/453–7172 or 877/702–4980 | fax 520/855–1685 | aztecinn.com | 16 suites | $54–$69 | MC, V.

Havasu Springs Resort. Rooms here are in four motel buildings. There are also an RV park and houseboat rentals. Some of the motel rooms offer views of Lake Havasu, on which the houseboats are located. There are several houseboat models available; each sleeps from 10 to 12 people. Restaurant. Some kitchenettes, some microwaves, some refrigerators, cable TV. Laundry facilities. Pets allowed (fee). | 2581 Hwy. 95, Parker | 520/667–3361 | fax 520/667–1098 | www.havasusprings.com | 44 rooms, 4 houseboat models | $85–$100 motel rooms, $901–$1,431 for 3 nights in houseboats (3–night minimum) | AE, D, MC, V.

Holiday Inn. This motel is about ½ mi from Lake Havasu, next to Lake Havasu State Park. Restaurant, bar, room service. In-room data ports, refrigerators, cable TV. Pool. Video games.

Laundry facilities. Business services, airport shuttle. Some pets allowed. | 245 London Bridge Rd. | 520/855–4071 or 888/428–2465 | fax 520/855–2379 | www.holiday-inn.com | 157 rooms, 5 suites | $57–$84 | AE, D, DC, MC, V.

Island Inn. This large motel offers large, immaculate, though basic rooms near a public beach. Many rooms have balconies. Pool. In-room data ports, cable TV. Hot tub. Laundry facilities. | 1300 W. McCulloch Blvd. | 520/680–0606 or 800/243–9955 | fax 520/680–4218 | 162 rooms | $65–$125 | AE, D, DC, MC, V.

London Bridge Resort. This 110-acre, all-suite waterfront resort offers a kitschy combination of Tudor- and southwestern-style buildings. Basic motel-style rooms have full kitchens on Lake Havasu near the Municipal Airport. Restaurant, bar, picnic area. Kitchenettes, microwaves, refrigerators, cable TV. 3 pools. Hot tub. 9-hole golf course, putting green, tennis court. Shops. Business services, airport shuttle. | 1477 Queens Bay Rd. | 520/855–0888 or 800/238–8808 | fax 520/855–5404 | www.londonbridgeresort.com | 118 suites | $99–$259 | AE, D, DC, MC, V.

LITCHFIELD PARK

MAP 3, D7

(Nearby town also listed: Glendale)

Litchfield Park is a growing Phoenix suburb of 3,200, 20 minutes west of the city. Its claim to fame is the Arizona Kitchen, an inventive Native American restaurant.

Information: **Tri-City West Chamber of Commerce** | 501 W. Van Buren, Suite K, Avondale, 85323 | 623/932–2260 | www.tricitywestcofc.org.

Attractions

Wigwam Resort Golfing Course. With three challenging, championship golf courses, this is considered one of the country's premier golfing venues. | 300 Wigwam Blvd. | 623/935–3811 | fax 623/856–1081. | www.wigwamresort.com | Daily 6 AM–5.

Wildlife World Zoo. On view at this zoo 3 mi west of Litchfield Park are camels, monkeys, antelope, kangaroos, and wallabies, among other species. | 16501 W. Northern Ave. | 623/935–9453 | www.wildlifeworld.com | $11 | Daily 9–5.

ON THE CALENDAR

JAN.: *Native American Festival.* Dozens of Native American tribes sell their wares at this event, and there's dancing and music. | 602/932–2260.
FEB.: *Goodyear Rodeo Days.* A rodeo is one of the highlights of this festival at Estrella Mountain Regional Park in Goodyear. | 602/932–2260.
OCT.: *Billy Moore Days.* A celebration of the founding of the community with Hispanic and western dances, burro races, and a barbecue in Avondale and Goodyear. | 602/932–2260.

Dining

Arizona Kitchen. Southwestern. This restaurant, well worth the 20-minute drive from downtown Phoenix, offers a bold, innovative southwestern menu. Try the smoked corn chowder, grilled sirloin of buffalo, or Chilean sea bass. | 300 Wigwam Blvd. | 623/935–3811 | Closed Sun.–Mon. and July–Aug. No lunch | $17–$27 | AE, D, DC, MC, V.

Vasta Pasta Ristorante. Italian. Most of the ingredients, as well as the pasta that is used at this cozy eatery, come from the northern Italian city of Parma. Pictures of Parma also adorn the walls. Try the scallops with Italian sausage and veal with marsala sauce. | 12345 W. Indian School Rd. | 623/535–5664 | Closed Sun. No lunch | $7–$13 | AE, D, DC, MC, V.

Lodging

Best Western Phoenix Goodyear Inn. This motel in Goodyear, 3 mi south of Litchfield Park, is 5 mi from the Desert Sky Pavilion and 15 mi from Sky Harbor International Airport. Restaurant, bar. In-room data ports, cable TV. Pool. Laundry service. Business services. Some pets. | 55 N. Litchfield Rd., Goodyear. | 623/932–3210 | fax 623/932–3210 | www.bestwestern.com | 85 rooms | $89–$119 | AE, D, DC, MC, V.

Holiday Inn Express. This chain motel in Goodyear, 3 mi south of Litchfield Park, is 10 mi from Wildlife World and 17 mi west of downtown Phoenix. Complimentary Continental breakfast. In-room data ports, microwaves, refrigerators, some in-room hot tubs, cable TV. Pool. Hot tub. Gym. Video games. Laundry facilities. Business services. Pets allowed. | 1313 Litchfield Rd., Goodyear | 602/535–1313 | fax 602/535–0950 | www.hiexpress.com | 60 rooms, 30 suites | $129, $149–$169 suites | AE, D, DC, MC, V.

The Wigwam. Built in 1918 as a retreat for executives of the Goodyear Company, this luxurious resort has two top-notch golf courses. Casita-style rooms are filled with local artwork, and in keeping with its origins, the business center is extensive and in a separate wing so as not to mix business with pleasure. Suites are breathtakingly large. Take Interstate 10, exit 128. 3 restaurants, 3 bars, room service. Some minibars, some refrigerators, cable TV. 2 pools. Barbershop, beauty salon, 2 hot tubs. 3 18-hole golf courses, putting greens, tennis courts. Basketball, gym, volleyball, bicycles. Library. Children's programs (ages 5–12), playground. Business services, airport shuttle. Some pets allowed. | 300 Wigwam Blvd. | 623/935–3811 or 800/327–0396 | fax 623/935–3737 | www.wigwamresort.com | 264 rooms in casitas, 67 suites | $330–$390, $390–$475 suites | AE, D, DC, MC, V.

MARBLE CANYON

MAP 3, E1

(Nearby town also listed: Page)

Marble Canyon, 38 mi southeast of Page, marks the geographical beginning of the Grand Canyon, although it is outside the National Park area. The small town here is a good stopping-off point if you are driving U.S. 89 to the North Rim. Also nearby is Lee's Ferry, a spot on a sharp bend of the Colorado River about 3 mi northeast of the town, where most river-rafting trips through the Canyon begin. Navajo Bridge, a terrifyingly narrow crossing traversing a 500-ft-deep gorge (for pedestrians only), is another local highlight.

Information: **Page/Lake Powell Chamber of Commerce** | Box 727, 644 N. Navajo, Tower Plaza, Page, 86040 | 520/645–2741 or 888/261–7243 | www.page-lakepowell.com.

Attractions

Lee's Ferry. At a sharp bend in the Colorado River, 3 mi northeast of the town of Marble Canyon, this is the place traditionally considered Mile Zero when referring to distances through the Grand Canyon by river. Named for John D. Lee, who constructed the first ferry across the Colorado here in 1872 under the direction of Brigham Young, the area is now where most Colorado River rafting trips through the canyon begin. An actual ferry ran here until 1928, when Navajo Bridge, the first bridge across this part of the river, was built over Marble Canyon. Since huge trout linger in this stretch of the river, it's a popular place for fishing as well. | Off U.S. 89A | No phone | Free | Daily.

Marble Canyon. The geographical beginning of the Grand Canyon was carved out by the Colorado River. You can see the Navajo Bridge here, which traverses a 500-ft-deep gorge in the canyon. It's now a pedestrian overpass. | U.S. 89A | No phone | Free | Daily.

Navajo Bridge Interpretive Center. This visitor center in the town of Marble Canyon is next to the pedestrian walkway across the old Navajo Bridge, which spans the Colorado River.

You can get information about the area and watch a video about the bridge. | Off Hwy. 89A | 520/608–6404 | Mid-Apr.–Oct., weekdays 9–5; early Apr., Nov., weekends 10–4.

Vermilion Cliffs. Alongside U.S. 89A west of Marble Canyon, on the right side of the highway, these sheer, spectacular cliffs are more than 3,000 ft high in many places. Watch for condors, which were reintroduced into the area in the winter of 1996–97. | U.S. 89A, west of Marble Canyon | No phone | Free | Daily.

Dining

Lee's Ferry Lodge Restaurant. American. Paintings and pictures of fishing, particularly of trout, adorn the walls of this rustic restaurant in Lee's Ferry Lodge. Try the filet mignon and BBQ pork ribs. | U.S. 89A, mile marker 54½ | 520/355–2231 | Breakfast also available | $7–$18. | MC, V.

Marble Canyon Lodge Dining Room. American. Set in the historic 1929 Marble Canyon Lodge ¼ mi west of Navajo Bridge, this rustic, casual restaurant has a multilevel dining room. Known for fresh seafood, steak, and chicken. Kids' menu. | U.S. 89A | 520/355–2225 or 800/726–1789 | $15–$27 | MC, V.

Lodging

Cliff Dwellers Lodge. An active trading post 10 mi west of Marble Canyon at the foot of the Vermilion Cliffs, this is one of the few lodgings in this remote area. Rooms in the motel are attractive and clean. Restaurant, bar. No room phones, no TVs. Business services. No pets. | U.S. 89A | 520/355–2228 or 800/433–2543 | fax 520/355–2229 | www.cliffdwellerslodge.com | 20 rooms | $57–$74 | D, MC, V.

Lee's Ferry Lodge. All the no-frills rooms in this lodge have a different theme; you'll find the bear room, the fish room, and the cowboy room, among others. The services here are geared toward trout-fishing groups. Restaurant. No room phones, no TVs. | Hwy. 89A, mile marker 54½ | 520/355–2231 | 11 rooms (baths with shower only) | $54 | MC, V.

Marble Canyon Lodge. This lodge opened in 1929 on the same day that Navajo Bridge was dedicated. You'll find historic rooms in the original lodge, more modern rooms in the newer motel across the street, and two-bedroom suites in a building from 1992. Popular with hikers, there are many trails within walking distance. It's ¼ mi west of Navajo Bridge. Restaurant, bar. Some kitchenettes. Laundry facilities. Business services. Pets allowed. | Hwy. 89A | 520/355–2225 or 800/726–1789 | 55 rooms, 7 suites | $55–$70, $134 suites | D, MC, V.

McNARY

MAP 3, H6

(Nearby towns also listed: Show Low, Springerville/Eagar)

McNary is a beautiful town in the White Mountains of eastern Arizona on the Apache Reservation. Its heyday was from the 1920s to the 1950s, when the McNary Lumber Company prospered and the town grew to 2,000 residents. Today, fewer than 500 people remain, and it's a ramshackle community. Slow down, however, if you see roadside stands advertising Indian fry bread; these are worth a stop.

Information: **Pinetop–Lakeside Chamber of Commerce** | Box 4220, 674 E. White Mountain Blvd., Pinetop, 85935 | 520/367–4290 | www.pinetoplakesidechamber.com.

Attractions

Fort Apache Museum. Come see Apache heritage and history on display here at this museum 30 mi south of McNary in the town of Fort Apache. Exhibits include traditional baskets, illustrations, and sculptures. | Hwy. 73, Fort Apache | 520/338–4625 | www.wmat.nsn.us | $3 | Weekdays 9–5.

Hawley Lake. Fishing, hiking, and picnicking are popular activities at this lake southeast of McNary stocked with rainbow, brown, and brook trout. This is also a popular ice-fishing spot in winter. From McNary, go 12 mi east on Highway 260, then south 11 mi on Highway 473. | Hwy. 473 | 520/335–7511 | Free | Daily.

Sunrise Park Resort. This is a popular ski area for both downhill and cross-country enthusiasts. The resort 17 mi southeast of McNary, on the Fort Apache Indian Reservation, has 11 lifts and 65 trails on 3 mountains rising to 11,000 ft. Eighty percent of the runs are for beginners and intermediates. Snowboarders, snowshoers, and snowmobilers are also welcome, and there are 13½ mi of cross-country trails. The resort also operates through the summer, offering horseback riding, hiking, biking, and fishing activities May through October. | Hwy. 273 | 520/735–7669 or 800/772–7669 | www.sunriseskipark.com | Ski season: late-Nov.–Apr., daily 8–4; summer season: May–mid-Nov., daily 7 AM–5:30.

ON THE CALENDAR
MAY: *White Mountain Apache Tribe Fair & Rodeo.* A powwow, full rodeo, art exhibitions, and Sunrise dances are all highlights of this event in the town of White River, 21 mi south of McNary. | 520/338–1230.

Dining
Brown Trout Cafe. American/Casual. You have an excellent view of Hawley Lake from the dining area of this small café. Burgers and Native American fry bread are the top sellers. From McNary, go 12 mi east on Highway 260, then south 11 mi on Highway 473. | Hwy. 473, Hawley Lake | 520/335–7511 | No dinner | $3–$7 | MC, V.

Lodging
Hawley Lake Lodge. Right on Hawley Lake and surrounded by towering pine trees, this lodge is perfect for a peaceful getaway. Guests can go fishing or hiking on the premises. From McNary, go 12 mi east on Highway 260, then south 11 mi on Highway 473. Restaurant. Kitchenettes, no room phones, no TV. | Hwy. 473, Hawley Lake. | 520/335–7511 | fax 520/335–7434 | 11 rooms | $75–$85 | MC, V.

Sunrise Resort Hotel. Convenient to the ski slopes, this lodge 20 mi east of McNary offers a ski shuttle every half hour during the season. Rooms have ski racks and are comfortable and not too small. Restaurant. Cable TV. Pool. Outdoor hot tub. Horseback riding, volleyball. Sleigh rides. | Hwy. 273 | 520/735–7669 or 800/772–7669 | fax 520/735–7315 | www.sunriseskipark.com | 95 rooms | $95–$225 | AE, D, DC, MC, V.

MESA

MAP 3, E7

(Nearby towns also listed: Chandler, Phoenix, Scottsdale, Tempe)

Founded as Lehi in 1878 by Mormons on their way to Salt Lake City, Utah, Mesa (population 405,000) is a large sprawling suburb east of Phoenix. Set in what is known as the East Valley, Arizona's third-largest city is starting to seem contiguous with the Phoenix sprawl. But true to its Mormon roots, it's still a deeply conservative place where people go to raise families, and still has the largest concentration of Mormons in Arizona. The Salt River, which runs right through Mesa, has formed several shimmering desert lakes, including Roosevelt Lake and, closer to Phoenix, Canyon Lake.

Information: **Mesa Convention and Visitors Bureau** | 120 N. Center, Mesa, 85201 | 480/827–4700 or 800/283–6372 | www.mesacvb.com.

Attractions

Arizona Mormon Temple Visitors' Center. Displays here chart the history of irrigation, which the Mormons used to create fertile farmland out of desert, while gardens contain a wide variety of trees. The whole place is beautifully illuminated for the Yuletide holidays. | 525 E. Main St. | 480/964–7164 | Free | Daily 9–9.

Arizona Museum for Youth. This fine-arts museum has rotating, hands-on exhibits for kids. Classes and workshops in painting and pottery are also offered. | 35 N. Robson St. | 480/644–2467 | $2 | Tues.–Sat. 9–5, Sun. 1–5.

Buckhorn Wildlife Museum. The museum features more than 400 mounted and displayed native bird and animal specimens that were collected by an expert taxidermist. | 5900 E. Main St. | 480/832–1111 | $2. | Tues.–Sat. 9–5.

Canyon Lake. This man-made lake 16 mi northeast of Apache Junction is a popular summer weekend destination for boating, fishing, waterskiing, and swimming. Surrounded by the towering Superstition Mountains, the 28 mi of shoreline boast spectacular red-rock cliffs, canyons, and cactus-dotted hills. Steamboat rides and boat rentals are available from the docks at Tortilla Flats, and all the campsites are lakeside. | 16802 N.E. Hwy. 88 | 602/944–6504 | fax 480/380–9301 | $10 day use fee per vehicle, camping $12–$25 | Daily.

Champlin Fighter Museum. An aircraft collection including examples from the two World Wars, as well as the Korean and Vietnam wars, is the focal point of this museum at Falcon Field airport. There's also a photo library. | 4636 Fighter Aces Dr. | 480/830–4540 | $6.50 | Daily.

Lost Dutchman State Park. Legend has it that miner Jacob Waltz hid gold in what is now a 300-acre park, 20 mi northeast of Mesa. Saturdays at 10, rangers lead a 3-mi nature hike through the desert landscape. | 6109 N. Apache Trail | 480/982–4485 | www.pr.state.az.us/parkhtml/dutchman.html | $5 per vehicle | Daily.

Mesa Southwest Museum. This museum traces local history from prehistoric times to the present. The interactive exhibits include one in which visitors pan for gold. | 53 N. Mac-Donald St. | 480/644–2230 | $6 | Tues.–Sat. 10–5, Sun. 1–5.

SIGHTSEEING TOURS/TOUR COMPANIES

Dolly Steamboat Cruises. This company provides narrated cruises on Canyon Lake, as well as dinner cruises. | Apache Junction | 480/827–9144 | www.dollysteamboat.com | $14–$40 | Weekdays 8–5, weekends 8–2.

Salt River Tubing and Recreation. This outfitter offers tube rentals for use on the Salt River in Tonto National Forest, 15 mi from Highway 60 in northeast Mesa. | Power Rd. | 480/984–3305 | www.saltrivertubing.com | $9 | Mid-Apr.–mid-Sept., daily 9–5.

ON THE CALENDAR

FEB.: *Mesa Territorial Days.* This is an Old West celebration of Arizona's statehood. | 520/644–2760.

FEB.–MAR.: *Arizona Renaissance Festival.* Reenactments of 16th-century European life, complete with music, jousting, vendors, and crafts, held 9 mi east of Apache Junction. | 520/463–2700.

MAR.: *Baseball Spring Training.* The Chicago Cubs and nine other major-league teams, including the Seattle Mariners, Arizona Diamondbacks, Chicago White Sox, San Diego Padres, Oakland A's, San Francisco Giants, Colorado Rockies, Anaheim Angels, and Milwaukee Brewers, play exhibition games throughout the month. | 480/827–4700 or 800/283–6372.

MAY: *Cinco de Mayo Celebrations.* This festival includes music, entertainment, food, and activities for the entire family in Pioneer Park. | 480/827–4700 or 480/644–2984.

OCT.: *Native American Pow Wow.* More than 300 Native American dancers from throughout the nation compete in this colorful event in Pioneer Park. | 480/827–4700.

Dining

Euro Cafe. Mediterranean. Portion sizes and flavor content are both very large at this restaurant. The southern Mediterranean fare is staggering, in every sense. Try the Chicken Palm, which is adorned with palm hearts and artichokes heaped over pasta and is enough to feed a small army, or the gyros platter, heaped with capers, sun-dried tomatoes, red peppers, and two kinds of Greek cheese. | 1111 S. Longmore | 480/962–4224 | $12–$19 | AE, D, DC, MC, V.

Joe's Real Barbecue. Barbecue. This family-oriented restaurant in Gilbert, just south of Mesa, is decorated with memorabilia from 1940s agricultural Arizona and has a park on the premises. Ten kinds of meat are served; popular items include ribs and pulled pork. | 301 N. Gilbert Rd., Gilbert | 480/503–3805 | Closed Sun. | $5–$16 | D, MC, V.

Landmark. American. Built in 1908, this former church has a large photo gallery of the history of Mesa. Try the prime rib, pot roast, or halibut. Salad bar. Kids' menu. No smoking. | 809 W. Main St. | 480/962–4652 | $11–$20 | AE, D, DC, MC, V.

Matta's. Mexican. This restaurant is especially lively and crowded on weekends, when a mariachi band entertains. Try the chimichangas. Kids' menu. | 932 E. Main St. | 480/964–7881 | $7–$15 | AE, D, DC, MC, V.

Michael Monty's Mesa Grill. American. On one of Mesa's main strips, this contemporary and casual restaurant in a shopping center serves good fresh fish dishes and steak. Try the Brazilian shrimp diablo, the ostrich fillet teriyaki, or a tender filet mignon. Kids' menu. No smoking. | 1233 S. Alma School Rd. | 480/844–1918 | No lunch Sun. | $16–$35 | AE, D, DC, MC, V.

Organ Stop Pizza. Italian. If you've got kids in tow, this is the place for dinner. The centerpiece of the operation is a Mighty Wurlitzer organ, on which talented organists play while the family munches on pizza, pasta, sandwiches, and salads. | 1149 E. Southern Ave. | 480/813–5700 | No lunch | $5–$15 | No credit cards.

Rosa's Mexican Grill. Mexican. This festive, family-friendly restaurant summons up images of a Baja beach "taqueria." The tacos are Rosa's true glory: beef, pork, and chicken marinated in fruit juices and herbs then slowly oven-baked, shredded, and charbroiled. | 328 E. University Dr. | 480/964–5451 | Closed Sun.–Mon. | $5–$11 | No credit cards.

Scarole's of New York. Italian. This New York–style bistro offers great Italian home cooking. Try the veal Parmesan and buffalo mozzarella for dinner, then top it off with some ricotta cheesecake for dessert. There is also a cigar and martini bar in the restaurant. | 830 W. Southern Ave. | 480/964–7771 | Reservations essential | Closed Sun. No lunch Sat. | $8–$19 | AE, D, DC, MC, V.

Sluggo's Sports Grill. American/Casual. Sports memorabilia enliven this crowded, friendly restaurant known for hamburgers and grilled chicken. Open-air dining with a waterfall view. | 161 N. Centennial Way | 480/844–8448 | $6–$9 | AE, DC, MC, V.

Zur Kate. German. Exuding homey congeniality, this spot is crammed with beer steins, flags, travel posters, and, on weekends, live oompah-pah music. Try the *kasseler* (smoked pork chops) or homemade bratwurst. | 4815 E. Main St. | 480/830–4244 | Reservations not accepted | Closed Sun. (Sun.–Mon., June–Sept.). No lunch | $5–$11 | MC, V.

Lodging

Arizona Golf Resort and Conference Center at Superstition Springs. This 150-acre resort, with a championship golf course and school, is very beginner-friendly. Many rooms have private balconies or patios. Restaurant, bar, picnic area. In-room safes, some kitchenettes, microwaves, refrigerators, cable TV. Pool. Driving range, 18-hole golf course, putting green, tennis courts. Gym. Laundry facilities. Business services. Pets allowed. | 425 S. Power Rd. | 480/832–3202 or 800/528–8282 | fax 480/981–0151 | www.azgolfresort.com | 89 rooms, 98 suites | $159, $259–$298 suites | AE, D, DC, MC, V.

Best Western Dobson Ranch Inn and Resort. This resort is on 10 acres. The Chicago Cubs stay here during spring training. Restaurant, bar, complimentary Continental breakfast, room service. In-room data ports, some refrigerators, cable TV. Pool. Hot tub. Gym. Video games. Laundry facilities, laundry service. | 1666 S. Dobson Rd. | 480/831–7000 or 800/528–1356 | fax 480/831–7000 | www.bestwestern.com | 200 rooms, 13 suites | $130–$165, $180–$200 suites | AE, D, DC, MC, V.

Best Western Mesa Inn. This chain motel is less than a mile from the Mormon Temple. Complimentary Continental breakfast. In-room data ports, cable TV, in-room VCRs (and movies). Pool. Outdoor hot tub. Laundry facilities, laundry service. Pets allowed (fee). | 1625 E. Main St. | 480/964–8000 | fax 480/835–1272 | www.bestwestern.com | 100 rooms | $80–$99 | AE, D, DC, MC, V.

Best Western Mezona Inn. This motel is just over a mile from the Mormon temple and 6 mi from Arizona State University. Restaurant, bar, room service. Cable TV. Pool. Business services. | 250 W. Main St. | 480/834–9233 or 800/528–8299 | fax 480/844–7920 | www.bestwestern.com | 136 rooms | $100–$110 | AE, D, DC, MC, V.

Best Western Superstition Springs Inn & Suites. A comfortable chain hotel 6 mi from the Mormon Temple and 18 mi from downtown Phoenix. Complimentary Continental breakfast. In-room data ports, some microwaves, some refrigerators, cable TV. Pool. Hot tub. Gym. Laundry facilities. Business services. | 1342 S. Power Rd. | 480/641–1164 or 800/528–1234 | fax 480/641–7253 | www.bestwestern.com | 59 rooms | $120–$139 | AE, D, DC, MC, V.

Courtyard Phoenix Mesa. This comfortable chain hotel is two blocks from the Fiesta Mall. Restaurant, bar. In-room data ports, some microwaves, some refrigerators, cable TV. Pool. Hot tub. Gym. Laundry facilities. Business services. | 1221 S. Westwood Ave. | www.courtyard.com | 480/461–3000 or 800/321–2211 | fax 480/461–0179 | 138 rooms, 11 suites | $159–$169 | AE, D, DC, MC, V.

Days Inn–East Mesa. This two-story motel is on the east side of Mesa, eight blocks from the municipal airport. Complimentary Continental breakfast. Cable TV. Pool. Hot tub. Business services. | 5531 E. Main St. | 480/981–8111 | fax 480/396–8027 | www.daysinn.com | 49 rooms, 12 suites | $80–$90, $95–$105 suites | AE, D, DC, MC, V.

Fairfield Inn Phoenix/Mesa. This chain hotel is 1 mi northeast of Gila River Casino and a few blocks from the Fiesta Mall. Complimentary Continental breakfast. In-room data ports, microwaves, some refrigerators, cable TV. Pool. Hot tub. Business services. | 1405 S. Westwood | 480/668–8000 | fax 480/668–7313 | www.fairfieldinn.com | 66 rooms, 18 suites | $99–$129 | AE, D, DC, MC, V.

Gold Canyon Golf Resort. This resort 7 mi east of Mesa has great views of the Superstitious Mountains. Many rooms have fireplaces and private patios. The two golf courses here are considered very good by enthusiasts. Restaurant, bar, room service. In-room data ports, refrigerators, some in-room hot tubs, cable TV. Pool. Hot tub. Driving range, 2 18-hole golf courses, putting green, tennis courts. Bicycles. Business services. Pets allowed (fee). | 6100 S. Kings Ranch Rd., Gold Canyon | 480/982–9090 or 800/624–6445 | fax 480/983–9554 | www.goldcanyongolfresort.com | 101 casitas | $160–$270 | AE, D, DC, MC, V.

Hampton Inn-Phoenix/Mesa. This four-story chain hotel is 4 mi east of downtown Mesa. Complimentary Continental breakfast. In-room data ports, refrigerators, cable TV. Pool. Hot tub. Laundry facilities. Business services. | 1563 S. Gilbert Rd. | 480/926–3600 or 800/426–7866 | fax 480/926–4892 | www.hamptoninn.com | 116 rooms | $99–$119 | AE, D, DC, MC, V.

Hilton Mesa Pavilion. This eight-story atrium-style hotel is located across the street from the Fiesta Mall. Rooms are medium size; the corner suites have the best views. Restaurant, bar. In-room data ports, some microwaves, refrigerators, cable TV. Pool. Hot tub. Gym. Business services. | 1011 W. Holmes Ave. | 480/833–5555 | fax 480/649–1886 | www.hilton.com | 201 rooms, 62 suites | $140–$200, $169–$229 suites | AE, D, DC, MC, V.

Motel 6 Mesa Main. This chain motel in central Mesa is less than 1 mi from the Mormon Temple and 10 mi from Papago Park. Cable TV. Laundry facilities. Pool. Some pets allowed.

| 630 W. Main St. | 480/969–8111 | fax 480/655–0747 | www.motel6.com | 102 rooms | $49 | AE, D, DC, MC, V.

Motel 6 Mesa South. Located in south Mesa, this chain motel is 1½ mi from the Fiesta Mall and ¼ mi from Golf Land Amusement Park. Cable TV. Some microwaves, some refrigerators. Pool. Laundry facilities. Some pets allowed. | 1511 S. Country Club Dr. | 480/834–0066 | fax 480/969–6313 | www.motel6.com | 91 rooms | $45 | AE, D, DC, MC, V.

Phoenix Days Inn–Mesa. This three-story chain motel is within walking distance of several restaurants. Complimentary Continental breakfast. Refrigerators, cable TV. Pool. Hot tub. Gym. Laundry facilities. Business services. | 333 W. Juanita Ave. | 480/844–8900 | fax 480/844–0973 | www.daysinn.com | 118 rooms, 6 suites | $79–$109, $129–$239 suites | AE, D, DC, MC, V.

Phoenix/Mesa Travelodge. This two-story standard chain motel built in 1964 is close to Arizona State University and Papago Park. In-room data ports, cable TV. Pool. Business services. | 22 S. Country Club Dr. | 480/964–5694 | fax 480/964–5697 | www.travelodge.com | 39 rooms | $82–$90 | AE, D, DC, MC, V.

Quality Inn. This chain motel is 2 mi north of the Fiesta Mall and 3 mi west of the Mormon Temple. Complimentary Continental breakfast. Some microwaves, some refrigerators, cable TV. Pool. Hot tub. Gym. Laundry facilities. Business services. | 951 W. Main St. | 480/833–1231 | fax 480/833–1231 | www.qualityinn.com | 96 rooms | $86–$155 | AE, D, DC, MC, V.

Ramada Inn Suites. This comfortable all-suite chain hotel is 12 mi east of Sky Harbor International Airport. Complimentary Continental breakfast. In-room data ports, kitchenettes, cable TV. Pool. Hot tub. Laundry facilities. | 1410 S. Country Club Dr. | 480/964–2897 or 800/272–6232 | fax 480/833–0536 | www.ramada.com | 121 suites | $116–$155 | AE, D, DC, MC, V.

Residence Inn Phoenix/Mesa. This three-story all-suite hotel is across the street from Fiesta Mall and 8 mi from Papago Park. Complimentary breakfast. In-room data ports, kitchenettes, microwaves, refrigerators, cable TV. Pool. Spa. Laundry service. Business services. Pets allowed (fee). | 941 W. Grove Ave. | 480/610–0100 | fax 480/610–6490 | www.residenceinn.com | 117 suites | $159–$199 | AE, D, DC, MC, V.

Sheraton Mesa Hotel and Conference Center. This 12-story hotel is 2 mi from the Fiesta Mall, 5 mi from Arizona State University. Restaurant, bar. Some refrigerators, cable TV. Pool. Hot tub. Driving range, putting green. Gym. Business services, airport shuttle. Some pets allowed (fee). | 200 N. Centennial Way | 480/898–8300 or 800/456–6372 | fax 480/964–9279 | www.sheraton.com | 265 rooms, 8 suites | $119–$159, $225–$300 suites | AE, D, DC, MC, V.

Travelodge Suites. This all-suite chain motel is near Arizona State University. Microwaves, refrigerators, cable TV. Pool. Hot tub. Laundry facilities. Business services. | 4244 E. Main St. | 480/832–5961 or 888/515–6375 | fax 480/830–9274 | www.travelodge.com | 77 suites | $85–$135 | AE, D, MC, V.

NOGALES

MAP 3, F10

(Nearby towns also listed: Tubac, Tucson)

Nogales, Arizona, was founded in 1880 as a customs control center between the United States and Mexico, primarily for cattle shipping. By 1910, its Mexican namesake just across the border had become the most important city in Sonora, both economically and socially. Nogales, both in Arizona and in Mexico, is still a crowded, bustling Mexican border town of 25,000, just an hour south of Tucson. On the Mexican side, it now reaps the rewards of NAFTA, with warehouses and trucking firms dedicated to distributing Mexican produce and other goods bound for the United States. Senior citizens drive down from the many Arizona retirement communities to buy their prescription drugs across the border, where they are much cheaper. The American side depends on Mexicans, who cross the border from Mexico to buy American goods. Shops line the streets, competing with homeless children selling gum or mints. The Sonoran food is great, of course, and there's good shopping for wool blankets, glassware, and tequila. Rather than risking your car by driving it across the border, park in one of the many guarded lots on the American side for a nominal amount (about $4 or $5) and walk across the border; most of the area of interest to tourists is within easy walking distance and can be covered in a day trip.

Information: **Nogales–Santa Cruz County Chamber of Commerce** | 123 W. Kino Park Way, Nogales, 85621 | 520/287–3685.

Attractions

Nogales, Sonora. You can shop or get great Mexican food just over the border in this Mexican city. The main shopping area on the Mexican side is Avenida Obregón, which begins a few blocks west (right) of the border entrance and runs north–south. Just follow the crowds. Except where signs indicate otherwise, bargaining is accepted and expected. | Avenida Obregón, Nogales, Sonora, Mexico | no phone | Free | Daily.

Patagonia Lake State Park and Sonoita Creek Natural Area. This lake 17 mi northeast of Nogales is a great place to see many species of desert scrub and lower canyon habitats plus waterfowl and other birds. Broad-billed hummingbirds and verdins are common also around the campground. You can take one-hour pontoon boat birding tours of the lake. It's a popular fishing and camping spot. | Off Hwy. 82, Patagonia. | 520/287–2791 | www.pr.state.az.us | Free | Visitor center daily 8:30–5.

Pimeria Alta Historical Society Museum. Displays in this museum in the city's 1914 former city hall document the varied past of this area and adjacent areas of southern Arizona and Sonora, Mexico. There are self-guided walking tours, as well as a photo collection. Guided tours are also available. | 136 N. Grand Ave. | 520/287–4621 | Free | Fri.–Sat. 10–4.

ON THE CALENDAR

MAY: *Cinco de Mayo Festivities.* This festival celebrates the city's Mexican heritage. | 520/287–3685.

© Corbis

A BRIEF GUIDE TO TEQUILA

Throughout southern Arizona, the landscape is crowded with agave, the plant from which fine tequila is made, and just across the border in Mexico, there are more than 50 tequila producers. So it's understandable that tequila is a popular drink in Arizona, especially alongside Mexican food. The heart of the tequila-making region is Tequila itself, some 30 mi west of Guadalajara, in the state of Jalisco. The hills around the town are responsible for its name, "tel" meaning "hill," and "quilla," a kind of lava around the dead volcanoes in the area.

To produce tequila the bulb of the agave plant is harvested (it may weigh up to 150 pounds), heated to break down the sugars, and fermented. The best brands, Herradura and El Tesoro, are fermented with wild yeasts that add distinctive flavors to the final product. The fermented tequila is then placed into pot stills, where it is double-distilled to 90 proof or higher. Bottles designated "añejo" have been aged for a minimum of a year in oak barrels and these tequilas are anything but cheap.

Dining

Elvira. Mexican. Every meal at this large, friendly restaurant comes with a free shot of tequila. The fish dishes are fine, as are the chicken mole and carne asada tacos. | Avenida Obregon 1, Nogales, Mexico | 631/24773 | Reservations not accepted | $12–$16 | MC, V.

El Balcon de la Roca. Mexican. East of the railroad tracks and off the beaten path, this is a lovely place—a series of tiled rooms on the sprawling second floor of a stately old stone house, with a balcony overlooking a charming patio. Try the *carne tampiqueña*, an assortment of grilled meats that comes with chiles rellenos and an enchilada. Entertainment nightly. | Calle Elias 91, Nogales, Mexico | 631/20760 or 631/20891 | $15–$25 | MC, V.

Zula's. Eclectic. Standard, old-fashioned border restaurant fare is served with Greek flair in this spot on the U.S. side, with Sonoran food (tortillas, cheese, refried beans) alongside gyros and American selections. | 982 N. Grand Ave. | 520/287–2892 | Breakfast also available | $7–$16 | MC, V.

Lodging

Americana Motor Hotel. This motel less than 1 mi from the Mexican border has basic amenities. Restaurant, bar, room service. Some refrigerators, cable TV. Pool. Business services. Some pets allowed (fee). | 639 N. Grand Ave. | 520/287–7211 or 800/874–8079 | fax 520/287–5188 | 97 rooms | $55–$79 | AE, D, DC, MC, V.

Best Western Siesta Motel. This motel is 1 mi from the Mexican border. Complimentary Continental breakfast. In-room data ports, cable TV. Pool. Hot tub. Laundry service. Business services. Some pets allowed. | 673 N. Grand Ave. | 520/287–4671 | fax 520/287–9616 | www.bestwestern.com | 47 rooms | $80 | AE, D, DC, MC, V.

Nogales Days Inn. This chain motel about 2 mi from the Mexican border offers casual, unpretentious border flavor. The small-town service is friendly. Restaurant, bar, room service. Some refrigerators, cable TV. Pool. Hot tub. Laundry facilities, laundry service. Business services. Pets allowed (fee). | 884 N. Grand Ave. | 520/287–4611 | fax 520/287–0101 | www.daysinn.com | 98 rooms | $60–$65 | AE, D, DC, MC, V.

Rio Rico Resort and Country Club. Atop a mesa 12 mi north of Nogales with panoramic views of the surrounding landscape, this deluxe resort has one of the best golf courses in southern Arizona. There's entertainment on weekends and special events such as cookouts on a regular basis. It's off Interstate 17, exit 17. Restaurant, bar, room service. Cable TV. Pool. Beauty salon, hot tub. Driving range, 18-hole golf course, putting green, tennis courts. Gym, horseback riding. Business services, airport shuttle. Pets allowed. | 1069 Camino Caralampi, Rio Rico | 520/281–1901 or 800/288–4746 | fax 520/281–7132 | www.rioricoresort.com | 181 rooms, 15 suites | $135–$175, $225–$700 suites | AE, D, DC, MC, V.

Super 8. This two-story motel is 3 mi from the Mexican border, next to a shopping mall. Restaurant, bar. Refrigerators, cable TV. Pool. Hot tub. Laundry facilities. Free parking. | 547 W. Mariposa Rd. | 520/281–2242 or 800/800–8000 | fax 520/281–2242 | www.super8.com | 116 rooms | $49–$74 | AE, D, DC, MC, V.

PAGE

INTRO
ATTRACTIONS
DINING
LODGING

PAGE

MAP 3, F1

(Nearby towns also listed: Marble Canyon)

Established in 1957 as a construction camp for construction crews building the Glen Canyon Dam, Page (population 9,830) was incorporated in 1974, and is the largest community in this section of far northern Arizona. It's also the most convenient base for exploring Lake Powell and parts of the Navajo Nation in northeastern Arizona. The John Wesley Powell Memorial Museum, whose namesake led some of the earliest Grand Canyon expeditions, is a compelling stop.

Information: **Page/Lake Powell Chamber of Commerce** | Box 727, 644 N. Navajo, Tower Plaza, Page, 86040 | 520/645–2741 or 888/261–7243 | www.page-lakepowell.com.

Attractions

Glen Canyon National Recreation Area. This huge preserve consists of more than a million acres in northeastern Arizona and southern Utah, including Lake Powell, which has over 1,900 mi of shoreline. Only a small portion of the park is in Arizona. There are opportunities for swimming, waterskiing, fishing, boating, hiking, and camping, and with only 8 inches of rainfall annually, the skies are almost always blue. South of Lake Powell, the landscape gives way to the Echo Cliffs, orange sandstone formations rising up to 1,000 ft above the Colorado River in some places. At Bitter Springs, the road ascends the cliffs and provides a spectacular view of the Arizona Strip and Vermilion Cliffs. The Carl Hayden Visitors Center at Glen Canyon Dam, 2 mi west of Page, features a three-dimensional map of the area; from May to October you can also take tours of the dam every hour on the half hour from 8 to 5. | Visitor Center: U.S. 89 and Scenic View Dr., | www.nps.gov/glca | 520/608–6404 | $5 per vehicle | Visitor center Memorial Day–Labor Day daily 7–7; Labor Day–Memorial Day daily 8–5.

John Wesley Powell Memorial Museum. Artifacts from the explorer's expeditions along the Colorado River are displayed in the museum along with artifacts of the Navajo and Pueblo cultures. Visitors can also get information here on local boating excursions and scenic flights. | 6 N. Lake Powell Blvd. | 520/645–9496 | www.powellmuseum.org | $1 | Memorial Day–Labor Day, weekdays 8:30–5:30; Labor Day–Memorial Day, weekdays 9–5. Closed mid-Dec.–mid-Feb.

Rainbow Bridge National Monument. This is the world's largest natural bridge, standing 290 ft high and 275 ft long. The bridge approximately 60 mi northeast of Page in Utah is only accessible only by boat (*see* tour information under Lake Powell Resorts and Marinas, *below*). *National Geographic* featured it in 1909, and it was declared a national monument the following year. The bridge is northwest of Navajo Mountain. | Lake Powell, Utah | 520/608–6404 or 602/645–2471 | www.nps.gov/rabr | Free | Year-round.

SIGHTSEEING TOURS/TOUR COMPANIES

Lake Powell Resorts and Marinas. Half- and full-day tours to Rainbow National Monument by boat are available through this tour operator. Call for directions and starting times, as departures vary according to demand. | Box 6909, | 520/645–1070 or 800/528–6154 | www.visitlakepowell.com | $75–$99 | Nov.–Apr., 1 tour daily at 11; May–Oct., multiple tours daily.

Wilderness River Adventures. This company offers a variety of tours, including a 4½-hour guided rafting trip down a smooth portion of the Colorado River between Glen Canyon Dam and Lee's Ferry. Call for directions and starting times, as departures vary according to demand. | 50 S. Lake Powell Blvd. | www.visitlakepowell.com | 520/645–3279 or 800/528–6154 | $55 and up | Closed late-Oct.–Feb.

ON THE CALENDAR

OCT.: *Lake Powell Air Affair.* Antique biplanes simulate dogfights, precision flight teams give stunning acrobatic displays, and impressive models with 20-ft wingspans are on display the first weekend in October at the Royce K. Knight Memorial Field. | 520/645–9373.

Dining

Bella Napoli. Italian. Standard Italian-American food is served in a casual setting. Try the shrimp scampi or chicken tetrazzini. | 810 N. Navajo Dr. | 520/645–2706 | No lunch | $7–$18 | AE, D, DC, MC, V.

Dam Bar and Grill. American. Pretzel-encrusted pork chops and prime rib are the best offerings at the hippest joint in Page. The interior is filled with images of the Glen Canyon Dam, including photographs and an impressive mural. Outdoor seating is also an option. | 644 N. Navajo | 520/645–2161 | $6–$24 | AE, MC, V.

Dos Amigos. Mexican. Folks rave about the arroz con pollo, but fajitas with spicy pico de gallo sauce are also a crowd pleaser. Bright sombreros and wooden parrots create a mirthful atmosphere. | 608 Elm St. | 520/645–3036 | $8–$12 | AE, MC, V.

Ken's Old West. American. A western ambience sets the tone at this restaurant. Known for steak and barbecued ribs. Open-air dining on patio with a horseshoe pit below. Salad bar. Country band. Kids' menu. | 718 Vista Ave. | 520/645–5160 | No lunch | $11–$25 | AE, D, DC, MC, V.

Zapata's. Mexican. The food here is very traditional, so you may find the dishes spicier than at more Americanized restaurants. Chiles rellenos and enchiladas are local favorites; ceramic tile floors and stucco walls lend an air of authenticity. | 614 Navajo Dr. | 520/645–9006 | $8–$14 | D, MC, V.

Lodging

Best Western Arizona Inn. This motel overlooks Glen Canyon Dam and Lake Powell. Some of the basic, southwestern-style rooms have views of the lake. Cable TV. Pool. Hot tub. Gym. Business services, airport shuttle. Pets allowed (fee). | 716 Rimview Dr. | 520/645–2466 or 800/826–2718 | fax 520/645–2053 | www.bestwestern.com | 101 rooms, 2 suites | $89–$113, $108–$128 suites | AE, D, DC, MC, V.

Best Western Weston Inn & Suites. This three-story motel overlooking the Glen Canyon Dam has some nice views of Lake Powell. The large rooms are functional and comfortable. Complimentary Continental breakfast. In-room data ports, cable TV. Pool. Hot tub. Business services, airport shuttle. Pets allowed (fee). | 207 Lake Powell Blvd., | 520/645–2451 | fax 520/645–9552 | www.bestwestern.com | 99 rooms, 9 suites | $55–$170, $170–$180 suites | AE, D, DC, MC, V.

Canyon Colors Bed and Breakfast. Each room here has a unique theme: one features sunflower motifs, another mauve and rose paisley designs, and another is based on southwestern imagery. There is a view of the Vermillion Cliffs, which are about 20 mi away. Complimentary breakfast. Some in-room hot tubs, cable TV, in-room VCRs. Pool. Pets allowed. No smoking. | 225 S. Navajo Dr. | 800/536–2530 | fax 520/645–5979 | www.canyoncountry.com/lakepowell/colors.htm | 3 rooms | $70–$90 | AE, D, DC, MC, V.

Courtyard by Marriott. This hotel is next to the Lake Powell National Golf Course. Some rooms have views of Lake Powell. Restaurant, bar, room service. Cable TV. Pool. Hot tub, sauna. Gym. Meeting rooms, data ports. | 600 Clubhouse Dr. | 520/645–5000 or 800/321–2211 | fax 520/645–5004 | www.marriott.com | 153 rooms | $109–$149 | AE, D, DC, MC, V.

Lake Powell Motel. Rooms at this quaint and basic motor inn have views of canyon, cliffs, or Lake Powell. Guests here have access to all of the facilities at the Wahweap Lodge and Marina, which is down the hill from the motel. Cable TV. Airport shuttle. Pets allowed. | 2505 U.S. 89 | 520/645–2477, 800/528–6154 outside AZ | 24 rooms | $58–$79 | Closed Nov.–Mar. | AE, D, DC, MC, V.

Ramada Inn, Page–Lake Powell. This hotel offers standard rooms with views of the Vermilion Cliffs and the adjacent golf course. Restaurant, bar, picnic area, room service. Cable TV. Pool. Laundry facilities. Business services, airport shuttle. Pets allowed. | 287 N. Lake Powell Blvd. | 520/645–8851 | fax 520/645–2523 | www.ramada.com | 129 rooms | $99–$109 | AE, D, DC, MC, V.

Red Rock Motel. This affordable motel is a good option for families traveling to Zion National Park, the Grand Canyon, and Monument Valley. All beds are queen size, and rooms feature plush couches and chairs. No air-conditioning in some rooms. Some kitchenettes, cable TV, no room phones. | 114 8th Ave. | 520/645–0062 | www.redrockmotel.com | 7 rooms, 5 suites | $59 rooms, $65 suites | AE, D, MC, V.

Thatcher's. This brick B&B is two blocks from a scenic overlook above Lake Powell. The inn includes a large porch, and rooms feature either four-poster cherry beds or contemporary Italian provincial furnishings. Some baths are shared. Complimentary breakfast. No room phones, no TV in some rooms. No pets. No smoking. | 7 N. 16th Ave. | 520/645-3335 | fax 520/645-6856 | 3 rooms | $69-$89 | No credit cards.

★ **Wahweap Lodge and Marina.** This resort on the shores of Lake Powell offers basic rooms of various sizes, and can accommodate larger groups and families. Half of the southwestern-style rooms are lakeside, and all rooms have patios or balconies. Lake tours and boat rentals are available through the lodge's own marina. Restaurant, bar. Refrigerators, cable TV. 2 pools. Hot tub. Gym, boating. Laundry facilities. Business services, airport shuttle. Pets allowed. | 100 Lakeshore Dr. | 520/645-2433 or 800/528-6154 | fax 520/645-1031 | www.visitlakepowell.com | 369 rooms, 2 suites in 8 buildings | $79-$160, $227 suites | AE, D, DC, MC, V.

World Host Empire House. Larger-than-average rooms decorated in southwestern tones are available at this affordable two-story motor inn 2 mi from Lake Powell and across the street from Page's only shopping center. Tours of the lake and surroundings can be booked in the lobby. Restaurant, bar. Cable TV. Pool. Pets allowed (fee). | 107 S. Lake Powell Blvd. | 520/645-2406 or 800/551-9005 | fax 520/645-2647 | eh@pageamerica.net | 69 rooms | $72 | AE, D, MC, V.

PARKER

MAP 3, B6

(Nearby towns also listed: Lake Havasu City, Yuma)

Parker is centered around a dam built between 1934 and 1938 (the barrier that forms Lake Havasu). A small cotton- and melon-farming community of 3,000 on the Colorado River at Arizona's border with California, Parker offers water recreation in summer. There's also Blue Water Casino, a joint venture of the Mohave, Chemehuevi, Navajo, and Hopi tribes.

Information: **Parker Chamber of Commerce** | 1217 California Ave., Parker, 85344 | 520/669-2174 | www.coloradoriverinfo.com/parker.

Attractions

Blue Water Casino. This casino is on the Colorado River Indian Reservation. | 11222 Resort Dr. | 520/669-7777 or 800/747-8777 | www.bluewatercasino.com | Free | Daily 24 hrs.

Buckskin Mountain State Park. Though this gorge 11 mi northeast of Parker is lined with mobile-home encampments, the park preserves some wilderness area, both along the Colorado River and in the Buckskin Mountains proper. There are both hiking trails and camping facilities. | Hwy. 95 | 520/667-3231 | $4-$7 | Daily 8-10.

Colorado River Indian Tribes Museum and Library. This small museum houses a collection of rare photographs that document the Native American presence in the region. There are also baskets and pottery on display. | 2nd Ave. at Mohave Rd. | 520/669-9211 ext. 1335 | Free | Weekdays 8-5, Sat. 10-3.

La Paz County Park. This park consists of 1 mi of beachfront along the Colorado River 8½ mi north of Parker. There are tennis courts and camping. | Hwy. 95 | 520/667-2069 | $2 | Daily.

ON THE CALENDAR

JAN.: *Parker-Whiplash 400 Off Road Race.* Trucks, buggies, motorcycles, and ATVs compete in specialized events over 400 mi of desert racing. | 520/669-2174.

MAR.: *Balloonfest.* Hot-air balloon races lift off at this annual event at the Parker Airport. | 520/669-2174.

MAR.: *Miss La Paz County Pageant.* This county fair holds a livestock auction. There's also a carnival and children's activities in Mantaba Park on the Colorado River Indian Reservation. | 520/669–2174.

MAY: *Enduro Boat Races.* High-speed boats race in this national competition on the Parker Strip section of the Colorado River. | 520/669–2174.

NOV.: *Holiday Lighted Boat Parade.* This is a contest among boats decorated for the holidays on the Parker Strip of the Colorado River, the Saturday after Thanksgiving. | 520/669–2174.

Dining

Early Bird Cafe. American. Tourists and locals mingle in this no-frills diner. Collectible plates depicting horses and pictures of the Wild West adorn the walls. Burgers and country-fried steak are the most popular dishes. | 904 California Ave. | 520/669–5355 | Breakfast also available; no dinner | $4–$7 | No credit cards.

Lodging

El Rancho Motel. You'll be right in the middle of downtown here, and you certainly can't beat the price. The small rooms feature southwestern motifs and paint schemes, and for the money they feature a lot of conveniences. Some kitchenettes, microwaves, refrigerators, cable TV. Pool. Pets allowed. | 709 California Ave. | 520/669–2231 | fax 520/669–2246 | 19 rooms | $35 | AE, D, MC, V.

Kofa Inn. A large 1960s-style neon sign marks the entryway at this palm-flanked motor inn. Rooms are clean and basic, and surround a poolside garden courtyard. Restaurant. Cable TV. Pool. | 1700 S. California Ave., | 520/669–2101 or 800/742–6072 | fax 520/669–6902 | 41 rooms | $39–$43 | AE, DC, MC, V.

KODAK'S TIPS FOR NIGHT PHOTOGRAPHY

Lights at Night
· Move in close on neon signs
· Capture lights from unusual vantage points

Fireworks
· Shoot individual bursts using a handheld camera
· Capture several explosions with a time exposure
· Include an interesting foreground

Fill-In Flash
· Set the fill-in light a stop darker than the ambient light

Around the Campfire
· Keep flames out of the frame when reading the meter
· For portraits, take spot readings of faces
· Use a tripod, or rest your camera on something solid

Using Flash
· Stay within the recommended distance range
· Buy a flash with the red-eye reduction mode

From Kodak Guide to Shooting Great Travel Pictures © 2000 by Fodor's Travel Publications

PATAGONIA

MAP 3, G10

(Nearby town also listed: Nogales, Tubac)

Patagonia, a turn-of-the-20th-century shipping center for cattle and ore about 20 mi northeast of Nogales, is now lively with art galleries and boutiques. There are still some real western saloons, though, along the tree-lined streets. Most people go to visit the state park (on a reservoir), popular with water-sport enthusiasts. But Patagonia-Sonoita Creek Preserve is also worth seeing: 1,400 acres of riparian habitat are home to more than 275 bird species and other desert fauna.

Information: Patagonia Visitor's Center | Box 241, 307 McKeown Ave., Patagonia, 85624 | 520/394–0060 or 888/794–0060.

Attractions

Patagonia Lake State Park. This man-made lake 11 mi south of town offers opportunities for water sports, camping, and picnicking. There are boat ramps, and a supply store at the marina rents water-sports equipment. Go 8 mi south on Route 82, then 4 mi north on Patagonia Lake Rd. | Patagonia Lake Rd. | 520/287–6965 | $5 | Daily 4 AM–10 PM.

Patagonia-Sonita Creek Preserve. More than 275 species of birds, as well as deer, javelina, and coatimundi, have been sighted in this 1,400-acre preserve on the southwest edge of town. There's a self-guided nature trail, and guided walks are given every Saturday at 9 AM. | Off Hwy. 82, on Blue Haven Rd. | 520/394–2400 | $5 donation accepted | Wed.–Sun. 6:30 AM–4 PM.

Sonoita Vineyard. Though 30 mi east of Patagonia, the wine is exceptional and the view is splendid. The vineyard is on a 5,000-ft elevation, and sits among grasslands, oak glades, and yucca patches. Bring a picnic lunch and dine on their balcony that overlooks the vineyards. It's 3 mi south of Elgin, off of Elgin Road; take a left onto Elgin Canello Road. | Elgin Canello Rd., Elgin | 520/455–5893 | www.sonoitavineyards.com | $1–$5 for wine tasting | Daily 10–4.

ON THE CALENDAR

OCT.: *Fall Festival.* Over 5,000 people attend this celebration. You can tap your toes to Mexican-American groups or country and western bands, or just peruse the 100 craft and food booths the second weekend in October. | 888/794–0060.

Dining

Marie's. Continental. This local favorite is one of the more sophisticated spots in Patagonia, with top-notch service. Try the homemade chicken pâté with pistachios or the roast pork in white wine and mustard sauce. | 340 Naugle Ave. | 520/394–2812 | Closed Mon.–Tues. No lunch Wed.–Sat. | $12–$15 | D, MC, V.

Lodging

Circle Z Ranch. This is the oldest continuously operating guest ranch in Arizona. It's 4 mi southwest of Patagonia. Rates include all meals and horseback riding. There's a special kids' cantina with video games, jukebox, and foosball, and the younger ones have their own restaurant. Dining room. Pool. Tennis court. Horseback riding. | Hwy. 82 | 520/394–2525 or 888/854–2525 | fax 520/394–2054 | www.circlez.com | 24 rooms | $990–$1,070 per person per wk (7–day minimum stay) | Closed mid-May–early Nov. | AP | No credit cards.

Duquesne House. This B&B offers rooms in a turn-of-the-20th-century adobe, with a private entrance for each, and a koi pond in the back. Complimentary breakfast. No room phones, no TV in rooms, TV in common area. Pond. | 357 Duquesne Ave. | 520/394–2732 | 4 rooms | $75 | No credit cards.

Rio Rico Resort. Seventeen miles from Patagonia in the rural town of Rio Rico, this luxurious resort sits on a mesa where there are both mountain and valley views. Rooms are filled with southwestern touches like metal and wood tables, armoires, and wrought-iron chairs. A central courtyard with a fountain and a flower and herb garden offers an idyllic spot to relax. Restaurant. Cable TV. Pool. Hot tub, sauna. 18-hole golf course, 4 tennis courts. Health club, hiking, horseback riding. Shops. | 1069 Camino Caralampi, Rio Rico | 520/281–1901 | fax 520/281–7132 | www.rioricoresort.com | 164 rooms, 16 suites | $165–$185, $225–$275 suites | AE, D, DC, MC, V.

Sonoita Inn. The owner of Secretariat used to own this home. The inn sits at the mile-high mark, with views of several mountain ranges, so the views of sunsets are great. The rooms are expansive with motifs ranging from florals to cowboys on bucking broncos. Complimentary Continental breakfast. Cable TV. Pets allowed (fee). No smoking. | 3243 Hwy. 82 | 520/455–5935 | fax 520/455–5069 | www.sonoitainn.com | 18 rooms | $99–$125 | AE, MC, V.

Stage Stop Inn. This rustic, family-owned and operated inn offers basic accommodations that surround a courtyard pool. Each room is individually named, and all are filled with western knickknacks and pictures of cowboys. Restaurant. Some kitchenettes, cable TV. Pool. Business services. Pets allowed. | 303 W. McKeown Ave. | 520/394–2211 or 800/923–2211 | fax 520/394–2211 | 54 rooms | $69–$125 | AE, D, DC, MC, V.

PAYSON

MAP 3, F6

(Nearby town also listed: Phoenix)

This mountain town of 13,000 takes its name from a senator who never set foot in Payson, but who managed to secure its residents a post office in 1884. At 5,000 ft, Payson is in Arizona rim country and is home to the world's oldest continuously running rodeo. Payson also offers a welcome escape from the desert heat, and it's one of the relatively few places in Arizona where there are four distinct seasons.

Information: **Payson Chamber of Commerce** | 100 W. Main St., Payson, 85541 | 520/474–4515 or 800/672–9766 | www.rimcountrychamber.com.

Attractions

Rim Country Museum. Exhibits that document the natural history of the rim country region are on display at this museum run by the Northern Gila County Historical Society. The museum includes the original forest ranger's residence, now the museum store, and a re-creation of the Herron, Payson's finest turn-of-the-19th-century hotel. | 700 Green Valley Pkwy. | 520/474–3483 | $3 | Wed.–Sun. noon–4.

Tonto National Forest. The draws here are hiking, camping, and fishing in the high country cloaked in piñon, ponderosa pine, and juniper, but also in Sonoran desert terrain. With more than 3 million acres, it's one of the largest national forests in the United States. The forest also contains several designated Scenic Byways and the Tonto National Bridge. There's a district ranger office in Payson that offers information on fire restriction, closed areas, and trails. | 1009 E. Hwy. 260 | 602/225–5200 | www.fs.fed.us/r3/tonto | Free | Ranger office weekdays 8–4:30.

ON THE CALENDAR
AUG.: *World's Oldest Continuous PRCA Rodeo.* This annual PRCA (Professional Rodeo Cowboy Association) rodeo first held in 1884 includes a parade, entertainment, and some of the best riders and ropers in the country. | 520/474–4515 or 800/672–9766.

Dining

La Casa Pequeña. Mexican. There's a collection of wheeled decanters on display at this casual restaurant. Try the house chimichangas, chicken Acapulco, or chicken fajitas. Entertainment Friday and Saturday. | 911 S. Beeline Hwy. (Rte. 87) | 520/474–6329 | $7–$14 | MC, V.

Macky's Grill. American. The menu choices here are extensive, but most folks go for hamburgers or steak. Cowboy gear such as chaps, boots, and spurs dominate the walls. | 1111 S. Beeline Hwy. | 520/474–7411 | $7–$22 | MC, V.

Mario's Villa. Italian. This typical Italian-American restaurant serves mostly southern Italian–style dishes, with homemade pizza, pasta, and bread. Kids' menu. | 600 E. Hwy. 260 | 520/474–5429 | AE, D, MC, V.

Lodging

Best Western Paysonglo Lodge. Accommodations are typical motel-style rooms, except that you can also get a fireplace. Complimentary Continental breakfast. Refrigerators, cable TV. Pool. Hot tub. Laundry facilities. Business services. Some pets allowed. | 1005 S. Beeline Hwy. | 520/474–2382 | fax 520/474–1937 | www.bestwestern.com | 47 rooms | $72–$130 | AE, D, DC, MC, V.

Holiday Inn Express. This three-story chain hotel is 1 mi from the Payson Visitor's Information Center and 2 mi from the rodeo grounds. Complimentary Continental breakfast. Some microwaves, some refrigerators, cable TV. Pool. Hot tub. Laundry facilities. Business services. Pets allowed (fee). | 206 S. Beeline Hwy. | 520/472–7484 or 800/818–7484 | fax 520/472–6283 | www.hiexpress.com | 42 rooms, 2 suites | $99–$129, $129–$169 suites | AE, D, DC, MC, V.

The Inn of Payson. This inn is surrounded by ponderosa pines. Each room has a patio or balcony and some rooms have a fireplace. Complimentary Continental breakfast. Refrigerators, some in-room hot tubs, cable TV. Pool. Hot tub. Gym. Business services. Pets allowed (fee). | 801 N. Beeline Hwy. | 520/474–3241 or 800/247–9477 | fax 520/472–6564 | www.innof-payson.com | 99 rooms | $49–$119 | AE, D, DC, MC, V.

Majestic Mountain Inn. This modern, comfortable hotel has a stone fireplace in the lobby. Picnic area. Refrigerators, some in-room hot tubs, cable TV. | 602 E. Hwy. 260 | 520/474–0185 or 800/408–2442 | fax 520/472–6097 | 37 rooms | $58–$140 | AE, D, DC, MC, V.

Mountain Meadows Cabins. All the cabins at this place 27 mi east of Payson have porches with swings, pine-paneled interiors, and fireplaces. You'll enjoy a fine view of the mountains. Kitchenettes, some in-room hot tubs, no room phones, cable TV. Pets allowed (fee). | Hwy. 260 | 520/478–4415 | www.rimcountry.com/mmeadow.htm | 6 cabins | $55–$180 | MC, V.

The Village at Christopher Creek. The largest cabin at this rustic place 22 mi east of Payson is 1,400 square ft. All the units feature faux log siding, pine cabinets, and oak floors. Kitchenettes, some in-room hot tubs, no room phones. Laundry facilities. | Hwy. 260 | 520/478–4255 | fax 520/478–4080 | www.thevillageatcc.com | 5 cabins | $190–$240 | AE, MC, V.

PHOENIX

MAP 3, E7

(Nearby towns also listed: Glendale, Litchfield Park, Mesa, Scottsdale, Tempe)

It's easy to understand why the setting of Phoenix, the nation's eighth-largest city, is called the Valley of the Sun. At this tip of the great Sonoran Desert, which stretches from central Arizona deep into northwestern Mexico, it rains fewer than 30 days a year on average, and summer temperatures often climb above 100°F for weeks at a time. That it's "a dry heat" isn't much consolation. But in spring, the dry desert soil responds magically to the touch of rain, and wildflowers display their brilliance.

As the Hohokam, who were the first settlers here more than 2,300 years ago, discovered, this miracle of spring can be enhanced by human hands. They cultivated cotton, corn, and beans, and established more than 300 mi of canals with very limited technology. No one knows why they disappeared 600 years ago, but it's thought that drought and famine simply took their toll. Until the U.S. army established Fort McDowell in the mountains to the east in 1865, the once fertile Salt River valley was forgotten. To feed the men and horses stationed in the area, the long dormant Hohokam canals were reopened in 1867, and a town, then called Punkinsville, grew up around the newly blooming region.

But by 1870, when the town site was plotted, the 300 inhabitants had decided that their new city would rise "like a phoenix" from the ashes of a vanished civilization. The new image—and the new name—stuck. Before the end of the 19th century, Phoenix wrested the title of territorial capital from Prescott. Its rise was assured in 1911, when the Roosevelt Dam cut off the Salt River 60 mi to the east. The artificial lakes created by the dam—13,000 square mi all told, an area larger than Belgium—ensured that Phoenix would remain verdant. The initial idea was to ensure the agricultural development of the area, but a huge network of canals served not only crops but a lush urban landscape. Yet, while then having a reliable water supply, Phoenix still didn't enter its real growth spurt for another 40 years, when air-conditioning made the desperately hot summers bearable.

In the 1950s and 1960s the growth of the city's manufacturing base furthered the growth in population. Between 1945 and 1960, more than 300 new industries moved into the Phoenix Valley. And the city has experienced the ups and downs of unbridled growth ever since. With so many changes, and so quickly, even long-term residents have trouble keeping up. Yet what has been good for the city's entrepreneurial zeal hasn't always been good for the residents.

Modern Phoenix is a city that's struggling to deal with the effects of increasing population and a lack of civic foresight. Once a place recommended to sufferers of asthma and other respiratory ailments, this is now a city where allergies are rampant (because of the importation of nonnative plants from the east, as well as pollution). And only now are civic leaders beginning to deal with ways to control automobile traffic and urban sprawl, and to maintain a reliable supply of drinking water for future generations. Though in truth, many cities in the American west must come to grips with these problems, and Phoenix is hardly the worst example.

For visitors, especially from November to April, when the weather is nicest, it isn't difficult to understand the lure of the desert. Residents, seldom clad in more than a light jacket, drive convertibles with the top down, eat lunch outside, and devote their spare time to outdoor pursuits. Golfers love it here, and there are more than 100 courses, several of them world-class, throughout the valley. Other recreational opportunities include hiking in the nearby mountains and swimming (up to six months out of the year). South Mountain Park is a must-see. The world's largest city park (at 17,000 acres) offers hiking and biking trails and horseback riding, an amazingly serene experience just outside this major metropolis.

However, the city's greatest allure is a way of life that keeps its own pace. Phoenix—indeed, all of central Arizona—is a low-key place where people take things easy and dress informally. And if things get a little hot in the middle of a summer day, well, at least life also slows down to an enjoyable speed. Its rapid growth in the 1980s and 1990s has also brought a revitalized downtown, a rapidly emerging culinary scene, and professional sports teams, all of which give visitors more reason to come and, perhaps, to stay. One might say that Phoenix is behaving like a city with a future.

Information: **Phoenix and Valley of the Sun Convention and Visitors Bureau** | 1 Arizona Center, 400 E. Van Buren St., Suite 600, Phoenix, 85004 | 602/254–6500 | www.phoenix-cvb.com.

NEIGHBORHOODS

It's hard to think of Phoenix in terms of traditional neighborhoods since the Valley of the Sun is made up of what were once over 20 individual communities that have now more or less sprawled into one another to form a single, large metropolitan area. Other cities that form the Valley metropolitan area include Glendale and Litchfield Park in the West Valley; Scottsdale to the northeast; and Chandler, Mesa, and Tempe in the East Valley.

Downtown Phoenix. Bordered by Thomas Road on the north, Buckeye Road on the south, 7th Street on the east, and 19th Avenue on the west, the downtown area has seen a major resurgence in the 1980s and 1990s. Major sporting events take place at America West Arena and Bank One Ballpark, and there are performing arts venues such as the Herberger and Orpheum theaters as well. Downtown museums include the Heard Museum and the Arizona Science Center.

SPRING TRAINING IN ARIZONA

One way for baseball fans to cure the wintertime blues is to visit one of Arizona's many ballparks to see teams at work during spring training—the months before they play in their regular venues around the country.

Most teams begin preliminary workouts in the middle of February, though actual games don't begin until March. Spring training continues to occupy the entire month of March with teams playing around 15 games through the first week of April.

This is a good time to meet and collect autographs from favorite players. While teams are definitely serious about spring training regimens, the atmosphere around parks is more relaxed than during the regular season. Players will often come up to the side of the field to greet fans as they leave the stadium.

Tickets for some teams go on sale as early as December. Brochures list game schedules and ticket information and are available from the teams' Arizona venues. Prices range from around $5 for bleacher seats to around $15 for reserved seats, which makes it affordable.

To obtain more information about spring training in Arizona, contact the following teams at their Arizona offices, which are either in the Phoenix or Tucson areas:

Anaheim Angels, Tempe Diablo Stadium, Tempe, AZ 602/784–4444

Arizona Diamondbacks, Tucson Electric Park, Tucson, AZ 888/777–4664

Chicago Cubs, Hohokam Park, Mesa, AZ 602/503–5555

Chicago White Sox, Tucson Electric Park, Tucson, AZ 800/638–4253

Colorado Rockies, Hi Corbett Field, Tucson, AZ 520/327–9467

Milwaukee Brewers, Maryvale Baseball Park, Phoenix, AZ 602/895–1200

Oakland A's, Phoenix Municipal Stadium, Peoria, AZ 602/392–0217

San Francisco Giants, Scottsdale Stadium, Scottsdale, AZ 602/990–7972

Seattle Mariners, Peoria Stadium, Peoria, AZ 602/412–9000

© Corbis

When it Comes to Getting Cash at an ATM, Same Thing.

Whether you're in Yosemite or Yemen, using your Visa® card or ATM card with the PLUS symbol is the easiest and most convenient way to get cash. Even if your bank is in Minneapolis and you're in Miami, Visa/PLUS ATMs make getting cash so easy, you'll feel right at home. After all, Visa/PLUS ATMs are open 24 hours a day, 7 days a week, rain or shine. And if you need help finding one of Visa's 627,000 ATMs in 127 countries worldwide, visit **visa.com/pd/atm**. We'll make finding an ATM as easy as finding the Eiffel Tower, the Pyramids or even the Grand Canyon.

It's Everywhere You Want To Be.®

The Biltmore District. Also known as the Camelback Corridor, Phoenix's main shopping district runs along Camelback Road between 24th and 44th streets. It's filled with modern office buildings and centered on the Biltmore Hotel and Biltmore Fashion Park mall.

Papago Salado. This region between Phoenix and Tempe contains Papago Park and the Pueblo Grande ruins. It's bounded by 44th Street and Scottsdale Road on the east and west, and by McDowell Road and Interstate 10 on the north and south.

Paradise Valley. This is the city's most upscale residential area. Visitors to the area like to drive through this neighborhood, northwest of downtown, to soak up contemporary architecture.

South Phoenix. A mostly residential area and home to much of Phoenix's substantial Hispanic population, South Phoenix is worth a visit to eat at one of the family-style Mexican restaurants here and to see South Mountain Park and Mystery Castle. It's the area south of Baseline Road, between 51st Street and Interstate 10.

TRANSPORTATION

Airports: Sky Harbor International Airport (8500 Peña Blvd. | 602/273–3300) is just 3 mi east of downtown Phoenix and surrounded by freeways linking it to almost every part of the metro area. It's the busiest airport in Arizona and the hub for America West Airlines.

Airport Transportation: It's easy to get from Sky Harbor to downtown Phoenix by car (3 mi west) or Tempe (3 mi east). The airport is only 20 minutes by freeway from Glendale (to the west) and Mesa (to the east). Scottsdale (to the northeast) can be reached via the Squaw Peak Parkway (Highway 51), but it's just as easy to get there using all surface streets (44th Street to Camelback Road is usually the easiest); either way, it's about 30 minutes.

Only a few taxi companies are licensed to pick up passengers at Sky Harbor. All add a $1 surcharge for airport pickups and are available 24 hours a day. A trip to downtown Phoenix costs $12–$15; the fare to Scottsdale averages about $18. **Checker/Yellow Cab** (602/252–5252) and **Courier Cab** (602/232–2222)) both charge about $3 for the first mile and $1.50 per mile thereafter, not including tips.

SuperShuttle (602/244–9000 or 800/258–3826) serves downtown and makes door-to-door trips to and from all Phoenix suburbs, with trips for $7–$25.

Train Lines: Amtrak (401 W. Harrison St. | 602/253–0121 or 800/872–7245) provides train service in Arizona with bus transfers to Phoenix from Flagstaff or Tucson. What used to be Phoenix's downtown train terminal is now the bus stop.

Bus Lines: The **Greyhound Bus Terminal** (2115 E. Buckeye Rd. | 602/389–4207 or 800/231–2222.) is a hub for service from all over the country.

DRIVING AND PARKING

In the Valley of the Sun, rain and fog are rare, and snow gets major headlines. Most metro-area streets are well marked and well lighted, and the freeway system is making gradual progress in linking valley areas.

Around downtown Phoenix, Highway 202 (Papago Freeway), Highway 143 (Hohokam Freeway), and Interstate 10 (Maricopa Freeway) make an elongated east–west loop, encompassing the state capitol area to the west and Tempe to the east. At mid-loop, Highway 51 (Squaw Peak Freeway) runs north into Paradise Valley. And from the loop's east end, Interstate 10 runs south to Tucson, 100 mi away (though it's still referred to as Interstate 10 east, as it is eventually headed that way); U.S. 60 (Superstition Freeway) branches east to Tempe and Mesa.

Roads in Phoenix and its suburbs are laid out on a single, 800-square-mi grid. Even the freeways run predominantly north–south and east–west. Central Avenue is the main north–south grid axis: all roads parallel to and west of Central are numbered *avenues*; all roads parallel to and east of Central are numbered *streets*. The numbering begins at Central and increases in each direction. (Grand Avenue, running about 20 mi from northwest downtown to Sun City, is the *only* diagonal.)

Camera devices are mounted on many street lights to catch speeders and red-light runners, and their location is constantly changing. You may think you've gotten away with a few miles over the limit and return home only to find a ticket waiting for you. Smart commuters know to avoid Paradise Valley, where incomes are sky high and speed limits ridiculously low; and locals swear that Indian School Road is a better street than Camelback for driving between Phoenix and Scottsdale. Average tickets for speeding 1–20 mi over the limit will range between $110–$140. If you go over 20 mi above the speed limit, you may be charged with criminal speeding and receive an even heftier fine. As Phoenix is one of the national leaders in red-light running and speeding, it pays to be a defensive driver while in town.

Weekdays 6 AM–9 AM and 4 PM–6 PM, the center or left-turn lanes on the major surface arteries of 7th Street and 7th Avenue become one-way traffic-flow lanes between McDowell Road and Dunlap Avenue. These specially marked lanes are dedicated mornings to north–south traffic (into downtown) and afternoons to south–north traffic (out of downtown).

Parking in Phoenix is plentiful, with over 31,000 spaces in the downtown area alone. Metered street parking will cost about 60¢ an hour; covered parking garages, which are also plentiful, will run about $1 an hour, except during special events, when charges range $5–$10. If you are planning to park in downtown Phoenix during an event at the America West Arena or the Bank One Ballpark, you may want to arrive early, as nearby parking fills up fast. Parking fines are fairly strictly enforced, and will run about $16.

Attractions

ART AND ARCHITECTURE

Heritage Square. Some of the oldest architecture in Phoenix is exhibited in a parklike setting along a city block. Buildings include the midwestern-style Stevens House, the California-style Stevens-Haugsten house, the Silda House, and a doll museum. There is an excellent 30-minute tour of the Victorian Rosson house. You can walk around the square any time, but call ahead to find out the individual hours of the homes and the doll museum. | 7th and Monroe Sts. | 602/262–5071 | Park and most homes free; Rosson house tour $4 | Park open daily dawn–midnight; Rosson house tour Wed.–Sat. 10–3:30, Sun. noon–3:30; call for specific hrs of other homes.

Mystery Castle. This "castle" at the foot of South Mountain is a curious dwelling fashioned from desert rocks, railroad refuse, and anything else its builder, Boyce Gulley, could get his hands on. He built the structure between 1930 and 1945. Guided tours are given by Boyce's daughter, Mary Lou. Go 7 mi south via Central Ave., east on Baseline Rd., south on 7th St., then east on Mineral Rd. | 800 E. Mineral Rd. | 602/268–1581 | $5 | Oct.–June, Thurs.–Sun. 11–4.

BEACHES, PARKS, AND NATURAL SIGHTS

Papago Park. Year-round sun allows locals and tourists alike to enjoy the 1,200 acres at this popular and widely used urban park and recreation area. Huge boulders and cacti cover the desert landscape here, and a variety of activities and sites include 10 mi of mountain bike trails, an 18-hole golf course, a zoo, a desert botanical garden, hiking paths, horseback riding, and, even in the desert, a stocked fishing lagoon. The "Hole in the Rock," a formation in the sandstone cliffs, is a sought-after destination for sunset viewing. | 625 N. Galvin Pkwy. | 602/256–3220 | Free; prices vary for individual attractions | Daily 6:30 AM–11 PM.

★ **Desert Botanical Garden.** Opened in 1939, the various gardens display local flora on more than 150 acres in Papago Park. There are also demonstration gardens, seasonal lectures, and children's activities. | 1201 N. Galvin Pkwy. | 480/941–1217 or 480/941–1225 | $7.50 | Oct.–Apr., daily 8–8; May–Sept., daily 7 AM–8 PM.

Phoenix Mountains Preserve. The Phoenix Mountains Preserve includes four major recreational areas all over Phoenix: Echo Canyon, North Mountain Recreation Area, South Mountain Park, and Squaw Peak Park. In all, it preserves 23,500 acres. The preserve has its own rangers to help plan hikes. | 602/262–6861 | www.cityofphoenix.org | Free | Daily.

Echo Canyon. Foothpaths climb through Echo Canyon up and around Camelback Mountain east of downtown Phoenix and south of Paradise Valley. Part of the Phoenix Mountains Preserve. | E. McDonald and Tatum Blvd. | 602/256–3220 | www.cityofphoenix.org | Free | Daily sunrise–sunset.

North Mountain Recreation Area. This recreation area in north Phoenix offers hiking and picnic facilities. Part of the Phoenix Mountains Preserve. | 10600 N. 7th St. | 602/262–7901 | www.cityofphoenix.org | Free | Daily 5 AM–11 PM.

South Mountain Park. At almost 17,000 acres, this is the world's largest city park. Just minutes from downtown Phoenix, it offers opportunities for hiking, biking, and horseback riding. The Environmental Center features a large model of the park as well as displays on its history. Look for ancient petroglyphs; try to spot a desert cottontail rabbit or chuckwalla lizard; or simply stroll among the vegetation. Part of the Phoenix Mountains Preserve. | Environmental Center: 10919 S. Central Ave. | Free | 602/495–0222 | www.cityofphoenix.org | Daily 5 AM–10:30 PM; Environmental Center daily 8–5.

Squaw Peak Park. The Summit Trail, a strenuous 1.2-mi hike, rewards you with fine Phoenix panoramas from the top of this peak northeast of downtown, just to the west of Paradise Valley. Try the 1.4-mi nature trail if you want to avoid crowds, and if you desire a slightly easier walk. Part of the Phoenix Mountains Preserve. | 2701 E. Squaw Peak Dr. | 602/262–7901 | www.cityofphoenix.org | Free | Daily 5 AM–11 PM.

CULTURE, EDUCATION, AND HISTORY

Burton Barr Central Phoenix Public Library. Local architect William Bruder designed this massive five-story glass, concrete, and copper building that opened in downtown Phoenix in 1995. Housing over 1 million volumes and multiple reading areas, the library also has lovely views of Margaret T. Hance Park with its sculpture gardens and Japanese teahouse and various mountain ranges that surround the valley. Free guided tours of the building are available by appointment. | 1221 N. Central Ave. | 602/262–4636 or 602/262–7930 for tour information | Free | Mon.–Thurs. 9–9, Fri.–Sat. 9–6, Sun. noon–9.

Orpheum Theatre. Built in 1929, this Spanish Revivalist carved stucco theater in the downtown area was reopened in 1997 after undergoing a massive $11.4-million restoration. On the National Register of Historic Places, this is the oldest theater left in spanking-new Phoenix, and today hosts a variety of performing arts and popular music concerts. To see the inside of the theater, you must either have a ticket for a performance or call ahead to find out the monthly tour schedule. | 203 W. Adams St. | 602/534–5600, 602/252–9678 for tour information | Performance prices vary | Tours daily (reservations required).

Pueblo Grande Museum and Cultural Park. Once the site of a 500-acre Hohokam village 1 mi northeast of Sky Harbor International Airport, this is Phoenix's only National Historic Landmark. Three galleries contain displays on Hohokam culture, archaeology, and other Southwest interests. A short trail leads to some of the excavated ruins. There are also children's activities. | 4619 E. Washington St. | 602/495–0901 | $2, free Sun. | Mon.–Sat. 9–4:45, Sun. 1–4:45.

MUSEUMS

Arizona Hall of Fame Museum. In the building that was the Carnegie Public Library, the first public library in Phoenix, this museum documents the ranchers, buffalo soldiers, Mexican miners, early government officials, and various other individuals who were instrumental in establishing Arizona. A section called the Arizona Women's Hall of Fame documents the roles of women in government throughout history, as well as having exhibits on the women's suffrage movement and women who shaped Arizona culture and politics. It also offers rotating exhibits by local and regional artists. | 1101 W. Washington St. | 602/255–2110 | Free | Weekdays 8–5.

Arizona Military Museum. This museum exhibits artifacts documenting Arizona's military past. There's also a photographic collection depicting the buffalo soldiers. | 5636 E. McDowell Rd. | 602/267–2676 | Donations accepted | Tues. and Thurs. 9–2, Sun. 1–4.

Arizona Mining and Mineral Museum. Rocks, minerals, and mining artifacts are on display at this small local museum, which focuses on the copper mining that brought thousands of individuals to Phoenix and surrounding areas. An old mining hoist and a mining car engine are also exhibited outside of the main building. | 1502 W. Washington St. | 602/255–3791 | Free | Weekdays 8–5, Sat. 11–4.

Arizona Science Center. This museum designed by Antoine Predock offers 350 hands-on exhibits on all manner of scientific subjects. Though the structure seems out of character with nearby Heritage Square, it's meant to suggest a mountain peak and mesa. Inside, you'll find a giant-screen theater, a planetarium, and rotating science exhibits. | 600 E. Washington St. | 602/716–2000 | $8 | Daily 10–5.

Arizona State Capitol Museum. This museum has comprehensive displays on Arizona's government and history, state symbols, and governors. The top floor has the original house and senate chambers. Other exhibits focus on territorial life. | 1700 W. Washington St. | 602/542–4581 or 602/542–4675 | Free | Weekdays 8–5.

Hall of Flame Firefighting Museum. The world's largest firefighting museum exhibits fire engines from all over the world. There are also a hall of heroes, a helmet display, and displays of other firefighting memorabilia. Retired firefighters lead tours. | 6101 E. Van Buren St. | 602/275–3473 | $5; special rates for senior citizens and children | Mon.–Sat. 9–5, Sun. noon–4.

Heard Museum. Early Phoenix settlers Dwight and Maie Heard built this Spanish Colonial–style building to house their significant collection of southwestern art. Today it's the nation's premier showcase of Native American art. More than 32,000 pieces of basketry, pottery, weaving, fine art, jewelry, and bead work are on display. Gallery space was doubled in 1999. | 2301 N. Central Ave. | 602/252–8848 or 602/252–8840 | www.heard.org | $7 | Daily 9:30–5.

Museo Chicano. Brilliantly colored paintings and folk-art pieces fill the rooms at this gallery that focuses on Mexican, Mexican-American, and Latin-American art, history, and culture. The museum resides on the first floor of a recently renovated six-story building, and a gift shop sells imported Mexican fine art and folk-art pieces, as well as bilingual books. | 147 E. Adams St. | 602/257–5536 | $2 | Tues.–Sat. 10–4.

Phoenix Art Museum. Displayed inside this museum's beautiful green quartz exterior are over 13,000 works of art. The significant American West collection includes pieces by Georgia O'Keeffe and Frederick Remington. Holdings of 18th- and 19th-century European art are also strong. | 1625 N. Central Ave. | 602/257–1222 | www.phxart.org | $7 | Tues.–Sun. 10–5 (Wed. until 9).

Phoenix Museum of History. This striking glass-and-steel museum documents regional history from the 1860s to the 1930s. Kids enjoy the interactive exhibits, which allow them to appreciate the city's multicultural heritage and understand its growth. | 105 N. 5th St. | 602/253–2734 | $5 | Mon.–Sat. 10–5, Sun. noon–5.

Pioneer Arizona Living History Museum. This re-created territorial town includes 28 original and reconstructed buildings from throughout Arizona. Costumed performers reenact frontier life and demonstrate pioneer crafts. It's in northern Phoenix, exit 225 off Interstate 17. | 3901 W. Pioneer Rd. | 623/465–1052 | $5.75 | Wed.–Sun. 9–5.

RELIGION AND SPIRITUALITY

St. Mary's Basilica. The oldest Catholic church in Phoenix, St. Mary's has stood on its present site since 1879. The current basilica, on the National Register of Historic Places, was completed in 1914 over the original church, which was built in 1881, though you can still see some of the old windows and frames. Built in the Mission Revival style out of adobe, the two bell towers, red-clay tiled roof, and numerous stained-glass windows are worth a visit. | 231 N. 3rd St. | 602/252–7651 | Free | Mon., Tues., Thurs., Fri. 10–2; Wed. 11:30–1.

SHOPPING

Arizona Center. The rejuvenation of downtown Phoenix owes as much to this 150,000-square-ft outdoor shopping mall as it does to the huge sports arenas that sprang up in the area in the late 1990s. A variety of specialty shops, bars, and restaurants are surrounded by walkways, fountains, gardens, sitting areas, and palm trees, and all are showered upon gently by a huge outdoor misting system, which makes summer heat bearable. | 400 E. Van Buren St. | 602/271–4000 | Free | Weekdays 10–9, Sat. 10–10, Sun. 10–6; restaurant hrs vary.

Biltmore Fashion Park. Biltmore has posh shops lining its open-air walkways, as well as some of the city's most popular restaurants and cafés. The lush gardens make it worth a visit by themselves. | 24th St. and Camelback Rd. | 602/955–8400 | www.shopbiltmore.com | Free | Weekdays 10–9, Sat. 10–6, Sun. noon–6.

Metrocenter. This huge mall is located on the west side of Phoenix and has more than 200 specialty stores and eateries. Anchor department stores include Macy's and Dillard's. | I–17, between Peoria and Dunlap Aves. | 602/997–2641 | Free | Mon.–Sat. 10–9, Sun. 11–6.

Paradise Valley Mall. This older mall in northeastern Phoenix has more than 150 stores and restaurants and a playground. There is also a movie theater and outdoor plaza. | 4568 E. Cactus Rd. | 602/996–8840 | www.westcor.com/pvm | Free | Mon.–Sat. 10–9, Sun. 11–6.

SPECTATOR SPORTS

Phoenix's professional football team, the Arizona Cardinals, actually plays in nearby Tempe, in one of the few sports arenas that hosts both a college and professional sports team (*see* Tempe).

Arizona Diamondbacks. One of the newest additions to Major League Baseball, the National League Western Division Champion Diamondbacks have accrued quite a following in sports-loving Phoenix. The team plays in the massive Bank One Ballpark (*see below*), which, because it was built specifically for baseball, offers a stadium full of great views. | Bank One Ballpark, 401 E. Jefferson St. | 602/462–6500 | Ticket prices vary | Apr.–Sept.; call for specific schedule.

Arizona Rattlers. Headed by former Dallas Cowboys quarterback Danny White, this indoor football club won the Arena Football League championship in 1994 and 1997. | America West Arena, 201 E. Jefferson St. | 602/514–8383 | Ticket prices vary | Late Mar.–late Aug.; call for specific schedule.

Phoenix Coyotes. Hockey is a growing sport here, even though the ice has to be manufactured. The Coyotes face off in America West Arena. | America West Arena, 201 E. Jefferson St. | 480/473–5600 | Ticket prices vary | Sept.–Apr.; call for specific schedule.

Phoenix Mercury. Phoenix's WNBA team, headed by coach Sheryll Miller, drew over 400,000 fans last year to America West Arena (*see below*), which is otherwise dominated by men's teams. | America West Arena, 201 E. Jefferson St. | 602/252–9622 | Ticket prices vary | May–Aug.; call for specific schedule.

Phoenix Suns. The America West Arena, home of the Suns NBA professional basketball team, seats 19,000 fans, and tip-off is usually at 7 PM. Call for ticket and game information. | America West Arena, 201 E. Jefferson St. | 602/379–7867 | Ticket prices vary | Oct.–mid-Apr.; call for specific schedule.

Turf Paradise Race Course. World-class thoroughbred horses race here, and betting is allowed. It's 1 mi east of Interstate 17 to the Bell Road exit. | 19th Ave. and Bell Rd. | 602/942–1101 | $2–$4 | Late Sept.–early May, Fri.–Tues. gates open at 11 AM; race times and closing hrs vary.

OTHER POINTS OF INTEREST

America West Arena. When Phoenix Suns owner Michael Colangelo teamed up with America West Airlines, the result was this 20,000-seat sports/entertainment arena in downtown Phoenix. As well as being home to the Suns, the arena hosts various other teams such as the WNBA Phoenix Mercury, the Phoenix Coyotes, and the Arizona Rattlers, and shows huge outdoor rock and popular music concerts. | 201 E. Jefferson St. | 602/379–2000, 602/379–2060 for tour reservations | Tours $3; event prices vary | Limited tours on weekdays (excluding event days) by appointment only; call for specific schedule of events.

Bank One Ballpark. This state-of-the-art stadium is home to the Arizona Diamondbacks Major League baseball team, and offers over 20,000 seats with panoramic views of the field, a mega-screen TV, a 9-million pound retractable roof that opens to symphonic music and sound effects, a pool, restaurants, and a high-quality sound system. Tours are available. | 401 E. Jefferson St. | 602/462–6500, 602/462–6799 for tour information | Tours $6; ticket prices vary | Call for tour schedule; call for specific schedule of events.

Phoenix Zoo. Five trails meander through this 125-acre zoo in Papago Park, which has replicas of several habitats, including an African savanna and a tropical rain forest. There are also special children's activities. The 30-minute narrated Safari train tour costs $2 and gives a good overview of the park. | 455 N. Galvin Pkwy. | 602/273–1341 | $8.50 | May–Labor Day, daily 7:30 AM–4 PM; Labor Day–Apr., daily 9–5.

SIGHTSEEING TOURS/TOUR COMPANIES

Gray Line Tours of Phoenix. This company offers a wide variety of seasonal, narrated motorcoach tours—everything from a three-hour narrated tour of Phoenix to a daylong excursion to the Grand Canyon. Most tours are seasonal, but sometimes operate on a reduced schedule outside of the high season. | 1243 S. 7th St., Suite 2 | 602/495–9100 or 800/732–0327 | www.graylinearizona.com | $30–$99 | Oct.–Apr., with a reduced schedule of tours the rest of the year.

Open Road Tours. This travel company, which offers package tours throughout the Southwest, also offers a range of sightseeing tours from half-day tours of Phoenix to daylong excursions to Sedona and the Grand Canyon. A few tours are seasonal. | 748 E. Dunlap, No. 2 | 602/997–6474 or 800/766–7117 | fax 602/997–2276 | www.openroadtours.com | $32–$99 for day trips, $185–$700 for multiday packages | Daily (some tours seasonal).

Vaughan's Southwest Custom Tours. This company offers tours for small groups in custom vans. Their five-hour city tours include a stop at the Heard Museum, but they also go out to such wide-ranging destinations as Sedona, the Grand Canyon (with an overnight option), and even Nogales, Mexico, for a shopping expedition. | Box 31250 | 602/971–1381 or 800/513–1381 | fax 602/992–5596 | www.southwesttours.com | $38–$89 | Daily (some tours seasonal).

WALKING TOUR

Downtown Phoenix Walking Tour (approximately 6 hours)
The renovated downtown area gives you a look at Phoenix's past and present, as well as a peek at its future. In moderate weather, this walk is a pleasant daylong tour, if you include time to eat lunch and visit museums; from late May to mid-October, it's best to break it up over two days.

Park your car in the garage on the southeast corner of 5th and Monroe streets or at any of the many nearby public parking garages (they're listed on a free map provided by Downtown Phoenix Partnership, which you can pick up at most local restaurants). Begin your tour in the blocks known as Heritage Square and Science Park.

Fifth to 7th streets between Monroe and Adams contain several places worth seeing. **Heritage Square** is lined with some of the oldest houses in Phoenix, and you can even tour some of them. If you have kids, the **Arizona Science Center** will be a big hit, with its hands-on displays. The **Phoenix Museum of History** is worth seeing for the building alone, but it's also a good museum.

From the corner of 5th and Monroe, walk two blocks west to **St. Mary's Basilica,** Phoenix's first Catholic church. Head north one block to Van Buren Street.

On the northeast corner of the intersection, you'll see two glass-clad office towers with a lane of royal palms between them. Follow the palm trees: they lead to the **Arizona Center,** a vibrant shopping and dining complex. This would be a good place to stop off and have lunch or a snack to fortify yourself.

Leaving the Arizona Center, from the corner of 3rd and Van Buren, walk a block west to 2nd Street and two blocks south on 2nd Street, passing the 24-story Hyatt Regency Hotel on your right, then another block and a half west on Adams Street to the **Museo Chicano.** You can then return to your car or continue on two more blocks west toward the striking facade of the **Orpheum Theatre.**

If you're really an indefatigable walker, continue south through the plaza on the Orpheum's east side to Washington Street; head east on Washington Street, passing Historic City Hall and the county courthouse on your right. At the intersection of Washington Street and 1st Avenue, you'll see Patriots Square Park on the southeast corner; cross diagonally (southeast) through the park to the corner of Jefferson Street and Central Avenue. Another block east on Jefferson and then a block south on 1st Street will take you to the **America West Arena.** From the arena, follow Jefferson Street east for two blocks to South 4th Avenue and **Bank One Ballpark,** affectionately nicknamed BOB by locals.

ON THE CALENDAR

MAR.: *Heard Museum Guild Indian Fair and Market.* Visitors can enjoy a juried show of Native American arts and crafts at the Heard Museum. There's also food, music, and dance. | 602/252–8848.

MAR.: *Phoenix Jaycees Rodeo of Rodeos.* Roping and riding contests for cowboys and cowgirls of all ages at Veterans Memorial Coliseum. | 602/263–8671.

MAR., APR.: *Yaqui Indian Holy Week Ceremonials.* Visitors are invited to watch ceremonial dances at this annual ritual in the Guadalupe town square, which begin on the Friday after Ash Wednesday. | 480/730–3080.

SEPT.–MAY: *The Phoenix Symphony.* Professional musicians perform various works in a beautiful, acoustically brilliant setting in Symphony Hall. | 602/495–1999.

OCT., NOV.: *Arizona State Fair.* At this large fair complete with livestock, visitors can soak up music, enjoy rides, and try their hand at games, all at the State Fairgrounds. | 602/252–6771.

OCT., NOV.: *Cowboy Artists of America.* Exhibits on western art and artists are offered at the Phoenix Art Museum. | 602/257–1222.

OCT.–MAR.: *Arizona Opera Company.* This professional company performs a variety of operas each season in Phoenix Symphony Hall. | 602/266–7464.

NOV.–JUNE: *Arizona Theatre Company.* The Arizona Theatre Company is a highly regarded troupe that performs plays of various kinds each season in the Herberger Theater. | 602/252–8497.

DEC.: *Fiesta Bowl Parade.* On Central Avenue in Phoenix, more than 400,000 people watch this annual parade, one of the nation's finest with 20 floats, 20 bands, and equestrian units. | 800/635–5748 or 480/350–0900.

Dining

INEXPENSIVE

Blue Burrito Grille. Mexican. This local chain, with its emphasis on fresh, heart-healthy south-of-the-border fare, has become a popular fast-food option in the valley. The chicken burritos, fish tacos, grilled veggie burritos, and blue-corn tacos are good options. All dishes are made without lard, and come with chips and salsa. Beer and wine only. | 3118 E. Camelback Rd. | 602/955–9596 | $5–$10 | AE, DC, MC, V.

Chompie's. Delicatessens. The Greenway Park Plaza branch of this local chain is a busy gathering place, especially on Sunday mornings when folks line up for very good bagels and coffee. Mile-high sandwiches are a major draw. Kids' menu. Wine, beer. | 3202 E. Greenway Rd. | 602/971–8010 | Breakfast also available | $9–$17 | AE, MC, V.

Duck and Decanter. American. A fancy sandwich shop with a lovely terrace for open-air dining. There's a guitarist Friday evening, and Saturday and Sunday afternoons. Kids' menu. No smoking. | 1651 E. Camelback Rd. | 602/274–5429 | Breakfast also available | $5–$8 | AE, D, DC, MC, V.

Ed Debevic's. American. Table-top jukeboxes set a nostalgic tone at this 1950s-style diner, part of the chain, in the Town and Country Shopping Center. The menu runs the gamut of diner basics, but the highlights are malts and burgers. Kids' menu. | 2102 E. Highland Ave. | 602/956–2760 | $5–$12 | AE, D, DC, MC, V.

El Bravo. Mexican. Although the modest decor may not be inspiring, the food makes up for it. Widely considered the best Sonoran fare in town, the tacos, chimichangas, enchiladas, and burritos are simple and well spiced; the huge meat burros are tender and filling, and a red chile popover will cure any spice-lover's cravings. Desserts such as the chocolate chimichanga are also great. | 8338 N. 7th St. | 602/943–9753 | Closed Sun. | $5–$12 | AE, D, DC, MC, V.

Hard Rock Cafe. American/Casual. Rock 'n' roll memorabilia decorate this branch of the national chain. Be warned—the restaurant is extremely loud at all hours. Stick with the burgers or chicken. A flower- and tree-lined patio is pleasant when the weather is not too hot. Kids' menu. | 2621 E. Camelback Rd. | 602/956–3669 | $9–$20 | AE, D, DC, MC, V.

Honey Bear's BBQ. Barbecue. Melt-in-your-mouth ribs are the specialty at this rustic, western-style restaurant that serves up authentic Tennessee-style barbecued ribs. If these slightly smokey sweet-and-tangy slabs of meat don't fill you, supplement your meal with homemade sausage beans, scallion potato salad, and sweet-potato pie. | 5012 E. Van Buren St. | 602/273–9148 | $5–$15 | AE, MC, V.

Indian Delhi Palace. Indian. Although this restaurant attracts locals, tourists often miss out on an authentic northern Indian meal. Brightly colored handmade tapestries decorate the walls, and Indian string music plays while you eat chana saag or lamb korma, perhaps with some of their popular garlic naan. | 5050 E. McDowell Rd. | 602/244–8181 | $7–$18 | AE, D, DC, MC, V.

Havana Cafe. Cuban. Colorful and friendly, this small place is very casual at lunchtime, a bit more dressed up in the evening. Try the *bacalaitos* (fried salt cod fritters), the *pollo Cubano* (boneless chicken in a lime juice and sweet onion marinade), or the Cuban sandwich (pork loin, ham, swiss cheese, and pickles, grilled). Dine outside under a large canopy. No smoking. | 4225 E. Camelback Rd. | 602/952–1991 | No lunch Sun. | $9–$19 | AE, D, DC, MC, V.

Marilyn's. Mexican. Toy Mexican villages sit atop the booths at this brightly colored and relaxed family-style eatery. Try the fajitas, *pollo fundido* (a thin flour tortilla stuffed with chicken and covered in a cream sauce), or *spinchada* (rice, spinach, and cheese in a tortilla covered with a white spinach sauce and almonds). Kids' menu. | 12631 N. Tatum Blvd. | 602/953–2121 | $8–$15 | AE, D, DC, MC, V.

Pizzeria Bianco. Pizza. A local favorite, this spot is known for its pizzas made in a wood-fired oven. Toppings include homemade fennel sausage, wood-roasted cremini mushrooms, imported cheeses, and the freshest herbs and spices. No smoking. | 623 E. Adams St. | 602/258–8300 | Closed Mon. No lunch weekends | $12–$22 | MC, V.

Silver Dragon. Chinese. Insist on sitting in the large dining room at the right of the entrance (where Asian customers are routinely seated) and ask for the Chinese menu (with brief English translations) and you will be rewarded with some of the most authentic, mouth-watering Hong Kong–style fare around. The "Crispy Hong-Kong style Chicken" is steamed, flash-fried, and cut into tender, plump pieces; the "Buddhist-style rolls" are a vegetarian's delight. Also try the hot pot and fresh seafood dishes. | 8946 N. 19th Ave. | 602/674–0151 | No lunch Sat. | $5–$15 | AE, MC, V.

Thai Lahna. Thai. You'll sit in red booths surrounded by Thai knickknacks at this cozy eatery. Owner Tom Thanom presents dishes from family recipes like pad Thai and *tom yum gai*, a chicken and coconut milk soup that is supposed to be good for colds. | 3738 E. Indian School Rd. | 602/955–4658 | $6–$10 | AE, MC, V.

MODERATE

Ayoko of Tokyo. Japanese. You can order sushi here or if you want something cooked, they'll do it right on your table, teppanyaki-style. Caterpillar and California rolls are two of the more popular sushis. | 2564 E. Camelback Rd. | 602/955–7007 | $10–$35 | AE, DC, MC, V.

Baby Kay's Cajun Kitchen. Cajun. This bustling restaurant in the Town and Country Shopping Center offers all the usual Cajun favorites, including gumbo, jambalaya, and crawfish étouffée. The entertainment is a big draw. There's blues/jazz at lunch Tuesday–Friday, and Friday–Saturday nights. | 2119 E. Camelback St. | 602/955–0011 | $12–$22 | AE, MC, V.

Eliana's Restaurant. Latin. El Salvadoran fare is the specialty at this simple, unpretentious gem in midtown Phoenix. Tasty appetizers like *pupusas* (corn patties stuffed with pork, pepper, and cheese), tamales, and *pasteles* (meat turnovers) are a meal in themselves. Huge, wonderfully prepared main dishes include *mojarra frita* (fried tilapia) and *pollo encebollado* (fried chicken with rice and beans). | 1627 N. 24th St. | 602/225–2925 | Closed Mon. | $10–$15 | AE, D, DC, MC, V.

Fish Market Restaurant. Seafood. This bi-level restaurant has a more formal upstairs and a more casual downstairs dining room, as well as a sushi bar. But fresh seafood is the key, and a variety of dishes like smoked tuna or trout, grilled halibut, and live Maine lobster tails are wonderfully prepared standards. You can also buy fish to cook at home because this is a genuine fish market, too. Raw bar. Kids' menu. | 1720 E. Camelback Rd. | 602/277–3474 | $14–$32 | AE, D, DC, MC, V.

George and Dragon. English. At this dark, cozy English pub, you can order standards like bangers and mash (traditional English sausage and mashed potatoes), shepherd's pie, and, of course, fish-and-chips. Kids' menu. | 4240 N. Central Ave. | 602/241–0018 | $6–$12 | AE, DC, MC, V.

Gourmet House of Hong Kong. Chinese. As well as serving the usual suspects, the menu at this standard restaurant in a shopping plaza is full of specialties like *chow fun* (thick noodles) with assorted meat, shrimp, or squid; lobster with black bean sauce; and five-flavor frog legs. The seafood and vegetarian selections are extensive. | 1438 E. McDowell Rd. | 602/253–4859 | $12–$25 | AE, DC, MC, V.

Greekfest. Greek. This lovely Greek taverna has stucco walls, cool marble floors, and white tablecloths. The moussaka is wonderful, as is the lamb *exohiko*, a phyllo-wrapped meat-and-cheese concoction. A tiled patio has trees and columns. Kids' menu. | 1940 E. Camelback Rd. | 602/265–2990 | No lunch Sun. | $14–$25 | AE, D, DC, MC, V.

Houston's. American/Casual. This noisy, very popular spot offers lively meals. On the menu: fresh fish, ribs, chicken, salads, and purportedly the best burgers in Phoenix. A more limited menu is served on the patio off the bar, which has a view of the Biltmore Fashion Park. | 2425 E. Camelback Rd. | 602/957–9700 | $9–$23 | AE, MC, V.

Little Saigon. Vietnamese. This serene, intimate restaurant in the Christown Mall with a tiled pool and footbridge in the foyer is a far cry from the surrounding strip malls. Try the *bahn khot* (pancakes with coconut and shrimp topping) for an appetizer, and the wonderful charboiled beef in grape leaves, lemongrass chicken, and prawns, all served in a hot pot. The superstrong Vietnamese coffee ends the meal with a kick. | 1588 N. Montebello Ave. | 602/864–7582 | $10–$20 | AE, D, MC, V.

Lombardi's at the Arizona Center. Italian. This good bet downtown has a contemporary Italian menu, an open kitchen, and a nice open-air courtyard, which is an oasis from downtown. It really hops when an event is going on at an arena nearby. Try the cioppino or risotto, and tiramisu. | 455 N. 3rd St. | 602/257–8323 | $14–$32 | AE, DC, MC, V.

Lon's at the Hermosa. American. Once home to cowboy artist Lon Megargee, this restaurant is in a 1930s adobe ranch house that is now the Hermosa Inn. The wide-ranging menu offers everything from grilled polenta pie with wild mushroom ragoût to wood-grilled filet mignon. Finish with the gingered crème brûlée tart. You can see Camelback Mountain from the romantic patio. Sunday brunch. No smoking. | 5532 N. Palo Cristi Rd. | 602/955–7878 | Reservations essential | No lunch Sat. | $12–$32 | AE, MC, V.

Los Dos Molinos. Mexican. Fire is the key word at this popular, brightly colored local eatery that specializes in New Mexico–style south-of-the-border fare. The root of each dish lies in the use of super-hot New Mexico chiles. Try the house specialty, adobada ribs (tender meat marinated in red chiles), or the green chile enchilada. A warm sopaipilla covered in cinnamon, sugar, or honey may be just the thing to soothe your taste buds at the end of the meal. | 8646 S. Central Ave. | 602/955–7878 | Closed Sun., Mon. | $12–$25 | AE, D, MC, V.

Monti's. Steak. Servers wear western dress at this relaxed, family-friendly steak house. The sirloin is the star of the menu. The patio has lovely mountain views. Kids' menu, early-bird dinners. | 12025 N. 19th Ave. | 602/997–5844 | $14–$29 | AE, D, DC, MC, V.

Rustler's Rooste. Steak. This casual family steak house in the Pointe Hilton on South Mountain has a rustic, country look. On the menu are favorites like southern fried chicken; porterhouse steak; marinated, broiled swordfish; and more esoteric choices, including rattlesnake. Kids enjoy the slide down to the dining room. Entertainment nightly. Kids' menu. | 7777 S. Pointe Pkwy. | 602/431–6474 | No lunch | $13–$22 | AE, D, MC, V.

Such Is Life. Mexican. In Moises Treves's corner of Phoenix you can taste cactus, chicken Maya, garlic shrimp—delicious regional Mexican food. | 3602 N. 24th St. | 602/955–7822 | Closed Sun. No lunch Sat. | AE, D, DC, MC, V.

Taste of India. Indian. The northern Indian fare here is well spiced and flavorful. The delicious breads—naan, poori, paratha—are appetizers in themselves. Try the chicken or lamb kashmiry or the flavorful chicken tikka masala. A large vegetarian selection includes vegetable korma and *benghan bhartha*, an eggplant dish. Desserts like rice pudding or *ras malai*, sweet milk and cheese with pistachios, are light and refreshing. | 1609 E. Bell Rd. | 602/788–3190 | $15–$20 | AE, D, DC, MC, V.

Texaz Grill. Steak. This place is true Texas, with cowboy-inspired artwork, booths, a jukebox, and huge down-home portions. It's been voted the best affordable steak house in the valley, and folks come here for the satisfying T-bone and the mammoth chicken-fried steak with fresh mashed potatoes. | 6003 N. 16th St. | 602/248–7827 | No lunch Sun. | $15–$25 | AE, MC, V.

Timothy Michael's Hideaway. Contemporary. Tucked off the main road, this elegant and intimate restaurant boasts white linens, candles, and French doors that overlook a koi pond in the back garden. For a romantic dinner, try to nab a seat on the outside patio, which stretches around the pond and has a stone fireplace. Try the homemade crab and shrimp ravioli or the Portobello pie. | 2999 N. 44th St. | 602/667–3001 | No lunch weekends | $14–$23 | AE, D, DC, MC, V.

Tomaso's. Italian. An unfussy neighborhood place known for its homey old-country dishes like osso buco, and *braciole*, a flank steak stuffed, rolled, and marinated. Kids' menu. | 3225 E. Camelback Rd. | 602/956–0836 | No lunch weekends | $14–$27 | AE, D, DC, MC, V.

Tucchetti. Italian. The large, open dining room here has a distinct rustic Tuscan feel, with colorful photographs of the Italian countryside and bustling waiters serving up steaming plates of food. Favorites include *mostaccolli*, chicken breast stuffed with prosciutto and spinach, and chicken *vesuvio*, a grilled half chicken in a garlic marinade. A covered stone-

and-brick patio is open most of the year. Kids' menu. | 2135 E. Camelback Rd. | 602/957–0222 | No lunch Sun. | $11–$27 | AE, D, DC, MC, V.

EXPENSIVE

Altos. Spanish. This intimate restaurant in a mid-Phoenix shopping center has an authentic Iberian touch. Try well-prepared tapas like *calamari di Pedro* (squid dipped in a saffron batter), or *combrilla Andaluza* (a marinated Portobello mushroom and serrano ham dish). Main courses like filet mignon with Spanish blue cheese are also inventive and tasty. | 5029 N. 44th St. | 602/808–0890 | No lunch weekends | $20–$35 | AE, D, DC, MC, V.

Avanti. Italian. This upscale local favorite features a snazzy black-and-white interior with white linen tablecloths. The menu is Italian but influenced with touches from around the world. Try *pappardelle boscaiola* (fettuccine in a wild mushroom sauce topped with arugula), chicken and sausage *scarpariello* (sautéed in olive oil with a white wine sauce), or the scampi and scallops combination. Known for seafood. Entertainment Wednesday–Saturday. | 2728 E. Thomas Rd. | 602/956–0900 | No lunch weekends | $25–$50 | AE, D, DC, MC, V.

Coup Des Tartes. French. Housed in a former antiques store, this cozy BYOB spot serves inspired French-Mediterranean fare like ginger pork tenderloin, fennel-tinged sea bass, and a signature braised lamb shank with couscous. Don't leave without trying one of the exquisite desserts—the chef-proprietor originally trained as a pastry chef. | 4626 N. 16th St. | 602/212–1082 | Closed Sun., Mon. No lunch | $15–$30 | AE, DC, MC, V.

Eddie Matney's Grill. Contemporary. This bistro in the Biltmore Financial Center has an elegant, cherrywood-trimmed dining room and one of the largest wine cellars in Arizona. Try the rock shrimp ravioli or the grilled veal chops. Entertainment nightly. No smoking. | 2398 E. Camelback Rd. | 602/957–3214 | No lunch | $16–$37 | AE, D, DC, MC, V.

Il Forno. Italian. Not only is this restaurant one of the most attractive in town, but it serves some of the most outstanding dishes around. Try the clams in white wine sauce, the squash ravioli, or the pappardelle Bolognese (wide pasta ribbons in a fresh ground-veal sauce). | 4225 E. Camelback Rd. | 602/952–1522 | Closed Sun. June–Aug. No lunch | $20–$35 | AE, MC, V.

La Fontanella. Italian. This family-owned, neighborhood Italian restaurant offers outstanding Roman cuisine. Try *suppli* (rice croquettes filled with cheese), escargot in bubbling garlic butter, or *agreassato* (a lamb shank braised in wine with raisins, pine nuts, and potatoes). Kids' menu. | 4231 E. Indian School Rd. | 602/955–1213 | No lunch weekends | $16–$32 | AE, D, DC, MC, V.

Norman's Arizona. Mexican. The Sonoran-style "Nueva Mexicana" cuisine at this intimate and bustling restaurant in east Phoenix attracts sophisticated locals tired of the usual Americanized fare. Try the *tamalitos* (red chile or sweet green corn baby tamales) for an appetizer, and the special chile mash, chiles stuffed with mashed potatoes and covered with a chicken breast in a mole sauce. Top off the meal with excellent chocolate chimichangas or banana squash pie. | 4410 N. 40th St. | 602/956–2288 | Closed Mon. No lunch weekends | $20–$30 | AE, D, DC, MC, V.

Richardson's. Mexican. Everything is spicy at this extremely popular neighborhood joint which focuses on New Mexican cuisine. Adobe booths and bright-color walls surround a noisy bar, and the open kitchen serves up enchiladas, tamales, and chiles rellenos. Some meat and seafood dishes are prepared on a wood-burning stove, and specialty dishes include cordon bleu, stuffed chicken breast (with spinach, sun-dried tomatoes, poblano chiles, and Asiago cheese), and a variety of spicy steaks. | 1582 E. Bethany Home Rd. | 602/265–5886 | $16–$24 | AE, DC, MC, V.

RoxSand. Eclectic. One of the most interesting restaurants in the state, in the Biltmore Fashion Park, offers up inspired combinations like tamales with curried lamb moistened in Thai-style peanut sauce, daily specialty soups, and the house specialty, air-dried duck served with buckwheat crêpes and a pistachio-onion marmalade. | 2594 E. Camelback Rd. | 602/381–0444 | $14–$32 | AE, MC, V.

Sam's Cafe. Mexican. This elegant and tasteful restaurant in the Biltmore Fashion Park, with candle- and linen-clad tables, serves basic and well-prepared south-of-the-border–inspired fish, pasta, steak, and seafood dishes. Try the poblano chicken chowder or Sedona spring rolls (tortillas wrapped around chicken and veggies). The chicken-fried tuna with jalapeño cream gravy is superb. | 2556 E. Camelback Rd. | 602/954–7100 | $16–$23 | AE, D, DC, MC, V.

Steamer's Genuine Seafood. Seafood. Dine on petrale sole or sesame-miso encrusted Chilean sea bass while you take in the mountain views from the large windows in the dining room or from the outdoor patio. Raw bar. Kids' menu. | 2576 E. Camelback Rd. | 602/956–3631 | $19–$32 | AE, D, DC, MC, V.

T-Bone Steak House. Steak. This rustic old western steak house about halfway up South Mountain has great views of the valley and downtown Phoenix. Cooking is done over mesquite wood. Try the monstrous 2-pound porterhouse, merely huge 1-pound T-bone, or more manageable 12-ounce sirloin. Salad bar. Kids' menu. | 10037 S. 19th Ave. | 602/276–0945 | No lunch | $15–$35 | AE, DC, MC, V.

T. Cook's. Contemporary. This restaurant in the Royal Palms Resort resembles an Italianate church with its brick walls, painted tile, and vaulted ceiling. The rustic-Mediterranean fare on the rotating menu has featured such delights as grilled lamb loin with wild mushrooms and Swiss chard, sea bass wrapped in Parma ham with olives and artichokes, and oven-baked John Dory. Desserts are luscious. Pianist June–August, Tuesday–Saturday, and September–May, nightly. Sunday brunch. | 5200 E. Camelback Rd. | 602/808–0766 | Breakfast also available | $21–$50 | AE, D, DC, MC, V.

Tarbell's. Contemporary. This sleek, glitzy restaurant distinguishes itself with a deftly prepared, constantly changing menu. Start with the smoked rock shrimp with plum tomato relish. If they're available, try the aromatic mussels, steamed in a heady broth of white wine and shallots, or the surprisingly good pizza from the wood-fired oven. Kids' menu. | 3213 E. Camelback Rd. | 602/955–8100 | No lunch | $16–$32 | AE, D, DC, MC, V.

VERY EXPENSIVE

Bistro 24. French. This smart and stylish bistro in the Ritz-Carlton Hotel offers a menu of especially tempting seafood choices. Grilled salmon, bouillabaisse, and crispy-skin whitefish are deftly done, but so is the steak au poivre. Dine inside or on a sidewalk patio. Sunday brunch is among the best in town. | 2401 E. Camelback Rd. | 602/952–2424 | Breakfast also available | $24–$60 | AE, D, DC, MC, V.

Christopher & Paola's Fermier Brasserie. French. The elegant restaurant in the Biltmore Fashion Park, headed by James Beard Award–winning Christopher Gross, has a luminous glow. Calling this a brasserie may seem modest when you taste the elegant Gallic-inspired dishes, which include an escargot-stuffed ravioli appetizer, delicately grilled vegetables in puff pastry, rack of lamb, and a lightly smoked sirloin steak marinated and rubbed with truffles. The wine selection is vast. | 2584 E. Camelback Rd. | 602/522–2344 | $25–$45 | AE, D, DC, MC, V.

Compass Restaurant. Continental. You can take in the whole city from this 24th-floor revolving restaurant on top of the Hyatt Regency Hotel. Try the skillet-seared pork, vegetable torta, or the honey-almond encrusted salmon fillet. Kids' menu. Sunday brunch. No smoking. | 122 N. 2nd St. | 602/440–3166 | $20–$30 | AE, D, DC, MC, V.

Different Pointe of View. American. This mountaintop restaurant just north of central Phoenix in the Pointe Hilton Resort at Tapatio Cliffs has breathtaking views of the valley, particularly on the patio at sunset (it's reserved for those wanting drinks and appetizers only). The American regional menu includes such dishes as herb-crusted rack of lamb, pan-roasted muscovy duck breast, and various other specialty veal, duck, pork, and lamb dishes that rotate regularly. There's also a spectacular vegetable and herb garden on the premises. Entertainment Wednesday–Saturday. | 11111 N. 7th St. | 602/863–0912 | Closed Sun.–Mon. mid-June–Oct. No lunch | $24–$40 | AE, D, DC, MC, V.

El Chorro Lodge. American. The large windows and a plant-surrounded outdoor patio offer excellent views of the Phoenix Mountain Preserve at this 60-year-old local favorite. Steak and lobster dishes are the specialties here, and the beef stroganoff and chateaubriand are tender and skillfully prepared. Leave room for the chocolate-chip pecan pie. | 5550 E. Lincoln Dr. | 480/948–5170 | $25–$50 | AE, MC, V.

Harris'. Steak. Dry-aged steaks are featured in this offshoot of the Ann Harris's San Francisco steak house. This place knows its meat. Try the signature steak, a bone-in sirloin. But other choices, such as grilled Atlantic salmon or chicken Victoria (with a mushroom ragoût and béarnaise sauce), are almost as good. The outdoor patio is heated. Pianist Tuesday–Saturday | 3101 E. Camelback Rd. | 602/508–8888 | www.harrisrestaurantphx.com | $21–$50 | AE, D, DC, MC, V.

Le Rhone. Continental. An elegant formal restaurant approximately 13 mi northwest of Phoenix, with a pianist on weekends June–September and nightly October–May. The menu features such classic dishes as rack of lamb, rock lobster tail medallions, and veal sweetbread. | 9401 W. Thunderbird Rd., Peoria | 623/933–0151 | Closed Mon. No lunch | $18–$32 | AE, D, DC, MC, V.

Morton's of Chicago. Steak. Across from the Biltmore Fashion Park in the Shops at the Esplanade center, this outlet of the national chain doesn't skip the details—steaks here are premium. Your waiter will go through your various options, which include double-cut fillet, New York sirloin, and a 24-ounce porterhouse steak. Nonmeat items include shrimp Alexander and lobster, and desserts such as the Godiva chocolate cake are divine. | 2501 E. Camelback Rd. | 602/955–9577 | No lunch | $40–$65 | AE, D, DC, MC, V.

Pronto Ristorante. Italian. Service is professional in this elegant restaurant that serves basic seafood, veal, and pasta dishes in a northern Italian style. Try the house lasagna or the veal Parmesan. Dinner theater Friday and Saturday. | 3950 E. Campbell Ave. | 602/956–4049 | $15–$30 | AE, D, DC, MC, V.

Ruth's Chris Steak House. Steak. This polished restaurant is part of the upscale chain known for its steaks served with melted butter on top. The service is top-notch. You can also dine on a patio with a fountain. | 2201 E. Camelback Rd. | 602/957–9600 | No lunch | $24–$50 | AE, DC, MC, V.

Vincent Guerithault on Camelback. Southwestern. It's hard to tell whether Chef Guerithault prepares French food with a southwestern flair, or southwestern fare with a French touch. The menu includes such delicious dishes as duck tamales, smoked salmon quesadillas, grilled wild boar loin, and sautéed veal sweetbreads with blue corn chips. The signature dessert is a triple crème brûlée. | 3930 E. Camelback Rd. | 602/224–0225 | Reservations essential | Closed Sun.–Mon. June–Sept. No lunch Sat. | $26–$46 | AE, DC, MC, V.

Lodging

INEXPENSIVE

Best Western Executive Park. Many rooms in this eight-story downtown hotel have mountain views. It's two blocks from the Phoenix Art Museum and four blocks from the Heard Museum. Restaurant, bar. Some refrigerators, cable TV. Pool. Hot tub, sauna. Gym. Laundry service. Business services, airport shuttle. | 1100 N. Central Ave. | 602/252–2100 | fax 602/340–1989 | www.bestwestern.com | 101 rooms, 6 suites | $119–$135, $210 suites | AE, D, DC, MC, V.

Best Western Grace Inn Ahwatukee. This six-story hotel is in south Phoenix, 1 mi from South Mountain and 10 mi from Arizona State University. Larger suites have full kitchens. Restaurant, bar, room service. In-room data ports, some microwaves, refrigerators, cable TV. Pool. Beauty salon, hot tub. Tennis courts. Basketball. Laundry service. Business services, airport shuttle. | 10831 S. 51st St. | 480/893–3000 | fax 480/496–8303 | www.bestwestern.com | 152 rooms, 8 suites | $100–$132, $120–$175 suites | AE, D, DC, MC, V.

Best Western InnSuites. This all-suite hotel in north Phoenix is west of Squaw Peak, 5 mi from the Paradise Valley Mall and Biltmore Fashion Park. Picnic area, complimentary Continental breakfast. In-room data ports, some kitchenettes, microwaves, refrigerators, cable TV. Pool. Hot tub. Gym. Playground. Laundry facilities. Business services. Some pets allowed (fee). | 1615 E. Northern Ave. | 602/997–6285 | fax 602/943–1407 | www.bestwestern.com | 124 rooms | $119–$169 | AE, D, DC, MC, V.

Hampton Inn. This inexpensive motel is right off Interstate 17 in central Phoenix, 1 mi from the Metrocenter Mall and within walking distance of many restaurants. The newly remodeled rooms are clean, modern, and comfortable. Complimentary Continental breakfast. In-room data ports, cable TV. Pool. Hot tub. Business services. Some pets allowed. | 8101 N. Black Canyon Hwy. | 602/864–6233 | fax 602/995–7503 | www.hamptoninn.com | 147 rooms | $54–$94 | AE, D, DC, MC, V.

La Quinta–Thomas Road. This two-story brick motel in central Phoenix is convenient to Interstate 17. The basic rooms are decorated in cream and hunter green, and are roomy and comfortable. Complimentary Continental breakfast. In-room data ports, some refrigerators, cable TV. Pool. Laundry facilities. Business services. Pets allowed. | 2725 N. Black Canyon Hwy. | 602/258–6271 | fax 602/340–9255 | www.laquinta.com | 139 rooms | $95–$110 | AE, D, DC, MC, V.

Los Olivos Executive Hotel and Suites. Some of the rooms at this downtown hotel face an inner, palm tree–filled courtyard. Accommodations are well decorated and clean, and suites are larger than average. Restaurant, picnic area. Some refrigerators, cable TV. Pool. Hot tub. Laundry facilities. Business services. | 202 E. McDowell Rd. | 602/258–6911 or 800/776–5560 | fax 602/258–7259 | losolivos@travelbase.com | 48 rooms, 15 suites | $99, $129 suites | AE, D, DC, MC, V.

Phoenix Inn. This three-story all-suite hotel is a block off popular Camelback Road, near the Biltmore Fashion Park. It's a remarkable bargain with amenities not often found in lodgings in this price category. Complimentary Continental breakfast. In-room data ports, microwaves, refrigerators, cable TV. Pool. Hot tub. Gym. Laundry facilities. Business services, airport shuttle. | 2310 E. Highland Ave. | 602/956–5221 or 800/956–5221 | fax 602/468–7220 | www.phoenixinn.com | 120 suites | $119–$239 | AE, D, DC, MC, V.

Premier Inn Phoenix. This large, southwestern-style motel is directly across from the Metro Center Mall and near Turf Paradise Race Track. Some refrigerators, cable TV. 2 pools, wading pool. Laundry facilities. Business services. Some pets allowed. | 10402 N. Black Canyon Hwy. | 602/943–2371 or 800/786–6835 | fax 602/943–5847 | www.premierinns.com | 249 rooms, 3 suites | $60–$90, $130 suites | AE, DC, MC, V.

Quality Hotel and Resort. With a 1½-acre lagoon ringed by palms and bamboo, this is one of central Phoenix's best bargains. The VIP floor has cabana suites and a private rooftop pool with skyline views. Restaurant, bar, picnic area. Refrigerators, cable TV. 4 pools, wading pool. Hot tub. Putting green, tennis court. Basketball, gym, volleyball. Video games. Playground, laundry facilities. Business services. Pets allowed (fee). | 3600 N. 2nd Ave. | 602/248–0222 | fax 602/265–6331 | www.qualityinn.com | 280 rooms, 33 suites | $79–$99, $210 suites | AE, D, DC, MC, V.

Quality Inn South Mountain. This four-story chain motel is in south Phoenix, 8 mi southeast of Sky Harbor International Airport. Restaurant. Some microwaves, some refrigerators, cable TV. Pool. Hot tub. Laundry facilities, laundry service. Business services. Pets allowed (fee). | 5121 E. La Puente Ave. | 480/893–3900 | fax 480/496–0815 | 189 rooms | $79–$129 | AE, D, DC, MC, V.

Les Jardins Hotel and Suites. A comfortable, four-story hotel accommodation in midtown Phoenix. Rooms are basic and comfortable, the lobby is pleasant, and a sundeck offers views of the surrounding valley. Restaurant, bar. In-room data ports, some refrigerators, cable TV. Pool. Hot tub. Business services. | 401 W. Clarendon Ave. | 602/234–2464 | fax 602/277–2602 | 106 rooms | $69–$130 | AE, D, DC, MC, V.

Ramada Phoenix, Camelback. This four-story motel is built around a courtyard. It's 3 mi from downtown. Restaurant, bar, room service. Refrigerators, cable TV. Pool. Hot tub. Gym. Laundry facilities. Business services, airport shuttle. | 502 W. Camelback Rd. | 602/264–9290 or 800/688–2021 | fax 602/264–3068 | www.ramada.com | 161 rooms, 5 suites | $59–$110, $120 suites | AE, D, DC, MC, V.

Ramada Plaza Hotel Metrocenter. This four-story hotel is 1 mi from the Metrocenter Mall and 17 mi from Sky Harbor airport. Restaurant, bar, room service. In-room data ports, some microwaves, some refrigerators, cable TV. Pool. Hot tub. Business services. | 12027 N. 28th Dr. | 602/866–7000 | fax 602/942–7512 | www.ramada.com | 163 rooms, 9 suites | $59–$99 rooms, $159–$179 suites | AE, D, DC, MC, V.

MODERATE

Courtyard–Phoenix Airport. This chain hotel is 2½ mi from the airport and 3 mi from Arizona State University. Some refrigerators, cable TV. Pool. Hot tub. Gym. Laundry facilities. Business services, airport shuttle. | 2621 S. 47th St. | 480/966–4300 | fax 480/966–0198 | www.courtyard.com | 145 rooms, 12 suites | $159–$169, $179–$189 suites | AE, D, DC, MC, V.

Courtyard–Phoenix North. This three-story hotel is 1 mi from the Metrocenter Mall and less than 1 mi from Castles & Coasters amusement park. Restaurant, bar, room service. In-room data ports, some refrigerators, some microwaves, TV. Pool. Hot tub. Gym. Laundry facilities. Business services. | 9631 N. Black Canyon Hwy. | 602/944–7373 | fax 602/944–0079 | www.courtyard.com | 134 rooms, 12 suites | $119, $139 suites | AE, D, DC, MC, V.

Courtyard–Phoenix/Camelback. This four-story hotel built in 1990 is in the Biltmore district, with many restaurants within six blocks. Room service is available Monday–Thursday for dinner only. Restaurant, bar, room service. In-room data ports, some refrigerators, cable TV. Pool. Hot tub. Gym. Laundry facilities. Business services. | 2101 E. Camelback Rd. | 602/955–5200 | fax 602/955–1101 | www.courtyard.com | 155 rooms, 11 suites | $165–$175, $185–$199 suites | AE, D, DC, MC, V.

Embassy Suites–Phoenix Airport West. Lush palms and olive trees surround bubbling fountains in the courtyard of this hotel. There's an evening social hour in the atrium lounge. Complimentary breakfast. Minibars, microwaves, refrigerators. Gym. | 2333 E. Thomas Rd. | 602/957–1910 | fax 602/955–2861 | www.embassy-suites.com | 183 suites | $149–$179 | AE, D, DC, MC, V.

Hilton Suites. This practical and popular downtown 11-story all-suite hotel is the model of excellent design within tight limits. The marble-floored, pillard lobby opens out to an atrium filled with boulder fountains and palms, with glass-walled elevators. Restaurant, bar, complimentary breakfast. Microwaves, refrigerators, cable TV, in-room VCRs (movies available). Pool. Hot tub. Exercise equipment. Business services. | 10 E. Thomas Rd. | 602/222–1111 | fax 602/265–4841 | 226 suites | $109–$239 | AE, D, DC, MC, V.

Holiday Inn Select–Airport. This 10-story hotel is seven minutes from Sky Harbor airport and has a 24-hour shuttle there. Restaurant, bar. In-room data ports, some microwaves, some refrigerators, cable TV. Pool. Hot tub. Gym. Laundry facilities. Business services, airport shuttle. Pets allowed. | 4300 E. Washington St. | 602/273–7778 | fax 602/275–5616 | www.holiday-inn.com | 301 rooms | $129–$139 | AE, D, DC, MC, V.

Holiday Inn–West. This chain hotel is 3 mi west of downtown. Restaurant, bar. In-room data ports, some refrigerators, cable TV. Pool. Hot tub. Driving range, putting green. Gym. Business services. | 1500 N. 51st Ave. | 602/484–9009 | fax 602/484–0108 | www.holiday-inn.com | 144 rooms, 3 suites | $156, $259 suites | AE, D, DC, MC, V.

Hotel San Carlos. This seven-story boutique hotel in the center of Phoenix has been open for over 70 years; it was the first air-conditioned hotel in the Southwest. It prides itself on affordable luxury. It's done up in Italian Renaissance style, though rooms are not large. 2 restaurants, bar, complimentary Continental breakfast. In-room data ports, some refrigerators, cable TV. Pool. Laundry service. Pets allowed. | 22 N. Central Ave. | 602/253–4121 | fax 602/253–6668 | www.hotelsancarlos.com | 133 rooms | $140–$200 | AE, D, DC, MC, V.

Lexington Hotel. This sports-themed hotel also gives you access to the huge, full-service City Square Sports Club in downtown Phoenix. Rooms range in size from average to small. Restaurant, bar. Some microwaves, cable TV. Pool. Barbershop, beauty salon, hot tub. Basketball, health club, racquetball. Business services. Some pets allowed. | 100 W. Clarendon Ave. | 602/279–9811 | fax 602/631–9358 | 180 rooms | $149–$169 | AE, D, DC, MC, V.

Maricopa Manor. Gardens and fountains enliven the landscaping at this Spanish-style B&B. About half the rooms have full kitchens, and some also have fireplaces. Breakfast is delivered to your door in a little basket, so you don't have to be social if that's not your style. Picnic area, complimentary Continental breakfast. In-room data ports, some kitchenettes, some microwaves, some refrigerators, some in-room hot tubs, cable TV, some in-room VCRs. Pool. Hot tub. Library. Business services. No smoking. | 15 W. Pasadena Ave. | 602/274–6302 or 800/292–6403 | fax 602/266–3904 | www.maricopamanor.com | 7 suites | $179–$189 | AE, D, DC, MC, V.

Radisson Phoenix Airport. This hotel is 2½ mi from Sky Harbor airport. Restaurant, bar, room service. Some refrigerators, cable TV, some in-room VCRs. Pool. Hot tub. Gym. Laundry service. Business services, airport shuttle. | 3333 E. University Dr. | 602/437–8400 | fax 602/470–0998 | www.radisson.com | 163 rooms | $169–$219 | AE, D, DC, MC, V.

Sheraton Crescent. This large hotel in west Phoenix is next to the Metrocenter Mall, with a free shuttle there. Restaurant, bar, room service. Refrigerators, cable TV. Pool. Sauna, steam room. 2 tennis courts. Basketball, health club, volleyball. Business services. Some pets allowed (fee). | 2620 W. Dunlap Ave. | 602/943–8200 | fax 602/371–2857 | www.sheraton.com | 328 rooms, 14 suites | $59–$239, $500 suites | AE, D, DC, MC, V.

Wyndham Garden Hotel–North Phoenix. This pleasing hotel boasts extra comforts like feather pillows, large working desks in the rooms, and a comfy lobby. Good if you want to get an early start in the morning. Restaurant, bar, room service. In-room data ports, some refrigerators, cable TV. Pool. Hot tub. Business services. | 2641 W. Union Hills Dr. | 602/978–2222 | fax 602/978–9139 | www.wyndham.com | 166 rooms | $159 | AE, D, DC, MC, V.

EXPENSIVE

Bed and Breakfast Guesthouse. Nestled in the Camelback Mountains, with an excellent views of Phoenix, this B&B is 15 minutes from Sky Harbor airport. The single guest house features flagstone floors and paintings of the desert. The home is set on 1½ acres of mountain cactus land. Complimentary breakfast. Kitchenette, refrigerator, microwave, in-room hot tub, cable TV, in-room VCR. Pool. Miniature golf. No kids under 6. No smoking. | 5319 E. Valle Vista Rd. | 602/955–9390 | fax 602/840–9475 | 1 room | $200 | No credit cards.

Crowne Plaza Phoenix Downtown. America West Arena is just a few blocks from this large, 19-story downtown hotel, which has Mediterranean decor. 2 restaurants. In-room data ports, cable TV. Pool. Beauty salon, hot tub, sauna. Gym. Laundry service. Business services. | 100 N. 1st St. | 602/333–0000 or 800/359–7253 | fax 602/333–5180 | 532 rooms | $189–$255 | www.phxcrowneplaza.com | AE, D, DC, MC, V.

Doubletree Suites–Phoenix Gateway Center. This six-story all-suite atrium hotel is 2 mi north of Sky Harbor International Airport in the Gateway Center. Restaurant, bar. Minibars, microwaves, refrigerators, cable TV. Pool. Hot tub. Exercise equipment. Business services, airport shuttle. | 320 N. 44th St. | 602/225–0500 | fax 602/225–0957 | 242 suites | $175–$275 | AE, D, DC, MC, V.

Embassy Suites–Biltmore. Across the street from the Biltmore Fashion Park, this large allsuite hotel has an airy lobby with huge palms, boulders, and waterfalls. The suites have small living rooms and larger bedrooms. Restaurant, bar, complimentary breakfast. In-room data ports, microwaves, refrigerators, cable TV. Pool. Hot tub. Gym. Laundry facilities. Business services. | 2630 E. Camelback Rd. | 602/955–3992 | fax 602/955–6479 | www.embassy-suites.com | 232 suites | $265–$325 | AE, D, DC, MC, V.

Embassy Suites–Camelback. All of the accommodations at this four-story all-suite hotel surround an expansive open atrium filled with trees and cozy sitting areas. The large two-room suites are decked in soft pastels, and have sofa sleepers as well as beds. Restaurant, bar, complimentary breakfast. Microwaves, refrigerators, cable TV. Pool. Hot tub. Laundry facilities. Business services, airport shuttle. | 1515 N. 44th St. | 602/244–8800 | fax 602/244–8114 | www.embassy-suites.com | 229 suites | $185–$209 | AE, D, DC, MC, V.

Embassy Suites–North. This stucco and red-tile-roofed all-suite hotel has an airy, bright atrium lobby with a waterfall, and boasts large two-room suites. Restaurant, bar, complimentary breakfast, room service. In-room data ports, refrigerators, cable TV. Pool, wading pool. Hot tub. Tennis court. Gym. Laundry facilities. Business services. | 2577 W. Greenway Rd. | 602/375–1777 | fax 602/375–4012 | www.embassy-suites.com | 314 suites | $189 | AE, D, DC, MC, V.

Four Points Barcelo Hotel Phoenix Metrocenter. This upscale hotel is next to the Metrocenter Mall and less than 1 mi from Castles N' Coasters amusement park. Restaurant, bar. In-room data ports, some refrigerators, cable TV. Pool. Hot tub, sauna. Tennis courts. Gym. Shops. Business services. | 10220 N. Metro Pkwy. E | 602/997–5900 | fax 602/943–6156 | www.fourpoints.com | 284 rooms, 5 suites | $248, $269–$349 suites | AE, D, DC, MC, V.

Hilton–Phoenix Airport. This four-story hotel is 1½ mi from Sky Harbor airport and 3 mi from Arizona State University. Restaurant, bar, room service. In-room data ports, minibars, cable TV. Pool. Hot tub. Gym. Business services, airport shuttle. | 2435 S. 47th St. | 480/894–1600 | fax 480/921–7844 | www.hilton.com | 253 rooms, 4 suites | $164–$314, $299–$425 suites | AE, D, DC, MC, V.

Legacy Golf Resort. After a long day of playing golf, you can retire to a large suite furnished in Spanish Mission style. The smallest bed you'll find here is king, with queen-size beds in pull-out couches. Restaurant. In-room data ports, kitchenettes, microwaves, refrigerators, some in-room hot tubs, cable TV. Pool. Massage. 18-hole golf course, 2 tennis courts. Health club. Kids' program (ages 4–17). Airport shuttle. | 6808 S. 32nd St., | 602/305–5500 or 888/828–3673 | fax 602/305–5501 | www.legacygolfresort.com | 328 suites | $200–$450 | AE, D, DC, MC, V.

Pointe Hilton at Squaw Peak. This family-oriented Pointe Hotel has a 9-acre water park, where man-made waterfalls feed swimming pools, a 130-ft water slide, and a 1,000-ft river that winds past a minigolf course and other recreational facilities. Accommodations in pink stucco buildings range from standard two-room suites to larger casitas. Some kitchenettes, some minibars, microwaves, some refrigerators, cable TV. 5 pools. Spa. Miniature golf, 4 tennis courts. Health club, volleyball. Shops. Kids' programs (ages 4–12). | 7677 N. 16th St. | 602/997–2626 or 800/876–4683 | fax 602/997–2391 | 430 suites, 133 casitas, 1 grand suite | $279 suites, $499 casitas, $899 grande suite | AE, D, DC, MC, V.

Pointe Hilton at Tapatio Cliffs. This large resort on 400 acres at the base of Phoenix North Mountain park has spectacular views. The lobby is open and airy, and rooms are boldly done up in purple with whitewashed furnishings. But the centerpiece of the resort is a 40-ft waterfall ending in 12 travertine pools, surrounded by terraces and gardens. 3 restaurants (see Different Pointe of View, above), bar, picnic area. Minibars, refrigerators, cable TV. Pool. Barbershop, beauty salon, hot tub, spa. Driving range, 18-hole golf course, putting green, 11 tennis courts. Health club, horseback riding, bicycles. Shops. Kids' programs (ages 3–12). Laundry facilities. Business services. | 11111 N. 7th St. | 602/866–7500 | fax 602/993–0276 | www.pointehilton.com | 600 rooms | $89–$179 rooms, $399 suites | AE, D, DC, MC, V.

Pointe Hilton on South Mountain. Sitting next to South Mountain Park, this is one of the largest resorts in the Southwest. Rooms are standard, but the four-story sports center is superb, and the golf course is one of Phoenix's best. The 750-acre property is lined with landscaped walkways and roads. Restaurant (see Rustler's Rooste, above), bar, room service. Minibars, cable TV. 6 pools, wading pool. Beauty salon, hot tub, massage, spa. 18-hole golf course, putting green, tennis courts. Health club, hiking, horseback riding, volleyball, bicycles. Kids' programs (ages

5–12). Laundry facilities. Business services. | 7777 S. Pointe Pkwy. | 602/438–9000 | fax 602/431–6535 | www.hilton.com | 643 suites | $249–$495 | AE, D, DC, MC, V.

VERY EXPENSIVE

Arizona Biltmore. The Biltmore has remained the premier luxury resort in Phoenix since it opened in 1920. The dramatic lobby and impeccably manicured grounds add to the sense of opulence. Rooms have marble baths and low-key elegance. 4 restaurants, bar, room service. Refrigerators, cable TV. 8 pools, wading pool. Beauty salon, hot tub. 18-hole putting green, 7 tennis courts. Health club, bicycles. Shops. Kids' programs (ages 4–12). | 24th St. and Missouri Ave. | 602/955–6600 or 800/950–0086 | fax 602/381–7600 | www.arizonabiltmore.com | 728 rooms, 12 one-bedroom suites, 61 two-bedroom suites | $330–$495, $650–$1,200 1–bedroom suites, $1,345–$1,695 2–bedroom suites | AE, MC, V.

Hermosa Inn. This ranch-style lodge, the former home and lodge of 1930s cowboy artist Lon Megargee, is on 6 acres of lush lawns mixed with desert landscaping. The hot tub is in a serene courtyard. Most rooms have fireplaces. The restaurant is one of Phoenix's best. Restaurant (*see* Lon's at the Hermosa, *above*), bar, complimentary breakfast. In-room data ports, some kitchenettes, some minibars, some in-room hot tubs, cable TV. Pool. Hot tub. 3 tennis courts. | 5532 N. Palo Cristi Rd. | 602/955–8614 or 800/241–1210 | fax 602/955–8299 | www.hermosainn.com | 4 villas, 3 haciendas, 11 casitas, 14 ranchos | $655 villas, $450 haciendas, $340 casitas, $265 ranchos | AE, D, DC, MC, V.

Hyatt Regency Phoenix at Civic Plaza. Rooms are spacious and comfortable, though not distinctive, in this 24-story convention hotel downtown. The seven-story, all-white atrium has a space-station feel, and there are huge sculptures and glass elevators. 3 restaurants, bar. In-room data ports, cable TV. Pool. Hot tub. Gym. Shops. Laundry service. Business services, parking (fee). | 122 N. 2nd St. | 602/252–1234 | fax 602/254–9472 | 685 rooms, 27 suites | $279–$350 | AE, D, DC, MC, V.

Ritz-Carlton, Phoenix. This hotel's sand-color neo-Federal facade faces the Biltmore Fashion Park and hides a graceful, well-appointed luxury hotel. Rooms have white-marble baths and views of either the mountains or the city. Restaurant, bar, room service. Minibars, some microwaves, cable TV, some in-room VCRs. Pool. Massage. Tennis courts. Gym, bicycles. Business services, airport shuttle. | 2401 E. Camelback Rd. | 602/468–0700 | fax 602/468–9883 | www.ritzcarlton.com | 270 rooms, 11 suites | $260–$315, $375–$425 suites | AE, D, DC, MC, V.

Royal Palms Hotel and Casitas. This beautiful Mediterranean-style resort in Paradise Valley, a Cunard executive's former home, has courtyards with antique fountains, a stately row of palms at the entrance, and stylish, individually designed guest rooms. Restaurant, bar. Minibars, cable TV. Pool. Tennis. Gym. Business services, airport shuttle. | 5200 E. Camelback Rd. | 602/840–3610 or 800/672–6011 | fax 602/840–6927 | www.royalpalmshotel.com | 52 rooms, 35 suites, 16 casitas, 3 villas | $300–$325, $385 suites, $3,500 presidential suite, $475 casitas, $1,200 villas | AE, D, DC, MC, V.

PINETOP/LAKESIDE

MAP 3, H6

(Nearby towns also listed: McNary, Show Low)

In 1540 Coronado passed through the White Mountains, an area inhabited by Native Americans, in search of gold, but the Mormons actually settled here, founding the towns of Pinetop and Lakeside when they arrived in the late 1800s. At an elevation of 7,200 ft, Pinetop/Lakeside, now a combined community of 4,500 year-round residents, is nestled among the largest stand of ponderosa pines in the world. This small community attracts city dwellers in summer with its cool temperatures and clean mountain air, and at these times the population swells to as much as 40,000. In winter, the Sunrise Park Ski Resort, 25 mi southeast, is also a draw (*see* McNary).

Information: Pinetop–Lakeside Chamber of Commerce | 674 E. White Mountain Blvd., Box 4220, Pinetop, 85935 | 520/367–4290 | www.pinetoplakesidechamber.com.

Attractions

A-1 Lake. This lake 22 mi east of Pinetop and surrounding area provide opportunities for camping, hiking, and fishing. There's wheelchair access. | Off Hwy. 260 | 520/367–4290 | Free | Mid-May–mid-Sept., daily.

Hon-Dah Casino. Black and red lights, wall-length mirrors, and deep red and black colors give a traditional Vegas quality to this gambling floor in the Hon-Dah Resort lodge, which offers video poker, video blackjack, video keno, and a variety of slot machines. No table games. Nightly entertainment Tuesday–Sunday. | 77 Hwy. 260 | 520/369–0299 | www.hon-dah.com | Free | Daily 24 hrs.

Show Low Lake. A popular fishing spot, Show Low Lake, off Highway 260 northeast of Pinetop, is known for walleye, trout, and bass in early spring. Campsites are available. | Show Lake Rd. | 520/367–4290 | Free | Daily sunrise–sunset.

White Mountain Country Club. This 18-hole course features steep fairways through ponderosa pine forests and several doglegs and is inarguably one of the most challenging courses in the area. | 3644 Country Club Circle, Pinetop | 520/367–4357 | Daily 7:30–5.

ON THE CALENDAR

AUG.: *Annual White Mountain Bluegrass Musical Festival.* This festival features lively music, food, and dance. | 520/367–4290.

OCT.: *Oktoberfest.* A biergarten is the site for polka music, bratwurst, and baked goods at this annual celebration of Germany at the Pinetop Lakes Country Club. | 520/367–4290.

Dining

Annie's Gift Shop and Tea Room. American. This intimate and homey bistro across the highway from the Lakeside Fire Department offers cozy lunch and breakfast fare like quiche, baked goods, scones, and specialty sandwiches and teas. Plan on an early meal—Annie's closes at 2:30 PM. | 2849 White Mountain Blvd., Lakeside | 520/368–5737 | Closed Sun.; closed Mon. Labor Day–Memorial Day. No dinner | $8–$11 | AE, D, MC, V.

The Chalet. American. This chalet-style restaurant is known for ribs and chicken. Salad bar. Kids' menu. | 348 White Mountain Blvd. | 520/367–1514 | Closed Sun.–Mon. No lunch | $15–$32 | D, MC, V.

Charlie Clark's Steak House. Steak. Cozy and casual, this log-cabin family restaurant has a congenial western-style interior filled with historic photographs of the area. Prime rib is the house specialty, as are a variety of other steak and chicken dishes (try the classic chicken-fried steak). Kids' menu. | 1701 E. White Mountain Blvd. | 520/367–4900 | $10–$19 | AE, DC, MC, V.

Christmas Tree. American. The home-cooked "Chicken and Dumplings" is one of the cornerstones at this down-home restaurant offering gourmet comfort food like broiled lamb chops, honey duck with fried apples, and a delectable fresh fruit cobbler. Kids' menu. | Woodland Rd. and White Mountain Blvd., Lakeside | 520/367–3107 | Closed Mon., Tues. No lunch | $18–$42 | D, MC, V.

Pasta House. Italian. A glassed-in porch in a converted house serves as the dining area for this casual, candlelit, and intimate restaurant. You'll find standard lasagna, manicotti, and ravioli dishes, all well prepared and served with soup or salad and a homemade garlic bread. Finish off with a made-from-scratch tiramisu or cannoli. | 2188 E. White Mountain Blvd., Pinetop | 520/367–2782 | Closed Sun., Mon. Labor Day–Memorial Day. No lunch | $14–$34 | AE, D, MC, V.

PINETOP/
LAKESIDE

INTRO
ATTRACTIONS
DINING
LODGING

Lodging

Best Western Inn. This chain motel is next to a restaurant and offers tea and hot choco-late on cool, mountain nights. In cold weather, opt for a room with a fireplace. Complimentary Continental breakfast. Some microwaves, some refrigerators, cable TV. Hot tub. Business services. | 404 Hwy. 260 | 520/367–6667 | fax 520/367–6672 | 41 rooms, 1 suite | $99, $199 suite | AE, D, DC, MC, V.

Comfort Inn–Lakeside. This chain motel is just north of Pinetop, 9 mi south of Show Low. Some rooms have fireplaces. Complimentary Continental breakfast. Refrigerators, cable TV. Hot tub. Business services. | 1637 Hwy. 260 | 520/368–6600 or 800/843–4792 | fax 520/368–6600 | 55 rooms | $49–$99 | AE, D, DC, MC, V.

Hon-Dah Resort. At an altitude of 7,400 ft, and in the midst of 1.7 million acres of ponderosa pine forest, this mountain resort boasts an extravagant lobby with a display of stuffed high-country animals, and a comfortable fireplace area with cushy chairs and couches. Rooms are oversize but basic. The property also includes a gambling floor and a heritage room, which gives an overview of area history, culture, and the White Mountain Apache tribe. 2 restaurants, bar. In-room data ports, minibars, refrigerators. Pool. Hot tub, sauna. | 77 Hwy. 269, | 520/369–0299 | 180 rooms | $79–$99 | AE, D, DC, MC, V.

Lakeview Lodge. Antique furnishings, stone fireplaces, and rustic decor fill this quaint inn, which is the oldest guest lodge in Arizona, 8 mi east of Show Low. Outside, cobblestone walkways wind through the surrounding pine groves and gardens, and a private stocked lake is available for fishing. The main sitting area features a huge fireplace, leather chairs, and plush sofas, all under a two-story cathedral ceiling. Restaurant, picnic area. No room phones, no TV in some rooms, TV in common area. Fishing. Some pets allowed (fee). | Hwy. 260 | 520/368–5253 | www.dynexgroup.com/lakeview | 9 rooms | $65–$90 | MC, V.

Northwoods Resort. Surrounded by mountain pines, each of these home-style cabins has a full kitchen, covered porch, barbecue grill, and homey interior. Some cabins have in-room hot tubs, and two-story cabins can accommodate up to 18 people; accommodations are perfect for groups or families. Picnic area. Refrigerators, no in-room phones. Pool. Hot tub. Playground. Pets allowed (fee). | 165 E. White Mountain Blvd. | 520/367–2966 or 800/813–2966 | fax 520/367–2969 | www.northwoodsaz.com | 14 cabins | $79–$269 | D, DC, MC, V.

Whispering Pines Resort. These cabin-style accommodations come with double or king-size beds. Located at 7,200 ft and surrounded by a sea of conifers, you'll be soothed to sleep with the fresh smells of mountain air and evergreens. There's little traffic nearby, so you'll be assured a tranquil stay. Some kitchenettes, some microwaves, some refrigerators, some in-room hot tubs, cable TV, no room phones. Laundry facilities. Pets allowed (fee). | 237 E. Mountain Blvd., Pinetop | 520/367–4386 or 800/840–3867 | fax 520/367–3702 | www.whis-peringpinesaz.com | 33 cabins | $70–$240 | AE, D, MC, V.

PRESCOTT

MAP 3, D5

(Nearby towns also listed: Clarkdale, Cottonwood, Jerome, Sedona)

Named the first capital of Arizona Territory in 1864, Prescott was settled by north-easterners with interests in local gold. They brought with them a New England archi-tectural style still visible today. Despite a devastating downtown fire in 1900, Prescott remains the Southwest's richest store of New England–style architecture; in fact, it's been called the "West's most Eastern town" by some. At an elevation of 5,300 ft, it's one refuge where Phoenix residents can escape the summertime heat, and it's also a popular retirement community, given the temperate climate and low cost of living. The Yavapai Indian Reservation is just outside the town limits.

Information: **Prescott Chamber of Commerce** | 117 W. Goodwin St., Box 1147, Prescott, 86302 | 520/445–2000 or 800/266–7534 | www.prescott.org.

Attractions

Arcosanti. Italian architect Paolo Soleri designed this futuristic community where architecture and ecology would function in harmony. The community was begun in 1970 and continues to be built today. About 100 people are in residence now, but the plan is to create a community that can house 6,000. The only time you're allowed to walk through the grounds is during tour hours. It's 36 mi southeast of Prescott on Highway 69 to Cordes Junction, then 2 mi east on an unnumbered road (follow the signs). | Off I–17, Cordes Junction | 520/632–7135 | $6 (suggested donation) for tour | Daily 10–4 (tours hourly).

Courthouse Plaza. In the heart of the city, this plaza is bounded by Gurley and Goodwin streets to the north and south and by Cortez and Montezuma streets to the west and east. The 1916 Yavapai County Courthouse is still standing tall, and it is protected by an equestrian bronze of turn-of-the-20th-century journalist and lawmaker Bucky O'Neill. | 520/445–2000 or 800/266–7534 | Free | Daily.

Phippen Museum of Western Art. This museum 5 mi north of downtown features the work of many prominent artists of the West in its permanent collection. But the focus is the paintings and bronze sculptures of George Phippen. | 4701 Hwy. 89 N | 520/778–1385 | www.phippenmuseum.com | Free | Wed.–Mon. 10–4.

★ **Prescott National Forest.** You can hike and camp on the million or more acres of forest land here that surround the town of Prescott, which is in the Bradshaw Ranger District. The winding road from Jerome to Prescott through the forest is one of Arizona's most breathtaking mountain drives. | Ranger District office: 344 S. Cortez St. | 520/445–1762 | Free | Forest daily; district office weekdays 8–4:30.

Prescott Zoo. This small but impressive facility houses both animals native to Arizona like the speedy pronghorn, and more exotic creatures like Bengal tigers. | 1403 Heritage Park Rd. | 520/778–4242 | www.prescottzoo.com | $5 | May–Oct., daily 9–5; Nov.–Apr., daily 10–4.

Sharlot Hall Museum. Named for historian and poet Sharlot Hall, three fully restored period homes and an original ponderosa pine cabin that once housed the territorial governor are in a parklike setting. | 415 W. Gurley St. | 520/445–3122 | $5 donation per group requested | Mon.–Sat. 10–5, Sun. 1–5.

Smoki Museum. This 1935 stone and log building houses a fine collection of Native American artifacts. Though the items on exhibit are genuine, the museum is named for a fictitious tribe, invented in 1921 by Anglos who wanted to draw visitors to Prescott. | 147 N. Arizona St. | 520/445–1230 | $2 | Hours are irregular; call before visiting.

Whiskey Row. This stretch of Montezuma Street flanks Courthouse Plaza's west side. In its heyday it held 20 saloons and houses of pleasure; nowadays the historic bars just provide a respite from the street's many boutiques. | Montezuma St. at Courthouse Plaza | Free | Daily.

Young's Farm. Family-run since 1947, this farm features hayrides, a nursery, and a petting zoo. The Farm Store offers fresh poultry, vegetables, and desserts. | Hwy. 69 at Hwy. 169, Dewey | 520/632–7272 | fax 520/632–7975 | www.youngsfarminc.com | Free | Daily 7–6.

ON THE CALENDAR

MAY: *George Phippen Memorial Western Art Show.* Many artists exhibit their work at this annual Memorial Day weekend show in Courthouse Plaza. | 520/445–2000 or 800/266–7534.

JUNE: *Territorial Prescott Days.* This festival includes arts and crafts, contests, and tours of the Courthouse Plaza area. | 520/445–2000 or 800/266–7534.

JUNE: *Bluegrass Festival.* Local, state, and national musicians perform both contemporary and traditional bluegrass in Courthouse Square. | 520/445–2000 or 800/266–7534.

JUNE–JULY: *Prescott Frontier Days and Rodeo.* A parade, food, vendors, dancing, and fireworks enliven this annual July 4th rodeo at the Yavapai County Fairgrounds. | 520/445–2000 or 800/266–7534.

AUG.: *Cowboy Poets Gathering.* Poetry readings, as well as contests and music, celebrate this annual gathering at the Sharlot Hall Museum and Yavapai College. | 520/445–2000 or 800/266–7534.

SEPT.: *Yavapai County Fair.* This old-fashioned fair offers rides, games, livestock, and special children's activities at the Yavapai County Fairgrounds. | 520/445–7820.

Dining

Coyote Joe's Bar and Grill. American. Exposed brick, sturdy wooden booths and bar, potted plants, and lots of light provide an inviting setting. Corn chip–crusted catfish and green chile chicken are a couple of the offerings. | 214 S. Montezuma St. | 520/778–9570 | $7–$14 | AE, D, MC, V.

© Corbis

RODEO LESSON

Rodeo is a sport involving a series of contests and exhibitions derived from riding, roping, and related skills developed by cowboys during the era of the range cattle industry in northern Mexico and the western United States between 1867 and 1887.

The five standard events in contemporary rodeo are calf roping, bull riding, steer wrestling, saddle bronc-riding, and bareback bronc-riding. ("Bronc" is short for bronco, an unbroken range horse chosen for its resistance to training and its tendency to buck, or throw, a rider.)

Two other events are recognized in championship competitions: single-steer roping and team roping. The barrel race, a saddle horse race around a series of barrels, is a popular contest for cowgirls.

The participants pay entry fees, and the prize money won is their only compensation. More than half of all rodeos are independent of state and county fairs, livestock shows, or other attractions, and many are held in arenas devoted to the purpose. The equipment, however, is simple and may be improvised.

Rodeo developed as an American sport, originating when cowboys gathered in the "cowtowns" at the end of cattle-driving trails and vied for the unofficial titles of best bucking-horse rider, roper, and so on. As the cowboys' day jobs were curtailed in scope by the railroads and by fencing, the contests became regular, formal programs of entertainment.

In 1929, the Rodeo Association of America, an organization of rodeo managers and producers, was formed to regulate the sport. The contestants themselves took a hand in 1936 after a strike in Boston Garden and organized the Cowboy Turtles Association—"turtles" because they had been slow to act. This group was renamed the Rodeo Cowboys Association (RCA) in 1945 and the Professional Rodeo Cowboys Association (PRCA) in 1975. Its rules became accepted by most rodeos.

Dinner Bell Café. American. A block and a half from the courthouse, you can have breakfast at the oldest café in town—and possibly the most reasonably priced one, too—while sitting on the patio beside Granite Creek. Or sit inside at the espresso bar and listen to jazz. Try eggs with fresh tomato and basil. | 321 W. Gurley St. | 520/445–9888 | Breakfast also available; closed Wed. | $3–$7 | No credit cards.

Doghouse Restaurant. American. Chicago-style hot dogs are the big draw at this casual sports bar and restaurant on the famous Whiskey Row. | 126 S. Montezuma Rd. | 520/445–7962 | $3–$6 | No credit cards.

Genovese. Italian. This small family-owned and -operated restaurant with exposed-beam ceilings and gold-stained walls serves lovingly prepared Italian country-style food. Favorites include calamari steak in a lemon butter and caper sauce, Portobello mushrooms stuffed with sun-dried tomatoes and spinach, and the veal Toscana (sliced veal with tiger shrimp). There's an extensive lunch salad menu, and the homemade desserts are worth saving room for. | 217 W. Gurley St. | 520/541–9089 | $8–$16 | AE, D, DC, MC, V.

Gurley Street Grill. American/Casual. This pub is in Arizona's first territorial capitol, a turn-of-the-20th-century building. The excellent rotisserie chicken is cooked daily, and the roasted potpie, vegetable stir-fry, and pistachio chicken are good bets. Many microbrews are on tap. Kids' menu. | 230 Gurley St. | 520/445–3388 | $8–$14 | AE, D, MC, V.

Juniper House. American. Whimsical rooster figurines and lots of plants brighten this modest spot. The huevos rancheros and breakfast burritos should satisfy you. | 810 White Spar Rd. | 520/445–3250 | No dinner | $4–8 | AE, D, MC, V.

Kendall's Famous Burgers and Ice Cream. American. This 1950s-style diner in downtown Prescott serves up some of the best home-cooked burgers in the area. Grab a booth and include a thick shake and some of the crispy homemade french fries in your order. | 113 S. Cortez St. | 520/778–3658 | $4–$7 | AE, MC, V.

Murphy's. American. Turn-of-the-20th-century artifacts decorate this former mercantile building that's on the National Register of Historic Places. The menu stars mesquite-grilled meats and house-brewed beer. Try baby-back ribs, fresh steamed clams, or fried catfish. Kids' menu, early-bird dinners (Sunday–Thursday). Sun brunch. | 201 N. Cortez St. | 520/445–4044 | $8–$25 | AE, D, MC, V.

The Palace. American. An ornate 1880s New Brunswick bar from Prescott's Whiskey Row serves as the centerpiece at this elegant restaurant in a restored turn-of-the-20th-century building. The high tin-pressed ceilings and original woodwork add to the old-world charm. Prime rib is the house specialty, as is the popular citrus salmon, and the Tom Mixed Grill, which includes sirloin steak, citrus salmon, and shrimp scampi, makes for a satisfying meal. | 120 S. Montezuma St. | 520/541–1996 | $15–$25 | AE, D, MC, V.

Pine Cone Inn. American. This family-style eatery is known for steak, chicken, lamb, and seafood dishes such as shrimp Louis, sirloin steak, and lamb chops. Entertainment Tuesday–Sunday. Early-bird dinners. | 1245 White Spar Rd. | 520/445–2970 | Closed Mon. | $7–$23 | AE, D, MC, V.

Prescott Brewing Company. American. Frontier steak fajitas with Portobello mushrooms or saguaro chicken (with jalapeño jack cheese) go great with one of the fine ales or porters that are brewed here. The room is very airy and open, with a large bar and displays of the many medallions the company has won for its beers. | 130 Gurley St. | 520/771–2795 | $7–$14 | AE, D, MC, V.

Zuma's Woodfire Café. Eclectic. Almond-encrusted salmon and tequila chicken are standouts at this establishment. The tables and bar feature unique copper exteriors, and the place is full of plants. Two patios provide outdoor seating. | 124 N. Montezuma Rd. | 520/541–1400 | $11–$17 | AE, D, MC, V.

PRESCOTT

INTRO
ATTRACTIONS
DINING
LODGING

Lodging

Best Western Prescottonian. This well-kept, comfortable motel is in the heart of Prescott, on one of the main streets. Restaurant, bar. In-room data ports, refrigerators, cable TV. Pool. Hot tub. Laundry facilities. Business services. Pets allowed. | 1317 E. Gurley St. | 520/445–3096 | fax 520/778–2976 | www.bestwestern.com | 121 rooms, 3 suites | $79–$95, $125–$200 suites | AE, D, DC, MC, V.

Chapel Suites. In a remodeled church building, this hotel is good if you like peace and quiet and are spending some time in the area. It's only five blocks from downtown Prescott. Rooms are simple, with pleasant blue and mauve tones. Kitchenettes, microwaves, refrigerators, cable TV. No pets. No smoking. | 146 N. Mount Vernon Ave. | 520/776–7030 | www.chapel-suites.com | $520–$570 for 1 wk (1–wk minimum) | No credit cards.

Comfort Inn. This reliable motel is on the southwest side of Prescott, 2 mi from Courthouse Square. Some kitchenettes, some refrigerators, cable TV. Hot tub. | 1290 White Spar Rd. | 520/778–5770 | fax 520/771–9373 | www.comfortinn.com | 61 rooms in 4 buildings | $90–$115 rooms | AE, D, DC, MC, V.

Cottages at Prescott Country Inn. These cottages date from the 1940s and retain many pre–World War II touches, including photographs from the era, older still life and landscape paintings, and rocking chairs. Most units provide a view of wooded areas. Complimentary Continental breakfast. Cable TV. No smoking. | 503 S. Montezuma St. | 520/445–7991 | www.cableone.net/cottages | 12 suites | $69–$129 | AE, D, MC, V.

Dolls and Roses Bed and Breakfast. Named for the display of antique dolls sitting in a 1870s baby carriage that greets you in the foyer, this 1883 Victorian inn is an elegant alternative to area motels. The house was moved from its original location at the corner of Pleasant and Gurley in 1903 and has been carefully restored. It has the largest Victorian rose garden in Prescott's historic district. Complimentary breakfast. Some kitchenettes, no room phones, no TV in some rooms, TV in common area. No smoking. | 109 N. Pleasant St. | 520/776–9291 | 4 rooms, 1 carriage house | $99–$139, $119 carriage house | MC, V.

Forest Villas. A magnificent winding staircase is the focal point of the lobby of this popular Mediterranean-style hotel, which was built in 1995. Regular rooms are hotel-standard, but suites have fireplaces and in-room hot tubs. Complimentary Continental breakfast. Some refrigerators, some in-room hot tubs, cable TV. Pool. Hot tub. Gym. Business services. | 3645 Lee Circle | 520/717–1200 or 800/223–3449 | fax 520/717–1400 | www.forestvillas.com | 62 rooms, 16 suites | $95–$109, $125–$208 suites | AE, D, DC, MC, V.

Hassayampa Inn. Built in 1927 and listed on the National Register of Historic Places, this hotel has great touches like the hand-painted ceiling in the lobby; some of the rooms still have their original furnishings. Restaurant, bar, complimentary breakfast. Some in-room hot tubs, cable TV. Business services. | 122 E. Gurley St. | 520/778–9434 or 800/322–1927 | fax 520/445–8590 | www.hassayampainn.com | 57 rooms, 10 suites | $99–195 | AE, D, DC, MC, V.

Hotel St. Michael On the busiest corner of the Courthouse Plaza, this hotel offers many rooms with views of the courthouse. The hotel dates from the turn of the 20th century, and the rooms feature furniture dating back to the 1930s. Complimentary Continental breakfast. Cable TV. | 205 W. Gurley St. | 520/776–1999 or 800/678–3757 | fax 520/776–7318 | 72 rooms | $49–$99 | AE, D, MC, V.

Hotel Vendome–A Clarion Carriage House Inn. The best moderately priced hotel in town, this World War I–era hostelry in downtown Prescott, just a block from Courthouse Square, has welcomed everyone from miners and health-seekers to cowboy star Tom Mix. And there are old-fashioned touches like claw-foot tubs. Complimentary Continental breakfast. Cable TV. Business services. | 230 S. Cortez St. | 520/776–0900 or 888/468–3583 | fax 520/771–0395 | www.vendomehotel.com | 17 rooms, 4 suites | $69–$159, $89–$189 suites | AE, D, DC, MC, V.

Lynx Creek Farm. Very private, freestanding rooms overlook Lynx Creek. Call for directions, as the property is quite secluded and difficult to find. Picnic area, complimentary breakfast. Some kitchenettes, no room phones. Pool. Hot tub. Airport shuttle. Some pets allowed (fee). No smoking. | Mile marker 291 (Onyx Dr.) | 520/778–9573 | www.vacation-lodging.com | 6 rooms, 2 suites | $85–$180, $105–$165 suites | AE, D, MC, V.

Mark's House. This Victorian B&B was once the home of Prescott's mayor, in territorial days. Rooms are furnished with period antiques. The circular turret contains a particularly impressive suite. Complimentary breakfast. Some air-conditioning, no room phones, no TV. No smoking. | 203 E. Union St. | 520/778–4632 or 800/370–MARK | www.themark-shouse.net | markshouse@cableone.net | 4 suites | $85–$135 | D, MC, V.

Pleasant Street Inn. This 1906 Victorian home has lots of windows and light. Furnishings are contemporary and comfortable rather than the antiques typical of a lot of B&Bs. Some rooms offer a view of Thumb Butte. Complimentary breakfast. No room phones, no TV. No smoking. | 142 S. Pleasant St. | 520/445–4774 or 877/226–7128 | fax 520/777–8696 | www.cwde-signers.com/pleasantstreet | 4 rooms | $89–$135 | AE, D, MC, V.

Prescott Resort and Conference Center. This property is on a hilltop above town with lovely views. It's one of only two hotel-casinos in Arizona. Restaurant, bar. Refrigerators, cable TV. Indoor-outdoor pool. Barbershop, beauty salon, hot tub. 4 tennis courts. Gym, racquetball. Business services. | 1500 Rte. 69 | 520/776–1666 or 800/967–4637 | fax 520/776–8544 | www.prescottresort.com | 161 rooms, 80 suites | $139, $159 suites | AE, D, DC, MC, V.

SAFFORD

MAP 3, H8

(Nearby towns also listed: Clifton, Willcox)

The largest city in Graham County in southeastern Arizona, Safford was founded in 1874 by four farmers who wanted to grow crops along the Gila River. Today it's a market town for cotton, alfalfa, grain, vegetables, and fruit.

Information: **Graham County Chamber of Commerce** | 1111 Thatcher Blvd., Safford, 85546 | 520/428–2511 | www.chamber.safford.az.org.

Attractions
Cluff Ranch. Formerly a working ranch, this expansive area 12 mi west of Safford now offers fishing, big-game hunting, archery, and hiking opportunities. | Off Hwy. 70 | 520/428–2511 | Free | Daily.

Roper Lake State Park. There's a rock-lined hot tub fed by a natural spring at this man-made lake 4 mi south of Safford. It's also a popular spot for hiking, fishing, and camping. There are 20 hookup sites for RVs and campers. | U.S. 191 | 520/428–6760 | www.roperlake.com | $4 per vehicle | Daily 6–10.

ON THE CALENDAR
MAY: *Fiesta de Mayo.* Fiesta de Mayo celebrates Mexico's independence day at St. Rose of Lima Church. | 520/428–2511.
JULY: *Pioneer Days.* This event at the fairgrounds, 3 mi south of Safford, commemorates the founding of the Mormon settlement at Thatcher. | 520/428–2511.
OCT.: *Graham County Fair.* A carnival and children's activities are the draw here, along with a livestock auction at the county fairgrounds, 3 mi south of Safford. | 520/428–2511.
OCT.: *Old West Highway Car Show.* This annual event at Roper Lake State Park attracts a modest crowd. Lots of vintage cars and hot rods are on display. | 520/428–6760. .

Dining
Casa Mañana. Mexican. Try the chimichangas or fajitas at this restaurant that also serves some American dishes. Beer only. | 502 1st Ave. | 520/428–3170 | $7–$19 | MC, V.

El Charro Restaurant. Mexican. All the familiar dishes come in generous portions here. The centerpiece of the room is a massive mural of the mountains and desert. | 601 Main St. | 520/428–4134 | Closed Sun. | $5–$9 | DC, MC, V.

Lodging

Best Western Desert Inn. This motel is on the northwest side of town. Bar. Refrigerators, cable TV. Pool. Laundry facilities. Business services, airport shuttle. | 1391 Thatcher Blvd. | 520/428–0521 | fax 520/428–7653 | 70 rooms | $65–$85 | AE, D, DC, MC, V.

Comfort Inn. This clean motel on the northwest side of Safford offers basic amenities. Complimentary Continental breakfast. Refrigerators, cable TV. Pool. Business services. | 1578 W. Thatcher Blvd. | 520/428–5851 | fax 520/428–4968 | 44 rooms | $50–$70 | AE, D, DC, MC, V.

Ramada Inn Spa Resort. This hotel is fairly isolated, but the mountain views are splendid. The inn looks like a sprawling Mexican hacienda. The rooms have the ad hoc cheer of a beach house and will suffice for a good night's sleep. Restaurant. In-room data ports, microwaves, refrigerators, some in-room hot tubs, cable TV, in-room VCRs. Pool. Sauna. Gym. Pets allowed. | 420 E. U.S. 70 | 520/428–3288 | fax 520/428–3200 | www.ramadainn-spare-sort.com | 102 rooms | $80–$150 | AE, D, DC, MC, V.

SAN CARLOS

MAP 3, G7

(Nearby town also listed: Globe)

The headquarters of the San Carlos Apache Indian Reservation makes a good day trip from nearby Globe, where you'll find the nearest accommodations.

Information: **San Carlos Recreation and Wildlife Dept.** | Box 97, San Carlos, 85550 | 520/ 475–2343.

Attractions

Apache Indian Reservation. This reservation covers over 1.8 million acres of mountain and desert terrain, with altitudes ranging 2,500 ft–8,000 ft. Fishing is offered in both high-country and desert lakes, or on the beautiful Black River; permits can be purchased from a variety of vendors in the Globe and San Carlos areas. The San Carlos Apaches sometimes invite outsiders to their tribal dances on their reservation. Call ahead for more information. | Hwy. 170 | 520/475–2361, 520/475–2653 recreation department | Free; fishing permit $7–$10 per day; camping fee $7 per night | Daily.

ON THE CALENDAR

NOV.: *Veteran's Day Parade, Fair, and Rodeo.* Many tribes, including the Apache, participate in a parade, powwows, rodeo, and carnival. Thousands attend this three-day Veteran's Day Weekend event. | 520/475–2361.

Lodging

Best Western Apache Gold. The rates are a bargain at this hotel 12 mi west of San Carlos near the junction of Highway 77 and Interstate 70, so you can save your pennies and slip next door to the Apache Gold Casino. Pleasant rooms feature a southwestern color scheme and pictures of Native American scenes. Restaurant, bar, room service. In-room data ports, some in-door hot tubs, cable TV. Pool. Gym. | I–70, | 520/402–5600 | fax 520/475–5601 | www.bestwestern.com | 145 rooms, 2 suites | $39–$95 | AE, D, DC, MC, V.

SCOTTSDALE

(Nearby towns also listed: Chandler, Mesa, Phoenix, Tempe)

A chic suburb northeast of Phoenix, Scottsdale is best known for its shopping (along 5th Avenue) and resorts (including the world-class Phoenician). Historic Old Town is a respite from the bustle of downtown Phoenix, and Main Street is home to innumerable art galleries geared toward collectors and browsers alike. The Scottsdale Center for the Arts is a good place to check on current cultural events.

Information: Scottsdale Chamber of Commerce | 7343 Scottsdale Mall, Scottsdale, 85251 | 480/945–8481 or 800/877–1117 | www.scottsdalecvb.com.

Attractions

SCOTTSDALE

INTRO
ATTRACTIONS
DINING
LODGING

Buffalo Museum of America. This quirky little museum pays homage to the American bison and its important role in American history. Contents range from a mounted shaggy beast to reflective works of art. | 10261 N. Scottsdale Rd. | 480/951–1022 | $3 | Weekdays 9–5.

5th Avenue. This stretch of shops is home to about 100 boutiques and specialty shops. Whether you seek handmade Native American arts and crafts, casual clothing, or cacti, you'll find it here—with colorful storefronts and friendly merchants. | 7121 5th Ave. | 480/946–7566 | Daily 10–6.

Main Street Arts District. Numerous galleries on Main Street and 1st Avenue, particularly on the blocks between Scottsdale Road and 69th Street, display artwork of various styles, from contemporary to Native American to traditional. Shops that specialize in elegant porcelains and oriental rugs, along with antiques shops, can also be found here. | Main St., 1st Ave., between Scottsdale Rd. and 69th St. | Free | Daily.

Marshall Way Arts District. Galleries that exhibit predominantly contemporary art line the blocks of Marshall Way north of Indian School Road. Upscale gift and jewelry shops can also be found here. | Marshall Way, north of Indian School Rd. | Free | Daily.

Old Town Scottsdale. Approximately half a dozen blocks constitute "Old Town," a cluster of early-20th-century buildings with rustic storefronts and wooden sidewalks. Jewelry, pots, and Mexican imports are sold alongside standard souvenirs. | Main St. | Free | Daily.

Scottsdale Center for the Arts. Although the galleries within this cultural and entertainment complex rotate exhibits frequently, they usually emphasize contemporary art. The Museum Store has a wonderful collection of jewelry and books. | 7380 E. 2nd St. | 480/994–2787 | www.scottsdalearts.org | Free | Wed.–Sat. 10–5, Sun. noon–4. Closed Mon.–Tues. and July–Aug.

Scottsdale Historical Museum. This redbrick structure was Scottsdale's first schoolhouse and it preserves the 1910 schoolroom. Photographs, original furniture from the city's founding fathers, and displays of other treasures from Scottsdale's early days are included in the collection. | 7333 Scottsdale Mall | 602/945–4499 | Free | Wed.–Sat. 10–5, Sun. noon–4. Closed Mon.–Tues. and July–Aug.

Scottsdale Museum of Contemporary Art. Adjacent to the Scottsdale Center for the Arts, this museum focuses on contemporary art, architecture, and design. The spacious outdoor sculpture garden is a highlight of the museum. | 7380 E. 2nd St. | 480/994–2787 | www.scottsdalearts.org/smoca | $5 | Mon.–Wed. and Fri.–Sat. 10–5, Thurs. 10–9, Sun. noon–5.

★ **Taliesin West.** This complex of buildings and garden courts linked by walls and terraces stands at the base of the McDowell Mountain range in northeast Scottsdale, overlooking the Phoenix metropolitan area. It was designed by famed architect Frank Lloyd Wright in 1937 and became his western headquarters. Tour times vary, so call ahead because visitors must be accompanied by a guide. | 12621 Frank Lloyd Wright Blvd. | 480/860–2700 or 480/860–8810 | www.franklloydwright.org | $12–$35 | Daily 8:30–5.

ON THE CALENDAR

JAN., FEB.: *Parada del Sol and Rodeo.* This annual rodeo at the Rawhide Rodeo Arena includes a parade. | 480/990–3179 or 480/502–5600.

MAR.: *Baseball Spring Training.* The San Francisco Giants get back in shape at Scottsdale Stadium. | 480/312–2586 or 480/312–2580.

MAR., APR.: *The Tradition at Desert Mountain.* This annual Senior PGA Tour golf tourney is at Cochise Golf Course at Desert Mountain. | 480/595–4070.

APR. *Annual Scottsdale Culinary Festival.* Food and wine tastings are the thing at this food festival at the Scottsdale Civic Center Mall to benefit local art education programs. | 480/994–2787.

Dining

Al Amir. Middle Eastern. This dark, intimate restaurant offers traditional well-prepared favorites like hummus, tabbouleh, falafel, and meat kabobs, as well as specialties like *ma'anek* (Lebanese sausage spiked with cloves), *kebbe bil sanyeh* (seasoned ground beef baked in bulgur wheat and pine nuts), and, for dessert, the excellent *knafeh* (warm cheese pastry). Belly dancing on Friday and Saturday nights. | 8989 E. Via Linda | 480/661–1137 | Closed Sun., Mon. | $10–$25 | AE, D, MC, V.

Avanti's of Scottsdale. Italian. The menu at this local downtown favorite is Italian with touches from around the world. Candles light every linen-draped table. Try the *osso buco* (braised veal shank), with tiramisu for dessert. The softly lit patio out front is a romantic spot. Entertainment Tuesday–Saturday. | 3102 N. Scottsdale Rd. | 480/949–8333 | No lunch | $21–$35 | AE, D, DC, MC, V.

Bandera. American/Casual. This casual and friendly family restaurant specializes in rotisserie chicken, but you can also get salads, fresh fish, and prime rib. The mashed potatoes are very good. Be prepared for a wait, especially weekends. Kids' menu. No smoking. | 3821 N. Scottsdale Rd. | 480/994–3524 | No lunch | $16–$30 | AE, DC, MC, V.

Buster's Restaurant, Bar & Grill. American. The antique-style furnishings and reproduction prints give this local neighborhood eatery an elegant yet casual quality. It specializes in steak and fresh seafood. Try the coconut shrimp, prime rib, lobster, or Caesar salad. You can dine on a patio overlooking a small man-made lake. Kids' menu, early-bird dinners. | 8320 N. Hayden | 480/951–5850 | Reservations not accepted | $11–$27 | AE, DC, MC, V.

Cafe Terra Cotta. Southwestern. Owners Donna Nordin and Don Luria are pioneers on the local culinary scene. The menu here focuses on inventive regional creations using sophisticated flavors. Try the large prawns stuffed with herb goat cheese or the tortilla-crusted chicken breast. It's in the Borgata Shopping Center. No smoking. | 6166 N. Scottsdale Rd. | 480/948–8100 | $12–$22 | AE, D, DC, MC, V.

Carlsbad Tavern. Mexican. The New Mexico–inspired fare at this family restaurant, filled with cozy booths and colorful artwork, has quite a kick. Wash down appetizers like red chile potato pancakes with a premium margarita; try the *carne adovada*, slow-roasted pork in a red chile sauce, or the *machaca* beef burrito, with spicy shredded beef, for added fire. An outside patio and deck with fireplace overlooks a small pond. | 3313 N. Hayden Rd. | 480/970–8156 | Reservations not accepted | $9–$20 | AE, D, DC, MC, V.

Chaparral Dining Room. American. The muted desert colors and southwestern decor at this formal restaurant in the Marriott Camelback Inn complement the gorgeous views of Camelback Mountain outside. Service is impeccable, and flavorful, carefully prepared entrées include beef Wellington, lobster bisque, sea bass, and salmon. End the meal with the light-as-air chocolate soufflé. Reservations are recommended. | 5402 E. Lincoln Dr. | 480/948–1700 | Closed Mon., Tues. June–mid-Oct. No lunch | $25–$47 | AE, D, DC, MC, V.

Chart House. Seafood. The menu at this outlet of the upscale seafood and steak chain includes such choices as sesame-crusted salmon and prime rib. You can dine on a patio overlooking Camelback Lake and the mountains. Salad bar. Kids' menu. | 7255 McCormick Pkwy. | 480/951–2550 | No lunch | $16–$40 | AE, D, DC, MC, V.

Chompie's. Delicatessen. A New York–style decor predominates at this local chain where bagels and mile-high sandwiches are the standard. Try the pastrami. Wine, beer. | 9301 E. Shea Blvd. | 480/860–0475 | Breakfast also available | $10–$12 | AE, MC, V.

Cowboy Ciao. Contemporary. You'll sense a festive mood as soon as you gaze up at the antique wrought-iron chandeliers draped with Mardi Gras beads. Exotic mushrooms over polenta and the bread pudding are a few of the special treats. | 7133 E. Stetson Dr. | 480/946–3111 | No lunch Sun., Mon. | $10–$32 | AE, D, DC, MC, V.

Don and Charlie's American Rib and Chop House. Steak. A favorite hangout for visiting baseball players during spring training, this venerable steak house specializes in prime beef and baseball memorabilia, which decorate every square inch of the walls. Try the New York sirloin, prime rib, or double-thick lamb chops; the best sides include au gratin potatoes and creamed spinach. Kids' menu. No smoking. | 7501 E. Camelback Rd. | 480/990–0900 | No lunch | $14–$35 | AE, D, DC, MC, V.

Franco's Trattoria. Italian. The Florence-born Franco assembles meals that practically sing out with the rich flavors of Italy. Risotto, veal, and venison are specialties. There is an extensive wine list from Italy and California. | 8120 N. Hayden Rd. | 480/948–6655 | Closed Sun. and July | $12–$27 | AE, MC, V.

Golden Swan. Southwestern. This restaurant in the Hyatt Regency at Gainey Ranch is especially good for a leisurely Sunday brunch. Try the herb-marinated free-range chicken baked in Arizona red clay, or grilled lamb chops glazed with jalapeño honey mustard. Sit outside under umbrellas or in a covered pavilion that juts out into a koi-filled pond. Sunday brunch buffet. Kids' menu. No smoking. | 7500 E. Doubletree Ranch Rd. | 480/991–3388 | Closed Mon. July–Aug. No lunch | $28–$36 | AE, D, DC, MC, V.

Gregory's Grill. Contemporary. It may be hard to get a table at this intimate bistro in the Papago Plaza shopping center, but the wait is worth it. Delicious appetizers include duck prosciutto and salmon ceviche, and main dishes like apple-crusted salmon and beer-marinated beef tenderloin are intricately spiced and perfectly cooked. You can bring your own wine or beer. | 7049 E. McDowell Rd. | 480/946–8700 | Reservations essential | Closed Sun.–Mon. No lunch | $25–$35 | AE, D, MC, V.

Grill at TPC. Continental. Dark wood tables, booths, and bars heighten the mood of elegance here in an upscale dining room at the Scottsdale Princess Resort. Some favorites are the dry-aged porterhouse steak and grilled mixed seafood. The sesame-crusted ahi tuna proves that the seafood is flown in fresh daily. Though jackets are not required, men may feel more comfortable if they are less casual. | 7575 E. Princess Dr. | 480/585–4848 | Reservations essential | Breakfast also available | $20–$40 | AE, D, DC, MC, V.

Hops! Bistro and Brewery. American/Casual. This family-oriented brewpub with wood tables and booths serves a variety of handcrafted ales, ambers, and stouts made daily on the premises. Upscale pub fare includes Alaskan cod fish-and-chips, Chinese chicken salad, and a sesame-seared ahi tuna. You can have drinks and appetizers on the patio. Kids' menu. | 8668 E. Shea Blvd. | 480/998–7777 | $11–$27 | AE, D, DC, MC, V.

Houston's. American. This is a popular restaurant, especially with the after-work crowd. Try the Chicago-style spinach dip, knife-and-fork barbecue ribs, or double-cut pork chops. A limited bar menu is served on the outdoor patio. Kids' menu. | 6113 N. Scottsdale Rd. | 480/922–7775 | $11–$24 | AE, MC, V.

Kyoto. Japanese. This spare and traditional Japanese restaurant features some tableside preparations. The menu includes a large selection of fresh sushi, filet mignon, vegetable tempura, and fried fish. | 7170 Stetson Dr. | 480/990–9374 | $12–$17 | AE, D, DC, MC, V.

L'Ecole. French. This restaurant is staffed by chefs from Arizona's premier cooking academy. For a very reasonable price, you get a six-course dinner. Look for such appetizers as ginger soy gravlax; main courses might include fillet Rossini. | 8100 E. Camelback Rd. | 480/990–7639 | Reservations essential | Closed weekends | $11–$29 | D, MC, V.

La Hacienda. Mexican. At this elegant restaurant in the Scottsdale Princess, the menu is heavily weighted with seafood. However, the signature dish is *cochinillo asado* (roasted suckling pig), which is carved at your table. Also consider the mixed grill (breast of chicken and shrimp). The patio overlooks a courtyard with a fountain. Kids' menu. | 7575 E. Princess Dr. | 480/585–4848 | No lunch | $22–$30 | AE, D, DC, MC, V.

Landry's Pacific Fish Company. Seafood. This local chain is known for fresh fish cooked over a mesquite grill, and features salmon, swordfish, ahi tuna, snapper, and halibut, all served with lemon butter. The menu also includes live Maine lobster, top sirloin, Alaskan king crab legs, and filet mignon. Eat in the dining room or on the patio. Entertainment weekends. Kids' menu. | 4321 N. Scottsdale Rd. | 480/941–0602 | $12–$57 | AE, D, DC, MC, V.

Leccabaffi Ristorante. Italian. A huge antipasto table with grilled vegetables greets you in the foyer at this lovely, jewel-tone restaurant specializing in northern Italian fare. The *costoletta alla Valdostana* (a bone-in veal chop with a pocket of fontina cheese), the wine-soaked quail, and the Roman-style semolina gnocchi are exquisite. All entrees come with pasta. Homemade biscotti and *vin santo* (Tuscan dessert wine) add a sweet touch to the end of the meal. | 9719 N. Hayden Rd. | 480/609–0429 | Closed Mon. No lunch | $14–$28 | AE, D, MC, V.

Los Olivos. Mexican. This relaxed, traditional Mexican restaurant has great sour-cream enchiladas, chimichangas, and fajitas. Entertainment Wednesday–Sunday. Kids' menu. | 7328 E. 2nd St. | 480/946–2256 | $7–$14 | AE, D, DC, MC, V.

Malee's on Main. Thai. An extremely popular and often crowded Old Town favorite, this eatery offers a serene candlelit interior filled with plants and Thai artwork, and sophisticated, creative cuisine. House favorites include the "spicy crispy *pla*," a white fish fillet with tempura batter in a jalapeño garlic sauce, and the *tom kha gai* soup, a hot-and-sour soup in a coconut broth. The spicy Thai barbecue chicken is also a knockout. | 7131 E. Main St. | 480/947–6042 | No lunch Sun. | $15–$25 | AE, DC, MC, V.

Mancuso's Northern Italian. Italian. All of the lustrous woodwork, lamps, sculptures, furniture, and tapestries were imported from Italy for this castlelike restaurant in north Scottsdale. The highly skilled staff serves up specialty dishes like frog legs, veal, duck breast, and a terrific eggplant Parmesan, and a wine steward will help with selections from one of Arizona's finest wine lists. | 6166 N. Scottsdale Rd. | 480/948–9988 | No lunch | $21–$38 | AE, D, DC, MC, V.

Marco Polo Dinner Club. Continental. Reminiscent of a 1930s Chicago steak house, with a large wood bar in the center of the dining room, this restaurant caters to the over-30 crowd, and serves from a vast menu of steak, seafood, and pasta dishes. Appetizers such as shrimp tempura and crab Rangoon have an Asian flair, but the prime rib and sirloin steak are pure American. There's an enclosed terrace and dance floor adjacent to the dining room. Live music Wednesday–Saturday. | 8608 E. Shea Blvd. | 480/483–1900 | Reservations essential | No lunch | $18–$35 | AE, D, DC, MC, V.

Maria's When in Naples. Italian. This standout neighborhood spot serves excellent housemade pasta and veal dishes. Try *salsiccia Pugliese* (fettuccine topped with sausage, leeks, porcini mushrooms, and white wine sauce), or *orecchiette Barese* (ear-shape pasta tossed with cauliflower, pancetta, sun-dried tomatoes, olive oil, and cheese). | 7000 E. Shea Blvd. | 480/991–6887 | No lunch weekends or Memorial Day–Labor Day | $13–$35 | AE, D, DC, MC, V.

Marquesa. Spanish. Images of Spanish kings hang on the walls at this Catalan restaurant in the Scottsdale Princess. Appetizers are extraordinary; try *pebrots del piquillo* (crab and fontina cheese baked into sweet red peppers). Good main dishes include a first-class paella and pan-roasted rack of lamb. The romantic patio has a fireplace. Kids' menu. Sunday brunch. | 7575 E. Princess Dr. | 480/585–4848 | No dinner Sun., Mon. mid-July–Aug. | $29–$41 | AE, D, DC, MC, V.

Mary Elaine's. French. This swanky, formal restaurant at the Phoenician resort (*see below*) has sweeping views of Phoenix. The chef creates scrumptious contemporary French dishes with organically grown ingredients. A rotating menu often includes favorites like monkfish medallions in orange-Burgundy sauce or turbot with fresh hearts of palm. Reservations are recommended. A live jazz duet play nightly. | 600 E. Camelback Rd. | 480/423–2530 | Jacket required | Closed Sun.; closed Mon. mid-June–Aug. No lunch | $75–$100 | AE, D, DC, MC, V.

Michael's at the Citadel. Contemporary. This idyllic restaurant on the side of Pinnacle Peak is the perfect place for a special occasion—an outdoor brick patio with fountains, a fireplace, and a small pond offers a serene setting, and the bar has magnificent nighttime views of the city. Excellent entrées include pan-seared duck with foie gras, sesame-crusted swordfish, and grilled lamb with a goat cheese potato tart. Leave room for one of the homemade desserts. | 8700 E. Pinnacle Peak Rd. | 480/515–2575 | $25–$55 | AE, D, DC, MC, V.

Mr. C's. Chinese. Chinese paintings, ceramics, and other art decorate this elegant, upscale restaurant. Try the macadamia chicken or the jade lobster. | 4302 N. Scottsdale Rd. | 480/941–4460 | $16–$35 | AE, D, DC, MC, V.

Oregano's. Italian. Sinatra often croons in the background at this extremely popular pizza-pasta-sandwich joint filled with 1950s memorabilia. The main attraction here, Chicago-style pizza, comes in two varieties—stuffed deep-dish and thin-crusted. The pizzookie, a hot chocolate-chip cookie topped with ice cream, literally melts in your mouth. | 3622 N. Scottsdale Rd. | 480/970–1860 | $5–$15 | AE, D, MC, V.

Original Pancake House. American/Casual. This landmark does one thing really well, but they do it to perfection: pancakes. The flapjacks are worshipped by locals who line up patiently for a table every weekend. The apple pancakes stand above the other offerings. Kids' menu. | 6840 E. Camelback Rd. | 480/946–4902 | $4–$8 | No credit cards.

P. F. Chang's China Bistro. Chinese. This dramatically decorated, always crowded contemporary Chinese restaurant serves food very loosely based on traditional recipes. Try the warm duck salad, salt-and-pepper shrimp, or Phillip's lemon chicken. | 7014 E. Camelback Rd. | 480/949–2610 | Reservations not accepted | $7–$13 | AE, DC, MC, V.

Palm Court. Continental. This stately, old-fashioned restaurant at the Scottsdale Conference Resort proudly serves classics like Caesar salad prepared tableside, steak au poivre, rack of lamb Diable (with English mustard and an herb crust), plus the best lobster bisque in town. It's all perfectly executed with high style. Kids' menu. Sunday brunch. No smoking. | 7700 E. McCormick Pkwy. | 480/596–7700 | Reservations essential | Jacket required (dinner) | Breakfast also available | $12–$29 | AE, D, DC, MC, V.

Pinnacle Peak Patio. Steak. "Big Marv" Dickson has been cooking the world-famous steaks and baby-back ribs at this restaurant mecca for over 40 years, having served over 2 million pounds of meat off the mesquite grill since 1961. The world's largest restaurant, with a seating capacity of 1,600 (another 1,400 can sit on the outdoor patio), this one is a favorite of tourists and hard-core steak lovers. The menu hasn't changed in years, and consists of five steak options or a hickory-roasted chicken. | 10426 E. Jomax Rd. | 480/585–1599 | No lunch Mon.–Sat. | $10–$25 | AE, D, MC, V.

Pischke's Paradise. American/Casual. A casual, busy family diner with a nautical theme, Pischke's is a popular breakfast spot. The menu is extensive and the portions huge, with over 30 different grilled sandwich options and over 19 salad plates. Try the Paradise shrimp pasta or the *lavosch*, a thin-crust pizza topped with artichoke hearts and tomatoes. Desserts include homemade pies and cakes. | 7217 E. 1st St. | 480/481–0067 | Breakfast also available | $9–$25 | AE, D, MC, V.

Quilted Bear. American. At this family restaurant, everything is quilted, even the seat cushions. The menu is straightforward American fare; try the prime rib or chicken. In spring or autumn you can dine on the patio outside. Salad bar. Kids' menu. | 6316 N. Scottsdale Rd. | 480/948–7760 | Breakfast also available | $9–$26 | AE, D, DC, MC, V.

Ra Sushi Bar and Restaurant. Japanese. This trendy Japanese restaurant in Old Town Scottsdale is a loud and popular spot, particularly at Happy Hour. In addition to sushi there's a full menu of yakisoba, tempura, shinsen salmon, and more. There are also teppanyaki tables in the dining room where you can watch your food cooked in front of you. Kids' menu. | 3815 N. Scottsdale Rd. | 480/990–9256 | $16–$35 | AE, D, DC, MC, V.

Rancho Pinot Grill. Contemporary. This is one of Scottsdale's favorite restaurants, and for good reason: the menu features high-quality, inventive dishes like posole (a soup with hominy, salt pork, and cabbage), quail with soba noodles, and grilled sea bass atop basmati rice. No smoking. | 6208 N. Scottsdale Rd. | 602/468–9463 | Reservations essential | $16–$29 | AE, D, DC, MC, V.

Remington. American. Subdued southwestern colors give this fine special-occasions restaurant a quiet elegance. Try the Colorado lamb chops or the Kansas City sirloin. If romance is in the air, ask for a table on the patio, which sits alongside a pool and offers mountain views. Jazz Monday–Saturday. | 7200 N. Scottsdale Rd. | 480/951–5101 | No lunch weekends | $19–$40 | AE, D, DC, MC, V.

★ **Restaurant Hapa.** Asian-American. Bamboo, teak, and wicker furniture give a Pacific Islands accent to this inspired restaurant that serves creative Asian-inspired cuisine. The signature dish is the Chinese mustard–caramelized beef tenderloin; the miso-marinated sea bass is another favorite. Leave room for dessert—the skillet of Asian pears with macadamia nut crust and the Saigon cinnamon ice cream are heavenly. | 6204 N. Scottsdale Rd. | 480/998–8220 | Closed Sun. No lunch | $25–$35 | AE, MC, V.

Restaurant Oceana. Seafood. Fresh seafood flown in daily makes this upscale and trendy seafood restaurant an oasis in the desert. Tastefully decorated, candlelit dining rooms are filled with original artwork, and an open wall allows for views into the bustling kitchen. The menu rotates daily, and often includes such specials as miso Chilean sea bass, Belon oysters from Washington, Copper River salmon, and Maine lobster. Desserts are inspired, and often include bing-cherry shortcake and jasmine rice pudding with pineapple soup. | 8900 E. Pinnacle Peak Rd. | 480/515–2277 | www.restaurantoceana.com | Closed Sun., Mon. No lunch Sat. and May–Sept. | $30–$50 | AE, D, DC, MC, V.

Roaring Fork. Contemporary. Everything about this friendly restaurant is western, and the menu reflects these western-American roots. Try the tea-smoked duck, or the oven-seared salmon, or the steak. The patio has a fireplace for chilly evenings. Kids' menu. | 7243 E. Camelback Rd. | 480/947–0795 | No lunch | $19–$29 | AE, D, DC, MC, V.

Roy's of Scottsdale. Pan-Asian. One of Roy Yamaguchi's many restaurants, this James Beard Award–winning chef continues to inspire sophisticated Pacific Rim cuisine with creative twists. The resort-inspired dining area here has bamboo and teak accents and the professional waitstaff are prepared to answer questions. Specialties of the house include oak-fired Chinese-style barbecued rack of lamb, hibachi barbecue grilled salmon, and Roy's original blackened ahi tuna. | 7001 N. Scottsdale Rd. | 480/905–1155 | No lunch | $25–$35 | AE, D, DC, MC, V.

Ruth's Chris Steak House. Steak. This polished restaurant is part of the upscale national chain that's known for prime beef topped with melted butter. The service is top-notch, and the terrace overlooks Camelback Mountain and Squaw Peak. | 7001 N. Scottsdale Rd., | 480/991–5988 | No lunch | $24–$55 | AE, D, DC, MC, V.

Salt Cellar. Seafood. This no-frills, subterranean restaurant has an especially busy happy hour, when things get crowded and noisy. Try the Yakimono Hawaiian ahi or king salmon with cucumber dill sauce. Kids' menu. | 550 N. Hayden Rd. | 480/947–1963 | No lunch | $20–$25 | AE, MC, V.

Sushi on Shea. Japanese. This spare, contemporary restaurant serves impeccably fresh sushi, but it's also known for *nabemono* (hot-pot dishes prepared tableside). No smoking. | 7000 E. Shea Blvd. | 480/483–7799 | No lunch | $9–$22 | AE, D, DC, MC, V.

Terrace Dining Room. Continental. This two-story restaurant at the Phoenician resort offers booth and table seating, but try to get a window seat overlooking the pool. Attention is paid to every lavish detail. Go to the elaborate Sunday brunch. In season, a patio allows outdoor dining. A pianist provides light entertainment most nights. | 6000 E. Camelback Rd. | 480/423–2530 | Reservations essential | Breakfast also available | $14–$40 | AE, D, DC, MC, V.

Windows on the Green. Southwestern. This links-view restaurant at the Phoenician is less formal than the Terrace, its other major restaurant, but still a bit stuffy. Try the campfire salmon or New York steak. Kids' menu. Sunday buffet. No smoking. | 6000 E. Camelback Rd. | 480/423–2530 | Closed Tues.–Wed. and mid-June–mid-Sept. | $30–$50 | AE, D, DC, MC, V.

Z'Tejas Grill. Southwestern. This outlet of the relaxed, contemporary chain offers the same favorites. Try the voodoo tuna, stuffed pork tenderloin, or wild mushroom enchilada. Kids' menu. Sunday brunch. | 7014 E. Camelback Rd. | 480/946–4171 | $12–$22 | AE, D, DC, MC, V.

Lodging

Best Western Papago Inn. This upscale motel 2 mi south of downtown Scottsdale, with a nice green courtyard, offers some "green" rooms, with filtered air and water and environmentally sensitive bath products. Restaurant, bar, complimentary Continental breakfast. Some microwaves, refrigerators, cable TV. Pool. Gym. Laundry facilities. Business services, airport shuttle. | 7017 E. McDowell Rd. | 480/947–7335 | fax 480/994–0692 | www.bestwestern.com | 56 rooms | $109–$179 | AE, D, DC, MC, V.

Chaparral Suites Hotel. This four-story all-suite hotel has a nice courtyard with a fountain. Restaurant, bar, complimentary breakfast. Microwaves, refrigerators, cable TV. 2 pools. Tennis court. Gym. Laundry facilities. Business services, airport shuttle. | 5001 N. Scottsdale Rd. | 480/949–1414 | fax 480/947–2675 | 311 suites | $199 suites | AE, D, DC, MC, V.

Country Inn and Suites. This chain hotel offers more homespun charm and less cookie-cutter rooms. Complimentary Continental breakfast. In-room data ports, microwaves, refrigerators, cable TV. Pool, wading pool. Hot tub. Gym. Laundry facilities. Business services. | 10801 N. 89th Pl | 480/314–1200 | fax 480/314–5868 | www.countryinns.com | 133 rooms, 30 suites | $84, $104–$114 suites | AE, D, DC, MC, V.

Courtyard Scottsdale/Mayo Clinic. This two-story chain hotel is across from the Scottsdale Mayo Clinic, 13 mi from Old Town Scottsdale. Restaurant, bar, room service. In-room data ports, some microwaves, refrigerators, cable TV. Pool. Hot tub. Gym. Laundry facilities, laundry service. Business services. | 13444 E. Shea Blvd. | 480/860–4000 | fax 480/860–4308 | www.courtyard.com | 113 rooms, 11 suites | $149–$179 | AE, D, DC, MC, V.

Doubletree Scottsdale Paradise Valley Resort. Meticulously manicured grounds surround this popular two-story hotel. There's complimentary transportation anywhere within 3 mi from 7 AM to 11 PM. 2 restaurants, bar, room service. In-room data ports, minibars, some microwaves, cable TV. 2 pools. Barbershop, beauty salon, hot tub, massage. 2 tennis courts. Gym. Business services. | 5401 N. Scottsdale Rd. | 480/947–5400 | fax 480/946–1524 | www.doubletree.com | 375 rooms, 12 suites | $205–$300, $390–$430 1–bedroom suites, $585–$685 2–bedroom suites | AE, D, DC, MC, V.

Econolodge Scottsdale. This three-story motel is within a short walk of Old Town Scottsdale and the Fifth Avenue shopping district. The oversize rooms are basic, and it's a friendly place. Complimentary Continental breakfast. Cable TV, refrigerators. Pool. Exercise room. Coin laundry. | 6935 E. 5th Ave. | 480/991–2400 | fax 480/994–9461 or 800/528–7396 | www.econolodge.com | 92 rooms | $99–$109 | AE, D, DC, MC, V.

Fairfield Inn Scottsdale North. This three-story hotel is on the north side of Scottsdale. Picnic area, complimentary Continental breakfast. Some refrigerators, cable TV. Pool. Hot tub. Laundry facilities, laundry service. Business services. | 13440 N. Scottsdale Rd. | 480/483–0042 | fax 480/483–3715 | www.fairfieldinn.com | 132 rooms | $90–$140 | AE, D, DC, MC, V.

Fairfield Inn Scottsdale Downtown. This two-story hotel is a half mile from both Old Town Scottsdale and the Fashion Square Mall. Restaurant, complimentary Continental breakfast. In-room data ports, cable TV. Pool. Hot tub. Laundry facilities, laundry service. Business services. | 5101 N. Scottsdale Rd. | 480/945–4392 | fax 480/947–3044 | 218 rooms | $149–$169 | AE, D, DC, MC, V.

Four Seasons Scottsdale at Troon North. You'll enjoy a view of the acclaimed True North golf course from any room at this luxurious resort. Each room has a balcony or patio and extra touches like double vanity mirrors in the bathrooms. Suites have their own plunge pools. 3 restaurants. In-room data ports, in-room safes, some kitchenettes, minibars, cable TV, some in-room VCRs. Pool. Beauty salon, hot tub, massage, sauna, spa, steam room. 4 tennis courts. Health club, bicycles. Baby-sitting, children's programs (ages 5–17). Laundry service. Business services, airport shuttle. Some pets allowed. No smoking. | 10600 E. Crescent Moon Dr. | 480/515–5700 | fax 480/515–5599 | www.fourseasons.com/scottsdale | 187 rooms, 23 suites | $475–$625 rooms, $850–$3,500 suites | AE, D, DC, MC, V.

Gainey Suites Hotel. The rooms at this all-suite hotel built in 1998 feature murals of the desert and southwestern color schemes. Complimentary Continental breakfast. In-room data ports, kitchenettes, microwaves, refrigerators, cable TV. Pool. Spa. Gym. Laundry service. Business services. | 7300 E. Gainey Suites Dr. | 480/922–6969 or 800/970–4666 | fax 480/922–1689 | www.gaineysuiteshotel.com | 164 suites | $165–$295 | AE, D, DC, MC, V.

Hampton Inn Phoenix-Scottsdale at Shea Blvd. This two-story inn is in the center of Scottsdale. Several restaurants are within six blocks. Complimentary Continental breakfast. In-room data ports, cable TV. Pool. Hot tub. Gym. Laundry facilities. Business services. | 10101 N. Scottsdale Rd. | 480/443–3233 | fax 480/443–9149 | www.hamptoninn.com | 132 rooms | $112–$180 | AE, D, DC, MC, V.

Hampton Inn Scottsdale-Old Town. This hotel is 1 mi north of Old Town and just a few blocks from the Fashion Square Mall. Complimentary Continental breakfast, room service. In-room data ports, cable TV. Pool. Laundry service. Business services. Pets allowed (fee). | 4415 N. Civic Center Plaza | 480/941–9400 | fax 480/675–5240 | www.hamptoninn.com | 126 rooms | $120–$150 | AE, D, DC, MC, V.

Holiday Inn Phoenix-Old Town Scottsdale. This hotel and conference center is right on the Civic Center Mall in Old Town Scottsdale. Restaurant, room service. In-room data ports, cable TV. Pool. Tennis court. Gym. Laundry service. Business services. Some pets allowed. | 7353 E. Indian School Rd. | 480/994–9203 or 800/695–6995 | fax 480/941–2567 | www.holiday-inn.com | 204 rooms, 2 suites | $145, $375 suites | AE, D, DC, MC, V.

Holiday Inn Hotel and Suites. This all-suite hotel is in north Scottsdale. All rooms have a pull-out couch in a separate living room, and some have great views of the McDowell Mountains. Restaurant, bar, complimentary Continental breakfast, room service. In-room data ports, kitchenettes, microwaves, refrigerators, cable TV. Pool. Hot tub. Gym. Laundry service. Business services. Some pets allowed. | 7515 E. Butherus Dr. | 480/951–4000 | fax 480/483–9046 | 120 suites | $149–$159 | AE, D, DC, MC, V.

Holiday Inn Sunspree. This three-story resort hotel is 3 mi from the Fashion Square Mall and 12 mi from Sky Harbor airport. Restaurant, bar, room service. In-room data ports, in-room safes, refrigerators, cable TV. Pool. Hot tub. 18-hole golf course, tennis. Basketball, health club, volleyball, bicycles. Children's programs (ages 5–13). Laundry service. Business services. | 7601 E. Indian Bend Rd. | 480/991–2400 | fax 480/998–2261 | 200 rooms | $145 | AE, D, DC, MC, V.

Hospitality Suite Resort. This all-suite hotel is on the southern edge of Scottsdale. All rooms have full kitchens. Restaurant, bar, picnic area, complimentary breakfast, room service. Kitchenettes, microwaves, refrigerators, room service, cable TV. 3 pools. Hot tub. Tennis. Basketball. Laundry facilities. Business services, airport shuttle. Some pets allowed. | 409 N. Scottsdale Rd. | 480/949–5115 or 800/445–5115 | fax 480/941–8014 | www.hospitality-suites.com | 210 suites in 3 buildings | $120–$169 | AE, D, DC, MC, V.

Hotel Waterfront Ivy. This hotel is made up primarily of suites and is located near 5th Avenue and the waterfront. Rooms are oversize with queen or king beds. Complimentary breakfast. In-room data ports, kitchenettes, microwaves, refrigerators, cable TV. 6 pools. Hot tub. 2 tennis courts. Basketball, gym. Laundry service. Pets allowed (fee). | 7445 E. Chapparal Rd. | 877/284–3489 or 480/994–5282 | fax 480/994–5625 | www.ivyfront.com | 35 rooms, 75 suites | $69–$369 | AE, D, DC, MC, V.

Hyatt Regency Scottsdale at Gainey Ranch. This family-oriented luxury resort is set on more than 560 acres. It has a large water park and three highly regarded golf courses. There's even a center for Hopi culture on the premises. 3 restaurants, bar, room service. In-room data ports, in-room safes, minibars, some microwaves, cable TV. 10 pools, wading pool. Massage, spa. Driving range, 3 9-hole golf courses, putting green, 8 tennis courts. Health club, bicycles. Baby-sitting, kids' programs (ages 3–12), playground. Laundry service. Business services. | 7500 E. Doubletree Ranch Rd. | 480/991–3388 | fax 480/483–5550 | 486 rooms, 7 casitas | $405–$515, $1,600–$2,965 casitas | AE, D, DC, MC, V.

Inn at the Citadel. Antiques-filled rooms offer desert views at this luxurious B&B. Complimentary Continental breakfast, room service. Some minibars, cable TV. Business services. Pets allowed. | 8700 E. Pinnacle Peak Rd. | 480/585–6133 or 800/927–8367 | fax 480/585–3436 | 11 suites | $229–$259 suites | AE, D, DC, MC, V.

La Hacienda Resort. This small boutique hotel near Scottsdale Fashion Square offers suite-style rooms with sitting areas that overlook a pool courtyard. Convenient to Old Town Scottsdale shops and restaurants. Minibars, microwaves, refrigerators, cable TV. Pool. | 7320 E. Camelback Rd. | 480/994–4170 | fax 480/994–7387 | www.suitedreamsaz.com | 22 rooms | $80–$240 | AE, D, DC, MC, V.

La Paz in Desert Springs. Each room at this B&B has its own western motif, which includes either Native American pottery and blankets or cowboy hats and gear. The home is a southwestern ranch built in the 1980s, situated in a suburban neighborhood. Complimentary Continental breakfast. Some kitchenettes, some microwaves, some refrigerators, cable TV, in-room VCRs. Pool. Outdoor hot tub. No smoking. | 6309 E. Ludlow Dr. | 888/922–0963 or 480/922–0963 | fax 480/905–0085 | www.bedandbreakfast.com/bbc/p603212.asp | 3 rooms | $85–$175 | MC, V.

La Quinta Inn and Suites. This motel is in central Scottsdale, 15 mi from Sky Harbor airport. Complimentary Continental breakfast. In-room data ports, some microwaves, some refrigerators, cable TV. Pool. Hot tub. Gym. Laundry facilities. Business services. Some pets allowed. | 8888 E. Shea Blvd. | 480/614–5300 | fax 480/614–5333 | www.laquinta.com | 140 rooms | $89–$129 | AE, D, DC, MC, V.

Marriott Suites. All rooms at this modern, eight-story, all-suite hotel in Old Town Scottsdale have separate living rooms and marble baths. 2 restaurants, bar, room service. In-room data ports, refrigerators, cable TV. Pool. Hot tub, sauna. Gym. Laundry facilities, laundry service. Business services. | 7325 E. 3rd Ave. | 480/945–1550 | fax 480/945–2005 | www.marriott.com | 251 suites | $209–$249 suites | AE, D, DC, MC, V.

Marriott's Camelback Inn Resort, Golf Club, and Spa. This historic 1930s resort set on 125 acres offers gracious service and has the best spa in Scottsdale. Rooms are notably spacious, some with fireplaces; a few suites have private pools. 5 restaurants, bar, room service. In-room data ports, minibars, microwaves, refrigerators, cable TV. 3 pools. Barbershop, beauty salon, hot tub, massage, spa. Driving range, 2 18-hole golf courses, putting greens, 6 tennis courts. Health club, hiking, bicycles. Kids' programs (ages 3–12). Laundry facilities. Business services. Pets allowed. | 5402 E. Lincoln Dr. | 480/948–1700 or 800/24–CAMEL | fax 480/951–8469 | www.marriott.com | 394 rooms, 59 suites in casitas, 1 house | $409, $700–$950 1–bedroom suites, $980–$1,600 2–bedroom suites, $2,050 house | AE, D, DC, MC, V.

Marriott's Mountain Shadows. Across the street from the more upscale Marriott Camelback Inn, this ranch-style resort, built in 1958, is family oriented and located right at the base of Camelback Mountain. Rooms are large and comfortable; the golf course is even open at night. 3 restaurants, bar, room service. Minibars, some microwaves, cable TV. 3 pools. Hot tub, massage, sauna. Driving range, 18-hole golf course, putting green, 8 tennis courts. Gym. Playground. Business services, airport shuttle. | 5641 E. Lincoln Dr. | 480/948–7111 | fax 480/951–5430 | 318 rooms, 19 suites | $249–$269, $300–$750 suites | AE, D, DC, MC, V.

Motel 6 Scottsdale. The best bargain in Scottsdale is easy to miss, but worth hunting for since it's near the specialty shops of 5th Avenue, and the Scottsdale Civic Plaza. Rooms are small and spare, with a small desk and wardrobe. Cable TV. Pool. | 6848 E. Camelback Rd., | 480/946–2280 | fax 480/949–7583 | 122 rooms | $45 | AE, D, DC, MC, V.

Orange Tree Golf and Conference Resort. At this popular golf resort, all accommodations are spacious suites. This was one of the earlier year-round resorts to open in Scottsdale, in 1957. 2 restaurants, bar (with entertainment), room service. In-room data ports, in-room safes, refrigerators, cable TV, in-room VCRs. Pool, wading pool. Hot tub, massage. 18-hole golf course. Gym. Laundry service. Business services, airport shuttle. | 10601 N. 56th St. | 480/948–6100 or 800/228–0386 | fax 480/483–6074 | www.orangetree.com | 160 suites | $220–$249 | AE, D, DC, MC, V.

★ **The Phoenician.** This is easily one of the finest resorts in Arizona, offering solicitous service and every amenity imaginable. The 2-acre cactus garden and nice spa are pluses. South-facing rooms have views of the pools and the city. The restaurants are among the finest in the Valley. 4 restaurants, bar, picnic area, room service. In-room data ports, minibars, some microwaves, some refrigerators, cable TV. 9 pools, 2 wading pools. Barbershop, beauty salon, hot tub, massage, spa. Driving range, 3 9-hole golf courses, putting green, 12 tennis courts. Gym, hiking, bicycles. Shops. Kids' programs (ages 5–12). Business services. | 6000 E. Camelback Rd. | 480/941–8200 or 800/888–8234 | fax 480/947–4311 | 468 rooms, 119 casitas, 7 villas | $415–$600, $1,225–$1,800 casitas, 2,800–$3,100 villas | AE, D, DC, MC, V.

Radisson Resort and Spa. This luxurious but low-key resort sprawls over more than 75 acres, and offers a lush property with jogging trails and parklike settings. Spacious rooms are in two-story buildings. Restaurant, bar, room service. Some minibars, some refrigerators, cable TV. 3 pools. Barbershop, beauty salon, spa. 21 tennis courts. Gym. Kids' programs (ages 3–12). Laundry service. Business services. | 7171 N. Scottsdale Rd. | 480/991–3800 | fax 480/948–1381 | www.radisson.com | 318 rooms, 45 suites | $225–$275, $375–$1,500 suites | AE, D, DC, MC, V.

Regal McCormick Ranch. This small boutique resort is on the shores of Camelback Lake. All rooms have private patios or balconies; villas have fireplaces. There's also a dock with sailboats and paddleboats. Restaurant, bar, room service. Some kitchenettes, minibars, cable TV. Pool. Hot tub. Driving range, 2 18-hole golf courses, putting green, tennis court. Volleyball, boating. Business services. | 7401 N. Scottsdale Rd. | 480/948–5050 or 800/243–1332 | fax 480/991–5572 | www.millenium-hotels.com | 125 rooms, 51 villas | $195–$325, $460–$625 villas | AE, D, DC, MC, V.

Renaissance Cottonwoods Resort. This 25-acre resort is across the street from the Borgata Shopping Center. The rooms are in adobe buildings spread out around the property; bathrooms are a bit small; villa suites, however, are grand in every way. Restaurant, bar, room service. Minibars, some microwaves, refrigerators, cable TV. 2 pools. Hot tub. Putting green, 4 tennis courts. Business services. Some pets allowed. | 6160 N. Scottsdale Rd. | 480/991–1414 | fax 480/951–3350 | 64 rooms, 107 suites | $285–$330, $345–$360 suites | AE, D, DC, MC, V.

Residence Inn Scottsdale. This two-story, all-suite hotel is in north Scottsdale, a half mile from the Borgata Shopping Center. All rooms have a sitting area and fully equipped kitchens. Complimentary Continental breakfast. In-room data ports, kitchenettes, microwaves, refrigerators, cable TV. Pool. Hot tub. Gym. Laundry facilities. Business services. | 6040 N. Scottsdale Rd. | 480/948–8666 | fax 480/443–4869 | www.marriott.com | 122 suites | $186–$289 | AE, D, DC, MC, V.

Resort Suites. This upscale condominium resort is popular with families because of the spacious apartments and full kitchens in each unit. Personal planners help you book your golf rounds. Restaurant, bar, room service. Kitchenettes, microwaves, refrigerators, cable TV. 4 pools. 2 hot tubs. Gym. Laundry facilities. Business services. | 7677 E. Princess Blvd. | 480/585–1234 or 800/541–5203 | fax 480/585–1457 | www.resortsuites.com | 296 condos | $225–$475 1– and 2–bedroom condos, $500–$735 3– and 4–bedroom condos | AE, DC, MC, V.

Rodeway Inn. This basic, two-story chain motel is on the south side of Scottsdale. Complimentary Continental breakfast. Microwaves, refrigerators, cable TV. Pool. Hot tub. Business services. | 7110 E. Indian School Rd. | 480/946–3456 | fax 480/874–8492 | 61 rooms, 4 suites | $109–$139, $150 suites | AE, D, DC, MC, V.

Sanctuary on Camelback Mountain. The casitas at this all-suite boutique tennis resort are terraced on the north slope of Camelback Mountain. The views are spectacular from all rooms; suites have fireplaces, sunrooms, and private balconies. Restaurant, bar, room service. Some kitchenettes, some microwaves, some refrigerators, cable TV. 3 pools. Massage, spa. 17 tennis courts. Health club. Parking (fee). | 5700 E. McDonald Rd. | 480/948–2100 or 800/245–2051 | fax 480/483–7314 | www.sanctuaryoncamelback.com | 41 rooms, 41 suites, 24 spa villas | $200–$925 | AE, D, DC, MC, V.

Scottsdale Plaza Resort. This 40-acre Spanish-Mediterranean resort has an old-world charm. Some of the rooms are arranged around a courtyard pool, with Arizona's largest hot tub. 5 restaurants, bar, room service. Minibars, refrigerators, cable TV. 5 pools. Beauty salon. 5 tennis courts. Gym, racquetball, bicycles. Business services. Some pets allowed (fee). | 7200 N. Scottsdale Rd. | 480/948–5000 or 800/832–2025 | fax 480/998–5971 | www.scottsdale-plaza.com | res@tspr.com | 230 rooms, 174 suites | $350, $395–$445 suites | AE, D, DC, MC, V.

Scottsdale Princess. This luxurious 450-acre resort is set against the splendor of the McDowell Mountains and has a wonderful, open feel. Rooms are all spacious and have huge, "walk-around" showers. It also boasts one of the top golf courses on the PGA Tour. A small, stocked lagoon and fishing equipment are available for kids. Entertainment is offered at the Cazadores Lounge nightly September–May. 5 restaurants, bar, room service. Minibars, cable TV. 3 pools. Barbershop, beauty salon, hot tub, massage. Driving range, 2 18-hole golf courses, putting green, 7 tennis courts. Basketball, health club, racquetball, squash. Shops. Kids' programs (ages 5–12, major holidays only). Business services. | 7575 E. Princess Dr. | 480/585–4848 or 800/223–1818 | fax 480/585–0091 | www.fairmont.com | 456 rooms, 75 suites, 119 casitas | $360–$445, $2,900 suites, $550–$650 casitas | AE, D, DC, MC, V.

Sonoran Suites of Scottsdale The rooms here are furnished with tasteful antiques that complement the southwestern color scheme. You can gaze out at the Camelback Golf Course from most rooms. Kitchenettes, microwaves, refrigerators, cable TV. 3 pools. Hot tub, sauna. Tennis court. Volleyball. Laundry facilities. No smoking. | 5335 E. Shea Blvd. | 480/607–6669 or 888/786–7848 | www.sonoransuites.com | 35 suites | $199–$329 | AE, D, MC, V.

Southwest Inn at Eagle Mountain. This inn between the Red and McDowell mountains combines the congeniality of a B&B and the services of a hotel. Several of the rooms have clever design themes, such as images of Frank Lloyd Wright architecture and Indian chiefs. Complimentary Continental breakfast. In-room data ports, refrigerators, microwaves, in-room VCRs, cable TV. Pool. Outdoor hot tub. No smoking. | 9800 N. Summer Hill Blvd. | 800/992–8083 | fax 480/816–3090 | www.southwestinn.com | 31 rooms, 11 suites | $195–$295 rooms, $345 suites | AE, D, DC, MC, V.

Sunburst Resort. This low-rise resort has grounds dotted with orange trees and Adirondack chairs. Rooms are in five two-story buildings and feature intricately carved pine furnishings. Restaurant, bar, picnic area, room service. In-room data ports, minibars, refrigerators, cable TV. 2 pools. Hot tub. Driving range, putting green. Exercise equipment. Business services. | 4925 N. Scottsdale Rd. | 480/945–7666 or 800/528–7867 | fax 480/946–4056 | www.sunburstresort.com | 205 rooms (7 with shower only), 5 suites | $200–$260, $425–$675 suites | AE, D, DC, MC, V.

SEDONA

MAP 3, E5

(Nearby towns also listed: Cottonwood, Flagstaff)

Sedona is one of the most unabashedly beautiful places in the state. To the east and south, just across Oak Creek, red rock formations with such evocative names as Cathedral Rock and Bell Rock jut up into the clear blue sky, their dazzling colors intensified by dark-green pine forests. It's a rugged landscape that has drawn visitors since the town's founding in 1902 by Carl and Sedona Schnebly. The area was a favorite of filmmakers in the 1940s and 1950s, when more than 80 westerns were shot here.

In the 1960s Sedona became an art colony, and art remains the town's primary industry. Of a population of around 9,200 full-time residents, there are at least 300 professional artists and around 50 galleries. There was an influx of retirees in the 1970s, and in the early 1980s psychics claimed that Sedona was surrounded by metaphysical vortices. In 1987 thousands of gullible New Agers were lured to Sedona to witness a "Harmonic Convergence," when, it was said, Bell Rock would depart for the galaxy of Andromeda. Needless to say, that didn't happen, but the New Age industry is still a strong sideline for many local entrepreneurs.

Since the early 1980s, overcrowding has become an issue. On summer weekends, when Sedona sees a large influx of Phoenix residents who seek relief from the intense heat, traffic can become a problem. City planners are even considering building a bridge over Oak Creek to help relieve the congestion. Despite these growing pains, Sedona's future—not to mention its allure to visitors—remains undiminished. Canyons, creeks, Indian ruins, and the red rocks themselves are readily accessible on foot or by Jeep.

Information: Sedona–Oak Creek Canyon Chamber of Commerce | Box 478, Sedona, 86339 | 520/282–7722 or 800/288–7336 | www.sedonachamber.com.

Attractions

Boynton Canyon. This canyon is sacred to the Yavapai Apache, who believe it was their ancient birthplace. A 3¼ mi trail offers breathtaking scenery and Native American ruins. | 525 Boynton Canyon Rd. | Free | Daily.

Chapel of the Holy Cross. Commissioned by Marguerite Brunwige Staude in 1956, this modern landmark south of town is one of the most stunning churches in the southwest. Set on a red-rock peak, the church and surroundings provide spectacular views of Sedona. | 780 Chapel Rd. | 520/282–4069 | Free | Daily.

★ **Oak Creek Canyon.** This wooded, primarily evergreen canyon, with Oak Creek gurgling through it, begins 1 mi north of Sedona and continues to Flagstaff. Here you'll find camping, fishing, and hiking. | Hwy. 89A | 520/282–7722 or 800/288–7336 | Free | Daily.

Rainbow Trout Farm. You'll get a cane pole, hook, and bait for a buck. Any trout under 8 inches is yours to keep for free. Bigger ones cost $3 to $6. The staff will clean and pack your fish for 50¢. | 3500 N. Hwy. 89A | 520/282–3379 | $1 | Labor Day–Memorial Day, daily 9–5; Memorial Day–Labor Day, daily 8–6.

Red Rock State Park. This 286–acre nature preserve is 2 mi west of Sedona on Highway 89A. Feel free to go on nature walks or a bird-watching excursion, but swimming is not permitted. | 4050 Red Rock Loop Rd. | 520/282–6907 | www.pr.state.az.us | $5 per vehicle | Daily 8–5.

Slide Rock State Park. A natural rock slide that deposits you into a swimming hole is the lure at this state park 6 mi north of town, along with an apple orchard and picnic tables for lunching (bring jeans if you plan to slide). In summer, traffic is extreme, and there will probably be a wait to get in. | 6871 N. U.S. 89A | 520/282–3034 | $5 per vehicle | Daily 8–7.

Tlaquepaque. Named for the Mexican village it resembles, Tlaquepaque's shops and restaurants are decidedly upscale, and the complex has been planned so you won't see endless rows of the same merchandise. | 336 Hwy. 179 | 520/282–4838 | www.tlaquepaque.net | Free | Daily 10–5.

ORGANIZED TOURS/TOUR COMPANIES

Jeep Tours. Guided tours through red-rock country are available through several operators, and they are a Sedona tradition. Almost all of these companies are headquartered along Sedona's main street, Highway 89A.

Pink Jeep Tours. One of the more popular companies in town, Pink Jeep has permits that allow them to use trails that other companies can't use. You can choose from a number of tours that highlight everything from the Mogollon Rim to Honanki, an ancient Native American cliff dwelling. | 204 N. Hwy. 89A | 520/282–5000 or 800/873–3662 | www.pinkjeep.com | $32–$75 | Daily 7–5.

Sedona Adventures. This company offers a variety of tours, ranging from rugged and adventurous to mild and scenic. | 276 N. Hwy. 89A | 520/282–3500 or 800/888–9494 | www.sedonaadventures.com | $35–$65; special rates for children | Daily 7–5.

Sedona Red Rock Jeep Tours. In addition to standard Jeep tours, Sedona Red Rock also offers horseback riding and Jeep-helicopter combination tours. For those who prefer to use their own two feet, there are also a number of archaeological adventure tours to choose from. | 270 N. Hwy. 89A | 520/282–6826 or 800/848–7728 | www.redrockJeep.com | $32–$165.

VORTEX TOUR

What is a vortex? The word "vortex" comes from the Latin "vertere," which means "to turn or whirl." In Sedona, a vortex is a funnel created by the motion of spiraling energy. Sedona has long been believed to be a center for spiritual power because of the vortices of subtle energy in the area. This energy isn't described as electricity or magnetism, though it is said to leave a slight residual magnetism in the places where it is strongest.

New Agers believe there are four major vortices in Sedona: Airport, Red Rock Crossing/Cathedral Rock, Boynton Canyon, and Bell Rock. Each manifests a different kind of energy, and this energy interacts with the individual in its presence. People come from all over the world to experience these various energy forms, hoping for guidance in spiritual matters, health, and relationships.

Juniper trees, which are all over the Sedona area, are said to respond to vortex energy in such a way that reveals where this energy is strongest. The stronger the energy, the more axial twist the junipers bear in their branches.

Airport Vortex is said to strengthen one's "masculine" side, aiding in self-confidence and focus. Red Rock Crossing/Cathedral Rock Vortex nurtures one's "feminine" aspects, such as patience and kindness. You'll be directed to Boynton Canyon Vortex if you're seeking balance between the masculine and feminine. And finally, Bell Rock Vortex, the most powerful of all, strengthens all three aspects: masculine, feminine, and balance.

These energy centers are easily accessed, and vortex maps are available at crystal shops all over Sedona.

© Corbis

Sedona Trolley. Tours last approximately one hour and cover Sedona's main attractions. Highlights include Tlaquepaque and the Boynton Canyon. | Cheers, Hwy. 89A and Forest Ave. | 520/282–5400 | www.sedonatours.com/trolley.htm | $7–$11 | Daily 10–5.

ON THE CALENDAR

MAR.: *Sedona Film Festival.* American and international films are previewed at the Harkins Theater. | 520/282–0747.

SEPT.: *Sedona Jazz on the Rocks.* Ensembles perform in a spectacular rock setting in Sedona Cultural Park. | 520/282–1985.

OCT.: *Fiesta del Tlaquepaque.* Arts-and-crafts displays, as well as food and music in Tlaquepaque. | 520/282–4838.

OCT.: *Annual Sedona Arts Festival.* This festival at Sedona Red Rock High School serves up arts, crafts, and entertainment. | 520/204–9456.

NOV.–JAN.: *Annual Red Rock Fantasy of Lights.* More than a million Christmas lights adorn the grounds of Los Abrigados Resort on Oak Creek. The displays, ranging from religious to commercial, compete with each other for the "people's choice" crown. The proceeds benefit charity. | 520/282–1777.

DEC.: *Annual Festival of Lights at Tlaquepaque.* More than 6,000 luminarias are set ablaze during this holiday season event. | 520/282–4838.

Dining

Cowboy Club. Southwestern. A lively Old West ambience with an overwrought, kitschy decor. Most diners order steaks, but you'll also find dishes made from cactus, like the Sonoran cactus fries. House specials include buffalo sirloin steak, cowboy gumbo with buffalo sausage, beef and shrimp, and campfire ribs with a raspberry plum sauce. For something a little different, try the southwestern crème brûlée, made with tequila and jalapeños. Kids' menu. | 241 N. U.S. 89A | 520/282–4200 | $11–$25 | AE, MC, V.

El Rincon. Mexican. This is old Mexican through and through, with its high ceilings and antique furniture. On the menu: enchiladas, burritos, quesadillas, and a host of other favorites, all made from scratch with traditional Navajo spices and Indian masa flour. The freshly prepared guacamole is excellent. There's a covered patio for outdoor dining. Kids' menu. No smoking. | Rte. 179 | 520/282–4648 | Closed Mon. No dinner Feb. | $9–$14 | MC, V.

Heartline Café. Southwestern. This casual restaurant is serious about its innovative southwestern cuisine. Try the pecan-crusted local trout with bijon cream sauce. In season, done on the garden patio. Kids' menu. | 1610 W. U.S. 89A | 520/282–0785 | $11–$32 | AE, D, DC, MC, V.

Hideaway. Italian. There's nothing pretentious about this southern Italian restaurant. The setting is eye-popping, with views of the mountains from a large outdoor patio overlooking Oak Creek. On the menu are traditional, hearty favorites like manicotti and lasagna, but don't forget the antipasti, salads, and pizza. | 179 Country Sq. | 520/282–4204 | $9–$11 | AE, D, DC, MC, V.

Joey Bistro. Italian. This restaurant in the casual Los Abrigados Resort offers great homemade fare like fettuccine primavera, chicken marsala over linguine, and a classic lasagna dish. If you're looking to really eat big, try the weekly Lotsa Pasta special Tuesday through Thursday nights—all you can eat for $7.95. No smoking. | 160 Portal La. | 520/204–5639 | No lunch | $16–$26 | AE, D, DC, MC, V.

Judi's Restaurant. American/Casual. This intimate American country restaurant is known for their lip-smacking baby-back ribs, as well as a variety of other steak dishes. The large salads and the pasta primavera are options for light eaters or vegetarians. No smoking. | 40 Soldier's Pass Rd. | 520/282–4449 | No lunch Sun. | $15–$35 | AE, D, DC, MC, V.

L'Auberge. French. This is one of the best restaurants in northern Arizona, known for its tranquil and relaxing atmosphere, great service, and food. Try the pâté, lobster fricassee, or the Dungeness crab ravioli. Dine on the creek-side terrace. Sunday brunch. No smoking. | 301 L'Auberge La. | 520/282–1667 | Reservations essential | Jacket required (dinner) Labor Day–Memorial Day | Breakfast also available | $17–$90 | AE, D, DC, MC, V.

Mesquite Grill and Barbecue. American. Tucked behind a strip of tourist shops and restaurants, this uptown Sedona barbecue joint serves up some of the best ribs in town. An outdoor mesquite-burning pit next to the patio lets off wonderful aromas of beef, pork, and chicken slowly roasting over the fire. The sauce is great, as are the homemade fries. | 250 Jordan Rd., #9 | 520/282–6533 | $8–$20 | No credit cards.

Pietro's. Italian. With a lively and casual atmosphere, this northern Italian restaurant is one of the most popular in Sedona. Try *gamberi giardinieri* (grilled shrimp with shiitake mushrooms in white wine), followed by fettuccine with duck and figs, or veal piccata. Sit out on the outdoor enclosed patio with marbleized tables and wrought-iron street lamps for a romantic dinner. Early-bird specials Sunday–Wednesday from 5:30 until 6:30 PM. No smoking. | 2445 W. Hwy. 89A | 520/282–2525 | www.pietrossedona.com | $13–$30 | AE, D, DC, MC, V.

René at Tlaquepaque. Continental. This elegant dining room with plush banquettes in the Tlaquepaque shopping center has superb service and classic, well-prepared food. Try the salad of baby spinach leaves and sautéed wild mushrooms in a hazelnut vinaigrette, or French onion soup. The house specialty is Colorado rack of lamb. No smoking. | 336 Rte. 179 | 520/282–9225 | $12–$34 | MC, V.

Rosebud's. American. Memorabilia from Orson Welles's classic movie *Citizen Kane* abound at this intimate restaurant (named for that famous line). The bright and airy dining room has hardwood floors, copper-top tables, and picture windows that overlook Schnebly Canyon. Try the ahi tuna salad, the southwestern pasta with chicken and chorizo, or the Argentine shrimp pasta in a white wine sauce with feta cheese. | 320 N. U.S. 89A | 520/282–3022 | $17–$35 | MC, V.

Sasaki. Japanese. The spare, clean architectural lines give a serene balance inside this upscale restaurant surrounded by Sedona's red rocks. As well as having an extensive sushi menu, a wide variety of traditional dishes are available. The *shogayaki*, lightly sautéed fish, chicken, or pork marinated with fresh ginger, sweet sake, and soy, is tender and well spiced, as is the *yakiniku*, shredded beef marinated in garlic sauce and sprinkled with sesame seeds and scallions. | 65 Bell Rock Blvd. | 520/284–1757 | No lunch | $15–$25 | AE, D, MC, V.

Sedona Swiss Restaurant and Café. Swiss. This European-style restaurant serves such classic dinner entrées as veal tenderloin Zurichoise (with a sauce of mushrooms, cream, and cognac). There are lighter alternatives, like pasta with fresh salmon. Lunch is a little hectic since groups often stop here. Wonderful European pastries are served for breakfast from the pastry shop. Kids' menu. No smoking. | 350 Jordan Rd. | 520/282–7959 | Breakfast also available; closed Sun. Nov.–Jan. (will open for large groups with reservation) | $11–$30 | AE, MC, V.

Shugrue's Hillside Grill. International. Named after its location with a view, this is one of the more reliable Sedona establishments. Try rack of lamb, filet mignon, paella, or sashimi. The salads are also good. Jazz Friday–Saturday. Kids' menu. | 671 Rte. 179 | 520/282–5300 | $11–$31 | AE, MC, V.

Takashi. Japanese. Traditional Japanese art helps instill Zen-like tranquility here. The light, healthy meals include combo dinners with sashimi, tempura, and teriyaki. | 465 Jordan Rd. | 520/282–2334 | Closed Mon. No lunch Sun. | $15–$22 | AE, DC, MC, V.

Yavapai Dining Room. Southwestern. The views of the red rocks from the Enchantment Resort's dining room are superb, and the traditional menu is also quite good. Try the grilled sea bass, the Colorado rack of lamb, or the filet mignon. The super-rich volcano cake is a good antidote for chocolate cravings. Pianist Friday, Saturday. Kids' menu. Sunday brunch. No smoking. | 525 Boynton Canyon | 520/282–2900 | Breakfast also available | $12–$42 | AE, D, MC, V.

Lodging

Adobe Hacienda Bed and Breakfast. This home is modeled on a Spanish hacienda and is decorated with Native American crafts and Mexican furniture. The 1-acre property is in a residential neighborhood and borders the Sedona Golf Resort. Complimentary breakfast. Some in-room hot tubs. No pets. No smoking. | 10 Rojo Dr. | 520/284–2020 or 800/454–7191 | fax 520/284–0247 | www.sedona.net/bb/adobe | 5 rooms | $140–$170 | AE, D, MC, V.

Alma de Sedona. Each of the rooms in this inn surrounded by pine, juniper, and cacti has a distinct theme. There are super views of the mountains, including Cathedral Rock. Complimentary breakfast. In-room hot tubs, cable TV. Pool. No kids under 14. No smoking. | 50 Hozoni Dr. | 800/923–2282 or 520/282–2737 | fax 520/203–4141 | www.almadesedona.com | 12 rooms | $150–$240 | AE, MC, V.

Apple Orchard Inn. All your stress will melt away as you stroll the inn's 2 tranquil acres with piñon pines and take a dip in the pool with a waterfall. Some rooms feature lodgepole pine furnishings; others are filled with Victorian antiques. The views of Steamboat Rock and the Wilson Mountain Range are majestic. Complimentary breakfast. In-room hot tubs, cable TV, in-room VCRs. Pool. Spa. No kids under 12. No smoking. | 656 Jordan Rd. | 800/663–6968 or 520/282–5328 | fax 520/204–0044 | www.appleorchardbb.com | 7 rooms | $135–$230 | AE, MC, V.

Bell Rock Inn & Suites. This adobe-style hotel is right off Interstate 17, about 6½ mi southeast of downtown Sedona. Rooms are built around a landscaped pool area. Some suites have private patios. Restaurant, bar. In-room data ports, some in-room safes, microwaves, refrigerators, some in-room hot tubs, cable TV, some in-room VCRs. 2 pools. Hot tub. Business services. | 6246 Hwy. 179 | 520/282–4161 or 800/881–7625 | fax 520/284–0192 | bell-rockinn.com | 96 rooms | $80–$140 | AE, D, DC, MC, V.

Best Western Inn of Sedona. Many rooms in this motel in West Sedona, which is ½ mi from the airport, have great views of the surrounding red rocks. Complimentary Continental breakfast. In-room data ports, some refrigerators, cable TV. Pool. Hot tub. Gym. Laundry service. Business services. Pets allowed (fee). | 1200 W. U.S. 89A | 520/282–3072 or 800/292–6344 | fax 520/282–7218 | www.innofsedona.com | 110 rooms | $115–$155 | AE, D, DC, MC, V.

Best Western Arroyo Roble Hotel & Creekside Villas. This hotel in Uptown Sedona overlooks Oak Creek Canyon. Rooms have views of the red rocks, and all have a private patio or balcony. The separate villas, which have two bedrooms and full kitchens, sit on the banks of Oak Creek. Restaurant. Some kitchenettes, some microwaves, some refrigerators, cable TV, some in-room VCRs. Indoor-outdoor pool. 2 hot tubs. 2 tennis courts. Gym. Laundry service. Business services. | 400 N. U.S. 89A | 520/282–4001 or 800/773–3662 | fax 520/282–4001 | www.bestwesternsedona.com | 56 rooms, 5 deluxe king rooms, 1 cottage, 7 villas | $109 rooms, $159 deluxe king, $199 cottage, $299 villas | AE, D, DC, MC, V.

★ **Briar Patch Inn.** These wooden cabins are set on 9 lush, green acres right on Oak Creek, 3½ mi north of town. Some have views of the red rocks, some have decks, and some have fireplaces. Picnic area, complimentary breakfast. Kitchenettes, refrigerators, no room phones. Massage. Fishing. Library. Business services. | 3190 N. U.S. 89A | 520/282–2342 | fax 520/282–2399 | 17 cottages (15 with shower only) | $149–$295 | AE, MC, V.

Canyon Portal. All the rooms at this standard wooden two-story motel in uptown Sedona have private patios overlooking the red-rock country. The inn is within walking distance of uptown shops, restaurants, and tourist attractions. Some microwaves, cable TV. Pool. Business services. | 280 N. U.S. 89A | 520/282–7125 or 800/542–8484 | fax 520/282–1825 | 20 rooms, 1 cottage | $59–$120, $140–$150 cottage | MC, D, V.

Canyon Villa Bed and Breakfast. This small modern inn 6½ mi south of downtown has views of Bell Rock and Courthouse Butte. Individually decorated rooms are large. Afternoon hors d'oeuvres are served year-round. Complimentary breakfast. Some in-room hot tubs, cable TV. Pool. Business services. No kids under 10. No smoking. | 125 Canyon Circle Dr. | 520/284–1226 or 800/453–1166 | fax 520/284–2114 | www.canyonvilla.com | 11 rooms | $160–$250 (2-night minimum weekends) | AE, MC, V.

Casa Sedona Bed and Breakfast. This secluded and quiet B&B in West Sedona has panoramic views of the surrounding red rocks from the second-floor redwood deck. All rooms have fireplaces, and all but one have a double jetted tub and a separate shower. Picnic area, complimentary breakfast. Refrigerators, in-room hot tubs, cable TV. Outdoor hot tub. Business services. No smoking. | 55 Hozoni Dr. | 520/282–2938 or 800/525–3756 | fax 520/282–2259 | www.casasedona.com | 16 rooms | $135–$225 | AE, MC, V.

Cathedral Rock Lodge. Rooms in this rambling country house are furnished with antiques and have quilts on the beds. Accommodations come in varying sizes, and all have full kitchens. Picnic area, complimentary breakfast. No air-conditioning, kitchenettes, microwaves, refrigerators, cable TV, in-room VCRs. No smoking. | 61 Los Amigos La. | 520/282–7608 or 800/352–9149 | fax 520/282–4505 | www.cathrockbnb.com | 3 cottages | $90–$140 cottage (3–night minimum) | D, MC, V.

Cedars Resort. This hotel is in the heart of downtown. Many rooms have balconies and views of Oak Creek. Cable TV. Pool. Hot tub. No smoking. | 20 E. Hwy. 89A | 520/282–7010 | fax 520/282–5372 | www.cedarsresortsedonaaz.com | 39 rooms | $66–$120 | AE, D, DC, MC, V.

Cozy Cactus Bed and Breakfast. This small B&B is about 6½ mi south of town. Though all the simply furnished rooms have private baths, there are two shared living room/kitchen areas, each shared by two rooms (these have a fireplace, TV, and VCR). The room in the main house has its own TV/VCR and a small private patio. Complimentary breakfast. No room phones, cable TV. No smoking. | 80 Canyon Circle Dr. | 520/284–0082 or 800/788–2082 | fax 520/284–4210 | www.cozycactus.com | 5 rooms | $105–$125 | AE, D, DC, MC, V.

Days Inn Sedona. This motel was built in 1988 and offers fine views of the red rocks from all rooms. Complimentary Continental breakfast. Some microwaves, some refrigerators, cable TV. Pool. Hot tub. No smoking. | 2991 W. Hwy. 89A | 520/282–9166 | fax 520/282–6208 | 56 rooms, 10 suites | $110–$140 | AE, D, DC, MC, V.

Desert Quail Inn. This motel is about 6½ mi south of Sedona, and some rooms have views of the red-rock formations. Some microwaves, refrigerators, some in-room hot tubs, cable TV. Pool. Laundry facilities. Business services. Some pets allowed (fee). | 6626 Hwy. 179 | 520/284–1433 or 800/385–0927 | fax 520/284–0487 | www.desertquailinn.com | 40 rooms, 1 suite | $54–$89, $150 suite | AE, D, DC, MC, V.

Enchantment Resort. This luxury resort has a beautiful setting in serene Boynton Canyon northwest of Sedona. Southwestern-style rooms are in casitas; separate haciendas have full kitchens. Many rooms have kiva-style fireplaces, and all have great views and private decks. 2 restaurants (see Yavapai Dining Room), bar, picnic area, room service. In-room data ports, some kitchenettes, cable TV. Pool. Hot tub, massage, spa. Miniature golf, putting green, tennis. Health club, hiking, bicycles. Children's programs (ages 4–12). Business services. | 525 Boynton Canyon Rd. | 520/282–2900 or 800/826–4180 | fax 520/282–9249 | www.enchantmentresort.com | enchant@sedona.net | 220 rooms (110 rooms can be rented as suites), 56 casitas | $295–$395, $525–$725 suites, $895 casitas | AE, D, DC, MC, V.

Garland's Oak Creek Lodge. Some of these cabins 8 mi north of Sedona date back to the turn of the 20th century and are constructed of either log or wood frames. The furniture is rustic, and many pieces are also made of logs. Breakfast and dinner are complimentary. Restaurant. No room phones, no TV. Tennis court. Volleyball, fishing. No smoking. | Hwy. 89A | 520/282–3343 | www.garlandslodge.com | 16 rooms | $168–$198 | Closed Nov.–Mar. | MAP | MC, V.

Graham Bed & Breakfast Inn and Adobe Village. This inn and its beautiful, one-of-a-kind casitas next door are all attractively decorated in southwestern style, but gracious and welcoming service really sets this place apart. Casitas have jetted tubs and separate showers, two fireplaces, plus a kitchenette. It's about 6½ mi south of town. Complimentary breakfast. Some kitchenettes, some microwaves, some refrigerators, some in-room hot tubs, cable TV, in-room VCRs (and movies). Pool. Hot tub, massage. Bicycles. Library. Laundry facilities. Business services. No smoking. | 150 Canyon Circle Dr. | 520/284–1425 or 800/228–1425 | fax 520/284–0767 | www.sedonasfinest.com | 6 rooms, 4 casitas | $159–$249, $339–$379 casitas | AE, D, MC, V.

Holiday Inn Express. This two-story motel is in the Village of Oak Creek, south of Sedona. Complimentary Continental breakfast. In-room data ports, cable TV. Pool. Hot tub. Laundry service. Business services. | 6175 Hwy. 179 | 520/284–0711 | fax 520/284–3760 | www.hiexpress.com | 104 rooms, 12 suites | $109, $129 suites | AE, D, DC, MC, V.

Inn on Oak Creek. This B&B, originally an art gallery, is on the banks of Oak Creek surrounded by red-rock mountains and has a private creek-side park. All rooms have gas fireplaces and marble baths. Complimentary breakfast. In-room data ports, in-room hot tubs, cable TV, in-room VCRs (and movies). Business services. No kids under 10. No smoking. | 556 Hwy. 179 | 520/282–7896 or 800/499–7896 | fax 520/282–0696 | www.sedona-inn.com | 11 rooms, 2 suites | $160–$250, $190–$245 suites | AE, D, MC, V.

Junipine Resort. This resort 8 mi north of Sedona on Oak Creek offers modern one- and two-bedroom wood-and-stone "creek houses," with full kitchens, stone fireplaces, and private redwood decks. Even the smallest will accommodate a family with two children. Some units have hot tubs on the decks. Restaurant. Kitchenettes, refrigerators. | 8351 N. U.S. 89A | 520/282–3375 or 800/742–7463 | fax 520/282–7402 | www.junipine.com | 32 creek houses | $170–$245 1–bedroom creek house, $230–$300 2–bedroom creek house | AE, D, DC, MC, V.

Kokopelli Inn. This hotel, just south of Bell Rock, offers southwestern-style rooms, many with panoramic, red-rock views. Complimentary Continental breakfast. In-room data ports, some in-room safes, some in-room hot tubs, refrigerators, cable TV, in-room VCRs. Pool. | 6465 Hwy. 179 | 520/284–1100 | www.kokopelliinn.com | 42 rooms | $130–$165 | AE, DC, D, MC, V.

Kokopelli Suites. This adobe-style, all-suite hotel in West Sedona offers rooms with southwestern decor and adjustable beds. Complimentary Continental breakfast. In-room safes, kitchenettes, microwaves, refrigerators, cable TV. Pool. Hot tub. Laundry facilities. | 3119 W. U.S. 89A | 520/204–1146 or 800/789–7393 | fax 520/204–5851 | www.kokopellisuites.com | 46 suites in 4 buildings | $119–$239 | AE, D, DC, MC, V.

L'Auberge de Sedona. This romantic resort in the Uptown area is perched on a hillside above Oak Creek. It offers large, hotel-style rooms in a hotel building or in a small lodge on Oak Creek (lodge rooms have more amenities), or private cottages with full kitchens and fireplaces, also along the creek. An inclined railway connects creek-side accommodations with the Orchards hotel rooms on the top of the hill. 2 restaurants. In-room data ports, some kitchenettes, minibars, some microwaves, some refrigerators, cable TV. Pool. Hot tub, massage. Horseback riding. Library. Business services, airport shuttle. | 301 L'Auberge La. | 520/282–1661 or 800/272–6777 | fax 520/282–2885 | www.lauberge.com | 39 Orchards rooms, 22 lodge rooms, 34 cottages | $175–$195 Orchards rooms, $190–$280 lodge rooms, $255–$425 cottages | AE, D, DC, MC, V.

Lodge at Sedona. On 2½ landscaped acres dotted with sculptures and gardens, plus a large rock-walled labyrinth, this intimate and friendly B&B is furnished with antiques. Some rooms have redwood decks, hot tubs, or fireplaces. Picnic area, complimentary breakfast. Some in-room hot tubs, no room phones, TV in common area. Massage. Library. Business services. No smoking. | 125 Kallof Pl. | 520/204–1942 or 800/619–4467 | fax 520/204–2128 | www.lodgeatsedona.com | 14 rooms | $125–$245 | AE, D, MC, V.

Los Abrigados Resort and Spa. This upscale, all-suite resort on the south side of Sedona has a great spa. Suites have partial kitchens; some have fireplaces. A two-bedroom stone house with full kitchen and Jacuzzi tub is also available. 3 restaurants (see Joey Bistro), bar. Microwaves, refrigerators, cable TV, in-room VCRs. 2 pools. Beauty salon, hot tub, spa. 2 tennis courts. Basketball, health club, volleyball, fishing. Video games. Playground. Laundry facilities. Business services. | 160 Portal La. | 520/282–1777 or 800/521–3131 | fax 520/282–2614 | www.ilxinc.com | 173 suites, 1 cottage | $225–$395 suites, $1,500 cottage | AE, D, DC, MC, V.

Poco Diablo. This family-oriented resort on 22 acres 2 mi south of town offers red-rock views from some rooms, which run the gamut from regular hotel-style rooms with two beds to large suites with fireplaces. 2 restaurants, bar, room service. Some in-room data ports, some minibars, refrigerators, some in-room hot tubs, cable TV. 2 pools. Hot tub, massage. 9-hole golf course, 4 tennis courts. Gym, racquetball. Video games. Playground. Business services. | 1752 S. Hwy. 179 | 520/282–7333 or 800/528–4275 | fax 520/282–2090 | www.pocodiablo.com | 135 rooms, 2 suites | $115–$245, $240–$360 suites | AE, D, DC, MC, V.

Quail Ridge Resort. One of the more affordable accommodations in the Sedona area, this small, family-oriented resort in the Village of Oak Creek is about 6½ mi south of town. It offers smaller rooms or separate, private A-frame chalets, all with kitchens. Picnic area. Some kitchenettes, some microwaves, cable TV. Pool. Hot tub. 2 tennis courts. Hiking, bicycles. Laundry facilities. Business services. No smoking. | 120 Canyon Circle Dr. | 520/284–9327 | fax 520/284–0832 | www.quailridgeresort.com | 4 rooms, 9 chalets | $79 rooms, $79–$169 chalets | AE, D, MC, V.

Quality Inn King's Ransom. Rooms at this motel 2 mi south of Sedona feature contemporary southwestern decor. Balconies offer views onto red rocks. Restaurant, bar. Some refrigerators, some in-room hot tubs, cable TV. Pool. | 771 Hwy. 179 | 520/282–7151 or 800/846–6164 | fax 520/282–5208 | www.qualityinn.com | 101 rooms | $89–$149 | AE, D, DC, MC, V.

Saddle Rock Ranch. This property perched on a hillside five minutes from Oak Creek and 1¼ mi from downtown Sedona shops and restaurants was originally a guest ranch in the 1930s and 1940s. Now, the main ranch house is a small, upscale B&B run by a former exec of the Ritz-Carlton company. Complimentary breakfast. No room phones, cable TV, in-room VCRs. Pool. Hot tub. Business services. No kids under 14. No smoking. | 255 Rock Ridge Dr. | 520/282–7640 | www.saddlerockranch.com | 3 rooms | $159–$179 | MC, V.

Sedona Reál Inn. This all-suite hotel is in West Sedona. Restaurant, complimentary Continental breakfast. In-room data ports, kitchenettes, microwaves, refrigerators, some in-room hot tubs, cable TV, in-room VCRs (and movies). Pool. Hot tub. Gym. Library. Business services. | 95 Arroyo Piñon Dr. | 520/282–1414 or 800/353–1239 | fax 520/282–0900 | www.sedonareal.com | 47 suites | $140–$250 | AE, D, MC, V.

Sky Ranch Lodge. This hotel near the top of Airport Mesa has the best views in Sedona. Some rooms have private patios or balconies, stone fireplace, or kitchenettes. The grounds are planted with flowers. Some kitchenettes, some refrigerators, cable TV. Pool. Hot tub. Laundry facilities. Business services. Some pets allowed (fee). | Airport Rd. | 520/282–6400 | fax 520/282–7682 | www.skyranchlodge.com | 94 rooms, 2 cottages | $75–$160, $180 cottages | AE, MC, V.

Southwest Inn at Sedona. All rooms at this well-maintained small hotel in West Sedona have fireplaces. Complimentary Continental breakfast. In-room data ports, refrigerators, some in-room hot tubs, cable TV, some in-room VCRs. Pool. Hot tub. Tennis. Business services. No smoking. | 3250 W. U.S. 89A | 520/282–3344 or 800/483–7422 | fax 520/282–0267. | www.swinn.com | 24 rooms, 4 suites | $149–$199 rooms, $199–$225 suites | AE, D, DC, MC, V.

Territorial House. A former ranch house constructed of cedar and red rock, this B&B is on the west side of Sedona, about 3 mi from downtown shops and attractions. Complimentary breakfast. No air-conditioning, some microwaves, refrigerators, cable TV, in-room VCRs (and movies). Hot tub. Business services. | 65 Piki Dr. | 520/204–2737 or 800/801–2737 | fax 520/204–2230 | oldwest@sedona.net | 4 rooms (2 with shower only), 1 suite | $115–$185, $205 suite | AE, D, MC, V.

A Touch of Sedona. This B&B in a contemporary home in Uptown offers quiet accommodations and personalized service. Picnic area, complimentary breakfast. Some kitchenettes, cable TV, no room phones. No smoking. | 595 Jordan Rd. | 520/282–6462 or 800/600–6462 | fax 520/282–1534 | www.touchsedona.com | 5 rooms (3 with shower only) | $109–$159 | AE, D, MC, V.

Wishing Well. You'll forget you're less than a mile from Uptown Sedona, due to the cascading waterfall, old Indian trail, and breathtaking views of Cathedral Rock. The rooms here are spacious, private, and ideal for a romantic getaway; some are furnished with Victorian antiques. Complimentary Continental breakfast. Some in-room hot tubs, no room phones, TV in common area. No smoking. | 995 N. Hwy. 89A | 520/282–4914 or 800/728–9474 | fax 520/204–9766 | www.sedonawishingwell.com | 5 rooms | $170–$195 | AE, D, MC, V.

SELIGMAN

MAP 3, D4

(Nearby town also listed: Williams)

Seligman was founded in 1866, when the Atchison, Topeka, and Santa Fe Railroad connected a long unused line to Prescott with their main line at this juncture. The railroad named the town after Jesse Seligman, one of the main financial backers of the railroad. It was also on the original Route 66 and was a popular stopping-off point for travelers. Today, it's a very sleepy town of 900 best known as a rest stop for visitors to nearby Grand Canyon Caverns, 25 mi away.

Information: **Seligman Chamber of Commerce** | Box 65, Seligman, 86337 | 520/422–3939.

Attractions

Grand Canyon Caverns. A tour through the cool, dark caverns 25 mi northwest of town is a welcome respite from summer heat. | Rte. 66 | 520/422–3223 | $9.50 | Weekdays 8–6, weekends 9–5.

Route 66 Gift Shop. From apparel to vanity license plates, this shop has all the Route 66 memorabilia and souvenirs that you could ever want. While it passes through quite a few major cities from Chicago to California, the heart of Route 66 lies in small towns such as Seligman. | 217 E. Rte. 66 | 520/753–5001 | www.route66giftshop.com | Free | Daily 9–6.

Dining

Copper Cart. American. Right on Route 66, this casual eatery is known for its choice western-fed beef and charbroiled steaks. There are also a number of Mexican items on the menu. Kids' menu. | 103 W. Chino Ave. at Rte. 66 | 520/422–3241 | Breakfast also available | $6–$14 | MC, V.

Lodging

Comfort Lodge of Seligman. This small roadside motel in downtown Seligman offers basic 1980s-style rooms, and is within walking distance of convenience stores and restaurants. Restaurant, complimentary Continental breakfast. Cable TV. Pets allowed. | 114 E. Chino St. | 520/422–3255 or 800/700–5054 | fax 520/422–3600 | www.rentor.com/seligman-hotel.htm | 16 rooms | $27 | AE, D, DC, MC, V.

Romney Motel. This single-story motel is on historic Route 66. There are a handful of restaurants and a bar within walking distance. Some microwaves, some refrigerators, cable TV. Business services. Some pets allowed. | 122 Rte. 66 | 520/422–3700 | fax 520/422–3680 | 28 rooms | $28–$40 | AE, MC, V.

SELLS

MAP 3, E10

(Nearby town also listed: Tucson)

Sells is the tribal capital of the Tohono O'odham Nation, the second-largest Indian reservation in the United States, covering 4,400 square mi between Tucson and Ajo. Baboquivari Peak (7,730 ft) is sacred to the tribe and the home of their deity, I'itoi ("elder brother"). An arts-and-crafts store on the main drag sells locally made handcrafts.

Information: **Tohono O'odham Nation Executive Office** | Box 837, Sells, 85634 | 520/383–2028.

Attractions

Kitt Peak National Observatory. Funded by the National Science Foundation and managed by more than 20 universities, this observatory 32 mi northeast of Sells is on the Tohono O'odham Reservation. At the visitor center, you can look through the world's largest solar telescope. | Rte. 386 | 520/318–8600 | $2 suggested donation | Daily 9–4.

ON THE CALENDAR

FEB.: *Tohono O'odham Rodeo and Fair.* Juniors and senior citizens alike buck broncos and rope calves at this annual event. There is also a carnival and arts-and-crafts booths for the less daring, all the first weekend in February. | 520/383–2588.

Dining

Basha's Deli and Bakery. American. This is a takeout-only joint, but for a deli, you can get some clever dishes such as green chile and rice. The two-piece chicken dinner is quite a bargain. | Topawa Rd. off Hwy. 86 | 520/383–2546 | Breakfast also available | $2–$5 | AE, MC, V.

SHOW LOW

MAP 3, G6

(Nearby towns also listed: McNary, Pinetop/Lakeside)

According to local legend, back in 1870, two homesteading partners, Cooley and Clark, wanted to dissolve their partnership, so they decided to play a round of cards to determine which one would buy the other out. Clark was winning when he said to Cooley, "Show low and you win." Cooley cut the deck and pulled the two of clubs, thereby winning the homestead, at the current site of this little resort town. Show Low, the commercial center for this high-country area, has little of the charm of nearby McNary or Pinetop/Lakeside, but it is a good stopping point on your way to the Painted Desert or Petrified Forest.

Information: **Show Low Regional Chamber of Commerce** | 951 W. Deuce of Clubs, Box 1083, Show Low, 85902 | 520/537–2326 or 888/746–9569.

Attractions

Rainbow Lake. Off Highway 260 and approximately 10 mi north of Show Low, good bass, trout, and bluegill fishing is available to anglers at this lake circled by vacation homes. Access from Rainbow Lake Road takes you right down to the dock and boat ramp. | Rainbow Lake Rd. | 520/367–4290 | Free | Daily.

Show Low Golf Club. This par 70 course has a back nine in the woods and front nine in a more open setting. | 860 N. 36 Dr. | 520/537–4564 | Daily 6:30–6:30.

ON THE CALENDAR

JULY: *Freedom Fest Activities.* This event includes the largest July 4th parade in northern Arizona, along with fireworks. | 888/746–9569.

Dining

High in the Pines Deli. American. An intimate coffeehouse and sandwich shop one block east of Deuce of Clubs, here you can find European-style charcuterie boards with fresh meats and cheeses served with baguettes, as well as a variety of specialty sandwiches. Try the garlic pepper loin sandwich with one of the many coffee drinks. | 1201 E. Hall | 520/537–1453 | Closed Sun. No dinner | $3–$13 | No credit cards.

Paint Pony Steakhouse. Steak. Brass railings, mounted game, and Tiffany-style lights give an elegant air to this restaurant. Filet mignon and prime rib are top drawer. | 571 W. Deuce of Clubs Dr. | 520/537–8220 | Closed Sun. No lunch Sat. | $10–$30 | AE, D, DC, MC, V.

Lodging

Best Western Paint Pony Lodge. Some of the rooms at this motel right in Show Low have fireplaces. Restaurant, bar, complimentary Continental breakfast, room service. In-room data ports, some microwaves, some refrigerators, cable TV. Business services. Pets allowed (fee). | 581 W. Deuce of Clubs Dr. | 520/537–5773 | fax 520/537–5766 | www.bestwestern.com | 50 rooms | $74–$84 | AE, D, DC, MC, V.

Days Inn. This motel is in the center of town. Restaurant. Microwaves, refrigerators, cable TV. Pool. Beauty salon. Laundry facilities. Business services, airport shuttle. Some pets allowed (fee). | 480 W. Deuce of Clubs | 520/537–4356 | fax 520/537–8692 | 122 rooms | $69–$74 | AE, D, DC, MC, V.

KC Motel. The rooms at this motel built in 1995 are generic and offer only standard conveniences. This is the place to go when you want to save a buck and spend time on outdoor excursions, rather than lounging about your room. Complimentary Continental breakfast. Cable TV. Hot tub. | 60 W. Deuce of Clubs Dr. | 520/537–4433 | fax 520/537–0106 | 35 rooms | $40–$55 | AE, D, DC, MC, V.

SIERRA VISTA

MAP 3, G10

(Nearby towns also listed: Benson, Bisbee)

A temperate climate has made Sierra Vista a draw for retirees. It's nestled at the base of the Huachuca Mountains. The city grew up around an army post established in 1877, now called Fort Huachuca. Sierra Vista is near bird-watchers' mecca Ramsey Canyon (at the northernmost point of the Sierra Madre), as well as the hiking trails throughout the San Pedro Valley and San Pedro riparian area. Although the town is fairly characterless, it's a good base from which to explore the area's sights.

Information: **Sierra Vista Chamber of Commerce** | 21 E. Wilcox, Sierra Vista, 85635 | 520/458–6940.

Attractions

Coronado National Forest. A fairly accessible chunk of this 1.7-million-acre preserve lies just southwest of Fort Huachuca. Camping, hiking, and fishing are available year-round. The Sierra Vista Ranger District office is actually southeast of the town of Sierra Vista in Hereford. | 5990 S. Hwy. 92, Hereford | 520/670–4552 | www.fs.fed.us | Free | Daily.

Coronado National Memorial. Francisco Vásquez de Coronado, the conquistador to whom this site 16 mi south of town is dedicated, made his way here in 1540. There's a visitor center and hiking trails. Views are best at the top of 7,000-ft Coronado Peak, which is ½ mi on foot from Montezuma Pass, 3 mi on a dirt road from the visitor center. The turnoff for the monument is 16 mi south of Sierra Vista on Highway 92, then it's another 5 mi to the visitor center. | 4101 E. Montezuma Canyon Rd., Hereford | 520/366–5515 | Free | Visitor center daily 8–5.

Fort Huachuca Museum. The colorful history of the Southwest and its military history are the focus of this museum at Fort Huachuca, west of Sierra Vista. The collection includes displays on an army outpost established in 1877, modern military items, and Buffalo Soldiers. | Corner of Grierson and Boyd Sts. on Fort Huachuca off Hwy. 90 | 520/533–5736 | huachuca-www.army.mil | Donations accepted | Weekdays 9–4, weekends 1–4.

Ramsey Canyon Preserve. Managed by the Nature Conservancy, this spectacular 300-acre site 6 mi south of Sierra Vista is superb for bird-watching, especially from April to October when 14 species of hummingbirds come to the area. Golden eagles have been spotted here, too. Parking is limited to 19 spaces, and is on a first-come, first-served basis. If you wish to attend one of the nature walks conducted on Tuesday, Thursday, or Saturday mornings between March and October, then you must make reservations. | 27 Ramsey Canyon Rd., Hereford | 520/378–2785 | www.tnc.org | $5; special rates for children | Mar.–Oct., daily 8–5; Nov.–Feb., daily 9–5.

ON THE CALENDAR

FEB.: *Cochise Cowboy and Music Gathering.* Cowboy poets and western musicians celebrate the ranching history of the area through songs and spoken-word performances. | 520/459–3868.

MAY: *Salute to the Buffalo Soldier.* This event commemorates the service rendered by African-American troops. Activities include educational programs, displays, a parade, and troop encampments. | 520/459–3868.

AUG.: *Southwest Wings Birding Festival.* Lectures by Audubon authorities and field trips are highlights of this bird-watchers' favorite. | 520/378–0233.

Dining

La Casita Mexican Restaurant and Cantina. Mexican. Glass chile peppers and little ladders draped with Mexican blankets are a couple of the precious touches in this fun restaurant. Fajitas and chimichangas are the big hits. | 465 E. Ferry Blvd. | 520/458–2376 | $6–$14 | AE, D, MC, V.

Mesquite Tree Restaurant. American/Casual. The patio at this restaurant 6 mi south of Sierra Vista has excellent views of the surrounding mountains, and the southwestern-style interior is filled with antiques and old potbellied stoves. Specialty dishes here include filet mignon stuffed with mushrooms, spinach, green onions, and garlic, and the Gilroy Striped Ravioli, filled with black beans, green chile, and corn. Fresh fish is also available. Kids' menu. | 6398 S. Rte. 92 at Carr Canyon, Hereford | 520/378–2758 | Closed Mon. No lunch | $11–$23 | AE, MC, V.

Lodging

Casa de San Pedro. Bird-watchers are drawn to this contemporary hacienda-style bed-and-breakfast abutting the San Pedro Riparian National Conservation area. Guest quarters are bright and modern, with handcrafted wooden furniture. The great room boasts a telescope to help you enjoy the spectacular view of the stars. Complimentary breakfast. No room phones, no TV. No kids under 12. No smoking. | 8933 S. Yell La. | 520/366–1300 | fax 520/366–9701 | www.naturesinn.com | 10 rooms | $105–$140 | MC, V.

Baxter's at Thunder Mountain Inn. Although this hotel rests at the foot of the Huachuca Mountains, the view is rather modest. Rooms feature copper and turquoise colors. Guests get $5 off breakfast at the hotel's restaurant, so you'll probably eat free. Restaurant. In-room data ports, kitchenettes, some microwaves, cable TV. Pool. Hot tub. Pets allowed. | 1631 S. Hwy. 92 | 520/458–7900 or 800/222–5811 | fax 520/458–7900 | 103 rooms, 2 suites | $55–$85 | AE, D, DC, MC, V.

Ramsey Canyon Inn. This charming country inn managed by the Nature Conservancy is next to the Ramsey Canyon Preserve in Hereford, and is sprinkled with antiques. More than 10 hummingbird species visit the inn's feeders during the year. The apartments with full kitchens are suitable for a family with two children. The conservancy runs a range of nature programs that can include inn guests. Complimentary breakfast (B&B rooms only). No air-conditioning, no room phones, no TV. No kids under 12. No smoking. | 29 Ramsey Canyon, Hereford | 520/378–3010 | fax 520/803–0819 | www.tnc.org | 6 rooms, 2 apartments | $110–$132 rooms, $135–$142 apartments | MC, V.

Super 8. This motel is right outside Fort Huachuca army base, west of Sierra Vista, within walking distance of downtown. Complimentary Continental breakfast. Refrigerators, cable TV. Pool. Business services. | 100 Fab Ave. | 520/459–5380 | fax 520/459–6052 | 52 rooms | $53 | AE, D, DC, MC, V.

Windemere Resort & Conference Center. This modern three-story hotel is right in town and a short drive from Ramsey Canyon. Restaurant, bar, complimentary breakfast, room service. Some refrigerators, cable TV. Pool. Hot tub. Laundry facilities. Business services, airport shuttle. Some pets allowed. | 2047 S. Hwy. 92 | 520/459–5900 or 800/825–4656 | fax 520/458–1347 | 148 rooms, 3 suites | $80 rooms, $150–$200 suites | AE, D, DC, MC, V.

SPRINGERVILLE-EAGAR

MAP 3, H6–I6

(Nearby town also listed: Alpine, Greer)

Founded by and named for Henry Springer, the proprietor of a late-1800s trading post, Springerville is the gateway to the White Mountains and Apache-Sitgreaves National Forest and home of the Springerville Volcanic Field. Just north of town are double volcanoes that erupted 700,000 years ago. Springerville has become a center for lumbering and cattle ranching, but with less snowfall and a milder climate than nearby Greer, this is also a popular spot for skiers to stay given the easy drive to the Sunrise Park Ski Resort here.

Information: **Round Valley Chamber of Commerce** | 318 E. Main St., Box 31, Springerville, 85938 | 520/333–2123.

Attractions

Apache-Sitgreaves National Forest. More than 2 million acres of hiking, biking, and fishing are available in the White Mountains region of this huge national forest. There's a forest service office in Springerville. | 165 S. Mountain Ave., Springerville | 520/333–4372 | www.fs.fed.us | Free | Daily.

Big Lake. There are a number of campgrounds scattered along the southeast shore of this lake, which is 30 mi southwest of Round Valley in the White Mountains area. | 24 mi south of Hwy. 260 on Hwy. 273 | 520/735–7313 or 877/444–6777 | Free | Daily.

Casa Malpais Archaeological Park. Built on a series of basalt terraces at an elevation of 7,000 ft, Casa Malpais spans 17 acres. Highlights include the Great Kiva—the largest Native American ceremonial chamber in North America—catacomb burials, and numerous solar petroglyph markers. | 318 E. Main St., Springerville | 520/333–5375 | www.casamalpais.com | $5 | Daily 8–4; guided tours from museum at 9, 11, and 2.

Lyman Lake State Park. When the Little Colorado River was dammed for irrigation in 1905, a 3-mi-long reservoir was created in this area about 18 mi north of Springerville. The reservoir has since become the park's centerpiece, with designated beaches for swimming and hiking trails that weave through the White Mountains. Waterskiing is permitted in some areas. There are also campsites for small parties or large groups. | U.S. 180/191 | 520/337–4441 | $4 per vehicle | Daily.

Madonna of the Trail. This 18-ft-tall statue celebrates the importance of pioneer women in the winning of the West. It's across from the post office and is one of 12 such monuments in the country. | Main St., Springerville | 520/333–2123 | Free | Daily.

Raven Site Ruins. Three prehistoric pueblos overlooking the banks of the Little Colorado River 12 mi north of Springerville contain several kivas, more than 800 rooms, and exhibit cultural features of the Mongollon and Anasazi peoples. | U.S. 180/191 | 520/333–5857 | www.ravensite.com | $4 | May–mid Oct., Mon.–Sat. 10–4; other times by appointment.

Renée Cushman Art Collection Museum. In a special wing of the meeting hall of the Mormon Church, this small collection includes an engraving attributed to Rembrandt and three Tiepolo pen drawings. It also houses an impressive collection of European antiques. It's open only by appointment through the Round Valley Chamber of Commerce; when you call ahead, they will give you the address. | 520/333–2123 | By appointment only.

Springerville Volcanic Field. The Twin Knolls, a pair of volcanoes, erupted twice here about 700,000 years ago. The spot affords impressive views of the surrounding area. | U.S. 180/191 and U.S. 60 | 520/333–2123 | Free | Daily.

ON THE CALENDAR
OCT.: *Indian Summer "Pow Wow."* An authentic Native American powwow, with a traditional dance and drum competition held the second week in October each year. | 520/333–2123.

Dining
Booga Reds. American. The home-style cooking here has a legion of local fans. Fish-and-chips and roast beef with mashed potatoes are options, as are several spicy Mexican dishes. Teal booths and Mexican tile give this spot a typical southwestern vibe. | 521 E. Main St., Springerville | 520/333–2640 | Breakfast also available | $6–$13 | MC, V.

Lodging
Paisley Corner Bed and Breakfast. This B&B is an impeccably restored 1910 Colonial Revival–style home, furnished with period antiques. It's a romantic setting. Complimentary breakfast. No room phones, TV in common area. | 287 N. Main St., Eagar | 520/333–4665 | 4 rooms | $65–$95 | MC, V.

Reed's Lodge. This lodge in the foothills of the White Mountains offers interesting accommodations with a decent view. Rooms have individually made Navajo print bedspreads on either queen- or king-size beds, and southwestern color schemes. Some in-room data ports, some microwaves, some refrigerators, cable TV. Shop, video games. Pets allowed. | 514 E. Main St., Springerville | 520/333–4323 | fax 520/333–5191 | 45 rooms, 5 suites | $40–$50 | AE, D, DC, MC, V.

South Fork Guest Ranch. This guest ranch on 38 forested acres, with its own stocked trout pond, offers basic to luxurious creek-side cabins with full kitchens off Highway 260. All cabins have fireplaces for chilly evenings. It's between MM 390 and MM 391. Kitchenettes, microwaves, refrigerators, no room phones, no TV. Pond. Fishing. | Off Hwy. 260 | 520/333–4455 or 888/333–3565 | 16 cabins | $35–$120 (2–night minimum stay) | MC, V.

SUPERIOR

MAP 3, F7

(Nearby towns also listed: Florence, Globe)

Superior is an old 1870s mining town of about 3,500 residents, whose winding roads reveal the dramatic vistas of the Mescal Mountains. Though it was founded by silver miners, the town's existence was ensured because of its location in one of the richest copper-mining areas of the state. It's only a few miles from Globe, Florence, and Boyce-Thompson Arboretum.

Information: **Superior Chamber of Commerce** | 151 Main St., Superior, 85273 | 520/689–0200 | www.superior-arizona.com/chamber.htm.

Attractions

Boyce Thompson Arboretum. A "living museum" about 3 mi west of Superior at the foot of Picketpost Mountain, this is a beautiful place to spend an afternoon. Native Sonoran Desert flora coexists alongside exotic specimens from all over the world. Well-marked, self-guided trails traverse 35 acres of varied desert habitats, from gravelly open desert to lush creek-side glades. The Smith Interpretive Center is a National Historic Landmark with two greenhouses and other exhibits. You can also buy desert plants, take in educational talks on regional flora, or have a picnic. It's administered by the University of Arizona in Tucson. | 37615 U.S. 60 | 520/689–2723 | ag.arizona.edu/BTA | $5 | Daily 8–5.

Dining

Buckboard Restaurant. American. This casual spot is adjacent to the World's Smallest Museum and sees a lot of customers who are traveling along the highway. Popular items include the charbroiled chicken breast and the taco salad. | 1111 W. U.S. Hwy. 60 | 520/689–5800 | Breakfast also available; no supper | $3–$8 | AE, D, DC, MC, V.

Lodging

El Portal Motel. Built in the 1950s, this single-story motel is within 1 mi of a number of hiking trails. There are a handful of restaurants within walking distance. Refrigerators, cable TV. Laundry facilities. | 577 W. Kiser St. | 520/689–2886 | fax 520/689–2886 | 16 rooms | $35 | No credit cards.

TEMPE

MAP 3, E7

(Nearby towns also listed: Chandler, Mesa, Phoenix, Scottsdale)

When Charles Trumbell Hayden arrived at the east end of the Salt River in the 1860s, he built a flour mill and began a ferry service to cross the river (then called the Rio Salado). The town he founded was called Hayden's Ferry. When other settlers began to arrive, they thought the butte, river, and fields of green mesquite looked like the Vale of Tempe in Greece. While Hayden disagreed with the name change, he finally relented in 1879, and Tempe was officially named.

Today, Tempe is Arizona's sixth-largest city and the home to its largest institution of higher learning, Arizona State University. A 20- to 30-minute drive southeast of Phoenix, the city's main street is Mill Avenue (where the Hayden mill still stands), and it's lined with student-oriented hangouts, bookstores, boutiques, and restaurants.

Information: **Tempe Chamber of Commerce** | 909 E. Apache Blvd., Box 28500, Tempe, 85285-8500 | 480/967–7891 | www.tempechamber.org.

Attractions

Arizona Cardinals. The Cardinals were one of the charter teams of the National Football League, and they are actually the oldest continuously run professional football franchise in the country, having begun playing in 1898 in Chicago. After 28 years in St. Louis, the team moved to Arizona in 1988 and now plays in the Sun Devil Stadium on the Arizona State University campus. | Stadium Dr. at 6th St. | 602/379–0102 | www.azcardinals.com.

Arizona State University. What started out in 1866 as the Tempe Normal School for Teachers, with a four-room redbrick building and a 20-acre cow pasture, is now the largest university in the Southwest and, with almost 50,000 students, the third-largest in the United States. Some campus highlights include an auditorium designed by Frank Lloyd Wright, a good art museum, and the impressive Sun Devil Stadium. You can pick up a brochure for a self-guided walking tour of the 750-acre campus at the ASU Visitor Information Center, which is a good place to begin your visit. | Visitor Information Center: 826 E. Apache Blvd., at Rural Rd. | 480/965–9011 | www.asu.edu | Free | Visitor center weekdays 9–5.

ASU Art Museum at the Nelson Fine Arts Center. This gray-purple building on the west end of campus, north of Gammage Auditorium, houses a nice collection of 19th- and 20th-century paintings and sculptures, including works by Edward Hopper, Georgia O'Keeffe, and Norman Rockwell. For a small museum, the collection is extensive. | Mill Ave. and 10th St. | 480/965–2787 | asuam.fa.asu.edu/homepage.htm | Free | Tues.–Sat. 10–5 (during school year, until 9 Tues.), Sun. 1–5; closed Mon.

Grady Gammage Memorial Auditorium. This auditorium is the last public structure completed by architect Frank Lloyd Wright. The stage is large enough to accommodate a full symphony orchestra. The hall is noted for its superior acoustics: Wright detached the rear wall from the grand tier and balcony sections to give every patron surround-sound. If you visit when classes are in session, free half-hour guided tours are offered weekdays. | Mill Ave. at Apache Blvd. | 480/965–3434 box office, 480/965–4050 tours | Tours free; performance costs vary | Tours weekdays 1–3:30.

Matthews Center—Institute for Studies in the Arts. The Matthews Center, at the center of the campus next to Hayden Library, is home to an art gallery and to ASU's Institute for Studies in the Arts, one of the premier arts and technology research sites in the country. The second-floor gallery displays rotating exhibits by up-and-coming visual and video artists. An "intelligent stage," which is able to "participate" in a performance through computer sensors, hosts various dance and performance arts pieces throughout the year. Call ahead for a schedule of events. | University Dr. at College St., next to Hayden Library | 480/965–9438 | Gallery free; performance prices vary | Weekdays 8–5; call for performance schedule.

Sun Devil Stadium. Built into an area of land between two Tempe buttes in 1958, this towering, over-74,000-seat stadium is home to both the Arizona State Sun Devil football team and to the Arizona Cardinals NFL team. It is the largest on-campus stadium in the PAC-10 conference, and hosts the Fiesta Bowl each January, as well as numerous concert and sports events throughout the year. | 500 E. Stadium Dr. | 480/965–2381 | Ticket prices vary | Call for schedule.

Niels Petersen House Museum. A Danish immigrant built this two-story Queen Anne Victorian in 1892. The house is on the National Register of Historic Places. | 1414 W. Southern Ave. | 480/350–5151 | $1 suggested donation | Tues.–Thurs. and Sat. 10–2; closed Mon., Fri., Sun.

Tempe City Hall. This three-story glass-and-copper structure stands in the shape of an upside-down pyramid with the top floor stretching out over the precarious-looking but solid base. You can stroll around the courtyard outside, or take a peek inside during business hours. It's in downtown Tempe, right off Mill Avenue. | 31 E. 5th St. | 480/967–2001 | Free | Weekdays 8–5.

Tempe Historical Museum. A community museum with permanent displays on Tempe city history, which includes a photo archive, artifacts of the early settlers who came to farm and work at Hayden's mill, and historical information. The two other galleries show rotating art exhibits. | 809 E. Southern Ave. | 480/350–5100 | Free | Mon.–Thurs. and Sat. 10–5, Sun. 1–5; closed Fri.

ON THE CALENDAR

JAN.: *Fiesta Bowl.* The two top-ranked college football teams square off in this annual sports classic in ASU Sun Devil Stadium. | 800/635–5748 or 480/350–0900.

MAR.: *Baseball Spring Training.* The Anaheim Angels train at Tempe Diablo Stadium every March. | 602/438–9300.

MAR.: *MAMA Spring Festival of the Arts.* More than 600 artists exhibit woodwork, pottery, jewelry, and paintings downtown, and live entertainment fills the streets. | 480/967–4877.

DEC.: *Fiesta Bowl Block Party.* *USA Today* named this celebration one of America's top eight places to spend New Year's Eve. The festivities in downtown Tempe include music, pyrotechnics, and plenty of opportunities to cheer for your favorite team. | 800/635–5748 or 480/350–0900.

Dining

Byblos. Mediterranean. Cushy, high-backed booths, plants, and Middle Eastern artwork fill the interior at this restaurant down the road from central Tempe. The lamb dish is baked over six hours in special sauces and stuffed with rice and pine nuts; fresh halibut and shrimp dishes are also well prepared. Belly dancing bimonthly on Sunday. Kids' menu. | 3332 S. Mill Ave. | 480/894–1945 | Closed Mon. and 1st 3 wks July. No lunch Sun. | $8–$23 | AE, DC, MC, V.

Cafe Lalibela. Ethiopian. Forget silverware: Ethiopians scoop up their food with *injera*, a spongy and slightly sour bread that is simply delicious. Combo platters let you sample several of the scrumptious meats and vegetables. Photographs and baskets from Ethiopia add an authentic mood. | 849 W. University Dr. | 480/829–1939 | Closed Mon. | $5–$11 | AE, D, MC, V.

Gordon Biersch. American. Hardly your typical college-town dive, this sophisticated brewpub, part of a San Francisco–based chain, offers a wide range of fine beers. The goat cheese ravioli and the garlic fries are dynamite. Big picture windows give a sweeping view of Tempe. | 420 S. Mill Ave. | 480/736–0033 | $8–$20 | AE, D, DC, MC, V.

House of Tricks. Contemporary. This rustic restaurant in a turn-of-the-20th-century house has an innovative menu of offbeat combinations, and is one of the prettiest places to eat in Tempe. Try the Portobello mushroom with goat cheese, grilled rack of pork with a jalapeño-orange marmalade, or the lavender-and-herb-encrusted ahi tuna served in a red curry sauce with risotto cakes and sautéed greens. There are plenty of seats at the outdoor patio bar. | 114 E. 7th St. | 480/968–1114 | Closed Sun. and first 2 wks Aug. | $14–$22 | AE, D, DC, MC, V.

Hunter Steakhouse. Steak. This casual, contemporary steak house has subdued lighting, dark-color walls and linens, and dried-flower arrangements on the tables. Filet mignon and porterhouse steaks are the stars here, other good choices are the beer-battered shrimp and the salmon. Kids' menu. | 4455 S. Rural Rd. | 480/838–8388 | No lunch | $12–$22 | AE, D, DC, MC, V.

Lo Cascio. Italian. One of the best Italian restaurants in the Valley, all the southern Italian cuisine here, down to the pasta, is made from scratch. Don't let the unassuming menu or dining room fool you—basics like homemade ravioli, gnocchi, and lasagna are fresh, flavorful, and pure heaven. Try the excellent rosemary rotisserie chicken, and leave room for the creamy tiramisu. Kids' menu. | 2210 N. Scottsdale Rd. | 480/949–0334 | Closed Mon. and June–Sept. | $10–$24 | AE, D, DC, MC, V.

Macayo's Depot Cantina. Mexican. Mesquite-grilled items and fajitas star on the menu in this former train station, which is always bustling. The Baja chimichanga with chicken, covered in a spicy cheese sauce, is a local favorite, as are the green tamales and chiles rellenos. You can eat out on the patio when the weather is nice. Entertainment Wednesday–Saturday. Kids' menu. | 300 S. Ash Ave. | 480/966–6677 | $9–$20 | AE, D, DC, MC, V.

Marcello's Pasta Grill. Italian. This comfortable neighborhood joint with huge wood tables and an open kitchen keeps regulars coming with dishes like shrimp fra diavolo, chicken Francese lightly battered and fried in a lemon pulp butter, and veal marsala. Kids' menu. | 1701 E. Warner Rd. | 480/831–0800 | Closed Mon. No lunch weekends | $9–$24 | AE, DC, MC, V.

Montis La Casa Vieja. Steak. You might feel like one of the cows yourself in this enormous dining room. But don't be daunted: the atmosphere is friendly, and the filet mignon and prime rib are tasty. Historic photographs of Tempe cover the walls. | 3 W. 1st St. | 480/967–7594 | $10–$30 | AE, D, DC, MC, V.

Siamese Cat. Thai. This ultracasual Thai spot has efficient service and is filled with Thai-inspired artwork, plants, and serene colors. Try the pad Thai, garlic chicken, or the Penang beef curry with bell peppers. Wine, beer. | 5034 S. Price Rd. | 480/820–0406 | $6–$10 | AE, MC, V.

★ **Tasty Kabob.** Middle Eastern. This unassuming little eatery in a shopping center draws locals and students from nearby ASU with its delectable Persian-inspired fare. Skewers of chicken, beef, lamb, or beef tenderloin are served with a perfumed basmati rice, and the *khoresht* stew is spicy but never overwhelming. | 1250 E. Apache Blvd. | 480/966–0260 | Closed Mon. | $10–$15 | AE, D, MC, V.

Top of the Rock. American. This beautiful restaurant atop Tempe Butte, in the Buttes Hotel, has panoramic views of Phoenix through its floor-to-ceiling windows as well as superior food. The signature appetizer is a lobster napoleon (lobster layered between crispy won tons lined with Boursin cheese); as a main course, try the sugar-spiced barbecue salmon or grilled Black Angus sirloin. It's often considered one of the most romantic restaurants in the Valley. The patio is open weekends when weather permits. Entertainment weekends. Kids' menu. Sunday brunch. | 2000 Westcourt Way | 480/225–9000 | No lunch | $21–$33 | AE, D, DC, MC, V.

Lodging

Best Western Inn of Tempe. The rooms at this motel are bright and feature impressionist paintings of the desert. There is a Denny's on the grounds, but not much else of note within walking distance. Tempe's Old Town is a bit over a mile to the south. Restaurant. In-room data ports, cable TV. Pool. Hot tub. Gym. Some pets allowed. | 670 N. Scottsdale Rd. | 480/784–2233 | www.innoftempe.com | 103 rooms | $60–$130 | AE, D, DC, MC, V.

The Buttes. Nestled in desert buttes near the intersection of Interstate 10 and Highway 60, this hotel set on 25 secluded acres has dramatic Valley views. Its architecture is dramatic (the lobby's back wall is the volcanic rock itself), and the hotel is decorated with works by major regional artists and furnished with pine and saguaro-rib furniture. The restaurant is one of Tempe's top spots. 2 restaurants (*see* Top of the Rock), 3 bars, room service. In-room data ports, minibars, some microwaves, cable TV. 2 pools. 4 hot tubs, massage, sauna. 4 tennis courts. Health club, hiking, volleyball, bicycles. Children's program (ages 3–12). Laundry service. Business services. | 2000 Westcourt Way | 602/225–9000 or 800/843–1986 | fax 602/438–8622 | www.wyndham.com | 353 rooms, 4 suites | $275–$329, $475–$700 1-bedroom suites, $600–$700 2-bedroom suites | AE, D, DC, MC, V.

Embassy Suites Phoenix-Tempe/ASU Area. This all-suite hotel is 3½ mi from ASU and surrounded by malls, including Arizona Mills and the Fiesta Mall, with free shuttle service for guests. Restaurant, bar, complimentary breakfast, room service. Kitchenettes, microwaves, refrigerators, cable TV. Pool. Hot tub. Tennis. Gym. Video games. Baby-sitting. Laundry service. Business services, airport shuttle. | 4400 S. Rural Rd. | 480/897–7444 | fax 480/897–6112 | www.embassy suites.com | 224 suites | $169–$189 | AE, D, DC, MC, V.

Fiesta Inn Resort. A scattering of period pieces enliven this Mexican-style hotel set on 33 acres about 10 minutes southeast of Sky Harbor airport. Restaurant, bar, room service. In-room data ports, refrigerators, cable TV. Pool. Hot tub. Driving range, putting green, 3 tennis courts. Gym. Video games. Laundry service. Business services, airport shuttle. | 2100 S. Priest Dr. | 480/967–1441, 800/528–6481 outside AZ, 800/528–6482 in AZ | fax 480/967–0224 | www.fiestainnresort.com | 200 rooms, 70 suites | $150, $225–$275 suites | AE, D, DC, MC, V.

Holiday Inn Express. This hotel 5 mi south of Sky Harbor airport is 1 mi from Arizona Mills Mall and 5 mi from downtown Tempe. Complimentary breakfast. In-room data ports, some microwaves, some refrigerators, cable TV. Pool. Hot tub. Laundry service. Business services, airport shuttle. Pets allowed. | 5300 S. Priest Dr. | 480/820–7500 | fax 480/730–6626 | www.hiexpress.com | 160 rooms | $90–$140 | AE, D, DC, MC, V.

Innsuites Tempe/Airport. This all-suite hotel is at the intersection if Interstate 10 and Highway 60, next to the Arizona Mills Mall. Restaurant, complimentary Continental breakfast. In-room data ports, some kitchenettes, some microwaves, some refrigerators, cable TV. Pool. Hot tub. 2 tennis courts. Gym. Playground. Laundry facilities. Business services, airport shuttle. Pets allowed (fee). | 1651 W. Baseline Rd. | 480/897–7900 or 800/842–4242 | fax 480/491–1008 | www.innsuites.com | 251 suites | $89–$139 | AE, D, DC, MC, V.

La Quinta Inn Phoenix/Tempe Sky Harbor Airport. This three-story motel is southeast of Sky Harbor airport, a few blocks south of University Avenue, and 3 mi from ASU. Complimentary Continental breakfast. In-room data ports, cable TV. Pool. Putting green. Laundry service. Business services, airport shuttle. Some pets allowed. | 911 S. 48th St. | 480/967–4465 | fax 480/921–9172 | www.laquinta.co | 129 rooms, 3 suites | $99–$129 | AE, D, DC, MC, V.

Residence Inn Tempe. This all-suite hotel is less than a half mile from the Arizona Mills Outlet Mall and 4 mi from Sun Devil Stadium. Complimentary Continental breakfast. In-room data ports, kitchenettes, microwaves, refrigerators, cable TV. Pool. Hot tub. Tennis court. Basketball, gym. Laundry facilities, laundry service. Business services. Pets allowed (fee). | 5075 S. Priest Dr. | 480/756–2122 or 800/331–3131 | fax 602/345–2802 | www.residenceinn.com | 126 suites | $130–$180 | AE, D, DC, MC, V.

Rodeway Inn Airport East. This motel is 2 mi west of Sky Harbor airport, 8 mi from downtown Phoenix, and 3 mi from ASU. Complimentary Continental breakfast. Microwaves, refrigerators, cable TV. Pool. Hot tub. Laundry facilities. Business services, airport shuttle. | 1550 S. 52nd St. | 480/967–3000 | fax 480/966–9568 | www.rodewayinn.com | 100 rooms, 1 suite | $55–$129, $129–$149 suite | AE, D, DC, MC, V.

Sheraton Phoenix Airport Hotel Tempe. This hotel is 3 mi from Sky Harbor Airport, 2 mi from the Arizona Mills Mall, and 3 mi from the ASU campus. Restaurant, bar, room service. Cable TV. Indoor-outdoor pool. Hot tub. Gym. Business services, airport shuttle. | 1600 S. 52nd St. | 480/967–6600 | fax 480/829–9427 | www.sheraton.com | 210 rooms | $99–$139 | AE, D, DC, MC, V.

Tempe Mission Palms Hotel. Between the ASU campus and Old Town Tempe, this four-story courtyard hotel has a handsome lobby and an energetic young staff. It's next to to Sun Devil Stadium, which is great if you are attending an ASU sports event. Restaurant, bar. In-room data ports, some refrigerators, some in-room hot tubs, cable TV. Pool. Hot tub. 3 tennis courts. Gym. Shops. Business services, airport shuttle. Pets allowed. | 60 E. 5th St. | 480/894–1400 or 800/547–8705 | fax 480/968–7677 | www.tempemissionpalms.com | 286 rooms, 17 suites | $189–$239, $395–$389 suites | AE, D, DC, MC, V.

Phoenix/Tempe-University Travelodge. This motel is near ASU, within walking distance of Sun Devil Stadium. Complimentary Continental breakfast. Some microwaves, some refrigerators, cable TV. 2 pools. Laundry facilities. Business services. Some pets allowed (fee). | 1005 E. Apache Blvd. | 480/968–7871 | fax 480/968–3991 | www.travelodge.com | 93 rooms | $49–$89 | AE, D, DC, MC, V.

Twin Palms Hotel. This modern, seven-story hotel is a few minutes from Old Town Tempe, across the street from ASU's Grammage Auditorium. Bathrooms are a little cramped here. Bar. In-room data ports, some microwaves, cable TV. Pool. Hot tub. Driving range, putting green. Laundry facilities, laundry service. Business services, airport shuttle. | 225 E. Apache Blvd. | 480/967–9431 or 800/367–0835 | fax 480/968–1877 | www.twinpalmshotel.com | 140 rooms | $109–$139 | AE, D, DC, MC, V.

TOMBSTONE

MAP 3, H10

(Nearby towns also listed: Benson, Bisbee, Sierra Vista)

Tombstone's hills, once rich with silver ore, created a booming mining economy here in the late 1800s, making it a western boomtown that was once larger than San Francisco. The town was founded in 1877 as a mining camp called Goose Flats. Along with silver wealth came outlaws and the problems they caused, including the famous shoot-out at the OK Corral. Tombstone is best remembered for its notorious saloons and the famous gunfight, all of which were centered on Allen Street. But those days are long gone. When the mines played out, the town persevered by embracing its past, notorious and otherwise, and now it lives on tourism. You'll find staged shoot-outs and souvenir shops aplenty.

Information: Tombstone Office of Tourism | Box 917, Tombstone, 85638 | 520/457–3421 or 800/457–3423.

Attractions

Allen St. This historic section of town features the old boardwalk-style sidewalks. You'll be able to pop into numerous tacky souvenir shops, but also some genuine historic landmarks like the Birdcage Theater. | Allen St. | Free | Daily.

Bird Cage Theater. Once a music hall where Sarah Bernhardt and Enrico Caruso, among others, performed, it was also the site of the longest recorded poker game, which went on continuously from 1881 to 1889 (eight years, five months, and three days). When the silver mines closed down in 1889, so did the Bird Cage. But the owners locked it up tight, threw nothing away, and finally reopened it as a tourist attraction in 1995. Even the basement, which was once a bordello, was reopened to the public for the first time since 1889. | 517 E. Allen St. | 520/457–3421 | $4.50 | Daily 8–6.

Boothill Graveyard. The victims of the OK Corral shoot-out are buried in this graveyard, in the northwest corner facing U.S. 80, along with many others, including Chinese laborers who came from San Francisco during the mining boom. About a third of the graves here are unmarked. You enter through a gift shop. | U.S. 80 W | 520/457–9344 | Free | Daily.

Crystal Palace Saloon. The beautiful mahogany bar, wrought-iron chandeliers, and tin ceilings at this working saloon date from Tombstone's heyday. Locals come on weekends, when there is live music. | 5th and Allen Sts. | 520/457–3611 | www.crystalpalacesaloon.com | Free | Sun.–Thurs. 10–10, Fri.–Sat. 10 AM–1 AM.

OK Corral. This is the famous site of the 1881 shoot-out, in which the Earp family and Doc Holliday battled to the death with the Clanton boys. A recorded voice-over details the town's most famous event, while life-size figures are posed in the gunmen's positions. A live shoot-out show is held daily at 2 PM. | 308 E. Allen St., between 3rd and 4th Sts. | 520/457–3456 | www.ok-corral.com | $2.50 | Daily 8:30–5; show daily at 2.

Fly Exhibit Gallery. This gallery showcases a collection of photographs taken by C. S. Fly, whose studio was next door to the OK Corral. Geronimo and his pursuers were among the historical figures he captured on camera. Admission is included with the OK Corral. | OK Corral, 308 E. Allen St. | 520/457–3456 | www.ok-corral.com | Free, with OK Corral admission | Daily 8:30–5.

Rose Tree Inn Museum. This museum was originally a boardinghouse and later a popular hotel. You can tour the 1880s period rooms and take a look at the giant rosebush, which may be the world's largest. Planted in 1885, the bush is 10 ft tall; its trunk has a circumference of 16 ft and shows almost 8,000 square ft of foliage when it blooms each April. | 116 S. 4th St. | 520/457–3326 | $2 | Daily 9–5.

Tombstone Chamber of Commerce and Visitor Center. Pick up a detailed map of the area that highlights all the attractions and unmarked sights in Tombstone. You can also obtain dining and lodging listings. | 4th and Allen Sts. | 520/457–3929 | www.cityoftombstone | Free | Weekdays 9–4, weekends 10–4.

Tombstone Courthouse State Historic Park. Displays here include a reconstruction of the original 1882 courtroom, area artifacts such as mining equipment and buggies, and photos of the town's earliest residents and mining-industry entrepreneurs. | Toughnut and 3rd Sts. off Rte. 80 | 520/457–3311 | $2.50 | Daily 8–5.

Tombstone Epitaph. Arizona's oldest continuously published newspaper printed its first issue in 1880. Now the monthly issues focus on themes and events in western history. In its office, you can see the original 19th-century printing presses. | 9 S. 5th St. | 520/457–2211 | Free | Daily.

Tombstone's Historama. Vincent Price narrates this half-hour multimedia presentation of Tombstone's history. The town fires, the mining boom, and of course the infamous gunfight, are featured. | 308 E. Allen St. | 520/457–3456 | fax 520/457–2211 | $2.50 | Daily 9–4.

ON THE CALENDAR

MAY: *Wyatt Earp Days.* Gunfights, chile cook-offs, a fiddling contest, food, and children's activities make up this annual Memorial Day weekend event. | 520/457–3421 or 800/457–3423.

SEPT.: *Rendezvous of Gunfighters.* Wild West reenactments, games, and food enliven this Labor Day weekend event. | 520/457–3421 or 800/457–3423.

OCT.: *Helldorado.* Three days of 1880 Tombstone events are reenacted here, including the infamous shoot-out at the OK Corral. | 520/457–3421 or 800/457–3423.

Dining

Longhorn. American/Casual. This busy, noisy family restaurant was originally the Bucket of Blood Saloon, back in the days of Wyatt Earp and Bat Masterson. Today it serves up a satisfying, eclectic menu of American, Mexican, and Italian dishes. Try the Saturday-night prime-rib special or the beef-back ribs. Wine, beer. | 501 E. Allen St. | 520/457–3405 | Breakfast also available | $9–$30 | MC, V.

Nellie Cashman. American. This restaurant has stuck to its historic roots, with a waitstaff dressed in period garb. Try the breaded liver or Arizona-grown pork chops. The building, which dates from 1879, is the oldest in Tombstone. | 117 S. 5th St. | 520/457–2212 | Breakfast also available | $7–$27 | AE, D, MC, V.

Lodging

Best Western Lookout Lodge. Touches like Victorian-style lamps and locally made wooden clocks give these rooms more character than the typical motel. Views of the Dragoon Mountains are spectacular. Complimentary Continental breakfast. Cable TV. Pool. Business services. Some pets allowed (fee). | U.S. 80 W | 520/457–2223 | fax 520/457–3870 | 40 rooms | $68–$84 | AE, D, DC, MC, V.

Priscilla's Bed and Breakfast. Two blocks from the OK Corral, this 1904 Victorian, furnished with period antiques, is the perfect place to stay if you want to experience the history and romance of the Wild West. The inn is the sole surviving two-story clapboard house in town, and it's just two blocks off Allen Street. Complimentary breakfast. No TV in some rooms, no room phone, TV in common area. No smoking. | 101 N. 3rd St. | 520/457–3844 | www.tombstone1880.com/priscilla | 3 rooms (with shared bath), 1 suite | $59 rooms, $69 suite | AE, MC, V.

Tombstone Boarding House Bed & Breakfast. These two meticulously restored 1880s adobe homes sit side by side in a quiet residential neighborhood, away from the bustle of Allen Street. Rooms are spotless and are furnished with period antiques. Restaurant, complimentary breakfast. No room phones, TV in common area. Library. Some pets allowed. No smoking. | 108 N. 4th St. | 520/457–3716 | fax 520/457–3038 | 6 rooms, 1 cabin | $65–$80 rooms, $60 cabin | MC, V.

Tombstone Bordello B&B. The last remaining bordello in town moved to Allen Street in the 1920s. It's now a B&B decorated in a restrained Victorian style. It's charming, yet small, with views of the Dragoon Mountains from the porch and balcony. Complimentary breakfast. Cable TV, no room phones. Some pets allowed. | 101 W. Allen St. | 520/457–2394 | 2 rooms | $59–$69 | No credit cards.

Tombstone Motel. Right on the town's main street, this comfortable and well-run motel with basic rooms is catercorner from the offices of the *Tombstone Epitaph*. It will remind you of motor courts of years past. Some refrigerators, cable TV. Some pets allowed. | 502 E. Fremont St. | 520/457–3478 or 888/455–3478 | www.tombstonemotel.com | 12 rooms, 1 suite | $45–$70, $90–$120 suite | MC, V.

TUBA CITY

(Nearby towns also listed: Flagstaff, Kayenta, Page)

With a population of about 12,000, Tuba City is the headquarters of the western portion of the Navajo Nation. Aside from a couple of motels and restaurants, there's not much in this isolated town about 80 mi northeast of Flagstaff, but it could be a base if you are visiting this region of northeastern Arizona and wish to venture farther than Wupatki National Monument (*see* Flagstaff). This is certainly one of the most beautiful regions of the Painted Desert.

Information: Navajoland Tourism Dept. | Box 663, Window Rock, 86515 | 520/871–7371 or 520/871–6436.

Attractions

Cameron Trading Post. Twenty-nine miles southwest of Tuba City stands this historic enterprise, now known as a great place to buy authentic Navajo and Hopi jewelry, rugs, baskets, and pottery. The post also includes a restaurant, a cafeteria, a post office, a motel, a grocery store, and a butcher shop. | U.S. 89 at AZ 64. | 520/679–2244 or 520/679–2231 | Free | Daily.

Dinosaur Tracks. Some well-preserved dilophosaurus tracks can be viewed at this site about 5½ mi west of Tuba City, between mileposts 316 and 317 of U.S. 160. | U.S. 160 | No phone | Free | Daily.

Tuba City Trading Post. Founded in the 1880s, this octagonal trading post sells authentic Navajo, Hopi, and Zuni rugs, pottery, baskets, and jewelry as well as groceries. | Main St. and Moenabe Rd. | 520/283–5441 | Free | Daily.

ON THE CALENDAR

JAN.–DEC.: *Swap Meet.* Each Friday, jewelry, rugs, pottery, and other arts and crafts are put up for sale behind the community center, next to the baseball field. | 520/283–5255.
OCT.: *Western Navajo Fair.* This colorful, week-long local event features performances of traditional Navajo songs and dances, a powwow, parades, concerts, arts and crafts displays, rodeos, a carnival, and a free barbecue. | 520/283–4716.

Dining

Hogan Restaurant. Southwestern. This spot next to the Quality Inn Tuba City offers a menu of mostly southwestern and Mexican dishes like chicken enchiladas and beef tamales. It has a nondescript western coffee shop atmosphere, but the food is good. | Main St./Hwy. 264 | 520/283–5260 | Breakfast also available | $7–$10 | AE, D, DC, MC, V.

Kate's Café. American/Casual. This all-American café is a local favorite. Though you might have to wait a bit, for local color and fine, reasonably priced food, this is the place. | Edgewater and Main Sts. | 520/283–6773 | Breakfast also availble | $7–$12 | No credit cards.

Tuba City Truck Stop Cafe. American. This conveniently located restaurant has fast service and hearty home cooking. Try the Navajo vegetarian taco, a mix of beans, lettuce, sliced tomatoes, shredded cheese, and green chiles served open-face on succulent fry bread. Or you might consider mutton stew served with fry bread and hominy. | Hwy. 264 at U.S. 160 | 520/283–4975 | Breakfast also available | $6–$12 | MC, V.

Lodging

Quality Inn Tuba City. The standard rooms at this motel are spacious and well maintained. The Tuba City Trading Post is also here. It's fine for an overnight stop before or after a visit to the Hopi Mesas between Tuba City and Kayenta. Restaurant. Some in-room data ports, some in-room safes, cable TV. Laundry facilities. Business services. Pets allowed. | Main St. and Moenabe Rd. | 520/283–4545 or 800/644–8383 | fax 520/283–4144 | www.qualityinn.com | 80 rooms | $102 | AE, D, DC, MC, V.

TUBAC

MAP 3, F10

(Nearby towns also listed: Nogales, Tucson)

About halfway between Tucson and Nogales, Tubac played several important roles in early Arizona history. Established in 1752, it was the site of the first European settlement in Arizona. Juan Batista de Anza led 240 colonists from here to establish San Francisco in 1776. In 1860 it was the largest town in Arizona; Arizona's first newspaper, the *Weekly Arizonan,* was started here in 1859. Today, it's a quiet little town of almost 1,100 that plays host to a small artists' community (there are about 30 local galleries) and a beautiful farming area that relies on agriculture and tourism for its livelihood. Six miles north of Tubac is the equally small town of Amado.

© Corbis

THE DESERT'S FRAGILE GIANT

Saguaro cacti punctuate the desert landscape. Easy to anthropomorphize because they have "arms," saguaros are thought to be the descendants of tropical trees that lost their leaves and became dormant during drought. Recognizably modern species of cactus came into being between 3 and 10 million years ago, and *Carnegiea gigantea* (the saguaro's scientific name) grows nowhere else on earth than the Sonoran Basin, an area that includes southern Arizona and northern Mexico.

Tourists are often amazed to find that these odd-looking plants actually bloom. But, in fact, the saguaro blossom is Arizona's state flower. Each bloom opens only for a few evening hours after sunset in May or June. The next afternoon, the creamy-white chalice closes forever. Each adult saguaro produces six or seven flowers a day for about a month. They are cross-pollinated by bees, Mexican white-winged doves, and brown bats.

Because the saguaro stores massive quantities of water (enough to conceivably last two years), it is often called the "cactus camel." New saguaros are born when the seeds of the flower take root, an arduous process. Late freezes and even high heat can kill a seedling in its first days. Once a seed is established, it grows up under the protection of a "nurse" tree, such as a paloverde. Fully grown, a saguaro can weigh as much as 7 tons.

The saguaro, like many wild plants, is protected by Arizona law. Without an Arizona Department of Agriculture permit, it is illegal to move a saguaro or sell one from private property. And the saguaro has its own means of protecting itself from would-be poachers or vandals. In the early 1980s, a hunter fired a shotgun at a large saguaro near Phoenix. It collapsed onto him, killing him instantly.

Information: **Tuba City Chamber of Commerce** | Box 1866, Tubac, 85646 | 520/398–2704 | www.tubacaz.com.

Attractions

Tubac Center for the Arts. This gallery and performance space was created by the Santa Cruz Valley Art Association to showcase the work of local artists. There are three galleries as well as a performance stage and a shop. | 9 Plaza Rd. | 520/398–2371 | az.arts.asu.edu/tubac | Free | Tues.–Sat. 10–4:30, Sun. 1–4:30 (also open Mon. from Thanksgiving–Apr. 15).

Tubac Presidio State Historic Park and Museum. Sections of an original 1752 Spanish presidio are displayed 20 mi north of Tubac at this site. Within walking distance is Tubac's 1855 original schoolhouse, as well as a picnic area. | Presidio Dr. | 520/398–2252 | www.pr.state.az.us | $2 | Daily 8–5.

Tumácacori National Historic Park. Although this site 3 mi south of Tubac was visited by missionary Father Eusebio Francesco Kino in 1691, the Jesuits didn't build a church here until 1751. You can still see some of its ruins, but the main attraction is the well-preserved mission of San José de Tumácacori, built by the Franciscans between 1709 and 1803, which became a national monument in 1908 to protect it from looters drawn by persistent rumors of the wealth left behind by the Franciscans and Jesuits. | I–19, exit 29 | 520/422–3223 | www.nps.gov/tuma | $2 | Daily 8–5.

ON THE CALENDAR
FEB.: *Tubac Festival of the Arts.* High-quality arts and crafts are exhibited and sold. | 520/398–2704.

Dining

Cantina Romantica. Southwestern. This restaurant is in an historic adobe hacienda on the grounds of Rex Ranch, 6 mi north of Tubac. Try the Guaymas shrimp or blackened chicken salad. Wine, beer. | 131 Amado Montosa Rd., Amado | 520/398–2914 | $11–$27 | AE, D, DC, MC, V.

Lodging

Amado Territory Inn. Handmade Mexican furniture enriches this B&B where balconies offer Santa Rita Mountain views. On the property, which was built in 1996, you'll find a nursery filled with plants, the office of a naturopathic doctor, and a certified massage therapist. A two-bedroom house with a full kitchen is also available for larger groups. Restaurant, complimentary breakfast, picnic area. No room phones, no TV. Putting green. Library. No smoking. No kids under 12. No pets allowed. | 3001 E. Frontage Rd., Amado | 520/398–8684 or 888/398–8684 | fax 520/398–8186 | www.amado-territory-inn.co | 9 rooms, 1 house | $105–$135, $350 house | MC, V.

Burro Inn. In the rolling hills just west of the village of Tubac, this small inn offers views of a reservoir that's popular with wild animals, and you'll be given complimentary carrots to feed the owner's two sweet burros. Though the atmosphere here is rustic, the rooms are modern, but not particularly stunning. Restaurant, bar. Kitchenettes, microwaves, refrigerators, cable TV. No pets. | 70 W. El Burro La. | 520/398–2281 | 4 suites | $124 | D, MC, V.

Tubac Golf Resort & Restaurant. This property just north of Tubac was originally the Otero Hacienda, which was established on the first land grant in Arizona issued by the King of Spain. The main hacienda has been restored, and accommodations are in casitas dotting the property. The pool area has mountain views, and many rooms have fireplaces. Restaurant, bar. Some kitchenettes, refrigerators. Pool. 18-hole golf course, putting green, tennis. Laundry facilities. | 1 Otero Rd. | 520/398–2211 or 800/848–7893 | fax 520/398–9261 | www.arizonaguide.com/tubac | 32 rooms, 9 suites | $135, $165–$225 suites | AE, MC, V.

TUCSON

MAP 3, F9

(Nearby towns also listed: Benson, Sells, Tubac)

Tucson is the oldest continuously inhabited city in the United States; the Hohokam settled here as early as AD 100. The Spanish were the first Europeans to settle here, and Tucson became part of Mexico when that colony declared its independence from Spain in 1820. It became part of the United States under the Gadsden Purchase of 1854. Its name is derived from the Pima Indian name "chuk son," which means "spring at the foot of a black mountain."

When the Butterfield stage line was extended to Tucson in the 1850s, it brought along adventurers, settlers, and more than a few outlaws. The railroad came in 1880, and the University of Arizona in 1891, though Arizona didn't become a state until 1912. The city's population really began to grow during World War II, when the Davis-Monthan Air Force Base was opened and brought with it an aerospace industry. However, as in Phoenix, folks could not live comfortably here year-round until the development of modern air-conditioning in the 1950s. Nowadays, more businesses and people relocate because of the lower cost of living here, the cleaner environment, and the spectacular scenery.

Although it's Arizona's second-largest city and a fast-growing metropolitan area of over 725,000 people, Tucson still feels like a small town. Perhaps this is because, while the city is a bustling center of business, it's also a laid-back university and resort town, popular for the warm sun and 320 days of clear weather a year. The population increases every winter, when average daytime temperatures are 65°F, and 38°F at night.

Tucson has a tri-cultural (Hispanic, Anglo, Native American) population and plenty of visitors. It's particularly popular among golfers, but it's also known as the home of world-class museums, a copper and cattle market, and the best Sonoran Mexican food north of the border. The recent influx of residents and visitors has given the city some growing pains, including questions regarding development and pollution control, which are now being addressed by city planners.

Information: **Metropolitan Tucson Convention and Visitors Bureau** | 130 S. Scott Ave., Tucson, 85701 | 520/624–1817 | www.visittucson.org.

NEIGHBORHOODS

Fourth Avenue. From University Boulevard to 9th Street, this is a colorful, vibrant, shopping district near the university. There are also several bars and restaurants around which Tucson nightlife centers.

Downtown Arts District. This is where you'll find the largest concentration of art galleries in Tucson. The Arts District encompasses Broadway and Congress Street from 4th Avenue to Stone Street; many galleries are also on 5th and 6th avenues between Broadway and Congress.

Armory Park. Bordered by 12th and 19th streets and Stone and 3rd avenues, this is the city's oldest historic district. It's mostly residential, but it's a nice place to walk on cool afternoons.

El Presidio. Named for the military garrison that once occupied the neighborhood, this neighborhood is bordered by Main and Church avenues, and Franklin and Alameda streets. Here you'll find the Tucson Museum of Art, along with shops and restaurants.

Barrio Historico. This historic neighborhood is characterized by adobe houses, many of which have been converted to office space. Revitalization of the area, bordered by Cushing Street, 18th Street, Stone Avenue, and the railroad tracks, is ongoing.

South Tucson. Home to the city's first-rate Mexican restaurants, this area of Tucson is home as well to many Mexican-American businesses.

TRANSPORTATION

Airports: Tucson International Airport | 7250 S. Tucson Blvd. is 8½ mi south of downtown, west of I–10 (520/573–8000). Check plane fares carefully if you are considering flying into Tucson. Though you may not want to spend time in Phoenix, it's sometimes much cheaper to fly into that city and then take a 1½-hour drive down Interstate 10.

Airport Transportation: Since a car is a virtual requirement if you want to explore Tucson, it makes sense to rent at the airport: all the major agencies are represented. The driving time from the airport to the center of town varies, but it's usually less than half an hour.

Taxi rates vary widely; they are unregulated in Arizona. It's always wise to inquire about the cost of a trip before getting into the cab. You shouldn't pay much more than $18 from the airport to central Tucson. A few of the more reliable cab companies are **ABC** (520/623–7979), **Airline Taxi** (520/977–7999), and **Fiesta Taxi** (520/622–7777).

Arizona Stagecoach (520/889–1000) takes groups and individuals to all parts of Tucson for $8.50–$26, depending on the location.

Train Lines: Amtrak (400 E. Toole St. | 520/623–4442) offers service to Tucson three times a week, going both eastbound and westbound.

Bus Lines: The **Greyhound Bus Terminal** | 4 S. 4th Ave. (520/792–3475 or 800/231–2222) is a hub for service from all over the country.

DRIVING AND PARKING

While downtown Tucson is laid out on a fairly regular grid, the system doesn't work much beyond this small area. In general, major streets are spaced at intervals of 1 mi, with smaller streets filling in the space in between. The city is sliced diagonally by Interstate 10 from northwest to southeast, but unlike Phoenix, Tucson is not ringed by major freeways, and most of your driving will be on surface streets.

A car is a necessity in Tucson since public transportation is fairly limited. Much of the year, traffic isn't especially heavy, but during the busiest winter months (December through March), streets in central Tucson can get congested. You should also consider adding a little extra driving time during rush hours (7:30 AM–9 AM and 4:30 PM–6 PM).

Parking is not a problem in most parts of town; you'll find it plentiful and free. Downtown is still not such a difficult place in which to find a parking space, and lots are relatively inexpensive. There are also plenty of metered spaces on the smaller downtown side streets to supplement the large lots near the Convention Center and garages underneath the public library and El Presidio Park. Virtually all Tucson hotels and resorts offer free parking.

Attractions

ART AND ARCHITECTURE

Pima County Courthouse. This beautiful Spanish Colonial–style building with its mosaic-tile dome was constructed in 1927 on the site of the original adobe court of 1869. A portion of the old presidio wall can be seen in the south wing of the courthouse's second floor. | 115 N. Church St. | 520/740–3505 | Free | Weekdays 8–5.

Sosa-Carillo-Frémont House Museum. One of Tucson's oldest residences and former home of John C. Frémont, the territorial governor, it was the only building spared when the surrounding barrio was torn down to build the Tucson Convention Center. It's now administered by the Arizona State Historical Society. | 151 S. Granada Ave. | 520/622–0956 | Free | Wed.–Sat. 10–4.

BEACHES, PARKS, AND NATURAL SIGHTS

"A" Mountain (Sentinel Peak). Just off Congress Street, you may drive around up to the top of this mountain for a great view of downtown Tucson. | Free | Daily.

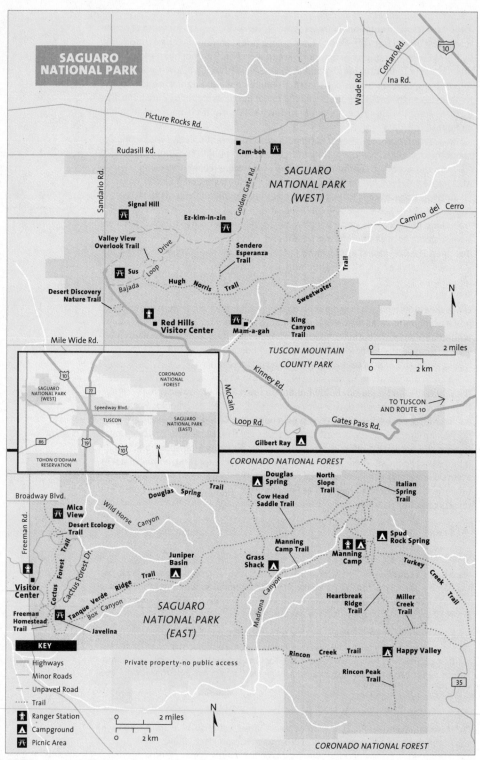

SAGUARO NATIONAL PARK

Picture Rocks Rd.

Wade Rd.

Cortaro Rd.

Ina Rd.

10

Rudasill Rd.

Cam-boh

SAGUARO
NATIONAL PARK
(WEST)

Golden Gate Rd.

Camino del Cerro

Sandario Rd.

Signal Hill

Ez-kim-in-zin

Valley View
Overlook Trail

Drive

Sendero
Esperanza
Trail

Sweetwater Trail

Loop

Sus

Bajada

Hugh Norris Trail

Desert Discovery
Nature Trail

Red Hills
Visitor Center

Mam-a-gah

King
Canyon
Trail

Mile Wide Rd.

TUSCON MOUNTAIN
COUNTY PARK

0   2 miles

0   2 km

Kinney Rd.

10

CORONADO
NATIONAL
FOREST

77

SAGUARO
NATIONAL PARK
(WEST)

Speedway Blvd.

TUCSON

SAGUARO
NATIONAL PARK
(EAST)

86

19

10

TOHON O'ODHAM
RESERVATION

McCain

Loop Rd.

Gates Pass Rd.

TO TUSCON
AND ROUTE 10

Gilbert Ray

CORONADO NATIONAL FOREST

Douglas
Spring

North
Slope
Trail

Italian
Spring
Trail

Broadway Blvd.

Douglas   Spring   Trail

Cow Head
Saddle Trail

Mica
View

Wild Horse   Canyon

Desert Ecology
Trail

Manning
Camp Trail

Spud
Rock Spring

Freeman Rd.

Cactus   Forest   Trail

Juniper
Basin

Grass
Shack

Manning
Camp

Turkey   Creek   Trail

Cactus Forest Dr.

Tanque Verde   Ridge   Trail

Visitor
Center

Madrona   Canyon

Box   Canyon

Heartbreak
Ridge
Trail

Miller
Creek
Trail

Freeman
Homestead
Trail

SAGUARO
NATIONAL PARK
(EAST)

Javelina

KEY

Private property-no public access

Rincon   Creek   Trail

Happy Valley

Highways

Rincon Peak
Trail

35

Minor Roads

Unpaved Road

Trail

Ranger Station

Campground

Picnic Area

0   2 miles

0   2 km

CORONADO NATIONAL FOREST

Catalina State Park. This 5,500-acre park 9 mi north of town draws people for hiking, birding, and picnicking. The park is crisscrossed with hiking trails; one of them, an easy two-hour walk, leads to the Romero Pools, a series of natural *tinajas*, or stone tanks, filled with water much of the year. | Hwy. 77 | 520/628–5798 | www.pr.state.az.us | $5 per vehicle | Daily 7 AM–10 PM.

Colossal Cave. This limestone grotto 20 mi east of Tucson (take Broadway Boulevard or East 22nd Street to Colossal Cave Road) is the largest dry cavern in the world, parts of which have not yet been explored. Guided tours take 45 minutes. | Colossal Cave Rd. and Old Spanish Trail Rd. | 520/647–7275 | www.colossalcave.com | $7.50 | Oct.–Mar. 15, daily 9–5; Mar. 16–Sept., Mon.–Sat. 8–6, Sun. 8–7.

Coronado National Forest. The mountainous, wooded area northeast of Tucson is just a fraction of this enormous forest. It has popular hiking and camping spots. There are also opportunities for fishing, birding, and, skiing. | 5700 N. Sabino Canyon Rd. | 520/749–8700 | www.fs.fed.us | $5 per vehicle | Daily.

Madera Canyon Recreation Area. Approximately 200 mi of scenic trails make this a popular destination for hikers. Bird-watchers also flock here year-round: more than 400 bird species have been spotted in the area. It's 6½ mi southeast of Tucson; take the Continental Rd. exit off I–19. | Madera Canyon Rd. | 520/625–8746 | Free | Daily.

Sabino Canyon Recreation Area. Year-round, but especially during summer, locals flock to this oasis in the Santa Catalina foothills in northwest Tucson, which is part of the Coronado National Forest. It's a good spot for hiking, picnicking, or enjoying the waterfalls, streams, swimming holes, and shade trees. | Sabino Canyon Rd. | 520/749–8700 | Free | Park daily; visitor center daily 8–4:30.

★ **Saguaro National Park East.** About 16 mi east of central Tucson, the larger of the two parts of this national park, at 67,000 acres, is also less developed and less accessible but still protects a substantial array of saguaro cacti. The park climbs through five climate zones, which can make for dramatic hiking in the backcountry. An 8-mi drive leads to a variety of hiking trailheads. The visitor center offers a slide show and has a cactus garden. Take Speedway Boulevard or 22nd Street East. | Old Spanish Trail | 520/733–5158 | www.nps.gov/sagu | $4 per vehicle | Visitor center daily 8:30–5.

★ **Saguaro National Park West.** Dedicated to the preservation of the fragile, stately saguaro cactus, this is the smaller of two sections of the park at 24,000 acres; it's also the more visited. Together, the two sections of the park are home to the world's largest concentration of the huge cactus, which is native to the Sonoran Desert and known for its towering height (sometimes as much as 50 ft). In spring (usually April or May), the cacti sport tiny party hats of white blossoms. The impressive visitor center offers a Native American perspective of the saguaro as well as lifelike displays of the region's flora and fauna. You can also take a loop drive through the park. | 2700 N. Kinney Rd. | 520/733–5158 | www.nps.gov/sagu | Free | Visitor center daily 8:30–5.

Tohono Chul Park. You can take an easy hike through 48 beautifully landscaped desert acres of Tohono Chul Park. A restaurant and teahouse are on the premises. | 7366 N. Paseo del Norte | 520/575–8468 | www.tohonochulpark.org | $2 suggested donation | Daily 7 AM–sunset.

Tucson Botanical Gardens. This 5-acre midtown oasis is home to a sensory garden, a greenhouse, and historical gardens begun in the 1930s. It is also the headquarters of Native Seeds/SEARCH, a group that helps farmers throughout the Southwest by collecting, growing, and selling seeds native to this dry region. | 2150 N. Alvernon Way | 520/326–9255 | www.tucsonbotanical.org | $4 | Daily 8:30–4:30.

CULTURE, EDUCATION, AND HISTORY

El Tiradito (The Castaway). In the Barrio Historico District, this shrine is on the National Register of Historic Places. A bronze plaque indicates that it is dedicated to a sinner who is buried here on unconsecrated ground. | Main Ave., just south of Cushing St. | Free | Daily.

Fort Lowell Park Museum. The site of this restful park was originally a Hohokam village; centuries later, Fort Lowell was built here to protect Tucson from the Apaches. Some of the ruins of the original fort, which was abandoned in the 1890s, are preserved here in Fort Lowell County Park along with re-creations of military officers' quarters. It's administered by the Arizona Historical Society. | 2900 N. Craycroft Rd. | 520/885–3832 | w3.arizona.edu/~azhist | Free | Wed.–Sat. 10–4.

St. Augustine Cathedral. Construction began in 1896 on this imposing pink building that was modeled after the Cathedral of Querataro in Mexico. The desert influence upon the designers becomes apparent when one notices the carvings of a saguaro cactus, yucca, and horned toad next to the bronze statue of St. Augustine. | 192 S. Stone Ave. | Free | Daily.

University of Arizona. The U of A, as the University of Arizona is known, covers 352 acres and with about 35,000 students, is a great economic influence on Tucson. Many of Tucson's fine museums are on the university's campus, including the world-class Center for Creative Photography and the Arizona State Museum. Volunteers lead free walking tours of the campus during the school year. | University Visitor Center, Cherry Ave. and University Blvd. | 520/621–5130 | www.arizona.edu | Free | Campus daily; tours Sept.–May, Thurs. and Sat. at 9:30; bus tour first Sat. at 9:30.

MUSEUMS

Arizona Historical Society's Museum. This museum on the University of Arizona campus houses the offices of the Arizona State Historical Society. Exhibits focus on the history of southern Arizona, the southwestern United States, and northern Mexico. There are also rotating exhibits. A research library devoted to Southwest history also houses the historical Arizona photography collection. | 949 E. 2nd St. | 520/628–5774 | w3.arizona.edu | $3 requested donation | Mon.–Sat. 10–4, Sun. noon–4.

Arizona State Museum. The oldest museum in the state, dating from 1893, is just inside the gates of the University of Arizona. Exhibits document the state's natural and cultural history, including such exhibits as "Paths of Life: American Indians of the Southwest," which explores the cultural traditions, origins, and contemporary lives of 10 tribes native to the region. | 1013 E. University Ave. | 520/621–6302 | www.statemuseum.arizona.edu | Free | Mon.–Sat. 10–5, Sun. noon–5.

Center for Creative Photography. In addition to the excellent collection of Ansel Adams's photographs (he donated most of his negative archives to this museum), the center on the University of Arizona campus has works by many other major 20th-century photographers, including Paul Strand, W. Eugene Smith, Edward Weston, and Richard Misrach. | 1030 N. Olive Rd. | 520/621–7968 | www.creativephotography.org | $2 suggested donation | Weekdays 9–5, weekends noon–5.

De Grazia's Gallery in the Sun. The late Arizona artist Ted De Grazia depicted Native American and Mexican life in his artwork. This gallery, which was constructed only from local natural materials, houses his work. Visitors can tour his workshop, former home, and grave. | 6300 N. Swan Rd. | 520/299–9191 | Free | Daily 10–4.

History of Pharmacy Museum. This museum is home to a variety of pharmacy artifacts spanning more than 100 years. Be sure to check out the elaborate mortar-and-pestle collection. | University of Arizona, 1703 E. Mabel St. | 520/626–1427 | www.pharmacy.arizona.edu/museum | Free | Weekdays 8–5.

International Wildlife Museum. The wildlife in this museum isn't alive. On exhibit are 400 taxidermy displays in re-creations of their habitats. There are also special children's activities, including interactive computer exhibits, and a theater showing nature movies daily. | 4800 W. Gates Pass Rd. | 520/617–1439 | www.thewildlifemuseum.org | $7 | Daily 9–5.

Pima Air and Space Museum. This huge facility covering 80 acres is one of the largest private collections of its kind in the world. You'll find more than 200 aircraft on display, including an exact replica of the Wright flyer (now in the Smithsonian in Washington, DC) and a former *Air Force One* used by Presidents Kennedy and Johnson. Take Interstate 19 to exit 267, southeast of Tucson. | 6000 E. Valencia Rd. | 520/574–0462 | fax 520/574–9238 | www.pimaair.org | $7.50; special rates for children and senior citizens | Daily 9–5.

Titan Missile Museum. During the Cold War, 18 Titan II missiles ringed Tucson. The only one left is here, in this former missile silo in Sahuarita, 25 mi south of Tucson; the rest were dismantled as part of the Salt II treaty with the Soviet Union. You can tour the command post where a ground crew of four once lived. It's 20 mi south of town; take Interstate 19, exit 69. One-hour guided tours start every half hour. | 1580 W. Duval Mine Rd., Sahuarita | 520/625–7736 | $7.50 | Nov.–Apr., daily 9–5; May–Oct. Wed.–Sun 9–5.

Tucson Children's Museum. Kids are encouraged to touch and explore the exhibits here, which are geared towards science, language, and history. They can also dress up and pretend to be involved in a variety of professions, from doctor to grocery store manager. | 200 S. 6th Ave. | 520/792–9985 | $5.50; special rates for children and senior citizens | Tues., Thurs. 9–5; Wed., Fri. 9:30–5; Sat. 10–5; Sun. noon–5.

Tucson Museum of Art and Historic Block. This downtown museum, which occupies the spot where the Spanish built their original presidio, houses a permanent collection of pre-Columbian art and also hosts traveling exhibits. It underwent a major 7,000-square-ft expansion in 1998, incorporating several historic buildings into a larger design, including an 1868 adobe, the Edward Nye Fish House, which now houses the museum's collection of western American art. Admission to the museum includes three historic houses on the same block. | 140 N. Main Ave. | 520/624–2333 | www.tucsonarts.com | $2, free Tues. | Mon.–Sat. 10–4, Sun. noon–4.

J. Knox Corbett House. This two-story Mission Revival–style home was built in 1907 and is furnished with American arts-and-crafts works. It was occupied by members of the Corbett family until 1963. | 180 N. Main Ave. | 520/624–2333 | Free with TMA admission | Mon.–Sat. 10–4, Sun. noon–4.

La Casa Cordova. Constructed in 1848, this Sonoran row house is now home to the Mexican Heritage Museum. Inside you'll find an exhibit on the history of the presidio and furnishings of the Indian and pioneer settlers of the period. | 175 N. Meyer Ave., | 520/624–2333 | Free | Mon.–Sat. 10–4, Sun. noon–4.

Stevens Home. This 1865 house was the site where wealthy politician and cattle rancher Hiram Stevens entertained many of Tucson's early leaders. | 150 N. Main Ave., | 520/624–2333 | Free with TMA admission | Mon.–Sat. 10–4, Sun. noon–4.

University of Arizona Museum of Art. This small museum on the University of Arizona campus houses a collection of European paintings from the Renaissance through the 17th century, and the world's second-largest collection of bronze, plaster, and ceramic sculptures by Jacques Lipschitz. In addition, there are rotating exhibitions of work by local, national, and international artists. | N. Park Ave. and E. Speedway Blvd. | 520/621–7567 | artmuseum.arizona.edu | Free | Oct.–May, weekdays 9–5, Sun. noon–4; June–Sept, Mon.–Fri. 10–3:30, Sun noon–4.

SHOPPING

4th Avenue. The stretch of 4th Avenue near the University of Arizona, particularly between 2nd and 9th streets, is a great place to shop in artsy boutiques and secondhand stores. | 4th Ave. | Most stores open daily 10–5.

Old Town Artisans. Art and crafts by local and national artists are for sale in this quaint shopping and dining complex downtown. | 186 N. Meyer Ave. | 520/623–5787 | Mon.–Sat. 9:30–5, Sun. noon–5.

Plaza Palomino. This shopping center has a stunning array of small shops and clothing boutiques. Maya Palace and The Strand both offer Mexican imports. | 2980 N. Swan Rd., at Ft. Lowell Rd. | 520/795–1177 | Mon.–Sat. 10–6.

Tucson Mall. The city's busiest mall has more than 200 specialty shops as well as departments stores like Dillard's and Macy's. | 4500 N. Oracle Rd., at Wetmore Rd. | 520/293–7330 | Mon.–Sat. 10–9, Sun. 11–6.

SIGHTSEEING TOURS

Arizona Historical Society. The friendly, knowledgeable docents of the society conduct walking tours of the El Presidio neighborhood, departing from the Sosa-Carillo-Frémont House. | 151 S. Granada Ave. | 520/622–0956 | $5 | Nov.–Mar., Sat. at 10.

Gray Line Bus Tours. Full- and half-day tours hit the highlights of the city. Specialized tours go to Old Tucson Studios, Saguaro National Park, Biosphere 2, and the Arizona Sonora Desert Museum. Full-day excursions outside of the Tucson area, to such places as Tombstone and Nogales, are also available. Most tours are conducted daily year-round. | 181 W. Broadway | 520/622–8811 | www.grayline.com/arizona | $35–$90 | Daily.

Sunshine Jeep Tours. This company arranges trips to the Sonoran Desert in open-air four-wheel-drive vehicles. There is a two-person minimum for all tours. | 9040 N. Oracle Rd., Suite D | 520/742–1943 | fax 520/544–2639 | info@sunshineJeeptours.com | www.sunshineJeeptours.com | $50; special rates for children | Daily 8–4.

Spectator Sports

Arizona Diamondbacks. The Phoenix National League baseball team conducts spring training at Tucson Electric Park. | 2500 E. Ajo Way | 520/434–1367 | fax 520/434–1361 | www.tucsonbaseball.com | $3–$14 | Mar. (call for game schedule).

Chicago White Sox. Chicago's National League baseball team conducts spring training at Tucson Electric Park. | 2500 E. Ajo Way | 520/434–1367 | fax 520/434–1361 | www.tucsonbaseball.com | $3–$14 | Mar. (call for game schedule).

Colorado Rockies. Denver's National League baseball team conducts spring training at the U.S. West Sports Complex at Hi Corbett Field. | 3400 E. Camino Campestre | 520/327–9467 or 303/762–5437 | fax 520/434–1361 | www.coloradorockies.com | $4–$12 | Mar. (call for game schedule).

Tucson Scorch. Tucson's professional minor league hockey team plays at the Tucson Convention Center. | 260 S. Church Ave. | 520/8–SCORCH | www.tucsonscorch.com | $7–$20 | Oct.–Mar. (call for game schedule).

Tucson Sidewinders. Tucson's AAA minor-league baseball team, a farm club for the Arizona Diamondbacks, plays at Tucson Electric Park. | 2500 E. Ajo Way | 520/434–1021 | fax 520/889–9947 | www.tucsonsidewinders.com | $4.50–$8 | Apr.–Sept. (call for game schedule).

OTHER POINTS OF INTEREST

Arizona-Sonora Desert Museum. This museum 12 mi west of town is actually a zoo where you can watch rattlesnakes, javelina, and other desert critters move about in re-creations of their natural habitats. There are good displays of local flora as well. On the premises are a gift shop and two restaurants. | 2021 N. Kinney Rd. | 520/883–1380 | www.desertmuseum.org | $8.95 ($9.95 Nov.–Apr.) | Mar.–Sept., weekdays and Sun. 7:30–5, Sat. 7:30–10; Oct.–Feb., daily 8:30–5.

Asarco Mineral Discovery Center. Exhibits in two connected buildings at this facility 15 mi south of Tucson include a walk-through model of an ore crusher and videos that explain various refining processes. The biggest draw at the center is the 2-mi-long open pit of Mission Mine. | 1421 W. Pima Mine Rd., Sahuarita | 520/625–0879 | www.mineraldiscovery.com | $6; special rates for children and senior citizens | Tues.–Sat. 9–5.

Biosphere 2. This self-contained miniature universe about 20 mi north of Tucson, a half-acre under glass, housed eight people for two years. The microclimates inside include a rain forest, a marsh, an ocean, and a savanna. Guided tours include a look into the former residential areas. Though the scientific project behind the Biosphere wasn't entirely successful, the structure is intriguing. There are guided tours every half hour. | Biosphere 2 Rd. (off Hwy. 77), Oracle | 520/896–6200 | $12.95 | Daily 8:30–5.

Flandrau Science Center and Planetarium. A 16-inch public telescope and the impressive Star Theater are the main attractions at this planetarium on the University of Arizona campus. There's also an interactive mineral exhibit and other hands-on exhibits. Laser shows are held in the evening. Special adapters allow you to take photographs through the telescopes. | N. Cherry Ave. and E. University Blvd. | 520/621–7827 | www.flandrau.org | Exhibits $3, planetarium $5; special rates for children and senior citizens | Mon.–Sat. 9–5 (Wed.–Sat. also 7 PM–9 PM), Sun. 1–5; call for show schedules.

University of Arizona Mineralogical Museum. Exhibits at this museum on the lower level of the Flandrau Science Center and Planetarium exhibit over 22,000 mineral samples, including a popular collection of meteorites. The focus of the collection is on minerals from Arizona and northern Mexico. | N. Cherry Ave. and E. University Blvd. | 520/621–4227 | $3; special rates for children | Mon.–Sat. 9–5, Sun. 1–5.

Old Tucson Studios. This film set/theme park displays many of the adobe structures that have been used as movie backdrops over the years. Adults usually enjoy the screenings of old westerns. Kids love the simulated gunfights, rides, and petting farm. | 201 S. Kinney Rd., | 520/883–0100 | www.oldtucson.com | $14.95; special rates for children | Mid- Apr.–Dec., Tues.–Sat. 10–6; Jan.–mid Apr., Tues.–Sat. 9–7.

Reid Park Zoo. This small but well-designed zoo in Reid Park is a manageable place to visit. The South American enclosure and the zoo's adorable newborn animals will win over the children. The animals are most active in the morning. | 22nd and Country Club Rd. | 520/791–3204, 520/791–4022 recorded info | $4 | Daily 9–4.

ON THE CALENDAR

JAN., FEB.: *Gem and Mineral Show.* This trade show at the Tucson Convention Center offers everything from precious stones to beads. Some sessions are open to the public, while others are wholesale only. | 260 S. Church Ave. | 520/624–1817.

FEB.: *La Fiesta de los Vaqueros.* The largest outdoor mid-winter rodeo in America takes place on the Tucson Rodeo Grounds. | 4825 S. 6th Ave. | 520/741–2233.

FEB.: *Touchtone Energy Tucson Open.* A PGA golf tournament at Starr Pass and Tucson National golf courses. | 520/297–2271.

FEB.: *Tucson Rodeo Parade.* The world's largest nonmotorized parade is at the Tucson Rodeo Grounds. | 520/741–2233.

FEB.–MAR.: *Baseball Spring Training.* The Arizona Diamondbacks, the Chicago White Sox, and the Colorado Rockies get their winter kinks out at Tucson Electric Park and Hi Corbett Field. | 520/325–2621.

MAR.: *PING/Welch's LPGA Championship.* More than 140 world-class women golfers compete for $450,000 in prize money in this LPGA tournament at the Randolph North Golf Course. | 520/791–5742.

APR.: *Pima County Fair.* Fire eaters, jugglers, and hypnotists entertain at the Pima County Fairgrounds, There's also food, concerts, arts and crafts, livestock, and soccer. | 520/762–9100.

APR.: *Yaqui Easter.* In Tucson, on Ash Wednesday, you'll find the Yaqui Easter festival and traditional Yaqui dances and ceremonies. | 520/791–4609.

SEPT.–MAY: *Arizona Theatre Company.* Classic and modern plays in the Temple of Music and Art. | 520/622–2823.

SEPT.–MAY: *Tucson Symphony Orchestra.* Professional symphony with a large local following at the Tucson Convention Center. | 520/882–8585.

OCT.: *La Fiesta de los Chiles in Tucson.* Stop by the Tucson Botanical Gardens for a chile plant (there are plenty for sale) or food, music, and educational programs. | 520/326–9686.

OCT.: *Tucson Heritage Experience Festival.* Native American dancing and other cultural exhibitions round out this citywide annual. | 520/624–1817.

OCT.–MAR.: *Arizona Opera.* This highly regarded company performs classic operas in the Convention Center Music Hall. | 520/293–4336.

Dining

INEXPENSIVE

Beyond Bread. American/Casual. Scents of fresh-baked goods waft from the kitchen at this intimate, cheery neighborhood bakery/sandwich shop that consistently draws crowds. The European-style breads are crispy on the outside and flaky on the inside and are the base of sandwiches like the Bart's Bag (turkey, brie, lettuce, and tomato on a baguette) and the Brad's Beef, with roast beef and green chiles. | 3055 N. Cambell Ave. | 520/322–9965 | Breakfast also available | $2–$6 | AE, D, DC, MC, V.

Buddy's Grill. American. In the Crossroads Festival Shopping Center in midtown, this friendly family restaurant is great for sandwiches or a quick bite and also has more substantial fare like steaks and seafood. Try the chicken Sonoma. Kids' menu. | 4821 E. Grant Rd. | 520/795–2226 | $6–$17 | AE, D, DC, MC, V.

Chad's Steakhouse. Steak. This popular midtown family steak house has a southwestern-style interior filled with Native American paintings. The New York strip, prime rib, and rib-eye steak are particularly good. Kids' menu. | 3001 N. Swan | 520/881–1802 | No lunch | $13–$26 | AE, D, MC, V.

Eclectic Cafe. American. In a strip mall on the east side of town, this casual restaurant is a favorite with locals—and a good value. Everything is homemade with fresh ingredients. It's known for Mexican fare, but the sandwiches and salads are more consistent. Kids' menu. Wine, beer. No smoking. | 7053 E. Tanque Verde Rd. | 520/885–2842 | Breakfast also available weekends | $5–$12 | AE, DC, MC, V.

Govinda's Natural Foods. Vegetarian. Numerous fountains, an aviary, and a koi pond provide a resortlike setting for this Hare Krishna–run vegetarian oasis. The full salad bar offers organic mixed greens and various fresh fruit and vegetable items, and a rotating menu often includes homemade rice, bean, and tofu dishes. | 711 E. Blacklidge Dr. | 520/792–0630 | Closed Sun., Mon. | $4–$9 | MC, V.

Lotus Garden. Chinese. While you'll find the typical standards like sweet and sour chicken and lo mein on this restaurant's menu, seek out the more unusual Szechuan dishes like walnut-glazed shrimp with lotus blossoms, or sautéed spicy scallops. | 5975 E. Speedway Blvd. | 520/298–3351 | $8–$25 | AE, D, DC, MC, V.

Millie's Pancake Haus. American. Pancakes are the specialty of this friendly neighborhood restaurant that features a German-influenced American menu. Also try the thick slices of French toast or the apple strudel. Kids' menu. | 6530 E. Tanque Verde Rd. | 520/298–4250 | Breakfast also available; closed Mon., no dinner | $5–$10 | No credit cards.

Nonie. Cajun/Creole. Nonie was a prominent costume maker in the Big Easy (New Orleans) and grandmother of the owner, who learned to cook at her knee. Pictures of her and posters of Mardi Gras abound. You'll enjoy friendly service and some rollicking Cajun music at this flamboyant restaurant. You can't go wrong with crawfish étoufée followed by bread pudding for dessert. | 2526 E. Grant Rd. | 520/319–1965 | Reservations essential | Closed Mon. No lunch weekends | $7–$14 | AE, MC, V.

Pinnacle Peak Steak House. Steak. Mesquite perfumes the air of this Wild West steak house in Trail Dust Town, where your meat is served with salad and pinto beans. Hold onto your hats—there are shoot-em-ups outside on weekends. Kids' menu. | 6541 E. Tanque Verde Rd. | 520/296–0911 | Reservations not accepted | No lunch | $7–$14 | AE, D, MC, V.

Seri Melaka. Malaysian. One of Tucson's best Asian restaurants serves great *satay* (skewered barbecue with peanut sauce), *sambal* (spicy onions and meat), and *rendang* (spicy marinated beef cooked in a rich sauce with a hint of coconut)—and Dungeness crab in season. Early-bird dinners weekdays. | 6133 E. Broadway | 520/747–7811 | $10–$42 | AE, D, DC, MC, V.

Taqueria Pico de Gallo. Mexican. This casual, friendly spot in south Tucson is known for fish tacos and ceviche. | 2618 S. 6th Ave. | 520/623–8775 | $7–$15 | AE, MC, V.

Tohono Chul Tea Room. Southwestern. This casual restaurant is surrounded by a cactus garden in Tohono Chul Park, north of downtown. House favorites include seafood corn chowder served with bread and butter scones, and chicken enchiladas with Monterey Jack cheese, corn, and green chiles. Afternoon tea is served between 2:30 PM and 5 PM daily. Kids' menu. Sunday brunch. | 7366 N. Paseo del Norte | 520/797–1222 | Breakfast also available; no dinner | $6–$17 | AE, MC, V.

Zemam. Ethiopian. Always crammed with locals, this tiny, bright restaurant is decked with African dresses, baskets, and artifacts. The rich, stewlike dishes are always served with a spongy bread and eaten with the hands. Try the *zigni* (a mild beef stew in a tomato sauce) or the *yesimir wat* (spicy lentils). You can fill up for a great price, especially since you bring your own alcohol. | 2731 E. Broadway | 520/323–9928 | Closed Mon. | $6–$8 | MC, V.

MODERATE

Athens on 4th Ave. Greek. Two small, lovely rooms in simple Greek country style welcome hungry diners in this downtown restaurant. Try the sea bass, stewed lamb, or *spanakopita* (a Greek spinach pastry) with a bottle of Greek wine. | 500 N. 4th Ave. | 520/624–6886 | Closed Sun. | $9–$19 | AE, D, MC, V.

Bistro Chartreuse. Continental. You can eat outside in this small, intimate foothills restaurant, which has won 38 awards over the last eight years for their chocolate desserts. Try the game mixed grill, Norwegian salmon, or steak Diane. Tableside preparations are a common feature. The patio and balcony have wonderful mountain views. Sunday brunch. | 7117 N. Oracle Rd. | 520/575–9277 | Closed Mon. | $13–$19 | AE, D, DC, MC, V.

Café Poca Cosa. Mexican. Rather than focusing on cheese-heavy Sonoran cuisine familiar to Americans, one of Tucson's most innovative Mexican restaurants pays homage to other regions of Mexico. The changing menu usually includes *pollo à mole* (chicken in a spicy cocoa-based sauce), or pork *pibil* (tangy Yucatan barbecue), all served in a colorful and bustling downtown spot. No smoking. | 88 E. Broadway | 520/622–6400 | Reservations essential | Closed Sun. and mid-July–early Aug. | $10–$23 | MC, V.

Capriccio. Italian. This eclectic Italian restaurant 3 mi north of downtown has an interesting menu with such favorites as *osso buco* (veal shank), and more adventurous dishes like roast duckling in Grand Marnier and green peppercorn sauce or a veal porterhouse braised in a white wine sauce. | 4825 N. 1st Ave. | 520/887–2333 | Closed Mon. No lunch | $13–$22 | AE, D, DC, MC, V.

City Grill. American. This hip, contemporary restaurant has a popular singles scene, perhaps because it's one of the few restaurants in Tucson open late. Known for wood-fired pizzas, prime rib, rotisserie chicken, and seafood. Try the spicy-sweet wok-charred salmon. Kids' menu. | 6464 E. Tanque Verde | 520/733–1111 | $9–$17 | AE, D, DC, MC, V.

Daisy Mae's Steak House. Steak. This casual western-style steak house has friendly service and is 2 mi west of downtown. A 9-ounce filet mignon and the rib-eye steak are house specials. Open-air dining. Kids' menu. | 2735 W. Anklam | 520/792–8888 | No lunch | $14–$29 | AE, D, MC, V.

Daniel's. Italian. You'll find a good selection of grappas at this romantic, Art Deco, northern-Italian restaurant on St. Philip's Plaza, north of downtown. Try the pork chops stuffed with feta and pine nuts or rack of lamb, but seafood also shines. The patio overlooks St. Philip's Plaza courtyard. | 4340 N. Campbell Ave. #107 | 520/742–3200 | $17–$32 | AE, D, DC, MC, V.

Delectables Restaurant. Eclectic. The oak furniture, exposed-beam ceiling, and old-fashioned lamps give this relaxed and friendly downtown option a warm glow. Asparagus and leek crêpes in a cheese-and-lemon sauce are hearty and flavorful, as is the spinach-and-chicken enchilada. Try the featherlight chocolate mousse for dessert. Open-air dining. Wine, beer. | 533 N. 4th Ave. | 520/884–9289 | $9–$19 | AE, D, DC, MC, V.

The Dish. Contemporary. This tiny, 12-table midtown restaurant has generally been a secret known only to the savviest locals. Hidden behind the Rum Runner wine shop, the menu offers both "small dishes," such as saffron mussels, and "big dishes," such as penne Piacenza. | 3200 E. Speedway Blvd. | 520/326–1714 | Closed Sun., Mon. | $15–$25 | AE, D, DC, MC, V.

El Charro Café. Mexican. Opened in 1922, this is the oldest Mexican restaurant in the United States. It still serves excellent Sonoran-Mexican staples like chimichangas and cheese crisps. Especially good is the *carne asada* (dried beef) chimichanga. In nice weather there's a beautiful outdoor patio. Kids' menu. | 311 N. Court Ave. | 520/622–1922 | $7–$16 | AE, D, DC, MC, V.

El Minuto Cafe. Mexican. Always busy, this brightly colored restaurant in Tucson's historic barrio is the place to come for world-renowned carne seca, a dried, cured beef which takes days to prepare. Also try the red chile and menudo soup, and the light and flaky sopaipillas for dessert. | 354 S. Main | 520/882–4145 | $10–$20 | AE, D, DC, MC, V.

Evangelo's. Continental. This elegant restaurant is in the foothills north of Tucson. Open-air dining. Kids' menu. | 4405 W. Speedway Blvd. | 520/792–3055 | Closed Mon. No lunch | $22–$32 | AE, D, DC, MC, V.

Kingfisher Bar and Grill. American. One of the best moderately priced restaurants in town has a loyal following, who come for the regional American cuisine and chic setting. It's known for seafood, including soft-shell crab flown in fresh in season. But also consider mesquite-grilled pork chops or crawfish étouffée. Blues/jazz band Monday. Kids' menu. | 2564 E. Grant Rd. | 520/323–7739 | No lunch weekends | $9–$27 | AE, D, DC, MC, V.

La Fuente. Mexican. This traditional Sonoran-Mexican restaurant north of downtown is a longtime local favorite, and it's always friendly and bustling. Try the mole poblano (with a spicy, chocolaty sauce), steak picado, or pastella steak. Kids' menu. Sunday brunch. | 1749 N. Oracle Rd. | 520/623–8659 | Closed Mon. June–Aug. | $9–$25 | AE, DC, MC, V.

La Placita Cafe. Mexican. This charming restaurant specializes in seafood, particularly the cuisine of Oaxaca and Guaymas. House specials include a grilled white fish with chiles, tomatoes, and onions; garlic shrimp; and stuffed jalapenos. | 2950 N. Swan Rd. | 520/881–1150 | No lunch Sun. | $6–$17 | AE, D, DC, MC, V.

Le Bistro. French. This small, quaint, plant-filled restaurant is one of the prettiest in town. It's known for such dishes as supreme of salmon with ginger crust, and roast duck with a raspberry vinaigrette. | 2574 N. Campbell Ave. | 520/327–3086 | No lunch Sat.–Mon. | $12–$22 | AE, D, MC, V.

Mariscos Chihuahua. Mexican. Specializing in Mexican seafood dishes, this lively and bright spot is usually hopping for lunch and dinner. The *tostadas ceviche,* loads of uncooked, marinated seafood piled on a tortilla and spiced with salsa, is light and refreshing, and the Seven Seas soup, full of fish and shellfish, is warm and hearty. No alcohol. | 1009 N. Grande Ave. | 520/623–3563 | $16–$19 | No credit cards.

Metropolitan Grill. Steak. There's an open kitchen at this casual foothills restaurant known for rotisserie-cooked meats, including prime rib, pork loin, and roasted chicken. In good weather you can dine on a covered patio. Kids' menu. | 7892 N. Oracle Rd. | 520/531–1212 | $10–$18 | AE, D, DC, MC, V.

New Delhi Palace. Indian. This nice Indian restaurant has a wide-ranging menu of tandoori dishes, curries, and breads. Try the shrimp vindaloo in a tangy tomato base with potatoes or *karhai aloo palak* (curried potatoes in a cream and spinach base). | 6751 E. Broadway, | 520/296–8585 | Reservations essential | $9–$22 | AE, DC, MC, V.

Saguaro Corners. American. This restaurant is at once kitschy and old world, with desert wildlife feeding right outside the window as you munch on seafood, prime rib, and filet mignon. It's ¼ mi south of Saguaro National Park East. Kids' menu. | 3750 S. Old Spanish Trail | 520/886–5424 | Closed Mon. | $9–$19 | AE, D, DC, MC, V.

Wildflower Grill. Contemporary. The chef at this trendy restaurant came from Wolfgang Puck's Spago, and the influence shows. Try the ahi sashimi, rack of lamb, or grilled quail with mushroom risotto. | 7037 N. Oracle Rd. | 520/219–4231 | $12–$29 | AE, D, DC, MC, V.

EXPENSIVE

Café Terra Cotta. Southwestern. Owners Donna Nordin and Don Luria were pioneers of southwestern cuisine at this restaurant 5 mi north of downtown in St. Phillip's Plaza shopping center. Try prawns stuffed with herbed goat cheese on a tomato coulis or tortilla-crusted chicken breast with garlic and goat cheese sauce, orzo, and black-bean corn salsa. There are great city views from the outdoor patio. | 3500 E. Sunrise Dr. | 520/577–8100 | fax 520/527–9015 | www.cafeterracotta.com | $12–$25 | AE, D, DC, MC, V.

Firecracker. Pan-Asian. Popular with young professionals, this bustling, bright, and airy restaurant serves inventive Chinese-influenced dishes. Try the special Fireworks Chicken with red peppers and chiles, or the perfectly fried Mongolian beef. Finish off with the mild macadamia nut tart, which balances the spicy entrées well. | 2990 N. Swan Rd. | 520/318–1118 | $14–$28 | AE, D, DC, MC, V.

Fuego Restaurant, Bar & Grill. Southwestern. Chef Alan Zeeman's restaurant has one of the most creative menus in town, known especially for his combinations of exotic ingredients and flavors, which are often spicy. Try the prickly-pear pork tenderloins or salmon Navajo, but also consider one of the ostrich or emu specials. Kids' menu. Entertainment Sunday evening. | 6958 E. Tanque Verde Rd. | 520/886–1745 | No lunch | $11–$28 | AE, MC, V.

Gold Room. Continental. This elegant restaurant in the Westward Look Resort (*see below*) has great views of the city and mountains from the dining room's large picture windows or the patio overlooking the pool. The continental menu now features southwestern touches, including a Caesar salad with spicy chipotle dressing. Try any of the rabbit specials. Kids' menu. No smoking. | 245 E. Ina Rd. | 520/297–1151 | Breakfast also available | $12–$37 | AE, D, DC, MC, V.

Grill at Hacienda del Sol. American. This restaurant at the Hacienda del Sol is known for its regional American menu featuring fresh fish and grilled meats. Try any of the specialties featuring pork loin, salmon, or duck, or the New York strip steak. | 5601 N. Hacienda del Sol Rd. | 520/299–1501 | fax 520/299–5554 | $6–$32 | AE, D, DC, MC, V.

Last Territory. American. A western motif prevails at this restaurant in the Sheraton El Conquistador Resort (*see below*). The ribs here are fall-off-the-bone tender, and the venison sausage, Colorado lamb, and American bison fillet are also well prepared. All entrées are served with salad, soup, fresh-baked bread, and the "pot-o-beans." Open-air dining. Entertainment nightly. Kids' menu, early-bird dinners. | 10000 N. Oracle Rd. | 520/544–5000 | No lunch | $14–$27 | AE, D, DC, MC, V.

Le Mediterranean. Mediterranean. The subtle colors and serene lighting at this standard contemporary restaurant hardly reflect the exotic menu, which includes standards like falafel, smokey baba ghanoush (eggplant paste), lamb kebab, beef moussaka, and *shawarma* (beef in tahini sauce). Live belly dancing on weekends. | 4955 N. Sabino Canyon Rd. | 520/ 529–1330 | Closed Mon. No lunch | $15–$28 | AE, D, DC, MC, V.

Le Rendez-Vous. French. This romantic restaurant has an intimate setting and a traditional French menu featuring such classics as duck à l'orange, veal mignons with Calvados, and beef Wellington. Don't forget the Grand Marnier soufflé. | 3844 E. Fort Lowell | 520/323–7373 | Reservations essential | Closed Mon. No lunch weekends | $15–$30 | AE, D, DC, MC, V.

Olive Tree. Greek. While this restaurant serves up fine versions of Greek standards like moussaka and stuffed grape leaves, there are also some more unusual dishes on the menu. Try the lamb chops or the salmon. The patio has a soothing fountain. | 7000 E. Tanque Verde Rd. | 520/298–1845 | No lunch | $18–$34 | AE, MC, V.

Presidio Grill. Southwestern. This chic bistro near the university with stylish black booths and Art Deco room dividers might be in New York, except for the organ pipe cacti flanking the window. Try the porcini and pistachio-nut-encrusted rack of lamb or the prickly-pear marinated pork tenderloin. Kids' menu. | 3352 E. Speedway Blvd. | 520/327–4667 | $11–$29 | AE, MC, V.

Sakura. Japanese. In Tucson's hopping "restaurant row," this contemporary and sleek restaurant is one of the best sushi spots in town. Expert teppan chefs put on quite a show with their fast and flashy knife work; dishes range from the familiar California rolls, tuna, and chicken teriyaki, to the huge sushi "boat" filled with fresh and interesting delights from the sea. | 6534 E. Tanque Verde Rd. | 520/298–7777 | $19–$26 | AE, DC, MC, V.

VERY EXPENSIVE

Anthony's in the Catalinas Restaurant Continental. Locals like to come here to celebrate special occasions. Dishes like seafood relleno and veal Sonoita put a contemporary spin on an otherwise continental menu. Pink tablecloths, fresh flowers, candlelight, and a pianist add up to a romantic evening. | 6640 N. Campbell Ave. | 520/299–1771 | No lunch weekends | $20–$38 | AE, DC, MC, V.

Arizona Inn Restaurant. Continental. The flower-decked patio at this historic inn's dining room overlooks the meticulous grounds and has views of surrounding mountains. Breast of chicken with smoked shrimp, grilled salmon, applewood-smoked bacon-wrapped lamb loin, and the Provençal vegetable tart are all succulent. | 2200 E. Elm St. | 520/325–1541 | $33–$45 | AE, DC, MC, V.

El Corral. American. Each of the six dining rooms has its own character in this rustic adobe ranch-style building, but most have fireplaces and you'll see a lot of Mexican tile. Known for prime rib, steak, and barbecue ribs. Kids' menu | 2201 E. River Rd. | 520/299–6092 | No lunch | $21–$40 | AE, D, DC, MC, V.

Elle. Contemporary. This elegant and trendy "wine country" restaurant serves northern California cuisine with French and Italian influences. Try the linguine with Portobello mushrooms and roasted shallots in a sun-dried tomato pesto, or the grilled chicken penne in a basil walnut pesto sauce. The flourless chocolate cake is superb. | 3048 E. Broadway | 520/327–0500 | Closed Sun. No lunch Sat. | $26–$36 | AE, DC, MC, V.

★ **Janos at La Paloma.** Southwestern. Chef-owner Janos Wilder, a pioneer of southwestern cuisine, performs magic in this elegant, understated desert-view restaurant in the Westin La Paloma (*see below*) in the foothills northeast of town. Try the brie and exotic mushroom relleno, salmon with crayfish tails in an anise-scented lobster broth, or the venison chop with chorizo-tortilla casserole. The wine list is exemplary. | 3770 E. Sunrise Dr. | 520/615–6100 | Reservations essential | Closed Sun. No lunch | $25–$35 | AE, D, DC, MC, V.

McMahon's Prime Steakhouse. Steak. This chic steak house manages to be both elegant and formal without being stuffy. Meat eaters come for the prime grade beef, grilled to order. The Steak Ellsworth (New York strip smothered with garlic, onion, mushrooms, and peppers) and the Chicken Oscar (grilled chicken with king crab legs in a béarnaise sauce) are also favorites. | 2959 N. Swan Rd. | 520/327–7463 | $21–$55 | AE, MC, V.

Pastiche. Contemporary. Trendy with sleek furnishings and linen tablecloths, this popular restaurant has a professional staff and a creative menu of interesting combinations. The Jamaican jerk–spiced chicken with a prickly-pear yogurt sauce wonderfully combines spicy and cool; the beef tenderloin medallions with yellow cornmeal and poblano waffles are equally stimulating. End with the Pastiche tiramisu, served in a martini glass, or the semi-flourless chocolate brownie. | 3025 N. Campbell Ave. | 520/325–3333 | $21–$33 | AE, D, DC, MC, V.

Rancher's Club. Steak. Each of the four wood-burning grills gives a different quality to the steaks at this upscale western restaurant with dark wood interior and mounted animal heads. Mesquite wood is used in the grill every day, and hickory, sassafras, and wild cherry alternate throughout the week as a second option. A large variety of butters and condiments enhance the huge, flavorful steaks, which you might want to share if you are a light eater. | 5151 E. Grant Rd. | 520/321–7621 | Closed Sun. No lunch Sat. No dinner Mon. | $26–$40 | AE, D, DC, MC, V.

Tack Room. Continental. The cuisine at this elegant old adobe restaurant can charm even though the service is overly fussy and the menu a little stuffy. Try the Arizona four-pepper steak, the roasted duckling with a pistachio crust in a jalapeño lime sauce, or the rack of lamb for two cooked with mesquite honey, cilantro, and southwestern limes. | 7300 E. Vactor Ranch Trail | 520/722–2800 | Closed Mon., and 1st 2 wks July. No lunch | $27–$36 | AE, D, DC, MC, V.

Ventana Room. Continental. This restaurant in the Loews Ventana Canyon Resort (*see below*) is a triumph of understated elegance. The French-, Asian-, and Italian-inspired menu reflects seasonally available ingredients, which might include buffalo tenderloin or seared ahi tuna. It's the kind of place where the dressed-down feel out of place, even though jackets are not required. No smoking. | 7000 N. Resort Dr. | 520/299–2020 | No lunch | $50–$60 | AE, D, DC, MC, V.

Lodging

INEXPENSIVE

Adobe Rose Inn. In the quiet residential neighborhood a few blocks east of the University of Arizona campus, this small B&B has lodgepole-pine-furnished rooms. Picnic area, complimentary breakfast. Some microwaves, refrigerators, cable TV, some in-room VCRs, some room phones. Pool. Hot tub. No kids under 12. No smoking. | 940 N. Olsen Ave. | 520/318–4644 or 800/328–4122 | fax 520/325–0055 | aroseinn@azstarnet.com | 6 rooms (2 with shower only), 3 suites | $65–$115, $95–$135 suites | AE, D, DC, MC, V.

Best Western Ghost Ranch Lodge. This 8-acre resort is populated by an orange grove, innumerable bleached-out cow skulls, and a garden that plays host to over 400 species of cacti. Established in 1941, this compound of adobe, Spanish-tile roofs is marked with a neon cow-skull sign. Guest rooms are decorated with modern motel furnishings but retain their original brick walls and sloped, wood-beam ceilings. Restaurant, bar, complimentary Continental breakfast. Pool. Hot tub. | 801 W. Miracle Mile | 520/791–7565 | fax 520/791–3898 | 83 rooms | $44–$65 | AE, D, DC, MC, V.

Best Western Inn at the Airport. This motel is next to the airport in south Tucson. Restaurant, bar, complimentary Continental breakfast. In-room data ports, refrigerators, cable TV. Pool. Hot tub. Putting green, tennis court. Laundry service. Business services, airport shuttle. | 7060 S. Tucson Blvd. | 520/746–0271 | fax 520/889–7391 | www.bestwestern.com | 149 rooms | $59–$129 | AE, D, DC, MC, V.

Best Western Innsuites–Catalina Foothills. This all-suite hotel is in the foothills in northwest Tucson. Restaurant, bar, complimentary breakfast, room service. Kitchenettes, microwaves, refrigerators, some in-room hot tubs, cable TV. Pool. Hot tub. Tennis court. Gym. Video games. Laundry service. Business services. Some pets allowed. | 6201 N. Oracle Rd. | 520/297–8111 | fax 520/297–2935 | www.bestwestern.com | 159 rooms, 74 suites | $109–$129, $129–$179 suites | AE, D, DC, MC, V.

Best Western Royal Sun Inn & Suites. This hotel is between the Convention Center and the university. Restaurant, bar, room service. Refrigerators, some in-room hot tubs, cable TV, in-room VCRs and movies. Pool. Hot tub. Gym. Laundry facilities, laundry service. Business services. | 1015 N. Stone Rd. | 520/622–8871 | fax 520/623–2267 | 58 rooms, 20 suites | $129–$149, $129–$179 suites | AE, D, DC, MC, V.

Car Mar's Southwest. This B&B is 7 mi southwest of town. A separate guest house has a full kitchen. Picnic area, complimentary breakfast. Some kitchenettes, some microwaves, some refrigerators, cable TV, some in-room VCRs, no TV in some rooms. Pool. Hot tub. Business services, airport shuttle. No smoking. | 6766 W. Oklahoma St. | 520/578–1730 or 888/578–1730 | fax 520/578–7272 | hometown.aol.com/carmarbb/carmarbb.htm | 3 rooms (2 with shared bath), 1 guest house | $65–$125 | MC, V.

Casa Alegre. The inn north of downtown in central Tucson is composed of two vintage bungalows filled with antiques. There are lovely gardens. Complimentary breakfast. Some kitchenettes, some refrigerators, cable TV, in-room VCRs (and movies), no room phones. Pool. Hot tub. No smoking. | 316 E. Speedway Blvd. | 520/628–1800 or 800/628–5654 | fax 520/792–1880 | alegre123@aol.com | 5 rooms (2 with shower only), 1 casita | $80–$135 | AE, D, MC, V.

Catalina Park Inn. This charmer is a 1927 Mediterranean-style home on a quiet residential street in the West University neighborhood. Two rooms have balconies. Complimentary breakfasts. Cable TV. No kids under 10. No smoking. | 309 E. 1st St. | 520/792–4541 or 800/792–4885 | fax 520/792–0838 | www.catalinaparkinn.com | 6 rooms | $104–$134 | AE, D, MC, V.

Clarion Hotel–Airport. An affordable hotel south of downtown, ½ mi from the airport. Restaurant, bar, picnic area, complimentary breakfast, room service. In-room data ports, some refrigerators, cable TV. Pool. Hot tub. Gym. Laundry service. Business services, airport shuttle. | 6801 S. Tucson Blvd. | 520/746–3932 | fax 520/889–9934 | www.clarionhotel.com | 187 rooms, 4 suites | $59–$129 | AE, D, DC, MC, V.

Clarion Hotel–Tucson Randolph Park. This hotel in midtown is southeast of the university. Picnic area, complimentary breakfast. Microwaves, refrigerators, cable TV. Pool, wading pool. Exercise equipment. Business services. | 102 N. Alvernon Way | 520/795–0330 or 800/227–6086 | fax 520/326–2111 | www.clarionhotel.com | 157 rooms | $59–$149 | AE, D, DC, MC, V.

Cliff Manor Inn. This unassuming hotel is an excellent base of operations if you plan to explore the hiking, birding, or day-tripping options in the area. The Cliff Manor offers pleasant, but not overwhelming amenities, and Oracle Road abounds with restaurants, two nearby malls, and a movie theater. Kitchenettes, cable TV. Pool. | 5900 N. Oracle Rd. | 520/887–4800 | fax 520/292–9861 | 61 rooms, 11 casitas | $79–$99 | AE, D, MC, V.

Country Suites by Carlson. Affordable all-suite hotel on the north side of town. Complimentary Continental breakfast. Kitchenettes, refrigerators, cable TV. Pool. Hot tub. Putting green. Laundry facilities. Business services, airport shuttle. | 7411 N. Oracle Rd. | 520/575–9255 or 800/456–4000 | fax 520/575–8671 | 157 suites | $49–$129 | AE, D, DC, MC, V.

Courtyard Tucson/Williams Center. This three-story hotel is built around a courtyard with a fountain. It's 1 mi from the El Con Mall. Restaurant, bar, room service. In-room data ports, cable TV. Pool. Hot tub. Gym. Laundry facilities, laundry service. Business services. | 201 S. Williams Blvd. | 520/745–6000 | fax 520/745–2393 | www.marriott.com | 153 rooms | $59–$140 | AE, D, DC, MC, V.

Doubletree Hotel at Reid Park. Only 8 mi from the airport and downtown, this midtown hotel is directly across from Reid Park. Some rooms have views of the park. Restaurant, bar, room service. In-room data ports, some kitchenettes, some minibars, some refrigerators, cable TV. Pool. Tennis court. Gym. Business services, airport shuttle. Some pets allowed (fee). | 445 S. Alvernon Way | 520/881–4200 | fax 520/323–5225 | www.doubletree.com | 288 rooms, 7 suites | $129, $150 suites | AE, D, DC, MC, V.

El Presidio Bed and Breakfast. This late-19th-century Victorian adobe house is sumptuously furnished with period antiques. The grounds surrounding it are carefully tended and have fountains, gardens, and courtyards. The inn is within easy walking distance of Old Tucson's restaurants, shops, and galleries. Complimentary breakfast. Some kitchenettes, cable TV. No smoking. | 297 N. Main Ave. | 520/623–6151 or 800/349–6151 | fax 520/623–3860 | 3 suites | $95–$115 | No credit cards.

Flamingo Hotel. This two-story pink motel is popular with families, who appreciate the affordable rates and proximity to downtown attractions. Complimentary Continental breakfast. Some refrigerators, cable TV. Pool. Hot tub. Laundry facilities. Business services. Some pets allowed. | 1300 N. Stone Ave. | 520/770–1910 | fax 520/770–0750 | 80 rooms | $50–$106 | AE, D, DC, MC, V.

Hampton Inn Tucson Airport. This hotel is at the entrance to the Tucson airport and has views of the Catalina Mountains. Complimentary Continental breakfast. Some refrigerators, cable TV. Pool. Hot tub. Laundry service. Business services, airport shuttle. | 6971 S. Tucson Blvd. | 520/889–5789 | fax 520/889–4002 | www.hampton-inn.com | 117 rooms, 9 suites | $49–$109, $79–$129 suites | AE, D, DC, MC, V.

Hawthorn Suites. This all-suite hotel in northeast Tucson is within walking distance of 30 restaurants. It's 6 mi from Saguaro National Park East. Complimentary breakfast. In-room data ports, some kitchenettes, some microwaves, some refrigerators, cable TV. Pool. Hot tub. Laundry facilities, laundry service. Business services. Pets allowed (fee). | 7007 E. Tanque Verde Rd. | 520/298–2300 | fax 520/298–6756 | www.hawthorn.com | 30 rooms, 60 suites | $100–$115, $120–$135 suites | AE, D, DC, MC, V.

Holiday Inn Tucson Airport. This large convention hotel is 8 mi south of downtown and 4 mi from the airport. Some suites are poolside. Restaurant, bar, room service. In-room data ports, some kitchenettes, some microwaves, some refrigerators, cable TV. Pool. Hot tub. Tennis court. Gym. Laundry facilities, laundry service. Business services, airport shuttle. | 4550 S. Palo Verde Blvd. | 520/746–1161 | fax 520/741–1170 | 257 rooms, 44 suites | $98–$175, $115–$185 suites | AE, D, DC, MC, V.

Hotel Congress. Loved by many for its eccentric charm, this downtown hotel was built in 1919 and has since been restored to its Art Deco glory. Each guest room is different, but all have black-and-white tile baths and original iron beds, and some have desks and tables. Within easy walking distance of the Sun Tran terminal and all the downtown restaurants, clubs, and galleries, this is a very convenient location, but it can be somewhat noisy on weekends. Restaurant, bar. Beauty salon. Shop. | 311 E. Congress St. | 520/622–8848 or 800/722–8848 | fax 520/792–6366 | 40 rooms | $48–$60 | AE, MC, V.

La Posada del Valle. This inn was designed by noted Swiss architect Josias Joesller in the Spanish Colonial–Territorial style he made popular in the Tucson area. Breezeways and gentle arches characterize the structure, which is of soothing-pink adobe and directly across from the university medical center. All rooms are individually decorated with antique and rustic modern pieces. Picnic area, complimentary breakfast. Some kitchenettes, cable TV, some room phones. Library. No smoking. | 1640 N. Campbell Ave. | 520/795–3840 | 5 rooms, 1 suite | $90–$110, $115–$145 suites | MC, V.

La Quinta Hotel. This hotel on the east side of Tucson, built in 1975, is close to restaurants, a mall, and movie theaters. Complimentary Continental breakfast. Cable TV. Pool. Hot tub. Laundry facilities. Business services. Some pets allowed. | 6404 E. Broadway | 520/747–1414 | fax 520/745–6903 | www.laquinta.com | 144 rooms | $49–$129 | AE, D, DC, MC, V.

Lodge on the Desert. This quiet, hacienda-style resort opened in 1936. It's on 3 landscaped acres in a residential area in the foothills. Many rooms have fireplaces. Restaurant, bar, complimentary Continental breakfast, room service. Some refrigerators, cable TV. Pool. Business services. | 306 N. Alvernon Way | 520/325–3366 or 800/456–5634 | fax 520/327–5834 | www.lodge-on-the-desert.com | 35 rooms | $79–$249 | AE, D, DC, MC, V.

Peppertrees Bed & Breakfast Inn. This 1905 home is in the West University historic district, within walking distance of the university. Rooms are individually decorated with family antiques. Picnic area, complimentary breakfast. Some kitchenettes, refrigerators. No smoking. | 724 E. University | 520/622–7167 or 800/348–5763 | travelassist.com/reg/az102.html | 6 rooms (2 with shower only), 2 suites | $108, $125–$175 suites | D, MC, V.

Plaza Hotel and Conference Center. This affordable seven-story hotel across from the University Medical Center was renovated in 1998. It's a basic, no-nonsense hotel with simple, modern modular furnishings and innocuous wall art. Restaurant, bar, room service. Some refrigerators, cable TV. Pool. Hot tub. | 1900 E. Speedway Blvd. | 520/327–7341, 800/843–8052 outside AZ, 800/654–3010 in AZ | fax 520/327–0276 | 150 rooms | $95–$169 | AE, DC, MC, V.

Presidio Plaza Hotel. This 14-story hotel is downtown, next to Tucson Convention Center. It's a five-minute walk to restaurants and museums. Restaurant, bar. Some microwaves, some refrigerators, cable TV. Pool. Gym. Business services. Some pets allowed. | 181 W. Broadway | 520/624–8711 | fax 520/623–8121 | 299 rooms, 10 suites | $99–$139, $185 suites | AE, D, DC, MC, V.

Ramada Inn Foothills Inn & Suites. This hotel is in northeast Tucson, near Sabino Canyon. Fuego Restaurant is next door. Complimentary Continental breakfast. In-room data ports, some refrigerators, cable TV. Pool. Hot tub, sauna. Laundry facilities, laundry service. Business services. | 6944 E. Tanque Verde Rd. | 520/886–9595 | fax 520/721–8466 | www.ramada.com | 63 rooms, 50 suites | $100–$120, $110–$140 suites | AE, D, DC, MC, V.

Rodeway Inn–Grant Road at I–10. This motel is 2 mi north of downtown, just off Interstate 10. Restaurant, bar, room service. Some refrigerators, cable TV. Pool. Hot tub. Laundry facilities, laundry service. Business services. Pets allowed (fee). | 1365 W. Grant Rd. | 520/622–7791 | fax 520/629–0201 | www.rodewayinn.com | 146 rooms | $60–$130 | AE, D, DC, MC, V.

Sheraton Tucson Hotel and Suites. This comfortable low-rise hotel is in northeast Tucson in the Carolina foothills, near "restaurant row." Restaurant, bar, complimentary breakfast. Some microwaves, refrigerators, cable TV. Pool. Hot tub. Gym. Laundry facilities, laundry service. Business services. | 5151 E. Grant Rd. | 520/323–6262 or 800/257–7275 | fax 520/325–2989 | www.sheraton.com | 216 rooms | $89–$104 | AE, DC, MC, V.

Smuggler's Inn. This comfortable hotel, popular with families, has easy access to the east side of Tucson and the "restaurant row" of Tanque Verde Road. The lushly landscaped courtyard has a lagoon with ducks, turtles, and fish. Rooms are basic. Restaurant, bar, room service. Some kitchenettes, some microwaves, some refrigerators, cable TV. Pool. Hot tub. Putting green. Laundry facilities, laundry service. Business services. | 6350 E. Speedway Blvd. | 520/296–3292 or 800/525–8852 | fax 520/722–3713 | www.smugglersinn.com | 122 rooms, 28 suites | $69–$119, $75–$135 suites | AE, D, DC, MC, V.

Viscount Suite Hotel. This four-story all-suite hotel in midtown has an atrium lobby. 3 restaurants, bar, room service. Some kitchenettes, some microwaves, some refrigerators, cable TV. Pool. Hot tub. Gym. Laundry service. Business services. | 4855 E. Broadway | 520/745–6500 | fax 520/790–5114 | www.viscountsuite.com | 215 suites | $70–$140 | AE, D, DC, MC, V.

Wayward Winds Lodge. This ranch-style lodge with oversize rooms is north of downtown, off Interstate 10. Picnic area, complimentary Continental breakfast (in season). Some kitchenettes, some microwaves, some refrigerators, cable TV. Pool. Laundry facilities. Business services. Some pets allowed. | 707 W. Miracle Mile | 520/791–7526 or 800/791–9503 | fax 520/791–9502 | 40 rooms | $30–$99 | AE, D, DC, MC, V.

MODERATE

★ **Casa Tierra.** For an authentic desert experience, head out to this bed-and-breakfast situated on 5 acres near the Arizona-Sonora Desert Museum and Saguaro National Park. All rooms have private baths and private patio entrances that look out onto a lovely central courtyard area set about with paloverde trees and desert foliage. Furnishings are rustic and reminiscent of the surrounding desert, with Mexican pigskin chairs, tiled floors, and viga-beam ceilings. A full vegetarian breakfast is served each morning. A two-night minimum stay is required. Kitchenettes. Hot tub. | 11155 W. Calle Pima | 520/578-3058 | fax 520/578-8445 | 3 rooms | $105–$165 | No credit cards.

Clarion Santa Rita. The lobby of this historic downtown hotel sports marble floors and comfortable antique couches. The rooms are somewhat unremarkable, but have coffeemakers, irons, and hair dryers. Some rooms have views of the outdoor pool, which is a gorgeous remnant of the original hotel. The excellent Cafe Poca Cosa is adjacent. Restaurant, complimentary Continental breakfast. Pool. Exercise room. Library. | 88 E. Broadway | 520/622-4000 or 800/622-1120 | fax 520/620-0376 | 152 rooms | $94–$114 | AE, D, DC, MC, V.

Courtyard Tucson Airport. This three-story chain hotel built around a courtyard is south of downtown, less than 1 mi from the airport. Rooms are spacious but otherwise unremarkable. Restaurant, bar, room service. In-room data ports, some microwaves, some refrigerators, cable TV. Pool. Hot tub. Gym. Laundry facilities, laundry service. Business services, airport shuttle. | 2505 E. Executive Dr. | 520/573-0000 | fax 520/573-0470 | www.marriott.com | 149 rooms | $144–$169 | AE, D, DC, MC, V.

Doubletree Guest Suites. This all-suite hotel is in northeast Tucson, about a mile from the Tanque Verde Drive "restaurant row." Restaurant, bar, picnic area, complimentary Continental breakfast. Some in-room data ports, refrigerators, cable TV. Pool. Hot tub. Gym. Laundry facilities. Business services. | 6555 E. Speedway Blvd. | 520/721-7100 | fax 520/721-1991 | www.doubletree.com | 304 suites | $167 | AE, D, DC, MC, V.

Embassy Suites Broadway. This reliable three-story all-suite hotel in midtown is 10 mi from the airport, 5 mi from downtown, and close to malls, theaters, and restaurants. All suites are two rooms and open onto an atrium lobby. Bar, complimentary breakfast. Kitchenettes, microwaves, refrigerators, cable TV. Pool. Hot tub. Laundry facilities. Some pets allowed (fee). | 5335 E. Broadway | 520/745-2700 | fax 520/790-9232 | www.embassysuites.com | 142 suites | $189 | AE, D, DC, MC, V.

Embassy Suites Hotel and Conference Center. This comfortable, three-story all-suite hotel is south of downtown, near the airport. Restaurant, bar, complimentary breakfast. Kitchenettes, microwaves, refrigerators, cable TV. Pool. Hot tub. Gym. Laundry facilities. Business services, airport shuttle. Pets allowed. | 7051 S. Tucson Blvd. | 520/573-0700 | fax 520/741-9645 | 204 suites | $139–$169 | AE, D, DC, MC, V.

Hacienda de Sol Guest Ranch Resort. This 34-acre property in the Santa Catalina foothills is part guest ranch and part resort. You can choose a room with a view of the mountains, city, or desert. All have fireplaces, and each has a unique decorative scheme, from bedding with cactus motifs to southwestern-style tile floors. Restaurant, complimentary Continental breakfast. Refrigerators, some in-room hot tubs, cable TV. Pool. Hot tub. Tennis court. Hiking. No smoking. | 5601 N. Hacienda del Sol Rd. | 520/299-1501 | fax 520/299-5554 | www.haciendadelsol.com | 22 rooms, 7 suites, 1 casita | $150–$200 rooms, $290 suites, $425 casitas | AE, MC, V.

Inn Suites Hotel and Resort. Despite being right off the St. Mary's Road exit of Interstate 10, this is a quiet place, just north of downtown Tucson and the historic district. The large, peach-and-green southwestern-theme rooms have large work areas and can thus double as offices on the road. Most rooms face a lush green interior courtyard with a sparkling pool and thatched gazebos. A complimentary breakfast and morning newspaper make this a haven for those traveling for business or pleasure. Restaurant, bar. Cable TV. Pool. | 475 N. Granada Ave. | 520/622-3000 or 800/446-6589 | fax 520/623-8922 | 277 rooms | $79–$109 | AE, D, MC, V.

Marriott University Park Hotel. This nine-story atrium hotel is two blocks from the university, close to downtown and next to several restaurants. Restaurant, bar. In-room data ports, some kitchenettes, some microwaves, some refrigerators, cable TV. Pool. Hot tub, sauna. Gym. Video games. Business services. | 880 E. 2nd St. | 520/792-4100 | fax 520/882-4100 | www.marriott.com | 234 rooms, 16 suites | $149–$189, $174–$214 suites | AE, D, DC, MC, V.

Suncatcher Bed & Breakfast. There are views of the Catalina Mountains from the individually decorated rooms (based on famous hotels from around the world) in this B&B in a residential neighborhood east of downtown. Picnic area, complimentary breakfast. Cable TV, in-room VCRs (and movies). Pool. Hot tub. Business services. No smoking. | 105 N. Avenida Javalina | 520/885–0883 or 877/775–8355 | fax 520/885–0883 | 4 rooms (1 with shower only) | $125–$165 | AE, DC, MC, V.

Sunstone Guest Ranch. At the base of the Santa Catalina Mountains, this is a great hideaway where you will be pampered amid the tranquil garden environment. Most rooms are furnished with antiques, and some of the older rooms have bathrooms with brass faucets and the original tiles. Some have views of the lush green lawn with water fountains and ponds, while others have desert views. Complimentary Continental breakfast. In-room data ports, some refrigerators, no TV in rooms, TV in common area. Pool. Hot tub. Tennis court. Hiking. | 2545 N. Woodland Rd., | 520/749–1928 | fax 520/749–2456 | www.azstarnet.com/~sunstone/ | 12 rooms | $145 | MC, V.

Tucson Hilton East. This reliable seven-story hotel, which was built in 1985, is 9 mi east of downtown in a quiet, residential neighborhood. Restaurant, bar, complimentary Continental breakfast. In-room data ports, minibars, cable TV. Pool. Hot tub. Gym. Laundry service. Business services. | 7600 E. Broadway | 520/721–5600 | fax 520/721–5696 | www.hilton.com | 224 rooms, 9 suites | $105–$205, $235–$425 suites | AE, D, DC, MC, V.

Varsity Clubs of America. Opened in 1998, this time-share facility doubles as a hotel, so it may have any or all of its suites available at any time. Its location is very handy, but can also be very noisy. The one- and two-bedroom suites are decorated with basic hotel furnishings and have whirlpool tubs and fully outfitted kitchens. If you'd rather not cook, the Stadium Grill is just downstairs, and the hotel is within easy walking distance of a score of restaurants. Cable TV. Pool. Hot tub. Exercise room. | 3855 E. Speedway Blvd. | 520/318–3777 or 888/594–2287 | fax 888/410–9770 | 59 suites | $75–$115 | AE, D, MC, V.

White Stallion Ranch. This family-run guest ranch on 3,000 acres next to Saguaro National Park has been going strong since 1965. Most rooms are rustic, with western furniture. Kids like the petting zoo. Dining room, bar. Some refrigerators, no room phones, no TV. Pool. 2 tennis courts. Basketball, horseback riding, volleyball. Library. Laundry facilities. Business services, airport shuttle. | 9251 W. Twin Peaks Rd. | 520/297–0252 or 888/977–2624 | fax 520/744–2786 | www.wsranch.com | 20 rooms, 14 suites | $120–$140 per person per night, $151–$170 person per night in suites (7–night minimum) | Closed June–Aug. | AP | No credit cards.

Windmill Inn at St. Philip's Plaza. This all-suite hotel is in the St. Philip's Plaza shopping center in the foothills section of north Tucson. The suites all have sleeper sofas and two TVs. It's one of the better chain options in town, and, yes, there is a windmill on the front lawn. Complimentary Continental breakfast. Microwaves, refrigerators, cable TV. Pool. Hot tub. Bicycles. Library. Laundry facilities. Business services. Some pets allowed. | 4250 N. Campbell Ave. | 520/577–0007 or 800/547–4747 | fax 520/577–0045 | www.windmillinns.com | 122 suites | $65–$139 standard suites, $135–$395 king and deluxe suites | AE, D, DC, MC, V.

EXPENSIVE

★ **Arizona Inn.** This hotel sprawls over 14 acres in central Tucson near the university and feels like an oasis in the middle of town. Spacious rooms are in pink stucco buildings, including three fully furnished homes. Restaurant, complimentary Continental breakfast (May–September only), room service. In-room data ports, microwaves, refrigerators, cable TV, in-room VCRs. Pool. 2 tennis courts. Gym. Library. Business services. | 2200 E. Elm St. | 520/325–1541 or 800/933–1093 | fax 520/881–5830 | www.arizonainn.com | 71 rooms, 15 suites, 3 houses | $195–$245, $247–$300 suites, $525–$1,500 houses | AE, MC, V.

La Tierra Linda Guest Ranch Resort. Off a quiet dirt road in the desert, this family-run ranch stands on 30 acres adjacent to Saguaro National Park West. Its adobe casitas, built in the 1930s, are done in typical southwestern style. This place is family friendly, and even offers a petting zoo for the kids. Restaurant, bar, complimentary breakfast. Refrigerators, cable TV. Pool. Hot tub. Tennis court. Hiking, horseback riding. No smoking. | 7501 N. Wade Rd. | 520/744–7700 | fax 520/579–9742 | www.latierralinda.com | 8 rooms, 6 suites | $165–$240 | AE, D,MC, V.

Sheraton El Conquistador Resort and Country Club. This luxury resort at the base of the Catalina mountains 15 mi northwest of Tucson draws a large family contingent. Rooms are in the main hotel or private casitas. Some suites have kiva-style fireplaces. 4 restaurants, 2 bars, room service. Minibars, some microwaves, cable TV. 4 pools. Beauty salon, hot tub, massage, sauna. Driving range, 2 18-hole golf courses, putting green, 3 tennis courts. Basketball, gym, hiking, horseback riding, racquetball, volleyball, bicycles. Shops. Children's programs (ages 5–12). Laundry service. Business services, parking (fee). Some pets allowed. | 1000 N. Oracle Rd. | 520/544–5000 or 800/325–7832 | fax 520/544–1228 | www.sheraton.com | 328 rooms, 100 suites | $130–$300, $160–$850 suites | AE, D, DC, MC, V.

Westward Look Resort. This hotel in the foothills has excellent city, desert, and mountain views. Built in 1912, it was originally a private residence but became a resort in 1943. The rooms are done up with mission-style furnishings and leather chairs. 2 restaurants, bar, room service. In-room data ports, minibars, some refrigerators, cable TV. 3 pools. 3 hot tubs, massage. 8 tennis courts. Gym, horseback riding, bicycles. Business services. Some pets allowed. | 245 E. Ina Rd. | 520/297–1151 or 800/722–2500 | fax 520/297–9023 | www.westwardlook.com | 244 rooms | $169–$369 | AE, D, DC, MC, V.

VERY EXPENSIVE

Canyon Ranch. Established in 1979, this luxe resort draws the well-funded masses with its superb spa facilities. Set on 70 acres of desert foothills, the resort's two main activity centers include a full-service spa complex and the Ranch's Health and Healing Center, where dieticians, exercise physiologists, massage therapists, and a host of others tend to your body and your mind. Guest rooms are decorated in high-desert chic, with lots of soothing sandy colors, rich textures, and minimalist furnishings. A four-night minimum stay is required. Guests may book standard accommodations or go for a luxury package that includes access to all spa facilities and services. 3 pools. Beauty salon, spa. 8 tennis courts. Basketball, health club, racquetball, squash. | 8600 Rockcliff Rd. | 520/749–9000 or 800/742–9000 | fax 520/749–1646 | www.canyonranch.com | 240 rooms | Per person: $2,050 standard, $3,550 luxury | AE, D, MC, V.

Lazy K Bar Guest Ranch. In the Tucson Mountains, 16 mi northwest of town at an altitude of 2,300 ft, this family-oriented guest ranch accommodates both greenhorns and rough riders. Mountain views and hearty ranch-style meals and cookouts deliver an authentic Wild West atmosphere. Rooms are simply decorated, with pictures of the desert and horses. Dining room. No room phones, no TV in rooms, TV in common area. Pool. Hot tub. 2 tennis courts. Hiking, horseback riding. Business services, airport shuttle. | 8401 N. Scenic Dr. | 520/744–3050 or 800/321–7018 | fax 520/744–7628 | www.lazykbar.com | 23 rooms | $270–$340 | AP | AE, D, MC, V.

Lodge at Ventana Canyon. This luxurious, all-suite resort in the Santa Catalina foothills northeast of Tucson is widely considered to be one of the best golf resorts in the Southwest. The smallest sumptuous suite is 800 square ft. 2 restaurants, bar, room service. Kitchenettes, minibars, microwaves, refrigerators, cable TV. Pool, wading pool. Hot tub, massage, sauna. Driving range, 2 18-hole golf courses, putting green, 12 tennis courts. Health club, bicycles. Laundry facilities, laundry service. Business services. | 6200 N. Clubhouse La. | 520/577–1400 or 800/828–5701 | fax 520/577–4065 | www.grandbay.com/properties/lodge | 50 suites | $299–$595 | AE, D, DC, MC, V.

Loews Ventana Canyon Resort. On a plateau overlooking Tucson, this luxurious 93-acre resort has sweeping views of the mountains and city, and an 80-ft waterfall, but it's a bit snootier than most Tucson properties. Rooms are spacious and modern. 4 restaurants, bar, picnic area, room service. In-room data ports, minibars, some microwaves, some refrigerators, cable TV. 2 pools. Beauty salon, hot tub, spa. Driving range, 18-hole golf course, putting green, 8 tennis courts. Health club, hiking, bicycles. Shops. Laundry service. Business services. | 7000 N. Resort Dr. | 520/299–2020 or 800/234–5117 | fax 520/299–6832 | loewshotels.com | 371 rooms, 27 suites | $305–$405, $254–$390 suites | AE, D, DC, MC, V.

Miraval Resort and Spa. This spa 20 mi north of Tucson is surrounded by the desert. You'll stay in extravagant southwestern rooms while viewing either the Santa Catalina Mountains or well-kept gardens. People come here for the myriad wellness programs, many of them based on Eastern philosophies. 2 dining rooms, bar. In-room data ports, minibars, microwaves, refrigerators, some in-room hot tubs, cable TV, in-room VCRs. 3 pools. Hot tub, sauna, spa. 2 tennis courts. Horseback riding, bicycles. No smoking. | 5000 E. Via Estancia Miraval, Catalina | 520/825–4000 or 800/825–4000 | fax 520/792–5870 | www.miravalresort.com | 106 rooms | $400–$900 | AP | AE, D, DC, MC, V.

Omni Tucson National Golf Resort and Spa. One of the premier golf resorts in the Southwest, this is also a full-service, European-style spa. In northwest Tucson, it's more centrally located than many other resorts. Oddly, hacienda rooms, the most expensive option, are the least attractive. 2 restaurants, 2 bars, room service. Minibars, cable TV. 2 pools. Barbershop, beauty salon, hot tub, massage, spa. Driving range, 27-hole golf course, putting green, 4 tennis courts. Basketball, gym, volleyball. Business services. | 2727 W. Club Dr. | 520/297–2271 or 800/528–4856 | fax 520/742–2452 | www.tucsonnational.com | 81 rooms, 86 suites | $229–$274, $254–$390 suites | AE, D, DC, MC, V.

Tanque Verde Guest Ranch. This rustic, family-oriented resort on 630 acres in the Rincon Mountains has great views. Rooms are in the ranch house or in private casitas and have views of the desert; some have fireplaces. Dining room. Some microwaves, some refrigerators, no TV. 2 pools, lake, wading pool. Hot tub, massage, 2 saunas. 5 tennis courts. Gym, hiking, horseback riding, fishing, bicycles. Kids' programs (ages 4–11). Laundry facilities. Business services, airport shuttle. | 14301 E. Speedway Blvd. | 520/296–6275 or 800/234–3833 | fax 520/721–9426 | www.tanqueverderanch.com | 71 rooms (in casitas) | $260–$390 | AP | AE, D, MC, V.

Westin La Paloma. Nestled in the Santa Catalina foothills, this sprawling family resort has the longest waterslide (at 177 ft) of any resort in Arizona. Considered one of the top family resorts in the United States, it specializes in golf, fitness, and top kids' programs, including a kids-only pool. 4 restaurants (see Janos at La Paloma), 2 bars, room service. Some microwaves, some refrigerators, some in-room hot tubs, cable TV. 3 pools. Beauty salon, hot tub, massage. Driving range, 27-hole golf course, putting green, 12 tennis courts. Health club, racquetball, volleyball. Shops. Kids' programs (ages 6 months–12 years). Laundry service. Business services. | 3800 E. Sunrise Dr. | 520/742–6000 | fax 520/577–5877 | www.westin.com | 455 rooms, 32 suites | $230–$440, $490–$1,990 suites | AE, D, DC, MC, V.

WICKENBURG

MAP 3, D6

(Nearby towns also listed Glendale, Phoenix, Prescott)

This town is named for Henry Wickenburg, whose Vulture Mine was the richest gold mine in the Arizona Territory. By the late 1800s, it was a booming mining town with a seemingly endless supply of gold, copper, and silver. Nowadays, Wickenburg, with a population of around 5,000, is known for dude ranches, antiques shops, and Old West atmosphere.

Information: **Wickenburg Chamber of Commerce** | 216 N. Frontier St., Wickenburg, 85390 | 520/684–5479 or 520/684–0977 | www.wickenburgchamber.com.

Attractions

Desert Caballeros Western Museum. This museum re-creates a turn-of-the-20th-century western store and street; there is also a display of minerals and Native American artifacts. | 21 N. Frontier St. | 520/684–2272 | $5 | Mon.–Sat. 10–5, Sun. noon–4.

Frontier Street. The main drag of Wickenburg, Frontier Street, is lined with historic buildings, including the Old Sante Fe Train Station (now the Chamber of Commerce) and the post office, which has a drive-up window once used by people on horseback. | Frontier St. | 520/684–5479 or 520/684–0977 | Free | Daily.

Hassayampa River Preserve. Self-guided trails wind through 333 mi of lush cottonwood-willow and mesquite forests, and around the 4-acre Palm Lake, 3 mi southeast of Wickenburg. Road signs around the preserve make it easy to find your way. | U.S. 60 | 520/684–2772 | Free | Wed.–Sun. 6 AM–noon.

The Jail Tree. This was the first "jail" in town. Prisoners were chained to this tree while the Wickenburg jail was being constructed, the desert heat sometimes finishing them off before their sentences could be served out. | Tegner St. and Wickenburg Way | 520/684–5479 or 520/684–0977 | Free | Daily.

Old 761 Santa Fe Steam Locomotive. Behind the town hall you can view this out-of-service locomotive and envision what it was like to travel by locomotive across the country almost a hundred years ago. | Apache Rd. and Tegner St. | 520/684–5479 | Free | Daily 10–4.

ON THE CALENDAR

FEB.: *Gold Rush Days.* Along with reenactments of the gold rush days and panning for gold, there's a rodeo and a parade the second week in February. The focal point of activities is Wickenburg Community Center. | 520/684–5479 or 520/684–0977.

SEPT.: *Septiembre Fiesta.* Wickenburg celebrates its Spanish history and heritage at the Wickenburg Community Center with mariachi music, folkloric dances, salsa contests, and an arts-and-crafts market on the first Saturday in September. | 520/684–5479 or 520/684–0977.

OCT.: *Wickenburg Fly-In.* You'll be able to view antique planes and models, as well as classic cars at the Wickenburg Municipal Airport on the last Saturday of October. | 520/684–5479.

NOV.: *Bluegrass Music Festival.* You'll find bluegrass competitions and food booths, along with a fiddle championship the second week in November. | 520/684–5479 or 520/684–0977.

DEC.: *Cowboy Christmas.* Cowboy poets gather for evening performances at the Wickenburg Community Center. | 520/684–5479 or 520/684–0977.

Dining

Anita's Cocina. Mexican. Fresh steaming tamales and dessert burritos have the locals storming in night after night. Don't let the Harley Davidson theme deter you: this is a warm and inviting place. | 57 N. Valentine St. | 520/684–5777 | $5–$10 | MC, V.

Cowboy Café. American. Photographs of local rodeos from years gone by will remind you that this is still the West. The local radio station that's always tuned in will help you feel like a local. Chicken-fried steak and Mexiburgers are yummy. | 686 N. Tegner St. | 520/684–2807 | Breakfast also available | $4–$6 | No credit cards.

March Hare. American/Casual. Feel free to curl up with a book at this cozy, antiques-filled tearoom. Take a chance on a unique special like a tortilla crab wrap, or play it safe with the grilled salmon. The classical music that fills the air adds to the overall mood. | 170 W. Wickenburg Way | 520/684–0223 | Breakfast also available; closed Sun., Mon.; no dinner | $5–$8 | No credit cards.

Lodging

Americinn. At this family-run hotel you'll find small-town hospitality and affordable, basic rooms, some with patios. Restaurant, bar, room service. Some microwaves, some refrigerators, cable TV. Pool. Hot tub. Business services. Pets allowed (fee). | 850 E. Wickenburg Way | 520/684–5461 | fax 520/684–5461 | 29 rooms | $66–$82 | AE, D, DC, MC, V.

Best Western Rancho Grande. This stucco motel downtown has southwestern decor. Complimentary Continental breakfast. Some kitchenettes, some microwaves, some refrigerators, cable TV. Pool. Hot tub. Tennis. Playground. Business services, airport shuttle. Pets allowed. | 293 E. Wickenburg Way | 520/684–5445 | fax 520/684–7380 | 80 rooms, 10 suites | $66–$80, $88–$99 suites | AE, D, DC, MC, V.

Flying E. Ranch. Breakfast cookouts and chuck-wagon dinners are part of your week at this dude ranch 4 mi west of town. There's occasional entertainment, such as square or line dancing. Refrigerators, cable TV, no room phones. Pool. Tennis court. Gym, horseback riding. | 2801 W. Wickenburg Way | 520/684–2690 | fax 520/684–5304 | www.flyingeranch.com | 17 rooms | $220–$285 | Closed May–Oct. | AP | No credit cards.

Kay El Bar Ranch. Tucked into a hollow by the Hassayampa River, this is what dude ranches used to be: personable, low-key, and away from it all. Some of the biggest mesquite trees in Arizona will shade your room. Compact quarters are made for sleeping, not spending time. Dining room, bar. No room phones, TV in common area. Pool. Hot tub. Hiking, horseback riding, volleyball. Library. | 37500 S. Rincon Rd., Box 2480 | 520/684–7593 | 9 rooms, 1 homestead house, 1 cottage | $275–$300 | Closed May–mid-Oct. | AP | MC, V.

Merv Griffin's Wickenburg Inn and Dude Ranch. This family-oriented resort 8 mi northwest of town is great for an authentic western experience. Enjoy great views of the Sonoran Desert and keep busy in the crafts center or at the nature programs. Casitas have fireplaces. Bar, dining room. Some kitchenettes, some refrigerators. 3 pools. Hot tub. Gym, horseback riding. Children's programs (ages 3–12), playground. Laundry facilities. | 34801 N. Hwy. 89 | 520/684–7811 or 800/942–5362 | fax 520/684–2981 | www.merv.com | 9 rooms, 54 casitas | $325–$430 rooms, $375–$430 casitas | AP | AE, D, DC, MC, V.

Owl Tree Inn. In the midst of the high Sonoran Desert and the Bradshaw Mountains, this B&B has the homey feel of a hacienda, with rooms containing family heirlooms or handmade Mexican furniture. You'll have access to the brightly colored Mexican patio, where there is an array of potted plants. Complimentary breakfast. No room phones, TV in common area. Library. No smoking. | 32415 W. Palo Verde Dr. | 877/684–1197 or 520/684–1197 | fax 520/684–1197 | www.owltreeinn.com | 3 rooms | $75–$125 | No credit cards.

Rancho de los Caballeros. This 20,000-acre guest ranch offers comfortable (and by guest ranch standards, particularly nice) accommodations as well as a wide range of activities. It's more like a resort, at least in the level of comfort offered; for example, guests are asked to dress for dinner (jackets for men). Dining room, bar. Some kitchenettes, some microwaves, some refrigerators. Pool. Massage. Driving range, 18-hole golf course, putting green, tennis. Hiking, horseback riding, volleyball, bicycles. Children's programs (ages 5–12), playground. Laundry facilities, laundry service. Business services, airport shuttle. | 1551 S. Vulture Mine Rd. | 520/684–5484 | fax 520/684–2267 | www.sunc.com | 112 rooms | $309–$499 | Closed mid-May–mid-Oct. | AP | No credit cards.

WILLCOX

MAP 3, H9

(Nearby towns also listed: Benson, Safford)

From picturesque landscapes and farmland to historic streets and museums, Willcox is a sleepy town where travelers can relax. Rex Allen's Cowboy Museum is a fun stop, but the history is in the land itself. This is where the Chiricahua Apaches and Fort Bowie troops battled so bitterly in the 1880s. Willcox is also known for its apples, and there are many orchards around town where you can pick your own.

Information: **Willcox Chamber of Commerce, Cochise Information Center** | 1500 N. Circle I Rd., Willcox, 85643 | 520/384–2272 or 800/200–2272 | fax 520/384–0293 | www.willcoxchamber.com.

Attractions

Amerind Foundation. This research facility and museum, whose name is a contraction of "American" and "Indian," is in a Spanish Colonial Revival building designed by Tucson architect H. M. Starkweather. Displays of archaeological materials, crafts, and photographs give an overview of Native American cultures in the Southwest and Mexico. | 2100 N. Amerind Rd., off Dragoon Rd., Dragoon | 520/586–3666 | $3 | Sept.–May, daily 10–4; June–Aug., Wed.–Sun. 10–4.

Apache Station Wildlife Viewing Area. The viewing area is open year-round, but from October to February you can spot birds like sandhill cranes. The wetlands 12 mi west of Willcox, off U.S. 191, attract numerous species. There is a public rest room for your convenience. | Off. U.S. 191 | 800/200–2272 | Free | Daily.

Chiricahua National Monument. The Chiricahua Apache Indians called this "The Land of Standing-up Rocks" for its dramatic vertical formations. These enormous outcroppings of volcanic rock have been eroded into dreamlike spires and pinnacles that look as though they could just as easily roll down the mountain. If you visit between July and September, you'll be treated to a thunderstorm almost every afternoon. Bird-watchers and hikers also gravitate to the monument. There are 17 mi of well-maintained hiking trails. The monument is 37 mi southeast of Willcox | U.S. 186 | 520/824–3560 | www.nps.gov/chir | $4 per vehicle | Daily 8–5.

Fort Bowie National Historic Site. Fort Bowie was a key player in the struggle between the expanding United States and the Apache, culminating in the surrender of Geronimo here in 1886. On the site you will also see a ruined stop of the Butterfield Stagecoach, which carried mail, passengers, and freight across the Southwest in the 1880s as well as the ruined fort. The site is about 37 mi from Willcox and accessible via a moderately strenuous 1½-mi walk that gives you a sense of the isolation of the fort as soldiers experienced it. | Off U.S. 186 | 520/847–2500 | www.nps.gov/fobo | Free | Daily 8–5.

Rex Allen Arizona Cowboy Museum and the Cowboy Hall of Fame. This downtown museum houses memorabilia of the famous cowboy, movie star, and entertainer, the late Rex Allen, who grew up in Willcox. You may remember him as the voice behind the Walt Disney nature films like *The Living Desert*. The Cowboy Hall of Fame is a portrait gallery of local cattle men and women. | 150 N. Railroad Ave. | 520/384–4583 | $2 | Daily 10–4.

ON THE CALENDAR

JAN.: *Wings Over Willcox/Sandhill Crane Celebration.* Celebration of over 20,000 cranes that arrive here every year from mid-October through mid-March. There are also workshops on wildlife and seminars the third weekend in January. | 520/384–2272 or 800/200–2272.

AUG.: *Peach Mania.* You'll find lots of sweet juicy peaches, along with an all-you-can-eat pancake breakfast starting at the crack of dawn, and free samples of various homemade peach foods about 6 mi north of Willcox. | 520/384–2084 or 800/840–2084.

OCT.: *Rex Allen Days.* A PRCA Rodeo, parade, fair and rides, turtle race, dancing, and activities for kids are highlights of this festival the first weekend in October. | 520/384–2272 or 800/200–2272.

Dining

Desert Rose Café. American. Fresh roses grace every table in the front room, and cowboy gear gives a more rugged mood in the back. Steaks, lobster, and tiger shrimp are popular here. | 706 S. Haskell | 520/384–0514 | No dinner Sun. | $4–$25 | D, MC, V.

Regal. American. This small, family-run place has been making everything from scratch since the 1960s. You won't have to break the bank at this affordable spot. Try any of the steaks, followed by the pie of the day. There is an adjoining bar with a jukebox and darts. | 301 N. Haskell Ave. | 520/384–4780 | Breakfast also available | $5–$10 | AE, D, DC, MC, V.

Stout's Cider Mill. American. This bakery across from the chamber of commerce makes local apple specialties, including cider and pie. There's a working cider mill. | 1510 N. Circle I Rd. | 520/384-3696 | $7–$15 | No credit cards.

Lodging

Best Western Plaza Inn. You'll have mountain views from this reliable motel 10 minutes from the Rex Allen Museum. Restaurant, bar, complimentary breakfast, room service. Some refrigerators, cable TV. Pool. Laundry facilities, laundry service. Business services. Some pets allowed (fee). | 1100 W. Rex Allen Dr. | 520/384-3556 | fax 520/384-2679 | 91 rooms | $59–$79 | AE, D, DC, MC, V.

Chiricahua Foothills B&B. Rooms are simple and comfortable at this ranch about 36 mi southeast of town, where people come for the peace and quiet. It's popular with bird-watchers and hikers. It's just ¼ mi southeast of the national monument entrance. Picnic area, complimentary breakfast. No air-conditioning, in-room VCRs (and movies), no room phones. No smoking. | 6310 Pinery Canyon Rd. | 520/824-3632 | 5 rooms | $70 | No credit cards.

Days Inn Willcox. This motel is right off Interstate 10 next to the Safeway shopping center. In-room data ports, cable TV. Pool. Laundry facilities. Business services. Some pets allowed. | 724 N. Bisbee Ave. | 520/384-4222 | fax 520/384-3785 | 73 rooms | $46–$65 | AE, D, DC, MC, V.

Grapevine Canyon Ranch. This guest ranch 30 mi west of Chiricahua National Monument is in the Dragoon Mountains next to a working cattle ranch. You get to watch and, in some cases, participate in, real day-to-day cowboy activities. Some rooms are a little plain, but others have striking southwestern-style decor. All meals and activities are included in the rates. Dining room. No room phones, no TV. Pool. Hot tub. Hiking, horseback riding. Laundry facilities. No kids under 12. | Pearce | 520/826-3185 | www.cowboys.com/grapevinecanyonranch | 12 rooms | $220–$260 (3-night minimum) | AP | AE, D, MC, V.

Muleshoe Ranch. The casitas, all of which have full kitchens, at this small property 30 mi northwest of Willcox are managed by the Arizona chapter of the Nature Conservancy. The primary draw here is the outdoors, on the thousands of starkly beautiful acres that have been preserved by the Nature Conservancy. There are hot natural springs on the property (for ranch guests' use only). Kitchenettes, no room phones, no TV. Hiking. | 6502 N. Muleshoe Ranch Rd. | 520/586-7072 | fax 520/586-7072 | www.tnc.org/arizona | 5 casitas | $88–$129 | AE, MC, V.

Sunglow Guest Ranch. This guest ranch in Cottonwood Canyon, about 15 mi south of Chiricahua National Monument, consists of mostly modern buildings. Rooms are around a courtyard and have views of the ponds or forest beyond. Unlike many guest ranches, no activities or meals are included in the room prices. Meals are available to ranch guests with 24 hours' notice. Dining room. Kitchenettes, refrigerators, no room phones, TV in common area. Lake. Hiking, horseback riding, fishing. | Turkey Creek Rd., Pearce | 520/824-3334 | 9 rooms, 1 house | $65–$89, $149 house | AE, MC, V.

WILLIAMS

MAP 3, E4

(Nearby town also listed: Flagstaff)

Named for the mountain man Bill Williams, a trapper in the 1820s and 1830s, Williams was founded when the railroad passed through in 1882. It's a small town less than an hour from the Grand Canyon (closer by an hour than Flagstaff) and is a reasonable place to stay if everything closer to the canyon is full. It's also where you catch the historic

Grand Canyon Railway for a slow, narrated ride to the canyon. Williams's Main Street is historic Route 66; in fact, the town wasn't bypassed by Interstate 40 until 1984. This is a popular area for hiking, hunting, and fishing. Tourism is its most important economic engine.

Information: **Williams and National Forest Service Visitors Center and Chamber of Commerce** | 200 W. Railroad Ave., Williams, 86046 | 520/635–4061.

Attractions

Grand Canyon Deer Farm. You can bond with precious critters like pygmy goats and trembling little fawns, which are born in June and July. More exotic specimens like llamas are also there for your petting pleasure at this place 8 mi east of Williams, off Interstate 40, exit 171. | 100 Deer Farm Rd. | 520/635–4073 | $5.50 | Jan.–Feb. and Nov.–Dec., daily 10–5; Mar.–May and Sept.–Oct., daily 10–6.

Grand Canyon Railway. In 1989 the railway re-inaugurated service that had first been established in 1901; railcars date from the 1920s. This scenic train route runs from the Williams Depot to the South Rim of the Grand Canyon (2½ hours each way). There are several classes of service; some tickets include food and beverages. The depot is worth a visit since there is a small railroad museum and a vintage train car to explore. | N. Grand Canyon Blvd. at Fray Marcos Blvd. | 800/843–8724 | $50–$120 plus national park admission fee of $6 per person. Depot free | Departs daily at 10 AM, returning to Williams at 3:30.

Kaibab National Forest. This huge national forest around the Grand Canyon encompasses more than 1.6 million acres. Wildlife unique to the land include the mule deer and Kaibab squirrel. Forested with pines and sycamores, the area offers hiking, fishing (trout), and camping. | Headquarters: 800 S. 6th St. | www.fs.fed.us/r3/kai | 520/635–2681 | Free | Daily.

Williams Ski Area. Four slopes include one for beginners only. There are also cross-country trails. Go 1½ mi south on 4th Street, then 1½ mi west on Ski Area Road. | Ski Area Rd. | 520/635–9330 | Mid-Dec.–Mar., Thurs.–Sun. 9–5.

ON THE CALENDAR

MAY: *Bill Williams Rendezvous Days.* A carnival, street dances, and pioneer arts and crafts each Memorial Day weekend. | 520/635–4061.

SEPT.: *Labor Day Rodeo.* A rodeo and Old West celebration each Labor Day weekend. | 520/635–4061.

DEC.: *Mountain Village Holidays.* Throughout December, you'll find craft sales, art shows featuring Native American jewelry, and hotel discounts, with a Parade of Lights on the first Saturday of the month. | 520/635–4061.

Dining

Cruisers Café 66. American. Icons from old Route 66 fill this renovated gas station. Steak platters and barbecue are the big sellers. In good weather you can sit outside. | 233 W. Rte. 66 | 520/635–2445 | No lunch | $6–$14 | AE, D, MC, V.

Pancho McGillicuddy's. Mexican. Dating from the late 1800s, this restaurant is on the National Register of Historic places. Wood tables, faux Mexican windows with iron bars, and a fountain add to the experience. Combination shrimp, chicken, and beef fajitas and chimichangas are on the menu. | 141 Railroad Ave. | 520/635–4150 | $6–$13 | AE, D, MC, V.

Rod's Steak House. Steak. You can't miss the huge plastic cow out front of this casual steak house known for charred steaks and prime rib. (They have a tendency to overcook.) Kids' menu. | 301 E. Bill Williams Ave. | 520/635–2671 | $7–$28 | MC, V.

Lodging

Best Western. This motel is nestled into a pine forest west of Williams on the edge of the Kaibab National Forest. Bar, complimentary Continental breakfast. In-room data ports, cable

TV. Pool. Hot tub. Laundry facilities, laundry service. Business services. | 2600 W. Bill Williams Ave. (Rte. 66) | 520/635–4400 | fax 520/635–4488 | www.bestwestern.com | 79 rooms, 10 suites | $89–$135, $125–$181 suites | AE, D, DC, MC, V.

El Rancho. This affordable motel is on the east side of Williams, ½ mi from the Grand Canyon Railway Depot. Some microwaves, some refrigerators, cable TV. Pool. | 617 E. Bill Williams Ave. | 520/635-2552 or 800/228–2370 | fax 520/635–4173 | www.thegrandcanyon.com/elrancho/ | 25 rooms, 2 suites | $62–$95, $95–$105 suites | AE, D, DC, MC, V.

Fray Marcos Hotel. Western art by a local artist decorates the grand lobby of this hotel, which has a huge flagstone fireplace. Southwestern-style rooms have large bathrooms. Restaurant, bar. Cable TV. Pool. Hot tub. Gym. Business services. | 235 N. Grand Canyon Blvd. | 520/635-4010 or 800/843–8724 | fax 520/635–2180 | 196 rooms | $79–$119 | AE, D, MC, V.

Holiday Inn. This family-friendly motel is three blocks from the Grand Canyon Railway Depot and a mile from Cataract Lake, which offers good fishing. Restaurant, bar, room service. Some refrigerators, cable TV. Pool. Hot tub. Gym. Laundry facilities, laundry service. Business services. Pets allowed. | 950 N. Grand Canyon Blvd. | 520/635–4114 | fax 520/635–2700 | 120 rooms, 12 suites | $79–$99, $99–$119 suites | AE, D, DC, MC, V.

Motel 6. This inexpensive motel is across the street from a Mexican restaurant and within walking distance of others on the west side of Williams. Cable TV. Pool. Hot tub. Laundry facilities. Business services. Pets allowed. | 831 W. Bill Williams Ave. | 520/635-9000 | fax 520/635–2300 | 52 rooms | $45–$69 | AE, D, DC, MC, V.

Norris Motel. It's ⅓ mi to the Grand Canyon Railway Depot from this comfortable motel on the west side of Williams that's popular with families. In-room data ports, some microwaves, refrigerators, cable TV. Pool. Hot tub. Business services. | 1001 W. Bill Williams Ave. | 520/635–2202 or 800/341–8000 | fax 520/635–9202 | ukgolf@primenet.com | 33 rooms | $59–$66 | AE, D, MC, V.

Mountainside Inn. This motel on 27 acres is one of the better maintained in town. There's a good steak house on the premises and country-and-western bands in summer. Hiking trails crisscross the property. Restaurant, bar, picnic area, room service. Some microwaves, some refrigerators, cable TV. Pool. Hot tub. Hiking. Some pets allowed (fee). | 642 E. Bill Williams Ave. | 520/635–4431 | fax 520/635–2292 | thegrandcanyon.com/mountainsideinn | 96 rooms | $86–$125 | AE, D, DC, MC, V.

Quality Inn Mountain Ranch and Resort. Just 6 mi east of town, this hotel is relatively convenient to Williams. Rooms are simple and predictable, but do offer views of the San Francisco Peaks. Restaurant, bar, complimentary Continental breakfast. Cable TV. Pool. Hot tub. 2 tennis courts. Horseback riding. Pets allowed (fee). | 6701 E. Mountain Ranch | 520/635–2693 | fax 520/635–4188 | www.qualityinn.com | 73 rooms | $75–$110 | AE, D, MC, V.

Red Garter. Built in 1897, this former bordello is now a bed-and-breakfast retaining an old-fashioned feel. Despite its location near railroad tracks, the rooms are quiet since the train runs infrequently. Rooms have 12-ft ceilings with skylights and Victorian antiques. Complimentary Continental breakfast. Cable TV, no room phones. No pets. No kids under 8. No smoking. | 137 W. Railroad Ave. | 520/635–1484 or 800/328–1484 | 4 rooms | $75–$110 | Closed Dec.–Jan. | AE, D, MC, V.

Sheridan House Inn. This bed-and-breakfast, nestled among pine trees just a few blocks off Route 66, provides a more soothing alternative to crowded Grand Canyon National Park lodgings. Hors d'oeuvres are served every afternoon, and the rates include both breakfast and dinner. Complimentary breakfast. Cable TV, in-room VCRs (and movies). Hot tub. Gym. Business services. | 460 E. Sheridan Ave. | 520/635–9441 or 888/635–9345 | www.thegrandcanyon.com/sheridan | 6 rooms, 2 suites | $95–$165, $175–$225 suites | MAP | AE, D, MC, V.

Terry Ranch. This modern log home at the base of Bill Williams Mountain has views of the surrounding mountains from the veranda. Baths have claw-foot tubs with showers; one room has a fireplace. Picnic area, complimentary breakfast. No air-conditioning, cable TV, in-room VCRs, no room phones. No smoking. | 701 Quarter Horse | 520/635–4171 or 800/210–5908 | fax 520/635–2488 | terryranch@workmail.com | 4 rooms | $100–$155 | AE, D, MC, V.

WINDOW ROCK

(Nearby town also listed: Ganado)

The headquarters of the Navajo Nation, Window Rock is named for the nearby natural sandstone bridge that looks like a window. With a population of fewer than 5,000, the town serves mainly as the business and social center for families living in the eastern part of the Navajo Nation. It's a good place to stop if you are traveling in this area.

Information: **Navajoland Tourism Dept.** | Hwy. 264 and Loop Rd., Box 663, Window Rock, 86515 | 520/871–6436 or 520/871–7371.

Attractions

Navajo Nation Council Chambers. This handsome building resembles a large hogan. Visitors can observe sessions of the council, where 88 delegates representing 100 reservation communities meet quarterly. | Off Hwy. 12 | 520/871–6436 | Free | 3rd Mon. in Jan., Apr., July, Oct.

Navajo Nation Museum. This small space in the Navajo Arts and Crafts Enterprise Center is devoted to the art, culture, and history of the Navajo people. There are rotating exhibits. Each season, the museum hosts Navajo artists. A store selling Navajo crafts is next door. | Hwy. 264 at Loop Rd. | 520/871–6673 | Free | Weekdays 8–5, Sat. 8–8.

Navajo Nation Zoological and Botanical Park. Set amid sandstone monoliths, this zoo northeast of the Navajo Nation Museum specializes in indigenous animals that are important in Navajo legend, including golden eagles, elk, and coyotes. Displays accentuate the relationship between local wildlife and Navajo culture. | Rte. 264 | 520/871–6573 | Free | Daily 8–5.

St. Michael's. This former mission 3 mi west of town is now a small museum with self-guided tours. | Hwy. 264 | 520/871–4171 | Free | Memorial Day–Labor Day, daily 9–5; Labor Day–Memorial Day, call for hours.

ON THE CALENDAR
JULY: *Powwow and PRCA Rodeo.* Rodeo, Native American arts and crafts, and entertainment at the Navajo Nation Fairgrounds. | July 4 | 520/871–6478.
SEPT.: *Navajo Nation Annual Tribal Fair.* A major event at the Navajo Nation Fairgrounds with a carnival, a rodeo, and a parade, beginning the Wednesday after Labor Day. | 520/871–6478.

Lodging
Navajo Land Days Inn. This motel is 2 mi west of Window Rock, in the neighboring town of St. Michaels. A Blimpie's sandwich shop is on the premises. Restaurant, complimentary Continental breakfast. In-room data ports, cable TV. Pool. Hot tub. Gym. Laundry service. Business services. | 392 W. Hwy. 264, St Michaels | 520/871–5690 | fax 520/871–5699 | www.daysinn.com | 73 rooms | $79–$99 | AE, D, DC, MC, V.

WINSLOW

MAP 3, F4

(Nearby towns also listed: Holbrook, Flagstaff)

Like many towns in the region, Winslow, about 51 mi east of Flagstaff, was born around the tracks of the railroad built through here in 1881. It's still somewhat of a railroad town and trade center, and it makes a good stopping point for an exploration of the Hopi Nation. Tourism has become its primary economic base.

Information: **Winslow Chamber of Commerce** | 300 W. North Rd., Winslow, 86047 | 520/289–2434 or 520/289–2435.

Attractions

Homolovi Ruins State Park. The ruins of a large complex of pueblos built by the Atsinom, ancestral Hopi people, are scattered in this area, including four late-14th-century sites; a few of the pueblos are well preserved. The Hopi consider that more than 300 archaeological sites are sacred. Ask about camping details. The park is 1 mi north of town on Highway 87. | Hwy. 87 | 520/289–4106 | $4 per vehicle (up to 4 people); $1 each additional person | Park daily; visitor center daily 8–5.

Hopi Indian Reservation. The Hopi Mesas in this vast reservation in northeastern Arizona and the small villages atop them are home to the Hopi, or "peaceful people," and they are so heavily touristed that you need advance permission to visit. Though all the villages are independent, you should call the Hopi Tribe Office of Public Relations in advance of your visit for the latest information regarding which permissions are necessary. Each of the three mesas offers a look at both ancient and contemporary Hopi tribal life; simple rock-and-adobe mortar structures share the space with satellite dishes. They are all along a 37-mile stretch of Highway 264 starting at Polacca and going west. | U.S. 264, Kykotsmovi | 520/734–2441 | www.hopi.nsn.us | Daily 9–5.

First Mesa. The largest community here is Polacca. Atop the mesa, there are three older villages: Hanoki, Sitsomovi, and Waalpi. These villages are known for their hand-coiled white pottery. Call the First Mesa Visitor's Center for permission and to arrange a guided tour

© Corbis

HOPI SNAKE DANCES

A Hopi village holds a snake dance every other year. Its purpose is to transmit prayers for rain to the spirits of the underworld. The elaborate ceremony takes place over 16 days.

The first four days of the ceremony involve collecting snakes, both poisonous and nonpoisonous, from the four cardinal directions. The next 11 days incorporate footraces and other tribal festivities.

On the final day of the ceremonies, the actual snake dance is performed by the Men of the Snake Society, tribal members who form pairs and dance with the snakes they've gathered. One dancer holds a snake in his mouth; the other hypnotizes it with an eagle feather.

Visitors are allowed by permission only. Inquire at the Hopi Tribal Council for more information (Box 123, Kykotsmovi, AZ 86039, 520/743–2441)

of the three older villages. | U.S. 264, Polacca | 520/737–2262 | www.hopi.nsn.us | Tours $5 | Guided tours daily 9–4 (by reservation only, except when ceremonies are being held).

Hopi Cultural Center. This center 68 mi north of Winslow via Highway 87 is a good place to learn about the Hopi people, their reservation, and their cuisine. A museum here displays local artifacts. Some of the colorful Hopi ceremonies with dancing are open to the public; all are free. | U.S. 264, Second Mesa | 520/734–2401 | www.hopi.nsn.us | $5 | Weekdays 8–5.

Second Mesa. The largest and oldest village here is Shongopovi; there are also two smaller villages, Mishongnovi and Shipaulovi. Inquire at the Hopi Cultural Center, in Second Mesa, about permission to visit these villages, which are known for remarkable silver jewelry and coiled plaques. | U.S. 264, Second Mesa | 520/734–2401 | www.hopi.nsn.us | Tours $5 | Guided tours daily 9–4 (by reservation only, except when ceremonies are being held).

Third Mesa. There are four villages on Third Mesa: Oraibi, Kykotsmovi, Hotevilla, and Bacavi. The tribal headquarters is in Kykotsmovi, which is known for its greenery and peach orchards. Contact the Office of Public Relations in advance of your visit for permission to visit these villages. | U.S. 264, Kykotsmovi | 520/734–2441 | www.hopi.nsn.us | Tours $5 | Guided tours daily 9–4 (by reservation only, except when ceremonies are being held).

Meteor Crater. An impressive hole in the ground that's 600 ft deep, 1 mi across, and 3 mi in circumference, the Meteor Crater was formed when a meteorite crashed here 50,000 years ago. One-hour guided tours are available. It's 37 mi east of town on Interstate 40, at exit 233, then 5 mi south on Meteor Crater Rd. | Meteor Crater Rd. | 520/289–2362 or 800/289–5898 | www.meteorcrater.com | $10 for tour | May–Sept., daily 6–6; Oct.–Apr. daily 8–5.

Old Trails Museum. You'll find the best collection of Route 66 memorabilia anywhere in the state at this small museum. | 212 N. Kinsley Ave. | 520/289–5861 | Donations accepted | Apr.–Oct., Tues.–Sat. 10–4; Nov.–Mar., Tues., Thurs., Sat. 10–4.

Dining

Casa Blanca Café. Mexican. The meals here lean towards down-home, traditional cooking. Blue-corn enchiladas, steak enchiladas, and steak à la Mexicano are the standouts, and the prices will leave you staring in disbelief. Ceramic floors, paintings of Mexican peasants, and a jukebox full of *musica latina* add to the authentic mood. | 1201 E. 2nd St. | 520/289–4191 | $6–$7 | AE, D, DC, MC, V.

Falcon. American. This casual and friendly 1950s-style diner offers home cooking. Try the chicken-fried steak or homemade pies. Kids' menu. | 1113 E. 3rd St. | 520/289–2342 | Breakfast also available | $4–$13 | AE, D, MC, V.

Lodging

Best Western Adobe Inn. This motel is right off Interstate 40. Restaurant, bar, room service. Cable TV. Pool. Hot tub. Laundry facilities. Business services. Some pets allowed (fee). | 1701 N. Park Dr. | 520/289–4638 | fax 520/289–5514 | www.daysinn.com | 70 rooms, 2 suites | $55–$70, $80 suites | AE, D, DC, MC, V.

Econo Lodge at I-40. This motel is right off Interstate 40 at exit 253, on the northeast side of Winslow. Some microwaves, some refrigerators, cable TV. Pool. Laundry facilities. Business services. Pets allowed (fee). | 1706 N. Park Dr. | 520/289–4687 | fax 520/289–9377 | 72 rooms | $45–$69 | AE, D, DC, MC, V.

Winslow Inn. This motel is dirt cheap, rooms are downright institutional, and you may be awakened by the trains that churn by. Cable TV. Pets allowed. | 701 W. 3rd St. | 520/289–9389 | fax 520/289–9197 | 63 rooms | $30 | AE, D, DC, MC, V.

YUMA

(Nearby town also listed: Gila Bend)

When the Spanish arrived in the 1500s looking for a shallow place to cross the Colorado River, Native Americans had been farming the area near Yuma for centuries, and agriculture still plays an important role in Yuma County's economy. (More than 202,145 acres were harvested in 1994.) But a town didn't really take root here until three centuries later, when Fort Yuma was established in 1850 to guard the community against Indian attacks; the building of the territorial prison here in 1876 stabilized the economy and allowed it to grow. And, in the late 1800s, this southwestern town bordering California and Mexico became an important river-crossing point into Mexico. The Laguna Dam, completed in 1909, assured the area a consistent supply of water and controlled the overflow of the Colorado River, which made further agricultural development possible. Isolated in the southwestern corner of the state, Yuma is Arizona's third-largest metropolitan area and the fourth-fastest-growing metropolitan area in the nation. Recreational activities include four-wheeling in the dramatic sand dunes and waterskiing in the Colorado River.

Information: Convention and Visitors Bureau | 377 S. Main St., Box 11059, Yuma, 85366 | 520/783–0071 | www.visityuma.com.

Attractions

Arizona Historical Society Century House Museum and Gardens. This museum, in a building built around 1870, exhibits artifacts from Yuma's territorial days and explains the military presence in the area. | 240 Madison Ave. | 520/782–1841 | Free | Tues.–Sat. 10–4.

Cocopah Casino. The Cocopah Indian tribe manages this full-service casino and bingo hall 5 mi southeast of Yuma in Somerton. | 15136 S. Ave. B, Somerton | 520/726–8066 | Free | Daily 24 hrs.

Fort Yuma Quechan Indian Museum. Once the mess hall for Fort Yuma and then a school for Indian children, this space now houses a small museum displaying historical photographs, Indian artifacts, archaeological finds, and art pieces. It's a mile north of Yuma. | 350 Picacho Rd. | 760/572–0661 | $1 | Daily 8–5.

Imperial National Wildlife Refuge. This 25,765-acre refuge 40 mi north of town via U.S. 95 is devoted to the protection of indigenous river and desert creatures, on land set aside after the building of the Imperial Dam. It has become an important nesting ground for migrating waterfowl. Mosquitoes are least active from October to May, which makes your visit more pleasant. The mile-long Painted Desert Nature Trail takes you through different levels of the Sonoran Desert. | Red Cloud Mine Rd. | 520/783–3371 | Free | Weekdays 8–4.

Yuma Crossing State Historic Park. Across the Colorado River from Fort Yuma, the historic home of riverboat captain G. A. Johnson is the centerpiece of this park, which opened in 1997. Yuma Crossing was an important distribution point for steamboat freight headed overland to Arizona forts. You can tour the home, a re-creation of the Commanding Officer's Quarters, and a transportation museum. | 4th Ave., between 1st St. and the Colorado River Bridge | 520/329–0471 | www.pr.state.az.us | $3 | Daily 10–5.

Yuma Territorial Prison State Historic Park. Built between 1876 and 1909 primarily by convicts, this prison is the most notorious sight in town. Closed in 1909, when the prison population outgrew the location, the prison was considered state-of-the-art for its time. The mess hall opened as a museum in 1940, and now you can take guided tours of the cell block (in winter only), mess hall, and grounds. Take the Giss Parkway exit off Interstate 8. | 1 Prison Hill Rd. | 520/783–4771 | www.pr.state.az.us | $3 | Daily 8–5.

Yuma Valley Railway. Short 34-mi excursions are offered around the Yuma area, including picnic rides. The ride takes about 3 hours. The depot is right behind City Hall. | 1st St. and 2nd Ave. | 520/783–3456 | $11 | Nov.–May, weekends 1pm. Closed June–Oct.

ON THE CALENDAR
MAR.: *Midnight at the Oasis Festival.* This three-day antique car show in Desert Sun Stadium on the first weekend in March also has live bands playing 1950s music. | 520/343–1715.
APR.: *Yuma County Fair.* Livestock, rides, games, and entertainment at the fairgrounds. | 520/726–4420.

Dining
Bella Vita Restaurant. Italian. There are no surprises on the menu; the big sellers are good old spaghetti Bolognese and lasagna. Red tablecloths and photographs of Italy add a little zest to the room. | 2755 South Ave. | 520/344–3989 | $5–$14 | No credit cards.

Chretin's Mexican Food. Mexican. This Yuma institution opened as a dance hall in the 1930s before becoming one of the first Mexican restaurants in town in 1946. The interior is nondescript, but the food, all made on the premises (including the chips and tortillas), is fresh and delicious. Try anything with *machaca* (shredded spiced beef or chicken). | 485 S. 15th Ave. | 520/782–1291 | Closed Sun. | $6–$12 | D, MC, V.

The Crossing. American/Casual. This casual and welcoming place is said to have the best buffalo wings in Yuma; you might also want to try the hot and spicy burger called the SMA. When it's not too hot, you can eat outside on a patio. Kids' menu. Margaritas, wine, beer. | 2690 S. 4th Ave. | 520/726–5551 | $7–$20 | AE, D, MC, V.

Hunter Steakhouse. Steak. A friendly, bustling steak house popular with locals. Try the prime ribs and the baby-back ribs. Kids' menu. | 2355 S. 4th Ave. | 520/782–3637 | No lunch weekends | $11–$30 | AE, D, DC, MC, V.

Mandarin Palace. Chinese. This restaurant serving the usual staples of Americanized Szechuan cuisine has a sort of China-meets-the-Southwest feel. Try the seafood dishes, beef stir-fry, or the kung pao chicken. | 350 E. 32nd St. | 520/344–2805 | $9–$30 | AE, DC, MC, V.

Lodging
Best Western Coronado Motor Hotel. This Spanish-style hotel was built in 1938, and it's still efficiently run by the same family who originally built it. (Bob Hope stayed here often during World War II, when he entertained the troops training in the area.) Rooms have always been well kept and are consistently refurbished. Restaurant, bar, complimentary Continental breakfast. In-room data ports, some kitchenettes, microwaves, refrigerators, cable TV, some in-room VCRs. 2 pools. Hot tub. Laundry facilities. | 233 4th Ave. | 520/783–4454 or 800/528–1234 | fax 520/782–7487 | www.bestwestern.com | 49 rooms | $69–$99 | AE, D, DC, MC, V.

Innsuites Yuma. This all-suite, low-rise hotel is close to the Colorado River Park and offers large rooms. It's one of the better chain options in Yuma. Complimentary Continental breakfast. In-room data ports, microwaves, refrigerators, cable TV. Pool. Hot tub. 2 tennis courts. Gym. Library. Laundry facilities, laundry service. Business services. Pets allowed. | 1450 Castle Dome Ave. | 520/783–8341 | fax 520/783–1349 | www.innsuites.com | 166 suites | $69–$139 | AE, D, DC, MC, V.

Interstate 8 Inn. This inexpensive, independent motel built in 1990 offers basic rooms within walking distance of several restaurants. It's right off Interstate 8. Picnic area. Some microwaves, refrigerators, cable TV. Pool. Hot tub. Laundry facilities. Business services. Some pets allowed. | 2730 S. 4th Ave. | 520/726–6110 or 800/821–7465 | fax 520/726–7711 | 120 rooms | $57 | AE, D, DC, MC.

La Fuente Inn. This motel near the airport, popular with military personnel, is unremarkable, but it's got good-size rooms and is well maintained. Complimentary Continental breakfast. Some microwaves, refrigerators, cable TV. Pool. Hot tub. Gym. Laundry facilities. Business services. | 1513 E. 16th St. | 520/329–1814 or 800/841–1814 | fax 520/343–2671 | 50 rooms, 46 suites | $49–$85, $88–$99 suites | AE, D, DC, MC, V.

Martinez Lake Resort. On Martinez Lake, 35 mi north of Yuma, this resort has spartan cabins, but people come here to waterski, fish for catfish, and spend time away from urban life rather than lounge about their rooms. The restaurant features live bands every Saturday. The resort is off U.S. 95, 13 mi down Martinez Drive, on the lake. Restaurant, bar. No room phones, no TV. Lake. Water sports, boating. Pets allowed (fee). | Martinez Dr. | 520/783–9589 or 800/876–7004 | fax 520/782–3360 | www.martinezlake.com | 8 cabins, 4 houses | $65 cabins, $135–$235 houses | D, MC, V.

Palms Inn. The rooms in this inexpensive motel may be bland, but the rosebushes and gardens growing outside add a little bit of character. Plus, it's close to several malls. All beds are queen size. Some microwaves, some refrigerators, cable TV. Pool. | 2655 S. 4th Ave. | 520/344–0082 | fax 520/344–6905 | 31 rooms | $55–$65 | AE, D, MC, V.

Radisson Suites Inn. This upscale all-suite hotel is 2 mi from the airport and within walking distance of several restaurants. It's a sprawling hotel, with a well-manicured courtyard. Complimentary Continental breakfast. Microwaves, refrigerators, cable TV. Pool. Hot tub. Laundry facilities, laundry service. Business services, airport shuttle. Pets allowed. | 2600 S. 4th Ave. | 520/726–4830 | fax 520/341–1152 | 164 suites | $58–$119 | AE, D, DC, MC, V.

Shilo Inn Yuma. On the outskirts of Yuma, this quiet, secluded hotel has a tropical courtyard. Despite being a conference center, it's popular with leisure travelers. Restaurant, bar, complimentary breakfast. In-room data ports, some kitchenettes, some microwaves, some refrigerators, cable TV. Pool. Hot tub, sauna, steam room. Gym. Laundry facilities, laundry service. Business services. Pets allowed. | 1550 S. Castle Dome Rd. | 520/782–9511 | fax 520/783–1538 | www.shiloinn.com | 134 rooms | $89–$260 | AE, D, DC, MC, V.

PACKING IDEAS FOR HOT WEATHER

- ❑ Antifungal foot powder
- ❑ Bandanna
- ❑ Cooler
- ❑ Cotton clothing
- ❑ Day pack
- ❑ Film
- ❑ Hiking boots
- ❑ Insect repellent
- ❑ Rain jacket
- ❑ Sport sandals
- ❑ Sun hat
- ❑ Sunblock
- ❑ Synthetic ice
- ❑ Umbrella
- ❑ Water bottle

*Excerpted from *Fodor's: How to Pack: Experts Share Their Secrets*
© 1997, by Fodor's Travel Publications

Yuma Airport Travelodge. This two-story motel is near the Yuma airport, 3 mi from downtown. Restaurant, bar, picnic area, complimentary Continental breakfast. Some in-room data ports, some microwaves, some refrigerators, cable TV. Pool. Hot tub. Laundry facilities, laundry service. Business services. Some pets allowed. | 711 E. 32nd St. | 520/726–4721 | fax 520/344–0452 | 80 rooms | $62 | AE, D, MC, V.

Colorado

If you like high places, Colorado is the spot for you. Split down the middle, north to south, by the majestic Rocky Mountain chain, the Centennial State's average elevation is 6,800 ft, and it claims 56 peaks that tower more than 14,000 ft above sea level. Even the lowest point in the state is not very low—well over ½ mi high, at 3,350 ft.

The name Colorado is derived from the Spanish word for red, and it was the reddish-color water in the region's namesake river that prompted the appellation. Covering a vast region by any measurement, Colorado's nearly 67 million acres make it the eighth-largest state in the Union.

Like other Rocky Mountain states, Colorado is a land of great geographical contrasts. Its terrain varies from the flat Great Plains of the east to the 2½-mi-high peaks clustered along the Continental Divide. Raging white-water rivers, such as the Gunnison and the Colorado in the mountainous west, give way to wide, shallow, placid waterways such as the Platte in the flatlands of the east.

Colorado is a vacationer's paradise regardless of the season. Full of historical attractions, natural wonders, scenic vistas, and quaint towns and villages, the state also offers some of the most outstanding skiing in North America. Two national parks, totaling more than 300,000 acres, are complemented by 8 national monuments and recreational centers, 15 national forests and grasslands, and 40 state parks, to bring the total acreage set aside by the federal or state government to several million.

History

Colorado's first residents were American Indians of the Paleo culture who arrived in the area as early as 10 to 15 thousand years ago. Big-game hunters who had crossed

CAPITAL: DENVER	POPULATION: 3,410,216	AREA: 103,598 SQUARE MI
BORDERS: NM, OK, KS, NE, WY, UT	TIME ZONE: MOUNTAIN	POSTAL ABBREVIATION: CO
WEB SITE: WWW.COLORADO.COM		

the Bering Strait from Siberia into Alaska, these wandering bands of men, women, and children had gradually migrated southward along the eastern front of the Rocky Mountains into today's states of Montana, Wyoming, Colorado, and New Mexico. There, they found vast herds of plains-dwelling mammals, including giant bison, woolly mammoths, mastodons, elk, and other long-extinct species. With this proliferation of big game, hunting was good for these early emigrants and they occupied the countryside for thousands of years.

Nearly 8,500 years ago a small band of Paleo hunters slaughtered hundreds of bison near Big Sandy Creek in southeastern Colorado. The kill site was discovered by amateur archaeologists in 1957, and today it represents one of the many places in the state where evidence of prehistoric life exists. Hundreds of years after the Big Sandy Creek hunters killed the 200 bison and carted off the meat, fat, and hides, another group of prehistoric people settled the vast canyon lands of the Four Corners region of southwestern Colorado. There they built a number of cliff dwellings in what is today Mesa Verde National Park and lived for hundreds of years farming the rich river bottoms by day and climbing to their homes hundreds of feet above the valley floor at night.

As early as 1807, an American army officer, Zebulon M. Pike, explored the headwaters of the Arkansas River in the Pueblo region before being arrested by Spanish soldiers and hauled off to Mexico. Although Colorado was frequented by Spanish military parties from neighboring New Mexico, no permanent Hispanic settlements were established within the area until the 19th century, when Mexicans occupied the San Luis Valley. In the meantime, much of the present-day state had been explored by mountain men, mostly American beaver trappers.

When the Mexican-American War ended in 1848, the southern portion of present-day Colorado, originally in the possession of Mexico, was ceded with most of the rest of the present-day Southwest to the United States. Not until a down-on-his-luck former "California 49er" named George Jackson discovered gold on Clear Creek near the newly settled village of Denver in early 1859 was much attention directed to the region that would one day become Colorado. But, when the word got out that placer gold was indeed to be found in the creeks rushing out of the Rocky Mountains, prospectors by the thousands converged upon the area with gold pan and pick in hand. The so-called "Pike's Peak" gold rush was on, and over the next 50 years more than $100 million of the precious metal was extracted from the region.

Rapidly declining North-South relations in the East and a means to finance what appeared to be a quickly approaching war galvanized political opinions in Washington, D.C., that the vast, gold-bearing region should become part of the Union. Accordingly, in February 1861, two months before the Civil War erupted in South Carolina, Congress bestowed territorial status on Colorado and immediately began to study ways to capitalize on Colorado's newly found wealth.

CO Timeline

6500 BC	AD 1300	1776	1807
Big-game hunters of the Paleo culture slaughter more than 200 bison near Big Sandy Creek in southeastern Colorado. The remains of the site will be discovered by archaeologists in 1957.	Indians of the Anasazi culture abandon Mesa Verde and other sites in the Four Corners region after an occupation there of nearly 700 years.	The Dominguez-Escalante Expedition sets out from Santa Fe, New Mexico, and explores much of southwestern Colorado.	Lieutenant Zebulon M. Pike, under orders to explore the far-western reaches of newly acquired Louisiana Territory, is arrested by Spanish soldiers on the headwaters of the Rio Grande River in southern Colorado.

INTRODUCTION
HISTORY
REGIONS
WHEN TO VISIT
STATE'S GREATS
RULES OF THE ROAD
DRIVING TOURS

Although no actual combat between Confederate and Union forces ever occurred on Colorado soil, authorities in the new territory kept a wary eye on what they feared would be an invasion by the Southerners. Instead, the duration of the war was occupied with various Indian skirmishes, primarily between the Colorado Volunteers, under the dubious command of Colonel John Chivington, culminating in Chivington's massacre of a peaceful Cheyenne Indian camp at Sand Creek in late November 1864.

The coming of the railroad to Colorado after the Civil War brought additional attention and new settlers to the territory, and by 1876 the region had fulfilled the population requirements for statehood. On August 1, 1876—during the centennial year of the United States, hence the nickname "Centennial State"—Colorado was officially admitted to the Union as the 38th state by a decree signed by President Ulysses S. Grant.

For almost 20 years, the vast amounts of gold that had been extracted from Colorado's mountains had made many people wealthy and had provided badly needed funds for the nation's treasury. Now, during the early days of statehood, the region once again found itself in the national limelight by the discovery of yet another precious metal: silver. Almost overnight, repeating the activity of the hectic days of the gold rush, prospectors and miners flocked to the Rocky Mountains by the thousands, hoping they would become the newest millionaires.

During the last part of the 19th century, Colorado also became known for its cattle industry. For years, trail drivers had herded cows out of Texas into New Mexico, then northward through Colorado to Wyoming and Montana. One of the best known of these cattle thoroughfares was the Goodnight-Loving Trail, which eventually connected Fort Belknap, Texas, with Cheyenne, Wyoming. Charles Goodnight himself became a prominent rancher in Colorado before moving back to Texas in the late 1870s.

Gold, silver, and cattle were all elements that prompted a large population increase in Colorado. By 1890, with a population approaching ½ million, the state had more than doubled in the number of residents during the past decade. It was also during this period of relative prosperity that much of the state's imposing Victorian architecture was created and its residents' cultural values firmly established. Both the Universities of Denver and of Colorado, as well as the Colorado School of Mines and several other institutions of higher learning were established in this era.

Although Colorado's population increase slowed considerably between 1920 and 1940, the region's attractiveness to industry and tourism have made it one of the nation's most rapidly growing states. The population now approaches 4 million people, many of them clustered along the Front Range of the Rocky Mountains between Pueblo in the south, northward through Colorado Springs and Denver, and on to the Wyoming border.

1821		**1822**	**1832**	**1835**
After hearing that Mexico had won its independence from Spain and was now anxious to trade with Americans, Missouri entrepreneur William Becknell charts the path of the Santa Fe Trail	through Colorado to Santa Fe.	Two American fur trappers, Hugh Glenn and Jacob Fowler, spend the winter on the site of present-day Pueblo.	The Bent brothers of St. Louis, Charles and William, along with their partner, Ceran St. Vrain, build Bent's Fort on the Arkansas River near present-day La Junta.	Louis Vasquez and Andrew Sublette build their fur post, Ft. Vasquez, near present-day Platteville.

The Regions

1. Northeast

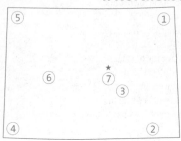

Colorado's Northeast Region is dominated by vast grasslands that seem to stretch all the way to the horizon. Sometimes called "the other Colorado," the area stands in stark contrast to the lofty, snow-covered peaks of the Rocky Mountains found far to the west. Agriculture is the primary industry here, and country flavor and rural attitudes abound. The largest town is Sterling, with close to 14,000 people. The sparseness of the population aside, there is still plenty to do and see in this region, including the site of the Beecher Island standoff between the U. S. army and some of the Cheyenne nation's best warriors, and the hometown of world-renowned band leader Glenn Miller.

Towns listed: Burlington, Fort Morgan, Limon, Sterling

2. Southeast

The Southeast Region is similar to the Northeast in that the landscape is one of endless panoramas. Sweeping grasslands stretch forever before your eyes, here and there punctuated by a farm or ranch building. While it was still part of Mexico, this part of Colorado was one of the first sections visited by merchants from the United States as they trekked across the newly routed Santa Fe Trail on their way to the rich markets of New Mexico. Pueblo, with a population of 123,000, is the largest community in this region and other sizable towns include La Junta, Trinidad, Walsenburg, and Lamar.

Towns listed: Cuchara, La Junta, Pueblo, Trinidad, Walsenburg

3. South Central

Colorado Springs, with a population of almost 362,000 people, is the largest city in the South Central Region. This is the section where the Great Plains in the east meet the Rocky Mountains in the west. It is a land of contrasts, ranging from the magnificent, glistening dunes at Great Sand Dunes National Monument to the towering, snow-covered heights of Pike's Peak that lent inspiration to the writing of "America, the Beautiful." The United States Air Force Academy, with its familiar chapel, lies nestled in the foothills north of Colorado Springs, and ghost towns and other deserted mining villages abound in the Sangre de Cristo (Blood of Christ) range of the Rockies.

Towns listed: Alamosa, Buena Vista, Cañon City, Colorado Springs, Cripple Creek, Fairplay, Leadville, Manitou Springs, Monte Vista, Salida South Fork

1851	1853	1859	1860	
Present-day Colorado receives its first white residents as natives of northern New Mexico settle in the San Luis River valley.	Captain John W. Gunnison of the U.S. Corps of Topographical Engineers surveys the land along the 38th parallel through Colorado to determine its feasibility for a transcontinental railroad route.	Gold is discovered in the Clear Creek region about 30 mi west of Denver. The site will ultimately yield more than $100 million of the precious metal.	In order to take care of all the gold being found in the region, Emanuel Gruber and brothers Austin and Milton Clark establish a private mint in Denver. More than $120,000 worth of gold coins are minted during	the first three months of operation.

INTRODUCTION
HISTORY
REGIONS
WHEN TO VISIT
STATE'S GREATS
RULES OF THE ROAD
DRIVING TOURS

4. Southwest

Mention Colorado's Southwest Region, and the first thing that comes to mind are the ancient cliff dwellings at Mesa Verde National Park. Named by readers of *Condé Nast Traveler* magazine as the world's number-one historic monument, these Anasazi ruins are more than one thousand years old. The region is also great for fly-fishing, mountain biking, hiking, and white-water sports and abounds with silver-mining history and lore. Several narrow-gauge railroads allow for some interesting side trips through the towering mountains. Durango, with a population over 21,000, and Montrose, with over 17,500, are the two largest towns.

Towns listed: Cortez, Crested Butte, Dolores, Durango, Gunnison, Lake City, Mesa Verde National Park, Montrose, Norwood, Ouray, Pagosa Springs, Silverton, Telluride

5. Northwest

Theodore Roosevelt liked Colorado's Northwest Region so much that he traveled there often on big-game hunting trips. Today, skiing vies with hunting and fishing as popular sports in these parts. Vail, Breckenridge, Aspen, and Steamboat Springs are just a few of the winter wonderlands you'll find in this region that combines "jet-set" fashions with "rural Americana" lifestyles. Mountains, lakes, canyons, and fast-flowing rivers all combine to make this area one of the most popular and most traveled sections of the state.

Towns listed: Aspen, Beaver Creek, Breckenridge, Cedaredge, Copper Mountain, Craig, Delta, Dillon, Dinosaur, Frisco, Georgetown, Glenwood Springs, Granby, Grand Junction, Grand Lake, Keystone, Kremmling, Meeker, Palisade, Rifle, Steamboat Springs, Vail, Winter Park

6. Front Range

Stretching from the Wyoming border down the eastern slope of the Rocky Mountains to just north of Denver, the Front Range Region is home to several medium-size cities, including Fort Collins (population, 109,000), Boulder (225,000), Greeley (76,500), Longmont (63,600), and Loveland (54,000). Also here are the world-famous Rocky Mountain National Park and beautiful Estes Park. There is a lot to see along the Front Range, from the historic fur post at Fort Vasquez to the oldest operating hotel in Colorado at Empire, which has hosted the likes of P. T. Barnum and General Ulysses S. Grant and his cohort, William T. Sherman.

Towns listed: Allenspark, Boulder, Estes Park, Fort Collins, Greeley, Longmont, Loveland, Lyons, Nederland, Rocky Mountain National Park

7. Denver Region

Denver and its outlying suburbs have a combined population of well over 1 million residents, making it one of the largest marketing areas in the entire West. Home to the

1861	1864		1866	1868
Colorado is created as a territory of the United States.	Despite the fact that he is flying the U.S. flag over his camp as a token of friendship, Cheyenne chief Black Kettle and his followers are attacked by Colonel John Chivington and his Third	Colorado Volunteers at Sand Creek in southeastern Colorado. Between 200 and 400 Cheyennes and Arapahoes— mostly women and children—are slaughtered.	Charles Goodnight and Oliver Loving blaze a cattle trail— afterward called the Goodnight-Loving Trail—from Texas through New Mexico to Denver.	The Battle of Beecher Island is fought on the Arikara Fork of the Republican River, resulting in the near annihilation of Major George A. Forsyth's command and the death of the Cheyenne warrior Roman Nose.

Super Bowl champion Denver Broncos, the "mile-high city" also boasts a brand-new airport, as well as a large variety of museums, parks, theaters, and sports venues. Denver sits astride Interstate 25 and as such is centrally located in Colorado and is on the direct route from New Mexico to Wyoming. Endless plains to the east are contrasted to the backdrop of the monumental Rocky Mountains to the west. Denver is a cultured, sophisticated city poised for its coming-of-age in the 21st century. Coloradans like to boast that if you can't find what you're looking for in Denver, you can't find it anywhere west of the Mississippi River.

Towns listed: Aurora, Central City, Denver, Englewood, Evergreen, Golden, Idaho Springs, Lakewood

When to Visit

Colorado is an all-year destination. Each of the four seasons, which are quite distinct, offers its own unique attractions ranging from sightseeing, hiking, boating, mountain biking, and fishing during warmer weather to downhill and cross-country skiing in the winter.

Many parts of Colorado average as many as 300 days of sunshine annually. The abundance of sun, however, does not mean that temperatures are constant. In fact, official records reveal that the highest temperature ever recorded in Colorado was 118°F on July 11, 1888, at Bennett, while the lowest was minus 61°F on February 1, 1985, at Maybell. The average high temperature across the state in July is 73°, while the average low in January is 26°. Temperatures fluctuate across the state and across the seasons, with warm summer days approaching the 90s, while evenings often fall off to the 40s and 50s. Winters can be long, cold, and snowy, with daytime highs barely approaching freezing, but with nighttime temperatures sometimes plunging to well below zero.

Likewise, the amount of precipitation received annually varies greatly as you go from east to west. Moisture is so sparse in some sections of the high plains that massive irrigation is required to support agriculture. In the mountains to the west, on the other hand, snowdrifts measuring several feet deep are common every winter.

The best rule of thumb for dressing—regardless of the type of weather you expect to encounter in Colorado—is to layer your clothing so that adjustments can be made to attain your own personal comfort level. By all means, if you intend to visit the state during the winter, bring warm clothing.

CLIMATE CHART
Average High/Low Temperatures (°F) and Monthly Precipitation (in inches)

	JAN.	FEB.	MAR.	APR.	MAY	JUNE
ALAMOSA	33/-4 .26	40/5 .29	49/16 .45	59/24 .49	68/33 .64	78/41 .67

1874
Alferd (sometimes spelled "Alfred") Packer, a down-on-his-luck prospector, gets lost in the midst of the Colorado Rockies; he walks out of the wilderness without his companions and it becomes clear that he has cannibalized them.

1876
Colorado becomes the 38th state of the Union on August 1.

1877
Leadville, at an altitude of 10,000 ft, is established and quickly becomes the center of Colorado's newfound silver rush.

1878
Two different railroads—the Atchison, Topeka, and Santa Fe, and the Denver and Rio Grande—reach central Colorado. The ATSF continues its road over Raton Pass into New Mexico.

INTRODUCTION
HISTORY
REGIONS
WHEN TO VISIT
STATE'S GREATS
RULES OF THE ROAD
DRIVING TOURS

COLORADO SPRINGS

	JULY	AUG.	SEPT.	OCT.	NOV.	DEC.
	82/48	79/45	73/37	63/25	47/12	35/-.5
	1.19	1.12	.89	.7	.43	.44
	JAN.	FEB.	MAR.	APR.	MAY	JUNE
	41/16	45/19	50/25	60/33	69/42	79/51
	.29	.4	.94	1.19	2.15	2.25

DENVER

	JULY	AUG.	SEPT.	OCT.	NOV.	DEC.
	84/57	81/55	74/47	64/36	51/25	42/17
	2.9	3.02	1.33	.84	.47	.46
	JAN.	FEB.	MAR.	APR.	MAY	JUNE
	43/16	47/19	52/25	62/33	71/42	81/51
	.5	.57	1.28	1.71	2.4	1.79

GRAND JUNCTION

	JULY	AUG.	SEPT.	OCT.	NOV.	DEC.
	88/57	86/55	77/47	66/36	53/25	45/17
	1.91	1.51	1.24	.98	.87	.64
	JAN.	FEB.	MAR.	APR.	MAY	JUNE
	36/15	45/24	56/31	66/39	76/48	88/57
	.56	.48	.9	.75	.87	.5

PUEBLO

	JULY	AUG.	SEPT.	OCT.	NOV.	DEC.
	94/64	91/62	81/53	68/42	51/29	39/19
	.65	.81	.82	.98	.71	.61
	JAN.	FEB.	MAR.	APR.	MAY	JUNE
	45/14	51/20	57/26	68/36	77/46	88/54
	.32	.31	.78	.88	1.25	1.25
	JULY	AUG.	SEPT.	OCT.	NOV.	DEC.
	93/61	90/59	81/50	71/37	57/24	47/16
	2.09	1.99	.9	.57	.43	.42

FESTIVALS AND SEASONAL EVENTS
WINTER

Dec.   **Victorian Christmas and Home Tour, Leadville.** The town's beautifully restored and rebuilt Victorian homes and businesses are all decorated for the holidays. | 719/486–3900 or 888/264–5344.

Jan.   **The National Western Livestock Show, Horse Show and Rodeo, Denver.** This two-week event includes one of the largest livestock competitions in the West. | 303/297–1166.

1880
Ouray, the celebrated chief of the Ute Indians, dies at the age of 60.

1892
Bob Ford, the killer of Jesse James, is himself murdered in his saloon in Creed.

1913
Mary Harris Johns, known to the world as "Mother Jones," arrives in Trinidad to the cheers of hundreds of local coal and iron miners. Before she is forced to leave the state, the 83-year-old labor organizer instigates a massive strike that eventually brings out the national guard.

1917
William F. (Wild Bill) Cody dies at his sister's home in Denver. Despite his instructions that he be buried in his namesake town of Cody, Wyoming, he is interred atop Lookout Mountain outside Denver.

SPRING

Mar.–June   **Dog Racing, Loveland.** The height of the dog-racing season is in spring, which brings nightly racing with pari-mutuel betting. No minors allowed. | 970/667–6211.

Mar.   **Monte Vista Crane Festival, Monte Vista.** At this festival you can observe thousands of sandhill cranes on their annual spring migration back north. | 719/852–3552.

May   **Mountain Film Festival, Telluride.** This ski town hosts photography exhibits and symposia and attracts filmmakers from all over the United States. | 888/783–0264.

SUMMER

June   **Glenn Miller Festival, Fort Morgan.** Relive the "Swing" era with the music of America's most famous band leader, Glenn Miller. | 970/867–6702 or 800/354–8660.

FIBArk Whitewater Festival, Salida. This 26-mi-long race on the Arkansas River brings together veteran kayakers from all over the world. | 719/539–2068.

June–Aug.   **Koshare Indian Dances, La Junta.** Native American Indian dances are performed on Saturday evenings by a world-renowned Boy Scout troop. | 719/384–4411.

July   **Rainbow Weekend, Steamboat Springs.** This colorful festival has arts-and-crafts exhibits, while overhead, 50 hot-air balloons fill the sky. | 970/879–0880 or 800/922–2722.

Aug.   **Artists' Alpine Holiday and Festival, Ouray.** Artists from all over the nation gather to compete in a one-week, all-media event. | 970/325–4746 or 800/228–1876.

Aug.–Sept.   **Colorado State Fair, Pueblo.** This large fair offers up lots of entertainment, PRCA (Professional Rodeo Cowboys Association) rodeo competition, livestock and agricultural exhibits, hi-tech displays, and more. | 719/561–8484.

FALL

Sept.   **The Scottish-Irish Highland Festival, Estes Park.** A full weekend of classic highland dancing, athletic competition, arts-and-crafts demonstrations, and authentic Celtic music. | 970/586–4431 or 800/443–7837.

1929
The 1,053-ft-high bridge spanning the Arkansas River at Royal Gorge is completed.

1935
Elizabeth McCourt Doe Tabor, the widow of millionaire Horace Tabor and famous in her heyday as "Baby Doe," is found frozen to death in a cabin at the Matchless Mine in Leadville.

1941
U.S. National Ski championships held for the first time in Aspen.

1954
U.S. Air Force Academy is established in Colorado Springs.

1962
Vail Ski Resort opens.

INTRODUCTION
HISTORY
REGIONS
WHEN TO VISIT
STATE'S GREATS
RULES OF THE ROAD
DRIVING TOURS

Oct. **Durango Cowboy Gathering, Durango.** This festival brings together cowboy poets, rodeo cowboys and cowgirls, and western artists and storytellers for a full weekend of entertainment and fun. | 970/259–2165.

Nov. **Christmas Mountain USA, Salida.** Usher in the Yule season as local designers outline a gigantic 700-ft Christmas tree on nearby Tenderfoot Mountain with nearly 4,000 lights. | 719/539–2068.

State's Greats

The two keywords for Colorado vacationers are "contrast" and "variety." The state's terrain runs the full gamut from high mountain peaks, to dry canyonland, to endless—and treeless—prairie. With such contrasts in its geography, Colorado offers plenty of outdoor activities to suit even the most discriminating adventurer's taste. But Colorado provides more than just outdoor fun. Denver is one of America's most cosmopolitan cities, ranking with the very best in the variety and quality of its cultural, educational, and business offerings.

Forests and Parks

Colorado is home to several units of the National Park Service, including **Rocky Mountain** and **Mesa Verde National Parks, Black Canyon of the Gunnison** and **Dinosaur National Monuments,** and **Bent's Old Fort National Historic Site,** among others. Literally millions of acres of pristine **wilderness** are protected by these properties, along with a number of **national forests,** including the Gunnison, San Juan, Rio Grande, Pike, Uncompahgre, Routt, Roosevelt, Grand Mesa, White River, and San Isabel, as well as the Comanche and Pawnee National Grasslands. Rocky Mountain National Park alone encompasses more than 265,000 acres and contains 355 mi of hiking and climbing trails. With assets like this, it is no wonder that 3 million vacationers find their way to this natural playground annually.

On most of these properties, passive recreational pursuits—hiking, backpacking, fishing in season, and water sports—are allowed. Keep in mind, however, these lands and the flora and fauna that inhabit them are national treasures. Indeed, they belong to everyone and should be treated with the utmost respect.

In addition to the federally owned parks and forests, the State of Colorado maintains 40 state parks, where fishing, water sports, skiing, hiking, picnicking, camping, nature-watching, and other activities are available.

Culture, History, and the Arts

Some of America's best-preserved cliff dwellings can be seen at **Mesa Verde National Monument** in southwestern Colorado. There, and at **Hovenweep National Monu-**

1985	1992	1998	1999
A temperature reading of −61°F, the coldest ever recorded in Colorado, is taken at Maybell on February 1.	Ben Nighthorse Campbell elected to the U.S. Senate, the first Native American to serve in over 60 years.	The Denver Broncos, led by renowned quarterback John Elway, win the Super Bowl.	The Broncos win their second Super Bowl, amid speculation that John Elway might retire. Later in the year, Elway does, in fact, announce his retirement.

ment, near Cortez, you can see what life in the Centennial State was really like more than a thousand years ago. But even before humans roamed the region, ancient dinosaurs and other reptiles frequented such places as **Florissant Fossil Beds** and **Dinosaur National Monuments. Bent's Old Fort National Historic Site** takes you back in time to the days when the first American fur traders plied the Santa Fe Trail in search of valuable beaver pelts, and later, buffalo hides. A great deal of mining history—and tales of fortunes made and fortunes lost—is preserved today in the many **ghost towns** scattered across the face of Colorado, especially in the vicinity of Ouray, Salida, and Silverton.

Denver and other large Colorado cities have museums galore, and their offerings range from fine, contemporary, modern, and western art, to historical exhibits depicting the history of the region, to natural history and scientific displays. Zoos, botanic gardens, performing-arts theaters, and specialty museums are also abundant. In short, you won't get bored trying to decide what to do or see next in Colorado, whether you're in Denver or Colorado Springs or miles away in the heart of the Rocky Mountains where your only neighbors are elk, deer, and black bear.

Sports

Skiing is arguably the number-one sport in Colorado. Each year, skiers from all over America flock to Aspen, Vail, Steamboat Springs, or one of the other countless ski resorts to try their hand at a new season of cross-country or downhill skiing or snowboarding. Colorado's rugged mountains, their immense altitude, and the abundance of snowfall have all combined to make the state the nation's most popular ski destination.

If you like **fishing,** Colorado is the place to go. Cutthroat, brown, rainbow, brook, and lake trout are all abundant in the cold streams and lakes of the highlands. And, if extreme cold weather catches up with you, you can even ice-fish in some locations.

Colorado maintains a number of **dude ranches,** which fall into two categories—guest ranches and working ranches. You are expected to share in the daily chores, such as roping and herding, on a working ranch, whereas at a guest ranch, you are just that and are not expected to do anything but enjoy yourself.

Denver is one of a few American cities to have major-league professional teams in four sports: baseball, basketball, football, and hockey. The **Colorado Rockies** baseball team is in the National League, the **Denver Nuggets** are part of the National Basketball Association, the **Colorado Avalanche** plays with the National Hockey League, while the world-champion **Denver Broncos** are in the National Football League. So, if you're a spectator-sports lover, you won't have a problem finding a game at just about any time of the year.

State Parks

Colorado has 40 state parks, which are generally open daily, though some visitor centers and activities are seasonal. All state parks charge $4 for day use or $40 for an annual pass, with additional fees for overnight camping. For a fee of $7, you can make campsite reservations by calling at least 3 days in advance (303/470–1144 or 800/678–2267); camping fees range from $6 for a primitive site to $16 for a full-service RV site. For further information, call the state park information number (303/866–3437), or check out the state park web site (www.parks.state.co.us).

Rules of the Road

License requirements: As a visitor driving an automobile in Colorado, you must have a valid driver's license from your home state.

Right turn on red: A driver can legally turn right on a red light after coming to a full stop.

Seat belt and children's safety seat laws: State law requires automobile drivers and passengers in the front seat of the vehicle to use seat belts. Children under four years old and under 40 pounds, regardless of where in the vehicle they are riding, must use an approved safety seat.

Speed Limits: Individual speed limits are posted along all major thoroughfares and in all municipalities. The interstate system, except where posted for lower rates, maintains a 75-mph speed limit.

For more information on highway laws, safety, and the condition of specific roads, call 303/239–4500. For medical emergencies, call 911.

INTRODUCTION
HISTORY
REGIONS
WHEN TO VISIT
STATE'S GREATS
RULES OF THE ROAD
DRIVING TOURS

Exploring South-Central Colorado Driving Tour

PUEBLO–LA JUNTA–TRINIDAD–ALAMOSA–CAÑON CITY TOUR

Distance: approximately 525 mi   Time: 2 days
Breaks: Overnight in Trinidad

This two-day driving tour carries you in a large, irregular circle from Colorado's fifth-largest city, Pueblo, to one of the most spectacular sights in North America, the breathtaking 1,053-ft-deep Royal Gorge. Along the way, you will view the reconstructed site of Colorado's first permanent settlement and one of America's most famous trading posts, Bent's Fort; travel across the original path of the fabled Santa Fe Trail; and stand in awe before massive sand dunes that look totally out of character amidst the majestic Sangre de Cristo Mountains. Although this tour is enjoyable during any season of the year, be prepared to get relatively warm, even hot, in the eastern part of it, around Bent's Fort and along the route of the Santa Fe Trail.

❶ Using **Pueblo** as your base of operations, have breakfast there and depart eastward along U.S. 50 into La Junta and on to Bent's Fort.

❷ **Bent's Fort** was built in the early 1830s as a fur post and way station on the Santa Fe Trail. Today, it's a national historic site.

❸ From Bent's Fort backtrack southwest on Route 109/194 into **La Junta,** a small town whose major attraction is its Indian museum. If you are arriving in the summer, see an Indian dance performance at the museum. Have lunch in La Junta.

❹ After lunch, travel southwest along U.S. 350 for about 80 mi until you reach **Trinidad.** This is the route of the original Santa Fe Trail, and although you won't meet many cars along the way, the trip is well worth the time just to see what the prairie looked like when the wagons rolled across the Trail. The town itself is well preserved, and its entire downtown area has been declared a national landmark, with many Victorian homes, churches, and gardens. Spend the night in Trinidad.

❺ Leaving Trinidad in the morning, take a small detour and travel south along Interstate 25 through picturesque **Raton Pass.** Here, Interstate 25 crosses the high mountains that separate Colorado from New Mexico. Turnoffs along the way allow you to view some magnificent scenery with sweeping vistas on all sides.

❻ On the far side of Raton Pass, turn around and follow Interstate 25 back north again until you reach exit 13. There, pick up Route 12 and follow the highway west and then

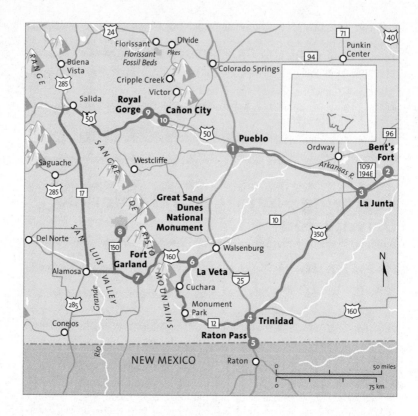

north for 65 mi until you reach **La Veta.** This expanse of Route 12 cuts through Colorado's coal country, and despite the number of coal trucks you meet along the way, it is very picturesque. Among the most interesting sights are the many lava dikes, mute vestiges from ancient volcano eruptions in the area. You will climb hundreds of feet in altitude along this highway, crossing Cucharas Pass at an altitude of nearly 10,000 ft.

7 Just beyond La Veta, turn west onto U.S. 160 and proceed for 36 mi to **Fort Garland** where U.S. 160 and Route 159 meet. Take a look at the historic fort for which the town was named.

8 From Fort Garland, continue west on U.S. 160 for about 12 mi to its junction with Route 150; proceed north on Route 150 for 16 mi to **Great Sand Dunes National Monument.** Take time to walk out into the dunes and witness for yourself the eerie beauty and mystery of this unique natural wonder.

9 From the Monument, return south on Route 150 to U.S. 160, turn west and proceed on U.S. 160 for 14 mi to Alamosa. There, turn north onto Route 17 and drive for 77 mi to Poncha Springs, turning east there on U.S. 50. At Salida, continue eastward on U.S. 50 for 44 mi to the turnoff to **Royal Gorge.** Here, the world's highest suspension bridge (1,053 ft) spans the Arkansas River. You can also go down into the gorge on an incline railway.

10 After you leave Royal Gorge, return to U.S. 50 and follow it for 10 mi into **Cañon City,** which is most famous for the former territorial prison located there (it's now a museum). Return the 39 mi to Pueblo traveling eastward on U.S. 50.

Exploring Colorado's Heartland Driving Tour

GOLD AND SILVER COUNTRY TOUR

INTRODUCTION
HISTORY
REGIONS
WHEN TO VISIT
STATE'S GREATS
RULES OF THE ROAD
DRIVING TOURS

Distance: approximately 275 mi   Time: 1 or 2 days
Break: Overnight in Breckenridge

To see Colorado's most beautiful countryside, begin near Colorado Springs with the Garden of the Gods, then move on to see the ancient fossil beds near Florissant. You will also drive though oxygen-thin passes in the mountains, explore the old gold-rush boomtowns of Breckenridge and Georgetown, watch Coors beer being made in Golden, and see the world-famous U.S. Air Force Academy.

In summer, you can make this trip in a single day if you leave early and plan on getting back to Colorado Springs late. However, that's too much of a stretch in winter, when an overnight in Breckenridge is in order and would also give ample time for more relaxed driving on potentially hazardous roads. Given the number of attractions to see on this tour, if you have the time, it would be best to make it a two-day trip, summer or winter.

❶ From **Colorado Springs** proceed northwest on U.S. 24 for 3 mi, then turn right on 30th Avenue and view the absolutely stunning **Garden of the Gods.** Take the time to follow the one-way drive completely though this geological wonderland, which has acres of fantastic, 300-million-year-old red sandstone formations.

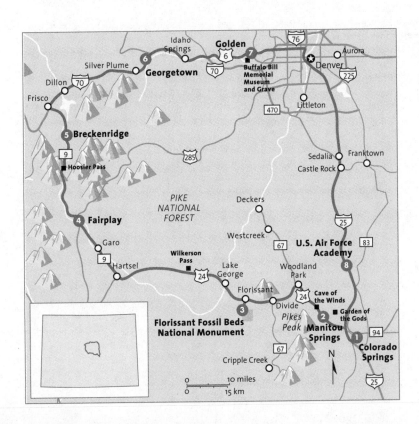

❷ Leaving the Garden of the Gods, follow U.S. 24 to **Manitou Springs,** located just outside the city limits of Colorado Springs. There, you will want to tour the Miramont Castle Museum, a late-19th-century mansion. If you're up to a brisk walk, you may want to visit the Cave of the Winds. An interesting 45-minute underground tour takes you by millions of years of local geology. You might get cool, even in the summertime, so bring a light jacket, and by all means, wear comfortable shoes.

❸ From Cave of the Winds, proceed west on U.S. 24 for another 21 mi until you enter the village of Florissant and see the sign pointing southward to **Florissant Fossil Beds National Monument,** where a Oligocene redwood forest and all its inhabitants were perfectly preserved. Enjoy a ranger-led or self-guided walk on one of the well-marked trails. This little-known wonder is a boon for fossil buffs.

❹ Leaving the Fossil Beds, continue westward on U.S. 24 for 30 mi to Hartsel. (On your way you will cross Wilkerson Pass at an elevation of 9,507 ft.) At Hartsel take Route 9 north for 17 mi to **Fairplay.** Here you may wish to visit the South Park City Museum, which contains 30 original buildings, mining exhibits, and 60,000 artifacts from the past.

❺ From Fairplay, proceed north on Route 9 for 22 mi and through the 11,541-ft-high Hoosier Pass to **Breckenridge.** You'll marvel at the snowcapped peaks on all sides, even in the summertime. There's plenty to do and see in Breckenridge, which had its beginnings in 1859 as a gold-rush boomtown, and which today is a mecca for vacationers and skiers. If your visit is on a weekday or Saturday, you can take a walking tour of the historic district and some of the outlying gold mines. If you're hungry, you might want to grab a bite to eat. This is also a good stopping point if you want to break your tour up into two days.

❻ Leaving Breckenridge, take Route 9 north for 10 mi to its junction with Interstate 70, and proceed east on Interstate 70 for about 38 mi to historic **Georgetown.** Georgetown dates from 1859, when gold was discovered in the area. Since then the area has produced more than $200 million worth of precious metals. If you have the time, try to visit the **Georgetown Loop Historic Mining and Railroad Park.** Featured at the park are reconstructed mining and railroad buildings dating from the town's heyday. After the gold strikes in the Georgetown region came the silver boom. See what life was like for one of the period's most successful silver moguls when you visit the Hamill House Museum, the restored home of Colorado state senator William A. Hamill. Nearby is the Hotel de Paris Museum. French immigrant Louis Dùpuy built this hotel in 1878 and watched it become one of the West's finest hostelries. Period furnishings re-create a period of wealth and influence.

❼ When you leave Georgetown, it's just a straight shot—and 29 mi—east along Interstate 70 into Denver, which is certainly worth a stay. But since you only have a short amount of time on this tour, **Golden** should be your next stop. Take exit 244, pick up U.S. 6, and proceed the 10 mi or so into the town that Coors beer and the Colorado School of Mines, both renowned throughout the world, put on the map. You can tour the Coors Brewing Company and watch as the ever-popular Coors beer is being brewed. Mineral and mining history exhibits are on display at the School of Mines' Geology Museum. The Buffalo Bill Memorial Museum and Grave, 5 mi west of town off U.S. 6, is the site of Buffalo Bill (William F.) Cody's grave. Nearby is an interpretive museum that portrays the life of the famous scout and entertainer.

❽ Leaving Golden, pick up U. S. 6 eastbound and follow it through Denver (about 12 mi) to its junction with Interstate 25. Turn south on Interstate 25 and proceed 50 mi to the

U. S. Air Force Academy (take exit 156B [North Gate] or exit 150B [South Gate]). This magnificent campus is the Air Force's answer to West Point and Annapolis. Be sure and visit the chapel, which is an architectural wonder in itself. After leaving the Academy, pick up Interstate 25 again and proceed south back to Colorado Springs.

ALAMOSA

(Nearby town also listed: Monte Vista)

Alamosa (population 8,964) is in the lovely San Luis River valley, a region first settled by Hispanic emigrants from nearby New Mexico in 1851. Impressed by the abundance of cottonwood trees that hugged the stream's banks, they named the town that soon sprang up "Alamosa," which means cottonwood in their native tongue, Spanish.

Today, Alamosa is a good jumping-off place for a trip to the nearby Great Sand Dunes National Monument or to Kit Carson's old army post, Fort Garland.

Information: Alamosa County Chamber of Commerce | Cole Park, Alamosa 81101 | 719/589–3681 or 800/BLU–SKYS | www.alamosa.org.

Attractions

Alamosa National Vista Wildlife Refuge. These natural and man-made wetlands 6 mi east of Alamosa are an important sanctuary for the nearly extinct whooping crane and its cousin, the sandhill. | 9383 El Rancho La. at U.S. 160 | 719/589–4021 | Free | Daily sunrise–sunset.

Cole Park. In this park on the Rio Grande River, you'll find picnicking areas, bicycle trails, tennis courts, and a narrow-gauge train on display. | 425 4th St. | 719/589–3681 or 800/BLU–SKYS | Free | Daily.

Cumbres and Toltec Scenic Railroad, Colorado Limited. You can take a round trip on this narrow-gauge railroad from Antonito to Osier, Colorado, or to Chama, New Mexico. The depot is located in Antonito, 28 mi south of Alamosa. | Junction U.S. 285 and Rte. 17, Antonito | 719/376–5483 or 505/756–2151 | fax 505/756–2694 | www.cumbresandtoltec.com | $38–$58 | Mid-May–mid-Oct.; call for exact times of individual trips.

Fort Garland Museum. Historic U.S. Army post, which was originally commanded by Kit Carson, with original adobe buildings and a very nice gift shop and museum depicting army life in the 1860s–70s. The fort is located in Fort Garland, 25 mi east of Alamosa. | Rte. 159 at U.S. 160, Fort Garland | 719/379–3512 | $3 | Apr.–Oct., daily 8–4; Nov.–Mar., Thurs.–Mon. 9–5.

Great Sand Dunes National Monument. This vast expanse of shifting sand dunes 35 mi northeast of Alamosa, some reaching a height of 700 ft, became trapped on the valley floor at the base of the Sangre de Cristo Mountains over millions of years. Here in the heart of the richly forested Rocky Mountains is a several-square-mile expanse of gleaming white desert that looks more like it should be in North Africa than in Colorado. A self-guided nature trail and picnic areas are on the premises. Also on-site are a Visitor Center, museum, and gift shop. | 11500 Rte. 150, Mosca | 719/378–2312 | www.nps.gov/grsa | $3 | Daily, visitor center daily 8–6.

ON THE CALENDAR

JULY–AUG.: *Summer Concerts.* Sunday jazz, blues, pop, and country/western performances in the outdoor amphitheater at Great Sand Dunes National Monument. 719/378–2312.

SEPT.: *Early Iron Festival.* This annual Labor Day weekend event in Cole Park features more than 300 antique (pre-1972) automobiles from all over the region vying in friendly competition. 719/589–3681 or 800/BLU–SKYS.

SIGHTSEEING TOURS/TOUR COMPANIES

Great Sand Dunes 4-Wheel-Drive Tour. A 20-mi, two-hour round-trip tour through the Great Sand Dunes offers spectacular scenery. Six-person minimum. | Great Sand Dunes Oasis, 5400 Rte. 150, Mosca | 719/378–2222 | $14 | May–Oct., by appointment only.

Dining

Taqueria Calvillo. Mexican. This informal eatery serves nine kinds of fresh salsa, along with authentic, homemade tortillas, fajitas, chiles rellenos, and slow-cooked carnitas. | 119 Broadway | 719/587–5500 | $4–$13 | No credit cards.

True Grits. Steak. More than a predictably good steak house. As the name implies, this is a shrine to the Duke, complete with all manner of John Wayne memorabilia. Kids' menu. | 100 Santa Fe Ave., at the junction U.S. 1, Rte. 160, and Rte. 17 | 719/589–9954 | $7–$19 | D, MC, V.

Truijillo's. American/Casual. Popular restaurant in downtown Alamosa, whose menu features such diverse fare as baby-back ribs, angel-hair pasta with sautéed prawns in a homemade cream sauce, and steak stuffed with green chile strips topped by jalapeno cheese and chipotle sauce. | 326 Main St. | 719/589–2641 | $10–$25 | AE, MC, V.

Lodging

Best Western Alamosa Inn. A sprawling, well-maintained motel complex near downtown Alamosa. The spacious rooms are the best bet in town. Restaurant, bar. Cable TV. Pool. Hot tub. Business services. Airport shuttle. | 1919 Main St. | 719/589–2567 | fax 719/589–0767 | www.bestwestern.com | 116 rooms, 2 suites | $52–$96, $96–$135 suites | AE, D, DC, MC, V.

Budget Host–Alamosa Lamplighter. Standard chain motel in downtown Alamosa. Restaurant. Some kitchenettes, some microwaves. Pool. Hot tub. Laundry facilities. | 425 Main St. | 719/589–6636 or 800/359–2138 | fax 719/589–3831 | 62 rooms, 12 apartments | $33–$55, $485–$550/month apartments | AE, D, DC, MC, V.

Conejos River Guest Ranch. This peaceful retreat, 14 mi south of Alamosa on the Conejos River, offers rooms and cabins that combine rustic style with modern conveniences. Restaurant, bar, complimentary breakfast. Horseback riding. Fishing. | 25390 Rte. 17, Antonito 81120 | 719/376–2464 | fax 719/376–2299 | www.conejosranch.com | 8 rooms, 6 cabins | $79–$95, $95–$115 cabins | D, MC, V.

Cottonwood Inn Bed and Breakfast. Work by local artists is on exhibit in this 1908 Craftsman house and an adjoining building with sunny rooms. Cooking workshops are offered regularly. Complimentary breakfast. Kitchenettes (in suites), TV in common area. Hot tub. Business services. No smoking. | 123 San Juan Ave. | 719/589–3882 or 800/955–2623 | fax 719/589–6437 | www.cottonwoodinn.com | 5 rooms in 2 buildings (2 with shared bath), 4 suites | $75–$125, $99–$125 suites | AE, D, DC, MC, V.

Days Inn Alamosa. Standard chain accommodations near downtown Alamosa. Complimentary Continental breakfast. Cable TV. | 224 Okeefe Pkwy. | 719/589–9037 or 800/325–2525 | fax 719/589–9037 | www.daysinn.com | 33 rooms | $37–$67 | AE, D, DC, MC, V.

Echo Canyon Guest Ranch. From Alamosa, 50 mi east. Located near West Spanish Peak Mountain and the Cucharas River, this is a working cattle ranch, with riding lessons for beginners and the promise of western adventure for riders who can "work cattle." Nature walks offered by a local naturalist. Restaurant, bar with entertainment. No air-conditioning, no TV, TV in common area. Hot tub. Hiking, horseback riding. Fishing. Video games. | 12507 Echo Canyon Creek Rd., La Veta | 719/742–5524 or 800/341–6603 | fax 719/742–5525 | www.coloradovacation.com/duderanch/echo | 9 rooms, 4 cabins | $1,050 per person, 4–day stay | Closed Oct.–mid-May | AP | AE, D, MC, V.

Holiday Inn. Located less than a mile from downtown Alamosa, this well-kept motor lodge is a Holidome and also has conference facilities. Restaurant, bar. In-room data ports, room service, some microwaves, cable TV. Pool. Hot tub, sauna. Video games. Laundry facilities. Business services. Airport shuttle. Pets allowed. | 333 Santa Fe Ave. | 719/589–5833 | fax 719/589–4412 | www.holiday-inn.com | 127 rooms, 3 suites | $86–$96 | AE, D, DC, MC, V.

Inn at Zapata Ranch. Bison graze outside this late-19th-century ranch house with rugged furniture and real western style 30 mi northeast of Alamosa and 4 mi south of Great Sand Dunes National Monument. Dining room, picnic area, complimentary breakfast. No room phones. Pool. Hot tub. Massage. Driving range, putting green. Gym. Business services. No smoking. | 5303 Hwy. 150, Mosca | 719/378–2356 or 800/284–9213 | fax 719/378–2428 | www.greatsanddunes.com | 14 rooms, 1 suite | $150–$180, $225 suite | Closed Jan.–mid-Mar. | AE, D, DC, MC, V.

Rainbow Trout Ranch. This historic lodge and cabin complex 55 mi southwest of Alamosa is at riverside in the Conejos River valley. There are square dances and western entertainers performing every week. Take Highway 285 to Highway 17, then go 21 mi west. Restaurant. No air-conditioning, no room phones, no TV. Pool. Hot tub. Basketball, hiking, horseback riding, volleyball. Fishing. Children's programs (ages 3–17), playground, laundry service. No smoking. | Box 458, 1484 FDR250, Antonito | 719/376–5659 or 800/633–3397 | fax 719/376–5659 | rainbow2@amigo.net | www.rainbowtroutranch.com | 16 cabins | $1,300 per person per wk; special rates for children | Closed late Sept.–mid-May | AP | No credit cards.

ALLENSPARK

MAP 6, F3

(Nearby towns also listed: Boulder, Estes Park, Grand Lake, Rocky Mountain National Park)

Allenspark's origins can be traced back to the 1850s, when Alonzo Allen's family settled the Taylor Mountain Ranch in the shadow of Long's Peak, 2 mi east of present-day Allenspark. Other homesteaders soon took an interest in the area, and a small mountain community began to emerge. Homesteading law in the late 19th century required that to retain the land a crop had to be grown, but seeds would not sprout in the high altitude. When government agents came to inspect the crops, they would find potatoes that the settlers had buried the night before. Destroyed by fire in 1894, all that stands of Taylor Mountain Ranch today is the stone chimney.

In the century that has passed, modern conveniences have afforded Allenspark's residents and guests a much higher level of comfort, but the sense of community and simplicity still prevails. You will not be bombarded with endless forms of entertainment here; rather, it will be up to you to create your own adventures. A horse can be rented from one of the many stables, but a hike around town or a drive on the Peak-to-Peak Highway are also worthy pursuits. Fill your canteen with icy water from Crystal Springs in the center of town, pack a lunch, and explore one of the six scenic trails originating in Allenspark. Try fishing one of the several pristine mountain streams and lakes nearby. At night, dance to live bluegrass, read a book, or play one of the locals in a game of chess. By the end of your stay, a clear head and rested body will be your reward.

Information: Estes Park Chamber of Commerce | 500 Big Thompson Hwy., Estes Park, 80517 | 970/586–4431 | www.estesnet.com.

Attractions
Allenspark Livery. Here you can rent a horse for any occasion. Hourly trail rides, moonlight rides, fishing trips, and guided Rocky Mountain National Park tours are all offered. All horses have park permits and park entry fees are included. | 211 Main St. | 303/747–2551 | $20–$55 for 1–4 hrs, $85 all day | May–Sept., daily.

Rocky Mountain National Park. Just to the northwest of Allenspark is Wild Basin, the south entrance to Rocky Mountain National Park (*see also* Rocky Mountain National Park). The park is best known for its remarkable geologic features resulting from glacial movement during the previous ice age. Take your time exploring, bring plenty of water, and be prepared for inclement weather. | Estes Park | 970/586–1206 | www.nps.gov/romo | $10 per vehicle, $5 per hiker or cyclist | Daily.

ON THE CALENDAR

JULY: *Fourth of July Parade.* Sponsored by the Hilltop Guild, the parade begins at 10 AM, and the festivities run all day. A free picnic is offered, and aerobatic biplanes from Longmont provide a spectacular show overhead. | July 4th.

Dining

Fawn Brook Inn. Continental. Cozy, warm, and slightly rustic in an alpine way, this restaurant is 16 mi south of Estes Park. Try the duckling or the venison. | Hwy. 7 | 303/747–2556 | Closed Jan.–Feb. No lunch | $29–$48 | AE, MC, V.

Meadow Mountain Café. American/Casual. This little café in the center of Allenspark serves travelers from all over the region. Try the omelet with avocado, Monterey jack, tomato, and home-grown sprouts, or you can have light fare such as sandwiches, soups, burgers, and even veggie burgers that some say are better than the real thing. The house-made baked goods are also popular. | 441 Business Rte. 7 | 303/747–2541 | Breakfast also available; no dinner | $5–$7 | No credit cards.

Millsite Inn. American/Casual. Located on Route 72 between Allenspark and Nederland, this isolated, rustic tavern is local favorite. Almost all the dishes on the menu are home-made—even the hamburger buns are fresh baked. Also try the pizzas and calzones, along with such hearty dinner entrées as "My Grandma's Mac & Cheese." Entertainment Saturday night. | 44365 Rte. 72, Ward | 303/459–3308 | No breakfast | $7–$14 | MC, V.

Wild Basin Lodge. Contemporary. Along the banks of the St. Vrain River, with a huge deck facing Rocky Mountain National Park, this is a wonderful outdoor dining experience. Try the venison osso buco, mint-rubbed Colorado red trout, or for some of everything, the "Taste of Colorado" dinner buffet. | 1130 County Rd. 84 W | 303/747–2545 | Reservations essential | No lunch | $10–$25 | MC, V.

Lodging

Allenspark Lodge. This sprawling, three-story lodge is made entirely of pine timbers, with unique rooms of every imaginable shape and configuration scattered throughout. An apartment is available with a full kitchen. Two of the units connect to sleep up to eight, or for a couple seeking a little more privacy, the hideaway room has a cozy gas fireplace. | 13 rooms (7 with shared bath). Complimentary breakfast. Hot tub. No kids under 14. No smoking. | 184 Main St. | 303/747–2552 | $65–$135 | AE, D, MC, V.

Alpine Mountain Ranch. Just across the road from Rocky Mountain National Park, this combination bed-and-breakfast and guest ranch is a beautiful setting for an outdoor-oriented vacation. Deer, elk, and bighorn sheep can often be viewed from the property. Expert riding instruction is a specialty. Pool. Hot tub. Basketball, hiking, horseback riding, volleyball. Fishing. Children's programs (ages 4–17). | 15747 Rte. 7, Allenspark | 303/747–2532 or 800/578–3598 | fax 303/747–0750 | www.alpinemountainranch.com | 15 rooms, 5 cabins | $1,185 per person per wk (1–week minimum) | AP | MC, V.

Pine Grove Cabins. Many of these secluded forest cabins, spread out over 7 acres, were built in the late 1800s to house local miners. Most cabins have a fireplace and a furnished patio complete with a grill. Rocky Mountain National Park trailheads are within walking distance, and a corral on the property can accommodate guests' horses. | 10 cabins. Laundry facilities. No smoking. | 60 County Rd. 90 | 303/747–2529 | $65–$138 | AE, D, MC, V.

ASPEN

(Nearby towns also listed: Glenwood Springs, Leadville)

Aspen became one of Colorado's early boomtowns when silver was discovered nearby in the early 1890s. Soon boasting a population of nearly 12,000, the village supported hundreds of prospectors and their families. Later, when the price of silver bottomed out, fewer than 700 residents remained in the ghost town. Aspen received a new lease on life in the 1940s when it was developed into a recreational destination with emphasis on skiing, and its year-round population is now back up to over 5,500. Its location on the western slope of the Continental Divide in central Colorado makes its ski facilities some of the best that the state has to offer. A magnet for cultural and counter-cultural types, the atmosphere is freewheeling and tolerant, but it is also a magnet for glittering celebrities, so a sense of wealth, style, and privilege runs almost as deep as the snow cover.

Snowmass is a development within the greater Aspen community. It consists of four ski areas, as well as an abundance of eateries, shops, and boutiques. It is a little more affordable and family oriented than some of the other glittery ski resorts nearby.

Information: Aspen Chamber Resort Association | 425 Rio Grande Pl., Aspen 81611 | 970/925–1940 or 800/26–ASPEN | www.aspenchamber.org.

Snowmass Resort Association | 38 Village Square, Snowmass 81615 | 970/923–2000 or 800/766–9627.

Attractions

Aspen Art Museum. Contemporary art museum featuring exhibits from local and national artists. The complimentary wine-and-cheese gallery tour, held Thursday at 5, is a lot of fun. | 590 N. Mill St. | 970/925–8050 | $3, free Sat. | Tues., Wed., Fri., Sat. 10–6; Thurs. 10–8; Sun. noon–6; closed Mon.

Aspen Historical Society Museum. Exhibits depict the early history of Aspen and the surrounding area. | 620 W. Bleeker St. | 970/925–3721 | fax 970/925–5347 | www.aspenhistory.org | $3 | June–Sept., daily 1–4; Jan.–mid-Apr., daily 1–4.

Skiing. Skiing is the name of the game in Aspen, though the resort is now becoming almost equally busy during the summer months once the snow is gone. Although there are many other activities going on year-round, the number one attraction is skiing. There are four separate ski areas in the immediate area owned by the Aspen Skiing Company, all sharing daily lift tickets. Snowboarding is allowed at Aspen Highlands, Buttermilk, and Snowmass only. | 970/923–3148 or 970/925–2145 | www.aspen.com.

Aspen Highlands. You'll find 81 runs (the longest is 3½ mi) spread out over 619 acres of terrain with a 3,635-ft vertical drop, located 1½ mi southwest of Aspen in White River National Forest. The Highlands offers thrilling descents at Steeplechase and Olympic Bowl, as well as the best views among the four Aspen mountains; 3 restaurants, snowmaking, 4 lifts. | Maroon Creek Rd. | 970/925–1220 or 800/525–6200 | www.aspen.com | Early Dec.–early Apr.

Aspen Mountain. You'll find 77 runs (the longest is 3 mi) spread out over 631 acres with a 3,267-ft vertical drop. This is the standard by which good skiers often test themselves; there are no novice runs on this mountain. There are four restaurants and eight lifts; snowboarding is not allowed. | 601 E. Dean St. | 970/925–1221 or 888/277–3676 for snow conditions; 970/925–1220 or 800/525–6200 for information | www.aspen.com | Late Nov.–mid-Apr.

Buttermilk. There are 45 runs (the longest is 3 mi) on these 410 acres 2 mi east of Aspen, with a vertical drop of 2,030 ft. Often called Aspen's "learning" area because of its gently rolling slopes for beginners and intermediates, you'll nevertheless find superb powder; cafeteria, 2 restaurants, 6 lifts, 45 runs. | Rte. 82 | 970/925–1220 or 800/525–6200 | www.aspen.com | Early Dec.–early Apr.

Snowmass. You'll find 72 runs (the longest is 5$\frac{1}{20}$ mi) at this sprawling ski area covering 2,655 acres 12 mi northwest of Aspen, with a vertical drop of 4,206 ft. Although more than half of the area here is designated intermediate, the area has triple the black and double black diamond terrain as Aspen Mountain; 9 restaurants, 20 lifts. | Rte. 82 | 800/332-3245 | www.aspen.com | Late Nov.–mid-Apr.

SIGHTSEEING TOURS/TOUR COMPANIES

Blazing Adventures. Offers guided, active outdoor trips year-round, including hiking, biking, jeep, and river-rafting excursions. | 45 Snowmass Village Mall, Snowmass Village | 970/923-4544 or 800/282-7238 | fax 970/923-4994 | www.blazingadventures.com | May–Oct., daily.

Blazing Adventures. The company has a second office in Aspen. | 407 E. Hyman Ave. | 800/282-7238 | www.blazingadventures.com | May–Oct., daily.

Krabloonik Husky Kennels. "Half-day" (approximately two hours, not including time for lunch) dogsled trips into the nearby forests, which include lunch at the Krabloonik Restaurant. During the summer months, kennel tours are available. | 4250 Divide Rd., Snowmass Village | 970/923-3953 | www.krabloonik.com | $195, kennel tours $4.50 | Dec.–Apr., daily 8:30 and 12:30, reservations required; mid-June–Labor Day, kennel tours daily 11 and 12:30, reservations required | No kids under 3.

ON THE CALENDAR

JAN.: *Winterskol Carnival.* A three-day winter carnival with skating parties, cross-country skiing parties, fireworks, and a parade. | 970/925-1940 or 800/26-ASPEN.

JUNE–AUG.: *Aspen Music Festival.* Symphonies, jazz, opera, chamber music, and lectures create an eclectic musical experience, utilizing various music venues in Aspen. | 970/925-3254.

JUNE–SEPT.: *JazzAspen.* An indoor and outdoor music festival with both American and Jazz music located at the Snowmass Village. | Brush Creek Rd. | 970/920-4996.

Dining

★ **Ajax Tavern.** Mediterranean. This establishment looks a little like an English tavern. Try the New York strip, or the seafood pastina risotto. Open-air dining on a large patio at the base of Aspen Mountain. Kids' menu. | 685 E. Durant Ave. | 970/920-9333 | Closed mid-Apr.–early June, and early Oct.–late Nov. | $15–$30 | AE, D, DC, MC, V.

Boogies on the Rocks. American/Casual. A 1950s-style diner with an authentic soda fountain serving burgers, fries, and other fast food. | 534 E. Cooper Ave. | 970/925-6610 | $4–$10 | AE, MC, V.

Cache Cache. French. This is one of Aspen's most elegant restaurants, with flawless service and heavenly food. The mostly Provençal menu offers such dishes as duck salad with candied walnuts and rotisserie chicken with kalamata olives and capers, but also an unmatched osso buco. Extensive wine list. Open-air dining on garden patio. | 205 S. Mill St. | 970/925-3835 | Closed mid-Apr.–May, Oct., Nov. No lunch | $16–$29 | AE, MC, V.

Campo De Fiori. Italian. Wall-climbing vines, hand-painted murals, and intimate tables provide a nice setting for the authentic Tuscan and Venetian fare. The fresh handmade pasta dishes and broad selection of lamb, beef, fresh fish, and marinated seafood antipasto define this Italian trattoria. | 205 S. Mill St. | 970/920-7717 | $12–$16 | AE, MC, V.

Cantina. Mexican. This busy restaurant decorated in contemporary southwestern style and with many windows is popular year-round with local residents. Specializing in enchiladas, burritos, and tacos. Open-air dining on large outdoor patio. Kids' menu. | 411 E. Main St. | 970/925-3663 | $7–$19 | AE, D, DC, MC, V.

Century Room. Continental. Eighteenth-century western period antiques fill this restaurant in the Hotel Jerome. The kitchen does a good job with trout and prime beef. Open-air dining on a patio overlooking the mountains. Live jazz guitarist Tuesday–Saturday. | 330 E. Main St., | 970/920–1000 | No lunch | $24–$34 | AE, DC, MC, V.

The Chart House. Steak. A comfortably elegant restaurant with beamed ceilings and two fireplaces. Known for prime rib, seafood, steak, chocolate lava cake. Salad bar. Kids' menu. | 219 E. Durant Ave. | 970/925–3525 | No lunch | $15–$30 | AE, D, DC, MC, V.

Crystal Palace Dinner Theater. Continental. This restaurant is absolutely elegant with its turn-of-the-20th-century fixtures, copious stained-glass windows, and crystal chandeliers. Rack of lamb, prime rib, duckling, and shrimp grace the menu. Dinner theater. Kids' menu. | 300 E. Hyman Ave. | 970/925–1455 | Reservations essential | Closed mid-Apr.–mid-June, Sept.– Nov., and Sun., Mon. June–Sept. No lunch | $55 | AE, D, DC, MC, V.

★ **Farfalla.** Italian. Specialties include tortellini with asparagus, ham in walnut pesto, and deboned quail in vegetable sauce on a bed of polenta and beans. | 415 E. Main St. | 970/ 925–8222 | No breakfast or lunch | $15–$30 | AE, D, MC, V.

Guido's. Swiss. Bright, high-ceilinged chalet-style restaurant, with cozy, pinewood accents and lots of windows with a stunning view of the Rocky Mountains. Fondue, lamb, and veal feature prominently on the menu here. Kids' menu. | 403 S. Galena St. | 970/925–7222 | Closed mid-Apr.–mid-June, mid-Oct.–late Nov. No lunch | $15–$35 | AE, D, MC, V.

Il Poggio. Italian. Try the dishes from the wood-burning oven, such as free-range chicken wrapped in pancetta and duck breast with polenta in honey grappa sauce. Pizzas and pastas are also fine. | Elbert La., Snowmass | 970/923–4292 | Closed May–June, Oct.–late Nov. No lunch | $20–$40 | MC, V.

Kenichi. Contemporary. Known for the bamboo salmon and the oriental roast duck. Blackened sea bass is very popular, as is the seared ahi tuna with Cajun spices. | 533 E. Hopkins Ave. | 970/920–2212 | Closed Mon. No lunch | $20–$30 | AE, MC, V.

★ **Krabloonik.** Continental. This rustic restaurant is on the premises of the dogsled company, right on the slope, though you can also drive there, and you'll dine on some of the best game in Colorado. Try carpaccio of smoked caribou with lingonberry vinaigrette or elk loin with marsala and sun-dried cherry glaze. No smoking. | 4250 Divide Rd., Snowmass Village | 970/923–3953 | Closed mid-Apr.–mid-June, mid-Oct.–late Nov. No lunch June–Sept. | $23–$50 | AE, MC, V.

La Cocina. Mexican. The salsa dip, margaritas, and inexpensive food have kept the locals coming for over 20 years. | 308 E. Hopkins Ave. | 970/925–9714 | Closed late Apr.–late May, late Oct.–early Nov. No lunch | $8–$14 | MC, V.

L'Hostaria. Italian. Sleek and elegant, with well-spaced tables and seamless service, this restaurant is known for its fresh pastas and such entrées as stewed rabbit and veal Milanese. | 620 E. Hyman Ave. | 970/925–9022 | Closed mid-Apr.–mid-May. No lunch | $20– $30 | AE, D, MC, V.

Main Street Bakery and Café. Contemporary. You'll feel like you're home in your own kitchen at this quaint, homey café with communal tables and kitchen accessories like cookie jars on the walls. Try the French toast, or the rainbow trout. Open-air patio garden area. Kids' menu. Beer and wine only. | 201 E. Main St. | 970/925–6446 | No dinner Mon.–Tues. and Apr.–mid-June, Labor Day–Dec. | $9–$25 | AE, MC, V.

Matsuhisa. Japanese. Mirrors hung about in the main dining room give it a spacious feel. Known for its lobster with wasabi pepper, king crab claw tempura, and baby abalone with a light garlic sauce. The menu also includes chicken and beef dishes, salads, and a wide variety of sashimi. This is another restaurant from celebrity chef Nobu Matsuhisa. | 303 E. Main St. | 970/544–6628 | Closed Sun., Mon. | $20–$30 | AE, MC, V.

Motherlode. Italian. This Victorian built in the 1880s displays portraits of the Victorian belles who lived here over 100 years ago. Try the beef tenderloin, Chilean sea bass, or the many varieties of pasta. Open-air dining on a brick patio surrounded by flowers and hanging plants. | 314 E. Hyman Ave. | 970/925–7700 | Closed mid-Apr.–May. No lunch | $14–$28 | AE, D, DC, MC, V.

Pacifica Seafood Brasserie. Contemporary. Located in a pedestrian mall, this establishment overlooks Wagner Park. Try charred ahi tuna steak, almond crusted halibut. Raw bar. Open-air dining in a fenced-in area on the cobblestone pedestrian walkway. | 307 S. Mill St. | 970/920–9775 | $15–$30 | AE, MC, V.

Pine Creek Cookhouse. Continental. In winter, to get to this mealtime experience high in the mountains you come either on cross-country skis or in a sleigh. What you find is some delicious food, including trout, wild game, and succulent quail. No smoking. | 312-G AABC, Ashcroft | 970/925–1044 | Reservations essential | Closed Apr.–May, Oct.–mid-Nov. | $19–$33 | AE, MC, V.

Piñons. Contemporary. Upholstered walls and leather-wrapped railings create a room that is subtly elegant. The creative menu features appetizers such as lobster strudel and pan-seared Canadian scallops with roasted vegetables. Also try the sesame-crusted ahi or the Parmesan-crusted loin of veal. | 105 S. Mill St. | 970/920–2021 | Closed Mon. No lunch | $30–$50 | AE, MC, V.

Poppies Bistro Café. Continental. One of the most romantic spots in Aspen, the cozy Victorian atmosphere here, combined with classic bistro cuisine, is only slightly updated from what you might find in France. The steak au poivre, Vietnamese lamb chops, and trout and pheasant dishes are local favorites, as is the crème brûlée. | 834 W. Hallam | 970/925–2333 | Closed mid-Apr.–mid-June, late Oct.–mid-Nov. No lunch | $19–$34 | AE, MC, V.

Red Onion. American. This lively, century-old saloon is known for its burgers and comfort food ranging from meat loaf to gigantic sandwiches, ribs, and chicken. There's also a Mexican menu, with a lineup of tacos, burritos, and enchiladas. | 420 E. Cooper St. | 970/925–9043 | Closed mid-Apr.–mid-May | $7–$15 | AE, MC, V.

★ **Renaissance.** Contemporary. The menu here sparkles with such creativity that your breath may be taken away. Try the crispy Chilean sea bass with crispy artichokes, seared foie gras with caramelized pears, or date-marinated rack of lamb. Kids' menu. | 304 E. Hopkins St. | 970/925–2402 | No lunch | $24–$32 | AE, D, DC, MC, V.

Restaurant at Little Nell. American. Located in the Little Nell Hotel, this restauraunt offers hearty, expressive American alpine cooking, high in the majestic Rockies. Try the charred tuna steak, the rack of lamb, or the mustard-crusted trout. Open-air terrace dining overlooking Aspen mountain. Sunday brunch. | 675 E. Durant Ave. | 970/920–6330 | Breakfast also available | $27–$36 | AE, D, DC, MC, V.

Rusty's Hickory House. Barbecue. Known for its baby-back ribs, homemade biscuits and gravy, salsa, and hand-cut onion rings. Any of the slow-smoked meats or chicken is a good bet. | 730 W. Main St. | 970/925–2313 | No dinner | $10–$20 | AE, MC, V.

★ **Syzygy.** Contemporary. The cuisine here is Asian influenced and exceptional. Try the elk tenderloin with ancho chile and fabulous tuna preparations. Exceptional wine list. Jazz Wednesday–Sunday. | 520 E. Hyman Ave. | 970/925–3700 | Closed mid-Apr.–May. No lunch | $17–$33 | AE, D, DC, MC, V.

Takah Sushi. Japanese. Murals and paper umbrellas make this place feel fun and casual—and it's popular with locals. There are two rooms, one with a sushi bar. If you don't feel like sushi, try the crispy duck. No smoking. | 420 E. Hyman Ave. | 970/925–8588 | Closed mid-Apr.–May. No lunch | $15–$25 | AE, D, DC, MC, V.

Tower. Continental. Traditional furnishings team up with mountain views in this dining room in Snowmass Village Mall. Try the mussels with garlic and basil or the roast blackberry duck. Open-air dining on patio. Comedy, magic. Kids' menu. No smoking. | 45 Village Sq., Snowmass Village | 970/923–4650 | Closed May. No lunch June–Sept. | $14–$24 | AE, D, DC, MC, V.

Ute City Bar and Grill. Contemporary. Ute is in a 19th-century former bank with an original tin ceiling and bank vaults against the walls. Try the crab cakes, the pork duet, or the home-smoked salmon. Entertainment Friday, Saturday. Kids' menu. | 501 E. Hyman Ave. | 970/920–4699 | $15–$25 | AE, D, DC, MC, V.

Wienerstube. Swiss. Cherry-wood furniture and flowers fill this Bavarian-style dining room. Try the Wiener schnitzel, debreziner sausage (a mild, smoked pork sausage), or veal bratwurst. Open-air dining on a covered patio. Kids' menu. | 633 E. Hyman Ave. | 970/925–3357 | Breakfast also available; closed Mon. | $8–$19 | AE, D, DC, MC, V.

Lodging

Aspen Meadows at the Aspen Institute. Located on 40 wooded acres near Sardy Field, this property borders the Roaring Fork River and there are great views of Aspen Mountain and Red Mountain from the balconies of its six Bauhaus-style buildings. Many conferences are held here in summer. Restaurant, bar, picnic area. No air-conditioning, in-room data ports, some microwaves, cable TV, in-room VCRs (and movies). Pool. Hot tub, massage. Tennis. Gym. Bicycles. Cross-country skiing, downhill skiing. Business services. Airport shuttle, parking (fee). | 845 Meadows Rd. | 970/925–4240 or 800/452–4240 | fax 970/925–7790 | www.aspen-meadows.com | 40 rooms, 58 suites in 6 buildings | $195–$395, $265–$695 suites | AE, D, DC, MC, V.

Aspen Mountain Lodge. This hostelry just west of downtown is built around a towering stone fireplace and is on a free shuttle bus route to the ski area. Complimentary Continental breakfast. In-room data ports, refrigerators, cable TV. Pool. Hot tub. | 311 W. Main St. | 970/925–7650 | fax 970/925–5744 | www.aspenmountainlodge.com | 38 rooms | $189–$249 | AE, D, DC, MC, V.

Aspen Square Hotel. Right in the heart of downtown, Aspen Square has apartment-style accommodations. Each unit has a full kitchen and fireplace. In-room data ports, kitchenettes, cable TV, in-room VCRs. Pool. Hot tub. Gym. Laundry facilities. Business services. | 617 E. Cooper Ave. | 970/925–1000 or 800/862–7736 | fax 970/925–1017 | www.aspensquarehotel.com | 103 apartments | $315 studio apartments, $405 1–bedroom apartments, $515 2–bedroom apartments | AE, MC, V.

The Beaumont. Just four blocks from downtown Aspen, the Beaumont has a casual lounge where you can have dinner and drinks in front of the fireplace. Some rooms are rustic, with German antiques, while others are more modern. Complimentary breakfast. In-room data ports, cable TV, some in-room VCRs (and movies). Pool. Hot tub. Laundry facilities. Business services. Some pets allowed (fee). | 1301 E. Cooper Ave. | 970/925–7081 or 800/344–3853 | fax 970/925–1610 | www.thebeaumont.com | 30 rooms | $140–$285 | AE, D, DC, MC, V.

Boomerang Lodge. This moderately priced lodge is one of Aspen's oldest hotels. The obvious influence of Frank Lloyd Wright is everywhere in the building. All rooms look out onto the quiet courtyard, with a secluded pool area. Complimentary Continental breakfast. In-room data ports, some kitchenettes, some microwaves, some refrigerators, cable TV, some in-room VCRs (and movies). Pool. Hot tub, sauna. Laundry facilities. Business services. | 500 W. Hopkins Ave. | 970/925–3416 or 800/992–8852 | fax 970/925–3314 | www.boomeranglodge.com | 34 rooms, 6 suites, 6 apartments | $208–$275, $298 suites, $480–$770 apartments | AE, DC, MC, V.

Crestwood. This ski-in, ski-out resort is at Snowmass Village, and almost all rooms have fireplaces. In-room data ports, kitchenettes, microwaves, refrigerators, cable TV, in-room VCRs (and movies). Heated outdoor pool. 2 hot tubs, sauna. Gym. Laundry services. Business services. Airport shuttle, free parking. | 400 Wood Rd., Snowmass Village | 970/923–2450 or 800/356–5949 | fax 970/923–5018 | www.thecrestwood.com | 124 apartments | $250 studios, $335 1 bedroom, $500 2 bedrooms, $665 3 bedrooms | AE, D, DC, MC, V.

The Gant. This condominium complex at the base of Aspen Mountain on 5 acres has one- to four-bedroom units that are comfortably and individually furnished by independent owners. Each unit has a fireplace, a full kitchen, multiple bathrooms, and a balcony. In-room data ports, kitchenettes, microwaves, refrigerators, cable TV, in-room VCRs. 2 outdoor pools. 3 hot tubs, 2 saunas. 5 tennis courts. Gym. Laundry. Airport shuttle. | 610 West End St. | 970/925–5000 or 800/345–1471 | fax 970/925–6891 | www.gantaspen.com | 141 units | $175–$835 | AE, D, DC, MC, V.

Hearthstone House. In downtown Aspen, rooms in this Frank Lloyd Wright–style lodge are spacious, offering understated luxury and privacy. But you can be sociable at the afternoon wine-and-cheese gathering in front of the lodge's main fireplace. Guests receive a complimentary pass for the Aspen Club and Spa. Complimentary Continental breakfast. Refrigerators, cable TV. Hot tub, steam room. | 134 E. Hyman Ave. | 970/925–7632 or 888/925–7632 | fax 970/920–4450 | www.hearthstonehouse.com | 17 rooms | $178–$310 | Closed mid-Apr.–mid-May | AE, D, DC, MC, V.

Hotel Aspen. This hotel is three blocks from downtown. Most of the southwestern-style rooms have a balcony or terrace and are comfortable, though not luxurious. Complimentary Continental breakfast. In-room data ports, some microwaves, refrigerators, cable TV. Pool. Hot tub. Business services. | 110 W. Main St. | 970/925–3441 or 800/527–7369 | fax 970/920–1379 | 45 rooms | $219–$319 | AE, D, DC, MC, V.

★ **Hotel Jerome.** A gold rush–era grand dame that's Victorian to the core, with lavishly patterned wallpaper and appropriately ornate guest rooms. 3 restaurants, 2 bars. In-room data ports, refrigerators, room service, some in-room hot tubs, cable TV, in-room VCRs (and movies). Pool. Hot tubs, massage. Gym. Business services. Airport shuttle. Pets allowed (fee). | 330 E. Main St. | 970/920–1000 or 800/331–7213 | fax 970/925–2784 | www.hoteljerome.com | 93 rooms, 16 suites | $485–$575, $885–$950 suites | AE, DC, MC, V.

Hotel Lenado. This downtown Aspen B&B is contemporary but features rustic, hand-carved, four-poster beds in each room. Bar, complimentary breakfast. In-room hot tubs, some refrigerators, cable TV, some in-room VCRs. Library. Free parking. | 200 S. Aspen St. | 970/925–6246 or 800/321–3457 | fax 970/925–3840 | www.aspen.com/sardylenado | 19 rooms | $299–$379 | AE, DC, MC, V.

Independence Square Bed and Breakfast. A B&B located in an historic landmark building on the mall in downtown Aspen, one block from the Silver Queen gondola. Complimentary health club pass. Complimentary Continental breakfast. Minibars, some microwaves, refrigerators, cable TV, some in-room VCRs. Outdoor hot tub. Laundry service. Free airport shuttle, free parking. | 404 S. Galena | 970/920–2010 or 800/633–0336 | fax 970/920–2020 | www.friasproperties.com | 28 rooms | $250–$385 | Closed mid-Apr.–late May and mid-Oct.–late Nov. | AE, MC, V.

Inn at Aspen. The slopeside lodging at Buttermilk Mountain, this inn is centrally located between the four ski mountains of Aspen/Snowmass. Each room has a private patio or balcony. Restaurant, bar, picnic area. In-room data ports, some microwaves, refrigerators, room service, cable TV. Pool. Hot tub, massage. Gym, hiking. Business services. Airport shuttle, free parking. | 38750 W. Hwy. 82 | 970/925–1500 or 800/952–1515 | fax 970/925–9037 | www.innataspen.com | 112 rooms, 10 suites | $150–$325, $210–$625 suites | AE, D, DC, MC, V.

Innsbruck Inn. Centrally located in downtown Aspen, this inn feels like a Swiss ski lodge. Free ski shuttle stops right out front. Complimentary Continental breakfast. No air-conditioning in some rooms, some microwaves, some refrigerators, cable TV. Pool. Hot tub. | 233 W. Main St. | 970/925–2980 | fax 970/925–6960 | www.preferredlodging.com | 28 rooms, 2 suites | $185–$275, $275 suites | AE, D, DC, MC, V.

Limelite Lodge. Located next to Wagner Park in the heart of Aspen, the Limelite Lodge offers traditionally furnished rooms and one- and two-bedroom apartments at reasonable prices. Complimentary Continental breakfast. No air-conditioning in some rooms, in-room data ports, refrigerators, cable TV, some in-room VCRs. 2 pools. 2 hot tubs, sauna. Laundry facilities. Pets allowed. | 228 E. Cooper Ave. | 970/925–3025 or 800/433–0832 | fax 970/

925–5120 | www.limelite.net | 63 rooms, 9 apartments | $68–$350, $250–$350 apartments | AE, D, DC, MC, V.

★ **Little Nell.** Colorado's only five-star, five-diamond property. Rooms are luxuriously furnished and have gas fireplaces; all the large bathrooms have a separate tub and shower; most have balconies. The hotel also has a ski concierge. Restaurant, bar (with entertainment). In-room data ports, in-room safes, minibars, refrigerators, room service, cable TV, in-room VCRs (and movies). Pool. Hot tub, massage. Health club. Shops. Business services. Airport shuttle. Pets allowed. | 675 E. Durant Ave. | 970/920–4600 or 800/843–6355 | fax 970/920–4670 | www.the-littlenell.com | 77 rooms, 14 suites | $550–$700, $1,025–$4,100 suites | AE, D, DC, MC, V.

Molly Gibson Lodge. A B&B three blocks from the town center, offering free shuttles to nearby mountains. Some rooms have wood-burning fireplaces. Bar, complimentary Continental breakfast. In-room data ports, some kitchenettes, refrigerators, some in-room hot tubs, cable TV, in-room VCRs (and movies). 2 pools. 2 hot tubs. Bicycles. Business services. Airport shuttle, free parking. | 101 W. Main St. | 970/925–3434 or 800/356–6559 | fax 970/925–2582 | www.mollygibson.com | 44 rooms, 6 apartments | $219–$365, $289–$389 apartments | AE, D, DC, MC, V.

Mountain Chalet. Since 1954, the same couple has owned and operated this property a block from the Silver Queen gondola. The two-bedroom units have basic furnishings and small bathrooms. Bunk rooms that sleep four in each room are available, as well as apartments with full kitchens that accommodate six. Complimentary Continental breakfast. Outdoor pool. Hot tub. Spa. Gym. Laundry facilities. Free parking. | 333 E. Durant Ave. | 970/925–7797 or 800/321–7813 | fax 970/925–7811 | www.apen.com/mtnchalet | 47 rooms, 4 apartments | $55–$400 | AE, D, DC, MC, V.

The Residence. In the Historic Aspen Block Building in the center of Aspen, this hotel contains individually designed one- and two-bedroom apartments. The apartments are lavishly furnished with antiques, and all have fireplaces. Each also has a fully equipped kitchen and dining room stocked with crystal, china, and silver. Kitchenettes, microwaves, refrigerators, cable TV. Spa. Health club. | 305 S. Galena St. | 970/920–6532 | fax 970/925–1125 | www.aspenresidence.com | 7 suites | $850–$2,975 | AE, DC, MC, V.

★ **Sardy House.** An elegantly decorated Gay Nineties house downtown full of modern conveniences. Bar, dining room, complimentary breakfast. In-room data ports, some refrigerators, room service, cable TV, some in-room VCRs (and movies). Pool. Hot tub, sauna. Business services. | 128 E. Main St. | 970/920–2525 or 800/321–3457 | fax 970/920–4478 | www.aspen.com/sardylenado | 14 rooms, 6 suites | $360–$420, $500–$700 suites | AE, DC, MC, V.

Shenandoah Inn. A B&B on the Frying Pan River, about 15 mi northwest of Aspen, in a turn-of-the-20th-century fully restored log house. Complimentary breakfast. No air-conditioning, refrigerators. Outdoor hot tub. Fishing. No kids under 12. No smoking. | 600 Frying Pan Rd., Basalt | 970/927–4991 or 800/804–5520 | fax 970/927–4990 | www.shenandoahinn.com | 4 rooms (2 with shower only), 1 two-bedroom cabin | $98–$120, $165 cabin | AE, MC, V.

Silvertree Hotel. A full-service slopeside hotel in the Snowmass Village Mall decorated in a contemporary mountain style and loaded with recreational facilities and amenities. Restaurant, bar (with entertainment). No air-conditioning, in-room data ports, refrigerators, room service, some in-room hot tubs. Cable TV. 2 pools. Beauty salon, 2 hot tubs, massage. Gym. Bicycles. Shops. Playground, laundry facilities. Business services. Airport shuttle, free parking. Pets allowed. | 100 Elbert La., Snowmass Village | 970/923–3520 or 800/525–9402 | fax 970/923–5192 | www.silvertreehotel.com | 247 rooms, 14 suites | $265–$435, $775–$1,680 suites | AE, D, DC, MC, V.

Skier's Chalet. Skier's Chalet has been under the same ownership for a half a century. The location—100 ft from the ticket office and Chairlift 1A—is ideal. The rooms are basic and well maintained. The complimentary Continental breakfast is offered during ski season only. Restaurant, complimentary Continental breakfast. Cable TV. Pool. | 233 Gilbert St. | 970/920–2037 or 800/262–7736 | fax 970/920–6504 | 16 rooms | $120–$170 | Closed late Apr.– early June, Sept.–late Nov. | MC, V.

Snowflake Inn. Three blocks from the Silver Queen gondola, this inn has regular rooms and suites, plus deluxe one-bedroom suites and two-bedroom suites. Some rooms and suites have full kitchens. The rustic lobby with its stone fireplace and wood beams is a convivial gathering place. Complimentary Continental breakfast (ski season). Some in-room data ports, cable TV. Pool. Hot tub, sauna. Laundry facilities. | 221 E. Hyman Ave. | 970/925–3221 or 800/247–2069 | fax 970/925–8740 | www.snowflakeinn.com | 29 regular rooms and suites, 6 deluxe 1-bedroom suites, 3 2-bedroom suites | $102–$249 rooms and 1–bedroom suites, $143–$305 deluxe 1–bedroom suites, $210–$585 2–bedroom suites | AE, D, DC, MC, V.

★ **Snowmass Club and Lodge.** Condo accommodations ¼ mi from the slopes (complimentary guest shuttle). The mountain golf course doubles as a cross-country ski center in winter. Restaurant, bar, room service. In-room data ports, some microwaves, refrigerators, cable TV, some in-room VCRs. 3 pools, wading pool. Hot tub. Driving range, 18-hole golf course, putting green, tennis. Health club. Cross-country skiing, sleigh rides, snowmobiling, tobogganing. Children's programs (ages 6 months–15), laundry facilities. Business services. Airport shuttle. | 0239 Snowmass Club Circle, Snowmass Village | 970/923–5600 or 800/525–0710 | fax 970/923–6944 | www.snowmassclub.com | 62 1- to 3-bedroom condos | $425–$750 | AE, D, DC, MC, V.

Stonebridge Inn. Only 50 yards from the slopes and two blocks below the Snowmass Village Mall, this inn prides itself on reasonable rates for lodge-style rooms. The Inn also has meeting space. Restaurant, bar, complimentary Continental breakfast. Refrigerators, cable TV. Pool. Hot tub, sauna. Laundry facilities. Business services. Airport shuttle, parking (fee). | 300 Carriage Way, Snowmass Village | 970/923–2420 or 800/922–7242 | fax 970/923–5889 | www.stonebridgeinn.com | 95 rooms, 5 suites | $225–$275, $305–$345 suites | AE, D, DC, MC, V.

★ **St. Regis at Aspen.** A luxury hotel that is memorable even by Aspen standards, from the overstuffed leather chairs in the lobby lounge to the rich dark woods and muted colors of the guest rooms. It's also close by the ski slopes. Restaurant, 2 bars. In-room data ports, in-room safes, minibars, room service, cable TV, some in-room VCRs (and movies). Pool. Beauty salon, hot tubs, massage, sauna, spa, steam room. Health club, hiking. Bicycles. Shops. Baby-sitting, children's programs (ages 3–16). Business services. Parking (fee). Pets allowed. | 315 E. Dean St. | 970/920–3300 | fax 970/925–8998 | www.stregisaspen.com | 257 rooms, 27 suites | $500–$600, $775–$1,000 suites | AE, D, DC, MC, V.

Wildwood Lodge. This rustic Snowmass ski lodge is 60 yards from the slopes overlooking the village mall. Some rooms have fireplaces, and you have access to the health club at the Silvertree Hotel, its sister property. Restaurant, bar, complimentary Continental breakfast. In-room data ports, some microwaves, refrigerators, room service, cable TV, some in-room VCRs. Pool. Hot tub. Laundry facilities. Business services. Airport shuttle, free parking. Pets allowed. | 40 Elbert La., Snowmass Village (mailing address: Box 5009) | 970/923–3550 or 800/525–9402 | fax 970/923–5192 | www.wildwood-lodge.com | 148 rooms, 6 suites | $69–$229, $89–$259 suites | Closed late Apr.–early May | AE, D, DC, MC, V.

AURORA

MAP 6, G4

(Nearby towns also listed: Denver, Englewood)

Founded in 1891, Aurora, with a population of slightly over 250,000, is today the third-largest city in Colorado and an eastern suburb of greater Denver, near the new Denver International Airport. The city, which claims nearly ¼ million residents, is also the home of the University of Colorado's Health Sciences Center and is less than a one-hour drive from the Rocky Mountains. Over 7,700 businesses in Aurora employ more than 64,000 people in fields ranging from construction and manufacturing to retail and service industries. Much of the economic development has occurred along the Interstate 225 corridor.

Information: Aurora Chamber of Commerce | 562 Sable Blvd, Suite 200, Aurora 80011 | 303/344–1500 | fax 303/344–1564 | www.aurorachamber.org.

Attractions

Aurora Reservior. Scuba area, fishing, boating, boat rental (paddle and canoe), picnic shelters, bike trails, general store, and a submerged plane wreck. | 5800 Powhaton Rd. | 303/690–1286 | $4 | Daily 5:30–9.

Cherry Creek State Park. Horseback riding, shooting, a model airplane field, fishing, boating, and more. | 4201 S. Parker Rd., Aurora | 303/690–1166 | $5 per vehicle | Oct.–Apr., daily 6–7; May–Sept., daily 5–10.

SIGHTSEEING TOURS/TOUR COMPANIES

Best Mountain Tours. Tour ghost towns, retrace stagecoach routes, and see spectacular mountain sunsets. Individual or group rates available. Reservations necessary. | 3003 S. Macon Circle | 303/750–5200 | fax 303/750–2949 | www.bestmountaintours.com | $40–$70. .

ON THE CALENDAR

SEPT.: *Gateway to the Rockies Parade.* Annual parade along E. Colfax Avenue in downtown Aurora with floats, clowns, and marching bands. After the parade, stay for the jazz festival in Fletcher Plaza. | 303/361–6169.

Dining

La Cueva. Mexican. For 25 years, La Cueva has been serving authentic Mexican dishes in downtown Aurora. The homemade tortillas are a great addition to the marinated pork loin with grilled onion and jalapeno or the red snapper fillet that is dipped in egg batter, fried, and topped with green or red chile. | 9742 E. Colfax Ave. | 303/367–1422 | fax 303/367–4071 | www.lacueva.net | $4–$10 | AE, MC, V.

Lodging

Doubletree-Southeast. This hotel is just off Interstate 225 at East Iliff, between Denver International Airport and the Denver Tech Center. Restaurant, bar. Some in-room hot tubs, cable TV, some in-room VCRs (and movies). Pool. Gym. Business services. | 13696 E. Iliff Pl. | 303/337–2800 | fax 303/752–0296 | www.doubletree.com | 224 rooms, 24 suites | $109–$119, $119–139 suites | AE, D, DC, MC, V.

Hampton Inn Denver–East–Aurora. A budget-oriented chain hotel located ½ mi off Interstate 225 (exit 7/Mississippi) and 18 mi from Denver International Airport. Complimentary Continental breakfast. In-room data ports, some microwaves, some refrigerators, cable TV. Pool. Gym. Baby-sitting. Laundry facilities. Business services. Free parking. | 1500 S. Abilene St. | 303/369–8400 or 800/426–7866 | fax 303/369–0324 | www.hamptoninn.com | 132 rooms | $69–$88 | AE, D, DC, MC, V.

Holiday Inn Southeast. This upscale chain motel is 5 mi from downtown Aurora. You get a complimentary pass to the adjacent health club. Restaurant, bar. In-room data ports, some refrigerators, cable TV. Pool. Hot tub. Laundry facilities, laundry service. Business services. | 3200 S. Parker Rd. | 303/695–1700 | fax 303/745–6958 | www.denversehotel.com | 475 rooms | $99–$129 | AE, D, DC, MC, V.

BEAVER CREEK

MAP 6, D4

(Nearby towns also listed: Dillon, Leadville, Vail)

Developed by the same corporate group that is responsible for Vail (Vail Resorts Inc.), Beaver Creek is the exclusive, ultraluxurious four-season resort you are looking for if you are very affluent and want the height of pampering. Only 10 mi down the valley from Vail, Beaver Creek is both quieter and more family oriented than its big sister. A shuttle bus connects the two resorts.

The village, which is perched on the slopes above the tiny hamlet of Avon, is a gated compound, where more than 40% of the accommodations offer direct access to the ski slopes in the winter. Although it opened only in 1980, it is giving Vail a run for the money when it comes to tourism.

Information: **Vail Valley Tourism and Convention Bureau** | 100 E. Meadow Dr., Vail 81657 | 970/476–1000 or 800/525–3875 | www.snow.com.

Attractions

Beaver Creek Resort. A sister resort to Vail, which is 10 mi away, is built on a plateau just above the small town of Avon. This is a real luxury ski area, precisely laid out, including the double-dome peaks of Grouse Mountain; newer, lower-level areas Bachelor Gulch and Arrowhead are set aside for novices and intermediates, respectively. The ski area features 6 high-speed quads, 3 triples, 4 doubles, 1 surface lift, 146 runs (the longest is 3½ mi), and a vertical drop of 3,340 ft. | U.S. 6 (Box 915), Avon | 970/949–5750 or 800/525–2257 | www.beavercreek.com | Late Nov.–mid-Apr.

Vilar Center for the Arts. A performing and visual arts center in Market Square hosting classical, jazz, blues, and folk concerts, as well as theatrical and dance performances. The gallery features exhibits from local and national artists. | 68 Avondale La. | 970/949–4348 or 888/920–ARTS | fax 970/949–5568 | www.vilarcenter.org | Mon.–Sat. 9–9.

ON THE CALENDAR

MAR.: *Vail/Beaver Creek American Ski Classic.* Hosted by former President Gerald Ford, highlights include the "Legends of Skiing" competition, honoring past national and world champs. Held on Golden Peak the second weekend in March. | 970/949–1999 or 888/VVF–VAIL.

AUG.: *Jerry and Betty Ford Artisan's Golf Classic.* This two-day tournament at the Beaver Creek and Cordillera Golf Courses benefits the Vilar Center for the Arts. | 970/949–1999.

Dining

Beano's Cabin. Continental. You take a sleigh in winter or, in summer, take a horse-drawn wagon, a van, or ride on horseback to get to this remote Beaver Creek restaurant (leaving from Beaver Creek Plaza). Try the brick-oven pizzas. Guitarist. Kids' menu. No smoking. | Larkspur Bowl | 970/845–5770 | Reservations essential | Closed mid-Apr.–1st wk June, late Sept.–Dec., and Mon.–Tues. June–Sept. No lunch | $45–$85 prix fixe | AE, D, DC, MC, V.

Cassidy's Hole in the Wall. American/Casual. Two-floor western saloon, where specialties include a 1-pound burger, chicken-fried steak, and a 2-ft-long rack of ribs. | 82 E. Beaver Creek Blvd., Avon | 970/949–9449 | $10–$20 | AE, D, MC, V.

Fiesta's. Southwestern. The New Mexican folk art and paintings create a perfect setting for the appetizing dishes. The chicken enchilada in a white jalapeno sauce, the chicken relleno, and the handmade corn tamales stuffed with pork and smothered in a chile sauce are among some of the house specialties. Located in Edwards, 6 mi west of Beaver Creek. | 57 Edwards Access Rd., Edwards | 970/827–4114 | $9–$12 | AE, D, DC, MC, V.

The Gas House. American. Local hangout in a 1930s log cabin with trophy-covered walls. Dine on steaks, ribs, fresh salmon, and wild game. Don't forget to try the Buffalo shrimp (a close cousin to the famous wings). | Rte. 6, Edwards | 970–926–2896 | $12–$20 | AE, MC, V.

Golden Eagle Inn. Contemporary. This European country restaurant is enclosed by shades of dark green and wood paneling. On the menu: roasted loin of elk, hazelnut bacon-crusted rainbow trout, roast duckling. Open-air dining on garden patio. Kids' menu. | 118 Beaver Creek Plaza | 970/949–1940 | $18–$34 | AE, MC, V.

★ **Mirabelle.** French. The chef's creations include Atlantic salmon with artichokes and roast peppers, crispy ricotta gnocchi, and Dover sole meunière with citrus white butter. Desserts include a caramelized cinnamon pear tart served with passion-fruit sorbet and vanilla ice cream. | 55 Village Rd. | 970/949–7728 | $23–$32 | AE, D, MC, V.

Restaurant Picasso. French. Original paintings by the eponymous artist hang on the walls at this elegant French restaurant with arched windows in the Lodge and Spa at Cordillera overlooking the mountains 6 mi west of Beaver Creek in Edwards. The kitchen takes a light approach to European classics such as seared Chilean sea bass and rack of Colorado lamb. Open-air dining with mountain views. Pianist Thursday–Saturday. No smoking. | 2205 Cordillera Way (I–70 W, exit 163), Edwards | 970/926–2200 | $23–$33 | AE, D, DC, MC, V.

Lodging

Beaver Creek Lodge. All rooms are suites at this small hotel located within 30 yards of two ski lifts. 2 restaurants, bar. In-room data ports, microwaves, refrigerators, cable TV, in-room VCRs (and movies). Indoor-outdoor pool. Hot tub, sauna, steam room. Gym. Shops, video games. Laundry facilities. Business services. | 26 Avondale La. | 970/845–9800 | fax 970/845–8242 | www.beavercreeklodge.net | 72 suites | $325–$525 | AE, MC, V.

Charter at Beaver Creek. Regular lodge rooms and condos are available in this ski-in, ski-out property; many have fireplaces and balconies. 2 restaurants, bar. In-room data ports, refrigerators, cable TV, in-room VCRs (and movies). 2 pools (1 indoor), wading pool. Beauty salon, hot tub, massage, sauna, spa, steam room. Health club. Sleigh rides, snowmobiling. Shops, video games. Business services. Free parking. | 120 Offerson Rd. | 970/949–6660 or 800/525–6660 | fax 970/949–6709 | www.thecharter.com | 65 lodge rooms, 115 1- and 2-bedroom condo apartments | $270–$350, $395–$495 1–bedroom apartment, $560–$675 2–bedroom apartment | AE, MC, V.

★ **Hyatt Regency–Beaver Creek Resort and Spa.** The lobby at this slopeside resort, with a magnificent antler chandelier and huge oriel windows opening into the mountain, manages to be both cozy and grand. 2 restaurants, bar (with entertainment). Some refrigerators, cable TV, some in-room VCRs. Pool. Barbershop, beauty salon, hot tub, spa. Baby-sitting, children's programs (ages 5–12), playground. Laundry facilities. Business services. Parking (fee). | 136 E. Thomas Pl. | 970/949–1234 | fax 970/949–4164 | www.hyatt.com | 271 rooms, 5 suites | $445–$615, $395–$725 1–bedroom suites, $500–$1,200 2–bedroom suites | AE, D, DC, MC, V.

Inn at Beaver Creek. This cozy, European-style lodge may be the most ski-accessible property in North America—the Strawberry Park chairlift is just 4 yards from the door. Bar, complimentary breakfast. In-room data ports, microwaves, refrigerators, cable TV, some in-room VCRs. Pool. Hot tub, sauna, steam room. Laundry facilities. Parking (fee). | 10 Elk Track La. | 970/845–7800 or 800/859–8242 | fax 970/845–5279 | 45 rooms, 1 apartment | $330–$395, $600–$865 apartment | AE, D, DC, MC, V.

Inn at Riverwalk. These comfortable rooms and condominiums are quite affordable. All have a queen- or king-size bed, and some have balconies with great views. The inn also offers ski and bicycle storage. Just 4 mi from Beaver Creek in Edwards. Restaurant, bar. Complimentary Continental breakfast. In-room data ports, some kitchenettes, some microwaves, some refrigerators, cable TV, some in-room VCRs (and movies). Pool. Hot tub. Gym. Laundry service. Pets allowed (fee). | 27 Main St., Edwards | 970/926–0606 or 888/926–0606 |

fax 970/926–0616 | www.vail.net/riverwalk | 60 rooms, 14 condos | $150–$250, $500–$700 condos | AE, D, DC, MC, V.

★ **Lodge at Cordillera.** Surrounded by pristine wilderness, this exclusive, luxurious lodge is only 15 minutes from the lifts at Beaver Creek, shuttle provided. It's located in Edwards, about 6 mi west of Beaver Creek. 4 restaurants (*see* Restaurant Picasso), bar. In-room data ports, minibars. Indoor-outdoor pool. 3 hot tubs, spa. 2 18-hole golf courses, 1 short course. Health club. Cross-country skiing. | 2205 Cordillera Way, Edwards | 970/926–2200 or 800/548–2721 | fax 970/926–2486 | www.cordillera-vail.com | 56 rooms | $335–$725 | AE, D, DC, MC, V.

The Pines Lodge. A small lodge that is both posh and unpretentious. Rooms are spacious and airy, several with balconies overlooking the ski slopes. Restaurant, bar (with entertainment). In-room data ports, some kitchenettes, refrigerators, cable TV, in-room VCRs (and movies). Pool. Hot tub. Tennis. Gym. Business services. | 141 Scott Hill Rd. | 970/845–7900 or 800/859–8242 | fax 970/845–7809 | www.vail.net/lodging/vbcr.properties/pines | 60 rooms, 7 apartments | $200–$425, $615–$970 apartments | AE, D, DC, MC, V.

Poste Montane Lodge. Directly on the Village Promenade, this small, modern, European-style lodge caters to you with large, comfortable rooms and an attentive staff. You are at the foot of all the shops, restaurants, and galleries in Beaver Creek. Restaurant, bar, complimentary Continental breakfast. In-room data ports, some kitchenettes, refrigerators, cable TV, in-room VCRs. Pool. Hot tub, outdoor hot tub, sauna, spa, steam room. Health club. Ice-skating. Laundry facilities. Business services, free parking. No smoking. | 76 Avandale La. | 970/845–7500 or 800/497–9238 | fax 970/845–5012 | www.eastwestresorts.com | 24 units | $475–$1,100 | Closed 1st wk May and 1st wk Oct. | AE, MC, V.

BOULDER

MAP 6, F3

(Nearby towns also listed: Allenspark, Denver, Longmont, Lyons, Nederland)

With a population of 85,000, Boulder, the home of the University of Colorado, sits nestled in the midst of the Rocky Mountains just a few miles northwest of Denver. Since 1998 it has been more widely known as the home of JonBenét Ramsey than for the many scientific and technological concerns—both governmental and private—that have their headquarters here. Indeed, much of the city's present-day economy is linked to these industries. Yet, Boulder still has the feel of a college town with an arty, liberal tradition. Locals are outdoor oriented (the city has 25,000 acres of parks and other green spaces) and are almost as likely to ride a mountain bike as drive an SUV.

Information: **Convention and Visitors Bureau** | 2440 Pearl St., Boulder 80302 | 303/442–2911 or 800/444–0447 | www.bouldercoloradousa.com.

Attractions

Boulder Museum of Contemporary Art. Located in a two-story former factory in downtown Boulder, BMoCA concentrates on contemporary art by both new and established artists. It's also a major performing space. | 1750 13th St. | 303/443–2122 | bmoca.org | $4 | Wed.–Fri. noon–8, Sat. 9–5, Sun. noon–5.

Boulder Museum of History. Housed in the 1889 Harbeck-Bergheim mansion, the museum's exhibits depict the history of Boulder and the surrounding region from 1858 to the present. | 1206 Euclid Ave. | 303/449–3464 | $3 | www.bcn.boulder.co.us/arts/bmh/ | Tues.–Fri. 10–4; weekends noon–4; closed Mon.

Boulder Reservoir. Picnicking, fishing, boating, and swimming are available. | 5100 N. 51st St. | 303/441–3461 | fax 303/441–1807 | Labor Day–May free, May–Labor Day $5 | Daily 6 AM–dusk.

Celestial Seasonings Guest Tours. Visitors to Boulder can take a 45-minute tour of the factory where herbal teas are created and packaged, including an art gallery and the "Mint Room." No kids under 5 permitted on tours. | 4600 Sleepytime Dr. | 303/530–5300 | www.celestialseasonings.com | Free | Tours hourly, Mon.–Sat. 10–3, Sun. 11–3.

Leanin' Tree Museum of Western Art. This is the corporate headquarters of "Leanin' Tree" greeting cards. The museum exhibits original paintings and bronzes by contemporary artists, including members of the Cowboy Artists of America, that illustrate cowboys, Indians, wildlife, and landscapes of the American West. | 6055 Longbow Dr. | 303/530–1442 ext. 299 | www.leanintree.com | Free | Weekdays 8–4:30, weekends 10–4.

National Center for Atmospheric Research. The sun, hazards of global warming, weather, and aviation hazards are exhibited and explained. Also maintained is a 400-acre nature preserve on the premises. | 1850 Table Mesa Dr. | 303/497–1174 | www.ncar.ucar.edu | Free | Weekdays 8–5, weekends and holidays 9–4; self-guided tours any time, 1-hr guided tour by appointment only.

Pearl Street Mall. Colorful shopping mall with fine shops, eateries, and street entertainment. A very popular local spot. | Pearl St., between 11th and 15th Sts. | Free | Daily during store hrs.

University of Colorado. Founded in 1876, UC's campus population nears 25,000 students. Wooded and open spaces separate the original stone buildings with red tile roofs. It's about a 60- to 90-min drive from Denver International Airport. | Broadway, between Arapahoe Ave. and Baseline Rd. | 303/492–1411 | www.colorado.edu | Free | Daily.

Fiske Planetarium. Astronomical exhibits are on hand as well as a new, computerized planetarium on the University of Colorado campus. Star shows are held on Friday evenings, usually at 7 or 7:30. Located next door to the Sommers–Bausch Observatory. | Regent Dr., University of Colorado campus | 303/492–5001 (recorded information) or 303/492–5002 | $4 | www.colorado.edu/fiske | Fri. evenings.

Macky Auditorium Concert Hall. Dating from 1914, this historic hall was totally renovated in 1986. Home of the Boulder Philharmonic Orchestra, with guest performers, and the University's Artist Series. | 17th St., University of Colorado campus at University Ave. | 303/492–8008 or 303/449–1343 | www.colorado.edu/macky | Prices vary | Call for concert dates.

Sommers–Bausch Observatory. The giant telescope provides excellent stargazing. Located next door to the Fiske Planetarium. | Regent Dr., University of Colorado campus | 303/492–6732 | Free | Fri. evenings when school is in session starting at dusk.

University of Colorado Museum. A variety of archaeological, geological, botanical, and zoological exhibits depict the history of the region. Located in the Henderson Building. | Broadway at 15th St. | 303/492–6892 | fax 303/492–4195 | www.colorado.edu/cumuseum | Free | Weekdays 9–5, Sat. 9–4, Sun. 10–4.

SIGHTSEEING TOURS/TOUR COMPANIES

Fair Winds Hot Air Ballon Flights. Enjoy Boulder's scenery as you float among the mountains. Flights include Continental breakfast, champagne, and souvenir. Takeoff is from the Gunbarrell area northeast of Boulder. | Box 4253, Boulder | 303/939–9323 | www.fairwindsinc.com | $200; special rates for children.

ON THE CALENDAR

MAY: *Bolder Boulder.* Several races are featured at this Memorial Day event, including 10K and world-class criterium races. | 303/444–7223.

MAY: *Kinetic Sculpture Challenge.* This people-powered sculpture race across both water and land is truly an extraordinary occurrence. | 303/442–2911 or 800/444–0447.

JUNE–JULY: *Colorado Dance Festival.* Dance workshops and performances by world-renowned artists. Performances are held on the University of Colorado Campus and locations throughout Boulder. | 303/442–7666.

JUNE–AUG.: *Colorado Music Festival.* Lectures and entertainment produce an enlightening experience in Chautauqua Park. | 303/449–1397.

JUNE–AUG.: *Colorado Shakespeare Festival.* A theater company assembled from all over the country performs Shakespeare's plays at the Mary Rippon Outdoor Theater on the University of Colorado campus. | 303/492–0554.

Dining

Caffe Antica Roma. Italian. Rustic tables and an indoor fountain make this feel almost like a courtyard in the old country. Try *zuppa di pesce* (a rich fish soup), saltimbocca alla romana (veal topped with sage and prosciutto), or simply grilled swordfish or salmon, but the pastas cannot be recommended. Open-air dining on patio on Pearl St. mall. No smoking. | 1308 Pearl St. | 303/442–0378 | $10–$20 | AE, D, DC, MC, V.

Dagabi Cucina. Italian. Great for candlelight and romance, or a nice place to meet a friend. Try the homemade black ravioli stuffed with salmon and served in tomato cream sauce, or the chicken breast in artichoke-heart cream sauce. | 3970 N. Broadway | 303/786–9004 | No lunch | $12–$18 | AE, DC, MC, V.

Dandelion. Contemporary. A sleek and elegant restaurant decorated in black and white. Try seared tuna with roasted new potatoes or roasted cervena venison with onions. Open-air dining on patio. Sunday brunch. No smoking. | 1011 Walnut St. | 303/443–6700 | No lunch Sat. | $13–$20 | AE, DC, MC, V.

Dolan's Restaurant. Seafood. If you like seafood, try Dolan's fish stew (fish, shrimp, clams, and mussels in a tomato broth) or the macadamia-crusted ahi. The vegetarian menu includes a roasted vegetable torte. Extensive wine list. | 2319 Arapahoe Ave. | 303/444–8758 | fax 303/786–7197 | $11–$35 | AE, D, DC, MC, V.

Dot's Diner. American. Dine among artwork created by some of the employees at this spot that specializes in homemade buttermilk biscuits with ham and gravy. | 2716 28th St. | 303/449–1323 | Breakfast also available; no dinner | $4–$7 | No credit cards.

European Café. Contemporary. A comfortable place decorated with artwork by local artists, faux marble walls, and pastel colors. Try the lamb chops or the *fruits de mer* (sautéed fresh scallops, shrimp, and steamed crab in sherry-butter sauce), or the salmon with a balsamic vinegar-butter sauce colored with pomegranate. | 2460 Arapahoe Ave. | 303/938–8250 | Closed Sun. No lunch Sat. | $14–$26 | AE, DC, MC, V.

★ **Flagstaff House.** Contemporary. This elegant aerie is high on Flagstaff Mountain, about 20 minutes from downtown Boulder with breathtaking city views. The cosmopolitan background of the chef shows up in dishes such as the rack of Colorado lamb or the ahi tuna. | 1138 Flagstaff Rd. | 303/442–4640 | Reservations essential | No lunch | $24–$65 | AE, D, DC, MC, V.

Full Moon Grill. Italian. Earth tones and faux marble walls provide a warm Mediterranean setting. Try the pan-seared ahi tuna or the grilled Colorado lamb T-bone. Open-air dining on small patio. No smoking. | 2525 Arapahoe Ave. | 303/938–8800 | No lunch | $10–$25 | AE, MC, V.

★ **Gold Hill Inn.** American. Log cabin 10 mi west of Boulder that serves a six-course set menu. Try the paella or lamb venison marinated for four days in buttermilk, juniper berries, and cloves. The inn also hosts occasional "murder mystery" nights using professional actors. | 401 Main, Gold Hill | 303/443–6461 | Closed Tues. No lunch | $24 prix fixe | No credit cards.

The Greenbriar Inn. Continental. This clubby retaurant 6½ mi north of Boulder, all dark wood and hunter green, offers views of a tranquil garden through its large picture window. The menu includes such dishes as beef Wellington, Caesar salad, and ostrich. Open-air dining on covered patio. Sunday brunch 11–2. | Hwy. 36 at Left Hand Canyon | 303/440–7979 | No lunch | $18–$32 | AE, DC, MC, V.

John's. Contemporary. A cozy, intimate restaurant in a turn-of-the-20th-century cottage. Try the filet mignon with Stilton-and-ale sauce, or the lamb chops peperonata. No smoking. | 2328 Pearl St. | 303/444–5232 | Closed Sun. No lunch Mon. | $16–$24 | AE, D, MC, V.

Laudisio. Italian. Two dining rooms—one with an open kitchen—are done in terra-cotta tones and Italian style. Try chicken and ricotta ravioli, salmon bouillabaisse, spinach gnocchi. | 2785 Iris Ave. | 303/442–1300 | No lunch weekends | $10–$24 | AE, D, DC, MC, V.

Mataam Fez. Moroccan. Lavish restauraunt serves a five-course dinner that features such dishes as lamb with honey and almonds, and hare paprika couscous. | 2226 Pearl St. | 303/440–4167 | No lunch | $25 prix fixe | AE, DC, MC, V.

Mediterranean Café. Mediterranean. The open kitchen turns out daily specials such as blue cheese–crusted filet mignon and horseradish-crusted tuna. There's an extensive wine list. | 1002 Walnut St. | 303/444–5335 | fax 303/444–6451 | www.themedboulder.com | $6–$22 | AE, DC, MC, V.

Q's. Contemporary. Modern paintings adorn this restaurant in the Hotel Boulderado. Try grilled tuna, rack of lamb, and grilled beef. Kids' menu. Sunday brunch. No smoking. | 2115 13th St. | 303/442–4880 | Breakfast also available | $17–$25 | AE, D, DC, MC, V.

Red Lion. Steak. Revered for its game. Start with wild game sausage, then try the elk or kangaroo. Or try the steak Diane or one of the changing specials such as crab legs, pheasant, buffalo, or caribou steak. | Boulder 38470 Hwy. 119 Dr. | 303/442–9368 | Reservations essential | No lunch | $13–$35 | AE, D, MC, V.

★ **Redfish New Orleans Brewhouse.** Cajun/Creole. Enjoy the gumbo, crawfish-stuffed grilled quail, and tuna seared with French spices and topped with Creole hollandaise. To accompany your meal, try one of the Brewhouse's own house-made ales. | 2027 13th St. | 303/440–5858 | $15–$24 | AE, MC, V.

Rhumba. Caribbean. Latin music, 45 rums, a Cuban drink called a *mojito,* ceviche, pulled pork, jerk chicken with black beans, coconut rice, and grilled pineapple all come together in this popular Boulder eatery. Open-air dining on a patio that opens onto Pearl St. | 950 Pearl St. | 303/442–7771 | fax 303/448–1185 | $7–$22 | AE, DC, MC, V.

Royal Peacock. Indian. Ceramic elephants and Hindu religious symbols embellish this popular restaurant specializing in the cuisine of northwest India. Vegetarian selections include lentil dishes, *paneer* (fresh cheese), and curries; you'll also find creative non-vegetarian options including Cornish hen curry and lamb tandoori. Open-air dining on patio. Buffet lunch. | 5290 Arapahoe Ave. | 303/447–1409 | No lunch weekends | $7–$22 | AE, D, DC, MC, V.

★ **Sushi Zanmai.** Japanese. Known for its seared tuna served with soy vinaigrette and organic baby greens and also the Z-no. 9 Roll (salmon, avocado, shrimp tempura, and eel sauce). The chefs periodically burst into song. | 1221 Spruce St. | 303/440–0733 | $6–$18 | AE, MC, V.

Trio's. Contemporary. Paintings by Joyce Lieberman (from the adjacent gallery) are on the walls in this elegant, dimly lit restaurant all done up in light brown, black, and natural wood tones. Menu changes seasonally but if they are offered, try seared ahi tuna, grilled mahi mahi, or grilled lamb loin chops. Live jazz. Sunday brunch. | 1155 Canyon Blvd. | 303/442–8400 | www.triosgrille.com | $15–$28 | AE, D, DC, MC, V.

★ **Zolo Grill.** Southwestern. Fresh, hip, and casual, with impeccable food. Try such specialties as tortilla-crusted tuna served with chipotle beurre blanc and smoked-chicken enchiladas. An open-air patio provides view of the Flatirons. | 2525 Arapahoe Blvd. | 303/449–0444 | fax 303/939–9277 | $9–$18 | AE, DC, MC, V.

Lodging

The Alps. The distinctive rooms in this 1870s-era inn 3 mi west of Boulder are furnished with real antiques and have working fireplaces; French doors open to the inn's gardens or patio or even a private patio. Complimentary breakfast. No air-conditioning, in-room data ports, some in-room hot tubs, no TVs in rooms, cable TV in common area. No kids under 12. Business services. No smoking. | 38619 Boulder Canyon Dr. | 303/444–5445 or 800/414–2577 | fax 303/444–5522 | www.bedandbreakfastinns.org/alps | 12 rooms | $125–$225 | AE, D, DC, MC, V.

Best Western Boulder Inn. This chain motel is in a quiet area near the University of Colorado campus, a mile from the Pearl Street Mall. Some of the rooms have balconies and amazing views of the Flatirons. Restaurant, complimentary Continental breakfast. In-room data ports, some microwaves, cable TV. Outdoor pool. Hot tub, sauna. Gym. Laundry service. Airport shuttle, free parking. | 770 28th St. | 303/449–3800 or 800/233–8469 | fax 303/402–9118 | www.boulderinn.com | 98 rooms | $84–$114 | AE, D, DC, MC, V.

Best Western Golden Bluff Lodge. This motel is at the foot of the Rocky Mountains, less than a mile away from the Pearl Street Mall, and next door to the Crossroads Mall. All rooms have king- or queen-size beds, and deluxe rooms have a 27-inch stereo television. Restaurant, bar, complimentary Continental breakfast. In-room data ports, some kitchenettes, some minibars, some microwaves, refrigerators, cable TV. Outdoor pool. Hot tub, sauna. Gym. Laundry facilities, laundry service. | 1725 28th St. | 303/442–7450 or 800/999–2833 | fax 303/442–8788 | www.bestwestern.com/goldenbluff | 112 rooms | $84–$119 | AE, D, DC, MC, V.

Briar Rose Bed and Breakfast. Period pieces furnish this quaint, turn-of-the-20th-century Victorian B&B. Five rooms are in the main house (two with fireplaces), with four in the adjacent carriage house. Complimentary Continental breakfast. Business services. Airport shuttle. No smoking. | 2151 Arapahoe Ave. | 303/442–3007 | fax 303/786–8440 | www.globalmall.com/brose | 9 rooms, 1 suite | $129–$154, $1,000 per wk suite | AE, DC, MC, V.

Broker Inn. This small hotel three blocks from the campus of the University of Colorado at Boulder offers many of the amenities of a larger, more expensive hostelry. Rooms are modern, but decorated in a Victorian motif. Restaurant, bar (with entertainment), complimentary Continental breakfast. In-room data ports, room service, cable TV. Pool. Hot tub. Business services. Airport shuttle. Pets allowed. | 555 30th St. | 303/444–3330 or 800/338–5407 | fax 303/444–6444 | www.boulderbrokerinn.com | 116 rooms, 4 suites | $120–$130, $160–$195 suites | AE, D, DC, MC, V.

Coburn House. A "green" hotel, the Coburn uses low-flush toilets, reduced-flow showerheads, and 100% cotton linens, offering the services of a hotel and the intimacy of a B&B. A rotating gallery of modern art leads into a coffee bar. Complimentary Continental breakfast. In-room data ports, some in-room hot tubs, cable TV. No pets. No smoking. | 2040 16th St. | 303/545–5200 or 800/858–5811 | fax 303/440–6740 | www.nilenet.com/~coburn | 12 rooms | $155–$195 | AE, D, MC, V.

Courtyard by Marriott. Traditional Marriott quality with a nod to business travelers (each room features a comfortable workspace and sitting area). Restaurant, bar. In-room data ports, some microwaves, refrigerators, cable TV. Pool. Hot tub. Gym. Laundry facilities. Business services. | 4710 Pearl E. Circle | 303/440–4700 | fax 303/440–8975 | www.courtyard.com | 137 rooms, 12 suites | $109–$129, $155–$165 suites | AE, D, DC, MC, V.

Earl House Historic Inn. 1882 stone Gothic Revival mansion four blocks from the Pearl Street Mall. Afternoon tea is served on marble-top tables near the fireplace. The rooms have down comforters and Victorian Revival furnishings, some have iron beds, and all are done in deep tones. Complimentary Continental breakfast. In-room data ports, some in-room hot tubs, cable TV. No smoking. | 2429 Broadway | 303/938–1400 | fax 303/938–9710 | 6 rooms | $139–$189 | AE, MC, V.

★ **Foot of the Mountain Motel.** This collection of wood cabin–style units is just a few minutes' walk from downtown Boulder and across the street from a city park with bike path. Each cabin has a mountain or stream view. Refrigerators, cable TV. Pets allowed (fee). | 200 Arapahoe Ave. | 303/442–5688 | 18 rooms | $65–$75 | AE, D, MC, V.

Hampton Inn. A budget-oriented chain hotel 10 mi southeast of Boulder and a mile off U.S. 36 in Louisville. Complimentary Continental breakfast. In-room data ports, microwaves, refrigerators, cable TV. Pool. Hot tub. Gym. Laundry facilities. Business services. | 912 W. Dillon Rd., Louisville | 303/666–7700 | fax 303/666–7374 | www.hamptoninn.com | 80 rooms | $68–$109 | AE, D, DC, MC, V.

★ **Hotel Boulderado.** Be sure to check out the stained-glass ceiling in the lobby of this historic hotel dating from 1909. Rooms in the old building have period charm, while those in the newer wing are more modern but lack character. 3 restaurants (*see* Q's), 2 bars (with entertainment). In-room data ports, some refrigerators, cable TV. Business services. Airport shuttle. | 2115 13th St. | 303/442–4344 or 800/433–4344 | fax 303/442–4378 | www.boulderado.com | 160 rooms, 25 suites | $139–$191, $204–$275 suites | AE, D, DC, MC, V.

Inn on Mapleton Hill. Redbrick Victorian, on a quiet residential street, a few blocks away from the Pearl Street Mall and the University of Colorado campus. Rooms are furnished with antiques, some with fireplaces. Complimentary breakfast. In-room data ports. | 1001 Spruce St. | 303/449–6528 or 800/276–6528 | fax 303/415–0470 | www.innonmapletonhill.com | 7 rooms (2 with shared bath) | $93–$159 | AE, MC, V.

★ **Regal Harvest House.** This modern hotel, built in a semicircle surrounding lovely gardens, offers beautiful mountain views from some rooms. Located just north of the University of Colorado campus. Restaurant, bar. Some refrigerators, cable TV, some in-room VCRs. 2 pools (1 indoor). Hot tub. Tennis. Gym. Laundry facilities. Business services. | 1345 28th St. | 303/443–3850 or 800/222–8888 | fax 303/443–1480 | www.millennium-hotels.com | 265 rooms, 4 suites | $112–$185, $195–$500 suites | AE, D, DC, MC, V.

Residence Inn by Marriott. Spacious rooms in this modern, all-suite property feature separate sleeping and living areas and fully equipped kitchens. Picnic area, complimentary Continental breakfast. In-room data ports, kitchenettes, microwaves, refrigerators, cable TV. Pool. Hot tub. Playground. Laundry facilities. Business services. Pets allowed (fee). | 3030 Center Green Dr. | 303/449–5545 | fax 303/449–2452 | www.residenceinn.com | 128 suites | $139–$199 | AE, D, DC, MC, V.

Sandy Point Inn. A modern, all-suite motel in a residential neighborhood. A full central kitchen is available for guests' use. Picnic area, complimentary breakfast. Kitchenettes, microwaves, refrigerators, cable TV, some in-room VCRs. Playground. Laundry facilities. No smoking. | 6485 Twin Lakes Rd. | 303/530–2939 or 800/322–2939 | fax 303/530–9101 | www.sandypointinn.com | 33 suites | $109–$130 | AE, D, DC, MC, V.

University Inn. This motel is three blocks from the Pearl Street Mall, a block from the city park, and near the University of Colorado campus. Rooms are relatively spacious and have a table for reading the complimentary local paper. Complimentary Continental breakfast. Refrigerators, Cable TV. Outdoor pool. Laundry facilities. Airport shuttle. | 1632 Broadway | 303/442–3830 or 800/258–7917 | fax 303/442–1205 | www.u-inn.com | 39 rooms | $85–$115 | AE, D, DC, MC, V.

★ **Victoria B&B.** All rooms in this 1870s Victorian have queen-size brass beds, down pillows and comforters, and antique furniture dating back to 1889. Some rooms have private patios, balconies, or luxurious steam showers. The Dwight Room has original leaded-glass windows. High tea served daily in a sunny parlor. Complimentary Continental breakfast. Cable TV. | 1305 Pine St. | 303/938–1300 | fax 303/938–1435 | www.bouldervictoria.com | 7 rooms | $129–$189 | AE, MC, V.

BRECKENRIDGE

MAP 6, E4

(Nearby towns also listed: Copper Mountain, Dillon, Fairplay, Frisco, Keystone)

Like so many other Colorado settlements, Breckenridge (population 1,804) had its beginnings in the mid-1800s as a gold-mining town. After the precious metal played out, prospectors moved on to greener pastures, leaving the once prosperous and heavily populated community almost deserted. Today, the town's 12-square-block historic downtown district contains 254 buildings listed on the National Register of

Historic Places. Many consider it one of Colorado's prettiest towns. Additionally, Breckenridge's location in the high Rockies on the western slope of the Continental Divide and its convenience to both Denver and Colorado Springs has blessed it with a new kind of wealth—coveted ski slopes—and each year brings thousands of enthusiastic followers of the sport to its doorstep.

Information: **Breckenridge Resort Chamber** | 311 S. Ridge St., Breckenridge 80424 | 970/453–2913 | www.gobreck.com.

Attractions

Breckenridge Golf Club. This is the only municipally owned golf course in the world that is designed by Jack Niklaus. Dramatically situated, it resembles a nature reserve, with woods and beaver ponds lining the fairways. | 200 Clubhouse Dr. | 970/453–9104 | May–Aug. 7 AM–6 PM; Sept. 8 AM–7 PM.

Breckenridge Ski Resort. America's second-most popular ski resort in terms of the number of visitors per year (a sister resort of Vail, Keystone, and Beaver Creek) is located 1 mi west of Breckenridge off Route 9. The 2,043 skiable acres here encompass peaks 7, 8, 9, and 10 of the Ten Mile Range. This was one of the first resorts in the United States to allow snowboarding. The ski area has 23 lifts, 139 runs (the longest 3½ mi), and a 23-km cross-country ski layout; there's a 3,398-ft vertical drop. More than half the terrain is advanced or expert. Summertime activities such as miniature golf, an alpine slide, horseback riding, hiking, and biking are also available. | Ski Hill Rd. | 970/453–5000 or 800/221–1091 | www.snow.com | Year-round, daily 8:30–4.

© Corbis

SKI CAPITAL OF AMERICA

Colorado is probably better known to vacationers for its extraordinary skiing facilities than it is for anything else. With dozens of peaks reaching skyward to thousands of feet in elevation, it is no wonder that practically everywhere you look you see snow clinging to the uppermost heights. It is the abundance of the white stuff, along with an ideal climate that maintains it even in comparatively warm weather, that makes the "Centennial State" one of North America's leading skiing and wintertime sports destinations.

The Rocky Mountains split Colorado from north to south right down the middle; consequently, no matter where you are in the state, you're not far from some kind of skiing activity. The Vail/Beaver Creek consortium, along with the Aspen/Snowmass complex, are probably the most recognizable names when it comes to skiing in Colorado. But, there are plenty of other resorts that are just as enjoyable, and in many cases, less expensive, than these two. Breckenridge, Crested Butte, Steamboat Springs, Telluride, Winter Park, Copper Mountain, and Keystone all provide exceptional skiing facilities to participants of all experience levels.

Whether you are a beginner, a veteran, or somewhere in between, Colorado has something to offer you. For the last word on the state's skiing situation at any time, contact **Colorado Ski Country U.S.A.** | 1560 Broadway, Suite 1440, Denver, CO | 303/837–0793.

Summit Historical Society. The society conducts guided walking tours of the historical homes and businesses of Breckenridge. Learn about the Victorian structures and get a chance to tour some of their interiors. | 309 N. Main St. | 970/453–9022 | www.summithistorical.org | Daily; reservations required for tours | $6.

SIGHTSEEING TOURS/TOUR COMPANIES

Mountain High Rentals. For some serious backcountry exploring, a late-model jeep with a cellular phone can be rented at the Lone Star Sports in the Blazing Saddles Center. Experienced staff provide trail maps and suggest drives tailored to your abilities. | Bottom of 4 O'clock Rd. and Park | 970/389–1739 or 800/955–0807 | www.mountainhighrentals.com | $125–$140 per day | Daily.

ON THE CALENDAR

JAN.: *Ullr Fest and World Cup Freestyle.* Honoring the Norse god of snow, this festival includes ski competitions, fireworks, and parades. | 970/453–2913 or 970/453–5579.

JUNE–AUG.: *Breckenridge Music Festival.* Highlighted at this festival in the Riverwalk Center are music workshops, classical music performances, children's programs, workshops, and Elderhostels. | 970/453–2120.

JULY–SEPT. AND DEC.–MAR.: *Backstage Theatre.* Comedy, melodramatic, and musical performances provide entertainment for all who attend this festival at the pond level in Breckenridge Village. | 970/453–0199.

AUG.: *No Man's Land Day Celebration.* A celebration of Breckenridge's past, including a look at Colorado's statehood. | 970/453–2913 or 970/453–5579.

DEC.: *International Snow Sculpting Championships.* Renowned artists judge the works created by 16 teams of snow sculptors from around the world during the week before Christmas. During the week, the teams shape 12-ft-tall, 20-ton blocks of snow at the Riverwalk Center. | 970/453–6018.

DEC.: *Lighting of Breckenridge.* The Victorian Village comes alive in early December for the holidays. Parade, choral singing, hot cocoa, and the lighting of the Town Tree. | Main St. | 970/453–6018.

Dining

Blue Moose. American/Casual. Breakfasts include eggs, oatmeal, pancakes, and more. Some lunch specials include sandwiches, burritos, or salad. Come early, though, because they close at 2. | 540 S. Main St. | 970/453–4859 | No dinner | $3–$7 | MC, V.

Breckenridge Brewery. American/Casual. The brewery equipment used to concoct the beers on tap dominates this brewpub. To go with your suds, try the ribs, fajitas, or a juicy burger. Open-air dining on a deck with great mountain view. Kids' menu. | 600 S. Main St. | 970/453–1550 | $8–$18 | AE, D, DC, MC, V.

Briar Rose. Continental. A swanky if fading place decorated with black-and-white photos of Breckenridge in the late 1800s. Known for prime rib, wild game, steak. Entertainment Saturday. Kids' menu. | 109 E. Lincoln St. | 970/453–9948 | No lunch | $15–$50 | AE, D, MC, V.

★ **Café Alpine.** Eclectic. Contemporary paintings and ceramics fill the rooms of this late 1880s three-story Victorian House with a tapas bar and fireplace. Menu changes seasonally. Open-air dining on deck with mountain view. Kids' menu. No smoking. Private dining also available. | 106 E. Adams St. | 970/453–8218 | $14–$27 | AE, D, MC, V.

Hearthstone. Continental. Lace curtains frame fabulous mountain views at this eatery in a late 19th-century house; walls are hung with antique barn wood. Try *tilapia pepita* (pumpkin seed–crusted tilapia filet) and elk chops. Four large decks overlook the Breckenridge ski mountain. Kids' menu. No air-conditioning. | 130 S. Ridge St. | 970/453–1148 | No lunch | $13–$22 | AE, MC, V.

Horseshoe II. American. An 1890s Brunswick Bar in mahogany and cherry wood anchors this popular restaurant in Breckenridge's historic district. Once a barber shop and candy store, now it's a place where you can enjoy such hearty fare as sirloin steak, teriyaki salmon, and the popular half-slab of pork ribs. Open-air dining on patio. Kids' menu. No air-conditioning. | 115 Main St. (Rte. 9) | 970/453–7463 | Breakfast also available | $5–$17 | AE, MC, V.

Mi Casa. Mexican. Located in downtown Breckenridge next to Peak 9 ski area. Adobe walls, plants, and oil paintings are the setting for basic fare plus a few neat twists like deep-fried ice cream. Open-air dining on a deck with views of the mountains and a pond. Kids' menu. | 600 Park Ave. | 970/453–2071 | $8–$15 | AE, MC, V.

Pierre's Riverwalk Café. French. You can watch the chefs at work through the open kitchen at this elegant café. Try the Rocky Mountain trout, or the Colorado rack of lamb. Open-air dining on deck overlooking the Blue River and the Rocky Mountains. | 137 S. Main St. | 970/453–0989 | Closed May and early Nov. | $20–$30 | DC, MC, V.

Poirrier's Cajun Café. Cajun/Creole. Green tables and red carpet provide the backdrop for paintings by Louisiana artists, photos of crawfish, and scenes from Louisiana life in this cozy, intimate place known for its catfish, seafood platters, crawfish, and gumbo. Open-air dining on patio. Kids' menu. No smoking. | 224 S. Main St. | 970/453–1877 | $10–$22 | AE, D, DC, MC, V.

Salt Creek. Steak. Have a New York strip steak or barbecue ribs in this Wild West pine-log dining room accented by mounted animal heads. Open-air dining on deck. Country-western dance hall located upstairs. Kids' menu. | 110 E. Lincoln Ave. | 970/453–4949 | $9–$24 | AE, D, DC, MC, V.

St. Bernard Inn. Continental. An historic building with old photos, a tin ceiling, and mining artifacts create a western mood. Try the herb-crusted rack of lamb or the seafood fra diavolo. Kids' menu. | 103 S. Main St. | 970/453–2572 | Closed May. No lunch | $14–$28 | AE, D, DC, MC, V.

Swan Mountain Inn Restaurant. Continental. In the Swan Mountain Inn, this former log-cabin home has a romantic candlelit dining room with a lovely fireplace. The menu, which changes daily, offers such dishes as crab-stuffed filet mignon with bernaise sauce. Open-air dining on deck with a view of Mt. Baldy. Kids' menu. | 16172 Rte. 9 | 970/453–7903 | Breakfast also available | $10–$28 | D, MC, V.

Lodging

Allaire Timbers Inn. There are fabulous views of the Ten Mile Range from the main deck of this stone-and-log B&B. All rooms have a private deck and king-size beds. Complimentary breakfast. Cable TV. Hot tub. Cross-country skiing, downhill skiing. No kids under 13. Business services. No smoking. | 9511 S. Main St. (Rte. 9) | 970/453–7530 or 800/624–4904 | fax 970/453–8699 | www.allairetimbers.com | 8 rooms, 2 suites | $165, $225–$250 suites | AE, D, MC, V.

Beaver Run. This large full-service resort and conference center at the base of Peak 9 is convenient for skiing (it's ski-in, ski-out) as well as for summer activities. Rooms are large, modern, and comfortable. Restaurant, bar (with entertainment). Kitchenettes, some in-room hot tubs, cable TV. 2 pools (1 indoor-outdoor). 8 hot tubs, massage, sauna. Tennis. Gym. Downhill skiing. Shops, video games. Playground, children's programs (ages 6 weeks to 12). Laundry facilities. Business services. | 620 Village Rd. | 970/453–6000 or 800/525–2253 | fax 970/453–2454 | www.beaverrunresort.com | 90 rooms, 460 suites | $190–$290, $305 1–bedroom suites, $475–$750 multiple–bedroom suites | AE, DC, MC, V.

★ **Bed and Breakfasts on North Main Street.** This unique property actually encompasses three separate buildings: two restored, historic cottages and a converted barn. The innkeepers will take skiers to their favorite spots. Picnic area, complimentary breakfast. No air-conditioning, some in-room data ports, some refrigerators, some room phones, no TV in some rooms, TV in common area. Hot tubs. No smoking. | 303 N. Main St. | 970/453–2975 or 800/795–2975 | fax 970/453–5258 | bnb@imageline.com | www.breckenridge-inn.com | 11 rooms | $89–$319 | AE, DC, MC, V.

Evans House. A B&B in an 1886 house two blocks from Main St. Picnic area, complimentary breakfast. No air-conditioning, cable TV. Hot tub. Exercise equipment. Business services. No smoking. | 102 S. French St. | 970/453–5509 | fax 970/547–1746 | www.coloradoevanshouse.com | 4 rooms, 2 suites | $100–$140, $118–$140 suites | AE, D, DC, MC, V.

Fireside Inn. An original Victorian that has been expanded to offer a bed-and-breakfast experience. Accommodations range from dormitory-style rooms (with four bunk beds) to suites. Two blocks from Main Street. Complimentary Continental breakfast. No TV in some rooms, cable TV in common area, some in-room VCRs. Hot tub. | 114 N. French | 970/453–6456 | fax 970/453–9577 | www.firesideinn.com | 4 rooms, 4 hostel rooms | $85–$140, $28–$35 per person for hostel rooms | No credit cards.

Great Divide. Located just 50 yards from the base of Peak 9 and two blocks from Main Street, this is one of the few full-service hotels in Breckenridge. Offers especially large guest rooms, some with private balconies, as well as meeting facilities. Bar. In-room data ports, refrigerators, cable TV. Pool. Hot tub, massage. Gym. Video games. Business services, airport shuttle. | 550 Village Rd. | 970/453–4500 or 800/321–8444 | fax 970/453–0212 | www.great-dividelodge.com | 208 rooms | $150–$225 | AE, D, DC, MC, V.

Hunt Placer Inn. This Bavarian chalet–style inn is tucked in the mountainside, surrounded by aspens, evergreens, and wildflowers. Rooms are simply furnished and comfortable. Complimentary breakfast. In-room data ports, no TV in rooms, cable TV in common area. Outdoor hot tub. Video games. No kids under 12. No smoking. | 275 Ski Hill Rd. | 970/453–7573 or 800/472–1430 | fax 970/453–2335 | www.huntplacerinn.com | 8 rooms, 3 minisuites | $149, $179–$199 suites | AE, D, DC, MC, V.

Lodge at Breckenridge. The lodge is on a cliff surrounded by trees, 2.2 mi from town. Some rooms have gas fireplaces or private balconies with stunning views of the mountains. Be sure to pamper yourself with an appointment at the full-service spa. Restaurant, complimentary Continental breakfast. Pool. 2 indoor hot tubs, spa. Health club, racquetball. Shops. | 112 Overlook Dr. | 970/453–9300 or 800/736–1607 | fax 970/453–0625 | www.thelodgeatbreck.com | 45 rooms | $190–$340 | AE, D, DC, MC, V.

Ridge Street Inn. A small 1890 Victorian located in the Breckenridge Historic District furnished with some antiques. Complimentary breakfast. No air-conditioning, no room phones. No kids under 6. No smoking. | 212 N. Ridge St. | 970/453–4680 or 800/452–4680 | www.colorado.net/ridge | 6 rooms (2 with shared bath) | $98–$150 | MC, V.

River Mountain Lodge. This condo-style lodge, just one block from Main Street, has a distinctive lobby and a bustling bar. Most apartments have fireplaces; some have washers and dryers. Restaurant, bar. Some kitchenettes, some microwaves, some refrigerators, some in-room hot tubs, cable TV, in-room VCRs (and movies). Pool. Hot tub, sauna, steam room. Gym. Business services. | 100 S. Park Ave. | 970/453–4711 or 800/627–3766 | fax 970/453–1763 | www.cfpbreck.com | 150 apartments | $189–$239 1–bedroom suites, $239–$419 2–bedroom suites, $379–$599 3– to 4–bedroom suites | AE, D, MC, V.

Swan Mountain Inn. A former log home converted into a B&B. Located between Frisco and Breckenridge. Restaurant, bar, picnic area, complimentary breakfast. Some in-room hot tubs, cable TV, in-room VCRs (and movies). Outdoor hot tub. Laundry facilities. No smoking. | 16172 Rte. 9, at Swan Mountain Rd. | 970/453–7903 or 800/578–3687 | swanmt@colorado.net | www.colorado-bnb.com/swanmtn | 4 rooms (1 with shared bath) | $70–$145 | MAP | D, MC, V.

Village at Breckenridge. This is really a town unto itself. The Village spans from Main Street to the mountains and has a beautiful central gazebo, Maggie pond (which serves as the area's only outdoor ice rink). You can reserve a hotel room that has a queen bed or a queen bed and bunk beds, a studio that has a full kitchen, or a condominium with a fireplace and a balcony. 9 restaurants, 3 bars. Some kitchenettes, cable TV. Indoor-outdoor pool, 2 outdoor pools. 9 hot tubs, sauna. Health club. Ice-skating. Shops. | 535 S. Park | 970/453–2000 or 800/800–7829 | fax 970/453–3116 | www.breckresort.com/village | 347 rooms | $150–$795 | AE, D, DC, MC, V.

The Wellington Inn. This inn is on Main Street and embodies the classic charm of Breckenridge. The picture windows are as inviting as the fireplace. The rooms have cathedral ceilings and are filled with family antiques, but the attention to detail seen in the goose-down comforters and robes and slippers in each room really make this place special. Some have private balconies with mountain views. Restaurant, bar, complimentary Continental breakfast. In-room hot tubs, cable TV, in-room VCRs. | 200 N. Main St. | 970/453–9464 or 800/655–7557 | fax 970/453–0149 | www.thewellingtoninn.com | 4 rooms | $179–$249 | AE, D, MC, V.

BUENA VISTA

MAP 6, E5

(Nearby towns also listed: Leadville, Salida)

Twelve mountain peaks exceeding altitudes of 14,000 ft (including the Collegiate Peaks named Yale, Harvard, Princeton, and Columbia by the alumni of these universities who first climbed them), along with 500 lakes and four rivers, lie within 20 mi of Buena Vista, situated less than 100 mi due west of Colorado Springs. The town, with a population of 2,219, had its beginnings as a mining community, but like so many of these places, when the ore dried up, the town turned to tourism to survive. Outdoor pursuits, including hiking, wildlife-watching, snowmobiling, and cross-country skiing, are the big draws to these parts.

Information: **Buena Vista Chamber of Commerce** | 343 S. U.S. 24, Buena Vista 81211 | 719/395–6612 | www.fourteenernet.com.

Attractions

Buena Vista Heritage Museum. Each of the four rooms is devoted to a different aspect of the region's history: one to mining equipment and minerals, another to fashions and household utensils, a third to working models of the three railroads that serviced the area, and the last to historical photos. | 511 E. Main St. | 719/395–8458 or 719/395–8453 | $2 | Memorial Day–Labor Day, daily 9–5.

Collegiate Peaks Wilderness Area. Encompassing 168,000 acres in three different national forests (the Gunnison, White River, and San Isabel), this huge wilderness is a good place if you want to hike, bike, or do rock climbing; in the winter you can do snowmobiling or cross-country skiing here. Groups of 10 or more must get a permit from the Salida Ranger District office for the San Isabel National Forest. | 325 W. Rainbow Blvd. | 719/539–3591 | www.fs.fed.us/r2/psicc/sal/index.htm | Daily.

Trailhead Ventures. You can purchase or rent equipment for outdoor activities here. | 707 Rte. 24 | 719/395–8001 | www.trailheadco.com | Memorial Day–Labor Day, daily 9–6; Labor Day–Memorial Day, daily 10–6.

SIGHTSEEING TOURS/TOUR COMPANIES

White-water Rafting Trips. Several rivers in the region offer outstanding white-water opportunities. You can spend one day or several on the many rivers that flow through this mountain region. The headwaters of the Arkansas and the Rio Grande, as well as the Colorado, North Platte, and Gunnison rivers, all provide mild to wild rapids for your white-water or rafting pleasure.

Arkansas River Tours. Offers 2-hour to 3-day outings on the spectacular Arkansas River. | Box 337, Cotopaxi | www.arkansasrivertours.com | 800/321–4352 or 800/332–7238 | May–Aug.

Bill Dvorak's Kayak and Rafting Expeditions. You can arrange ½- to 12-day excursions on the Arkansas, Colorado, Gunnison, and other wild rivers in the region from this outfitter. | 17921 U.S. 285, Nathrop | 719/539–6851 or 800/824–3795 | www.dvorakexpeditions.com | Mid-Apr.–early Oct.

Noah's Ark Whitewater Rafting Company. This outfitter arranges ½- to 3-day trips on the Arkansas River. | Box 850, Buena Vista | 719/395–2158 | Mid-May–late Aug.

Wilderness Aware. Runs ½- to 10-day trips on five Colorado rivers—the Arkansas, Colorado, Gunnison, Dolores, and North Platte. | Box 1550, Buena Vista | www.inaraft.com | 719/395–2112 or 800/462–7238 | May–Sept.

ON THE CALENDAR

AUG.: *Gold Rush Days.* Parade, burro race, food, entertainment, gunfighters, western dancers, and arts-and-crafts exhibits on Main Street. | 2nd weekend | 719/935–6612 | www.fourteenernet.com/goldrush.

Dining

Bongo Billy's High Country Coffees and Café. Café. Enjoy the soups, salads, and sandwiches. The bakery goods are made on-premises. Try the sour-cream coffee cake. Coffee, in 15 varieties, is roasted on-site. | 713 S. U.S. 24 | 719/395–2634 or 800/738–0622 | www.bongobillys.com | $4–$8 | AE, D, MC, V.

Buffalo Bar and Grill. Continental. Photos of buffaloes and mountains hang on the walls along with Rocky Mountain antiques, including skis, cameras, and snowshoes. Try the prime rib, fresh grilled salmon, or beef Wellington. | 710 U.S. 24 N | 719/395–6472 | $5–$17 | D, DC, MC, V.

Casa Del Sol. Mexican. This popular restaurant is in an old miner's cabin. Try the *pechuga suiza* (a fried then baked flour tortilla with chicken and sour cream), chicken mole, or the enchiladas. Open-air dining in a garden courtyard with a fountain. Kids' menu. | 333 N. U.S. 24 | 719/395–8810 | Closed Oct.–mid-Dec and Apr. | $10–$15 | D, MC, V.

The Elkhorn Woodfired Grill. Italian. At this casual spot, try the wood-fired pizzas or one of the calzones. Have a drink at the upstairs sports bar or dine on the garden patio. | 301 E. Main St. | 719/395–2231 | $6–$17 | MC, V.

Lodging

Adobe Inn. A restored adobe hacienda built in the 1880s with fireplaces and a solarium. Rooms are decorated in various motifs, but all are comfortable and furnished with antiques; one room has a fireplace. Complimentary breakfast. Cable TV, no room phones. Hot tub. No smoking. | 303 N. U.S. 24 | 719/395–6340 or 888/343–6340 | www.bbonline.com/co/adobe | 3 rooms, 2 suites | $75–$95 | MC, V.

Elk Mountain Ranch. Surrounded by aspen and evergreen in the San Isabel National Forest, 17 mi southeast of Buena Vista, this guest ranch is remote, secluded, and cozy. The rustic though comfortable cabins are big enough for a family of four–six. Seven-day minimum stay. Picnic area. No room phones, no TV. Hot tub. Hiking, horseback riding. Fishing. | 13000 Rte. 185B | 719/539–4430 or 800/432–8812 | fax 719/539–4430 | www.elkmtn.com | 11 rooms, 7 cabins | $1,275 per wk | Closed late-Sept.–May | AP | AE, MC, V.

Great Western Sumac Lodge. This small motel is economically priced, with mountain views. Picnic area. Cable TV. In-room data ports. Some kitchenettes. | 428 U.S. 24 S | 719/395–8111 | fax 719/395–2560 | 30 rooms | $56–$68 | AE, D, DC, MC, V.

Meister House. Located on the quiet east end of Main Street—just three blocks from the Arkansas River—this inn was built in the late 1890s as a hotel. The sitting room has a wood-burning stove, 13-ft ceilings, and large windows. Patios provide views of the Rockies. Picnic area, complimentary breakfast. Sauna. Business services. No smoking. | 414 E. Main St. | 719/395–9220 or 888/395–9220 | fax 719/395–9455 | www.meisterhouse.com | 6 rooms (2 with shared bath) | $80–$115 | AE, D, MC, V.

Super 8 Motel–Buena Vista. Standard inexpensive chain accommodations at this small motel with views of the Rocky Mountains' Collegiate Peaks. Complimentary Continental breakfast. Cable TV. Pool. Hot tub. Laundry facilities. | 530 N. U.S. 24 | 719/395–8888 or 800/800–8000 | fax 719/395–4090 | www.super8.com | 38 rooms | $75–$95 | AE, D, DC, MC, V.

Topaz Lodge. This small motel is next to downtown Buena Vista, near a park and a launch point for white-water rafting trips on the Arkansas River. No air-conditioning, cable TV. Some pets allowed. | 115 U.S. 24 N | 719/395–2427 | 18 rooms, 1 two-bedroom apartment | $65–$110 | AE, D, DC, MC, V.

Vista Inn. Motel whose mountain views add to its convenient location in Buena Vista. Complimentary Continental breakfast. Cable TV. 3 outdoor hot tubs. Laundry facilities. | 733 N. U.S. 24 | 719/395–8009 or 800/809–3495 | fax 719/395–6025 | www.vtinet.com/vistainn | 41 rooms | $85–$95 | AE, D, DC, MC, V.

BURLINGTON

MAP 6, K4

(Nearby towns also listed: Lamar, Limon)

Burlington lies in the valley formed by tributaries of the Smoky Hill and Republican rivers, right off Interstate 70 just 12 mi inside the Colorado border from Kansas. The town was organized back in the 1880s by farmers who had settled along the Kansas City–Denver railroad line. Today, the community is the largest in the east-central part of the state (with a population of 3,193), and the local economy is boosted by the extensive wheat farming in the area.

Information: **Burlington Chamber of Commerce** | 415 15th St., Burlington 80807 | 719/346–8070.

Attractions

Bonny Lake State Park. A beautiful 1,900-acre reservoir provides fishing, boating, water-skiing, and swimming. Located 23 mi north of Burlington on U.S. 385, near Idalia. | 30010 County Rd. 3, Idalia | 970/354–7306 | $4 per vehicle, overnight camping $10–$14 | Daily.

Kit Carson County Carousel. This national historic landmark is the nation's oldest wooden merry-go-round. It's located at the Kit Carson County Fairgrounds. | Colorado Ave. and 15th St. | 719/346–8070 | 25¢ | Memorial Day–Labor Day, daily 1–8.

Old Town. Gunfights and outdoor play-acting highlight the events at this late-19th-century restored town. | 420 S. 14th St. | 719/346–7382 or 800/288–1334 | $6 | Memorial Day–Labor Day, daily 9–6; Labor Day–Memorial Day, Mon.–Sat. 9–5, Sun. noon–5.

Wray Museum. Small historical museum exhibiting about 900 archaeological artifacts as well as a diorama of the Battle of Beecher Island (1868) and a cannon from the battle. The museum is also the local tourist information office. | 203 E. 3rd St., at U.S. 34 | 970/332–5063 | $1 | Tues.–Sat. 10–noon and 1–5; closed Sun., Mon.

Beecher Island Battlefield. Site of the 1868 battle where the legendary Cheyenne warrior Roman Nose was killed. The site has two churches, a theater, and a trail. Located 17 mi south of Wray, about 44 mi north of Burlington off U.S. 385. Watch for signs. | Colorado Rd. KK, off U.S. 385 | 970/332–5063 | Free | Daily dawn to dusk.

ON THE CALENDAR

MAY: *Little Britches Rodeo.* A parade and rodeo competition for boys and girls between the ages of 8 and 18 at the Kit Carson County Fairgrounds. | 719/346–8070.

AUG: *Kit Carson County Fair and Rodeo.* This county fair, PRCA rodeo, and parade is an anticipated annual event. Held at the Kit Carson Country Fairgrounds. | 719/346–8133.

SEPT.: *Oktoberfest.* Enjoy all that is German at this fall festival in downtown Burlington. Sample the food, hear the music, watch the traditional dances, and take home some of the crafts. | 719/346–5526.

Dining

Mitten's Interstate House. American/Casual. Locals frequent this spot off Interstate 70. Generous portions. Enjoy the chicken-fried steak, biscuits and gravy, or green chile. | 415 Lincoln St. | 719/346–7041 | $6–$14 | D, MC, V.

Lodging

Budget Host Chaparral Motor Inn. A budget motel located one block from the intersection of Interstate 70 (exit 437) and U.S. 385, near several restaurants. Cable TV. Pool. Hot tub. Playground. Some pets allowed. | 405 S. Lincoln St. | 719/346–5361 | fax 719/346–8502 | 39 rooms | $45 | AE, D, DC, MC, V.

Comfort Inn–Burlington. Inexpensive chain accommodations a few blocks from downtown. Complimentary Continental breakfast. In-room data ports, some in-room hot tubs, cable TV. Pool. Hot tub. Gym. | 282 S. Lincoln | 719/346–7676 or 800/228–5150 | fax 719/346–7780 | www.comfortinn.com | 57 rooms | $64–$106 | AE, D, DC, MC, V.

Sloans. This small independent motel is less than a mile from Old Town and the Kit Carson County Carousel. Some microwaves, cable TV. Pool. Playground. Business services. | 1901 Rose Ave. | 719/346–5333 | fax 719/346–9536 | 29 rooms | $40–$44 | AE, D, DC, MC, V.

CAÑON CITY

MAP 6, F6

(Nearby towns also listed: Colorado Springs, Cripple Creek, Manitou Springs)

Situated at the mouth of the spectacular Royal Gorge, Cañon City (population 16,076) is the home of Colorado Territory's first prison—the town's residents voted for building the prison rather than a university when given the choice. The famous poet Joaquin Miller was once the town's mayor and judge. When the wordy writer suggested that the village be renamed Oreodelphia, the townspeople quickly shot down the idea and opted to leave the appellation as it was. Much of Cañon City's present-day economy is linked to its popularity among visitors of Royal Gorge, but much of its vitality can be linked to the 10 prisons in the vicinity.

Information: Cañon City Chamber of Commerce | 403 Royal Gorge Blvd., Cañon City 81212 | 719/275–2331 or 800/876–7922 | www.canoncitychamber.com.

Attractions

Buckskin Joe Frontier Town and Railway. An Old West theme park that includes a restaurant, a saloon, 30 original buildings, and a railroad that runs along the edge of Royal Gorge, and features shoot-outs, trolley rides, and more. The film *Cat Ballou* was filmed here. Located 8 mi west of Cañon City on U.S. 50. | U.S. 50 | 719/275–5149 or 719/275–5485 | fax 719/275–5149 | www.buckskinjoes.com | $13 | Railroad: May–Sept., daily 8–8. Frontier Town: May–Sept., daily 9–6.

Cañon City Municipal Museum. Features of the museum include a Fremont County historical collection, historic firearms, and a mineral and rock collection. | 612 Royal Gorge Blvd. | 719/269–9018 | $2 | Early May–Labor Day, Tues.–Sun. 10–4; Labor Day–early May, Tues.–Sat. 10–4.

Fremont Center for the Arts. A community art center that has exhibits and cultural programs. | 505 Macon Ave. | 719/275–2790 | Free | Tues.–Sat. 10–4.

Museum of Colorado Prisons. Prison memorabilia are displayed in Colorado's original women's prison. | 201 N. First St. | 719/269–3015 | $5 | May–Sept., daily 8:30–6; Oct.–Apr., Fri.–Sun. 10–5.

Red Canyon Park. Go rock climbing, hike among the sandstone spires, camp, or just relax and have a picnic 12 mi north of Cañon City. The unique formations are the perfect setting for outdoor activities. | Off U.S. 50 N (exit Field Ave.) | 719/269–9028 | Free | Daily.

Royal Gorge. The world's highest suspension bridge crosses the Arkansas River at a height of 1,053 ft. An incline railway and an aerial tramway are operated daily. A restaurant and gift shop are also available. Located 12 mi west of Cañon City. | 4 mi south of U.S. 50, Box 549, Cañon City | 888/333–5597 or 719/275–7507 | www.royalgorgebridge.com/ | $14 | Daily dawn to dusk.

Skyline Drive. Not for the faint of heart, this short, one-way road goes high above Cañon City, giving you breathtaking views—and on either side—sheer drops. It was built by chain gangs from the area's prisons in the early part of the 20th century. Buses and RVs are not allowed. Enter off U.S. 50, 3 mi west of Cañon City. | Off U.S. 50 | No phone | Free | Daily.

ON THE CALENDAR

MAY: *Music and Blossom Festival.* A spring celebration of music and flowers the first weekend in May. | 719/275–2331 or 800/876–7922.
MAY: *Royal Gorge Rodeo.* This parade and rodeo is an enjoyable event during the first weekend in May. Held at the Fremont County Fairgrounds. | 719/275–2331 or 800/876–7922.
JULY–AUG: *Entertainment in the Park.* Live Tuesday-night concerts in an outdoor band shell in Veterans' Park. The repertoire includes rock, pop, country/western, and jazz. | 719/275–2331.

Dining

Janey's Chile Wagon. Mexican. Founded by a former New Yorker who got tired of the Big Apple, Janey's serves huge portions of basic fare such as chile and burritos. | 807 Cyanide Ave. | 719/275–4885 | Closed Sun., Mon. | $3–$8 | No credit cards.

Le Petit Chablis. Creole. Built in 1880, this Victorian is now the elegant home of Le Petit Chablis. On the menu are fresh seafood, crawfish pie, and duck. Try the seafood gumbo. | 512 Royal Gorge Blvd. | 719/269–3333 | Closed Sun., Mon. | $16–$25 | AE, D, DC, MC, V.

Merlino's Belvedere. Italian. Stained and etched glass and murals suggesting views from a veranda add character to this establishment where you can tuck into pastas made on the premises or order a juicy steak. Kids' menu. | 1330 Elm Ave. | 719/275–5558 | No lunch Mon.–Sat. | $9–$19 | AE, D, DC, MC, V.

Lodging

Best Western Royal Gorge. Located just minutes from the Royal Gorge. Enjoy trout fishing at the motel's pond. Restaurant, bar, picnic area. In-room data ports, some microwaves, some refrigerators, cable TV. Pool. Hot tub. Playground. Laundry facilities. | 1925 Fremont Dr. | 719/275–3377 or 800/231–7317 | fax 719/275–3931 | www.bestwestern.com | 67 rooms | $65–$99 | AE, D, DC, MC, V.

Cañon Inn. A two-story motel just 8 mi from Royal Gorge Bridge. Spacious rooms abound in this comfortable motel. Conveniently located just off of Highway 50. Restaurant, bar. Some microwaves, some refrigerators, room service, cable TV. Pool. 6 hot tubs. Laundry facilities. Business services, airport shuttle. Pets allowed (fee). | 3075 E. U.S. 50 | 719/275–8676, 800/525–7727 in Colorado | fax 719/275–8675 | www.canoninn.com | 152 rooms | $65–$100 | AE, D, DC, MC, V.

St. Cloud Hotel. This historic building is in downtown Cañon City. The lobby's grand piano and tin ceiling add to its charm. The coffeehouse, restaurant, and western-style bar & grill are quite popular with locals. Restaurant, bar. Cable TV. | 631 Main St. | 719/276–2000 or 800/405–9666 | fax 719/276–9317 | www.stcloudhotel.com | 35 rooms | $69–$169 | AE, MC, V.

CEDAREDGE

(Nearby towns also listed: Delta, Grand Junction, Palisade)

The town site of Cedaredge was originally the headquarters of a cattle spread, the Bar-I Ranch. The town got its name from Sophie Kohler, the wife of the Bar-I foreman, who dubbed the small western hamlet Cedar Edge because the ranch was bordered by a large grove of cedar trees. The name was shortened to one word when the post office was established in 1894.

Today, Cedaredge is known as the "Gateway to the Grand Mesa," the world's largest flat-topped mountain boasting over 300 lakes. The basis for the town's economy is agriculture. With an elevation of 6,200 ft, the mild climate is perfect for growing apples, peaches, and cherries, not to mention ranching. This tourist-friendly destination of 1,800 full-time residents is also home to many art galleries, gift shops, antiques stores, and wineries. For the avid outdoorsman, there are also hunting, camping, fishing, and great mountain biking trails.

Information: Cedaredge Area Chamber of Commerce | Box 278, Cedaredge, 81413 | 970/856–6961 | www.cedaredgecolorado.com.

Attractions

The Apple Shed. Once an apple-packing shed, the 1922 building has been restored and remodeled into a series of quaint little gift shops and galleries featuring local artists. | 250 S. Grand Mesa Dr. | 970/856–7007 or 888/856–7008 | Free | Mon.–Sat. 10–5, Sun. noon–4.

Deer Creek Village Golf Club. A unique 18-hole golf course tucked at the foot of the Grand Mesa National Forest. The course features two distinct nines with water, elevated tees, numerous hazards, and rolling terrain; greens fees are reasonable. | 500 S.E. Jay Ave. | 970/856–7781 | fax 970/856–7292 | Free | Daily 7–dusk.

Pioneer Town. Take a step back in time and discover how the early settlers of Colorado once lived. You'll find a country chapel, the Lizard Head Saloon, original silos from the Bar-I Ranch, and a working blacksmith shop. | 315 S.W. 3rd St. | 970/856–7554 | $3 | Memorial Day–Labor Day, Mon.–Sat. 10–4, Sun. 1–4.

ON THE CALENDAR

OCT.: *Apple Fest.* Celebrate Cedaredge's apple harvest with home-baked food, fine wine, and live entertainment in the Cedaredge Town Park. | 1st full weekend | 970/856–6961.

Dining

The Divot at DeerCreek Village. American. After a day of sightseeing or playing golf, this casual restaurant offers Italian- and European-influenced cuisine. The dining room overlooks the golf course, or you can dine outside on the patio. Try the steaks, seafood, and pasta dishes (especially seafood pasta). | 500 S.E. Jay Ave. | 970/856–7782 | Reservations essential weekends | No dinner Mon. | $5–$15 | D, DC, MC, V.

Highway 65 Burgers. American/Casual. Good old-fashioned hamburgers cooked just the way you like them, also chicken, some Mexican food, and fresh-baked cookies; all meat is fresh, and the burgers are hand-pressed. Local favorites include the bacon cheeseburger and hickory burger, and the thick, frosty malts. | 1260 S. Grand Mesa Dr. | 970/856–4465 | $3–$7 | No credit cards.

The Loading Dock Deli. Delicatessen. This informal deli and espresso bar is located inside the Apple Shed. Whether you're dining in or eating out on the patio, you can enjoy menu favorites like turkey club salad, cheeseburger with oven fries, chicken enchiladas, or cauliflower quiche. There is also a soup and salad bar for those wanting lighter fare. | 250 S. Grand Mesa Dr. | 970/856–7070 | No dinner | $5–$6 | AE, D, MC, V.

Lodging

Cedars' Edge Llamas Bed & Breakfast. This quaint bed-and-breakfast is a good place to recharge your batteries. The working llama ranch provides an opportunity to get to know these unusual creatures one-on-one while relaxing on the grounds. Beds feature hand-made quilts. Complimentary breakfast. No room phones, no TVs in rooms. No smoking. | 2169 Hwy. 65 | 970/856–6836 | fax 970/856–6846 | www.llamabandb.com | 4 rooms | $60–$85 | AE, MC, V.

Log Cabin Bed & Breakfast. This pioneer log home was built in 1891 and is a Colorado State Historic Site. Rooms are decorated with antique tools, cowboy collectibles, and original art. Guests are also treated to afternoon snacks of popcorn, fresh fruit, or cookies and evening sherry or wine. Complimentary breakfast. No room phones, no TV, TV in common area. Hot tub. No smoking. | 210 N. Grand Mesa Dr. | 970/856–7585 | fax 970/856–7586 | log-cabin@gjct.net | 3 rooms | $75–$85 | MC, V.

Super 8 Motel. Cedaredge's newest economy motel has the only pool in town and is located just a few minutes south of downtown. Complimentary Continental breakfast. Cable TV. Pool. Hot tub. Laundry facilities. | 530 S. Grand Mesa Dr. | 970/856–7824 | fax 970/856–7826 | www.super8.com | 31 rooms | $62 | AE, D, DC, MC, V.

CENTRAL CITY

MAP 6, F3

(Nearby towns also listed: Evergreen, Georgetown, Golden, Idaho Springs, Nederland)

The site of Colorado's first measurable gold strike, this onetime boomtown, just west of Denver, was called the richest square mile on earth during the period of its greatest activity in the mid- and late-1800s. Within recent years, gambling has been reintroduced to this small town of 302 full-time residents, and today many of the town's historic buildings house gambling parlors, yet manage to retain their original dignity thanks to strict local zoning laws.

Information: Gilpin County Chamber of Commerce | Box 343, Blackhawk 80422 | 303/582–5077 or 800/331–5825 | www.peaknet.org/webpages/gilchamber/.

Attractions

Central City Opera House. Opera has been staged here almost every year since opening night in 1878. Lillian Gish has acted, Beverly Sills has sung, and many other greats have performed in this 550-seat space. | 200 Eureka St. | 303/292–6700 | fax 303/292–2221 | www.centralcityopera.org | Performances in summer only.

Gilpin County Historical Society and Museum. Exhibits feature the history of Gilpin County and paint a vivid portrait of life in a rowdy mining town. | 228 E. High St. | 303/582–5283 | $3 | Memorial Day–Labor Day, daily 11–4.

ON THE CALENDAR

JUNE: *Lou Bunch Day.* In honor of the town's last madam. Festivities include bed races and a formal costume ball. | June 17 | 303/582–5251.
AUG.: *Central City Music Festival.* This festival is a three-day affair, with outstanding music by regional and national musicians. | 303/582–5077 or 800/331–5825.

Dining

Ponderosa Restaurant. Mexican. In the Famous Bonanza Casino. Specialties include spicy pork chile verde or a milder red chile sauce. | 107 Main St. | 303/582–5914 | fax 303/582–0447 | www.famousbonanza.com | $5–$7 | D, MC, V.

Lodging

Harvey's Wagon Wheel Hotel/Casino. In the heart of all the action, this casino hotel boasts that it has the "most jackpots in Colorado," so try your luck at the slot machines or other games on the premises. Enjoy live entertainment or take a twirl on the dance floor. The rooms are spacious, have minibars, and come in a variety of styles. Restaurant, 2 bars. Minibars, some refrigerators, some in-room hot tubs, cable TV. | 321 Gregory St. | 303/582–0800 or 800/WAGONHO | fax 303/582–5860 | www.harveys.com | 118 rooms | $110–$175 | AE, D, DC, MC, V.

COLORADO SPRINGS

(Nearby towns also listed: Cañon City, Cripple Creek, Manitou Springs, Pueblo)

Colorado Springs, with a population of 344,719, is the state's second-largest city, being surpassed in population only by Denver. Conveniently located on Colorado's primary north–south thoroughfare, Interstate 25, the city is positioned along the Front Range of the magnificent Rocky Mountains, with lofty peaks to the west and spacious plains and prairie to the east. The most notable of the peaks visible from the city is Pike's Peak (*see* Manitou Springs); you can take a cog railway trip to the top of the mountain or simply drive.

The city was founded in the 1870s as a health resort and spa by the president of the Denver and Rio Grande Railroad, General William Palmer. For years, wealthy easterners flocked to the cool, dry climate that blessed the town, eventually earning the community the nickname, "Saratoga of the West."

Tourism is still high on Colorado Springs' list of industries, but the area also gets a healthy shot in the arm from military and governmental sources. Personnel from the army's nearby Fort Carson, the U.S. Air Force Academy, and Peterson Air Force Complex contribute to nearly one-half of the region's overall economy.

Information: Colorado Springs Convention and Visitor Bureau | 104 S. Cascade Ave., Suite 104, Colorado Springs 80903 | 719/635–7506 or 800/368–4748 | www.coloradosprings-travel.com.

Attractions

American Numismatic Association. Many exhibits of American coinage, paper money, and tokens are displayed. | 818 N. Cascade Ave. | 719/632–2646 | www.money.org | Free | Weekdays 9–4, Sat. 10–4.

★ **The Broadmoor.** Even if you're not staying here, it's worth passing by the pink-stucco, Italianate Broadmoor complex, built in 1918 and still one of the world's great luxury resorts (*see* Lodging, *below*). You can also drop in on original owner Spencer Penrose's collection of antique carriages. | 1 Lake Ave. (I–25, exit 138) | 719/634–7711 or 800/634–7711 | fax 719/577–5700 | www.broadmoor.com | Free | Daily.

El Pomar Carriage Museum. This museum at the Broadmoor resort has a collection of 1890s carriages and other Americana that were collected by the resort's original owner, Spencer Penrose. | Broadmoor Resort, 16 Lake Circle | 719/634–7711 ext. 5353 | www.broadmoor.com | Free | Mon.–Fri. 10–5, Sat. 10–4, closed Sun.

Cheyenne Mountain Zoological Park. America's highest zoo is perched at 6,800 ft and has 800 animals, including primates, giraffes, and felines. The zoo also has an antique carousel and "tot train"; during the summer a zoo tram helps you get up and down the mountain. Admission includes the Will Rogers Shrine. | 4250 Cheyenne Mountain Zoo Rd. | 719/633–

9925 | www.cmzoo.org | $8.50, carousel $2, tot train $1, zoo tram $1 | June–Sept., daily 9–6; Oct.–May, daily 9–5.

Will Rogers Shrine of the Sun. A memorial to humorist Will Rogers built by Spencer Penrose, constructed of pink granite and steel. Has great views of Pike's Peak and Colorado Springs. Located 1.4 mi farther up Cheyenne Mountain from the Cheyenne Mountain Zoo. Admission included with the zoo. | Cheyenne Mountain Zoo Rd. | Free with a zoo ticket | Memorial Day–Labor Day, daily 9–4; Labor Day–Memorial Day, daily 9–3.

★ **Colorado Springs Fine Arts Center.** American Indian art, Latin American textiles, and 19th–20th century western art dominate this excellent museum. | 30 W. Dale St. | 719/634–5581 | $4 | Tues.–Fri. 10–5, Sat. 9–5, Sun. 1–5.

Colorado Springs Pioneers Museum. Located in the former El Paso County Courthouse, this museum contains exhibits on the history of the Pike's Peak region. | 215 S. Tejon St. | 719/385–5990 | www.colorado-springs.com/fmp/cspm/ | Free | May–Oct., Tues.–Sat. 10–5, Sun. 1–5; Nov.–Apr., Tues.–Sat. 10–5.

Flying W Ranch. This ranch, 8 mi northwest of Colorado Springs, located between the Air Force Academy and the Garden of the Gods, has a chuck-wagon dinner meal and live music show. | 3330 Chuckwagon Rd. | 719/598–4000 or 800/232–3599 | www.flyingw.com | Prices vary with shows | Memorial Day–late Sept., daily; hrs vary with shows.

May Natural History Museum. At this site 9 mi southwest of Colorado Springs you'll find exhibits on more than 7,000 varieties of tropical invertebrates and an area devoted to outer space, where hundreds of NASA photos and movies are on view. | 710 Rock Creek Canyon Rd. | 719/576–0450 or 800/666–3841 | $4.50 | May–Sept., daily 8–5.

COLORADO'S HALLS OF FAME

Seems like nowadays there is a "Hall of Fame" to commemorate just about everything. Colorado has its share of Halls of Fame that give insight into such varied subjects as rodeoing and figure skating. In fact, the state boasts five such institutions with interesting information and exhibits about their subjects. Appropriately located at Leadville is the National Mining Hall of Fame and Museum, which honors among other notables in the mining and related professions, Herbert Hoover (U.S. president whose profession was mining engineer), Levi Strauss (originator of blue jeans which were actually created for and extensively worn by miners), and Horace Tabor (Denver millionaire who made his fortune in silver). The Pro Rodeo Hall of Fame and Museum of the American Cowboy in Colorado Springs pays homage to such rodeo greats as Casey Tibbs, Bill Pickett, Larry Mahan, Ben Johnson, and many others. Olympic medalists Scott Hamilton, Peggy Fleming, Dick Button, Katarina Witt, and Dorothy Hamill are among the champion figure skaters featured at the World Figure Skating Museum and Hall of Fame, also in Colorado Springs. At the Colorado Ski Museum and Hall of Fame in Vail, you'll learn about such skiing greats as Hank Kashiwa, Billy Kidd, Warren Miller, Andy Mill, and Jimmie Heuga. And, finally, the Mountain Bike Hall of Fame and Museum in Crested Butte details the history of mountain biking and tells the stories of Mike Sinyard, Gary Fisher, Charles Kelly, Chris Chance, and many others.

McAllister House Museum. An 1873 Gothic-style cottage with Victorian furnishings. | 423 N. Cascade Ave. | 719/635–7925 | www.oldcolo.com/hist/mcallister | $4 | May–Aug., Wed.–Sat. 10–4, Sun. noon–4; Sept.–Apr., Thurs.–Sat. 10–4.

Old Colorado City. On the west side of Colorado Springs, this is where Colorado Springs had its beginnings; though today it's part of the greater metropolitan area, in the 1880s it was the only settlement around. The restored historic district includes immaculately restored buildings housing shops, boutiques, restaurants, and B&Bs. | West Colorado Ave. | www.oldcoloradocity.com | Free | Daily.

The Old Colorado City History Center. Located at Pike's Peak Ave., this small center has historical displays on the beginnings of Colorado Springs, as well as a research library. | 1 S. 24th St. | 719/636–1225 | history.olcolo.com | Free | Tues.–Sat. 11–4.

Palmer Park. A 710-acre park perched high above the surrounding countryside. There are picnicking sites. | Maizeland Rd. off N. Academy Blvd. | 719/385–6504 | Free | Daily.

Pike National Forest. Pikes Peak sits in the midst of the 1,100,000-acre forest and offers picnicking, hiking, and camping. | 601 S. Weber St., Colorado Springs | 719/636–1602 | Free | Daily; main office weekdays 8–5.

Pikes Peak Ghost Town. An authentic 1800s town built under one roof in an old railroad building. | 400 S. 21st St. | 719/634–0696 | $4.50 | Labor Day–Memorial Day, Mon.–Sat. 10–5, Sun. noon–5; Memorial Day–Labor Day, Mon.–Sat. 9–6, Sun. noon–6.

Pro Rodeo Hall of Fame and American Cowboy Museum. Displays of western art, photos, and memorabilia focusing on the professional rodeo cowboy. | 101 Pro Rodeo Dr., Rockrimmon Blvd. (I–25, exit 147) | 719/528–4764 | fax 719/548–4874 | $6 | Daily 9–5.

Rock Ledge Ranch Historic Site. Exhibits portray life at an 1868 homestead and an 1895 working ranch. A Braille nature trail is also included. Located across the street from the Garden of the Gods Visitor Center. | 3202 Chambers Way | 719/578–6777 | $5 | June–Labor Day, Wed.–Sun. 10–5.

★ **Seven Falls.** Either walk the 224 steps to the top of this natural wonder, or ride the elevator; you can also hike a 1-mi trail. The view from the top encompasses the entire city of Colorado Springs. At night there is a light show. | S. Cheyenne Canyon Rd. | 719/632–0765 | www.sevenfalls.com | $7 | Memorial Day–Labor Day, daily 8 AM–11 PM; Labor Day–Memorial Day, daily 9–4.

U.S. Air Force Academy. Since its establishment in 1954, the academy has graduated thousands of career Air Force men and women; for the Air Force, this is the equivalent to West Point. Be sure and visit the chapel, which is an architectural wonder in itself. Though much of the campus is off-limits to civilians, the gift shop, hiking trails, and beautiful scenery are not to be missed. | I–25, exit 150B (South Gate) or 156B (North Gate) | 719/333–2025 or 800/955–4438 | www.usafa.af.mil | Free | Memorial Day–Labor Day, daily 9–5; Labor Day–Memorial Day, daily 9–6.

U.S. Olympic Complex and Visitor Center. The national headquarters of the U.S. Olympic Committee has a training season that accommodates 25,000 athletes annually. Both guided and walking tours are available. | 1 Olympic Plaza, at Union Blvd. | 719/578–4618 or 888/659–8687 | fax 719/578–4728 | Free | Daily 9–5; call for tour schedule.

Van Briggle Art Pottery Co. This high-end pottery studio has been in production since the turn of the 20th century. Free tours are available. | 600 S. 21st St., at U.S. 24 W | 719/633–7729 or 800/847–6341 | fax 719/633–7720 | www.vanbriggle.com | Free | Mon.–Sat. 8:30–5, Sun. 1–5.

Western Museum of Mining and Industry. At this 27-acre mountain site, the history of mining is represented through comprehensive exhibits of equipment, techniques, and hands-on demonstrations including gold panning. | 225 Gate Rd. (I–25, exit 156A) | 719/488–0880 | www.wmmi.org | $6 | June–Sept., Mon.–Sat. 9–4, Sun. noon–4.

World Figure Skating Hall of Fame and Museum. Exhibits tell the story of figure skating through the years. Featured are a library, art, and skating memorabilia. The museum is located adjacent to the U.S. Figure Skating Association headquarters. | 20 First St. | 719/635–5200 | www.worldskatingmuseum.org | $3 | June–Aug., Mon.–Sat. 10–4; Sept.–May, weekdays and 1st Sat. of each month 10–4.

SIGHTSEEING TOURS/TOUR COMPANIES

Academy Riding Stables. Tour the Garden of the Gods on horseback. Your guide will show you the beauty of the park and some of the distinct rock formations. | 4 El Paso Blvd. | 719/633–5667 or 888/700–0410 | fax 719/475–9183 | www.academyridingstables.com | $25–$40 | May–Labor Day, daily 8–6; Labor Day–Apr., daily 8–5.

Gray Line. This bus tour company offers several tours of the Colorado Springs area. | 3704 W. Colorado Ave. | 719/633–1747 or 800/345–8197 | fax 719/633–9643 | Call for schedules.

ON THE CALENDAR

APR.–SEPT.: *Greyhound racing.* Some of the best dog racing west of the Mississippi is on hand at the Rocky Mountain Greyhound Park, off Interstate 25 at exit 146. | 719/632–1391 or 800/444–7297.

MAY–AUG.: *Motor sports.* All kinds of automobile racing are featured at the Pikes Peak International Raceway, located approximately 15 mi south of Colorado Springs on I–25 (exit 123). | 719/382–RACE or 800/955–RACE.

AUG.: *Pikes Peak or Bust Rodeo.* Weeklong rodeo competition offers plenty of fun for all who attend at Spencer Penrose Stadium. | 719/635–3547.

SEPT.: *Colorado Springs Balloon Classic.* Entrants from all over the region gather for this large balloon display each Labor Day weekend at Memorial Park. | 719/471–4833 or 800/368–4748.

Dining

County Line Smoke House & Grill. Barbecue. Ribs are the major draw, but the steaks and seafood are equally delicious. | 3350 N. Chestnut Ave. | 719/578–1940 | $8–$19 | AE, D, DC, MC, V.

Edelweiss. German. This quaint restaurant in the southern part of town has cozy fireplaces and strolling musicians. Try the Wiener schnitzel or the sauerbraten. Homemade soups. Open-air dining on patio with a garden view. Entertainment Friday, Saturday. | 34 E. Ramona Ave. | 719/633–2220 | No lunch Sun. | $12–$23 | AE, D, DC, MC, V.

★ **El Tesoro.** Southwestern. Turn-of-the-20th-century building. Enjoy the *posole* (hominy with pork and red chile), the green chile, the mango quesadillas, or a margarita made with fresh-squeezed lime juice and a large selection of tequilas. | 10 N. Sierra Madre | 719/471–0106 | Closed Sun. No dinner Mon. No lunch Sat. | $10–$16 | AE, D, MC, V.

Fish Market. Seafood. You'll enjoy great views of downtown Colorado Springs and mountains here. Try the seafood collage, live Maine lobster, or the grilled filet mignon. Kids' menu. | 775 W. Bijou St. | 719/520–3474 | Reservations essential Fri., Sat. | $17–$26 | AE, D, DC, MC, V.

Giuseppe's Old Depot. American. This family-friendly restaurant in an old train station displays railroad memorabilia in several dining areas, each different. The menu offers lasagna, pizza, prime rib, and Reuben sandwiches. Salad bar. Kids' menu. | 10 S. Sierra Madre | 719/635–3111 | $9–$22 | AE, D, DC, MC, V.

Joseph's Hatch Cover. Continental. The dining room at this upscale restaurant is home to a number of aquariums and the roster of flaming desserts prepared tableside makes it festive. Try the flaming pepper steak, Dover sole, swordfish. Open-air dining on patio with view of Pike's Peak. Kids' menu. | 252 E. Cheyenne Mountain Blvd. | 719/576–5223 | No lunch weekends | $13–$40 | AE, D, DC, MC, V.

King's Chef. American/Casual. Pink and purple turrets have been added to make this restaurant resemble a castle. For the bold, there is "The Thing" (Texas toast, hash browns, green chile, eggs, and your choice of meat). Green chile is served with local color. | 110 E. Costilla Ave. | 719/634–9135 | Breakfast also available. No dinner | $2–$9 | No credit cards.

La Crêperie. French. This vintage stable is cozy despite the lofty ceilings. Crêpes star on the menu for both meals and dessert. Beer and wine only. | 204 N. Tejon St. | 719/632–0984 | $11–$23 | AE, DC, MC, V.

La Petite Maison. Contemporary. In this romantic restaurant in a restored Victorian cottage Parisian posters hang against pale pink walls, and there are bouquets of fresh flowers on the tables as in a French country home. Try the curried shrimp with banana chutney or the pork chops with Peruvian mashed potatoes. Early-bird supper. No smoking. | 1015 W. Colorado Ave. | 719/632–4887 | Reservations essential | Closed Sun., Mon. No lunch | $15–$25 | AE, D, DC, MC, V.

Maggie Mae's. American. This homey restaurant is popular for breakfast all day long. The casual environment and varied menu are great for families. Known for omelets, pork chops, fajitas. Kids' menu. | 2405 E. Pikes Peak Ave. | 719/475–1623 | Breakfast also available | $9–15 | AE, D, MC, V.

The Mason Jar. American. Home-style cooking at this diner includes an appetizing chicken-fried steak. | 2925 W. Colorado Ave. | 719/632–4820 | fax 719/632–0392 | $5–$20 | D, MC, V.

Old Chicago Pasta and Pizza–Colorado Springs North. Pizza. Part of a chain of moderately priced restaurants, this lively restaurant has a sports bar in front and a pleasant enclosed atrium. On the menu: deep-dish pizza, pasta, burgers. Video games, pool table. Kids' menu. | 7115 Commerce Center Dr. | 719/593–7678 | $8–$20 | AE, DC, MC, V.

Old Chicago Pasta and Pizza–Downtown. Pizza. This downtown member of the lively chain is housed in an historic building. Known for pizza, homemade pasta, salads. Open-air dining with front and back patios. Kids' menu. | 118 N. Tejon St. | 719/634–8812 | $9–$16 | AE, DC, MC, V.

Penrose Room. French. One of the finest restaurants in the state, the Broadmoor Hotel's famed Penrose Room is a luxurious place with its grand chandeliers, rich velvet draperies, and majestic views of the city and mountains. Try the *Chateaubriand Bouquetiére*, the grilled duck breast Bigarade, and the restaurant's signature sweet soufflées. Entertainment nightly. | 1 Lake Ave., in the Broadmoor Hotel | 719/634–7711 | Reservation essential | Jacket required | No lunch | $25–$35 | AE, D, DC, MC, V.

Pepper Tree. Continental. On a hilltop, this restaurant has a great view of the city. Table-side preparations include the pepper steak with Indian-mango chutney. Specials include calamari stuffed with crabmeat and bacon. | 888 W. Moreno Ave. | 719/471–4888 | fax 719/471–0997 | Jacket required | Closed Sun. No lunch | $15–$30 | AE, MC, V.

Phantom Canyon Brewing Co. American/Casual. Microbrews on tap and English fare (fish-and-chips, shepherd's pie) doled out in a restored turn-of-the-20th-century building. | 2 E. Pikes Peak Ave. | 719/635–2800 | www.phantomcanyon.com | $6–$17 | AE, D, DC, MC, V.

Trattoria De Angelo's. Italian. In downtown Colorado Springs, next door to the Peak Theater. Try the shrimp and cannolini (white beans) or the three-mushroom calzone. | 123 Pikes Peak Ave. | 719/227–7400 | fax 719/227–7390 | Closed Sun. | $6–$15 | AE, MC, V.

Lodging

Antlers Adam's Mark. There has been an Antlers Hotel in Colorado Springs since 1883, but the present building dates from 1964. Some rooms have excellent views of nearby Pikes Peak, and there's a microbrewery on the premises. 2 restaurants, bars. Some microwaves, cable TV, some in-room VCRs. Pool. Hot tub. Gym. Business services. | 4 S. Cascade Ave. (I–25, exit 142), | 719/473–5600 or 800/444–2326 | fax 719/389–0259 | www.antlers.com | 286 rooms (41 with shower only), 6 suites | $79–$176, $200–$825 suites | AE, D, DC, MC, V.

Best Western Le Baron Hotel. This mid-priced full-service motor hotel is built around a central courtyard with a large pool. Its convenient location in downtown Colorado Springs is a plus. The rooms are well kept and comfortably furnished. Restaurant, bar, complimentary Continental breakfast. In-room data ports, some minibars, some microwaves, some refrigerators, some in-room hot tubs, cable TV. Pool. Gym. Laundry service. Business services, free airport shuttle. | 314 W. Bijou | 719/471–8680 or 800/477–8610 | fax 719/471–0894 | www.bestwestern.com | 202 rooms | $119–$199 | AE, D, DC, MC, V.

Black Forest Bed and Breakfast Inn. A modern log home complex on 20 acres, surrounded by Ponderosa pines in the foothills of the Rockies. Rooms are in the main house, the "Haven," or the "Barn." Breakfast is brought to your room. Complimentary breakfast. In-room data ports, kitchenettes, cable TV, in-room VCRs (and movies). Hiking. Playground. Laundry facilities. No smoking. | 11170 Black Forest Rd. | 719/495–4208 or 800/809–9901 | fax 719/495–0688 | www.blackforestbb.com | 5 rooms | $75–$200 | AE, D, MC, V.

★ **The Broadmoor.** One of the most noteworthy hotels in the United States, the Broadmoor sprawls over 3,500 acres, which include a private lake. Although all the rooms are exceptional, those in the historic main building have the most character (and are the most inexpensive). A full-service resort, the Broadmoor has several award-winning golf courses. 9 restaurants, 4 bars (some with entertainment). In-room data ports, minibars, some refrigerators, room service, cable TV, some in-room VCRs. 4 pools (1 indoor). Beauty salon, hot tub, massage, sauna, spa, steam room. Driving range, 3 18-hole golf courses, 12 tennis courts. Health club, horseback riding. Boating, fishing, bicycles. Shops. Children's programs (ages 4–12). Business services. Airport shuttle. | 1 Lake Ave. (I–25, exit 138) | 719/634–7711 or 800/634–7711 | fax 719/577–5700 | www.broadmoor.com | 593 rooms, 107 suites | $280–$425, $485–$950 1–bedroom suites, $975–$2,250 2–bedroom suites, $2,395–$2,525 3–bedroom suites | AE, D, DC, MC, V.

The Cheyenne Cañon Inn. B&B in a 1918 Mission-style mansion. Most rooms have a special feature: a fireplace, rooftop view, antique soaking tub, or private deck. Daily wine and appetizer reception. Trails from the property lead directly into Cheyenne Cañon Park; located 5 mi from Downtown. Complimentary breakfast. In-room data ports, some kitchenettes, some minibars, some in-room hot tubs, cable TV, in-room VCRs (and movies). Hot tub, massage, spa. Library. No smoking. | 2030 W. Cheyenne Blvd. | 719/633–0625 or 800/633–0625 | fax 719/633–8826 | www.cheyennecanoninn.com | 8 rooms, 2 suites | $95–$200 | AE, D, MC, V.

Colorado Springs Fairfield Inn North by Marriott. This moderately priced chain hotel offers clean, reasonably sized rooms between the Air Force Academy and downtown with little extras like free HBO. Complimentary Continental breakfast. Some microwaves, some refrigerators, cable TV. Pool. Hot tub. Business services. | 7085 Commerce Center Dr. (I–25, exit 149) | 719/533–1903 or 800/228–2800 | fax 719/533–1903 | www.fairfieldinn.com | 67 rooms | $84–$91 | AE, D, DC, MC, V.

Comfort Inn–Airport. Reliable budget motel located near Municipal Airport that offers a few extras like a free newspaper. Complimentary Continental breakfast. In-room data ports, cable TV, some in-room VCRs. Pool. Hot tub. Gym. Business services. Airport shuttle. | 2115 Aerotech Dr. | 719/380–9000 | fax 719/596–4738 | www.comfortinn.com | 44 rooms | $50–$129 | AE, D, DC, MC, V.

Doubletree World Arena. Conveniently located across from a shopping mall and the World Arena, this upscale chain hotel has large, comfortable rooms. Restaurant, bar (with entertainment). In-room data ports, room service, cable TV. Pool. Hot tub. Gym. Business services. Airport shuttle. Pets allowed. | 1775 E. Cheyenne Mountain Blvd. | 719/576–8900 or 800/222–8733 | fax 719/576–4450 | www.doubletree.com | 299 rooms, 6 suites | $109–$498, $299 suites | AE, D, DC, MC, V.

Drury Inn. This reasonably priced chain motel is on the north side of Colorado Springs, near a shopping mall and the Air Force Academy. Complimentary Continental breakfast. In-room data ports, some microwaves, some refrigerators, cable TV, some in-room VCRs. Indoor-outdoor pool. Hot tub. Gym. Laundry facilities. Business services. Some pets allowed.

| 8155 N. Academy Blvd. (I–25, exit 150) | 719/598–2500 or 800/378–7946 | fax 719/598–2500 | www.drury-inn.com | 118 rooms | $74–$109 | AE, D, DC, MC, V.

Embassy Suites. Glass elevators shoot through the atrium of this four-story upscale, all-suite property on the city's north side. Families will appreciate the sofa bed in each suite. Restaurant, bar, complimentary breakfast. In-room data ports, microwaves, refrigerators, room service, cable TV. Pool. Hot tub. Gym. Video games. Laundry facilities. Business services. | 7290 Commerce Center Dr. (I–25, exit 149) | 719/599–9100 or 800/362–2779 | fax 719/599–4644 | www.embassy-suites.com | 207 suites | $125–$149 | AE, D, DC, MC, V.

Fairfield Inn South by Marriott. This three-story, moderately priced chain hotel is across the street from the World Arena in southern Colorado Springs and offers clean, reasonably sized rooms. Complimentary Continental breakfast. Some microwaves, some refrigerators, some in-room hot tubs, cable TV. Pool. Hot tub. Gym. Business services. | 2725 Geyser Dr. | 719/576–1717 or 800/228–2800 | fax 719/576–4747 | www.fairfieldinn.com | 85 rooms | $89–$129 | AE, D, DC, MC, V.

Fireside Suites. Have all the comforts of home while you travel. Each suite has a living/dining area, a spacious work station, a bedroom with a king- or queen-size bed, a kitchen, a closet, and a bath. Some of the suites have a private balcony/patio with views of Pikes Peak. Complimentary Continental breakfast. In-room data ports, kitchenettes, microwaves, refrigerators, cable TV, in-room VCRs. Outdoor pool. Gym. Laundry facilities. Pets allowed (fee). | 620 N. Murray | 719/597–6207 | fax 719/597–7483 | www.firesidesuites.com | 70 rooms | $79–$149 | AE, D, MC, V.

Garden of the Gods Motel. This small moderately priced motel is 2 mi from the Garden of the Gods. Some microwaves, some refrigerators, cable TV. Pool. Sauna. | 2922 W. Colorado Ave. (I–25, exit 145) | 719/636–5271 | fax 719/477–1422 | 32 rooms, 2 cottages | $49–$89, $90–$120 cottages | AE, D, DC, MC, V.

Hearthstone Inn. This sprawling late-19th-century Victorian home is full of period furnishings. Some of the rooms, which are simply furnished, have views, porches, or a fireplace. Complimentary breakfast. No room phones. No smoking. | 506 N. Cascade Ave. (I–25, exit 143) | 719/473–4413 or 800/521–1885 | fax 719/473–1322 | www.hearthstoneinn.com | 25 rooms (2 with shared bath) | $69–$199 | AE, D, MC, V.

Holden House 1902. You can warm yourself in front of your own fireplace in some rooms in this stately, antiques-filled Victorian B&B, which consists of two separate houses and a carriage house. Bathrooms are especially opulent. Complimentary breakfast. Cable TV in common area, no TV in rooms. No kids allowed. No smoking. | 1102 W. Pikes Peak Ave. (I–25, exit 141) | 719/471–3980 or 888/565–3980 | fax 719/471–4740 | www.holdenhouse.com | 5 suites | $120–$135 suites | AE, D, DC, MC, V.

Holiday Inn Express–Airport. Located 3 mi north of the airport, this motor hotel provides the consistently good rooms typical of this chain. Complimentary Continental breakfast. In-room data ports, some microwaves, some refrigerators, cable TV. Gym. Laundry facilities. Business services. Airport shuttle. | 1815 Aeroplaza Dr. (I–25, exit 139) | 719/591–6000 or 800/465–4329 | fax 719/591–6100 | www.holiday-inn.com | 94 rooms, 15 suites | $89–$109, $149 suites | AE, D, DC, MC, V.

Maple Lodge. Set on 2 acres a quarter-mile from the Garden of the Gods, this small lodge offers traditional suites and separate two-room units. Picnic area. Some kitchenettes, some microwaves, refrigerators, cable TV. Pool. Miniature golf. Pets allowed. | 9 El Paso Blvd. | 719/685–9230 | www.colorado-springs.com | 17 rooms | $30–$159 | AE, D, MC, V.

Mel-Haven Lodge. This motel is between Colorado Springs and Manitou Springs, and conveniently located near many of Pike's Peak attractions. Picnic area. Some kitchenettes, some microwaves, refrigerators, cable TV. Pool. Hot tub. Playground. Laundry facilities. | 3715 W. Colorado Ave., | 719/633–9435 or 800/762–5832 | fax 719/633–9345 | melhavenlodge@pikes-peak.com | melhavenlodge.pikes-peak.com | 3 rooms, 17 suites | $55–$105, $110–$150 suites | AE, D, MC, V.

Quality Inn. This comfortable mid-priced chain hotel is located at the Interstate 25 exit for Garden of the Gods Road. Complimentary Continental breakfast. Some microwaves, cable TV. Pool. Gym. Laundry facilities. Business services. | 555 W. Garden of the Gods Rd. (I–25, exit 146) | 719/593–9119 | fax 719/260–0381 | www.qualityinn.com | 156 rooms | $99–$125 | AE, D, DC, MC, V.

Radisson Inn North. This upscale chain hotel near the Air Force Academy offers above-average facilities and amenities. Restaurants, bar. In-room data ports, some microwaves, room service, cable TV, some in-room VCRs. Pool. Hot tub, sauna. Gym. Laundry facilities. Business services. Airport shuttle. Some pets allowed. | 8110 N. Academy Blvd. (I–25, exit 150) | 719/598–5770 or 800/333–3333 | fax 719/598–3434 | www.radisson.com | 188 rooms, 12 suites | $144–$154, $159–$259 suites | AE, D, DC, MC, V.

Radisson Inn and Suites–Airport. Near the airport, reasonably priced suites make this a good choice for business travelers. Restaurant, bar, complimentary breakfast. In-room data ports, some microwaves, room service, cable TV. Pool. Hot tub. Gym. Video games. Laundry facilities. Business services. Airport shuttle. Some pets allowed (fee). | 1645 Newport Dr. | 719/597–7000 or 800/333–3333 | fax 719/597–4308 | www.radisson.com | 200 rooms, 44 suites | $100–$140, $160 suites | AE, D, DC, MC, V.

Ramada Inn North. This full-service budget hotel is just off Interstate 25, one exit south of Garden of the Gods. Restaurant, bar. In-room data ports, room service, cable TV, Pool. Video games. Laundry facilities. Airport shuttle. Pets allowed. | 3125 Sinton Rd. | 719/633–5541 or 888–298–2054 | fax 719/633–3870 | www.ramada.com | 220 rooms, 4 suites | $99–$109, $175–$225 suites | AE, D, DC, MC, V.

Red Roof Inn. This simple, budget motel is located near the Air Force Academy on the city's north side. In-room data ports, cable TV. Pool. | 8280 Hwy. 83 (I–25, exit 150) | 719/598–6700 or 800/733–7663 | fax 719/598–3443 | www.redroof.com | 117 rooms | $30–$105 | AE, D, DC, MC, V.

Red Stone Castle. Built in the 1880s, the Castle is built on a private 20-acre estate overlooking Manitou Springs, with views of Colorado Springs and the Garden of the Gods. You can have a turret of your own. Complimentary breakfast. Minibar, no TV in rooms. | 601 S. Side Rd. | 719/685–5070 | 1 suite | $140 | No credit cards.

Residence Inn by Marriott–North. An all-suite hostelry near the Air Force Academy, with fireplaces in some units. Complimentary Continental breakfast. In-room data ports, kitchenettes, microwaves, refrigerators, cable TV, some in-room VCRs. Pool. Hot tub. Laundry facilities. Business services. Airport shuttle. Some pets allowed (fee). | 3880 N. Academy Blvd. (I–25, exit 146) | www.residenceinn.com | 719/574–0370 or 800/228–9290 | fax 719/574–7821 | 96 suites | $127–$185 | AE, D, DC, MC, V.

Residence Inn by Marriott–South. An all-suite hostelry near downtown Colorado Springs, across from the World Arena. Some units have fireplaces. Complimentary Continental breakfast. In-room data ports, kitchenettes, microwaves, refrigerators, cable TV, some in-room VCRs. Pool. Hot tub. Gym. Laundry facilities. Business services. Some pets allowed (fee). | 2765 Geyser Dr. | 719/576–0101 or 800/228–9290 | fax 719/576–4848 | www.residenceinn.com | 72 suites | $119–$195 | AE, D, DC, MC, V.

Rodeway Inn. This moderately priced chain motel is popular with older travelers, perhaps because of its large-button TV remote control and telephone and brighter lighting; it is conveniently 2 mi north of downtown Colorado Springs. Some rooms have fireplaces. Bar, complimentary Continental breakfast. In-room data ports, some kitchenettes, cable TV. Pool. Business services. Airport shuttle. | 2409 E. Pikes Peak Ave. | 719/471–0990 or 800/228–2000 | fax 719/633–3343 | www.rodewayinn.com | 110 rooms, 3 suites | $75–$85, $135 suites | AE, D, DC, MC, V.

Room at the Inn. A romantic turret tops this turn-of-the-20th-century antiques-furnished mansion with an expansive wraparound porch. Fresh-cut flowers are placed in each room daily. Complimentary breakfast and afternoon tea. Some in-room hot tubs, some in-room VCRs. No kids under 12. No smoking. | 618 N. Nevada Ave. | 719/442–1896 or 888/442–1896 | fax 719/442–6802 | www.roomattheinn.com | 7 rooms (1 with shower only) | $90–$150 | AE, D, DC, MC, V.

Sheraton Colorado Springs Hotel. This upscale chain hotel is just 4 mi from Seven Falls and has several recreational facilities. Restaurant, bars (with entertainment). In-room data ports, some microwaves, some refrigerators, room service, cable TV, some in-room VCRs (and movies). 2 pools (1 indoor), wading pool. Hot tub, sauna, steam room. Putting green, 2 tennis courts. Basketball, gym. Video games. Playground. Business services. Airport shuttle. Pets allowed. | 2886 S. Circle Dr. (I–25, exit 138) | 719/576–5900 or 800/981–4012 | fax 719/576–7695 | www.asgusa.com/scsh | 500 rooms, 16 suites | $105–$155, $250 suites | AE, D, DC, MC, V.

Spurs N' Lace. A lovely B&B in a completely restored 1886 three-story Victorian. The third-floor balcony has tables and a view of Pike's Peak. Reasonable rates. Dining room, complimentary breakfast. No TV in rooms. Laundry facilities. | 2829 W. Pikes Peak Ave. | 719/227–7662 or 800/378–9717 | fax 719/227–8701 | www.colorado-bnb.com/spursnlace | 5 rooms | $68–$88 | AE, D, MC, V.

Victoria's Keep. Turreted 1891 Queen Anne B&B. Each room has its own fireplace and some distinguishing feature—a hot tub or a claw-foot tub, stained-glass windows, or views of Miramont Castle. Evening wine and cheese. Complimentary breakfast. No TV in rooms, TV in common area. No smoking. | 202 Ruxton Ave. | 719/685–5354 or 800/905–5337 | fax 719/685–5913 | www.victoriaskeep.com | 6 rooms | $80–$175 | AE, D, MC, V.

Wyndham Colorado Springs. Upscale chain hotel near the Air Force Academy and Garden of the Gods on the north end of Colorado Springs. Manages to be stylish without being stuffy. Restaurant, bar. Cable TV, some in-room VCRs. 2 pools (1 indoor). Gym. Laundry facilities. Business services. | 5580 Tech Center Dr. | 719/260–1800 or 800/996–3426 | fax 719/260–1492 | www.wyndham.com | 311 rooms, 9 suites | $129–$179, $275–$350 suites | AE, D, DC, MC, V.

COPPER MOUNTAIN

INTRO
ATTRACTIONS
DINING
LODGING

COPPER MOUNTAIN

MAP 6, E4

(Nearby towns also listed: Breckenridge, Dillon, Frisco, Keystone, Leadville)

One of the leading resorts in Summit County—Colorado's prime skiing country—Copper Mountain shares the terrain of the scenic Ten Mile Range with Keystone, Breckenridge, and Arapahoe Basin. In spite of a mix-and-match condo village and a homogenized approach to the hotels and restaurants, this resort is pleasant and offers an abundance of good skiing on trails that are among the best laid-out in the country.

When not on the slopes, most skiers will spend their time in the recently updated Village Square, Copper's main hub. Here shops, restaurants, and bars are perched along the serpentine banks of Ten Mile Creek amid the stunning scenery of Arapaho National Forest. Most facilities are within walking distance, and two high-speed quads provide fast access to mid-mountain.

To the west is the Union Creek base area with standard condos and town houses providing immediate access to the excellent novice ski slopes on this part of the mountain. Union Creek is ideal for families, although it's a shuttle ride from the Central Village.

At Copper's east end is the Super Bee lift base area, which tends to draw a younger, more reckless crowd seeking fast access to the steeper, bumpier terrain. A 40,000-square-ft day lodge also brings skiers to the east river area.

Information: **Copper Mountain Resort Chamber** | Box 3003, Copper Mountain 80443 | 970/968–6477 | www.copperchamber.com.

Attractions

Copper Creek Golf Club. At 9,650 ft, this is the highest 18-hole course in North America. Designed by Pete and Perry Dye, the par-70, 6,094-meter course follows the twisting, narrow terrain of Copper's Valley. | Wheeler Circle | 970/968–2339 | Free | June–Oct., daily.

Copper Mt. Resort Ski Area. Of the mountain's 118 trails covering 2,433 acres, 21% are rated for beginners, 25% for intermediates, 36% for advanced skiers, and 18% for experts. The 21 lifts include one kids' conveyor lift, five surface tows, five doubles, five triples, four high-speed quads, and one six-person high-speed lift. There are several snowboarding pipes and parks, along with 25 km of groomed cross-country trails. | 209 Ten Mile Circle (junction Rte. 91 and I–70) | 970/968–2882 or 800/458–8386 | www.ski-copper.com | Mid-Nov.–Apr., daily.

ON THE CALENDAR

SEPT.: *Copperfest.* This three-day country/western music and arts festival at the Copper Mountain Resort each Labor Day weekend is the big summer event here. | 970/968–2318, ext. 6301 or 800/458–8386.

Dining

The Commons. American/Casual. This market-style cafeteria is usually the busiest spot on the mountain, but an efficient layout gets you in and out quickly. Chile and burgers are the most popular items, but the pizza has been voted the county's best. | Copper Commons Building, base of American Eagle lift | 970/968–2318 ext. 6574 | Closed June–Oct. | $4–$8 | AE, D, DC, MC, V.

Dining in the Woods. Contemporary. Take a horse-drawn sleigh ride to a heated miners' tent in the woods, enjoy live country and folk music, and dine on smoked trout appetizers, New York strip steak, or mesquite smoked chicken, and chocolate mousse for dessert. Departures 5:30–8. | Mountain Plaza Building | 970/968–2882 ext. 6320 | Reservations essential | Closed June–Oct. No lunch | $59 | AE, MC, V.

Imperial Palace. Chinese. This is a good spot to satisfy your hunger for egg rolls, fried rice, wok-cooked vegetables, and sweet-and-sour anything. It's not adventurous Chinese cooking, but it's reliable, familiar, and tasty. Spicy Szechuan and Hunan dishes are also on the menu. | Village Sq | 970/968–6688 | $9–$14 | MC, V.

Lizzie's Bagelry and Coffeehouse. Café. Here you can grab a cup of coffee and a bagel as you head for the American Flyer lift, or you can take a seat, enjoy cappuccino, and chat with locals about the best places to ski. Fresh-baked bagels, sandwiches, and espresso drinks make up the bill of fare. | Village Sq. West Building | 970/968–2036 | No dinner | $5–$7 | MC, V.

Molly B's Saloon. Contemporary. Located at the Copper Creek Golf Club, this American bistro serves contemporary dishes with a fresh, flavorful twist. Try the rotisserie chicken, pork loin with ancho chile and peach glaze, Thai beef salad, and pan-roasted mussels. The 60-ft bar is the longest in Summit County and serves premium well drinks. | 102 Wheeler Circle | 970/968–2318 ext. 6514 | Closed May, Oct. | $13–$24 | AE, D, DC, MC, V.

Solitude Station. American/Casual. The heavy lunchtime crowds can usually be avoided here during the ski season, and it's a convenient rendezvous spot. The food is basic cafeteria fare, with hamburgers and chicken sandwiches coming off the outdoor grill. | Solitude Station Building, top of American Eagle lift | 970/968–2882 ext. 6522 | Closed May–Oct. | $6–$11 | AE, D, MC, V.

Lodging

Club Méditerranée. Club Med's first-floor lobby is a great place to relax, with a big fireplace, comfortable armchairs, and floor-to-ceiling windows overlooking the slopes. The small but comfortable rooms are in neutral tones and decorated with southwestern art. Expert ski or snowboard instruction is included in the rate. 2 restaurants, 2 bars (with entertainment). 4 hot tubs, 2 saunas, health club. Laundry facilities. Video games. | 50 Beeler Pl., Copper Mountain | 970/968–7000 or 800/258–2633 | fax 970/968–2216 | www.clubmed.com | 236 rooms | $1,000–$1,500 per person per wk, includes lift tickets and instruction | Closed May–Oct. | AP | AE, MC, V.

Copper Mountain Central Village. This is the largest complex on the resort, covering over 250 acres, all of which are reserved through a central reservations office. The village is divided into three parts (East, Center, and West), of which only the East is open year-round. Accommodations are available in modern hotel rooms, somewhat larger studios, and one- to two-bedroom condos. Two high-speed quads provide quick access to any part of the ski area, and there are numerous shops, restaurants, and bars to explore when you're not on the slopes. Restaurants, bars, picnic area. In-room data ports, some microwaves, some refrigerators, cable TV, in-room VCRs (and movies). Pool. Hot tub, massage. Driving cages, putting green, tennis. Health club, boating, bicycles. Ice-skating, cross-country skiing, downhill skiing, sleigh rides. Children's programs (ages 3–12), playground. Laundry facilities. Business services. Free parking. | 209 Ten Mile Circle | 970/968–2882 or 800/458–8386 | fax 970/968–2733 | www.ski-copper.com | 467 rooms, 432 condos, in 19 buildings | $89–$225 hotel rooms & studios, $129–$545 1– to 2–bedroom condos | AE, D, DC, MC, V.

Woods and Legends Town Homes. The two small subdivisions of town houses contain some of the largest and most upscale accommodations in Copper. The beautifully decorated three- and four-bedroom units have full kitchens, dining areas, patios, garages, and in some cases private hot tubs. | 54 units. Kitchenettes, refrigerators, microwaves, cable TV. Health club. Laundry facilities. | 209 Ten Mile Circle | 970/968–2882 or 800/458–8386 | fax 970/968–6227 | $490–$650 | AE, D, DC, MC, V.

CORTEZ

MAP 6, A8

(Nearby towns also listed: Dolores, Durango, Mesa Verde National Park)

A onetime market center for sheep and cattle ranchers in the area, Cortez (population 8,274) is situated in the Four Corners region of Colorado, where the states of Colorado, New Mexico, Arizona, and Utah all meet. The town's proximity to two well-preserved pueblos, Hovenweep National Monument and Mesa Verde National Park *(see* Mesa Verde National Park), which is one of the nation's premier parks and best-preserved examples of cliff dwellings, as well as other archaeological sites, makes it a popular base for your visit to southwestern Colorado and a good starting point for a tour of that area.

Information: **Cortez/Mesa Verde Visitor Information Bureau** | 928 E. Main St., Cortez 81321 | 970/565–8227 or 800/253–1616 | www.swcolo.org.

Attractions

Crow Canyon Archaeological Center. One-day archaeology program gives insight into the excavation process and the ancestral Puebloan (Anasazi) culture through hands-on learning, laboratory tour, site visit, lunch included. Weeklong excavation program requires reservation. | 23390 Rd. K | 970/565–8975 or 800/422–8975 | www.crowcanyon.org | $50 and $900 | Closed Nov.–Feb.

Hovenweep National Monument. These pueblo ruins, 12 of which are easily accessible near the visitor center (there are more in the interior of the monument), date back to prehistoric times. The most impressive is the Castle, and it underscores the site's uncanny resemblance to a medieval fiefdom. The monument is located 43 mi east of Cortez. Overnight camping $10. | McElmo Rte., Cortez | 970/749–0510 | www.nps.gov/hove | $6 per vehicle | Daily 8–4:30.

Ute Mountain Tribal Park. Part of the Ute Mountain Indian Reservation, this large archaeological site has been set aside to preserve Anasazi ruins, including many cliff dwellings that feature wall paintings and petroglyphs. Entry is by reservation only, and primitive camping trips are also available. Tours begin at the Ute Mountain Tribal Complex. | Hwy. 160 at Rte. 666 | 970/565–3751 ext. 282 or 800/847–5485 | $20 for ½-day tour, $30 for full-day tour, per person | Apr.–Oct. guided tours only; Visitor Center daily 8–3.

ON THE CALENDAR

MAY–SEPT.: _Native American Dances._ The Cortez Cultural Center invites performers from the Ute, Navajo, and Hopi tribes to perform traditional dances from their respective cultures. | 970/565–1151.

JUNE: _Ute Mountain Round Up Rodeo._ A parade and rodeo competition at the Legion Arena. | 970/565–4485.

AUG.: _Montezuma County Fair._ A county fair the first week in August with an agricultural competition as well as arts and crafts. | 970/565–1000.

Dining

Francisca's. Mexican. Sample the _sopaipilla_ (slightly sweet, fried bread served with honey) or the _chimichangas_ (fried, flour tortilla filled with beef or chicken). Accompany your meal with margaritas served by the quart. | 125 E. Main St. | 970/565–4093 | Closed Sun., Mon. | $5–$10 | AE, D, MC, V.

Homesteaders. Southwestern. Vintage photographs and a collection of license plates from every state decorate the walls of this rustic downtown restaurant. Known for omelets, BBQ chicken, baby-back ribs, and other southwestern specialties. Kids' menu. | 45 E. Main St. | 970/565–6253 | Closed Sun. June–Aug. | $5–$16 | AE, D, MC, V.

M and M Family Restaurant and Truck Stop. American. The parking lot is packed day and night at this 24-hour truck-stop restaurant with a great bargain menu of oversize breakfasts, ribs, and chicken-fried steak. Kids' menu. No smoking. | 7006 U.S. 160 S | 970/565–6511 | $8–$15 | AE, D, DC, MC, V.

Mainstreet Brewery and Restaurant. American/Casual. The tin roof and the wood floors bring back the old-world charm of the building. The beer is brewed on-site. The dining room serves prime rib that keeps the locals coming back for more. | 21 E. Main St. | 970/564–9112 | $6–$18 | AE, MC, V.

Lodging

Anasazi Motor Inn. This motor inn with large rooms is a mile from the intersection of U.S. Highways 160 and 666. Restaurant, bar (with entertainment). Room service, cable TV, some in-room VCRs. Pool. Hot tub. Business services. Airport shuttle. Pets allowed. | 640 S. Broadway | 970/565–3773, 800/972–6232 outside CO | fax 970/565–1027 | iyp.uswestdex.com/anasazimotorinn/ | 87 rooms | $57–$71 | AE, D, DC, MC, V.

A Bed and Breakfast on Maple Street. A cozy antiques-filled inn built in the early 1900s in downtown Cortez, 9 mi west of Mesa Verde National Park. Complimentary breakfast. No room phones, no TVs in rooms, TV in common area. Hot tub. No smoking. | 102 S. Maple St. | 970/565–3906 or 800/665–3906 | fax 970/565–2090 | www.cortezbb.com | 4 rooms (3 with shower only) | $89–$129 | D, MC, V.

Best Western Turquoise Inn and Suites. This chain motel is 10 mi from Mesa Verde National Park. Complimentary Continental breakfast. In-room data ports, microwaves, some refrigerators, cable TV. Pool. Hot tub. Laundry facilities. Business services. Airport shuttle. Some pets allowed. | 535 E. Main St. | 970/565–3778 or 800/547–3376 | fax 970/565–3439 | www.cortezbestwestern.com | 46 rooms, 31 suites | $79–$150, $99–$129 suites | AE, D, DC, MC, V.

Comfort Inn. This mid-priced motel is on Cortez's east side. Complimentary Continental breakfast. In-room data ports, some in-room hot tubs, satellite TV. Pool. Hot tub. Laundry facilities. Pets allowed. | 2321 E. Main St. | 970/565-3400 | fax 970/564-9768 | www.comfortinn.com | 148 rooms | $89–$99 | AE, D, DC, MC, V.

East Valley Accommodations Bed & Breakfast. Large property with a solarium, a greenhouse, private interior and exterior entrances, and a balcony. Area wildlife includes hawks, eagles, and blue herons. Located 5 mi from downtown Cortez and 8 mi from Mesa Verde National Park. Complimentary breakfast. Microwaves, refrigerators. Hot tub. Gym. Laundry facilities. | 30031 Rd. L | 970/564-9851 or 800/889-7180 | www.subee.com/eva/home.html | 6 rooms | $69–$75 | AE, MC, V.

Holiday Inn Express. This clean and comfortable chain motel is on the outskirts of Cortez, about 9 mi from Mesa Verde National Park. Complimentary Continental breakfast. In-room data ports, cable TV. Pool. Hot tub. Gym. Business services. Airport shuttle. Some pets allowed. | 2121 E. Main St. | 970/565-6000 | fax 970/565-3438 | www.holiday-inn.com | 100 rooms | $48–$109 | AE, D, DC, MC, V.

National 9 Inn–Sand Canyon. Motel in downtown Cortez that is walking distance to area shops, city parks, and restaurants. Kids stay free. Restaurant, bar, complimentary Continental breakfast. In-room data ports, some microwaves, cable TV. Outdoor pool. Laundry facilities. | 301 W. Main St. | 970/565-8562 or 800/524-9999 | fax 970/565-0125 | www.sandcanyon.com | 28 rooms | $45–$68 | AE, D, MC, V.

CRAIG

MAP 6, C2

(Nearby towns also listed: Meeker, Steamboat Springs, Dinosaur)

Situated in Colorado's sparsely populated northwest, Craig (population 9,082) is the home of Colorado's largest coal-processing plant, the Colorado-Ute Power Station. The surrounding area is a favorite for big-game hunters (antelope, elk, and deer) as well as a fisherman's paradise. Guided trips to the best fishing spots are available along with horseback pack trips into the wilderness.

Information: **Crested Butte Vacations** | 500 Gothic Rd., Mount Crested Butte 81225 | 800/544-8448 | www.crestedbutteresort.com.

Attractions

Elkhead Reservoir. A man-made reservoir with camping, picnic areas, boat launching ramp, beach area, fishing, and 11 mi of recreational trails. Located 10 mi northeast of Craig. | Moffat County Rd. 29 | 970/824-8151 | www.colorado-go-west.com/elkhead | Free | Daily.

Marcia Car. This museum in City Park features the private Pullman car of Colorado mining magnate David Moffat, who at one time either owned or held interest in more than 100 gold and silver mines. | U.S. 40 | 970/824-5689 | Free | Memorial Day–Labor Day, weekdays 8–5.

Museum of Northwest Colorado. Housed in a former state armory in the center of town, this museum's eclectic collection has everything from arrowheads to a fire truck, including Bill Mackin's collection of cowboy artifacts, the largest private collection in the world. Also housed here is memorabilia from former governor and U.S. senator Edward Johnson. | 590 Yampa Ave. | 970/824-6360 | www.museumnwco.org | Free | Mon.–Sat. 10–5.

Save Our Sandrocks Nature Trail. This hiking trail features American Indian petroglyph art. | On the 900 block of Alta Vista Dr. | 970/824-5689 | Free | May–Nov., daily.

MAY: *Grand Olde West Days.* This Memorial Day weekend fair has musicians, rides, arts and crafts, western history displays, quickdraw shooters, bull riding, a rodeo, and a parade at the Moffat County Fairgrounds. | 970/824–5689 or 800/864–4405.

Dining
Golden Cavvy. American/Casual. A lively coffee shop on the site of the old Baker Hotel. Known for hearty breakfasts, homemade pies, and anything deep-fried. Kids' menu. | 538 Yampa Ave. | 970/824–6038 | $6–$21 | MC, V.

Lodging
Holiday Inn Hotel and Suites. This full-service hotel 1 mi south of town center is the only place to stay between Steamboat Springs and the state line. Restaurant, bar. Some microwaves, room service, cable TV, some in-room VCRs. Pool. Hot tub. Gym. Video games. Laundry facilities. Business services. Pets allowed. | 300 S. Colorado Hwy. 13 | 970/824–4000 | fax 970/824–3950 | www.holidayinn.com | 152 rooms, 20 suites | $69–$89, $84–$109 suites | AE, D, DC, MC, V.

Taylor Street Bed and Breakfast. Rooms have individual decoration motifs, from the wolf room or the cowboy room to the sweetheart room. In downtown Craig, near hunting, snowmobiling, and ice skating. Dining room, complimentary breakfast. No TV in some rooms, TV & VCR in common area. | 403 Taylor St. | 970/824–5866 | fax 970/824–1713 | www.texasguides.com/taylor.html | 8 rooms (3 with shared bath) | $32–$65 | D, MC, V.

CRESTED BUTTE

MAP 6, D5

(Nearby town also listed: Gunnison)

Located in the heart of the Gunnison National Forest, Crested Butte lies in a cul-de-sac surrounded by towering, snowcapped peaks, lush hillsides, and green forests. Here, where Highway 135 ends, any memory of the big city quickly evaporates. The locals come off as more neighborly and laid-back than their Vail and Aspen counterparts. As one of the nation's largest National Historic Districts, Crested Butte brims with brightly colored, Victorian-era architecture. A stroll down Elk Avenue evokes a bustling boomtown from the late 19th century, but the trading posts are now occupied by upscale art dealers, restaurants and pottery studios.

Just 3 mi north of the town of Crested Butte you'll find the Crested Butte Mountain Resort. Here, snaking its way down from the 12,000-ft jagged peak, is one of the most revered ski areas in the world. The terrain is more rugged than most other ski areas in Colorado, and many runs are geared toward expert skiers and snowboarders. The nightlife at the resort is as colorful as a run down the slopes is exciting. At the top of Mount Crested Butte, you can see the awe-inspiring sight of the Ruby Range and Elk Mountains.

In summer, the sport of choice is mountain-biking. Countless trails are but a few pedals out of town, amidst bountiful fields of Indian paintbrushes and other native wildflowers.

Information: Crested Butte Vacations | 500 Gothic Rd., Mount Crested Butte 81225 | 800/544–8448 | www.crestedbutteresort.com.

Attractions
The Alpineer. This shop rents bikes and leads free guided mountain bike tours, which start from their shop and lead to the surrounding area. They use a Level I and Level II rental system for advanced riders. They also have tents, sleeping bags, backpacks, kid carriers, and

rock-climbing shoes available to rent. | 419 6th St. | 970/349–5210 | www.alpineer.com | Front suspension bike $25, full day; Level I $35, full day; Level II $45, full day | June–Sept., daily.

Crested Butte Country Club. This 18-hole course designed by Robert Trent Jones, Jr., is open to the public. The par 72 has 84 bunkers and 14 holes with water hazards. Nine-hole and junior rates are available. It is regarded as one of the most beautiful courses on the Western slope. | 385 Country Club Dr. | 970/349–6127 or 800/628–5496 | www.golfcolorado.net | Free | Mid-Sept.–Apr., daily.

Crested Butte Mountain Heritage Museum. Exhibits cover the history of the town, particularly mining in the region and the development of skis and skiing. Admission includes the Mountain Bike Hall of Fame, which is in the same building. | 200 Sopris Ave. | 970/349–1880 | www.discovercolorado.com/crestedbuttemuseum | $2 | Late Nov.–mid-Apr., 2–7; early June–late Sept. 1–6; Oct., weekends, 1–6; closed mid-Apr.–early June.

Mountain Bike Hall of Fame and Museum. A must-see for any bike enthusiast, this museum within the Crested Butte Heritage Museum is home to many pieces of early mountain biking equipment, as well as historic race highlights, photos, and press clippings. | 200 Sopris Ave. | 970/349–1880 | $2 | Late Nov.–mid-Apr., 2–7; early June–late Sept. 1–6; Oct., weekends, 1–6; closed mid-Apr.–early June.

Crested Butte Mountain Resort Ski Area. At this ski resort 3 mi north of Crested Butte (30 mi north of Gunnison), there are 85 runs with a vertical drop of 3,062 ft. Snowmobiling and wilderness hiking are also popular winter activities at the resort. | Rte. 317, Mount Crested Butte | 970/349–2333 | www.crestedbutte-ski.com | $52 full day, $38 half-day | Nov. 24–Apr. 16, daily.

SIGHTSEEING TOURS/TOUR COMPANIES

Alpine Outside. Call here to book sleigh-ride dinners at Lazy F Bar Ranch or guided fishing trips by Willowfly Anglers in nearby Almont. Willowfly Anglers offers float and walk trips on the fantastic Gunnison and East rivers, and Taylor and Cebolla creeks. | 315 6th St. | 970/349–5011 | Sleigh Ride Dinner $50, guide service $100 per day | Lazy F Bar Ranch Apr.–mid-Nov., daily.

ON THE CALENDAR

AUG.: *Crested Butte Reel Fest-Short Film Festival.* At this decade-old film festival at the Crested Butte Center for the Arts, screening categories include animation, comedy, drama/narrative, experimental, student, and documentary film. There are also film workshops. | 970/349–2600.

Dining

The Bacchanale. Italian. Beautiful stained-glass windows and antique furniture make this house-turned-restaurant a lovely place to dine. The northern Italian menu includes the requisite pasta selections as well as excellent veal and seafood dishes. Try the *coquille St. Jacques* (scallops baked in a light pastry with a creamy mushroom sauce) or the savory eggplant parmesan. | 208 Elk Ave. | 970/349–5257 | Closed May–Nov. | $9–$17 | AE, D, MC, V.

Bakery at Mount Crested Butte. Café. During the ski season, this is the spot for some of the best coffee on the mountain, along with homemade muffins, breads, nut bars, cookies, pastries, and veggie pockets. Located at the bus center, it's a local favorite. | Bus Center, Mountain Village | 970/349–1419 | No dinner | $5–$7 | No credit cards.

Donita's Cantina. Tex-Mex. Donita's is housed in an eye-grabbing hot pink building—a former hotel replete with the original pressed-tin ceiling. The fare is a notch above the norm and includes dishes like mahi mahi fajitas, chiles rellenos with homemade sauce, and sopaipilla sundaes, not to mention great margaritas. It's also a good bet for families. Kids' menu. | 330 Elk Ave. | 970/349–6674 | Reservations not accepted | No lunch | $8–$18 | AE, D, MC, V.

Idle Spur Brewery and Pub. Steak. Crested Butte's first microbrewery is also a rollicking nightspot, built with massive log beams and centered around a huge stone fireplace. The bar serves handcrafted brews, including the refreshing White Buffalo and the hearty Rodeo Stout. The restaurant is reputed to have the best steaks in town, all aged Colorado beef. | 226 Elk Ave. | 970/349–5026 | $8–$28 | AE, MC, V.

Karolina's Kitchen. American. The menu here includes a variety of hearty dishes, with a series of daily blue plate specials such as meat loaf or fresh fish. Huge sandwiches and hamburgers are a specialty, and entrées include fish-and-chips, Cajun chicken, kielbasa with sauerkraut, and beef bourguigonne. | 127 Elk Ave. | 970/349–6756 | $5–$10 | MC, V.

Le Bosquet. French. Decorated with lacy curtains, fine linens, and plush carpeting, Le Bosquet offers traditional country French fare in a romantic setting. House specials include roast duckling, rack of lamb, tofu piccata (tofu in a lemon butter and caper sauce), and a four-onion risotto cake with Portobello mushrooms. Open-air dining on their shady patio is available in summer months. No smoking. | 525 Red Lady Ave., in Majestic Plaza | 970/349–5808 | Reservations essential | Closed mid-Apr.–mid-May. No lunch | $15–$30 | AE, D, MC, V.

★ **Powerhouse.** Mexican. This enormous barnlike structure contains an antique 1890s bar, where the bartenders mix more than 100 tequilas into the best margaritas in town. The burritos are popular, as is the mesquite-roasted *cabrito* (succulent baby goat). | 130 Elk Ave. | 970/349–5494 | Reservations not accepted | No lunch | $8–$20 | AE, D, DC, MC, V.

★ **The Slogar.** American. This renovated 1882 Victorian restaurant's specialty is skillet-fried chicken, served with all-you-can-eat sweet-and-sour coleslaw, mashed potatoes, fresh baked biscuits, and sweet corn, with homemade ice cream as the finale. Steak dinners are also available. Kids' menu. | 517 2nd St. | 970/349–5765 | Closed mid-Apr.–May. No lunch | $13–$20 | MC, V.

★ **Soupçon.** French. Tucked away off the main street in a tiny log cabin, the Soupçon (pronounced "soup's on") is renowned for its creative menu, which changes daily but might include standouts like roast duckling with Michigan cherry sauce or petrale sole with black bean, ginger, and sake sauce. Only 35 seats are available, and they're always in high demand. | 127A Elk Ave. | 970/349–5448 | Reservations essential | Closed mid-Apr.–May | $17–$35 | AE, MC, V.

Swiss Chalet. Swiss. This mountain chalet-style restaurant features cheese and meat fondues and *raclette* (melted cheese served over boiled potatoes) with either traditional Buendnerfleisch or beef tenderloin. Many German specialties are also offered, including schnitzel and grilled venison medallions with lingonberry sauce. | 620 Gothic Rd. | 970/349–5917 | Reservations essential | Closed Mon. and June–Aug. | $15–$25 | AE, MC, V.

Timberline Restaurant. Contemporary. This restored miner's cabin offers intimate dining upstairs with a lively bar scene below. The seasonal menu focuses on Rocky Mountain interpretations of Continental dishes. Entrées may include venison with wild mushrooms or pheasant braised with ginger sauce. Sunday brunch. | 201 Elk Ave. | 970/349–9831 | Reservations essential | $10–$30 | AE, MC, V.

Wooden Nickel. American. This saloon/restaurant is adorned with dark wood and artwork depicting local scenes. The 100-year-old back bar offers a late-night menu and a happy hour from 3 to 6 daily. The menu covers a variety of tastes, including steak, ribs, lamb, and pork chops, sandwiches, burgers, fresh fish, and many other staples. | 222 Elk Ave. | 970/349–6350 | Reservations not accepted | $8–$31 | AE, D, DC MC, V.

Lodging

Claim Jumper. This unique B&B is filled with an outrageous collection of memorabilia and antiques, ranging from wall-to-wall Coca Cola trinkets to a bow-to-stern nautical motif. One room is a replica of a 1950s service station complete with a gas pump. The suites, with a queen and two twins, perfectly accommodate a family. Complimentary breakfast. Cable TV, in-room VCRs. Hot tub, sauna. | 704 Whiterock Ave. | 970/349–6471 | fax 970/349–7756 | www.visitcrestedbutte.com/claimjumper | 5 rooms, 2 suites | $99–$139 | D, MC, V.

★ Crested Butte Club. A small, Victorian-style hotel that's a National Historic Landmark, the Club is furnished with antiques and reproductions. All rooms have a gas fireplace and a copper bathtub; some have canopy beds. Complimentary Continental breakfast. Cable TV. Pool. Hot tub. Gym. Business services. No smoking. | 512 2nd St. | 970/349–6655 or 800/815–2582 | fax 970/349–7580 | cbclub@crestedbutte.net | 8 rooms | $180–$275 | D, MC, V.

Crested Butte Marriott Resort. This ski-in, ski-out resort on the slopes of Mount Crested Butte has very large rooms complete with wet bars and private balconies; some rooms have fireplaces. The bar here is boisterous during the ski season. Restaurant, bar (with entertainment), picnic area. In-room data ports, refrigerators, some in-room hot tubs, cable TV. Pool. Hot tub. Gym. Cross-country skiing, downhill skiing. Business services. | 6 Emmons Rd., Mount Crested Butte | 970/349–4000 | fax 970/349–4466 | www.marriott.com | 261 rooms, 51 suites | $189–$344, $241–$425 suites, $480–$847 deluxe suites | AE, D, DC, MC, V.

Crested Mountain Village. This modern condominium complex adjacent to the slopes in the mountain village is comprised of five different buildings. Modern, comfortable units range in size from studios to three bedrooms, all with fireplaces and balconies. Furnishings and ornamentation vary by tastes of owner. Cable TV. Pool. Hot tub, sauna. | 500 Gothic Rd., Mount Crested Butte | 970/349–4747 or 800/950–2133 | fax 970/349–2144 | www.crestedbutte.com | 11 rooms, 66 condominiums | $76–$100, $98–$299 studios, $245–$465 2 bedrooms, $325–$635 3 bedrooms | AE, D, MC, V.

Cristiana Guesthaus. This European-style lodge offers hospitality and comfort without sacrificing peace and privacy. Some of the simple, individually decorated rooms will accommodate up to four. Complimentary Continental breakfast. No TV in rooms, TV in common area. Hot tub, sauna. No smoking. | 621 Maroon Ave. | 970/349–5326 or 800/824–7899 | fax 970/349–1962 | www.visitcrestedbutte.com/cristiana | 21 rooms | $65–$87 | AE, D, MC, V.

Elk Mountain Lodge. The miners who originally stayed in this turn-of-the-20th-century hotel certainly never enjoyed the kind of luxury it now offers. The elegant lobby, with its chintz-covered furniture and grand piano, sets the tone, and the peerless good taste continues in the individually decorated rooms. Children may not stay in the same room with their parents. Bar, complimentary breakfast. In-room data ports, cable TV. Hot tub. Library. No kids under 12. | 129 Gothic Ave. | 970/349–7533 or 800/374–6521 | fax 970/349–5114 | www.elk-mountainlodge.net | 19 rooms | $90–$120 | AE, D, MC, V.

Gateway at Crested Butte. These slopeside condominiums next to the Peach Tree lift are among Crested Butte's nicest. Units range from one to three bedrooms and can accommodate up to eight. All apartments have a full kitchen, fireplace, washer/dryer, and two balconies, most of which overlook the slopes. Kitchenettes, microwaves, refrigerators, cable TV. Hot tub, sauna. | 400 Gothic Rd., Mount Crested Butte | 970/349–5705 | fax 970/349–7520 | www.highcountry.com | 17 units | $195–$395 1 bedroom, $205–$595 2 bedrooms, $360–$745 3 bedrooms | AE, D, MC, V.

Last Resort. This unpretentious bed-and-breakfast in downtown Crested Butte has a wood, stucco, and brick facade. The most interesting room is the Miner's Cabin, the original dwelling around which the existing house is built. The sunny rooms and suites have skylights and balconies, and the suites come equipped with hot tubs. Complimentary breakfast. Some in-room hot tubs. Steam room. Library. | 213 3rd St. | 970/349–0445 or 800/349–0445 | 4 rooms, 2 suites | $95–$105 | MC, V.

Manor Lodge. The European-style Manor Lodge, about 250 yards from the lifts, is an alternative to the usual condominium complexes on the mountain. The rooms are comfortable and fairly large, and some have fireplaces. Restaurant, bar, complimentary Continental breakfast. Cable TV. Hot tub. Laundry facilities. | 650 Gothic Rd., Mount Crested Butte | 970/349–5365 or 800/826–3210 | fax 970/349–5360 | 53 rooms, 4 suites | $73–$135 | AE, DC, MC, V.

Nordic Inn. A Norwegian stucco fireplace anchors the lobby of this ski-oriented property just one block from the lifts. Complimentary Continental breakfast. In-room data ports,

some kitchenettes, cable TV. Hot tub. Downhill skiing. Business services. | 14 Treasury Rd. | 970/349–5542 | fax 970/349–6487 | www.nordicinncb.com | 27 rooms, 2 cabins | $111–$152, $286–$365 cabins | Closed mid-Apr.–May | AE, MC, V.

Old Town Inn. This in-town roadside motel is 3 mi from the ski slopes. Picnic area, complimentary Continental breakfast. Some microwaves, cable TV. Hot tub. Laundry facilities. | 201 6th St. | 970/349–6184 | fax 970/349–1946 | brifley@gunnison.com | 33 rooms | $58–$137 | AE, D, DC, MC, V.

Pioneer Guest Cabins. Only 10 minutes out of town, in the Gunnison National Forest, these rustic log cabins from the 1930s have been updated to include full kitchens, wood-burning stoves or fireplaces, down comforters, and antique furnishings. A resident guide organizes mountain bike, snowshoe, and cross-country ski tours. Kitchenettes, refrigerators. Hiking, bicycles. Cross-country skiing. | Cement Creek Rd. | 970/349–5517 | fax 970/349–5517 | www.thepioneer.net | 8 cabins | $75–$90 | MC, V.

Sheraton Crested Butte Resort. Located in the heart of the mountain village, this modern hotel has a luxuriant lobby of giant pine logs and river stone. Comfortable, overstuffed furniture surrounds the massive hearth. The comprehensive and casual amenities make it perfect for families. Restaurant, bar, room service. Refrigerators, cable TV. 2 pools (1 outdoor). 2 outdoor hot tubs, sauna. Gym. Shops. Laundry facilities. Business services, parking (fee). | 6 Emmons Rd., Mount Crested Butte | 970/349–8000 or 888/223–2469 | fax 970/349–2397 | www.sheraton.com | 143 rooms, 109 suites | $93–$150 rooms, $150–$320 suites | AE, D, MC, V.

Village Center Properties. These five condo buildings, about 50 ft from the lifts, are an excellent slopeside value. The rooms are not overly large, but they are well laid out and modern with high ceilings, white walls, and contemporary furnishings. Every unit has a fireplace and balcony. Cable TV. Hot tub. | 600 Gothic Rd., Mount Crested Butte | 970/349–2111 or 800/521–6593 | fax 970/349–6370 | 30 units | $130–$485 | D, MC, V.

CRIPPLE CREEK

MAP 6, F5

(Nearby towns also listed: Cañon City, Colorado Springs, Manitou Springs)

Touring Cripple Creek today, with a population of 584, it is difficult to appreciate that the town, at the height of its glory, was home to more than 25,000. Gold was the attraction, and when the precious metal was discovered nearby, prospectors frantically operated more than 500 mines at one time. An inferno destroyed much of the old town

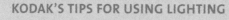

KODAK'S TIPS FOR USING LIGHTING

Daylight
· Use the changing color of daylight to establish mood
· Use light direction to enhance subjects' properties
· Match light quality to specific subjects

Dramatic Lighting
· Anticipate dramatic lighting events
· Explore before and after storms

Sunrise, Sunset, and Afterglow
· Include a simple foreground
· Exclude the sun when setting your exposure
· After sunset, wait for the afterglow to color the sky

From Kodak Guide to Shooting Great Travel Pictures © 2000 by Fodor's Travel Publications

in the late 1890s, but many of the period's buildings have been rebuilt. Cripple Creek is a few miles south of U.S. 24, just west of Colorado Springs. Today the town's economy is driven by gambling, which is legal here.

Information: Cripple Creek Chamber of Commerce | Box 650, Cripple Creek 80813 | 719/689–2169 or 800/526–8777 | www.cripple-creek.co.us.

Attractions
Cripple Creek District Museum. The museum focus on the local history of the region, with emphasis on the mining and railroads. | East end of Bennett Ave. | 719/689–2634 | $2 | Memorial Day–mid-Oct., daily 10–5; mid-Oct.–Memorial Day, weekends noon–4.

Cripple Creek–Victor Narrow Gauge Railroad. Runs the 6 mi between Cripple Creek and Victor, a deserted mining town, from its depot at the Cripple Creek District Museum. | East end of Bennett Ave. | 719/689–2640 | $6 | Memorial Day–Oct., daily 10–5; train departs every 45 mins.

Golden Loop Historic Parkway. Self-guided driving tour tracing the abandoned mining districts of Cripple Creek and Victor. Focuses on gold rush–era history and includes some of the ghost towns and abandoned mines in the area. Get a map at the Cripple Creek Welcome Center. | Hwy. 67 and Bennett Ave. | 719/689–3315 or 800/858–GOLD | www.cripple-creek.co.us/attr.html | 50¢.

Imperial Hotel. Dating from 1896, this still-active hotel offers gambling, not to mention a peek into the town's golden era. | 123 N. 3rd St. | 719/689–2922, 719/689–7777, or 800/235–2922 | Free | Daily.

Mollie Kathleen Gold Mine. A 40-minute guided tour takes you 1,000 ft underground into this once-productive gold mine, which is located 1 mi north of town. | Rte. 67 | 719/689–2465 | $11 | May–Oct., daily 9–5.

ON THE CALENDAR
JUNE: *Donkey Derby Days.* Donkey and burro races are a lively happening the last full weekend in June. | 719/689–2169.
SEPT.: *King of the Hill Rodeo and BBQ Blaze-off.* The rodeo is held 1 mi from downtown in the County Fairgrounds, while the barbecue contestants, barbecue vendors, and other entertainment line Bennett Avenue in Cripple Creek the last weekend in September. | 719/689–3315 or 877/858–GOLD.

Dining
Golden Grille Restaurant. American/Casual. Popular dishes include burgers, chicken, fish, and the 8-ounce New York strip steak. In the Gold Rush Hotel and Casino. | 209 E. Bennett Ave. | 719/689–2646 or 800/235–8239 | $7–$13 | AE, D, DC, MC, V.

Lombard's Grill. American. In the Double Eagle Hotel in downtown Cripple Creek. Try the 8-ounce fillet, served with potatoes or rice, and a soup and salad buffet. | 442 E. Bennett Ave. | 719/689–5000 or 800/711–7234 | $11–$17 | AE, D, MC, V.

Maggie's. American. In the Colorado Grande Casino. Specialties include prime rib, with a rotating menu every Sunday. | 300 E. Bennett Ave. | 719/689–3517 | www.cripple-creek.co.us/grand.html | $8–$18 | AE, D, MC, V.

Stratton Dining Room. American. The more formal of two restaurants in the vintage Imperial Hotel, the Stratton offers a varied menu of steaks, chicken, salmon, and salads. On weekends, you can opt for seafood on Fridays or prime rib and crab legs on Saturdays at a buffet. Sunday brunch during summer. | 123 N. 3rd St. | 719/689–7777 | $9–$15 | AE, D, MC, V.

Lodging
Cripple Creek Hotel. A schoolhouse built in 1899 is now a hotel a block away from gaming in downtown Cripple Creek. The spacious rooms have the original blackboards that

once held algebraic equations, plus a private bath, and one to three double beds. Transform the memory of your high-school years into a nostalgic trip to this two-story brick hotel. Cable TV, no room phones. | 350 E. Carr | 719/689–3709 | fax 719/689–3731 | www.cripple-creek.co.us/cchotel.htm | 13 rooms | $55–$85 | AE, D, MC, V.

Double Eagle. This is a modern place with an on-site casino. Restaurant, complimentary breakfast. Some minibars, cable TV. Business services. | 442 E. Bennett Ave. | 719/689–5000 or 800/711–7234 | fax 719/689–5050 | 147 rooms, 10 suites | $59–$119, $129–$500 suites | AE, D, DC, MC, V.

Holiday Inn Express. This chain hotel is on the eastern edge of Cripple Creek, just off Route 67. Picnic area, complimentary Continental breakfast. Cable TV. Pool. Gym. Laundry facilities. | 601 E. Galena Ave. | 719/689–2600 | fax 719/689–3426 | www.holiday-inn.com | 67 rooms | $80–$109 | AE, D, DC, MC, V.

Hotel St. Nicholas. On a hilltop, this converted 1898 hospital has great views of the Sangre de Cristo Mountains from the rooftop. Some rooms have enclosed balconies; shuttle to downtown casinos. Bar, complimentary Continental breakfast. Cable TV. Outdoor hot tub, sauna. | 303 N. Third St. | 719/689–0856 or 888/786–4257 | fax 719/689–2877 | www.cripple-creek.co.us/stnick.html | 15 rooms | $68–$100 | AE, MC, V.

Imperial Casino Hotel. A Victorian hotel built in 1896, furnished with antiques; it has its own casino. Restaurant, bar. No air-conditioning, cable TV. Free parking. | 123 N. 3rd St. | 719/689–7777 or 800/235–2922 | fax 719/689–0416 | www.cripple-creek.co.us/impl.html | 27 rooms (16 with shared bath), 2 suites | $50–$125 | AE, D, MC, V.

Independence Hotel. Less than a block from the downtown casinos, this century-old brick building boasts original woodwork and mouldings in the huge lobby. Rooms are basic, but have large bathrooms and old-fashioned ceiling fans. Complimentary Continental breakfast. Cable TV. | 151 E. Bennett Ave. | 719/689–2744 | 8 rooms | $40–$80 | AE, D, MC, V.

Last Dollar Inn. This two-story 1898 Victorian brownstone in downtown Cripple Creek is said to be the most haunted house in town. Some rooms have fireplaces. Dining room, complimentary breakfast. Some in-room hot tubs, no TV in rooms, TV in common area. No smoking. | 315 E. Carr Ave. | 719/689–9113 or 888/429–6700 | fax 719/689–0868 | www.cripple-creek.co.us/lastdinn.htm | 6 rooms | $60–$100 | MC, V.

Tarryall River Ranch. Located on the border of the Lost Creek Wilderness area 35 mi northwest of Cripple Creek, this cozy western ranch has stunning views of Pikes Peak. Accommodations are in comfortable, though rustic, log cabins. Three home-cooked meals are included in rates. No air-conditioning, no room phones, no TV in rooms. Pool. Hot tub. Volleyball. Fishing. Children's programs (ages 3–17), playground. Laundry facilities. | 27001.5 County Rd. 77, Lake George | 719/748–1214 or 800/408–8407 | fax 719/748–1319 | www.tarryallranch.com | 8 cabins | $1,300 per person per wk | Closed Oct.–Apr. | AP | No credit cards.

Victor Hotel. A former bank 6 mi from Cripple Creek is an historic landmark built in 1899, though guest rooms have a more modern feel. Many guests claim that there is a ghost residing in the hotel. Restaurant, complimentary Continental breakfast. Cable TV. Business services. Pets allowed. | 4th St. and Victor Ave., Victor | 719/689–3553 or 800/748–0870 | fax 719/689–3979 | www.indra.com/fallline/vh/vh.htm | 30 rooms | $89–$99 | D, MC, V.

CUCHARA

MAP 6, G8

(Nearby towns also listed: Trinidad, Walsenburg)

People of the Ute and Comanche tribes were the first to inhabit this secluded valley, describing it as a paradise on earth. In the 16th century, Spanish explorers appropriately named it Cuchara, or "spoon." Early traders and settlers frequented the area, using the nearby Spanish Peaks as a guidepost along their travels. Colorful legends permeate the Cuchara Valley and its numerous surrounding rock formations.

Today, the Cuchara Valley is widely considered to be an undiscovered gem. Predominantly a summer resort, it is known for its cool temperatures and stunning scenery. Located in the San Isabel National Forest between the Spanish Peaks and Sangre de Cristo Mountains, Cuchara is the perfect starting point for any summer outdoor experience.

Information: **La Veta–Cuchara Chamber of Commerce** | Box 32 (131 E. Ryus Ave.), La Veta, 81055 | 719/742–3676 | www.ruralwideweb.com/lvec.htm.

Attractions

Cuchara Mountain Resort. Its remote location and quiet setting make this an ideal winter ski destination for the family. Out of the 28 runs on 230 acres, 40% are oriented toward the beginner. With four chairlifts and one surface tow, the wait for a ride is usually minimal. About 20% of the mountain is dedicated to expert terrain, with 45 acres of gladed area to accommodate more advanced skiers. There are children's programs during ski season, as well as summer activities. | 946 Panadero Ave. | 888/282–4272 | www.cuchara.com | $30 1-day lift tickets | Nov.–Apr.

Ft. Franciso Museum. This adobe-and-timber plaza, built in 1862, was the first settlement in the upper Cuchara Valley. Today it houses many historical accounts, photos, and artifacts, most of which were donated by local residents. | 308 N. Main St., La Veta | 719/742–5501 | $2 | Memorial Day–late Oct., Wed.–Sun.

San Isabel National Forest. This 1-million-acre forest is home to the Spanish Peaks, Collegiate Peaks, and the Sangre De Cristo range, which boasts Colorado's highest peak, 14,433-ft Mt. Elbert. Many options for wildlife viewing, hiking, camping, fishing, and horseback riding originate near Cuchara. | U.S. Forest Service, San Isabel Ranger District, 1920 Valley Rd., Pueblo | 719/545–8737 | Free | Daily.

ON THE CALENDAR

JULY: _Hermosa Art Show._ For almost 40 years, local and international artists have gathered in Cuchara, at the Cuchara Community Center, during the third weekend of July each summer to display and sell paintings, sculptures, ceramics, glasswork, jewelry, and mixed media pieces. | 719/742–3676.

Dining

Boardwalk Saloon and Restaurant. American/Casual. Locals affectionately call this "The Dog Bar"; a friendly St. Bernard has been at the saloon for years. It's an expansive space, with dance floor and backyard deck, where live blues is presented in the summer. The pizza is outstanding, all homemade including the sausage. Burgers, steaks, and trout round out the dinner menu. | 34 Cuchara Rd. | 719/742–6366 | $6–$15 | AE, MC, V.

The Silver Spoon Restaurant. American. A little footbridge takes you across the Cuchara River to this sunny, elegant restaurant that has earned a reputation for serving the best food in southern Colorado. Steaks, chicken, seafood, and pasta dishes are all served with the chef's famous pepper sauces. During the summer months lighter fare is also served at lunchtime on the backyard river peninsula. | 16984 Rte. 12 | 719/742–3764 or 888/680–3764 | www.silverspoonrestaurant.com | Reservations essential | No lunch Tues., Wed. or Nov.–Apr. | $10–$22 | AE, D, MC, V.

The Timbers Restaurant. Italian. This old-fashioned storefront hides a rustic Victorian interior, with consigned local artwork lining the walls. The dinner menu includes trout, salmon, chicken, pasta, and an excellent pepper steak. For lunch, sandwiches and salads are offered. | 23 E. Cuchara Ave. | 719/742–3838 | Reservations essential | Closed mid-Oct.–Apr. | $11–$19 | MC, V.

Lodging

Cuchara Central. This office arranges short-term rentals of privately owned lodges, cabins, and condominiums throughout the Cuchara Valley. Anything from a small rustic cabin for couples to a lodge that sleeps 30 is available. They also arrange fishing trips, horseback tours, and hiking trips. | 30 E. Cuchara Ave. | 719/742–5258 or 800/282–4272 | www.cucharacentral.com | 20 cabins and condominiums | $95–$300 | AE, MC, V.

River's Edge Bed & Breakfast. This modern, two-story cabin is finely appointed with log furniture and local southwestern art. The Cuchara River runs right through the backyard, where a terrace of furnished patios is perfectly positioned for wildlife viewing and relaxing. Two rooms have private baths and the suite sleeps up to five. Complimentary breakfast. In-room data ports, cable TV. | 90 E. Cuchara Ave. | 719/742–5169 | fax 719/742–3111 | www.ruralwideweb.com/rebb.htm | 3 rooms (2 with shared bath), 1 suite | $110–$138, $188 suite | AE, D, MC, V.

Yellow Pine Guest Ranch. Hidden in the pine groves just north of Cuchara, these 1920s cabins are a true getaway; only the lulling sound of nearby Cuchara River intrudes on your quiet. The cabins are on spacious, private lots, have full kitchens, and are individually decorated in country fashion. Many have fireplaces and porches and some can accommodate up to eight guests. Kitchenettes, refrigerators. No room phones, no TV. Horseback riding. Fishing. Laundry facilities. Pets allowed (fee). | 15880 Rte. 12 | 719/742–3528 | www.coloradodirectory.com/yellowpineranch | 9 cabins | $75–$120 | Closed Nov.–Apr. | AE, MC, V.

DELTA

MAP 6, B5

(Nearby towns also listed: Cedaredge, Grand Junction, Montrose)

The site of an early fur-trading post, Fort Uncompahgre, Delta (population 6,253) is along the banks of the Gunnison River in the midst of Colorado's fruit-growing region. Every year, millions of dollars worth of apples, cherries, and peaches are produced by farmers of the fertile area. The town's proximity to several national forests (it's the location for the headquarters of the Grand Mesa, Gunnison, and Uncompahgre national forests) makes it a good jumping-off point for a journey into the wilds of western Colorado. Delta is often called the "City of Murals," after the seven murals decorating local buildings, which were painted by local artists in the late 1980s. It's near the Black Canyon of the Gunnison National Park *(see* Montrose), a spectacularly deep and narrow canyon whose north rim can be reached via Highway 92 out of Delta.

Information: **Delta Area Chamber of Commerce** | 301 Main St., Delta 81416 | 970/874–8616 | www.deltacolorado.org.

Attractions

Confluence Park–Fort Uncompahgre. The primary feature of the park is the replica of historic Fort Uncompahgre, an early fur-trading post built in 1826. Employees at the fort are attired in period dress, and the experience sends you back more than 150 years to when trapping beaver was the only occupation around. | 205 Gunnison River Dr. | 970/874–8349 | Park free, fort $4 | June–Aug., Tues.–Sat. 10–5; Mar.–May and Sept.–mid Dec., Tues.–Sat. 10–4.

Grand Mesa National Forest. Nearly 350,000 acres of alpine forest await the hiker, boater, fisherman, skier, and nature-lover. The office in Delta is also the headquarters for Gunnison and Uncompahgre national forests. | 2250 Hwy. 50 | 970/874–6600 | fs.fed.us/r2/gmug | Free | Daily.

JULY: *Deltarado Days.* A parade, mud volleyball, booths, games, arts and crafts, and a PRCA rodeo are featured at this event in Confluence Park. | 970/874–7566.

SEPT.: *Council Tree Pow Wow and Cultural Festival.* Different groups of American Indians gather to share their heritage and culture through dance, music, and song in Confluence Park during the last week in September. | 970/874–1718 or 800/874–1741.

Dining

Fireside Inn. American/Casual. A favorite Sunday dinner spot. Specialties include prime rib and *jaeger schnitzel* (breaded veal in a brown mushroom sauce). It has a lounge and banquet facilities. | 820 Hwy. 92 | 970/874–4413 | $12–$16 | AE, D, MC, V.

Lodging

Best Western Sundance. This chain motel is centrally located near the heart of town. Restaurant, bar, complimentary breakfast. In-room data ports, room service, cable TV. Outdoor pool. Hot tub. Gym. Laundry facilities. Business services. Pets allowed. | 903 Main St. | 970/874–9781 or 800/626–1994 | fax 970/874–5440 | www.bestwestern.com | 41 rooms | $55–$70 | AE, D, DC, MC, V.

Comfort Inn–Delta. This chain motel is on the north end of Delta alongside the Gunnison River. Complimentary Continental breakfast. In-room data ports, some microwaves, refrigerators, cable TV, some in-room VCRs (and movies). Video games. | 180 Gunnison River Dr. | 970/874–1000 | fax 970/874–4154 | www.comfortinn.com | 47 rooms, 4 suites | $69–$79, $89–$109 suites | AE, D, DC, MC, V.

Riverwood Inn and RV Park. In the motel, some rooms have views of the Gunnison River. The RV park has separate laundry and shower facilities and is cable-ready. A 3-acre island space is available for tent sites if you want to camp. Restaurant, picnic area. In-room data ports, cable TV. Hiking. Fishing. Laundry facilities. | 677 Hwy. 50 | 970/874–5787 | fax 970/874–4872 | www.riverwoodn.com | 12 rooms. | $50–$66 | D, DC, MC, V.

DENVER

(Nearby towns also listed: Aurora, Boulder, Englewood, Evergreen, Golden, Lakewood)

Universally known as the Mile-high City, Denver's official altitude is exactly 5,280 ft. Settled in 1858, shortly after gold was discovered in the nearby mountains, the town grew rapidly after silver was found in the region as well. By 1890, Denver supported a population of more than 100,000 people, many of them still engaged in prospecting and mining but many also involved in businesses that supplied the mining industry.

Although the Colorado mining boom made Denver an important transportation and financial center, it was not until the 1930s that Denver's importance really came about. The reason was cattle. Until then, western ranchers simply let their cattle roam the range, eating whatever grass was handy. The Monfort family, who came to Denver in 1930, decided that it might be more efficient if the cattle were restricted to pens and fattened with hay, corn, and grain. With cattle feedlots concentrated in the area, the city's railroad yards expanded to get them out to the rest of a hungry nation. While never as centrally important as Chicago, by the 1940s Denver had grown to be a major city with a real social and cultural base.

Today, Denver and its suburbs are the focal point of Colorado's growth. With a greater metropolitan area population of nearly 1½ million, the Denver region contains almost one-half of the entire state's people. The financial industry is more important now to the city's economy than cattle ever were. Many visitors are surprised to find that Denver is vibrant and fun filled, with something to offer everyone—from a variety of professional sports to nearby skiing at world-class resorts, museums and galleries, and sightseeing. The restaurants and hotels are some of the finest in the Rocky Mountain region.

Those who don't know Denver may be in for another small shock. Despite its mile-high moniker, the city itself is quite flat (its other name is "Queen City of the Plains." Looking east, you might almost imagine you can see Kansas in the distance—the view is that uninterrupted. The Rocky Mountains are a backdrop, and as such, Denver has a remarkably mild climate (over 300 days of sunshine a year), something its residents take for granted as they actively pursue outdoor recreation to their heart's content.

Information: Denver Metro Convention and Visitors Bureau | 1555 California St., Suite 300, Denver 80202 | 303/892–1112 or 800/645–3446 | www.denver.org.

NEIGHBORHOODS

Despite being a sprawling city of endless highways and suburbs, many of Denver's most popular attractions are concentrated in a fairly manageable area centered on downtown Denver, which can itself be divided up into three parts, and the neighborhoods directly east and south of downtown.

Lower Downtown (LoDo) is the oldest part of Denver. Keeping in mind that downtown Denver is a grid, but turned at a 45-degree angle, LoDo is the area of downtown more or less south of Union Station, from Wynkoop on the northwest to Larimer on the southeast and from 14th Street on the southwest to 20th Street on the northeast. This is a vibrant area, which has been revived of late by the Coors Field, which opened in 1995; on the other side of Cherry Creek from LoDo is Elitch Gardens, a popular amusement park. Trendy new restaurants and shops are opening up in restored, historic buildings, and no high-rises are allowed here, which keeps the area on a more human scale.

The **Central Business District** is a triangular area of very tall buildings, many of which run in a corridor from 16th to 18th streets between Larimer and Broadway. This area was built up in the 1980s and is sandwiched between LoDo and the Civic Center.

The state and city government buildings and many of Denver's important museums and public buildings are built around **Civic Center,** a small, two-square-block green space at downtown's southeast corner, south of the intersection of Broadway and Colfax.

Capitol Hill is the area south and east of downtown, extending roughly from Civic Center Park to East 6th Avenue, east of Broadway to Cheesman Park. Here, you'll find many of the Victorian mansions that resulted from the mining fortunes made in the late 19th century, including the Molly Brown House.

Cherry Creek is an affluent, primarily residential neighborhood to the south and east of downtown, where you'll find the Denver Country Club. Its boundaries extend from East 8th Avenue to East 1st Avenue between Downing and Steele streets. Many of Denver's wealthiest families have lived here for generations.

While there are certainly many other neighborhoods in Denver, they will be important primarily to residents who live, work, and shop there. Other important areas to keep in mind are Denver's suburbs, including **Aurora** to the east (*see* Aurora), **Englewood,** Littleton, and the Denver Tech Center to the south (*see* Englewood), **Lakewood** to the west (*see* Lakewood), and Arvada to the northwest.

TRANSPORTATION

Airports: Denver International Airport | 8500 Peña Blvd. 24 mi northeast of downtown Denver (800/247–2336), is served by most major domestic carriers and is a major hub for United.

Airport Transportation: There are several options for getting to the airport. A taxi ride costs $45–$50. **Metro Taxi** (303/333–3333), **Yellow Cab** (303/777–7777), or **Zone Cab** (303/444–8888).

SuperShuttle (303/342–5450) serves downtown and makes door-to-door trips for $10–$19.

The region's public bus service, the **Regional Transportation District** (RTD | 303/299–6000. for route and schedule information | 303/299–6700. for other inquiries | www.rtd-denver.com/skyride) runs SkyRide to and from Denver. The main transportation center is at the old Stapleton Airport (Martin Luther King Boulevard and Syracuse Street); the trip takes 55 minutes and costs $4–$8 one-way, $10–$13 round-trip, depending on where you are coming from. Buy SkyRide tickets at RTD Market Street Station, Market and 16th Street; RTD Civic Center Station, Broadway and 16th Street; RTD Boulder Transit Center, 14th and Walnut Street, Boulder; RTD Sales Counter at DIA's West Terminal, Level 5; and King Soopers and Safeway supermarkets throughout the metro area.

Public Transit: The region's **public bus service** (RTD | 303/299–6000) is comprehensive and offers many routes throughout the metropolitan area, linking to such outlying towns as Boulder and Nederland. Fares depend on time and distance traveled; within the city limits it's $1.25 during peak hours (6 AM–9 AM, 4 PM–6 PM), 75¢ other times.

A **light-rail service** (303/299–6000) links downtown Denver with southwest and northeast sections. The fare is $1.25 peak, 75¢ off-peak. A loop connects popular downtown stops.

A **free shuttle bus** operates about every 10 minutes until 11 PM, stopping every two blocks along the 16th Street Mall, which roughly bisects downtown.

A **Cultural Connection Trolley** (303/299–6000) runs between 18 prime cultural attractions about every half hour. Tickets, good for the entire day, cost $3 and can be purchased either on the bus or from hotel concierges.

Driving and Parking: If you are going beyond downtown, you'll probably need your car to get around. Interstate 25 runs north–south through Denver; Interstate 70 runs east–west across the northern part of the city. Interstate 225 is the major highway around the southeast part of Denver; it connects Aurora to the Denver Tech Center. The morning rush hour begins early (perhaps as early as 7), but is usually tapering off by 9; evenings, traffic picks up again at 3:30 and goes strong until at least 7. The Mousetrap, the most congested part of the city, is the intersection of I–25 and Interstate I–70. A **24-hour hot line** gives recorded road condition information (303/639–1111).

Avoid driving downtown if you can. It's congested, and most streets are one-way. Since public transportation downtown is quite good and walking is almost as fast as driving, consider leaving your car at your hotel. Parking can also be a problem downtown, but it's not impossible and actually cheaper than in most big cities. There are both on-street meters and parking lots; expect to pay between $4 and $8 for a morning or afternoon of shopping or sightseeing. Beyond downtown, parking is usually plentiful and free.

Attractions

ART AND ARCHITECTURE

Daniels & Fischer Tower. This 330-ft-high clock tower was built to emulate the campanile of San Marco in Venice, and when it was built in 1909 it was the tallest structure west of the Mississippi. If you take the free walking tour of 16th Street that starts here in summer, you can sometimes take a look inside. | 16th & Arapahoe Sts. | 303/892–1505 | Daily; walking tours Jun.–Aug., Thurs. and Sat. at 10:30 AM.

State Capitol. Built in 1886 of Colorado granite and topped with a dome covered in gold from Colorado mines, Colorado's state capitol is one of the nation's most striking. Climb to the balcony for a panoramic Rocky Mountain view or just to the 18th step, which is exactly 1 mi above sea level. Tours are offered. | Broadway and 200 E. Colfax Ave. | 303/866–2604 | Free | Weekdays, tours offered 9:30–2:30.

United States Mint. Established in 1862 to accommodate the Colorado gold rush, this mint now produces over 10 billion coins each year. | 320 W. Colfax Ave., at Cherokee St. | 303/405–4761 | Free | Weekdays 8–3; tours every 10–20 mins.

CULTURE, EDUCATION, AND HISTORY

Arvada Center for the Arts and Humanities. A performing arts center 2½ mi north of Interstate 70 in Arvada with concerts, theater, and art in a 1,200-seat amphitheater. There's also an historical museum. | 6901 Wadsworth Blvd., Arvada | 303/431–3939 | fax 303/431–3083 | www.arvadacenter.org | Free; performance costs vary | Weekdays 9–6, Sat. 9–5, Sun. 1–5.

Chicano Humanities and Arts Council. This gallery and performance space offers a venue for visual artists, writers, dancers, poets, filmmakers, and other local artists and performers of Chicano and Latino heritage. Visual arts exhibits in the gallery are often accompanied by performance pieces, and the schedule rotates every two to three weeks. | 772 Santa Fe Dr. | 303/571–0440 | www.chacweb.org | Gallery free; performance costs vary | Fri. 7 PM–10 PM, Sat. 1–4.

Denver Performing Arts Complex. Shops, restaurants, several theaters, and a futuristic concert hall fill this complex, the second-largest performing-arts complex in America. The Galleria, an 80-ft-high soaring glass archway, connects all the theaters. | 1245 Champa St., between Speer Blvd. and Arapahoe St. | 303/893–4100 or 800/641–1222 | www.denvercenter.org.
Auditorium Theatre. This theater dating from 1908 is the home of Colorado Contemporary Dance. Guided tours are conducted by appointment only. | 1245 Champa St., between Speer Blvd. and Arapahoe St. | 303/640–7113 | Free | Guided tours by appointment only.
Boettcher Concert Hall. Home to the Colorado Symphony Orchestra and Opera Colorado, this concert hall was the first fully surround theater in the nation. All of its 2,630 seats are within 75 ft of the stage. Opera Colorado is the only major opera company in the country that performs in the round. | 1245 Champa St., between Speer Blvd. and Arapahoe St. | 303/640–2862.
The Helen Bonfils Theatre Complex. This complex within the Denver Performing Arts Complex houses four separate smaller theaters—the Stage, the Source, the Space, and the Ricketson Theater, as well as the Donald R. Seawell Grand Ball Room. | 303/893–4000 or 303/893–4100.
Temple Hoyne Buell Theatre. This 2,800-seat auditorium is home to the Colorado Ballet as well as several other performance groups. | 1245 Champa St., between Speer Blvd. and Arapahoe St. | 303/640–2862.

Denver Public Library. This library, containing more than 4 million items, is the largest public library in the Rocky Mountains. Its historical photograph collection is outstanding. | 10 W. 14th Ave. Pkwy. | 303/640–6200 | Free | Mon.–Wed. 10–9, Thurs.–Sat. 10–5:30, Sun. 1–5.

University of Denver. Nine thousand students attend classes at this university established in 1864. Some notable buildings on its 124-acre campus in southeast Denver are the Penrose Library, Harper Humanities Gardens, Shwayder Art Building, and the Law School. Daily campus tour are available at the University Admissions Office. | 2199 S. University Blvd. | 303/871–2711 or 303/871–6400 | www.du.edu | Free | Campus daily; tours Sept.–May, weekdays 11 and 3, Sat. 11.

Chamberlin Observatory. The telescope here is more than 100 years old. Lectures are offered. | Observatory Park, 2930 E. Warren Ave. | 303/871–5172 | $2 | Oct.–Mar., Tues., Thurs. 7–9:30 PM; Apr.–Sept., Tues., Thurs. 8:30–10:30 PM.

MUSEUMS

Black American West Museum and Heritage Center. Exhibits here document the contributions that black Americans have made to the history of the American west. One floor is devoted to black cowboys, who made up nearly a third of all the cowboys; another floor is devoted to military history, including the Buffalo soldiers; other exhibits focus on black homesteaders and black churches in the west. | 3091 California St., at Downing | 303/292–2566 | $5 | May–Sept., daily 10–5; Oct.–Apr., Wed.–Fri. 10–2, weekends 10–5.

Byers-Evans House. This red-brick Victorian mansion was once the home of William N. Byers, who founded the *Rocky Mountain News*. Built in 1883, it was restored in the 1980s and is furnished in period style. In the former carriage house you'll find the Denver History Museum; combined admission gets you into both. | 1310 Bannock St. | 303/620–4933 | $5 (includes the Denver History Museum) | Tues.–Sun. 11–3.

Charles C. Gates Planetarium. This huge planetarium in City Park has a screen that's nearly five stories high and seven stories wide. It's currently closed until late 2001 or early 2002 for a major renovation. | 2001 Colorado Blvd. | 303/322–7009 or 303/370–6351.

The Children's Museum of Denver. Hands-on exhibits lure kids into learning about nature, science, and history. One of the most popular exhibits is a working television studio. There's also an outdoor park with climbing equipment. | 2121 Children's Museum Dr. (I–25, exit 211) | 303/433–7433 | www.cmdenver.org | $5 | Memorial Day–Labor Day, weekdays 9–4, weekends 10–5; Labor Day–Memorial Day closed Mon.

Colorado History Museum. Dioramas and other exhibits cover state history from prehistoric times to the present. On display are Conestoga wagons and an artifact-packed timeline exhibit that surveys Colorado history in a little over 112 ft, devoting 9 inches to each year. The museum is located near the state capitol complex. | 1300 Broadway | 303/866–3682 | www.coloradohistory.org | $4.50 | Mon.–Sat. 10–4:30, Sun. noon–4:30.

Comanche Crossing Museum. This collection of historic buildings, including two schoolhouses (one dating from 1891), a depot, and a barn, includes exhibits on the history of the area as well as the transcontinental railroad. It's 30 mi east of Denver on I–70 in Strasburg. | 56060 E. Colfax Ave., Strasburg | 303/622–4322 | Free | June–Aug., daily 1–4.

★ **Denver Art Museum.** The Asian, pre-Columbian, Spanish Colonial, and Native American holdings are the strengths of this highly accessible and well-designed museum. Rotating special exhibits and dazzling mountain views are a bonus. A floor devoted to "Adventures in Art" will delight children. | 100 W. 14th Ave. Pkwy. | 303/640–2793 | www.denverartmuseum.org | $4.50, free Sat. | Tues. 10–5, Wed. 10–9, Thurs.–Sat. 10–5, Sun. noon–5.

Denver Firefighters Museum. The museum building began its life in 1909 as Fire Station No. 1. Today it displays original firefighting equipment, some of which dates from the late 1800s. | 1326 Tremont Pl. | 303/892–1436 | $3 | Memorial Day–Labor Day, Mon.–Sat. 10–4; Labor Day–Memorial Day, Mon.–Sat. 10–2.

Denver History Museum. The highlight is the Ann Evans collection of southwestern art. You'll also find interactive exhibits covering local history. | 1310 Bannock St. | 303/620–4933 | $5 (includes Byers-Evans House) | Tues.–Sun. 11–3.

Denver Museum of Miniatures, Dolls, and Toys. This 19th-century house, the Pearce-McAllister Cottage, houses eight rooms full of porcelain dolls, teddy bears, Mickey Mouse toys, trains, and many more. | 1880 Gaylord St. | 303/322–1053 | $4 | Tues.–Sat. 10–4, Sun. 1–4.

★ **Denver Museum of Science and Nature.** In City Park, you'll find this rich collection of natural history exhibits from all over the world, which includes gems, minerals, Egyptian artifacts, and dinosaur bones. There are also intriguing hands-on exhibits, including a "Hall of Life," where you can test your health and fitness, and an IMAX Theater. It's very kid-friendly. | 2001 Colorado Blvd. | 303/322–7009 or 800/925–2250 | www.dmnh.org | $7, Phipps IMAX Theater $7 | Daily 9–5.

Forney Transportation Museum. This eccentric museum houses 300 antique autos, coaches, locomotives, carriages, and bicycles. Though not always well-thought-out, the displays offer enough amusement to keep a car or train enthusiast amused. | 4303 Brighton Blvd. | 303/297–1113 | www.forneymuseum.com | $4 | Mon.–Sat. 9–5, Sun. 11–5.

Molly Brown House Museum. This Victorian mansion between East 13th and 14th Avenues was the home of the "Unsinkable" Molly Brown, who survived the *Titanic* disaster. Costumed guides take you through the period-furnished rooms and tell you about Denver history. | 1340 Pennsylvania St. | 303/832–4092 | www.mollybrown.com | $6 | Sept.–May, Tues.–Sat. 10–3:30, Sun. noon–3:30; June–Aug., Mon.–Sat. 10–3:30, Sun. noon–3:30.

Museo de las Americas. Exhibits at this museum depict the achievements of generations of America's Latino men and women in the fields of art, literature, and politics. | 861 Santa Fe Dr. | 303/571–4401 | $3 | Tues.–Sat. 10–5.

Museum of Western Art. This former bordello now houses some of the finest artworks by Remington, Russell, and other renowned artists known for their depictions of the American west. | 1727 Tremont Pl | 303/296–1880 | $3 | Tues.–Sat., 10–4:30.

Trianon Museum and Art Gallery. This tranquil museum houses a collection of 18th- and 19th-century European furnishings and objets d'art, with pieces dating from the 17th century onward. Guided tours are offered on the hour. | 335 14th St. | 303/623–0739 | $1 | Mon.–Sat. 10–4.

PARKS

Cheesman Park. Providing excellent views of the Rockies, this 80-acre Denver park was originally a cemetery. Now it is a place for lounging, sunbathing, dog-walking, and picnicking. It's also a favorite gathering place for Capitol Hill's gay community. In the summer, folks flock to see the beautiful flowers. The Memorial Pavilion, resembling a Greek temple, provides some of the only shade. The park is next to the Denver Botanic Gardens and Boettcher Memorial Conservatory. | E. 8th Ave. and Franklin St. | 303/964–2500 | Free | Daily.

★ **City Park.** At 320 acres—a mile long and ¾ mi wide—Denver's largest public space contains the Denver Zoo, the Denver Museum of Science and Nature, and an 18-hole municipal golf course, as well as a rose garden, two lakes, and tennis courts. It's a favorite spot for in-line skating, jogging, bike-riding, and Sunday evening summer jazz concerts in the park's bandshell; the latter are reputedly the best summer deal in Denver. | Between 17th and 26th Aves., York St. and Colorado Blvd. | 303/964–2500 | Free | Daily.

Civic Center. Many of the city's cultural institutions, including the public library, the Denver Art Museum, and the state capitol are located on the perimeter of this extensive downtown park, containing an amphitheater and a lovely flower garden. | Bannock St. to Broadway south of Colfax Ave. and north of 14th Ave. | No phone | Free | Daily.

Denver Botanic Gardens. These beautifully landscaped gardens include the Boettcher Memorial Conservatory that contains nearly 900 species of tropical plants. | 1005 York St. | 303/331–4000 | $4.50 | Daily 9–5.

Red Rocks Park. Easter sunrise services and summer concerts are held in this magnificent 9,500-seat amphitheater off Route 26, between Interstate 70 exit 259 and U.S. 259. | 303/964–2500.

Washington Park. Southeast of the Cherry Park neighborhood, this large park is criss-crossed with hiking and biking trails and surrounded by historic residential neighborhoods. It's a favorite spot for soccer and volleyball games in the spring and summer. There's also a replica of George Washington's Mt. Vernon garden. | 701 S. Franklin St., between E. Louisiana and E. Virginia Aves | 303/964–2500 | Free | Daily.

SHOPPING

Larimer Square. A shopping district that grew up around Denver's first street, which was about all there was of the city back in 1858. The Victorian buildings of the area house shops and restaurants. | Larimer St., between 14th and 15th Sts. | 303/534–2367 | Free | Daily.

★ **16th Street Mall.** A beautifully landscaped pedestrian shopping mall downtown. Notable landmarks are the 34-ft-high, computer-controlled fountain and the cast-iron antique clock. | 16th St., between Market St. and Tremont Pl | No phone | Free | Daily.

The **Shops at Tabor Center.** Part of the 16th Street Mall, this state-of-the-art shopping center has close to 60 shops as well as restaurants, artisans, and pushcarts. It's named after Horace Tabor, Denver's silver king. | 16th St., between Larimer and Arapahoe Sts. | 303/572–6868 | Free | Daily.

The Tattered Cover is a must for all bibliophiles. It may be the best bookstore in the United States, not only for the near-endless selection of volumes (more than 400,000 on four stories at the Cherry Creek location and 300,000 in LoDo) and helpful, knowledgeable staff, but also for the incomparably refined atmosphere: over-stuffed armchairs, reading nooks, and afternoon reading and lectures. | 1st Ave. at Milwaukee St. | 303/322–7727 | 1628 16th St. | 303/436–1070.

Union Station. The 1914 Italian Romanesque building that was the Union Depot now houses shops, restaurants, and bars. Amtrak's California Zephyr stops here. The largest model railroad collection in the state is on the basement level. | 1701 Wynkoop St. | 303/534–1012 | Free | Station daily 6 AM–2 AM; model railroad last Fri. of each month.

SPECTATOR SPORTS

Denver is one of the few cities in the United States that has teams in all four major-league professional sports (hockey, basketball, football, and baseball).

Colorado Avalanche. Denver's professional hockey team plays at the state-of-the-art Pepsi Center in downtown Denver. The Avalanche is in the Northwest Division of the Western Conference of the National Hockey League (NHL). | 901 Auraria Pkwy. | 303/405–1100 | www.pepsicenter.com | Oct.–Apr.

Colorado Rockies. Baseball finally came to Denver with the arrival of the Rockies, a National League expansion team, in 1993. They play at Coors Field, which is just beyond the reenergized LoDo section of downtown Denver. | 2001 Blake St. | 303/762–5437 | www.coloradorockies.com | Apr.–Oct.

Denver Broncos. Denver's professional football franchise plays at Mile High Stadium, just west of downtown Denver. It's in the West Division of the National Football League (NFL). | 1900 Eliot St. | 303/433–7466 | www.denverbroncos.com | Sept.–Dec.

Denver Nuggets. Denver's professional basketball team, part of the Midwest Division of the National Basketball Association (NBA), plays in the state-of-the-art Pepsi Center in downtown Denver. | 901 Auraria Pkwy. | 303/405–1100 | www.pepsicenter.com | Oct.–Apr.

SIGHTSEEING TOURS/TOUR COMPANIES

Gray Line Denver. Guided bus tours of Denver as well as excursions to nearby places like Rocky Mountain National Park and Colorado Springs, are offered by this company. | Box 17646 | 303/289–2841 or 800/348–6877 | www.coloradograyline.com | $28–$70 | Office hrs daily 7–5; tour times vary.

OTHER POINTS OF INTEREST

Colorado's Ocean Journey. On the west side of the Platte River, across from Six Flags Elitch Gardens is the million-gallon aquarium that focuses on aquatic and animal life in two distinct areas, the Colorado River and Indonesia's Kampar River. In addition, you can visit Sea Otter Cove. Tickets offer a timed admission; buy them in advance if possible because lines can be long, but this carries an extra service charge. | 700 Water St. | 303/561–4450 | www.oceanjourney.org | $14.95 | Memorial Day–Labor Day, daily 9–6; Labor Day–Memorial Day, daily 10–6.

Sakura Square. The Japanese Cultural and Trade Center of Denver contains Asian restaurants, shops, gardens, and a Buddhist temple. | 19th St., between Lawrence and Larimer Sts. | 303/295–0305 | Free | Daily.

Six Flags Elitch Gardens. This large amusement park in downtown Denver, which was first opened in 1889, is one of the oldest in the U.S. It moved to its present location in 1995. More than 100 rides, shows, and attractions speak to almost everyone. At nearly 100 ft, Twister II is one of the highest wooden roller coasters in the country; the Ferris wheel is even taller and offers sensational views of downtown. Access to the Island Kingdom Water Park is included with admission price. | Speer Blvd. (I-25, exit 212A) | 303/595-4386 | www.sixflags.com/elitchgardens | $29.99 for unlimited access | Early June–late Aug., daily 10-10; late Apr.–May and late Aug.–Oct. reduced hours and days; closed Nov.–late Apr.

ON THE CALENDAR

JAN.: *National Western Livestock Show, Horse Show, and Rodeo.* During this two-week event at the National Western Complex and Coliseum, one of the largest in the West, you can catch a livestock competition, rodeos, and more. | 303/297–1166.

MAR.: Denver March Pow Wow. More than 70 tribes convene for dance competitions and celebtations of Native American traditions. | 303/934–8045.

JUNE: *Cherry Blossom Festival.* Colorful blossoms are everywhere at this two-day event in Sakura Square. Taiko drummers, martial artists, Japanese cultural performances, a food bazaar, Japanese craft booths, and bonsai and flower exhibits. | 303/295–0305.

JUNE–JULY: City Park Jazz. Considered by many the best free live music series in Denver, concerts are Sundays at 7 all summer long. | 303/964–2500.

JUNE–FEB.: *Greyhound Racing.* Features satellite "off-track" dog betting year-round. Mile High Greyhound Park is located 7 mi northeast of Denver at the junction of Interstate 270 and Vasquez Boulevard. | 303/288–1591.

Dining

INEXPENSIVE

Annie's Café. American/Casual. Housed in an old-fashioned drugstore east of downtown, with retro advertisements on the walls and classic 1950s music playing all day long. Burgers, Mexican specialties, and shakes are favorites here. Kids' menu. No smoking. | 4012 E. 8th Ave. | 303/355–8197 | No supper Sun. | $7–$13 | D, MC, V.

Bluebonnet Café and Lounge. Mexican. The fantastic jukebox sets an upbeat tone for margaritas, burritos, and green chile. Though out of the tourist loop, in a fairly seedy neighborhood southeast of downtown, crowds line up early. | 457 S. Broadway | 303/778–0147 | $5–$13 | MC, V.

Chipotle Mexican Grill. Mexican. South-of-the-border fast food in an airy loftlike space east of downtown. Open-air dining on a patio. | 745 Colorado Blvd., at 8th Ave. | 303/333–2121 | $7–$10 | MC, V.

Empress. Chinese. Cantonese preparations, with good seafood and dim sum in an elegant dining room decorated with Chinese art. | 2825 W. Alameda Ave. | 303/922–2822 | $9–$18 | AE, D, MC, V.

India's. Indian. Casual and intimate, in the Tarmarac Square Mall in southeast Denver. You'll find exceptional Indian cuisine; try the samosas and the lamb with spinach. | 3333 S. Tamarac Dr. | 303/755–4284 | No lunch Sun. | $9–$16 | AE, D, DC, MC, V.

McCormick's Fish House and Bar. Seafood. In the historic Oxford Hotel (on the National Register of Historic Places) in LoDo, this formal seafood restaurant, with silver chandeliers, dark oak paneling, and white-jacketed waiters, has a top-notch menu of exceptionally fresh fish. Bar. Kids' menu. Sunday brunch. | 1659 Wazee St. | 303/825–1107 | Closed Sun. | $10–$21 | AE, D, DC, MC, V.

Old Spaghetti Factory. Italian. This old-time family favorite is in an antique-filled vintage commercial building downtown that's full of antiques. Your best bet is one of the pastas.

Kids are drawn to the full-size replica trolley car. Kids' menu. | 1215 18th St., at Lawrence | 303/295–1864 | No lunch weekends | $6–$10 | AE, D, DC, MC, V.

Pasquini's Pizzeria. Pizza. This informal spot serves fresh, homemade pastas, pizzas, and calzones. Individual pizzas are the house specialty. The Italian bread here is fresh baked and great. | 1310 S. Broadway | 303/744–0917 | No lunch Sun. | $5–$13 | AE, D, MC, V.

Qdoba. Mexican. Vintage photographs of Mexico decorate this outlet of the local fast-food Mexican chain, which can be crowded during lunch. The burritos are giant; the poblano pesto burrito is the best of the lot. (The pesto's green comes from the chiles and cilantro.) | 550 Grant St., off of Speer Blvd. | 303/765–5878 | $5–$6 | MC, V.

Rocky Mountain Diner. American. This lively western saloon has a popular bar scene. Try the panfried chicken, but you might also consider the buffalo meat loaf or the rainbow trout fillet. There's a small sidewalk patio for alfresco dining. Kids' menu. | 800 18th St. | 303/293–8383 | $8–$24 | AE, D, DC, MC, V.

Wahoo's Fish Taco. Mexican. This simple *Taqueria* (taco stand) has burritos and soft tacos made with grilled or blackened fish of the day (or chicken, beef, or grilled vegetables) and served with black beans, rice, and salsa with plenty of cilantro. | 1521 Blake St. | 303/623–0263 | $3–$7 | MC, V.

Wazee Supper Club. Pizza. Denverites flock here for the jazz and the pizza, which is crisp yet gooey and bursting with flavor. | 1600 15th St. | 303/623–9518 | $4–$20 | AE, MC, V.

★ **Wynkoop Brewing Company.** American/Casual. Colorado's oldest brewpub, established in 1988, is downtown in trendy LoDo near Coors field. Try the shepherd's pie, buffalo meat loaf, or the Portobello mushroom sandwich, and shoot some pool upstairs after dessert. There's also an improvisational theater downstairs. The open-air patio has views of Coors Field and the Union Station. Kids' menu. | 1634 18th St., at Wynkoop St. | 303/297–2700 | $6–$16 | AE, D, DC, MC, V.

Zaidy's Deli. Delicatessen. Cherry Creek's New York–style deli offers both sit-down and take-out service. Signature homemade soups include matzoh ball and vegetable barley. Eat out front on a small open-air patio. Kids' menu. No smoking. | 121 Adams St. | 303/333–5336 | Breakfast also available; no dinner Mon., Tues. | $4–$12 | AE, MC, V.

MODERATE

Aubergine Café. Mediterranean. This creative menu of this tiny café draws on the cuisines of many different Mediterranean countries. Try specialties that come from not only Provence and Tuscany but also Morocco and Greece. Open-air dining on sidewalk patio. | 225 E. 7th Ave. | 303/832–4778 | Closed Mon. No lunch weekends | $17–$25 | AE, D, DC, MC, V.

Baby Doe's Matchless Mine. American. This large, comfortable restaurant west of downtown re-creates Leadville's Matchless Mine. An extensive collection of photographs and memorabilia is on display, and the views are fantastic. Known for pasta, seafood, steak. Kids' menu. Sunday brunch. | 2520 W. 23rd Ave. | 303/433–3386 | $15–$39 | AE, D, DC, MC, V.

Bistro Adde Brewster. Contemporary. This busy basement bistro in Cherry Creek is sleek and stylish. The menu is diverse, with heavy Swiss and Swedish influences. Try Wiener schnitzel, salmon salad, bistro burger, and Swedish gravlax. Open-air dining on a patio. No smoking. | 250 Steele St. | 303/388–1900 | Closed Sun. | $11–$35 | AE, DC, MC, V.

Café Brazil. Brazilian. In an outlying neighborhood known as the Highlands (just over the viaduct from LoDo) this is the spot to try *feijoada completa*, the Brazilian national dish made of black bean stew and smoked meats, accompanied with fried plantains. Try the sautéed shrimp and scallops in white wine, garlic, and coconut milk, or the grilled chicken breast in a sauce of ginger, raisins, shallots, and coconut milk. | 3611 Navajo St. | 303/480–1877 | Reservations essential | Closed Sun., Mon. No lunch | $14–$21 | No credit cards.

Coos Bay Bistro. Contemporary. Dried vines and stone archways fill this trendy restaurant next to the University of Denver. A creative menu offers tapas, seafood, and homemade pastas. | 2076 S. University Blvd. | 303/744–3591 | $10–$21 | AE, DC, MC, V.

Denver Chophouse and Brewery. Steak. Housed in the old Union Pacific Railroad warehouse, this restaurant and microbrewery is a clubby place with its dark paneling and exposed brick. Convenient to Coors Stadium, which is nearby. | 1735 19th St. | 303/296–0800 | $12–$25 | AE, DC, MC, V.

Highland's Garden Café. American. Housed in two Gay Nineties Victorians with hardwood floors, exposed brick walls, lovely murals, and extensive gardens, this restaurant offers a rotating menu emphasizing the freshest seafood, fish, lamb, and veal, not to mention fresh herbs from the garden. Make reservations at least one week in advance. | 3927 W. 32nd Ave. | 303/458–5920 | Closed Mon. | $18–$28 | Reservations essential | Closed Sun., Mon. No lunch | AE, MC, V.

Hugh's New American Bistro. Contemporary. The dining areas are decorated with the work of local artists and feature large windows overlooking South Pearl Street. Try the Argentine grass-fed beef, the roasted ostrich, or the wild Alaskan salmon. No smoking. | 1469 S. Pearl St. | 303/744–1940 | Closed Sun., Mon. | $19–$25 | AE, DC, MC, V.

Imperial Chinese. Chinese. Papier-mâché lions greet you at the entrance of this Szechuan stunner west of downtown. Try the scallion pancakes and sesame chicken or salmon with ginger, and leave room for the ginger ice cream. No smoking. | 431 S. Broadway | 303/698–2800 | No lunch Sun. | $9–$21 | AE, DC, MC, V.

Japon. Japanese. Steel fixtures give this busy restaurant an industrial look. Eat at the sushi bar, or order from the full menu. The soy sauce is house-made. No smoking. | 1028 S. Gaylord St. | 303/744–0330 | No lunch Sun. | $15–$30 | AE, D, MC, V.

★ **Le Central.** French. This affordable Provençal bistro is always busy. Mussels are a specialty, but also try the steak *au poivre*, salmon à la moutarde (in a mustard sauce), or Denver's best salade niçoise. Enclosed patio. Sunday brunch. No smoking. | 112 E. 8th Ave., corner Lincoln St. | 303/863–8094 | $12–$20 | AE, MC, V.

Mel's Bar and Grill. Contemporary. A pianist performs in this North Cherry Creek spot with a covered patio in front for open-air dining in summer and a wine list that's more extensive than you might expect. The food is simple, straightforward bistro cuisine. Try the goat-cheese salad with walnuts and dried cherries or the grilled pork tenderloin with achiote sauce. Entertainment nightly. | 235 Fillmore St. | 303/333–3979 | No lunch Sun. | $14–$30 | AE, D, DC, MC, V.

Normandy French Restaurant. Continental. This Victorian house decorated with period furnishings is a little stuffy, but folks come for consistently well-prepared classics, such as rack of lamb, filet mignon, châteaubriand. | 1515 Madison St. | 303/321–3311 | Closed Mon. No lunch weekends | $16–$35 | AE, D, DC, MC, V.

Starfish. Seafood. A reliable place in North Cherry Creek, east of downtown, with good fish dishes, creatively conceived. Try the Caesar salad with fried oysters, lobster bisque, or seared salmon. There's open-air dining on a patio. Pianist nightly. | 300 Fillmore St. | 303/333–1133 | Closed Sun. | $17–$33 | AE, D, DC, MC, V.

Trinity Grille. Seafood. This downtown favorite across from the Brown Palace Hotel is modeled after a traditional English men's club, with lots of dark wood and brass accents. Known for crab cakes, fresh seafood, bread pudding. A popular spot for a business lunch. | 1801 Broadway | 303/293–2288 | Closed Sun. No lunch Sat. | $15–$30 | AE, D, DC, MC, V.

Tuscany. Italian. Fresh flowers, a glowing fireplace, and frescoes adorn this peaceful and romantic dining room in the Loews Giorgio Hotel. One of the finest restaurants in Denver is known for pasta, seafood specials, steak. In good weather, dine outside on the cobblestone piazza. Pianist Friday–Sunday, harpist Sunday. Kids' menu. Sunday brunch. No smoking. | 4150 E. Mississippi Ave. | 303/782–9300 | Reservations essential Sun. | Breakfast also available | $14–$32 | AE, D, DC, MC, V.

Zenith. Southwestern. A cool high-tech look unusual among Denver restaurants sets the scene for creative southwestern fare like a smoked sweet corn soup with barbecued shrimp, and macadamia-crusted sea bass over pepper stir-fry. No smoking. | 815 17th St., between Champa and Stout Sts. | 303/293–2322 | Closed Sun. No lunch weekends | $14–$24 | AE, DC, MC, V.

EXPENSIVE

★ **Barolo Grill.** Italian. Dried flowers in brass urns, Tuscan dishes, and fresh flower arrangements decorate this upscale favorite. The house specialty is roast duckling in Barolo wine. Extensive wine list. | 3030 E. 6th Ave. | 303/393–1040 | Closed Sun. No lunch Mon. | $20–$30 | AE, D, DC, MC, V.

Brittany Hill. Continental. Antiques and fireplaces fill this hilltop Victorian, and wraparound windows offers lovely views of the city. Try the prime rib or the coconut shrimp. Kids' menu. Sunday brunch. | 9350 Grant St. | 303/451–5151 | $19–$33 | AE, D, DC, MC, V.

★ **The Fort.** Steak. This replica of historic Bent's Fort comes complete with flickering luminarias and a piñon bonfire in the courtyard. Buffalo meat and game are the specialties; try the elk with huckleberry sauce and tequila-marinated quail, or if you are more adventurous, consider the buffalo bone-marrow appetizer, jalapenos stuffed with peanut butter, or Rocky Mountain oysters. | U.S. 285 and Rte. 8 | 303/697–4771 | $18–$40 | AE, D, DC, MC, V.

The Palm Restaurant. Steak. On the ground level of the Westin Hotel in downtown Denver, this upscale steak chain serves up juicy and grand portions. Try the popular New York strip steak. | 1672 Lawrence St. | 303/825–7256 | No lunch weekends | $19–$35 | AE, DC, MC, V.

Papillon. Contemporary. This warm café has a varied menu with Asian and French influences. Try the lobster ravioli or the ahi tuna. Kids' menu. No smoking. | 250 Josephine St. | 303/333–7166 | $21–$32 | AE, DC, MC, V.

Strings. Contemporary. This light, airy restaurant is a place to see and be seen. The pastas are consistently good, and you should try some of the spicier choices. It's known for pan-roasted sea bass in a citrus-cashew crust and penne with chicken, mushrooms, and broccoli in a tomato-cream sauce. In the front, there's an open-air patio. | 1700 Humbolt St. | 303/831–7310 | No lunch Sun. | $18–$25 | AE, D, DC, MC, V.

Tante Louise. French. This longtime Denver favorite, 15 minutes east of downtown by car, resembles an intimate French country home. The preparations utilize many American ingredients but are classic French. A third of the offerings are low-fat. Try the Maine sea scallops served with caramelized foie gras butter or any of the superlative lamb specials. Kids' menu. | 4900 E. Colfax Ave., at Eudora St. | 303/355–4488 | Closed Sun. No lunch | $20–$32 | AE, D, DC, MC, V.

Tommy Tsunami's. Pan-Asian. This hip Larimer Square establishment has a happening singles scene and a sometimes deafening sound level. Try the grilled Hawaiian swordfish or the macadamia-crusted Chilean sea bass. Tables sprout on the sidewalk in summer. No smoking. | 1432 Market St. | 303/534–5050 | No lunch Sat., Sun. | $19–$31 | AE, D, DC, MC, V.

Wellshire Inn. Continental. An opulent restaurant in a Tudoresque former country club south of downtown. Try the marinated rack of Colorado lamb, spice-crusted New York steak, or one of the seasonal specials. Open-air dining on the golf course patio with a mountain view. Sunday brunch. No smoking. | 3333 S. Colorado Blvd. | 303/759–3333 | Breakfast also available weekdays | $20–$35 | AE, D, DC, MC, V.

VERY EXPENSIVE

The Broker. Continental. In the vault of the old Denver National Bank building, this fine restaurant has dark, cherry-wood furnishings. The vault's huge door is on display. Known for prime rib and fillet Wellington. Also, you receive a complimentary bowl of steamed gulf shrimp to begin your meal. | 821 17th St. | 303/292–5065 | No lunch weekends | $26–$49 | AE, D, DC, MC, V.

Buckhorn Exchange. American. Buffalo Bill was reportedly a regular at this 1893 Denver landmark with red-checked tablecloths, and rodeo photos, shotguns, and hunting trophies on the walls. Try one of the exotic game dishes, which are the house specialty—everything from buffalo and quail to alligator and rattlesnake. A roof garden is the place to sit in the summer. Live western music Wednesday–Saturday. | 1000 Osage St. | 303/534–9505 | No lunch Sat., Sun. | $22–$46 | AE, D, DC, MC, V.

Fresh Fish Company. Seafood. In the Tiffany Plaza Shopping Center, southeast of downtown, this family-friendly place serves straightforward preparations of marine fare flown in from all over. Kids especially like the 19 aquariums. Kids' menu. Sunday brunch. | 7800 E. Hampden Ave. | 303/740–9556 | No lunch Sat. | $19–$46 | AE, D, DC, MC, V.

Morton's of Chicago. Steak. The Denver outlet of the upscale chain across from Union Station has an elegant, dimly lit dining room and an adjacent lounge. Expense account holders and others who appreciate fine steaks flock here for the consistently good cuts of beef. | 1710 Wynkoop St. | 303/825–3353 | No lunch | $26–$40 | AE, DC, MC, V.

Palace Arms. Continental. The fanciest, most formal restaurant in Denver is in the Brown Palace Hotel. Try the rack of lamb, lobster, or buffalo. If you fancy wine, ask for the expert help of the sommelier. | 321 17th St. | 303/297–3111 | Jacket required | No lunch weekends | $29–$48 | AE, D, DC, MC, V.

Lodging

INEXPENSIVE

Drury Inn–Denver East. The rooms in this inexpensive chain motel, 12 mi from downtown Denver and 15 mi from Denver International Airport, are quiet and comfortable and have a desk with chair and an in-room coffee machine. Complimentary breakfast. In-room data ports, some microwaves, some refrigerators, cable TV. Indoor-outdoor pool. Hot tub. Gym. Laundry facilities, laundry service. Business services. Free parking. Pets allowed. | 4400 Peoria St. | 303/373–1983 or 800/378–7946 | fax 303/373–1983 | www.druryinn.com | 138 rooms | $70–$80 | AE, D, DC, MC, V.

La Quinta–Downtown. This economical chain motel with simply furnished yet comfortable rooms is on the northwest side of downtown Denver. Complimentary Continental breakfast. In-room data ports, cable TV. Pool. Business services. Free parking. Pets allowed. | 3500 Park Ave. W (I–25, exit 213) | 303/458–1222 or 800/687–6667 | fax 303/433–2246 | www.laquinta.com | 105 rooms | $70–$85 | AE, D, DC, MC, V.

Quality Inn West. A reasonably priced chain motel 13 mi west of downtown Denver on Tabor Lake in Wheat Ridge. Restaurant, bar. Room service, cable TV. Gym. Business services. Some pets allowed (fee). | 12100 W. 44th Ave., Wheat Ridge | 303/467–2400 or 800/228–5151 | fax 303/467–0198 | www.qualityinn.com | 108 rooms | $54–$79 | AE, D, DC, MC, V.

MODERATE

Best Western Executive. One of the closest properties to Denver International Airport, this chain motel is geared for business travelers. Restaurant, bar. In-room data ports, room service, cable TV, some in-room VCRs. Pool. Gym. Laundry facilities. Business services. Free parking. Some pets allowed (fee). | 4411 Peoria Way | 303/373–5730 or 800/848–4060 | fax 303/375–1157 | www.bestwestern.com | 186 rooms, 12 suites | $80–$85, $99 suites | AE, D, DC, MC, V.

Castle Marne Urban Inn. This 1889 historic stone mansion, furnished with Victorian antiques and reproductions, is a family-owned and -operated B&B, three blocks north of Cheesman Park. Complimentary breakfast. In-room data ports, some in-room hot tubs, TV in common area. Library. No kids under 10. Business services. Free parking. No smoking. | 1572 Race St. | 303/331–0621 or 800/926–2763 | fax 303/331–0623 | www.castlemarne.com | 10 rooms | $90–$235 | AE, D, DC, MC, V.

Four Points Hotel Denver Central. This mid-priced chain hotel is in east Denver, 17 mi from Denver International Airport. Restaurant, bar. Some microwaves, room service, cable TV, some in-room VCRs. Pool. Hot tub. Gym. Laundry facilities. Business services. Airport shuttle, free parking. | 3535 Quebec St. | 303/333–7711 or 888/625–5144 | fax 303/322–2262 | 185 rooms | $94–$109 | AE, D, DC, MC, V.

Haus Berlin. This landmarked redbrick Victorian town house near Capitol Hill has been turned into an upscale inn with all the amenities. All rooms have a work desk, some have fireplaces, and there is a nice garden out back to sit in. Complimentary breakfast. In-room data ports, some cable TV. | 1651 Emerson St. | 303/837–9527 or 800/659–0253 | fax 303/837–9527 | www.hausberlinbandb.com | 4 rooms, 1 suite | $100, $140 suite | AE, D, DC, MC, V.

La Quinta Airport–South. A chain hotel on the east side of Denver, just north of Aurora, about 15 mi from both the airport and downtown. Complimentary Continental breakfast. In-room data ports, microwaves, some refrigerators, cable TV. Pool. Laundry facilities. Business services. Airport shuttle, parking (fee). Some pets allowed. | 3975 Peoria Way (I–70, exit 281) | 303/371–5640 or 800/687–6667 | fax 303/371–7015 | www.laquinta.com | 112 rooms | $69–$89 | AE, D, DC, MC, V.

La Quinta Inn–Denver Cherry Creek. Moderately priced chain hotel next to many restaurants, and minutes away from Cherry Creek State Park. Complimentary Continental breakfast. In-room data ports, some refrigerators, cable TV. Outdoor pool. Laundry facilities,

KODAK'S TIPS FOR PHOTOGRAPHING PEOPLE

Friends' Faces
- Pose subjects informally to keep the mood relaxed
- Try to work in shady areas to avoid squints
- Let kids pick their own poses

Strangers' Faces
- In crowds, work from a distance with a telephoto lens
- Try posing cooperative subjects
- Stick with gentle lighting—it's most flattering to faces

Group Portraits
- Keep the mood informal
- Use soft, diffuse lighting
- Try using a panoramic camera

People at Work
- Capture destination-specific occupations
- Use tools for props
- Avoid flash if possible

Sports
- Fill the frame with action
- Include identifying background
- Use fast shutter speeds to stop action

Silly Pictures
- Look for or create light-hearted situations
- Don't be inhibited
- Try a funny prop

Parades and Ceremonies
- Stake out a shooting spot early
- Show distinctive costumes
- Isolate crowd reactions
- Be flexible: content first, technique second

From *Kodak Guide to Shooting Great Travel Pictures* © 2000 by Fodor's Travel Publications

laundry service. Business services. | 1975 S. Colorado Blvd. | 303/756–8886 or 800/531–5900 | fax 303/756–2711 | www.laquinta.com | 128 rooms | $69–$109 | AE, D, DC, MC, V.

Quality Inn and Suites. This northeast Denver chain hotel provides easy access to Interstate 70, 1 mi away, and the airport, 16 mi away. Restaurant, bar. In-room data ports, room service, cable TV. Outdoor pool. Hot tub. Gym. Laundry service. Business services. Airport shuttle, free parking. Pets allowed. | 4590 Quebec St. (I–70, exit 278) | 303/320–0260 or 800/228–5151 | fax 303/320–7595 | www.qualityinn.com | 164 rooms, 18 suites | $75–$85, $89–$135 suites | AE, D, DC, MC, V.

Quality Inn South. This chain hotel is 2 mi from the Denver Tech Center and 12 mi south of downtown. Bar, picnic area, complimentary Continental breakfast. In-room data ports, some refrigerators, cable TV. Pool. Hot tub, gym. Laundry facilities. Business services. Pets allowed (fee). | 6300 E. Hampden Ave., at I–25 | 303/758–2211 or or 800/228–5151 | fax 303/753–0156 | www.qualityinn.com | 185 rooms | $75–$120 | AE, D, DC, MC, V.

Stapleton Courtyard by Marriott. This chain hotel, near the former Denver airport on the northeast side of Denver, appeals to business travelers (and others), with large work desks and comfortable sitting areas in each room. Restaurant, bar. In-room data ports, some microwaves, some refrigerators, cable TV. Pool. Hot tub. Gym. Laundry facilities. Business services. Free parking. | 7415 E. 41st Ave. | 303/333–3303 or 800–321–2211 | fax 303/399–7356 | www.courtyard.com | 136 rooms, 10 suites | $49–$82, $95–$105 suites | AE, D, DC, MC, V.

Victoria Oaks Inn. This turn-of-the-20th-century mansion in the Wymann historic neighborhood, now a comfortable B&B, is 1 mi east of downtown Denver and decked to the nines with period furnishings. Complimentary Continental breakfast. In-room data ports, no TV in rooms, TV in common area. Laundry facilities. | 1575 Race St. | 303/355–1818 | fax 303/331–1095 | vicoaksinn@aol.com | 9 rooms (2 with shared bath) | $60–$95 | AE, D, DC, MC, V.

EXPENSIVE

Adagio. Suites are named for composers in this B&B in an attractive Victorian house in Capitol Hill. Rooms are comfortable and quiet, most with ceiling fans. Complimentary breakfast. No smoking, some in-room hot tubs, cable TV, in-room VCRs. Business services. | 1430 Race St. (I–25, exit Speer Blvd.) | 303/370–6911 or 800/533–3241 | www.adagiobb.com | 5 rooms, 2 suites | $95–$130, $150–$170 suites | AE, D, DC, MC, V.

Cambridge Club Hotel. This small, luxurious 1960s-era all-suite hotel is on a tree-lined street one block from the capitol. Restaurant, complimentary Continental breakfast. In-room data ports, microwaves, some refrigerators, room service, cable TV. Business services. Parking (fee). | 1560 Sherman St. | 303/831–1252 or 800/877–1252 | fax 303/831–4724 | 31 suites | $129–$139 | AE, D, DC, MC, V.

Capitol Hill Mansion. This historic 1891 mansion, with its original furnishings, is downtown, near the convention center, museums, and restaurants. Some rooms have fireplaces. Complimentary breakfast. No air-conditioning, in-room data ports, some in-room hot tubs, cable TV. Business services. No smoking. | 1207 Pennsylvania St. | 303/839–5221 or 800/839–9329 | fax 303/839–9046 | www.capitolhillmansion.com | 8 rooms, 3 suites | $95–$175, $145–$175 suites | AE, D, DC, MC, V.

Comfort Inn–Downtown. This chain hotel is downtown, within walking distance of Coors Field and many attractions. Bar, complimentary Continental breakfast. In-room data ports, room service, cable TV, some in-room VCRs. Barbershop, beauty salon. Business services. | 401 17th St. (I–25, exit Lincoln St.) | 303/296–0400 or 800/228–5150 | fax 303/297–0774 | www.comfortinn.com | 209 rooms, 20 suites | $85–$130, $150–$300 suites | AE, D, DC, MC, V.

Holiday Chalet. A B&B in an 1896 Victorian brownstone in the Wyman neighborhood north of Capitol Hill, a few blocks south of City Park. Complimentary Continental breakfast. Kitchenettes, some microwaves, in-room data ports, cable TV, in-room VCRs (and movies). Library. Pets allowed. No smoking. | 1820 E. Colfax Ave. | 303/321–9975 or 800/626–4497 | fax 303/377–6556 | www.bbonline.com/co/holiday/index.html | 10 suites | $94–$160 | AE, D, DC, MC, V.

Holiday Inn–Northglenn. This upscale chain motel is next to Interstate 25, about 10 mi north of downtown. Restaurant, bar. In-room data ports, cable TV. Pool. Hot tub. Gym. Business services. | 10 E. 120th Ave., Northglenn | 303/452–4100 or 800/465–4329 | fax 303/457–1741 | www.holiday-inn.com | 223 rooms, 12 suites | $89–$125, $150–$175 suites | AE, D, DC, MC, V.

Lost Valley. This working guest ranch in Sedalia, 27 mi south of Denver, has beautiful mountain views and an all-season roster of activities, including a fishing school. Each cabin is large and comfortable—even luxurious—and has a fireplace with wood delivered to your door daily. No air-conditioning, refrigerators, no room phones, no TV. Pool. Hot tubs. Tennis. Baby-sitting, children's programs (ages 3–18), playground. Laundry facilities. Business services. | 29555 Goose Creek Rd., Sedalia | 303/647–2311 | fax 303/647–2315 | www.ranchweb.com/lost | 24 1- to 3-bedroom cabins | $1,740 per person per wk | Closed Dec. 1–early Mar. | AP | No credit cards.

Marriott–Denver Tech Center. A large chain hotel, south of downtown, near the Denver Tech Center. 4 restaurants, bar. In-room data ports, refrigerators, room service, cable TV, some in-room VCRs. 2 pools (1 indoor). Barbershop, beauty salon, hot tub. Gym. Shops. Laundry service. Business services. Free parking. Pets allowed. | 4900 S. Syracuse St. | 303/779–1100 or 800/321–2211 | fax 303/740–2523 | www.marriott.com | 614 rooms, 12 suites | $87–$169, $260–$500 suites | AE, D, DC, MC, V.

Marriott–Southeast. Located immediately east of Interstate 25 in south Denver, this chain hotel has rooms with balconies and a luxury level. Restaurant, bar. In-room data ports, some refrigerators, cable TV. 2 pools (1 indoor). Barbershop, beauty salon, hot tub. Gym. Video games. Shops. Laundry facilities. Business services. Airport shuttle. Some pets allowed. | 6363 E. Hampden Ave. (I–25, exit Hampden Ave.) | 303/758–7000 or 800/321–2211 | fax 303/691–3418 | www.marriott.com | 280 rooms, 10 suites | $59–$154, $250–$450 suites | AE, D, DC, MC, V.

Merritt House. This 1889 mansion in the Swallow Hill Historic District was built for Colorado Senator Elmer Merritt. Now a B&B furnished in period Victorian style, the glow of its 81 chandeliers can light the way for you. Complimentary breakfast. Minibars, cable TV, some in-room hot tubs. | 941 E. 17th Ave. | 303/861–5230 or 877/861–9009 | fax 303/861–9009 | www.merritthouse.com | 10 rooms | $100–$145 | AE, D, MC, V.

★ **Queen Anne Inn.** This B&B is full of antiques and has a beautiful garden; some rooms have fireplaces. Located in east Denver five blocks southeast of the state capitol, these two side-by-side historic Victorians are within walking distance of downtown Denver. Complimentary breakfast. In-room data ports, some in-room hot tubs, some cable TV. Business services. No smoking. | 2147-51 Tremont Pl. | 303/296–6666 or 800/432–4667 | fax 303/296–2151 | www.queenannebnb.com | 14 rooms, 4 suites | $99–$165, $175 suites | AE, D, DC, MC, V.

Ramada Inn–Airport. A chain motel 5 mi from downtown Denver and 17 mi from Denver International Airport. Restaurant, bar. In-room data ports, some refrigerators, room service, cable TV. Pool. Gym. Laundry facilities. Business services. Airport shuttle, free parking. Pets allowed (deposit). | 3737 Quebec St. (I–70, exit 278) | 303/388–6161 or 888/298–2054 | fax 303/388–0426 | www.ramada.com | 148 rooms | $87–$145 | AE, D, DC, MC, V.

Residence Inn by Marriott–Downtown. In this all-suite motor hotel in downtown Denver, many rooms have fireplaces. Complimentary Continental breakfast. Kitchenettes, microwaves, refrigerators, cable TV, some in-room VCRs. Outdoor pool. Hot tub. Gym. Business services. Free parking. Pets allowed (fee). | 2777 Zuni St. (I–25, exit Speer Blvd.) | 303/458–5318 or 800/321–2211 | fax 303/458–5318 | www.residenceinn.com | 156 suites | $89–$155 suites | AE, D, DC, MC, V.

VERY EXPENSIVE

Adam's Mark. This large, upscale hotel is in the heart of downtown Denver's shopping district, just off the 16th Street Mall and within walking distance of the U.S. Mint and the Convention Center. Rooms are spacious and modern; there is a concierge level. Restaurants, bar (with entertainment). In-room data ports, some microwaves, room service, cable TV, some VCRs (with movies). Pool. Sauna. Gym. Laundry facilities, laundry service. Business services. Airport shuttle, parking (fee). | 1550 Court Pl. | 303/893–3333 | fax 303/626–2544 | www.adamsmark.com | 1,225 rooms, 92 suites, in 2 buildings | $175–$185, $250–$600 1–bedroom suites, $700–$1,200 2–bedroom suites | AE, D, DC, MC, V.

★ **Brown Palace.** This historic hotel, which opened in downtown Denver in 1892, was built to offer the kind of luxurious accommodations that could only be found "back east," and it's still the premier hotel in the city. The dramatic nine-story lobby is topped with a glorious stained-glass ceiling. Rooms are decorated with Victorian flair, using sophisticated wainscoting and Art Deco fixtures. Restaurants (*see* Palace Arms), bar (with entertainment). In-room data ports, some refrigerators, room service, cable TV, some in-room VCRs. Barbershop. Gym. Shops. Business services. | 321 17th St. (I–25, exit E. Colfax Ave.) | 303/297–3111 or 800/321–2599 (outside CO) or 800/228–2917 (CO) | fax 303/312–5900 | www.brown-palace.com | 237 rooms, 25 suites | $169–$279, $379–$479 suites | AE, D, DC, MC, V.

Burnsley All Suite Hotel. This all-suite boutique hotel is near the state capitol in a residential area. Since the hotel was originally an apartment building, all rooms have full kitchens. Restaurant, bar. Kitchenettes, microwaves, room service, cable TV. Pool. Business services. Some pets allowed (fee). | 1000 Grant St. (I–25, exit 6th St.) | 303/830–1000, 800/231–3915 outside CO | fax 303/830–7676 | www.burnsley.com | 82 suites | $159–$189 | AE, DC, MC, V.

Doubletree Denver. This large upscale chain hotel is across from the former Stapleton Airport, between downtown Denver and Denver International Airport. Some rooms have views of the Rocky Mountains. Restaurant, bar. In-room data ports, some refrigerators, room service, cable TV, some in-room VCRs. Pool. Hot tub. Gym. Business services. Airport shuttle, free parking. Pets allowed. | 3203 Quebec St. | 303/321–3333 | fax 303/329–5233 | www.doubletree.com | 557 rooms, 6 suites | $169, $350–$500 suites | AE, D, DC, MC, V.

Embassy Suites–Denver Southeast. This all-suite hotel is north of the Denver Tech Center and near shopping malls and movie theaters, 10 mi south of downtown Denver. Restaurant, bar, complimentary breakfast. In-room data ports, minibars, microwaves, refrigerators, cable TV. Pool. Hot tub. Gym. Laundry service. Business services. | 7525 E. Hampden Ave. (I–25, exit 201) | 303/696–6644 or 800/362–2779 | fax 303/337–6202 | www.embassy-suites.com | 206 suites | $180–$200 | AE, D, DC, MC, V.

Holtze Hotel. In the renovated 1906 American Bank Building, this hotel has large, modern rooms in the heart of Denver. Complimentary van service to restaurants, shops, and sporting events within 3 mi is a plus for those without cars. Complimentary Continental breakfast. In-room data ports, some kitchenettes, some microwaves, refrigerators, cable TV. Steam room. Health club. Laundry service. Business services. | 818 17th St. | 303/607–9000 or 888/446–5893 | fax 303/607–0101 | www.holtzedenver.com | 244 rooms | $159–$299 | AE, D, DC, MC, V.

Hotel Monaco. In the completely renovated 1917 Railway Exchange Building in downtown Denver, this upscale and elegant boutique hotel offers such extra amenities as in-room fax machines and pet treats (if you are traveling with Rover). Each evening there is a wine and cheese reception. Restaurant, bar. In-room data ports, minibars, some in-room hot tubs, cable TV. Beauty salon, spa. Gym. Laundry service. Business services. Pets allowed. | 1717 Champa St. | 303/296–1717 or 800/397–5380 | fax 303/296–1818 | www.monaco-denver.com | 189 rooms | $185–$990 | AE, D, DC, MC, V.

Hyatt Regency–Denver. This full-service luxury high-rise with panoramic views from the higher floors is on the south edge of downtown Denver, an easy walk to the state capitol and the U.S. Mint. Restaurant, bar. In-room data ports, minibars, some refrigerators, cable TV, some in-room VCRs. Pool. Tennis. Gym. Baby-sitting. Laundry service. Business services. Airport shuttle, parking (fee). | 1750 Welton St. | 303/295–1234 or 800/633–7313 | fax 303/292–2472 | www.hyatt.com | 486 rooms, 25 suites | $165–$195, $350–$1,500 1–bedroom suites, $525–$2,500 2–bedroom suites | AE, D, DC, MC, V.

Hyatt Regency–Tech Center. This large modern chain hotel is in the Denver Tech Center, 10 mi south of downtown. Restaurant, bar. In-room data ports, some microwaves, refrigerators, cable TV, some in-room VCRs (and movies). Pool. Hot tub. Gym. Business services. Airport shuttle. | 7800 Tufts Ave. | 303/779–1234 or 800/633–7313 | fax 303/850–7164 | www.hyatt.com | 438 rooms, 12 suites | $195–$220, $350–$1,500 suites | AE, D, DC, MC, V.

★ **LoDo Inn.** Luxury B&B in Lower Downtown. Some rooms have balconies, and some of the rooms have sports themes. Hotel-style amenities keep business travelers flocking here. Restaurant, complimentary Continental breakfast. In-room data ports, cable TV, in-room VCRs (and movies). Business services. No smoking. | 1612 Wazee St. | 303/572–3300 | fax 303/623–0773 | www.lodoinn.com | 14 rooms | $129–$249 | AE, D, MC, V.

★ **Loews Giorgio.** This 12-story luxury hotel is modern on the outside but has an unexpected Italian Baroque interior. Restaurant (see Tuscany), bar. Minibars, some refrigerators, cable TV, some in-room VCRs (and movies). Gym. Library. Business services. Free parking. Some pets allowed. | 4150 E. Mississippi Ave. | 303/782–9300 or 800/235–6397 | fax 303/758–6542 | www.loewshotels.com | 183 rooms, 19 suites | $199–$249, $259–$1,000 suites | AE, D, DC, MC, V.

Lumber Baron. Lumber magnate John Mouat built this romantic and beautifully restored inn as his family home in 1890. Each room is furnished with antiques and has the original, restored woodwork. The inn is known for its regular murder-mystery dinners. Complimentary breakfast. Some in-room VCRs (and movies). Business services. No smoking. | 2555 W. 37th Ave. | 303/477–8205 | fax 303/477–0269 | www.lumberbaron.com | 5 rooms | $125–$210 | AE, D, MC, V.

Marriott–City Center. A large chain hotel in downtown Denver is a block from the 16th Street Mall and 1.5 mi from Coors Field. Restaurant, bar. In-room data ports, some refrigerators, room service, cable TV, some in-room VCRs. Pool. Hot tub. Gym. Shops. Business services. Some pets allowed. | 1701 California St. | 303/297–1300 or 800/321–2211 | fax 303/298–7474 | www.marriott.com | 615 rooms, 20 suites | $169–$179, $550–$680 suites | AE, D, DC, MC, V.

★ **Oxford.** This LoDo hotel, now on the National Register of Historic Places, is right next to Union Station. The rooms are uniquely furnished with French and English period antiques. Restaurant, bar. In-room data ports, minibars, room service, cable TV, some in-room VCRs. Barbershop, beauty salon, hot tub. Gym. Business services. Parking (fee). | 1600 17th St., at Wazee | 303/628–5400, 800/228–5838 outside CO | fax 303/628–5413 | 71 rooms, 9 suites | $125–$179, $149–$359 suites | AE, D, DC, MC, V.

Radisson Stapleton Plaza Hotel and Fitness Center. Glass elevators speed you to your room through the atrium of this modern, 11-story upscale hotel. All rooms have balconies. Restaurant, bars. In-room data ports, cable TV. Pool. Hot tub. Gym. Shops. Business services. Airport shuttle. | 3333 Quebec St. | 303/321–3500 or 800/333–3333 | fax 303/322–7343 | www.radisson.com | 296 rooms, 4 suites | $125–$159, $205–$395 suites | AE, D, DC, MC, V.

Renaissance Denver. An immense atrium dominates this 12-story upscale hotel, which is 20 minutes from Denver International Airport and 15 minutes away from most city attractions. Restaurant, bar. In-room data ports, refrigerators, room service, cable TV. 2 pools (1 indoor). 2 hot tubs (1 indoor). Gym. Business services. | 3801 Quebec St. | 303/399–7500 or 800/228–9290 | fax 303/321–1966 | www.renaissancehotels.com | 388 rooms, 12 suites | $155–$165, $225–$600 suites | AE, D, DC, MC, V.

The Teatro. This hotel, once the 1911 Tram Tower for the Tri-system Railway, has a theater motif. Costumes and theater props decorate the hallways, and theater photos are on the walls in the elegant rooms. Extra amenities include down pillows and comforters, CD players, terry-cloth robes, and marble baths. Some rooms have porcelain soaking tubs. Next to the Denver Performing Arts Complex. 2 restaurants, bar. In-room data ports, refrigerator, cable TV. Gym. Laundry service. | 1100 14th St. | 303/228–1113 | fax 303/228–1101 | 116 rooms | $195–$245 | AE, D, DC, MC, V.

The Warwick. This stylish hotel on the east side of downtown is three blocks northeast of the state capitol. The large rooms are furnished with antique reproductions. Restaurant, bar, complimentary Continental breakfast. In-room data ports, some microwaves, some refrigerators, room service, cable TV. Pool. Business services. Airport shuttle, parking (fee). Some pets allowed. | 1776 Grant St. | 303/861–2000 or 800/525–2888 | fax 303/832–0320 | www.warwickhotels.com | 220 rooms, 49 suites | $165–$175, $200–$800 suites | AE, D, DC, MC, V.

★ **Westin Tabor Center.** This large, sleek high-rise hotel downtown is next to the 16th Street Mall. Restaurant, bar. In-room data ports, minibars, refrigerators, room service, cable TV, some in-room VCRs. Indoor-outdoor pool. Hot tub. Gym. Shops. Business services. Some pets allowed. | 1672 Lawrence St. | 303/572–9100 or 800/325–3589 | fax 303/572–7288 | www.westin.com | 417 rooms, 13 suites | $222–$237, $390–$1285 suites | AE, D, DC, MC, V.

DILLON

MAP 6, E4

(Nearby towns also listed: Breckenridge, Copper Mountain, Frisco, Georgetown, Keystone, Leadville)

When Dillon Lake was created in the early 1960s to provide water for the greater Denver area, the old town of Dillon was moved to its present location and given a face-lift. Today, the town (population 739) is a popular resort just beyond the point where Interstate 70 crosses the Continental Divide. Locals visit the outlets in nearby Silverthorne.

Information: Summit County Chamber of Commerce | Box 214, Frisco 80435 | 800/530–3099 | www.summitchamber.org.

Attractions

Lake Dillon. This popular lake in White River National Forest offers 3,300 acres of fishing, boating, rafting, hiking, picnicking, and camping. | U.S. 6, ½ mi south of Dillon | 970/468–5400 | Free | Daily.

Prime Outlets at Silverthorne. Over 70 outlet stores 2 mi north of Dillon. | 145 Stevens Way (I–70, exit 205), Silverthorne | 970/468–9440 | fax 970/468–2936 | Free | Mon.–Sat. 10–8, Sun. 10–6.

ON THE CALENDAR

JUNE–JULY: *Nature Nights.* Weekly programs dedicated to nature and culture in the Lake Dillon Ampitheatre. Wildlife exhibits, dancers, performers, storytellers, and more | 970/262–3403.

JULY: *Mountain Community Fair.* Arts-and-crafts exhibits, a rodeo, and plenty of good food and entertainment for all ages. Held in Blue River Park in Silverthorne during the second weekend in July. | 970/513–8081.

Dining

Blue Moon Bakery. Delicatessen. You can get excellent bagels, deli sandwiches, and other light fare here. Located in the Summit Plaza Shopping Center. | 253 Summit Place Shopping Center, Silverthorne | 970/468–1472 | Breakfast also available; no dinner | $1–$6 | MC, V.

Dillon Dam Brewery. American/Casual. One of the house specialties is the Chicken Pilsner, a chicken breast that is breaded and sautéed, covered in a light Portobello mushroom cream sauce, and served over rice. | 100 Little Dam Rd. | 970/262–7777 | $6–$19 | AE, D, DC, MC, V.

Historic Mint Steakhouse. American. Once a bar and brothel, this 1862 place is full of antique charm. But now you cook your own meat or fish on lava rocks, though if you aren't in the mood you can leave the cooking to the chef. There's also a salad bar. | 347 Blue River Pkwy., Silverthorne | 970/468–5247 | No lunch | $10–$26 | MC, V.

Lodging

Best Western Ptarmigan Lodge. This chain motel on the west side of town overlooks Lake Dillon. Complimentary Continental breakfast. No air-conditioning, some kitchenettes, some microwaves, cable TV. Hot tub, sauna. Boating. Business services. Pets allowed (fee). | 652 Lake Dillon Dr. | 970/468–2341 or 800/842–5939 | fax 970/468–6465 | ptarmigan-lodge@colorado.net | 69 rooms | $110–$140 | AE, D, DC, MC, V.

Home and Hearth. B&B in a private home with five simply furnished bedrooms. All share three baths and three common areas. The two bunk-bed rooms are ideal for families with kids. Complimentary breakfast. No TVs in rooms, TV in common area. Outdoor hot tub. Video games. | 1518 Rainbow Dr. | 970/468–5541 or 800/753–4386 | fax 970/262–6242 | www.colorado-bnb.com/hhearth | 5 rooms | $30–$75 | No credit cards.

The Lodge at Carolina in the Pines. At over 9,000 ft, this is the place for mountain seclusion. The lodge is within walking distance of the Dam Brewery and some of Dillon's factory outlets. Complimentary breakfast. In-room data ports, cable TV, in-room VCRs. Outdoor hot tub, sauna. Gym. No smoking. | 64 E. Anemone Trail | 970/262–7500 | fax 970/262–9377 | www.carolinainthepines.com | 10 rooms | $150–$190 | MC, V.

Silverthorne Days Inn. This chain motel is just off I–70. Some rooms have fireplaces. Complimentary Continental breakfast. Some kitchenettes, some microwaves, cable TV. Wading pool. Hot tub, sauna. Laundry facilities. Business services. Pets allowed (fee). | 580 Silverthorne La., Silverthorne | 970/468–8661 | fax 970/468–1421 | www.daysinn.com | 73 rooms | $139–$229 | AE, D, DC, MC, V.

Western Skies. Twenty-two acres along the Snake River provides a tranquil retreat. Some rooms and cabins have fireplaces; one cabin has a private outdoor hot tub. Complimentary breakfast. Some kitchenettes, some microwaves, some refrigerators, cable TV. Outdoor hot tub. No smoking. | 5040 Montezuma Rd. | 970/468–9445 | fax 970/262–6466 | www.colorado-bnb.com/westernskies | 4 rooms, 3 cabins | $115–$190 | AE, D, MC, V.

DINOSAUR

MAP 6, A3

(Nearby towns also listed: Craig, Meeker)

Dinosaur, a town of 350, offers little more than pit stops and independent motels. However, it is the Colorado gateway to Dinosaur National Monument and internationally known for the world-class hang-gliding at nearby Cliff Ridge. The town even hosts an annual international competition. Rangely, 19 mi south with 2,700 residents, has more to offer in the way of places to stay and eat.

Information: **Dinosaur Area Chamber of Commerce** | Box 202, Dinosaur, 81610 | 800/864–4405 | www.colorado-go-west.com.

Attractions

Dinosaur National Monument. Dinosaurs roamed this region 150 million years ago; today, many fossilized remains show what life was like back then. The monument covers 325 square mi and lies partially in Colorado and partially in Utah. In addition to its fascinating fossil displays, the monument provides hiking, picnicking, camping, fishing, river rafting, and other outdoor activities. The park headquarters lies 1 mi east of Dinosaur; this is the entrance to the monument's scenic canyon area, where there are no fossils. The fossil quarry is 20 mi west of Dinosaur and includes exhibits, a paleontology lab, and fossil exhibits. |

4545 E. U.S. 40 | 970/374–3000 | fax 435/789–2270 | www.nps.gov/dino | $10 per vehicle | Memorial Day–Labor Day, daily 8–7; Labor Day–Memorial Day, daily 8–4:30.

Dining

B&B Family Restaurant. American/Casual. The only place in town with Brontosaurus burgers and Stegosaurus sirloins. Kids' menu. | 123 E. Brontosaurus Blvd. | 970/374–2744 | $5–$14 | MC, V.

Cowboy Corral. American/Casual. Chicken-fried steaks and hamburgers and the best choices at this restaurant in Rangely, 19 mi from Dinosaur. Salad bar. Kids' menu. | 202 W. Main St., Rangely | 970/675–8986 | $4–$13 | AE, D, MC, V.

Miner's Café. Mexican. Best known for its Mexican dishes, this small café also has some American dishes on its menu. Kids' menu. | 420 E. Brontosaurus Blvd. | 970/374–2020 | Closed Sun. | $4–$11 | AE, MC, V.

Lodging

Budget Host. This small chain motel is 18 mi from Dinosaur in Rangely. Microwaves, refrigerators, cable TV. Laundry facilities. | 117 S. Grand, Rangely | 970/675–8461 or 800/283–4678 | fax 970/675–8463 | 29 rooms | $36–$49 | AE, D, MC, V.

Four Queens Motel. Rooms are small in this spartan motel 18 mi from Dinosaur. Refrigerators, cable TV. Laundry facilities. Pets allowed. | 206 E. Main, Rangely | 970/675–5035 | fax 970/675–5037 | 32 rooms | $40–$48 | AE, D, DC, MC, V.

Hi Vu Motel. This low-priced family motel is in downtown Dinosaur and has a picnic barbecue area. No room phones, cable TV. Pets allowed. | 122 E. Brontosaurus Blvd. | 970/374–2267 or 800/374–5332 | fax 970/374–2249 | www.cmn.net/~whtrvn | 8 rooms | $28–$36 | AE, MC, V.

DOLORES

MAP 6, B8

(Nearby towns also listed: Cortez, Mesa Verde National Park)

Dolores is rich in railroad history. The Dolores River valley's first colonial settlement came in 1877 at Big Bend, just a stone's throw from where the town is located today. For 60 years, the large Victorian-style structure on Railroad Avenue housed the train depot that was a major Rio Grande Southern station between Durango and Ridgway. The Galloping Goose, a restored passenger railcar sits proudly in front of the depot which is now the Rio Grande Southern Railroad Museum.

Another claim to fame for the small town of 1,051 residents, located near the Four Corners area of Colorado, is water. The Dolores River gave the town its name and continues to be a vital water supply offering many recreational opportunities. Dolores is also home to McPhee Reservoir, the second-largest lake in Colorado. You can enjoy boating, waterskiing, and fishing, not to mention camping, hunting, rafting, and winter sports.

Information: **Dolores Chamber of Commerce** | Box 602, Dolores, 81323 | 800/807–4712 | www.doloreschamber.com.

Attractions

★ **Anasazi Heritage Center.** Discover the Anasazi heritage through a hands-on journey that lets you tour a replica Anasazi dwelling, grind corn, weave on a loom, and touch real artifacts. | 27501 Hwy. 184 | 970/882–4811 | www.co.blm.gov:80/ahc/hmepge.htm | $3 | Mar.–Oct., daily 9–5; Nov.–Feb., daily 9–4.

Lowry Pueblo Ruins. An Anasazi pueblo built around 1075, with several kivas, about 20 mi northwest of Dolores (30 mi northwest of Cortez) near Pleasant View. | Rte. CC | 970/247–4874 | Free | Daily 8–sunset.

McPhee Reservoir. The second-largest lake in Colorado is home to some of the state's best boating, waterskiing, and fishing—minus the crowds. To date, McPhee Reservoir has been stocked with 4½ million fish. The Marina is located 8 mi north of Dolores. | Hwy. 184 | 970/882–7296 | Free | Daily 7–9; closed winter.

Rio Grande Southern Railroad Museum. You don't have to be a train buff to enjoy a stroll through the Galloping Goose railcar and museum situated next to the spot where the railroad once ran. | Railroad Ave. & 5th St. | 970/882–7082 | Free | Tues.–Sat. 12:30–4:30.

ON THE CALENDAR

AUG.: *Escalante Days*. A parade down Main Street kicks off this full day of fun. Other activities include a pancake breakfast, bike race, fireman's barbecue, arts-and-crafts booths, and live music in Flanders Park. | 970/882–4018.

Dining

German Stone Oven Restaurant Bakery. German. This restaurant and bakery serves authentic German fare straight from Munich. Favorites include Wiener schnitzel and sauerbraten as well as a few American dishes like sirloin steak and pork chops, and some vegetarian dishes. You can also dine on the garden patio. The room is decorated with antiques and collectibles from Germany, France, and Italy. Not recommended for children. | 811 Railroad Ave. | 970/882–7033 | Closed Tues., Wed. and Jan.–Apr. | $6–$16 | No credit cards.

Line Camp Chuckwagon Supper and Western Stage Show. Barbecue. The menu features barbecue beef, campfire baked potatoes, dryland pinto beans, sourdough biscuits with honey, and spicy applesauce cake. The evening is capped off with live entertainment by "The Trail-hands," who put on a family-friendly comedy and music show. Located 9 mi east of Dolores. | 22374 Hwy. 145 | 970/882–4158 | Reservations essential | Closed Labor Day–Memorial Day and every Mon. No lunch | $7–$14 | MC, V.

The Naked Moose Restaurant. American. Feast on an array of steaks including the Macho Moose and the Lady Moose. This casual, family-friendly restaurant also serves up chicken, pasta, and seafood, and prime rib dinners on Friday and Saturday nights. | 104 Second St. S | 970/882–7540 | No lunch | $5–$22 | MC, V.

Lodging

Dolores Mountain Inn. Located right in the heart of downtown Dolores, this mountain inn, which consists of three separate buildings, offers comfortable accommodations at an affordable price. | 14 rooms, 16 suites. Cable TV, some kitchenettes. Pets allowed (fee). No smoking. | 701 Railroad Ave. | 970/882–7203 or 800/842–8113 | fax 970/882–7011 | www.dminn.com | $68 | AE, D, MC, V.

The Lodge. A modern log building nestled away on 30 acres with rustic charm but all the amenities; rooms are in the main lodge or the separate bunkhouse (these rooms sleep four). Steak dinners are offered Wednesday through Saturday and a six-course dinner is offered on Sunday (reservations required). | 17 rooms, 1 suite. Complimentary breakfast. No TV in rooms, TV in common area. Laundry facilities. No smoking. | 19581 Rd. 31 (Norwood/Groundhog Rd.) | 970/882–3333 or 877/882–3335 | fax 970/882–3334 | www.lodgecolorado.com | $70–$90 | Closed Feb. | MC, V.

DURANGO

MAP 6, C8

(Nearby towns also listed: Cortez, Pagosa Springs, Silverton)

Durango became a town more than one hundred years ago when the Denver & Rio Grande Railroad pushed its tracks across the neighboring San Juan Mountains. When nearby Animus City refused to donate land for a railroad depot, General William Palmer (the president of the Denver & Rio Grande) established a brand-new town; within 10 years, Durango had absorbed its main rival, becoming the region's main municipality and the gateway to the American Southwest. Today, it's a nice-size town of almost 15,000 people. Nestled between the San Juan National Forest and the Southern Ute Indian Reservation, Durango offers unparalleled sightseeing, hunting in season, and service by one of America's oldest narrow-gauge railroads.

Information: **Durango Area Chamber Resort Association** | 111 S. Camino Del Rio, Durango 81301 | 970/247–0312 or 800/GO–DURANGO | durango.org.

Attractions

Diamond Circle Theatre. Turn-of-the-20th-century vaudeville and melodrama performances are held here, in the Strater Hotel. | 699 Main Ave. | 970/247–4431 or 970/247–3400 | $17 | June–Sept., Mon.–Sat. 8 PM.

Durango Arts Center. The gallery's exhibits rotate monthly and feature regional and national artists. Also home to a children's museum, repertory theater company, and the local arts council. | 802 E. Second Ave. | 970/259–2606 | fax 970/259–6571 | www.durangoarts.org | Free | Tues.–Sat. 10–5.

Durango and Silverton Narrow Gauge Railroad. This train has been in service since 1882 and makes daily 3½-hour runs between Silverton and Durango along a spectacularly scenic mountain route. Advance reservations required. | 479 Main Ave. | 970/247–2733 | $53 round-trip | Mid-May–Oct., daily; call for winter schedule.

Purgatory Resort. The most prominent feature of this popular ski resort in the San Juan National Forest is the stepped terrain, with lots of bumps and dips to keep skiers on their guard. The clientele here runs the gamut from families to college kids on spring break, but it is definitely not an upscale resort. Available at the ski area are 1 quad, 3 triple, 5 double chairlifts, 70 runs (the longest is 2 mi), and a vertical drop of 2,029 ft. Rental equipment, patrols, five restaurants and five bars are also included. The resort offers summer activities such as mountain biking, an alpine slide, and various festivals. | U.S. 550, 25 mi north of Durango | 970/247–9000 or 800/525–0892 | Year-round; ski season, late Nov.–early Apr.

San Juan National Forest. Several peaks in this almost-2-million-acre wilderness exceed 14,000 ft. Activities include hiking, boating, white-water rafting, biking, camping, and four-wheel driving. The visitor center is in Durango, the forest entrance 13 mi north of Durango on U.S. 550. | 15 Burnett Court | 970/247–4874 | www.fs.fed.us/sanjuan | Free | Daily.

Southern Ute Indian Cultural Museum. An historical museum that exhibits Ute artifacts, clothing, tools, and archival photos located 23 mi southeast of Durango via U.S. 160 and Route 172. | 14826 Hwy. 172, Ignacio | 970/563–9583 | fax 970/563–4641 | $1 | Mid-May–mid-Oct., weekdays 10–6, weekends 10–3; mid-Oct.–mid-May, Tues.–Fri. 10–5:30.

ON THE CALENDAR

JAN.: *Snowdown Winter Carnival.* A parade, musical follies, and good food the last week in January. | 970/382–3737 or 800/525–8855.

MAY: *Iron Horse Bicycle Classic.* An annual Memorial Day bicycle race that pits cyclists against the Durango and Silverton narrow-gauge railroad train. | 970/259–4621.

JULY: *Durango Fiesta Days.* Annual festival that started in 1935, with a barbecue, street dance, pie auction, rodeos, and a parade. At the La Plata County Fair Grounds | 970/247–8835.

OCT.: *Durango Cowboy Gathering.* A rodeo, western art exhibitions, cowboy poetry, storytelling, and a dance the first weekend in October. | 970/259–2165.

Dining

Ariano's. Italian. This popular restaurant occupies a softly lit room hung with local art. No smoking. | 150 E. College Dr. (6th St.) | 970/247–8146 | No lunch | $10–$26 | AE, MC, V.

Carver's Brewing Company. Southwestern. This local microbrewery has a coffeehouse-bakery up front and a hopping sports bar in the back, with a large patio. There are about eight original beers on tap at any given time. Try the fajitas or the homemade bread bowls filled with soup or salad. Open-air dining with live music on Thursday and Saturday. Kids' menu. | 1022 Main Ave. | 970/259–2545 | Breakfast also available | $5–$11 | AE, MC, V.

Cyprus Café. Mediterranean. In an old Victorian with a patio and private garden in the heart of downtown Durango. The menu offers a selection of lamb, chicken, vegetarian, and seafood dishes. No smoking. | 725 E. 2nd St. | 970/385–6884 | $6–$15 | AE, D, MC, V.

Durango Diner. American/Casual. Enjoy sandwiches and burgers in a casual spot frequented by locals. Breakfast is served all day. | 957 Main Ave. | 970/247–9889 | $2–$6 | No credit cards.

Edgewater Grill. American. In the Doubletree Inn on the banks of the Animas River. Breakfast and lunch fare are served on the patio and more elaborate dinners in the dining room. Try the crab cakes, the salmon, or the T-bone steak. Sunday brunch. | 501 Camino del Rio | 970/259–6580 | $8–$24 | AE, D, MC, V.

Farquarhts. American/Casual. The eclectic menu has something for everyone. Enjoy the baked, soft tortilla enchilada, or the pizza. | 725 Main Ave. | 970/247–5440 | $8–$11 | AE, D, MC, V.

Francisco's. Mexican. Traditional Mexican atmosphere enlivens this large, family-owned restaurant. The bar is a good spot for margaritas and microbrews. Best bets: the combination plate with beef enchiladas, a beef taco, and green chile, or the chicken Francisco. Kids' menu. Sunday brunch. | 619 Main Ave. | 970/247–4098 | $8–$20 | AE, D, DC, MC, V.

Gazpacho. Mexican. A lively crowd gathers for the sopaipillas (deep-fried dough), steak fajitas, and margaritas. | 431 E. Second Ave. | 970/259–9494 | $6–$11 | MC, V.

Griego's. Mexican. Drive-in restaurant in an old A&W with sweat-producing chile. | 2603 N. Main Ave. | 970/259–3558 | $2–$7 | No credit cards.

Henry's at the Strater Hotel. Contemporary. Utilizes the historic hotel dining room. Try the pepper steak Herbert, pepper mango chutney sauce over a pan-seared fillet of beef, topped with cognac. Hosts an elegant Sunday brunch buffet. | 699 Main Ave. | 970/247–4431 | www.strater.com | $10–$24 | AE, D, DC, MC, V.

Lori's Family Dining. American. Comfortable and homey, this downtown diner's fresh-baked daily specials draw a large crowd. Salad bar. Kids' menu. | 2653 Main Ave. | 970/247–1224 | Breakfast also available | $5–$14 | MC, V.

Olde Tymer's Café. American. Locals flock to this former drugstore, which still has the feel of days gone by. The tin ceiling, artifacts, and photos that cover the walls combine to give it the appearance of a 1920s dance hall. The burgers are a hit. | 1000 Main Ave. | 970/259–2990 | $6–$9 | AE, MC, V.

Ore House. Steak. The aroma of beef fills the air. Order one of the enormous slabs of aged Angus that are cut daily. | 1022 Main Ave. | 970/247–5707 | $15–$35 | AE, D, DC, MC, V.

Red Snapper. Seafood. It takes more than 200 gallons of saltwater to fill the aquariums in this lively restaurant housed in one of the town's older buildings. On the menu: oysters Durango, with jack cheese and salsa. Salad bar. Kids' menu. No smoking. | 144 E. 9th St. | 970/259–3417 | No lunch | $9–$38 | AE, D, MC, V.

★ **Sow's Ear.** Steak. You'll get great beef at the best steak house in the Durango area, in the Silver Pick Resort at Purgatory 24 mi north of Durango. Once you take in the dramatic mountain views, try the jalapeño-cheese rolls. Known for blackened filet mignon and the "hodgeebaba" (an 18-ounce rib eye smothered in sautéed mushrooms and onions), but the menu also includes a range of salads and pastas. | 48475 U.S. 550, Purgatory | 970/247–3527 | No lunch | $8–$28 | AE, D, MC, V.

Steamworks Brewing Co. Southwestern. The brewing operation is visible in the large warehouse-type building, offering eight house-brewed beers. The enchiladas are a great accompaniment to the beers. | 801 E. Second Ave. | 970/259–9200 | $9–$18 | AE, MC, V.

Lodging

Adobe House. This motel is 10 blocks from the downtown shopping district with two adjacent properties. The quiet and comfortable rooms all have coffeemakers, queen-size beds, and average-size baths. Some rooms have soaking tubs and balconies. Complimentary Continental breakfast. Some kitchenettes, microwaves, refrigerators, some in-room hot tubs, some cable TV. Outdoor pool. Outdoor hot tub. Laundry facilities. | 2178 Main Ave. | 970/247–2743 or 880/251–8773 | fax 970/247–2743 | 51 rooms | $60–$90 | AE, D, DC, MC, V.

Alpine Motel. This small motel is on the north side of Durango, 2½ mi north of the center near several restaurants and grocery stores. Some microwaves, cable TV. Some pets allowed. | 3515 N. Main Ave. | 970/247–4042 or 800/818–4042 | fax 970/385–4489 | 25 rooms | $74–$84 | AE, D, DC, MC, V.

★ **Apple Orchard Inn.** The main farmhouse anchors 4½ acres in an old apple orchard 8 mi north of Durango; there are also six separate cottages, all with covered porches facing a pond, and a peaceful garden area. Rooms are comfortable and large. Dining room, picnic area, complimentary breakfast. Refrigerators, some in-room VCRs. No smoking. | 7758 County Rd. 203 | 970/247–0751 or 800/426–0751 | www.appleorchardinn.com | 4 rooms, 6 cottages | $125–$145, $145–$180 cottages | AE, D, MC, V.

Best Western Durango Inn and Suites. This chain motel is set on 56 acres, a mile west of downtown Durango and 36 mi east of Mesa Verde National Park. Restaurant, bar, complimentary Continental breakfast. In-room data ports, cable TV, some in-room VCRs (and movies). Pool. Hot tub, sauna. Video games. Playground. Business services. | 21382 U.S. 160 W | 970/247–3251 or 800/547–9090 | fax 970/385–4835 | www.durangoinn.com | 44 rooms, 28 suites | $92–$105, $109–$139 suites | AE, D, DC, MC, V.

Best Western Purgatory. In this chain motel just 150 yards from the Purgatory ski lift you stay either in a suite or in traditional motel rooms. Restaurant, bar, picnic area, complimentary Continental breakfast. Some kitchenettes, cable TV, some in-room VCRs (and movies). Pool. Hot tub. Gym. Business services. Pets allowed (fee). | 49617 Hwy. 550 N, Purgatory | 970/247–9669 | fax 970/247–9681 | www.purgatorylodge.com | 31 rooms, 18 suites | $99–$109, $119–$129 suites | AE, D, DC, MC, V.

Caboose Motel. Family-owned and -operated for over 20 years. One mile from the central shopping district and across the street from Christina's restaurant. Some kitchenettes, some microwaves, refrigerators, cable TV. | 3363 Maine Ave. | 970/247–1191 | 18 rooms | $58–$68 | AE, MC, V.

Colorado Trails Ranch. This expansive ranch next to the San Juan National Forest 12 mi northeast of Durango has a lively activity program with hayrides, extensive horseback riding and fly-fishing instruction, and kids and teen programs. There are both archery and shooting ranges. Dining room, snack bar. No room phones. Pool. Hot tub. Tennis. Hiking. Fishing. Children's programs (ages 5–18), laundry facilities. Business services. Airport shuttle. | 12161 County Rd. 240 | 970/247–5055 or 800/323–3833 | fax 970/385–7372 | www.coloradotrails.com | 33 rooms in 12 cabins | $1,175–$1,665 per-person, 7-day minimum | Closed Oct.–May | AP | AE, D, DC, MC, V.

Country Sunshine. Nestled in the piney Animas Valley, 10 mi north of Durango, this cozy inn is filled with antiques. An outdoor deck provides mountain views. Picnic area, complimentary breakfast. No room phones. Hot tub. Library. No kids under 6. Business services. No smoking. | 35130 U.S. 550 N | 970/247–2853 or 800/383–2853 | fax 970/247–1203 | www.countrysunshine.com | 6 rooms | $85–$105 | AE, D, DC, MC, V.

Days Inn. A versatile mid-priced chain motel located 4 mi north of downtown Durango off U.S. 550 North. Complimentary Continental breakfast. In-room data ports, cable TV. Pool. Hot tub. Gym. Business services. | 1700 County Rd. 203, off U.S. 550 N | 970/259–1430 | fax 970/259–5741 | www.daysinn.com | 95 rooms | $89–$99 | AE, D, DC, MC, V.

Doubletree Durango. This upscale, full-service chain hotel is located one block from downtown, next to the Animas River, an easy walk from the train station and the shopping and dining districts. Restaurant, bar. In-room data ports, room service, cable TV. Pool. Beauty salon, hot tub. Gym. Laundry facilities. Business services. Airport shuttle. Pets allowed. | 501 Camino Del Rio | 970/259–6580 | fax 970/259–4398 | www.doubletree.com | 157 rooms, 2 suites | $119–$154, $300 suites | AE, D, DC, MC, V.

Durango Lodge. This economical motel is just a block from the train station downtown. Some of the simple rooms have balconies. Complimentary Continental breakfast. Some refrigerators, cable TV. Hot tub. Pool. Free parking. | 150 E. 5th St. | 970/247–0955 or 888/440–4489 | fax 970/385–1882 | www.durangolodge.com | 39 rooms | $57–$102 | AE, D, MC, V.

Econo Lodge. A simple, inexpensive chain motel about a mile north of downtown. Complimentary Continental breakfast. Some microwaves, cable TV. Pool. Hot tub. Business services. | 2002 Main Ave. | 970/247–4242 | fax 970/385–4713 | www.econolodge.com | 40 rooms, 1 suite | $84–$96, $97 suite | AE, D, DC, MC, V.

Gable House. This 1892 Queen Anne Victorian B&B is seven blocks from the historic downtown district. The location is a quiet area near all the shopping and town activity. Complimentary breakfast. No TV in rooms, TV in common area. Gym. Laundry facilities. | 805 E. Fifth Ave. | 970/247–4982 | www.creativelinks.com/gablehouse | 3 rooms | $85–$135 | MC, V.

General Palmer Hotel. Bed-and-breakfast in a restored Victorian building, next door to the Durango and Silverton Narrow Gauge Depot. Complimentary Continental breakfast. In-room data ports, some minibars, some refrigerators, some in-room hot tubs, cable TV. Laundry service. No smoking. | 567 Main Ave. | 970/247–4747 | fax 970/247–1332 | 39 rooms | $98–$275 | AE, D, DC, MC, V.

Hampton Inn. This mid-priced chain hotel is 2 mi north of downtown Durango. Complimentary Continental breakfast. In-room data ports, cable TV, some in-room VCRs (and movies). Pool. Hot tub. Laundry facilities. Business services. | 3777 N. Main St. | 970/247–2600 | fax 970/259–8012 | www.hamptoninn.com | 72 rooms, 4 suites | $107–$129, $159 suites | AE, D, DC, MC, V.

Hawthorn Suites. The rooms are two-room suites with balconies with patio furniture. Next to the Animas River, a block from the Durango and Silverton Narrow Gauge Train Depot, 16 mi from La Plata County Airport. Complimentary breakfast. Microwaves, refrigerators, cable TV, some in-room VCRs. Pool. Hot tub, sauna. Gym. Laundry service. Airport shuttle. | 401 E. Second Ave. | 970/385–4985 or 888/245–4466 | fax 970/385–4980 | www.durango-hawthorn.com | 36 suites | $110–$190 | AE, D, DC, MC, V.

Iron Horse Inn. This property on the north edge of town has many two-story suites with fireplaces, making it a great choice for larger families. Restaurant. Some refrigerators, cable TV. Pool. Hot tub, sauna. Video games. Laundry facilities. Business services. Airport shuttle. Pets allowed. | 5800 N. Main Ave. | 970/259–1010 or 800/748–2990 | fax 970/385–4791 | www.durango.com/ironhorseinn/ | 144 suites | $99–$129 suites | AE, D, DC, MC, V.

Jarvis Suite. This former theater in the center of downtown became a hotel in 1984, about a century after its curtain went up for the first time, and it's loaded with historic western charm. In-room data ports, kitchenettes, microwaves, cable TV, some in-room VCRs. Laundry facilities. Business services. | 125 W. 10th St. | 970/259–6190 or 800/824–1024 | fax 970/259–6190 | www.durangohotel.com | 22 suites | $94–$174 suites | AE, D, DC, MC, V.

Lake Mancos Ranch. Situated in the San Juan Mountains at 8,000 ft in a ponderosa pine forest near Jackson Lake, this guest ranch 35 mi west of Durango on Highway 160 was established in 1956 by the Sehnert family, who operate it to this day. There are many weekly activities, among them Jeep tours, hayrides, and other entertainment. Dining room. No air-conditioning, refrigerators, no room phones. Pool. Hot tub. Children's programs (ages 4–17), laundry facilities. Business services. Airport shuttle. | Hwy. 160 | 970/533–7900 or 800/325–9462 | fax 970/533–7858 | www.lakemancosranch.com | 13 cabins, 4 ranch-house rooms | $1,300 per person per wk | Closed Nov.–May | AP | D, MC, V.

Leland House B&B and Suites. The building was built in 1927 and is located one block east of the historic downtown. Gas fireplaces are in all suites. Complimentary breakfast. Kitchenettes, some microwaves, refrigerators, cable TV, some in-room VCRs. | 721 E. Second Ave. | 970/385–1920 or 800/664–1920 | fax 970/385–1967 | www.leland-house.com | 5 rooms, 6 suites | $95–$109, $135–$300 suite | AE, D, DC, MC, V.

Lightner Creek Inn. A wildlife preserve on Lightner Creek surrounds this country manor inn in a 1903 homestead, 3 mi west of Durango. Rooms are spacious and comfortable; suites are large and luxurious. Complimentary breakfast. No air-conditioning, in-room data ports, some in-room hot tubs, no TVs in rooms. Business services. No smoking. | 999 County Rd. 207 | 970/259–1226 or 800/268–9804 | fax 970/259–9526 | www.lightnercreekinn.com | 10 rooms | $85–$205 | AE, D, DC, MC, V.

Logwood Bed and Breakfast. A large cedar log building with comfortable rooms, 8 mi north of Durango; the only bed-and-breakfast on the Animas River, with spectacular views. Complimentary breakfast. No TV in some rooms. No smoking. | 35060 U.S. 550 N | 970/259–4396 or 800/369–4082 | fax 970/259–9670 | www.durango-logwoodinn.com | 7 rooms, 1 suite | $100–$125, $145 suite | AE, MC, V.

★ **Purgatory Village Condominium Hotel at Durango Mountain Resort.** This luxurious ski-in/ski-out resort offers both rooms and condo apartments. The condos include full kitchens, washer/dryers, and fireplaces. 2 restaurants, bar. Pool. Some kitchenettes, some microwaves, some refrigerators, some in-room hot tubs, cable TV. 3 hot tubs, massage, sauna. Downhill skiing. Business services. | 5 Skier Pl., Purgatory | 970/385–2100 | fax 970/382–2248 | 9 rooms, 124 suites | $119, $129–$545 suites | AE, D, MC, V.

Ramada Limited. This limited-service chain motel is on the north side of Durango, convenient to both downtown and Purgatory Village. Complimentary Continental breakfast. In-room data ports, cable TV. Pool. Hot tub, sauna. Business services. | 3030 N. Main Ave. | 970/259–1333 or 800/252–8853 | fax 970/247–3854 | www.ramada.com | 48 rooms | $76–$108 | AE, D, DC, MC, V.

★ **New Rochester Hotel.** Many films have been made in these parts, and the rooms in this small, 19th-century hotel take their cue from the moviemakers' vision, from their names to the artifacts inside. Strives for a chic but funky atmosphere, with mismatched furniture and wagon-wheel chandeliers. Complimentary breakfast. Some kitchenettes, refrigerators, cable TV, some in-room VCRs (and movies). Business services. Some pets allowed (fee). No smoking. | 726 E. 2nd Ave. | 970/385–1920 or 800/664–1920 | fax 970/385–1967 | www.rochester-hotel.com | 12 rooms, 3 suites | $139–$179, $179–$199 suites | AE, D, DC, MC, V.

Rodeway Inn. This small-budget chain motel is on Durango's north side. Complimentary Continental breakfast. Some microwaves, cable TV. Pool. Hot tub. Laundry facilities. Business services. | 2701 N. Main Ave. | 970/259–2540 or 800/752–6072 | fax 970/247–9642 | www.rodewayinn.com | 31 rooms | $50–$90 | AE, D, DC, MC, V.

★ **Sheraton Tamarron Resort.** On 750 acres within the San Juan National Forest 18 mi north of Durango, this luxurious resort offers large, Southwestern-style rooms. The Cliffs golf course is considered one of the best in the U.S. 2 restaurants, bar. Some kitchenettes, some microwaves, some refrigerators, cable TV. Indoor-outdoor pool. Hot tub, massage, sauna, spa. 18-hole golf course, 3 tennis courts. Health club, hiking, horseback riding. Shops. Children's programs (ages 5–12). | U.S. 550, Purgatory | 970/259–2000 or 800/678–1000 | fax 970/259–0745 | www.tamarron.com | 55 rooms, 245 suites | $99–$179, $209–$479 suites | AE, D, DC, MC, V.

Silver Spur Inn and Suites. John Wayne once stayed at this motel, and in his honor the rooms are named after his films. Three miles from the train station. Restaurant, bar. Some microwaves, some refrigerators, cable TV. Outdoor pool. | 3416 Main Ave. | 970/247–5552 or 800/748–1715 | fax 970/247–1592 | www.silver-spur.com | 33 rooms | $68–$84 | AE, D, DC, MC, V.

★ **Strater Hotel.** This is a classic, elegant western Victorian hotel, from its unusual bar to its exquisite rooms filled with the finest Victorian-era antiques. Restaurant, bar (with entertainment). In-room data ports, room service, cable TV. Hot tub. Business services. | 699 Main Ave. | 970/247–4431 or 800/247–4431 | fax 970/259–2208 | www.strater.com | 93 rooms | $129–$235 | AE, D, DC, MC, V.

Tall Timber Resort. This luxury resort 25 mi north of Durango lies in the midst of millions of acres of national forest. This is the ultimate private retreat as there are no roads in or out; the resort can only be reached by helicopter or train. Accommodations are in modern, condominium-style apartments. Dining room. No air-conditioning, refrigerators, no room phones. Indoor-outdoor pool. Hot tubs, massage, sauna. Driving range, 9-hole golf course, putting green, tennis. Hiking, horseback riding. Fishing. Cross-country skiing. Library. No smoking. | 1 Silverton Star, Silverton | 970/259–4813 | www.talltimberresort.com | 10 suites | $4,100–$5,000 per person per wk | Closed Nov.–mid-May | AP | MC, V.

Wilderness Trails Ranch. A mountain guest ranch surrounded on three sides by wilderness area. Hayrides and four-wheel-drive trips are available. Cabins are rustic but comfortable. Dining room, picnic area. No air-conditioning, no room phones. Pool. Hot tub. Water sports, boating, fishing. Children's programs (ages 3–17), playground. Laundry facilities. Airport shuttle. No smoking. | 23486 Rte. 501, Bayfield | 970/247–0722 or 800/527–2624 | fax 970/247–1006 | www.wildernesstrails.com | 20 rooms in 10 cabins | $1,600 per person per wk | Closed Oct.–May | AP | D, MC, V.

Wit's End. In a stream-crossed valley about 40 mi northeast of Durango. Cabins are large, luxurious, and well appointed. Bar (with entertainment), dining room. No air-conditioning, in-room data ports, kitchenettes, some microwaves, room service, some in-room VCRs (and movies). Pool. Hot tub. Tennis. Horseback riding. Fishing, bicycles. Cross-country skiing, sleigh rides, snowmobiling. Children's programs (ages 5–17). Laundry facilities. Business services. Airport shuttle. No smoking. | 254 Rte. 500, Vallecito | 970/884–4113 | fax 970/884–3261 | www.witsendranch.com | 35 cabins | $4,800 per couple per wk | AP | AE, D, MC, V.

ENGLEWOOD

MAP 6, G4

(Nearby towns also listed: Aurora, Denver, Evergreen, Golden, Lakewood)

In the mid 1800s, the Englewood area was inhabited by Ute Indians and buffalo, antelope, and other wildlife. In 1858, William Green Russell led a small group of Georgia miners on an expedition of the South Platte River valley and discovered gold in Little Dry Creek (today is intersection of Dartmouth and Santa Fe streets). A plaque in C.E. Cushing Park marks the site of the first gold-mining camp. Present-day Englewood is a suburb of Denver, on the south side of the city, and has a population of nearly 33,000. The Denver Technological Center is located here.

Information: **Greater Englewood Chamber of Commerce** | 3501 S. Broadway, Englewood 80110 | 303/789–4473 | www.greatenglewoodchamber.com.

Attractions

Bellview Park. This park features a minitrain ride and a children's farm that houses chickens, ponies, pigs, and more. | 5001 S. Inca St. | 303/762–2680 | 75¢ | Tues.–Sun. 10–4.

Chatfield State Park. Swimming, waterskiing, fishing, boating, and other water activities. | 11500 N. Roxborough Park Rd., Littleton | 303/791–7275 | $4 per vehicle | Daily 5 AM–10 PM.

The Museum of Outdoor Arts. A 400-acre outdoor sculpture garden with facilities for the performing arts. Located 5 mi southeast of Englewood. | 7600 E. Orchard Rd., Suite 160N | 303/741–3609 | www.fine-art.com/museum/moa.html | $3 | Weekdays 8:30–6.

Fiddlers Green Amphitheatre. An outdoor theater on the grounds of the Museum of Outdoor Arts that hosts summer concerts. | 6350 Greenwood Plaza Blvd. | 303/220–7000 | www.fiddlers.com | Admission varies by performance | May–early Oct.; call for performance schedules.

Prime Outlets at Castle Rock. An outlet mall approximately 20 minutes south of Englewood containing around 100 shops and stores, plus a food court. | Castle Rock (I–25, exit 184) | 303/688–4494 | Free | Mon.–Sat. 10–9, Sun. 11–6.

ON THE CALENDAR

AUG.: *Englewood Funfest/Olde Tyme Fair.* The whole town comes out for this festival of arts and crafts, games, and live musical entertainment at Miller Field. Hot-air balloon rides are also offered. | 303/762–2300.

Dining

County Line Barbecue. Barbecue. Vintage artifacts and ephemera from the World War II and postwar eras decorate this casual eatery. Folks come for the barbecue and the ice cream, which is made on the premises. Kids' menu. No smoking. | 8351 Southpark La., Littleton | 303/797–3727 | $9–$18 | AE, D, DC, MC, V.

Fratelli's. Italian. This popular Italian restaurant has a bar from the 1800s that was originally from the Old Tabor Hotel. Antiques are also displayed. Kids' menu. | 1200 E. Hampden Ave., west of I–25 | 303/761–4771 | Breakfast also available | $7–$15 | AE, D, DC, MC, V.

Grady's American Grill. Continental. Dark wood and brass fill the three dining areas of this large bi-level restaurant known for prime rib and mesquite grilled salmon. Open-air dining on a patio with mountain views. Kids' menu. | 5140 S. Wadsworth Blvd., at U.S. 285, Littleton | 303/973–5140 | $8–$25 | AE, D, DC, MC, V.

India Grill. Indian. Look no further than India Grill for the finest Indian cuisine in Englewood. The dishes are predominantly North Indian. Try the chicken tikka marsala or chicken kurma. | 6014 S. Holly St. | 303/290–8883 | $9–$13 | AE, D, DC, MC, V.

The Swan. Contemporary. An elegant bistro in the Inverness Hotel and Golf Club where many items, including the Châteaubriand and specialty desserts, are prepared tableside. Try the rack of lamb rosemary pesto, or the wild boar rib chops. Music Tuesday–Saturday. | 200 Inverness Dr. W | 303/799–5800 | Closed Sun., Mon. No lunch | $28–$45 | AE, D, DC, MC, V.

Lodging

Best Western–Denver Tech Center. Conveniently located in the Denver Technological Center, this chain hotel is just minutes away from malls, museums, theaters, and restaurants. Complimentary Continental breakfast. In-room data ports, microwaves, refrigerators, cable TV. Laundry service. Business services, free parking. | 9799 E. Geddes Ave. | 303/768–9300 | fax 303/768–0958 | www.bestwestern.com | 62 rooms | $79–$89 | AE, D, DC, MC, V.

Courtyard by Marriott. A two-story chain hotel at the southern edge of the Denver metropolitan region. Bar, picnic area. In-room data ports, some microwaves, some refrigerators, cable TV, some in-room VCRs. Pool. Hot tub. Gym. Video games. Laundry facilities. Business services. | 6565 S. Boston St. | 303/721–0300 or 800/228–9290 | fax 303/721–0037 | www.marriott.com | 143 rooms, 12 suites | $109, $139 suites | AE, D, DC, MC, V.

Embassy Suites–Denver Tech Center. This all-suite chain hotel is next to Interstate 25, just north of Arapahoe Road, and convenient to the Denver Tech Center. Restaurant, bar, complimentary breakfast, room service. In-room data ports, microwaves, refrigerators, cable TV. Pool. Hot tub. Gym. Video games. Business services. | 10250 E. Costilla Ave. (I–25, exit Arapahoe Ave.) | 303/792–0433 or 800/326–2779 | fax 303/792–0432 | www.embassysuites.com | 236 suites | $109–$199 | AE, D, DC, MC, V.

Hampton Inn–Denver Southeast. Easy access to Interstate 25, the Denver Tech Center, and Fiddler's Green. Complimentary Continental breakfast. In-room data ports, cable TV. Pool. Gym. Laundry facilities. Business services. Some pets allowed. | 9231 E. Arapahoe Rd. | 303/792–9999 or 800/426–7866 | fax 303/790–4360 | www.hamptoninn.com | 152 rooms | $89–$99 | AE, D, DC, MC, V.

Hilton–Denver Tech South. Centered around a six-story atrium, this upscale chain hotel is in the middle of the Denver Tech Center. Restaurant, bars, room service. In-room data ports, some refrigerators, cable TV, some in-room VCRs. Indoor-outdoor pool. Gym. Business services. | 7801 E. Orchard Rd. | 303/779–6161 or 800/327–2242 | fax 303/689–7080 | www.hilton.com | 300 rooms, 5 suites | $117–$169, $195–$275 suites | AE, D, DC, MC, V.

Homestead Village. Rooms at this sprawling, inexpensive motel are perfect if you are doing business in Inverness, Denver Tech Center, or Meridian Office Parks. Rates become lower if you stay for one week. In-room data ports, kitchenettes, microwaves, refrigerators, cable TV. Laundry facilities. | 9650 E. Geddes Ave. | 303/708–8888 | fax 303/708–1620 | 142 rooms | $69 | AE, D, DC, MC, V.

Inverness Hotel and Golf Club. Overlooking a private golf club with an 18-hole championship course, this is one of the Denver area's most exclusive resorts. Many rooms and suites have excellent mountain views. Restaurant (*see* The Swan), bar. In-room data ports, minibars, cable TV, some in-room VCRs. 2 pools (1 indoor). Hot tub. Driving range, 18-hole golf course, putting green, tennis. Gym. Business services, airport shuttle. | 200 Inverness Dr. W (I–25, exit Dry Creek Rd.) | 303/799–5800 or 800/346–4891 | fax 303/799–5873 | www.invernesshotel.com | 302 rooms, 19 suites | $149–$269, $199–$309 suites | AE, D, DC, MC, V.

Ramada Limited–Denver Tech Center. All guest rooms are richly appointed with the comforts of home at this moderately priced, limited-service motor hotel. The hotel is only minutes away from professional football, baseball, basketball, and hockey, as well as the Denver Tech Center. In-room data ports, microwave, refrigerator, cable TV. Laundry services. Free parking. | 9719 E. Geddes Ave. | 303/768–9400 | www.ramada.com | 135 rooms | $80 | AE, D, DC, MC, V.

Residence Inn by Marriott–South. This all-suite chain hotel provides easy access to the Denver Tech Center. All suites have full kitchens; many rooms have fireplaces. Complimentary Continental breakfast. In-room data ports, kitchenettes, microwaves, refrigerators, cable TV. Pool. Hot tub. Laundry facilities. Business services. Pets allowed (fee). | 6565 S. Yosemite | 303/740–7177 or 800/331–3131 | fax 303/741–9426 | www.residenceinn.com | 128 suites | $129–$165 | AE, D, DC, MC, V.

Sheraton–Denver Tech Center. This upscale chain hotel is conveniently located in the Denver Tech Center area, next to several restaurants. It has a luxury level. Restaurant, bar. In-room data ports, some microwaves, cable TV. Pool. Hot tub. Gym. Business services, airport shuttle. | 7007 S. Clinton St. | 303/799–6200 or 800/937–8461 | fax 303/799–4828 | www.sheraton.com | 263 rooms | $59–$149 | AE, D, DC, MC, V.

ESTES PARK

MAP 6, F2

(Nearby towns also listed: Allenspark, Boulder, Fort Collins, Grand Lake, Longmont, Loveland, Rocky Mountain National Park)

Joel Estes settled this region in 1859, but ownership of the entire valley soon passed to a British nobleman, the Earl of Dunraven. Later, Freelan Stanley, the inventor of the "Stanley Steamer" automobile, purchased a large chunk of the park and built his world-famous Stanley Hotel. Although situated in a parklike setting at an altitude of more than 7,500 ft, Estes Park is surrounded by even higher mountain peaks. The town, whose current population is 10,000, lies at the gates of Rocky Mountain National Park, and as such sees tens of thousands of visitors annually and is one of Colorado's most visited resorts. Containing 114 peaks exceeding 10,000 ft, this national park is one of America's finest. Nearly 800 varieties of plant life, 260 species of birds, and scores of species of mammals (deer, elk, bighorn sheep, beaver) call this wilderness home.

Information: Information Center at the Chamber of Commerce | 500 Big Thompson Ave., Estes Park 80517 | 970/586–4431 or 800/443–7837 | www.estesparkresort.com.

Attractions

Aerial Tramway. This suspended tramway moves at 1,000 ft per minute and offers spectacular views of the Continental Divide. | 420 E. Riverside Dr. | 970/586–3675 | $8 | Mid-May–mid Sept., daily 9–6:30.

Baldpate Inn. This historic inn is home to a collection of over 20,000 keys. Notable keys include ones from Mozart's wine cellar and the White House. | 4900 Hwy. 7 | 970/586–6151 | www.baldpateinn.com | Free | June–Sept., daily 8–noon.

Enos Mills Original Cabin. Enos Mills, the "father" of Rocky Mountain National Park, once lived in this cabin 8 mi south of Estes Park. Built in 1885, it is on 200 undeveloped acres in the shadow of Long's Peak. A nature guide and self-guided nature trails are also available. | 6760 Rte. 7 | 970/586–4706 | Free | Memorial Day–Labor Day, Tues.–Sun. 11–4; Labor Day–Memorial Day, by appointment only.

Estes Park Area Historical Museum. Historical exhibits tell the story of Estes Park and the surrounding area. | 200 Fourth St. | 970/586–6256 | www.estesnet.com/museum | $2.50 | May–Oct., Mon.–Sat. 10–5, Sun. 1–5; Nov.–Apr., Fri.–Sat. 10–5, Sun. 1–5.

Estes Park Ride-a-Kart. Casey's Silverstreak Train, batting cages, miniature golf, go-carting, and bumper boats are a few of the activities designed for kids and adults at this small amusement park 2 mi east of Estes park on U.S. 34. | 2250 Big Thompson Ave. | 970/586–6495 | Free (activities are individually priced) | Memorial Day–Labor Day, daily 9:30 AM–10 PM.

MacGregor Ranch Historic Trust and Museum. The MacGregor Ranch is one of Estes Park's original homesteads, dating back to 1873. The ranch house has been preserved, furnished with original antiques, china, silver, paintings and diaries. | 180 MacGregor La. | 970/586–3749 | Free | June–Aug., Tues.–Fri. 10–4.

Rocky Mountain National Park. *(See also* Rocky Mountain National Park.) One of America's finest, this is 3 mi west of Estes Park on U.S. 34/36. | Rocky Mountain National Park, Estes Park | 970/586–1206 | www.nps.gov/romo | $10 per car | Daily.

Roosevelt National Forest. Nearly 800,000 acres of mountain vistas, forests, and lovely scenery await the hiker, camper, picnicker, and angler visiting this natural paradise. The national forest surrounds Estes Park on the north, east, and south. | 1311 S. College Ave., Ft. Collins | 970/498–1100 | www.fs.fed.us/arnf/png/ | Free | Daily.

JUNE: *Father's Day Celebration.* Kids dress their fathers up for the Father's Day Fashion show at Yogi Bear's Jellystone Park of Estes. All dads also eat free at Sunday's Pancake Breakfast. | 970/586–4230.

JUNE–AUG.: *Estes Park Music Festival.* Chamber and symphonic music and choral arrangements are presented at the Rocky Ridge Music Center. | Rocky Ridge Music Center | 970/586–4431 or 800/443–7837.

JUNE–SEPT.: *Horse shows.* Several shows are held throughout the region. | 970/586–4431 or 800/443–7837.

JULY: *Rooftop Rodeo.* Parade, PRCA rodeos, kids' exhibits, and dancing. | 5 days in mid-July | 970/586–4431 or 800/443–7837.

SEPT.: *Scottish–Irish Highland Festival.* Classic highland dancing, athletic competitions, arts-and-crafts demonstrations, and Celtic music are all part of the fun the weekend after Labor Day. | 970/586–4431 or 800/443–7837.

Dining

Andrea's of Estes. Continental. Diners can enjoy a great view of downtown Estes Park while they eat from the rooftop beer garden and dining room. The specialty is wild game; the ostrich tenderloin is quite popular. | 145 E. Elkhorn Ave., 3rd floor | 970/586–0886 | Closed Tues. | $7–$25 | AE, D, DC, MC, V.

Big Horn Restaurant. Barbecue. A family-style dining spot renowned for hearty breakfasts; definitely try the BBQ ribs for dinner. | 401 W. Elkhorn Ave. | 970/586–2792 | Breakfast also available; no dinner Jan.–Apr. | $6–$16 | D, DC, MC, V.

Candy's Mountaineer Restaurant. American/Casual. Inside a rustic log cabin, this restaurant overlooks a golf course. Standard American fare including burgers and fish-and-chips. | 540 S. Saint Vrain Ave. | 970/586–9001 | No dinner | $4–$8 | MC, V.

Ed's Cantina & Grill. Mexican. Lighthearted antiques adorn the walls here. Huge burritos and tasty enchiladas are reliable choices at this popular local hangout. | 362 E. Elkhorn Ave. | 970/586–2919 | Breakfast also available | $7–$10 | AE, D, DC, MC, V.

Grubsteak Restaurant. American. Outdoor dining under a covered patio is available at this popular, upscale spot. The big beef, buffalo, and elk burgers are very popular. Kids' menu. | 134 W. Elkhorn Ave. | 970/586–8838 | $9–$20 | D, MC, V.

Grumpy Gringo. Mexican. The homemade Mexican food here is prepared from scratch. Six different homemade sauces are used to complement dishes such as chiles rellenos and chimichangas. | 1560 Big Thompson Ave. | 970/586–7705 | $5–$12 | AE, D, MC, V.

Mama Rose's. Italian. The Victorian decor and large fireplace make this local favorite especially inviting. Known for veal Parmesan, chicken Parmesan, and fettuccine Alfredo. Open-air dining on a patio overlooking the Big Thompson River. Kids' menu. No smoking. | 338 E. Elkhorn Ave. | 970/586–3330 | Breakfast also available; closed Mon., Tues. in Jan., Feb. | $7–$18 | AE, D, MC, V.

Molly B Restaurant. American. A comfortable, homey atmosphere and a great view of Longs Peak await patrons at this eatery. Try the Rocky Mountain trout, and top it off with a delicious mud pie. Outdoor dining on the patio is available. Kids' menu. | 200 Moraine Ave. | 970/586–2766 | fax 970/586–7341 | Breakfast also available; closed Wed.; no dinner Nov.–Apr. | $5–$14 | AE, MC, V.

Nicky's Resort. Steaks. Elegant wood beams and oak paneling frame the beautiful mountain and river views at this sophisticated dining spot. Known for prime rib, steak, and seafood. Open-air dining on a redwood deck that crosses the river. Salad bar. Kids' menu. | 1350 Fall River Rd. | 970/586–5376 | Breakfast also available | $9–$25 | AE, D, DC, MC, V.

ESTES PARK

INTRO
ATTRACTIONS
DINING
LODGING

Oasis Grill. American. The walls of the dining room in this restaurant are covered with memorabilia recounting the old days of Estes Park. The buffalo and elk burgers are very tasty and popular. | 110 W. Elkhorn Ave. | 970/586–1757 | $7–$25 | AE, D, DC, MC, V.

Penelope's World Famous Burgers and Fries. American/Casual. Patrons here can enjoy an old-fashioned atmosphere and the "Best Burger in Estes Park." Old-fashioned malts and flavored sodas are also served. Kids' menu. | 229 Elkhorn Ave. | 970/586–2277 | fax 970/586–1965 | $3–$7 | D, DC, MC, V.

Twin Owls Steakhouse at Black Canyon Inn. Steaks. Built in 1927 of rough-cut, hand-assembled logs, the rustic mountain restaurant has a huge moss-and-rock fireplace, high beamed ceilings, and original oak floors. Known for steaks and seafood. Kids' menu. No smoking. | 800 MacGregor Ave. | 970/586–9344 | Closed Jan.; Nov.–Dec., closed Mon.; Feb.–Mar., closed Mon., Tues. | $10–$22 | AE, D, MC, V.

Wild Rose. Contemporary. This restaurant in the Old Church Shop occupies a former church. The back room is done up in old English style; the front room is contemporary with fine art. Known for fresh seafood, beef tenderloin, mako shark. Open-air dining on the patio. Salad bar. Kids' menu. | 157 W. Elkhorn Ave. | 970/586–2806 | $8–$16 | AE, MC, V.

Lodging

All Budget Inn. Just a few feet away from the Rocky Mountain Park entrance, this inexpensive inn is a great place if you want to see wildlife, including elk and mule deer, roaming about. There are restaurants nearby. Some kitchenettes, some microwaves, cable TV. | 945 Moraine Ave. | 970/586–3485 or 800/628–3438 | www.allbudgetinn.com | 23 rooms | $69–$160 | MC, V.

Alpine Trail Ridge Inn. This reliable motel is about 2 mi from the north entrance to Rocky Mountain National Park. Some rooms offer panoramic mountain views. Restaurant, bar. No air-conditioning, some kitchenettes, refrigerators, cable TV. Pool. Business services, airport shuttle. | 927 Moraine Ave. | 970/586–4585 or 800/233–5023 | fax 970/586–6249 | www.alpinetrailridgeinn.com | 46 rooms, 2 suites | $81–$108, $125–$149 suites | Closed mid-Oct.–Apr. | AE, D, DC, MC, V.

★ **Aspen Lodge Ranch Resort and Conference Center.** This resort is set on 82 wooded acres 7 mi south of downtown Estes Park, near the north entrance of Rocky Mountain National Park. Rooms and cabins are done up in a rustic, western motif. Known for loads of entertainment—including lectures, line and square dancing, and concerts. Bar, dining room, picnic area. No air-conditioning, cable TV in common area. Pool. Hot tub. Tennis. Gym. Horseback riding, bicycles. Ice-skating, cross-country skiing. Video games. Children's programs (ages 3–12), playground. Business services, airport shuttle. | 6120 Hwy. 7 N | 970/586–8133 or 800/332–6867 | fax 970/586–3419 | www.aspenlodge.com | 36 rooms, 23 cabins | $300 per adult per 2–night stay (2–night minimum in summer) | AP (in summer) | AE, D, DC, MC, V.

Aspen Winds. Each spacious room has a gas fireplace at this inn 25 ft from the edge of the Fall River and 3 mi west of Estes Park. Picnic area. Microwaves, refrigerators, in-room hot tubs, cable TV, in-room VCRs. | 1051 Fall River Ct | 970/586–6010 or 800/399–6010 | fax 970/586–3626 | www.estes-park.com/aspenwinds | 16 suites | $139–$179 | AE, D, MC, V.

Best Western Lake Estes Resort. All the well-maintained rooms are good size and outfitted with a hodgepodge of furniture at this mid-priced motel resort. Ask for a unit with a lake view. Restaurant. Refrigerators, some in-room hot-tubs, cable TV. Pool. Sauna, spa. Babysitting, playground. Laundry service. | 1650 Big Thompson Hwy. | 970/586–3386 | fax 970/586–9000 | www.bestwestern.com | 58 rooms | $120–$130 | AE, D, DC, MC, V.

Big Thompson Timberlane Lodge. Many different styles of accommodations—from motel-style rooms to log cabins—on the Big Thompson River. Picnic area. Some kitchenettes, some microwaves, refrigerators, cable TV, some in-room VCRs. Pool, wading pool. Hot tub. Playground. Laundry facilities. | 740 Moraine Ave. | 970/586–3137 or 800/898–4373 | fax 970/

586–3719 | www.estes-park.com/bigthompson | 13 rooms, 45 cabins | $135 rooms, $99–$335 cabins | AE, D, MC, V.

Black Dog Inn Bed and Breakfast. Built in 1910, this small B&B offers you a splendid view of the various mountain ranges. Each guest room is named for a peak in Rocky Mountain National Park. Complimentary breakfast. Some in-room hot tubs. No kids under 18. | 650 S. Saint Vrain Ave. | 970/586–0374 | www.blackdoginn.com | 4 rooms | $85–$150 | MC, V.

Boulder Brook. This modern, upscale all-suite lodge is between Estes Park and the north entrance to Rocky Mountain National Park on the river. The choice is between a "spa suite," which is a studio with a river view, or a one-bedroom suite, which offers more room and a separate sleeping area. Picnic area. In-room data ports, some microwaves, some in-room hot tubs, cable TV, some in-room VCRs (and movies). Hot tub. Business services, airport shuttle. | 1900 Fall River Rd. | 970/586–0910 or 800/238–0910 | fax 970/586–8067 | www.estes-park.com/boulderbrook/index.html | 16 suites | $169–$199 | AE, D, MC, V.

Columbine Inn. This friendly, old-fashioned mountain inn caters to senior citizens. It is 1 mi east of Lake Estes Marina and within walking distance of golfing and horseback riding. Some kitchenettes, some refrigerators, cable TV. Outdoor hot tub. Some pets allowed. | 1540 Big Thompson Ave. | 970/586–4533 or 800/726–9049 | fax 970/586–4363 | www.estes-park.com/columbine | 19 rooms | $81–$98 | MC, V.

Comfort Inn. This chain motel east of downtown offers easy access to the highways and Rocky Mountain National Park. Picnic area, complimentary Continental breakfast. Some microwaves, some refrigerators, cable TV. Pool. Hot tub. Playground. Business services, airport shuttle. | 1450 Big Thompson Ave. | 970/586–2358 or 800/228–5150 | fax 970/586–4473 | www.comfortinn.com | 75 rooms | $87–$176 (2–night minimum stay) | Closed Nov. 1–Apr. 1 | AE, D, DC, MC, V.

Deer Crest. This secluded motel offers rooms with balconies overlooking Fall River or a poolside patio. Picnic area. Some kitchenettes, microwaves, refrigerators, cable TV. Pool. Hot tub. Airport shuttle. No kids under 18. No smoking. | 1200 Fall River Rd. | 970/586–2324 or 800/331–2324 | fax 970/586–8693 | www.estes-park.com/deercrest | 26 rooms, 8 suites | $89, $94–$125 suites | MC, V.

Estes Park Center/YMCA of the Rockies. Both the lodge rooms and the 200 cabins are simple, clean, and attractive, and all are constructed of sturdy oak. This property is so huge it has its own zip code. Restaurant. Some kitchenettes. Pool. Basketball, gym. Playground. Some pets allowed. | 2515 Tunnel Rd. | 970/586–3341 | 730 rooms | $64–$92 | No credit cards.

Fawn Valley Inn. This inn is on 8 wooded acres just east of Rocky Mountain National Park and 3½ mi west of Estes Park. All rooms have fireplaces; some have hot tubs. Picnic area. No air-conditioning, microwaves, refrigerators, cable TV. Pool. Hot tub. | 2760 Fall River Rd. | 970/586–2388 or 800/525–2961 | fax 970/586–0394 | www.fawnvalleyinn.com | 25 1- to 2-bedroom apartments | $130–$175 per person per day (3–night minimum stay) | AE, D, MC, V.

4 Seasons Inn. Catering to couples, this inn provides clean rooms and a romantic setting. From the deck, you can enjoy a breathtaking river view. Grills for outdoor cooking are also available. Picnic area. Microwaves, refrigerators, cable TV. Outdoor hot tub. Fishing. | 1130 W. Elkhorn Ave. | 970/586–5693 or 800/779–4616 | www.estes-park.com/4seasons/index.html | 8 rooms | $95–$138 | D, MC, V.

Glacier Lodge. Surrounded by mountains and along the Big Thompson River, the rustic cabins and lodge at this resort have the basics, including electricity, but little else. There is also a corral on the premises. Picnic area. Kitchenettes. Pool. Horseback riding, fishing. Library. Baby-sitting, playground. No pets. | 2166 State Hwy. 66 | 970/586–4401 or 800/523–3920 | www.glacierlodge.com | 26 cabins | $98–$142 | Closed Dec.–Apr. | D, MC, V.

Holiday Inn–Rocky Mt. Park. A four-story Holidome 4 mi from Rocky Mountain National Park. The combination of amenities and location make this a great family choice for a national park visit. Restaurant, bar, room service. Cable TV. Pool. Gym. Video games. Laundry facilities. Business services. | 101 S. St. Vrain St. | 970/586–2332 or 800/803–7837 | fax 970/586–2038 | www.holiday-inn.com | 145 rooms, 5 suites | $99–$139, $239 suites | AE, D, DC, MC, V.

Idlewilde by the River. On the banks of the Big Thompson River 3 mi west of Estes Park, the split-log cottages at this property are paneled with shiny knotty-pine inside, with carpeting and screened-in porches, many fronting the water. It's 1 mi south of the entrance to Rocky Mountain National Park. Picnic area. No air-conditioning, kitchenettes, refrigerators, cable TV, no room phones. Hot tub. Fishing. Library. Playground. | 2282 Hwy. 66 | 970/586–3864 or 303/651–7846 (winter) | www.estes-park.com/idlewilde | 13 1- to 3-bedroom cottages | $75–$230 | Closed mid-Oct.–mid-May | No credit cards.

Machin's Cottages in the Pines. These cottages nestled within a shady pine forest, with big windows, porches, patios, and fireplaces, are on private property within the boundaries of Rocky Mountain National Park. Picnic area. Kitchenettes, microwaves, cable TV. Hiking. Playground. Some pets allowed. | 2450 Eagle Cliff Rd. | 970/586–4276 | www.estes-park.com/machins | 17 1- to 3-bedroom cottages | $82–$178 | Closed Oct.–late May | AE, MC, V.

McGregor Mountain Lodge. The lodge adjoins Rocky Mountain National Park, which is accessible via a footpath; the main entrance is ½ mi away via Highway 34, and Estes Park is 3½ mi east. Bighorn sheep, newly reintroduced in the park, often wander onto the property, and the lobby with its south-facing windows is a pleasant place to gather year-round. Picnic area. No air-conditioning, some microwaves, refrigerators, cable TV, in-room VCRs, no room phones. Hot tub. Playground. Business services, airport shuttle. | 2815 Fall River Rd. | 970/586–3457 or 800/835–8439 | fax 970/586–4040 | www.mcgregormountainlodge.com | 9 suites, 10 cottages | $155–$185 suites, $165–$210 cottages | D, MC, V.

Olympus Lodge. Seclusion and stunning views of Longs Peak can be found at this small lodge, 2 mi east of downtown Estes Park. Restaurant, picnic area. No air-conditioning in some rooms, some microwaves, some refrigerators, cable TV. Airport shuttle. | 2365 Big Thompson Ave. | 970/586–8141 or 800/248–8141 | fax 970/586–8143 | 17 rooms | $85–$175 | AE, D, DC, MC, V.

Ponderosa Lodge. Set among the pines on the Fall River, between Castle Mountain and Deer Mountain, at the end of a one-lane road halfway between Estes Park and the north entrance to Rocky Mountain National Park. Many rooms have private balconies, and all have either a wood-burning or gas fireplace. Picnic area. No air-conditioning, some kitchenettes, microwaves, refrigerators, cable TV, no room phones. Fishing. Playground. | 1820 Fall River Rd. | 970/586–4233 or 800/628–0512 | www.estes-park.com/ponderosa | 16 rooms, 3 cabins | $148–$430 (2–night minimum stay) | AE, D, MC, V.

Romantic Riversong Inn. No two rooms are alike in this inn built by a wealthy family in the 1920s on 27 acres next to Rocky Mountain National Park, though all are loaded with charm. You may sleep in a swing bed, a brass bed, or a log four-poster, for example. All tubs are oversize, and there are fireplaces in all guest quarters. Picnic area, complimentary breakfast. No air-conditioning, some refrigerators, some in-room hot tubs, no room phones. Airport shuttle. No kids under 12. No smoking. | 1765 Lower Broadview | 970/586–4666 | fax 970/577–0699 | www.romanticriversong.com | 9 rooms, 5 suites | $150–$275, $170–$275 suites | D, MC, V.

Silver Saddle Lodge. Many of the motel-style rooms in this modern lodge have balconies with fantastic views of the peaks of the Front Range. Picnic area, complimentary Continental breakfast. In-room data ports, some kitchenettes, microwaves, refrigerators, cable TV, some in-room VCRs. Pool. Hot tub. Playground. Laundry facilities. Business services. No smoking. | 1260 Big Thompson Ave. | 970/586–4476 or 800/578–7878 | fax 970/586–5530 | www.estesresort.com | 50 rooms, 5 suites | $89–$159, $139–$189 suites | AE, D, DC, MC, V.

★ **The Stanley Hotel.** This classic sparkling white hotel, built in 1909 by the same F.O. Stanley who developed the famous Stanley Steamer automobile, is renowned for its Georgian elegance and awesome natural setting, cupped by rocky cliffs. Accommodations range from spacious to quirky rooms under the eaves. This is the place that inspired Stephen King to pen *The Shining*, though the film was shot elsewhere. Restaurant, bar (with entertainment). Some refrigerators, cable TV. Pool. Tennis. Playground. | 333 Wonderview Ave. | 970/586–3371 or 800/976–1377 | fax 970/586–3673 | www.grandheritage.com | 134 rooms | $159–$299 | AE, D, DC, MC, V.

Streamside Cabins. Situated on 16 pine-filled acres on the slope of Old Man Mountain, each cabin has a private porch or deck. Fall River runs through the property. Picnic area. Some kitchenettes, microwaves, cable TV, in-room VCR (and movies). Pool. Hot tub. Hiking. Playground. Business services. | 1260 Fall River Rd. | 970/586–6464 or 800/321–3303 | fax 970/586–6272 | www.streamsidecabins.com | 19 cabins | $115–$175 | AE, D, MC, V.

Sunnyside Knoll. Nestled in the Fall River valley, overlooking huge rock formations and a pine and aspen forest. Each room has a fireplace; many have hot tubs. Caters mostly to couples. Picnic area. No air-conditioning, some kitchenettes, some in-room hot tubs, cable TV, in-room VCRs, no room phones. Pool. 3 outdoor hot tubs. Gym. No kids under 12. | 1675 Fall River Rd. | 970/586–5759 or 800/586–5212 | www.sunnysideknoll.com | 4 rooms, 5 suites, 6 cabins | $92, $139–$172 suites, $129–$279 cabins (3–night minimum stay May–Sept.) | D, MC, V.

Trappers Motor Inn. A small, economical motel just off U.S. 34 ½ mi west of downtown Estes Park. Picnic area. No air-conditioning, some microwaves, some refrigerators, cable TV. Hot tub. Playground. | 553 W. Elkhorn (U.S. 34 business) | 970/586–2833 or 800/552–2833 | www.estes-park.com/trappers | 20 rooms | $55–$80 | AE, MC, V.

Wind River Ranch. Set on 110 aspen- and pine-laden acres facing majestic Longs Peak, 7 mi south of Estes Park, this Christian guest ranch has a lively program of activities, including authors, speakers, pastors, and evangelists, who mingle with guests and preside over fireside chats and other events. The daily camp for kids includes Bible study. A favorite for family reunions. Dining room. No room phones, no TV. Pool. Hot tub. Basketball, hiking, horseback riding, volleyball, fishing. Children's programs (ages 4 to 17), playground. | 5770 S. St. Vrain | 970/586–4212 or 800/523–4212 | fax 970/586–2255 | www.windriverranch.com | 28 1- to 3-bedroom cottages | $1,199–$1,369 per person for 6 days (6–night minimum stay) | Closed Oct.–May | AP | D, MC, V.

EVERGREEN

(Nearby towns also listed: Denver, Englewood, Golden, Idaho Springs, Lakewood)

At more than 7,040 ft elevation, Evergreen encompasses approximately 130 square mi of pine-and aspen-laden hills, with a population of some 34,000. Residents include artists, engineers, scientists, carpenters, retailers, homemakers, and heads of corporations, many of whom work in downtown Denver, which is only 20 mi east via Routes 8 and 74. Many residents prefer to work in the city but choose to make their homes in this tranquil mountain community.

From a community that was once merely a summer resort destination, Evergreen began to be transformed in the 1960s to one of Denver's many bedroom communities. While present-day Evergreen is composed of a large working class, the residents still enjoy watching the elk and buffalo roam about. Beautiful mountain vistas, thick pine forests, wildlife, and an abundance of recreational activities await visitors to Evergreen.

The arts, whether fine art, pottery, music, or fine crafts, hold a strong presence in Evergreen, as is evidenced by the numerous artistic associations which operate in the area. The annual Rodeo Weekend is also a huge draw and community tradition.

Information: Evergreen Area Chamber of Commerce | 29029 Upper Bear Creek Rd. #202, Box 97, Evergreen, 80439 | 303/674–3412 | www.evergreenchamber.org.

Attractions

Hiwan Homestead Museum. A restored 1880 mountain lodge housing Native American and regional history artifacts. | 4208 S. Timbervale Dr. | www.heartbeat-of-evergreen.com/homestead/homestead.html | 303/674–6262 | fax 303/670–7746 | Free | Memorial Day–Labor Day, daily 11–5.

Maxwell Falls. This splendid waterfall is a very popular local attraction. Take Highway 73 to Brook Forest Rd., then go west for 2½ mi. | Brook Forest Rd. | 303/964–2522 | Free | Daily.

ON THE CALENDAR

JUNE: *Rodeo Weekend.* A parade and PRCA rodeo competition at the Elpinal Rodeo Arena the third weekend in June. | 303/298–0220.

JULY: *Summerfest.* This two-day event at Heritage Grove, next to the Hiwan Homestead Museum, is a showcase of art and crafts by artists from all across the United States. Live music is also provided. | 303/674–4625.

AUG.: *Mountain Rendezvous.* An interpretation of the era of the mountain men at the Hiwan Homestead Museum, with arts, crafts, cooking demonstrations, games, and trapping exhibits the first Saturday in August. | 303/674–6262.

Dining

Key's on the Green. Steak. Perched on the shore of Evergreen Lake, this classy spot serves the best steaks in town. Try the teriyaki sirloin or steak David. Kids' menu. Sunday brunch | 29614 Upper Bear Creek Rd. | 303/674–4095 | fax 303/670–6973 | $12–$23 | AE, D, DC, MC, V.

Lodging

Bears Inn Bed and Breakfast. Formerly a mountain lodge hotel resort, this B&B is perfect for romantic getaways. You can relax by the fireplace in the great room or take in breathtaking mountain views from the deck. Complimentary breakfast. Cable TV. Outdoor hot tub. Business services. No kids under 12. No smoking. | 27425 Spruce La. | 303/670–1205 or 800/863–1205 | fax 303/670–8542 | www.bearsinn.com | 11 rooms | $95–$125 | AE, MC, V.

Highland Haven Creekside Inn. On the banks of Bear Creek, this inn has mountain cottages with modern conveniences. Complimentary Continental breakfast. In-room data ports, no air-conditioning, some kitchenettes, some microwaves, cable TV. Massage. | 4395 Independence Trail | 303/674–3577 or 800/459–2406 | fax 303/674–9088 | www.highland-haven.com | 4 rooms, 6 suites, 6 cottages | $90–$100, $150–$230 suites, $170–$220 cottages | AE, D, MC, V.

FAIRPLAY

MAP 6, E5

(Nearby towns also listed: Breckenridge, Buena Vista)

Located on the headwaters of the South Platte River, the town of Fairplay (population 600) was organized in 1859, when gold was discovered in the region. However, for scores of years before its formal establishment, all of the surrounding area was a favorite haunt for the Ute Indians and French and American fur trappers. A restored mining town shows how life was lived during the early days of the Colorado gold rush. Today, the town is most noted for its easy access to the large variety of recreational opportunities in the region.

Information: **Town Clerk** | 400 Front St., Box 267, Fairplay 80440 | 719/836–2622.

Attractions

Monument to Prunes, a Burro. A monument to a faithful burro who hauled supplies to area mines for more than 60 years. | Between 16th and 17th Sts. | 719/836–2622 | Free | Daily.

Pike National Forest. *(See* Colorado Springs.) Fairplay is surrounded on three sides by national forest, and by following U.S. 285 in either direction, you will soon come to the entrance of Pike National Forest. This wilderness wonderland of more than 1 million acres, offers hiking, fishing, and other outdoor activities. Stop by the South Park Ranger station for more information. | Junction U.S. 285 and Rte. 9 | 719/836–2031 | www.fs.fed.us/r2/psicc | Free | Daily.

South Park City Museum. A re-creation of an old mining town features 30 buildings and more than 60,000 artifacts dating from 1860 to 1900. | 100 4th St. | 719/836–2387 | $5 | Mid-Oct.–mid-May, by appointment only.

ON THE CALENDAR
JUNE: *Fair Folk Festival.* This one-day event is a family-oriented arts and music festival, all in Cohen Park. | 719/836–2698.
JULY: *World's Championship Pack Burro Race.* An annual event that honors the lowly burro, the lifesaver of many miners and prospectors in the region the last full weekend in July. The race course is 29 mi long. | 719/836–1535.

Dining
Front Street Café. Contemporary. A casual atmosphere in a bistro-type setting awaits diners at this café. All of the food is freshly prepared; the grilled Portobello mushroom sandwich and sesame-seared salmon are highly recommended. The weekend brunch is very popular. | 435 Front St. | 719/836–7031 | Breakfast also available weekends | $10–$13 | D, MC, V.

Lodging
American Safari Ranch. You will enjoy breathtaking views of the Rocky Mountains. Rooms are clean and comfortable. Special horseback riding packages are available. No room phones, no TV in rooms, TV in common area. Horseback riding. | County Rd. 7 | 719/836–2431 | www.americansafariranch.com | 12 lodge rooms, 6 two-room cabins | $75–$95 | MC, V.

The Hand Hotel Bed and Breakfast. Overlooking the Middle Fork of the South Platte River and surrounded by the Rocky Mountains, this B&B offers warm and friendly hospitality. All the rooms have a theme, such as "the Miner," "the Rancher," and "the Indian." Complimentary Continental breakfast. | 531 Front St. | 719/836–3595 | fax 719/836–1799 | www.hand-hotel.com | 11 rooms | $45–$60 | AE, D, MC, V.

North Fork Ranch. The views are panoramic at this guest ranch, near the South Platte River in the Pike National Forest 50 mi southwest of Evergreen on Highway 285. There is daily entertainment, including square dances and campfire sing-alongs. Dining room, picnic area. No air-conditioning, some refrigerators, no room phones, no TV. Pool. Hot tub. Horseback riding, hiking, fishing. Children's programs (ages 0–6). Laundry facilities. Airport shuttle. | 55395 Hwy. 285, Shawnee | 303/838–9873 or 800/843–7895 | fax 303/838–1549 | www.northforkranch.com | 9 rooms, 3 1- to 3-bedroom cottages | $1,395 per person per wk (1–wk minimum stay) | Closed mid-Sept.–mid-May | AP | No credit cards.

Tumbling River Ranch. This family-oriented ranch near the South Platte River is 37 mi southeast of Evergreen, and about an hour from Denver. Cabins and historic ranch houses with fireplaces provide lodgings for guests. White-water rafting on the Arkansas River is available. No air-conditioning, no room phones, no TV. Pool. Hot tub, sauna. Basketball, hiking, horseback riding, volleyball, fishing. Children's programs (ages 3–17). | 3715 Park County Rd. 62, Grant | 303/838–5981 or 800/654–8770 | fax 303/838–5133 | www.tumblingriver.com | 9 rooms, 16 cabins, 3 suites | $1,600–$1,800 per person per wk (1–wk minimum stay) | Closed Oct.–Apr. | AP | No credit cards.

FORT COLLINS

(Nearby towns also listed: Estes Park, Greeley, Longmont, Loveland)

Fort Collins was established in 1864 to protect area traders from the natives, while the former negotiated the treacherous Overland Trail. Unexpectedly, however, the town grew on two industries: education (Colorado State University was founded here in 1879) and agriculture (rich crops of alfalfa and sugar beets).

Today, with a population approaching 90,000 (23,000 coming from CSU), Fort Collins is one of Colorado's most progressive cities. It has all the amenities of a big city with a touch of small-town charm and an abundance of outdoor recreation. Some of the activities that you can engage in include hiking, rock climbing, mountain biking, camping, trout fishing, and white-water rafting. The headquarters for the Roosevelt and Arapaho National forests are also located here.

Information: **Fort Collins Convention and Visitors Bureau** | 420 S. Howes St. #101, Fort Collins 80521 | 970/482–5821 or 800/274–3678 | fax 970/493–8061 | www.ftcollins.com.

Attractions

Colorado State University. Founded in 1879, this is an agricultural and mechanical university, meaning that the college was originally founded as a place for farmer-scientists to expand their knowledge of agricultural and engineering processes. The elm-lined Oval at the center of campus is its heart, and it's ringed by the older campus buildings (many dating from the 1920s), as well as some newer ones. Today, more than 23,000 students attend, and its mission has been greatly extended, including a very well-regarded veterinary school and occupational health program. | W. Laurel and Howes Sts., west of College Ave. | 970/491–1101 | www.colostate.edu/ | Free | Daily.

Discovery Center Science Museum. This museum houses over 90 educational exhibits, including a variety of science and technology displays. | 703 E. Prospect Rd. | 970/472–3990 | www.dcsm.org | $4 | Tues.–Sat. 10–5, Sun. noon–5.

Fort Collins Museum. Houses a model of the old Fort Collins army post, three historic pioneer cabins, turn-of-the-20th-century schoolhouse, as well as Indian artifacts and exhibits of local history. | 200 Mathews St. | 970/221–6738 | www.ci.fort-collins.co.us | Free | Tues.–Sat. 10–5.

Lincoln Center. A performing-arts complex with a sculpture garden, art gallery, and concert hall. | 417 W. Magnolia | 970/221–6730 | www.ci.fort-collins.co.us | Free (charges for performances) | Daily (performance hrs vary).

Lory State Park. Biking, hiking, horseback riding, and picnicking are available at this 2,500-acre preserve 9 mi west of Fort Collins. | County Rd. 25G | 970/493–1623 | parks.state.co.us/lory | $4 per vehicle, $2 per person | Daily.

Swetsville Zoo. This "zoo" is the unique creation of a dairy farmer insomniac who stayed up nights fashioning more than 100 dinosaurs and other creatures from old farm equipment. | 4801 E. Harmony Rd. | 970/484–9509 | Free | Daily dawn to dusk.

ON THE CALENDAR
JUNE: *Colorado Brewers Fest*. This weekend festival brings together the best brewers from across the state for some friendly competition and merriment in Old Town. | 970/484–6500.

Dining
Bisetti's Italian Restaurant. Italian. This family-owned eatery provides a warm setting and great authentic Italian cuisine. Almost all the pasta is made from scratch. Popular dishes

include chicken olive bisetti and the basil chicken. Kids' menu. | 120 S. College Ave. | 970/493–0086 | No lunch weekends | $7–$13 | D, MC, V.

Coopersmith's Pub & Brewing. American. One of Colorado's original brewpubs—they even put their brews in some of the dinner entrées. Blackboard specials change daily. Try the homemade root beer, ginger ale, or cream soda. Known for burgers, appetizers. Open-air dining on patio with evening concerts in summer. Kids' menu. | 5 Old Town Sq | 970/498–0483 | $7–$18 | MC, V.

Lone Star Steakhouse & Saloon. Steak. Mesquite-grilled delights and a lively atmosphere remind you of a Texas roadhouse. Known for Cajun rib eye, grilled shrimp. Open-air dining on small patio in front. Kids' menu. | 100 W. Troutman Pkwy. | 970/225–6284 | $12–$22 | AE, D, MC, V.

Rio Grande. Mexican. Colorful Mexican decorations add to the festive atmosphere, and the 99¢ margaritas will start you off to a great Mexican dinner. Known for Mexican steak, burritos, and sopaipillas. | 143 W. Mountain Ave. | 970/224–5428 | $8–$15 | MC, V.

Silver Grill Cafe. American. Opened in 1933, this remains a popular spot with locals for breakfast and lunch. Homemade baked goods and desserts. Known for giant cinnamon rolls. Kids' menu. | 218 Walnut St. | 970/484–4656 | Breakfast also available | $3–$8 | D, MC, V.

Lodging

Best Western Kiva Inn. This chain motel is about halfway between Interstate 25 and the Colorado State University campus. Complimentary Continental breakfast. Cable TV. Pool. Business services. | 1638 E. Mulberry St. | 970/484–2444 or 888/299–5482 | fax 970/221–0967 | www.bestwestern.com | 62 rooms | $89–$105 | AE, D, DC, MC, V.

Best Western University Inn. An ideal resting spot for visiting parents, this chain motel is across the street from the Colorado State University campus. In-room data ports, cable TV. Pool. Business services. | 914 S. College Ave. | 970/484–1984 or 888/299–5482 | fax 970/484–1987 | www.bestwestern.com | 74 rooms | $60–$75 | AE, D, DC, MC, V.

Budget Host Inn. Just 1 mi north of Old Town and other attractions, this budget-price motel offers clean rooms and affordable rates. Complimentary Continental breakfast. Cable TV. Outdoor hot tub. | 1513 N. College Ave. | 970/484–0870 | fax 970/224–2998 | 30 rooms | $59–$69 | AE, D, MC, V.

Cherokee Park Ranch. First opened in 1886, this family-friendly ranch 42 mi northwest of Fort Collins offers a plethora of outdoor activities. Located on 300 acres bordering the Roosevelt National Forest, its rustic cabins have an authentic western feel. Dining room. No air-conditioning, no room phones, no TV. Pool. Hot tub. Basketball, hiking, horseback riding, volleyball, fishing. Children's programs (ages 3–12). Airport shuttle. | 436 Cherokee Hills Drive, Livermore | 970/493–6522 or 800/628–0949 | fax 970/493–5802 | www.ranch-web.com/cherokeepark/index.html | 4 suites, 6 cabins | $900–$1,100 per person per wk (1–wk minimum stay) | Closed mid-Sept.–mid-May | AP | MC, V.

Elizabeth Street Guest House Bed & Breakfast. Family antiques and folk art pieces decorate the walls and rooms of this cozy B&B. Be sure to note the intricate three-story miniature house in the entry hall. Complimentary breakfast. No room phones, TV in common area. Airport shuttle. No smoking. | 202 E. Elizabeth St. | 970/493–2337 | fax 970/493–6662 | sheryl.clark@juno.com | 3 rooms | $70–$90 | AE, MC, V.

Holiday Inn Fort Collins–I–25. This reliable, mid-priced chain hotel is just east of downtown Fort Collins. Restaurant, bar, room service. Cable TV, some in-room VCRs. Pool, wading pool. Hot tub, sauna. Gym. Video games. Laundry facilities. Business services. Pets allowed. | 3836 E. Mulberry St. | 970/484–4660 or 800/465–4329 | fax 970/484–2326 | www.holiday-inn.com | 197 rooms | $89–$99 | AE, D, DC, MC, V.

Fort Collins Marriott. This upscale chain hotel is in southeast Fort Collins, about 2 mi from the CSU campus. Restaurant, bar. In-room data ports, cable TV. Indoor-outdoor pool. Gym.

Laundry facilities. Business services, airport shuttle. | 350 E. Horsetooth Rd. | 970/226–5200 or 800/228–9290 | fax 970/226–9708 | www.marriott.com | 206 rooms, 23 suites | $129–$149, $185 suites | AE, D, DC, MC, V.

Residence Inn Fort Collins. Rooms at this all-suite chain hotel are comfortable and spacious. It is ideal for business travelers and there is a meeting room. Complimentary breakfast. In-room data ports, kitchenettes, refrigerators, cable TV. Pool. Gym. Laundry service. Business services. Pets allowed (fee). | 1127 Oakridge Dr. | 970/223–5700 | fax 970/266–9280 | www.residenceinn.com | 78 suites | $89–$109 | AE, D, DC, MC, V.

Sky Corral Guest Ranch. This small ranch, 23 mi northwest of Fort Collins, is surrounded by the high mountain trails of the Roosevelt National Forest. Rodeos and square dancing provide hearty family entertainment. Dining room. No air-conditioning, no room phones, no TV in rooms, TV (with VCR) in common area. Tennis. Basketball, hiking, horseback riding, volleyball. Fishing, bicycles. Laundry service. | 8233 Old Flowers Rd. (Hwy. 285), Bellvue | 970/484–1362 or 888/323–2531 | fax 970/484–0331 | www.skycorral.com | 5 rooms, 6 cabins | $1,200 per person for 6 nights (6–night minimum stay) | Closed Nov.–May | AP | MC, V.

FORT MORGAN

MAP 6, H2

(Nearby towns also listed: Greeley, Sterling)

Originally a U.S. Army post during the 1860s, Fort Morgan's primary claim to fame is the fact that the great American band leader of the 1930s and 40s, Glenn Miller, was born here. In the prairie country of eastern Colorado, the town, with a population of 11,700, sits astride Interstate 76 between Denver and Sterling. Agriculture is the primary occupation in these parts with sugar beets, wheat, corn, and alfalfa being popular crops.

Information: Fort Morgan Area Chamber of Commerce | 300 Main St., Fort Morgan, 80701 | 970/867–6702 | www.fortmorganchamber.org.

Attractions

Fort Morgan Museum. The history of northeastern Colorado is displayed through a variety of permanent and rotating exhibits. Glenn Miller memorabilia is also displayed. | 414 Main St. | 970/867–6331 | www.ftmorganmus.org | Free | Mon. and Fri. 10–5, Tues.–Thurs. 6–8, Sat. 11–5.

Jackson Lake State Park. Swimming, waterskiing, fishing, boating, camping, biking, hiking, and picnicking are available at the park, which is 20 mi north and west of Fort Morgan. | Rte. 144 | 970/645–2551 | Free | Daily.

Rainbow Arch Bridge. The longest concrete arch bridge of its type in the United States, this unique structure measures 1,110 ft long and contains 11 arches. | Rte. 52 at Riverside Park | 970/867–6331 | Free | Daily.

ON THE CALENDAR
JUNE: *Glenn Miller Festival.* Relive the "Big Band" era with the sounds of Colorado's favorite musical son the third weekend in June. | 970/867–6702 or 800/354–8660.
JULY: *Festival in the Park.* Arts-and-crafts booths and local musical performers highlight this family-oriented event in City Park. | 970/867–6484.
JULY: *Rodeo.* The world's largest amateur rode is held in Brush, 10 mi east of Fort Morgan in early July. | 970/867–6702 or 800/354–8660.

Dining
Country Steak-Out. Steak. Fort Morgan's first steak house—a combination diner and barn—looks as if it hasn't changed since the Dust Bowl era. The steaks, however, are suc-

culent. Kids' menu. | 19592 E. 8th Ave. | 970/867–7887 | Closed Mon. No dinner Sun. | $9–$30 | AE, D, DC, MC, V.

Fergie's West Inn Pub. American/Casual. This small, simple restaurant and bar in the heart of town is comfortable and has a no-nonsense menu. Known for chicken wings and pizza. | 324 W. Main St. | 970/522–4220 | Closed Sun. | $8–$15 | MC, V.

Lodging

Best Western Park Terrace. This simple chain motel is four blocks south of Interstate 76. Picnic area. In-room data ports, cable TV. Pool. Hot tub. Pets allowed (fee). | 725 Main St. | 970/867–8256 or 888/593–5793 | fax 970/867–8256 | www.bestwestern.com | 24 rooms | $49–$70 | AE, D, DC, MC, V.

Central Motel. This independently owned budget motel is in downtown Fort Morgan. Microwaves, refrigerators, cable TV, some in-room VCRs. Some pets allowed. | 201 W. Platte Ave. | 970/867–2401 | fax 970/867–2401 | 13 rooms, 6 suites | $40–$55, $60 suites | AE, D, DC, MC, V.

Fort Morgan Days Inn. This budget chain motel offers clean rooms and is great for travelers on a tight budget who still want a comfortable room. Refrigerators, cable TV. Pool. | Exit 80 S off I-76 and Hwy. 52 | 970/542–0844 | fax 970/867–4657 | www.daysinn.com | 33 rooms | $55–$65 | AE, D, DC, MC, V.

FRISCO

MAP 6, E4

(Nearby towns also listed: Breckenridge, Copper Mountain, Dillon, Keystone)

Surrounded by the many corporate ski resorts in Summit County, Frisco (population 2,767) has long strived to retain its individuality and small-town charm. There are no manufactured mountain villages or high-speed chairlifts here, but the winter sports are more varied than they are at most of the big ski resorts. In the center of a wide mountain valley, the Frisco area has terrain perfectly suited for Nordic skiing; the Frisco Nordic Center is considered to be one of the country's best. When temperatures drop, the frozen surface of Lake Dillon comes alive with pickup hockey games, ice-boat races, and ice fishing.

When the snow melts and other resorts turn into just another place to shop, Frisco becomes even more popular. The Frisco Bay Marina on Lake Dillon provides full services for boating enthusiasts, and the Ten Mile Creek inlet is a great place to fish for brown, rainbow, and brook trout. A great way to explore the area on foot, blade, or bike is the Ten Mile Recreational Pathway, which follows Ten Mile Creek for some 50 mi. Many interesting shops and restaurants line Main Street and Summit Boulevard, and the Frisco Historic Park gives a glimpse into the past with its museum and historical buildings.

Information: **Summit County Chamber of Commerce** | Box 214, Frisco 80435 | 800/350–3099 | www.summittchamber.org.

Attractions

Breckenridge and Frisco Nordic Center. This center has 27 mi of one-way loops for cross-country skiing. | 18545 N. Summit Blvd. | 970/668–0866 | $12 per day | Nov.–May, daily.

SIGHTSEEING TOURS/TOUR COMPANIES

Timber Ridge Adventures. Ride snowmobiles with a professional guide on endless miles of groomed trails and through fields of open powder along Ten Mile Canyon. Tours can be tailored for families and riders of all experience levels and overnight camping rides are available. | Box 330, Frisco | 970/668–8349 | www.trsnowmobile.com | $75–$120 | Nov.–Apr. daily.

ON THE CALENDAR

AUG.: *Colorado Barbecue Challenge.* Every year Colorado's official barbecue cook-off draws hundreds of gourmet grillmasters from all over the state to downtown Frisco. | 800/350–3099.

Dining

Blue Spruce Inn. Continental. This 1940s log cabin in downtown Frisco houses a spacious restaurant and dining room. The attached saloon dates back to the 1860s when it catered to thirsty miners. Game specials are offered nightly, along with lamb chops in a pesto demi-glace, and steak Diane with mushroom-mustard cream sauce. | 20 Main St. | 970/668–5900 | No lunch | $14–$26 | AE, D, DC, MC, V.

Barkley's Margaritaville. Mexican. Prime rib, fajitas, and burritos are available in numerous configurations at this lively Mexican-American restaurant. There's plenty of meal-size appetizers on the bar menu. Kids' menu. | 620 S. Main St. | 970/668–3694 | $6–$20 | AE, D, MC, V.

Claimjumper. American/Casual. Large windows and hanging plants provide a bright, comfortable dining area, which has counter and booth seating. Smoked meat and fish plates are the specialty; the owner does his own hickory smoking out back. Also available are Mexican and vegetarian dishes, pastas, prime rib, and chicken. | 805 N. Summit | 970/668–3617 | $8–$17 | AE, D, DC, MC, V.

El Rio. Mexican. On a sunny deck overlooking Ten Mile Creek and Gore Range, you can enjoy great margaritas and fresh south-of-the-border specialties, such as blackened Chilean sea bass tacos, or Taos tacos—a soft flour tortilla with cheese, pinto beans, and roasted vegetables. Try the handmade tamales. | 450 W. Main St. | 970/668–5043 | No lunch Sept.–May | $7–$13 | AE, D, MC, V.

Frisco Bar & Grill. American. Burgers, ribs, and prime rib are presented in myriad forms at prices that even locals can afford. Daily specials and appetizers are an even cheaper alternative. A Frisco tradition. | 720 Granite St. | 970/668–5051 | Reservations not accepted | $4–$14 | AE, D, DC, MC, V.

Lodging

Creekside Inn. This modern bed-and-breakfast has an amazing view of Mt. Royal, with individually decorated rooms and southwestern accents. The forested backyard has a furnished patio facing Ten Mile Creek. A suite is available with a fireplace and hot tub. Complimentary breakfast. Some room phones, no TV in rooms, TV in common area. Outdoor hot tub. Business services. No kids under 12. No smoking. | 51 W. Main St. | 970/668–5607 or 800/668–7320 | fax 970/668–8635 | www.creeksideinn-frisco.com | 7 rooms | $100–$185 | D, MC, V.

Frisco Lodge Bed & Breakfast. Built in 1885 this renovated stagecoach stop has relatively small rooms furnished with some antiques and a comfortable feel. Many of the rooms have private baths and efficiency kitchens, making them more than adequate for couples. Some can be connected to accommodate small families. Complimentary breakfast. Some kitchenettes, some microwaves, some refrigerators, some in-room hot tubs, cable TV, no TV in some rooms, TV in common area. Outdoor hot tub. No smoking. | 321 Main St. | 970/668–0195 or 800/279–6000 | fax 970/668–0149 | www.friscolodge.com | 19 rooms (9 with shared bath) | $75–$100 | AE, D, MC, V.

Galena Street Mountain Inn. This pink stucco inn is furnished with stylish reproduction Mission pieces. Decorated with a southwestern motif, the rooms have curved moldings, washed-oak window trim, down comforters, and either king or queen beds. Complimentary breakfast. Cable TV. Hot tub, sauna. | 106 Galena St. | 970/668–3224 or 800/248–9138 | fax 970/668–5291 | 15 rooms | $85–$165 | AE, D, DC, MC.

Holiday Inn Summit County. This large, modern hotel on Lake Dillon provides excellent family lodging. In addition to the many facilities there is an extensive game room with pool, darts, and video games. Proximity to the lake makes this a fishing and boating hot spot. Restaurant, bar, room service. Some refrigerators, cable TV. Pool. Hot tub, massage. Gym. Laundry facilities. Business services. | 1129 N. Summit Blvd. | 970/668–5000 | fax 970/668–0718 | www.holiday-inn.com | 216 rooms | $99–$139 | AE, D, DC, MC, V.

Hotel Frisco. This three-story log structure, built in 1987, is modeled after neighboring historic buildings in downtown Frisco. The rooms are filled with antiques and, although no two are alike, they all share a casual country feel. Complimentary Continental breakfast. In-room data ports, cable TV, in-room VCRs. Hot tub. Library. | 308 Main St. | 970/668–5009 or 800/262–1002 | www.hotelfrisco.com | 14 rooms | $90–$145 | AE, D, MC, V.

Lark Mountain. This B&B near Main Street is the largest log building in town. The common areas include a movie room, living room with fireplace, dining room, and outdoor picnic area. Bikes are provided free of charge for getting around town. Picnic area, complimentary breakfast. In-room data ports, some microwaves, no room phones. Outdoor hot tub. No smoking. | 109 Granite St., Frisco | 970/668–5237 or 800/668–5275 | fax 970/668–1988 | lark-inn@toski.com | www.toski.com/lark | 7 rooms (2 with shared bath, 2 with shower only) | $120–$150 | MC, V.

New Summit Inn. One of the more economical places to stay in Frisco, it is relatively quiet and offers many amenities. Close to Lake Dillon and downtown, almost everything is a walk away. Complimentary Continental breakfast. Some microwaves, cable TV. Hot tub, sauna. Gym. Laundry facilities. Pets allowed (fee). | 1205 N. Summit Blvd. | 970/668–3220 or 800/745–1211 | fax 970/668–0188 | www.newsummitinn.com | 31 rooms | $99–$109 | AE, D, DC, MC, V.

Sky Vue Motel. Here you'll find clean and comfortable rooms with sturdy, bleached oak furnishings. About half have small efficiency kitchens. Complimentary Continental breakfast. Some kitchenettes, cable TV. Pool. Hot tub. Laundry facilities. | 305 S. 2nd St. | 970/668–3311 or 800/672–3311 | fax 303/668–5787 | www.skyvuemotel.com | 26 rooms | $59–$98 | AE, D, MC, V.

Snowshoe Motel. In historic downtown Frisco, this quaint little motel is walking distance to restaurants and shops and 2 blocks from Lake Dillon. Complimentary Continental breakfast. Some microwaves, refrigerators, cable TV, some in-room VCRs. Hot tub, sauna. Business services. | 521 Main St. | 970/668–3444 or 800/445–8658 | fax 970/668–3883 | www.toski.com/snowshoe | 37 rooms | $90–$97 | AE, D, MC, V.

Ten Mile Creek Condominiums. This pleasant and comfortable condo complex is modestly priced for the level of luxury it offers. Two to four bedroom units are well-equipped with full kitchens, balconies, and fireplaces. Cable TV. Pool. Hot tub, sauna. Laundry facilities. | 200 Granite St., Frisco | 970/668–3100 or 800/530–3070 | fax 970/668–3273 | 40 units | $145–$185 | AE, D, MC, V.

GEORGETOWN

MAP 6, F4

(Nearby towns also listed: Central City, Dillon, Golden, Idaho Springs, Keystone, Winter Park)

The area around Georgetown has produced nearly $200 million worth of gold, silver, zinc, and lead since gold was first discovered there in 1859. George Griffith, the prospector who found the gold, is the town's namesake. Located some 50 mi west of Denver along Interstate 70, this picturesque town of just over 1,000, with its restored historic district, is typical of the scores of mining villages that punctuated the Rockies during the mid- to late-1800s.

Information: Georgetown Visitor Center | Box 426, Georgetown, 80444 | 800/472–8230.

Attractions

Georgetown Energy Museum. This museum provides a thorough look at hydro-electric generators. You can witness the actual mechanics of how electricity is created as you stand a few feet away from spinning generators. | 600 Main St. | 303/569–3557. | www.historic-georgetown.org | Free. | Mon.–Sat. 10–4, Sun. noon–4.

Georgetown Loop Railroad and Historic Mine. Featured on the tour are reconstructed mining and railroad buildings from the late 1800s. The railroad travels 6 mi to Silver Plume. | 100 Loop Dr. | 800/691–4386 or 303/569–2403 | fax 303/569–2894 | www.gtownloop.com | Train trip $13, mine tours $5 | Late May–early Oct., daily 9–4; call for schedule.

Hamill House Museum. The restored home of Colorado state senator William A. Hamill, who made his fortune in silver. Period (1860s–70s) furnishings are displayed. | 305 Argentine St. | 303/569–2840 | www.historicgeorgetown.org | $5 | Late May–Sept., daily 10–4; Oct.–Dec., weekends noon–4.

Hotel de Paris Museum. French immigrant Louis Dupuy built this hotel in 1878 and watched it become one of the West's finest hostelries. Period furnishings re-create a period of wealth and influence. | 409 6th St. | 303/569–2311 | www.colostate.edu/depts/hist/hdp | $4 | Memorial Day–Sept., daily 10–5; Oct.–Memorial Day, weekends noon–4.

Loveland Ski Area. The ski area 12 mi west of Georgetown features 3 quads, 2 triple and 4 double chairlifts, 1 Pomalift, 1 Mighty-mite, 60 runs (the longest is 2 mi), and a vertical drop of 2,410 ft. | I–70, exit 216 | www.skiloveland.com | 303/569–3203 or 303/571–5580 | Mid-Oct.–May, weekdays 9–4, weekends 8:30–4.

ON THE CALENDAR

DEC.: *Georgetown Christmas Market.* This outdoor, Scandinavian-style celebration features arts-and-crafts booths and food vendors the first two weekends in December | 303/569–2840.

Dining

Happy Cooker. American/Casual. This popular local restaurant is homey and comfortable. The waffles and cinnamon buns are locally famous. Open-air dining with great views of Rocky Mountains. Kids' menu. | 412 6th St. | 303/569–3166 | Breakfast also available. No dinner | $4–$8 | D, MC, V.

The Red Ram. American. An almost half-century-old restaurant housed in a century-old building. Known for its great hamburgers, ribs, and Mexican dishes. | 606 6th St. | 303/569–2300 | $6–$14 | AE, D, DC, MC, V.

Victorian Lady Restaurant. Contemporary. Housed in a Victorian-era building dating from 1869, this restaurant serves up salads, burgers, and seafood. Known, appropriately, for "Victorian" chicken and also halibut. | 415 Rose St. | 303/569–2208 | Closed Thurs. | $9–$14 | MC, V.

Lodging

Alpine Hideaway B&B. On a hillside above Georgetown Lake, this B&B is perfect for couples who need a private, romantic getaway. Rooms are spacious, luxurious, and contain fireplaces. Complimentary breakfast. In-room hot tubs, no room phones, no TV. No kids under 18. | Box 788 | 303/569–2800 or 800/490–9011 | www.entertain.com/wedgwood/hide.html | 3 rooms | $145–$165 | MC, V.

Mad Creek Bed and Breakfast. An impressive fireplace dominates the parlor of this 1881 Victorian on Highway 40, 2 mi north of Georgetown in the even tinier town of Empire. Complimentary breakfast. No air-conditioning, no room phones, no TV in rooms, TV in common area. Hot tub. No kids under 10. No smoking. | 167 Park Ave., Empire | 303/569–2003 | 3 rooms (2 with shared bath) | $55–$85 | MC, V.

GLENWOOD SPRINGS

(Nearby towns also listed: Aspen, Meeker, Rifle)

Glenwood Springs (population 8,202), which is 41 mi northwest of Aspen, is surrounded on three sides by White River National Forest and is noted for its hot springs where the water hovers around 100°F year-round. You can participate in practically any kind of outdoor sport you can think of here, including hunting, fishing, biking, golf, and horseback riding. John Henry "Doc" Holliday survived the gunfight at the OK Corral, only to die in bed in Glenwood Springs.

Information: Chamber Resort Association | 1102 Grand Ave, Glenwood Springs, 81601 | 970/945–6589 or 888/445–3696 | www.glenscape.com.

Attractions

Frontier Historical Society Museum. This museum captures the history of Glenwood Springs and Garfield County. It features an exhibit on Doc Holliday, a turn-of-the-20th-century kitchen, and an exhibit on the Ute Indians. | 1001 Colorado Ave. | 970/945–4448 | $3 | May–Oct., Mon.–Sat. 11–4.; Nov.–Apr., Mon. and Thurs.–Sat. 1–4.

Glenwood Hot Springs Pool. Warm mineral water keeps two outdoor pools, one measuring two city blocks long, at a constant temperature of 90°F and 104°F. | 401 N. River Rd. | 970/945–6571 or 800/537–7946 | www.hotspringspool.com | $9 | Memorial Day–Labor Day, daily 7:30 AM–10 PM; Labor Day–Memorial Day, daily 9 AM–10 PM.

Sunlight Mountain Resort. This ski area has 64 runs (the longest is 2½ mi) and a vertical drop of 2,010 ft. | 10901 County Rd. 117 | 970/945–7491 or 800/445–7931 | www.sunlightmtn.com | Late Nov.–early Apr., daily.

White River National Forest. This wilderness consists of 2¼ million acres in the heart of the Rocky Mountains, completely enveloping the town of Glenwood Springs. Seventy developed sites offer boating, picnicking, camping, fishing, birding, and more. | Old Federal Building, 9th Ave. and Grand St. | 970/945–2521 | www.fs.fed.us/r2/whiteriver | Free | Daily.

ON THE CALENDAR
JUNE: *Strawberry Days Festival.* Rodeo competition, music, and arts-and-crafts exhibits are part of the fun the third weekend in June. | 970/945–6589 or 888/445–3696.
AUG.: *Garfield County Fair and Rodeo.* A traditional county fair and rodeo are featured. | 970/945–6589 or 888/445–3696.
SEPT.: *Tri-G Tri-Athalon.* Competitors compete in three events: swimming, bicycling, and running to raise money for the Colorado Animal Rescue (CARE). Held at the Hot Springs Pool. | 970/945–6589.

Dining
★ **The Bayou.** Cajun. This casual eatery has a frog awning that somehow beckons you in. Choose from lip-smacking gumbo, étouffée, and blackened fish, or lethal Cajun martinis. On summer weekends live music is played on the patio. | 52103 U.S. 6, at Rte. 24 | 970/945–1047 | No lunch | $5–$15 | AE, MC, V.

Crystal Club Café. Italian. You can have your meal on the patio or in the garden at this mountain-rustic spot on the Crystal River. Try the Italian wedding soup, chicken marsala, or homemade pizza. It's about 30 mi south of Glenwood Springs in Redstone. There's open-air dining by the river under a tent-covered patio and on picnic tables. Kids' menu. | 467 Redstone Blvd., Redstone | 970/963–9515 | Closed Mon.–Thurs. Nov.–May | $6–$16 | MC, V.

Daily Bread Café. American/Casual. Wooden floors and booths, stained-glass windows, and art by local artists set the scene for homey fare in this casual place. Known for bacon, turkey, and avocado sanwiches, homemade biscuits and gravy, and salads. | 729 Grand Ave. | 970/945-6253 | Breakfast also available; no dinner; no lunch Sun. | $4–$7 | D, MC, V.

Florinda's. Italian. Exhibits by local artists hang on the russet-and-salmon walls of this popular Italian restaurant. Expect garlic in everything; try veal chops grilled with shiitake mushrooms in marsala, garlic, and sun-dried tomatoes. Kids' menu. No smoking. | 721 Grand Ave. | 970/945-1245 | Closed Sun. | $10–$18 | MC, V.

Juicy Lucy's Steakhouse. Steak. This upscale steak house is decked out in late 19th-century finery. Lucy's is renowned for unique salads, savory steaks, and fresh fish and seafood. Try the Alaskan king crab legs. | 308 7th St. | 970/945-4619 | $9–$26 | MC, V.

Los Desperados. Mexican. A southwestern-style place with adobe walls and all your south-of-the-border favorites. Open-air dining on patio surrounded by water fountains and flowers. Kids' menu. | 0055 Mel Rey Rd. | 970/945-6878 | No lunch Mon. | $6–$15 | AE, D, MC, V.

Rivers. Continental. You'll look out on the Roaring Fork River through the windows of this airy, high-ceilinged dining room with white linens on the tables. Try smoked trout pâté or elk medallions. Open-air dining on deck overlooking the river. Kids' menu. Sunday brunch. | 2525 S. Grand Ave. | 970/928-8813 | No lunch | $7–$33 | AE, D, MC, V.

Lodging

Avalanche Ranch. Many of the cozy, carpeted, pine-paneled cabins have lofts and fireplaces at this ranch on the Crystal River about 30 mi south of Glenwood Springs. Each cabin has its own yard with a picnic table and charcoal grill as well as a full kitchen. Down comforters on all the beds keep you warm and comfortable. Picnic area. No air-conditioning, kitchenettes, some in-room VCRs, no room phones, TV in common area. Hot tub. Playground. Business services. Some pets allowed (fee). No smoking. | 12863 Hwy. 133, Redstone | 970/963-2846 or 877/963-9339 | fax 970/963-3141 | www.avalancheranch.com | 12 cabins, 1 3-bedroom ranch house | $95–$175 cabins, $395 ranch house (3–night minimum stay in summer) | D, MC, V.

Best Western Antlers. A chain motel convenient to downtown and the highway. Picnic area. Cable TV. Pool, wading pool. Hot tub. Playground. Laundry facilities. Business services. | 171 W. 6th St. | 970/945-8535 or 800/626-0609 | fax 970/945-9388 | www.bestwestern.com | 87 rooms, 13 suites | $69–$129, $110–$170 suites | AE, D, DC, MC, V.

Glenwood Motor Inn. This motel is located within easy walking distance of downtown restaurants and shopping. No air-conditioning in some rooms, in-room data ports, some microwaves, some refrigerators, cable TV. Hot tub, sauna. Laundry facilities. Business services. | 141 W. 6th St. | 970/945-5438 or 800/543-5906 | fax 970/945-5438 | 45 rooms | $64–$98 | AE, D, DC, MC, V.

Hotel Colorado. The exterior of this building is simply exquisite, with graceful sandstone colonnades and Italian campaniles. In its halcyon days everybody from Doc Holliday to Al Capone stayed here. Rooms are decorated in somewhat updated period fashion. Restaurant, bar. Cable TV. Beauty salon. Gym. Pets allowed (fee). | 526 Pine St. | 970/945-6511 or 800/544-3998 | fax 970/945-7030 | www.hotelcolorado.com | 128 rooms, 32 suites | $122–$178 | AE, D, DC, MC, V.

Hotel Denver. Although this hotel was originally built in 1806, its most striking features are the numerous Art Deco touches throughout. The rooms are neat and comfortable, ranging in size from small to quite large. Restaurant, bar. Some kitchenettes, cable TV. Beauty salon. Gym. Pets allowed. | 402 7th St. | 970/945-6565 or 800/826-8820 | fax 970/945-2204 | www.thehoteldenver.com | 60 rooms | $89–$129 | AE, D, DC, MC, V.

Hot Springs Lodge. Most rooms have a private patio or balcony at this lodge (across the street from the Glenwood Hot Springs pool). Those who stay here get a discount on pool fees. Picnic area. In-room data ports, some refrigerators, cable TV. Pool. Hot tub. Miniature golf. Gym. Laundry facilities. Business services, airport shuttle. | 415 E. 6th St. | 970/945-

6571 or 800/537–7946 (in CO only) | fax 970/947–2950 | www.hotspringspool.com | 107 rooms | $90–$115 | AE, D, DC, MC, V.

Mt. Sopris. Perched on the edge of a 40-ft bluff, this tranquil, upscale B&B affords lovely panoramic mountain and valley views. The buildings are modern log construction; the two-story great room has a beautiful river rock fireplace and grand piano. The inn is in Carbondale, 12 mi south of Glenwood Springs. Complimentary breakfast. Pool. Hot tub. Business services. No kids under 18. No smoking. | 0165 Mt. Sopris Ranch Rd., Carbondale | 970/963–2209 or 800/437–8675 | fax 970/963–8975 | www.mtsoprisinn.com | 14 rooms in 3 buildings | $85–$175 | MC, V.

Redstone Inn. This inn was built as quarters for bachelor miners at the turn of the 20th century and is the centerpiece of Redstone, 29 mi south of Glenwood Springs. Restaurant, bar. Cable TV. Pool. Beauty salon, hot tub. Tennis. Gym. Business services. | 82 Redstone Blvd., Redstone | 970/963–2526 or 800/748–2524 | fax 970/963–2527 | www.redstoneinn.com | 30 rooms, 5 suites | $65–$185, $149–$210 suites | AE, D, MC, V.

Sunlight Mountain Inn. This traditional ski lodge brims with European country charm, from the delightful lounge to the cozily rustic rooms. Sunlight is a true get-away-from-it-all place. Restaurant, bar, complimentary breakfast. TV in common area. Outdoor hot tub. Video games. No smoking. | 10252 County Rd. 117 | 970/945–7428 | 20 rooms | $70–$120 | AE, D, DC, MC, V.

GOLDEN

MAP 6, F4

(Nearby towns also listed: Central City, Denver, Evergreen, Idaho Springs, Lakewood)

This almost-150-year-old town was once a fierce rival of its neighbor, Denver, and in fact, Golden served as the Colorado territorial capital from 1862 to 1867. Today, with a population of nearly 15,000, the town is famous as the home of Coors Brewing Company and the gravesite of William F. "Buffalo Bill" Cody. But its economy is fueled more and more by high tech, in addition to Coors and the Colorado School of Mines.

Information: **Greater Golden Chamber of Commerce** | Box 1035, Golden, 80402 | 303/279–3113 or 800/590–3113 | www.goldenchamber.org.

Attractions

Astor House Museum. Displaying period furnishings, this was the first stone hotel west of the Mississippi, built in 1867. Now it is in the process of a complete restoration to its original condition. | 822 12th St. | 303/278–3557 | astorhousemuseum.org | $3 | Tues.–Sat. 10–4:30.

Buffalo Bill Memorial Museum and Grave. Despite what the museum here might want you to believe, it was never Buffalo Bill Cody's request that he be buried on top of Lookout Mountain. Nevertheless, here he is, along with a small museum and gift shop, but the admission price is more than paid for by the beauty of the drive up the mountain. | 987½ Lookout Mountain Rd. | 303/526–0747 | www.buffalobill.org | $3 | May–Oct., daily 9–5; Nov.–Apr., Tues.–Sun. 9–4.

Colorado Railroad Museum. Located just outside the Golden city limits, this is a must for any railroad buff. A replica of a depot from the 1880s houses railroad memorabilia, artifacts, and a working model railroad. | 17155 W. 44th Ave. | 303/279–4591 or 800/365–6263 | www.crrm.org | $4 | June–Aug., daily 9–6; Sept.–May, daily 9–5.

Colorado School of Mines. Founded in 1874, this is one of the world's foremost mining engineering schools. More than 3,100 students attend annually. The lovely campus houses an outstanding geology museum, as well as the National Earthquake Information Center. |

16th and Maple Sts. | 303/273–3000 | www.mines.edu | Free | Late Aug.–early May, Mon.–Sat. 9–4, Sun 1–4; early May–late Aug., Mon.–Sat., 9–4.

USGS National Earthquake Information Center. Located on the campus of the Colorado School of Mines, the main job of this center is to record data gathered and transmitted by the Earthquake Early Alerting Service. Free tours are given by appointment. | 1711 Illinois St. | 303/273–8500 | wwwneic.cr.usgs.gov/ | Free | Tues.–Thurs., by appointment only.

Geology Museum. Minerals, ore, and gemstones from around the world, not to mention mining history exhibits, are on display at this informative museum on the campus of the Colorado School of Mines. | 16th St. and Maple St. | 303/273–3815 | Free | Late Aug.–early May, Mon.–Sat. 9–4, Sun 1–4; early May–late Aug., Mon.–Sat., 9–4.

Coors Brewing Company. Thousands of beer-lovers make the pilgrimage to this venerable brewery each year. It's actually one of the largest breweries in the world, founded well over 100 years ago (in 1873) by German immigrant Adolph Coors. Daily output exceeds 1½ million gallons a day. The tour includes an informal tasting for those 21 and over at the end of the tour. | 13th St. and Ford Sts. | 303/277–BEER | Free | Mon.–Sat. 10–4.

Foothills Art Center. This arts center is housed in a 19th-century church. It has numerous galleries and sponsors one of the country's leading watercolor exhibitions. | 809 15th St. | 303/279–3922. | fax 303/279–9470 | www.foothillsartcenter.org | Free | Mon.–Sat. 10–5, Sun. 1–5.

Golden Gate Canyon State Park. More than 10,000 acres feature hiking trails, cross-country skiing, picnicking, camping, and more at this park 2 mi north of Golden via Route 93. | Golden Gate Canyon Rd. | 303/582–3707 | $4 per vehicle | Daily.

Golden Pioneer Museum. More than 4,000 artifacts depict the history of Golden from its earliest days. | 923 10th St. | 303/278–7151 | www.henge1.henge.com/~goldenpm/ | Free | Mon.–Sat. 10–4:30.

Heritage Square. A re-creation of an 1880s frontier town. You'll find rides, including a Ferris wheel, a narrow-gauge railway, and bumper cars, shops, and shows. | U.S. 40 at Rte. 93 (I–70, exit 257) | 303/279–2789 | Free for park, admission varies for rides | Mon.–Sat. 10 AM–9 PM, Sun. noon–7.

Rocky Mountain Quilt Museum. Housing more than 120 quilts; at any given time approximately 20 to 25 are on display. The museum also has a quilting gift shop. | 1111 Washington Ave. | 303/277–0377 | $3 | Mon.–Sat. 10–4.

ON THE CALENDAR

JULY: *Buffalo Bill Days.* A golf tournament, carnival, and parade honoring "Buffalo Bill" Cody are the main attractions. | 303/279–3113 or 800/590–3113.

SEPT.: *Goldenfest.* A parade, music, kids' activities, and food concessions highlight this annual event in downtown Golden the first weekend after Labor Day. | 303/279–3113 or 800/590–3113.

DEC.: *Olde Golden Chritmas.* **Candlelight Walk.** Everybody comes out to walk through downtown Golden with candles in hand the first Friday in December. Santa Claus, carolers, and New Foundland dogs are all on hand. | 303/279–3113.

Dining

Chart House. Seafood. This upscale chain, which started its life in Aspen as a single steak house, is a Colorado favorite. You can still get the Chart House Cut steak, but fresh fish and other seafood dishes now predominate. Salad bar. Kids' menu. | 25908 Genesee Trail | 303/526–9813 | No lunch | $15–$27 | AE, D, DC, MC, V.

Hilltop Café. Mediterranean. A restaurant in a 1900 Victorian that's known for its five-cheese stuffed chicken breast, ricotta and zucchini fritters, and triple-decker strawberry shortcake. Open-air dining on patio in the garden. No smoking. | 1518 Washington Ave. | 303/279–8151 | fax 303/278–1583 | Closed Sun. | $10–$17 | AE, D, DC, MC, V.

Simms Landing. Continental. This restaurant has a marvelous Denver panorama. Look for its prime rib, steak, and seafood. Open-air dining on upper and lower patios. Buffet lunch. Kids' menu. Sunday brunch. | 11911 W. 6th Ave. | 303/237–0465 | $8–$35 | AE, D, DC, MC, V.

Table Mountain Inn Restaurant. Southwestern. You dine in southwestern style here in a stucco room warmed by a fireplace in winter. Known for buffaloaf (buffalo meatloaf), pan-seared fillets, and smoked pork loin chop. Open-air dining on patio on Main Street. Kids' menu. Sunday brunch. | 1310 Washington Ave. | 303/277–9898 | Breakfast also available | $10–$22 | AE, D, DC, MC, V.

Lodging
Denver-Days Inn & Suites West/Golden. Tucked away in the foothills of the Rockies, this Days Inn is just west of downtown Denver. Restaurant, room service. In-room data ports, cable TV. Pool. Hot tub. Gym. Laundry services. Some pets allowed (fee). | 15059 W. Colfax Ave. | 303/277–0200 | fax 303/279–2812 | www.daysinn.com | 133 rooms, 24 suites | $79–$119, $109–$179 suites | AE, D, DC, MC, V.

La Quinta. A reliable, mid-priced chain motel 4 mi east of downtown Golden. Complimentary Continental breakfast. In-room data ports, cable TV. Pool. Laundry facilities. Business services. Pets allowed. | 3301 Youngfield Service Rd. | 303/279–5565 or 800/687–6667 | fax 303/279–5841 | www.laquinta.com | 129 rooms | $79–$99 | AE, D, DC, MC, V.

Table Mountain Inn. This five-story hotel in downtown Golden was bult in the early 1900s, but three floors were added in 1999. Most rooms have either a private balcony or patio. Restaurant, bar, room service. In-room data ports, some microwaves, refrigerators, cable TV, some in-room VCRs. Business services, airport shuttle. | 1310 Washington Ave. | www.table-mountaininn.com | 303/277–9898 or 800/762–9898 | fax 303/271–0298 | 65 rooms, 9 suites | $99–$109, $138–$168 suites | AE, D, DC, MC, V.

GRANBY

(Nearby towns also listed: Grand Lake, Kremmling, Rocky Mountain National Park, Winter Park)

Located near the southwestern entrance to Rocky Mountain National Park, Arapaho National Forest, and Arapaho National Recreational Area, the small town of Granby (population 535) offers a vast variety of outdoor sports, including big-game hunting and skiing.

Information: **Greater Granby Area Chamber of Commerce** | Box 35, Granby 80446 | 970/887–2311 or 800/325–1661 | www.rkymtnhi.com/granbycoc.

Attractions
Arapaho National Recreation Area. The National Forest Service has set aside a large portion of the Arapaho and Roosevelt national forests that are especially suitable for recreation; the entrance is 6 mi northeast of Granby. Boating, fishing, hunting, camping, and picnicking are available. Information is available from the Sulphur Ranger District office in Granby. | 9 Ten Mile Dr., Box 10 | 970/887–4100 | www.fs.fed.us/r2/arnf/vvc | Free | Daily.

Grand County Museum. This small museum is 10 mi west of Granby via Highway 40 in Hot Sulphur Springs. Exhibits depict the history of skiing, ranching, and Rocky Mountain railroads in the region. | 110 E. Byers Ave., Hot Sulphur Springs | 970/725–3939 | fax 970/725–0129 | www.grandcountymuseum.com | $4 | Memorial Day–Labor Day, daily 10–5; Labor Day–Memorial Day, Wed.–Sat. 11–4.

Reach Out and Touch the Past Museum. Eleven miles west of Granby in Hot Sulphur Springs, this museum features six historic buildings, including a jailhouse that dates back to 1897, a courthouse, a ranch house, and a blacksmith's shop. | 110 E. Byers Ave., Hot Sulphur Springs | 970/725–3939 | $4 | Memorial Day–Labor Day, Mon.–Sat. 10–5, Sun. noon–5; Labor Day–Memorial Day, Wed.–Sat. 11–4.

Silver Creek Ski Area. This resort 3 mi southeast of Granby has 33 runs (the longest is 1½ mi) with a vertical drop of 1,000 ft. There's one quad, one triple, one double, one Pomalift, and one surface lift. You'll also find a health club and sleighing. | Just off U.S. 40 | 303/629–1020 or 970/887–3384 or 800/448–9458 | www.silvercreekresort.com | Dec.–mid-Apr.

ON THE CALENDAR
FEB. & MAR.: Ice-Fishing Contest. This competition at Granby Lake, 2 mi northeast of Granby, on the first weekend in both February and March draws participants of all ages from all over Colorado. Prizes are awarded for the biggest catches and raffles are held. | Granby Lake | 970/887–2311.

Dining
Columbine Café. American. Mounted animal heads, stuffed fish, and pictures of local mountain ranges adorn the walls of this café. The local favorites are the chicken-fried steak and perch basket. | 395 E. Agate Ave. | 970/887–3812 | Breakfast also available; no dinner; no lunch Sun. | $4–$8 | No credit cards.

Longbranch Restaurant. German. Although the restaurant sports an Old West look, the cuisine here is German. Try the Wiener schnitzel, sauerbraten, or bratwurst. Kids' menu. No smoking. | 165 E. Agate Ave. | 970/887–2209 | Closed mid-Apr.–mid-May, mid-Oct.–mid-Nov. No lunch Sun. | $6–$18 | D, MC, V.

Schatzi's Pizza and Pasta. Italian. Housed in the same building as Longbranch restaurant and separated from it by a stained-glass window, this casual Italian restaurant serves up pizza and decent pasta dishes that include hearty standards like lasagna, spinach ravioli, spaghetti with meatballs, and garlic bread. Kids' menu. No smoking. | 165 E. Agate Ave. | 970/887–2209 | Closed mid-Apr.–mid-May, mid-Oct.–mid-Nov. No lunch Sun. | $8–$18 | D, MC, V.

Sunrise Grill. American. A casual atmosphere and rustic setting await diners at this restaurant. Breakfast is served all day long, and the eggs Benedict are very popular. For lunch try the steak burrito or bagel club sandwich. | 729 W. Agate Ave. | 970/887–9466 | Breakfast also available; no dinner | $5–$7 | No credit cards.

Lodging
Bar Lazy J Guest Ranch. This guest ranch 15 mi west of Granby in a valley along the Colorado River has been in operation since 1912. Many activities are available, including sightseeing trips to Rocky Mountain National Park. Accommodations are in rustic log cabins. Picnic area. No air-conditioning, no room phones, no TV. Pool. Hot tub. Horseback riding, volleyball, fishing, bicycles. Children's programs (ages 3–12). | 447 Rte. 3, Parshall | 970/725–3437 or 800/396–6279 | fax 970/725–0121 | www.barlazyj.com | 12 cabins | $1,195 per adult per wk | Closed Oct.–mid-May | AP | MC, V.

★ **C Lazy U Ranch.** Situated in the peaceful Willow Creek Valley about 10 mi west of Granby, the C Lazy U is a family-owned ranch resort with just the right amount of sophistication, comfortable cabin accommodations, and all kinds of activities, from rafting and fly-fishing to hayrides, dances, barbecues, and outdoor buffets. Dining room, bar. No air-conditioning, no room phones, no TV in rooms, TV in common area. Pool, lake. Hot tub, massage. Tennis. Gym, hiking, horseback riding. Boating, fishing. Ice-skating, cross-country skiing, sleigh rides, tobogganing. Library. Children's programs (ages 3–18), playground. Laundry facilities. Business services. | 3640 Hwy. 125 | 970/887–3344 | fax 970/887–3917 | www.clazyu.com | 41 cottages, 4 rooms in lodge | $1,800–$3,200 per person per wk (1–wk minimum stay) | Closed Apr.–May | AP | No credit cards.

Casa Milagro B&B. In Parshall, 15 mi south of Granby, this modern log building is situated amid the pine trees above the Williams Fork Road. Various packages including recreational activities are offered. Complimentary breakfast. Some in-room hot tubs, cable TV, some room phones, in-room VCRs (and movies). Outdoor hot tub. Business services. Some pets allowed (fee). | 13628 County Rd. 3, Parshall | 970/725–3640 or 888–632–8955 | fax 970/725–3617 | www.casamilagro.com. | 4 rooms | $145–$220 | AE, D, DC, MC, V.

Drowsy Water Ranch. In the mountains 7 mi west of Granby, this family-friendly ranch borders the Arapaho National Forest and other great equestrian terrain. Weekly activities include hayrides, square dancing, and cookouts. Dining room. No air-conditioning. Pool. Hot tub. Hiking, horseback riding. Fishing. Children's programs (ages 1–13), playground. Business services. | County Rd. 219 | 970/725–3456 or 800/845–2292 | fax 970/725–3611 | www.drowsywater.com | 9 cottages, 8 rooms in lodge | $1,100–$1,350 per person per wk (1–wk minimum stay) | Closed Oct.–May | AP | No credit cards.

Homestead Motel. This small, economical motel offers a significant money-saving opportunity in winter, since it is less than 5 mi from activities such as snowboarding, ice fishing, and ice biking. Some refrigerators, cable TV. Some pets allowed. | 851 W. Agate Ave. | 970/887–3665 or 800/669–3605 | fax 970/887–2426 | 10 rooms | $57–$65 | AE, D, DC, MC, V.

Inn at Silver Creek. This large inn is located next to the Silver Creek ski area, about 2 mi south of Granby. Most rooms at have a fireplace and a private patio. Seasonal hot-air balloon rides can be arranged at the front desk. Bar. No air-conditioning, in-room data ports, some kitchenettes, refrigerators, in-room hot tubs, cable TV. Pool. Hot tub. Tennis. Gym, racquetball. Fishing, bicycles. Downhill skiing, sleigh rides. Shops. Laundry facilities. Pets allowed (fee). | 62927 U.S. 40, Silver Creek | 970/887–2131 or 800/926–4386 | fax 970/887–4083 | www.innatsilvercreek.com | 342 rooms | $89–$299 | AE, D, DC, MC, V.

Trail Riders. A small, economical motel just off of U.S. 40 in Granby. Microwaves, refrigerators, cable TV. Airport shuttle. Some pets allowed. | 215 E. Agate Ave. | 970/887–3738 | 11 rooms, 5 suites | $35–$45, $49–$75 suites | AE, D, MC, V.

GRAND JUNCTION

MAP 6, B5

(Nearby towns also listed: Cedaredge, Delta, Montrose, Palisade, Rifle)

Grand Junction gets its name naturally, since the town of 43,000 is situated at the junction of the Colorado and Gunnison rivers. It is also the site of the joining in 1882 of the railroad that connected Salt Lake City and Denver. Altitudes are lower in this region and the rich soil found here is ideal for the growing of all kinds of fruit, including grapes, which have spawned a local wine industry.

Information: **Grand Junction Visitor and Convention Bureau** | 740 Horizon Dr., Grand Junction 81506 | 970/244–1480 or 800/962–2547 | www.grand-junction.net.

Attractions

Colorado National Monument. Just after its confluence with the Gunnison River, the rapid-flowing Colorado River has cut a magnificent canyon studded with monolithic rock formations along much of its length. A 23-mi drive covers 1 billion years of prehistory as depicted by the colorful rocks, canyons, and rugged chasms. Abundant wildlife, spectacular geological features, and a variety of hiking and cross-country skiing trails combine to make this area an outstanding destination for the nature-lover. The monument headquarters is about 10 mi west of Grand Junction. | Fruita | 970/858–3617 | www.nps.gov/colm | $4 per vehicle | Daily.

Highline Lake State Park. Waterfowl hunting in season, waterskiing, swimming, and camping are all available at the park 19 mi northwest of Grand Junction. | Rte. 139 | 970/858–7208 | $4 per vehicle | Daily.

Museum of Western Colorado. Exhibits depict the natural and social history of the western slopes of the Rocky Mountains from the 1880s. The museum also operates the Cross Orchards Historic Farm and Dinosaur Discovery; each museum has a separate admission. | 462 Ute. Ave. | 970/242–0971 or 888/488–3466 | www.wcmuseum.org | $5 | Apr.–Sept., Mon.–Sat. 9–4; Oct.–Mar., Tues.–Sat. 10–4.

Cross Orchards Historic Farm. This historic apple orchard (1896–1923) was once operated by the owners of the Red Cross Shoe Company; it's now a part of the Museum of Western Colorado. Exhibits depict western Colorado's agricultural heritage and the history of farming in the region. Farm buildings and equipment are on display. | 3073 F Rd. | 970/434–9814 | www.wcmuseum.org | $4 | Memorial Day–Labor Day, Tues.–Sat. 9–3.

Museum of Western Colorado's Dinosaur Journey. The paleontological history of western Colorado is exhibited through this branch in Fruita, 10 mi west of Grand Junction. Robotic dinosaurs and one-half and full-scale models of dinosaurs and related animal life are the main draw. In summer, you can participate in one-day dinosaur digs. | 550 Jurassic Ct., at Hwy. 340, Fruita | 970/241–9210 | www.dinosaurjourney.com | $6 | Memorial Day–Labor Day, daily 9–4; Labor Day–Memorial Day, daily 10–4.

Rabbit Valley Trail Through Time. A 1½-mi self-guided walking trail through fossilized flora and fauna remains. It's 30 mi west of Grand Junction, 2 mi from the Utah border. Trail brochures are available at Colorado's Dinosaur Journey in Fruita. | I–70 (exit Rabbit Valley) | 970/241–9210 | www.dinosaurjourney.com | Free | Daily.

Riggs Hill Trail. A ¾-mi trail through fossilized remains, south of Fruita on 24 Road to the Riggs Hill sign. Trail brochures are available at Colorado's Dinosaur Journey in Fruita. | Junction S. Broadway and Meadows Way | 970/241–9210 | Free | Daily.

Powderhorn Ski Resort. At this ski resort with 500 skiable acres 15 mi east of Grand Junction, you'll find 29 runs (the longest is 2⅕ mi) with a vertical drop of 1,650 ft. There are also 6 mi of snowshoe trails, and summer activities. Restaurants and lodging also available. | Rte. 65 | 970/268–5700 or 800/241–6997 | fax 970/268–5351 | www.powderhorn.com | Early Dec.–early Apr.

Western Colorado Botanical Gardens. The botanical garden contains several outdoor gardens, a butterfly house, and a greenhouse. | 641 Struthers Ave. | 970/245–3288 | $3 | Wed.–Sun. 10–5.

Western Colorado Center for the Arts. A nice permanent collection of Native American and contemporary western art. Be sure to check out the doors carved by a WPA artist during the Great Depression. | 1803 N. 7th St. | 970/243–7337 | $2 | Tues.–Sat. 9–4.

TOURS AND TOUR COMPANIES

Adventure Bound. Adventure Bound offers two- to five-day white-water rafting excursions on the Colorado, Yampa, and Green rivers. | 2392 H Rd. | 970/241–5633 or 800/423–4668 | www.raft-colorado.com | May–Sept.

ON THE CALENDAR

JUNE: *Colorado Stampede.* A parade and PRCA rodeo competition highlight this event the third week in June. | 970/244–1480 or 800/962–2547.

SEPT.: *Colorado Mountain Winefest.* Outdoor exhibits and events are featured, along with wine tasting the third week in September. | 800/704–3667.

SEPT.: *Valley Pride Festival.* This event is a multicultural gathering of artisans, arts, and culture organizations at Cross Orchards Historic Farm. Highlights include performing arts demonstrations, a children's melodrama, and gardening demonstrations. | 970/242–0971.

Dining

Crystal Café and Bake Shop. Cafés. Locals flock to this European-style café for its apple pancakes and homemade granola at breakfast. The oriental chicken salad and grilled vegetable sandwiches are lunch favorites. | 314 Main St. | 970/242–8843 | No dinner | $5–$9 | No credit cards.

Dolce Vita. Italian. This Northern Italian restaurant with its outdoor patio fronting on Main Street provides consistently wonderful cooking. Try the veal piccata or Portobella mushrooms marinated in Chianti. Both the cannoli and tiramisu are good dessert choices. | 336 Main St. | 970/242–8482 | Reservations essential | Closed Sun. | $10–$18. | AE, D, DC, MC, V.

Far East. Chinese. Authentic Cantonese, Szechuan, and Mandarin dishes, and some additional Asian dishes served in a palatial setting. Try the almond chicken or teriyaki chicken, as well as pork and beef dishes. Kids' menu. | 1530 North Ave., at U.S. 6 | 970/242–8131 | $5–$10 | AE, D, DC, MC, V.

Starvin' Arvin's. American. Whitewashed walls hung with antique photographs and an oak buffet highlight this casual place. You won't starve—try the chicken-fried steak or the beef. Homemade pastries. Kids' menu. | 752 Horizon Dr. | 970/241–0430 | Breakfast also available | $5–$11 | AE, D, MC, V.

The Winery. American. This is the place you go for a special occasion in Grand Junction. It's a pretty room, with barn-wood beams, exposed brick, stained glass, and lots of plants. Try the steak, chicken, prime rib, or shrimp. Salad bar. No smoking. | 642 Main St. | 970/242–4100 | No lunch | $8–$27 | AE, D, DC, MC, V.

Lodging

Adam's Mark Grand Junction. This is by far the nicest hotel in town, and for the level of amenities prices are reasonable. Rooms are large and have such welcome extras as a phone and a TV in the bathroom. 2 restaurants, bar. Cable TV. Pool. Hot tub. Tennis. Gym. Video games. Playground. Business services, airport shuttle. | 743 Horizon Dr. | 970/241–8888 or 800/444–2326 | fax 970/242–7266 | www.adamsmark.com | 243 rooms, 21 suites | $89–$129, $159–$295 suites | AE, D, DC, MC, V.

Best Western Horizon Inn. Some of the rooms at this chain motel offer exquisite views of Grand Mesa and Colorado National Monument. Complimentary Continental breakfast. In-room data ports, cable TV. Pool. Hot tub. Playground. Laundry services. Business services. Pets allowed. | 754 Horizon Dr. | 970/245–1410 | fax 970/245–4039 | www.bestwestern.com | 99 rooms | $59–$72 | AE, D, DC, MC, V.

Best Western Sandman. Geared for business travelers, this chain motel is just south of Grand Junction's Walker Field Airport and Interstate 70. In-room data ports, refrigerators, cable TV. Pool. Hot tub. Laundry facilities. Business services, airport shuttle. | 708 Horizon Dr. | 970/243–4150 | fax 970/243–1828 | www.bestwestern.com | 80 rooms | $54–$72 | AE, D, DC, MC, V.

Budget Host Inn. A budget chain motel 1 mi south of Walker Field Airport. Cable TV. Pool. Playground. Laundry facilities. | 721 Horizon Dr. | www.budgethost.com | 970/243–6050 or 800/283–4678 | fax 970/243–0310 | 54 rooms | $41–$55 | AE, D, DC, MC, V.

Days Inn. Rooms at this Days Inn are spacious and bright. The hotel restaurant, Good Pastures, is a popular local spot in Grand Junction. Restaurant. In-room data ports, cable TV. Pool. Laundry services. Airport shuttle. Some pets allowed. | 733 Horizon Dr. | 970/245–7200 or 800/790–2661 | fax 970/243–6709 | www.daysinn.com | 104 rooms, 4 suites | $64–$71, $85–$103 suites | AE, D, DC, MC, V.

Grand Vista Hotel. This hotel, while mid-priced, offers upscale amenities and service. Rooms have old-fashioned charm and are decorated in dark mountain colors. The hotel is convenient to Interstate 70. Restaurant, bar, room service. In-room data ports, cable TV. Pool. Hot tub. Business services, airport shuttle. Pets allowed. | 2790 Crossroads Blvd. | 970/

241–8411 or 800/800–7796 | fax 970/241–1077 | 158 rooms, 19 suites | $89–$99, $109–$119 suites | AE, D, DC, MC, V.

Holiday Inn–Grand Junction. This mid-priced chain motel, just south of Walker Field Airport, is reliably clean and comfortable. Restaurant, bar (with entertainment), room service. Cable TV, some in-room VCRs. 2 pools. Hot tub. Gym. Video games. Laundry facilities. Airport shuttle. Pets allowed. | 755 Horizon Dr. | 970/243–6790 or 888/489–9796 | fax 970/243–6790 | www.holiday-inn.com | 292 rooms, 9 suites | $74–$79, $83–$89 suites | AE, D, DC, MC, V.

Los Altos B&B. Enjoy breathtaking views of the Grand Mesa and Bookcliffs from this modern, upscale B&B. All the rooms have wraparound decks. Complimentary breakfast. No kids under 3. No smoking. | 375 Hillview Dr. | 970/256–0964 or 888/774–0982 | fax 970/256–0964 | www.colorado-bnb.com/losaltos | 7 rooms | $80–$150 | AE, D, MC, V.

Ramada Inn. Less than a mile south of Walker Field Airport, this chain motel has rooms with private patios or balconies. Restaurant. In-room data ports, some microwaves, cable TV, some in-room VCRs (and movies). Pool. Laundry facilities. Business services, airport shuttle. Pets allowed (fee). | 752 Horizon Dr. | 970/243–5150 or 888/298–2054 | fax 970/242–3692 | www.ramada.com | 100 rooms | $54–$91 | AE, D, DC, MC, V.

West Gate Inn. An economical motel on the western edge of Grand Junction. Restaurant, bar. Cable TV. Pool. Laundry facilities. Business services. Pets allowed. | 2210 U.S. 6 | 970/241–3020 or 800/453–9253 | fax 970/243–4516 | www.gj.net/wgi | 100 rooms | $49–$76 | AE, D, DC, MC, V.

GRAND LAKE

MAP 6, E3

(Nearby towns also listed: Allenspark, Estes Park, Granby, Rocky Mountain National Park)

The town of Grand Lake is located on the northern shore of a glacial lake (of the same name)—Colorado's largest natural lake—which was formed tens of thousands of years ago when this part of the country was covered with ice. The town serves as the western gateway to the Rocky Mountain National Park (*see* Rocky Mountain National Park), and each summer its population swells from 350 year-round residents to 5,000. You wouldn't expect to find a yacht club at 8,380 ft, but Grand Lake has one, in addition to great facilities for hiking, fishing, and horseback riding. The region offers a wide variety of summertime outdoor sports and activities, including backpacking, day hiking, horseback riding, and a full array of water sports.

Information: **Grand Lake Area Chamber of Commerce** | Box 57, Grand Lake 80447 | 970/627–3402, 800/531–1019, 970/627–3220 (boating information), or 970/627–3514 (horseback riding information) | www.grandlakechamber.com.

Attractions

Grand Lake, Granby Lake, and Shadow Mountain Lake. These three bodies of water—the former the largest natural body of water in Colorado, the latter two comprising an even larger series of man-made reservoirs—offer plenty of varied water sports and boating opportunities. | Grand Lake | 800/325–1661 | Free | Daily.

Rocky Mountain National Park. *(See* Rocky Mountain National Park.) Grand Lake serves as the western gateway to the Rocky Mountain National Park. The park entrance is just north of Grand Lake on U.S. 34. | 970/586–1206 | www.nps.gov/romo | $10 per vehicle | Daily.

ON THE CALENDAR

JAN.–FEB.: *Winter Carnival.* Ice-fishing competition, ice-golf, snow sculptures, and ice-skating are among the winter activities featured at this annual event held at Town Hall the last weekend in January and first weekend in February. | 970/627–3402 or 800/531–1019.

JUNE: *Grand Festival of the Arts.* This festival in Town Park showcases the unique work of local artists. | 970/627–3402.

JUNE–AUG.: *Rocky Mountain Repertory Theatre.* Performances of musicals in repertory at the Grand Lake Community Building. | 970/627–3421.

JULY: *Buffalo Barbecue and Western Week Celebration.* A celebration of the mountain-man era, with food, exhibits, a rendezvous, and a parade the third week in July. | 970/627–3402 or 800/531–1019.

AUG.: *Lipton Cup Sailing Regatta.* A colorful parade of boats on Grand Lake and nearby Granby Lake are enjoyed by all spectators. | 970/627–3402 or 800/531–1019.

Dining

Caroline's Cuisine. Continental. This upscale restaurant at Soda Springs Ranch has three dining rooms downstairs and an art gallery upstairs. Try steak Diane, escargot Provençale. Open-air dining on deck with mountain views. Pianist Saturday. Kids' menu. | 9921 U.S. 34 #27 | www.sodaspringsranch.com | 970/627–9404 | Closed 2 wks in Apr., 2 wks in Nov. No lunch | $14–$22 | AE, D, DC, MC, V.

Mountain Inn. American. When it is time to have a meal after a long day in Rocky Mountain National Park, this rustic restaurant is a convenient place to go on the west side. Specialties include fried chicken, prime rib, and giant chicken potpie. Vegetables and potatoes are served family-style in big bowls. Kids' menu. | 612 Grand Ave. | 970/627–3385 | Reservations essential in summer | Closed Apr. and Nov. | $11–$20 | D, MC, V.

Pancho and Lefty's. Mexican. Housed in a round building that dates back to 1915, this family-oriented spot is known for fajitas and fiesta salad. Everything is made from scratch, and margaritas are always on tap. | 1120 Grand Ave. | 970/627–8773 | Reservations not accepted | $7–$20 | D, MC, V.

Lodging

Best Value Inn–Bighorn Lodge. This small, rustic motel is located right in Grand Lake's historic downtown area, just two blocks from the water, and close to Rocky Mountain National Park. Cable TV. Hot tub. Business services. | 613 Grand Ave. | 970/627–8101 or 800/341–8000 | fax 970/627–3771 | 20 rooms | $120 | AE, D, DC, MC, V.

Driftwood Lodge. This lodge overlooks Shadow Mountain Lake and is convenient to hiking and fishing. Picnic area. No air-conditioning, in-room data ports, some kitchenettes, some refrigerators, cable TV. Pool, wading pool. Hot tub, sauna. Playground. Business services. | 12255 U.S. 34 | 970/627–3654 | fax 970/627–3654 | www.rkymtnhi.com/driftwood | 17 rooms, 9 suites | $75, $82–$125 suites | D, DC, MC, V.

Grand Lake Lodge. Built of lodgepole pine in 1921, the lodge is known as "Colorado's favorite front porch." You can enjoy the vista of both Grand and Shadow Mountain lakes below or simply enjoy the seclusion of your rustic cabin in the hills. Restaurant, bar. No air-conditioning, some kitchenettes, some refrigerators, no room phones, no TV in rooms, TV in common area. Pool. Hot tub. Horseback riding. Video games. Playground. | 15500 Hwy. 34, Grand Lake | 970/627–3967 | fax 970/627–9495 | www.grandlakelodge.com | 56 cabins | $75–$154 | mid-Sept.–early July | AE, D, MC, V.

Lazy Moose Cabins. These simple cabins are near Grand Lake. Some kitchenettes, refrigerators, cable TV. Hot tub. Business services. | 1007 Lake Ave. | 970/627–1881 | 10 cabins | $65–$110 a night (3–night minimum stay) | AE, D, DC, MC, V.

Mack's Shadow Mountain Motel. Across the street from Shadow Mountain Lake and across the lake from Rocky Mountain National Park, this small motel offers up some wonderful views. Moose and elk can often be seen grazing on the hotel grounds. Picnic area. Microwaves, refrigerators, cable TV. Playground. | 12365 U.S. 34 | 970/627–8546 | www.grandlakecolorado.com/lodging/macks | 18 rooms | $65 | MC, V.

Spirit Mountain Ranch. A secluded B&B just minutes from several national forests between Granby and Grand Lake, and in 70 acres of aspen forest. Picnic area, complimentary breakfast. No room phones, no TV. Hot tub. Business services. No kids under 10. No smoking. | 3863 County Rd. 41 | 970/887–3551 | fax 970/887–3551 | www.fcinet.com/spirit | 4 rooms | $130–$175 | D, MC, V.

Waconda Motel. This small, two-story motel provides a serene setting and a respite from hectic city life. "Waconda" translated is a Kansas Sioux name for running water; the Lake and public beach are only two blocks away. Restaurant, bar. Cable TV. Hot tub. Pets allowed (fee). | 725 Grand Ave. | 970/627–8312 | fax 970/627–8312 | www.grandlakecolorado.com/waconda | 10 rooms | $50–$80 | AE, D, DC, MC, V.

Western Riviera Motel. This small motel on the southern side of the town of Grand Lake has views of the lake and mountains. Refrigerators, cable TV. Hot tub. Business services. | 419 Garfield Ave. | 970/627–3580 | fax 970/627–3320 | 15 rooms | $75–$95 | AE, D, DC, MC, V.

GREELEY

MAP 6, G2

(Nearby towns also listed: Fort Collins, Fort Morgan, Loveland)

Named in honor of Horace Greeley, the New Yorker who urged America's youth to "Go West, young man, go West," Greeley was founded in 1870 by Nathan Meeker, an editor for Horace's newspaper, the *New York Tribune*. Originally organized as a utopian colony, today's city of 72,000 is the center of the rich agricultural region of north-central Colorado.

Information: Greeley Convention and Visitors Bureau | 902 7th Ave., Greeley, 80631 | 970/352–3566 or 800/449–3866 | www.greeleycvb.com.

Attractions

Centennial Village. This reconstructed village reflects Greeley and Weld County history from 1860 to 1920. | 1475 A St., at N. 14th Ave. | 970/350–9220 or 970/350–9224 | www.greeleycvb.com/centennial.html | $3.50 | Memorial Day–Labor Day, Tues.–Sat. 9–4; mid-Apr.–Memorial Day and Labor Day–mid-Oct., Tues.–Sat. 10–3.

Fort Vasquez. A reconstructed fur post originally built in the 1830s 18 mi south of Greeley near Platteville on U.S. 85. | U.S. 85 | 970/785–2832 | Free | Memorial Day–Labor Day, Mon.–Sat. 9:30–4:30, Sun. 1–4:30; Labor Day–Memorial Day, Wed.–Sat. 9:30–4:30, Sun. 1–4:30.

Meeker Home. An 1870 adobe house that was the home of Greeley's founder, Nathan Meeker. Meeker's personal belongings and other historical artifacts from the region are on display. | 1324 9th Ave. | 970/350–9220 | Free | Memorial Day–Labor Day, Tues.–Fri. 10–5; Labor Day–mid-Oct. and mid-Apr.–Memorial Day, Tues.–Sat. 10–3.

Municipal Archives. The facility contains the Weld County archives, a research library, documents, and photographic archives. | 919 7th St. | 970/350–9220 | fax 970/350–9470 | Free | Weekdays 10–4.

University of Northern Colorado. Established in 1889, UNC now has a student body of 11,000 and a campus of 236 acres covering the area from 16th Street to 24th Street between 8th and 14th Avenues. | 501 20th St. | 970/351–1890 or 970/351–1889 | www.univnorthco.edu | Free | Daily.

Mariani Art Gallery. This gallery is actually a multipurpose center on the University of Northern Colorado campus that features student and faculty exhibitions. It's in Guggenheim Hall. | 8th Avenue | 970/351–2184 | www.univnorthco.edu | Free | Varies; call for schedule.

Michener Library. Colorado's largest university library was named in honor of James A. Michener, the author of *Centennial*. Michener's research papers are deposited here on the campus of the University of Northern Colorado. This is also the home of the university archives and the Mari Michener Art Gallery. | 14th Avenue | 970/351–2671 | www.univnorthco.edu | Free | Mon.–Thurs. 7:30–midnight, Fri. 7:30–6, Sat. 10–6, Sun. noon–midnight; reduced hrs mid-May–late Aug.

ON THE CALENDAR

JUNE–JULY: *Independence Stampede Greeley Rodeo.* A rodeo and parade are the featured events that start in late June. | 970/352–3566 or 800/449–3866.

JULY: *Weld County Fair.* A county fair, arts and crafts, and food are all part of the fun the last week in July. | 970/352–3566 or 800/449–3866.

AUG.: *Supercross Race.* Greeley is home to the only "supercross" track between the Mississippi River and Las Vegas. Come watch more than 300 participants compete and display their prized motorcycles at the Island Grover Regional Park. | 970/350–9392.

Dining

Cables End Italian Grille. Italian. This cozy spot uses cable spools for tables; the fireplace and lounge also contribute to the homespun atmosphere. Cables is known for its homemade pasta and pizza. Wine is available. | 3780 W. 10th St. | 970/356–4847 | $5–$8 | AE, D, DC, MC, V.

New York Burrito. Mexican. Huge burritos are the trademark of this eatery. Large pictures of New York City streets and former U.S. presidents adorn the walls. Be sure to try the smothered burrito (smothered with green chile) or plain handheld variety, with marinated chicken. | 2411 8th Ave. | 970/346–9227 | Closed Sun. | $5–$7 | MC, V.

Texas Road House. Steak. Friendly service and a comfortable atmosphere keeps diners coming back to the Texas Road House. Rib-eye steaks and BBQ ribs are recommended. Wash your meal down with their notorious 46-ounce margarita. | 2451 W. 28th St. | 970/330–3668 | No lunch Mon.–Thurs. | $8–$18 | AE, MC, V.

Lodging

Best Western Ramkota Inn. This mid-priced motel is the closest place to stay near the University of Northern Colorado campus. Restaurant, bar, room service. Cable TV. Pool. Video games. Business services. Pets allowed. | 701 8th St. | 970/353–8444 | fax 970/353–4269 | www.bestwestern.com | 144 rooms, 4 suites | $69–$104, $135–$195 suites | AE, D, DC, MC, V.

Days Inn. This three-story budget motel offers spacious and well-lit rooms. Restaurant, complimentary Continental breakfast. In-room data ports, some microwaves, refrigerators, cable TV. Pool. Beauty salon, hot tub. Laundry services. Business services. | 2467 W. 29th St. | 970/330–6380 | fax 970/330–6382 | www.daysinn.com | 50 rooms | $70 | AE, D, DC, MC, V.

Fairfield Inn Greeley. This chain hotel is less than 2 mi from the University of Northern Colorado. There are many restaurants within walking distance. Complimentary Continental breakfast. In-room data ports, cable TV. Pool. Laundry service. Business services. Some pets allowed. | 2401 W. 29th St. | 970/339–5030 | fax 970/339–5030 | www.marriot.com. | 62 rooms, 8 suites | $71–$74, $85 suites | AE, D, DC, MC, V.

German House Bed and Breakfast. An extensive collection of German antiques and collectibles fills this 1885 brick Victorian mansion near downtown and the University of Northern Colorado. Rooms are comfortably furnished (some are singles). Bar, complimentary breakfast. Cable TV, some in-room VCRs. Pool. Hot tub. | 1305 6th St. | 970/356–1353 | www.germanhousebnb.com | 4 rooms (2 with shared bath) | $84–$89 | No credit cards.

Motel 6. This budget motel is located 2 mi south of Greeley on U.S. 85. Cable TV. Pool. Pets allowed. | 3015 8th Ave., Evans | 970/351–6481 or 800/466–8356 | www.motel6.com | 94 rooms | $32–$40 | AE, D, DC, MC, V.

Sod Buster Inn Bed and Breakfast. A modern octagonal home built in 1997 and decorated in country style; the location between downtown and the University of Northern Colorado is convenient. Complimentary breakfast. Some in-room hot tubs. In-room data ports, cable TV. | 1221 9th Ave. | 970/392–1221 or 888/300–1221 | fax 970/392–1222 | www.sodbus-terinn.com | 10 rooms | $94–$124 | AE, DC, MC, V.

GUNNISON

MAP 6, D6

(Nearby towns also listed: Crested Butte, Lake City, Montrose, Salida)

Named after the U.S. Army engineer who first mapped the area in 1853, Gunnison (population 5,392) is situated near the headwaters of the river of the same name. The town was founded in 1874. Gunnison offers within easy reach more than 2,000 mi of pristine trout streams as well as Colorado's largest lake, Blue Mesa Reservoir. Nearby Gunnison National Forest contains 27 peaks that soar over 12,000 ft high.

Information: Gunnison County Chamber of Commerce | 500 E. Tomichi Ave., Gunnison, 81230 | 970/641–1501 or 800/274–7580 | www.gunnisonchamber.com.

Attractions

Alpine Tunnel. This nearly 2,000-ft long railroad tunnel, at an altitude of more than 11,500 ft, was used between 1881 and 1910. It's 36 mi northeast of Gunnison via U.S. 50 and Route 765, then 3 mi east of Pitkin on a dirt road. | Rte. 765, Pitkin | 970/641–1501 | Free | July–Oct., daily.

Blue Mesa Reservoir. Almost 20 mi long, the largest man-made lake in Colorado is 10 mi west of Gunnison. Known for its good fishing waters; rainbow and brown trout can be caught here. | U.S. 50 | 970/641–1501 | Free | Daily.

Cumberland Pass. A gravel road through the pass, situated at 12,200 ft, connects the towns of Pitkin and Tincup; Pitkin is 36 mi northeast of Gunnison via U.S. 50 and Route 765. | Rte. 765, Pitkin | 970/641–1501 | Free | July–Oct., daily.

Curecanti National Recreation Area. The area was named in honor of the Ute Indian chief of the same name. This park has an outdoor activity for everyone. You can go camping, hiking, boating, windsurfing, fishing, ice fishing, cross-country skiing, or take a boat tour of the reservoir. Inside the park, you can also find the Cimarron Railroad Exhibit that has 1940s railroad cars on display. Get information from the visitor center in Elk Creek, 15 mi west of the town of Gunnison on U.S. 50, or Lake Fork, 18 mi east of Cimarron; there is another visitor center in the town of Cimarron. | 102 Elk Creek | 970/641–0406 or 970/641–2337 | www.nps.gov/cure/ | Free | Daily, visitor center daily mid-May–Nov.

Gunnison National Forest. This forest of nearly 1,700,000 acres surrounds Gunnison on the north, east, and south, and has 27 peaks with an altitude of more than 12,000 ft. All varieties of outdoor sports and activities are offered. There is a ranger district office in Gunnison. | 216 N. Colorado | 970/641–0471 | www.fs.fed.us/r2/gmug | Free | Daily.

Gunnison Pioneer Museum. Exhibits at this museum on the eastern edge of Gunnison depict early and pioneer history of the region. Also contains over 40 vintage automobiles. | U.S. 50, at S. Adams St. | 970/641–4530 | $7 | Memorial Day–Labor Day, Mon.–Sat. 9–5, Sun. noon–4.

Taylor Park Reservoir. Fishing, hunting, boating, and camping are available at this lake in Gunnison National Forest about 35 mi northeast of Gunnison. | Rte. 742 at Rte. 59 | 970/641–0471 | Free | Memorial Day–Labor Day, daily.

Tincup. Located 40 mi northeast of Gunnison, this is one of several old, deserted mining towns in this region. The town is reached via the Cumberland Pass road, a dirt road open only during the summer (July–October); this road is accessed from Pitkin, 36 mi northeast of Gunnison via U.S. 50 and Route 765. | Visitor Center: 500 E. Tomichi Ave. | 970/641–1501 | Free | Daily.

Western State College of Colorado. Twenty-five hundred students attend WSC, established in 1901. The library has a good collection of local history books. | 600 N. Adams St., between N. Adams St. and N. Colorado St. | 970/943–0120 | www.western.edu | Free | Daily.

ON THE CALENDAR
JULY: *Cattlemen's Days Celebration.* This celebration at the Gunnison Fairgrounds features a PRCA Rodeo, horse and cattle shows, a county fair, and a parade. When the sun sets there are dances and live musical entertainment. | 970/641–1501.

Dining

Cattlemen Inn. Steak. This country-style steak house is decorated with pictures of area mountains and cowboys. Enjoy the prime rib or chicken-fried steak, and then get your hair cut at the barbershop, which is within the restaurant. | 301 W. Tomichi Ave. | 970/641–1061 | Breakfast also available | $5–$18 | AE, D, DC, MC, V.

Firebrand Delicatessen. Delicatessen. This homey deli is a popular local hangout. All the furniture is secondhand, giving it a funky feel. The Reuben and vegetarian sandwiches are recommended. | 108 N. Main St. | 970/641–6266 | No dinner | $5–$8 | No credit cards.

Garlic Mike's. Italian. For upscale Italian and a nightly changing menu, give this spot a try. Go for the homemade meat ravioli, pizzas, and eggplant Parmesan. The marinated sirloin steak carbonara wins as the house favorite. Kids' menu. | 2674 Hwy. 153 | 970/641–2493 | No lunch | $9–$21 | AE, D, MC, V.

Palisades Saloon and Restaurant. American. San Francisco pasta (vegetarian or nonvegetarian) and the rib-eye steaks are favorites here. As you enjoy your meal look around at the various drawings and mounted animals for an informal history lesson about Gunnison. Full bar. | 820 Main St. | 970/641–9223 | $6–$14 | AE, D, MC, V.

Quarter Circle Restaurant. American. This family-oriented eatery is decorated with hand-printed local artwork. Renowned for their house-smoked barbecued meats. Finish the meal off with delicious homemade pie. | 323 E. Tomichi Ave. | 970/641–0542 | Breakfast also available; closed Sun. | $6–$15 | D, MC, V.

The Trough. Continental. Fine dining in a restaurant built with barn wood, situated about 2 mi west of Gunnison. Known for steak, prime rib, fresh seafood, wild game. Kids' menu. No smoking. | 37550 W. U.S. 50 | 970/641–3724 | Closed Sun. Nov.–Apr. No lunch | $11–$32 | AE, D, MC, V.

Lodging

Best Western Tomichi Village. Corral facilities are available during hunting season at this chain motel 1 mi east of Gunnison. Restaurant, complimentary Continental breakfast. Cable TV, some in-room VCRs (and movies). Pool. Hot tub. Gym. Laundry facilities. Airport shuttle. | 41883 E. U.S. 50 | 970/641–1131 | fax 970/641–9954 | www.bestwestern.com | 51 rooms | $79–$119 | AE, D, DC, MC, V.

Days Inn Gunnison. This Days Inn was renovated in 1998 and offers clean and modern rooms. Room service. In-room data ports, microwaves, refrigerators, cable TV. Hot tub. Laundry services. Business services. Pets allowed (fee). | 701 W. U.S. 50 | 970/641–0608 or 888/641–0608 | fax 970/641–2854 | www.bestwestern.com | 45 rooms | $69–$79 | AE, D, DC, MC, V.

Econo Lodge. This one-story budget motel is 20 mi from skiing facilities and 2 mi from whitewater rafting. Ideal for travelers on a tight budget. Restaurant, complimentary Continental breakfast. Cable TV. Outdoor hot tub. Business services. | 37760 W. U.S. 50 | 970/641–1000 | fax 970/641–5648 | www.econolodge.com | 37 rooms | $68–$70 | AE, D, DC, MC, V.

Harmel's. A 300-acre guest ranch surrounded by the Gunnison National Forest, at the confluence of three rivers about 20 mi north of Gunnison. Hayrides, square dancing, and river rafting fill the days. Bar, dining room, picnic area. No air-conditioning, refrigerators, no room phones, no TV in rooms, TV in common area. Pool. Horseback riding, fishing, bicycles. Video games. Children's programs (ages 5–12), playground. Laundry facilities. Airport shuttle. | 6748 County Rd. 742, Almont | 970/641–1740 or 800/235–3402 | fax 970/641–1944 | www.harmels.com | 38 rooms, 11 suites, 19 cottages | $100 per person per day (3–night minimum) | Closed Nov.–mid-May | AP | MC, V.

Holiday Inn Express. This limited-service chain motel is on the east side of town, near the city parks and the campus of Western State College. Complimentary Continental breakfast. In-room data ports, cable TV. Pool. Hot tub. Gym. Laundry facilities. Business services, airport shuttle. | 400 E. Tomichi Ave. | 970/641–1288 or 800/486–6476 | fax 970/641–1332 | www.holiday-inn.com | 54 rooms | $54–$99 | AE, D, DC, MC, V.

Hylander Motel. This small, basic motel is next to the City Park and across the street from miniature golf. All the rooms are decorated with intricate handmade quilts. Cable TV. Some pets allowed. | 412 E. Tomichi Ave. | 970/641–0700 | 24 rooms | $58–$78 | AE, D, DC, MC, V.

Lake Fork Resort. Overlooking picturesque Blue Mesa Lake, all six cabins at this small resort-style B&B have a private porch. Vacation activity packages are available for all seasons, including mountain biking, waterskiing, and snowboarding. Located 25 mi west of Gunnison off U.S. 50. Complimentary Continental breakfast. Kitchenettes. Volleyball. Playground. Laundry facilities. Business services. No smoking. | 940 Cove Rd. | 970/641–3564 or 800/368–9421 | fax 970/641–0623 | 6 cabins | $85 | AE, D, MC, V.

Mary Lawrence. This former boardinghouse, where once no men were allowed, is filled with period pieces. Complimentary breakfast. No air-conditioning, no room phones, no TV in some rooms, TV in common area. Airport shuttle. No kids under 6. No smoking. | 601 N. Taylor St. | 970/641–3343 | fax 970/641–6719 | www.commerceteam.com/mary.html | 5 rooms, 2 suites | $79–$85, $99–$129 suites | MC, V.

Powderhorn Guest Ranch. A very secluded guest ranch surrounded by the Gunnison National Forest, with accommodations in carpeted log cabins, each with a front porch. It is located 36 mi south of Gunnison via U.S. 50 and County Road 149, on County Road 27. Dining room, picnic area. Refrigerators. Pool, pond. Hot tub. Hiking, horseback riding, fishing. Playground. Laundry facilities. Airport shuttle. | 1525 County Rd. 27, Powderhorn | 970/641–0220 or 800/786–1220 | www.powderhornguestranch.com | 13 1- to 2-bedroom cabins | $1,200 per person per wk (1–wk minimum stay) | Closed late Sept.–June | AP | AE, V.

Ramada Limited. This limited-service chain motel is on the west side of Gunnison, convenient to Western State College. Complimentary Continental breakfast. Cable TV. Pool. Hot tub. | 1011 W. Rio Grande Ave. | 970/641–2804 or 888/298–2054 | fax 970/641–1420 | www.ramada.com | 36 rooms | $69–$89 | AE, D, DC, MC, V.

Super 8. Budget motel, near the county airport and Western State College. Cable TV. Airport shuttle. | 411 E. Tomichi Ave. | 970/641–3068 or 800/800–8000 | fax 970/641–1332 | www.super8.com | 52 rooms | $36–$70 | AE, D, DC, MC, V.

Water Wheel Inn. Four ponds punctuate the grounds of this secluded motel west of Gunnison. Complimentary Continental breakfast. Cable TV. Hot tub. Gym. Business services, airport shuttle. | 37478 U.S. 50 | 970/641–1650 or 800/642–1650 | fax 970/641–1650 | www.gunnison-co.com/main/lodging/waterwheel.htm | 52 rooms, 2 suites | $85, $100 suites | AE, D, DC, MC, V.

Waunita Hot Springs. A group of hot springs heat the pool at this guest ranch, on the edge of a mountainous pine forest. Entertainment includes square dances, cookouts, western music shows, hayrides, and jeep, camping, and rafting trips. A petting zoo delights younger guests. No alcohol permitted. Take U.S. 50 to County Rd. 887. Dining room. No room phones, no TV in rooms, TV in common area. Pool. Hot tub. Fishing. Video games. Laundry facilities. Airport shuttle. | 8007 County Rd. 887 | 970/641–1266 | www.waunita.com | 22 rooms | $1,150 per person for 6 nights (6–night minimum stay) | Closed Apr.–May | AP | MC, V.

Wildwood Motel. Away from the main streets and highways, the Wildwood is the ideal place for those who want the convenience of town and the tranquility of a Rocky Mountain day. Rooms at this small, simple motel are clean and comfortable, while the service is very friendly. Kitchenettes, refrigerators, cable TV. | 1312 W. Tomichi Ave. | 970/641–1663 | www.gunnison-co.com/main/lodging/wildwood.htm. | 18 rooms | $52–$59 | D, MC, V.

IDAHO SPRINGS

(Nearby towns also listed: Central City, Denver, Dillon, Evergreen, Georgetown, Golden)

The Ute Indians were the first to appreciate the healthy waters that flowed freely from the region's hot springs. In 1859, gold was discovered nearby, and Idaho Springs was settled soon afterward. Today, the area still relies on its mineral wealth, but more so on uranium, tungsten, and molybdenum than on the old favorites, gold and silver. Idaho Springs (population 2,063) is just west of Denver along Interstate 70. Be sure and take a look at the National Historic Landmark district along downtown's Miner Street.

Information: **Idaho Springs Visitors Center** | Box 97, Idaho Springs, 80452 | 303/567–4382 or 800/685–7785 | www.clearcreekcounty.com.

Attractions

Arapaho National Forest. Camping, hiking, picnicking, and winter sports on 1,000,000 acres north of Interstate 70, along Highway 60. The area around Idaho Springs and Dillon is administered by the Clear Creek Ranger District, whose office is in Idaho Springs. | 101 Chicago Creek Rd. | 303/567–3000 | www.fs.fed.us/r2/arnf/ccrd/vvc.htm | Free | Daily.

Argo Gold Mine, Mill, and Museum at Argo Town, USA. A reproduction of a western mining town on the National Register of Historic Places that tells the story of mining in Colorado. You can pan for gold and mine for gemstones here, see the historic mill at work grinding stones, and visit the historic mines. The museum displays mining artifacts, old payrolls, and photographs of the miners who worked here. | 2350 Riverside Dr. | 303/567–2421 | $9 | May–Sept., daily 9–6; Oct.–Apr. by appointment only.

Charlie Tayler Water Wheel. This distinctive wooden waterwheel, the largest in the state, is at the base of Bridal Veil Falls. It was built in the 1890s by a single miner. Park behind City Hall. | Downtown Idaho Springs | 303/567–4382 | Free | Daily.

Colorado School of Mines—Edgar Mine. Operated by the Colorado School of Mines in Golden, this experimental mine provides hands-on experience for aspiring mining engineers. Wear old shoes and a warm sweater; you must make a reservation in advance. | Colorado Ave. and 8th St. | 303/567–2911 | www.mines.edu | $6 | Mid-June–mid Aug., Tues.–Sat., tours at 9, 11, 1, 3 by appointment only.

Mount Evans Wilderness Area. The northern half of this wilderness area is in Arapahoe National Forest; the southern half is in Pike National Forest—a total of about 115 square mi. Some of the wildlife that can be seen are bighorn sheep, mountain goat, elk, marmot, pikas, and ptarmigan. You'll find many hiking trails, lakes, ponds, and mountains to enjoy along Highway 103; the entire area is administered by the Clear Creek Ranger District. While the area is free, there is a $10 toll to drive on the Mount Evans Scenic Byway, where the popular Echo and Summit lakes can be found. | Clear Creek Ranger District, Hwy. 103, Idaho Springs | 303/567–2901 | www.fs.fed.us/arnf | Free | Daily.

Echo Lake. Just off the Mount Evans Scenic Byway, Echo Lake is a great spot for fishing, but there is no boating allowed. A great trail goes around the lake and will interest hikers. Not far down the trail is a picnic area with pavilions and barbecue pits. Although the lake itself is free, there is a $10 toll to enter the Mount Evans Scenic Byway. The Echo Lake Lodge is a good place to stop for a meal. | Mount Evans Hwy. (Hwy. 5) at Hwy. 103 | 303/567–2901 | www.fs.fed.us/arnf | Free | Daily.

Mount Evans Scenic Byway. To get to the top of Mount Evans, you could take America's highest paved road, which was completed in 1927. The road extends 14 mi from the entrance station to the Mount Evans summit parking area and rises to an elevation of 14,130 ft. | Mount Evans Hwy. (Hwy. 5) | 303/567–2901 | www.fs.fed.us/arnf | $10 per vehicle | Daily.

Summit Lake. If you travel along the Mount Evans Scenic Byway, be sure to visit this glacial cirque that sits 12,830 ft in the mountains. The lake is somewhat of a bowl that catches the melting snow from Mount Evans and Mount Spaulding. You can access the lake from the Summit Lake parking area, which is a few hundred feet away. Although the lake itself is free, there is a $10 toll to enter the Mount Evans Scenic Byway. You can get souvenirs and lunch at the Echo Lake Lodge. | Mount Evans Hwy. (Hwy. 5) | 303/567–2901 | www.fs.fed.us/arnf | Free | Daily.

Phoenix Gold Mine. The only working gold mine in Colorado that can be visited by the public. You can take a tour, then dig or pan for gold using 19th-century tools (you keep anything you find). Approximately 2½ mi southwest of Idaho Springs via Stanley Road to Trail Creek Road. | Off Trail Creek Rd. | 303/567–0422 or 800/685–7785 | www.phoenixmine.com | $9 | Daily 10–6.

Saint Mary's Glacier. Great summertime picnicking around an alpine lake near Idaho Springs in Arapahoe National Forest. Skiing on the glacier is permitted in winter. Take Interstate 70 2 mi northwest of Idaho Springs, then exit 238, and drive up Fall River Road to St. Mary's Lake. | 303/567–2901 | Free | Daily.

ON THE CALENDAR

JUNE: *Gold Rush Days.* Commemorates the great gold strikes with footraces, food, a parade, a mining competition, and crafts. | 303/567–4382 or 800/685–7785.

JUNE: *Horseshoe Tournament.* This competition draws participants from all over Colorado. | 16th St. and Colorado Blvd. | 303/567–9996.

Dining

Buffalo Restaurant and Bar. American. Western artifacts decorate the walls in this bar and grill; the bar is more than 100 years old. A wide variety of buffalo entrées as well as beef, chicken, pasta, and pizza dishes fill the menu. Kids' menu | 1617 Miner St. | 303/567–2729 | $8–$15 | AE, D, DC, MC, V.

Echo Lake Lodge. American. Stop at this 1926 log lodge on your trip up the Mount Evans Highway for a quick bite. This restaurant offers spectacular views of Echo Lake from its wood-lined interior and specializes in trout, buffalo chile, and homemade pies. | 13264 S. Hwy. 103 | 303/567–2138 | No dinner | $6–$13 | AE, MC, V.

Wildfire. American. Known for their smoked brisket and chicken, Wildfire also features a wide selection of Mexican dishes. Feel free to inspect the collection of over 1,000 tin cans. | 2910 Colorado Blvd. | 303/567–2775 | Breakfast also available | $6–$15 | D, DC, MC, V.

Lodging

Brookside Inn. Originally a hydroelectric plant, the boxy building housing this B&B was built in 1910. Fall River runs right through the property and will sing you to sleep. All the rooms are uniquely decorated and have a private entrance. Picnic area, complimentary breakfast. Cable TV, in-room VCRs. Outdoor hot tub. No kids under 18. No smoking. | 2971 Fall River Rd. | 303/567–9610 | fax 303/567–9611 | www.brookside-inn.com | 4 rooms | $135 | MC, V.

St. Mary's Glacier Bed and Breakfast. Outside the town of Idaho Springs, this remote B&B is a three-story log building. At 10,000 ft it's the highest-altitude B&B in North America. The public areas are built around a stone fireplace; a large deck provides views of the Continental Divide and St. Mary's Glacier. Complimentary breakfast. No air-conditioning, no room phones, no TV in rooms, TV/VCR in common room. No smoking. | 336 Crest Dr. | 303/567–4084 | fax 303/567–4084 | 6 rooms, 1 suite | $89–$139, $159 suite | AE, D, DC, MC, V.

KEYSTONE

(Nearby towns also listed: Breckenridge, Dillon, Frisco, Georgetown)

In 1859 gold was discovered in Summit County, attracting prospectors to the mountain valleys. The first silver vein in the state was found at nearby Montezuma, and settlers from Pennsylvania, the Keystone State, gave this valley its name. After the mining boom the area remained dormant for many years until the Eisenhower Tunnel was completed in the 1950s. This brought an influx of people seeking winter recreation to the area, and in 1970 Keystone Mountain Resort was born.

As a ski resort, Keystone's reputation was originally that of a family destination, with only one mountain consisting of mostly beginner and intermediate trails and fairly limited summer activities. Beginning in 1984, a series of expansion projects has made it a more respectable ski area, catering to first-time skiers and serious thrill seekers alike. Options for summer activities have been expanded greatly as well, with water sports on Keystone Lake and a top-ranked golf course.

Keystone is now a standout among the other Summit County resorts, with some of the best groomed trails in the state, some very challenging mogul skiing on North Peak, and one of the largest night skiing operations in the country. Keystone is also renowned for its expansion policy with concern to environmental impact. In summer or winter, seasoned skier or first-timer, Keystone will more than suit your needs.

Information: Summit County Chamber of Commerce | Box 214, Frisco 80435 | 970/668–2051 | www.summitnet.com/chamber/index.html.

Attractions

Keystone Ranch Golf Course. One of the top 50 resort courses in America. With a par of 72, the course is more than 7,000 yards long and was designed by Robert Trent Jones, Jr. Reservations are necessary. | 22010 U.S. 6 | 970/496–4250 | Free | Mid-May–late Oct.

Keystone Lodge Skating Rink. At 5 acres, this is the largest outdoor Zamboni-groomed rink in the country. During the holidays childrens' events and shows are featured, usually with costumed characters. | U.S. 6 | 970/468–2316 | $10 | Nov.–Apr., daily.

Keystone Resort Ski Area. The area contains three ski mountains, each varying in overall difficulty level. Keystone Mountain is geared towards beginners and intermediate skiers, while North Peak has more advanced terrain. The Outback has the most challenging terrain, including over 600 acres of above-timberline bowls for expert skiers. Summer activities include horseback riding, golf, bicycling, boating and tennis. | U.S. 6, Keystone | 877/734–4480 | www.snow.com | Daily.

Keystone Mountain. The main ski area at Keystone Resort offers 2 triple, 8 double, 4 quad, 2 high-speed chairlifts, and 4 surface lifts. There are 53 runs (the longest is 3 mi) and a vertical drop of 2,340 ft. During the summer, the mountain offers hiking and horseback-riding. | U.S. 6, Keystone | 877/734–4480 | www.snow.com | Daily.

North Peak. This mountain is open year-round, with both summer and winter activities. For skiing, the mountain has 19 runs (the longest is 2½ mi), a vertical drop of 1,620 ft, and offers quad and triple chairlifts. | U.S. 6, Keystone | 877/734–4480 | www.snow.com | Daily.

The Outback. During ski season, this mountain has a high-speed quad chairlift, 17 runs (the longest is 2½ mi), and a vertical drop of 1,520 ft. It's also open year-round. | U.S. 6, Keystone | 877/734–4480 | www.snow.com | Daily.

ON THE CALENDAR

APR.: *Festival of Fools Snowsports Triathlon.* At this zany April Fool's Day event, entrants compete in events on snowshoes, skis, snowboards, and mountain bikes while wearing some really bizarre costumes. Everyone is welcome to watch the spectacle, but there is a $20 entry fee to compete. | 877/734–4480.

Dining

★ **Alpenglow Stube.** German. Located at 11,444 ft above sea level, this elegant restaurant is truly one of a kind. You will enjoy breathtaking views of the Continental Divide as a gondola takes you up to the Outpost on North Peak. Award-winning chefs prepare Bavarian-influenced dishes designed to complement this unique and rich setting. No smoking. | Outpost Lodge at the North Peak | 970/496–4132 or 800/354–4386 | Reservations essential | Closed Mon., Tues. No lunch Sept.–May | $78 prix fixe | AE, D, DC, MC, V.

Der Fondue Chessel. Swiss. The prix-fixe four-course traditional fondue meal includes cheese fondue, Caesar salad, your choice of entrée plate for raclette (melted cheese served over boiled potatoes), grilling, and chocolate fondue for dessert. Choose from scallops, shrimp, chicken breast, veal sausage, or beef tenderloin. Entertainment. | Timber Ridge Room, Outpost Lodge, top of North Peak | 970/496–4386 | Reservations essential | Closed Apr.–May, Oct.; closed Sun. Nov.–Mar.; closed Mon., Tues. June–Sept. | $42 prix fixe | AE, D, DC, MC, V.

Gassy's Food and Spirits. American/Casual. Named after late 1800s miner/swindler Gassy Thompson, this reputable tavern is filled with Colorado mining memorabilia. Barbecued ribs are the specialty, along with burgers and huge sandwiches. Other hearty American fare rounds out the menu. | Mountain House, base of Keystone Mountain, Keystone Rd. | 970/496–4130 | Closed Feb.–Aug. | $5–$18 | AE, D, DC, MC, V.

Great Northern Tavern. Modern American. The exceptional dinner menu makes this upscale brewpub the perfect spot for a leisurely, intimate meal. The creative menu features wild game, such as venison with roasted-shallot juniper-berry demi-glace. For an appetizer, try the rock shrimp cakes. | River Run Village Base | 970/262–2202 | Reservations essential | $8–$26 | AE, D, DC, MC, V.

Ida Belle's Bar and Grill. Tex-Mex. In keeping with its former incarnation as a gold mine, the dining room is reached through the old mineshaft entrance. Chile and fajitas are the highlights, and barbecue ribs and half-pound burgers are also offered. The Mal Brown sundae will more than satisfy your sweet tooth. | Lakeside Condominiums, next to skating pond, Keystone Village | 970/496–4289 | $6–$15 | AE, D, DC, MC, V.

★ **Keystone Ranch.** Continental. This 1930s log cabin was once part of a working cattle ranch. You'll find cowboy memorabilia, stylish throw rugs, a massive stone fireplace, and great views. Six-course dinners include a Ranch Kettle Soup and many wild game entrées. Kids' menu. | Keystone Rd. | 970/468–4161 | Reservations essential | No lunch | $68 prix fixe | AE, D, DC, MC, V.

Kickapoo Tavern. American/Casual. This stylish sports bar and grill features handcrafted brews and home-style American food. TVs constantly beam sports and sports news while the kitchen turns out chile and chicken potpie. Enjoy the spectacular views from the huge outdoor patio. | Jackpine Lodge, River Run Village | 970/468–4601 | $8–$20 | AE, D, DC, MC, V.

The Outpost. Contemporary. At this magnificent log and glass structure on the top of North Peak you will find some of the best vistas in Keystone. The upscale ski cafeteria serves popular pasta, meat, and poultry dishes. The deck barbecue is a favorite on warm days. | Outpost Lodge, top of North Peak | 970/496–4386 | $8–$20 | AE, D, DC, MC, V.

Razzberry's. American/Casual. Fill up on steak and eggs, hash browns, pancakes, and fruit at the all-you-can-eat breakfast bar overlooking the mountain before you head out to ski. The bistro-style dinner features grilled items and fresh pasta. | The Inn, 23044 U.S. 6 | 970/496–1334 | Breakfast also available; no lunch | $16–$26 | AE, D, DC, MC, V.

Lodging

Chateaux d'Mont. This is a classy slopeside complex with views overlooking the ski area. All units have a balcony or terrace, fireplace, and washer and dryer. Units have either two or three bedrooms. Some kitchenettes, some microwaves, some refrigerators, in-room hot tubs, cable TV. Gym. | Bldg. 21996, U.S 6, Keystone | 970/496–2316 or 800/222–0188 | fax 970/496–4343 | 14 units | $245–$1,175 | AE, D, MC, V.

Inn at Keystone. This seven-story redbrick tower overlooking the Snake River valley houses a modern full-service hotel with modest, comfortable rooms. Two suites have hot tubs. You have access to the resort's gym. Restaurant, bar. Some in-room hot tubs, cable TV. 3 outdoor hot tubs. | 23044 U.S. 6 | 970/496–1334 or 800/222–0188 | fax 970/496–4343 | 103 rooms, 17 suites | $115–$338 | AE, D, MC, V.

Keystone Condominiums. Anything from a studio to a five-bedroom house can be reserved for you at one of four different scattered complexes. Mountain Premium has the more extravagant units and slopeside convenience, while Village, Resort II, and Resort I offer more modest rates. Most units come with a kitchen and fireplace, and all guests have access to Keystone Fitness Center. Restaurant, bar, complimentary Continental breakfast. Some kitchenettes, some microwaves, some refrigerators, cable TV. Hot tub. Laundry facilities. | U.S. 6 | 970/496–2316 or 800/222–0188 | fax 970/496–4343 | 1,300 units | $105–$1,095 | AE, D, DC, MC, V.

★ **Keystone Lodge.** This large, modern hotel is situated between Keystone Lake and U.S. 6. The standard double rooms and suites are luxurious if not overly large. Try for one with a balcony lakeside. Restaurant, bar. Cable TV. Outdoor pool. Hot tub, massage, spa. 2 tennis courts. Health club. Shops. Baby-sitting. Laundry facilities. | U.S. 6, Keystone | 970/468–2316 or 800/222–0188 | 152 rooms | $150–$350 | AE, D, DC, MC, V.

★ **Ski Tip Lodge.** Just east of Keystone, about 12 mi north of Breckenridge, this faux chalet was a stagecoach stop in the mid-1800s. It's an inn with a definite personality of its own, with uneven floors, wooden beams, and a vast collection of regional antiques. The restaurant serves a four-course dinner, and guests receive privileges at the nearby Keystone Fitness Center. Restaurant, bar, complimentary breakfast. No air-conditioning, no room phones. Hot tub. Tennis. Business services. No smoking. | 0764 Montezuma Rd., Keystone | 970/496–4950 or 800/222–0188 | fax 970/496–4940 | 11 rooms (2 with shared bath), 2 suites | $70–$174, $144–$204 suites | AE, D, DC, MC, V.

KREMMLING

MAP 6, E3

(Nearby towns also listed: Dillon, Frisco, Granby)

Kremmling is on the scenic highway between the Rocky Mountain National Park and Steamboat Springs. Surrounded by national forests, the town of nearly 1,500 enjoys a brisk business from tourists, both winter and summer, enjoying the many outdoor activities in the area.

Information: Greater Granby Chamber of Commerce | Box 35, Granby 80446 | 970/887–2311 or 800/325–1661 | www.rkymtnhi.com/granbycoc.

Attractions

Green Mountain Reservoir. Waterskiing, camping, fishing, boating, and picnicking are available at this man-made lake 16 mi south of Kremmling on Route 9. A grocery store is nearby. | Rte. 9, Heeney | 970/468–5400 | Free | Daily.

Wolford Mountain Reservoir. Activities at this man-made lake 6 mi north of Kremmling include fishing, jet skiing, boating, swimming, and wildlife watching. | U.S. 40 | 800/416–6992 | $3 | Daily.

FEB.: *Ididarace.* This sled-dog race mimics the famous Iditarod that is held in Alaska. | 970/724–3472.

Dining

Lone Moose Restaurant and Lounge. Steak. Mounted deer heads help contribute to the Old West feel at the Lone Moose, where you'll find the best prime rib in town; the New York steak is also very popular. | 115 W. Park Ave. | 970/724–9987 | $7–$14 | MC, V.

Lodging

Hotel Eastin. Constructed in 1906, the Eastin is a quaint little hotel with natural woodwork and some Art Deco touches. Unmodernized European-style rooms are available for those who want to escape the 1990s. Cable TV. No smoking. | 105 S. Second St. | 970/724–3261 or 800/546–0815 | www.coloradovacation.com/bed/eastin | 27 rooms | $30–$50 | AE, DC, MC, V.

Latigo Ranch. Contemporary log guest cabins, each with a view of the Continental Divide, on a heavily forested mountainside. There is entertainment nightly. Dining room, picnic area. Refrigerators. Pool, pond. Hot tub. Hiking, horseback riding. Fishing. Cross-country skiing, sleigh rides. Children's programs (ages 3–13), playground. Laundry facilities. Business services. | 201 County Rd. 1911 | 970/724–9008 or 800/227–9655 | www.dude-ranch.com | 10 cabins | $1,600 per person per wk (1–wk minimum stay) | Closed Apr.–May, Oct.– Nov. | AP | AE, MC, V.

LA JUNTA

MAP 6, I7

(Nearby towns also listed: Lamar, Pueblo)

Although La Junta (population 8,169) lies on the route of the historic Santa Fe Trail, the town itself was not established until around 1875, some years after the Trail's heyday. The surrounding countryside is irrigated farm land and produces a large variety of commercial vegetables and melons.

Information: Chamber of Commerce | 110 Santa Fe Ave., La Junta, 81050 | 719/384–7411 | www.lajunta.net.

Attractions

Bent's Old Fort National Historic Site. This magnificent reconstruction of one of the largest and most important fur posts in all of the United States was built in the early 1830s by the Bent brothers, Charles and William, and their partner, Ceran St. Vrain. The fort was a hub of influence among several southern Great Plains tribes as well as an important resting place on the Santa Fe Trail. The fort is located 8 mi northeast of La Junta on Route 194 East. | 35110 Rte. 194 E | 719/383–5010 | www.nps.gov/beol | $2 | June–Aug., daily 8–5:30; Sept.–May, daily 9–4.

Comanche National Grassland. The Grasslands are home to the Santa Fe National Historic Trail sites and Picket Wire Canyonlands. The Canyonlands feature a Dinosaur Tracksite, ancient rock art, and more. The visitor center is in La Junta. | 1420 E. 3rd St. | 719/384–2181 | www.fs.fed.us/r2 | Free | Daily.

Koshare Indian Kiva Museum. Home of the world-renowned Koshare Indian dancers, this dome-shaped building exhibits an extensive collection of Native American artifacts (Navajo silver, Zuni pottery, Shoshone buckskin clothing) and western paintings by artists like Remington, who are known for their depictions of Native Americans. | 115 W. 18th St. | 719/384–4411 | www.ruralnet.net/koshare | $2, dance presentations $5 | Daily 10–5; dances June–early Aug., Fri., Sat. 8 PM.

Otero Museum. The museum provides a good overview of Otero County history. | 3rd and Anderson Sts. | 719/384–7500 | Free | June–Sept., Mon.–Sat. 1–5.

ON THE CALENDAR
JUNE–AUG.: *Koshare Indian Dances.* American Indian dances are performed at the Koshare Kiva Museum by a world-acclaimed Boy Scout troop weekend evenings at 8pm. | 719/384–4411.
AUG.: *Arkansas Valley Fair and Exposition.* This event is Colorado's oldest continuous fair, with free watermelons and other daily highlights at the Rocky Ford Fairgrounds. | 719/254–7483.
SEPT.: *Early Settlers Day.* Arts and crafts, a parade, and a fiddlers' contest provide a day of historic activities on the Saturday after Labor Day. | 719/384–7411.
DEC.: *Koshare Winter Night Ceremonial.* Nightly Native American performances present a memorable experience at the Koshare Kiva Museum. | 719/384–4411.

Dining

Chiaramonte's. Continental. Cedar walls and mirrors decorate the upstairs dining room of this popular spot across from the courthouse; downstairs, there's a wood-and-brick bar. Known for steak, seafood, and homemade soups. Kids' menu. | 208 Santa Fe St. | 719/384–8909 | Closed Sun. No lunch Sat. | $7–$15 | D, MC, V.

K-Bob Steak House. Steak. Lassos and intricate rugs line this family-oriented chain steak house. The T-bone and rib-eye steaks are recommended. Salad bar. Kids' menu. | 27866 Frontage Rd. W | 719/384–7338 | $5–$15 | AE, D, DC, MC, V.

Lodging

Best Western Bent's Fort Inn. This chain motel is in the tiny berg of Las Animas, 20 mi east of La Junta via U.S. 50. Restaurant, bar, room service. Cable TV. Pool. Business services, airport shuttle. Some pets allowed. | 719/456–0011 | fax 719/456–2550 | www.bestwestern.com | 38 rooms | $49–$59 | AE, D, DC, MC, V.

Quality Inn. Located on La Junta's east side, offering reliable chain motel amenities. Restaurant, bar, room service. Some refrigerators, cable TV, some in-room VCRs (and movies). Indoor-outdoor pool. Hot tub. Gym. Business services, airport shuttle. Some pets allowed. | 1325 E. 3rd St. | 719/384–2571 or 800/228–5151 | fax 719/384–5655 | www.qualityinn.com | 60 rooms, 16 suites | $59–$89, $89–$95 suites | AE, D, DC, MC, V.

Mid-Town Motel. This affordable motel provides clean and comfortable rooms, though little else. The Comanche National Grasslands are only 7 mi away. Cable TV. | 215 E. 3rd St. | 719/384–7741 | 26 rooms | $34–$40 | AE, D, DC, MC, V.

Stagecoach Motel. This economical roadside motel is on the western outskirts of La Junta. In-room data ports, cable TV. Pool. Pets allowed. | 905 W. 3rd St. | 719/384–5476 | fax 719/384–9091 | 31 rooms | $35–$65 | AE, D, DC, MC, V.

LAKE CITY

MAP 6, C7

(Nearby towns also listed: Gunnison, South Fork)

Lake City is situated smack in the middle of four of Colorado's national forests: Uncompahgre, Gunnison, Rio Grande, and San Juan. With neighbors like that, you know the area has got to be rich in all varieties of outdoor attractions. But the town of nearly 400 residents has its own charms. Lake City has a large collection of gingerbread-trim houses as well as the largest National Historic Landmark District in the state of Colorado. But the area is perhaps best known for a more lurid interlude: Alferd (sometimes

LAKE CITY

INTRO
ATTRACTIONS
DINING
LODGING

misspelled Alfred) Packer, while guiding gold prospectors through these parts in 1873–74, is supposed to have murdered and eaten some of his companions when winter marooned the party in the high mountains near Lake San Cristobal without food.

Information: Lake City Chamber of Commerce | Box 430, Lake City 81235 | 970/944–2527 or 800/569–1874 | www.lakecity.net.

Attractions

Alpine Triangle Recreation Area. A true wilderness experience can be had in this area administered jointly by the Bureau of Land Management and the U.S. Forest Service. Primitive and motorized recreational activities abound. Wildlife is abundant. The recreation area extends south and west of Lake City; access is by the Alpine Loop National Backcountry Byway (four-wheel drive necessary in some places). | www.co.blm.gov/gra/gra-rec.htm | 970/641–0471 | Free | June–mid-Oct.

Slumgullion Earth Slide. This huge mass of volcanic rock caused the formation of Lake San Cristobal. Movement on the flow ranges from 5 to 20 ft per year. | Hwy. 149, south of downtown Lake City | 970/944–2527 | Free | Daily.

ON THE CALENDAR

MAY: *Alferd Packer Barbeque Cook-off.* This may be the world's only event celebrating a convicted cannibal. Packer was prosecuted for dining on some of his fellow travelers way back in the 1800s when he was caught in a blizzard with nothing else to eat. | 970/944–2527 or 800/569–1874.
JULY–AUG.: *Ghost Town Narration Tours.* Guided and narrated tours of the old ghost towns that lay silent in the surrounding mountains are available. | 970/944–2527 or 800/569–1874.

Dining

Mother Lode. American. Decorated with antiques and turn-of-the-20th-century furnishings, this eatery serves up standard American fare. Featured are prime rib and a surprisingly extensive vegetarian menu. | 310 Gunnison Ave. | 970/944–5044 | Breakfast also available | $10–$17 | MC, V.

Lodging

Crystal Lodge. A western mountain lodge in the San Juan Mountains with panoramic views from its many decks. Restaurant. No air-conditioning, no room phones, no TVs in some rooms. Business services. No smoking. | 2175 Hwy. 149 S | 970/944–2201 or 877/465–6343 | fax 970/944–2503 | 18 rooms, 5 suites, 4 cabins | $65, $75–$95 suites, $110 cabins | MC, V.

Matterhorn Motel. This small motel is in the majestic San Juan Mountains and just two blocks from the Lake City Historical District. Rooms are comfortable and affordable. Some kitchenettes, some refrigerators, cable TV. Some pets allowed. No smoking. | 409 N. Bluff | 970/944–2210 | 12 rooms, 2 cabins | $65–$80 | MC, V.

LAKEWOOD

MAP 6, F4

(Nearby towns also listed: Aurora, Denver, Englewood, Golden)

Although Lakewood's roots stretch back into the Colorado gold rush days of the 1860s, when it was established as a mining settlement, the city's fortunes are quite a bit higher and brighter than they once were. Encompassed in the greater Denver metropolitan area, Lakewood is now an affluent suburb of Denver, and with a population of 135,000, the fourth-largest city in the state. Lakewood is home to the capital city's rich and famous who want to live away from the hubbub of the city.

Information: **West Chamber Serving Jefferson County** | Box 280748, Lakewood, 80228-0748 | 303/233–5555.

Attractions

Bear Creek Lake Park. A nice park with hiking, fishing, boating, cycling, picnicking, a water-skiing school, and more. | Morrison Rd. | 303/697–6159 | $3 per vehicle | Daily.

Crown Hill Park. A 242-acre park that provides fishing, hiking, cycling, and horseback riding. The park also contains a wildlife sanctuary. | W. 26th Ave., at Kipling St. | 303/271–5925 | Free | Wildlife Sanctuary closed Mar.–June.

Lakewood's Heritage Center. This historic and social center in Belmar Park features a look at early 20th-century lifestyles, especially rural life. The center encompasses more than 10 historic structures and preserves a collection of over 30,000 artifacts. | 797 S. Wadsworth Blvd. | 303/987–7850 | www.ci.lakewood.co.us | Free | Tues.–Fri. 10–4, weekends noon–4.

ON THE CALENDAR

AUG.: *Irish Fest.* This celebration of all things Irish is held in Belmar Park. | 303/987–7850.

Dining

Carnation Restaurant. American. Providing a very casual and relaxed atmosphere, the Carnation is a great place to bring the whole family. The taco salad and chicken-fried steak are popular with the locals. Breakfast is served all day. Kids' menu. | 1395 Wadsworth Blvd. | 303/238–3045 | Breakfast also available | $4–$8 | D, DC, MC, V.

Casa Bonita of Denver. Mexican. This Lakewood outlet of the midwest chain is one of the largest Mexican restaurants in the state. Housed in a pink stucco castle, this place offers loads of entertainment such as cliff diving, puppet shows, and gunfights. Open-air dining on patio. Kids' menu. | 6715 W. Colfax Ave. | 303/232–5115 | $7–$9 | AE, D, DC, MC, V.

Chowda House. Seafood. This New England–style clam shack serves up the best seafood in town. Be sure to try the whole clams or crown salmon. Kids' menu. | 11104 W. Colfax Ave. | 303/237–1555 | $6–$24 | AE, D, DC, MC, V.

Dardano's. Italian. Set on the side of a hill, this casual, family-style restaurant has many windows overlooking the foothills; it has been in business since 1976. In addition to pizza and homemade pasta, you can get great prime rib and even lobster. Kids' menu. | 11968 W. Jewell Ave. | www.dardanosrestaurant.com | 303/988–1991 | Closed Mon. No lunch | $6–$16 | AE, DC, MC, V.

The Fort. Southwestern. In a southwestern-style building modeled after Bent's Old Fort in La Junta, this local favorite is in Morrison, 7 mi from Lakewood, with fine views of Denver. Best bets: bison steaks, Rocky Mountain oysters, rattlesnake. Kids' menu. | 19192 Rte. 8, Morrison | 303/697–4771 | No lunch | $18–$40 | AE, D, DC, MC, V.

Lodging

Comfort Inn–Southwest Denver. This upper-budget motel is located just north of a thriving retail area. Complimentary Continental breakfast. Microwaves, refrigerators, cable TV. Pool. Hot tub. Gym. Laundry facilities. Business services. Pets allowed (fee). | 3440 S. Vance St. | 303/989–5500 or 800/228–5150 | fax 303/989–2981 | www.comfortinn.com | 123 rooms, 4 suites | $72–$83, $117 suites | AE, D, DC, MC, V.

Four Points by Sheraton. This upscale chain hotel sits in the middle of Lakewood, convenient to both Denver and Golden. Restaurant, bar. In-room data ports, some refrigerators, cable TV. Pool. Hot tub. Gym. Business services. | 137 Union Blvd. | 303/969–9900 or 800/937–8461 | fax 303/989–9847 | www.fourpoints.com | 170 rooms | $99–$139 | AE, D, DC, MC, V.

Hampton Inn–Denver Southwest. This upper-budget chain hotel is just south of U.S. 285. Complimentary Continental breakfast. In-room data ports, some microwaves, some refrigerators, cable TV. Pool. Gym. Laundry facilities. Business services. | 3605 S. Wadsworth Blvd. | 303/989–6900 or 800/426–7866 | fax 303/985–4730 | www.hamptoninn.com | 150 rooms | $72–$75 | AE, D, DC, MC, V.

Holiday Inn–Denver-Lakewood. This motel is a reliable choice for both business and pleasure travelers. Restaurant, bar, room service. In-room data ports, some refrigerators, cable TV. Pool. Gym. Laundry facilities. Business services. | 7390 W. Hampden Ave. | 303/980–9200 or 800/737–5253 | fax 303/980–6423 | www.holiday-inn.com | 185 rooms, 5 suites | $105, $150 suites | AE, D, DC, MC, V.

Residence Inn Denver Southwest/Lakewood. Just 13 mi from downtown Denver, this upscale all-suite hotel provides professional, friendly service and comfortable, spacious rooms. Complimentary Continental breakfast. In-room data ports, kitchenettes, refrigerators, cable TV. Pool. Laundry services. Business services. | 7050 W. Hampden Ave. | 303/985–7676 or 800/331–3131 | fax 303/985–1257 | www.residenceinn.com | 102 suites | $119–149 | AE, D, DC, MC, V.

Sheraton–Denver West. This upscale hotel is situated near the Denver Federal Center. Restaurant, bar. In-room data ports, some refrigerators, cable TV. Pool. Barbershop, beauty salon, hot tub, massage. Gym. Business services, free parking. | 360 Union Blvd. (I–25, exit 6th Ave. W) | 303/987–2000 or 800/937–8461 | fax 303/969–0263 | www.sheraton.com | 242 rooms | $140–$175 | AE, D, DC, MC, V.

LAMAR

(Nearby town also listed: La Junta)

Lamar sits astride the old Santa Fe Trail and on the banks of the historic Arkansas River as it works itself toward the Kansas border. The town actually came to be established through a land dispute with the Atchison, Topeka, and Santa Fe railroad company, which was looking to establish a new town along its route in southeastern Colorado. The town might have been called "Blackwell", but rancher A.R. Black, who owned a substantial amount of land in the area, would not sell some of it to the railroad for a new townsite; thus, the railroad purchased land 3 mi away, naming the new townsite "Lamar" after Lucius Quintius Lamar, President Grover Cleveland's Secretary of the Interior. The naming of the town made securing a land office an easy task. The town of Lamar (population 8,748) is now the county seat of Prowers County, and its major economic base is the rich agricultural land surrounding it.

Information: **Lamar Chamber of Commerce** | 109A E. Beech St. 81052 | 719/336–4379.

Attractions

Big Timbers Museum. The museum is named for the giant cottonwood trees that once lined the nearby Arkansas River. Exhibits depict local history, art, and artifacts. | 7517 U.S. 50 | 719/336–2472 | Free | Memorial Day–Labor Day 10–5.

ON THE CALENDAR

MAY: *Lamar Days.* This celebration brings the entire town together. The senior pro rodeo, car show, and parade are big draws. | 719/336–4379.

Dining

Blackwell Station. Steak. Check out the miniature train that runs around the perimeter of the restaurant. From T-bones to rib eyes, the steaks are succulent. Many seafood dishes are also served. Kids' menu. | 1301 S. Main St. | 719/336–7575 | $7–$14 | D, MC, V.

Lodging

Best Western–Cow Palace Inn. This mid-priced motel has several hunting-themed events a year. Restaurant, bar, room service. Cable TV, some in-room VCRs. Pool. Barbershop, beauty salon. Hot tub. Driving range. Business services, airport shuttle. Pets allowed. | 1301 N. Main St. | 719/336–7753 or 800/678–0344 | fax 719/336–9598 | www.bestwestern.com | 102 rooms | $75–$95 | AE, D, DC, MC, V.

Blue Spruce. An inexpensive roadside motel across the street from Lamar College on the south side of town. Complimentary Continental breakfast. Cable TV. Pool. Airport shuttle. Pets allowed. | 1801 S. Main St. | 719/336–7454 | fax 719/336–4729 | 30 rooms | $32–$44 | AE, D, DC, MC, V.

Days Inn. This simple chain motel offers clean rooms and professional service. Complimentary Continental breakfast. In-room data ports, microwaves, refrigerators, cable TV. Pool. Hot tub. Gym. Business services. | 1306 N. Main St. | 719/336–5340 or 800/544–8313 | fax 719/336–8438 | www.daysinn.com | 35 rooms, 2 suites | $64–$69, $96–$125 suites | AE, D, DC, MC, V.

LEADVILLE

MAP 6, E4

LEADVILLE

INTRO
ATTRACTIONS
DINING
LODGING

(Nearby towns also listed: Aspen, Buena Vista, Copper Mountain)

Born in the early days of the Colorado gold rush and raised in the later and richer silver-boom years, Leadville was once temporary home to many self-made millionaires. Horace Tabor, millionaire mine owner and U.S. senator, whose name adorns the Leadville Opera House, was one such resident. At times, it rivaled Denver as most important city in Colorado. After the gold rush years, however, the town (as well as Tabor) went broke and became a ghost village. Today it has been restored and reconstructed to its former glory. Its present-day economy is centered around tourism, and Leadville maintains a year-round community of 3,449 people. Leadville is 113 mi west of Denver, high in the Rockies and on the eastern slope of the Continental Divide; at 10,152 ft, it's actually the highest incorporated town in the United States.

Information: Greater Leadville Area Chamber of Commerce | 809 Harrison Ave., Leadville, 80461 | 719/486–3900 or 888/264–5344 | www.leadvilleusa.com.

Attractions

Healy House-Dexter Cabin. A restored Victorian house and "gentleman's" cabin, both dating from the late 1800s. Period furnishings are included. | 912 Harrison Ave. | 719/486–0487 | $3.50 | Memorial Day–Labor Day, daily 10–4:30.

Heritage Museum and Gallery. Exhibits depict local history and display mining memorabilia. | 120 E. 9th St. | 719/486–1878 | $3.50 | Memorial Day–Sept., daily 10–6.

Leadville, Colorado, and Southern Railroad Train Tour. Provides a 23-mi round-trip journey along the headwaters of the Arkansas River. | 326 E. 7th St. | 719/486–3936 | www.leadville-train.com | $23 | Memorial Day–mid-June, daily 1 PM; mid-June–Labor Day, daily 10 AM and 2 PM; Labor Day–Oct. 1 daily 1 PM.

Leadville National Fish Hatchery. Nearly 25 tons of cutthroat trout are hatched annually at this hatchery 7 mi southwest of Leadville via U.S. 24. Hiking and ski-touring trails are available nearby. | 2844 Hwy. 300 | 719/486–0189 | Free | Memorial Day–Labor Day, daily 7:30–5; Labor Day–Memorial Day, daily 7:30–4.

The Matchless Mine. This is the mine that Horace Tabor thought would revive his lost fortune; it didn't. In 1935, Tabor's widow, "Baby Doe," was found frozen to death in a cabin near this mine. She had lived in poverty, a forgotten recluse since her husband's death in 1899. | E. 7th St., 1 mi east of Leadville | 719/486–1899 | $3 | June–Labor Day, daily 9–4:45.

Mt. Massive Golf Course. At an elevation of 9,680 ft, this is the highest golf course in North America. Tee off on greens that are surrounded by towering peaks and tall trees. | 259 County Rd. 5 | 719/486–2176 | Free | Daily 8–8.

National Mining Hall of Fame and Museum. Exhibits depict the history and technology of mining. | 120 W. 9th St. | 719/486–1229 | www.leadville.com/miningmuseum/mine.htm | $4 | May–Oct., daily 9–5.; Nov.–Apr., weekdays 10–3.

Ski Cooper. You'll find triple and double chairlifts, a Pomalift, T-bar, and 26 runs (the longest is 1½ mi) with a vertical drop of 1,200 ft at this ski resort 10 mi north of Leadville. Groomed cross-country ski trails are also available. | U.S. 24 | 719/486–3684 | www.ski-cooper.com | Late Nov.–early Apr., daily.

Tabor Opera House. This beautifully restored opera house was built in 1879 by Colorado's "silver king," Horace Tabor. The Metropolitan Opera and the Chicago Symphony, as well as most of the actors and actresses of the era, played in this facility during its heyday. Guided tours cover all the important areas of the building. | 308 Harrison Ave. | 303/471–0984 | www.home1.gte.net/tabor | $4 | Memorial Day–Sept., daily 8–5:30.

ON THE CALENDAR
AUG.: *Boom Days Celebration.* A parade, street race, and mining demonstrations highlight this celebration of Leadville's Victorian heritage in downtown Leadville the first week in August. | 719/486–3900.
DEC.: Victorian Christmas and Home Tour, Leadville. The town's beautifully restored and rebuilt Victorian homes and businesses are all decorated for the holidays. | 719/486–3900 or 888/264–5344.

Dining
The Grill. Mexican. This local favorite has been run by the Martinez family since 1965. Traditional Mexican specialties are homemade, from the hand-roasted green chile to the stuffed sopaipillas. | 715 Elm St. | 719/486–9930 | No lunch weekdays | $4–$9 | MC, V.

High Country Restaurant. American. Mounted trout and deer hang from the walls of this casual eatery. Chicken-fried steaks and cod sandwiches are popular items. | 115 Harrison Ave. | 719/486–3992 | $6–$9 | MC, V.

© Artville

RECORD HIGHS

The words to the popular song "On a clear day, you can see forever" were never truer than in Colorado. Seeing forever is, indeed, the name of the game here, and the lofty average altitudes found across the state do their share in providing hundreds of vantage points from which to view the surrounding beauties of Colorado. Fifty-two mountain peaks exceed 14,000 ft, with the highest one, Mt. Elbert, located southwest of Leadville, clocking in at 14,443 ft. In fact, Leadville itself, situated 10,152 ft above sea level, is North America's highest incorporated city, and the Mt. Evans Highway, which reaches an altitude of 14,270 ft, is the world's highest paved road. Even the giant city of Denver is perched exactly 1 mi high (5,280 ft). Other high-altitude records claimed by Colorado are the world's highest automobile tunnel (the Eisenhower Tunnel on Interstate 70) at 11,158 ft; the nation's highest railroad tunnel (Alpine Tunnel near Gunnison) at 11,546 ft; and the country's highest railroad (the Pike's Peak Cog Railroad) at 14,110 ft.

Wild Bill's Restaurant. American. Facing Colorado's two highest peaks, Mt. Elbert and Mt. Massive, Wild Bill's provides a lovely backdrop for your dining experience. The charbroiled bacon and guacamole burger is a must-try. Kids' menu. | 200 Harrison Ave. | 719/486–0533 | $3–$8 | AE, D, DC, MC, V.

Lodging

Appleblossom. A late-19th-century Victorian home-turned-inn, where each room is individually decorated with antiques. Complimentary breakfast. No room phones, no TV. No smoking. | 120 W. 4th St. | 719/486–2141 or 800/982–9279 | fax 719/486–0994 | www.bbonline.com/co/appleblossom | 5 rooms | $99–$145 | AE, MC, V.

Delaware Hotel. This 1886 hotel on the National Register of Historic Places is downtown, within walking distance of the Tabor Opera House. Rooms are done up in restored Victorian splendor but with modern conveniences. It's known for its annual murder mystery parties. Complimentary breakfast. Cable TV. Hot tub. Business services. | 700 Harrison Ave. | 719/486–1418 or 800/748–2004 | fax 719/486–2214 | www.delawarehotel.com | 36 rooms (32 with shower only), 4 suites | $75–$100, $120–$140 suites | AE, D, DC, MC, V.

Ice Palace Inn. The Leadville Ice Palace, built from 5,000 tons of ice and 307,000 board ft of lumber in 1895–96, was the inspiration for this building, which dates from 1899 and includes some lumber from the original. All the rooms are named after rooms from the original Ice Palace and are decorated with Victorian antiques. Complimentary breakfast. Cable TV, in-room VCRs. No smoking. | 813 Sprice St. | 719/486–8272 or 800/754–2840 | www.icepalaceinn.com | 7 rooms | $79–$139 | AE, D, DC, MC, V.

Leadville Country Inn Bed and Breakfast. Built in 1892, this downtown inn offers a friendly common room and a lovely backyard gazebo (with an inviting hot tub). The style may be Victorian, but the rooms in both the main house and the carriage house have many modern conveniences. Complimentary breakfast. Cable TV in some rooms, some in-room VCRs, some room phones. No kids under 10. No smoking. | 127 E. 8th St. | 719/486–2354 or 800/748–2354 | fax 719/486–0300 | www.leadvillebednbreakfast.com | 9 rooms | $67–$160 | AE, D, MC, V.

Peri and Ed's Mountain Hideaway. This B&B is housed in a large Victorian, formerly a boardinghouse, and is surrounded by pine trees. The parlor and porch are perfect for meeting friends. Complimentary breakfast. No TV in rooms, TV in common area. No smoking. | 201 W. 8th St. | 719/486–0716 or 800/933–3715 | www.mountainhideaway.com | 10 rooms | $49–$159 | AE, D, MC, V.

Super 8. Traditional Super 8 quality and reliability, just south of downtown Leadville. No air-conditioning, cable TV. Sauna. Video games. | 1128 S. Hwy. 24 | 719/486–3637 or 800/800–8000 | www.super8.com | 55 rooms | $75–$95 | AE, D, DC, MC, V.

LIMON

MAP 6, H4

(Nearby towns also listed: Burlington, Colorado Springs)

The small agricultural town of Limon, situated on the Great Plains 66 mi northeast of Colorado Springs, started as a work camp for the Chicago & Rock Island Railroad, which was laying tracks from Kansas through Colorado in 1888. John Limon was a foreman for the railroad working in the area, and the town was eventually named after him.

In 1990, the town of 2,315 people was virtually destroyed by a ferocious tornado. Today, it has been lovingly restored to its pre-storm beauty and charm. The town has been called the "Hub City" of eastern Colorado, as it is an intersection for Interstate 70 U.S. 24, 40, and 287.

Information: **Limon Chamber of Commerce** | 1062 Main St., Limon, 80828 | 719/775–9418.

Attractions

Limon Heritage Museum and Railroad Park. The museum features a Union Pacific caboose, an 1890 boxcar, and a railroad lunch-counter diner. | 899 1st St. | 719/775–2373 | Free | June–Aug., Mon.–Sat. 1–8.

The Old Firehouse Art Center. This downtown gallery was once a firehouse but now displays rotating art exhibits from local, regional, national, and international artists. It offers workshops in photography and oil painting, and classes for kids. | 667 4th. Ave. | 303/651–2787 | www.oldfirehouseartcenter.org | Free | Wed.–Fri. 11–4, Sat. 10–2.

ON THE CALENDAR

JUNE: *Western Festival.* The festival features horse-drawn carriages, cowboys, a barbecue, and special museum exhibits the second weekend in June. | 719/541–2736.
AUG.: *Limon Heritage Celebration.* This festival in Railroad Park, next to the Limon Heritage Museum, showcases local arts and crafts, especially weaving, and has a display of antique engines, a quilt show, and a railroad dining car selling homemade pies the first Saturday in August. | 719/775–2373.

Dining

Fireside Junction. Mexican. A casual family restaurant known for Mexican food as well as such American fare as chicken-fried steak and barbecue brisket. Kids' menu. | 2295 9th St. | 719/775–2396 | Breakfast also available | $7–$14 | AE, D, MC, V.

Flying J. Husky. American/Casual. Stop into this family restaurant for a hamburger, steak, or any of the short order selections. | 198 E. Main St. | 719/775–2725 | $4–$6 | MC, V.

Rip Griffin's Country Fare. American. Help yourself at the buffet or try the chicken-fried steak. Located next door to the Comfort Inn. | I–70 and Hwy. 24 | 719/775–2811 | $6–$9 | AE, D, DC, MC, V.

Lodging

Best Western–Limon Inn. This reliable chain motel is just west of the town center, convenient to area highways. Complimentary Continental breakfast. In-room data ports, cable TV. Pool. Pets allowed (fee). | 925 T Ave. (I–70, exit 359) | 719/775–0277 | fax 719/775–2921 | www.bestwestern.com | 48 rooms | $50–$75 | AE, D, MC, V.

Limon Comfort Inn. Comfortable chain motel with a pool and a hot tub, 1 mi from downtown at the intersection of U.S. 24 and Interstate 70. Complimentary Continental breakfast. In-room data ports, some microwaves, some refrigerators, some in-room hot tubs, cable TV. Pool. Hot tub. Gym. | 2255 9th. St. | 719/775–2752 | fax 719/775–8891 | www.comfortinn.com | 50 rooms | $75–$113 | AE, D, DC, MC, V.

Econo Lodge of Limon. This budget-priced motel is 1 mi from downtown, close to the interstate, and within walking distance to fast-food restaurants. Complimentary Continental breakfast. Some microwaves, some refrigerators, cable TV. | 985 Hwy. 24, at I–70 | 719/775–2867 | fax 719/775–2485 | www.econolodge.com | 47 rooms | $55–$70 | AE, D, DC, MC, V.

Midwest Country Inn. In summer, blooming flowers surround this family-run inn in downtown Limon. The rooms are individually decorated with antiques, stained-glass mirrors, and comfortable quilts. Cable TV. | 795 Main St. | 719/775–2373 | 32 rooms, 1 suite | $42–$46, $60 suite | AE, D, DC, MC, V.

Preferred Motor Inn. In eastern Limon, this motel is next to restaurants and a market. Cable TV. Pool. Hot tub. Airport shuttle. Pets allowed. | 158 E. Main St. | 719/775–2385 | fax 719/775–2901 | 57 rooms, 2 suites | $28–$62, $65–$100 suites | AE, D, DC, MC, V.

Safari Motel. A small one- and two-story downtown motel. In-room data ports, cable TV. Pool. Playground. Laundry facilities. Pets allowed (fee). | 637 Main St. | 719/775–2363 | fax 719/775–2316 | 28 rooms, 2 suites | $36–$58, $68 suites | AE, D, DC, MC, V.

LONGMONT

(Nearby towns also listed: Boulder, Denver, Loveland)

Founded in 1871 by an expedition headed by Major Stephen H. Long. The town's name comes from Longs Peak, which is clearly visible from most anywhere in town (it was named after Major Long). Longmont today has a population approaching 64,000. Located along the Front Range, in the heavily populated Interstate 25 corridor between Denver and Fort Collins, the town sits pleasantly with mountains to the west and the Great Plains to the east. Two of the strongest engines of the town's economy have been computers (a large IBM plant is located nearby) and the U.S. government (which built an air traffic control center here in the 1960s).

Information: **Longmont Area Chamber of Commerce** | 528 Main St., Longmont, 80501 | 303/776–5295 | www.longmontchamber.org.

Attractions

Longmont Museum. Exhibits depict the history of Longmont and the St. Vrain valley, as well as space and science. | 375 Kimbark St. | 303/651–8374 | www.ci.longmont.co.us/museum.htm | Free | Weekdays 9–5, Sat. 10–4.

ON THE CALENDAR

JUNE: *Annual Police Fair.* Enjoy canine demonstrations, helicopter lights, games, and pie-eating contests in Centennial Park the third Saturday in June. | 1100 Lashley | 303/651–8511.
JULY: *Rhythm on the River.* This well-attended event at Roger's Grove hosts various concerts with all types of music, good food, and arts-and-crafts exhibits. | 303/776–6050.
AUG.: *Boulder County Fair and Rodeo.* An annual, nine-day event at the local fairgrounds that features a parade, rodeo, and county fair. | 303/441–3927.

Dining

Wet Stone Steak House. Steak. A waterfall rolling over a wet stone stands at the entrance to this western-style steak house. You can choose from a wide range of steaks, as well as burgers and some specialty fare like cajun salmon, chipotle pasta, and shredded chicken enchiladas with tomatoes and goat cheese. | 1940 Ken Pratt Blvd. | 303/776–3543 | $8–$25 | AE, D, DC, MC, V.

Lodging

Ellen's Bed and Breakfast. This 1904 Victorian home on the historic east side of town, one block from Main St., has two comfortable guest rooms. Complimentary breakfast. No TV in rooms, TV in common area. Outdoor hot tub. | 700 Kimbark St. | 303/776–1676 | fax 303/684–0139 | 2 rooms | $75 | No credit cards.

Raintree Plaza Hotel Suites and Conference Center. This full-service two-story hotel also houses the largest conference center in northern Colorado. All rooms feature small sitting areas with a couch and/or chairs. Restaurant, bar, complimentary Continental breakfast, room service. Some kitchenettes, refrigerators, cable TV. Pool. Gym. Laundry service. Business services, airport shuttle. Pets allowed. | 1900 Ken Pratt Blvd. | 303/776–2000 or 800/843–8240 | fax 303/678–7361 | www.raintree.com | 211 rooms, 84 suites | $89–$265, $109–$265 suites | AE, D, DC, MC, V.

LOVELAND

MAP 6, G2

(Nearby towns also listed: Estes Park, Fort Collins, Greeley, Longmont, Lyons)

Although named in honor of the Colorado Central Railroad's president, W.A.H. Loveland, the town today is more associated with being a "love" land. To clinch the claim of being called the "Sweetheart City," the Loveland Post Office re-mails more than 300,000 Valentines annually so that the forwarded mail carries the town's unique "lovers'" postmark.

Today, Loveland's strategic location along the Interstate 25 corridor north of Denver places it in an enviable position as an agricultural and shipping center, and it supports a population of 47,150.

Information: Loveland Chamber of Commerce | 5400 Stone Creek Cr., Suite 100, Loveland, 80538 | 970/667–5728 or 800/258–1278 | www.loveland.org.

Attractions

Boyd Lake State Park. The park and its associated 1,800-acre lake offer swimming, water-skiing, boating, fishing, camping, and picnicking 1 mi east of Loveland off U.S. 34. | 3720 N. County Rd. | 970/669–1739 | www.parks.state.co.us/boyd | $4 per vehicle | Daily.

Loveland Museum & Gallery. A local history museum and a contemporary visual art gallery, with a permanent collection and rotating exhibits from regional, national and international artists. | 503 N. Lincoln | 970/962–2410 | www.ci.loveland.co.us | Free | Tues., Wed., Fri. 10–5; Thurs. 10–9; Sat. 10–4; Sun. noon–4.

ON THE CALENDAR
MAR.–JUNE: *Dog racing.* You can watch nightly dog racing, with pari-mutuel betting at the Cloverleaf Kennel Club, 4 mi east of Loveland at the junction of U.S. 34 and Interstate 25. | 970/667–6211.

AUG.: *Sculpture in the Park.* The largest juried sculpture show in the country occurs in Benson Sculpture Garden in Loveland the second week in August. 175 artists from around the globe present approximately 1,400 sculptures that are also available for purchase. | 970/663–2940.

AUG.: *Larimer County Fair and Rodeo.* An annual event, with a rodeo and the county fair, at the Larimer County Fairgrounds. | 970/667–5728 or 800/258–1278.

Dining
Cactus Grill North. American. This is more of a sports bar, with 18 TVs and 21 beers on tap, than a restaurant. Try the fajitas and taco buffet. Open-air dining on front patio. Kids' menu. | 281-A E. 29th St. | 970/663–1550 | $6–$9 | AE, D, MC, V.

Country Junction Restaurant. American. Antiques in the dining room provide a comfortable setting for the home cooking. Try the meat loaf or the prime rib. | 119 E. 4th St. | 970/613–0068 | $8–$13 | MC, V.

Perkin's Restaurant and Bakery. American. Start off with the appetizer sampler that includes onion rings, chicken fingers, and cheese sticks, then have the steak and shrimp platter. Treat yourself to the fresh strawberry pie. | 222 E. Eisenhower Blvd. | 970/663–1944 | $6–$11 | AE, D, DC, MC, V.

The Savoy. French. This romantic and warm wood-paneled restaurant is in the Berthoud, 6 mi south of Loveland. Try *fruits de mer* Savoy, or the *carre d'agneau*. No smoking. | 535 1st St., Berthoud | 970/532–4095 | Closed Mon. | $20–$30 | AE, MC, V.

Summit. Continental. The interior of this restaurant looks like an old country inn, with wood and brick accents and plenty of windows, complete with breathtaking mountain views.

Known for steak and seafood. Open-air dining on covered patio. Kids' menu. Sunday brunch. | 3208 W. Eisenhower Blvd. | 970/669–6648 | No lunch | $6–$21 | AE, D, DC, MC, V.

Lodging

Cattail Creek Inn. Bronze sculptures and private art adorn the rooms and public areas of this inn, on the seventh tee of Cattail Creek Golf Course. Each room was designed with an eye on the needs of business travelers, so you'll find two phone lines. It is within walking distance of the renowned Benson Sculpture Park and offers golf and arts packages. Complimentary breakfast. In-room data ports, cable TV. No kids under 14. No smoking. | 2665 Abarr Dr. | 970/667–7600 or 800/572–2466 | fax 970/667–8968 | www.cattailcreekinn.com | 8 rooms | $105–$170 | AE, D, MC, V.

Derby Hill Inn B&B. The rooms at this small B&B 1 mi from downtown Loveland are elegantly decorated and comfortable. You have breakfast on a covered redwood patio that overlooks the garden. Golf packages for local courses are available. Complimentary breakfast, in-room data ports. No smoking. | 2502 Courtney Dr. | 970/667–3193 or 800/498–8086 | fax 970/667–3193 | www.guestinns.com | 2 rooms | $70–$90 | AE, MC, V.

Lovelander. This Victorian inn, within walking distance of galleries, museums, and theaters in downtown Loveland, is furnished with splendid antiques. Picnic area, complimentary breakfast. Cable TV, no TV in some rooms. Business services, airport shuttle. No kids under 10. No smoking. | 217 W. 4th St. | 970/669–0798 or 800/459–6694 | fax 970/669–0797 | www.lovelander.com | 11 rooms | $90–$155 | AE, D, MC, V.

Sylvan Dale Guest Ranch. The simply but neatly furnished cabins at this working ranch, which adjoins the Roosevelt National Forest 7 mi west of Loveland on U.S. 34, have a comfortable country feel with the occasional genuine antique thrown in. There is a lively program of square dancing, cookouts, breakfast rides, and overnight pack trips, plus a Native American Living History Week in August. Dining room. No air-conditioning, no room phones, no TV. Pool, lake. Tennis. Horseback riding. Children's programs (ages 5–12). | 2939 N. County Rd. 31D (U.S. 34) | 970/667–3915 or 877/667–3999 | fax 970/635–9336 | www.sylvandale.com | 13 rooms, two 3- to 4-bedroom guest houses | $979 per person per wk (1–week minimum stay) | AP | No credit cards.

Wild Lane Bed and Breakfast Inn. This small B&B is in a Victorian mansion that dates from 1905. Enjoy sitting on the patio, which is surrounded by a garden, or take a stroll on the 3½-mi nature trail. Complimentary breakfast. In-room data ports, some in-room hot tubs, TV in common area. No smoking. | 5445 Wild La. | 970/669–0303 or 800/204–3320 | fax 970/663–9100 | www.wildlane.com | 5 rooms | $89–$119 | AE, D, MC, V.

LYONS

MAP 6, F3

(Nearby towns also listed: Allenspark, Boulder, Estes Park, Longmont, Loveland)

Located just a stone's throw from the beautiful Roosevelt National Forest, tiny Lyons (population 1,516) shares the beauty of the Rockies' Front Range with its larger neighbors, Longmont and Loveland. Bikers, hikers, climbers, and fishermen love the area for its many trails and streams, and there's no dearth of shopping and dining nearby.

Information: Lyons Chamber of Commerce | Box 426, Lyons 80540 | 303/823–5215 or 303/440–9062 | www.ben.boulder.co.us/lyons/.

Attractions

Lyons Historic District. Fifteen lovely sandstone buildings, all listed on the National Historic Register, comprise this historic downtown section of Lyons. | 340 High St. | 303/823–5215 or 303/440–9062 | Free | Daily.

ON THE CALENDAR

JUNE: *Good Old Days Celebration.* Arts and crafts, a flea market, carnival rides, and food highlight this annual affair the last weekend in June. | 303/823–5215.

AUG: *Rocky Mountain Folk Festival.* This three-day music festival along the St. Vrain River is a gathering of both established and emerging folk artists. | 303/823–0848 or 800/624–2422.

Dining

Andrea's. German. You'll enjoy German favorites at this quaint Bavarian-style restaurant. Try the pepper steak or sauerbraten. Bavarian folk music Friday and Saturday. | 216 E. Main St. | 303/823–5000 | Breakfast also available; closed Wed. | $7–$19 | AE, D, MC, V.

Black Bear Inn. Continental. The setting recalls something from Switzerland in this restaurant just outside town known for its veal, châteaubriand, and fresh seafood; the apple strudel is homemade. Open-air dining on a terrace with shaded tables. | 42 E. Main St. | 303/823–6812 | Reservations essential | Closed Jan.–mid-Feb. and Mon., Tues. | $23–$32 | AE, D, DC, MC, V.

La Chaumière. Continental. This restaurant with a warming fireplace and beautiful mountain views is in Pinewood Springs, 9 mi north of Lyons. Known for lavender-rubbed rack of lamb, duck breast with blood orange sauce, and homemade ice creams. | 12311 N. Saint Vrain Dr., Pinewood Springs | 303/823–6521 | Closed Mon. No lunch | $13–$24 | AE, MC, V.

Oskar Blues Grill and Brew. Cajun. This is a great spot for beer, food, and entertainment. The brewery offers six house brews on tap, the kitchen serves dishes such as shrimp étouffée, blackened redfish on red beans and rice, and an assortment of pizzas. Entertainment Wednesday, Thursday, and weekends. | 303 Main St. | 303/823–6685 | www.oskarblues.com | $9–$15 | D, MC, V.

Lodging

Stone Mountain Lodge and Cabins. Go hiking, feed the ducks in the pond, or grab a pole for some fishing at this mountain resort set on 45 acres of land, 2 mi from downtown Lyons. If you're roughing it, the campground has room for 10 small RVs and five small tents. Picnic area, complimentary Continental breakfast. No air-conditioning, some kitchenettes, some microwaves, refrigerators, some in-room hot tubs, cable TV. Pool, pond. Hiking, fishing. No smoking. | 18055 N. St. Vrain Dr. | 303/823–6091 or 800/282–5612 | fax 303/823–5108 | www.stonemountainlodge.com | 15 rooms, 6 cabins | $75–$150 rooms and cabins | MC, V.

MANITOU SPRINGS

MAP 6, G5

(Nearby towns also listed: Colorado Springs, Cripple Creek)

Located just outside Colorado Springs, Manitou Springs actually contains the many mineral springs from which Colorado Springs took its name. Before the Americans arrived, the entire area around Manitou Springs was considered sacred ground to the local Ute Indians; in fact, the word "manitou" means Great Spirit in the Ute languages. Today's town of 5,420 residents is listed as a National Historic District.

Information: **Manitou Springs Chamber of Commerce** | 354 Manitou Ave., Manitou Springs, 80829 | 719/685–5089 or 800/642–2567 | www.manitousprings.org.

Attractions

Cave of the Winds. This cave was discovered by two boys in 1880 and has been a popular regional tourist attraction ever since. A 45-minute underground guided tour re-creates millions of years of local geology; though blatantly commercial, the cave itself is truly impressive. Wear comfortable shoes and bring a light jacket. | U.S. 24 | 719/685–5444 | www.cave-ofthewinds.com | $12 | May–Labor Day, daily 9–9; Labor Day–Apr., daily 10–5.

Florissant Fossil Beds National Monument. In this 6,000-acre, federally owned and maintained property, you can see the remains of a 35-million-year-old lake that was gradually filled in with volcanic ash, which in turn fossilized all of the life in the lake. Nearby are the remains of a once-mighty redwood forest that was likewise covered by the ash and mud flows and similarly transformed. The grounds include picnic areas, nature trails, and a restored 19th-century farmstead; located 22 mi west of Manitou Springs on U.S. 24. | County Rd. 1, Florissant | 719/748–3253 | www.nps.gov/flfo | $2 Apr.–Nov.; free Dec.–Mar. | June–Sept., daily 8–7; Oct.–May, daily 8–4:30.

Garden of the Gods. Acres of fantastic, 300-million-year-old red sandstone formations are 3 mi northwest of Colorado Springs. | 1805 N. 30th St. | 719/634–6666 or 719/385–5940 | www.gardenofgods.com | Free | Sept.–May, daily 9–5; June–Aug., daily 8–8.

Garden of the Gods Trading Post. This 100-year-old trading post at the south end of the park near Balanced Rock sells southwestern art, jewelry, pottery, and kachinas and has a café with casual fare. | 324 Beckers La., Manitou Springs | 719/685–9045 or 800/874–4515 | Free | Daily.

Iron Springs Chateau. This dinner theater stages comedy melodrama and offers a family-style dinner. | 444 Ruxton Ave. | 719/685–5104 | www.pikes-peak.com/theatre | $21.50 dinner and show, $11.50 show only | Memorial Day–Labor Day, Tues.–Sat.; Labor Day–Memorial Day, Fri.–Sat.; dinner at 6, show at 8:30.

Manitou Cliff Dwellings Museums. You can see 40 rooms of prehistoric cliff dwellings dating to AD 1100. Exhibits of artifacts are also exhibited, and in summer (June–August) traditional Native American dance performances are held several times a day. | On U.S. 24 | 719/685–5242 | www.cliffdwellingsmuseum.com | $7 | June–Aug., daily 9–8; May and Sept., daily 9–6; Jan.–Apr. and Oct.–Dec. daily 9–5.

Miramont Castle Museum. Built in 1895, this 46-room mansion, once owned by French priest Jean-Baptiste Francolon, features nine separate styles of architecture. On display you'll find everything from a railroad collection to dolls, plus a tearoom and a soda fountain. | 9 Capitol Hill Ave. | 719/685–1011 | www.pikes-peak.com/castle | $4 | June–Aug., Tues.–Sun. 10–5; Sept.–May, Tues.–Sun. 11–4; closed Mon.

Pikes Peak. The best-known landmark in entire state is 14,110-ft Pikes Peak, which was named after Zebulon Pike; though the mountain is named after him, Pike never climbed it. Views from the top are expansive and inspired Katharine Lee Bates to write "America the Beautiful." Go 10 mi west of Colorado Springs on U.S. 24 to Cascade, then 19 mi on a toll road to the summit. | Hwy. 24, exit 141, Cascade | 719/385–7325 or 800/318–9505 | www.pike-speakcolorado.com | $10 per person; $35 per car | May–Sept., daily 7–7; Oct.–Apr. 9–3 (weather permitting).

Pikes Peak Cog Railway. Dating from the 1880s, this is the highest railroad in the United States. It makes the round-trip up to the summit in about three hours, including some time at the top. The railroad makes up to eight round-trips daily during peak season from its depot in Manitou Springs, 5 mi west of Colorado Springs. | 515 Ruxton Ave., Manitou Springs | 719/685–5401 | www.cograilway.com | $25 round-trip | Daily 8–5; call for exact train schedules).

ON THE CALENDAR

JULY: *Pikes Peak Auto Hill Climb.* The endurance of automobile and driver are tested as they strive to ascend Pike's Peak each July 4th. | 719/685–4400.

AUG.: *Pikes Peak Marathon.* A hearty footrace from the cog-railroad station to the top of Pike's Peak and back again. | 719/473–2625.

Dining

Briarhurst Manor. Continental. This former Victorian inn is now a restaurant, where you can dine well on such classic dishes as rack of lamb and Châteaubriand. Open-air dining with a view of mountains. Kids' menu. | 404 Manitou Ave. | www.briarhurst.com | 719/685–1864 or 877/685–1448 | No lunch | $11–$39 | AE, DC, MC, V.

Craftwood Inn. Contemporary. A romantic, historic Arts and Crafts Tudor building dating from 1912. Known for game dishes, including elk, wild boar, and pheasant. Open-air dining with a view of Pikes Peak. No smoking. | 404 El Paso Blvd. | 719/685–9000 | No lunch | $12–$32 | AE, D, DC, MC, V.

Adam's Mountain Café. Contemporary. This popular restaurant is known for culinary creations such as shiitaki-crusted tuna with wasabi and potato cakes topped by a miso apricot glaze, or lemon rustic chicken, a lemon- and rosemary-infused leg and thigh that is slow-roasted and garnished with spinach and sun-dried tomatoes. | 1100 Cañon Ave. | 719/685–1430 | $9–$15 | MC, V.

Historic Stagecoach Inn. Steak. Dine by the banks of Fountain Creek in a rustic setting. Try the popular sirloin steak, prime rib, or slow-roasted buffalo. | 702 Manitou Ave. | 719/685–9400 | $12–$18 | AE, D, MC, V.

Mission Bell Inn. Mexican. Quaint and casual place for traditional Mexican fare. Open-air dining tucked in a valley with trees. | 178 Crystal Park Rd. | 719/685–9089 | Closed Oct.–May and Mon. No lunch | $9–$11 | MC, V.

Lodging

Black Bear Inn. With a panoramic view of the Rockies, this eclectically decorated mountain inn, sits on 10 acres bordering the Pike National Forest. It is a mere 300 yards from the tollgate to Pikes Peak in Cascade, 5 mi north of Manitou Springs, and the only lodging located on the highway itself. Guests can enjoy complimentary bottles of the inn's microbrew, Black Bear Lager. Complimentary breakfast. Cable TV. Hot tub. Cross-country skiing. No kids under 10. No smoking. | 5250 Pikes Peak Hwy., Cascade | 719/684–0151 or 877/732–5232 | fax 719/684–8161 | www.blackbearinnpikespeak.com | 9 rooms (shower only), 3 cottages | $85, $120 cottages | D, MC, V.

Blue Skies Inn. A B&B in a cluster of buildings on the former estate of Manitou Springs' founder, Dr. William Bell, centered around the estate's original carriage house. This is an all-suite property, and each room has a private sitting area, some with fireplaces, and private entrances. Though in the heart of Manitou Springs, the estate feels like a tranquil oasis. Complimentary breakfast, room service. In-room data ports, some microwaves, some refrigerators, some in-room hot tubs, cable TV, in-room VCRs. Hiking, fishing. No smoking. | 402 Manitou Ave. | 719/685–3899 or 800/398–7942 | fax 719/685–3099 | www.blueskiesbb.com | 10 rooms | $125–$225 | AE, D, MC, V.

Cascade Hills. This inn on the border of the Pike National Forest in Cascade, 5 mi north of Manitou Springs, is just a few miles from many attractions at the foot of Pikes Peak. Rooms are basic; the hot tub is nestled in a mountain grove. Picnic area, complimentary Continental breakfast. No air-conditioning, some kitchenettes, some refrigerators, cable TV. Hot tub. | 7885 U.S. 24 W, Cascade | 719/684–9977 | fax 719/684–0966 | 14 rooms, 2 cottages | $65–$125, $129–$179 cottages | D, MC, V.

Cliff House Inn. This historic, Queen Anne Victorian structure was begun in 1873 and later expanded to its current 200 rooms. It sits at the base of Pike's Peak, one block from downtown Manitou Springs. The large, elegantly furnished rooms have been modernized with fast Internet connections and even heated toilet seats; suites have special steam showers and two-person hot tubs. Restaurant, bar, complimentary Continental breakfast. In-room data ports, in-room safes, refrigerators, some in-room hot tubs, cable TV, in-room VCRs. Massage. Gym. Laundry service. Business services, airport shuttle. No smoking. | 306 Cañon

Blvd. | 719/685–3000 or 888/212–7000 | fax 719/685–3913 | www.thecliffhouse.com | 57 rooms | $189–$399 | AE, D, MC, V.

Eastholme in the Rockies. An 1885 Victorian building on the National Register of Historic Places, this inn and two cottages are furnished with period antiques, some original to the building. In Cascade, 5 mi west of Manitou Springs. Complimentary breakfast. No air-conditioning, no room phones, no TV. Outdoor hot tub. No smoking. | 4445 Haggerman Ave., Cascade | 719/684–9901 or 800/672–9901 | www.eastholme.com | 6 rooms (3 with shower only, 1 with shared bath), 2 cottages | $79–$109, $150 cottages | AE, D, MC, V.

Red Crags. This B&B is a four-story, 1875 Victorian loaded with heirloom furnishings. Rooms are large and elegant and have private baths, but these are sometimes down the hall. Complimentary breakfast and evening wine. No TV in some rooms. No kids under 10. No smoking. | 302 El Paso Blvd. | 719/685–1920 or 800/721–2248 | fax 719/685–1073 | www.redcrags.com | 8 rooms | $80–$180 | AE, D, MC, V.

Red Wing. This small motel is one block from the entrance to the Garden of the Gods. Some kitchenettes, microwaves, refrigerators, cable TV. Pool. Playground. Some pets allowed. | 56 El Paso Blvd. | 719/685–5656 or 800/733–9547 | fax 719/685–9547 ext. 42 | 27 rooms | $49–$120 | AE, D, DC, MC, V.

Silver Saddle. This modern, two-story, upscale motel is right in the thick of historic Manitou Springs. Some in-room hot tubs, cable TV, some in-room VCRs. Pool. Outdoor hot tub. | 215 Manitou Ave. | 719/685–5611 | www.silver-saddle.com | 54 rooms, 10 suites | $69–$84, $100–$130 suites | AE, D, DC, MC, V.

Villa Motel. This very popular, family-run motel is in downtown Manitou Springs, offering easy access to both the Rocky Mountains and Colorado Springs. Reservations are essential far in advance. Picnic area. Some kitchenettes, cable TV. Pool. Hot tub. Laundry facilities. Business services. | 481 Manitou Ave. | 719/685–5492 or 800/341–8000 | fax 719/685–4143 | www.villamotel.com | 47 rooms | $83–$103 | AE, D, DC, MC, V.

MEEKER

MAP 6, C3

(Nearby towns also listed: Craig, Rifle, Dinosaur)

Once an outpost for the U.S. Army, Meeker (population 2,466), in the northwest corner of Colorado, is the site of the Meeker Massacre of the Ute Indian Tribe by the U.S. Army on September 29, 1879. The gateway to the White River National Forest and the Flat Tops Wilderness, Meeker now is a favorite spot for hunting, fishing, snowmobiling, caving, and other outdoor activities.

Information: **Meeker Chamber of Commerce** | Box 869, Meeker, 81641 | 970/878–5510 | www.meekerchamber.com.

Attractions

White River Museum. Read articles about the "real" facts behind the Meeker Massacre, and about the Meeker Bank robbery of 1896 in downtown Meeker. | 565 Park St. | 970/878–9982 | fax 435/789–2270 | Free | May–Oct., weekdays 9–5, weekends 10–5; Nov.–Apr., weekdays 11–3.

ON THE CALENDAR
SEPT.: *Meeker Sheepdog Trials.* Watch professional sheepdogs in action as they compete in the nation's most prestigious sheepdog trials that annually draws international competition the weekend after Labor Day. | 970/878–5510 or 970/878–5483.

Dining

Meeker Café. American. A collection of vintage photographs and lively stories of Meeker's past are included in the menu of this Old West restaurant in a historic building. Known for its homemade soup and salad bar, chicken-fried steak, and real mashed potatoes with creamy gravy. Open on Sunday only during hunting season. Kids' menu. Full bar. | A560 Main St. | 970/878–5255 | www.meekerhotel.com | Dec.–Sept., closed Sun. | $4–$23 | MC, V.

Market Street Bar and Grill. American/Casual. Country furnishings on hardwood floors, complete with antiques and paintings of the local area decorate this country-style restaurant and bar. Well known for its steaks, baked trout, homemade fruit pies, and bread baked daily. Kids' menu. Full bar. | 173 First St. | 970/878–3193 | $6–$25 | AE, D, MC, V.

Sleepy Cat. Steak. Enjoy the country log-cabin surroundings with large stone fireplace and mounted wildlife. Known best for its steaks, prime rib, baby-back ribs, and seafood. Bring your fishing pole and catch your trout or white fish, as the Sleepy Cat will cook what you catch right outside the restaurant's doors. Kids' menu. | 16064 County Rd. 8 | 970/878–4413 | www.colorado-west.com/sleepycat | Breakfast also available; mid-Nov.–May, closed Mon.–Thurs. and no dinner on weekends | $4–$13 | D, MC, V.

Lodging

Rambullinn Bed and Breakfast. Cozy, rambling home with treasures and sheep memorabilia from around the world. Comfortable rooms. Bunkhouse apartment sleeps one to 10. Complimentary breakfast. Microwaves, refrigerators, some room phones, cable TV, TV in common area. Laundry facilities. | 789 Eighth St. | 970/878–5483 | fax 970/878–5482 | gus@meekerco.com | 4 rooms, 1 apartment | $45–$55 | MC, V.

White River Inn. Remodeled motel rooms on the eastern edge of Meeker. One, two, and three queen-size beds are available. Cable TV. | 219 E. Market St., Box 299 | 970/878–5031 or 888/878–486 | fax 970/878–0366 | whiteriverinn@flattops.net | 20 rooms | $40–$80 | MC, V.

MESA VERDE NATIONAL PARK

MAP 6, B8

(Nearby towns also listed: Cortez, Dolores, Durango)

In Colorado's southwestern corner, the perfectly preserved Mesa Verde ruins were discovered by two ranchers in 1888, though before that some southwestern Colorado cliff dwellings had been discovered as early as the 1870s. Mesa Verde today stands as one of the premier prehistoric cliff-dwelling complexes in the entire Southwest (other well-known sites are in Canyon de Chelly in Arizona and Chaco Canyon in New Mexico) and one of the world's most recognizable archaeological sites. These particular dwellings were probably occupied for about 700 years, from approximately AD 500 to 1300, by a people the Navajos called Anasazi. The ruins have provided a wealth of knowledge about some of the "Four Corners" region's earliest inhabitants. Named a national park in 1906, due to the tireless efforts of Virginia McClurg and Lucy Peabody, Mesa Verde was the first national park created primarily to preserve man-made structures. But Mesa Verde is more than just an archaeological site. The lush area, blanketing the flat-topped mountain is covered in a piñon pine–juniper forest, and you'll have sweeping vistas of the Mancos and Montezuma valleys as you drive up the park's twisting roads. In 1978 Mesa Verde was one of the first places to be named a UNESCO World Heritage Site. There is one campground in the national park, which costs $16 (tent site) or $23 (RV site) per night.

Information: **Superintendent** | Box 8, Mesa Verde National Park 81330 | 970/529–4465 or 970/529–4461 | www.nps.gov/meve.

Attractions

Chapin Mesa Archaeological Museum. The museum tells the entire story of the cliff-dwelling people and gives a complete understanding of this interesting culture at Mesa Verde. It's located 21 mi south of the park entrance. | Chapin Mesa | 970/529-4465 or 970/529-4461 | www.mesaverde.org | Free | Daily 8-6:30.

Cliff Dwellings. Mesa Verde is one of the world's most renowned architectural wonders. Because of the fragility of both the ruins and the landscape, you are not permitted to wander beyond the sanctioned park trails. You can visit some of the ruins themselves only when a ranger is present, and several of the tours have limited capacity. Similarly, some ruins are not open all year. Therefore, you should plan your trip around a flexible schedule and call ahead to determine which tours are available during the time you will be present and

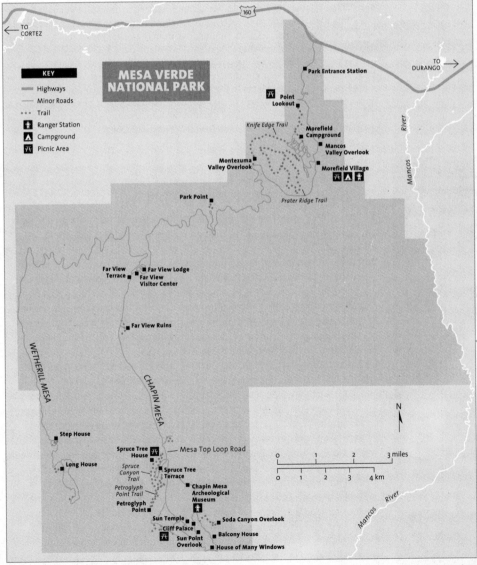

whether reservations are necessary. Several dwellings can be visited on self-guided tours, however. There are over 4,000 archaeological sites in the confines of Mesa Verde National Park, of which 35 are open to the public. The sites described below are some of the major cliff dwellings. The park entrance is 8 mi east of Cortez, 36 mi west of Durango, on U.S. 160; from there it is an additional 15 mi south to the visitor center. Tickets for tours to Balcony House, Cliff Palace, and Long House may be purchased up to one day in advance, but only in person. | Off U.S. 160 Mesa Verde National Park | 970/529–4465 or 970/529–4461 | www.nps.gov/meve | $10 per vehicle (for 7 days); $1.75 for a tour of Balcony House, Cliff Palace, or Long House | Visitor center mid-Apr.–mid-Oct, daily 8–5.

Balcony House. This medium-size cliff dwelling, which originally housed 40 or 50 people, is accessible only by a 32-ft-long ladder. It is about a 25-minute drive from the Far View Visitor Center, and can only be visited on a guided tour; reservations required. | Cliff Palace Loop Rd., Chapin Mesa | 970/529–4465 or 970/529–4461 | www.nps.gov/meve | $1.75 | Mid-May–mid-Oct., daily 9–5:30.

Cliff Palace. This was the first major Mesa Verde dwelling to be discovered in 1888; it contains about 150 rooms on three levels, with 14 rooms on the uppermost level believed to have been storage units. It's a 20-minute drive from the visitor center. It can only be visited on a guided tour; reservations required. | Cliff Palace Loop Rd., Chapin Mesa | 970/529–4465 or 970/529–4461 | www.nps.gov/meve | $1.75 | Mid-Apr.–early Nov., daily 9–6.

Long House. This is the second-largest cliff dwelling in Mesa Verde National Park, containing one of two large central plazas in the area. It was excavated in 1959–1961 to help divert crowds from Chapin Mesa. Perhaps 150 or 160 people lived here. It can only be visited on a guided tour; reservations required. | Wetherill Mesa | 970/529–4465 or 970/529–4461 | www.nps.gov/meve | $1.75 | Memorial Day–Labor Day, daily 10–5.

© Corbis

ANASAZI HISTORY AND MESA VERDE

A rudimentary culture first got underway on Mesa Verde about the time the Western World went from BC to AD. This first group is now called the "Basketmakers," and for about 450 years they eked out a meager existence, foraging for desert plants, hunting with spears, and making baskets. Eventually this culture evolved into what is now called the "Modified Basketmaker Period" (AD 450 to 750), identified by the use of the bow and arrow, the making of pottery, cultivation of crops such as beans and corn, and the creation of underground pit houses. Then came the houses and communal buildings erected from stone and adobe built from 750 to 1100; these are the dwellings you explore at Mesa Verde National Park. This classic Pueblo period lasted at Mesa Verde until the late 13th century.

In short, the Ancestral Pueblans who moved into the cliffs at Mesa Verde didn't just pop from behind some sagebrush with all their spiritual and cultural refinement intact. Rather, they were taking advantage of centuries of history and experience. And they used every shard of it in such monuments to their culture and skill, such as the Cliff Palace. It's uncertain what made the Anasazi abandon the dwellings at Mesa Verde, though scarcity of water may have been an important factor; there was a massive and long-lasting drought in the late 13th century, when many believe Mesa Verde was abandoned. Some archaeologists theorize that the increasing number of kivas at Mesa Verde suggests a turn toward religion in the face of adversity.

When the Ute Indians first migrated into this area they looked at the ruined pueblos, decided they were haunted, and afterwards avoided them. Indian tribes farther south in New Mexico also had seen evidence of the vanished culture as they'd migrated through southern Colorado into New Mexico. They were the ones who first referred to these ancient people as "Anasazi," or "enemy ancestors."

Spruce Tree House. This dwelling, in the canyon behind the Chapin Mesa Museum, is the best-preserved site in Mesa Verde National Park, containing 114 living rooms and eight kivas. This is the only dwelling where you can actually enter a kiva, via a short ladder, just as the original Anasazi inhabitants did. The dwelling is located ¼ mi off Mesa Top Loop Road. Self-guided tour. | Spruce Tree House Entrance Trail, Chapin Mesa | 970/529–4465 or 970/529–4461 | www.nps.gov/meve | Free | Daily 8:30–6:30 (weather permitting).

Step House. So-named because of a crumbling prehistoric stairway leading up from the dwelling, Step House is reached via a paved, though steep, trail, so it's a bit more accessible than some of the other dwellings. It can also be visited on a self-guided tour. | Wetherill Mesa | 970/529–4465 or 970/529–4461 | www.nps.gov/meve | Free | Memorial Day–Labor Day, daily 10–5.

Far View Visitor Center. Visitors should stop here for directions and orientation for the Cliff Dwelling Tours. Tickets for the Cliff Palace, Balcony, and Long House tours can only be purchased here, 15 mi south of the park entrance. | Chapin Mesa Rd. | 970/529–4465 or 970/529–4461 | www.nps.gov/meve | Free | Mid-Apr.–mid-Oct., daily 8–5.

Mesa Top Loop. A 6-mi self-guided scenic drive that allows visits and views of 10 to 30 cliff-dwelling sites. Enter at crossroads near the Chapin Mesa Archaeological Museum. | Chapin Mesa | 970/529–4465 or 970/529–4461 | www.nps.gov/meve | Free | May–Sept., daily 8–sunset.

Park Point Fire Lookout. The lookout, reached by a short trail, offers spectacular views of parts of Utah, Arizona, Colorado, and New Mexico. It's located about halfway between the park entrance and the Far View Visitor Center. | Chapin Mesa Rd. | 970/529–4465 or 970/529–4461 | www.nps.gov/meve | Free | Mid-May–late Oct., daily.

Soda Canyon Overlook. One of the easiest and most rewarding strolls in the park, the trail to this overlook stretches 1½ mi round-trip through the forest on almost completely level ground. It's an excellent place from which to photograph the cliff dwellings. The trailhead is about ¼ mi past the Balcony House parking area. | Chapin Mesa | 970/529–4465 | www.nps.gov/meve | Daily 8–sunset.

SIGHTSEEING TOURS/TOUR COMPANIES

Aramark Mesa Verde. This national park concession company offers several half- or full-day motor-coach tours of Mesa Verde, which generally leave from either the Far View Lodge or the Moorefield Campground. A variety of tours include visits to major cliff dwellings and promise many good photographic possibilities as well as background lectures. Tours are offered that cover all three dwellings that normally require tickets, and reservations for these tours may be made far in advance. | Box 277, Mancos | 970/533–7731 or 800/449–2288 | fax 970/533–7831 | www.visitmesaverde.com | $31–$51 | Daily (but not all areas of the park open year-round); call for tour schedules.

ON THE CALENDAR

AUG: *Hopi Dances.* Fascinating cultural dances, performed in traditional Hopi costumes at the Old Amphitheatre, 21 mi south of the Mesa Verde National Park headquarters. Performances are subject to the dance troupe's availability but usually take place in early August. | 970/529–4475.

Dining

Far View Terrace. American/Casual. Full-service cafeteria. Blueberry pancakes are often on the breakfast menu. Dinner options might include a heaping Navajo taco made with shredded chicken, pizza, or fried chicken. Desserts include ice cream, pies, and fudge. | Chapin Mesa Rd. | 970/529–4444 | Closed late Oct.–early Apr. | $4–$8 | AE, D, MC, V.

Millwood Junction. Continental. The entire restaurant, 7 mi east of Mesa Verde in Mancos, is made out of barn wood, so this is definitely a casual, rustic place. Features an outstanding Friday-night seafood buffet. Open-air dining on garden patio surrounded by 30-ft

MESA VERDE
NATIONAL PARK

INTRO
ATTRACTIONS
DINING
LODGING

aspens. Salad bar. | Main St. and Hwy. 160, Mancos | 970/533–7338 | No lunch weekends | $7–$22 | AE, DC, MC, V.

Lodging

Far View Lodge. This lodge in Mesa Verde National Park, 15 mi south of the park entrance, boasts a spectacular view of Shiprock Canyon and offers educational programs, campsites, trailer facilities, and Mesa Verde tours. The lodge is operated by Aramark, the official park concessionaire. Restaurant, bar, dining room, picnic area. No air-conditioning, no room phones, no TV. Hiking. Laundry facilities. Some pets allowed. | Chapin Mesa Rd. | 970/529–4421 or 800/449–2288 | fax 970/533–7831 | www.visitmesaverde.com | 150 rooms | $96–$106 | Closed mid-Oct.–mid-Apr. | AE, D, DC, MC, V.

MONTE VISTA

MAP 6, E8

(Nearby towns also listed: Alamosa, South Fork)

Located near the Monte Vista National Wildlife Refuge, Monte Vista (population 4,733) and its environs offer excellent outdoors and nature activities. The name is Spanish for "mountain view" and was bestowed upon this part of the picturesque San Luis Valley when Hispanics migrated from New Mexico before the American Civil War.

Information: Monte Vista Chamber of Commerce | 1035 Park Ave., Monte Vista 81144 | 719/852–2731 or 800/562–7085 | www.monte-vista.org.

Attractions

Monte Vista National Wildlife Refuge. Created as a nesting, migration, and wintering habitat for waterfowl and other federally protected species of birds, including sandhill and whooping cranes. It's 6 mi south of Monte Vista. *See* Alamosa National Wildlife Refuge *in* Alamosa, where there is a visitor center at 9383 El Rancho Lane, U.S. 160. | Hwy. 15 | 719/589–4021 | www.r6.fws.gov/alamosanwr | Free | Daily.

Rio Grande National Forest. Mountain ranges within the forest include the Sangre de Cristo and the San Juan. The Rio Grande del Norte (northern portion of the Rio Grande River) is also in the park. Enjoy hiking, cycling, backpacking, camping, and horseback riding. The closest entrance is 2 mi west of Monte Cristo via U.S. 160. | 1803 W. U.S. 160 | 719/852–5941 | www.ff.fed.us/r2/riogrande | Free | Daily.

ON THE CALENDAR

MAR.: *Monte Vista Crane Festival.* Thousands of sandhill cranes on their way back north are visible, as well as a variety of other wildlife, at this festival in Ski-Hi Park. | 719/589–4021.
JUNE: *Sunshine Festival.* A Spring event in Chatman Park with a pancake breakfast, arts and crafts, horse rides, and more the first full weekend in June. | U.S. 160 | 719/589–3681 or 800/258–7597.
JULY: *Ski-Hi Stampede.* Arts-and-crafts fair, barbecue, western dancing, rodeo, carnival, and concert are featured at this annual event in Ski-Hi Park the last weekend in July. | 719/852–2055.
AUG.: *San Luis Valley Fair.* The local 4-H club participates in this annual event which includes agricultural and ranching exhibits, arts-and-crafts displays, food, and entertainment in Ski-Hi Park. | 719/589–2271.

Dining

Restuarante Dos Rios. Mexican. This restaurant's authentic dishes include *filete a la tampiqueña* (sirloin steak) and a *combinacion* (includes enchiladas, chile relleno, taco, refried beans, and rice). | 1635 N. Hwy. 285 | 719/852–0545 | $5–$13 | MC, V.

Lodging

Best Western–Movie Manor. From May through September, guests at this motel about 2½ mi from the Monte Vista town center enjoy a view of a drive-in movie screen from their rooms; most rooms have speakers for the movies' sound. Restaurant, bar. Cable TV. Gym. Playground. Business services. Pets allowed (fee). | 2830 W. Hwy. 160 | 719/852–5921 or 800/771–9468 | fax 719/852–0122 | www.bestwestern.com | 60 rooms | $77–$95 | AE, D, DC, MC, V.

Comfort Inn. Chain motel on the east side of town, just off U.S. 160. Complimentary Continental breakfast. In-room data ports, cable TV. Pool. Hot tub. Business services. Pets allowed. | 1519 Grand Ave. | 719/852–0612 or 800/228–5150 | fax 719/852–3585 | www.comfortinn.com | 45 rooms | $60–$90 | AE, D, DC, MC, V.

Monte Villa Inn. This historic inn in downtown Monte Vista was built in 1930. Although the exterior is Spanish-style stucco, it's furnished in high Victorian style. Restaurant, bar, complimentary Continental breakfast. Cable TV. | 925 First Ave. | 719/852–5166 or 719/852–5166 | fax 719/852–2232 | www.montevista.com/villainn | 35 rooms | $50–$75 | AE, MC, V.

MONTROSE

MAP 6, B6

(Nearby towns also listed: Delta, Ouray)

The legendary Ute Indian chief Ouray and his wife, Chipeta, lived near here in the mid-19th century. Today, Montrose (population 12,585) straddles the important agricultural and mining regions along the Uncompahgre River and provides shopping outlets for the farming and mining families in the region. It also stands as a gateway to several natural wonders in the region.

Information: Montrose Chamber of Commerce | 1519 E. Main St., Montrose 81401 | 970/249–5000 or 800/923–5515 | www.montrose.org/chamber2.

Attractions

★ **Black Canyon of the Gunnison National Park (South Rim).** Here, the rapid-flowing Gunnison River cuts a canyon nearly 2,700 ft deep into the surrounding rock layers, creating a spectacular 14-mi stretch of scenery. Piñon trees almost 1,000 years old line the canyon walls, and they help support a sizable mule deer herd that frequents the region. The south rim entrance is approximately 6 mi east of Montrose via U.S. 50 and Route 347. | Rte. 347 | 979/249–1914 | www.nps.gov/blca | $7 per vehicle | Late May–late Sept., daily 8–6; late Sept.–late May, daily 8:30–4.

Montrose County Historical Museum. Collections at this museum in the Depot Building include antique farm machinery, a pioneer cabin, railroad caboose, pioneer memorabilia, a toy collection, and archaeological artifacts. | 21 N. Rio Grande, at W. Main St. | 970/249–2085 | www.montrose-colo.com/virtual/museum.htm | $2.50 | May–Sept., Mon.–Sat. 9–5.

Ute Indian Museum and Ouray Memorial Park. This museum commemorates the life of the famed Ute Indian chief Ouray and his wife, Chipeta, and depicts the history of the Ute tribe with artifacts and dioramas. Located 2 mi south of Montrose. | 17253 Chipeta Rd., at U.S. 550 | 970/249–3098 | $3 | Mon.–Sat. 9–5.

ON THE CALENDAR

JULY–AUG.: *Montrose County Fair.* Complete with a rodeo, pie-eating contests, livestock shows, tractor pulls, and food vendors, all at the Montrose County Fairgrounds in late July and early August. | 970/249–8884.

Dining

Glenn Eyrie. Continental. A cozy eatery where you can get good shrimp scampi, lightly blackened salmon, and game dishes. Kids' menu. | 2351 S. U.S. 550 | 970/249–9263 | Closed Sun., Mon. No lunch | $12–$28 | AE, D, DC, MC, V.

JoJo's Windmill. American/Casual. Start off your day with a hearty omelet at this restaurant. There are 15 different types of burgers, and the specialty is the homemade soup (beef noodle is popular). | 2133 E. Main St. | 970/240–8678 | Breakfast also available; no dinner | $3–$8 | No credit cards.

Red Barn Restaurant & Lounge. Steak. Next door to the Colorado Inn on the east side of town. Try the club steak or juicy prime rib steak. | 1413 E. Main St. | 970/249–9202 or 970/249–8100 | $6–$20 | AE, D, DC, MC, V.

Sally's Café. American/Casual. Gum-cracking waitresses serve up huge portions of food. The menu has it all, from the popular Mexi-burgers, patty melts, and chicken-fried steak, to grilled peanut butter–and–jelly sandwiches. | 715 Townsend Ave. | 970/249–6096 | Breakfast also available. Closed Wed., Thurs. No dinner | $3–$7 | No credit cards.

The Whole Enchilada. Mexican. An open-air dining spot surrounded by shade trees, for basic Mexican fare like tacos and burritos. | 44 S. Grand Ave. | 970/249–1881 | $4–$10 | AE, D, MC, V.

Lodging

Best Western Red Arrow Motor Inn. On the east side of Montrose, within walking distance of downtown, this upscale motel has many rooms with a private patio or a balcony. In-room data ports, refrigerators, some in-room hot tubs, cable TV, some in-room VCRs. Pool. Hot tub. Gym. Playground, laundry facilities. Business services, airport shuttle. | 1702 E. Main St. (U.S. 50) | 970/249–9641 or 800/468–9323 | fax 970/249–8380 | www.bestwestern.com | 58 rooms, 2 suites | $99–$109, $109–$125 suites | AE, D, DC, MC, V.

Black Canyon Motel. This inexpensive motel is named after the nearby Black Canyon of the Gunnison National Park and is on the east side of Montrose. Rooms are large, clean, and modern. Complimentary Continental breakfast. Some microwaves, cable TV. Pool. Hot tub. Business services. Some pets allowed. | 1605 E. Main (U.S. 550) | 970/249–3495 or 800/348–3495 | fax 970/249–0990 | www.innfinders.com/blackcyn | 49 rooms, 5 suites | $45–$75, $95 suites | AE, D, DC, MC, V.

Canyon Trails Inn. Near the Montrose County Airport on the north side of town, this motel is next to several restaurants. Complimentary Continental breakfast. Some microwaves, some refrigerators, cable TV. | 1225 E. Main (U.S. 550) | 970/249–3426 or 800/858–5911 | fax 970/240–6965 | 27 rooms | $36–$55 | AE, D, MC, V.

Colorado Inn. This motel offers fair-size rooms with all the usual amenities. An inexpensive alternative in a tourist-oriented town. Complimentary Continental breakfast. Cable TV. Pool. Hot tub, sauna. Laundry facilities. | 1417 E. Main St. | 970/249–4507 | fax 970/249–1828 | 71 rooms | $51–$64 | AE, D, DC, MC, V.

Country Lodge. This small budget motel on Montrose's east side offers a variety of rooms. Some kitchenettes, some microwaves, some refrigerators, cable TV. Pool. Playground. | 1624 E. Main (U.S. 550) | 970/249–4567 | fax 970/249–3082 | 22 rooms | $56–$98 | AE, D, DC, MC, V.

Holiday Inn Express–Hotel and Suites. The fireplace in the lobby lets you know that this is not your ordinary chain motel. Some of the spacious rooms and suites have fireplaces. There are many amenities for business travelers and families at this limited-service motor hotel. Enjoy the oversize lap pool and the sundeck. Bar, complimentary Continental breakfast. In-room data ports, some microwaves, some refrigerators, some in-room hot tubs, cable TV. Pool. 2 hot tubs. Gym. Laundry facilities, laundry service. Business services, airport shuttle. Pets allowed. | 970/240–1800 | fax 970/240–9093 | www.holidayinnexpmontrose.com | 122 rooms, 25 suites | $99–$149 | AE, D, DC, MC, V.

San Juan Inn. This inexpensive motel is located on the south side of Montrose. Some microwaves, cable TV. Pool. Hot tub. Playground. Airport shuttle. Pets allowed. | 1480 S. Townsend Ave. | 970/249–6644 | fax 970/249–9314 | www.sanjuaninns.com | 51 rooms | $48–$61 | AE, D, DC, MC, V.

Uncompahgre Bed and Breakfast. This B&B 5½ mi south of Montrose was once a country schoolhouse, built in 1904 in Frank Lloyd Wright's Prairie Style of architecture. Enjoy your breakfast in the dining room that has space for 50, or sit around the fireplace. Complimentary breakfast. Some microwaves, some in-room hot tubs, cable TV, some in-room VCRs (and movies). Gym. Laundry facilities. Pets allowed. No smoking. | 21049 Uncompahgre Rd. | 970/240–4000 or 800/318–8127 | fax 970/249–5124 | www.uncbb.com | 7 rooms | $75–$95 | AE, D, MC, V.

Western Motel. This small, clean, and simple motel is convenient to the county airport and several restaurants on the east of downtown Montrose. Some microwaves, cable TV, some in-room VCRs. Pool. | 1200 E. Main (U.S. 550) | 970/249–3481 or 800/445–7301 | fax 970/249–3471 | 25 rooms, 3 suites | $38–$58, $65–$90 suites | AE, D, DC, MC, V.

Whistling Acres Guest Ranch. This working cattle ranch offers a scenic Rocky Mountain location and pine-paneled rooms with down-filled comforters on the beds, either in a central lodge or in separate cabins. Square dances, musical shows, and cookouts are held weekly. In summer, children enjoy swimming in Minnesota Creek, which runs through the ranch property. The ranch is about an hour's drive northeast of Montrose via U.S. 50 to Highway 92, to Highway 122. Dining room. No room phones, no TV, cable TV in common area. Hot tub. Basketball, hiking, horseback riding, volleyball, bicycles. Snowmobiling. | 4397 050 Dr., Paonia | 970/527–4560 or 800/346–1420 | fax 970/527–6397 | www.whistlingacres.com | 6 rooms, 2 cabins | $690–$780 per person for 3 nights (3–night minimum stay) | AP | MC, V.

NEDERLAND

MAP 6, F3

(Nearby towns also listed: Allenspark, Boulder, Central City)

When silver was discovered in 1860 at Caribou, up Coon Track Creek, a mining settlement was founded in the valley below. The small town underwent a series of name changes including Dayton, Brownsville, and Middle Boulder. In 1873, a group of Dutch investors paid $3 million for Caribou Mine and renamed it "Mining Company Nederland." In the following years, Nederland became a major mining center, surrounded by some of the richest gold and silver veins in the state. In the early 1900s, large tungsten deposits were found in the surrounding mountains. When America entered World War I, the tungsten market boomed, further developing the area.

The old prospectors and settlers would hardly recognize Nederland if they saw it today. What was once a primarily industrial community is now one of Boulder County's great cultural centers. The music scene is enormous for such a small town (population 1,284), with styles ranging from folk and bluegrass to blues rock and acid jazz. With Eldora Ski Area's recent expansion and the growing popularity of nearby casinos, Nederland is facing another economic boom. There is a beautiful town park with a grass amphitheater, pavilion/picnic shelter, and childrens' fishing pier and playground. Hiking, biking, camping, and fishing options are numerous, and Barker Reservoir on the town's eastern edge is a popular boating spot.

Information: Nederland Area Chamber of Commerce | 45 W. 1st St., Box 396, Nederland, 80466 | 303/258–3266 | fax 303/258–1240 | www.townofnederland.com.

Attractions

Eldora Mountain Resort. This ski area on 680 acres 6 mi west of Nederland, offers 7 chair-lifts, 4 surface lifts, 43 runs (the longest being 2 mi), snowmaking, cafeteria, bar, and nursery. | Rte. 119 | 303/440–8700 | fax 303/440–8797 | www.eldora.com | Nov.–mid-Apr., daily 9–4.

Roosevelt National Forest. Just to the west of Nederland the Continental Divide crosses the Indian Peaks, where ponderosa, conifer, and lodgepole pines surround hidden aspen groves. Many fishing, horseback riding, and hiking opportunities abound. From the Hessie trailhead, a moderate hike will take you up to Lost Lake, where remnants of the area's mining history still remain. The Switzerland Trail follows an old rail bed and is great for beginners. | U.S. Forest Service Ranger District, 2140 Yarmouth Ave., Boulder | 303/444–6600 | www.fs.fed.us/r2 | Free | Daily.

ON THE CALENDAR

JULY: *Old Timer's and Miner's Days.* As many as 3,000 visitors are drawn to this unique festival near Wolf Tongue Mine in west Nederland, where many local artisans display their works and innkeepers share their culinary creations. Do not, however, miss the main event: daily "handmucking" exhibitions. There is also a parade through town and many nighttime festivities the last weekend in July. | 303/258–3423.

AUG.: *Nederland Music and Arts Festival.* This two-day outdoor concert at Barker Reservoir in Jeff Guercio Memorial Baseball Park features local and national artists performing bluegrass, jazz, and world-beat music. | 303/415–5665.

Dining

Black Forest Restaurant. German. This Swiss chalet in downtown Nederland provides four rooms, some of which are more casual, some more formal. Seasonal game dishes are a specialty, including elk, duck, and pheasant. Bavarian-style soups, salads, and sandwiches round out the menu. Try the German apple strudel for dessert. Kids' menu. | 24 Big Springs Dr. | 303/582–9971 | $10–$25 | AE, D, DC, MC, V.

Neapolitan's. Italian. This tiny, rustic restaurant is a real local's favorite. The meat-filled and vegetarian calzones are likely the largest you will ever see. Included in the price are fresh Italian rolls and a salad dripping with Gorgonzola. Homemade desserts are also a specialty. | 1 First St. | 303/258–7313 | No lunch weekdays | $7–$13 | MC, V.

Wolf Tongue Brewery. American/Casual. Near the entrance to the Wolf Tongue Mine, this old rough-timber building houses a fine restaurant and bar. From the expansive patio you can take in the views while enjoying hand-tossed pizza, a specialty, along with homemade soups and fish-and-chips. Kids' menu. | 35 E. 1st St. | 303/258–7001 | $6–$13 | AE, D, MC, V.

Lodging

Best Western Lodge. Built in 1994, this timber lodge in downtown Nederland combines modern convenience with a rustic, comfortable feel. Units on the top floor have cathedral ceilings, and those on ground level have gas fireplaces. Complimentary Continental breakfast. Cable TV. Hot tub. Laundry facilities. | 55 Lakeview Dr. | 303/258–9463 or 800/279–9463 | fax 303/258–0413 | www.ned-lodge.com | 23 rooms, 1 suite | $85–$125 | AE, D, DC, MC, V.

Sundance Lodge. This hotel is in Roosevelt National Forest, about 2 mi south of Nederland. Constructed of rough-hewn lumber, the building resembles an old mine. A café and lounge are on the main floor, and from the large west-facing balcony there is an incredible view of the Continental Divide. The rooms are small and comfortable. Complimentary breakfast. Cable TV. | 23942 Rte. 119 | 303/358–3797 | www.sundance-lodge.com | 12 rooms | $80–$100 | AE, D, MC, V.

Nederhaus Hotel. Just to the south of downtown Nederland, this quaint little hotel offers affordable rooms uniquely decorated with antiques and collectibles. A wonderful alpine backyard with goldfish ponds faces the Great Divide. There's a free shuttle service to nearby ski areas during ski season and to local casinos in summer. Restaurant. Cable TV, in-room VCRs. Pets allowed. | 686 Rte. 119 | 303/258–3585 | fax 303/258–3850 | 9 rooms, 1 apartment, 2 suites | $55–$85, $85–$100 apartment and suites | AE, D, MC, V.

Peaceful Valley Ranch and Conference Center. This large, modern ranch resort is perched in the mountains of the Roosevelt National Forest. A stay includes many activities—backcountry tours, overnight pack trips, dancing, picnics, barbecues, and more. All cabins have fireplaces and private hot tubs. Located about 12 mi north of Nederland. Dining room. No air-conditioning, some in-room hot tubs, some room phones, no TV in rooms, TV in common area. Pool, wading pool. Hot tub. Hiking, horseback riding, fishing. Cross-country skiing, downhill skiing, sleigh rides, snowmobiling. Children's programs (ages 3–18), playground. Laundry facilities. Business services, airport shuttle. | 475 Peaceful Valley Rd. (County Rd. 72) | 303/747–2881 | fax 303/747–2167 | www.peacefulvalley.com | 10 cabins, 42 rooms | $1,334–$1,612 per adult per wk (3–night minimum stay in summer) | AP | AE, D, DC, MC, V.

NORWOOD

(Nearby town also listed: Telluride)

Situated between two sections of the Uncompahgre National Forest, this small (population 500) ranching village and its environs offer some outstanding big-game hunting opportunities. Ranching and tourism are the major industries here.

Information: Norwood Chamber of Commerce | Box 116, Norwood, 81423 | 800/282–5988 | www.norwoodcolorado.com.

Attractions
Miramonte Reservoir. Fishing, boating, and windsurfing are just a few of the summertime outdoor activities available at this man-made lake 18 mi south of Norwood. | Lone Cone Rd. | 800/282–5988 | Free (inquire locally for fishing, licensing, and permit information) | Daily.

Uncompahgre National Forest. Nearly 1,000,000 acres of alpine forest lie within the boundaries of this huge national forest that literally surrounds Norwood, where you can hike, fish, cross-country ski, and hunt in season. Several peaks exceed 13,000 ft in height. | U.S. Forest Service, 1760 Grand Ave. | 970/327–4261 | www.fs.fed.us/r2/gmug | Free | Daily. **Lone Cone Mountain.** One of Norwood's signature peaks, standing 12,613 ft high; it is in Beaver Park (within the Uncompahgre National Forest), 17 mi south of the city limits. | U.S. Forest Service, 1760 Grand Ave. | 970/327–4261 | www.fs.fed.us/r2/gmug | Free | Daily.

ON THE CALENDAR
JULY: *San Miguel County Fair.* Highlights include a rodeo and the 4-H Club fair, all at the San Miguel County Fairgrounds the last full weekend in July. | 970/327–4393.
DEC: *Winter Carnival.* Nighttime Parade of Lights along Grand Avenue the first weekend in December. | 970/327–4833.

Dining
Lone Cone Restaurant. Steak. Here, you can spend some time with the locals and enjoy the steak and prime rib. | 1580 Grand Ave. | 970/327–4286 | $6–$18 | MC, V.

Lodging
Back Narrows Inn & Lodge. Inexpensive accommodations in a 100-year-old inn in downtown Norwood. The modern, six-room lodge has private baths and more amenities, such as room phones and TVs. Restaurant, bar. Some room phones, cable TV in some rooms. Pets allowed.

| 1515 Grand Ave. | 970/327–4417 or 970/327–4260 | www.norwoodcolorado.com/bnarrows.html
| 13 rooms (7 with shared bath) | $25–$60 | Restaurant closed Sept. | AE, D, DC, MC, V.

OURAY

MAP 6, C7

(Nearby towns also listed: Montrose, Silverton, Telluride)

Ouray is on U.S. 550 about halfway between Durango and Montrose, in southwestern Colorado. Named in honor of the Ute Indian chief Ouray, this town of 832 residents had its beginnings in 1876 when gold and silver were still being mined in the area. At an elevation of nearly 8,000 ft, Ouray is surrounded by peaks that reach 12,000 to 14,000 ft. Most of Ouray's permanent buildings were built between 1880 and 1900, and virtually all of them are still standing; the entire town is on the National Register of Historic Places.

Information: Ouray Chamber Resort Association | Box 145, Ouray, 81427 | 970/325–4746 or 800/228–1876 | www.ouraycolorado.com.

Attractions

Bachelor-Syracuse Mine. This mine 1 mi north of Ouray via U.S. 550 has been in continuous operation for more than 115 years. A mine train travels deep within a mountain to show visitors mining equipment, work areas, and explosives demonstrations. | County Rd. 14 (U.S. 550, exit Dexter Creen Rd.). | 970/325–0220 | $13 | Mid-May–mid-Sept., daily 9–5.

Bear Creek Falls. These imposing, 227-ft waterfalls are a fascinating sight 3 mi south of Ouray. | U.S. 550, 3 mi south of Ouray | 970/325–4746 or 800/228–1876 | Free | Daily.

Box Cañon Falls Park. From the floor of a 400-ft-deep canyon ¼ mi south of Ouray, the view of thundering waterfalls is awesome. The canyon floor is reached via stairs and a steel bridge. | U.S. 550 | 970/325–4464 | $2.50 | Daily.

Ouray County Historical Museum. A former hospital dating from 1887 houses exhibits depicting artifacts related to local and Ute Indian history, mining, and ranching. | 420 6th Ave. | 970/325–4576 | $3.50 | June–Aug., daily 10–5.

Ouray Hot Springs Pool. It's hard to tell which is more revivifying at this natural hot springs on the north side of Ouray: the 104°F waters or the views of the surrounding peaks. | 1200 Main St. | 970/325–4638 or 970/325–0611 | $7 | Daily 10–10.

Owl Creek Pass. A well-marked, 85-mi round-trip drive that provides a lot of scenic vistas of the mountains and meadows and passes by Silver Jack Reservoir. John Wayne filmed scenes from *True Grit* in this area. Enter the road 3 mi north of Ridgway, off U.S. 550; the road intersects with U.S. 50 a few miles east of Cimarron, near the south rim of the Black Canyon of the Gunnison. Allow three hours for driving, not including stopping time. | 970/249–5000 | Free | Daily (weather permitting).

Ridgway State Park. A 2,320-acre park 12 mi north of Ouray on U.S. 550 containing three recreational areas and a lake. Swimming, waterskiing, camping, boating, hiking, cycling, and more are offered. | 28555 U.S. 550, Ridgway | www.coloradoparks.org/ridgway | 970/626–5822 | $4 per vehicle | Daily.

ON THE CALENDAR

JUNE: *Music In Ouray.* Chamber music is presented at this event at Wright Opera House the second week in June. | 970/325–4746 or 800/228–1876.
AUG.: *Artists' Alpine Holiday and Festival.* Artists working in all media compete in this national event at the Ouray Community Center. | 970/325–4746 or 800/228–1876.

SEPT.: *Imogene Pass Mountain Marathon.* An 18-mi footrace that begins in Ouray and ends in Telluride the Saturday before Labor Day. | 970/325–4746.

SEPT.: *Ouray County Fair and Rodeo.* A regional favorite at the Ouray County Fairgrounds, 12 mi north of Ridgway each Labor Day weekend. | 970/325–4746 or 800/228–1876.

OCT.: *Octoberfest.* Fall celebration for the whole family at the Ouray Community Center. Sample German food, beer, and wine. Door prizes, live music, dancing, and traditional German costumes. | 970/325–4742 or 800/228–1876.

Dining

Bon Ton. Steak. This casual eating establishment is in the St. Elmo Inn. Try the beef Wellington, veal piccata, double bone pork chops. Open-air dining on covered patio. Kids' menu. Sunday brunch. No smoking. | 426 Main St. | 970/325–4951 | No lunch | $11–$24 | AE, D, MC, V.

Buen Tiempo. Mexican. A casual place for carne asada, fajitas, and fresh fish. Open-air dining on patio with mountain views. No smoking. | 513 Main St. | 970/325–4544 | No lunch Sept.–Apr. | $9–$16 | AE, D, MC, V.

Cecilia's. American. Comfort food in a former cinema. Try the trout, liver and onions, chicken-fried steak. Kids' menu. | 630 Main St. | 970/325–4223 | Breakfast also available; closed Nov.–Apr. | $6–$15 | No credit cards.

Ground's Keeper Coffee House & Eatery. Café. Have a cup of coffee, or try one of the cinnamon rolls or a bowl of fresh fruit cobbler. The vegetarian menu includes a vegetarian lasagna. Four homemade soups are prepared daily; the Texas chile is a popular item. | 524 Main St. | 970/325–0550 | $5–$9 | D, MC, V.

The Outlaw Restaurant. Steak. Outdoor barbecue and lunch available during the summer. The Duke (John Wayne) left his hat here during the filming of *True Grit,* so now everyone does. Try the cowboy rib-eye steak. | 610 Main St. | 970/325–4366 or 970/325–4458 | $12–$13 | MC, V.

Pa Pa's Goldbelt Bar & Grill. American/Casual. During the summer months you can dine out on the front patio and enjoy the views. Try the grilled chicken sandwich. | 800 Main St. | 970/325–7242 | $2–$15 | No credit cards.

GHOST TOWNS GALORE

When one considers that, by today's standards, hundreds of millions of dollars worth of gold and silver have been extracted from Colorado's Rocky Mountains, it is no wonder that the state has a great number of deserted mining towns. Prospecting during the region's early days was a precarious business, and many individuals—and villages—went from rags to riches almost overnight as the result of a lucky gold or silver strike. Today, no matter where you are in Colorado, you're not too far from one of these ghost towns. Many of these ghost towns still remain and can be visited, either on your own or on a guided tour. There are several ghost towns in the areas around Cripple Creek, Gunnison, Lake City, Ouray, Salida, and Silverton. If you are lucky, you'll get to see one of the villages that prospered for a few months, or even a few years, before the mines petered out and the residents moved on to try to strike it rich again.

© Artville

The Piñon Restaurant & Tavern. Contemporary. In the downstairs dining room enjoy salmon, trout, seafood, duck, and elk. In the upstairs tavern, the boneless BBQ rib sandwich is popular. Downstairs patio and upstairs tavern deck. | 737 Main St. | 970/325–4334 | $14–$22 | AE, MC, V.

Silver Nugget Café. American. Belly up to the counter and enjoy some unpretentious food and conversation with the locals. Order a hamburger, or just have a cup of coffee. | 746 Main St. | 970/325–4100 | $5–$10 | MC, V.

Lodging

Alpine Inn. A small, pleasant motel in downtown Ouray. Complimentary Continental breakfast. No air-conditioning, cable TV. No smoking. | 645 Main St. (U.S. 550) | 970/325–4546 | 12 rooms | $68 | D, MC, V.

Box Canyon Lodge and Hot Springs. Named for the eponymous canyon near the Uncompaghre River, with magnificent views, this comfortable inn has large, pleasant rooms. There are geothermal hot springs on the property. No air-conditioning, cable TV. Outdoor hot tub. | 45 3rd Ave. | 970/325–4981 or 800/327–5080 | fax 970/325–0223 | www.ouraycolorado.com/boxcanyn.html | 36 rooms, 2 suites | $85–$95, $145–$160 suites | AE, D, MC, V.

China Clipper Inn. Newly constructed in 1995, this bed-and-breakfast with a clipper-ship motif is furnished with many Victorian antiques. Some rooms have fireplaces. Complimentary breakfast. In-room data ports, some microwaves, some refrigerators, some in-room hot tubs, cable TV. Hot tub. Cross-country skiing. Laundry facilities. No kids under 15. No smoking. | 525 2nd St. | 970/325–0565 or 800/315–0565 | fax 970/325–4190 | www.chinaclipperinn.com | 10 rooms (3 with shower only), 2 suites | $90–$165, $115–$125 suites | AE, D, MC, V.

★ **Chipeta Sun Lodge and Spa.** This striking, southwestern-style adobe inn has handmade log beds, Mexican tiles, and breathtaking views. The two-story, plant-filled solarium is a wonderful place to enjoy breakfast. There is complimentary wine and cheese each afternoon. Guests in condos get only a complimentary Continental breakfast. Complimentary breakfast. Some refrigerators, some in-room hot tubs, cable TV. Pool. Hot tub, massage, spa. Health club. Laundry facilities. No smoking. | 304 S. Lena St., Ridgway | 970/626–3737 or 800/633–5868 | www.chipeta.com | 12 rooms, 8 condos | $95–$165, $165–$215 condos | D, DC, MC, V.

The Christmas House. This B&B is a Victorian home built in 1889. The inn has antiques, fireplaces, balconies, and patios that provide views of the San Juan Mountains, as well as private entrances to most of the rooms, which have modern amenities. Complimentary breakfast. In-room data ports, some kitchenettes, microwaves, refrigerators, in-room hot tubs, Cable TV, in-room VCRs (and movies). Sauna. No smoking. | 310 Main St. | 970/325–4992 or 888/325–XMAS | fax 970/325–4992 | www.ouraycolorado.com/xmasbb.html | 5 rooms | $80–$150 | MC, V.

Circle M. A small, inexpensive family-friendly motel one block off Main Street in Ouray. Picnic area. No air-conditioning, microwaves, refrigerators, cable TV. Playground. | 120 6th Ave. | 970/325–4394 or 888/466–8729 (in CO only) | 19 rooms | $49–$95 | Closed mid-Oct.–mid-May | D, MC, V.

Comfort Inn. This chain motel is one block west of U.S. 550 in Ouray's downtown. Complimentary Continental breakfast. Cable TV. Hot tub. Laundry facilities. | 191 5th Ave. | 970/325–7203 or 800/228–5150 | fax 970/325–4840 | www.comfortinn.com | 33 rooms | $64–$109 | AE, D, DC, MC, V.

The Damn Yankee Country Inn. One block from Main Street and next to a river, this three-story inn offers large rooms at reasonable rates. Complimentary Continental breakfast. In-room data ports, some in-room hot tubs, cable TV, in-room VCRs. Outdoor hot tub. No kids under 18. No smoking. | 100 6th St. | 970/325–4219 or 800/845–7512 | fax 970/325–4339 | www.damnyankeeinn.com | 10 rooms | $81–$190 | D, MC, V.

Historic Western Hotel. This three-story Victorian building was built in 1891; it offers one of the best views in town. Relax on the front or back porch, and enjoy the garden surrounding the property. Rooms are done up in period style. Restaurant, bar, complimentary Continental breakfast. No TV in rooms, TV in common area. No smoking. | 210 7th Ave. | 970/325–4645 or 888/624–8403 | www.ouraycoloradocom/histwest.html | 14 rooms (12 with shared bath) | $45–$85 | D, MC, V.

Matterhorn Motel. In the center of town, this mid-priced motel is within easy walking distance to several restaurants. Some in-room hot tubs, cable TV. Pool. Hot tub. Business services. | 201 6th Ave. | 970/325–4938 or 800/334–9425 | fax 970/325–7335 | www.ouraycolorado.com/matterhorn.html | 22 rooms, 3 suites | $75, $108 suites | Closed Nov.–Mar. | D, DC, MC, V.

Ouray Hotel. This 2-story hotel, which dates to 1893, was completely restored in 1993, including all its original woodwork and skylights (which make the building particularly light and airy). Rooms are clean, spacious, and fully air-conditioned. Cable TV. No smoking. | 303 6th Ave., at Main St. | 970/325–0500 or 800/216–8729 | fax 970/325–0500 | www.ourayhotel.com | 14 | $45–$100 | Closed mid-Oct.–early May | MC, V.

Ouray Victorian Inn. On the Uncompaghre River, this pretty and inviting two-story motel offers year-round comfortable rooms. Packages offer half-price Telluride lift tickets. Picnic area. No air-conditioning, cable TV. Hot tub. Playground. Business services. | 50 3rd Ave. | 970/325–7222 or 800/443–7361 | fax 970/325–7225 | www.ouraylodging.com | 38 rooms, 4 suites | $84–$89, $95 suites | AE, D, DC, MC, V.

Plain Jane Sack and Snack. Children are welcome at this small, friendly B&B with a park and sundeck on the river and a playground. The mining theme, including artifacts and art, makes your stay unique. There's also croquet on the lawn. Complimentary Continental breakfast. Some kitchenettes, no room phones, no TV. Massage. Basketball, horseshoes. Playground. No pets. No smoking. | 3 Munn Ct | 970/325–7313 | fax 970/325–7250 | www.plainjanebnb.com | 4 rooms | $45–$95 | MC, V.

St. Elmo. A turn-of-the-20th-century B&B with rooms decorated in period style with a scattering of antiques. Manages to be slightly elegant without much stuffiness. Restaurant, bar, complimentary breakfast. No TV, cable TV in common area. Hot tub, sauna. Business services. No smoking. | 426 Main St. (U.S. 550) | 970/325–4951 | fax 970/325–0348 | www.colorado-bnb.com/stelmo | 9 rooms, 1 suite | $100–$110, $115 suites | AE, D, DC, MC, V.

San Juan Guest Ranch. Six miles north of Ouray in the aspen and pine groves of the San Juan Valley, this guest ranch offers a wide variety of outdoor activities. Wagon rides and overnight camping trips are available weekly, as are cookouts and four-wheel-drive trips to local ghost towns and mines. There is also an on-site shooting range. Guests receive free passes to the nearby Ouray Hot Springs. Dining room. No room phones, no TV. Hot tub. Horseback riding, volleyball, fishing. Cross-country skiing. Children's programs (ages 5–12). | 2882 County Rd. 23, Ridgway | 970/626–5360 or 800/331–3015 | fax 970/626–5015 | www.sjgr.com | 9 rooms | $1,250 per person for 6 nights (6–night minimum stay June–Sept.) | Closed Apr., May, Nov.–mid-Dec. | AP | MC, V.

Super 8. Traditional Super 8 reliability and reasonable prices, 10 mi north of Ouray in Ridgway. Complimentary Continental breakfast. Cable TV. Pool. Hot tub, sauna. Video games. Laundry facilities. Business services. | 373 Palomino Trail (U.S. 550), Ridgway | 970/626–5444 or 800/800–8000 | fax 970/626–5898 | www.super8.com | 52 rooms | $73–$94 | AE, D, DC, MC, V.

Wiesbaden Hot Springs Spa and Lodgings. Combine a vapor cave, hot springs pool, and massage with comfortable rooms, and you have a great stress-reduction package. Accommodations, either in the lodge or in rooms lining an adjoining courtyard, are elegant and furnished with antiques; all guests have 24-hour access to the lovely lodge lobby. Some kitchenettes, some refrigerators, cable TV. Massage, spa. No smoking. | 625 5th St. | 970/325-4347 | fax 970/325-4358 | www.geocities.com/wiesbadenspa | 18 rooms | $110–$175 | D, MC, V.

PAGOSA SPRINGS

MAP 6, D8

(Nearby towns also listed: Durango, South Fork)

Mineral springs, whose healing waters reach 153°F, made Pagosa Springs a popular place back in 1880 when it was first settled. Today, lots of wilderness provided by the nearby San Juan National Forest makes the area around this small town (population 1818) popular to hunters and nature-lovers. It's also close to the excellent but under-utilized Wolf Creek Ski Area.

Information: **Pagosa Springs Area Chamber of Commerce** | 402 San Juan St., Pagosa Springs, 81147 | 970/264-2360 or 800/252-2204 | www.pagosa-springs.com.

Attractions

Chimney Rock Archaeological Area. Four guided tours daily take you through these Anasazi ruins and to a fire tower, from the top of which is a fabulous view. It's 17 mi west of Pagosa Springs. You must be on a ranger-led tour to enter the site, and reservations are mandatory. | Hwy. 151, Chimney Rock | 970/883-5359 or 970/385-1210 | www.chimney-rockco.org | Free | Daily, reservations required.

Fred Harman Art Museum. Original paintings from the hand of Fred Harman, the creator of the famous comic strip "Red Ryder," are on display at this small museum 2 mi west of Pagosa Springs on U.S. 160. | 2560 W. U.S. 160 | 970/731-5785 | www.harmanartmuseum.com | $2 | Memorial Day–Labor Day, weekdays 10:30–5, weekends noon–5; Labor Day–Dec., weekdays 10:30–5; Jan.–Memorial Day, by appointment only.

Navajo State Park. The park offers fishing, camping, boating, picnicking, and waterskiing on a large man-made lake. A café is also on site. The lake is about 37 mi southwest of Pagosa Springs, off Highway 151. | County Rd. 982, Arboles | 970/883-2208 | www.col-oradoparks.org/navajo | $4 per vehicle | Daily.

San Juan Historical Society and Museum. This museum has a collection of Native American artifacts as well as pioneer exhibits, including a general store, a weaving loom, pioneer attire, and a blacksmith shop. | 1st. and Pagosa Sts. | 970/264-4424 | $3 | Memorial Day–Labor Day, weekdays 9–4, weekends noon–4.

Wolf Creek Pass. This scenic drive along a portion of U.S. 60 from Pagosa Springs to South Fork goes across the Continental Divide at an altitude of 10,857 ft. The drive takes about 1 hour and 20 minutes. | U.S. 160, between Pagosa Springs and South Fork | 970/264-2268 | Free | Daily (weather permitting).
Treasure Mountain Trail. Legend has it that there is $5 million worth of gold bars lost in the vicinity. The trail is marked at the top of Wolf Creek Pass, just east of the summit. Begin at the top of Wolf Creek Pass, just east of summit marked where the Continental Divide Trail winds southward and connects with Treasure Mountain Trail. | No phone | Free | Daily (weather permitting).

Wolf Creek Ski Area. The ski area contains 1 quad, 2 triple, 2 double chairlifts, 50 runs (the longest is 2 mi), with a vertical drop of 1,097 ft. Shuttle bus service is available from Pagosa Springs. This is an excellent but underused ski area, due partly to the lack of on-site

accommodations. | U.S. 160, at Wolf Creek Pass | www.wolfcreekski.com | 970/264–5639 |
Early Nov.–early Apr., daily 9–4.

ON THE CALENDAR
FEB.: *Winter Fest.* A winter carnival with hot-air balloons as well as adult and kids' indi-
vidual and team events. | 970/264–2360 or 800/252–2204.
AUG: *Archuleta County Fair.* This annual fair includes a carnival, 4-H livestock show,
kids' rodeo, Saturday-night chuck wagon, music, and weekend dance the first full week
in August. Held at the Archuleta County Fairgrounds. | 970/264–5931.

Dining

Bob's Cabin. American/Casual. Put on your hard hat and try the construction burger, a half-
pound burger served on a deli roll with chile peppers, cheese, bacon, and avocado. The taquitos
(eight tightly rolled tacos with salsa and sour cream) are also tasty. | 165 N. Pagosa | 970/
731–2627 | $5–$17 | AE, D, MC, V.

Elkhorn Café. Mexican. Fiery Mexican fare and American standards draw crowds from miles
around to this popular restaurant. Try the breakfast burritos or stuffed sopaipilla. Kids'
menu. | 438C Pagosa St. | 970/264–2146 | Breakfast also available | $3–$8 | AE, D, MC, V.

Riverside. Southwestern. A casual western place with a view of the river and hot springs.
On the menu are breakfast burritos, chicken Monterey, and oriental chicken salad. Open-
air dining overlooking the San Juan River. Kids' menu. Beer and wine only. No smoking. |
439 San Juan St. | 970/264–2175 | Breakfast also available | $8–$13 | AE, D, MC, V.

Lodging

Davidson's Country Inn B&B. This three-story log building is on a 32-acre working ranch,
2 mi east of Pagosa Springs and 22 mi from Wolf Creek Ski Area. Rooms are comfortable
and decorated with family heirlooms and antiques, and many are large enough to accom-
modate a family of four. Dining room, complimentary breakfast. No room phones, no TV.
Hiking, horseshoes, volleyball. Cross-country skiing. No smoking. | 2763 U.S. 160 E | 970/264–
5863 | fax 970/264–5492 | www.coloradolodging.com/davidsons.html | 8 rooms (4 with shared
bath), 1 cabin | $65–$100 | AE, D, MC, V.

Fireside Inn. This "inn" actually provides accommodations in 15 private cabins with gas
fireplaces along the San Juan River, 1 mi from downtown Pagosa Springs. The property has
horse corrals so you can bring your own horses. No air-conditioning, in-room data ports,
kitchenettes, microwaves, refrigerators, cable TV, some in-room VCRs. Hot tub. Laundry facil-
ities. Pets allowed (fee). | 1600 E. Hwy. 160 | 970/264–9204 or 888/264–9204 | fax 970/264–
9204 | www.websites.pagosa.net/firesideinn | 15 cabins | $99–$159 | AE, D, MC, V.

High Country Lodge. High in the San Juan mountains 3 mi east of Pagosa Springs, this wood-
land lodge has motel-style rooms and cabins. Complimentary Continental breakfast. No
air-conditioning in some rooms, some kitchenettes, cable TV. Hot tub. Gym. Video games.
Laundry facilities. | 3821 U.S. 160 W | 970/264–4181 or 800/862–3707 | www.highcountry-
lodge.com | 25 rooms, 5 cabins | $55–$71, $85–$100 cabins | AE, D, DC, MC, V.

Pagosa Lodge. Situated in a picturesque mountain forest, this resort offers extensive
recreational activities and the closest accommodations to the Wolf Creek ski area; it's also
next to a 6,500-ft private airstrip. The lodge can arrange white-water rafting trips, hot-
air balloon rides, and jeep tours. Ski packages are available. Restaurants, bar, picnic area.
Cable TV. Pool, lake. Sauna, steam room. Driving range, putting green, tennis. Gym. Boating, bicycles. Cross-country skiing, sleigh rides. Playground. Business services, airport shut-
tle. | 3505 U.S. 160 W | 970/731–4141 or 800/523–7704 (outside CO) | fax 970/731–4343 |
www.pagosalodge.com | 95 rooms, 5 suites | $115–$120, $170 suites | AE, D, DC, MC, V.

Pagosa Springs Inn. A comfortable motel on the western side of Pagosa Springs. Some
microwaves, refrigerators, some in-room hot tubs, cable TV. Pool. Hot tub. Video games.

Business services. Pets allowed. | 3565 U.S. 160 W | 970/731–3400 or 888/221–8088 | fax 970/731–3402 | 97 rooms | $80–$99 | AE, D, DC, MC, V.

Spring Inn. In downtown Pagosa Springs, this comfortable, homey inn has 15 natural hot springs on the premises, which guests can use free of charge. Some microwaves, cable TV. Massage. Video games. | 165 Hot Springs Blvd. | 970/264–4168 or 800/225–0934 | fax 970/264–4707 | www.pagosasprings.net/springinn | 49 rooms, 1 suite | $83–$150 | D, DC, MC, V.

PALISADE

MAP 6, B5

(Nearby towns also listed: Cedaredge, Grand Junction, Rifle)

Victorian homes nestled against a backdrop of peach orchards is what you'll find in this town named for the dramatic palisades of Mancos Shale. The first inhabitants of the Grand Valley were the Ute Indians; white settlers followed in 1881. Three years later, the first fruit orchards were planted, and these have paved the way for the rich economy of today.

The basis for the town's economy has always been agriculture, but more innovative farmers are trying their hand at growing a new crop almost unheard of in Colorado: grapes. Nearly a dozen wineries have sprung up over the past few years, making it possible to buy fine wine with a Colorado label. The population of 2,392 continues to grow, but Palisade still maintains its small-town friendliness with Victorian homes laced with gingerbread trim and quaint little shops and a bakery dotting Main Street. The central location also serves as a convenient headquarters to experience the wealth of outdoor opportunities in the Grand Mesa area, which include hiking, mountain biking, rafting, fishing, hunting, and camping.

Information: Palisade Chamber of Commerce | Box 279, Palisade, 81526 | 970/464–7458 | www.palisadecoc.com.

Attractions

Canyon Wind Cellars. This winery's unique location allows it to produce wines of great distinction. Chardonnay, merlot, and cabernet sauvignon are available. The tasting room is on the banks of the Colorado River. | 3907 N. River Rd. | 970/464–0888 | Free | May–Oct., Mon.–Sat. 10–4; Nov.–Apr., by appointment only.

Carlson Vineyards. Carlson produces fruit wine as well as grape varieties. Specialties are the Prairie Dog series and the mythical Dinosaur series. Formerly, the entire property was an apricot orchard and the tasting room was an old packing shed. Group tours by appointment. | 461 35 Rd. | 970/464–5554 | Free | Daily 11–6.

Colorado Cellars Winery. Colorado Cellars is the state's oldest winery, producing over 20 varieties of wine and 24 wine-based food items. The winery's magnificent grounds include a picnic area and grassy knoll that provide a panoramic view of the Grand Valley. There is a tasting room in the retail sales outlet. Group tours by appointment. | 3553 E Rd. | 800/848–2812 | Free | Weekdays 9–4, Sat. noon–4.

Grande River Vineyards. Grande River features award-winning, premium Colorado-grown wines, including chardonnay, merlot, red and white meritage, syrah, and viognier. An annual concert series is also held on the premises. Group tours by appointment. | 787 Elberta Ave. | 970/464–5867 | Free | Daily 9–5.

Island Acres State Park. Fishing, picnicking, and swimming are offered at the park, about 4 mi northeast of Palisade. Campgrounds and a grocery store are nearby. | I–70, exit 47 | 970/464–0548 or 970/434–3388 | $4 per vehicle | Daily.

Little Bookcliffs Wild Horse Range. The Little Bookcliffs Wild Horse Range is just one of three in the United States specifically set aside for wild horses. Trails, which vary in difficulty, are available to hike, bike, or ride on horseback. Discover the mystique of the Wild, Wild West, at this unique site located approximately 8 mi north of Grand Junction. | 2815 H Rd. St. | 970/244-3000 | Free | Daily.

Plum Creek Cellars. Lovely lavender flowers and trees adorn the grounds of this winery. Plum Creek offers a full selection of fine wines from 100% Colorado-grown grapes. Chardonnay and riesling are among the wines available. Group tours by appointment. | 3708 G Rd. | 970/464-7586 | Free | Daily 9:30-6.

Riverbend Park. Walk or bike your way along the trails of Palisade's Riverbend Park. Along the way, you may spot nesting geese, wild turkeys, beavers, great horned owls and blue herons, along with the occasional mule deer with fawns. There are picnic areas along the ¾-mi surfaced trail. The biking trailhead is at the end of Brentwood Drive. | 319 Main St. | 970/464-7458 | fax 970/464-4757 | www.palisadecoc.com | Free | Daily.

Rocky Mountain Meadery/Rocky Mountain Cidery. Rocky Mountain is Colorado's exclusive producer of honey wine (mead) and carbonated hard cider made from Colorado fruits and honey. Savor the styles and blends of the Renaissance Era Honey Wines while overlooking Grand Mesa. Group tours by appointment. | 3701 G Rd. | 970/464-7899 | Free | Daily 10-5.

St. Kathryn Cellars. Come visit one of Colorado's newest wineries and event centers. Enjoy complimentary samples of Colorado varietal and fruit wines while browsing the spacious gift shop and artists' corner. Later, picnic on 3 acres of grass. | 785 Elberta Ave. (I-70, exit 42) | 970/464-9288 | Free | Daily 10-5.

Two Rivers Winery. Opened in November 1999, Two Rivers offers chardonnay, cabernet sauvignon, and merlot. Sip these fine wines while enjoying views of the Colorado National Monument and basking in the beautiful country-French setting in the Redlands. | 2087 Broadway, Grand Junction | 970/255-1471 | Free | Mon.-Sat. 10:30-6, Sun. noon-5.

SIGHTSEEING TOURS/TOUR COMPANIES

Wine Country Tours. Palisade is home to the largest concentration of wineries in the state. Take a tour of all eight of the region's wineries and learn about the wine-making process, talk with local experts, and taste a variety of Colorado wines. Reservations are required. | 740 Horizon Dr. | 970/244-1480 | fax 970/243-7393 | www.grand-junction.net | $20 | Wed., Sat., Sun. 1-5.

ON THE CALENDAR

AUG.: *Peach Festival.* Celebrate a bountiful peach harvest with a parade, pancake breakfast, barbecue, arts-and-crafts booths, and live entertainment in the Palisade town park. | 970/464-7458.

Dining

Ann Marie's Country Cottage Café. American. This casual, friendly country cottage café is the perfect place for breakfast, lunch, or dinner. Look for blue-plate specials like chicken-fried steak and the biscuits and gravy. Other menu favorites include breakfast burritos and hamburgers. | 349 W. 8th | 970/464-4600 | No dinner Sun. | $3-$8 | MC, V.

Slice O' Life Bakery. Café. Yummy is the only word to describe this down-home style bakery, which is known around the region for its melt-in-your mouth pastries, sweet rolls, muffins, and berry cups. Cold sandwiches, cookies, pies, and a full line of fresh baked breads are also available. | 105 W. 3rd St. | 970/464-0577 | Closed Sun., Mon.; Sat. at 3. No dinner | $1-$8 | No credit cards.

Antonios Pizza. Pizza. Pizzas and submarine sandwiches are the name of the game at Antonios Pizza. Check out the "All the Way" pizza loaded with every kind of topping you can imagine. Pizza is also available by the slice. How about a sub sandwich? Menu favorites include a club, turkey, ham and provolone, or salami plus ham and provolone. | 309 W. 8th | 970/464–7966 | Closed Sun. | $2–$16 | No credit cards.

Lodging

The Garden House Bed & Breakfast. Elegant country charm is what you'll find at this comfortable B&B tucked inside a small fruit orchard. All guest rooms offer designer linens for a cozy night's sleep. Breakfast is brought to your door, and afternoon snacks and evening turndown service are available. Complimentary breakfast. No TV in rooms, TV in common area. No smoking. | 3587 G Rd. | 970/464–4686 or 800/305–4686 | fax 970/464–4686 | www.colorado-bnb.com/gardnhse | 4 rooms | $68–$112 | D, MC, V.

Palisade's Bewelcome Bed and Breakfast. This delightful B&B is centrally located off Interstate 70 at the Palisade exit. Rooms are simply decorated in country, rustic, and just plain cozy styles. Two of the guest rooms have private baths. Enjoy afternoon tea, coffee, and snacks. Complimentary breakfast. No TV, cable TV and VCR in common area. No smoking. | 649 Aldrea Vista Ct | 970/464–0884 | 3 rooms (1 with shared bath) | $50 | No credit cards.

PUEBLO

MAP 6, G6

(Nearby towns also listed: Cañon City, Colorado Springs, Walsenburg)

The first non-native view of the Pueblo area was beheld by a fur trapper named Jacob Fowler, who on January 6, 1822, "Went up to the Warm Spring Branch and Soot [set] two traps." The famous black mountain man James P. Beckwourth is credited with being the first permanent settler in present-day Pueblo, arriving there in October, 1842. Today, the city is home to nearly 103,000 people and serves as a hub for many transportation, manufacturing, and agricultural facilities. A working-class steel town, it nevertheless has some lovely historic neighborhoods, but it is overshadowed by Colorado Springs, 42 mi to the north.

Information: **Pueblo Chamber of Commerce** | Box 697, Pueblo, 81002 | 719/542–1704 | www.pueblochamber.org.

Attractions

El Pueblo Museum. A full-size replica of the 1840s fort that served as base of operations for fur trappers in the region. Exhibits depict the early history of the area, from prehistoric days on. | 324 W. First St. | 719/583–0453 | $3 | Mon.–Sat. 10–4:30, Sun. noon–3.

Fred E. Weisbrod Aircraft Museum. An open-air museum 6 mi east of Pueblo on U.S. 50 at the Pueblo Memorial Airport. A huge collection of vintage aircraft are exhibited on what was originally the Pueblo Army Air Base during WWII. The adjoining B-24 Aircraft Memorial Museum tells the story of the famous World War II bomber, which was built here. | 31001 Magnuson Ave. | 719/948–3355 or 719/948–9219 | www.co.pueblo.co.us/pwam | Free | Weekdays 10–4, Sat. 10–2, Sun. 2–4.

The Greenway and Nature Center of Pueblo. Thirty-six miles of hiking and biking trails wind through a small reptile and raptor garden 5 mi west of Pueblo, off U.S. 50. There's a café in the park. | 5200 Nature Center Rd. | 719/549–2414 | www.uscolo.edu/gnc | Free | Grounds: daily dawn–10 PM; raptor center: Tues.–Sat. 11–4; interpretive center/nature shop: Tues.–Sun. 9–5.

Lake Isabel. A 310-acre recreational site in San Isabel National Forest, with boating, camping, and picnicking, but no swimming. The lake is in San Isabel, 43 mi southwest of Pueblo via I-25 South. | Rte. 165, San Isabel | 719/545–8737 | Free | Daily.

Pueblo State Park. Swimming, biking, fishing, boating, hiking, and camping at a large, man-made reservoir. It's one of Colorado's most popular parks. Located 6 mi west of Pueblo, via Route 96. | 640 Pueblo Reservoir Rd. | 719/561–9320 | www.coloradoparks.org/pueblo | $4 per vehicle | Daily.

Pueblo Zoo in City Park. The animals at this 25-acre zoo are housed in habitats that simulate their natural environment. There are over 300 animals of over 110 different species from around the world. Don't miss the lion exhibit and the black-footed penguins. | 3455 Nuckolls Ave. | 719/561–9664 | fax 719/561–8686 | www.pueblozoo.org | $4 | Memorial Day–Labor Day, daily 10–5; Labor Day–Memorial Day, daily 9–4.

Rosemount Museum. One of Colorado's premier historic homes, which once belonged to the wealthy Thatcher family. It's an immense American palace filled with period furnishings; includes the Andrew McClelland Collection, an eclectic and eccentric collection of objects accumulated from a lifetime of travel, including an Egyptian mummy. | 419 W. 14th St. | 719/545–5290 | www.rosemount.org | $5 | Sept.–May, Tues.–Sat. 1–4, Sun. 2–4.

San Isabel National Forest. More than 1,100,000 acres that includes Colorado's highest peak (Mt. Elbert, 14,433 ft). You'll find picnicking and camping among other outdoor activities. | 1920 Valley Dr. (I–25, exit San Isabel) | 719/545–8737 | Free | Daily.

Sangre de Cristo Arts and Conference Center. A well-thought-out space that includes an art gallery, workshops, dance studios, a theater, and a children's museum. Arts performances are hosted here, and there is also a gift shop. | 210 N. Santa Fe Ave. | 719/542–1211 or 719/543–0130 | Galleries free, children's museum $1 | Galleries: Mon.–Sat. 11–4; children's museum: Mon.–Sat. 11–5.

Union Avenue Historic District. During the 1880s, this street unified the separate towns of South and Central Pueblo. After the consolidation, this area became the hub of business and entertainment. Today, the commercial district is still vibrant. Many of the over 80 merchants in the area can give you copies of a self-guided walking tour map. | Union Ave. (I–25, exit 98) | 719/543–5804 | www.puebloonline.com/unionave | Free | Daily.

University of Southern Colorado. Established in 1975, the school now enrolls 4,500 students. Visitors can stop by the geology museum full of displays of rocks and minerals. | 2200 Bonforte Blvd. | 719/549–2461 | www.uscolo.edu | Free | Campus tours weekdays, by appointment.

ON THE CALENDAR

JULY: *Festival Friday.* Every Friday night in July, the Sangre de Cristo Arts Center hosts a dance featuring a different band. | 719/543–0130.
AUG.–SEPT.: *Colorado State Fair.* This is the state of Colorado's annual fair, with entertainment, PRCA rodeo competition, livestock and agricultural exhibits, and hi-tech displays. Held at the Colorado State Fairgrounds from late August to early September. | 719/561–8484.
OCT.–MAR.: *Pueblo Greyhound Park.* The park offers pari-mutuel betting on live racing January–April, via satellite May–December. | 719/566–0370.

Dining

Café Del Rio. American. The café is in the Greenway Nature Center in a southwestern-style building. Known for regional American dishes and homemade soups. Try the stuffed orange roughy, grilled salmon, New York strip steak. Open-air dining on a deck overlooking the Arkansas River. Kids' menu. Sunday brunch | 5200 Nature Center Rd. | 719/545–2009 | Closed Mon. | $10–$19 | AE, D, DC, MC, V.

DJ's Steak House. Steak. A popular restaurant whose baby-back ribs are a local favorite. This is a great place to sit down and enjoy the prime rib or savor the tasty lobster. North of downtown, on Interstate 25. | 4289 N. Elizabeth St. | 719/545–9354 | $9–$60 | AE, D, DC, MC, V | No lunch. Closed Sun.

Gaetano's. Italian. A casual place for lasagna, chicken florentine, or perhaps veal Oscar. Open-air dining in front. Kids' menu, early-bird suppers. No smoking. | 910 U.S. 50 W | 719/546–0949 | Closed Sun. No lunch Sat. | $8–$18 | AE, D, DC, MC, V.

Irish Brew Pub and Grill. American. In downtown Pueblo, this is one of the few places in America where you can order a mixed wild game sandwich. Alternatively, try the buffalo burgers, the great smoked duck sausage appetizer, and the seven varieties of beer brewed on the premises. | 108 W. 3rd St. | 719/542–9974 | Closed Sun. | $8–$20 | AE, D, DC, MC, V.

La Renaissance. Continental. This converted church and parsonage is the most imposing and elegant space in town, and the impeccably attired, unfailingly courteous waitstaff completes the picture. Try the filet mignon in mushroom sauce, superb baby-back ribs, and New Zealand deep sea fillet. No smoking. | 217 E. Routt Ave. | 719/543–6367 | Closed Sun. No lunch Mon., Fri., Sat. | $12–$26 | AE, D, DC, MC, V.

Lodging

Abriendo Inn. This B&B in a converted 1906 Victorian house is within walking distance of Pueblo's historic district. Complimentary breakfast. In-room data ports, some in-room hot tubs, cable TV, some in-room VCRs. Business services. No kids under 6. No smoking. | 300 W. Abriendo Ave. | 719/544–2703 | fax 719/542–6544 | www.bedandbreakfast.org/abriendo | 9 rooms, 1 suite | $69–$120, $84–$89 suite | AE, DC, MC, V.

Baxter Inn. This B&B is in a 1893 Victorian house that was once the home of O.H.P. Baxter, a notable figure in Pueblo's history. The Inn has a beautiful piano in the music room and a comfortable library. The three-course breakfast begins with a "wake-up" course that is served outside your room. Rooms are elegantly furnished with period antiques. It's next door to the Rosemount Museum. Complimentary breakfast. In room-data ports, some in-room hot tubs, cable TV. Library. Laundry service. No smoking. | 325 W. 15th | 719/542–7002 | fax 719/583–1560 | www.puebloonline.com/baxterinn | 5 rooms | $85–$120 | AE, DC, MC, V.

Best Western Inn at Pueblo West. This chain motel is just off U.S. 50 in Pueblo West, a small town 8½ mi west of Pueblo. Restaurant. Cable TV. Pool. Gym. Business services. | 201 S. McCulloch Blvd., Pueblo West | 719/547–2111 or 800/448–1972 | fax 719/547–0385 | www.best-western.com | 80 rooms | $64–$84 | AE, D, DC, MC, V.

Comfort Inn. A comfortable, mid-priced chain motel next to Interstate 25 on the north side of town. Complimentary Continental breakfast. In-room data ports, some in-room hot tubs, cable TV. Pool. Business services. | 4645 I–25 N | 719/542–6868 or 800/228–5150 | fax 719/542–6868 | www.comfortinn.com | 60 rooms | $60–$85 | AE, D, DC, MC, V.

Days Inn. This chain motel is on the north side of Pueblo, just off the interstate. Some suites have Jacuzzi tubs. Complimentary Continental breakfast. Some refrigerators, some in-room hot tubs, cable TV. Pool. Hot tub. Business services. | 4201 N. Elizabeth St. | 719/543–8031 or 800/544–8313 | fax 719/546–1317 | www.daysinn.com | 58 rooms, 7 suites | $46–$85, $75–$135 suites | AE, D, DC, MC, V.

Hampton Inn. This hotel is on the northern edge of town. Complimentary Continental breakfast. Cable TV, some in-room VCRs. Pool. Laundry facilities. Business services, free parking. | 4703 N. Fwy. | 719/544–4700 or 800/426–7866 | fax 719/544–6526 | www.hamptoninn.com | 111 rooms | $75–$109 | AE, D, DC, MC, V.

Holiday Inn–Pueblo. North of downtown Pueblo, this hotel offers many amenities, including an indoor pool, which makes it a family favorite. Restaurant, bar, room service. In-room data ports, some microwaves. Pool. Gym. Video games. Laundry facilities. Business services, airport shuttle. | 4001 N. Elizabeth St. (I–25, exit 101) | 719/543–8050 | fax 719/545–2271 or 800/465–4329 | www.holiday-inn.com/puebloco | 189 rooms, 2 suites | $59–$115, $150–$250 suites | AE, D, DC, MC, V.

La Quinta Inn. The rooms and suites in this four-story hotel are spacious and comfortable. Relax in the pool or outdoor hot tub. Just off of Interstate 25 at the north end of Pueblo, 10 mi from downtown. Complimentary Continental breakfast, room service. In-room data ports, some microwaves, some refrigerators, cable TV. Pool. Outdoor hot tub. Gym. Laundry facilities, laundry service. Business services. | 4801 N. Elizabeth St. | 719/542–3500 or 800/531–5900 | fax 719/542–3535 | www.laquintainn.com | 101 rooms | $69–$129 | AE, D, DC, MC, V.

Wingate Inn–Pueblo. Comfortable motor hotel in a four-story building, with oversized rooms and suites. The spacious lobby, the hot tub, and the exercise room help make your stay here as pleasant as possible. It's 5 mi from downtown Pueblo and 10 mi from Pueblo airport. Complimentary Continental breakfast. In-room data ports, some kitchenettes, some microwaves, refrigerators, cable TV. Hot tub. Gym. | 4711 N. Elizabeth St. | 719/586–9000 | fax 719/586–9000 or | www.wingateinns.com | 84 rooms | $69–$89 | AE, D, DC, MC, V.

RIFLE

(Nearby towns also listed: Glenwood Springs, Grand Junction, Meeker, Palisade)

Incorporated in 1905, Rifle is the only town in the United States with that name. Some say Rifle got its unique name after a soldier in 1880 left his rifle at camp on the bank of the stream. Upon returning for it, he named the stream Rifle Creek. Others say a rusty rifle was found at a creek. Regardless, Rifle (population 6,367) is best known for world-class technical climbing at Rifle Mountain Park, north of town off Highway 325. Other popular activities include hunting, skiing, and snowmobiling. Rifle Gap, Harvey Gap, and Rifle Falls state parks are also nearby.

Information: Rifle Chamber of Commerce | 200 Lions Park Circle, Rifle, 81650 | 970/625–2085 or 800/842–2085 | fax 970/625–4757 | www.riflechamber.com.

Attractions

Rifle Falls State Park. The 60-ft triple-fluke Rifle Falls is the centerpiece of this state park. Water cascades down moss-covered cliffs, concealing caves that can be explored. The sea of emerald trees is a great place to go camping, hiking among the limestone cliffs, or picnicking. | Rte. 325 | 970/625–1607 | www.parks.state.co.us/rifle_gap | $4 per vehicle | Daily.

Rifle Falls Fish Hatchery. Huge schools of rainbow trout are raised here to stock the ponds and lakes of Colorado. | 11466 Hwy. 325 | 970/625–1865 | Free | Daily.

Rifle Gap State Park. This recreation area along Route 325 North, at 6,000 ft in elevation and 1,305 acres of land (350 of which are water), has a variety of activities for the outdoor enthusiast. During the summer you can go scuba diving, boating, swimming, waterskiing, windsurfing, fishing, camping, hiking, and picnicking. In the winter you can go ice fishing, cross-country skiing, snowmobiling, and ice skating. Rifle Gap is a huge rock window that once inspired the famed installation artist Christo to create his *Valley Curtain* piece. The road wraps around a reservoir before reaching Rifle Falls. | 0050 County Rd. 219 | 970/625–1607 | www.parks.state.co.us/rifle_gap | $4 per vehicle | Daily.

Rifle Mountain Park. In this park, 13 mi north of Rifle and owned by the town of Rifle, you can barbecue or go picnicking and camping. Rifle Mountain itself offers some of the most challenging sport climbing in these parts, perhaps in the country. There are about 200 routes to climb on the mountain, many with exhilarating views. | Rte. 325 | 970/625–2121 | www.rifleco.org | $4 | Daily.

ON THE CALENDAR

AUG.: *The Rifle Rendezvous.* Experience an old-fashioned rendezvous with buckskinners, mountain men, cavalrymen, and Indians in a re-creation of an 1800s rendezvous. Held at the Garfield County Fairgrounds the weekend before Memorial Day. | 970/625–2085 or 800/842–2085.

Dining

Buckaroo's Family Restaurant. American. Family-style restaurant with photographs and maps of Rifle at the turn of both the 19th and 20th centuries. Steaks, chicken-fried steaks, and hearty breakfasts. Salad and homemade soup bar with fresh bread. Full bar. Kids' menu. | 1214 Access Rd. | 970/625–2233 | www.glenwoodguide.com/buckaroos | Breakfast also served | $3–$15 | MC, V.

Burgerworks. American/Casual. Antique Americana decorates this western diner. Specializing in buffalo burgers, hamburgers, and Mexican food. Beer and wine served. | 2178 Railroad Ave. | 970/625–2620 | $5–$9 | MC, V.

Sammy's on Park Avenue. Continental. With wood paneling and plant baskets throughout the dining room accented by a deep green carpet, the peach walls are covered with pictures of Switzerland where Sammy grew up. Known for steaks, seafood, pasta, and veal with a European flair. Full bar. | 412 Park Ave. | 970/625–8008 | Closed Sun. | $6–$28 | AE, D, MC, V.

Lodging

Buckskin Inn. A quiet country inn surrounded by a tree-lined lawn with picnic tables and outdoor grills just west of Rifle. Some rooms are decorated in knotty pine, some in country wallpaper. In-room data ports, some kitchenettes, microwaves, refrigerators, cable TV. Laundry facilities. Pets allowed. | 101 Ray Ave. | 970/625–1741 or 877/282–5754 | fax 970/625–4325 | www.buckskininn.com | 24 rooms | $40–$65 | AE, MC, V.

Coulter Lake Guest Ranch. This family-oriented guest ranch is surrounded by aspen woods, wildflower meadows, and the White River National Forest. It's 21 mi from Rifle, 56 mi from Glenwood Springs. Hiking, horseback riding, volleyball, fishing. Cross-country skiing, snowmobiling. | 80 County Rd. 273, Rifle | 970/625–1473 or 800/858–3046 | fax 970/625–1473 | www.ranchweb.com | 7 cabins | $1,248 per adult per wk, $654 per adult for 3 nights (3–night minimum in summer) | Closed Oct.–mid-Dec., Apr.–May | AP | AE, D, MC, V.

Red River Inn. A simple motel just south of Interstate 70, across the street from McDonald's. Complimentary donuts in the morning, hot beverages throughout the day in the lobby. In-room data ports, some kitchenettes, some microwaves, some refrigerators, cable TV. Some pets allowed. | 718 Taughenbaugh Blvd. | 970/625–3050 or 800/733–3152 | fax 970/625–0848 | www.redriverinnmotel.com | 65 rooms | $40–$85 | AE, D, MC, V.

Rusty Cannon Motel. A clean, basic motel just south of Interstate 70 next to McDonald's. In-room data ports, some refrigerators, cable TV. Pool. Sauna. Laundry facilities. Some pets allowed (fee). | 701 Taughenbaugh Blvd. | 970/625–4004 or 800/341–8000 | fax 970/625–3604 | www.imalodging.com | 88 rooms | $44–$92 | AE, D, MC, V.

ROCKY MOUNTAIN NATIONAL PARK

MAP 6, F2

(Nearby towns also listed: Allenspark, Estes Park, Granby, Grand Lake, Lyons, Nederland)

When Joel Estes built his log cabin on Fish Creek, he couldn't have known that far off in the future all of the vast mountain land to the west of his house would become one of America's most popular tourist destinations (over 3 million visitors annually). Estes is remembered today for the bestowal of his name on the nearby community of Estes Park, and Rocky Mountain National Park is best remembered for the fact that more than 114 peaks within its boundaries reach more than 10,000 ft in elevation.

The park is home to more than 750 species of wildflowers and nearly 300 varieties of birdlife. Elk, beaver, bighorn sheep, and other mammals round out the animal popu-

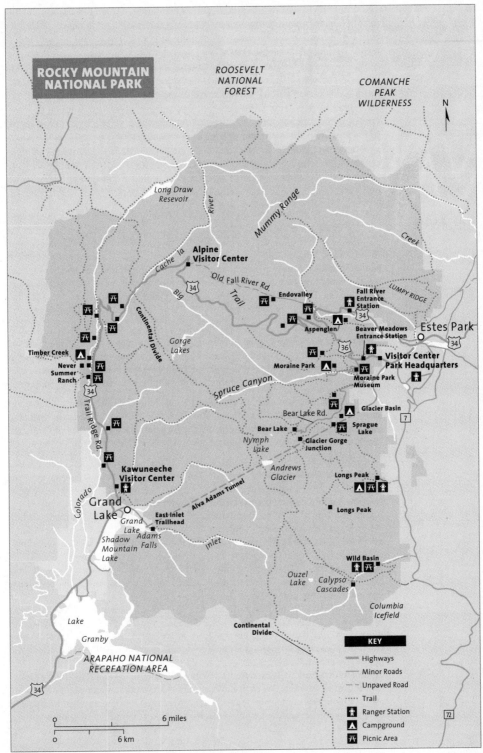

ROCKY MOUNTAIN NATIONAL PARK

ROOSEVELT NATIONAL FOREST

COMANCHE PEAK WILDERNESS

N

Long Draw Reservoir

Mummy Range

Cache la Poudre River

Alpine Visitor Center

Old Fall River Rd.

Trail

Big Thompson River

Endovalley

Fall River Entrance Station

LUMPY RIDGE

Creek

Aspenglen

Beaver Meadows Entrance Station

Estes Park

Gorge Lakes

Continental Divide

Moraine Park

Moraine Park Museum

Visitor Center Park Headquarters

Timber Creek

Never Summer Ranch

Spruce Canyon

Bear Lake Rd.

Glacier Basin

Bear Lake

Nymph Lake

Sprague Lake

Kawuneeche Visitor Center

Glacier Gorge Junction

Andrews Glacier

Alva Adams Tunnel

Longs Peak

Trail Ridge Rd.

Colorado River

Grand Lake

Grand Lake

East Inlet Trailhead

Adams Falls

Longs Peak

Shadow Mountain Lake

Inlet

Ouzel Lake

Calypso Cascades

Wild Basin

Columbia Icefield

Lake Granby

ARAPAHO NATIONAL RECREATION AREA

Continental Divide

KEY

Highways
Minor Roads
Unpaved Road
Trail
Ranger Station
Campground
Picnic Area

0   6 miles

0   6 km

lation. With few developed areas (there are only three paved roads in the park and few historic buildings or other man-made structures), this is a real wilderness area. Despite the summer crowds, you can still find relatively unspoiled and uninhabited wilderness by just getting off the beaten path.

Visitor centers at Park Headquarters, on U.S. 36 at the eastern side of the park, and Kawuneeche, on U.S. 34 north of Grand Lake on the park's southwest side, offer orientation exhibits and movies. You can also visit the Alpine Visitor Center, on Trail Ridge Road; the Lily Lake Visitor Center, off Route 7, at the Longs Peak entrance on the eastern side of the park; and the Sheep Lakes information station, at the far southeast corner of the park, near the Wild Basin entrance.

There is no lodging within Rocky Mountain National Park, but there are many possibilities in the vicinity of both Grand Lake and Estes Park; there is only one place to get food inside the park, the snack bar at the Alpine Visitor Center, but there are many restaurants in and around Grand Lake and Estes Park.

Information: **Superintendent, Rocky Mountain National Park** | Estes Park, 80517-8397 | 970/586–1206 | www.nps.gov/romo.

Attractions

Bear Lake Road. A beautiful 9-mi drive with views of 12,000–14,000-ft elevations including a self-guided nature trail. Offers superlative views of Long's Peak and the glaciers surrounding Bear Lake. The road dead-ends at the lake. The drive takes an hour round-trip. | Off Hwy. 36, near Park Headquarters | 970/586–1206 | Free, park admission $10 per vehicle per wk | Daily.

Beaver Meadows Visitor Center. Houses the information center, publications sales, and illustrated programs. The building was designed by the Frank Lloyd Wright School of Architecture at Taliesin West. | U.S. 36, just inside the eastern entrance to the park | 970/586–1206 | www.nps.gov/romo | Free, park admission $10 per vehicle per wk | Daily 9–5.

Moraine Park Museum. Full of natural history exhibits and other information about Rocky Mountain National Park. You can also get visitor information here, and there is a bookstore. The museum is about 1 mi inside the park from the Beaver Meadows entrance. | Bear Lake Rd. | 970/586–1206 | www.nps.gov/romo | Free, park admission $10 per vehicle per wk | May–Sept., daily 9–5.

Nature Trails and Short Walks. There are numerous possibilities for taking easily accessible walks and hikes in Rocky Mountain National Park. | 970/586–1206 | www.nps.gov/romo | Free, park admission $10 per vehicle per wk | Daily.

Adams Falls Trail. This very short (⅓-mi) trail climbs only 79 ft in elevation to the falls, which is a lovely picnic spot. The walk begins at the East Inlet Trailhead on the western boundary of the park. | Near Grand Lake | 970/586–1206 | www.nps.gov/romo | Free, park admission $10 per vehicle per wk | Daily.

Nymph Lake Trail. This short ½-mi trail leads from Bear Lake to the much smaller Nymph Lake. The elevation gain is only 225 ft. | Bear Lake | 970/586–1206 | www.nps.gov/romo | Free, park admission $10 per vehicle per wk | Daily.

Sprague Lake Nature Trail. A self-guided nature trail that begins at the Sprague Lake Picnic Area on Bear Lake Road and runs around the lake for ½ mi. This trail is easily accessible to those with disabilities; there are picnic tables, livery stables, and rest rooms at the trailhead. | Bear Lake Rd. | 970/586–1206 | www.nps.gov/romo | Free, park admission $10 per vehicle per wk | Daily.

Tundra Nature Trail. This paved trail is a ½-mi walk that teaches about the fragile ecosystem above the tree line. The trailhead is on Trail Ridge Road, approximately 4 mi southeast of the Alpine Visitor Center. | Trail Ridge Rd. | 970/586–1206 | www.nps.gov/romo | Free, park admission $10 per vehicle per wk | Daily.

Never Summer Ranch. This is the site of the Holzworth homestead, which was built at the turn of the 20th century as a cattle ranch and later used as a dude ranch until the 1920s. The ranch has been restored and is now used as an interpretive center. You can take free guided or self-guided tours to view the original lodge, workshop, icehouse, and taxidermy building. It's located off Trail Ridge Road, near the western boundary of the park. | Off Trail Ridge Rd. | 970/586–1206 | www.nps.gov/romo | Free, park admission $10 per vehicle per wk | Mid-June–Labor Day, daily 10–5.

Old Fall River Road. This breathtaking 9-mi, one-way road (uphill) is unpaved and filled with switchbacks. Completed in 1921, it was the first road leading into the high country of Rocky Mountain National Park; it's generally open from July to September. The road leads from Horseshoe Park, a short distance west of the Fall River park entrance, to the Trail Ridge Road, near the Alpine Visitor Center; take the Trail Ridge Road back down. | West of the Fall River entrance | 970/586–1206 | www.nps.gov/romo | Free, park admission $10 per vehicle per wk | Early July–Sept., daily.

Trail Ridge Road. An above-the-timberline road (45 mi) with fantastic scenery follows one once used by the Utes and Arapahos. The drive from the east side of the park to the west is a minimum of two hours. The road opens around Memorial Day and closes in mid-October, when the first heavy snows fall, but you might see snow in July at these elevations. Self-guided tours are available. | U.S. 36 | 970/586–1206 | Free, park admission $10 per vehicle per wk | Late May–mid-Oct., daily.

SIGHTSEEING TOURS/TOUR COMPANIES

Bus Tours. Several companies offer guided bus tours of Rocky Mountain National Park. These tours might leave from Denver, Aurora, Estes Park, or another surrounding community.

Best Mountain Tours. This sightseeing van service conducts tours of Rocky Mountain National Park with eight or more passengers. The individually tailored tours allow you to create the ideal trip, with an informed guide. There are a variety of tours from which to choose (including half-day and full-day); pickups at Denver and Aurora area hotels. | 3003 S. Macon, Aurora | 303/750–5200 | fax 303/750–2949 | www.bestmountaintours.com | $40–$70 | Office hrs daily 7 AM–9 PM; call for tour times.

Estes Park Shuttle and Mountain Tours. This shuttle company also runs tours in the park. Take a more intimate drive on Trail Ridge Road. The tours are generally three hours, but there are a variety of tour types. Three-person minimum. Reservations essential. | 875 Moraine Ave., Estes Park | 970/586–5151 | www.estesparkco.com | $135 (3-passenger minimum), $45 each additional passenger | Memorial Day–Labor Day, daily; call for tour times.

Gray Line Tours. Gray Line offers a 10-hour comprehensive tour of Rocky Mountain National Park. You get to follow Clear Creek stream through a canyon, stop for lunch in Grand Lake, and climb Trail Ridge Road. Tour departs from Cherry Creek Shopping Center, as well as from various Denver hotels. Reservations essential. | 5855 E. 56th. Ave., Commerce City | 303/289–2841 or 800/348–6877 | www.coloradograyline.com | $60 | June–Sept., daily; call for tour times.

Scenic Mountain Tours. Take a seven- to eight-hour sightseeing tour of Rocky Mountain National Park. There are visits to the major sites, a lunch stop, and many photo opportunities. The tour leaves from pickup sites at designated Denver area hotels. Reservations essential. | 973 Vetch Circle, Lafayette | 303/665–7625 | $70 | Office hrs daily 7 AM–10 PM; call for tour times.

Horseback Riding. Within Rocky Mountain National Park, there are two stables where you can rent horses or go on an organized trail ride (near Sprague Lake on Bear Lake Road and in Moraine Park, near the park's east entrance). There are other stables that will take you on organized rides in the surrounding national forest areas.

ROCKY MOUNTAIN
NATIONAL PARK

INTRO
ATTRACTIONS
DINING
LODGING

Glacier Creek Stables. Take a tour of Rocky Mountain National Park as the original settlers would have, on a horse. You can choose from two-hour to eight-hour tours that are led by informed guides. Reservations essential. | Near Sprague Lake | 970/586–3244 | www.sombrero.com | $35–$80 | Office hrs daily 8–4; call for tour times.

Moraine Park Stables. Enjoy the scenery of the park on horseback. Take a two-hour or a four-hour guided tour through the mountains and meadows to see wildlife, lakes, and all of nature's beauty. Let the Old West rider in you emerge. Reservations essential. | Moraine Park | 970/586–2327 | www.sombrero.com | $35–$55 | Office hrs daily 8–4; call for tour times.

Sombrero Stables. You can take in views of Grand Lake and ride trails in Rocky Mountain National Park. Take a breakfast ride, go on a steak fry ride, or let the kids take a half-hour pony ride. There is a tour for everyone. | 304 Portal Rd., Grand Lake | 970/627–3514 | www.sombrero.com | $20–$80; special rates for children | Office hrs daily 8–4; call for tour times.

Sombrero Stables. Sombrero also offers rides on trails on a cattle ranch and trails in the National Forest. Choose from a number of tours, and select a horse that is suitable to your riding ability. The knowledgeable staff will help make your ride memorable. Reservations essential. | 1895 Big Thompson Dr., Estes Park | 970/586–4577 | www.sombrero.com | $20–$150 | Office hours daily 7–4; call for tour times.

ON THE CALENDAR

JULY: *Buffalo Barbecue Weekend.* The festivities include a 5K run and walk, musical entertainment, a parade, fireworks, and barbecued buffalo in the town of Grand Lake in mid-July. | 970/627–3402.

SALIDA

MAP 6, E6

(Nearby towns also listed: Buena Vista, Cañon City, Gunnison)

Salida (population 5,909), 25 mi south of Buena Vista via U.S. 285 and Route 291 in South Central Colorado, is sometimes called the "banana belt" of the state because of its unusually mild climate. The town's proximity to the Arkansas Headwaters State Recreational Area allows visitors to pursue white-water rafting, canoeing, and kayaking on one of America's pristine "wild" rivers.

Information: **Heart of the Rockies Chamber of Commerce** | 406 U.S. 50 W, Salida, 81201 | 719/539–2068 | www.salidacolorado.com.

Attractions

Arkansas Headwaters Recreation Area. A 5,000-acre wilderness area that has deep canyons cut by the infant Arkansas River. Fishing, boating, hiking, horseback riding, and picnicking are available. The Arkansas River here provides some of the nation's finest white water for rafting and kayaking. | Headquarters: 307 W. Sackett St. | 719/539–7289 | www.parks.state.co.us/arkansas | Free | Daily.

Monarch Scenic Tram. Fabulous vistas of the Rockies are seen from the 12,000-ft-high observatory at the end of this tram which runs continuously. The tram starts about 22 mi west of Salida. | U.S. 50 at Monarch Pass | 719/539–4091 | $7 | May–Sept., daily 8–6:30.

Monarch Ski and Snowboard Area. The ski area 18 mi west of Salida includes 1 quad, 4 double chairlifts, 54 runs (the longest is 2 mi), with a vertical drop of 1,160 ft. A cafeteria, restaurant, bar, and nursery are also available. | U.S. 50 at Monarch Pass | 719/539–3573 or 888/996–7669 | fax 719/539–7652 | www.skimonarch.com | Mid-Nov.–mid-Apr., daily 9–4.

Mt. Shavano Fish Hatchery. This is a state-operated hatchery ½ mi west of Salida via Highway 291 that you can visit and tour. | 7725 Hwy. 154 | 719/539–6877 | Free | Daily 7:30–4.

Salida Museum. The museum has Native American, pioneer, mining, mineral, and railroad exhibits. | 406½ W. Rainbow Blvd. | 719/539–2068 | $1 | Late May–early Sept., Mon., Tues., Thurs.–Sat. 9–5.

SIGHTSEEING TOURS/TOUR COMPANIES

Mountain High Rentals. For some serious backcountry exploring, a late-model jeep with a cellular phone can be rented from this company. Experienced staff provide trail maps and suggest drives tailored to your abilities. | 334 E. Hwy. 50 | 719/539–1338 or 800/955–0807 | www.mountainhighrentals.com | $125–$140 per day | Daily.

River Runners Ltd. Some of the best white-water rafting can be experienced on the Arkansas River. There is a variety of trips that can be specifically tailored to you and your experience level. The outfitters offer half-day trips, full-day trips, and multiday trips through Brown's Canyon and Royal Gorge. Fishing and specialty trips are also available. Reservations are necessary. | 11150 U.S. 50 | 719/539–2144 or 800/525–2081 | fax 719/539–6113 | www.riverrunnersltd.com | $35–$86 | D, MC, V | May–Sept.; call for specific trip information.

ON THE CALENDAR

JUNE: *FIBArk Whitewater Festival.* This 26-mi-long kayak race, starting from Riverside Park in downtown Salida, brings experts from all over the world each Father's Day weekend. | 719/539–2068.

JULY: *Chaffee County Fair.* A five-day county fair complete with arts and crafts, food, and agricultural exhibits; held at the Chaffee County Fairgrounds. | 719/539–2068.

JULY: *Salida Art Walk.* Music, art, and fun. Local galleries, craftspeople, and artists display and sell their pieces in stores and galleries in downtown Salida. | 877/772–5432.

NOV.: *Christmas Mountain USA.* To usher in the Christmas holidays, local designers outline a gigantic 700-ft tree on nearby Tenderfoot Mountain and string up nearly 4,000 lights in downtown Salida in late November. | 719/539–2068.

Dining

Antero Grill. Contemporary. Known for its Antero Mixed Game Grill—venison medallions, smoked boar sausage, barbecue buffalo short ribs, sage polenta, braised chard, and smoked onion marmalade. Other popular dishes include the pecan-crusted catfish with green chile cheese grits, calabacitas (summer squash), and crawfish; and the Wrangler's Meatloaf made with green chile, wild mushrooms, and applewood-smoked bacon. Children's menu. | 114770 U.S. 285 | 719/530–0301 | $10–$18 | MC, V.

Country Bounty. American. This country-style restaurant serves the basics: hamburgers, steaks, hot sandwiches, pastas, all in plentiful amounts. The dining room has large picture windows overlooking a perennial flower garden. Aspen trees and quince bushes make up the striking collection of plants. A fireplace and tin-topped tables add to the country feel. Kids' menu. No smoking. | 413 W. Rainbow Blvd. | 719/539–3546 | Breakfast also available | $5–$12 | D, MC, V.

Windmill. Tex-Mex. The dining room is decorated with a variety of old road signs and vintage advertisements. An extensive menu includes such standard favorites as enchiladas, tacos, and chiles rellenos, as well as a variety of American dishes. Salad bar. Kids' menu. | 720 E. U.S. 50 | 719/539–3594 | $6–$15 | AE, D, DC, MC, V.

Lodging

Best Western Colorado Lodge. Right off U.S. 50, this chain motel provides a good base for skiers visiting the nearby Monarch ski area. Complimentary Continental breakfast. Cable TV. Pool. 2 hot tubs, sauna. Laundry facilities. Business services, airport shuttle. | 352 W. Rainbow Blvd. | 719/539–2514 | fax 719/539–4316 | www.bestwestern.com | 35 rooms | $70–$102 | AE, D, DC, MC, V.

Gazebo Country Inn. This B&B, in a 1901 Victorian style home four blocks from the downtown historic district, was built by one of Salida's first railroad families. The rooms are spacious, and some have fireplaces. Relax on one of the porches, sit under the gazebo in the garden, or unwind in the hot tub surrounded by willows. Complimentary breakfast. In-room data ports, no room phones, no TV in rooms, TV in common area. Hot tub. No pets. No smoking. | 507 E. Third St. | 719/539–7806 or 800/565–7806 | www.gazebocountryinn.com | 4 rooms | $85–$90 | AE, MC, V.

River Run Inn. Built in 1892 of Salida brick and once used as the county Poor Farm, this B&B is now the antithesis of its origins. Some of the rooms have a private bath and a footed tub, a mountain view, or a queen-size bed. The Lupine Meadow room is dorm style and accommodates five or more. Along the Arkansas River, on 5 acres of land with fabulous views, 3 mi from downtown. Picnic area, complimentary breakfast. No room phones, no TV in rooms, TV in common area. Pond. Fishing. No kids under 10. No smoking. | 8495 County Rd. 160 | 719/539–3818 or 800/385–6925 | fax 801/659–1878 | www.riverruninn.com | 7 rooms, 1 dorm room | $65–$150 | AE, MC, V.

Travelodge. An economical highway-side motel just west of Salida, with both cabins and rooms. Complimentary Continental breakfast. Some in-room hot tubs. Cable TV. Pool. Hot tub. Business services. Some pets allowed. | 7310 U.S. 550 W | 719/539–2528 or 800/515–6375 | fax 719/539–2528 | www.travelodge.com | 27 rooms (10 with shower only), 3 cottages | $65–$79, $75–$97 cottages | AE, D, DC, MC, V.

Tudor Rose. This stately Tudor building is on 37 mountainous acres. The "Wolf Den," a common area, is casual and rugged, while the living room and dining room are decorated with formal queen Anne furnishings. A large multilevel back deck offers panoramic views. Complimentary breakfast. No TV in rooms, TV in common room. Hot tub. Hiking. No kids under 10. | 6720 County Rd. 104 | 719/539–2002 or 800/379–0889 | fax 719/530–0345 | www.thetudorrose.com | 4 rooms, 2 suites | $60–$90, $110–$145 suites | AE, D, MC, V.

SILVERTON

MAP 6, C7

(Nearby towns also listed: Durango, Ouray)

Situated in the beautiful San Juan Mountains, Silverton's mines produced marketable gold for more than 100 years—from the town's founding in 1874 until 1991. Today, with a population of 515, the town's primary claim to fame is as a tourist attraction where a visitor can discover for himself what it was like to have been a 19th-century prospector in the wilds of Colorado.

Information: **Silverton Chamber of Commerce** | Box 565, Silverton, 81433 | 970/387–5654 or 800/752–4494 | www.silverton.org.

Attractions

Christ of the Mines Shrine. The 12-ton statue is made of Carrera marble. It stands as a tribute to all the people who worked in the mines around Silverton. The monument can be reached on foot by going up 10th Street or by vehicle on Shrine Road. | Anvil Mountain | 970/387–5654 or 800/752–4494 | www.silverton.org | Free | Daily.

Old Hundred Gold Mine Tour. A one-hour guided tour of this underground mine 5 mi east of Silverton via Route 110 offers views of crystal pockets, mining equipment, and artifacts. | Rte. 4A | 970/387–5444 or 800/872–3009 | www.minetour.com | $13 | May–mid-Oct., daily 10–4.

San Juan County Historical Society Museum. Mining and railroad artifacts from Silverton's early days are displayed in the old jail building. | Courthouse Sq | 970/387–5838 | www.silverton.org/attract/sjcm.html | $2.50 | Memorial Day–mid-Sept., daily 9–5; mid-Sept.–mid-Oct., daily 10–3.

ON THE CALENDAR
MAY: *Iron Horse Bicycle Classic.* This race on Highway 550 between bicyclists and the Silverton narrow-gauge train is an exciting spectacle in late May. | 970/387–5654 or 800/752–4494.
JUNE: *Silverton Jubilee Folk Music Festival.* The festivities celebrate American folk music and its musicians at the Kendall Mountain Recreation Area. | 970/387–5654 or 800/752–4494.
JUNE: *Step Back in Time Celebration.* This summer festival takes you back to Silverton's days as a mining town. | 970/387–5522.
AUG.: *Brass Band Festival.* Festivities in Memorial Park abound with music, music, and more music. | 970/387–5654 or 800/752–4494.
AUG.: *Hardrockers Holiday.* This activity allows newcomers and oldtimers alike to test their mining skills at the Kendall Mountain Recreation Area. | 970/387–5654 or 800/752–4494.

Dining
Handlebar's. American. As much a museum as an eatery, this restaurant has mining artifacts, antiques, and animal mounts—including a full-size elk. Baby-back ribs are the specialty, basted with the restaurant's own barbecue sauce (bottled to go). The hearty menu also includes steaks, hamburgers, mashed potatoes, and the like. Live entertainment weekends. | 117 13th St. | 970/387–5395 | Closed Nov.–Apr. | $4–$20 | D, MC, V.

Lodging
Alma House. Victorian furnishings decorate this 1898 mountain inn one block west of the Silverton train depot. Complimentary breakfast. Cable TV, no room phones. Business services. Some pets allowed. No smoking. | 220 E. 10th St. | 970/387–5336 or 800/267–5336 | fax 970/387–5974 | www.subee.com/alma/home.html | 10 rooms (2 with shared bath), 2 suites | $69–$99, $119–$129 suites | Closed Nov.–May | AE, MC, V.

Wingate House Bed & Breakfast. In a fully restored 1886 Victorian home, original art and Civil War photos adorn the walls. The front porch overlooks Kendall Mountain, a "thirteener" (higher than 13,000 ft). Large sunny rooms have down pillows and comforters on the beds. Two blocks from downtown. Complimentary breakfast. Some in-room hot tubs. No room phones, no TV in rooms, TV in common area. Library. Laundry services. No smoking. | 1045 Snowden St. | 970/387–5520 | www.silverton.org/wingate | 5 rooms | $74–$110 | MC, V.

Wyman Hotel and Inn. This wonderful 1902 red-sandstone Victorian, across the street from City Hall downtown, is listed in the National Register of Historic Places. The rooms are all decorated with period antiques, as well as modern conveniences. Complimentary breakfast. Cable TV, in-room VCRs (and movies). Business services. No smoking. | 1371 Greene St. | 970/387–5372 | fax 970/387–5745 | 17 rooms | $90–$175 | Closed Nov.–Dec., Mar.–Apr. | AE, D, MC, V.

SOUTH FORK

MAP 6, D7

(Nearby towns also listed: Lake City, Monte Vista, Pagosa Springs)

You won't find J.R. Ewing at this South Fork, but you will behold some of the most beautiful countryside in Colorado. Perched at 8,200 ft, South Fork, a town of only 661, is practically surrounded by the rugged Rio Grande National Forest, which offers a variety of recreational opportunities, including skiing, hiking, camping, and snowmobiling.

Information: **South Fork Visitors Center** | Box 1030, South Fork 81154 | 719/873–5512 or 800/571–0881 | www.southfork.org.

Attractions

Rio Grande National Forest. Fishing and hunting in season, as well as hiking, boating, and downhill and cross-country skiing are all available in this vast wilderness area. The town of South Fork is bordered by the forest on the north, south, and west approaches. The Scenic Thread Scenic Byway begins in South Fork. | Supervisor: 1803 W. Hwy. 160, Monte Vista | 719/852–5941 | www.fs.fed.us/r2/riogrande | Free | Daily.

Silver Thread Scenic Byway. Brochures for this self-guided driving tour can be obtained at the Silver Thread Interpretive Center. Gain a historical perspective of the South Fork, Creede, and Lake City communities. See some of the area's abandoned mining structures in the mountains. It's 75 mi in length, requiring a driving time of two hours. | Intersection of Hwy. 160 and Hwy. 149 | 719/873–5512 or 800/571–0881 | www.southfork.com | $1 | Road daily; interpretive center, weekdays 9–5.

ON THE CALENDAR

JUNE: *Rio Grande Raft Races.* A 13-mi white-water course that tests the skills of the participants is the featured event at this happening. | 719/658–2663.

JUNE–SEPT.: *Creede Repertory Theater.* Presented here are all types of theater entertainment, including classic and modern musicals and comedies, as well as dramatic works. Buy tickets in advance. Creede is 21 mi northwest of South Fork via Route 149. | 719/658–2541.

JULY: *Logger Days.* Come out and watch the two-day logging competitions held at the South Fork Community Building and Grounds the third weekend in July. | 166 Hwy. 149 | 719/873–5512 or 800/571–0881.

Dining

Hungry Logger. American. There's a rustic, lodge atmosphere at this popular local eatery. Known for steaks and also home-baked pastries. Salad bar. Kids' menu. No smoking. | 00011 Vista St. (U.S. 160) | 719/873–5504 | $4–$15 | AE, D, MC, V.

RockAway Café and Steak House. Steak. After touring the Silver Thread Scenic Byway or spending a day in the forest, come to this popular restaurant that has people coming back for the filet mignon and the rib-eye steak. | 30333 Hwy. 160 | 719/873–5581 | $7–24 | MC, V.

Lodging

South Fork Lodge. This lodge property includes cabins with full kitchens and separate bedrooms. The main lodge has a recreation room with two pianos, one of which is a player piano. There are also 27 RV sites. All of this is located 300 yards from the Hungry Logger restaurant. Kitchenettes, some microwaves, refrigerators, cable TV, TV in common area. Outdoor hot tub. Playground. Laundry facilities. Pets allowed (fee). | 0364 Hwy. 149 | 719/873–5303 or 877/354–2345 | fax 719/873–5305 | 12 cabins | $50–$75 | AE, MC, V.

Wolf Creek Ranch Ski Lodge. This roadside lodge is 18 mi east of the Wolf Creek Ski Area, on the eastern side of Wolf Creek Pass. Some rooms have mountain views. Bar. Some kitchenettes, some microwaves, cable TV. Hot tub. Hiking, fishing. Playground. Business services. Pets allowed. | 31042 U.S. 160 W | 719/873–5371 or 800/522–WOLF | www.wolfcreekco.com/ranch | 8 rooms, 6 cabins | $40–$70, $50–$125 cabins | AE, D, DC, MC, V.

STEAMBOAT SPRINGS

(Nearby towns also listed: Craig, Kremmling)

Steamboat Springs, a town of about 8,700 on the western slope of the Continental Divide in northwestern Colorado, is sometimes called "Ski Town U.S.A." because of the emphasis paid there to the sport. Several national ski-jumping records have been set at Steamboat Springs, and nearly 50 Winter Olympic champions call the area home. Skiing is the town's main employer nowadays. Unlike Aspen and Breckenridge, though, Steamboat Springs was never a mining town; it was established and grew in importance as a ranching and farming community. You'll find historic Victorian buildings, especially fronting Lincoln Avenue, but the result isn't as impressive as in some other Colorado towns since these buildings were built to be functional, rather than ornamental. The town got its name from the more than 100 springs in the immediate vicinity; apparently, they sounded like a steamboat chugging up the nearby Yampa River to the French trappers who first inhabited the area.

Information: **Steamboat Springs Chamber Resort Association** | Box 774408, Steamboat Springs, 80477 | 970/879–0880 or 800/922–2722 | www.steamboat-chamber.com.

Attractions

Bud Werner Memorial Library. This library is dedicated to the three-time Olympic skier Buddy Werner. The Library houses a collection of Werner memorabilia and a western heritage collection that has an array of books and materials that give insight into life in the west, as well as local history. | 1289 Lincoln Ave. | 970/879–0240 | www.steamboatlibrary.org | Free | Mon.–Thurs. 9–8, Fri. 9–6, Sat. 9–5, Sun. noon–5.

Routt National Forest. Winter sports, hiking, fishing, and hunting in season are available in this 1³/₁₀-million-acre wilderness on the north, east, and south sides of Steamboat Springs, along U.S. 40. | 925 Weiss Dr. | 970/879–1870 | www.fs.fed.us/mrnf | Free | Daily.

Skiing. Soon after Norwegian skiing champion Carl Howelsen built the first ski jump in Steamboat Springs in 1914, the roundabout region has been high on the list of favorite skiing sites in the state. Today, the town is among the most popular places in Colorado for skiing and other wintertime activities. While there are many skiing opportunities for novices and even children, the terrain is nearly perfect for intermediates and upper intermediates. The resort is also a popular snowboarding spot.

Howelsen Hill Ski Complex. Howelsen Hill is an international ski-jump complex, with a double chairlift, Pomalift, rope tow, and five jumping hills. | River Rd., off U.S. 40 | 970/879–4300 | Dec.–Mar., daily.

Steamboat Ski Resort. Offers 2 high-speed quads, 7 triple and 7 double chairlifts, and 2 surface tows. There are 113 runs (the longest is 3 mi), and the vertical drop of 3,668 ft. Cross-country skiing is also available. | U.S. 40, 3 mi east of Steamboat Springs | 970/879–6111 | www.steamboat-ski.com | Dec.–Mar., daily.

Steamboat Health and Recreation Assn. Three hot pools with water averaging 103°F, mineral water, saunas, massage, weight room, exercise classes, and tennis courts are featured. On the premises is a Hot Slide Hydrotube, a 350-ft tube slide of hot water. | 136 Lincoln Ave. | 970/879–1828 | $5 | Daily 7 AM–9:45 PM.

Steamboat Lake State Park. Fishing, boating, camping, picnicking, swimming, and water-skiing are featured at the park 26 mi north of Steamboat Springs. | Rte. 129 | 970/879–3922 | www.parks.state.co.us/steamboat | $4 per vehicle | Daily.

Strawberry Park Natural Hot Springs. Mineral springs 7 mi north of Steamboat Springs feed four pools with 160°F water that is cooled to 105°F. Picnicking, camping, and cabins are available. | 44200 Rte. 36 | 970/879–0342 | $5 weekdays, $10 weekends | Daily 10 AM–midnight; last admission is at 10:30 PM.

Tread of Pioneers Museum. Exhibits include Native American, early ranching, and pioneer artifacts and antique skiing equipment. The museum is housed in the old Zimmerman Home. | 800 Oak St., at 8th St. | 970/879–2214 | $5 | May, June, Sept.–Dec., Tues.–Sat. 11–5; July, Aug., daily 11–5; Jan.–Apr., Mon.–Sat. 11–5.

ON THE CALENDAR

FEB.: *Winter Carnival.* This annual event at the Winter Sports Club celebrates wintertime, snow, and skiing. It includes a parade and competitions. | 970/879–0880 or 800/922–2722.

JULY: *Cowboy Roundup Days.* A rodeo, parade, pancakes, fireworks, and plenty of western hospitality dominate this annual event at the Winter Sports Club. | 970/879–0880 or 800/922–2722.

JULY: *Rainbow Weekend.* Arts-and-crafts exhibits highlight the downtown area, while overhead, 50 colorful hot-air balloons fill the sky. Held at River Queen Park, at the base of the ski area | 970/879–0880 or 800/922–2722.

SEPT: *Classic Labor Day Weekend.* This four-day event features activities such as a vintage airplane fly-in, professional bull riding, a free outdoor concert, and more. | 970/879–0880.

Dining

★ **Antares.** Continental. In a 1906 building with a stone fireplace, tin ceiling, and stained-glass windows. Try the tournedos of beef, ahi tuna steak, or Thai chile prawns. Kids' menu. | 57½ 8th St., Steamboat Springs | 970/879–9939 | No lunch | $10–$25 | AE, MC, V.

★ **Harwig's Grill.** Eclectic. This popular eatery next door to L'Apogée, is run by the same team. The menu reflects specialties from around the world: home-cured salmon pastrami, raclette (melted cheese over boiled potatoes), jambalaya, and dim sum. The bar offers 40 wines by the glass, including many lesser-known labels, and you can also order from L'Apogée's wine list. | 911 Lincoln Ave. | 970/879–1980 | No lunch | $8–$18 | AE, MC, V.

L'Apogée. French. Former saddle-repair shop (circa 1886), with rustic furnishings including a bar paneled with wine-crate ends, handmade chairs and tables, and a color scheme that recalls an old tavern. The elegant dining room has stained glass, linen, and crystal tableware. Try oysters Rockefeller, wild mushrooms, or filet mignon. Open-air dining on sidewalk patio. Extensive wine list. Kids' menu. No smoking. | 911 Lincoln Ave. | 970/879–1919 | No lunch | $20–$32 | AE, MC, V.

★ **La Montaña.** Southwestern. The bar in this spot in the Village Center was part of a pavilion at the 1904 St. Louis World's Fair. Photographs of southwestern locales adorn the walls. Try the elk loin with pecans, the fajitas, or the red chile pasta. Kids' menu. | 2500 Village Dr. | 970/879–5800 | No lunch | $10–$29 | AE, D, MC, V.

Ore House at the Pine Grove. Steak. A western-style steak house 1½ mi east of Steamboat Springs where you will find steak, prime rib, and fresh seafood on the menu, as well as open-air dining on a deck with views of Steamboat Ski Mountain. Kids' menu. Salad bar. | 1465 Pine Grove Rd. | 970/879–1190 | No lunch | $12–$30 | AE, D, MC, V.

Riggio's. Italian. This local favorite has an industrial look that has been muted by delicate accents like tapestries and murals. The menu includes such dishes as pollo piccata (strips of chicken sautéed in a white wine and lemon butter sauce with capers) and melanzana (grilled eggplant with spinach, roast peppers, fontina and ricotta cheese, baked to perfection). | 1106 Lincoln Ave. | 970/879–9010 | No lunch | $8–$20 | AE, DC, MC, V.

Steamboat Smokehouse. Barbecue. Try the barbecue or hickory-smoked brisket and turkey. Occasional live music turns this restaurant into a loud, raucous scene. However, it is the food that really keeps people coming back. | 912 Lincoln Ave. | 970/879–5570 | $8–$14 | AE, D, MC, V.

Winona's. American/Casual. Wooden tables, with fresh flowers on every one, make a pleasant setting for good deli sandwiches and pastries. Choose your desserts from the deli cases. Open-air dining on Main Street with shaded tables. Kids' menu. Beer and wine only. No smoking. | 617 Lincoln Ave. | 970/879–2483 | Breakfast also available; no dinner | $6–$10 | MC, V.

Lodging

Alpiner Lodge. An economical motel 3 mi west of the ski slopes. In-room data ports, some microwaves, cable TV. Business services. Pets allowed. | 424 Lincoln Ave. | 970/879–1430 or 800/538–7519 | fax 970/879–0054 | www.steamboat-lodging.com/alpiner_ph2.html | 33 rooms | $70–$100 | AE, D, DC, MC, V.

Best Western Ptarmigan Inn. Many rooms at this ski-in, ski-out property have balconies that offer great views of Mt. Wernery. Restaurant, bar, room service. No air-conditioning in some rooms, in-room data ports, refrigerators, cable TV. Pool. Hot tub, sauna. Laundry facilities. Business services. Pets allowed (fee). | 2304 Apres Ski Way | 970/879–1730 or 800/538–7519 | fax 970/879–6044 | www.bestwestern.com | 77 rooms | $179–$209 | Closed early Apr.–late May | AE, D, DC, MC, V.

Fairfield Inn & Suites by Marriott. The rooms and suites at this mid-priced hotel 3 mi from downtown Steamboat Springs are affordable and well maintained. Some of the suites have fireplaces and hot tubs. Complimentary Continental breakfast. In-room data ports, some microwaves, some refrigerators, some in-room hot tubs, cable TV, Pool. Hot tub. Gym. Laundry facilities. Free parking. No pets. | 3200 S. Lincoln Ave. | 970/870–9000 or 800/228–2800 | fax 970/870–9191 | www.cha-colorado.com | 65 rooms | $119–$149 | AE, D, DC, MC, V.

Glen Eden Resort. A short drive (18 mi) north of Steamboat Springs, this mountain resort is designed for families and longer stays. Each cottage has a private porch. Bar, dining room, picnic area. Kitchenettes, microwaves, cable TV, some in-room VCRs (and movies). Pool. Hot tub. Tennis. Bicycles. Cross-country skiing. Playground. Laundry facilities. Business services. | 54737 County Rd. 129 | 970/879–3907 or 800/882–0854 | fax 970/870–0858 | www.glenedenresort.com | 28 cottages | $95–$165 | AE, D, MC, V.

★ **Harbor Hotel and Condominiums.** This completely refurbished 1940s hotel is in the middle of Steamboat's historic district, and filled with period artifacts, such as the old switchboard. Each room is individually decorated with antique furnishings and most have views of the surrounding mountains. The property also runs an adjacent motel and condo complex. Restaurant, bar. In-room data ports, some kitchenettes, some microwaves, some refrigerators, cable TV. Hot tub, sauna, steam room. Laundry facilities. Pets allowed (fee). | 703 Lincoln Ave. | 970/879–1522 or 800/543–8888 | fax 970/543–8888 | 113 rooms | $100–$200 | AE, D, DC, MC, V.

Holiday Inn. This chain motel can be found just southeast of the town of Steamboat Springs. It offers many amenities and facilities for skiers. Restaurant, bar, room service. In-room data ports, some microwaves, some refrigerators, cable TV. Pool, wading pool. Hot tub. Gym. Video games. Laundry facilities. Business services. Some pets allowed (fee). | 3190 S. Lincoln Ave. | 970/879–2250 or 800/654–3944 | fax 970/879–0251 | www.holiday-inn.com | 82 rooms | $99–$159 | AE, D, DC, MC, V.

★ **Home Ranch.** There is a fieldstone fireplace in the living room, and each cottage has an outdoor hot tub at this ranch resort 20 mi north of Steamboat Springs. You'll also find a petting zoo for children, and the activities program includes trips to the rodeo and cookouts weekly in summer. Dining room. Refrigerators, no room phones, no TV. Pool. Hot tub, sauna. Hiking, horseback riding, fishing. Cross-country skiing. Library. Children's programs (ages 6–16), playground. Business services, airport shuttle. | 54880 Hwy. 129 | 970/879–1780 | fax 970/879–1795 | www.homeranch.com | 8 cottages, 6 lodge rooms | $3,500–$4,600 per person per wk (1–wk minimum stay) | Closed Oct.–Dec., Apr., May | AP | AE, MC, V.

Rabbit Ears Motel. The playful pink neon bunny sign has been a local landmark since 1952. It is across the street from the hot springs, the town bus stops outside to go to the ski areas, and it is near the downtown shops, bars, and restaurants. All the rooms are equipped with coffeemakers; most have balconies and views of the Yampa River. Complimentary Continental breakfast. In-room data ports, some microwaves, refrigerators, cable TV. Laundry facilities. | 201 Lincoln Ave. | 970/879–1150 or 800/828–7702 | fax 970/870–0483 | www.rabbitearsmotel.com | 65 rooms | $79–$135 | AE, D, DC, MC, V.

Ranch at Steamboat Springs. Situated on a quiet hill overlooking the ski area, this 35-acre deluxe condominium resort offers moderate prices and spectacular views. Each room has a full kitchen and a private balcony. Picnic area. No air-conditioning, in-room data ports, kitchenettes, microwaves, cable TV, in-room VCRs (and movies). Pool. Hot tub, sauna. Tennis. Gym. Children's programs (ages 3–13). Laundry facilities. Business services. | 1 Ranch Rd. | 970/879–3000 or 800/525–2002 | fax 970/879–5409 | www.ranch-steamboat.com | 88 1- to 4-bedroom condos | $260–$285 1- to 2–bedrooms, $375–$450 3- to 4–bedrooms | AE, D, MC, V.

Scandinavian Lodge. You can ski-in and ski-out at this lodge. The rooms on the lower level have views of the valley, and other rooms have views of the woods. In-room data ports, kitchenettes, microwaves, refrigerators, cable TV, in-room VCRs. Pool. Hot tub, sauna. Laundry facilities. Pets allowed (fee). No smoking. | 2883 Burgess Creek Rd. | 970/879–0517 | fax 970/879–0943 | www.steamboat-springs.com | 21 rooms | $89–$699 | AE, D, MC, V.

Sheraton Steamboat Resort. This ski-in, ski-out resort offers a multitude of recreational opportunities in both winter and summer. The rooms' private patios offer great mountain views. Restaurant, bar, picnic area, room service. Some kitchenettes, some microwaves, refrigerators, cable TV. Pool. Hot tub. Gym. Cross-country skiing, downhill skiing. Shops. Video games. Laundry facilities. Business services. | 2200 Village Inn Ct. | 970/879–2220 or 800/848–8878 | fax 970/879–4988 | www.steamboat-sheraton.com | 299 rooms, 3 suites, 23 condos | $295–$340; $510–$1,079 suites; $1,065–$1,200 2–bedroom apartments, $1,275–$1,500 3–bedroom apartments, $1,485–$1,800 4–bedroom apartments | Closed mid-Apr.–mid-May, mid-Oct.–mid-Nov. | AE, D, DC, MC, V.

Sky Valley. This ski lodge is tucked in a valley overlooking Steamboat Springs. Decorated with a floral motif and country charm, exposed pole beams and a moss rock fireplace adorn the lobby. Bar, dining room, complimentary Continental breakfast. No air-conditioning, in-room data ports, cable TV, some in-room VCRs. Hot tub, sauna. Business services. No smoking. | 31490 E. U.S. 40 | 970/879–7749 or 800/499–4759 | fax 970/879–7752 | www.steamboat-lodging.com | 24 rooms | $100–$170 | AE, D, DC, MC, V.

Steamboat Bed and Breakfast. A former church, this blue-and-cream Victorian still has its large arched doorway and stained-glass windows. Rooms have lace curtains and floral wallpaper and are filled with potted geraniums and period antiques. Complimentary breakfast. No TV in rooms, TV and VCR in common area. Hot tub. | 442 Pine St. | 970/879–5724 | www.steamboatb-b.com | 7 rooms | $119–$199 | AE, D, MC, V.

★ **Vista Verde Guest Ranch.** This luxurious guest ranch sits on 540 acres and offers woodstoves and patios in each cabin. Backpacking, gold-panning, and guided rock climbing expeditions can be arranged, as well as seasonal hot-air balloon rides, dogsledding trips, hayrides, and cattle drives. Dining room. No air-conditioning, refrigerators. Lake. Massage. Gym, hiking, fishing, bicycles. Cross-country skiing, sleigh rides, tobogganing. Children's programs (ages 5–17), playground. Laundry service. Business services, airport shuttle. | 31100 Seedhouse Rd. | 970/879–3858 or 800/526–7433 | fax 970/879–1413 | www.vistaverde.com | 8 cabins, 3 rooms in lodge | $1,850–$2,000 per person per wk (1–wk minimum stay) | Closed Apr. and Nov. | AP | No credit cards.

STERLING

(Nearby town also listed: Fort Morgan)

The peaceful, prosperous town of Sterling (population 11,424), on the Great Plains in the northeastern part of Colorado, is noted for the numerous tree carvings and sculptures found within its limits. In fact, it is sometimes called, "The City of Living Trees," as a tribute to Brad Rhea, a local artisan who carved many of the trees. It's a town of graceful whitewashed houses with porch swings and shady trees that fringe neighborhood streets.

Information: Logan County Chamber of Commerce | 109 N. Front St., Sterling, 80751 | 970/522–5070 or 800/544–8609 | www.logancountychamber.com.

Attractions

Julesburg. Julesburg is in the extreme northeastern corner of Colorado, about 60 mi east of Sterling via Interstate 76, astride the South Platte River as the stream is about to cross the border into Nebraska. A 14-year-old Buffalo Bill Cody signed on with the Pony Express at nearby Fort Sedgwick. Mark Twain once called Julesburg the "wickedest city in the West," but today the town's economy gravitates around agriculture. | Julesburg Chamber of Commerce, 114 E. First St. | 970/474–3504 | Free | Daily.

Outdoor Sculptures. Throughout Sterling, you can't help but notice the myriad trees that have been carved and sculpted: towering giraffes, festive clowns, minutemen. The town has 16 unique works sculpted by a local artisan. Obtain a map from the Chamber of Commerce to locate these examples. | Chamber of Commerce, 109 N. Front St. | 970/522–5070 or 800/544–8609 | Free | Daily.

Overland Trail Museum. This very attractive museum documents Native American and early pioneer life and has a collection of agricultural artifacts. The local history of the area is highlighted. A park and picnic area are on the grounds. | 21053 County Rd. 26 | 970/522–3895 | Free | Apr.–Oct., daily 9–5, Sun. 1–5; Nov.–Mar., Tues.–Sat. 10–4.

ON THE CALENDAR

AUG: *Logan County Fair.* This five-day summer event at the Logan County Fairgrounds has a rodeo, a tractor pull, a demolition derby, 4-H exhibits, food vendors, and two evening concerts. | 970/522–0888.

Dining

Fergie's West Inn Pub. Pizza. This small, simple restaurant-bar serves pizza and hot wings. | 324 W. Main St. | 970/522–4220 | Closed Sun. | $3–$7 | MC, V.

River City Grill. American/Casual. This restaurant on Main Street has a dish for everyone. You can enjoy the rib-eye or porterhouse steaks, the roast chicken dish, the fajitas, or a hearty salad. Dine on the side patio among decorative topiaries. | 1116 W. Main | 970/521–7648 | $6–$19 | AE, MC, V.

T.J. Bummer's. American. A rustic dining room filled with antiques 2 mi north of Sterling. On the menu: prime rib, barbecue ribs. Guitarist Friday–Sunday. Kids' menu. No smoking. | 203 Broadway (Hwy. 6) | 970/522–8397 | Breakfast also available | $6–$15 | AE, D, MC, V.

Lodging

Best Western Sundowner. This chain motel is immediately off Interstate 76, across the South Platte River from Sterling. Picnic area, complimentary Continental breakfast. In-room data ports, cable TV. Pool. Hot tub. Gym. Laundry facilities. Business services. Pets allowed. | 125 Overland Trail St. | 970/522–6265 or 800/848–4060 | fax 970/522–6265 | www.bestwestern.com | 30 rooms | $74–$94 | AE, D, DC, MC, V.

Colonial Motel. This quiet roadside motel sits four blocks west of downtown Sterling. Some microwaves, some refrigerators, cable TV. Pets allowed. | 915 S. Division Ave. | 970/522–3382 or 888/522–2901 | fax 888/522–2901 | 14 rooms | $32–$44 | AE, D, MC, V.

Crest Motel. You'll receive friendly, thoughtful treatment at this small, inexpensive motel. The rooms are simple and have full-size beds. Microwaves, refrigerators, cable TV. Laundry facilities. Pets allowed. | 516 Division Ave. | 970/522–3753 | 8 rooms | $25–$35 | AE, D, DC, MC, V.

Elk Echo Ranch. This log B & B sits on a 2,000- acre elk ranch about 25 mi west of Sterling. Homemade pie and ranch tours are complimentary to the guests. Take Hwy. 14 to County Rd. 15. Complimentary breakfast. No room phones, no TV. No smoking. | 47490 W. County Rd. 155, Stoneham | 970/735–2426 | fax 970/735–2427 | www.elkecho.com | 4 rooms | $99 | MC, V.

Oakwood Inn. This small motel has clean, quiet rooms that have oak furnishings and queen or full-size beds. It is in a quiet area of town, three blocks from downtown Sterling. Some kitchenettes, microwaves, refrigerators, cable TV. Pets allowed (fee). | 810 S. Division Ave. | 970/522–1416 | fax 970/521–0759 | 15 rooms | $40–$50 | AE, D, DC, MC, V.

Ramada Inn. Immediately next to Interstate 76, this mid-priced chain motel offers basic amenities. Restaurant, bar. Cable TV. Pool. Hot tub. Gym. Video games. Business services. Some pets allowed. | 22246 E. Hwy. 6 | 970/522–2625 or 888/298–2054 | fax 970/522–1321 | www.ramada.com | 102 rooms | $60–$81 | AE, D, DC, MC, V.

TELLURIDE

MAP 6, C7

(Nearby towns also listed: Dolores, Norwood, Ouray, Silverton)

Telluride (population 1,958) is one of Colorado's best-kept secrets. Remote in the midst of Uncompahgre National Forest at an altitude of 8,800 ft, the onetime boomtown has preserved its late 1800s image, thereby providing the visitor with a look at what it was like to live in the wilds of Colorado in the 19th century. Once so inaccessible that it was a favorite hideout for desperadoes (including Butch Cassidy), the rough terrain now attracts mobs of snowboarders, mountain bikers, and freewheeling four-wheelers. Even skiers tend to be hardier souls since the slopes here are challenging, though there are plenty of slopes for beginners—just not much for intermediates.

Information: **Telluride Visitor Services** | 700 W. Colorado Ave., Telluride, 81435 | 970/728–4431 or 888/783–0257 | www.gotelluride.org.

Attractions

Bear Creek Trail. A 2-mi canyon walk with a great view of a lovely waterfall is featured. | South end of Pine St. | 970/728–4431 or 888/783–0257 | Free | May–Oct., daily.

Bridal Veil Falls. This is the highest free-falling waterfall in Colorado, located 2½ mi east of Telluride. | Rte. 145 | 970/728–4431 or 888/783–0257 | Free | Daily.

Sheridan Opera House. Listed on the National Register of Historic Places, this 1913 former vaudeville house is now home to the Sheridan Arts Foundation. Its 240-seat theater is a popular venue for visiting musicians and also theater productions, including those of the local Telluride Repertory Theatre Company. | 110 N. Oak St., | 970/728–6363 | fax 970/728–6966 | www.sheridanoperahouse.com | Free; performance costs vary | Daily 9–5; call for performance schedules.

Telluride Historical Museum. After four years of restoration work, this historical museum (formerly the San Miguel County Historical Society) reopened in spring 2000, telling the story of Telluride and the mining history of the region. It's housed in the old Miner's Hospital Building. | 317 N. Fir St. | 970/728–3344 | fax 970/728–6757 | www.telluridemuseum.com | $5, free after 6 Wed. | Tues.–Sun. 10–6 (Wed. until 9).

Telluride Ski Resort. This can be one of Colorado's toughest ski areas, and the element of danger has drawn extreme skiers, but you'll also find one of the best beginner areas around here. The mountain is broken into three pretty distinct areas: the mountain's front face, which is good for experts and hot-shots; a mid-area directly above the ski village, which is good for intermediates; and on the north side, a marvelous novice area. Snowboarders have access to the entire mountain and all its runs. This resort has 66 runs (the longest 2.85 mi) with a vertical drop of 3,522 ft. There are gondola, two high-speed quads, one gondola, two triples, five doubles, one Pomalift, and one Magic Carpet lift. You'll also find a health club and sleighing. | 565 Mountain Village Rd., Box 11155, | 970/728–6900 | fax 970/728–6228 | www.telski.com | Thanksgiving–early Apr.

ON THE CALENDAR
MAY: *Mountain Film Festival.* Picnics, photography exhibits, and symposiums bring together filmmakers from all over America each Memorial Day weekend. | 888/783–0264.

JUNE: *Balloon Rally.* Scores of hot-air balloons are on display. | 970/728–4431 or 888/783–0257.

JUNE: *Bluegrass Festival.* The event in Town Park has folk, country, and bluegrass musicians from across the nation. | 888/783–0264.

AUG.: *Chamber Music Festival.* Chamber music is performed indoors at the historic Sheridan Opera House or outside in Town Park. | 888/783–0264.

AUG.: *Jazz Celebration.* Jazz musicians gather to put on an outstanding performance in Town Park. | 888/783–0264.

AUG.: *Telluride Airmen's Rendezvous and Hang Gliding Festival.* Pilots from around the world attend this event on Gold Hill at the Telluride Ski Mountain. Hosts the World Aerobatic Championships. | 888/783–0264.

AUG: *Mushroom Festival.* This four-day summer event honors the fungi that everyone knows and loves. Primary location of activities is the Telluride Middle/High School. | 303/296–9359.

Dining
★ **Campagna.** Italian. Be transported to a Tuscan farmhouse with its open kitchen, oak and terra-cotta floors, and vintage photos of the Italian countryside. Some of the dining possibilities include the *Tortelli con burro e salvia* (handmade Tuscan cheese ravioli with butter and sage), wild mushrooms (porcini or Portobello), and wild boar chops. | 435 W. Pacifica Ave. | 970/728–6190 | Reservations essential | No lunch | $16–$33 | MC, V.

Cosmopolitan. Contemporary. Known as the "Cosmo," this elegant restaurant overlooks the slopes. The culinary creations include coriander-crusted tuna with mango, fillet with horseradish mashed potatoes, barbecue salmon with potatoes, and spinach ravioli in a corn broth. | 300 W. San Juan Ave. | 970/728–1292 | Reservations essential | No lunch | $20–$30 | AE, MC, V.

Fat Alley's BBQ. Barbecue. This popular spot has family-style tables and benches. The specialties include mouthwatering beef ribs, barbecue pork ribs, and sandwiches. The side dishes include sweet potato fries, snap-pea and feta salad, and coleslaw. | 122 S. Oak | 970/728–3985 | $6–$16 | AE, MC, V.

Floradora. Southwestern. Named for two turn-of-the-20th-century ladies of the evening, this rustic restaurant is decorated with pennants donated by patrons over the years. Try the chipotle teriyaki, New York strip steak, or the avocado- and spinach-stuffed trout. Kids' menu. No smoking. | 103 W. Colorado Ave. | 970/728–3888 | $7–$19 | AE, D, MC, V.

★ **La Marmotte.** French. This bistro seems to be transplanted from Provence, with its lace curtains and exposed brick walls. The specials include a grilled salmon with citrus risotto and the roasted loin of venison in a hazelnut wine sauce. | 150 W. San Juan Ave. | 970/728–6232 | Reservations essential | No lunch | $35–$45 | AE, D, MC, V.

Leimgruber's Bierstube. German. This restaurant offers a casual, traditionally German setting. Try Wiener schnitzel, bratwurst, or Jäegerschnitzel. Open-air dining on covered patio with view of mountains. No smoking. | 573 W. Pacific Ave. | 970/728–4663 | $8–$20 | AE, MC, V.

★ **The PowderHouse.** Italian. Wild game from around the area is incorporated into the best dishes here. Try pheasant ravioli, smoked buffalo sausage, stuffed quail, or marinated elk. | 226 W. Colorado Ave. | 970/728–3622 | $12–$30 | AE, MC, V.

Roma Bar and Café. Italian. In operation since 1897, this restaurant has had quite a history. The 1860 Brunswick bar with 12-ft mirrors has seen everything from cowboys to flappers brewing rotgut whisky during Prohibition. Try the grilled salmon in a white wine sauce over risotto. | 133 E. Colorado Ave. | 970/728–3669 | $10–$21 | AE, MC, V.

South Park Café. Contemporary. Try the Char Siu barbecue duckling or the crab-crusted catch of the day in a mango relish with a Thai curry sauce. The landscape photos that adorn the walls are for sale at this restaurant. | 300 W. Colorado Ave. | 970/728–5335 | $13–$24 | AE, MC, V.

221 South Oak Bistro. Contemporary. The blond-wood bar and the soft music contribute to a pleasant dining experience. Try the sea scallops with cauliflower mousse or the Mediterranean striped bass with saffron pasta. | 221 S. Oak St. | 970/728–3622 | $18–$30 | MC, V.

Lodging

Bear Creek Bed & Breakfast. This European-style B&B has a fireplace in the lobby and is in the heart of Telluride. Some rooms have a "wall of windows" with breathtaking mountain views, others have balconies and skylights. The rooftop garden has a spectacular 360-degree view. Complimentary breakfast. In room-data ports, cable TV, in-room VCRs. Hot tub, sauna, steam room. No kids under 12. No smoking. | 221 E. Colorado Ave. | 970/728–6681 | fax 970/728–3636 | www.bearcreektelluride.com | 9 rooms | $147–$245 | MC, V.

Alpine Inn. Built in 1903, this Victorian bed-and-breakfast is within walking distance of the ski gondola and downtown Telluride. Each room is individually decorated with antiques; there are two massage rooms. Complimentary breakfast. Cable TV. Hot tub, massage. No kids under 10. No smoking. | 440 W. Colorado Ave. | 970/728–6282 or 800/707–3344 | fax 970/728–3424 | www.alpineinn.com | 5 rooms, 1 suite | $135–$195, $170–$235 suite | D, MC, V.

Camel's Garden Hotel. You can ski-in, ski-out to the Oak Street lift and gondola from these rooms and condominiums. The spacious rooms have marble bathrooms with oversize tubs, gas fireplaces, CD players, and balconies. Restaurant, bar, complimentary Continental breakfast. In-room data ports, some kitchenettes, some minibars, some refrigerators, some in-room hot tubs, cable TV, in-rooms VCRs. Hot tub, steam room. Laundry service. No smoking. | 250 W. San Juan Ave. | 970/728–9300 or 888/772–2635 | fax 970/728–0433 | www.camels-garden.com | 30 rooms, 6 condos | $230–$375 rooms, $485–$905 condos | AE, D, DC, MC, V.

Franklin Manor. This luxurious B&B, named after the late artist Richard Franklin, has an art gallery with several of the artist's neoclassical and Renaissance-style works. The intimate setting has afternoon wine tastings, comfortable rooms furnished with iron beds and antiques, and private balconies with magnificent views. Some rooms have fireplaces. Great for romantic getaways. Complimentary breakfast. Some in-room hot tubs, cable TV, some room phones, no TV in some rooms. Outdoor hot tub. No kids under 10. No smoking. | 627 W. Colorado Ave. | 970/728–4241 or 888/728–351 | fax 970/728–9668 | www.franklin-manor.com | 5 rooms | $125–$310 | AE, MC, V.

Ice House Lodge. Situated 50 yards from Telluride's ski slopes, this modern lodge is centered around a mezzanine with a television, library, and fireplace. All rooms have balconies and are decorated with a southwestern motif. Complimentary Continental breakfast.

Minibars, cable TV, some in-room VCRs. Pool. Hot tub, steam room. Business services. | 310 S. Fir St. | 970/728–6300 or 800/544–3436 | fax 970/728–6358 | www.icehouselodge.com | 42 rooms, 7 suites | $175–$250, $250–$335 suites | AE, D, DC, MC, V.

Inn at Lost Creek. This elegant inn is right next to the lifts and trails, so you can ski in, ski out of your room or suite. The lobby has a cozy fireplace and timbered beams. Each uniquely designed room has a CD player, terry-cloth robes and slippers, a marble bath, a steam shower, a kitchen, and a fireplace. Most of the rooms have balconies. Restaurant, bar. In-room data ports, in-room safes, kitchenettes, microwaves, refrigerators, in-room hot tubs, cable TV, in-room VCRs (and movies). 2 hot tubs, massage. Gym. Laundry facilities. No smoking. | 119 Lost Creek La. | 970/728–5678 or 888/601–5678 | fax 970/728–7910 | www.innat-lostcreek.com | 32 rooms | $225–$1,095 | AE, D, DC, MC, V.

Johnstone. A former rooming house for miners, the rooms in this B&B are furnished with antique iron or brass beds and other antiques, and all have private answering machines. Baths are marble and brass. Complimentary breakfast. Hot tub. No kids under 9. No smoking. | 403 W. Colorado Ave. | 970/728–3316 or 800/752–1901 | fax 970/728–0724 | www.johnstoneinn.com | 8 rooms (with showers only) | $80–$125 | Closed mid-Apr.–late May, mid-Oct.–late Nov. | AE, D, MC, V.

Manitou Hotel. In downtown Telluride, this inn was built in 1972 and has many antiques. Each room sports a unique western theme, including mining and cowboys. Complimentary Continental breakfast. No air-conditioning, refrigerators, cable TV. Hot tub. | 666 W. Colorado Ave. | 970/728–4011 | fax 970/728–6160 | 12 rooms | $145–$170 | AE, D, DC, MC, V.

New Sheridan Hotel. The only hotel on Telluride's Main Street on the National Register of Historic Places is definitively Victorian. The rooms are decorated in period style, but they've been discreetly updated. Restaurant, bar, complimentary breakfast. In-room data ports, some in-room hot tubs, cable TV. Hot tub. Gym. Video games. Business services. No smoking. | 231 W. Colorado Ave. | 970/728–4351 or 800/200–1891 | fax 970/728–5024 | www.new-sheridan.com | 18 rooms (8 with shared bath), 8 suites, 6 condos | $100–$180, $180 suites, $220 condos | Closed mid-Apr.–mid-May, late Oct.–mid-Nov. | AE, DC, MC, V.

Wyndham Peaks Resort and Golden Door Spa. In Telluride Mountain Village, this ski-in, ski-out property offers a wide variety of luxury accommodations. Some rooms have balconies with a view of either the village or the Wilson Mountain Range. This resort also has the only golf course in Telluride. Restaurant, bar, room service. In-room data ports, minibars, some microwaves, refrigerators, cable TV, in-room VCRs (and movies). 2 pools (1 indoor-outdoor). Hot tub. Driving range, 18-hole golf course, putting green, tennis. Gym, hiking. Children's programs (ages 8 weeks–12 years). Business services, airport shuttle, parking (fee). Some pets allowed. | 136 Country Club Dr. | 970/728–6800 or 800/789–2220 | fax 970/728–6175 | www.thepeaksresort.com | 174 rooms, 28 suites | $385–$435, $685–$785 suites | AE, DC, MC, V.

Pennington's Mountain Village Inn. When you look out the windows here, you see the mountains off beyond the expanse of the Wyndham Resort's golf course. The huge, luxurious rooms have private decks, handcrafted furniture, and concierge service. Complimentary breakfast. No air-conditioning, minibars, cable TV. Hot tub, steam room. Library. Laundry facilities. Business services. No smoking. | 100 Pennington Ct. | 970/728–5337 or 800/543–1437 | fax 970/728–5338 | www.telluridemm.com/penn.html | 12 rooms | $185–$200 | Closed 3 wks in early Nov., 3 wks in May | AE, MC, V.

★ **San Sophia Bed and Breakfast.** Located just four blocks from Colorado Avenue, this modern inn with large, comfortable rooms features an observatory where you have a great view of the San Juan Mountains, as well as the town of Telluride. Complimentary breakfast. In-room data ports, cable TV, in-room VCRs (and movies). Hot tub. Business services. No smoking. | 330 W. Pacific Ave., at Aspen St. | 970/728–3001 or 800/537–4781 | fax 970/728–6226 | www.sansophia.com | 16 rooms | $145–$200 | Closed Apr., Nov. | AE, MC, V.

Skyline Guest Ranch. This guest ranch 8 mi south of Telluride originally served as a base camp for the Telluride Mountaineering School. Family owned, its secluded mountain

(9,600-ft elevation) location provides easy access to the town of Telluride. The simple cabins are cozy. Complimentary breakfast, dining room. Lake. Hot tub. Hiking, horseback riding, fishing, bicycles. Cross-country skiing. | 7214 Hwy. 145 | 970/728–3757 or 888/754–1126 | fax 970/728–6728 | www.ranchweb.com/skyline | 10 rooms, 6 cottages | Dec.–Apr.: $135, $225 cabins; June–Oct.: $1,400 per person per wk (1–wk minimum stay in summer) | Closed mid-Apr.–early June, Oct.–mid-Dec. | AP | AE, MC, V.

Victorian Inn. Located just one block from both Main Street and the gondola, this property has modern rooms with elegant Victorian common areas. Complimentary Continental breakfast. No air-conditioning, some kitchenettes, refrigerators, cable TV. Hot tub, sauna. No smoking. | 401 W. Pacific | 970/728–6601 | fax 970/728–3233 | www.tellurideinn.com | 31 rooms | $63–$230 | AE, D, DC, MC, V.

TRINIDAD

MAP 6, G8

(Nearby towns also listed: Cuchara, La Junta, Walsenburg)

Located on the historic Santa Fe Trail at the northern approach to Raton Pass, Trinidad was once the home of famed mountain man "Uncle Dick" Wootton, who built the first road over the pass into New Mexico. Today, the town of 9,800 is the hub of the widespread farming and ranching communities in the neighborhood.

Information: Trinidad–Las Animas County Chamber of Commerce | 309 Nevada Ave., Trinidad, 81082 | 719/846–9285 | www.trinidadco.com.

Attractions

A.R. Mitchell Memorial Museum of Western Art. The museum has western art by several eminent American painters, as well as Indian and pioneer artifacts. Hispanic folk art is also included. | 150 E. Main St. | 719/846–4224 | $2 | Apr.–Sept., Mon.–Sat. 10–4, or by appointment.

Raton Pass. Here, Interstate 25 crosses the high mountain pass from Colorado into New Mexico. Turnoffs along the way allow you to view some magnificent scenery. | I–25 between Trinidad and Raton | Free | Daily.

Trinidad History Museum. The museum complex, administered by the Colorado Historical Society, consists of the Baca House (1870), a nine-room, two-story adobe owned by a noted Hispanic sheep rancher; the Santa Fe Trail Museum; and the Bloom Mansion (1882), built by rancher Frank Bloom. | 300 E. Main St. | 719/846–7217 | $5 | May–Sept., daily 10–4; Oct.–Apr., by appointment only.

Trinidad Lake State Park. A 2,300-acre park with a 900-acre lake, 3 mi west of Trinidad. Fishing, waterskiing, mountain biking, camping, nature trails, a playground, and picnicking are all available. | Hwy. 12 | 719/846–6951 | www.parks.state.co.us/trinidad | $4 per vehicle | Daily.

ON THE CALENDAR
JUNE: *Santa Fe Trail Festival.* This celebration honors the history of the Santa Fe Trail that once ran through the town of Trinidad. | 719/846–9285.

Dining
Chef Liu's. Chinese. A popular local restaurant with traditional Asian style. | 1423 Country Club Dr. | 719/846–3333 | Closed Mon. late Nov.–Mar. | $5–$17 | AE, D, MC, V.

Main Street Bakery. American/Casual. This popular café is in a century-old building. The locals come for the fresh bread, the desserts, the potpie, and the roast-beef dinners. Among the other items on the menu are a Branding Iron Sandwich (roast beef and melted brie on focaccia) and the Michiganer (turkey breast salad with dried cherries). | 121 E. Main St. | 719/846–8779 | No dinner Sun.–Wed. | $6–$13 | AE, MC, V.

Nana and Nano Monteleone's Deli and Pasta House. Italian. Red lamps on every table and authentic photos of the owner's parents and grandparents on the walls add to the family-style, homey feeling. Known for fettuccine Alfredo, gnocchi Bolognese, and wonderful gourmet sandwiches. No alcohol. Kids' menu | 418 E. Main St. | 719/846–2696 | Closed Sun., Mon. | $7–$10 | AE, D, MC, V.

Lodging

Best Western Trinidad Inn. The rooms at this mid-priced chain motel, four blocks from the downtown historic district and museums, are comfortable and clean; some connecting rooms are available. Restaurant, bar. In-room data ports, microwaves, refrigerators, cable TV. Pool. Hot tub. Gym. Laundry facilities. Pets allowed. | 900 W. Adams St. | 719/846–2215 | fax 719/846–2480 | www.bestwestern.com | 55 rooms | $79–$99 | AE, D, DC, MC, V.

Budget Host. This economical chain motel 2 mi south of downtown is home to a local landmark: a 107-ft oil derrick. Picnic area. Some microwaves, some refrigerators, cable TV. Hot tub. Pets allowed (fee). | 10301 Santa Fe Trail Dr. | 719/846–3307 or 800/283–4678 | fax 719/846–3309 | www.budgethost.com | 26 rooms | $50–$70 | AE, D, MC, V.

Budget Summit Inn. An economical roadside hotel south of Trinidad, immediately off Interstate 25. Complimentary Continental breakfast. In-room data ports, some microwaves, some refrigerators, cable TV. Hot tub. Laundry facilities. Business services. Pets allowed (fee). | 9800 Santa Fe Trail Dr. | 719/846–2251 | fax 719/846–2251 ext. 30 | 39 rooms (21 with shower only) | $40–$80 | AE, DC, MC, V.

Chicosa Canyon Bed and Breakfast. This century-old stone home is in 64 acres of land, 12 mi from Trinidad. Enjoy the great solarium, the hot tub, or curl up with a book near the central fireplace. The rooms are generously sized and the cabin has a wood-burning stove and canyon views. Complimentary breakfast. Some kitchenettes, some microwaves, some refrigerators, no room phones, no TV in some rooms, TV in common area. Hot tub. Hiking. Pets allowed. No smoking. | 32391 County Rd. 40 | 719/846–6199 | fax 719/846–6199 | www.bbonline.com/co/chicosa | 3 rooms (2 with shared bath), 1 cabin | $88–$128 | MC, V.

Holiday Inn–Trinidad. Located just north of the Raton Pass, this chain motel offers a variety of amenities on the edge of a wooded area, 2 mi south of downtown Trinidad. Restaurant, bar, room service. Some microwaves, refrigerators, cable TV, some in-room VCRs. Pool. Video games. Laundry facilities. Business services. Some pets allowed. | 3125 Toupal Dr. | 719/846–4491 or 800/465–4329 | fax 719/846–2440 | www.holiday-inn.com | 113 rooms | $89–$119 | AE, D, DC, MC, V.

VAIL

(Nearby towns also listed: Beaver Creek, Copper Mountain, Dillon, Frisco, Leadville)

Until U.S. 6, the forerunner of today's Interstate 70, was built over 10,666-ft-high Vail Pass in 1939, the region around the town was devoted primarily to sheep ranching. It was only after World War II that the area's skiing potential was realized and efforts got underway to convert the sleepy town of Vail into one of the country's premier resort communities. A faux European village soon sprang up on the base of the mountains, complete with clock tower. Today, Vail is one of Colorado's most visited towns, particularly in winter when skiing rules and the population explodes; its permanent residents number a bit fewer than 4,500. Located on heavily traveled Interstate 70, Vail is easily accessible in all seasons. The rest of the Vail Valley is composed of solid, working-class towns such as Avon, Eagle, Edwards, and Minturn. Twelve miles west of Vail is Beaver Creek, its exclusive sister resort. As fashionable ski resorts go, Vail seems to draw the politicians (those who are merely fabulous go to Aspen).

Information: **Vail Valley Tourism and Convention Bureau** | 100 E. Meadow Dr. #34, Vail, 81657 | 970/476–1000 or 800/525–3875 | www.visitvailvalley.com.

Attractions

Betty Ford Alpine Gardens. Named after the former first lady, these luxurious alpine gardens in Ford Park are the highest public botanic gardens in North America. | Ford Park | 970/476–0103 | www.vailalpinegarden.org | Free | Mid-May–mid-Sept., daily dawn to dusk.

Colorado Ski Museum and Ski Hall of Fame. The museum, in the Vail Village Transportation Center, houses skiing artifacts and photos tracing the history of skiing, with particular emphasis on Colorado's contributions. On display are antique skis and skiing equipment and fashions. | 231 S. Frontage Rd. | 970/476–1876 | www.vailsoft.com/museum | $1 | Tues.–Sun. 10–5; closed May and Oct.

Vail Nature Center. Seven acres of natural mountain flora and fauna occupy this wild region that stretches along Gore Creek. | 841 Vail Valley Dr. | 970/479–2291 | $1 suggested | Memorial Day–Sept., daily 9–5.

Vail Ski Resort. One of Vail's former owners, George Gillett, once called the resort, "one of God's special works," and a brief look at the accommodations offered at this state-of-the-art ski resort confirms the statement. Vast in scope (there are 5,200 acres of skiable terrain), Vail is the most popular skiing destination in the United States. Though known as a playground for the ultra-moneyed set, Vail can still provide a vacation for most anyone, regardless of income. With several well-defined areas for novices and back bowls for the experienced skier, Vail has a bit of everything; however, it has a bit more for the intermediate skier, where you'll find perhaps the most variety in intermediate slopes in the country. You'll find 174 runs, the longest run being 4½ mi, and a vertical drop of 3,360 ft. There are 13 high speed quads, 9 fixed-grip quads, 1 gondola, and 9 surface lifts. During the summer, you can hike, go mountain biking, play golf, or just relax. | Vail (I–70, exit 176) | 970/476–5601 or 800/525–2257 | www.vail.com | Nov.–Apr., daily 8:30–4.

ON THE CALENDAR
JUNE–AUG.: *Vail Valley Rodeo.* An evening barbecue kicks off this weekly rodeo held at The Ranch at Berry Creek in Edwards. | 970/926–3679.

Dining

Alpen Rose Restaurant. Continental. Rich, luscious dishes such as schnitzels but also fresh seafood specials are served in a frilly, pink dining room at this restaurant that developed from a bakery and tearoom. Open-air dining on a terrace. | 100 E. Meadow Dr. | 970/476–3194 | Closed mid-Apr.–late-May, mid-Oct.–mid-Nov., and Tues. | $19–$25 | AE, D, DC, MC, V.

Blu's. American. The menu is eclectic and affordable at this busy Vail institution. The food is always fresh—from the California chicken relleno to the smoked duck. Open-air dining on the Gore Creek. Kids' menu. | 193 E. Gore Creek Dr. | 970/476–3113 | Breakfast also available | $8–$20 | AE, MC, V.

Bully Ranch. American/Casual. This western saloon has cowboy memorabilia on the walls and a large bar for all the wranglers. Regulars favor the prime rib, the fish-and-chips, and the burgers. In the Sonnenalp Resort. | 20 Vail Rd. | 970/476–5656 | $9–$28 | D, DC, MC, V.

Chili Willy's. Tex-Mex. This is the rustic option in the old railroad and mining town of Minturn, 7 mi west of Vail. The walls are covered in license plates from all over the world. Open-air dining on patio with view of Eagle River. Kids' menu. | 101 Main St., Minturn (I–70 W, exit 171) | 970/827–5887 | No lunch Labor Day–early July | $9–$17 | AE, D, MC, V.

Hubcap Brewery and Kitchen. Steak. Vail's first microbrewery offers five house beers (Beaver Tail Brown Ale and Vail Pale Ale are popular). The locals enjoy such kitchen specialties as porterhouse steak and Colorado rack of lamb. Don't forget to take a look at the chrome hubcaps that hang from the walls; you never know if one of them could have been yours. | 143 E. Meadow Dr. | 970/476–5757 | $14–$35 | AE, MC, V.

Kaltenberg Castle Brewhouse. German. Licensed by His Royal Highness Prince Luitpold of Bavaria, this brewhouse is at the base of Eagle Bahn Gondola. Dine among suits of armor and Prince Luitpold's coat of arms. Try the roast pork in Kaltenberg dark beer sauce, or the Wiener schnitzel with potato salad. The beers are fit for a king (or a prince at least). | 600 Lionshead Mall | 970/479–1050 | $9–$25 | AE, MC, V.

Lancelot Inn. Continental. A casual place for prime rib or Atlantic salmon in the center of Vail Village. Open-air dining on patio overlooking the Gore Creek. Kids' menu. No smoking. | 205 E. Gore Creek Dr. | 970/476–5828 | Closed May | $15–$25 | AE, MC, V.

La Tour. French. French paintings lend an air of culture to two comfortable dining rooms. Try the sautéed imported Dover sole, the crusted venison loin, or the whole Maine lobster. Families and businessmen alike frequent this eatery. | 122 E. Meadow | 970/476–4403 | Reservations essential | $20–$36 | AE, MC, V.

Left Bank. French. In the Sitzmark Lodge, this cozy candlelit restaurant serves traditional French cuisine with a Mediterranean touch. Try the pepper steak, shrimp in puff pastry, or *bouillabaise* (seafood stew in lobster broth). The rack of Colorado lamb for two is good for a romantic dinner. | 183 Gore Creek Dr. | 970/476–3696 | Closed mid-Apr.–mid-June, Oct.–mid-Nov., and Wed. No lunch | $24–$37 | Reservations essential | No credit cards.

Ludwig's. Continental. This elegant, formal restaurant is in the Sonnenalp Resort of Vail. Try Muscovy duck or stuffed veal tenderloin. Open-air dining with view of Gore Creek. Pianist. Kids' menu. | 20 Vail Rd. | 970/479–5429 | Reservations essential | Breakfast also available; no lunch | $8–$38 | AE, DC, MC, V.

Montauk Seafood Grill. Seafood. This restaurant has two sections: a dark, rustic bar, and a brighter, more festive main dining room. The kitchen is open, so you can watch as your seafood is being prepared—that is, if you can take your eyes off the mountains outside. Try the Hawaiian ahi, crispy calamari, or tempura shrimp. No smoking. | 549 W. Lionshead Mall | 970/476–2601 | No lunch | $21–$29 | AE, D, MC, V.

Minturn Country Club. Steak. This is one of the favorite hangouts of racers during World Cup ski competitions. The food varies in its preparation since you cook it yourself on a grill. Enjoy steaks, prime rib, chicken, and fish in the rustic surroundings. Minturn is about 15 mi west of Vail. | 131 Main St., Minturn | 970/827–4114 | $10–$25 | MC, V.

Ore House. Steak. The western mining theme, with overturned mining carts as tables, is sure to take you back to a time when raucous was a way of life. Try the fillet Ore House, the prime rib, or the tuna. | 232 Bridge St. | 970/476–5100 | $14–$47 | AE, DC, MC, V.

★ **Sweet Basil.** Contemporary. Towering floral arrangements and abstract art dominate this understated place done in buff and teal. Try the sesame seared tuna (served on a bed of lettuce and Asian vegetables), or the Portobello mushroom and goat-cheese tart drizzled with basil-pepper and balsamic vinaigrette. Open-air dining in front overlooking the walking streets of the village. No smoking. | 193 E. Gore Creek Dr. | 970/476–0125 | $23–$35 | AE, MC, V.

★ **Terra Bistro.** Contemporary. In the Vail Athletic Club, this airy space has a fireplace and sleek black wood chairs with black-and-white photographs adorning the walls. The menu features such specials as grilled Maine lobster with Prince Edward mussels accompanied by chipotle corn cakes, French beans, and tomato basil butter; or you might try roast rack-and-loin of Colorado lamb over Israeli couscous with almonds and harissa. Organic produce and free-range meat and poultry are used whenever possible. | 352 E. Meadow Dr. | 970/476–6836 | $19–$28 | AE, D, DC, MC, V.

The Tyrolean. Continental. Crisp white linens and shining silver place settings prepare you for polished cuisine at this restaurant. Continental fare has a lighter twist here: you might find elk medallions with forest mushrooms and black-pepper spaetzle or roasted duck breast with a Chambord-perfumed demi-glace. Open-air dining. Kids' menu. | 400 E. Meadow Dr. | 970/476–2204 | Closed late Apr.–May. No lunch | $21–$41 | AE, MC, V.

Up the Creek. Contemporary. This restaurant 5 yards from Gore Creek has intimate tables and no pretense, just serious food at prices quite reasonable by Vail standards. The herb-crusted halibut in a citrus burre blanc and the rack of Colorado lamb in a merlot shallot reduction are popular entrées. | 223 Gore Creek Dr., Suite 103 | 970/476–8141 | $16–$20 | AE, D, DC, MC, V.

Lodging

Best Western Vailglo Lodge. Located 200 yards from the Lionshead Gondola and a shopping and dining area, this small, cozy lodge exudes the luxurious feel of a private alpine retreat. Rooms, outfitted in white ash furnishings, are attractive and comfortable. Complimentary Continental breakfast. In-room data ports, refrigerators, cable TV. Pool. Hot tub. Free parking. | 701 W. Lionshead Circle | 970/476–5506 or 800/541–9423 | fax 970/476–3926 | www.bestwestern.com | 34 rooms | $225–$250 | AE, D, DC, MC, V.

Black Bear. A B&B in a log cabin on the banks of Gore Creek, 3 mi from the ski slopes. Rooms are cozily outfitted with log furnishings. Complimentary breakfast. In-room data ports, no TV, cable TV in common areas. Hot tub. Video games. Business services. No smoking. | 2405 Elliott Rd. | 970/476–1304 | fax 970/476–0433 | www.bedandbreakfastinns.org | 12 rooms | $120–$245 | Closed mid-Apr.–mid-May | D, MC, V.

Christiania at Vail. Each room in this Bavarian-style inn is distinct, with antiques and hand-carved furnishings. A cold breakfast buffet is available for a fee. Minibars, some microwaves, cable TV, some in-room VCRs. Pool. Sauna. Business services. No smoking. | 356 E. Hanson Ranch Rd. | 970/476–5641 or 800/530–3999 | fax 970/476–0470 | www.christiania.com | 10 rooms, 6 suites, 70 apartments | $165–$350; $250–$500 suites; $300–$850 2–bedroom apartments, $525–$1,300 3–bedroom apartments, $775–$2,400 4–bedroom apartments | AE, D, DC, MC, V.

Gasthof Gramshammer. This slopeside lodge recalls the Austrian homeland of owner and former international ski racer Pepi Gramshammer and his wife, Sheika. The comfortable suites and apartments have fireplaces. Restaurant, bar, complimentary Continental breakfast. No air-conditioning, some kitchenettes, some microwaves, some refrigerators, cable TV, some in-room VCRs. Hot tub, massage, sauna, spa. Shops. Business services, parking (fee). | 231 E. Gore Creek Dr. | 970/476–5626 or 800/610–7374 | fax 970/476–8816 | www.pepis.com | 32 rooms, 4 suites, 3 apartments | $195, $225–$495 suites, $335–$350 apartments | Closed mid-Apr.–mid-May | AE, D, DC, MC, V.

Lion Square Lodge. On Gore Creek and next to the gondola, this ski-in, ski-out lodge offers hotel-style rooms and condominium units. The condos are individually owned and all have various personal touches. Picnic area. No air-conditioning, microwaves, refrigerators, cable TV, some in-room VCRs. Pool. Hot tub, sauna. Children's programs (ages 5–12). Laundry facilities. Business services, free parking. | 660 W. Lionshead Pl. | 970/476–2281 or 800/525–5788 | fax 970/476–7423 | www.lionsquare.com | 28 rooms, 82 condos | $215–$280; $300–$630 1 bedroom, $485–$670 2 bedrooms, $810–995 3 bedrooms | AE, D, MC, V.

Lodge at Vail. In addition to luxury, this hotel is in a prime location at the base of Vail Mountain, allowing ski-in, ski-out status. The medium-size rooms have marble baths, and mahogany and teak furnishings. Some rooms have soaking tubs and gas fireplaces. The individually owned suites have balconies and wood-burning fireplaces. 2 restaurants, bar. In-room data ports, some kitchenettes, some microwaves, some refrigerators, some in-room hot tubs, cable TV, in-room VCRs. Pool. Hot tub, sauna. Gym. Laundry facilities, laundry service. Business services, free parking. | 174 E. Gore Creek Dr. | 970/476–5011 or 800/331–5634 | fax 970/476–7425 | www.lodgeatvail.com | 76 rooms, 49 suites | $400–$5,000 | AE, D, DC, MC, V.

Manor Vail. At this condominium complex at the base of Golden Peak, you can choose a lodge room or a studio, one-, two-, or three-bedroom apartment. All are individually owned and furnished; all have fireplaces and balconies. Complimentary breakfast. Some kitchenettes, some microwaves, some refrigerators, cable TV, in-room VCRs. 2 pools. 2 hot tubs, sauna, 2 steam rooms. Gym. Laundry facilities, laundry service. Business services, free parking. | 595 E. Vail Valley Dr. | 970/476–5000 or 800/950–8245 | fax 970/476–4982 | www.manorvail.com | 143 rooms, 93 condos | $80–$200 rooms, $100–$1,700 condos | AE, D, DC, MC, V.

★ **Roost Lodge.** Economical rates, comfortable rooms, and a heated pool are draws at this establishment on Interstate 70. Many of the airy rooms feature four-poster beds and all have basic amenities. Complimentary Continental breakfast. Cable TV. Pool. Hot tub, sauna. | 1783 N. Frontage Rd. | 970/476–5451 or 800/873–3065 | fax 970/476–9158 | 70 rooms, 2 suites | $80 rooms, $150 suites | AE, D, DC, MC, V.

Sitzmark Lodge. Conveniently in the center of Vail Village, this lodge is small, warm, and contemporary. Some rooms have fireplaces. Restaurant, bar, complimentary Continental breakfast. No air-conditioning, in-room data ports, some kitchenettes, refrigerators, cable TV. Pool. Hot tub, sauna. Shops. Laundry facilities. Business services. | 183 Gore Creek Dr. | 970/476–5001 | fax 970/476–8702 | www.sitzmarklodge.com | 36 rooms | $187–$269 | D, MC, V.

Sonnenalp Resort. Right in the heart of Vail Village and 200 ft from the base of the ski mountain, the ultraluxurious Sonnenalp is an all-suite, Bavarian-style resort that almost transports you to the Alps. The hotel is quaint; rooms have European touches like down comforters and Bavarian pine armoires. Restaurant (*see* Ludwig's, Bully Ranch), bar, room service. Air-conditioning, in-room data ports, cable TV, some in-room VCRs (and movies). 2 indoor-outdoor pools. Hot tub. Driving range, putting green. Gym. Video games. Children's programs (ages infant–6). Business services, free parking. | 20 Vail Rd. | 970/476–5656 or 800/654–8312 | fax 970/476–1639 | www.sonnenalp.com | 90 suites | $775–$815 1–bedroom suites, $1,120–$1,280 2–bedroom suites | AE, DC, MC, V.

Tivoli Lodge. This reasonably priced, Bavarian-style lodge has bright, spacious rooms, most of which come with multiple beds, making it ideal for families or groups. Some rooms have views of the peaks. Bar, complimentary breakfast. Refrigerators, cable TV. Pool. Hot tub. Laundry facilities, laundry service. No smoking. | 442 N. Main St. | 970/476–5615 or 800/451–4756 | fax 970/476–6601 | www.tivolilodge.com | 50 rooms | $69–$289 | D, DC, MC, V.

Vail Cascade Resort. This ski-in, ski-out property has a courtyard on Gore Creek. Some rooms have a private patio or balcony. Because of a top-notch staff, this rather large resort maintains an intimate feel, which creates a mood that is at once glamorous but also down to earth. Restaurants, bar (with entertainment), room service. In-room data ports, minibars, refrigerators, cable TV, some in-room VCRs (and movies). Pool. Beauty salon, hot tub, spa. Tennis. Gym, bicycles. Shops. Business services. | 1300 Westhaven Dr. | 970/476–7111 | fax 970/479–7020 | www.vailcascade.com | 266 rooms, 25 suites | $435–$525, $775–$975 suites | AE, D, DC, MC, V.

Vail Mountain Lodge & Spa. In Vail Village, just steps from the ski slopes, this small resort houses a full-service boutique, hotel, athletic club, and health spa. Private balconies provide stunning mountain views. Restaurant, bar, complimentary Continental breakfast, room service. In-room data ports, cable TV, some in-room VCRs. Hot tub, spa. Gym. Hiking. Children's programs (ages 2–16). Laundry facilities. Business services, free parking. | 352 E. Meadow Dr. | 970/476–0700 or 800/822–4754 | fax 970/476–6451 | www.vail.net/lodging/vac | 30 rooms, 8 condos, 2 penthouses | $275–$400, $600–$1,000 suites, $1,150–$1,450 penthouse suites | AE, D, DC, MC, V.

Vail Village Inn. The Bavarian-style architectural details add to the charm of the inn. Accommodations range from basic to luxury, but all are comfortable and well maintained. The condominiums have views and fireplaces. The property is arranged around a quad, three sides of which are lodgings, the fourth comprised of retail stores and restaurants. Restaurant, bar. Some kitchenettes, some refrigerators, cable TV. Pool. Laundry facilities. Shops. No smoking. | 100 E. Meadow Dr. | 970/476–5622 or 800/445–4014 | fax 970/476–4661 | www.vailvillageinn.com | 70 rooms, 12 condos | $79–$400 rooms, $250–$1,400 condos | AE, DC, MC, V.

The Willows. These condominiums are minutes from the Vista Bahn lift. The one-bedroom units have a queen bed, a twin sleeper sofa, two televisions, a fireplace, a good-size kitchen, and a VCR. In-room data ports, kitchenettes, microwaves, refrigerators, cable TV, in-room VCRs. Hot tub. Laundry facilities. | 74 Willow Rd. | 970/476–2233 or 888/945–5697 | fax 970/476–5714 | www.vailskishop.com/lodging/willows | 42 condos | $270–$360 | AE, MC, V.

WALSENBURG

MAP 6, G7

(Nearby towns also listed: Cuchara, La Junta, Pueblo, Trinidad)

A small Spanish village named La Plaza de los Leones once occupied the site of present-day Walsenburg (population 3,950). Located on Interstate 25 about halfway between Pueblo and Trinidad, the town once thrived on, and still depends upon, southern Colorado's coal-mining industry.

Information: **Walsenburg Chamber of Commerce** | 400 Main St., Walsenburg 81089 | 719/738–1065.

Attractions

Blackhawk State Trustland. Explore this 1,511-acre area that can only be accessed on horseback or on foot. You can see black bear, mountain lions, deer, elk, rabbits, turkey, and antelope in their natural environment. It's located 20 mi south of Walsenburg. | Rouse Rd. (I-25, exit 42) | 719/738–1065 | www.sangres.com/stateco/huerfano.htm#blackhawk | Free | Sept. 1–May, daily.

Lathrop State Park. Waterskiing, swimming, boating, golf, and picnicking are featured at the park 3 mi west of Walsenburg. | U.S. 160 | 719/738–2376 | www.parks.state.co.us/lathrop | $4 per vehicle | Daily.

Walsenburg Mining Museum. Exhibits on the history of coal mining in the region are displayed in the old County Jail building. | 101 W. 5th St. | 719/738–1065 | $2 | May–Sept., Mon. 9–noon, Tues. 1–5, Thurs., Fri. 9–noon.

ON THE CALENDAR

JUNE: *Black Diamond Jubilee.* This festival commemorates the coal-mining era during which Huerfano County and Walsenburg were founded on the first weekend each June. | 719/738–1065.

Dining

Alpine Rose Café. Mexican. This intimate restaurant is relaxed and inexpensive. Try the enchilada dinner or perhaps your choice of tacos. | 522 Main St. | 719/738–1157 | $6–$8 | No credit cards.

Lodging

Best Western Rambler. This small chain motel is less than 2 mi north of Walsenburg, near Lathrop State Park. Restaurant. Cable TV, some in-room VCRs. Pool. Some pets allowed. | I–25 (exit 52) | 719/738–1121 | fax 719/738–1093 | www.bestwestern.com | 32 rooms | $62–$87 | AE, D, DC, MC, V.

La Plaza de los Leones Inn. This B&B was formerly a hotel, originally built in 1907. The pink stucco building has an Art Deco–influenced interior, and there is a garden in the rear. The rooms feel larger due to high ceilings. Complimentary Continental breakfast. No room phones, no TV in rooms, TV in common area. No pets. No smoking. | 118 W. 6th St. | 719/738–5700 | 16 rooms | $55–$95 | MC, V.

WINTER PARK

MAP 6, F3

(Nearby towns also listed: Central City, Georgetown, Granby, Idaho Springs)

The Winter Park ski area, on the western slope of Berthoud Pass in the Arapaho National Forest, is actually owned by the city of Denver as a part of its Denver Mountain Park System and is a favorite weekend destination for Denverites looking for an affordable and easily reachable place to ski. You won't see the fabulous faces you might see at Aspen or Vail, but what you will find are a lot of locals and increasingly nonlocals coming for reasonably priced skiing and accommodations. It's also a popular summer destination for hiking and one of the top mountain biking destinations in the Rockies. The small town of Winter Park (population 596) is about 2 mi away.

WINTER PARK

INTRO
ATTRACTIONS
DINING
LODGING

Information: **Winter Park/Fraser Valley Chamber of Commerce** | Box 3236, Winter Park, 80482 | 800/903–7275 | www.winterpark-info.com.

Attractions

Amaze'N Mazes. Try to find your way through the labyrinth; those with the fastest time win a prize. This intricate human maze, constructed of 4x4-ft wooden planks, is fun for everyone. At the base entrance of Winter Park mountain. | Hwy. 40 | 970/726–0214 | $5 | May–Oct., daily.

Winter Park Resort. At this resort you'll find 2,886 skiable acres with 134 runs (the longest is 5⁵/₁₀ mi) and a vertical drop of 3,060 ft; there are seven high-speed quad, eight double, and five triple lifts. There are actually three different mountains in the resort. Vasquez Ridge is more appropriate for intermediates; Mary Jane is the slope for experienced skiers; and Winter Park has something for both groups. The program for disabled skiers is one of the best in the country. Summer activities include biking, miniature golf, and indoor and outdoor climbing walls. | 239 Winter Park Dr., off U.S. 40 | 970/726–5514 | www.skiwinterpark.com | Mid-Nov.–mid Apr., June–mid Sept., daily.

The Children's Center. Winter Park has excellent ski programs for children beginning at three years, including special kids' slopes, equipment rentals, and even day care for infants and toddlers who won't be skiing. There are snowboarding schools for older kids. | 239 Winter Park Dr., off U.S. 40 | 970/726–5514 | www.skiwinterpark.com | Mid-Nov.–mid Apr., June–mid-Sept., daily.

ON THE CALENDAR

JUNE: *High Altitude Chile Cook-off.* This competition in Cooper Creek Square is the first step in qualifying for the World Finals in Las Vegas. There are also magicians, children's events, face painters, live entertainment, and artisans. | 800/903–7275.

Dining

Crooked Creek Saloon. American/Casual. This saloon is filled with photographs documenting the settling of Fraser and Winter Park. As you take a trip through history, dine on the selection of sandwiches including chicken breast, grilled cheese, or grilled vegetables. Some other favorites are the steaks, pastas, or ribs. | 401 Zerex, Fraser | 970/726–9250 | $6–$15 | D, MC, V.

Deno's Mountain Bistro. American/Casual. The large portions are sure to satisfy after a day on the slopes. Try the chicken *saltimbocca* (a pan-seared chicken breast with prosciutto and spinach in a white wine, sage, and cream sauce), the Rocky Mountain trout, or the ever-popular burgers. | 78911 Hwy. 40 | 970/726–5332 | $8–$30 | AE, D, DC, MC, V.

★ **Dining Room at Sunspot.** Continental. This striking log-and-stone structure at the top of the Xephyr Express lift at Winter Park ski area can be reached only by gondola, and the view alone is to die for—it looks like a million peaks. Try the elk medallion with Dungeness crab and white asparagus, the shiitake mushroom and Chilean sea bass, or the vegetarian Wellington. Kids' menu. No smoking. | 677 Winter Park Dr. | 970/726–1446 | Reservations essential | Closed May–Oct. and Sun.–Wed. No lunch | $49–$59 | AE, D, DC, MC, V.

Divide Grill. American/Casual. You can take in the views of the Continental Divide while dining on elk medallions, steaks, seafood (the king crab and salmon are popular), or one of the pasta dishes. | Cooper Sq., Suite 305 | 970/726–4900 | Closed Oct. No lunch | $15–$20 | AE, D, DC, MC, V.

Fontenot's Cajun Café. Cajun. The emphasis at this restaurant is on the seafood, and you can enjoy the catch of the day blackened and served with raspberry sauce. But you could also try the crawfish étouffée, the gumbo, the jambalaya, or the po'boy sandwich. | 78711 Hwy. 40 | 970/726–4021 | $8–$20 | AE, D, MC, V.

Gasthaus Eichler. German. This romantic candlelit chalet feels almost Bavarian with its antler chandeliers and stained-glass windows. On the menu: Wiener schnitzel, jägerschnitzel, and rindsrolladen. Open-air dining on a deck along a mountain stream. Kids' menu, early-bird suppers. | 78786 Hwy. 40 | 970/726–5133 | $15–$45 | AE, MC, V.

The Last Waltz. Mexican. Hanging plants, a fireplace, and piano music set the scene at this homey restaurant with a huge menu of Mexican basics. Kids' menu. Sunday brunch. | 78336 Winter Park Dr. (U.S. 40) | 970/726–4877 | Reservations not accepted | $8–$15 | AE, D, DC, MC, V.

Rudi's. Delicatessen. A traditional deli that also offers soups, chile, stews, and fresh baked bread. While you are here, try the holiday-on-a-bun made with turkey, cream cheese, and cranberry sauce. | Park Plaza Center | 970/726–8955 | $5–$8 | No credit cards.

Smokin' Mo's. Barbecue. The log walls and the decorative farm tools provide a suitably rustic setting for the hickory-smoked meats. Don't be afraid to get a little messy with the BBQ ribs, which you should try; there is always a napkin handy. | Cooper Creek Sq | 970/726–4600 | $6–$16 | AE, D, DC, MC, V.

Winston's at the Vintage. English. This restaurant is built around a 19th-century English bar that is said to have been in Winston Churchill's favorite pub in London. Today, you too can enjoy the beef Wellington and a pint, just as Churchill himself might have. In the Vintage Hotel. | 100 Winter Park Dr. | 970/726–8801 | $13–$20 | AE, D, DC, MC, V.

Lodging

Arapahoe Ski Lodge. This family-run, European-style ski lodge offers simple, motel-style rooms and a modified American meal plan during ski season. Transportation to and from the Winter Park slopes, 3 mi away, is also free. Dining room, bar, picnic area, complimentary breakfast. In-room data ports. No air-conditioning, no room phones, no TV in rooms, TV in common area. Pool. Hot tub, sauna. Business services. No smoking. | 78594 U.S. 40 | 970/726–8222 or 800/754–0094 | fax 970/726–8222 | www.winterpark-info.com/arapahoe | 11 rooms | $120–$176 | Closed Apr.–mid-June, Sept.–Oct. | MAP (ski season) | AE, D, MC, V.

Beaver Village Condominiums. These accommodations range from hotel-style rooms to three-bedroom units and are priced accordingly. The hotel-style units have a spacious sleeping area and a bath, but no phone or TV. The larger condo units have a balcony, dishwasher, multiple baths, a kitchen, and a fireplace. In-room data ports, some kitchenettes, some microwaves, some refrigerators, some in-room VCRs, some room phones, no TV in some rooms. Hot tub, sauna. | 50 Village Dr. | 970/726–8813 or 800/824–8438 | fax 970/726–5313 | www.beavercondos.com | 130 condos | $110–$530 | AE, D, MC, V.

Crestview Place. At this condo complex 2 mi from the slopes, all units have balconies, high ceilings, bathrooms, and full kitchens. The units with two bedrooms or more have fireplaces and jet tubs. The Winter Park shuttle bus stops at the front door. Kitchenettes, microwaves, refrigerators, some in-room hot tubs, cable TV, some in-room VCRs. 2 hot tubs. Laundry facilities. | 78737 Hwy. 40 | 970/726–9421 or 800/228–1025 | www.vacationsinc.com | 19 condos | $92–$576 | AE, D, MC, V.

★ **Gasthaus Eichler Lodge.** European flags flutter outside this Bavarian-style lodge in downtown Winter Park, about 2 mi from the ski area. There's a pleasant garden. Restaurant (see Gasthaus Eichler), bar. In-room hot tubs, cable TV. Business services. | 78786 U.S. 40 | 970/ 726–5133 | fax 970/726–5175 | 15 rooms | $110–$149 | AE, MC, V.

Grand Victorian. This luxury inn looks like a gingerbread house that might be nestled deep in a forest, yet it is right in downtown Winter Park. Each room is individually decorated with high-end reproductions, and the bathroom fixtures are gold plated. Some rooms have cathedral ceilings and fireplaces or private terraces with panoramas of the Continental Divide. Complimentary breakfast. In-room data ports, some in-room hot tubs, no TV in some rooms. No kids under 12. | 78542 Fraser Valley Pkwy. | www.vacationspot.com | 970/726–5881 or 800/204–1170 | fax 970/726–5602 | 10 rooms | $155–$235 | Closed May | AE, D, DC, MC, V.

Hi Country Haus Resort Condominiums. This condominium complex is just off U.S. 40 in Winter Park, 3 mi from the slopes. Picnic area. Some microwaves, refrigerators, cable TV. Pool, pond. Hot tub, sauna. Video games. Playground. Laundry facilities. Business services. | 78415 U.S. 40 | 970/726–9421 or 800/228–1025 | fax 970/726–8004 | www.vacationsinc.com | 306 1- to 3-bedroom condos | $68–$186 1–bedroom apartment, $114–$336 2–bedroom apartment, $152–$448 3–bedroom apartment | AE, D, MC, V.

High Mountain Lodge. This simple but comfortable lodge with dark paneling and beams is perched on a hill overlooking 40 wooded acres with great sunset views of the Rockies. Rooms come with either a pool or mountain view. Take U.S. 40 to County Rd. 5. Bar, picnic area, complimentary breakfast. Microwaves, refrigerators, cable TV in common area. Pool. Hot tub, massage, sauna. Library. Gym. Laundry facilities. Some pets allowed. | 425 County Rd. 5001, Fraser | 970/726–5958 or 800/772–9987 | fax 970/726–9796 | www.himtnlodge.com | 14 rooms | $79–$99 per person | Closed May | MAP (ski season) | D, MC, V.

Iron Horse Resort. An upscale, ski-in, ski-out condominium complex near the head of the Fraser River. This is one of the deluxe choices in Winter Park. Each unit has a full kitchen. Restaurant, bar (with entertainment), picnic area. Kitchenettes, microwaves, cable TV. Indoor-outdoor pool. Hot tub. Gym, hiking. Cross-country skiing, downhill skiing. Laundry facilities. Business services. | 257 Winter Park Dr. | 970/726–8851 or 800/621–8190 | fax 970/ 726–2321 | www.ironhorse-resort.com | 126 apartments | $99–$499 | AE, D, DC, MC, V.

Sundowner Motel. This motel in downtown Winter Park has larger-than-average rooms with one queen or two double beds and a spacious bathroom. Some of the larger rooms can accommodate six people. The hot tub under the gazebo is a great place to unwind. In-room data ports, microwaves, refrigerators, cable TV. Pool. Hot tub. | 78869 Hwy. 40 | 970/ 726–9451 or 800/521–8279 | 32 rooms | $100–$170 | AE, D, MC, V.

Viking Lodge. In the middle of Winter Park, within walking distance to the area's restaurants and nightlife, this lodge offers everything from small economy rooms to deluxe suites and condos. Complimentary Continental breakfast. Some kitchenettes, cable TV. Hot tub, sauna. Pets allowed. | Hwy. 40 and Vasquez Rd. | 970/726–8885 or 800/421–4013 | 22 rooms, 3 condos | $60–$595 | AE, D, MC, V.

The Vintage Hotel. Despite the name, this is a contemporary lodge located right at the main entrance to the Winter Park Ski Resort. One of the most upscale properties in the area, the hotel offers large rooms with upscale features. Restaurant, bar (with entertainment), picnic area, complimentary Continental breakfast (summer only), room service. In-room data ports, some kitchenettes, cable TV. Pool. Hot tub, sauna. Gym. Cross-country skiing, downhill skiing. Video games. Laundry facilities. Business services. Pets allowed. | 100 Winter Park Dr. | 970/726–8801 or 800/472–7017 | fax 970/726–9230 | 118 rooms, 30 suites | $90–$185, $310–$525 suites | AE, D, DC, MC, V.

Woodspur Lodge. This rustic, cozy lodge sits within the boundaries of the Arapaho National Forest, a mile from downtown Winter Park. Many furnishings are handmade, and there are fireplaces in the bar and living room. Rooms are simple and pine paneled. Bar, picnic area. Cable TV in common areas. Hot tub, sauna. Business services. | 111 Van Anderson Dr. | 970/726–8417 or 800/626–6562 | fax 970/726–8553 | www.toski.com/woodspur | 32 rooms (16 with shower only) | $164 | MAP (ski season only) | D, MC, V.

KODAK'S TIPS FOR TAKING GREAT PICTURES

Get Closer
- Fill the frame tightly for maximum impact
- Move closer physically or use a long lens
- Continually check the viewfinder for wasted space

Choosing a Format
- Add variety by mixing horizontal and vertical shots
- Choose the format that gives the subject greatest drama

The Rule of Thirds
- Mentally divide the frame into vertical and horizontal thirds
- Place important subjects at thirds' intersections
- Use thirds' divisions to place the horizon

Lines
- Take time to notice lines
- Let lines lead the eye to a main subject
- Use the shape of lines to establish mood

Taking Pictures Through Frames
- Use foreground frames to draw attention to a subject
- Look for frames that complement the subject
- Expose for the subject, and let the frame go dark

Patterns
- Find patterns in repeated shapes, colors, and lines
- Try close-ups or overviews
- Isolate patterns for maximum impact (use a telephoto lens)

Textures that Touch the Eyes
- Exploit the tangible qualities of subjects
- Use oblique lighting to heighten surface textures
- Compare a variety of textures within a shot

Dramatic Angles
- Try dramatic angles to make ordinary subjects exciting
- Use high angles to help organize chaos and uncover patterns, and low angles to exaggerate height

Silhouettes
- Silhouette bold shapes against bright backgrounds
- Meter and expose for the background illumination
- Don't let conflicting shapes converge

Abstract Composition
- Don't restrict yourself to realistic renderings
- Look for ideas in reflections, shapes, and colors
- Keep designs simple

Establishing Size
- Include objects of known size
- Use people for scale, where possible
- Experiment with false or misleading scale

Color
- Accentuate mood through color
- Highlight subjects or create designs through color contrasts
- Study the effects of weather and lighting

From *Kodak Guide to Shooting Great Travel Pictures* © 2000 by Fodor's Travel Publications

New Mexico

Much of the New Mexico's allure stems from the extreme contrasts found there. From the 13,000-ft, snow-covered Sangre de Cristo Mountains in the north, to the stark, blanched landscape of White Sands National Monument farther south, to the ancient pueblo towns of Acoma and Zuni to the west, the state's natural and man-made wonders are almost too varied and majestic to comprehend.

Nearly 500 years ago, when Spanish conquistadors headed out of Mexico to view what treasures they might uncover in the northern reaches of the vast, windswept region they called New Spain, they couldn't have imagined that the extreme frontier of that dry, forsaken desert would one day become a mecca for tourists from all over the world. New Mexico, which did not become one of the United States until 1912, now receives millions of visitors annually, and the range of attractions that bring them there— natural wonders like the Carlsbad Caverns, historic towns such as Santa Fe and Taos, the urban sophistication of Albuquerque, to name a few—equals or surpasses any found in North America.

New Mexico is a state for nature and history lovers. Millions of acres of mountain forests, arid grassland, and remote wilderness areas have been set aside by the federal and state governments so that current and future generations can enjoy the magnif- icence of the great outdoors. The state has an abundance of national historical monu- ments, history parks, museums, and other facilities that preserve and protect the heritage of the region. Fully one third of New Mexico is held in public lands; in many places you can hear the whisper of the past as you explore the many layers of New Mexican history.

Modern New Mexico offers something for everybody; art, dance, opera, fine dining, and theater rival those in any other American region. If you simply enjoy shopping—

CAPITAL: SANTA FE	POPULATION: 1,729,751	AREA: 121,999 SQUARE MI
BORDERS: MEXICO, TX, OK, CO, AZ	TIME ZONE: MOUNTAIN	POSTAL ABBREVIATION: NM
WEB SITE: WWW.NEWMEXICO.ORG		

for clothes, antiques, books, fine jewelry, arts and crafts, souvenirs, or just about anything else you can think of—then New Mexico is the place for you. The residents of New Mexico's many towns and villages, including Albuquerque, Santa Fe, and Taos in the north and Mesilla, Las Cruces, and Carlsbad in the south, await your visit, eager to lay out their wares.

The presence of three separate and diversified cultures in New Mexico is one of the reasons it's such a rewarding travel destination. Over hundreds of years, Indian, Spanish, and "Yankee" Anglo cultures have grown, imparted their own characteristics, and intermingled to form a culture different from any other in America. Whether it be the food you eat, the handicrafts or jewelry that you purchase, or the accommodations you utilize, the chances are excellent that during your visit to the Land of Enchantment, you will savor—and never forget—a variety of experiences that are uniquely New Mexican.

History

On February 22, 1540, a young conquistador named Francisco Vásquez de Coronado left the small Spanish town of Compostela, located northwest of Mexico City near the Pacific Ocean. Coronado was at the head of an army of 225 mounted soldiers and 62 footmen, accompanied by at least three women. They were bound for Cíbola, a fabled place far to the northeast, rumored to be rich in gold, silver, and all manner of riches. Before the small army returned empty-handed to Mexico two years later, its quest had carried it on the first documented journey by Europeans into present-day New Mexico.

Coronado had barely crossed the majestic Rio Grande before learning that his conquistadors were not the first humans to make a mark on the expansive landscape. Evidence of a long occupation by various tribes of Pueblo Indians, who lived up and down the river and its tributary system, was everywhere. The apprehensive Spaniards, having already been confronted with hostility in practically every other place they had visited, braced themselves for battle.

Normally peaceful, the Pueblo people, for most of their existence, had led defensive lives, protecting themselves from the more warlike southern Plains tribes—the Comanches, Kiowas, and Apaches. After the Apaches acquired horses from the Spanish during the 16th century, they frequently preyed upon the Pueblos, who were content to live in one spot and raise corn, beans, squash, and other agricultural produce. The Pueblos lived in multilevel apartment houses, many of which are still in existence. Descended from the Anasazi, or "ancient ones," their population in the region just before the arrival of the Spanish may have reached 40,000.

It was one of these Pueblo tribes that Coronado visited at their primary town of Hawikul in 1540. Another Spaniard, Fray Marcos, had visited this area the previous year and had brought back reports to Spanish authorities that he had seen a town "larger than the city of Mexico." According to Marcos, Cibola possessed "a great store of gold and a hill of silver."

NM Timeline

12,000–6,000 BC		AD 1100–1300	1350–1400
Bands of prehistoric Indians roam the face of New Mexico, concentrating in three areas—on the Sandia slopes, near Clovis, and around Folsom—and leave behind their chipped flint work that identifies each	as a separate culture, named after the site of discovery.	The "golden age" of Anasazi culture reigns in northern New Mexico.	The extinction of many cliff-dwelling villages is complete, paving the way for the rise of the multistoried pueblo towns throughout New Mexico.

INTRODUCTION
HISTORY
REGIONS
WHEN TO VISIT
STATE'S GREATS
RULES OF THE ROAD
DRIVING TOURS

Unsuccessful in his search for the fabulous riches that Fray Marcos had reported, a disappointed Coronado found only a dusty pueblo, manned by several hundred hostile warriors anxiously perched atop the roofs of the adobe houses. Instead of a town whose inhabitants "wear silk clothing down to their feet," and that contained "a temple of their idols the walls of which . . . were covered with precious stones," Coronado and his tired command found only scantily clad natives working about their sunbaked apartment houses. Coronado was disappointed at his first view of Hawikul, now called Zuni Pueblo, still occupied and located about 40 mi south of Gallup, New Mexico.

After Coronado's fruitless expedition to New Mexico and beyond, the region was little visited by the Spanish again for nearly 60 years. Then, in 1598, Juan Oñate, the newly appointed governor of the province, led about 500 soldiers and settlers, along with 7,000 head of cattle, to the area around San Juan Pueblo, where he founded San Gabriel, the first Spanish town in New Mexico.

Oñate's successor, Pedro de Peralta, established New Mexico's capital at Santa Fe, perhaps as early as 1607 if recent archaeological findings are accurate. Situated on the extreme northern frontier of the province, the tiny settlement represented the only Spanish influence in the region for many years. Two of the town's oldest buildings, the Palace of the Governors and San Miguel Chapel, still stand on their original foundations and are open to visitors.

Soon after Coronado, Oñate, and Peralta had introduced the ways of Europeans to the frightened natives, they were followed by missionaries anxious to save the souls of the "lost" Pueblo peoples. The army and the Church worked hand in hand, and before many years had passed, the landscape of present-day New Mexico was dotted with missions, churches, and presidios. By 1625 padres had completed a church compound at Pecos, the remains of which are still visible. About 300,000 adobe bricks, each weighing 40 pounds, were used in the construction. Some of the walls were 22 ft thick, and the church itself had six separate bell towers. The ways of the Pueblo and the other indigenous peoples were changing dramatically as Spanish influences spread from tribe to tribe.

By 1680 the Pueblo people had grown tired of the Spanish yoke, and they attempted to drive the hated Europeans back to Mexico. They succeeded when Pope, a Tewa Indian, organized the warriors of most of the northern villages into a powerful force. The Pueblo Revolt, as the rebellion was called, pitted Indian against Spaniard, and when the insurrection was over, soldier and priest alike had been expelled from New Mexico. Retreating to the area around today's El Paso, the disfranchised Spanish could do little about their situation as they listened to the many rumors that their onetime neighbors to the north had destroyed all vestiges of the Spanish presence in the region.

For 12 years, the Pueblo people lived as they had before the arrival of the Spanish. At the end of that time, their foes from the south returned under the command of

1540	1598	1607	1680	1692
The Spanish conquistador Coronado crosses the Rio Grande from Mexico and for the next two years explores many sites throughout the Southwest, including several pueblos in New Mexico.	Juan de Oñate leads a colony of Spanish soldiers and priests into New Mexico and in April declares all of the region drained by the Rio Grande for Spain.	New Mexico's royal governor, Pedro de Peralta, establishes the town of Santa Fe and designates it as the territory's capital. (The previous estimate for the founding of Santa Fe was 1610.)	Residents of several northern pueblos revolt and push the Spanish back south to the region around present-day El Paso, Texas.	Don Diego de Vargas reconquers New Mexico for the Spanish, and the Pueblo Revolt is officially over.

General Diego de Vargas. Soon more villages were taking hold around the northern region; one of them, Albuquerque, eventually grew to become the largest city in the territory, and later, the state. With de Vargas's appearance, the Spanish reasserted themselves as the masters of New Mexico, and this time they were back for good.

Spanish authorities in Mexico City and Santa Fe were rigorously possessive of their New Mexican colony, and they frowned on outside influence or visitation. For a brief time in the 1700s, French traders from Louisiana made attempts to open commercial relations with the colony, with minimal success. In 1739, two French brothers, the Mallets, made it to Santa Fe, where they did a brief business before being deported.

The first merchants from the United States to reach the secluded town of Santa Fe were probably Jeannot Metoyer and Baptiste Lalande, two traders employed by William Morrison of Kaskaskia, Illinois, then Indiana Territory. They arrived in 1804, to be followed the next year by Lorenzo Durocher and Jacques d'Eglise. Lalande liked the land and the people so much that he stayed on in Santa Fe as a permanent resident, bilking the hapless Morrison of his profits for the mission. James Purcell, a Kentucky trapper, also visited and relocated to Santa Fe in 1805. Two years later, the American explorer Zebulon Pike was arrested near the headwaters of the Rio Grande, taken to Santa Fe, sent to Chihuahua, and briefly held prisoner before being released.

Mexico won its independence from Spain in 1821, and the attitude of the Mexican government changed almost overnight. Instead of prohibiting commerce with the Americans, the newly installed Mexican officials welcomed any and all trade. William Becknell, a Missouri merchant, made the first trip to New Mexico that same year, following what became the Santa Fe Trail, hopeful of making a fortune in the remote village of Santa Fe. His dreams came true; he returned to Missouri several months later boasting of the vast profits he had made among the friendly natives of New Mexico. The stage was now set for a lively commerce across the Santa Fe Trail that, over 30 years, resulted in the annual exchange of American-manufactured needles, thread, nails, tools, dry goods, pants, suspenders, dresses, scissors, razors, and a thousand other items in return for Mexican mules, donkeys, gold, silver, and fine furs coveted by Americans back East. During the 1830s and 1840s, many American fur trappers and mountain men made Taos their headquarters, and the small town became an important hub for the disposal of the pelts of beaver and other fur-bearing animals.

In time, however, Mexican authorities became disenchanted with their American neighbors, particularly after United States immigrants in Texas declared their independence from Mexico in 1836. A decade later, when the United States annexed Texas, war was declared between the two countries. In mid-1846, shortly after the first shots were fired, Colonel Stephen Watts Kearny of the United States Army was commanded to lead an "Army of the West" down the Santa Fe Trail, with explicit orders to occupy New Mexico and California.

Kearny arrived in Santa Fe on August 18, 1846, and occupied the town "without firing a gun or spilling a drop of blood." Leaving part of his command behind and appoint-

1739	1807	1821		1822–44
Two Frenchmen, Peter and Paul Mallet, reach Santa Fe and unsuccessfully attempt to establish trade relations with authorities there.	American army lieutenant Zebulon M. Pike is arrested on the headwaters of the Rio Grande and taken to Santa Fe for questioning. He is later released.	Mexico wins its independence from Spain at about the same time Missouri trader William Becknell heads west to New Mexico over the Santa Fe Trail. Mexican authorities, now in control, welcome	the Americans with open arms.	These two decades, the "golden age" of the Santa Fe Trail, witness trade goods worth millions of dollars being exchanged between American merchants in Missouri and Mexican citizens of Santa Fe.

INTRODUCTION
HISTORY
REGIONS
WHEN TO VISIT
STATE'S GREATS
RULES OF THE ROAD
DRIVING TOURS

ing Charles Bent, a well-known American resident of Taos and an owner of Bent's Fort on the Santa Fe Trail, the new governor of the territory, Kearny proceeded to California to fulfill the rest of his mission.

In January 1847 Governor Bent took leave of his duties in Santa Fe and proceeded to his home in Taos, located about 60 mi north of the capital. In the meantime, an undercurrent of dissatisfaction with the American occupation had been steadily growing among the native Mexicans and the Indians who lived at the nearby Taos Pueblo, 3 mi north of town. During the early morning hours of January 19, Bent and his family were awakened from their sleep by a mob of Mexicans and Indians, who proceeded to kill Bent and terrify his hysterical family. The unruly mob also murdered several other Americans along with Mexicans who had American loyalties.

Colonel Sterling Price was dispatched to Taos from Santa Fe with orders to quell the revolt. Traveling through a deep snow that made his army's movement difficult, Price and his command arrived at the Taos Pueblo on February 3, and for the next two days pounded the pueblo with artillery and small arms fire. The ringleaders of the uprising were arrested and eventually tried and found guilty. Most of them were hanged in Taos the following spring.

As New Mexico became more and more Americanized after the Mexican-American War, new problems faced its residents. The issue of whether the new territory should or should not allow slavery was vigorously argued in the halls of the Palace of the Governors, as well as in the United States Congress. When the Civil War broke out, neighboring Texans were quick to seize the opportunity to attempt to make New Mexico a Confederate holding. After a short, successful run at capturing several Union-held properties in the territory, the Texans were finally expelled from New Mexico after their defeat at the Battle of Glorieta Pass just east of Santa Fe, an affair that is sometimes called the Gettysburg of the West.

After the Civil War, New Mexico joined many other western regions in becoming heavily involved in the cattle industry. At one time John Chisum, a rancher in the east-central section of the territory along the Pecos River, owned the largest herd of cattle in the United States, with more than 80,000 head carrying his "Jinglebob" brand. The famous Goodnight-Loving Trail traversed part of New Mexico during this period. The cattle business brought with it a variety of marginal characters, and the outlaw-lawman era of the 1870s–1890s witnessed the arrival—and sometimes quick departure—of such notables as Billy the Kid; his killer, Sheriff Pat Garrett; "Black Jack" Ketchum; Clay Allison; and many others. Territorial governor Lew Wallace, who is most remembered as the author of the classic novel *Ben Hur,* wrote large portions of the book at his desk in the Palace of the Governors in Santa Fe when he wasn't hot on the trail of Billy the Kid.

The 20th century brought with it statehood for New Mexico (1912). Robert Goddard, the rocket pioneer, found the clear, clean air of the state to be a perfect place to test his pioneering ideas of attaining ultrarapid speed in space. At the same time, a large gathering of eastern painters and novelists had discovered Taos, and in the early part

1846	1847	1850	1851	1862
The United States and Mexico go to war (May 13) over Texas annexation. Colonel Stephen Watts Kearny takes his Army of the West across the Santa Fe Trail and occupies Santa Fe "without firing a gun."	Angry residents of the town of Taos and the neighboring Taos Pueblo murder newly appointed New Mexican governor Charles Bent at his home in Taos.	New Mexico Territory is created (September 9).	Construction begins on Fort Union, and when the final version of the structure is completed more than a decade later, the post will be the largest U.S. Army installation in the Southwest.	Confederate and Union forces clash at Glorieta Pass. The Confederate defeat leaves New Mexico under U.S. control for the remainder of the Civil War.

of the century turned the town into an internationally acclaimed artists' and writers' colony.

The World War Two years in New Mexico were dominated by the presence of the atomic energy laboratory at Los Alamos and the testing of an atomic bomb at White Sands, near Alamogordo. The world's most noted UFO sighting occurred near Roswell in 1947, and to this day the incident remains one of the most bizarre in New Mexico history.

New Mexico's noted native sons and daughters, along with its famous transplanted residents, include folk singer John Denver; cartoonist Bill Mauldin; race-car drivers Al and Bobby Unser; actress Greer Garson; novelists Lew Wallace, D. H. Lawrence, Tony Hillerman, Max Evans, and Norman Zollinger; artists Georgia O'Keeffe and Joseph Sharp; frontiersmen Kit Carson and Charles Bent; and socialite Mabel Dodge Luhan.

Regions

1. CENTRAL

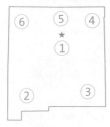

The central region of New Mexico consists of the counties of Sandoval, Bernalillo, Valencia, and Torrance, and includes the state's largest city, Albuquerque. Although Albuquerque is a large metropolis and its suburbs spread over many square miles, there is still an abundance of pristine surrounding land that offers all sorts of recreational opportunities. If you want to take a vacation that combines big-city sights, nightlife, and fine dining—yet will allow you to hit the great outdoors within minutes—the central region is the place to go.

Towns listed: Albuquerque, Belén, Bernalillo, Jémez Springs

2. SOUTHWESTERN

The southwestern region includes the counties of Catron, Socorro, Sierra, Grant, Hidalgo, Luna, and Doña Ana; it is bordered on the west by Arizona and on the south by Mexico. Much of the region is covered by the Gila and Cibola national forests, and the Rio Grande is the major water feature. The region's proximity to the international border gives it a Spanish-Mexican flair that best expresses itself in the annual chile celebration held in Las Cruces, New Mexico's second-largest city.

Towns listed: Deming, Las Cruces, Lordsburg, Silver City, Socorro, Truth or Consequences

3. SOUTHEASTERN

The southeastern region of New Mexico spans the ancient formation of Carlsbad Caverns millions of years ago and space-age technology that was harnessed near Alamogordo with the explosion of the world's first atomic bomb. Otero, Eddy, Lea, Roosevelt,

1866	1879	1881	1891	1898
"Uncle Dick" Wootton begins work on his toll road over Raton Pass.	The Atchison, Topeka, and Santa Fe Railroad reaches Las Vegas, New Mexico (July).	Billy the Kid is killed (July 14) at Pete Maxwell's ranch in Fort Sumner by Sheriff Pat Garrett.	Fort Union is officially abandoned by the U.S. Army.	Artists Ernest Blumenschein and Bert Phillips stop to change a wheel on their wagon a short distance out of Taos. Their brief delay in the town, and their immediate attraction to it, provides the catalyst for the

INTRODUCTION
HISTORY
REGIONS
WHEN TO VISIT
STATE'S GREATS
RULES OF THE ROAD
DRIVING TOURS

Curry, Chaves, Lincoln, and De Baca counties lie within this region; the Guadalupe Mountains run along its western flank, and the Pecos River bisects it from north to south. It is bordered on the east by Texas and on the south by Texas and Mexico. The region is noted for two other superlatives: the world's largest gypsum dune field, White Sands, makes up a large part of it, and Ruidoso Downs plays host to the All American Futurity, the world's richest quarter-horse race.

Towns listed: Alamogordo, Artesia, Carlsbad, Carrizozo, Cloudcroft, Clovis, Hobbs, Lincoln, Mescalero, Portales, Roswell, Ruidoso

4. NORTHEASTERN

New Mexico's northeastern region is bordered on the east by Texas and Oklahoma and on the north by Colorado. It includes the counties of Quay, Guadalupe, San Miguel, Harding, Colfax, and Union. The primary water features are the Canadian River and two streams that are each called the Cimarron River. Both the Cimarron Cutoff and the Mountain branches of the Santa Fe Trail crossed this region on their final approaches to Santa Fe, and during the mid-1800s thousands of wagons made their way across the parched high plains.

Towns listed: Cimarron, Clayton, Las Vegas, Raton, Santa Rosa, Tucumcari

5. NORTH CENTRAL

This region contains the oldest permanent Spanish communities in New Mexico, parts of it settled as early as 1598. Santa Fe, Taos, and Rio Arriba counties make up the region, which is bordered on the north by Colorado, with Santa Fe, Taos, and Española being the larger towns. A large part of the north-central region is public land, either the Carson or the Santa Fe national forests or the Jicarilla Apache Indian Reservation, so all types of outdoor recreation, including skiing in winter, are popular among residents and visitors alike. Santa Fe is a major art center and home to several world-class museums. Dining and lodging accommodations are excellent.

Towns listed: Angel Fire, Cerrillos, Chama, Chimayó, Dulce, Española, Los Alamos, Red River, Santa Fe, Taos

6. NORTHWESTERN

Cibola, McKinley, and San Juan counties comprise the northwestern region of New Mexico. With Arizona and Colorado and their rich Native American heritage bordering the region on the west and north, the Native American influences are strong. Nearly half the region is part of the huge Navajo Indian Reservation, and the cultural attractions there, coupled with the large number of prehistoric ruins in the area, make a trip to northwestern New Mexico an expedition into the distant past.

Towns listed: Acoma Pueblo, Aztec, Farmington, Gallup, Grants, Laguna Pueblo, Zuni Pueblo

	1901	**1912**	**1916**	**1945**
formation of the Taos art colony.	The notorious train robber, "Black Jack" Ketchum, is hanged (April 26) in Clayton, New Mexico.	New Mexico becomes the nation's 47th state (January 6).	The Mexican revolutionary and freedom fighter Pancho Villa raids Columbus, New Mexico (March 9).	Nuclear scientists explode the country's first atomic bomb at the Trinity Site, 60 mi northwest of Alamogordo (July 16).

When to Visit

There is no bad time to visit New Mexico; each of the four distinct seasons offers its own attractions, ranging from sightseeing, hiking, boating, and fishing during warmer weather to skiing and ice fishing in winter. The sun shines an average of 256 days a year in New Mexico, with some locales in the southern part of the state reaching 300 days annually. The abundance of sun, however, does not mean that temperatures and precipitation are constant. For example, the thermometer sometimes drops to 3°F in such northern towns as Chama and Red River in January, yet frequently reaches 100° and more in Albuquerque, Hobbs, and Deming during July and August. Likewise, a normal winter's snow in the Santa Fe National Forest might reach nearly 300 inches, while far to the south, along the lower Rio Grande, 2 inches is more the norm. The average high altitude of most of New Mexico makes temperature extremes between day and night vary greatly, in winter or summer. The best rule for dressing in New Mexico is to layer your clothing so that you can make adjustments for comfort.

Rainfall in New Mexico is infrequent. Average precipitation across the state ranges only between 8 and 26 inches. The humidity is practically always low and rarely exceeds 55% at any locale.

CLIMATE CHART
Average high/low Temperatures (°F) and monthly precipitation (in inches)

	JAN.	FEB.	MAR.	APR.	MAY	JUNE
ALBUQUERQUE	47/22	54/27	61/32	71/40	80/49	90/58
	.44	.46	.54	.52	.5	.59
	JULY	AUG.	SEPT.	OCT.	NOV.	DEC.
	93/64	89/63	82/55	71/43	57/31	48/23
	1.37	1.64	1.	.89	.43	.5
	JAN.	FEB.	MAR.	APR.	MAY	JUNE
CLAYTON	47/19	50/23	57/28	66/37	74/46	84/56
	.24	.31	.55	.94	1.99	2.27
	JULY	AUG.	SEPT.	OCT.	NOV.	DEC.
	88/61	85/59	78/52	69/41	57/29	48/21
	2.7	2.61	1.77	.9	.52	.29
	JAN.	FEB.	MAR.	APR.	MAY	JUNE
ROSWELL	54/25	60/29	68/36	77/45	85/55	94/62
	.35	.46	.33	.46	1.04	1.61
	JULY	AUG.	SEPT.	OCT.	NOV.	DEC.
	95/67	92/65	86/59	77/47	66/35	56/26
	1.71	2.58	2.02	1.05	.52	.45

1947
The "Roswell Incident," which many people believe proved once and for all the presence of UFOs and aliens from outer space, occurs near Roswell (July 3). The discovery of parts of strange-looking spacecraft, curious machine parts, and even corpses of aliens was reported at the time.

1950
Smokey the Bear, the official mascot for the U.S. Forest Service for more than a quarter of a century, is rescued as a cub by forest firefighters near Capitan, New Mexico.

1964
Noted Hollywood actress Greer Garson and her husband, oilman E. F. Fogelson, donate 279 acres of their Forked Lightning Ranch as a protective buffer zone around the Pecos Pueblo ruins.

1987
The Santa Fe Trail is designated part of the National Trail System.

WINTER

Jan.: **The Winter Wine Festival.** This festival in Taos is a weeklong wine and food-tasting event. | 505/776–2291.

Mar.: **The Winter Special Olympics.** This sporting event in Angel Fire pays tribute to scores of physically and mentally challenged athletes who compete in a number of winter sports. | 505/377–4237.

Go Fly a Kite Rally. In Carlsbad, this is a colorful display of hundreds of varieties of kites as they glide across the desert skies. | 505/457–2384.

SPRING

May: **The Silver City Blues Festival.** Locally and nationally acclaimed blues musicians, along with arts and crafts exhibits and plenty to eat and drink, are featured at this celebration in Silver City. | 505/538–2505 or 888/758–7289.

Mescal Roast and Mountain Spirit Dances. At Carlsbad, this several-day-long event features traditional Mescalero Apache dancing, interpretive talks, tribal ceremonies, and mescal tastings. | 505/887–5516.

SUMMER

June: **Blue Grass Festival.** Locally and nationally known bluegrass artists assemble to present a full day of music in Cloudcroft. | 505/682–2733.

Heritage Days Rodeo and Celebration. Two days of fun and excitement—including a 4-H–sponsored rodeo, arts and crafts exhibits, and plenty of entertainment—are part of the two-day festivities at Portales. | 505/356–8541.

Santa Fe Plaza Arts and Crafts Festival. More than 200 artists and craftspeople gather in Santa Fe. | 505/988–7621.

Wild, Wild West Pro Rodeo. This Professional Rodeo Cowboys Association–sanctioned rodeo, held at Silver City, features a five-day competition for cowboys and cowgirls from all over the region. | 505/538–3785.

July: **Traditional Spanish Market.** Held at the downtown Plaza in Santa Fe, this is a celebration of New Mexico's Spanish heritage. | 505/983–4038.

The Taos Powwow. You'll find Indian arts and crafts, as well as tribal dancing, music, and ceremonies at this Taos festival. | 800/732–8267.

Aug.: **Santa Fe Indian Market.** This Santa Fe market emphasizes a large variety of Indian wares from all over the Southwest, including jewelry, pottery, basketry, and more. | 505/983–5220.

Annual Inter-tribal Indian Ceremonial. This huge ceremony at Red Rock State Park near Gallup brings tribal representatives from all over the Four Corners region and beyond. | 505/722–2228.

Mountain Man Rendezvous, Buffalo Roast and Trade Fair. This event at the Palace of the Governors in Santa Fe features exhibits of leather goods and furs, as well as reenactments of historic events. | 800/777–2489.

FALL

Sept.: **New Mexico State Fair.** This once-a-year fair in Albuquerque offers good food, entertainment, a rodeo, livestock judging, agricultural exhibits, and concerts. | 505/265–1791.

The Southern New Mexico State Fair. This popular fair at Las Cruces provides a neat way to usher in autumn weather, with displays of agricultural and ranching produce, arts and crafts, a rodeo, music, and entertainment. | 505/541–2444.

Oct.: **Albuquerque International Balloon Fiesta.** Albuquerque's festival brings together hundreds of balloons and their pilots for a fabulous display of color high above the desert. | 505/842–9918 or 800/733–9918.

Oct. & Apr.: **Trinity Site Tour.** Near Alamogordo, this tour, featuring a guided tour of the first atomic bomb detonation site, is one of only two occasions annually that the site is open to the public; the other time is in April. | 800/826–0294.

Nov.: **Christmas in New Mexico.** Held at the New Mexico State Fair Grounds in Albuquerque, this festival features artisans and their wares from all over the region. | 505/823–1092.

Festival of the Cranes. The Bosque del Apache wildlife preserve near Socorro is the site for seminars, tours, workshops, and ample bird-watching, as observers from all over the country gather annually to watch the arrival of tens of thousands of migratory cranes and other birds. | 505/835–0424.

Dec.: **Luminaria Tour.** Old Town Albuquerque comes alive with the colorful lights of the holiday season during this event. | 505/842–9918 or 800/733–9918.

State's Greats

It's an often-repeated statement, but there is something for everybody in New Mexico, whether your interests lie in history, the great outdoors, sports, entertainment, or just plain relaxing.

Beaches, Forests, and Parks

The great outdoors has always been one of New Mexico's preeminent lures. Millions of acres of pristine forests, deserts, and high plains grasslands have been set aside by the federal government as parks for current and future generations to enjoy, among them **Apache, Carson, Cibola, Gila, Lincoln, and Santa Fe national forests and Kiowa National Grassland.** On most of these properties, passive recreational pursuits—hiking, backpacking, fishing in season, and water sports—are allowed. Keep in mind, however, that these lands and the flora and fauna that inhabit them are national treasures—they belong to everyone and should be treated with the utmost respect.

New Mexico is also home to two unique national parklands. **Carlsbad Caverns National Park,** in southeastern New Mexico, has one of the world's largest underground chambers and includes the nation's deepest limestone cave; it's also one of only two

INTRODUCTION
HISTORY
REGIONS
WHEN TO VISIT
STATE'S GREATS
RULES OF THE ROAD
DRIVING TOURS

cave systems that have been granted national park status. **White Sands National Monument** is part of the world's largest gypsum dunefields. The glistening white dunes here rise to 60 ft in places. More than 40 New Mexico state parks and recreational areas are scattered across the state as well, and they, too, offer a variety of outdoor activities to suit just about every taste and season. Whether your interest is water-skiing on **Elephant Butte Lake** near Truth or Consequences, hiking in the high mountains of the **Santa Fe National Forest** between Santa Fe and Taos, or looking for fossils at **Rock Hound State Park** near Deming, you will find an outdoor activity that satisfies your desires in New Mexico.

Culture, History, and the Arts

Because New Mexico is such a melting pot for the three major cultures found there—**Indian, Hispanic, and Anglo-American**—the state offers some of the most outstanding historical attractions found anywhere. New Mexico has the fourth-largest American Indian population in the United States. The many pueblos and reservations—along with the cultural activities, most of them open to the public, conducted there—offer an insight into native customs and lifestyles that can be found nowhere else.

The real problem in exploring New Mexico's Indian past is deciding which of the many pueblos and reservations to visit. For example, located along both banks of the Rio Grande from the vicinity of Albuquerque northward to the Colorado border are 13 separate and distinct **pueblos,** each with its own distinct culture. Added to that number are five other pueblos situated generally west of Albuquerque and the reservations, belonging to the Navajo, Mecalero, and Jacarilla Apache tribes.

It would be impossible to visit all of these villages and reservations during a single trip, so for starters the following give a pretty good idea of the overall picture. **Taos Pueblo,** located just 3 mi outside Taos, is a prime example of the classic "apartment house" dwelling that was once common in this region. **Laguna,** on the other hand, looks simply like the small village that it is, spread out across the landscape and punctuated with individual houses along Interstate 40 west of Albuquerque. **Acoma Pueblo,** a few miles west of Laguna off Interstate 40, is perched atop a high mesa and clearly demonstrates the lengths to which the Pueblo people would go to provide safety for their families. The **Mescalero Apache Reservation** is interesting to visit, not only for the insight it provides on these resourceful people, but on the lengths to which they have gone to assimilate themselves to the 21st century.

One word of caution: remember, the pueblos and reservations are private property, belonging to the people of the tribe who live there. When you visit, be respectful, observe the rules, ask before you take photographs, and do not trespass.

Likewise, the abundance of federally preserved archaeological sites throughout the state allows you to take a look at the past lives of New Mexico's original inhabitants. Most of these historical parks have visitor centers, and many provide a free film at the beginning of your visit that puts the place and its time frame in perspective. By all means, take advantage of these educational features to learn more about our continent's first residents. Some of the more popular sites are **Pecos National Historical Park,** located 30 mi east of Santa Fe just off Interstate 25; **Bandelier National Monument,** a few miles south of Los Alamos; and the **Gila Cliff Dwellings National Monument,** situated in the Gila National Forest some 30 mi north of Silver City. Pecos National Historical Park features the ruins of the ancient Pecos Pueblo as well as the remains of the Catholic church built by the Spanish soon after their arrival. Bandelier National Monument contains a number of prehistoric ruins that document early life in this area. Adolph Bandelier's historical novel, *The Delight Makers,* was set in one of the remote canyons in this park. Gila National Monument contains the only ruins in the region dating from the Mongollon culture period, dating back over 1,000 years.

It doesn't take too close a look at a highway map to appreciate the fact that New Mexico has been, and still is, heavily molded by its Hispanic past. The foods, the decor of the hotels and motels in which you lodge, the subject matter of a great many of the museums, cultural centers, and art galleries—all these reveal the area's Hispanic heritage. Nowhere in America outside New Mexico can you learn so much about the strong influences that Spain and Mexico had on the formation of the southwestern United States.

Sports

Within recent years, **hot-air ballooning, hang-gliding, and soaring** have become increasingly popular in New Mexico. An unusual number of days during which the air is clear and dry and the weather is sunny makes these activities naturals for many parts of the state. New Mexico hosts at least 15 hot-air balloon festivals annually, many of them concentrated in the Albuquerque area. Likewise, the warm wind currents, helped along by the state's average altitude, have made this a favorite destination for long-range hang-gliding.

White-water rafting and kayaking are other sports that have gained momentum over the past few years. The upper reaches of the Rio Grande offer some spectacular rapids, as does the Chama River. The best time for shooting the rapids in most streams is late May through late July, but parts of the larger rivers such as the Rio Grande can be traversed all year long.

Skiing in New Mexico is also popular. Sprinkled all over the state are many outstanding areas. The season generally lasts from late November until late March or early April. Combined with visits to local cultural and historical attractions nearby, a ski trip is a vacation not soon to be forgotten.

Rules of the Road

License requirements: As a visitor driving an automobile in New Mexico you must have a valid driver's license from your home state.

Right turn on red: A driver can turn right on a red light after coming to a full stop.

Seat belt and helmet laws: A state law requires automobile drivers and passengers to use seat belts. Although bikers are not required by law to wear helmets, they are strongly urged to do so. Children riding in automobiles must be restrained in the back seat, and if they are age four or under, they must be restrained in a children's car seat secured in the back seat.

Speed limits: Individual speed limits are posted in all municipalities. Most interstates maintain a 75-mph speed limit, depending on location.

For more information: Contact the New Mexico Highway Hotline at 800/432–4269. For medical emergencies, call 911.

Circling Northern New Mexico

SANTA FE, TAOS, AND THE FRONTIERS OF NEW SPAIN

INTRODUCTION
HISTORY
REGIONS
WHEN TO VISIT
STATE'S GREATS
RULES OF THE ROAD
DRIVING TOURS

Distance: Approximately 500 mi   Time: 4 days

Breaks: Overnights in Santa Fe, Taos, and Raton

On this tour through historic and scenic northern New Mexico, you'll be spending the night in the towns of Santa Fe, Taos, and Raton. Several stops are planned for each day of the actual driving part of the tour, including the old Spanish village of Chimayó; the scenic Rio Grande Gorge; the ski resort town of Red River; Cimarron, the administrative seat of the 2-million-acre Maxwell Land Grant; historic Fort Union; and Pecos National Historical Park.

Although the 16th- and 17th-century Spanish conquistadors traversed hundreds of miles of present-day Mexico and southern New Mexico to reach the northern frontiers of what they called New Spain, they elected to settle this remote northern section soon after the establishment of the first towns around Mexico City. Consequently, the history of this region dates back to the very beginnings of the Spanish *entrada.* This tour covers some of the most historic territory north of the Rio Grande and features attractions of the Spanish, Mexican, and American periods of occupation. A lot of this tour is on two-lane state highways, which can be treacherous when snow and ice are about. Spring and fall are great times to travel, from the standpoints of both temperature and the beauty of the natural scenery.

❶ Arrive in **Santa Fe** early and spend the entire day sightseeing. The abundance of shops, museums, art galleries, and other attractions will take the full day and then some if you have more time. Finding a great place to spend the night will not be difficult either— there are scores of hotels and B&Bs nearby.

❷ Enjoy a leisurely breakfast and leave Santa Fe around 10 AM, which will give you plenty of time to get to Chimayó, where you will have lunch. Take U.S. 84/U.S. 285 north out of Santa Fe. When you reach Pojoaque, turn right and take Route 503 to its junction with Route 98. Turn left and follow Route 98 to **Chimayó.** After lunch, save enough time to visit the **Santuario de Chimayó Church** and **Ortega's Weaving Shop,** both located within walking distance of each other. Eight generations of the Ortega family have been weaving here, and their works of textile art are breathtaking.

❸ Pick up Route 98 again to Route 76, turn right, and proceed through the ageless Hispanic towns of Truchas and Las Trampas to the road's junction with Route 75. The scenery through here is stunning. Turn left and follow Route 75 through Dixon to Route 68. Turn right (north) and follow Route 68 to **Ranchos de Taos,** with much-photographed **San Francisco de Asís Mission Church** on your right.

❹ Follow Route 68 into **Taos** and the town Plaza. With the Plaza as your base of operations, tour this sleepy Spanish town with its many museums, historic residences, and art galleries.

Taos was famous for many years during the early part of the 20th century as an artists' colony, and the village is full of references to those noted painters (Ernest Blumenschein, Bert Phillips, Irving Couse, Joseph H. Sharp, Oscar Berninghaus, among others) and writers (D. H. Lawrence, Frank Waters, and Mabel Dodge Luhan) who made their homes here. Famed mountain man Kit Carson lived in Taos for several years, and today the **Kit Carson Home and Museum** has been preserved much as it was during his lifetime.

The **Bent House** is the site of the murder of Governor Charles Bent by enraged Mexicans and Taos Indians in January 1847, soon after the American occupation of New Mexico.

Don't miss **Taos Pueblo**, where Governor Bent's attackers were confronted by an American army several weeks later under the command of Colonel Sterling Price. The

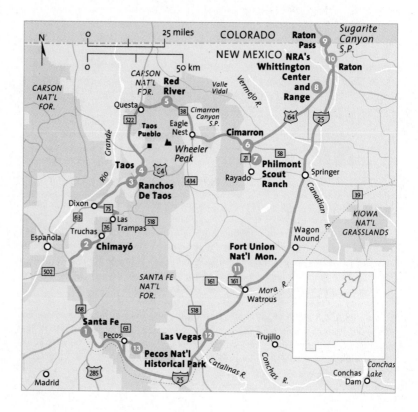

original church (the ruin of which is today a cemetery) was destroyed in the battle that followed. Spend the night in Taos.

⑤ Leave Taos and travel north on U.S. 64. At the split of U.S. 64 and Route 522, take U.S. 64 to the bridge crossing the Rio Grande. This view is a spectacular one of the wild Rio Grande Gorge, and parking the car and strolling across the bridge on foot is well worth the time (if you're wearing a hat, look out; the winds are brisk on the bridge). Return on U.S. 64 the way you came to Route 522, turn north and continue to the town of Questa. Take Route 38 east to **Red River,** a resort town known primarily for its nearby ski slopes.

⑥ Continuing on Route 38 brings you to the village of **Eagle Nest,** where you will pick up U.S. 64 East and proceed through the beautiful Cimarron Canyon to the town of **Cimarron.** Cimarron was once the administrative seat for the gigantic Maxwell Land Grant, which spread over 2 million acres of northern New Mexico and southern Colorado. Take a look at the historic **St. James Hotel,** which was started in 1880 as a saloon by Henri Lambert, onetime personal chef to both President Abraham Lincoln and General Ulysses S. Grant. Over the next several years, legend has it that as many as 26 men were killed within its walls. See the **Old Aztec Mill Museum** (across the street from the hotel) and other nearby attractions.

⑦ If you have ever been a Boy Scout, or are close to someone who is or was, you'll want to make a short side trip to see the historic **Philmont Scout Ranch.** The original land in Philmont Ranch (nearly 36,000 acres) was given to the Boy Scouts in 1938 by Waite Phillips, an Oklahoma oilman. Three years later, more acreage was donated, and today the ranch consists of around 140,000 acres. After visiting Philmont, return to Cimarron and proceed back to U.S. 64 toward Raton.

⑧ Just before reaching Raton, on your left, is the **National Rifle Association's Whittington Center and Range.** The range, situated on 52 square mi, offers hunting in season, an impressive variety of fully equipped shooting ranges, camping and recreational facilities, and a training center.

⑨ Pick up Interstate 25 at Raton and head toward the Colorado border and through historic and beautiful **Raton Pass.** Turn around on the other side of the Pass and proceed back along Interstate 25 to Raton.

⑩ You should allow yourself some time to visit historic downtown **Raton** and its sights. The town offers an impressive walking tour that highlights the **Santa Fe Railroad Depot,** one of the few remaining vestiges of Raton's once thriving rail facilities, as well as a number of commercial buildings, theaters, hotels, and saloons, dating from the mid to late 19th century and all remarkably well preserved. There are a number of fine hotel/motel facilities in Raton, so plan on dining and spending the night there.

⑪ Leave Raton early and proceed south on Interstate 25 through Maxwell and Springer until you arrive at exit 366. Follow Route 161 to **Fort Union National Monument.** Fort Union is an impressive sight, and after stopping by the visitor center, you must walk among its ruins to fully appreciate what military life on the southwestern frontier must have been like. Save some time to view the museum and visit the book and gift shop.

⑫ Leaving Fort Union, follow Route 161 back to Interstate 25 and continue southwest to **Las Vegas.** Visit the many shops clustered around the town Plaza. Return to Interstate 25 and continue toward Santa Fe.

⑬ At Route 63 (exit 307), leave the interstate and head north to **Pecos National Historical Park.** As in the case of Fort Union, you must hike the short trail to fully appreciate this deeply moving and spiritual place. The visitor center maintains a theater, a fine museum, a well-stocked bookstore, and squeaky-clean rest rooms.
Leaving Pecos, return south on Route 63 to Interstate 25 and proceed to **Santa Fe.**

On the Trail of Billy the Kid
FROM LAS CRUCES TO THREE RIVERS

Distance: Approximately 500 mi   Time: 4–5 days
Breaks: Overnights in Las Cruces, Alamogordo, and Ruidoso.

This tour through south-central New Mexico takes you through a large slice of New Mexico history, from the days of Billy the Kid to the Space Age. You'll visit the historic towns of Las Cruces, Cloudcroft, Tularosa, and Alamogordo, among others. There is a lot to see on this trip, and other stopovers include the historic town of Lincoln, site of the infamous Lincoln County War, and Smokey the Bear State Park, wherein lies the body of the U.S. Forest Service's most prominent spokesman.

Of all the infamous outlaws associated with the history of New Mexico, the one who stands out above all the rest is Billy the Kid. This tour is full of places associated with the Kid, including the towns of Mesilla, Lincoln, and White Oaks. But there's more to this trip than Billy the Kid; you'll also see the White Sands National Monument, the Space Hall of Fame, the stunning Apache-owned Inn of the Mountain Gods at Mescalero, one of America's premier horse-racing facilities at Ruidoso, and lots of the natural beauty of New Mexico along the way. Weather conditions in this part of the state are pretty mild year-round, except for periods in winter in the highlands, so you can plan your trip at your convenience.

❶ The tour begins in the morning in **Las Cruces,** New Mexico's second-largest city. Las Cruces was established in 1848, when the U.S. Army placed a small military post there. Five years later, when the Gadsden Purchase was ratified, the entire region became American territory. There's plenty to see in Las Cruces, and a good place to get your bearings is the **Las Cruces Museum of Natural History.**

❷ Located on the outskirts of Las Cruces is the historic village of **Mesilla.** Founded shortly after Las Cruces, in 1850, when the region was still owned by Mexico, the village later became, for a brief period during the Civil War, the unofficial capital of the Confederate Territory of Arizona. Billy the Kid was once incarcerated for murder in Mesilla, but escaped before his sentence could be carried out. Today the cluster of unique shops and restaurants that line the **Old Mesilla Plaza** offers everything from arts and crafts to antiques to fine food.

INTRODUCTION
HISTORY
REGIONS
WHEN TO VISIT
STATE'S GREATS
RULES OF THE ROAD
DRIVING TOURS

❸ Leaving Las Cruces, take U.S. 70 northeast out of town and drive the 25 mi to the entrance of the **White Sands Missile Range.** You will pass through a security station there and will need to inform the guard that you wish to visit the museum and/or the missile park. If you happen to be there on the first Saturday in either April or October, you will be able to tour the Trinity Site, where America's first atomic bomb was detonated.

❹ After you leave the range, turn back northeast on U.S. 70 and drive until you see the entrance (about 30 mi) to **White Sands National Monument** on your left. This natural wonder encompasses nearly 200,000 acres of glistening gypsum dunes.

❺ After viewing the dunes, follow U.S. 70 into **Alamogordo,** where you will spend the night. A must-see in Alamogordo is the **International Space Hall of Fame,** a four-story cube perched on the side of a mountain overlooking the town and containing a wide variety of space exhibits. It also honors men and women who have made their marks on space research and exploration, and even offers simulated space walks on Mars, along with many other attractions. **The Alameda Park Zoo** is one of the oldest animal parks in the Southwest and features hundreds of domestic and foreign species.

6 Leaving Alamogordo northward on U.S. 54, proceed until you arrive at the highway's junction with U.S. 82, which you will take to the town of **Cloudcroft.** In the early 1900s surveyors gave the romantic name to the town after spying a single white cloud hovering over a nearby meadow, which in the Old English vernacular is "croft." Today it's a mountain retreat that boasts great year-round temperatures and one of the nation's highest golf courses, along with antiques and arts-and-crafts shopping galore. While there, visit the **National Solar Observatory at Sacramento Peak,** the national center for the study of the sun. Pick up Route 244 at Cloudcroft and follow it through the Mescalero Apache Indian Reservation to its junction with U.S. 70.

7 Follow U.S. 70 eastward into **Ruidoso** and spend the next night. But get up bright and early in Ruidoso, for there's plenty to see and do in this resort village perched high in the picturesque Sacramento Mountains. If your tour is between May and Labor Day, then you must visit **Ruidoso Downs,** claimed by many to be the premier horse-racing facility in America. Nearby is **Hubbard Museum of the American West,** which displays a wide variety of Indian artifacts, horse-drawn vehicles, original art, antiques, and the Ruidoso Downs Horse Hall of Fame. Don't resist the pleasure of parking the car and just strolling down the main street, shopping or eating as you go.

8 Just outside Ruidoso, on the Mescalero Apache Indian Reservation, is the world-famous **Inn of the Mountain Gods.** Called New Mexico's most distinguished resort, the Apache-owned inn offers luxurious accommodations, fine dining, golf, tennis, boating, fishing, and several varieties of gambling, including poker and bingo.

9 Leave Ruidoso on Route 48 and drive north to **Capitan,** the home of the **Smokey Bear Historical Park** and Smokey's grave site. Nearby is the **Smokey Bear Museum,** which contains a nice exhibit of Smokey memorabilia.

10 Proceed east on U.S. 380 to **Lincoln.** Prepare to spend at least half a day in Lincoln and maybe more. This is Billy the Kid country, and there is plenty to see and do in the town's historic area. Tour the restored frontier town and site of Billy's last escape from the law. Depending on the time—and how absorbed in the Billy the Kid sites you became—you might consider spending the night at the Wortley-Pat Garrett Hotel before continuing your trip in the morning.

11 Backtrack on U.S. 380 to Capitan and then continue until you reach the town of **Carrizozo.** Twelve miles northeast of here, via U.S. 54 and Route 349, lies the legendary ghost town of **White Oaks,** which once boasted a population of 4,000, supporting three churches, two hotels, four newspapers, and quite a number of saloons. Finally abandoned in the 1950s, the town has undergone some restoration and renovation, but is still only a shadow of what it once was.

12 Returning to Carrizozo, continue southward along U.S. 54 through the village of Oscuro to the community of **Three Rivers** and the turnoff to **Three Rivers Petroglyph National Recreation Site** on your left. Here, more than 500 ancient drawings and rock carvings grace the cliffs overlooking the Tularosa basin. You should spend as much time as you can spare here, since the site offers an interpretive trail and other outdoor activities. Return to U.S. 54 and proceed southward on your way back to **Las Cruces.**

ACOMA PUEBLO

(Nearby town also listed: Grants)

Acoma Pueblo, sometimes called Sky City, once contained several hundred natives, and even today is a thriving village, providing home to a couple of dozen or so Native American families. Isolated atop a nearly 400-ft-high mesa, the pueblo's residents must haul in all supplies and daily necessities from below. You can get a sense of what that is like by hiking up the steep mesa via a primitive trail from the museum and gift shop. Acoma is one of the oldest continuously occupied villages in America, tracing its first habitation back to the 11th century. After nearly five decades of fruitless attempts, Spanish conquistadors finally conquered Acoma Pueblo in 1599, during an expedition led by Governor Don Juan de Oñate. As you listen to your tour guide explaining the Spanish conquest, you can almost see the glint of the approaching conquistadors' steel armor from far across the desert. If you like to gamble, be sure and visit Sky City Casino nearby.

Information: **Acoma Tourist Visitor Center** | Box 309, Acoma, 87034 | 505/470–4966 or 800/747–0181.

Attractions

★ **Acoma Pueblo.** You can ride a trolley or hoof it to the top of the 367-ft mesa upon which the pueblo of Acoma sits. Check in at the visitor center and museum first to orient yourself to what you are about to see at the top. The pueblo is located approximately 13 mi south of Interstate 40, exit 102, which is 12 mi east of Grants. | 505/470–4966 or 800/747–0181 | $9 | Apr.–mid-Oct., daily 8–6; mid-Oct.–Mar., daily 8–4.

Sky City Casino. The first high-stakes bingo facility in New Mexico, this newly refurbished casino features blackjack, roulette, craps, poker, bingo, and 350 slot machines. Take Interstate 40, exit 102, 12 mi east of Grants. | 888/759–2489 | www.skycitycasino.com | Free | Mon.–Thurs. 8 AM–4 PM, Fri.–Sun. 24 hrs.

ON THE CALENDAR

FEB.: *Governor's Feast.* This feast at Acoma Pueblo honors Acoma's newly elected governor and other elected officials and features men's dancing. | 505/740–4966 or 800/747–0181.

MAY: *Santa Maria Feast.* Santa Maria Feast is a celebration of McCarty's church in McCarty's Village. | 505/740–4966 or 800/747–0181.

AUG.: *Fiesta (St. Lorenzo's) Day.* This feast in the village of Acomita honors one of Acoma's patron saints, St. Lawrence, and features food and dancing. | 505/740–4966 or 800/747–0181.

SEPT.: *Feast of St. Estevan.* This is an annual celebration commemorating Acoma's patron saint, featuring food, dancing, and the harvest festival at Acoma Pueblo. | 505/740–4966 or 800/747–0181.

DEC.: *Christmas Festivals.* Acoma's four-day Christmas Festivals, from December 25 to 28, feature dancing in the San Estevan del Rey Mission. | 505/740–4966 or 800/747–0181.

ALAMOGORDO

(Nearby towns also listed: Cloudcroft, Las Cruces, Ruidoso)

Alamogordo, which means "large cottonwood" in Spanish, was first settled in the late 1890s, when the railroads opened the surrounding countryside to cattle, mining, and timber interests. Today the town is best remembered for its proximity to the White Sands Missile Range, created during World War Two as a training facility for B-17 bomber pilots. After the war, German rocket scientists were interned here to assist in the development of America's rocket and missile program. Also located nearby is the Trinity Site, where the first experimental atomic bomb was detonated in July 1945, and Holloman Air Force Base, where group tours are available by appointment. The Alameda Park Zoo is the oldest such facility in the Southwest and is home to 300 species of birds and mammals from around the world.

Information: **Alamogordo Chamber of Commerce** | Box 1301 N. White Sands Blvd., Alamogordo, 88311-0518 | 505/437-6120 or 800/826-0294.

Attractions

Alameda Park Zoo. More than 90 different displays show both domestic and foreign wildlife in natural settings. | 1021 N. White Sands Blvd. (U.S. 54/70) | 505/439-4290 or 505/437-1292 | $2.20 | Daily 9–5.

Eagle Ranch. You'll find the largest grove of pistachio trees in New Mexico here—some 12,000 trees—4 mi north of the White Sands Mall. Tour the farm, linger in the art gallery, or buy some nuts to take home. | 7288 Hwy. 54, at Hwy. 70 | 505/434-0035 or 800/432-0999 | www.eagleranchpistachios.com | Free farm tours | Sept.–May, weekdays at 1:30; June–Aug., weekdays at 10 and 1:30.

Lincoln National Forest. (*See* Ruidoso.) More than 1 million acres of native evergreens are included in this public land that covers parts of Lincoln, Otero, Eddy, and Chaves counties. The forest is divided into three sections, which lie northeast, east, and southeast of Alamogordo. The Forest Service supervisor's office is in Alamogordo. | 1101 New York Ave. | 505/434-7200 | fax 505/437-7218 | www.fs.fed.us/r3/lincoln | Free | Daily.

Oliver Lee Memorial State Park. Located in Dog Canyon, 10 mi south of Alamogordo off U.S. 54, this 180-acre park was once a stronghold for warring Apache Indians. Included in the park is a fully restored, 19th-century ranch house. | 409 Dog Canyon Rd. | 505/437-8284 | www.emnrd.state.nm.us/nmparks | $4 per vehicle | Daily; visitor center, daily 9–4.

Space Center–International Space Hall of Fame. This state-of-the-art facility 2 mi east of downtown Alamogordo features a simulated walk on Mars and lots of space and early rocketry exhibits, as well as a theater and planetarium, outdoor displays and parks, and the Space Hall of Fame. | Top of NM Hwy. 2001 | 505/437-2840 or 877-333-6589 | $2.50 | Weekdays 9–5.

Clyde W. Tombaugh Omnimax Theater and Planetarium. Adjacent to the Space Center, this theater and planetarium offers IMAX movies and laser shows. | Top of NM Hwy. 2001 | 505/437-2840 or 877-333-6589 | $5.50 for 1 movie, $9 for 2 movies | Daily 9–5.

Three Rivers Petroglyph National Recreation Site. Ancient Indians, who lived in the area between AD 1000 and 1350, carved thousands of pictures on the surrounding rocks here about 35 mi north of Alamogordo. It's one of the largest petroglyph sites in the United States. | County Rd. B30 | 505/525-4300 | $2 per vehicle | Daily.

Toy Train Depot. This model train museum at the north end of Alameda Park features hundreds of model and toy trains, plus a 2½-mi miniature train ride. | 1991 N. White Sands Blvd. | 505/437-2855 | $2 | Wed.–Sun. 12:30–4:30.

★ **White Sands National Monument.** Looking around at these huge white sand dunes 15 mi southwest of Alamogordo (some as high as 60 ft), you might think you were in the middle of the Sahara Desert. Actually it's White Sands National Monument, a vast expanse of brilliant white gypsum dunes lying 15 mi southwest of Alamogordo, between the San Andre and Sacramento mountains. Encompassing 275 square mi, this is the largest deposit of gypsum in the world. | Off I-70 | 505/679-2599 or 505/479-6124 | $3 | Memorial Day–mid-Aug., daily 7–10; mid-Aug.–Memorial Day, daily 7–5.

APR. AND OCT.: *Trinity Site Tour.* Twice a year, on the first Saturday of the month, you can visit the site of the first atomic bomb explosion. | 505/437–6120 or 800/826–0294.
SEPT.: *White Sands Annual Hot Air Balloon Invitational.* Colorful hot-air balloons drift over the gypsum sand dunes during this desert spectacle the third week in September | 505/682–3785.

Dining

Compass Rose. Continental. Patterned after a European-style pub, this unusual establishment has wooden bench seating and cozy surroundings, along with selections of cheese, meat, bread, salads, and hot sandwiches. The tasty food, including Reubens, pepper steaks, and the "ultimate ham and cheese," is a nice change of pace from Southwest fare. | 2203 E. 1st St. | 505/434–9633 | $6–$9 | AE, D, MC, V.

Margo's Mexican Food. Mexican. *Chalupas* (beans, meat, and cheese served on crisp tortillas) are the specialty at this casual, family-owned spot. In winter try *menudo,* made of hominy and tripe and served steaming hot. | 504 1st St. | 505/434–0689 | $5–$11 | AE, D, MC, V.

Palm Side Restaurant. Chinese. This popular Chinese restaurant offers a buffet at both lunch and dinner, including such favorites as dumplings, chow mein, and chicken wings. | 905 S. White Sands Blvd. | 505/437–8644 | $6–$10 | D, MC, V.

Ramona's Restaurant. Mexican. This casual family eatery with murals lining the walls is a favorite of locals, who appreciate good food at good prices. Try the chimichangas or huevos rancheros. | 2913 White Sands Blvd., 88310 | 505/437–7616 | $5–$10 | AE, MC, V.

Lodging

Best Western Desert Aire. This motel is an attractive adobe-and-brick building, with larger than average rooms. Complimentary Continental breakfast. Some microwaves, cable TV. Pool. Hot tub, sauna. Laundry facilities. Some pets allowed. | 1021 S. White Sands Blvd. | 505/437–2110 | fax 505/437–1898 | www.bestwestern.com | 100 rooms | $62–$109 | AE, D, DC, MC, V.

Days Inn. A late-1980s inexpensive motel that is clean and comfortable. Microwaves available, refrigerators, cable TV. Pool. Laundry facilities. | 907 S. White Sands Blvd. | 505/437–5090 | fax 505/434–5667 | www.daysinn.com | 40 rooms | $52–$65 | AE, D, DC, MC, V.

Holiday Inn Express. At this comfortable, two-story motel two blocks from the junction of highways 54 and 70, rooms are entered from an interior hallway, cutting down on noise. Complimentary Continental breakfast. In-room data ports, cable TV. Pool. Beauty salon. Laundry facilities, laundry service. Business services. Pets allowed. | 1401 S. White Sands Blvd. | 505/437–7100 or 800/465–4329 | fax 505/437–7100 | www.hiexpress.com | 108 rooms | $59–$75 | AE, D, DC, MC, V.

Satellite Inn. Medium-size budget motel on Alamogordo's main street. Some microwaves, refrigerators, cable TV, some in-room VCRs (and movies). Pool. Pets allowed. | 2224 N. White Sands Blvd. | 505/437–8454 or 800/221–7690 | fax 505/434–6015 | 40 rooms | $32–$46 | AE, D, DC, MC, V.

Super 8 Motel. This comfortable if spartan two-story motel on the northern edge of Alamogordo is located across the street from a shopping mall. Cable TV. Some pets allowed. Business services. | 3204 N. White Sands Blvd. | 505/434–4205 or 800/478–7378 | fax 505/434–4205 | www.super8.com | 57 rooms | $36–$60 | AE, D, DC, MC, V.

White Sands Inn. This lovely two-story motel is on Alamogordo's main street, within walking distance of three restaurants. It's a favorite of business travelers, who appreciate being only five minutes from downtown Alamogordo. Views are of the Sacramento Mountains. | 96 rooms. Complimentary Continental breakfast. Some microwaves, refrigerators, cable TV. Pool. Hot tub. Laundry facilities. Business services. | 1020 S. White Sands Blvd. | 505/434–4200 or 800/255–5061 | fax 505/437–8872 | $42–$65 | AE, D, DC, MC, V.

ALBUQUERQUE

MAP 9, D5

(Nearby towns also listed: Belén, Bernalillo, Laguna Pueblo)

With an end-of-the-millennium metropolitan population approaching 600,000, Albuquerque is the largest city in New Mexico. Strategically located at the crossroads of two of the nation's most traveled interstate highways, Interstate 40 and Interstate 25, the city is easily accessible by air, train, and motor vehicle.

Albuquerque was founded in 1706 and named in honor of its patron, Viceroy Francisco Fernandez de la Cueva, the Duke of Alburquerque. The first *r* in the name was dropped in later years. Old Town, the original settlement area, is a treasure to behold, and today contains shops, restaurants, and art galleries, as well as several nearby museums. The section's centerpiece, the historic San Felipe de Neri Church, is more than 200 years old. Take time to spend at least a half day just strolling through Old Town and reliving its historic past.

Clustered around Albuquerque are scores of pueblos, national monuments, state parks, and national forests, all of which are worth a visit. The nearby Sandia Mountains offer a wonderful ski area as well as a view of 15,000 square mi on a clear day. Temperatures range from an average low of around 22° in January to an average high of 93° in July. The humidity rarely exceeds 56% regardless of season, making for easy breathing.

ALBUQUERQUE, SANTA FE, AND TAOS

Probably the most popular and easily reached vacation destination in New Mexico is the skinny triangle anchored at each of its corners by the cities of Albuquerque, Santa Fe, and Taos. Set in the middle of the natural wonderland created by the Santa Fe and Carson national forests, the region is also close to several archaeological sites that highlight the prehistory of the Rio Grande valley, as well as 18 pueblos that still provide homes to thousands of Keres and Tanoan-speaking Indians. Albuquerque, the most accessible point by air, should be the starting point for any holiday that includes the three towns. Large, urban, and modern by anyone's definition, Albuquerque features hundreds of lodging, dining, cultural, and entertainment facilities, as well as a large number of outdoor attractions in the nearby national forests and along the Rio Grande. Santa Fe is one of the world's foremost art centers and is home to dozens of galleries that promote the work of both internationally known and local artisans. The Santa Fe Opera and other musical and performing arts attractions are among the best in the Southwest. Taos will remind you of a Mexican frontier town, yet it offers fine cuisine, above-average lodging facilities, and outstanding cultural and artistic attractions. A trip to the Albuquerque–Santa Fe–Taos "magic triangle" will provide you with a look at 500 years of history, spawned by three different cultures, not counting the stunning countryside that you will pass through to get there.

© Artville

More than 160 lodging choices are available in Albuquerque, plus hundreds of restaurants, ranging from those serving fast food to gourmet establishments that serve the very best in southwestern cuisine. Albuquerque truly blends the best of two worlds—yesterday and today—in a tradition that is not soon forgotten.

Information: Albuquerque Hispano Chamber of Commerce | 202 Central SE, Albuquerque, 87102 | 505/842–9003 | www.ahcnm.org.

Attractions
Albuquerque Biological Park. The park consists of the Albuquerque Aquarium, the Rio Grande Botanic Garden, and the Rio Grande Zoo, featuring sharks, sea lions, walled gardens, and a glass conservatory. The zoo contains 900 animals and 200 species. Opening 2001 is the Tingley Aquatic Park, which will replicate a wetland area and be home to both plants and wildlife. Gardens contain plants from the Southwest and Mediterranean climate zones. A combined ticket allows entrance to all three major exhibits. | 2601 Central Ave. NW | 505/764–6200 | www.cabq.gov/biopark | Park free; combined ticket for aquarium, botanic garden, and zoo $8 | Tues.–Sun. 9–5.

Albuquerque Aquarium. On the grounds of the Rio Grande Botanic Garden, the aquarium features a spectacular shark tank among its most popular exhibits. You can also watch a video following the path of a drop of water from the Rockies to the Gulf of Mexico. | 2601 Central Ave. NW | 505/764–6200 | www.cabq.gov/.biopark | Combined ticket for botanic garden and aquarium $4.50 | Tues.–Sun. 9–5.

Rio Grande Botanic Garden. The botanic garden features three walled gardens as well as a glass conservatory featuring exhibits of desert and Mediterranean flora. | 2601 Central Ave. NW | 505/764–6200 | www.cabq.gov/biopark | Combined ticket for aquarium and botanic garden $4.50 | Tues.–Sun. 9–5.

Rio Grande Zoo. An oasis of waterfalls, cottonwood trees, and naturalized animal habitats, the Rio Grande Zoo is one of the best-managed and most attractive facilities of its kind in the nation. More than 200 species of wildlife live here. | 903 10th St. SW | 505/764–6200 | www.cabq.gov.biopark | $4.50 | Tues.–Sun. 9–5.

Albuquerque Museum. This superb museum documents 400 years of Rio Grande history, culture, and art, including children's exhibits, a sculpture garden, and a complete gift shop. | 2000 Mountain Rd. NW | 505/242–4600 | fax 505/764–6546 | www.cabq.gov/museum | Free | Tues.–Sun. 9–5.

American International Rattlesnake Museum. Includes both exhibits on rattlesnakes and live specimens. The collection includes the largest number of different species of rattlesnake in the world. | 202 San Felipe St. NW | 505/242–6569 | www.rattlesnakes.com | $2.50 | Daily 10–6.

Cibola National Forest. In any direction you travel out of Albuquerque, you are bound to run into the 1.625-million-acre Cibola National Forest, which is headquartered in the city. The national forest includes the popular Sandia Peak ski area. Beyond that there is hiking, fishing, and hunting all over the forest, as well as old logging roads that can be used by four-wheelers, mountain bikers, and motorcyclists. | Supervisor: 2113 Osuna Rd. NE, Suite A | 505/346–2650 | fax 505/346–2663 | Free | Daily.

Sandia Peak Aerial Tramway. The view from atop Sandia Peak is breathtaking, and riding the 2.7-mi tramway to get there is even more exciting. The tram is located 5 mi northeast of Albuquerque via Interstate 25 or Interstate 40. | 10 Tramway Loop NE | 505/856–7325 or 505/856–1532 | fax 505/856–6490 | www.sandiapeak.com | $14 | Labor Day–Memorial Day, Thurs.–Tues. 9–8, Wed. 5–8; Memorial Day–Labor Day, daily 9 AM–10 PM.

Sandia Peak Ski Area. Sandia is one of the most popular ski areas in New Mexico, with 30 trails and a vertical drop of 1,800 ft. You'll find four chairlifts, one surface lift, and one children's mitey mite. The area contains novice, intermediate, and experienced trails, as well as cross-country trails; snowboarding is allowed throughout the ski area, which is located in the Cibola National Forest 6 mi east of Albuquerque. | Hwy. 536 | 505/242–9133 or 505/

242–9052 | www.sandiapeak.com | $34; special rates for children and senior citizens | Mid-Dec.–mid-Mar., daily 9–4.

★ **Indian Pueblo Cultural Center.** This cooperative center showcases the cultural life of the region's 19 pueblos via cultural displays and a children's museum. | 2401 12th St. NW | 505/843–7270 or 800/766–4405 | fax 505/842–6959 | $4 | Museum: daily 9–5:30; restaurant: daily 7:30–3:30.

Isleta Pueblo. The fourth-largest pueblo in New Mexico, with more than 200,000 acres, located 13 mi south of Albuquerque, is one of only two Tiwa-speaking communities in the middle Rio Grande Valley. The community's church, St. Augustine, is perhaps the oldest church in New Mexico, built about 1613. While the economic base of the pueblo is agriculture, the residents here also create polychrome pottery with red-and-black designs on a white background. Camera use is restricted within the pueblo; only the church may be photographed. | Tribal Rd. 40 off U.S. 85 | 505/869–3111 or 800/766–4405 | Free | Daily.

Isleta Gaming Palace. New Mexico's largest Indian gambling casino features blackjack, craps, high-stakes bingo, roulette, and 800 slot machines. | 11000 Broadway SE (I–25, exit 215) | 505/869–2614 or 800/460–5686 | isletagamingpalace.com | Free | Mon.–Thurs. 7 AM–3 AM, Fri.–Sun. 24 hrs.

National Atomic Museum. The only national museum of its kind in the United States features B-29 and B-52 bomber exhibits, a Titan II missile, and nuclear medicine and robotics displays. The museum also contains the world's largest display of unclassified nuclear weapons. It's located on Kirtland Air Force Base, about 2½ mi south of Albuquerque, at the Wyoming Gate, where you must stop and check in before parking. | 5 Wyoming Blvd. | 505/284–3243 | www.atomicmuseum.com | $3 | Daily 9–5.

New Mexico Museum of Natural History and Science. A simulated volcano, complete with bubbling lava flows, and an Ice Age cave are two of the highlights of Albuquerque's most popular museum. A large exhibit of dinosaurs and fossils shows what New Mexico was like millions of years ago. The Dynamax theater pulls you into the action during IMAX films. | 1801 Mountain Rd. NW | 505/841–2802 | fax 505/841–2866 | www.nmmnh-abq.mus.nm.us | $5, Dynamax theater $6, combined ticket to museum and Dynamax theater $9 | Daily 9–5.

Old Town Plaza. Almost 200 shops, restaurants, and galleries are located around this plaza, the oldest part of Albuquerque, which dates from 1706. San Felipe de Neri church faces the square. | Bounded by Rio Grande Blvd., Central Ave., and Mountain Rd. | No phone | Free | Daily.

Old Town Visitors Center. Event schedules and maps are available here, across the street from San Felipe de Neri Catholic Church. | 303 Romero St. NW | 505/243–3215 | Free | Labor Day–Memorial Day, daily 9:30–4:30; Memorial Day–Labor Day, daily 9–5.

Petroglyph National Monument. Thousands of years ago, New Mexico's prehistoric residents executed more than 17,000 petroglyphs (rock carvings) on the escarpment walls of this area 9 mi west of Albuquerque. Walking trails (one paved) lead past the carvings | Visitor center: 6001 Unser Blvd. NW | 505/899–0205 or 505/839–4429 | $2 per vehicle | Daily 8–5.

Rio Grande Nature Center State Park. This nature reserve in a portion of the nation's largest cottonwood forest (called "The Bosque") is a haven for migratory waterfowl and all manner of other birds. The history, ecology, and geology of the Rio Grande Valley are told in a partially underground visitor center on the east bank of the Rio Grande. | 2901 Candelaria Rd. NW | 505/344–7240 | $1 | Daily 10–5.

San Felipe de Neri Catholic Church. Erected in 1793, this is still an active parish church. Though expanded over time, its adobe walls and other original features remain. The small museum displays relics dating to the 17th century. | 2005 N. Plaza NW | 505/243–4628 | Free | Church: Mon.–Sat. 7–6; museum: weekdays 9–noon and 1–4:30, Sat. 9–1.

Telephone Pioneer Museum of New Mexico. Housed in a 1906 building in downtown Albuquerque, this museum's exhibits document the history of the telephone, especially in New Mexico. The collection includes such artifacts as the switchboard used to warn New Mexicans of Pancho Villa's attack. | 110 4th St. NW | 505/842–2937 | www.nmculture.org | $1 | Weekdays 10–2, tours by appointment.

Turquoise Museum. A museum devoted to the semiprecious stone, including displays on how it is formed and mined. You can learn some of the ancient uses of, and mythology associated with this stone, and how to tell fakes from the real deal. | 2107 Central Ave. NW | 505/247–8650 or 800/821–7443 | $2 | Mon.–Sat. 9:30–5:30.

University of New Mexico. Brown pueblo buildings give this institution a historic look; the architecture itself is noteworthy as one of the early examples of the 20th-century Pueblo Revival style as interpreted by John Gaw Meem, who designed the old wing of the Zimmerman Library and the Alumni Chapel. The university was established in 1889 and is the state's leading educational institution. The grounds, with a duck pond, waterfalls, and benches, are lovely and peaceful. | University Blvd. at Central Ave. | 505/277–0111 | www.unm.edu | Free | Daily 8–5.

Center for the Arts. A library, a theater, and an immense collection of fine art are contained in this complex that is also the home of the New Mexico Symphony Orchestra. | University of New Mexico, at the end of Stanford Dr. | 505/277–4569 or 505/277–4001 | fax 505/277–7315 | Free | Tues.–Fri. 9–4, Sun. 1–4.

Ernie Pyle Branch Library. This house is the smallest branch library of the Albuquerque Public Library system, which was built by Pulitzer Prize–winning reporter Ernie Pyle. It contains displays on Pyle's life. | 900 Girard Blvd. SE | 505/256–2065 | Free | Tues.–Wed. 10–8, Thurs.–Sat. 10–6.

Institute of Meteoritics Meteorite Museum. This small museum showcases highlights of the institute's meteorite collection. | University of New Mexico, 200 Yale Blvd. NE, in Northrop Hall | 505/277–1644 | fax 505/277–3577 | Free | Weekdays 9–4.

Jonson Gallery. This gallery houses important paintings by modernist Raymond Jonson and contemporaries. | 1909 Las Lomas NE | 505/277–4967 | fax 2773188 | www.unm.edu/~jonson | Free | Tues. 9–8, Wed.–Fri. 9–4.

Maxwell Museum of Anthropology. An important institution at the University of New Mexico, the Maxwell museum highlights cultures from around the world, but focuses on those of the Southwest. It's the only museum in the Southwest that offers a comprehensive overview of human culture. | University of New Mexico, Redondo Dr., in the Anthropology Building | 505/277–4404 | fax 505/277–1547 | www.unm.edu/~maxwell | Free | Tues.–Fri. 9–4, Sat. 10–4.

Tamarind Institute. This world-famous institution played a major role in reviving the fine art of collaborative lithographic printing. A gallery exhibits prints, lithographs and monotypes made by visiting artists. Guided tours (reservations essential) are conducted on the first Friday of each month at 1:30. | 108 Cornell Dr. SE | 505/277–3901 | www.unm.edu/~Etamarind/ | Free | Tues.–Fri. 9–5.

University of New Mexico Library. This library contains more than 1 million books, including those in the Western Americana Collection, the New Mexicana Collection, and the John Gaw Meem Archive of Southwest Architecture. | University of New Mexico, Center for the Arts | 505/277–4241 | Free | Mon.–Thurs. 8 AM–12 AM, Fri. 8 AM–9 PM, Sat. 9 AM–6 PM, Sun. 10 AM–12 AM.

SIGHTSEEING TOURS/TOUR COMPANIES

Gray Line Albuquerque. This national company offers tours of many of the sights in and around Albuquerque. Options include "Discover Albuquerque," a half-day tour of the city; "Acoma Indian Pueblo," a partial-day tour of the pueblo east of town; and "A Day in Santa Fe," which is a full-day tour of the nearby state capital. | 8401 Jefferson NE | 505/242–3880 or 800/256–8991 | fax 505/243–0692 | www.grayline-abq.com/ | $23–$39 | Tour offices: 5:30 AM–10 PM; some tours not offered every day, so call for times.

ON THE CALENDAR

JAN.: *Kings' Day.* This dance festival held at most of the pueblos in the Albuquerque area celebrates the buffalo, elk, deer, and eagle. | 505/843–7270.

APR.: *Founders Day.* A spring festival celebrating the founding of Albuquerque in 1706, held in Old Town Albuquerque. | 505/338–2399.

JUNE: *New Mexico Arts and Crafts Fair.* Craftsmen from all over the region gather to display their handiwork. | 505/265–1791.

JUNE: *San Antonio Feast Day.* The corn dance is featured at this festival at Sandia and Taos pueblos. | 505/867–3317 or 505/758–9593.

JUNE: *San Pedro Feast Day.* The corn dance is featured at this feast day at Santa Ana Pueblo. | 505/867–3301.

JULY: *Santa Ana Feast Day.* This feast day held at the Old Village features the corn dance, food, and other festivities. | 505/867–3301.

AUG.: *St. Augustin's Feast Day.* Mass in the morning is followed by dancing in the afternoon at Isleta Pueblo. | 505/869–3111.

AUG.–MAY: *Albuquerque Little Theatre.* This community theater has brought live theatrical performances to the Albuquerque community since 1930; the theater is located at 224 San Pasquale Southwest. | 505/242–4750.

SEPT.: *New Mexico State Fair.* This is New Mexico's annual exposition of its agricultural, ranching, and handicraft heritage held at the state fairgrounds on San Pedro Drive, between Lomas and Central boulevards. | 505/265–1791.

SEPT.–MAY: *New Mexico Symphony Orchestra.* The state's largest professional orchestra provides exceptional musical enrichment and enjoyment for New Mexicans and visitors alike. Concerts are held in the Center for the Arts on the University of New Mexico campus. | 505/881–9590 or 800/251–NMSO, 505/881–8999 for ticket info.

OCT.: *Kodak Albuquerque International Balloon Fiesta.* More than 850 hot-air balloons from all over the world compete for prizes in Balloon Fiesta Park in northwest Albuquerque. | 800/284–2282.

NOV. 12.: *San Diego Feast Day.* Corn is honored on this feast day in Jemez and Tesuqe pueblos. | 505/834–7235.

Dining

Antiquity. Continental. This quiet, romantic restaurant has intimate, private booths. Try the filet mignon on a bed of artichoke leaves topped with artichoke hearts and béarnaise sauce. Beer and wine only. | 112 Romero St. NW | 505/247–3545 | No lunch | $16–$25 | AE, D, MC, V.

★ **The Artichoke Café.** Contemporary. In a century-old building, the two-tiered dining room of this French-American bistro spills out onto a small courtyard. Known for grilled duck, breast of free-range chicken with wild mushrooms, and a menu heavy on organic ingredients. | 424 Central SE | 505/243–0200 | Closed Sun. No lunch Sat. | $12–$23 | AE, D, DC, MC, V.

Avalon. Contemporary. A white-linen, New American restaurant that is spacious and softly lit. Try the pork tenderloin, Atlantic salmon, or roast chicken. | 515 Central Ave. NW, 87102 | 505/924–1537 | Closed Sun., Mon. | $7–$20 | AE, DC, MC, V.

Barelas Coffee House. Mexican. Diners come from all over the city to sup in this old-fashioned chile parlor in the Hispanic Historic Route 66 neighborhood south of downtown. Looking like a movie set in search of a script, this spot is filled with dedicated chile eaters eager to dive into a bowl of Barelas potent red. | 1502 4th St. SW, 87102 | 505/843–7577 | Reservations not accepted | Closed Sun. No dinner | $2–$6 | D, MC, V.

Barry's Oasis. Mediterranean. This simple but romantic café-style restaurant specializes in lamb, shrimp, and chicken. The menu is a mix of France, Italy, Spain, and Greece. Belly dancer Friday–Saturday. Kids' menu. | 5400 San Mateo NE | 505/884–2324 | No lunch Sun., Mon. | $8–$20 | D, DC, MC, V.

Café De Las Placita. Continental. Cool adobe surrounds this tall-ceiling charmer scattered with potted plants. Try the wood-roasted pork chop with barbecue sauce or one of the other beef or lamb dishes. In the secluded, brick-walled garden you can hear the crickets chirping. Beer and wine only. | 664 Hwy. 165, Placitas | 505/867–1610 | Closed Sun., Mon. | $12–$21 | AE, D, MC, V.

Café Spoleto. Italian. Quiet, candlelight dining. Try the *saltinboca forestiera*. Beer and wine only. No smoking. | 2813 San Mateo NE | 505/880–0897 | Closed Sun., Mon. No lunch | $12–$18 | AE, D, DC, MC, V.

Casa De Benivadez. Mexican. This local favorite with a romantic patio serves some of the best fajitas in town. The chile is faultless, which may explain the dedicated clientele. | 8032 4th St. NW | 505/898–3311 | No dinner Sun. | $8–$24 | AE, D, DC, MC, V.

Chef Du Jour. Contemporary. At this small café with an open kitchen, a popular lunch spot, you'll find an eclectic menu of everything from garden burgers and tamales to salmon tacos (pan-seared salmon wrapped in a tortilla with citrus slaw and a black-bean relish. Try the ice cream–filled chocolate burrito with house-made caramel sauce for dessert. Known for fresh, seasonal foods and great house-made condiments. Outdoor tables are shaded by an awning. No smoking. | 119 San Pasquale SW | 505/247–8998 | Closed Sun. No lunch Sat. No dinner except Fri. and Sat. | $10–$20 | MC, V.

Christy Mae's. American/Casual. A nice, inexpensive, down-home restaurant known for its chicken potpie. Kids' menu. | 1400 San Pedro NE | 505/255–4740 | Closed Sun. | $6–$10 | AE, D, MC, V.

Conrad's Downtown. Southwestern. This cheerful, sunny restaurant in the Posada de Albuquerque Hotel offers such choices as blue cornmeal–encrusted calamari, a sugar-cured Black Angus tenderloin, and braised lamb empanada with cucumber raita. Entertainment weekends. | 125 2nd St. NW | 505/242–9090 | $10–$22 | AE, D, DC, MC, V.

The Cooperage. Steak. This dark, elegant dining room is good for romance and a quiet conversation. Known for prime rib in cuts from 7 to 14 ounces or the lightly breaded, deep-fried shrimp. A wide variety of other steaks and seafood is on the menu. | 7220 Lomas Blvd. NE | 505/255–1657 | $13–$28 | AE, D, DC, MC, V.

County Line BBQ. American. This popular and cheerful outlet of the nationally acclaimed barbecue chain overlooks Albuquerque. Known for their smoked brisket; also try the beef and pork ribs and smoked sausage. Kids' menu. | 9600 Tramway Blvd. NE | 505/856–7477 | Reservations not accepted | No lunch | $10–$20 | AE, D, DC, MC, V.

Duran Central Pharmacy. Mexican. This expanded Old Town lunch counter with a dozen tables and a tiny patio just might serve the best tortillas in town. A favorite of old-timers who know their way around a blue-corn enchilada, Duran is an informal place whose patrons give their food the total attention it deserves. | 1815 Central Ave. NW | 505/247–4141 | No dinner weekends | $4–$8 | No credit cards.

El Norteño. Mexican. The interior of this casual, home-style restaurant recalls Old Mexico, as does the food. If you've never tried goat, this is the place to do it, also the mole and menudo. Kids' menu. Beer and wine only. | 6416 Zuni SE | 505/255–2057 | $6–$10 | AE, D, MC, V.

El Patio. Mexican. A university-area hangout, this sentimental favorite among alums has consistently great food served on the funky patio. Try the green-chile chicken enchiladas, some of the best in town, or any of the heart-healthy and vegetarian selections. Watch out for the fiery green chiles served at harvest time. | 142 Harvard St. NE | 505/268–4245 | Reservations not accepted | $5–$9 | MC, V.

El Pinto. Mexican. Hanging plants, original art, and several waterfalls decorate the interior of this sprawling restaurant. Dine in one of several cozy rooms or on one of the two patios. Try the enchiladas, chiles rellenos, or tamales, and enjoy the homemade tortillas and house-roasted chiles. Open-air dining on a romantic patio with plants and a fountain. Kids' menu. | 10500 4th St. NW | 505/898–1771 | $7–$14 | AE, D, DC, MC, V.

Fajitaville. Mexican. An innovative addition to the Albuquerque scene, this restaurant in a converted drive-in serves healthful, greaseless, cooked-to-order fajitas with fabulous fresh salsa. Try the chicken fajita with the roasted tomato-chipotle salsa. | 6313 4th St. NW | 505/341–9683 | Reservations not accepted | $6–$8 | AE, D, MC, V.

Garcia's Kitchen. Mexican. Authentic Mexican cooking makes the Old Town location of this local chain a good stop for smooth red chile and daily lunch specials like flautas or chicken enchiladas. With colorful clowns, chiles, and bright piñatas hanging from the ceiling, the decor might best be described as early carnival toy. | 1736 Central Ave. SW | 505/842–0273 | Reservations not accepted | $2–$7 | AE, D, DC, MC, V.

Garduño's. Mexican. This chain restaurant is a festive, elaborately decorated spot for moderately priced, middle-of-the-road Mexican fare and tangy margaritas. Outdoor dining in a plazalike setting, complete with fountain. Entertainment Thursday–Sunday. Kids' menu. Sunday brunch. | 10551 Montgomery NE | 505/298–5000 | $8–$13 | AE, D, DC, MC, V.

High Finance Restaurant and Tavern. Continental. This high-in-the-clouds restaurant is atop Sandia Mountain, overlooking Albuquerque, and you must take the Sandia Peak Tramway to get here. The food is okay, but the view is stupendous. Try the prime rib, stir-fried vegetables, or the Szechuan chicken. | 40 Tramway Rd. | 505/243–9742 | Reservations essential | No lunch Wed. | $16–$35 | AE, D, DC, MC, V.

High Noon. Contemporary. Located in a historic adobe building with viga ceilings, formerly a woodworking shop, this sophisticated restaurant offers such dishes as a bison rib eye, grilled dry-aged lamb chops, and smoked duck tamales. Great margaritas. Guitarist Thursday–Saturday. | 425 San Felipe St. NW | 505/765–1455 | $12–$26 | AE, D, DC, MC, V.

Il Vicino. Italian. The gourmet pizzas here are baked in a European-style, wood-fired oven and come with 25 possible toppings. A favorite is the rustica, a buttery cornmeal crust topped with roasted garlic, artichokes, calamata olives, and capers. Good salads, pastas, and micro-brewery beers are also served. | 3403 Central Ave. NE | 505/266–7855 | Reservations not accepted | $5–$8 | MC, V.

La Crêpe Michelle. French. Next to San Felipe de Neri Church, this intimate country café serves traditional French dishes and innovative crêpes filled with chicken, beef, seafood, and vegetables, in addition to the standard dessert crêpes. | 400 C-2 San Felipe St. NW | 505/242–1251 | Closed Mon. No dinner Sun. | $8–$20 | MC, V.

La Hacienda Dining Room. Southwestern. This casual restaurant, decorated with south-western-style paintings by regional artists, is popular with tourists who come for the combination platters of hearty Mexican fare (taco, enchilada, tamale, and chiles rellenos) and fajitas. Entertainment Wednesday–Sunday. Open-air dining on a patio. Kids' menu. | 302 San Felipe NW | 505/243–3131 | $8–$10 | AE, D, DC, MC, V.

La Placita. Southwestern. Housed in a historic hacienda dating from 1706 just off Central Avenue (Route 66), this restaurant's six dining rooms double as art galleries, filled with outstanding Native American and southwestern paintings. The menu includes chiles rellenos, enchiladas, tacos, and sopaipillas as well as some American standards. | 208 San Felipe St. NW | 505/247–2204 | $5–$14 | AE, D, DC, MC, V.

Le Café Miche. French. A little bit of France in a shopping center, this quiet, romantic spot is a favorite place for a special night out. Try piccata-style veal, and the lamb shank braised in rosemary and garlic. Considered one of the best restaurants in New Mexico. | 1431 Wyoming NE | 505/299–6088 | Reservations essential | Closed Mon. No lunch weekends | $13–$19 | AE, D, DC, MC, V.

Los Cuates. Mexican. Frequently voted the best Mexican restaurant in local polls, this is a classic. The soft chicken taco smothered with green chiles and the chiles rellenos are tops. The roast beef burrito could be a contender for the best burrito in town. Fresh chips and spicy salsa are brought immediately to your table or red-vinyl booth. Portions are gargantuan. | 5016B Lomas Blvd. NE, 87110 | 505/268–0974 | Reservations not accepted | $5–$6 | AE, D, DC, MC, V.

M & J's Sanitary Tortilla Factory. Mexican. Nice and inexpensive, this small, casual lunch spot serves home-style Mexican favorites such as chiles rellenos, but also some good veal and chicken dishes. Kids' menu. | 403 2nd St. SW | 505/242–489 | Closed Sun. No dinner | $5–$9 | No credit cards.

Maine-Ly Lobster and Steakhouse. Seafood. This restaurant maintains a New England atmosphere, complete with antique lobster traps, buoys, painted lobster claws. Beer and wine only. | 300 San Pedro NE | 505/878–0070 | $11–$33 | AE, DC, MC, V.

Manhattan on the Rio Grande. American/Casual. A restaurant and pub with a deli serving overstuffed sandwiches as well as pasta and pizza. There is patio seating next to refreshing fountains, but this Manhattan sleeps, closing at 10 PM. | 901 Rio Grande St. | 505/248–1514 | $6–$10 | AE, MC, V.

Maria Teresa Restaurant & 1840 Bar. Continental. This elegant, romantic eatery in a 19th-century hacienda is full of original art and built around a fountain courtyard. Try the rack of Colorado lamb. Outside dining in a courtyard. Kids' menu. Sunday brunch. | 618 Rio Grande Blvd. NW | 505/242–3900 | $13–$25 | AE, DC, MC, V.

Monte Vista Fire Station. Southwestern. In an old fire station (circa 1936), complete with brass fire pole and a bar upstairs in the former sleeping quarters. There's also a great view of the mountains. Try the grilled sea scallops with roasted corn and cilantro pancakes, or the herb-crusted lamb loin. Open-air dining on a small patio surrounded by bushes and flowers. | 3201 Central NE | 505/255–2424 | No lunch weekends | $11–$20 | AE, D, DC, MC, V.

New Chinatown. Chinese. Look for the red and green pagoda to recognize this bustling, moderately priced Chinese restaurant, which also has a more intimate romantic room. Known for Szechuan cuisine; try the spicy chicken and shrimp. Buffet lunch. Piano bar. | 5001 Central Ave. NE | 505/265–8859 | $7–$15 | AE, D, DC, MC, V.

Portobello: A Taste of Tuscany. Italian. At the Courtyard Shopping Center, at San Mateo and Lomas, simple northern Italian dishes are prepared with fresh ingredients. Favorites include steak Portobello topped with fried leeks, veal scaloppine, and a daily fresh fish special. | 1100 San Mateo NE, Suite 50, 87110 | 505/232–9119 | No lunch Sat. | $11–$22 | AE, D, DC, MC, V.

Scalo Northern Italian Grill. Italian. An informal spot serving fine Italian food and wine. Try *salmon alla como* (a marinated, grilled salmon fillet) or one of the daily fresh fish specials. The homemade pastas and desserts are mighty fine as well. Open-air dining on a patio. | 3500 Central Ave. SE | 505/255–8782 | No lunch Sun. | $8–$17 | AE, D, DC, MC, V.

Seasons Rotisserie-Grill. Contemporary. Upbeat and elegant, this Old Town eatery is conveniently located near museums and shops. Try the spit-roasted half-chicken or the double-cut pork rib chop. | 2031 Mountain Rd. NW | 505/766–5100 | $13–$29 | AE, D, DC, MC, V.

66 Diner. American/Casual. A roadside diner hung with vintage photographs. A good place for a burger or an old-fashioned milk shake. You can dine outside on the patio. Kids' menu. Beer and wine only. | 1405 Central Ave. NE | 505/247–1421 | $3–$7 | AE, D, DC, MC, V.

Souper Salad. American/Casual. You can get a quick meal at this spot in the Montgomery Plaza Center. Salad bar. | 4411 San Mateo NE | 505/883–9534 | $3–$6 | No credit cards.

Trattoria Trombino. Italian. This casual family-friendly restaurant recalls an Italian piazza. Known for modestly priced seafood and pasta dishes. Kids' menu. Sunday brunch. | 5415 Academy Blvd. NE | 505/821–5974 | No lunch weekends | $6–$17 | AE, D, DC, MC, V.

Yanni's Mediterranean Bar and Grill. Greek. The Nob Hill district, ¼ mi east of the University of New Mexico, is where you can find excellent Greek dining. This airy and popular spot has wood floors, arched windows, and an outdoor patio where you can enjoy souvlakis, gyros, grilled lamb chops, and fresh halibut. Vegetarian options are the meatless moussaka, spanikopita, and stuffed grape leaves. | 3109 Central NE | 505/268–9250 | $9–$22 | AE, D, MC, V.

Yester-Dave's Grill, Bar and Bakery. American/Casual. This 1950s-style diner is something out of Wally Cleaver's days, complete with a soda fountain. There's a small patio where you can eat outside if it's not too hot. Good for burgers and other light fare. | 10601 Montgomery NE | 505/293–0033 | $7–$13 | AE, D, DC, MC, V.

Lodging

Adobe and Roses B&B. You're "in the country" here, about 15 minutes from downtown Albuquerque, with a great view of the western slopes of the Sandia Mountains. Should you wish to fix your own breakfast in your room, 10% will be deducted. Complimentary breakfast. Kitchenettes, cable TV. Pets allowed. No smoking. | 1011 Ortega St. NW | 505/898–0654 | 1 room, 2 suites | $60–$95 (2-day minimum stay) | No credit cards.

Albuquerque Hilton Hotel. This upscale chain hotel successfully marries southwestern style with comtemporary sophistication: Native American rugs, western and Native American art, and Santa Fe–style furniture. Only 4 mi from the airport. Restaurants, bar (with entertainment). In-room data ports, some refrigerators, cable TV. 2 pools (1 indoor). Hot tub. Tennis. Gym. Business services. | 1901 University Blvd. NE | 505/884–2500 | fax 505/889–9118 | www.hilton.com | 264 rooms, 6 suites | $69–$139 rooms, $175–$425 suites | AE, D, DC, MC, V.

Albuquerque Howard Johnson Express. An inexpensive chain motel near the Convention Center and Old Town. Complimentary Continental breakfast. In-room data ports, cable TV. Pool. Hot tub. Business services, airport shuttle. | 411 McKnight Ave. NW | 505/242–5228 or 800/446–4656 | fax 505/766–9218 | 100 rooms | $50–$64 | AE, D, DC, MC, V.

Albuquerque I-40 Tramway Travelodge. This two-story budget motel was built in 1989. Complimentary Continental breakfast. Cable TV. Some pets allowed. | 13139 Central Ave. NE | 505/292–4878 | fax 505/299–1822 | www.travelodge.com | 41 rooms | $40–$60 | AE, D, DC, MC, V.

Albuquerque Travelodge. This inexpensive two-story motel has nicely landscaped gardens and ample free parking. Complimentary Continental breakfast. Some refrigerators, cable TV. Pool. Laundry facilities. Business services, airport shuttle. | 2120 Menaul Blvd. NE | 505/884–0250 or 800/444–7378 | fax 505/883–0594 | www.travelodge.com | 200 rooms, 33 suites | $55–$76, $76–$135 suites | AE, D, DC, MC, V.

Amberly Suite Hotel. This full-service, all-suite hotel near Balloon Fiesta Park has spacious rooms with full kitchens. They will even do grocery shopping for you. Restaurant, bar, complimentary breakfast. In-room data ports, kitchenettes, microwaves, refrigerators, cable TV. Pool. Hot tub. Gym. Laundry facilities. Business services, airport shuttle. Pets allowed (fee). | 7620 Pan American Fwy. NE | 505/823–1300 or 800/333–9806 | fax 505/823–2896 | www.calav.com/amberley | $99–$138 | 170 suites | AE, D, DC, MC, V.

Barcelona Suites Uptown. With tile floors and wrought-iron railings, this colorful mauve and turquoise hotel has stained-glass windows in the ceiling and fountains in the atrium. The furnishings are contemporary southwestern, and rooms are spacious and have galley kitchens. Complimentary breakfast. Kitchenettes, minibars, microwaves, some in-room hot tubs, cable TV. 2 pools. Sauna. | 900 Louisiana Blvd. NE | 505/255–5566 | fax 505/266–6644 | www.barsuites.com | 164 suites | $79–$89, $189 Jacuzzi suite with fireplace | AE, MC, V.

Best Western Inn at Rio Rancho. On 2 acres of manicured, well-landscaped grounds, this inexpensive, resort-style motel is 10 mi northwest of Albuquerque in Rio Rancho. Restaurant, bar (with entertainment), picnic area, room service. In-room data ports, some kitchenettes, some microwaves, refrigerators, cable TV, some in-room VCRs. Pool. Hot tub. Exercise equipment. Laundry facilities. Business services, airport shuttle. Some pets allowed (fee). | 1465 Rio Rancho Dr. | 505/892–1700 | fax 505/892–4628 | 121 rooms | $55–$67 | AE, D, DC, MC, V.

Best Western Rio Grande Inn. This bright motel has a tiled lobby and a vaulted ceiling depicting the open sky. It's just off exit 157A of Interstate 40, a ¼-mi walk from Old Town and 1 mi from the Albuquerque Zoo and Botanical Gardens. Rooms are decorated with regional authenticity using custom-made furnishings, handcrafted wood furniture, tin sconces, and locally produced art for the walls. Restaurant, some refrigerators, cable TV, room phones. Pool. Hot tub. Free parking. | 1015 Rio Grande Blvd. NW | 505/843–9500 or 800/959–4726 | fax 505/843–9238 | www.riograndeinn.com | 171 rooms, 2 suites | $79–$125, $199 suites | AE, D, DC, MC, V.

Best Western Winrock Inn. Adjacent to Winrock Mall and its theaters and restaurants and just off Interstate 40, this quiet, two-story motel surrounds a lovely pool area. Complimentary breakfast. Some refrigerators, cable TV. Pool. Laundry facilities. Business services. | 18 Winrock Center NE | 505/883–5252 | fax 505/889–3206 | www.bestwestern.com | 173 rooms | $69–$125 | AE, D, DC, MC, V.

Böttger Mansion B&B. A restored Victorian mansion in historic Old Town, complete with lace, antiques, and a quiet courtyard to escape the Old Town crowds. Some of the rooms have their original pressed-tin ceilings. Complimentary breakfast. Cable TV, in-room VCRs. | 110 San Felipe NW | 505/243/–3639 or 800/758–3639 | fax 505/243–4378 | 8 rooms | $89–$179 | AE, D, DC, MC, V.

Brittania and W.E. Mauger Estate B&B. This redbrick Queen Anne Victorian is conveniently located downtown within walking distance of Old Town, making it popular with businesspeople and tourists alike. Complimentary breakfast. In-room data ports, refrigerators, cable TV. Laundry service. Business services. Pets allowed. | 701 Roma Ave. NW | 505/242–8755 or 800/719–9189 | fax 505/842–8835 | www.maugerbb.com | 8 rooms (with shower only) | $79–$189 | AE, D, DC, MC, V.

Casa del Granjero. This romantic, historic adobe hacienda offers large Spanish-style rooms, many with adobe fireplaces. Complimentary breakfast. Some microwaves, some refrigerators, no room phones, no TV, TV in common area. Hot tub, massage, sauna. Business services. No smoking. | 414 C de Baca La. NW | 505/897–4144 or 800/701–4144 | fax 505/897–9788 | www.innewmexico.com | 8 rooms (2 with shower only), 5 suites in 2 buildings | $79–$159 | D, DC, MC, V.

Casas de Sueños. Old-world antiques fill this sprawling Mexican-style compound with many private casitas surrounding a lovely courtyard, just a block from Old Town. The main building was designed by Albuquerque architect Bart Prince. Complimentary breakfast. In-room data ports, some kitchenettes, cable TV. Business services. No kids under 12. No smoking. | 310 Rio Grande SW | 505/247–4560 or 800/242–8987 | fax 505/842–8493 | 26 rooms, 15 one-bedroom casitas, 6 two-bedroom casitas | $85–$250, $135–$170 1–bedroom casitas, $155–$225 2–bedroom casitas | AE, D, DC, MC, V.

Casita Chamisa. In the village (now an Albuquerque suburb) of Los Ranchos, 15 minutes north of Old Town, this B&B is the former home of Jack Schaefer, author of the best-selling western *Shane*. The house sits atop an active archaeological site, and one of the owners is an archaeologist. Both units have fireplaces and access to a greenhouse, sundeck, and gardens. Complimentary Continental breakfast. Some kitchenettes. Pool. Hot tub. Pets allowed. | 850 Chamisal Rd. NW | 505/897–4644 | www.casitachamisa.com | 1 room, one 2-bedroom casita | $95 room, $135 casita | AE, MC, V.

Chocolate Turtle. This B&B in Corrales, 15 mi north of Albuquerque and 16 mi from the airport, is an adobe building decorated in southwestern style. Guests share a great room with views of the Sandia Mountains. A common refrigerator is stocked with cold drinks. Complimentary breakfast. Some in-room VCRs (and movies) available, no room phones, no TV in some rooms, TV in common area. Hot tub. Business services. No kids under 6. No smoking. | 1098 W. Meadowlark La., Corrales | 505/898–1800 or 800/898–1842 | www.collectorsguide.com/chocturtle | 4 rooms (3 with shower only), 1 suite | $60–$80, $95 suite | AE, D, MC, V.

Clubhouse Inn. Some rooms have private patios and balconies at this chain hotel 5 mi from the airport. Rooms are in several buildings surrounding a landscaped courtyard with a pool. Complimentary Continental breakfast. Some kitchenettes, cable TV. Pool. Hot tub. Business services. | 1315 Menaul Blvd. NE | 505/345–0010 | fax 505/344–3911 | www.clubhouse-inn.com | 136 rooms | $89–$133 | AE, D, DC, MC, V.

Comfort Inn Airport. This serviceable establishment is 1 mi from the airport. The rooms here have an uninspired but acceptable decor and furnishings. Complimentary Continental breakfast. In-room data ports, cable TV. Pool. Hot tub. Airport shuttle. | 2300 Yale Blvd. SE, 87106 | 505/243–2244 or 800/221–2222 | fax 505/247–2925 | www.comfortinn.com | 118 rooms | $70–$86 | AE, D, DC, MC, V.

Comfort Inn East. This basic, two-story, budget motel is 10 mi from the airport and just off Interstate 40. Restaurant, complimentary breakfast. Cable TV. Pool. Hot tub. Laundry facilities. Business services. Pets allowed (fee). | 13031 Central Ave. NE (I–40, exit 167) | 505/294–1800 | fax 505/293–1088 | www.comfortinn.com | 122 rooms | $52–$67 | AE, D, DC, MC, V.

Courtyard by Marriott. This mid-price chain hotel is geared to the needs of business travelers, with special attention paid to the work area in each room, but the beautiful gazebo and courtyard are appealing to all. Plus, it's just 2 mi from the airport. Restaurant, bar, picnic area, room service. Some refrigerators, cable TV. Pool. Hot tub. Gym. Business services, airport shuttle. | 1920 Yale Blvd. SE | 505/843–6600 | fax 505/843–8740 | www.marriott.com | 150 rooms | $94–$125 | AE, D, DC, MC, V.

Crowne Plaza Pyramid. There's a waterfall in the 10-story atrium of this upscale chain hotel in the Journal Center business complex. Restaurant, bar. In-room data ports, some refrigerators, cable TV. Indoor-outdoor pool. Hot tub. Gym. Shops. Business services. | 5151 San Francisco Rd. NE | 505/821–3333 or 800/227–6963 | fax 505/828–0230 | www.basshotels.com/crowneplaza | 311 rooms | $85–$200 | AE, D, DC, MC, V.

Days Inn West. This basic two-story budget motel is 3 mi from Old Town. Complimentary Continental breakfast. Cable TV. Pool. Hot tub, sauna. Business services. Pets allowed (fee). | 6031 Iliff Rd. NW | 505/836–3297 | fax 505/836–1214 | www.daysinn.com | 81 rooms | $55–$80 | AE, D, DC, MC, V.

Doubletree Albuquerque. A well-appointed upscale high-rise in downtown Albuquerque with attractive rooms and a brisk convention trade. It's connected directly to the Albuquerque Convention Center. Restaurant, bar. In-room data ports, cable TV. Pool. Gym. Business services. | 201 Marquette Ave. NW | 505/247–3344 | fax 505/247–7025 | www.hilton.com/doubletree | 295 rooms | $125–$475 | AE, D, DC, MC, V.

Elaine's, A Bed and Breakfast. This antiques-filled three-story log home 17 mi east of Albuquerque is in the evergreen folds of the Sandia Mountain foothills. Four acres of wooded grounds beckon just outside the back door. The top two floors have rooms with balconies and big picture windows. The third-floor room has a cathedral ceiling and king-size bed. Breakfast is served in a plant-filled kitchen next to the fireplace, or outside on a patio with a fountain. Complimentary breakfast. Some room phones. Hot tub. | 72 Snowline Rd., Cedar Crest | 505/281–2467 or 800/821–3092 | www.elainesbnb.com | 5 rooms | $85–$139 | AE, D, DC, MC, V.

Fairfield Inn. This three-story motor hotel offers simple, comfortable rooms at budget prices, with extras like free coffee and local calls that appeal to business travelers on a budget. Complimentary Continental breakfast. In-room data ports, cable TV. Pool. Hot tub, sauna. Gym. Laundry facilities, laundry service. Business services. | 1760 Menaul Rd. NE | 505/889–4000 or 800/228–2800 | fax 505/872–3094 | 188 rooms | www.fairfieldinn.com | $59–$64 | AE, D, DC, MC, V.

Hacienda Antigua. A lovely 200-year-old hacienda with kiva fireplaces and oriental rugs in the room and a warm beamed ceiling in the lobby. The large, landscaped courtyard has a pool. Complimentary breakfast. Refrigerators, no room phones, no TV, TV in common area. Pool. Hot tub. Business services. Some pets allowed. | 6708 Tierra Dr. NW | 505/345–5399 | fax 505/345–3855 | www.haciendantigua.com | 6 rooms | $100–$190 | MC, V.

Hampton Inn Albuquerque-North. This inexpensive southwestern-style motor inn is near the Balloon Fiesta Park. Complimentary Continental breakfast. In-room data ports, refrigerators, cable TV. Pool. Pets allowed. | 5101 Ellison NE | 505/344–1555 | fax 505/345–2216 | www.hamptoninn.com | 124 rooms | $64–$69 | AE, D, DC, MC, V.

Holiday Inn Express Albuquerque (I–40 Eubank). Simple clean rooms are offered in this mid-price limited-service motor hotel. Some rooms have balconies and views of the Sandia Mountains. Complimentary Continental breakfast. Some microwaves, some refrigerators, some in-room hot tubs, cable TV, some in-room VCRs. Pool. Hot tub, sauna. Gym. Laundry facilities. Pets allowed (fee). | 10330 Hotel Ave. NE | 505/275–8900 or 800/465–4329 | fax 505/275–6000 | www.basshotels.com/hiexpress | 104 rooms | $75–$100 | AE, D, DC, MC, V.

Holiday Inn-Mountain View. This large, southwestern-style motor hotel has clean, comfortable rooms. It is located just off Interstate 40 and a couple of miles from Interstate 25, 6 mi from the airport. Restaurant, bar, room service. Cable TV. Pool. Hot tub. Gym. Laundry facilities, laundry service. Business services. | 2020 Menaul Blvd. NE | 505/884–2511 | fax 505/884–5720 | www.basshotels.com/holiday-inn | 363 rooms | $99–$109 | AE, D, DC, MC, V.

Howard Johnson Hotel. Just 7 mi from the Albuquerque Airport, this chain motel offers basic, pleasant rooms. Restaurant, room service. In-room data ports, some refrigerators, cable TV. Pool. Hot tub. Gym. Laundry facilities, laundry service. Business services, airport shuttle. | 15 Hotel Circle NE | 505/296–4852 | fax 505/293–9072 | www.hojo.com | 150 rooms | $48–$88 | AE, D, DC, MC, V.

★ **Hyatt Regency Albuquerque.** Rooms at this upscale hotel, next to the Albuquerque Convention Center in downtown Albuquerque, offer panoramic views of the city and nearby mountains. Restaurant, bar (with entertainment). Some microwaves, refrigerators, cable TV, some in-room VCRs. Pool. Beauty salon. Gym. Shops. Business services, parking (fee). | 330 Tijeras NW | 505/842–1234 | fax 505/766–6710 | www.hyatt.com | 395 rooms, 14 suites | $185, $335–$375 suites | AE, D, DC, MC, V.

Inn at Paradise. Next to the first tee at the Paradise Hills Golf Club, this swank B&B atop West Mesa is a golfer's paradise. Rooms offer views of the mountains and are decorated with works and furnishings made by local artists and craftspeople. Complementary Continental breakfast. Cable TV. Spa. Library. Some pets allowed. No smoking. | 10035 Country Club La. NW | 505/898–6161 or 800/938–6161 | fax 505/890–1090 | www.innatparadise.com | 16 rooms, 2 suites, 1 apartment | $55–$110 | AE, D, DC, MC, V.

Jazz Inn Bed and Breakfast. Get your kicks 20 ft from Route 66 at this creatively restored 19th-century house in the Huning Highland Historic District. Rooms are themed after jazz musicians and have a mix of contemporary and antique furnishings. Browse the music library's 5,000 CDs, tapes, and records, or create your own music on the grand piano. Complementary breakfast. Some room phones. | 111 Walter NE, 87102 | 505/242–1530 or 888/529–9466 | fax 505/242–1530 | www.jazzinn.com | 5 rooms | $69–$99 | AE, D, DC, MC, V.

★ **La Posada de Albuquerque.** Conrad Hilton, an Albuquerque native, built this downtown hotel with southwestern charm in 1939, and it is now listed in the National Register of Historic Places. Rooms range from small to spacious. Restaurant (*see* Conrad's Downtown), bar, room service. Some in-room data ports, some refrigerators. Shops. Laundry service. Business services. | 125 2nd St. NW | 505/242–9090 or 800/777–5732 | fax 505/242–8664 | www.laposadadealbuquerque.net | 99 rooms | $99–$275 | AE, D, DC, MC, V.

La Quinta Inn Albuquerque Airport. This moderately priced motor hotel with large, comfortable rooms is ¼ mi from the Albuquerque airport. Complimentary Continental breakfast. In-room data ports, some microwaves, cable TV. Pool. Laundry facilities. Business services, airport shuttle. Some pets allowed. | 2116 Yale Blvd. SE | 505/243–5500 | fax 505/247–8288 | www.laquinta.com | 105 rooms | $69–$99 | AE, D, DC, MC, V.

Plaza Inn. Views of nightime Albuquerque are stunning from this attractive 5-story hotel, perched on a hill 2 mi from the airport. All of the rooms are decorated in southwestern pastels and have private balconies. Restaurant, bar, complimentary Continental breakfast. Some refrigerators. Pool. Hot tub. Gym. Laundry facilities. Business services, airport shuttle. Pets allowed. | 900 Medical Arts Ave. NE | 505/243–5693 or 800/237–1307 | fax 505/843–6229 | www.plazainnabq.com | 120 rooms | $85–$130 | AE, D, DC, MC, V.

Radisson Inn Albuquerque Airport. This mid-price chain hotel built around a landscaped courtyard with a pool is 5 mi from the Albuquerque airport. Restaurant, bar, room service. In-room data ports, cable TV. Pool. Hot tub. Gym. Airport shuttle. Pets allowed. | 1901 University Blvd. SE | 505/247–0512 | fax 505/843–7148 | www.radisson.com | 148 rooms | $79–$119 | AE, D, DC, MC, V.

Ramada Inn East Albuquerque. This upscale motel complex consists of seven southwestern-style buildings built around a courtyard. Restaurant, bar, room service. Cable TV. Pool. Hot tub. Video games. Laundry service. Business services, airport shuttle. Some pets allowed. | 25 Hotel Circle NE | 505/271–1000 | fax 505/291–9028 | www.ramada.com | 205 rooms | $65–$150 | AE, D, DC, MC, V.

Ramada Limited. This limited-service motor hotel is located adjacent to the Albuquerque airport and offers views of both the mountains and the city Complimentary Continental breakfast. In-room data ports, cable TV. Pool. Hot tub, sauna. Gym. Laundry facilities, laundry service. Airport shuttle. | 1801 Yale Blvd. SE | 505/242–0036 or 800/272–6232 | fax 505/242–0068 | www.ramada.com | 76 rooms | $55–$105 | AE, D, DC, MC, V.

Sheraton Old Town Hotel. A modern, 11-story upscale hotel in the Old Town district of Albuquerque. Rooms are large with large bathrooms. Restaurant, bar. In-room data ports, some refrigerators, cable TV. Pool. Barbershop, beauty salon, hot tub. Gym. Shops. Business services. | 800 Rio Grande Blvd. NW | 505/843–6300 or 800/237–2133 | fax 505/842–9863 | www.sheraton.com | 188 rooms | $110–$150 | AE, D, DC, MC, V.

Sheraton Albuquerque Uptown. This attractive, upscale hotel is located across from one of New Mexico's largest malls. Restaurant, bar. Refrigerators, cable TV. Pool. Hot tub, sauna. Gym. Laundry facilities. Business services. | 2600 Louisiana Blvd. NE | 505/881–0000 or 800/252–7772 | fax 505/881–3736 | 10556133@compuserve.com | www.sheraton.com | 296 rooms | $129–$300 | AE, D, DC, MC, V.

Sumner Suites. This inexpensive, all-suite hotel offers large rooms with a kitchenette and separate living area. Complimentary Continental breakfast. Kitchenettes, cable TV. Pool. Gym. Laundry facilities. Business services. | 2500 Menaul Blvd. NE | 505/881–0544 or 800/747–8483 | fax 505/881–0380 | www.sumnersuites.com | 125 suites | $89 | AE, D, DC, MC, V.

Wyndham Albuquerque Hotel. This upscale hotel is less than a mile from the Albuquerque airport, giving speedy access to early-morning flights. The nice-size, southwestern-style rooms have large work desks. Restaurant, bar. In-room data ports, some refrigerators, cable TV. Pool. Tennis. Gym. Business services, airport shuttle. | 2910 Yale Blvd. SE | 505/843–7000 | fax 505/843–6307 | www.wyndham.com | 276 rooms | $139–$300 | AE, D, DC, MC, V.

Wyndham Garden. This upscale hotel is adjacent to the Journal Center business park. Restaurant, bar, room service. In-room data ports, cable TV. Indoor-outdoor pool. Hot tub. Gym. Laundry facilities. Business services, airport shuttle. | 6000 Pan American Fwy. NE | 505/821–9451 | fax 505/798–4305 | www.wyndham.com | 150 rooms | $109–$119 | AE, D, DC, MC, V.

Yours Truly. This hillside inn 14 mi north of Albuquerque in Corrales has awesome views and plenty of windows through which to enjoy them. The modern adobe rooms are not large, but they are comfortable, each with a king-size bed and a fireplace. Other special touches include plush robes, afternoon wine and snacks, and praline French toast for breakfast. Complimentary breakfast. Cable TV. | 160 Paseo De Corrales, Corrales | 505/898–7027 or 800/942–7890 | fax 505/898–9022 | www.yourstrulybb.com | 4 rooms | $98–$130 | AE, D, DC, MC, V.

ANGEL FIRE

(Nearby town also listed: Taos)

Angel Fire, nestled in the midst of the Carson National Forest, is not only one of New Mexico's most popular winter ski resorts, it has established itself as a favorite for year-round luxury living as well. A multimillion-dollar, state-of-the-art ski lift speeds down-hillers to the heights in only nine minutes. Visitors and permanent residents alike enjoy a variety of clear, clean highland lakes, scores of miles of hiking trails, and the unparalleled beauty of the surrounding snowcapped mountains.

Information: Angel Fire Chamber of Commerce | Box 547, Angel Fire, 87710 | 800/446–8117 or 505/377–6661 | www.angelfirechamber.org

Attractions

Angel Fire Resort. At this family-oriented ski resort, you'll like the 68 trails with a 2,000-ft vertical drop, all of which are open to snowboarders, and two high-speed quads; many trails are suitable for beginners. In summer you can play golf on the 18-hole course, fish in the resort's lake, hike, mountain bike, and ride horses in the resort's acreage, or just enjoy a tennis match. There are also chairlift rides, minigolf, and a human maze. | North Angel Fire Rd. off U.S. 64 | 505/377–6401 or 800/633–7463 | www.angelfireresort.com | Daily.

DAV Vietnam Veterans National Memorial. This 6,000-square-ft monument 5 mi northeast of the ski slopes at Angel Fire rises dramatically over the beautiful Rocky Mountain valleys and stands to honor the men and women who gave their lives to serve their country and as a promise of hope for the future of peace. There is a visitor center and also resources that veterans can use to seek information about loved ones. A chapel is open 24 hours. | U.S. 64 | 505/377–6900 | fax 505/377–3223 | Free | Labor Day–Memorial Day, daily 9–5; summer, Memorial Day–Labor Day 9–7.

Eagle Nest Lake. Every year 60,000 fishermen visit this 2,200-acre lake 12 mi north of Angel Fire. There's ice fishing in winter. | U.S. 64, Eagle Nest | 800/494–9117 | www.eaglenest.org/village | Free | Daily 5 AM–10 PM.

ON THE CALENDAR

JULY: *Wings over Angel Fire.* Colorful hot-air balloons and an air show are the centerpiece of this day's events at the Angel Fire Airport. Other attractions are parachute jumps; an array of vintage airplanes are on display. | 505/377–6661 or 800/446–8117.

Dining

Aldo's Café and Bar. American. Aldo's is situated at the base of the ski slopes and is part of the Angel Fire Resort complex. | N. Angel Fire Rd. | 505/377–6681 | Closed Tues. | $7–$15 | AE, MC, V.

The Roasted Clove. Continental. This is the most upscale restaurant in Angle Fire and is right in the center of town. The rustic tile-and-slate walls set off the wrought-iron antique furniture and copper cooking hoods, yet the dining has a certain elegance, with white tablecloths. Outdoors there is deck seating with the same charm. For dinner, try the steaks, chops, or seafood, but for a lighter fare, or lunch, there are gourmet sandwiches and wraps. Beer and wine are served. For dessert, try the diablo à la mode (a brownie covered with ice cream and hot fudge) and the white-chocolate bread pudding. | 48 N. Angel Fire Rd. | 505/377–0636 | fax 505/377–1957 | Closed Tues. | $15–$28 | AE, D, MC, V.

Lodging

Angel Fire Resort Hotel. Rooms in this modern resort hotel are large, and some have fireplaces. Suites have kitchenettes. Restaurant, bar. Some kitchenettes, refrigerators, cable TV. Pool. Hot tub, sauna. 18-hole golf course. Pets allowed. | N. Angel Fire Dr. | 505/377–6401 or 800/633–7463 | fax 505/377–4200 | 139 rooms, 16 suites, 18 condos | $80–$160 rooms, $125–$255 suites, $135–$345 condos | AE, D, DC, MC, V.

Rustic Retreat Lodge. To reach this retreat, go 3 mi south of Angle Fire to the edge of Carson National Forest. Here you'll find 10 small cabins scattered around a main lodge on 13 acres of land. Each cedar cabin has a porch furnished with aspen chairs. The interior has a gas fireplace, tile and carpeted floors, and is furnished with pine and aspen furnishings, including the queen-size aspen bed. Cable TV. Laundry facilities. No smoking. | 3080 Hwy. 435 | 505/377–6741 or 877/777–4740 | 10 cabins | $65–$170 1–bedroom cabin, $100–$205 2–bedroom cabin | AE, D, MC, V.

ARTESIA

MAP 9, G8

(Nearby towns also listed: Alamogordo, Carlsbad, Cloudcroft, Hobbs, Roswell)

Artesia, at various points in its history called Blake's Spring, Miller's Siding, and Stegman, was given its present name in 1903, when artesian wells were created nearby. The water was a welcome relief to farmers and ranchers in this parched region of southeastern New Mexico, who wasted no time implementing a system of irrigation on their spreads. Soon after underground water was discovered, oil was generated from one of the wells, thereby bringing another source of income to some of the lucky landowners.

Today Artesia draws visitors who delight in the Heritage Walkway, a colorful mural that chronicles Artesia's interesting history, as well as the outdoor activities offered at nearby Brantley Lake State Park (*see* Carlsbad).

Information: Artesia Chamber of Commerce | Box 99, Artesia, 88210 | 505/746–2744 or 800/658–6251 | www.artesiachamber.com.

Attractions

Historical Museum and Arts Center. Collections include artifacts, family histories, and photographs documenting the history of the region from 1900 to the present. | 510 W. Main St. | 505/748–2390 | Free | Tues.–Sat. 8–5.

ON THE CALENDAR

MAR.: *ACE Car Show.* This two-day event is run by the Artesia Car Enthusiasts (ACE), a local car club. Culminates in a car parade and cruise down Main Street complete with a fireworks display. | 505/746–9477.

AUG.: *Eddy County Fair.* This annual event at the Eddy County Fairgrounds in Artesia features the area's best agricultural and ranching products. | 505/746–2744 or 800/658–6251.

Dining

Kwan Den Restaurant. Chinese. This mid-size restaurant with booths and tables serves both Szechuan and Mandarin favorites and can offer a welcome change of pace from the standard Mexican fare. | 2207 Main St. | 505/746–9851 | fax 505/746–8818 | $8–$11 | AE, D, MC, V.

KODAK'S TIPS FOR PHOTOGRAPHING LANDSCAPES AND SCENERY

Landscape
- Tell a story
- Isolate the essence of a place
- Exploit mood, weather, and lighting

Panoramas
- Use panoramic cameras for sweeping vistas
- Don't restrict yourself to horizontal shots
- Keep the horizon level

Panorama Assemblage
- Use a wide-angle or normal lens
- Let edges of pictures overlap
- Keep exposure even
- Use a tripod

Placing the Horizon
- Use low horizon placement to accent sky or clouds
- Use high placement to emphasize distance and accent foreground elements
- Try eliminating the horizon

Mountain Scenery: Scale
- Include objects of known size
- Frame distant peaks with nearby objects
- Compress space with long lenses

Mountain Scenery: Lighting
- Shoot early or late; avoid midday
- Watch for dramatic color changes
- Use exposure compensation

Tropical Beaches
- Capture expansive views
- Don't let bright sand fool your meter
- Include people

Rocky Shorelines
- Vary shutter speeds to freeze or blur wave action
- Don't overlook sea life in tidal pools
- Protect your gear from sand and sea

In the Desert
- Look for shapes and textures
- Try visiting during peak bloom periods
- Don't forget safety

Canyons
- Research the natural and social history of a locale
- Focus on a theme or geologic feature
- Budget your shooting time

Rain Forests and the Tropics
- Go for mystique with close-ups and detail shots
- Battle low light with fast films and camera supports
- Protect cameras and film from moisture and humidity

Rivers and Waterfalls
- Use slow film and long shutter speeds to blur water
- When needed, use a neutral-density filter over the lens
- Shoot from water level to heighten drama

Autumn Colors
- Plan trips for peak foliage periods
- Mix wide and close views for visual variety
- Use lighting that accents colors or creates moods

Moonlit Landscapes
- Include the moon or use only its illumination
- Exaggerate the moon's relative size with long telephoto lenses
- Expose landscapes several seconds or longer

Close-Ups
- Look for interesting details
- Use macro lenses or close-up filters
- Minimize camera shake with fast films and high shutter speeds

Caves and Caverns
- Shoot with ISO 1000+ films
- Use existing light in tourist caves
- Paint with flash in wilderness caves

From Kodak Guide to Shooting Great Travel Pictures © 2000 by Fodor's Travel Publications

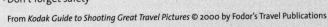

★ **La Fonda.** Mexican. For decades, residents of Carlsbad and Roswell have driven to this modest Mexican restaurant to dine on celebrated specialties like the Guadalajara (beef, cheese, and guacamole on a corn tortilla). Buffet lunch. Kids' menu. | 206 W. Main St. | 505/746–9377 | $5–$10 | AE, D, MC, V.

Lodging

Artesia Inn. This is a redbrick single-story motel on the outskirts of town on Highway 285 South. The southwestern-style rooms have a small dressing area next to the bathroom but are otherwise a bit cramped and unremarkable. Refrigerators, cable TV. Pool. Pets allowed. | 1820 S. 1st St. | 505/746–9801 or 800/682–4598 | fax 505/746–9801 | 33 rooms | $34–$52 | AE, D, DC, MC, V.

Best Western Pecos Inn. This mid-price motel offers more amenities than any other place in Artesia. Restaurant, bar, room service. Refrigerators, cable TV. Pool. Hot tub, sauna. Laundry facilities. | 2209 W. Main St. | 505/748–3324 | fax 505/748–2868 | www.bestwestern.com | 81 rooms | $56–$110 | AE, D, DC, MC, V.

AZTEC

MAP 9, C2

(Nearby town also listed: Farmington)

Early visitors to the ancient Indian ruins lying along the Rio de las Animas, the present-day Animas River, were certain that the original builders of the deserted and nearly disintegrated pueblos must be related to Mexico's Aztec Indians. Unaware that members of the Anasazi culture were the real guiding spirits behind the complex, the Anglos simply used the word "Aztec" to describe both the site and the vanished people who built it. Archaeologists were quick to appreciate the value of the ruins at Aztec, and in 1923 the area containing the 800-year-old pueblo was bestowed federal protection and named Aztec Ruins National Monument. A restored kiva within the site is the largest such structure in the entire Southwest.

The town of Aztec, situated just across the river from the monument, was first settled in the 1880s and borrowed its name from the pueblo when a post office was established there a few years later.

Sights to see today, in addition to the Aztec Ruins National Monument, are Historic Main Street, a downtown district consisting of several restored late-19th-century buildings, and the well-maintained Aztec Museum.

Information: **Aztec Chamber of Commerce** | 110 N. Ash St., Aztec, 87410 | 505/334–9551 | www.aztecnm.com.

Attractions

Aztec Museum and Pioneer Village. This museum offers a good collection of authentic Americana, historical photos, newspapers, and artifacts dating from the late 19th century, plus a great exhibit of farm machinery and oil- and gas-drilling equipment round out the collection. More than a dozen historic structures fill the village. | 125 N. Main St. | 505/334–9829 | $2 | Memorial Day–Labor Day, Mon.–Sat. 9–5; Labor Day–Memorial Day, Mon.–Sat. 10–4.

Aztec Ruins National Monument. Aztec Ruins National Monument, 1½ mi north of Aztec, has nothing to do with the Aztec Indian culture of Mexico, although some of its architectural features, such as the Great Kiva, are equally impressive. The Anasazi people occupied this site during the 11th and 12th century, and many of their material remains are still visible in the museum. It was designated a World Heritage Site in 1987. | 84 County Rd. 2900, off U.S. 550 | 505/334–6174 | www.nps.gov/azru | $4 | Memorial Day–Labor Day, daily 8–6; Labor Day–Memorial Day, daily 8–5.

Aztec Speedway. Owner Jack Nelson has a ⅓-mi oval dirt track ½ mi south of Aztec on Highway 544. Here local and regional contestants race sprint cars (with inverted wings to keep them on the ground), modified stock cars, minis, and dwarves (they look like old-time jalopies). | 420 Legion Rd. | 505/327–6314 | www.aztecspeedway.com | $9 | Apr.–Sept., Sat. (and sometimes Fri.).

Navajo Lake State Park. This 15,000-acre lake with a 150-mi shoreline, 28 mi east of Aztec, is northwest New Mexico's most prominent water feature. Swimming, fishing, waterskiing, and boating are popular sports in summer. The park itself comprises three separate recreation areas—Pine River, Sims Mesa, and the San Juan River Recreation Area—all of which are included in the price of the park admission. | NM 511 off NM 173 | 505/632–2278 | $4 per vehicle | Daily.
Pine River Site. On the west side of the lake, this is a good spot for swimming, fishing, boating, and other water sports. This is the most developed part of the lakeshore, and you'll find a visitor center with interpretive exhibits, as well as a campground with hot showers. Admission includes the Sims Mesa and San Juan River sections of the park. | NM 511 off NM 173 | 505/632–2278 | $4 per vehicle | Daily.
Sims Mesa Site. On the east side of Navajo Lake, there's a boat ramp and campgrounds here. Admission includes the Pine River and San Juan River sections of the park. | NM 527 | 505/632–2278 | $4 per vehicle | Daily.
San Juan River Recreation Area. The San Juan River, whose cottonwood-lined banks wind through the high-mesa country of northwestern New Mexico, is one of the top trout-fishing spots in the country. Many areas are catch and release only; the area just below Navajo Dam is the prime fishing grounds. There's a campground here with rest rooms but no showers. Admission includes the Pine River and Sims Mesa sites. | NM 173 | 505/632–2278 | $4 per vehicle | Daily.

ON THE CALENDAR

JUNE: *Aztec Fiesta Days.* There is an adult and children's carnival, music performances, and three parades. | 505 334–9551.

Dining

Aztec Restaurant. American/Casual. Good, all-round eating spot for the entire family. Try the chicken-fried steak, tiger burger, or the Mexican chile—and save room for the homemade pies. Salad bar. Entertainment Friday. Kids' menu. | 107 E. Aztec Blvd. | 505/334–9586 | $6–$12 | A, D, MC, V.

Highway Grill. American. This 1950s-style diner has a large, shady outdoor patio and an even bigger interior. The menu ranges from burgers to prime rib and includes malted milk shakes and caramel-covered apple pie. Look for the big blue 1958 DeSoto Firehawk on Highway 550 near the north end of town. Entertainment weekends. | 401 N.E. Aztec Blvd. | 505/334–6533 | Closed Sun. | $5–$18 | AE, D, DC, MC, V.

Lodging

Miss Gail's Inn. Built in 1907 and registered as a state historic site, this inn is in downtown Aztec, within walking distance of most major amenities. Restaurant. Cable TV. | 300 S. Main St. | 505/334–3452 or 888/834–3452 | fax 505/334–9664 | 5 rooms, 3 suites | $55–$60, $70–$90 suites | AE, D, MC, V.

Step Back Inn. This modern inn in Aztec's historic district is furnished with an array of antiques. Each room has two queen-size beds and is named after a founding family of the town of Aztec. Wall plaques in each room give a brief history of the town. Cable TV, some in-room VCRs. Business services. | 103 W. Aztec Blvd. | 505/334–1200 or 800/334–1255 | fax 505/334–9858 | 40 rooms | $58–$72 | AE, MC, V.

BELÉN

(Nearby towns also listed: Albuquerque, Socorro)

Belén is located just south of Albuquerque and is best known for the thousands of migratory sandhill cranes that frequent Senator Willie Chavez State Park nearby. The El Camino Real Visitors' Center tells the story of the age-old trail—perhaps the oldest "highway" in the United States—that ran from Mexico City to Taos.

Information: **Belén Chamber of Commerce** | 712 Dalies Ave., Belén, 87002 | 505/864–8091. | www.belennm.com.

Attractions

El Camino Real Visitors Center. Exhibits tell the story of the Spanish *entrada* along this ageless highway to empire. | 201 Rio Communities Blvd. | 505/864–8091 | Free | Daily 10–2.

Salinas Pueblo Mission National Monument. Belén is a good base of operations for a visit to Salinas Pueblo Missions National Monument, southeast of Belén off Routes 47 and 55 between Mountainair and Carrizozo. The monument actually consists of three separate archaeological sites: Quarai, Gran Quivira, and Abó. There is a lot to see, so allow plenty of time. The monument headquarters is located in the small town of Mountainair. | Broadway & Ripley, Mountainair | 505/847–2585 | www.nps.gov/sapu | Free | Labor Day–Memorial Day, daily 9–5; Memorial Day–Labor Day, daily 9–6.

Abó. Abó, 9 mi west of Mountainair, was a thriving pueblo when first visited by the Spanish in 1581, but less than 100 years later the entire site was abandoned, and even today remains largely unexcavated. The ruins of the old Spanish mission here are especially interesting; an interpretive trail visits both the mission and unexcavated pueblo. | U.S. 60 | 505/847–2400 | www.nps.gov/sapu | Free | Labor Day–Memorial Day, daily 9–5; Memorial Day–Labor Day, daily 9–6.

Gran Quivira. The Las Humanas Pueblo 8 mi north of Mountainair, the largest of the Salinas pueblos, had been an important trade center even before the Spanish entered the area. Its heyday was from AD 800 to around 1672, when it was abandoned because of drought and famines. Gran Quivira's 21 individual sites are linked by an interpretive trail, and the monument's visitor center is located here. | Hwy. 55 | 505/847–2770 | www.nps.gov/sapu | Free | Labor Day–Memorial Day, daily 9–5; Memorial Day–Labor Day, daily 9–6.

Quarai. The Quarai Pueblo, 8 mi north of Mountainair on Route 55, was thriving when Juan de Oñate passed through the region in 1598. During the 1600s, three of the Spanish priests at the church here headed New Mexico's Inquisition. A trail winds through the ruins of the mission, its gardens, and the adjacent pueblo. | Hwy. 55 | 505/847–2290 | www.nps.gov/sapu | Free | Labor Day–Memorial Day, daily 9–5; Memorial Day–Labor Day, daily 9–6.

Senator Willie M. Chavez State Park. Bird-watching and hiking are popular pastimes in this lovely park that borders the Rio Grande. | 1617 E. River Rd. | 505/864–3915 | $4 per vehicle | Daily.

ON THE CALENDAR

JUNE: *Hub City Music Fest and Annual Rio Valley Festival.* This event has an art show, craft booths, and good old-fashioned American food served from outdoor stalls. | 505/864–8091.

Dining

Montano's. Mexican. The small dining room has a homey, south-of-the-border feel. The most popular items on the menu are stuffed sopaipillas and the *carne adovada* (red chile–marinaded pork). | 317 S. Main St. | 505/864–3370 | No dinner Sun. | $4–$7 | D, MC, V.

Lodging

Casitas at Mountain View. Each of these cozy suites has a small living room, a kitchen, and small backyard. The walls are painted by a local artist, each with a unique border of flowers, plants, and trailing ivy. This family-run operation is at the southern end of town. Kitchenettes, refrigerators, cable TV. Some pets allowed. | 1304 S. Main St. | 505/861–1144 | 9 rooms | $39–$59 | AE, D, DC, MC, V.

BERNALILLO

(Nearby towns also listed: Albuquerque, Jemez Springs)

Tradition, church, and family have, for four centuries, structured life in this quaint Hispanic village on the Camino Real. Nearby Indian pueblos of Jemez, Santa Ana, Zia, and Sandia have ensured its place as a market center. Storefronts have recently filled with galleries, antiques shops, and western-wear and gift emporiums, making Bernalillo something of a browsing stop without altering the character of the town.

Information: **Sandoval County Visitor Center** | 243 Camino del Pueblo, Bernalillo, 87004 | 505/867–8687 or 800/252–0191 | www.sctourism.com.

Attractions

Coronado State Monument. Prehistoric Kuaua Pueblo ruins perch atop a bluff overlooking the Rio Grande, with a restored kiva, a small museum, a campground, and picnic tables on the site where conquistador Francisco Coronado camped in the winter of 1540–41. | 485 Kuaua Rd. | 505/867–5351 | www.nmculture.org | May–Sept. $3; Sept.–May $2 | Daily 8:30–5.

ON THE CALENDAR

AUG.: *Las Fiestas de San Lorenzo.* Ancient Matachine dances performed to honor town's patron saint. | 505/867–TOUR.

SEPT.: *New Mexico Wine Festival.* Each Labor Day weekend, there are wine tastings from New Mexico wineries, live music, dancing, and food. | 505/867–3311.

Dining

Abuelita's New Mexican Restaurant. Southwestern. Locals love the house special Enchiladas Abuelita and the Tacopilla, a giant taco on a sopaipilla, doused with piquant red chile, all savored in a homey pink dining room. | 621 Camino del Pueblo | 505/867–9988 | $5–$8 | No credit cards.

Prairie Star. Contemporary. A 1940s hacienda is the gracious setting for anniversaries, birthdays, and entertaining out-of-town guests. Albuquerque residents even consider the drive up worth it. "Santa Fe South" chefery brings forth bison in a Pinot Noir reduction and glazed lamb chops. The Prairie Star Chocolate Fetish is a knockout dessert. | 255 Prairie Star Rd. | 505/867–3327 | fax 505/827–2108 | Closed Mon. No lunch | $15–$29 | AE, D, DC, MC, V.

Range Café & Bakery. American. Hearty home cooking and New Mexican food served in a restored mercantile building. Known for meat loaf and chicken-fried steak with garlic mashed potatoes, Portobello mushroom burgers, and a signature dessert, Death by Lemon. | 925 Camino del Pueblo | 505/867–1700 | fax 505–867–7275 | $6–$15 | AE, D, MC, V.

Lodging

Days Inn Bernalillo. Spanking-clean standard motel at the crossroads of two highways, convenient to both the "fast-food" and "historic" sides of town. Complimentary Continental breakfast. Cable TV. Pool. Hot tub. Laundry facilities. Business services. | 107 Camino del Pueblo | 505/771–7000 | fax 505/771–7000 | www.daysinn.com | 52 rooms | $50 | AE, D, DC, MC, V.

Hacienda Vargas. Five miles north of Bernalillo, with lots of historical charm, the Hacienda Vargas was, in its day, a stage-coach stop, an Indian trading post, and a train depot. It's now a B&B. Most rooms have a fireplace, private courtyard, and private hot tub. Complimentary breakfast. Some in-room hot tubs. | 1431 Old U.S. 66 | 505/867–9115 or 800/261–0006 | fax 505/867–0640 | www.swcp.com/hacvar | 8 rooms | $89–$149 | AE, MC, V.

La Hacienda Grande. Classic New Mexicana in a 250-year-old home with central courtyard, covered portico, and beamed ceilings. Five of the six rooms have fireplaces. Complimentary breakfast. Some in-room hot tubs, some in-room VCRs, some room phones, no TV in some rooms. Business services. | 21 Barros La. | 505/867–1887 | fax 505/771–1436 | www.lahaciendagrande.com | 6 rooms | $99–$129 | AE, MC, V.

CARLSBAD

MAP 9, G9

(Nearby towns also listed: Artesia, Hobbs)

When local spring water was proclaimed to be as good as any in Europe, the 30-year-old town of Eddy changed its name in 1918 to Carlsbad, after the famous Karlsbad Springs in Czechoslovakia. Shortly thereafter the large cave network about 27 mi southeast of town, which had been locally explored since the early part of the 20th century, was designated the Carlsbad Caverns National Park by the U.S. Department of the Interior.

Today the town of 27,800 on the Pecos River is best known for the nearby caverns and as a place where travelers rest their weary heads after a day of cave-exploring. But much of the economy is driven by agriculture, particularly by the cotton and hay fields and pecan groves nearby.

Information: **Carlsbad Convention and Visitors Bureau.** | Box 910, Carlsbad, 88220 | 800/221–1224 or 505/887–6516 | www.caverns.com/~chamber.

Attractions

Brantley Lake State Park. In addition to the 42,000-acre Brantley Lake, this park 12 mi north of Carlsbad (5 mi off U.S. 285) offers primitive camping areas, nature trails, a visitor center, more than 51 fully equipped campsites, and fine fishing for largemouth bass, bluegill, crappie, and walleye pike. | Hwy. 30 | 505/457–2384 | www.emnrd.state.nm.us/nmparks | $4 per vehicle | Daily.

★ **Carlsbad Caverns National Park.** It took percolating water millions of years to create these magnificent caverns 27 mi southwest of Carlsbad. Carlsbad Cavern is one of the largest caverns in the world. The caverns are also known for the nightly bat flight from late May through mid-October, when tens of thousands of bats go out in search of food at sunset; this is actually how they were rediscovered in the 19th century, when the locals looked for the source of the nightly bat flights. Although the park boundaries include about 80 caves, many of these have not been explored, and only two are open to the public: Carlsbad Cavern and Slaughter Canyon Cave. A third, Lechuguilla Cave, is open to scientific expeditions. There are two self-guided tours, which are included in the entrance fee, and several guided tours, which are not and which require reservations. | 3225 National Parks Hwy., off U.S. 62/U.S. 180 | 505/887–6516 or 800/967–2283 (reservations for guided cave tours) | www.nps.gov/cave | $6 | Mid-Aug.–Memorial Day, daily 8–5; Memorial Day–mid-Aug., daily 8–7.

Carlsbad Cavern (self-guided tours). The main cavern can be visited on two self-guided tours, the Natural Entrance Route, which winds into the cavern for about a mile, takes approximately one hour to complete and is fairly strenuous; the Big Room Route is reached after a descent by high-speed elevator then covers about a mile underground, taking about an hour. The Big Room itself is impressive, large enough to hold 14 football fields and 225 ft high. | 3225 National Parks Hwy., off U.S. 62/U.S. 180 | 505/887–6516 | www.nps.gov/cave | $6 | Natural Entrance Route: June–mid-Aug., daily 8:30–3:30 (last entry to the caverns); mid-Aug.–May, daily 8:30–2 (last entry to the caverns). Big Room Route: June–mid-Aug., daily 8:30–5 (last elevator down); mid-Aug.–May, daily 8:30–3:30 (last elevator down).

Carlsbad Cavern (ranger-led tours). Five ranger-led tours go into the less-developed reaches of the main cavern that require more stamina and commitment than a simple walk around the Big Room, but the payoff is that you are able to see passages that the majority of visitors never get near. The Kings Palace Guided Tour, for example, goes into the deepest part of the cavern that is open to the public, some 830 ft underground and it requires some climbing. The Left Hand Tunnel tour goes to a less-visited part of the cavern, but is not very strenuous. The Lower Cave tour descends into the cavern, requiring an initial climb down a very tall ladder. The Spider Cave tour starts with a hike out into the wilderness and descent into a wild cave, requiring you to crawl through some very tight, bug-infested passages. Finally, the Hall of the White Giant tour goes into some narrow passages and requires some crawling as well. All these tours require reservations and payment of the $6 general admission, sturdy walking shoes; some require gloves and batteries for headlamps. No kids under 4 for Kings Palace, under 6 for Left Hand Tunnel, under 12 for Lower Cave, Spider Cave, or Hall of the White Giant. | 3225 National Parks Hwy., off U.S. 62/U.S. 180 | 800/967–2283 (reservations), 505/887–6516 (main park telephone) | www.nps.gov/cave | In addition to the general entrance fee of $6: Kings Palace $8; Left Hand Tunnel $7; Lower Cave, Spider Cave, and Hall of the White Giant $20 each | Kings Palace: Memorial Day–mid-Aug., daily hourly 9–3; mid-Aug.–late May, daily at 9, 11, 1, and 3. Left Hand Tunnel: daily at 9 AM. Lower Cave, weekdays at 1. Spider Cave, Sun. at 1. Hall of the White Giant, Sat. at 1.

Rattlesnake Springs. A picnic and recreation site in the park's backcountry with a view of the Black River, this is a good bird-watching spot. It's accessed via the Desert Loop Drive, part of the Walnut Canyon Desert Drive. | Off Desert Loop Dr. | 505/887–6516 | www.nps.gov/cave | Free | Daily.

Slaughter Canyon Cave. This ranger-led tour takes you into a completely wild cave with no modern conveniences, just the dazzling formations. The cave entrance is 25 mi from the main cavern The two-hour tour goes 1¼ mi and also visits the long-abandoned guano-mining excavations. You must first make a strenuous, ½-mi hike to the cavern entrance, which is high on a cliff face; the tour begins here. Bring water, sturdy walking shoes, and a flashlight. No kids under six. | Hwy. 418 off U.S. 62/U.S. 180, | 800/967–2283 (reservations) or 505/887–6516 (main park telephone) | www.nps.gov/cave | $15 | Memorial Day–mid-Aug., daily at 10 and 1; mid-Aug.–late May, weekends at 10 and 1.

Walnut Canyon Desert Drive. This 9½-mi scenic drive begins ½ mi from the Carlsbad Cavern Visitor Center and winds along the edge of Rattlesnake Canyon and back down through upper Walnut Canyon, intersecting with the main park road. The best time to go is late in the afternoon or early in the morning, to get the best light. | Off the main park road | 505/887–6516 | www.nps.gov/cave | Free | Daily.

Carlsbad Museum and Art Center. Fossils of the region's prehistoric life, pueblo pottery, meteorites, and pioneer and Apache artifacts make up the historical collection here, but the museum's real treasures are paintings in the McAdoo collection, which features works from the members of the Taos Society of Artists. | 418 W. Fox St. | 505/887–0276 | Free | Mon.–Sat. 10–5.

Lake Carlsbad Water Recreation Area. This large lake on the Pecos River provides opportunities for swimming, boating, fishing, and other water sports. To get there, go east on Church Street; the lake is at the east end. | Church St. | No phone | Free | Memorial Day–Labor Day, daily.

Lincoln National Forest, Guadalupe Ranger District. The Guadalupe District ranger office for this huge national forest covering more than 1 million acres in Lincoln, Otero, Eddy, and Chaves Counties is in Carlsbad, though the forest itself is almost 50 mi southwest of town via Route 137. | Federal Building, Room 159 | 505/885–4181 | Free | Daily.

Sitting Bull Falls. This 150-ft-high waterfall in Lincoln National Forest, 45 mi southwest of Carlsbad, cascades into sparkling pools below, creating an emerald oasis in the midst of

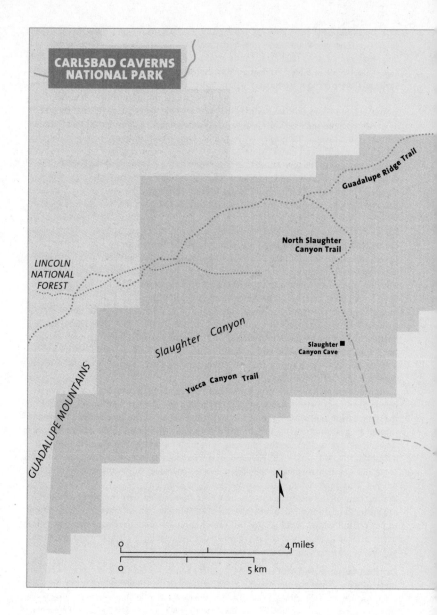

CARLSBAD CAVERNS
NATIONAL PARK

Guadalupe Ridge Trail

North Slaughter
Canyon Trail

LINCOLN
NATIONAL
FOREST

Slaughter ■
Canyon Cave

Slaughter   Canyon

Yucca Canyon Trail

GUADALUPE MOUNTAINS

N

0   4 miles

0   5 km

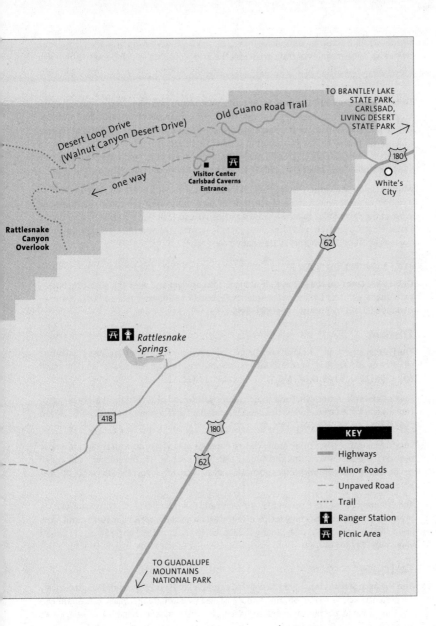

Desert Loop Drive
(Walnut Canyon Desert Drive)

Old Guano Road Trail

TO BRANTLEY LAKE
STATE PARK,
CARLSBAD,
LIVING DESERT
STATE PARK

180

← one way

Visitor Center
Carlsbad Caverns
Entrance

White's
City

Rattlesnake
Canyon
Overlook

62

Rattlesnake
Springs

418

180

62

KEY

Highways
Minor Roads
Unpaved Road
Trail
Ranger Station
Picnic Area

TO GUADALUPE
MOUNTAINS
NATIONAL PARK

the desert, with accommodations for hiking, picnicking, and viewing from the picturesque overlooks. Sixteen miles of trails crisscross the area. Route 137, which begins 12 mi north of Carlsbad, leads right to the falls. | Hwy. 137 | 505/885–4181 | $5 per vehicle, free Wed. | Daily dawn to dusk.

Living Desert Zoo and Gardens State Park. This nature preserve on the northwestern edge of Carlsbad focuses on the biology of the Chihuahuan Desert. It's an indoor/outdoor living museum, with more than 40 animal species and hundreds of cacti and other succulents, all native to the surrounding desert. There are also dioramas and nocturnal exhibits to visit. | 1504 Mielhs Dr., off U.S. 285 | 505/887–5516 | www.emnrd.state.nm.us/nmpark | $4 | Memorial Day–Labor Day, daily 8–8; Labor Day–Memorial Day, daily 9–5.

Million Dollar Museum. This homespun museum 20 mi southwest of Carlsbad displays a hodgepodge of Americana and a little bit of everything else, from the first automobile west of the Pecos River, to a two-headed rattlesnake, to 32 antique European dollhouses. | 21 Carlsbad Caverns Hwy., White's City | 505/785–2291 | $3 | Memorial Day–Labor Day, daily 7 AM–9 PM; Labor Day–Memorial Day, daily 7 AM–7 PM.

ON THE CALENDAR

DEC.: *Christmas on the Pecos.* Ride along the Pecos River and view the glittering backyard displays put up by the local residents. Reservations are essential, and tickets are usually sold out by August. | 505/887–6516.

Dining

The Flume. American. This local favorite in the Best Western Stevens Inn offers good prime rib, steaks, and seafood in comfortable surroundings. Salad bar. | 1829 S. Canal St. | 505/887–2851 | $8–$16 | AE, D, DC, MC, V.

Furr's Cafeteria. American. For a chain cafeteria, the food at this roomy eatery is exceptionally good. The fare includes fried chicken, roast beef, and lasagna. | 901 S. Canal St., 88220 | 505/885–0430 | $5–$6 | AE, D, MC, V.

Lucy's. Mexican. An informal family-owned eatery that is a favorite with the locals, whose motto is "the best margaritas and hottest chile in the world." Try the chicken fajita burritos or Tuscon-style chimichangas. | 701 S. Canal St. | 505/887–7714 | $4–$12 | AE, D, DC, MC, V.

Red Chimney. Barbecue. If you hanker for sweet and tangy barbecue, try this casual restaurant. Sauce from an old family recipe is slathered on chicken, pork, beef, turkey, and ham. Fried catfish is a popular dish among the locals. | 817 N. Canal St. | 505/885–8744 | Closed weekends | $7–$9 | MC, V.

Lodging

★ **Best Western Stevens Inn.** Here you will find carefully landscaped grounds and attractively decorated, spacious rooms, offering a touch of elegance at bargain prices. Restaurant (*see* The Flume), bar (with entertainment), room service. Some refrigerators, cable TV, in-room VCRs (and movies). Pool. Playground. Business services. Pets allowed. | 1829 S. Canal St. | 505/887–2851 | fax 505/887–6338 | www.bestwestern.com | 204 rooms | $59–$85 | AE, D, DC, MC, V.

Continental Inn. This two-story brick motel is just south of Carlsbad. The rooms are simple comfortable, and the grounds are well kept. In-room data ports, some refrigerators, cable TV. Pool. Business services, airport shuttles. Some pets allowed (fee). | 3820 National Parks Hwy. | 505/887–0341 | fax 505/885–1186 | 58 rooms | $35–$80 | AE, D, DC, MC, V.

Days Inn. This hotel is 2 mi southeast of the center of downtown. Rooms have southwestern decor, king-size beds, and sofa beds. Complimentary Continental breakfast. In-room data ports, cable TV. Pool. Hot tub. Business services, airport shuttle. Pets allowed. | 3901 National Parks Hwy. | 505/887–7800 or 800/329–7466 | fax 505/885–9433 | www.daysinn.com | 42 rooms, 8 suites | $55–$70 | AE, D, DC, MC, V.

Holiday Inn-Carlsbad. This southwestern-style, two-story chain motel in downtown Carlsbad has large, well-kept rooms opening onto exterior corridors. Restaurants, picnic area, room service. In-room data ports, some refrigerators, cable TV, some in-room VCRs (and movies). Pool. Hot tub. Gym. Playground. Business services. Pets allowed. | 601 S. Canal | 505/885–8500 or 800/472–9578 | fax 505/887–5999 | www.basshotels.com/holiday-inn | 100 rooms | $86–$115 | AE, D, DC, MC, V.

Quality Inn. One mile from the airport, this stone-face inn surrounds a landscaped patio with a pool and sundeck about as large as an aircraft hanger. Rooms are comfortable, with dull modern furnishings. Restaurant, bar with entertainment, complimentary breakfast. Some in-room data ports, cable TV. Pool. Hot tub. Video games. Laundry service. Airport shuttle. Some pets allowed. | 3706 National Parks Hwy. | 505/887–2861 or 800/321–2861 | fax 505/887–2861 | www.qualityinn.com | 120 rooms | $60–$70 | AE, D, DC, MC, V.

Stagecoach Inn. This family-oriented motor inn has basic rooms. Outside is a tree-shaded park with a playground and picnic area. Restaurant, complimentary Continental breakfast. Cable TV. Pool, wading pool. Hot tub. Laundry service. Some pets allowed. | 1819 S. Canal St. | 505/887–1148 | 57 rooms | $30–$46 | AE, D, DC, MC, V.

Super 8. This three-story motel is 2 mi from the Carlsbad airport and one block from the Carlsbad convention center. The southwestern-style rooms have generic furnishings. Complimentary Continental breakfast. Cable TV. Pool. Hot tub. Laundry facilities. Business services. | 3817 National Parks Hwy. | 505/887–8888 | fax 505/885–0126 | www.super8.com | 60 rooms | $41–$64 | AE, D, DC, MC, V.

CARRIZOZO

MAP 9, E7

(Nearby towns also listed: Lincoln, Ruidoso)

Named for the carrizo grass that grew in the area, Carrizozo got its start when the railroad came through in the early days of the 20th century. Today, standing at the well-traveled juncture of U.S. 54 and U.S. 380, this tiny town (population 1,000) is the Lincoln county seat and the center of a vast ranching district. For the traveler roaming the wide open spaces of the West, Carrizozo is a place to pull off the road, rest, and refuel.

Information: Carrizozo Chamber of Commerce | Box 567, Carrizozo, 88301 | 505/648–2732 | zozoccc@nm.net.

Attractions
Sierra Blanca Brewing Co. This local microbrewery is actually New Mexico's largest, offering samples and free tours. | 503 12th St. | 505/648–2732 | fax 505/648–6607 | www.sierrablanca.com | Free | Daily 9–4.

Valley of Fires Recreation Area. After the lava from an erupting volcano flowed here 1,500 years ago, it cooled and formed a jagged black landscape called the Malpais, now home to bald and golden eagles, many varieties of cactus, and a remarkable variety of wildlife. Hiking is permitted on the nature trail. There is a gift and souvenir shop in the visitor center. The area is 4 mi west of Carrizozo. | U.S. 380 | 505/648–2241 | $5 per vehicle | Visitor center daily 8–4.

Dining
Four Winds Restaurant. American/Casual. Made-from-scratch cinnamon rolls, Mexican food, soups, hefty steaks, and burgers draw truckers, bikers, and travelers from all directions to this family-run diner. | U.S. 54/U.S. 380 | 505/648–2964 | fax 505/648–0028 | $6–$14 | AE, D, MC, V.

Gift Gallery. Café. Known locally as "Roy's," named for the owner, Roy Dow, this old-fashioned ice-cream parlor dishes out malts and sundaes at a 1935 working soda fountain. Store fixtures date to the 1880s. | 1200 Ave. E | 505/648–2921 | Closed Sun. | $1–$3 | No credit cards.

Outpost Bar & Grill. American. One of New Mexico's venerable green chile hamburger joints, the Outpost is a well-weathered bar decorated with elk racks and the mounted heads of every critter that ever roamed these parts. Big-screen TVs, billiards, and pinballs make this the place to watch the game and indulge in a brew and an order of hand-cut fries. | 415 Central | 505/648–9994 | $4–$10 | No credit cards.

Lodging
Four Winds Motel. Basic roadside comforts; it's nothing fancy, but an adequate place to get a night's rest. Restaurant, microwaves, refrigerators, cable TV. | U.S. 54/U.S. 380 | 505/648–2356 | fax 505/648–0028 | 23 rooms | $38 | AE, D, MC, V.

Rainbow Inn. Small, upgraded motel that's just fine if you're passing through. Has the same comforts as a national chain. Microwaves, refrigerators, cable TV. | U.S. 54/U.S. 380 | 505/648–4006 | fax 505/648–2959 | 11 rooms | $40–$50 | AE, D, MC, V.

CERRILLOS

MAP 9, E4

(Nearby towns also listed: Albuquerque, Santa Fe)

As early as 1680 Spanish dons forced enslaved Indians to mine the rocky outcrops along today's New Mexico Highway 14 for the prized turquoise. In the 19th century, coal, silver, zinc, and gold were discovered in the region, and numerous boomtowns, among them Cerrillos, sprang up almost overnight. Once the home of four hotels and 21 saloons, Cerrillos has reverted to its pre-boomtown atmosphere and is a sleepy little village—almost a ghost town—astride the 52-mi-long Turquoise Trail.

Information: **Turquoise Trail** | Box 303, Sandia Park, 87047 | 505/471–1054 or 505/281–5233.

Attractions
Garden of the Gods. The elevation here is 6,000 ft, and nearby beds of sandstone were deposited in streams 70 million years ago, where they were later tilted, thus creating the unique rock formations seen here. | Hwy. 14 (the Turquoise Trail) | 505/281–5233 | Free | Daily.

Lodging
Heart Seed B&B and Spa. You'll see beautiful views here, amid 80 acres of land along the famous Turquoise Trail, a half-hour drive (about 20 mi) south of Santa Fe in the Ortiz Mountains between Madrid and Cerrillos. Rooms are a decent size, one with a private deck. Complimentary breakfast. Some kitchenettes. Hot tub, massage, spa. | 63 Corazon de Oro (County Rd. 55) | 505/471–7026 | fax 505/ 438–2416 | www.heart-seed.com | 6 rooms, 2 casitas | $95–$102, $125–$185 casita | AE, MC, V.

CHAMA

MAP 9, D2

(Nearby town also listed: Dulce)

Chama (population 1,250), had its heyday in the 1880s, when the railroad arrived in the region. The village, almost on the Colorado border, quickly became a mining, timber, and commercial center for much of northern New Mexico. Today you can still visit some of the original "railroad" houses built for the families of the men who worked along the rail line. The altitude here is nearly 8,000 ft, and the vistas of the surrounding mountains are lovely. The area contains several cozy B&Bs, as well as a number of quality motels and restaurants, and it offers a variety of outdoor recreational pursuits.

Information: **Chama Chamber of Commerce** | Box 306, Chama, 87520 | 800/477–0149 or 505/756–2306 | www.chama.com.

Attractions

Cumbres and Toltec Scenic Railroad, New Mexico Express. Relive the times when miners and loggers roamed the mountains by taking a ride on a steam-driven, narrow-gauge train from Chama to Antonito, Colorado, through the Cumbres Pass of the San Juan Mountains. Trips begin and end at the Chama Railroad Station | 15 Terrace Ave., 87520 | 505/756–2151 or 719/376–5483 | fax 505/756–2694 | www.cumbresandtoltec.com | $38–$58 | Mid-May– mid-Oct., daily.

El Vado Lake State Park. At this lake about 13 mi southwest of Chama is popular for boating, sailing, waterskiing, and windsurfing—and in winter cross-country skiing. A 5½-mi scenic trail connects El Vado and Heron lakes (*see* Heron Lake State Park, *below*). From U.S. 64/84, take Hwy. 112 13 mi south to State Park Road; then follow the signs 4 mi on State Park Road to the lake. | Hwy. 112, El Vado | 505/588–7247 | www.emnrd.state.nm.us/nmparks | $4 per vehicle; $8–$14 per night for camping | Daily.

Heron Lake State Park. A majestic lake 10 mi south of Chama surrounded by pine-studded hills, Heron Lake features sailing, hiking, picnicking, and ice fishing in winter. A 5½-mi scenic trail connects Heron and El Vado lakes (*see* El Vado Lake State Park, *above*). It's off Hwy. 64/84, on Hwy. 95 just past Tia Maria. | Hwy. 95 | 505/588–7470 | www.emnrd.state.nm.us/nmparks | $4 per vehicle | Daily.

Tierra Wools, Los Ojos Handweavers. This cooperative weaver-, spinner-, grower-owned company features on-site demonstrations of age-old textile techniques. It's a showroom and weaving school 15 mi south of Chama. | 91 Main St., Los Ojos | 505/588–7231 or 888/ 709–0979 | www.handweavers.com | Free | Memorial Day–mid Oct., Mon.–Sat. 9–6; mid-Oct.–Memorial Day, Mon.–Sat. 10–5.

ON THE CALENDAR

AUG.: *Chama Days Rodeo and Softball Tournament.* This three-day rodeo has all the competition categories of a professional event. The softball tournament includes juniors and senior citizens, professionals and amateurs alike. | 505/756–2306.

Dining

Biva Vera's Mexican Kitchen. Mexican. Some folks declare that Vera's has the best New Mexican food around these parts. Try the delightful enchiladas or burritos at this simple restaurant. | 2202 Hwy. 17 | 505/756–2557 | $3–$8 | AE, D, MC, V.

Whistle Stop Café. American. "We serve real food here," says the proprietor of this small café across from the charming train station in Chama. Eat inside or outside in the courtyard. Entrées include fresh roasted turkey and fresh seafood. Try the twice-baked duck with honey-almond sauce, the blackened salmon, and halibut in lemon-dill sauce. | 425 Main St. | 505/756–1833 | Closed Nov.–Apr. | $8–$15 | MC, V.

Lodging

Cardin's Crossing B&B. Have a cup of tea on a Victorian porch filled with white wicker furniture or stroll through a lovingly tended flower garden. As you might expect, apple pie is served every night as a snack. The narrow-gauge room has a model train running overhead, and a Victorian dollhouse complete with canopy bed and dollhouse of its own. Complimentary breakfast. No kids under 12. No smoking. | 551 Maple Ave. | 505/756–2542 or 800/852–6400 | 2 rooms | $85 | MC, V.

Elk Horn Lodge. This complex of rustic log cabins overlooks the Chama River. Some cabins have private porches. Restaurant, picnic area. Kitchenettes (in cottages), cable TV. Pets allowed. | 263 U.S. 84 | 505/756–2105 or 800/532–8874 | fax 505/756–2638 | www.elkhornlodge.net | 23 rooms, 10 cabins | $50–$72, $80–$125 cabins | AE, D, DC, MC, V.

Gandy Dancer B&B Inn. Named after the slang term for a railroad laborer, this 1913 Victorian home is now a B&B with large, attractive, antiques-furnished rooms with private baths. Relax on the wooden deck and watch the feeding of over 400 hummingbirds during the summer months. Complimentary breakfast. Cable TV, some in-room VCRs. Hot tub. Library. No smoking. No kids. | 299 Maple Ave. | 505/756–2191 or 800/424–6702 | fax 505/756–9110 | www.gandydancerbb.com | 7 rooms | $95–$125 | AE, D, DC, MC, V.

The Lodge at Chama. An outdoor vacation can also be luxurious at this lodge and working ranch owned by the Jicarilla Apache tribe. Two miles south of Chama, on the Colorado border at elevations between 9,000 and 11,000 ft, this 32,000-acre ranch has 10 lakes and is nothing short of idyllic. Go horseback riding, trophy fishing, tour the ranch, or relax by the huge stone fireplace inside this high-class lodge furnished with leather couches and cowhide chairs. Restaurant, bar. In-room data ports, TV in some rooms. Hot tub, sauna. Some pets allowed. | 16253 Hwy. 84 S | 505/756–2133 | fax 505/756–2519 | www.lodgeatchama.com | 9 rooms, 2 suites | $225–$450, $550 suites | AP | D, MC, V.

River Bend Lodge. This comfortable yet simple lodge has one of the only hot tubs in town. Right on the Chama River, you can walk out your door and cast a fly. But be careful—you might surprise a black bear and her cub. Cabins are ideal for families, with two queen-size beds, and a double bed in the loft, and cooking facilities. Management here is especially sensitive and accommodating, particularly for groups or family reunions. Kitchenettes, refrigerators, cable TV. Hot tub. Some pets allowed. | Hwy. 84, 87520 | 505/756–2264 or 800/288–1371 | fax 800/288–1371 | www.chamaleisure.com | 15 rooms, 4 cabins | $53–$90, $100 cabins | AE, D, DC, MC, V.

Spruce Lodge. If you like roughing it but not too rough, these 12 little cabins beside the Rio Chama are the perfect balance of rustic but comfortable. You know you're away from it all when you can hear the river and the wind sifting through the pines. Some kitchenettes, cable TV. Some pets allowed. No smoking. | Hwy. 84/Hwy. 64 | 505/756–2593 | 12 cabins | $47–$95 | Closed Nov.–Apr. | D, MC, V.

CHIMAYÓ

(Nearby towns also listed: Española, Taos)

Chimayó today is the home of the Ortega family's textile business. For many generations, members of this early Spanish family have produced high-quality woven goods. Nearby, the Santuario de Nuestro, world renowned for its healing powers, brings thousands of visitors on pilgrimages. Chimayó is a stop on the "High Road to Taos," nestled into hillsides where gnarled piñon pines seem to grow from bare bedrock. The town is also famous for its delicious New Mexican cuisine.

Information: **Santuario de Chimayó Church** | Box 235, Chimayó, 87522 | 505/351–4889.

Attractions

Galeria Ortega. The premier gallery in the region features art, gifts, music, southwestern books, and foods of New Mexico. It's next door to Ortega's Weaving Shop. | County Rd. 98 at Hwy. 76 | 505/351–2288 | Free | Mon.–Sat. 9–5:30 (late Mar.–late Oct., also Sun. 11–5).

Ortega's Weaving Shop. The Ortega family of Chimayo has been weaving outstanding products for eight generations; their shop displays samples of their best wares, and there are daily demonstrations of the weaving process. | County Rd. 98 at Hwy. 76 | 505/351–4215 | Free | Mon.–Sat. 9–5.

★ **Santuario de Chimayó.** This small frontier adobe church has a beautifully carved altar. Legend states that a mysterious light came from the ground here on Good Friday in 1810, giving the site healing properties. The shrine is a National Historic Landmark and is pleasantly free of much crass commercialism. Thousands come here each Holy Week. | County Rd. 98 | 505/351–4889 | Free | Daily 9–5:30.

Chapel of Santo Niño de Atocha. Just 200 feet away from the main church, this small chapel built in 1857 is also said to have miraculous healing powers. Named after a boy saint brought from New Mexico who, it is said, lost one of his shoes as he wandered the countryside helping people; it is tradition to place shoes at the foot of his statue as an offering. | Free | Daily 9–5:30.

ON THE CALENDAR

MAR.–APR.: *Chimayó Pilgrimage.* Thousands of New Mexico and out-of-state pilgrims trek on foot to the Santuario de Chimayó, a small frontier adobe church north of Santa Fe. Built on the site where a mysterious light is said to have come out of the ground on Good Friday in 1810, the chapel holds a sacred *posito* (a small well), the dirt from which is believed to have miraculous healing properties. People line U.S. 285 for miles en route to this sacred spot. | 505/753–2831.

Dining

Leona's de Chimayó. Mexican. This fast-food burrito-and-chile stand at one end of the Santuario de Chimayó parking lot has only a few tables, but it's always crowded in summer. The specialty is flavored tortillas—everything from jalapeno to blueberry chocolate and pesto. The tortillas are such a hit that the owner opened a tortilla factory in Chimayó's Mansana Center. | 4 Medina La. | 505/351–4569 | Closed Nov.–Apr. No dinner | $2–$3 | AE, DC, D, MC, V.

★ **Rancho De Chimayó.** Mexican. This is one of New Mexico's premier eateries, in a late-19th-century antiques-filled adobe hacienda. The margaritas are great. Open-air dining on two landscaped terraces. Entertainment June–August. Kids' menu. | Hwy. 98, Chimayó | 505/351–4444 | Closed Mon. and Nov.–May | $6–$13 | AE, D, DC, MC, V.

Lodging

Casa Escondida. Intimate and serene, this adobe inn has sweeping views of the Sangre de Cristo range. Rooms are decorated with antiques, especially American Mission period pieces. Ask for the Sun Room, in the main house, which has a private patio with French doors, viga ceilings (with exposed wood beams), and a brick floor. The separate one-bedroom Casita Escondida has a kiva-style fireplace, tile floors, and a sitting area. Complimentary breakfast. Hot tub. Some pets allowed. | Country Rd. 0100 | 505/351–4805 or 800/643–7200 | fax 505/351–2575 | www.casaescondida.com | 8 rooms, 1 casita | $80–$140 | AE, MC, V.

Hacienda de Chimayó Inn. This inn occupies an adobe hacienda with an enclosed courtyard, right on Chimayó's main street. The antiques-furnished rooms are large and have fireplaces. You can have your breakfast there or in the courtyard. Complimentary Continental breakfast. | Hwy. 98, Chimayó | 505/351–2222 | fax 505/351–2222 | 7 rooms | $52–$105 | AE, MC, V.

Inn at the Delta. A lovely adobe inn filled with regional artisanal furnishings. There are also fireplaces and hot tubs in all rooms. Complimentary breakfast. In-room hot tub, cable TV. | 304 Paseo de Oñate | 505/753–9466 or 800/995–8599 | fax 505/753–9446 | 10 rooms | $100–$150 | AE, D, DC, MC, V.

CIMARRON

MAP 9, F2

(Nearby towns also listed: Raton, Red River, Taos)

Cimarron was established soon after Carlos Beaubien was given a huge land grant by the Mexican government in 1841. Ownership of the grant passed to his son-in-law, Lucien B. Maxwell, who along with business partners soon increased the size of the grant's area until it had reached almost 2 million acres. The town of Cimarron became the site of Maxwell's home and the headquarters for his varied land operations. Over the years Maxwell's grant has been broken up, and today the Boy Scout Ranch at Philmont and the nearby National Rifle Association's Whittington Center (*see* Raton) occupy portions of it. You can take a downtown walking tour, which features 14 historical sites and markers.

Information: Cimarron Chamber of Commerce | 104 N. Lincoln Ave., Cimarron, 87714 | 505/376–2417 | chamber@cimarron.springercoop.com.

Attractions

Cimarron Canyon State Park. Palisades Sills, a 400-ft granite formation, dominates this state park 12 mi west of Cimarron on U.S. 64. There's superb rainbow and brown trout fishing here, not to mention an abandoned mine. It's a good place to stop for a morning or afternoon hike. | U.S. 64 | 505/377–6271 | www.emnrd.state.nm.us/nmparks | Free | Daily.

Old Aztec Mill Museum. First operated in 1864, this Old Town mill was built by Lucien Maxwell at a cost of $50,000. Today the mill houses four floors of vintage photos, clothing, tools, and memorabilia depicting life in Colfax County from the 1860s on. | Hwy. 21 | 505/376–2913 | $2 | May–Sept., Mon.–Wed. and Fri.–Sat. 9–5, Sun 1–5. Closed Thurs.

Philmont Scout Ranch. The 140,000-acre Philmont Ranch, 4 mi south of Cimarron on Route 21, is the world's largest private youth camp and was a gift to the Boy Scouts of America by Texas oilman Waite Phillips. If you visit the ranch, you can visit the two museums there, the Kit Carson Museum and the Philmont Museum, as well as the Villa Philmonte, Waite Phillips's original summer home. | Hwy. 21 | 505/376–2281 | Free; Villa Philmonte $4 | Weekdays 9–4; Jun.–Aug., weekends 9–4.

Kit Carson Museum. Built on a portion of the original fort founded by Kit Carson and Lucien Maxwell, which is 2 mi south of the main Philmont offices, this interpretive museum has both hands-on exhibits and displays that demonstrate turn-of-the-century mountain man life. Hosts, dressed in 1880s period costumes, talk about the history and legends of the area, and you can try your hand at blacksmithing or black powder rifle shooting. | Hwy. 21 | 505/376–2281 | Free | Jun.–Aug., daily 8–5. Closed Sept.–May.

The Philmont Museum and Seton Memorial Library. Across the street from Philmont's main offices and base camp, this museum exhibits photographs, artifacts, and information about the history of the area and the ranch; it also houses the extensive book collection of Ernest Thompson Seton, famed naturalist and founder of the Boy Scouts. A gift shop sells Native American jewelry, books, and area memorabilia. | Rte. 21 | 505/376–2281 | Free | Jun.–Aug., daily 8–6; Sept.–May, weekdays 8–5.

Villa Philmonte. This lavish Mediterranean-style villa, built in 1927, was the summer home of oil tycoon Waite Phillips until 1941. The collection here includes brilliantly colored oriental rugs, intricate tilework, antique furnishings, and numerous works of art, as well as photographs of regular guests like Theodore Roosevelt. Reservations for tours must be made at the Philmont Museum and Seton Memorial Library next door. | Rte. 21 | 505/376–2281 | $4 | Jun.–Aug. daily 8–5, tours every ½ hour; Sept.–May tours by appointment only.

St. James Hotel. The St. James, in addition to being an active downtown hotel, is in the National Register of Historic Places. Dating back to 1872, the hotel has sheltered such luminaries as Zane Grey, Wyatt Earp, Doc Holliday, Annie Oakley, Clay Allison, and Buffalo

Bill. Sightseeing in the lobby is free if you partake in dinner or drinks at the hotel, and full of memorabilia of the area. Ask about the ghost in Room 18. | 17th and Collinson Sts. | 505/376–2664 | $2 | Daily.

JULY: *Maverick Club Rodeo.* This combination parade and rodeo in the Maverick Club Arena is sponsored by the Maverick Club, a group of the region's prominent citizens. | 505/376–2417.
SEPT.: *Cimarron Days.* This Labor Day weekend festival in Village Park celebrates the arts-and-crafts heritage of the Santa Fe Trail. | 505/376–2417.

Dining

Colfax Tavern. American/Casual. Also known as Cold Beer, New Mexico, this tavern 11 mi east of Cimarron has been open since Prohibition. In addition to an ongoing card game and Shiner Bock on tap, there are Saturday-night dances and a winter *Jeopardy!* tournament. The menu includes excellent green-chile burgers, pizza, spaghetti on Monday, and brisket on Wednesday. | U.S. 64 | 505/376–2229 | $4–$6 | No credit cards.

Lodging

Casa del Gavilan. This World War I–era hacienda 6 mi south of Cimarron is completely surrounded by the Philmont Scout Ranch. The southwestern adobe structure, built around a central courtyard lies on 22½ acres, with carefully selected antique furnishings in the rooms. Complimentary breakfast. No air-conditioning, no room phones, no TV. Business services. No smoking. | Rte. 21 | 505/376–2246 or 800/428–4526 | fax 505/376–2247 | www.casadelgavilan.com | 6 rooms | $70–$125 | AE, D, MC, V.

Cimarron Inn. A small, homey, economical motel. Picnic area. Some microwaves, refrigerators, cable TV. Business services. | 212 E. 10th St. | 505/376–2268 or 800/546–2244 | fax 505/376–4504 | 12 rooms (5 with shower only) | $40–$62 | AE, D, MC, V.

Kit Carson Motel. This serviceable motel is nothing special, but it will do the job if you are after shelter and a hot shower. Restaurant, bar. Cable TV. Some pets allowed. | 31039 U.S. 64 E | 505/376–2288 or 800/293–7961 | fax 505/376–9214 | 38 rooms | $54–$66 | AE, D, DC, MC, V.

St. James Hotel. This adobe hotel, built in 1872 by a former chef for presidents Lincoln and Grant, is in the National Register of Historic Places. Everything in the main building, which was restored in 1985, is done up in period Victoriana. Rooms in the annex built in the 1960s are more modern and include TVs and phones. Although the formal dining room is open only on the weekends, a café is open daily. Bar, dining room. No TV in some rooms, some room phones. | 17th and Collinson Sts. | 505/376–2664 or 800/748–2694 | fax 505/376–2623 | 24 rooms in 2 buildings | $60–$120 | AE, D, DC, MC, V.

CLAYTON

MAP 9, H2

(Nearby town also listed: Raton)

Clayton had its beginnings as a watering hole on the Santa Fe Trail. In time a settlement took hold and by 1888, when the railroad came through, it counted several hundred residents. In 1901 the notorious outlaw Thomas E. "Blackjack" Ketchum was hanged there. Legend has it that when the trapdoor of the gallows was sprung open and Blackjack dropped through, the weight of his body snapped his neck, and his head rolled away into the mob of curious onlookers.

Clayton lies close to what was known as the Cimarron Cutoff of the Santa Fe Trail. Nearby is a natural stone formation called the Rabbit Ears, which was used by early travelers as a landmark. Clayton also serves as the gateway to the vast Kiowa National Grasslands. It bills itself as the carbon-dioxide capital of the world, but the gas lies underground in the sandstone west of town, not in smog on the surface. Other important economic forces are the cattle ranches in the surrounding area.

Information: **Clayton/Union County Chamber of Commerce** | Box 476, Clayton, 88415 | 800/390–7858 or 505/374–9253.

Attractions

Clayton Lake State Park. Five hundred dinosaur tracks crisscross the mud rock along the edge of Clayton Lake. These can be viewed from a ½-mi boardwalk and self-guided tour that gives information on the rich prehistory of this park, 15 mi north of Clayton on Highway 370. Also a popular fishing spot among locals. There are seven electrical hookups and 30 campsites throughout the site's 402 acres. | Hwy. 370, 88437 | 505/437–7100 | www.emnrd.state.nm.us/nmparks | $4 per vehicle | Daily 6 AM–9 PM.

Kiowa National Grasslands. Wide-open prairie vistas and fresh air are the main benefits of this vast expanse of prairie that stretches into Oklahoma and Texas. A 2-mi portion of the Santa Fe Trail passes through the portion closest to Clayton; look carefully, and you can see the wagon ruts. The area offers hiking, fishing, and camping opportunities, but no hiking trails. The grasslands are off U.S. 56, north and south of Clayton. | Administrative office: 614 Main St. | 505/374–9652 | www.fs.fed.us/grasslands | Free | Daily.

ON THE CALENDAR

JUNE: *Rabbit Ears Roundup Rodeo.* This is a combination of closed (for locals only) and open (anyone can enter) rodeo at the Clayton fairgrounds. The rodeo is accompanied by a barbecue and a street dance with live western music. | 505/374–9253.

Dining

Eklund Hotel Dining Room and Saloon. American. Good fare is served in both the dining room and saloon with splendid Victorian chandeliers, apricot tufted-velvet booths, and marble fireplaces. Hand-cut steaks are a specialty, or you can order hamburgers, beef stew, chicken-fried steak, some Mexican dishes, and a decent club sandwich. | 15 Main St. | 505/374–2551 | $6–$31 | MC, V.

Lodging

Best Western Kokopelli Lodge. When locals have out-of-town guests they can't put up for the night, they send them to this motel located 12 mi north of Clayton State Park. The pleasant lobby is full of fresh flowers and warmed with a gas stove. The rooms are spacious and clean. Complimentary Continental breakfast. Some in-room hot tubs, cable TV. Pool. Pets allowed. | 702 S. 1st St., 88415 | 505/374–2589 or 800/528–1234 | fax 505/374–2551 | www.bestwestern.com | 47 rooms, 6 suites | $57–$74 | AE, D, DC, MC, V.

CLOUDCROFT

MAP 9, E8

(Nearby towns also listed: Alamogordo, Artesia)

Cloudcroft, a quiet resort town nestled in the Sacramento Mountains and within the boundaries of the Lincoln National Forest, has become popular for its desirable high-altitude location and its proximity to nature. You can play golf on one of the loftiest courses in America, or pass the time observing the bears, deer, elk, antelope, and mountain lions known to inhabit the area. Clark Gable, Pancho Villa, and Judy Garland vacationed here.

Information: **Cloudcroft Chamber of Commerce** | Hwy. 82, Box 1290, Cloudcroft, 88317 | 505/682–2733 | www.cloudcroft.net.

Attractions

Lincoln National Forest, Sacramento Ranger District. This large reserve offers day hiking, backpacking, fishing, and other outdoor activities. | 61 Curlew St. | 505/682–2551 | www.fs.fed.us/links/forests.shtml | Free | Daily.

National Solar Observatory. At an altitude of 9,200 ft, the National Solar Observatory hosts research scientists from all over the world, who come to use the state-of-the-art solar facilities. It's located on Sacramento Peak, 18 mi south of Cloudcroft. During daylight hours you can take a self-guided tour and wander around the grounds and make observations through one of the telescopes. | Hwy. 6563 | 505/434–7000 | www.sunspot.noao.edu | Free | Visitor center daily 10–4; observatory daily dawn–dusk.

Sacramento Mountains Historical Museum. This small museum, housed in a restored log cabin, displays pioneer and railroad artifacts from the region. | U.S. 82 | 505/682–2932 | $2 | Mon.–Tues. and Fri.–Sat. 10–4, Sun. 1–4.

ON THE CALENDAR
JUNE: *Western Roundup.* A parade highlights this weekend festival in Zenith Park that includes a pie auction, barbecue, and fund-raising events for the local Chamber of Commerce. | 505/682–2733.
JULY, OCT., DEC.: *Cloudcroft Light Opera Company.* This community theater group performs both melodramas and vaudeville and runs several outdoor performances per year. There are also several weekend murder mysteries at the Cloudcroft Lodge in February and November. | 505/682–2765.

Dining

Rebecca's. Continental. Dine in a turn-of-the-20th-century atmosphere with a mountain view in The Lodge's restaurant. Try the shrimp, steak, or châteaubriand for two. Pianist nightly. Kids' menu. Sunday brunch. | 1 Corona Pl | 505/682–2566 | $13–$33 | AE, D, DC, MC, V.

The Western Bar and Café. American. Alleged to have the best omelets in New Mexico (try the Mexico omelet with green chile, cheese, tomatoes, and ham), this local landmark has served locals and visitors for half a century. Bring the family for a hearty meal, or come for karaoke night on a Thursday and get to know the locals. | 86 Burro St. | 505/682–2445 | $7–$14 | No credit cards.

Lodging

Eagle Eyrie Vacation Manor. Built on Grand Avenue in 1897 by Major William H. Long, this 2,800-square-ft house has retained its rustic grandeur and is rented out as a complete unit. The stone fireplace and majestic staircase are the centerpieces of the large interior and are surrounded by antiques that hark back to another age. There are five bedrooms, two baths, and a full kitchen; it can sleep 16 people. Cable TV. Pets allowed. No smoking. | 609 Grand Ave. | 505/522–1787 | www.cloudcroft.com/eagle/index.htm | 1 house | $325 | AE, D, DC, MC, V.

The Lodge. A meticulously restored turn-of-the-20th-century Bavarian lodge that has seen such illustrious guests as Judy Garland, Clark Gable, and Pancho Villa. Restaurant (*see* Rebecca's), bar (with entertainment). Cable TV, some in-room VCRs. Pool. Hot tub, massage, sauna. 9-hole golf course, putting green. Gym, volleyball, bicycles. Cross-country skiing, snow-mobiling. Business services. | 1 Corona Pl | 505/682–2566 or 800/395–6343 | fax 505/682–2715 | www.thelodge-nm.com | 61 rooms, 12 suites in 3 buildings | $99–$135, $149–$305 suites | AE, D, DC, MC, V.

CLOVIS

(Nearby towns also listed: Portales, Tucumcari)

Clovis is the commercial and service hub for more than 100,000 residents of eastern New Mexico and West Texas. The town's high altitude, dry air, and almost ideal climate make it a relaxing and enjoyable place. Perhaps its most notable role was as the site of Norman Petty's recording studio, where Buddy Holly recorded most of his greatest hits, including "That'll Be the Day" and "Peggy Sue." One of North America's most ancient archaeological sites, Blackwater Draw, is located nearby where you can get an idea of what everyday prehistoric Indian life was like almost 12,000 years ago.

Information: Clovis/Curry County Chamber of Commerce | 215 N. Main St., Clovis 88101 | 505/763–3435 or 800/261–7656 | www.clovis.org.

Attractions

Blackwater Draw Museum and Archaeological Site. This lovingly put-together museum is full of information about the nearby archaeological site, where one of the oldest prehistoric Indian cultures in North America has been discovered. Exhibits are informative and well presented, including special exhibits for kids. It's 12 mi south of Clovis; the archaeological site is on Highway 467, south of Clovis. | U.S. 70 | 505/562–2202 | $2 | Mon.–Sat. 10–5, Sun. noon–5.

Clovis Depot Model Train Museum. Nine working model-train layouts and a large collection of railroad memorabilia are displayed in the restored Santa Fe Railroad passenger depot. | 221 W. 1st St. | 505/762–0066 or 888/762–0064 | www.clovisdepot.com | $4; special rates for children, senior citizens, and families | Wed.–Sun. noon–5; closed Feb., Sept.

Hillcrest Park Zoo. More than 500 animals in their native habitats are housed in this 22-acre park, the region's largest such facility. | 10th St. and Sycamore St. | 505/769–7873 | $1 | Late Oct.–late Mar., daily 9–4; late-Mar.–late-Oct., Tues.–Sun. 9–5.

Lyceum Theater. This early-20th-century theater has been restored and now presents a full season of stage productions. | 411 Main St. | 505/763–6085 | Tour free | Sept.–June, daily.

ON THE CALENDAR

JUNE: *Pioneer Days and PRCA Rodeo.* This PRCA-sanctioned rodeo in the Curry County Mounted Patrol Arena is accompanied by a parade and a Little Buckaroo Rodeo. | 505/763–3435.

JUNE: *The Norman Petty Music Festival.* The Norman Petty Recording Studio is where Buddy Holly and others recorded hits in the 1950s. A tour of this facility is the main draw for this two-day music festival at the Curry County Fairgrounds. | 505/762–0515 or or 505/356–6422.

AUG.: *Curry County Fair.* Agricultural and ranching products are featured at this annual event at the Curry County Fairgrounds. | 505/763–3435.

Dining

Guadalajara Café. Mexican. It's hard to beat the prices or the food in this down-home chile palace. Try the Librabo. | 916 L. Casillas Blvd. | 505/769–9965 | Closed Sun. | $3–$8 | MC, V.

Kripple Creek. American. This restaurant is decked out with old license plates, railroad ties, and washboards to create a turn-of-the-20th-century feel. There's a spaghetti special on Thursday, or try the taco salad or fajita salad any night. For dessert try the Dutch apple pie, blackberry cobbler, or homemade cheesecake that comes in a plethora of flavors from crème brûlée or banana split to M&M or brownie bottom. | 2417 N. Prince St. | 505/762–7399 | $6–$10 | AE, D, DC, MC, V.

Leal's Mexican Food. Mexican. Leal's is a reasonably priced traditional Mexican restaurant. Known for enchiladas, tacos, tamales. Kids' menu. | 3100 E. Mabry Dr. | 505/763–4075 | $4–$10 | AE, D, MC, V.

Poor Boy's Steakhouse. American. A good, all-around steak house furnished with antiques. Salad bar. Kids' menu. | 2115 N. Prince | 505/763–5222 | $4–$21 | AE, D, DC, MC, V.

Lodging

Best Western La Vista Inn. This is a nicely maintained small chain motel. Complimentary Continental Breakfast. Refrigerators, cable TV. Pool. Video games. Laundry service. Business services. | 1516 Mabry Dr. | 505/762–3808 or 800/528–1243 | fax 505/762–1422 | www.bestwestern.com | 47 rooms | $41–$54 | AE, D, DC, MC, V.

Bishops Inn. This clean southwestern motel has room entrances on an inside hallway. The rooms are mid-size but well appointed and colorful. Complimentary Continental breakfast. Cable TV, refrigerators, room phones. Pool. Hot tub. Some pets allowed. | 2920 Mabry Dr. | 505/769–1953 or 800/643–9239 | fax 505/762–8304 | 57 rooms | $33–$43 | AE, D, DC, MC, V.

Clovis Inn. A basic, reasonably priced motel conveniently located near the municipal airport as well as a mall and several restaurants. Picnic area, complimentary Continental breakfast. Some refrigerators, cable TV. Pool. Hot tub. Laundry facilities. Business services. | 2912 Mabry Dr. | 505/762–5600 or 800/535–3440 | fax 505/762–6803 | 97 rooms | $43–$60 | AE, D, DC, MC, V.

Comfort Inn. Clean, comfortable, and inexpensive lodgings not far from the rodeo and fairgrounds. In-room data ports, cable TV. Pool. Business services. | 1616 E. Mabry Dr. | 505/762–4591 or 800/228–5150 | fax 505/763–6747 | www.comfortinn.com | 50 rooms | $39–$69 | AE, D, DC, MC, V.

Days Inn. Basic but reliable lodging near Clovis Community College. Cable TV. Pool. Business services. Pets allowed. | 1720 E. Mabry Dr. | 505/762–2971 | fax 505/762–2735 | www.daysinn.com | 94 rooms | $35–$57 | AE, D, DC, MC, V.

Holiday Inn. This well-maintained, moderately priced motel is the largest in Clovis. Restaurant, bar, room service. In-room data ports, cable TV. 2 pools. Hot tub, sauna. Gym. Video games. Business services. | 2700 Mabry Dr. | 505/762–4491 or 800/HOL–IDAY | fax 505/769–0564 | www.basshotels.com/holiday-inn | 120 rooms | $50–$90 | AE, D, DC, MC, V.

Westward Ho Motel. On the corner of 1st Street, a block off of Prince, you will see this motel that bears a resemblance to the Alamo, with its yellow clay adobe-style exterior. Only six blocks from downtown, with individual apartments as well as rooms, this place is convenient, quiet, and clean. Some kitchenettes, cable TV. | 616 E. 1st St., 88101 | 505/762–4451 | 36 rooms | $25–$180 | MC, V.

DEMING

MAP 9, C9

(Nearby towns also listed: Las Cruces, Lordsburg, Silver City)

In March 1881, railroad officials traveled to Deming to witness the completion of the country's second transcontinental railroad, when tracks of the Southern Pacific line and those of the Atchison, Topeka, and Santa Fe were joined by a silver spike. The railroad gave an economic boost to this small, desolate town; ranching and small industry continue to drive the economy of this town, which has a population of almost 15,000.

The beauty of the nearby Florida Mountains, the restored historic downtown section of Deming, the outstanding prehistoric ruins in the neighborhood, and the hometown spirit of the town's residents make a stopover in Deming well worth your time.

Information: Deming/Luna County Chamber of Commerce | Box 8, Deming, 88031 | 505/546–2674 or 800/848–4955 | www.demingchamber.com.

Attractions

City of Rocks State Park. This park 28 mi northwest of Deming preserves a series of monolithic blocks of ash, the product of an ancient volcanic eruption more than 33 million years ago. Hiking trails weave between the formations. A picnic area, 50 campsites, showers, and rest rooms are available. | Hwy. 61 | 505/536–2800 | www.emnrd.state.nm.us/nmparks | $4 per vehicle | Daily.

Columbus Historical Society Museum. Columbus, 32 mi south of Deming, was the last place in the continental United States to be invaded by a foreign power. The museum in the restored Southern Pacific railroad depot displays memorabilia and artifacts associated with Pancho Villa's raid on the village in 1916. | Hwy. 11 at Hwy. 9, Columbus | 505/531–2620 | Free | Sept.–May, daily 10–4; Jun.–Aug., weekdays 10–1, weekends 10–4.

Deming-Luna Mimbres Museum. The armory that houses this museum was completed two months after Pancho Villa's raid on the border town of Columbus, 32 mi south of Deming, in 1916. Its vast collections include antique cars, a cowboy exhibit, art gallery, gem and mineral room, a Hispanic Room, dolls, and an excellent assemblage of ancient Mimbres Indian basketry and pueblo pottery. | 301 S. Silver St. | 505/546–2382 | Free | Mon.–Sat. 9–4, Sun. noon–4.

Old Courthouse. One of the original buildings in Deming, built in 1910 and used continually ever since, it houses all judicial offices and serves as the focal point of town. The brick

© Artville

PANCHO VILLA ATTACKS

In the troubled days of the early 20th century, Mexico was in turmoil. A number of insurrectionists, dissatisfied with the manner in which their country was ruled, roamed the remote expanses of the country, drumming up support for their rebel causes. One of the most eminent of these revolutionaries was Pancho Villa, who was born a peasant in 1878 and was as an adult a leading critic of Mexico's government. For reasons that even today are not entirely clear, Villa hypothesized that if he could get the attention of the United States focused on his plight, perhaps his task of reforming the government would be made easier.

Accordingly, during the early hours of March 9, 1916, Villa, accompanied by several dozen of his compatriots, crossed the international border at Columbus, New Mexico, and descended on the tiny town. Members of the United States 13th Cavalry were stationed nearby, and as soon as the first shots were fired, they quickly mounted and responded to the village's cry for help. After two hours of brisk fighting, Villa and his men retreated across the border, leaving six U.S. soldiers and nine Columbus residents dead. Villa's small army had also destroyed the railroad station and two other buildings, looted three stores, and stolen seven American cavalry horses. The Mexicans lost 50 men in the skirmish. A week later, General John J. "Blackjack" Pershing led a sizable expeditionary force across the Mexican border, but after spending almost a year trying to track down and punish Villa, he returned empty-handed, having nonetheless run up a $130 million bill to American taxpayers.

After the raid on Columbus, Villa was immortalized in his own country, but for his efforts he was assassinated seven years later. Even today his name is spoken in whispers in remote areas of southern New Mexico.

walls are 2 ft thick in places, and the structure stands about six stories to the top of the clock tower. | 700 S. Silver St. | 505/546–0491 | Free | Closed weekends.

Pancho Villa State Park. This 49-acre state park is on the grounds of old Camp Furlong, 32 mi south of Deming near Columbus, where troops taking part in the futile invasion of Mexico in search of Pancho Villa in 1916 were based. The visitor center houses exhibits documenting Villa's raid on nearby Columbus and the search. Another major attraction is a desert botanical garden. | Hwy. 11 at Hwy. 9, Columbus | 505/531–2711 | $4 per vehicle | Daily.

Rockhound State Park. This geologically unique park 14 mi southeast of Deming is nestled in the foothills of the Florida Mountains. You can find all kinds of rocks and minerals, and you are encouraged to discover and keep up to 15 pounds of rocks. | Hwy. 497 | 505/546–6182 | $4 per vehicle | Daily.

ON THE CALENDAR
MAR.: *Deming Rock and Gem Society Rockhounding Trips.* Guided field trips, exhibits, and demonstrations at the Deming Courthouse Park. | 505/544–4158.
AUG.: *Great American Duck Race.* This event in Deming Courthouse Park features a live duck race, parade, tortilla toss, and an outhouse race. | 505/546–2674 or 800/848–4955.
OCT.: *Southwestern New Mexico State Fair.* A parade, livestock show, and midway highlight this annual event at the Deming fairgrounds. | 505/546–2674 or 800/848–4955.

Dining
Si Señor. Mexican. Tasty, spicy Mexican food in various combinations is served at this family-owned restaurant. It isn't fancy, but the food's good, and the prices are reasonable. The house special pairs a New York steak with rice and beans; also try the enchiladas. | 200 E. Pine St. | 505/546–3938 | $4–$10 | AE, D, MC, V.

Veranda Deli. Delicatessen. This quaint deli and bakery is located in Deming's old power plant, built at the turn of the 20th century. The meats in the sandwiches, including roast beef, ham, and turkey, are prepared on the premises, not commercially bought, so they are served fresh and hot every day. Soups, salads, and desserts are also available. | 110 S. Silver Ave. | 505/546–8585 | Closed weekends | $4–$6 | AE, D, DC, MC, V.

Lodging
Anselments Butterfield Stage Motel. These spacious rooms, the largest in town, are almost like suites, some equipped with up to four double beds. The 1960s motel-retro furniture is a treat for the nostalgic soul, and the neon sign out front is an original from 1963. The lobby is decked with an old-fashioned rifle, antique map of the United States, and an authentic Native American tomahawk. Refrigerators, cable TV, room phones. Laundry facilities. Some pets allowed. | 309 W. Pine St. | 505/544–0011 | fax 505/544–0614 | 13 rooms | $33–$56 | AE, D, DC, MC, V.

Deming Days Inn. This two-story motel, last remodeled in 1998, provides basic but comfortable rooms at reasonable prices. Restaurant, complimentary Continental breakfast. In-room data ports, some microwaves, refrigerators, cable TV. Pool. Some pets allowed (fee). | 1601 E. Pine St. | 505/546–8813 | fax 505/546–7095 | www.daysinn.com | 57 rooms | $38–$53 | AE, D, DC, MC, V.

Grand Motor Inn. This budget motel on Deming's main street is located near the visitor center and golf club. Restaurant, bar, room service. In-room data ports, cable TV. Pool. Business services, airport shuttle. Pets allowed. | 1721 E. Spruce St. | 505/546–2631 | fax 505/546–4446 | 62 rooms | $32–$38 | AE, D, DC, MC, V.

Holiday Inn. This two-story motel offers standard-size rooms decorated in a southwestern style. Right off I-10 and 2 mi from downtown shops and restaurants, this is a good place for a short stop-over. Restaurant. In-room data ports, in-room safes, refrigerators, some in-room hot tubs, cable TV. Pool. Gym. Laundry facilities. Business services. Pets allowed. | I-10, exit 85 | 505/546–2661 | fax 505/546–6308 | www.holiday-inn.com/demingnm | 116 rooms | $59–$99 | AE, D, DC, MC, V.

DULCE

(Nearby towns also listed: Chama, Farmington)

Dulce, just south of the Colorado border, is the capital of the Jicarilla Apache Indian Reservation, which abuts the town on the north, south, and west. The name of the community means "sweet" and tradition has it that the name refers to a spring of sweet water nearby. The 870,000-acre reservation is covered in evergreen forests and dotted with lakes that provide wonderful fishing and hiking.

Information: **Jicarilla Apache Indian Reservation** | Box 507, 87528 | 505/759–3242.

Attractions

Jicarilla Museum. This small museum operated by the Jicarilla Apache Tribal Council exhibits mostly arts and crafts, including basketry, beadwork, paintings, and leatherwork. | U.S. 64 | 505/759–3242 | Free | Weekdays 8–5.

Stone Lake. The Jicarilla Reservation is known for its fishing, particularly on Stone Lake, where you can fish from the banks or off the docks, but no swimming allowed due to the thick reeds near the shore. Sit on the banks and have a picnic or do some bird-watching; there are also nice hiking trails. A fishing permit is required and can be purchased from the Jicarilla Game and Fish Department (number below), from the Best Western Jicarilla, or from the Conoco station across from the Best Western. The lake is about 30 mi south of Dulce. | County Rd. J-8 | 505/759–3255 | Free | Daily.

ON THE CALENDAR

FEB.: *Jicarilla Day.* The powwow and talent show allow the native people to show off their hidden skills, while the traditional Native American fashion show (for adults and tots) is a rainbow of buckskin, feathers, and beads. | 505/759–3242.
JULY: *Little Beaver Roundup.* A parade, dances, and arts-and-crafts exhibits on the Jicarilla Apache Reservation. | 505/759–3242.
SEPT.: *Go-Gee-Yah.* A rodeo, footraces, and a powwow at Stone Lake. | 505/759–3242.

Dining

Hillcrest Restaurant. Mexican. Located in the Best Western Jicarilla Inn, this large restaurant has booths in the café and white linen–clad tables in the restaurant. Try the Jicarilla stew (a mild stew with meat and potatoes) or the Jicarilla taco (refrigerator bread with pinto beans with red or green chile smothered with cheese, lettuce, and tomato), or even a Jicarilla grilled cheese (the standard made with Texas toast smothered with red or green chile sauce). | U.S. 64 and Hawks Dr., 87528 | 505/759–3663 | fax 505/759–3170 | $5–$16 | AE, D, DC, MC, V.

Lodging

Best Western Jicarilla Inn. A stucco building with great views of the Rocky Mountains, this motel also houses a large casino (*see* Apache Nugget Casino). It's the only lodging option in Dulce, ¼ mi from the reservation conference center and museum, and 25 mi from the Cumbres and Toltec Scenic Railroad (*see* Chama). Restaurant, bar. Some refrigerators, cable TV. Airport shuttle. Some pets allowed. | Jicarilla Blvd. at U.S. 64 | 505/759–3663 | fax 505/759–3170 | 42 rooms | $65–$95 | AE, D, DC, MC, V.

ESPAÑOLA

MAP 9, E3

(Nearby towns also listed: Chimayó, Los Alamos, Santa Fe)

The region around Española was one of the first parts of New Mexico explored by the Spanish when conquistadors pushed north in the late 1500s. At that time Pueblo Indians had been settled there for hundreds of years. Today the area around Española offers a large variety of cultural and recreational activities for every age group, such as the nearby pueblos; the sights of Taos, Chimayó, Los Alamos, and Chama; some art galleries, restaurants, and hostelries; the white water of the Rio Grande; and the pristine beauty of the surroundings. While Española itself is more of a crossroads than a destination, it does have a few outstanding restaurants serving New Mexican cuisine.

Information: **Española Valley Chamber of Commerce** | 417 Big Rock Center, Española, 87532 | 505/753–2831.

Attractions

Georgia O'Keeffe Home and Studio. Painter Georgia O'Keeffe moved to Abiquiu, New Mexico, in 1949, living there in a Spanish Colonial home until 1984, two years before her death. The house and painting studio, since 1999 a national historic landmark, is open to the public for a limited season of tours by appointment only (made well in advance), which are conducted by the owners, the Georgia O'Keeffe Foundation. Visitors are taken to the house from the tour reservations office in Abiquiu by shuttle. From Española, go 22 mi northwest on U.S. 84 to Abiquiu; the reservations office is next to the Abiquiu Inn. | U.S. 84, Abiquiu | 505/685–4539 | $22 (minimum donation) | Apr.–Nov., Tues., Thurs., Fri. by appointment only.

Puyé Cliff Dwellings. This 740-room cliff dwelling, where the ancestors of the Tewa people once lived, is 2 mi south of Española on Santa Clara Pueblo tribal lands. An exploration of the ruins, as well as Top House, the deserted pueblo village on top of the mesa, gives an unparalleled glimpse into life in the region more than a millennium ago. The dwellings are off Hwy. 30; take the paved, marked road 7 mi south into Santa Clara Pueblo. | Santa Clara Pueblo | 505/753–7326 | $5, use of cameras $5 | Daily 8–4:30.

ON THE CALENDAR

JUNE: *San Juan Feast Day.* Food and dancing at San Juan Pueblo. | 505/852–4400.
JULY: *Fiesta del Valle de Española.* Street dancing, mariachi bands, arts and crafts, and food. | 505/753–2831.
AUG.: *Santa Clara Feast Day.* A market, dancing, and food at Santa Clara Pueblo, 2 mi south of Española. | 505/753–7330.
OCT.: *Española Valley Arts Festival.* Displays of works by local artisans at Northern New Mexico Community College. | 505/753–2831.
DEC.: *Main Street Electric Light Parade.* This evening parade lasts 2½ hours and is now the biggest in the state. With over 75 floats, this is a holiday treat for the eyes not to be missed. | Christine Bustos, 505/763–2258.

Dining

Anthony's at the Delta. Mexican. This adobe-and-log restaurant is loaded with locally made Native American Indian pottery, rugs, kachina dolls, and hand-crafted chairs and tables. A hand-carved staircase and bar and fresh flowers from the shop next door add to the charm. Nightly specials include broiled salmon, prime rib, a variety of Mexican dishes, and a fantastic flan. American. | 228 Oñate N.W. Chama Hwy. | 505/753–4511 | No lunch. Closed Mon. | $11–$32 | AE, D, DC, MC, V.

El Paragua. Mexican. Period furnishings fill this late-19th-century stone structure dominated by a fireplace. Try tacos or carne adovada. Live music weekends. Kids' menu. | 603 Santa Cruz Rd. | 505/753–3211 | $8–$28 | AE, D, MC, V.

JoAnn's Ranch O Casados. Mexican. JoAnn learned to grow squash and chiles growing up on the ranch that still provides many of the fresh ingredients used to create the great chiles rellenos, *posole* (corn with pork in a broth), and enchiladas served here. The restaurant's casual decor includes brightly striped Mexican blankets on the walls. | 418 N. Riverside Dr. | 505/753–2837 | $5–$15 | AE, D, DC, MC, V.

Lodging

Abiquiu Inn. This beautiful country inn 18 mi northwest of Española is in the middle of the Santa Fe and Carson national forests, with a restaurant serving Mediterranean and southwestern cuisine. There are fireplaces in some casitas. Restaurant. Some kitchenettes, cable TV. | U.S. 84, Abiquiu | 505/685–4378 or 800/447–5621 | fax 800/447–5621 | www.abiquiuinn.com | 19 rooms, 5 casitas | $55–$90, $120–$135 casitas | AE, D, DC, MC, V.

Best Western Holiday Motel. On Highway 285 just south of town, this friendly motel has all rooms at the ground level so loading and unloading is a breeze. Its claim to fame was as the set for the grade-B movie *Vampires* starring James Woods. Some kitchenettes, cable TV. Pool. Some pets allowed. | 1215 S. Riverside Dr. | 505/753–2491 or 800/653–9847 | fax 505/753–0191 | www.bestwestern.com | 26 rooms | $40–$60 | AE, D, DC, MC, V.

Chamisa Inn. At the center of Española's main drag, this brick one-story motel offers clean, standard-sized rooms and friendly service. Its lounge hosts dancing to live Spanish, country, and rock music on Wednesday, Friday, and Saturday nights. Bar, complimentary Continental breakfast. Cable TV. Pool. Pets allowed (fee). | 920 Riverside Dr. N (Hwy. 68) | 505/753–7291 or 800/766–7943 | fax 505/753–1218 | 51 rooms | $54–$60 | AE, D, MC, V.

Rancho de San Juan. Rooms at this elegant hacienda-inn are large, with tiled floors and exposed-beam ceilings, many with kiva fireplaces; furnishings are eclectic, sometimes antique, sometimes modern. The hacienda itself is built around a central courtyard filled with flowers, trees, and a trickling fountain on 225 acres overlooking the Ojo Caliente River and Jemez Mountains. Restaurant, complimentary breakfast. Some kitchenettes, microwaves, refrigerators, some in-room hot tubs. No kids under 12. No smoking. | U.S. 285 | 505/753–6818 or 800/726–7121 | wolftracks.8m.com/clients/ranchodesanjuan | 10 rooms, 5 suites | $175–$350 | AE, MC, V.

Super 8. This two-story motel with interior hallways has a small lobby and friendly staff. However, on the southern end of town, it is a 2-mi drive in nearly any direction from groceries, shopping, and convenience stores. The rooms are generally large with white walls and bright colors on the bedspreads and curtains. Complimentary Continental breakfast. Cable TV. | 811 S. Riverside Dr. | 505/753–5374 or 800/800–8000 | fax 505/753–5347 | 46 rooms, 2 suites | $50–$95, $90–$135 suites | AE, D, DC, MC, V.

FARMINGTON

MAP 9, C2

(Nearby town also listed: Aztec)

The area around Farmington was called *Totah* (Among the Waters) by the Navajo, probably because it lies at the confluence of the Animas, La Plata, and San Juan rivers. But the town got its modern name in 1879, when the railroad pulled into "Farmingtown" (later shortened to Farmington) which had built up as rich agricultural center. As the name indicates, the community's economy once relied primarily on agriculture, but with the discovery of oil and natural gas during the late 1940s, petroleum production has taken the lead in the region's boom and bust economy.

During the last decade, the local government has made more of an attempt to popularize the town's historic past. With several lovely riverfront parks, not to mention a historic downtown district that still thrives, this town of almost 37,000 people is the natural gateway to the Four Corners region and the largest town in northwestern New Mexico.

Most locals think of Farmington as the gateway to the area's natural and cultural treasures. Various Indian arts-and-crafts festivals, hot-air ballooning, Connie Mack amateur baseball play-offs, and some world-class fishing waters make Farmington a great place to visit, especially in summer.

Information: Farmington Convention and Visitors Bureau | 3042 E. Main St., Farmington, 87401 | 505/326–7602 or 800/448–1240 | www.farmington.nm.us.

Attractions

Bisti/De-Na-Zin Wilderness. Petrified logs and other fossils are among the natural wonders found in this 44,000-acre wilderness area 37 mi south of Farmington. The mushroom-shape rock formations, called hoodoos, are reminiscent of a moonscape; the best of these can be seen on a 3-mi hike east of the parking area. As there are no on-site facilities or formal hiking trails, make sure to bring plenty of water; the best time to visit these exposed "badlands" are in the spring and fall, when temperatures drop. | Off Hwy. 371 | 505/599–8900 | Free | Daily.

Chaco Culture National Historical Park. Located near Nageezi, in southeastern San Juan County between Farmington and Gallup, Chaco Culture National Historical Park is 60 mi from the nearest town, and parts of this park are remote and difficult to reach, and even then are reached by a miles-long dirt road—you should check with rangers for road conditions before setting out for unknown territory. But it contains some of the most important and interesting prehistoric Indian remains in the entire Southwest and is a World Heritage Site. Some 1,200 years ago, during the complex's heyday, the site's largest pueblo, Pueblo Bonito, was where the Anasazi carried out their sacred ceremonies in 30 kivas. Each year thousands of visitors come to study the 1,200-year-old architecture that dominates this park. The easiest access to the park is northeast of the park, via U.S. 550; take County Road 7900 to County Road 7950. | County Rd. 7950, Nageezi | 505/786–7014 | fax 505/786–7061 | www.nps.gov/chcu | $8 per vehicle | Visitor center: Memorial Day–Labor Day, daily 8–6; Labor Day–Memorial Day, daily 8–5. Trails and sites: daily.

Fifth Generation Trading Company. Five generations of the Tanner family have been involved with trading with the Indians of northwest New Mexico. Here they offer the best and largest selection of arts and crafts in the region. | 232 W. Broadway | 505/326–3211 | Free | Mon.–Sat. 9–5:30.

Four Corners Monument. About 64 mi west of Farmington you can see the exact spot where New Mexico, Colorado, Utah, and Arizona meet; it's the only place in the United States where this is possible. The site features a visitor center, Indian marketplace, crafts booths, and more. Take U.S. 64 from Farmington to U.S. 160, then north. | U.S. 160 | 520/871–6647 | $2 | May–Aug., daily 7 AM–6 PM, Sept.–Apr., daily 8–5.

San Juan County Archaeological Research Center/Library at Salmon Ruin. Named after George Salmon, a homesteader whose family protected the ruins for over 90 years, Salmon Ruin is a large, 11th-century Chacoan Anasazi dwelling along the San Juan River between Farmington and Bloomfield. The research center and museum at this complex 12 mi east of Farmington houses more than 1 million artifacts from the Chaco and Mesa Verde cultures. | 6131 U.S. 64 | 505/632–2013 | $3 | Weekdays 8–5, Sat., Sun. 9–5.

Shiprock Pinnacle. Shiprock Pinnacle, called Tse Bida'hi (Rock with Wings) by the Navajo, sticks out above the surrounding countryside like a tall ship at sea. Towering more than 1,700 ft, this hardened lava plug of a once-active volcano more than 3 million years old once served as a beacon to lost travelers in the arid desert of northwestern New Mexico. It's located about 7 mi southwest of the town to which it has given its name, 29 mi west of Farmington. You can't actually approach the monument very closely without tribal permission, nor is climbing allowed. | Off U.S. 666, south of the town of Shiprock | 505/325–0279 (Shiprock Chamber of Commerce) | Free | Daily.

ON THE CALENDAR

MAY: *Farmington Invitational Balloon Rally.* More than two dozen balloons compete for prizes from the launch site at Farmington Lake on Memorial Day weekend. This event also features hare and hound races. | 505/326–7602 or 800/448–1240.

JUNE–AUG.: *Anasazi, the Ancient Ones.* The region's first inhabitants are the subject of this summer outdoor musical drama in Lions Wilderness Park Amphitheater, off Piñon Hills Boulevard. | 505/327–9336.

AUG.: *Connie Mack World Series Baseball Tournament.* During this one-week event amateur teams from all over the country converge on Ricketts Park on Fairgrounds Road. | 505/326–7602 or 800/448–1240.

AUG.: *San Juan County Fair.* This old-time county fair in McGee Park is highlighted by a parade, chile cook-off, and fiddler's contest. | 505/326–7602 or 800/448–1240.

Dining

Clancy's Pub and Irish Cantina. American/Casual. Described by the owner as a "Mexican-style Irish" pub, this casual eatery, decked out with green leprechauns, offers a variety American and Tex-Mex favories. Try the mountain mushroom or old-English burgers, or the fish tacos. Open-air dining on a patio with trees and flowers. Kids' menu. | 2701 E. 20th St. | 505/325–8176 | $3–$12 | AE, D, DC, MC, V.

El Charro Cafe. Mexican. Don't be put off by the shabby carpet or out-of-the-way location on the west side of town. Locals who demand authentic fare head here regularly for lunch. The pulse of life beats within their red chile. Order a combination plate—a tamale, an enchilada, and a taco with guacamole, rice, and beans, and you won't go hungry. You won't go thirsty either, since it comes with a tall glass of iced tea. | 737 W. Main St. | 505/327–2464 | $4–$7 | AE, D, MC, V.

K.B. Dillon's. American. Fresh fish, beef, steamed vegetables, and pasta dishes are on the menu at this clubby steak house with a rough-and-ready western cowboy feel. The house specialty, steak Dillon, is a fillet topped with crab and béarnaise sauce served with fresh steamed vegetables; or try the shrimp Dillon, five jumbo shrimp stuffed with green chiles and provolone cheese, wrapped in bacon, grilled, and served over rice. | 101 W. Broadway | 505/325–0222 | Closed Sun. No lunch Sat. | $13–$40 | AE, MC, V.

La Fiesta Grande. Mexican. An economical and conveniently located restaurant serving traditional Mexican food. Salad bar. Buffet lunch. Kids' menu. | 1916 E. Main St. | 505/326–6476 | No dinner Sun. | $3–$9 | D, MC, V.

The Spare Rib. Barbecue. The look here is nothing fancy, just plastic tablecloths over picnic tables for indoor or outdoor patio dining. The whole family can fill up on generous portions of delicious smoked barbecue or deep-fried catfish served with a side order of fries and coleslaw. The fruit cobblers are all homemade and all come highly recommended. | 1700 E. Main St. | 505/325–4800 | Reservations not accepted | Closed Sun. | $4–$11 | AE, D, DC, MC, V.

Three Rivers Eatery and Brewhouse. American. The building housing this popular brewpub was formerly a drugstore; now it's on the National Register of Historic Places, decorated with period advertising signs and known for its barbecue pork ribs, hamburgers, steaks, and seafood. One tap are 12 different house-made brews, from light to dark, lagers and ales, as well as hard cider. | 101 E. Main St. | 505/324–2187 | www.threeriversbrewery.com | $7–$17 | AE, MC, V.

Lodging

Anasazi Inn. This quiet, well-kept roadside motel on the edge of town offers spacious rooms with ancient Native American accents. Restaurant, bar. Cable TV. Laundry service. Airport shuttle. | 903 W. Main St. | 505/325–4564 | www.cyberport.com/thriftynickel/anasazi_inn | 68 rooms | $40–$55 | AE, D, DC, MC, V.

Best Western Inn & Suites. This is Farmington's largest hotel, with a covered courtyard featuring a large pool. Rooms are large, clean, and well kept. The Animas River Walk is just behind the hotel. Restaurant, bar, complimentary breakfast, room service. Some in-room data ports, some kitchenettes, some refrigerators, cable TV, some in-room VCRs (and movies). Pool. Hot tub, sauna. Gym. Video games. Laundry service. Business services, airport shuttle. Pets allowed. | 700 Scott Ave. | 505/327–5221 | fax 505/327–1565 | www.best-western.com | 194 rooms | $79 | AE, D, DC, MC, V.

Casa Blanca Inn. This B&B is a postwar Mission-style home on a bluff overlooking the town of Farmington. The large rooms are in the main house or in an adjacent casita. The inn will pack lunches and even make dinner for you. Complimentary breakfast. Some in-room hot tubs, cable TV, in-room VCRs (and movies). Business services, airport shuttle. No kids under 12. No smoking. | 505 E. La Plata St. | 505/327–6503 | fax 505/326–5680 | www.farmington-nm-lodging.com | 6 rooms | $68–$128 | AE, D, MC, V.

Comfort Inn. Friendly and functional, this inexpensive motel offering basic, clean rooms is good for an overnight stay. Complimentary Continental breakfast. In-room data ports, some refrigerators, cable TV. Pool. Business services. Pets allowed. | 555 Scott Ave. | 505/325–2626 | fax 505/325–7675 | www.comfortinn.com | 60 rooms, 18 suites | $47–$69, $60–$66 suites | AE, D, DC, MC, V.

Holiday Inn. This moderately priced, two-story motel offers reliable lodgings with a large outdoor heated pool. Restaurant, bar, room service. Refrigerators, cable TV. Pool. Hot tub. Gym. Business services, airport shuttle. Pets allowed. | 600 E. Broadway | 505/327–9811 | fax 505/325–2288 | www.holiday-inn.com/farmingtonnm | 149 rooms | $55–$139 | AE, D, DC, MC, V.

Knight's Inn. This bare-bones budget motel is ½ mi from the airport. Cable TV. | 701 Airport Dr. | 505/325–5061 | fax 505/325–5061 | www.knightsinn.com | 21 rooms | $27–$35 | AE, D, MC, V.

Kokopelli's Cave Bed and Breakfast. This luxury cave dwelling in a cliff face overlooks the Four Corners area and is anything but a hole in the ground. Excavated by a geologist, this subterranean labyrinth is accessible only via a ladder and a set of sandstone steps carved into the cliff face. The interior is comprised of a 1,650-square-ft single-bedroom home complete with a flagstone porch, carpeting, a waterfall-style shower, and a hot tub. Complimentary Continental breakfast. Hot tub. No smoking. | 206 W. 38th St. | 505/325–7855 | fax 505/325–9671 | www.bbonline.com/nm/kokopelli | 1 suite | $180 | Closed Dec.–Feb. | AE, MC, V.

La Quinta Inn Farmington. This modern, moderately priced two-story motor inn offers decent-size, well-kept rooms. Picnic area, complimentary Continental breakfast. In-room data ports, some refrigerators, cable TV. Pool. Video games. Laundry service. Pets allowed. | 675 Scott Ave. | 505/327–4706 | fax 505/325–6583 | www.laquinta.com | 106 rooms | $59–$74 | AE, D, DC, MC, V.

Ramada Inn. Located in the heart of town, this full-service motor hotel is a good value. Rooms come with ceiling fans as well as air-conditioning and plenty of space to stretch out. The king deluxe rooms come with a convertible couch and coffee table. Suites have hot tubs and a double-head deluxe shower. Restaurant, bar. In-room data ports, cable TV. Pool. Hot tub. Laundry facilities. Airport shuttle. | 601 E. Broadway | 505/325–1191 or 888/325–1191 | fax 505/325–1223 | 73 rooms, 2 suites | $65–$69, $175 suites | AE, D, DC, MC, V.

Silver River Adobe Inn. The red-roof adobe bed-and-breakfast sits on a sandstone cliff, 30 ft above where the San Juan River meets the La Plata. Rough-hewn timbers, fluffy quilts, and complete privacy make this rustic getaway ideal for romance or rumination. Complimentary breakfast. Some kitchenettes, some room phones. No smoking. | 3151 W. Main St. | 505/325–8219 or 800/382–9251 | www.cyberport.com/silveradobe | 2 rooms, 1 suite | $65–$85, $105 suite | AE, MC, V.

GALLUP

MAP 9, B4

(Nearby towns also listed: Farmington, Grants, Zuni Pueblo)

Gallup, located on Interstate 40 less than 30 mi from the Arizona border, is situated in the middle of Navajo Indian country. When the railroad was being built through the unnamed community, the paymaster was a man by the name of Gallup. On Fridays, when rail workers announced that they were "going to Gallup's," they meant they were going to pick up their pay. The name caught on, and Gallup has been Gallup ever since.

Though now another exit off Interstate 40, Gallup was a favorite stop on historic Route 66. Today, with its more than 100 jewelry and crafts shops, the town offers shopping galore. You'll find Navajo silver and rugs, turquoise jewelry, and exquisite basketry and pottery to fit every budget. Gallup residents like to boast that their town is where the Indian Southwest really begins.

Information: Gallup Convention and Visitors Bureau | 701 E. Montoya Blvd., Gallup, 87301 | 505/863–3841 or 800/242–4282 | www.gallupnm.org.

Attractions

Gallup Cultural Center. Housed in the restored Santa Fe Railroad train and bus station, this cultural center features a screening room running documentaries about the Southwest, a small museum, a bookstore, art galleries, and a café. | 201 E. Historic Rte. 66 | 505/863–4131 | Free | Memorial Day–Labor Day, daily 9–9; Labor Day–Memorial Day, daily 9–6.

McGaffey Recreation Area. McGaffey Lake, about 22 mi southeast of Gallup, is the focal point of this area in Cibola National Forest, with fishing, camping, and picnicking. | Hwy. 400, McGaffey | 505/287–8833 | $5 | May–Nov., daily.

Red Rock State Park. The park 10 mi east of Gallup offers a visitor center, campsites, the Heritage Canyon display of ancient agricultural techniques, and the Red Rock Museum, housing Indian artifacts. You'll find hiking trails, stables, and plenty of scenic vistas set against the red sandstone buttes. Several times per year the outdoor amphitheater plays host to various events such as bull-riding and team-roping competitions, square-dancing festivals, and the annual Inter-Tribal Powwow and Gallup Inter-Tribal Indian Ceremonial. | Historic Rte. 66 | 505/722–3839 | Park $4 per vehicle, museum $2 | Daily.

Red Rock Museum. This superb museum in Red Rock State Park has exhibits of jewelry, pottery, rugs, silver, and other Anasazi, Zuni, Hopi, and Navajo artifacts, both modern and ancient. | Historic Rte. 66 | 505/863–1337 | $2, $4 per vehicle park admission | Memorial Day–Labor Day, weekdays 7–6, weekends 9–6; Labor Day–Memorial Day, Mon.–Sat. 8–4.

Rex Museum. Clothing, furniture, tools, and typewriters are among the artifacts from the coal-mining era on display. Operated by the Gallup Historical Society, the museum is inside the former Rex Hotel. | 300 W. Historic Rte. 66 | 505/863–1363 | $2 (suggested) | Weekdays 8–4, Sat. 8–3.

ON THE CALENDAR

AUG.: *Inter-Tribal Indian Ceremonial.* Representatives from more than 50 U.S. tribes gather at Red Rock State Park for parades, rodeos, and arts-and-crafts exhibits. | 505/863–3896 or 800/233–4528.

Dining

Baker's Hearth. American. The Giant Travel Center is the largest truck stop in the United States and is 17 mi east of Gallup. A little microcosm unto itself, the restaurant here serves breakfast, lunch, and dinner buffets fit for a trucker, a king, or a weary traveler. The selection includes fruit and salad bars; it's an all-you-can-eat affair. | I–40, exit 39 | 505/863–1116 | $4–$13 | AE, D, DC, MC, V.

The Butcher Shop. Continental. Ensconced in the Rodeway Inn, this hideaway is a pleasant surprise, complete with tablecloths and candles. This is a wonderful place to order prime rib and a glass of fine wine. Prime rib, steaks, seafood, and pasta are served with flair in a most romantic setting. | 2003 W. Historic Rte. 66 | 505/722–4711 | Closed Sun. No lunch | $10–$25 | AE, D, MC, V.

Eagle Café. American. For a glimpse of the past, slide into a red-vinyl booth in this 80-year-old café, where you can watch trains chug past as you munch on lamb stew, enchiladas, or a burger. Not much has changed through the years at this tasty piece of living history. | 220 W. Historic Rte. 66 | 505/722–3220 | Closed Sun. | $4–$12 | No credit cards.

Earl's Restaurant. American. Always busy, this homestyle restaurant serves favorites like rib-eye steak, chopped sirloin, liver and onions, and burgers. For lighter fare, you can try one of the hand-pressed gourmet sandwiches or something from the low-calorie menu. Casual family dining. Kids' menu. Salad bar. | 1400 E. U.S. 66 | 505/863–4201 | $5–$10 | AE, DC, MC, V.

The Ranch Kitchen. American. A western-theme restaurant with an emphasis on chile, with barbecue cooked in an open pit on the premises and some Mexican and Native American selections. Kids' menu. Beer and wine only. | 3001 W. U.S. 666 | 505/722–2537 | Breakfast also available. | $6–$17 | AE, D, DC, MC, V.

Lodging

Best Western Inn and Suites. With nice-size rooms arranged around an enclosed courtyard that includes a heated pool, this is probably the best full-service hotel in Gallup. Restaurant, bar, complimentary breakfast, room service. In-room data ports, some microwaves, cable TV. Pool. Hot tub, sauna. Gym. Video games. Laundry service. Some pets allowed. | 3009 W. U.S. 66 | 505/722–2221 | fax 505/722–7442 | www.bestwestern.com/gallupnm | 126 rooms | $64–$72 | AE, D, DC, MC, V.

Best Western Royal Holiday. This well-run two-story motel is on the west side of downtown. Rooms are large, but if you are traveling with kids, consider a family room with three beds, a microwave, and a refrigerator. Complimentary Continental breakfast, room service. Some microwaves, some refrigerators, cable TV. Pool. Hot tub, sauna. Playground. | 1903 U.S. 66 W/Historic Rte. 66 | 505/722–4900 | www.bestwestern.com | 50 rooms | $50–$79 | AE, D, DC, MC, V.

Days Inn East. This inexpensive two-story motel has a country-barn exterior, with larger-than-average, earth-tone-painted rooms offering all the basics. It was last remodeled in 1998. Complimentary Continental breakfast. In-room data ports, cable TV. Pool. Playground. Laundry facilities. Business services. | 1603 U.S. Hwy. 66 W | 505/863–3891 | fax 505/863–3891 ext. 300 | www.daysinn.com | 78 rooms | $50–$60 | AE, D, DC, MC, V.

EconoLodge. This basic but comfortable two-story motel is located on the west end of Gallup, beyond the municipal airport. Basic accommodations in a convenient location. Cable TV. Airport shuttle. Pets allowed (fee). | 3101 U.S. 66 W | 505/722–3800 | www.econolodge.com | 51 rooms | $39–$52 | AE, D, DC, MC, V.

El Rancho. This historic hotel, built in 1937, was a favorite stop for stars filming westerns in the area. Rooms are done up in Old West style, and some are quite large and have a certain nostalgic style, though others are more motel style. Bathrooms tend to be small. Restaurant, bar. Some kitchenettes, cable TV. Pool. Laundry facilities. Business services. Pets allowed. | 1000 U.S. Hwy. 66 E | 505/863–9311 or 800/543–6351 | fax 505/722–5917 | www.elranchohotel.com | $43–$76 | AE, D, MC, V.

Holiday Inn. This motel on the west end of Gallup, 2 mi east of the municipal airport, has a Holidome recreation area and is the largest hostelry in Gallup. Restaurant, bar, room service. In-room data ports, cable TV. Pool. Hot tub. Gym. Laundry service. Business services, airport shuttle. Pets allowed. | 2915 U.S. 66 W | 505/722–2201 | fax 505/722–9616 | www.holiday-inn.com/gallupnm | 212 rooms | $65–$73 | AE, D, DC, MC, V.

Red Roof Inn. Basic budget lodgings, with discounts for those over 50. Some refrigerators, cable TV. Pool. | 3304 U.S. 66 W | 505/722–7765 or 800/843–7663 | fax 505/722–4752 | 102 rooms | $36–$66 | AE, D, DC, MC, V.

Rodeway Inn. No-frills lodging, near the municipal airport. Cable TV. Pool. Hot tub, sauna. Business services. | 2003 U.S. 66 W | 505/863–9385 or 800/454–5444 | fax 505/863–6532 | www.rodewayinn.com | 92 rooms | $33–$44 | AE, D, DC, MC, V.

Sleep Inn. This quiet motel is just off exit 26 of Interstate 40. You'll get a reasonably priced room with all the basics. Cable TV. Pool. Pets allowed. | 3820 E. Historic Rte. 66 | 505/863–3535 | fax 505/722–3737 | www.sleepinn.com | 61 rooms | $39–$54 | AE, D, DC, MC, V.

Stauder's Navajo Lodge. About as close as you can get to B&B-style accommodations in the Gallup area, the lodge is 20 mi east of town, just 3 mi west of the Continental Divide. The cottages here are roomy and private, with a queen-size bed and Native American and Mexican decor. Breathtaking views of red rocks can be had from the Great Room of the main residence, a replica of a Spanish hacienda. Complimentary breakfast. Cable TV. No smoking. | Mile 44, Old Rte. 66, Coolidge | 505/862–7769 | 2 cottages | $89 | Closed Oct.–Feb. | No credit cards.

Zuni Mountain Lodge. This Territorial-style lodge is on the edge of the Zuni Mountain Range only one mi from Bluewater Lake State Park, and 35 mi east of Gallup. Peaceful rooms of white and natural woods induce tranquillity, as do their views of the lake and Cibola National Forest. Surrounded by piñon and ponderosa pines at almost 8,000 ft, this is a great base for hiking, mountain biking, and fishing. Dining room, complimentary breakfast, picnic area. No room phones, TV in common area. Volleyball, basketball. Library. Laundry facilities. Business services. | 40 Perch Dr. | 505/872–7769 | fax 505/862–7616 | www.cia-g.com/~zuniml | 9 rooms | $85 | MAP | No credit cards.

GRANTS

(Nearby towns also listed: Acoma Pueblo, Farmington, Gallup)

Cibola County, of which Grants is the county seat, didn't exist until 1981, but by then people had been living in the town for more than 100 years. The railroad provided the first boom, followed by the discovery of uranium in the Four Corners region in the 1950s. But Grants has been struggling since the early 1980s, and the bust is evident in tattered motel signs and vacant storefronts. Today Grants, located on historic Route 66, does provide a good starting point for touring such natural wonders as El Morro National Monument, Chaco Culture National Historical Park, El Malpais National Monument, and Acoma Pueblo.

Information: **Grants/Cibola County Chamber of Commerce** | Grants, 87020 | 505/287–4802 or 800/748–2142 | www.grants.org.

Attractions

Bluewater Lake State Park. It's a rare treat to find a lake as large as Bluewater to be as clean as it is. Fed by fresh snowmelt from the nearby Zuni Mountains, this local favorite about 25 mi southwest of Grants (southeast of the town of Prewitt), in the Cibola National Forest, is not to be missed if you love good fishing, winter and summer; it's also popular for boating and bird-watching. | Hwy. 412 | 505/876–2391 | $4 per vehicle | Daily.

El Malpais National Monument and National Conservation Area. El Malpais, Spanish for "the badlands," is a vast expanse of lava flows, volcanic tubes, and ice caves about 23 mi south of Grants, that was first visited by humans 10,000 years ago. You can hike a section of the ancient trail between the Zuñi and Acoma pueblos that could be 1,000 years old;

the monument encompasses the Cebolla Wilderness and La Ventana Arch. The park entrance is at the junction of Highway 53 and Route 177. | 11000 Ice Caves Rd., Grants | 505/783–4774 | www.nps.gov/elma | Free | Visitor center: daily 8:30–4:30. Monument and Conservation Area: daily.

El Morro National Monument. El Morro National Monument, 43 mi southwest of Grants near the Arizona border in western New Mexico, is also sometimes known as Inscription Rock. Even before the English had established their first permanent settlement at Jamestown, Virginia, in 1607, Spanish travelers were carving their initials into this sandstone mesa, which juts more than 200 ft above the desert floor. Two self-guided trails begin at the visitor center. | Hwy. 53, Ramah | 505/783–4226 | www.nps.gov/elmo | $4 per vehicle | Late Mar.–late Oct., daily 9–7; late Oct.–late Mar., daily 9–4.

Ice Cave and Bandera Volcano. These two sites are referred to as the "Land of Fire and Ice" and are located on the Continental Divide, 28 mi south west of Grants. The ultimate contrast in hot and cold, the caves are part of a collapsed lava tube, accessible via an ancient lava trail that cuts through an old-growth juniper and fir forest. On a hot day, walk the ½-mi volcano trail first, then cool off in an ice cave with a 20-ft-thick floor of ice. | Hwy. 53 | 505/783–4303 or 888/ICE–CAVE | www.icecaves.com | $7 | Daily, 8 AM until 1 hr before sunset.

New Mexico Mining Museum. This is the only uranium mining museum in the world. You actually go underground, into a re-created uranium mine, and there are also exhibits documenting the history of mining in the area. | 100 N. Iron St. | 505/287–4802 or 800/748–2142 | $3 | May–Sept., Mon.–Sat. 9–5, Sun. 9–4; Oct.–Apr., Mon.–Sat. 9–5.

ON THE CALENDAR
JULY: *Wild West Days.* Along with a parade down Santa Fe Avenue, there is an art show, crafts, and old-fashioned games like a pie-eating contest, watermelon-seed-spitting contest, and tug of war. | 505/287–4802 or 800/748–2142.

Dining
El Jardin Palacios. Mexican. Original art and plants adorn this stucco building. Try the tacos, chimichangas, fajitas, or enchiladas. | 319 W. Santa Fe Ave. | 505/285–5231 | Closed Sun. No lunch Sat. | $4–$10 | MC, V.

INSCRIPTION ROCK

People have been writing or carving graffiti in public places since the world began. To the explorers and later travelers who passed Inscription Rock in northwestern New Mexico (now in El Morro National Monument near Grants), the temptation to leave something behind was just too much. Don Juan de Oñate was the first to leave a message and his name on the side of the sheer, 200-ft-high mesa. On April 16, 1605, he inscribed, "Passed by here the Governor Don Juan de Oñate, from the discovery of the Sea of the South." Oñate was soon followed by a later colonial governor of New Mexico, Don Juan de Eulate, who scratched in the stone that he was "a most Christian-like gentleman extraordinary and gallant soldier of enduring and praised memory." Americans later added their names and comments to Inscription Rock. Two of them, Lieutenant J. H. Simpson of the U.S. Corps of Topographical Engineers and the artist R. H. Kern, inscribed that they "visited and copied these inscriptions, September 17th 18th 1849." Today you can read the names of scores of Spanish adventurers, U.S. soldiers, westward-bound emigrants, Indian agents, and settlers.

© Artville

La Ventana Steakhouse. American. This cozy local establishment has a casual feel with plenty of booths for intimate dining. Order the shepherder (a roast beef burrito with green chile) or go for a steak or lobster dinner. Fresh seafood on the weekends includes seasonal fare from Albuquerque, such as salmon, halibut, or red trout. The apple crunch is served with ice cream, and the white-chocolate raspberry cheesecake is a big draw with the locals. | 110½ Geis St. | 505/287–9393 | Closed Sun. | $6–$32 | AE, D, DC, MC, V.

Lodging

Best Western Inn and Suites. Rooms are nicely kept and comfortably large; there is a central courtyard filled with attractive plants and a pool. Restaurant, bar, room service. Some refrigerators, cable TV. Pool. Hot tub, sauna. Gym. Video games. Laundry facilities. Business services. Some pets allowed. | 1501 E. Santa Fe Ave. | 505/287–7901 | fax 505/285–5751 | www.bestwestern.com | 126 rooms | $66–$97 | AE, D, DC, MC, V.

Cimarron Rose Bed and Breakfast. Just below the Continental Divide and 30 mi southwest of Grants on Highway 63 is a pine-board house set on 20 acres in a grove of ponderosa pines, adjacent to Cibola National Forest and in between El Malpias and El Morro national monuments. The interior is post-and-beam construction, so there are no interior load-bearing walls, creating a large open space. Each suite has ponderosa-pine beam ceilings with saltillo tile floors (natural sun-baked tiles made in a town in Mexico of the same name). The bathrooms are accented with brightly colored glazed ceramic tiles, also from Mexico. Complimentary breakfast. No smoking. | 689 Oso Ridge Rte. | 505/783–4770 | www.cimarronrose.com | 2 suites | $60–$105 | No credit cards.

Holiday Inn Express. Just ¼ mi off Interstate 40, this limited-service motor hotel provides comfortable, moderately priced rooms. Complimentary Continental breakfast. Pool. Hot tub. Laundry service. Business services. Pets allowed. | 1496 E. Santa Fe Ave. (I–40, exit 85) | 505/285–4676 | fax 505/285–6998 | www.hiexpress/grantsnm | 58 rooms | $54–$70 | AE, D, DC, MC, V.

HOBBS

MAP 9, I8

(Nearby towns also listed: Artesia, Carlsbad)

Hobbs, in extreme southeastern New Mexico near the Texas border, was founded in 1907, when James Hobbs and his family settled there and built a dugout house at the corner of present-day First and Texas streets. Within four years, 25 more immigrant families had arrived. The population of the town boomed in 1927 when oil was discovered in the area, and the rapid expansion caused two more villages—New Hobbs and All Hobbs—to be organized. Today Hobbs is a popular retirement center; its recreational and cultural attractions, such as the Lea County Cowboy Hall of Fame, and its facilities for outdoor pursuits, like fishing and golf, blend to make Hobbs and the surrounding area a nice place to visit, but oil still drives the local economy.

Information: **Hobbs Chamber of Commerce** | 400 N. Marland, Hobbs, 88240 | 505/397–3202.

Attractions

Confederate Air Force Museum. This unique museum at Lea County Airport on the western edge of town features several models of aircraft from the World War II era. | U.S. 62/U.S. 180 | 505/392–7918 | Free | By appointment only.

Lea County Cowboy Hall of Fame and Western Heritage Center. This interesting museum on the campus of New Mexico Junior College has displays documenting the area's natural history, Indian life, and early ranching in southeast New Mexico. | Off Hwy. 18 | 505/392–1275 or 505/392–5518 | Free | Weekdays 10–5, Sat. 1–5.

ON THE CALENDAR

FEB.: *Lea County Cowboy Celebration.* This old-fashioned cowboy celebration is held in Lovington, the county seat 21 mi north of Hobbs. Top cowboy singers, storytellers, artists, and plenty of real cowboys abound during this four-day event. | 505/393–6176 (ask for John Harrison).

MAY: *Cinco de Mayo.* Arts and crafts and native food booths in City Park, at Jefferson and Clinton streets, celebrate Mexican independence. | 505/397–3202.

AUG.: *Lea County Fair.* Agricultural and ranching products and a 4-day PRCA rodeo are emphasized at this annual event in Lovington, 20 mi northwest of Hobbs. | 505/396–5344.

Dining

Cattle Baron Steak and Seafood. Steak. A branch of the fine American-style steak-house chain. Salad bar. Kids' menu. | 1930 N. Grimes St. | 505/393–2800 | $8–$25 | AE, D, DC, MC, V.

Rock House Grill and Cantina. Cajun. Cajun food is the highlight in this full-service family friendly bar and restaurant across from the main shopping center. The walls are a busy collage of antique hardware (stoves and frontier tools) as well as old town memorabilia such as the local high school sports jerseys and team photos. Try the crawfish fetuccini, Cajun Alfredo stir-fry, or the Cajun poor boy (a grilled hoagie with fried fish or shrimp and topped with Cajun mayo). | 1801 N. Turner, 88240 | 505/393–4575 | No dinner Sun. | $6–$24 | AE, D, MC, V.

Lodging

Best Inn. One of Hobbs's largest motels, this is popular with leisure and business travelers. Restaurant, bar (with entertainment). In-room data ports, room service, cable TV. Pool. Business services. Some pets allowed. | 501 N. Marland Blvd. | 505/397–3251 or 800/635–6639 | fax 505/393–3065 | 75 rooms | $39–$69 | AE, D, DC, MC, V.

Comfort Inn. The large rooms in this two-story motel have lots of windows and muted wallpaper that create a bright, welcoming feel. Complimentary Continental breakfast. In-room data ports, cable TV. Pool. Hot tub. Gym. | 5020 Lovington Hwy. | 505/392–2161 or 800/228–5150 | www.comfortinn.com | 27 rooms, 12 suites | $53–59, $88 suites | AE, D, DC, MC, V.

Leawood Travelodge. This reasonably priced, one-floor motel is seven mi from the Lea County Airport, offering basic rooms. Restaurant, complimentary breakfast. Cable TV. Pool. Business services. Pets allowed. | 1301 E. Broadway | 505/393–4101 or 888/532–9663 | fax 505/393–4101 | www.travelodge.com | 72 rooms | $40–$54 | AE, D, DC, MC, V.

JEMEZ SPRINGS

MAP 9, D3

(Nearby towns also listed: Bernalillo, Los Alamos)

Only an hour from Albuquerque, the pretty little village of Jemez Springs is a popular year-round getaway destination, with an assortment of B&Bs, hiking, cross-country skiing, and hot springs. The area has what many believe is a spiritual quality, with many Catholic and Buddhist retreat centers and the nearby Jemez Pueblo.

Information: Sandoval County Visitor Center | 243 Camino del Pueblo, Bernalillo, 87004 | 505/867–8687 or 800/252–0191 | www.sctourism.com.

JEMEZ SPRINGS

INTRO
ATTRACTIONS
DINING
LODGING

Attractions

Jemez Pueblo. The state's only Towa-speaking pueblo (as opposed to Tiwa- and Tewa-speaking), Jemez is set along the Jemez River, bordered on one side by the Jemez Mountains and the other by soaring cliffs of red rock. The pueblo itself is closed to the public except during certain feast days, but much can be learned from a visit to the Walatowa Visitors Center. The polychrome pottery made here is well known. Photography, sketching, and videography are prohibited. | Trading Post Rd. off Hwy. 4 | 505/834–7235 | www.jemezpueblo.org | Free | Visitor center daily 10–4.

Jemez Springs Bath House. Restored Victorian bathhouse with mineral soaks in the geothermal waters, massage, and herbal treatments. | Hwy. 4 | 505/829–3303 | www.jemez.com/baths | $9–$60 | Memorial Day–Labor Day, daily 9–9; Labor Day–Memorial Day, daily 10–7:30.

Jemez State Monument. The site of a 600-year-old pueblo, Guisewa, "place of the boiling waters," where the Spanish then built a mission church, San Jose de los Jemez. The monument includes the ruins of both. | Hwy. 4 | 505/829–3530 | Apr.–Oct. $3, Nov.–Mar. $2 | Tues.–Sun. 8:30–5.

ON THE CALENDAR

JUNE: *Red Rocks Arts & Crafts Show.* An opportunity to purchase fine polychrome pottery and artwork from the potters of Jemez Pueblo, taste bread baked in *hornos* (beehive ovens), fresh hot fry bread, and fantastic red chile. | 505/834–7235.

Dining

Deb's Deli Delights. American/Casual. Espresso, ice cream, and hearty breakfasts of blueberry pancakes and huevos rancheros are the thing here. | 17607 Hwy. 4 | 505/829–3829 | Breakfast also available. No dinner | $2–$8 | MC, V.

Los Ojos. American. Century-old must-see bar with huge stone fireplace, elk racks, and billiards tables. This rustic, local hangout is known for "famous Jemez" green chile cheeseburgers and weekend prime-rib specials. | 17596 Hwy. 4 | 505/829–3547 | $5–$12 | MC, V.

San Diego Canyon Bakery. American/Casual. Delicious fresh-baked pastries and huge omelets make this a wait on Sunday mornings. Known for wholesome, fresh breakfasts and lunches. | 17502 Hwy 4 | 505/829–3956 | Breakfast also available. No dinner | $4–$8 | MC, V.

Lodging

Dancing Bear. A glass-fronted great room faces the Jemez River and the mesa. Handmade pottery and original art decorate this comfortable modern inn. Complimentary breakfast. Cable TV, in-room VCRs. Laundry facilities. | 314 San Diego Dr. | 505/829–3336 or 800/422–3271 | www.dancingbearbandb.com | 4 rooms | $80–$125 | AE, D, MC, V.

Jemez Mountain Inn. A remodeled rock and mud adobe that is one of the oldest buildings in the village, this inn boasts a brook running through the property, a large deck area and patio, and is only a block from the Jemez Bath House. Cable TV, in-room VCRs. | Hwy. 4 | 505/829–3926 or 888/819–1075 | fax 505/829–9170 | www.jemezmtninn.com | 10 rooms | $85 | MC, V.

River Dancer B&B and Retreat Center. This adobe casita built in 1902 is right on the banks of the Jemez River. Rooms open onto a courtyard with a fountain, fruit trees, and seasonal flowers and are simply and comfortably decorated. A full range of spa treatments, hiking, and quiet relaxation are available. The breakfast is mostly vegetarian. Picnic area, complimentary breakfast. Some microwaves, some refrigerators, some in-room hot tubs, cable TV, some in-room VCRs (and movies). Massage, sauna. No smoking. | 16445 Hwy. 4 | 505/829–3262 or 800/809–3262 | fax 505/829–3262 | www.riverdancer.com | 7 rooms, 1 suite | $109–$124, $160 suite | D, MC, V.

LAGUNA PUEBLO

(Nearby towns also listed: Acoma Pueblo, Albuquerque, Grants)

Laguna Pueblo, 33 mi east of Grants, actually consists of six separate villages: Encinal, Laguna, Mesita, Paguate, Paraje, and Seama. People have lived in this area for 5,000 years, and the pueblo itself was first occupied around AD 1400. St. Joseph of the Lake Mission Church at Laguna, built in 1699, is a widely recognized landmark, visible from Interstate 40. The pueblo's pottery is highly prized and can be purchased in many shops in Laguna. There are no accommodations in Laguna Pueblo, though there is one isolated bed-and-breakfast a few miles away; the other closest accommodations are in Grants or Albuquerque.

Information: **Laguna Pueblo** | Box 194, Laguna, 87026 | 505/552–6654.

Attractions

Dancing Eagle Casino. This casino offers over 300 slot and video-poker machines, as well as craps, blackjack, and roulette tables, plus a gift shop and restaurant. | Casa Blanca (I–40, exit 108) | 505/552–9042 or 877/440–9969 | fax 505/552–0944 | www.dancingeagle-casino.com | $4–$13 | AE, D, DC, MC, V.

Saint Joseph's of the Lake Mission Church. This church was built in 1699 by the resident Native Americans at the request of the early Catholic missionaries. The architecture and interior

LOS HERMANOS PENITENTES

As you drive the back roads of northern New Mexico, you can't help noticing from time to time wooden crosses that have been erected on the side of the road, or more likely, atop a nearby hillside that overlooks the highway. These crosses were erected by members of Los Hermanos Penitentes (the Pentinent Brothers); they honor an ancient tradition among New Mexico's Hispanic peoples, whose roots go back to the earliest days of history.

In earlier times, neighbors gathered in a local church at Eastertime and recreated the events that surrounded Christ's crucifixion. After the ceremonies, the crowd gathered outside the church, where one of the brotherhood picked up a heavy cross and dragged it behind him, much as tradition says Christ did on his way to Calvary. While the man labored with the cross, his brethren walked beside him, flogging both him and themselves with whips. Sometimes the cross bearer died from his injuries and was buried on the spot. The cross was erected over the grave. The ancient Easter celebrations of the Penitent Brothers don't result in death anymore. But you can bet that in the remote recesses of New Mexico's Sangre de Cristo Mountains the ceremonies, albeit in milder form, are still being observed today.

© Artville

incorporate designs of both Spanish and Native American cultures. The floors are packed dirt, and the walls are still repaired using a traditional adobe plaster. You'll be able to see the church from Interstate 40. | Laguna Pueblo | 505/552–9330 | Free | Weekdays 9–3.

ON THE CALENDAR

SEPT. *Saint Joseph's Feast Day.* The Navajos sell traditional Native American foods such as mutton stew, roasted corn, and fried bread, and perform traditional dances. | 505/552–6654.

Dining

The Restaurant at Dancing Eagle Casino. Southwestern. This pueblo-style restaurant in the Dancing Eagle Casino offers a creative menu with an emphasis on southwestern flavors. Try the *pollo relleno* (a stuffed green chile stuffed in a chicken breast) or *shrimp capelin* (artichoke hearts with wild Portobello and shiitake mushrooms in a vegetable cream sauce). Gourmet pizzas come in a rainbow of toppings from Jamaican shrimp to Thai chicken. | Cara Blanca (I–40, exit 108) | 505/552–9042 or 877/440–9969 | fax 505/552–0944 | www.dancingeaglecasino.com | Breakfast also available. | $4–$13 | AE, D, DC, MC, V.

Lodging

Apache Canyon Ranch. Some rooms have a fireplace in this isolated, pueblo-style B&B near Laguna Pueblo, 26 mi west of Albuquerque. Large and sunny rooms have tile floors and whitewashed walls. There are spectacular views of the mountains and a telescope to observe the stars. Picnic area, complimentary breakfast. Some kitchenettes, some microwaves, some refrigerators, some in-room hot tubs, some in-room VCRs (and movies). Massage. Putting green. Hiking, horseback riding. Business services. No kids under 12. No smoking. | 4 Canyon Dr., To'hajiilee | 505/836–7220 or 800/808–8310 | fax 505/836–2922 | www.apachecanyon.com | 4 rooms, 5 suites in 2 buildings | $90–$126, $180–$265 suites | AE, MC, V.

LAS CRUCES

MAP 9, D9

(Nearby towns also listed: Alamogordo, Deming, Mesilla)

Las Cruces celebrated its 150th anniversary in 1999, dating its beginnings to an early U.S. Army survey that created the new town when nearby Dona Ana became overcrowded with Mexican settlers and American soldiers. With a variety of state parks, horse racing, and myriad outdoor attractions nearby, Las Cruces, New Mexico's second-largest city (with approximately 78,000 people), is a popular visitor destination. Las Cruces' cultural offerings have kept pace with its growth, and the town is known for its lyric opera, symphony, ballet, and community chorus. It's within an hour's drive of White Sands National Monument (*see* Alamogordo).

Las Cruces itself is one of the fastest-growing metropolitan areas in the United States, with an economy closely linked to the border factories of El Paso, Texas, and Ciudad Juárez, Mexico, to the southeast.

Information: **Las Cruces Chamber of Commerce** | Drawer 519, Las Cruces, 88004 | 505/524–1968 | www.lascruces.org.

Attractions

Aguirre Spring Recreation Site. Hiking, picnicking, and camping, about 20 mi southeast of Las Cruces beneath the towering spires of the Organ Mountains. From Las Cruces, take U.S. 70 12 mi northeast, then head south at the road marked "Aguirre Springs" for an additional 5 mi. | Off U.S. 70 | 505/525–4300 | $3 per vehicle | Daily.

Fort Selden State Monument. Some 16 mi north of Las Cruces, Fort Selden was built after the Civil War to protect settlers in the Mesilla Valley. As a boy, General Douglas MacArthur learned to ride and shoot here when his father was the post commander. The connection of the Santa Fe Railroad with the Southern Pacific made the fort obsolete, and it was abandoned in 1890. | I–25 (exit 19), Radium Springs | 505/526–8911 | $2 | Daily 8:30–5.

Historical Museum of Lawmen. This small museum is housed in the front lobby of the Sheriff's Office and displays interesting police memorabilia like weapons used by law-enforcement officers and criminals alike. Out front are nifty buggies like an 1865 horse buggy and an 1880s hay wagon, as well as a 1949 classic Ford police car in mint condition. Billy the Kid was found guilty here in 1881 and detained in this town's jail before his transfer to Lincoln County for execution, where he later escaped. | 1725 Marquess St. | 505/525–1911 | Free | Mon–Fri. 8–5.

Las Cruces Museum of Natural History. Hands-on nature exhibits and flora and fauna from the Chihuahuan desert highlight this museum in the Mesilla Valley Mall. | 700 S. Telshor | 505/522–3120 | Free | Mon.–Thurs. 10–5, Fri. 10–8, Sat. 10–5, Sun. noon–5.

New Mexico Farm and Ranch Museum. Agricultural and ranching exhibits cover the history, heritage, and science of farming and ranching in New Mexico in this museum that opened in 1998, 1½ mi east of Las Cruces. The goal of the gallery and farm exhibits is to document 3,000 years of agricultural history in New Mexico and the Southwest. | 4100 Dripping Springs Rd. | 505/522–4100 | $4 | Tues.–Sat. 9–5, Sun. noon–5.

New Mexico State University. This university began in 1888 as an agricultural college. It is now a major educational institution with an enrollment of over 15,000 at the main campus in Las Cruces and over 8,000 at branch campuses. NMSU is best known for its engineering and agricultural programs. The southwestern-style buildings are oriented around a horseshoe drive, though the university president's home, Nason House on University Drive, is in the Prairie style of Frank Lloyd Wright. | University Ave. and Locust St. | 505/646–3739 | www.nmsu.edu | Free | Daily.

New Mexico State University Museum. The museum's collections in Kent Hall focus on the multicultural heritage of the Southwest, particular Native American artifacts and a regional history collection. | Kent Hall, University Ave. at Solano | 505/646–3739 | www.nmsu.edu/~museum | Free | Tues.–Sat. noon–4.

University Art Gallery. This gallery on the first floor of Williams Hall is the largest gallery of contemporary art in south-central New Mexico and houses the largest public collection of 19th-century Mexican *retablos* (religious paintings on tin) in the U.S. It also exhibits prints and historic and contemporary photographs. | Williams Hall, University Ave. at Solano | 505/646–2545 | www.nmsu.edu/Campus_Life/artgal.html | Free | Jun.–Aug., Wed.–Sat., 10–5; Sept.–May, Tues., Wed., Fri., Sat., 10–5, Thurs. 10–7, Sun. 1–5. Closed Mon.

Corbett Center Art Gallery. This gallery on the second floor of the the Corbett Center Student Union hosts rotating exhibits by students and local artists. | International Mall, on Breland Dr. | 505/646–3235 | www.nmsu.edu/campus_life/upc_art.html | Free | Daily 8 AM–10 PM.

White Sands Missile Range. Some 25 mi east of Las Cruces is the southern entrance to the missile complex where you will find the Trinity Site, the place where the world's first atomic bomb was detonated in 1945, though that is on the far northern edge of the missile range (enter through the Stallion Range Center, 12 mi east of San Antonio, New Mexico, on Trinity Site visitation days, only twice a year). You can always visit the Range Museum, much closer to Las Cruces, which features historical exhibits and missiles and rockets outside; enter the Las Cruces Gate and tell the guard where you are going. | U.S. 70, 25 mi east of Las Cruces | 505/678–1134 | Free | www.wsmr.army.mil | Museum: weekdays 8–4:30, Sat. 10–3. Trinity site: 1st Sat. in Apr. and 1st Sat. in Oct., 8–2.

ON THE CALENDAR

MAY: *New Mexico Wine and Chile War Festival*. Eat great chile and drink New Mexico wine at this annual festival each Memorial Day weekend in the Southern New Mexico State Fairgrounds, 11 mi west of Las Cruces. | 505/646–4543.

SEPT.–OCT.: *Southern New Mexico State Fair and Rodeo.* Livestock, rides, food, and entertainment are features of this annual fair at the Dona Ana County Fairgrounds. | 505/524–8612.

OCT.: *Whole Enchilada Fiesta.* The world's largest enchilada is featured at this event at the Downtown Mall, accompanied by street dancing, games, and rides. | 505/524–6832.

NOV.: *Renaissance Craftfaire.* This unique fair in Young Park re-creates life during Renaissance times. | 505/523–6403.

Dining

Cattle Baron Steak and Seafood. Steak. This outlet of the reasonably priced regional chain serves the same good prime rib and steaks you have come to expect, along with seafood and pasta. The outdoor patio has city views. Kids' menu. Salad bar. | 790 S. Telshor Blvd. | 505/522–7533 | $8–$25 | AE, D, DC, MC, V.

The Durango Bagel. Café. All are welcome at this gourmet coffee and bagel shop, which caters to the college crowd from nearby New Mexico State University. In addition to apple-walnut and cranberry-orange bagels, muffins, cookies and sandwiches are also served. | 2460 S. Locust St. | 505/522–3397 | No dinner | $4–$6 | No credit cards.

Lorenzo's. Italian. A block from the New Mexico State University campus, this is the larger of the three Lorenzo's in the area. Grilled fish and chicken are served here, along with Sicilian sandwiches, pizza, pasta, and salads. | University Plaza, 1753 E. University Ave. | 505/521–3505 | fax 505/521–3753 | $7–$14 | AE, D, DC, MC, V.

Mesilla Valley Kitchen. Delicatessens. This casual deli is in the Arroyo Plaza on the east side, in the newer part of town. Try a gourmet sandwich like the "wrecker-decker" (fresh smoked turkey, ham, bacon, lettuce, tomato on grilled whole wheat), lunch quesadilla (turkey, cheese, sliced mushrooms, diced bacon, and green chile between two flour tortillas), or a beefburger accompanied by spud chips. Homemade specialties in this southwestern eatery include cinnamon rolls, cookies, and muffins. | 2001 E. Lohman Ave. | 505/523–9311 | No dinner | $4–$7 | AE, D, DC, MC, V.

My Brother's Place. Mexican. This exceptionally good restaurant serves *tostadas compuestos* (a concoction of red or green chile, meat, pinto beans, and cheese in a crispy tortilla cup) and pitchers of wine or several varieties of Mexican beer to wash down the fire. For dessert, try an *empanada* (Mexican pastry) or a crème caramel flan. The upstairs lounge is a pleasant watering hole. | 334 S. Main St. | 505/523–7681 | Closed Sun. | $6–$12 | AE, D, DC, MC, V.

Nellie's. Mexican. Its tough to find seating in this tiny, diner-style restaurant, but that's because the food is incredible. You wouldn't give this place a second look if you judged it only by its plain appearance, but the locals eat here in droves. The restaurant has gained national recognition for its mouthwatering dishes, such as chiles rellenos and a combination of enchiladas and tacos. | 1226 Hadley Ave. | 505/524–9982 | No dinner | $4–$8 | No credit cards.

Scoopy's. American/Casual. On the premise of an abandoned hamburger stand, this old-fashioned joint offers all manner of delectable sundaes and sodas using homemade custard-style ice cream. The low-fat treats can be supplemented with specialty hot dogs, mesquite-smoked turkey sandwiches, or prime rib on a sourdough bun. | 590 S. Valley Dr. | 505/647–5066 | $2–$6 | No credit cards.

Si Señor. Mexican. A popular business lunch and dinner spot, this immaculate restaurant has pleasant and spacious southwestern-style rooms. Entrées emphasize three distinct chile sauces—Las Cruces green (mild and flavorful), Deming red, and a variety described as "smoke," also known as Hatch green. | 1551 E. Amador Ave. | 505/527–0817 | Reservations not accepted | $6–$13 | AE, D, MC, V.

Lodging

Baymont Inn and Suites. This hotel is at exit 140 off Interstate 10 on the west side of Las Cruces. The overstuffed chairs and iron-framed love seats in the lobby surround a decorative fireplace. The spacious, southwestern-style rooms feel like home, some with a recliner chair or an extra-large work desk. Complimentary Continental breakfast. Cable TV. Pool. | 1500 Hickory Dr., 88005 | 505/523–0100 or 800/301–0200 | fax 505/523–0707 | www.baymontinns.com | 74 rooms, 13 suites | $44–$59, $59–$89 suites | AE, MC, D, DC, V.

Day's End Lodge. Well priced and conveniently located, this local 2-story motel with southwestern-style rooms is less than 1 mi from both I–10 and the downtown area, and it's good for an overnight stop. Complimentary Continental breakfast. Cable TV. Pool. Business services. | 755 N. Valley Dr. | 505/524–7753 | fax 505/523–2127 | 32 rooms | $31–$50 | AE, D, MC, V.

Days Inn. This economical chain motel tends to attract groups—it offers meeting rooms for 150—but it also offers simple, clean rooms at good prices. Restaurant, bar, room service. Some in-room data ports, some refrigerators, cable TV. Pool. Sauna. Laundry facilities. Business services. Some pets allowed (fee). | 2600 S. Valley Dr. | 505/526–4441 | fax 505/526–1980 | www.daysinn.com | 130 rooms | $45–$65 | AE, D, DC, MC, V.

Economy Inn. This basic, budget-minded motel is on the highway to Deming. Picnic area. Some kitchenettes, cable TV. Pool. Laundry facilities. Business services. | 2160 W. Picacho St. | 505/524–8627 | fax 505/523–2606 | www.innsofamerica.com | 96 rooms | $25–$50 | AE, D, DC, MC, V.

Fairfield Inn by Marriott. This three-floor motor hotel offers relatively inexpensive rooms with amenities, such as phones with data ports and free newspapers, that appeal to budget-minded business travelers. Complimentary Continental breakfast. In-room data ports, some microwaves, refrigerators, cable TV, some in-room VCRs. Gym. Pool. Laundry facilities, laundry service. Business services. | 2101 Summit Court | 505/522–6840 | fax 505/522–9784 | www.fairfieldinn.com | 78 rooms | $55–$65 | AE, D, DC, MC, V.

Hilltop Hacienda B&B. This inn with mountain views and lovely gardens sits on 20 acres, just minutes from downtown Las Cruces. Rooms are furnished with family heirlooms, and an extra private kitchen is available for guests. Complimentary breakfast. No TV in rooms, TV and VCR in common area. Library. No children under 12. No smoking. | 2600 Westmoreland | 505/382–3556 | fax 505/382–3556 | www.zianet.com/hilltop | 3 rooms | $75–$85 | AE, D, MC, V.

Holiday Inn de las Cruces. The lushly planted, Spanish-style courtyard at this hotel is as open as a plaza in some Mexican towns; common areas are decorated with antiques. It's definitely not your typical Holiday Inn. Restaurant, bar, room service. Cable TV. Pool, wading pool. Video games. Laundry facilities. Business services, airport shuttle. Some pets allowed. | 201 E. University Ave. | 505/526–4411 | fax 505/524–0530 | www.holidayinnlc.com | 114 rooms | $59–$150 | AE, D, DC, MC, V.

★ **Inn of the Arts.** Built in 1890, this adobe hotel is furnished with antiques, and there's an art gallery on the property; each room is named for an artist. There are fireplaces in the suites. Picnic area, complimentary breakfast. Some kitchenettes, some microwaves, some refrigerators, cable TV, some in-room VCRs. TV in common area. Gym. Library. Business services. Pets allowed. | 618 S. Alameda | 505/526–3326 | fax 505/647–1334 | www.innofthearts.com | 21 rooms, 7 suites | $77–$125, $125–$175 suites | AE, D, DC, MC, V.

Las Cruces Hilton. This upscale, modern, seven-story hotel has a view of the city and the Organ Mountains, not to mention large rooms and a great deal of southwestern charm and elegance, with a fountain in the lobby and lots of Mexican tilework. Restaurant, bar (with entertainment), room service. In-room data ports, some refrigerators, cable TV, some in-room VCRs (and movies). Pool. Hot tub. Gym. Business services, airport shuttle. Pets allowed. | 705 S. Telshor Blvd. | 505/522–4300 | fax 505/522–7657 | lchilton@zianet.com | www.weblife-pro.com/lchilton | 195 rooms, 7 suites | $77–$90, $120–$300 suites | AE, D, DC, MC, V.

LAS CRUCES

INTRO
ATTRACTIONS
DINING
LODGING

Mesón de Mesilla B&B. Most rooms in this boutique hotel are decorated with antiques. The location is well situated if you wish to soak in some of the charm in Mesilla; it's the closest lodging to the Mesilla Plaza. Some rooms have fireplaces, most have ceiling fans, but they range greatly in size and price (the least-expensive rooms are singles with twin beds). Restaurant (see Mesón de Mesilla), bar, picnic area, complimentary breakfast. Cable TV. Pool. | 1803 Avenida de Mesilla | 505/525–9212 or 800/732–6025 | fax 505/527–4196 | 15 rooms | $45–$145 | AE, D, DC, MC, V.

Springhill Suites by Marriot. These modern and comfortable suites are ideal for families on the road looking for a touch of home. Each is equipped with a kitchenette for some home cooking, as well as either a king or two double beds and a sofa bed. The Old Mesilla Historic District is about a mile away, New Mexico State University is about 2 mi away. Complimentary Continental breakfast. In-room data ports, kitchenettes, refrigerators, minibars, microwaves, cable TV. Pool. Hot tub. Gym. Laundry facilities, laundry service. | 1611 Hickory Loop, 88005 | 505/541–8887 or 888/772–8887 | fax 505/541–8837 | www.springhillsuites.com/lruss | 101 suites | $69–$129 | AE, D, DC, MC, V.

T.R.H. Smith Mansion Bed and Breakfast. This historic B&B is located in the center of Las Cruces, yet offers a quiet retreat within its spacious and elegant domain. Each room has a regional theme to represent different parts of the world visited by the owner. Relax in the glass porch or enjoy a game of billiards. Complimentary Continental breakfast. In-room data ports. No TV, TV in common area. Some pets allowed. No smoking. | 909 N. Alameda Blvd., 88005 | 505/525–2525 or 800/526–1914 | fax 505/524–8227 | www.smithmansion.com | 4 rooms | $70–$90 | AE, D, MC, V.

Western Inn. This inexpensive, family-run single-floor motel has big, sunny rooms and is about 4 mi from Main Street on the west side of Las Cruces. Restaurant. Kitchenettes, cable TV. | 2155 W. Picacho Ave. | 505/523–5399 | fax 505/523–5399 | 46 rooms, 2 suites | $22–$50 | AE, D, DC, MC, V.

LAS VEGAS

MAP 9, F4

(Nearby town also listed: Santa Fe)

In August 1846, before several hundred Mexican residents, General Stephen Watts Kearny stood on a rooftop in the small village of Las Vegas and declared that from that time forward all of New Mexico belonged to the United States. The town had its beginnings as a settlement along the Santa Fe Trail, but by the 1880s, when most of the commerce along the trail had shifted to the railroad, it blossomed into a sizable community. With an improvement in the economy came an increase in lawlessness, and during the latter part of the 19th century, Las Vegas was known as a wild and woolly town. Several movies have been filmed in the Las Vegas area, including *Easy Rider* and *Red Dawn*.

Today, this town of 15,000 is the antithesis of its namesake in Nevada. It's a quiet, historic place. The town plaza provides a place to spend several hours shopping, while history buffs will enjoy nearby Fort Union, the Rough Riders Museum, and the architectural beauty of the Plaza Hotel. Las Vegas lists more than 900 buildings in the National Register of Historic Places. You can pick up walking tour maps at the chamber of commerce office.

Information: **Las Vegas/San Miguel County Chamber of Commerce** | Box 128, 727 Grand Ave., Las Vegas, 87701 | 800/832–5947 or 505/425–8631 | www.lasvegasnewmexico.com.

Attractions

Armand Hammer United World College of the American West. Students from around the world study at this high-school created by industrialist Armand Hammer to promote international understanding. One of the main campus buildings is Montezuma Castle, a former resort hotel developed by the Santa Fe Railroad in the 19th century. The grounds, 5 mi north of Las Vegas, are open to the public (guests must register at the administration building before viewing the school), and cultural events are often held on the campus. | Hwy. 65, Montezuma | 505/454–4200 | fax 505/454–4274 | www.uwc-usa.org | Free | Weekdays 8–5.

Fort Union National Monument. During its heyday, Fort Union—located at a critical point along the Santa Fe Trail about 30 mi north of Las Vegas—was the largest U.S. military establishment in the entire Southwest. Completed in 1869, it served as a supply center for smaller installations across the region. The arrival of the Santa Fe Railroad in the 1880s put the fort out of business, as trains began to bypass the fort and speed much-needed army equipment directly to its destinations. Today the remains of the third and last army post built at the site are there for visitors to explore. | Hwy. 161 | 505/425–8025 | $4 per vehicle | Memorial Day–Labor Day, daily 8–6; Labor Day–Memorial Day, daily 8–5.

Las Vegas National Wildlife Refuge. Observe American eagles, waterfowl, and a large variety of other wildlife species from your vantage point in this refuge 6½ mi southeast of Las Vegas. It's one of the premier birding sites in the Southwest. | Hwy. 281 | 505/425–3581 | Free | Daily.

Morphy Lake State Park. Primitive camping, fishing, and picnicking are the primary pastimes pursued at Morphy Lake, which is about 27 mi north of Las Vegas. | Hwy. 94 | 505/387–2328 | $4 per vehicle for day use; $8 camping fee | Daily.

New Mexico Highlands University. This liberal arts college has about 3,000 students and is a community resource for concerts, theater productions, sporting events, and lectures. | 901 University Ave. | 505/425–7511 | www.nmhu.edu | Free | Daily.

Storrie Lake State Park. The lake 6 mi north of Las Vegas has a visitor center and offers windsurfing, fishing, boating, waterskiing, camping, and picnicking facilities. It's a favorite place to catch rainbow and German brown trout. | Hwy. 518 | 505/425–7278 | $4 per vehicle | Daily.

Theodore Roosevelt Rough Riders' Memorial and City Museum. Teddy Roosevelt recruited many members of his Rough Rider regiment from New Mexico and the surrounding territory. After the Spanish-American War, Roosevelt's veterans chose Las Vegas as their reunion site, and over the years the town became the depository for many Rough Rider artifacts, most of them collected in the Municipal Building. | 727 Grand Ave. | 505/454–1401 | Free | Weekdays 9–12 and 1–4, Sat. 10–3.

ON THE CALENDAR
JUNE: *Santa Fe Trail Heritage Days.* This yearly celebration in Plaza Park of life on the Santa Fe trail offers demonstrations and reenactments in costume of cooking, weaving, soap making, and sheep shearing, along with other entertainment and a crafts fair. | 505/425–8631 or 800/832–5947.

Dining

Blackjack's Grill. Italian. This award-winning menu will delight all the senses. The steaks are the best in town, or try the Old Mexico pork tenderloins or seafood enchiladas. Homemade flan and New York cheesecake are favorite desserts. Take a table outside on the patio by the garden or inside the romantic dining room full of old-world charm to enjoy the outstanding food. | 1133 Grand Ave. | 505/425–6791 or 888/448–8438 | fax 505/425–0417 | Closed Mon. | $10–$20 | AE, D, MC, V.

El Rialto Restaurant & Lounge. Mexican. In an historic 1890s building furnished with antiques, this popular restaurant offers perfectly blended margaritas to set the mood for fajitas, enchiladas, and chiles rellenos. The menu also offers American dishes and seafood. Salad bar. Kids' menu. | 141 Bridge St. | 505/454–0037 | Closed Sun. | $4–$20 | AE, D, MC, V.

Estella's Restaurant. Mexican. This is one of the best places to eat in the Las Vegas area, and has been smothering burritos in green chile since 1950. Don't be put off by the modest appearance of this legendary stop. | 148 Bridge St. | 505/454–0048 | Closed Sun. No dinner Mon.–Wed. | $5–$15 | AE, D, MC, V.

Landmark Grill at the Plaza Hotel. American. This Victorian dining room is off the lobby of the landmark Plaza Hotel, serving New Mexican cuisine with Mexican influences. It has a large wine selection. Try the quail, green chile posole, and *arroz con pollo.* | 230 Old Town Plaza | 505/425–3591 | $8–$20 | AE, D, DC, MC, V.

Pino's. American/Casual. This casual diner has an eclectic Mexican and American menu. Try the enchilada plate or the super burger. Salad bar. Kids' menu. Beer and wine only. | 1901 N. Grand Ave. | 505/454–1944 | $7–$24 | MC, V.

Lodging

Carriage House Bed and Breakfast. This simple but elegant three-story Queen Ann Victorian was built in 1893 in the residential Carnegie Library Historic District. Comfortably appointed country Victorian rooms are named after famous past owners. There is a second-floor side porch and a full front porch with plenty of comfortable chairs. Complimentary Continental breakfast. No smoking. | 925 6th St. | 505/454–1784 or 888/221–9689 | www.newmexicocarriagehouse.com | 5 rooms | $55–$75 | AE, D, DC, MC, V.

Comfort Inn. From the patio of this comfortable budget motel, you'll get great views of the distant mountains. Rooms offer basic amenities. Restaurant, complimentary Continental breakfast. Cable TV. Pool. Hot tub. Gym. Business services. | 2500 N. Grand Ave. | 505/425–1100 | fax 505/454–8404 | www.comfortinn.com | 101 rooms | $54–$70 | AE, D, DC, MC, V.

Hartley Guest Ranch. This is a working cattle ranch owned and operated by the Hartley family, 25 mi southwest of Roy, which is some 80 mi northeast of Las Vegas. Accommodations are in a comfortable but rustic guest house. It's surrounded by 2,500 acres of canyon and forest and 200 mi of trails that contain ancient Native American sites, dinosaur bones, and interesting geological formations. The ranch picks you up from the Albuquerque airport if you are flying in; river-rafting trips are available for an additional charge. Hiking, horseback riding, fishing. Airport shuttle. | HCR 73, Roy | 505/673–2245 or 800/687–3833 | fax 505/673–2216 | hartly@plateau.tel.net | www.guestranches.com/hartley | 6 rooms | $650 (3–day minimum stay) | Closed Oct.–Mar. | AP | No credit cards.

Inn of Santa Fe Trail. All rooms face the courtyard of this lovely hacienda-style motel. The grounds are well manicured, the rooms simple and unfussy but clean and comfortable. Picnic area, complimentary Continental breakfast. In-room data ports, some microwaves, some refrigerators, cable TV, some in-room VCRs. Pool. Hot tub. Business services. Pets allowed. | 1133 Grand Ave. | 505/425–6791 or 888/448–8438 | fax 505/425–0417 | www.innon-thesantafetrail.com | 33 rooms, 2 suites, 2 casitas | $64–$79 rooms, $105 suites, $140 casitas | AE, D, MC, V.

Pendaries Village Lodge. In the tiny mountain hamlet of Rocaida, 20 mi northwest of Las Vegas, this is an exquisite place to relax. While the mood here is Holiday Inn meets Kit Carson, the standard motel room decor in no way detracts from the thrill of high-altitude golfing. The course begins at 7,500 ft with a par 72. The rustic lodge has a well-esteemed restaurant and a lounge usually crowded with locals. Restaurant, bar. Cable TV. 18-hole golf course. | 1 Lodge Rd., Rocaida | 505/425–3561 or 800/733–5267 | fax 505/425–3562 | www.pendaries.net | 18 rooms | $69–$79 | Closed Oct. 16–Apr. 14 | AE, D, MC, V.

Plaza Hotel. This fully restored 1880 western Italianate hotel overlooks the downtown Las Vegas Plaza Park. Rooms continue the Victorian theme and are furnished with antiques and modern amenities. Interior rooms are quieter but have no views. Restaurant (*see* Landmark Grill at the Plaza Hotel), bar. Cable TV. Business services, airport shuttle. Pets allowed (fee). | 230 Plaza | 505/425–3591 or 800/328–1882 | fax 505/425–9659 | www.lasvegas-newmexico.com/plaza | 36 rooms | $79–$129 | AE, D, DC, MC, V.

Regal Motel. This very basic budget motel offers clean, comfortable rooms on U.S. 85, Las Vegas's main north–south thoroughfare. Some pets allowed (fee). | 1809 N. Grand | 505/454–1456 | fax 505/454–1456 | 50 rooms | $30–$49 | AE, D, DC, MC, V.

Scottish Inn. This inexpensive budget motel is known for its clean, simple rooms. Cable TV. Some pets allowed. | 1216 N. Grand Ave. | 505/425–9357 | fax 505/425–9357 | 45 rooms | $28–$60 | AE, D, DC, MC, V.

Town House. This inexpensive, locally owned motel is well located in the center of Las Vegas, easily accessible to everything. Picnic area. Cable TV. Some pets allowed (fee). | 1215 N. Grand Ave. | 505/425–6717 or 800/679–6717 | fax 505–425–9005 | 42 rooms | $27–$44 | AE, D, DC, MC, V.

LINCOLN

MAP 9, F7

(Nearby towns also listed: Carrizozo, Roswell, Ruidoso)

LINCOLN

INTRO
ATTRACTIONS
DINING
LODGING

This entire one-street town is a living history museum; in fact, the whole town is a designated National Historic Landmark, best known for its notorious resident, Henry McCarty, aka William Bonney, or more popularly Billy the Kid, who met his end at the hand of Sheriff Pat Garrett near here in the town of Fort Sumner. This quiet, gracious, well-preserved village was the site of the bloody Lincoln County War and is now the home of several museums commemorating that infamous era.

Information: Ruidoso Valley Chamber of Commerce | Box 698, Ruidoso, 88355 | 505/257–7395;800/253–2255 | www.ruidoso.net.

Attractions

Lincoln State Monument. The town of Lincoln is the location of many original sites of the Lincoln County War, including the Lincoln County Courthouse Museum, from which Billy the Kid made his legendary escape; Tunstall Mercantile Store Museum; Montano Store; as well as the San Juan Mission. Eleven individual sites around town make up the monument; one admission gets you into all of them. | Lincoln | 505/653–4372 | www.museumofnewmexico.org | $6 for all sites in Lincoln State Monument | Daily 8:30–5.

Historic Lincoln Visitors Center. The center houses exhibits on Native Americans, buffalo soldiers, and the history of the "Five Day Battle," as the Lincoln County War is known locally. | 505/653–4025 | fax 505/653–4627 | www.museumofnewmexico.org | $6 for all sites in Lincoln State Monument | Daily 8:30–5.

Lincoln County Courthouse Museum. This is the building from which Billy the Kid escaped as he was awaiting his execution. Exhibits contain historical documents, including a letter from Billy to Governor Lew Wallace. | Main St. | 505/653–4372 | www.museumofnewmexico.org | $6 for all sites in Lincoln State Monument | Daily 8:30–5.

Tunstall Store Museum. When the state of New Mexico purchased this store in the 1950s, boxes of old inventory—some dating back to the 19th century—were discovered and are now on display. John Chisum and Alexander McSween had their law offices here as well. | Main St. | 505/653–4049 | www.museumofnewmexico.org | $6 for all sites in Lincoln State Monument | Daily 8:30–5.

ON THE CALENDAR

AUG.: *Old Lincoln Days.* Historic reenactments, arts and crafts, with the Billy the Kid Pageant, a dramatization of the original shoot-out, highlighting the weekend. | 505/653–4025.

Dining

Ellis Store Country Inn. Contemporary. Wild game is the specialty here, but a choice of 10 entrées and several delicious desserts are available nightly to be enjoyed on fine china and crystal in an intimate setting in the oldest house in Lincoln County. Dinner is six courses, prix fixe in this award-winning B&B's dining room. | U.S. 380, Mile Marker 98 | 505/653–6460 | fax 505/653–4610 | Reservations essential | $50 prix fixe | AE, D, DC, MC, V.

Wortley Pat Garrett Hotel. American. Pot roast and real mashed potatoes that the original chef, Sam Wortley, would have loved, also meat loaf, quiche, green-chile stew, chicken salad, cobblers, and pineapple upside-down cake, served in the historic dining room of this hotel, which reopened in 1999. | U.S. 380, 88338 | 505/653–4300 | Closed Nov. 1–Apr. 27. No dinner | $5–$7 | No credit cards.

Lodging

Casa de Patrón B&B Inn. Legend has it that many a notorious character, including Billy the Kid, spent the night in this mid-19th-century adobe home. Today, travelers appreciate the whitewashed rooms, simply furnished with antiques, including a large washboard collection; rooms in the main house have viga ceilings, while casitas have full kitchens. Picnic area, complimentary breakfast. No air-conditioning, some kitchenettes, some refrigerators, no room phones. Business services. | U.S. 380 E, Lincoln | 505/653–4676 or 800/524–5202 | fax 505/653–4671 | www.casapatron.com | 5 rooms (3 with shower only) in 2 buildings, 2 casitas | $87–$117 | MC, V.

Ellis Store Country Inn. The main house here is an old adobe dating to 1850. Two smaller cottages are in the back, and there are lovely gardens. Rooms are furnished with 19th-century antiques. Complimentary breakfast. Cable TV, in-room VCRs. | U.S. 380, Mile Marker 98 | 505/653–4609 or 800/653–6460 | fax 505/653–6460 | ellistore@pvtnetworks.net | 10 rooms (4 with shared bath), 2 suites | $79–$109 | AE, D, DC, MC, V.

Wortley Pat Garrett Hotel. This historic hotel was established in 1874 and reopened in 1999. Rooms have antique furnishings and fireplaces. The 70-ft-long log porch is well supplied with rocking chairs. Restaurant. Cable TV. | U.S. 380 | 505/653–4300 or 877/967–8539 | fax 505/653–4686 | www.lincolnnewmexico.com | 7 rooms | $65 | Closed Nov. 1–late Apr. | AE, MC, V.

LORDSBURG

MAP 9, B9

(Nearby towns also listed: Deming, Silver City)

Situated on the western slope of the Continental Divide in New Mexico's southwestern-most county, Lordsburg is the center for excursions into the desert country along the New Mexico-Arizona border.

A visit to the nearby ghost towns of Shakespeare and Steins will carry you into the past, as guides dressed in authentic clothing of the period offer tours and reenactments of the towns' past. You can go day hiking, camping or fishing in season in the nearby Gila National Forest.

Even Charles Lindbergh visited Lordsburg. In 1927 the man who earned the nickname "Lone Eagle" and his *Spirit of St. Louis* stopped over to dedicate the local airport following his New York–to–Paris flight. But otherwise, this quiet town of about 3,000 is inching along into the 21st century.

Information: **Lordsburg/Hidalgo County Chamber of Commerce** | 128 E. Motel Dr., Lordsburg, 88045 | 505/542–9864 | www.gilanet.com/lordsburgcoc.

Attractions

Shakespeare Ghost Town. This authentic ghost town, 2½ mi south of downtown on Main Street, is complete with a saloon, general store, blacksmith shop, and stables. Billy the Kid was its most famous inhabitant and allegedly washed dishes in the Stratford Hotel to earn his keep as a boy. | Main St. | 505/542–9034 | $3 | 2nd weekend of each month, or by appointment.

ON THE CALENDAR

APR., JUNE, OCT., DEC. *Wild West Reenactment and Living History.* The ghost town of Shakespeare is on land that is part of a working ranch, but four times a year the owner invites the public in and puts on a show. With real *pistolleros* to help stage this western reenactment, there could be a shoot-out or a demonstration of how life was lived over a hundred years ago. | 505/542–9034.

Dining

Kranberry's. American. Near all the major chain motels in town, one block south of exit 22 off Interstate 10, this family-style restaurant serves steaks, catfish, and cod among other simple but hearty meals offered. There is also a genuine western mine shaft on the premises, and ore carts at the entrance as a reminder of the history of this region. | 1405 S. Main St. | 505/542–9400 | fax 505/542–9440 | $6–$14 | AE, D, DC, MC, V.

Lodging

Days Inn and Suites. This two-story motel is a relatively new structure, built in 1998 in southwestern style. It's a convenient and inexpensive place to stop over. Complimentary Continental breakfast. In-room data ports, some microwaves, some refrigerators, cable TV. Pool. Hot tub. Gym. Pets allowed. | 1100 W. Motel Dr. | 505/542–3600 | www.daysinn.com | 44 rooms, 12 suites | $55–$62, $65–$72 suites | AE, D, DC, MC, V.

Holiday Inn Express. A pared-down version of the full-service Holiday Inns, this simple location still offers well-appointed rooms with two queen beds, a desk, chair, and dresser. For families, there are oversize rooms with a living area and queen sleeper. All of this is two blocks south of exit 22 on Interstate 10. Complimentary Continental breakfast. In-room data ports, some kitchenettes, cable TV. Pool. Pets allowed. | 1408 S. Main St. | 505/542–3666 | fax 505/542–3665 | www.hiexpress.com | 40 rooms | $59–$79 | AE, D, DC, MC, V.

LOS ALAMOS

MAP 9, E3

(Nearby towns also listed: Española, Jemez Springs, Santa Fe)

In 1942, when the U.S. government found it, Los Alamos was a tiny community whose main claim to fame was the Los Alamos Ranch School, a boys' facility that taught the classics while allowing its students to live a strenuous outdoor life among the surrounding Jemez Mountains. Almost overnight the school was closed, and a top-secret atomic laboratory was established that eventually was responsible for the development of the first atomic bomb. Today the facility, operated by the University of California, pursues peacetime nuclear research, including environmental cleanup, nuclear security, and nonnuclear defense.

Visitors will enjoy strolling along Main Street, which is lined with interesting shops and restaurants. Nearby are several Rio Grande pueblos, which are usually open to tourists, as well as the captivating Bandelier National Monument.

Information: **Los Alamos Chamber of Commerce** | Box 460, Los Alamos, 87544 | 505/662–8105 or 800/444–0707 | www.vla.com/chamber.

Attractions

Bandelier National Monument. Bandelier National Monument, about 12 mi south of Los Alamos, displays evidence of a once-thriving population center, remnants of which can be seen in Frijoles Canyon. Its name derives from Adolph F. Bandelier, the man most responsible for what we know today about this ancient pueblo. Studying the ruins between 1880 and 1886, Bandelier made the vanished town even more visible with his novel, *The Delight Makers,* which was based on everyday life in the region during its heyday. | Hwy. 4 | 505/672–3861 | www.nps.gov/band | $10 per vehicle | Daily dawn to dusk.

Bradbury Science Museum. This museum, featuring high-tech exhibits about the Manhattan Project and the development of the atomic bomb, is part of the Los Alamos National Laboratory. | 15th St. and Central Ave. | 505/667–4444 | Free | Tues.–Fri. 9–5, Sat.–Mon. 1–5.

Fuller Lodge. This massive log building in the center of town was erected in 1918 as a dining and recreation hall for the small private boys' school that occupied this site. In 1943 the school was purchased by the federal government to serve as the base of operations for the Manhattan Project. Part of the lodge is an art center that shows the works of Northern New Mexican artists and hosts temporary exhibits. | 2131 Central Ave. | 505/662–9331 or 505/662–8405 | www.rt66.com/~laartsculturalcalendar.html | Free | Mon.–Sat. 10–4., Sun. 11–5.

Los Alamos Historical Museum. The building that now houses the museum, which adjoins Fuller Lodge, was originally built in 1918 as the guest house for a small, private boys' school. Today it offers displays about the region's history, as well as exhibits about the nuclear laboratory's wartime days. There is a well-supplied bookstore. | 1921 Juniper St. | 505/662–4493 or 505/662–6272 | Free | Late Mar.–late Oct., Mon.–Sat. 9:30–4:30, Sun. 1–5; late Oct.–late Mar., Mon.–Sat. 10–4, Sun. 1–4.

ON THE CALENDAR
AUG.: *Los Alamos County Fair and Rodeo and Summer Fair.* The combination of both an art and crafts fair and the traditional state fair. | 505/662–8173 or 555/662–9331.

Dining

Blue Window. Continental. This colorful, comfortable bistro is a nice place to grab a quick bite. Try the duck, shrimp pasta, or any of the salmon dishes. Kids' menu, No smoking. | 813 Central Ave. | 505/662–6305 | Closed Sun. | $8–$16 | AE, D, DC, MC, V.

Hill Diner. American/Casual. This large and friendly establishment serves some of the finest burgers in town, along with chicken-fried steak, homemade soup, and heaps of fresh vegetables. | 1315 Trinity Dr., 87544 | 505/662–9745 | fax 505/662–9745 | $6–$11 | AE, D, DC, MC, V.

Lodging

Best Western Hilltop House Hotel. This hotel and conference center within a few blocks of most of the town's major attractions, including the Los Alamos labs, has a magnificent view of the mountains. Its location makes it popular with both visiting scientists and tourists. Restaurant, complimentary Continental breakfast, room service. In-room data ports, some kitchenettes, some microwaves, some refrigerators, cable TV. Pool. Sauna. Gym. Laundry facilities, laundry service. Business services, airport shuttle. Pets allowed (deposit). | 400 Trinity Dr. (Hwy. 502) | 505/662–2441 or 800/462–0936 | fax 505/662–5913 | www.los-alamos.com/hilltophouse | 98 rooms | $76–$275 | AE, D, DC, MC, V.

Los Alamos Inn. This sprawling, one-story hotel offers modern, southwestern rooms and sweeping views of the canyon. Restaurant, bar. Cable TV. Pool. Hot tub. Business services. | 2201 Trinity Dr. | 505/662–7211 or 800/279–9279 | fax 505/661–7714 | www.losalamosinn.com | 116 rooms | $48–$79 | AE, D, DC, MC, V.

Renta's Orange Street B&B. This unremarkable wood-frame house sits in a quiet residential neighborhood, offering southwestern-style rooms with forest views. Picnic area, complimentary breakfast. Cable TV, TV in common area. Business services. No kids under 2. No smoking. | 3496 Orange St. | 505/662–2651 or 800/662–3180 | fax 505/661–1538 | www.los-alamos.com/orangestreetinn | 9 rooms (5 with bath) | $49–$99 | AE, D, DC, MC, V.

MESCALERO

(Nearby town also listed: Ruidoso)

Mescalero serves as the administrative headquarters for the nearby Mescalero Native American Reservation. The reservation comprises nearly 500,000 acres and lies between the northern and southern units of the Lincoln National Forest. The Mescalero-owned Inn of the Mountain Gods is a nearby luxury resort that offers all kinds of outdoor recreation.

Information: **Mescalero Apache Indian Reservation Tribal Office** | U.S. 70, Mescalero | 505/671–4494.

Attractions

Mescalero Apache Reservation. The Mescalero reservation 6 mi south of Ruidoso is one of the largest Native American holdings in New Mexico. In addition to providing fine hunting and fishing for its residents and visitors, it offers the Inn of the Mountain Gods, an upscale resort that features golf, horseback riding, tennis, and whirlpool baths. Casino Apache offers all kinds of gambling, including Caribbean stud, craps, and more than 500 slots. | U.S. 70 | 505/671–4494 | Free | Daily.

Mescalero Cultural Center. Pictures of the Mescalero Apaches at the turn of the 20th century and examples of traditional Native American dress are on display as well as traditional medicinal herbs used today. The center is directly east of the Mescalero tribal office. | U.S. 70, Mescalero | 505/671–4494 ext. 254 | Free | Weekdays 8–4:30.

Mescalero National Fish Hatchery. Three hundred and fifty thousand trout are hatched and raised here on the reservation annually. This fish hatchery works to preserve rare and endangered species of fish and is the only place in the world that spawns the endangered Gila Trout. | Off U.S. 70 (exit 246, ½ mi east) | 505/671–4401 | Free | Daily.

ON THE CALENDAR

MAY: *Mescalero Powwow.* Tribes from all over the United States come together to celebrate their similarities and differences through traditional song, music, and dance. Festivities are held in the tribal office gymnasium. | 505/671–4494.

JULY: *Mescalero Apache Maidens' Ceremonial.* The Mountain Spirits Dance on the Mescalero Apache Reservation honors young Mescalero women at their puberty rights ceremony each July 4th. | 505/671–4494.

Dining

Dan-Li-Ka. Continental. With a name that translates from Apache into "good food," this is the best restaurant at the Inn of the Mountain Gods. Overlooking Lake Mescalero and the Sacrament Mountains, this elegant, spacious and candlelit restaurant also offers stunning views. Try the veal medallions sautéed with wild mushrooms and marsala wine or sterling salmon maltese poached in court bouillon. | Carrizo Canyon Rd. | 505/630–7555 | $17–$25 | AE, D, DC, MC, V.

Old Road. New Mexican. On the reservation for over 18 years, this is one of the few restaurants in the town of Mescalero. Classics such as enchiladas and chiles rellenos are made daily by the owner himself. By request of the reservation, there is no advertising other than an "Open" sign. The red adobe building is located on the Old Road through town and stands alone. Ask anyone you see to point it out. | Old Rd. | 505/671–4674 | Reservations not accepted | Closed Mon. | $4–$6 | No credit cards.

Lodging

★ **Inn of the Mountain Gods.** This sprawling resort on the shores of Lake Mescalero, 3½ mi southwest of Ruidoso, has its own casino and offers just about any recreational activity you can think of. Rooms are attractive and large. 2 restaurants, bars (with entertainment), room service. Cable TV. Pool, lake, wading pool. Sauna. 18-hole golf course, putting green. Hiking, horseback riding, fishing, bicycles. Business services, airport shuttle. | Carrizo Canyon Rd., Mescalero | 505/257–5141 or 800/545–9011 | fax 505/257–6173 | 252 rooms | www.innofthemountaingods.com | $120–$150 | AE, D, DC, MC, V.

Mescalero Inn. This small condominium resort is also owned by the Mescalero Apaches, operators of Inn of the Mountain Gods, and a free shuttle travels between the resorts, 1 mi apart. The condo studio units are comfortable and have balconies overlooking Carrizozo Creek. Guests have total access to all of the facilities at the Inn of the Mountain Gods. Microwaves, cable TV. | Carrizo Canyon Rd., Mescalero | 800/545–6040 | fax 505/257–6173 | www.innofthemountaingods.com/mescinn.htm | 12 condos | $80–$120 | AE, D, DC, MC, V.

MESILLA

MAP 9, D9

(Nearby towns also listed: Alamogordo, Deming)

Some say that Mesilla occupies the spot that Don Juan de Oñate declared to be "the first pueblo of this kingdom." For many years, Mesilla stood opposite Las Cruces on the Mexican side of the international boundary line, until the river changed its course in 1865, leaving both villages east of the Rio Grande, but by this time, the United States had already annexed the town.

For a brief time in 1861, Mesilla, 2 mi southwest of Las Cruces, served as the Confederate capital of the Arizona Territory. The plaza in Mesilla has been the site of many historic events, including the transfer of the surrounding territory from Mexico to the United States in 1854, the raising of the Confederate flag for a brief period in 1861, and the confinement of Billy the Kid at the local jail. It was finally eclipsed by Las Cruces in 1881, when the Santa Fe Railroad extended its line into the neighboring town, bypassing Mesilla and making Las Cruces the area's major transportation hub. Today Mesilla's dozens of unique shops provide hours of shopping for the tourist.

Information: **Las Cruces Chamber of Commerce** | Drawer 519, Las Cruces, 88004 | 505/524–1968 or 800/343–7827 | www.lascruces.org.

ATTRACTIONS

Gadsden Museum. This museum three blocks from the Mesilla Plaza displays a variety of Native American and early Spanish artifacts relating to the area in the former home of the Fountain family. A painting commemorating the Gadsden Purchase is a highlight. | W. Barker Rd. at Hwy. 28 | 505/526–6293 | $2 | Mon.–Sat. 9–11 and 1–5.

Stahmann Farms. With over 4,000 acres, this is the largest family-owned pecan orchard in the world, 6 mi south of Mesilla. You can drive through the orchard on Highway 28 or stop by the farm store to sample and buy products made from pecans. | 22505 Hwy. 28 S., La Mesa | 505/526–8974 or 800/654–6887 | Free | Store: Mon.–Sat. 9–6, Sun. 11–5.

ON THE CALENDAR

DEC.: *Our Lady of Guadalupe Fiesta.* Native American dances, vespers, mass, and a fiesta round out activities at this event in Mesilla Park. | 505/526–8171.

Dining

Double Eagle. Continental. This restored Territorial-style hacienda on the east side of Mesilla Plaza dating from the mid-19th century, complete with a gold-leaf ceiling and century-old wall coverings, is hung with original art and decorated with period pieces. The Sunday champagne brunch is worth a special trip. Eat in the skylight-covered courtyard with trees and plants. Sunday brunch. | 308 Calle Guadalupe | 505/523–6700 | $11–$25 | AE, D, DC, MC, V.

El Comedor. Southwestern. At this simple and casual spot, try green chile con carne, taco ranchero. Beer and wine only. | 2190 Avenida de Mesilla | 505/524–7002 | $5–$8 | AE, D, MC, V.

★ **La Posta de Mesilla.** Mexican. This restaurant is housed in the former stagecoach stop for the Butterfield Overland Mail and Wells Fargo stages. The chefs here follow recipes dating back more than 100 years. The menu includes such southwestern favorites as chiles rellenos and red or green enchiladas, as well as a variety of well-prepared steak dishes. | 2410 Calle de San Albino | 505/524–3524 | Closed Mon. | AE, D, DC, MC, V.

Lorenzo's. Italian. A hand-painted mural of the Mesilla covers the wall while red-checked tablecloths cover the tables at this intimate Italian spot. Try any of the pizzas, pastas, or salads based on old Sicilian recipes. | Mesilla Plaza, 2000 Hwy. 292 | 505/525–3170 | $7–$18 | AE, D, MC, V.

★ **Mesón de Mesilla.** Continental. People drive from all over southern New Mexico and even west Texas to dine in this restaurant in the Mesón de Mesilla B & B. Known for seared sturgeon in pesto, châteaubriand for two, and filet mignon. If you stay in the inn, you enjoy the restaurant's gourmet breakfasts. Guitarist on weekends. | 1803 Avenida de Mesilla | 505/525–2380 | $20–$24 | AE, D, DC, MC, V.

★ **Old Mesilla Pastry Cafe.** Café. Known for delicious baked goods but also for specialty foods such as buffalo and ostrich meat and delicious pizzas, this café is a good stop for breakfast or lunch. | 2790 Avenida de Mesilla | 505/525–2636 | Closed Mon., Tues. No dinner | $5–$8 | AE, MC, V.

Lodging

Best Western Mesilla Valley Inn. This pleasant, two-story motel built around a courtyard with a pool offers southwestern hospitality ½ mi from Mesilla Plaza. Restaurant, bar (with entertainment), room service. Some in-room data ports, some microwaves available, some refrigerators, cable TV. Pool. Hot tub. Video games. Laundry facilities, laundry service. Business services. Pets allowed. | 901 Avenida de Mesilla | 505/524–8603 or 800/528–1234 | fax 505/526–8437 | www.bestwestern.com | 152 rooms, 8 suites | $59, $69–$79 suites | AE, D, DC, MC, V.

Meson de Mesilla. The views of the jagged Organ Mountains and lower mesas from the back patio and second-floor balcony are among this inn's lures. Rooms are done in Southwest tones and furnished with light-wood furniture and some antiques. They also have TVs, clock radios, and ceiling fans. The lower-priced single rooms are a good option for businesspeople on a budget. Restaurant, pool. Full breakfast. | 1803 Avenida de Mesilla | 505/525–9212 or 800/732–6025 | fax 505/527–4196 | 13 rooms | AE, D, DC, MC, V.

PORTALES

MAP 9, H6

(Nearby towns also listed: Clovis, Roswell)

The first settler in the Portales area was Doak Good, a cowboy who lived in the surrounding caves until he could get a permanent house built. The caves reminded Good of Mexican porches, or *portales,* so he named his new village accordingly. Today

Portales is a heavily agricultural community, with peanuts, cotton, and corn among the leading crops.

One of the state's larger institutions of higher learning, Eastern New Mexico University, is located here. The surrounding region is famous for its mineral and fossil finds, not to mention the Dalley Windmill Collection, which features 75 distinctive windmills from all over the world.

Information: **Portales/Roosevelt County Chamber of Commerce** | 206 E. 7th St., Portales, 88130 | 505/356–8541 or 800/635–8036 | www.portales.com.

Attractions

Dalley Windmill Collection. Portales resident Bill Dalley has put together the nation's largest collection of windmills. He has upwards of 80 windmills and is president of the International Windmillers' Trade Fair Association. Mr. Dalley says, "Come by and take a look." | Kilgore St., near 18th St. | 505/356–6263 | Free | Daily anytime for just a look; Mr. Dalley will show you around if he's home.

Eastern New Mexico University. The third-largest university in New Mexico offers a full four-year curriculum from its Portales campus. The university department of anthropology operates the Blackwater Draw Museum and its related archaeological site northeast of Portales. | 1200 W. University St. | 505/562–2131 or 505/562–1011 | www.enmu.edu | Free | Daily.

Blackwater Draw Museum. Featuring some of the first evidence that humans lived in the Portales region over 11,300 years ago, the exhibits in this roadside museum—operated by the Eastern New Mexico University Anthropology Department—7 mi northeast of town are well maintained. Prehistoric artifacts from Clovis, Folsom, and Native American civilizations are displayed along with photographs of the archaeological digs. There is an active dig (called Locality #1) that can also be toured by visitors; one admission gets you into both. | 42987 Hwy. 70 | 505/356–5235 | www.enmu.edu | $2 (includes Blackwater Locality #1 site) | Memorial Day–Labor Day, Mon.–Sat. 10–5, Sun. noon–5; Labor Day –Memorial Day, Tues.– Sat. 10–5, Sun. noon–5.

Blackwater Locality #1. A National Historic Landmark archaeological site being excavated by the Blackwater Draw Museum, 5 mi north of Portales. Clovis, the culture that resided here, is the oldest currently defined culture in the Americas. | 508 Hwy. 467 | 505/356–5235 | www.enmu.edu | $2 (includes Blackwater Draw Museum) | Memorial Day–Labor Day, Mon.–Sat. 10–5, Sun. noon–5; Labor Day–Oct. 31 and Mar. 1–Memorial Day, Sat. 10–5, Sun. noon–5.

Golden Library. This library on the Eastern New Mexico University campus houses 275,000 volumes, including titles in the Jack Williamson Science Fiction Collection and the Southwest Collection. | South Ave. K | 505/562–2624 | Free | Mon.–Thurs. 7:30 AM–11 PM, Fri. 7:30 AM–8 PM, Sat. 10–7, Sun. noon–11 PM.

Natural History Museum. Located in Roosevelt Hall on the Eastern New Mexico University campus, this small exhibit focuses on the plants and animals of southeastern New Mexico, including many live specimens. | South Ave. K | 505/562–2723 or 505/562–2307 | www.enmu.edu | Free | Weekdays 8–5, Sat. 10–12.

Roosevelt County Museum. Exhibits at this museum on the Eastern New Mexico University campus have been donated by county residents and focus on the region's history. | W. University Dr. | 505/562–2592 | www.enmu.edu | Free | Weekdays 8–5, Sat. 10–4, Sun. 1–4.

Oasis State Park. Hiking, picnicking, camping, and playing in the sand dunes are a few of the attractions offered at this state park 7½ mi northeast of Portales. | Off Hwy. 467 | 505/356–5331 | $4 per vehicle | Daily.

ON THE CALENDAR

JUNE: *Roosevelt County Heritage Days.* A rodeo, dancing, a barbecue, and a parade are all attractions at this affair at the Roosevelt County Fairgrounds. | 505/356–8541 or 800/635–8036.

AUG.: *Roosevelt County Fair.* Livestock shows, agricultural displays, and arts-and-crafts exhibits highlight this county fair at the county fairgrounds. | 505/356–8541 or 800/635–8036.

SEPT.: *Air Expo and Fly In.* Static displays and demonstrations of both private and military modern aircraft as well as an air show by the New Mexico State Police. There are even hot-air balloons. | 505/478–2863.

OCT.: *Peanut Valley Festival.* This annual festival celebrates the peanut harvest with arts-and-crafts exhibits on the Eastern New Mexico University campus. | 505/356–8541 or 800/635–8036.

Dining

Cattle Baron Steak and Seafood. Steak. This was the original outlet of the regional chain offering reliable steaks at reasonable prices. Known for the prime rib and fresh salad bar. | 1600 South Ave. D | 505/356–5587/ | $8–$25 | AE, D, DC, MC, V.

Mark's Eastern Grill. American. Tasty and fresh breakfast omelets, steaks, and sandwiches attract the hungry college crowd from nearby Eastern New Mexico University. This diner has a fun feel, with tile inlaid tables, brightly colored vinyl chairs, and a few fake parrots thrown in for color. | 1126 W. 2nd St., 88130 | 505/359–0857 | $6–$14 | AE, D, DC, MC, V.

Lodging

Classic American Economy Inn. This inexpensive motel offering standard rooms is downtown, next to Eastern New Mexico University. Picnic area, complimentary Continental breakfast. In-room data ports, refrigerators, cable TV, some in-room VCRs. Pool. Playground. Laundry facilities. Airport shuttle. Pets allowed. | 1613 W. 2nd St. | 505/356–6668 or 800/901–9466 | fax 505/356–6668 | 40 rooms | $30–$50 | AE, D, DC, MC, V.

Morning Star Bed and Breakfast. Antiques and brass highlights accent the fresh, bright look of this adobe-style bed-and-breakfast in downtown Portales. The bridal suite is a two-bedroom apartment with its own bath and kitchen. The other three rooms share a common area, which has a refrigerator, and 2 baths. Complimentary Continental breakfast. No TV, no room phones, TV in common area. | 620 W. 2nd St., 88130 | 505/356–2994 | www.pdr-pip.com./morningstarb&b | 3 rooms (2 with shared bath), 1 suite | $50–$80 | MC, V.

Super 8. Contemporary furnishings and pastel colors in the large rooms and bathrooms are a distinguishing feature of this budget motel, which is only two blocks away from the Eastern New Mexico University campus. Complimentary Continental breakfast. Cable TV. Indoor hot tub. | 1805 W. 2nd, 88130 | 505/356–8518 or 800/800–8000 | fax 505/359–0431 | www.super8.com | 40 rooms, 4 suites | $49–$54, $78 suites | AE, D, DC, MC, V.

RATON

MAP 9, G2

(Nearby towns also listed: Cimarron, Clayton)

Raton serves as the southern entrance to the fabled Raton Pass, a large gap in the southern Sangre de Cristo Mountains, which divide New Mexico from Colorado. The old Santa Fe Trail wove its tortuous way through the pass before dropping down into Raton. During the mid-1800s, a local entrepreneur named "Uncle Dick" Wootton built a toll road over Raton Pass and charged everyone—Native American, Mexican, or American settler—who used it.

Raton, the seat of Colfax County and a town of about 10,000, runs on ranching, mining, and railroading. It is the gateway to northern New Mexico and maintains a distinctive restored historic district. Besides its beautiful natural surroundings, Raton is located close to the National Rifle Association's Whittington Center, the Capulin Volcano, and the Maxwell National Wildlife Refuge.

Information: **Raton Chamber of Commerce** | Box 1211, Raton, 87740 | 800/638–6161 or 505/445–3689 | www.raton.com.

Attractions

Capulin Volcano National Monument. Walking along the rim of Capulin Mountain, about 35 mi east of Raton, jutting up more than 1,000 ft above the rolling plains that it dominates, you can see forever—or at least parts of five states. And whether your eyes are searching north, east, south, or west, the majestic 360° vista provides a breathtaking panorama. Capulin Mountain is young—only about 60,000 years old—but it has been dormant long enough for you to descend into its crater for a look around. The volcano is 29 mi east of Raton on U.S. 64/U.S. 87 to Capulin, then 3½ mi north. | Off Hwy. 325 | 505/278–2201 | www.nps.gov/cavo | $4 | Memorial–Labor Day, daily 7:30–6:30; Labor Day–Memorial Day, daily 8–4:30.

Folsom Museum. The Folsom Museum documents life in eastern New Mexico during the late 19th and early 20th centuries. Nearby, but on private property, is the site of the discovery of flint points belonging to Folsom Man, one of the earliest humans known to occupy North America, but the museum does not contain any authentic Folsom points. Folsom is 7 mi north of Capulin. | Main St., Folsom | 505/278–2122 or 505/278–3616 | $1 | Memorial Day–Labor Day, daily 10–5; May, Sept., weekends 10–5 or by appointment; Oct.–Apr. by appointment only.

Maxwell National Wildlife Refuge. Home to dozens of species of waterfowl, plus bald eagles and deer, this is the site of some of the best trout fishing in northern New Mexico. It's 23 mi south of Raton, 4 mi northwest of Maxwell. | Off Hwy. 505 | 505/375–2331 | southwest.fws.gov/refuges/newmex/maxwell.html | Free | Daily.

National Rifle Association Whittington Center. The country's largest and most complete shooting facility, with ranges for pistol, large- and small-bore rifles, and shotguns, is located 10 mi southwest of Raton. There are also campsites and cabins. Hunts are organized on the ranges, which can close various ranges, so call in advance to check the schedule and make sure you can shoot. | U.S. 64 | 505/445–3615 | www.nrawc.org | $10 | Daily; call for range times.

Raton Museum. Artifacts from Raton's past, a fine photo collection, regional artwork, and old musical instruments are just a few of the varied items housed in this museum. | 218 S. 1st St. | 505/445–8979 | Free | Memorial Day–Labor Day, Tues.–Sat. 9–5; Labor Day–Memorial Day, Wed.–Sat. 10–4.

Sugarite Canyon State Park. The site of an early coal mining camp that drew miners from all over the world, this park 10 mi northeast of Raton allows you to learn from the past by actually visiting one of the mine sites. | Hwy. 526 | 505/445–5607 | $4 per vehicle | Daily.

ON THE CALENDAR

JULY: *International Santa Fe Trail Balloon Rally.* This annual event is a spectacular display of color and flight. The festivities include a parade, a chuck-wagon dinner, music, dancing, fireworks, and kids' activities. | 505/445–3689 or 800/638–6161.

Dining

The Grapevine. Italian. By far the best place to eat in Raton, this cheery restaurant prepares excellent pizzas, calzones, and eggplant dishes. One specialty of the house is chicken with artichokes, fresh tomatoes, and basil in a marinara sauce. | 120 N. 2nd St. | 505/445–0969 | Closed Sun. | $8–$18 | AE, D, DC, MC, V.

Hot Dog Depot. American/Casual. Cute, clean, and smoke-free, this café inside a bright turquoise vintage house serves hearty, homemade chile, soup, and salads. The fresh coffee is a bargain and an eye-opener. | 100 S. 3rd St. | 505/445–9090 | Closed Sun. No dinner | $4–$6 | MC, V.

Pappas' Sweet Shop. American. Pappas' is furnished with many collectibles and antiques, exuding a sense of history and pleasant nostalgia. Known for steaks, pasta, seafood. Kids' menu. | 1201 S. 2nd St. | 505/445–9811 | Closed Sun. | $9–$28 | AE, D, MC, V.

Lodging

Best Western Sands. A renovated, late-1950s motel with southwestern decor. Rooms are a good size and comfortable. Restaurant. In-room data ports, some refrigerators, cable TV. Pool. Hot tub. Playground. Business services. | 300 Clayton Rd. | 505/445–2737 or 800/518–2581 | fax 505/445–4053 | www.bestwestern.com | 50 rooms | $71–$99 | AE, D, DC, MC, V.

Budget Host Melody Lane Motel. This establishment is unpretentious but squeaky clean and affordable. Complimentary Continental breakfast. Refrigerators, cable TV. Some pets allowed. | 136 Canyon Dr. | 505/445–3655 or 800/421–5210 | fax 505/445–3461 | www.budgethost.com | 27 rooms | $36–$49 | AE, D, DC, MC, V.

El Portal. This downtown building was erected in 1885 as a livery stable but has been a hotel since 1912. For years a rowdy railroad hotel, the now more sedate establishment contains antiques throughout. It closely resembles the interior of the original, and ghosts allegedly abound, roaming the hallways. Restaurant. Some kitchenettes. Cable TV. Pets allowed. | 101 N. 3rd St. | 505/445–3631 or 888/362–7345 | 15 rooms, 39 apartments | $35–$55, $105–$245 weekly for apartments | MC, V.

Morning Star. This 1885 Victorian near downtown is also the home of the owner's antiques business. It's a relaxed and pleasant change from the strictly motel accommodations elsewhere. Snacks are served in the evening. Complimentary breakfast. No TV in rooms, TV in common area. Pets allowed. No smoking. | 301 S. 3rd St. | 505/445–1000 | 4 rooms (with shared baths), 1 suite (with private bath) | $50 | MC, V.

Oasis. A basic old-fashioned roadside motel off Interstate 25, this is a perfectly fine place to stay. It is no frills but comfortable. Restaurant. Cable TV. | 1445 S. 2nd St., 87740 | 505/445–2221 | 14 rooms | $35–$54 | Closed late Jan.–early Feb. | AE, D, MC, V.

RED RIVER

MAP 9, F2

(Nearby towns also listed: Angel Fire, Cimarron, Taos)

Though Red River got its start as a mining town, it's now better known as a resort community whose primary business is skiing. An Old West flavor endures, with country dancing a favorite nighttime entertainment. The downtown bustles with shops and boutiques, and the ski area is right in the middle of town. This vacation destination is located on the Enchanted Circle, an 85-mi-long loop road encircling Wheeler Peak, which is the highest point in New Mexico. Its nickname of "mountain playground of the Southern Rockies" says it all.

Information: **Red River Chamber of Commerce** | Box 870, Red River, 87558 | 800/348–6444 or 505/754–2366 | www.redrivernewmex.com.

Attractions

Pioneer Canyon Trail. This 3-mi-long auto trail will carry you back in time more than 100 years, to the days when gold and copper were mined in the surrounding mountains. The trip length is two–three hours if you stop at all of the marked sites. The trail starts behind the Arrowhead Lodge at the end of Pioneer Road. | Pioneer Rd. | 505/754–2366 | Free | Daily.

Red River Ski Area. This ski area has 58 trails and a 1,600-ft vertical drop. It's the big winter draw for tourists in the immediate area. | Pioneer Rd. | 505/754–2223 or 800/348–6444 | taoswebb.com/redriver | Thanksgiving–Apr. for skiing.

ON THE CALENDAR

FEB.: *Mardi Gras in the Mountains.* Cajun food and a parade highlight this Red River Ski Area celebration. | 505/754–2366 or 800/348–6444.

MAY: *Red River Run Memorial Day Motorcycle Rally.* This four-day event is a must for cycle enthusiasts. There are various competitions, ceremonies, and bike shows. | 505/745–2366 or 800/348–6444.

SEPT.: *Enchanted Circle Century Bike Tour.* This bike tour, beginning and ending in downtown Red River, covers 100 mi and features more than 700 bikers. | 505/754–2366 or 800/348–6444.

Dining

Brett's Homestead Steakhouse. American. This cozy restaurant in a vintage Victorian house is filled with memorabilia from the early mining era, has a fireplace in the dining room and a pond in the lush yard. The rotating menu includes fresh trout, seafood, lamb and veal dishes, and standards like the shrimp Rio Grande (jumbo shrimp sautéed with chiles and exotic mushrooms in a sherry-butter sauce), and the herb-crusted rack of spring lamb. Kids' menu. Beer and wine only. | W. Main St. at High Cost Trail | 505/754–6136 | Closed Apr.–mid-May, Nov. No lunch | $15–$40 | AE, D, DC, MC, V.

Capos Corner. Italian. The two fireplaces are perfect for those winter nights. The home-made sauces are made daily. Try the lasagna or the *Capo Grande*, made of baked rigatoni, roast beef, mushrooms, green chile, meat sauce, and cheese. Kids' menu. | 110 Pioneer Rd. | 505/754–6297 | $9–$16 | AE, D, DC, MC, V.

Redwood Café. American/Casual. You can start your day with fresh biscuits, French toast, or an omelet at this restaurant on Main Street. The lunch menu includes BBQ beef brisket sandwiches, chile dogs, and hamburgers. Kids' menu. | 210 Main St. | 505/754–2951 | Breakfast also available; no dinner | $3–$8 | MC, V.

Shotgun Willie's. Barbecue. The all-you-can eat breakfast is popular. The meat here is smoked over hickory and mesquite and then served with Willie's own barbecue sauce. Try the BBQ chicken sandwich, the sliced brisket, or the charbroiled burger. | Main St. and Pioneer St. | 505/754–6505 | Breakfast also available | $2–$8 | No credit cards.

Sundance. Mexican. This southwestern-style restaurant with a large fireplace in the dining room serves good Mexican fare. Try the fajitas or burritos. Kids' menu. Beer and wine only. | 401 High St. | 505/754–2971 | Closed Apr.–mid-May. No lunch | $8–$16 | AE, D, DC, MC, V.

Texas Red's Steak House. American. At this two-story western-style steakhouse locals and tourists pack into long wooden tables, the waitstaff cheerfully gabs and banters, and signs along the walls encourage noise, tall-tales, and general old-West etiquette. It feels like a classic saloon. Specialties of the house include filet mignon, teriyaki pork tenderloin, and a variety of trout and catfish dishes. Kids' menu. | 111 E. Main St. | 505/754–2964 | No lunch | $6–$39 | AE, D, DC, MC, V.

Lodging

Alpine Lodge. This rustic-looking lodge on the banks of the Red River offers modern rooms, a cabin, and apartments. Plus, you're steps away from the ski lift. Restaurant, bar. No air-conditioning, some kitchenettes, cable TV. Hot tubs. Playground. Business services. | 417 W. Main St. | 505/754–2952 or 800/252–2333 | fax 505/754–6421 | www.redrivernm.com | 30 rooms, 16 apartments, cabin | $39–$72, $52–$148 apartments, $118 cabin | D, MC, V.

Arrowhead Lodge. At this small, unpretentious ski lodge you'll find easy access to the slopes in winter (they are right across the street), and a sundeck and easy access to the Pioneer Canyon Trail in summer. Picnic area. No air-conditioning, some kitchenettes, cable TV. Cross-country skiing, downhill skiing. Airport shuttle. | 405 Pioneer Tr | 505/754–2255 | fax 505/754–2588 | www.arrowheadlodge.com | 19 rooms | $45–$209 | AE, D, MC, V.

Best Western River's Edge Lodge This small chain hotel is right on the Red River in the heart of town. Stores and restaurants are within walking distance. The lobby has a fireplace and an inviting common area. The winter offers ski-in/ski-out capabilities. The rooms are spacious, and some have balconies and full kitchens. Children under 12 stay free. Complimentary Continental breakfast, in-room data ports, some kitchenettes, microwaves, refrigerators, cable TV. Hot tub. Laundry facilities. Free parking. Pets allowed (fee). | 301 W. River St. | 505/754–1766 or 877/600–9990 | fax 505/754–2388 or 505/754–2408 | www.bestwestern.com | 31 rooms | $90–$120 | AE, D, DC, MC, V.

Lifts West Condominium Resort Hotel. This modern, condominium resort offers modern, comfortable suites and apartments with a full kitchen, fireplace, and balcony or deck. The atrium lobby has a dramatic stone fireplace and direct access to a shopping mall. Restaurant, picnic area. Kitchenettes, cable TV, in-room VCRs (and movies). Pool. 2 hot tubs, sauna. Laundry facilities. Cross-country skiing, downhill skiing. Shops. Business services. | 201 W. Main St. | 505/754–2778 or 800/221–1859 outside NM | fax 505/754–6617 | www.redrivernm.com | 75 rooms | $60–$375 | AE, D, DC, MC, V.

The Lodge at Red River This hotel is one of the oldest buildings in town. The lobby has a beautiful fireplace for those cold winter nights. Common phones and a television are located in the entertainment center. The restaurant and nightclub (often featuring live entertainment) are very popular with the locals. The rooms are comfortable and well maintained. Restaurant, bar. No room phones, no TV, TV in common area. Library. Business services. No smoking. | 400 E. Main St. | 505/754–6280 | fax 505/754–6304 | www.redrivernm.com | 26 rooms | $68–$96 | AE, D, DC, MC, V.

Ponderosa Lodge. This lodge offers both pine-paneled, motel-style rooms and larger, more elaborate suites with stone fireplaces and full kitchens. One suite has five bedrooms and can accommodate a large family. No air-conditioning, cable TV. Hot tub. Sauna. | 200 Main St. | 505/754–2988 or 800/336–7787 | www.redrivernm.com | 17 rooms, 17 suites | $51–$350 | AE, D, DC, MC, V.

Red River Inn. This small, family-owned resort offers decent, inexpensive rooms year-round. There is also a spa, offering yoga classes, and a theater on the premises. Picnic area. No air-conditioning, some kitchenettes, cable TV. Hot tub, massage, sauna. Cross-country skiing, downhill skiing. Shops. No smoking. | 300 W. Main St. | 505/754–2930 or 800/365–2930 | fax 505/754–2943 | rrin@newmex.com | www.redrivernm.com | 13 rooms | $54–$64 | AE, D, MC, V.

River Ranch. These rustic housekeeping cabins are at the west end of Red River. The property has a lake and a stream for fishing. The cabins are comfortable, and linens can be provided for a fee. The apartments have a full kitchen, a fireplace, and cable TV. Kitchenettes, some microwaves, refrigerators, some cable TV, no room phones. Lake. Fishing. Video games. No pets. No smoking. | 1501 W. Main St. | 505/754–2293 | www.redrivernm.com | 13 cabins, 50 RV sites, 5 apartments | $37–$69 cabins, $16–$20 RV sites, $57–$67 apartments | Cabins closed Oct.–Memorial Weekend | No credit cards.

Riverside Lodge & Cabins. Located in the heart of Red River, right across from the Community Center and adjacent to a ski lift, this lodge is on 2 landscaped acres, with lovely mountain views. Some rooms have fireplaces or a patio area. Cabins have full kitchens. Picnic area. No air-conditioning, some kitchenettes, cable TV, in-room VCR. Hot tub. Playground. Business services. | 201 E. Main St. | 505/754–2252 or 800/432–9999 | fax 505/754–2495 | www.redrivernm.com | 8 lodge rooms, 30 cabins | $55–$150 | D, MC, V.

Tall Pine Resort. Surrounded by national forest and about 1½ mi into the mountains, the basic, well-spaced log cabins here are set in 40 acres of woods along the Red River and are perfect for those wanting peace, seclusion, and an outdoorsy setting. Picnic area. No air-conditioning, kitchenettes, no room phones. Playground. Pets allowed. | 1929 Hwy. 578 | 505/754–2241 or 800/573–2241 | fax 505/754–3134 | www.tallpineresort.com | 24 cabins | $75–$120 cabins | Closed Oct.–Apr. | MC, V.

Terrace Towers Lodge. This all-suite lodge offers a magnificent view of the Red River valley and spacious rooms. All units have a kitchenette or full kitchen, as well as a sleeper sofa, which makes them ideal for families. Hot tub. Kitchenettes, cable TV, some in-room VCRs (and movies). Playground. Laundry facilities. Pets allowed. | 712 W. Main St. | 505/754–2962 or 800/695–6343 | fax 505/754–2989 | www.redrivernm.com | 26 suites | $55–$160 | AE, D, MC, V.

Timberline Lodge. These rooms and apartments have the Red River ski slopes as a backdrop. All have queen-size beds; some have bunk beds, sofa sleepers, and balconies. The playground and picnic area are great for families. Picnic area. No air-conditioning, kitchenettes, some microwaves, refrigerators, cable TV. Hot tub. Playground. | 100 N. Independence Trail | 505/754–6267 or 800/262–6679 | fax 505/754–3234 | www.redrivernm.com | 17 rooms | $42–$90 | D, MC, V.

ROSWELL

MAP 9, G7

(Nearby towns also listed: Artesia, Portales, Ruidoso)

Roswell became a household word in 1947, when reports of a downed alien spaceship nearby hit the country's radio airwaves. Ironically, almost two decades before the bizarre news, Dr. Robert Goddard, the father of American rocketry, had already become a resident of Roswell and was busy conducting experiments with high-altitude missiles. To his chagrin, Goddard could interest no one, including the U.S. government, in the future of outer space and its value to mankind.

But Roswell isn't just a UFO mecca. It's actually a rather conservative city of 50,000 with an economy based on agriculture, manufacturing, oil, and gas. Roswell is conveniently located, with quick access to Lincoln National Forest, the Mescalero Apache Reservation, several wildlife refuges, and Billy the Kid country.

Information: **Roswell Convention and Visitors Bureau** | 912 N. Main St., Roswell, 88201 | 505/624–6860 | www.roswell-usa.com.

Attractions

Bitter Lake National Wildlife Refuge. Migratory waterfowl flock to this area 8 mi east of Roswell, off U.S. 380, during their annual migrations in spring and fall. Sandhill cranes winter here and are most numerous in mid-November. An 8½-mi self-guided tour takes you around the lake. There are also designated hunting and fishing areas. | 4065 Bitter Lakes Rd. | 505/622–6755 | southwest.fws.gov/refuges/newmex/bitter.html | Free | Daily.

Bottomless Lakes State Park. The so-called "bottomless" lakes of this state park 13 mi east of Roswell are actually sinkholes created after salt and gypsum deposits dissolve in ground water and then collapse. Swimming is permitted at Lea Lake, where you'll also find picnicking, camping, showers, and bathrooms. Go east of Roswell on U.S. 380 to Hwy. 409; follow the signs 5 mi south to park entrance. | Hwy. 409 | 505/624–6058 | www.emnrd.state.nm.us/nmparks | $4 per vehicle | Daily.

Dexter National Fish Hatchery and Technology Center. This place 15 mi southeast of Roswell (1 mi east of Dexter) will teach you how all those fish get stocked in New Mexico mountain lakes and streams. It's been working to save endangered fish species since 1931. | Hwy. 285, Dexter. | 505/734–5910 | Free | Daily 7–4.

Historical Center for Southeast New Mexico. This beautiful, former private home is stocked with antiques, artifacts from the region, and rotating exhibits. | 200 N. Lea Ave. | 505/622–8333 | Free | Daily 1–4.

The International UFO Museum and Research Center. This is probably Roswell's "must-see" attraction, a homespun museum and research center devoted to UFOs in general and the infamous "Roswell Incident" of 1947 in particular. | 114 N. Main St. | 505/625–9495 or 800/822–3545 | www.iufomrc.com | Free | Daily.

New Mexico Military Institute. The Institute is a prep school and junior college with an emphasis on both military and academic preparation. Founded in 1891, it now has over 1,000 cadets. You'll find the General Douglas L. McBride Museum on the campus grounds. To tour the campus you must make an appointment. | 101 W. College Blvd. | 800/421–5376 | www.nmmi.cc.nm.us/ | Free | Weekdays 8–5.

General Douglas L. McBride Museum. On the campus of New Mexico Military Institute, this museum houses a fine display of military artifacts, plus interesting exhibits relating to the history of the school. | 101 W. College Blvd. | 505/624–8220 or 800/421–5376 | $2 | Sept.–May, Tues.–Fri. 8:30–11:30 and 1–3; Jun.–Aug., call for hours.

New Mexico Military Institute Library. This well-stocked library on the campus of New Mexico Military Institute houses the Paul Horgan and the Napoleonic Archival Collections. | 101 W. College Blvd. | 505/622–6250 | Free (included in tour) | Weekdays 8–5.

Roswell Museum and Art Center. You'll find outstanding artwork by Peter Hurd, Georgia O'Keeffe, Henriette Wyeth, and others in this well-regarded art museum, which also houses the Robert H. Goddard rocketry workshop and additional space and historical displays. | 100 W. 11th St. | 505/624–6744 | www.roswellmuseum.org | Free | Mon.–Sat. 9–5, Sun. 1–5.

Robert H. Goddard Planetarium. This is the largest planetarium in the state of New Mexico, offering star talks and other multimedia programs. | 100 W. 11th St. | 505/624–6744 | www.roswellmuseum.org | $3, $5 for special shows | Call for hours.

Spring River Park and Zoo. This small zoo has a lake where kids can fish, a carousel, and a miniature train, as well as a collection of live animals, mostly from the region, including a prairie-dog town. | 1306 E. College Blvd. | 505/624–6760 or 505/624–6700 | Free | Memorial Day–Labor Day, daily 10–8; Labor Day–Memorial Day, daily 10–5:30.

ON THE CALENDAR

JULY: *Encounter Festival.* Lectures about UFOs, science-fiction writers workshops, and events such as alien-costume competitions. | 505/624–6860.

OCT.: *Eastern New Mexico State Fair and Rodeo.* Livestock, agricultural goods, arts and crafts, and plenty of good food and entertainment are elements of this annual event at Fair Park. | 505/623–9411.

Dining

Cattle Baron. Steak. This outlet of the reliable, regional chain offers a pleasing menu of steaks and seafood. Known for prime rib and an impressive salad bar. The dark wood of the furnishings and rooms are offset by ample windows and a skylight. | 1113 N. Main St. | 505/622–2465 | fax 505/623–2252 | $9–$20 | AE, D, DC, MC, V.

The Golden Corral. American. Come in and place your order for steak, chicken or burgers, or choose something from the all-you-can-eat buffet, and sample from the salad bar, bakery, and a dessert bar as well. | 2624 N. Main St. | 505/622–5102 | $7–$8 | AE, D, MC, V.

Lodging

Best Western Sally Port Inn and Suites. This standard motel in the middle of town, close to the New Mexico Military Institute, is a favorite of the cadets' parents. Restaurant, bar, room service. In-room data ports, refrigerators, cable TV. Pool. Beauty salon, hot tub. Tennis. Gym. Laundry facilities. Business services, airport shuttle. Pets allowed. | 2000 N. Main St. | 505/622–6430 | fax 505/623–7631 | www.bestwestern.com | $79–$119 | AE, D, DC, MC, V.

Budget Inn. A clean, no-frills motel, offering very basic rooms at reasonable prices two blocks north of the New Mexico Military Institute. Some microwaves, some refrigerators, cable TV. Pool. Hot tub. Some pets allowed (fee). | 2200 W. 2nd St. | 505/623–3811 or 800/806–7030 | fax 505/623–7030 | 29 rooms | $27–$45 | AE, D, MC, V.

Frontier. This is an older motel on the north side of town, but comfortable. Complimentary Continental breakfast. Some refrigerators, cable TV. Pool. Hot tub. Pets allowed. | 3010 N. Main St., at U.S. 70 | 505/622–1400 or 800/678–1401 | fax 505/622–1405 | 38 rooms | $28–$40 | AE, D, DC, MC, V.

Holiday Inn Express Roswell. This three-story hotel has many nice amenities, including larger-than-average rooms and good work tables. Free Continental breakfast. In-room data ports, some microwaves, some refrigerators, cable TV. Pool. Hot tub, sauna. Gym. Laundry facilities, laundry service. | 2300 N. Main St. | 505/627–9900 or 800/465–4329 | fax 505/627–9903 | www.roswell-online.com/holidayinn/ | 80 rooms | $71–$129 | AE, D, DC, MC, V.

Ramada Inn. This is a comfortable, well-maintained chain hotel with large rooms near the golf course. Restaurant, complimentary breakfast. Cable TV. Pool. Business services, airport shuttle. Pets allowed. | 2803 W. 2nd St. | 505/623–9440 | fax 505/622–9708 | www.ramada.com | 61 rooms | $53–$70 | AE, D, DC, MC, V.

Super 8. One mi from the Roswell Mall, this two-story motel has interior hallways and a small lobby with a white-and-green Spanish-style living room suite. The rooms are spacious and simple. Complimentary Continental breakfast. Cable TV. Pool. Hot tub. Laundry facilities. | 3575 N. Main St. | 505/622–8886 or 800/800–8000 | fax 505/622–3627 | www.super8.com | 59 rooms, 4 suites | $49–$56, $77 suites | AE, D, DC, MC, V.

© Corbis

THE CRASH AT ROSWELL

Following a severe storm during the night of July 2, 1947, a local rancher, while checking the next day on possible damage that the storm might have done to his operation, stumbled upon a pile of strange-looking metallic and plasticlike material in a remote pasture near Roswell. He reported his findings to military authorities at nearby Roswell Army Air Field, who soon released information to the public stating that the debris represented the remains of a "flying object." After causing consternation in the national press, the army quickly retracted the statement and took possession of all the strange material. The rancher was held for several days, undergoing intense interrogation, before he was released with the admonition not to discuss his findings with anyone.

The foreign material was taken back to Roswell Field, where it was kept under wraps and studied. In the meantime, government press releases insisted that the debris was simply part of a weather balloon that had gone down in the storm. Rumors soon began to circulate that alien bodies were discovered at the site. Over the years, reports of autopsies of the bodies and strange chemical and physical analysis results of the plasticlike material have surfaced, none of which is acknowledged by official sources. To this day the official government position on the episode is one of denial. As affairs turned out, the "Roswell Incident" was the first in a long line of "Unidentified Flying Object" (UFO) sightings that occurred with alarming regularity in the Western Hemisphere for more than 50 years. No doubt it was the single incident most responsible for starting the vast interest in the United States about UFOs, alien abductions, and life on other planets.

Zuni Motel. Clean and quiet rooms can be had at this family-run motel half a block from the bus station and several restaurants. Cable TV. Pool. | 1201 N. Main St. | 505/622–1930 | fax 505/622–1939 | 35 rooms | $22–$28 | AE, D, DC, MC, V.

RUIDOSO

MAP 9, F7

(Nearby towns also listed: Carrizozo, Lincoln, Mescalero, Roswell)

Nestled in the mountains of south-central New Mexico, Ruidoso offers a pleasant year-round climate. The town is surrounded by the Lincoln National Forest, thereby providing all kinds of outdoor activities, including hiking, camping, and fishing, and skiing in winter. The area is replete with unique arts-and-crafts shops, fine restaurants, and good choices for overnight lodging.

Ruidoso is perhaps best known for its horse-racing track, where the world's richest quarter-horse race is held at the end of each summer, with a purse of $2½ million. Ruidoso Downs is also considered a separate town.

You might also want to use Ruidoso as a jumping-off point for exploring such nearby towns and attractions as Alamogordo, the Mescalero Apache Reservation, Cloudcroft, Tularosa, Capitan, or Lincoln, which is in the heart of Billy the Kid country.

Information: Ruidoso Valley Chamber of Commerce | Box 698, Ruidoso, 88355 | 800/253–2255 or 505/257–7395 | www.ruidoso.net.

RUIDOSO

INTRO
ATTRACTIONS
DINING
LODGING

Attractions

Billy the Kid National Scenic Byway Visitor Center. This is the headquarters for information about Lincoln County, Billy the Kid, and the Scenic Byway. It is adjacent to the Hubbard Museum of the American West. | Hwy. 70 E, Ruidoso Downs | 505/378–5318 | www.byways.org | Free | Memorial Day–Labor Day, daily 9–5:30; Labor Day–Memorial Day, daily 10–5.

Hubbard Museum of the American West. This modern museum at Ruidoso Downs celebrates the heritage of the horse and contains 10,000 horse-related artifacts, as well as exhibits documenting the history of the American West, with a focus on culture, people, and technology. A special feature is one of the world's largest equine sculptures, 255 ft long, by local artist Dave McGary. | 841 U.S. 70 W, Ruidoso Downs | 505/378–4142 or 800/263–5929 | $6 | Labor Day–Memorial Day, daily 10–5.

Lincoln National Forest, Smokey Bear Ranger District. The Smokey Bear Ranger District Headquarters in Ruidoso manages approximately 375,000 acres of the more than 1 million acres of pristine Lincoln National Forest. Semi-desert plants, piñon pine, and juniper mingle with high-elevation grasses and flowering plants for a spectacular four-season display of colors. The forest covers four New Mexico counties and is popular for hiking, camping, and fishing. There are many access points around town. | Ruidoso Headquarters: 901 Mecham Dr. | 505/257–4095 | Free | Daily.

Ruidoso Downs Racetrack and Casino. Each Labor Day, this historic quarter-horse track holds one of the richest races in the world, for $2½ million. The races run from afternoon to early evening, wrapping up by 7 most nights. | 1461 U.S. 70 W, Ruidoso Downs | 505/378–4431 | www.ruidownsracing.com | Open seating free, reserved seating $2.50–$8.50, parking $3–$5 | Mid-May–Labor Day, Fri.–Sun., Thurs.–Fri. 3:30–end of last race, Sat.–Sun. 1:30–end of last race.

Billy the Kid Casino. This large casino, which opened in 1999, also features simulcast horse racing from around the country. | U.S. 70, Ruidoso Downs | 505/378–4431 | Free | Sun.–Thurs. 11–11, Fri.–Sat. noon–12.

Ski Apache Resort. Located 16 mi northwest of Ruidoso in Lincoln National Forest, this is one of the southern Rockies' best ski areas, and is home of New Mexico's only four-passenger gondola. Looking out from the top of 12,000-ft Sierra Blanca Peak gives you a breathtaking 360° view. You'll find 55 trails on 750 acres with skiing for all skill levels. There are no overnight accommodations at the resort. | Hwy. 532 (Ski Run Rd.) | 505/257–9001 or 505/336–4356 | www.skiapache.com | Late Nov.–Mar.

Smokey Bear Historical State Park. Dedicated to Smokey the Bear, the real bear cub who grew up to become a mascot of the National Forest Service after he was saved from a forest fire near Capitan, this park 22 mi north of Ruidoso in Capitan features a picnic area and a museum documenting the life and times of Smokey, whose grave is nearby and can be visited. Smokey lived out his life in the National Zoo in Washington, DC, and died in 1976. | 118 Smokey Bear Blvd., Capitan | 505/354–2748, 505/354–2298 (museum) | www.emnrd.state.nm.us/forestry/smokey.htm | $1 | Daily 9–5.

ON THE CALENDAR

MAY–SEPT.: *Horse racing.* The season at Ruidoso Downs. | 505/378–4431.

JULY: *Arts Festival.* Fine paintings from contemporary artists, pottery, arts and crafts, and photographs are highlighted at this festival of the arts at the Ruidoso Convention Center. | 505/257–7395 or 800/253–2255.

JULY: *Smokey Bear Stampede.* Smokey is honored annually with a parade, dancing, and a barbecue in Capitan. | 505/354–2748.

OCT.: *Aspenfest.* An antique car show, the official state chile cook-off, and arts-and-crafts exhibits are featured at this festival. | 505/257–7395 or 800/253–2255.

OCT.: *Ruidoso Oktoberfest.* The second-largest Oktoberfest celebration in New Mexico. Enjoy German food, beer, wine, dancing, arts and crafts, live entertainment, games, and kids' activities at the Ruidoso Convention Center. | 505/257–6171 or 877/877–9322.

Dining

Cattle Baron Steak and Seafood. Steak. Part of the regional chain, this local favorite serves up steak and seafood. Known for delicious prime rib and a mammoth fresh salad bar. | 657 Sudderth Dr. | 505/257–9355 | $10–$25 | AE, D, DC, MC, V.

La Lorraine. French. The French Colonial interior with flower arrangements and chandeliers set the perfect mood for traditional French cuisine—châteaubriand, beef bourguignon, sausage-stuffed quail, and the like. Select your favorite wine from a comprehensive list. | 2523 Sudderth Dr. | 505/257–2954 | Closed Sun. | $13–$29 | AE, MC, V.

Lincoln County Grill. American/Casual. The locals come here for quick service and good, inexpensive food. Step up to the counter to order hearty Texas chile, old-fashioned hamburgers, or chicken-fried steak. At breakfast you can grab eggs served with fluffy, homemade "Lincoln County" biscuits. Vinyl-covered tables are decorated with old coffee, tea, and tobacco tin images. | 2717 Sudderth Dr. | 505/257–7669 | fax 505/630–8012 | Breakfast also available | $4–$10 | AE, D, MC, V.

Pub 48. American/Casual. This happening place for hip families was opened by the Sierra Blanca Brewing Company in early 1999. An adobe brick fireplace, wood ceiling, and a play station for kids help create a cozy, mountain-cabin feel. Try some of their excellent microbrews, such as the nut-brown ale, while sampling pizzas or barbecued brisket. | 441 Mechem Dr. | 505/257–9559 | Reservations not accepted | Closed Tues. | $6–$11 | AE, D, MC, V.

Victoria's Romantic Hideaway. Italian. Reserve a table for the entire evening at this intimate place, which accommodates only 14 people, and is geared towards couples. Each diner is served a seven-course meal from a set menu. Known for traditional Sicilian cuisine. Beer and wine only. | 2117 Sudderth Dr. | 505/257–5440 | Reservations essential | $75 prix fixe | MC, V.

Lodging

Best Western Swiss Chalet Inn. This charming, simple resort hotel in the mountains 3 mi north of Ruidoso, with sweeping forest views, looks like a Swiss chalet. It's a 16-minute drive from Ski Apache slopes. The on-premises restaurant serves German and American food. Restaurant, bar, complimentary breakfast, room service. Cable TV, some in-room VCRs (and movies). Pool. Hot tub, sauna. Laundry facilities. Business services. Some pets allowed. | 1451 Mechem Dr. | 505/258–3333 or 800/477–9477 | fax 505/258–5325 | www.ruidoso.net/swiss-chalet | 82 rooms | $68–$150 | AE, D, DC, MC, V.

Days Inn Ruidoso Downs. This standard, contemporary motel with basic rooms is next to the Sierra Blanca Mountain foothills and ½ mi from the Ruidoso Downs Racetrack in Ruidoso Downs, just south of the town of Ruidoso. Restaurant, complimentary Continental breakfast. Some in-room hot tubs, cable TV. Pool. Laundry service. | 2088 Hwy. 70 W, Ruidoso Downs | 505/378–4299 or 800/329–7466 | fax 505/378–4299 | www.daysinn.com | 46 rooms, 4 suites | $46–$120, $160 suites | AE, D, DC, MC, V.

Enchantment Inn. Rooms and suites are spacious in this clean, pleasant motel. Restaurant, bar, picnic area, room service. Some kitchenettes, cable TV. Pool. Hot tub. Gym. Laundry facilities. Business services. | 307 U.S. 70 W | 505/378–4051 or 800/435–0280 | fax 505/378–5427 | magical@lookingglass.net | 40 rooms, 40 suites | $65–$89, $99–$195 suites | AE, D, MC, V.

High Country Lodge. Tucked beside a quiet mountain lake 5 mi north of Ruidoso, this mountain resort features large two-bedroom cabins, all with fully equipped kitchens and front porches, some with fireplaces. Picnic area. No air-conditioning, kitchenettes, cable TV. Pool. Hot tub, sauna. Tennis. Video games. Playground. Business services. Pets allowed (fee). | Hwy. 48, Alto | 505/336–4321 or 800/845–7265 | www.ruidoso.net/hcl | 32 two-bedroom cabins | $119 cabins | AE, D, DC, MC, V.

Innsbruck Lodge. This motel in Ruidoso, across from the city park, offers somewhat small, basic rooms with no frills. No air-conditioning in some rooms, cable TV. Business services. | 601 Sudderth Dr. | 505/257–4071 or 800/680–4447 | fax 505/257–7536 | www.ruidosonm.com/innsbruck | 47 rooms (17 with shower only) | $29–$85 | AE, D, DC, MC, V.

Park Place Bed and Breakfast. Guests at this cozy lodge have access to a variety of recreational activities such as fishing along the nearby Rio Ruidoso. One of the three rooms has its own marble-and-gold hot tub. Ask for your free passes to some local museums. Complimentary breakfast. Some in-room hot tubs, cable TV. Hot tub. Tennis court. No smoking. | 137 Reese Dr. | 505/257–4638 or 800/687–9050 | fax 505/630–0127 | www.ruidoso.net/parkplace | 3 rooms | $85–$125 | MC, V.

Ruidoso Lodge Cabins. In the heart of a gorgeous, tree-filled canyon, there is a placid retreat of 1920s knotty-pine cabins. The immaculate cabins have hot tubs, and some have fireplaces and decks with gas grills. Bring your own gear and go trout fishing along the Rio Ruidoso. Kitchenettes. | 300 Main St. | 505/257–2510 or 800/950–2510 | 10 cabins | $89–$160 | D, MC, V.

Shadow Mountain Lodge. In Upper Canyon, this is a couples-oriented resort hotel. Views of the forest are lovely, and fieldstone fireplaces in all the rooms add to the romantic feeling. Some rooms have full kitchens. Some kitchenettes, microwaves, refrigerators, cable TV. Hot tub. Business services. No kids under 15. | 107 Main St. | 505/257–4886 or 800/441–4331 | fax 505/257–2000 | www.smlruidoso.com | 19 suites | $67–$97 | AE, D, DC, MC, V.

Super 8. This budget motel at the junction of U.S. 70 and Highway 48 offers basic, comfortable rooms. Picnic area. In-room data ports, in-room safes, cable TV, some in-room VCRs (and movies). Hot tub, sauna. Laundry facilities, laundry service. Business services. | 100 Cliff Dr. | 505/378–8180 | fax 505/378–8180 | www.super8.com | 63 rooms | $47–$86 | AE, D, DC, MC, V.

Village Lodge. Nestled among tall pines, this small, all-suite lodge offers nice rooms at moderate prices. Kitchenettes, microwaves, refrigerators, cable TV. Hot tub. Business services. |1000 Mechem Dr. | 505/258–5442 or 800/722–8779 | fax 505/258–3127 | 25 suites | $79–$109 | AE, D, MC, V.

West Winds Lodge and Condominiums. This property east of Route 48 offers single rooms for a short stay or condominiums with up to three bedrooms for a longer stay. No air-conditioning, no room phones, cable TV. Pool. Hot tub. | 208 Eagle Dr. | 505/257–4031 or 800/421–0691 | www.wwlodge.com | 21 rooms, 15 condos | $30–$69 rooms, $75–$225 condos | D, MC, V.

SANTA FE

MAP 9, E4

(Nearby towns also listed: Cerrillos, Española, Los Alamos)

Santa Fe justifiably claims to be the second-largest art center and one of the top three tourist destinations in the United States. Founded around 1610 on the site of a deserted pueblo, the city is the oldest state capital in the country. With 300 days of sunshine, a terrific average humidity of only 40% or less, and temperatures that average between 41 and 91°F, it's no wonder that visitors flock to the town in droves all seasons.

La Villa Real de la Santa Fe de San Francisco de Asís was founded by Don Pedro de Peralta, who planted his banner in Spain's name. By 1680, the pueblos in the region rose up in revolt of the Spanish rulers, burning churches and killing hundreds of Spaniards. After an extended siege, the Spanish in Santa Fe were driven out of New Mexico, but the city was recaptured 12 years later by General Don Diego de Vargas with a new army. Once New Mexican territory was safely under Spanish control again, settlers poured in, first over the grand Camino Real from Mexico City to Santa Fe, later from the eastern United States over the Santa Fe Trail. When the Atchison, Topeka, and Santa Fe Railroad arrived in 1880, so did the city. Only later did the artists (and tourists) arrive.

By 1900 Santa Fe had begun to cultivate a reputation among artists, who easily fell in love with the city's cultural diversity, history, and beautiful colors and light. One could hear talk of the "Santa Fe style" as early as 1916. By the 1920s, dozens of prominent painters and other artists had made Santa Fe their home, including Georgia O'Keeffe, who settled in nearby Abiquiu. At that time, one of the draws was that Santa Fe was such an inexpensive place to live and work. How times change.

Today Santa Fe offers some of the finest (and most expensive) hotels, restaurants, museums, and shops found anywhere. More than 6,000 hotel, motel, and bed-and-breakfast rooms are available to weary travelers, while 225 restaurants await to please their palates. Add to these figures a total of 13 world-class museums, 250 art galleries, and 70 fine-jewelry shops, and you've got yourself a substantial destination. Easily accessible by air or car, the city is conveniently situated on Interstate 25, the north–south interstate highway that runs from Las Cruces, near the Mexican border, to Buffalo, Wyoming, almost the Montana state line.

Information: **Santa Fe Chamber of Commerce** | Box 1928, Santa Fe, 87504 | 505/983–7317 | fax 505/984–2205 | www.santafechamber.com.

Santa Fe Convention and Visitors Bureau. | Box 909, Santa Fe, 87504–0909 | 505/984–6760 or 800/777–CITY | fax 505/984–6679 | www.santafe. org.

NEIGHBORHOODS

Santa Fe Plaza. Like many Spanish cities, Santa Fe grew up around a plaza, which is the heart of its downtown and most of its most historic sights. Bounded on three sides (north, east, and south) by the horseshoe-shape Paseo de Peralta and on the west by Guadalupe, the downtown area straddles the Santa Fe River. The state capitol and official buildings are mostly on the south side of the river; the sights of most interest to visitors, such as the Palace of the Governors and Museum of Fine Arts, as well as the plaza itself, are on the north. This is an area of narrow streets, best negotiated on foot.

Canyon Road. Stretching off to the east from Paseo de Peralta, on the south side of the Santa Fe River, narrow Canyon Road is lined with some of the city's best art galleries, shops, and restaurants. It's often called the "art and soul of Santa Fe." Many of these galleries and shops are in authentic, historic adobe structures. This street is also best negotiated on foot.

Old Santa Fe Trail. Following the original route of the trail, this street begins at the Plaza. In its "lower" sections, you'll find many of Santa Fe's most historic buildings, including the state capitol. Along the "upper" (uphill) sections, you'll find some of the major museums that are not in the older part of the city, including the Wheelwright Museum, the Santa Fe Children's Museum, and the Museum of International Folk Art. Since you'll still be downtown, the lower stretches of Old Santa Fe Trail are best negotiated on foot, but you'll need a car to get out to the other museums.

Historic Guadalupe Railroad District. This warehouse district, where the old Santa Fe Railroad Depot is located, is now home to artists' studios, shops, bookstores, and restaurants. And the parking lot of the depot itself is turned into a colorful Farmer's Market on Saturday mornings in summer.

Cerrillos Road. Certainly not one of the more quaint strips in Santa Fe, Cerrillos Road (also U.S. 85) veers off to the southwest from Guadalupe Street to the Villa Linda Mall, the city's southern boundary. This is home to many of the cheaper hotels and motels in Santa Fe.

TRANSPORTATION

Airports: Santa Fe Municipal Airport on Airport Road (505/995–4708) is served by United Express to and from Denver and also accommodates small private, corporate, and charter planes. **Albuquerque International Sunport** (505/842–4366) is an hour's drive and is served by most major airlines.

   Airport Transportation: Shuttle buses (505/982–4311) are available for the trip to and from Albuquerque. The **Lamy Shuttle** (505/982–8829) provides shuttle service to and from selected Santa Fe hotels.

Train: Amtrak's "Southwest Chief" makes daily stops in Lamy, 18 mi south of Santa Fe, but does not enter Santa Fe itself. The **Santa Fe Southern Railway** | 410 S. Guadalupe St. (505/989–8600 or 888/989–8600) connects outbound only with Amtrak at Lamy.

Bus Lines: Greyhound and **TNM&O** buses stop at the Santa Fe Bus Station (858 St. Michael's Dr. | 505/471–0008).

Intra-city Transit: Ponyman Pedal-cabs (505/440–9309) are available for short rides about town from the Plaza. **Bear Creek Adventures** (505/757–6229) offers trail rides, chuck-wagon dinners, and special-event carriage services. **Santa Fe Trails** (505/438–1464 | fax 505/438–1470) runs on 11 intercity routes; schedules are available from most downtown hotels.

Driving and Parking: Two major highways pass through Santa Fe. Interstate 25 cuts east–west through the southern part of the city. U.S. 85/U.S. 285, which is also called St. Francis Drive, cuts through Santa Fe going north–south. Cerrillos Road was once the main highway going to Albuquerque; it's now a motel strip. The main street through the city's historic plaza section is Paseo de Peralta, which is horseshoe shaped, heading back toward St. Francis at both ends. Traffic is heavier than it once was, and it is advisable to park your car whenever possible and take public transportation or a taxi, or simply to walk since most of the restaurants, museums, galleries, and sights in the downtown area are within walking distance of the Plaza.

Because of the scarcity of parking spaces and narrow streets, not to mention the compact size of the most interesting part of the city, walking is by far the best way to get around the Plaza area.

Street parking is difficult to find, particularly in summer months. Your best bet is to park in one of the lots downtown, on West San Francisco, between Sandoval and Galisteo, or on Water Street, between Don Gaspar and Shelby streets. If you are visiting the Canyon Road galleries and need a place to park, there is a pay lot in the 800 block of Canyon Road, across from El Farol. The Santa Fe Convention and Visitors Bureau publishes a guide to parking (both lots and street parking).

Attractions

ART AND ARCHITECTURE

El Rancho de las Golondrinas. This site in La Cienega, 15 mi south of Santa Fe, is an attractively executed reconstruction of an early Spanish rancho. Sheep, goats, chickens, cows, and other domestic animals roam the barnyard much as they did hundreds of years ago. There is also a living history museum on the premises. You take a self-guided tour. | 334 Los Pinos Rd., La Cienega | 505/471–2261 | www.golondrinas.org | $5–$7 | June–Sept., Wed.–Sun. 10–4.

La Fonda. A *fonda* (inn) has stood on this site facing the southeast corner of the Plaza since 1610, though the current structure dates to 1922. Architect Isaac Hamilton Rapp, whose Rio Grande–Pueblo Revival structures put Santa Fe style on the map, was the original architect; it was remodeled in 1926 by another luminary of Santa Fe architecture, John Gaw Meem. Because of its proximity to the Plaza, La Fonda has been a gathering place for such historical luminaries as Errol Flynn, John F. Kennedy, and even Kit Carson. It is appropriately referred to as "The Inn at the End of the Trail." Even if you are not staying here, you will not be the only tourist milling about the lobby and grounds. | 100 E. San Francisco St. | 505/982–5511 or 800/523–5002 | fax 505/988–2952 | www.lafondasantafe.com | Free | Daily.

New Mexico State Capitol. Sometimes called the Roundhouse, New Mexico's capitol building is built in the shape of a Zia sun symbol. Artwork by regional artists adorns the lobby. | Paseo de Peralta and Old Santa Fe Trail | 505/986–4589 | Free | Weekdays 8–5.

United States Court House. This building, a fine example of unaltered Greek Revival architecture at the mouth of Lincoln Street, took 36 years to build and was completed in 1889. A monument to mountain man Kit Carson graces the front entrance. | S. Federal Plaza | Free | Weekdays 8–4:30.

BEACHES, PARKS, AND NATURAL SIGHTS

Hyde Memorial State Park. Camping and picnicking under majestic aspen and pine trees are just a few of the amenities offered at Hyde Memorial State Park. Go backpacking, or in winter make the park a jumping-off point if you wish to hike to the Santa Fe Ski Basin. A full-service restaurant is on the premises. The park is 12 mi northeast of Santa Fe via Hyde Park Road and Route 475. | 740 Hyde Park Rd. | 505/983–7175 | www.emnrd.state.nm.us/nmparks | $4 per vehicle | Daily.

Santa Fe National Forest. The huge Santa Fe National Forest, along with its neighbor, Carson National Forest (which is headquartered in nearby Taos), extend for miles on all sides of Santa Fe. In practically any direction you drive out of town, you're bound to enter one part of the forests or another. Superb hiking, fishing, backpacking, horseback riding, and sightseeing are available in both forests. If you are unfamiliar with the region, contact forest headquarters in Santa Fe before you plan a trip. | 1474 Rodeo Rd. | 505/438–7840 or 505/438–7840 | www.fs.fed.us/r3/sfe | Free | Daily.

Pecos Wilderness. In the heart of the Santa Fe National Forest, this was one of the country's first wilderness areas. Stop by the U.S Forest Service office for camping information. It is administered jointly by the Santa Fe National Forest and the Carson National Forest. | Hwy. 63 | 505/757–6121 | Free; camping fees vary | Daily.

Santa Fe Ski Area. The high desert's sunny days and deep powder (about 250 inches per year) delight skiers. One of the highest ski areas in the United States at a little more than 12,000 ft, it offers 500 skiable acres with a vertical drop of 1,650 ft. You'll find more than 40 trails with sections for all skill levels. It's 16 mi northeast of Santa Fe. | Hwy. 475 | 505/982–4429 information, 800/776–7669 accommodations | www.skisantafe.com | Late Nov.–early Apr.

CULTURE, EDUCATION, AND HISTORY

College of Santa Fe. The college, 3 mi southwest of Santa Fe Plaza, was founded in 1874 as a traditional liberals arts institution affiliated with the Catholic Church, focusing on the arts, business, and education. Its library, including the Southwest Collection, contains more than 100,000 volumes. | 1600 St. Michael's Dr., at Cerrillos Rd. | 505/473–6011 or 800/456–2673 | www.csf.edu | Free | Daily.

Glorieta Battlefield. In the Civil War battle that has been called the Gettysburg of the West, Colorado volunteers forever dashed Southern hopes of a Confederate New Mexico. Route 50, the road reached by exiting Interstate 25 at the Glorieta exit, goes to the town of Pecos, about 16 mi southeast of Santa Fe. The drive from the interstate to Pecos traverses the battlefield. There is no formal signage. | Off I–25, Glorieta exit | No phone | Free.

Pecos National Historical Park. On land donated by actress Greer Garson, 2 mi south of Pecos and 26 mi southeast of Santa Fe, this park presents the fascinating story of one of the largest prehistoric pueblos in the Southwest. The facility features an interesting walking tour, visitor center, bookstore, and museum. | Hwy. 63 (I–25, exit 299), Pecos | 505/757–6414 | $4 per vehicle | Memorial Day–Labor Day, daily 8–6; Labor Day–Memorial Day, daily 8–5.

San Ildefonso Pueblo. The name of this Tewa village, about 25 mi northwest of Santa Fe and 6 mi west of Pojoaque, means "where the water cuts down through." The black-on-black pottery that is made here is legendary and is best represented by the work of the late Maria Martinez, whose pots today command thousands of dollars each. Visitors are welcome, but you must register at the visitor center and follow tribal regulations. | Hwy. 502 | 505/455–2273 | $3 | Visitor center daily 8–5.

Santa Fe Opera. One of the most renowned opera companies in the United States, founded in 1956, performs each summer in Santa Fe, in a beautiful, modern open-air amphitheater 7 mi north of Santa Fe. The views of the city are tremendous. The repertory includes old favorites as well as new and neglected works. Book tickets far in advance unless you don't mind standing. | U.S. 84/U.S. 285 | 505/986–5955 or 800/280–4654 | www.santafeopera.org | Tickets $20–$128, standing room $8–$10 | Late June–late Aug.

St. John's College in Santa Fe. An adjunct campus to St. John's College of Annapolis, Maryland, just east of Camino del Monte Sol, the Santa Fe branch hosts St. John's summer classics program during July and August, featuring discussions on great books, opera, Shakespeare, T. S. Eliot, medieval art, and cowboy classics, among many other topics. | 1160 Camino Cruz Blanca | 505/984–6104 | Free | Daily.

MUSEUMS

Georgia O'Keeffe Museum. One of many painters who moved to Santa Fe in the early part of the 20th century, Georgia O'Keeffe settled near Santa Fe and focused some of her most famous paintings on southwestern themes. This private museum devoted to her art opened in 1997 and contains 120 of her works. O'Keeffe's favorite foods are for sale in the café. | 217 Johnson St. | 505/995–0785 | www.okeeffemuseum.org | $5 | Nov.–July, Mon., Tues., Thurs., Sat. 10–5, Fri. 10–8; Aug.–Oct., also open Wed. noon–8.

Museum of Fine Arts. Santa Fe's oldest art museum opened in 1917 and contains one of the finest regional collections in the United States, displaying the work of many early New Mexico artists who settled and worked around Santa Fe and Taos, as well as excellent examples of Spanish Colonial furniture. The building itself is a Pueblo Revival structure inspired by Acoma Pueblo. A combined ticket will grant admission for four days to the four State of New Mexico museums in Santa Fe, of which this is one. | 107 W. Palace Ave. | 505/476–5072 | www.nmculture.org | $5 single admission, $10 4-day pass to all 4 state museums in Santa Fe | Tues.–Sun. 10–5.

Museum of Indian Arts and Culture. Contemporary and traditional artifacts are on display at this institution, which also features a multimedia exhibition telling the story of Native American history in the Southwest. A neighboring, noncirculating library is open to the public. A combined ticket will grant admission for four days to the four State of New Mexico museums in Santa Fe, of which this is one. | 710 Camino Lejo | 505/827–6344 | www.nmculture.org | $5 single admission, $10 4-day pass to all 4 state museums in Santa Fe | Tues.–Fri. 10–5.

Museum of International Folk Art. This is one of the few museums in the world dedicated to global folk art and the premier institution of its kind. The vast collection of inventive handmade objects contains 125,000 toys, textiles, and handicrafts from around the world; one wing focuses on Spanish Colonial artifacts, including a large collection of *bultos* (carved, wooden saints) and *retablos* (holy images painted on wood or tin). A combined ticket will grant admission for four days to the four State of New Mexico museums in Santa Fe, of which this is one. | 706 Camino Lejo | 505/827–6350 | www.state.nm.us/moifa | $5 single admission, $10 4-day pass to all 4 state museums in Santa Fe | Tues.–Sun. 10–5.

Institute of American Indian Arts Museum. In contrast to those museums specializing in ancient Native American artifacts, this one features contemporary Native American art from a range of cultures, including those from Alaska as well as the Southwest. Inside the handsomely renovated former post office you'll find paintings, photography, sculptures, prints, and other crafts. The Institute itself has opened its own campus 3 mi south of Santa Fe Community College. | 108 Cathedral Pl | 505/983–8900 | www.iaiancad.org | $4 | Daily 9–5.

★ **Palace of the Governors.** This humble-looking one-story adobe structure is the oldest public building in continuous use in the United States. Now, it's the headquarters of the Museum of New Mexico and houses the main section of the State History Museum. Part of the fun in visiting Santa Fe is to walk under the portals of the palace and view all the wonderful handmade jewelry, the work of native New Mexicans, for sale on blankets lining the street. The museum, bookstore, and printing shop on the premises are all must-sees. A combined ticket will grant admission for four days to the four State of New Mexico museums in Santa Fe, of which this is one. | Palace Ave. (north side of the Plaza) | 505/476–5100 | www.nmculture.org | $5 single admission, $10 4-day pass to all 4 state museums in Santa Fe | Tues.–Sun. 10–5.

Santa Fe Children's Museum. If you have children, this is a must-see, with stimulating hands-on exhibits featuring everything from a solar greenhouse to a simulated 18-ft mountain-climbing wall. | 1050 Old Pecos Trail | 505/989–8359 | $3 | Sept.–May, Thurs.–Sat. 10–5, Sun. noon–5; June–Aug., Wed.–Sat 10–5, Sun. noon–5.

Santuario de Guadalupe. This old mission church dedicated to Our Lady of Guadalupe (the patron saint of Mexico), built by Franciscan friars between 1776 and 1795, is now a museum. The architecture is striking, with its altarpiece made in 1783 by Joseph Deehlzidar. | 100 Guadalupe St. | 505/988–2027 | Free | Late Mar.–late Oct., Mon.–Sat. 9–4.

SITE Santa Fe. A popular museum of contemporary art in Santa Fe. There's a biennial exhibition in odd-numbered years and occasional performances and lectures. | 1606 Paseo de Peralta | 505/989–1199 | www.sitesantafe.org | $5, free Fri. | Wed., Thurs., Sat., Sun., 10–5; Fri. 10–7.

Wheelwright Museum of the American Indian. The Wheelwright Museum, built in the octagonal shape of a Navajo hogan (designed by William Penhallow Henderson), opened in 1937 as the "House of Navajo Religion," to house ceremonial materials (many of which have been returned to the Navajo Nation). But as its collection expanded and developed into a full-fledged museum, a large range of traditional Southwest Native American artifacts and handicrafts were put on display and opened to the public. | 704 Camino Lejo | 505/982–4636 | www.wheelwright.org | Free | Mon.–Sat. 10–5, Sun. 1–5.

RELIGION AND SPIRITUALITY

Cathedral of St. Francis. This French Romanesque-style cathedral one block east of the Plaza, completed in 1884, is the tallest building in Santa Fe; local zoning laws prohibit any taller structures. Jean Baptiste Lamy, Santa Fe's first archbishop and the inspiration for Willa Cather's novel *Death Comes for the Archbishop,* is buried in the crypt behind the high altar. Mass is celebrated several times a day here. | 213 Cathedral Pl | 505/982–5619 | Free | Daily.

Cristo Rey Church. This church, the largest adobe structure in the United States, is considered by many the finest example of pueblo-style architecture anywhere. It was completed in 1940 to commemorate the 400th anniversary of Francisco Vásquez de Coronado's exploration of the Southwest. | Canyon Rd and Christo Rey St. | 505/983–8528 | Free | Daily 8–7.

Loretto Chapel. This gothic church is modeled after Saint-Chapelle in Paris. The carpenter who arrived out of nowhere in the late 1800s to build the freestanding spiral staircase in Loretto Chapel has never been identified. A Santa Fe landmark for more than a century, Loretto, which is privately owned and operated, is still used for occasional weddings and other special events. | 207 Old Santa Fe Trail | 505/982–0092 | www.lorettochapel.com | $2.50 | Mon.–Sat. 9:30–4:30, Sun. 10:30–4:30.

★ **San Miguel Mission.** This is probably the oldest church building still in use in the United States. Originally built in 1610, the roof was burned during the Pueblo Revolt of 1680; the church was restored and enlarged in 1710. The mission served as a place of worship for Spanish soldiers and settlers and Native American converts. Mass is held on Sunday only. | 401 Old Santa Fe Trail | 505/983–3974 | $1 | Weekdays 9–4:30.

SHOPPING

Canyon Road. Art galleries and arts and handicraft specialty stores abound on Canyon Road. The best way to see it all is to walk from one end of the road to the other; allow several hours.

Gerald Peters Gallery. Santa Fe's leading gallery moved to this suave, pueblo-style space in 1998. The focus here is on 19th- and 20th-century American and European art, including such luminaries as Georgia O'Keeffe, Charles M. Russell, and Pablo Picasso. | 1011 Paseo de Peralta | 505/954–5700 | www.gpgallery.com | Free | Mon.–Sat. 10–5.

Sena Plaza. This plant- and tree-filled plaza in the heart of downtown, complete with songbirds, has old-world charm and is filled with modern shops and eateries. | Between E. Palace Ave. and Nusbaum St., and between Washington and Otero Sts.

SIGHTSEEING TOURS/TOUR COMPANIES

Aboot About. This 2-hour walking tour covers mostly the architecture and history of the older buildings in downtown Santa Fe. An evening "spook about," which departs from the El Dorado Hotel, tours buildings around the Plaza that have a history of ghosts. Daily tours depart from the El Dorado and St. Francis Hotels; one tour departs from La Posada Hotel on Saturday mornings at 10. | 624 Galisteo St. #32 | 505/988–2774 | $10 | Regular historical tours, daily 9:30 and 1:30; tour from La Posada, Sat. 10AM; ghost walks, Tues., Fri., and Sat. at 5:30 PM.

Afoot in Santa Fe Tours. Santa Fe's oldest walking tour service, based in the Hotel Loretto, takes two hours to visit the most significant landmarks in the downtown area. Tours by tram are also offered by this company daily. | 211 Old Santa Fe Trail | 505/983–3701 | $10 walking tour; $9 trolley tour | Walking tours daily 9:30 AM; trolley tours daily 10–3, leaving hourly.

Gray Line Tours of Santa Fe. In addition to 2½-hour Santa Fe city tours, Gray Line offers full-day excursions to Taos and some surrounding Indian pueblos, 4-hour excursions to Bandelier National Monument and Los Alamos, and an all-day combination that includes Santa

Fe, Bandelier, and Los Alamos. Reservations are advisable. | 1330 Hickox St. | 505/983–9491 | www.grayline.com | $25–$72 | Mon.–Sat.; tour times vary, so call ahead.

Santa Fe Detours. In addition to bus, river, rail, and walking tours, this company fashions rafting and ski packages. Historic plaza walking tours depart from their office daily at 9:30 and 1:30 (reservations are requested); call about various other theme trips and multi-day tours that are offered throughout the year. | 54½ E. San Francisco St. (above Häagen Dazs) | 505/983–6565 or 800/338–6877 | www.sfdetours.com | $10 walking tours; $60–$100 bus tours; $38–$58 rail tours; $40–$100 river rafting tours | Daily 9–5.

Storytellers and the Southwest. Guide Barbara Harrelson has fashioned a tour of Santa Fe that explores the city through its literary history. The two-hour walking tour explores landmarks and historic sites as illuminated by authors who have written about them. Tours are by appointment only, with a minimum of two people; when you make your reservation, Barbara will set up a meeting place. | 505/989–4561 | barbarah@newmexico.com | $15 per person | By appointment only.

OTHER POINTS OF INTEREST

Camel Rock Casino. This convenient Indian casino, operated by the Tesuqe Pueblo Tribe, 10 mi north of Santa Fe has a fine restaurant as well as blackjack, poker, bingo, and lots of slots and video-poker machines for fun. | U.S. 84/U.S. 285 | 800/462–2635 | www.camel-rockcasino.com | Free | Sun.–Wed. 8AM–2AM; Thurs.–Sat., open 24 hours.

National Park Service (Southwest Regional Office). Stop by the Southwest Regional Office to get maps, brochures, and other information about the scores of national park properties throughout New Mexico. | 1100 Old Santa Fe Trail | 505/988–6011 | Free | Weekdays 8–4:30.

Santa Fe Southern Railway. You can take a scenic train ride from Santa Fe to the sleepy town of Lamy on these restored train coaches on a 120-year-old spur line of the famous Atchison, Topeka, and Santa Fe Railroad. After a picnic lunch at the quaint train station in Lamy (bring your own food and drinks, or buy them from the caterer that meets the train), you return to Santa Fe. There are also occasional nighttime dinner and special-events trains. | 410 S. Guadalupe St. | 505/989–8600 or 888/989–8600 | www.sfsr.com | Day trips $25–$40; call for schedules for night and special trips | Apr.–Oct., Tues.–Thurs. and Sat. depart 10:30 and return 3, Mon. and Sun. depart 1 and return 5 (no lunch layover); Nov.–Mar., Tues., Thurs. and Sat. depart 11 and return 3:30, Sun. depart 1 and return 5 (no lunch layover). Closed Wed. and Fri.

ON THE CALENDAR

JAN.: *Buffalo and Comanche Dances.* A traditional pueblo winter fiesta, with dancing at San Ildefonso Pueblo. | 505/455–2273.

MAY: *Fiesta and Green Corn Dance.* Traditional dancing dominates this celebration of spring at San Felipe Pueblo. | 505/867–3381.

MAR.–APR.: *Spring Corn Dances.* An Easter celebration of spring renewal with traditional dancing at Cochiti, San Felipe, Santo Domingo, and other pueblos. | 505/465–2244, 505/867–3382, or 505/465–2214.

JUNE: *St. Anthony's Feast-Green Corn Dance.* Homage to St. Anthony with dances at San Juan Pueblo. | 505/852–4400.

JULY: *Northern Pueblo Artists and Craftsman Show.* Native arts and crafts are displayed and sold on a rotating basis at one of the eight pueblos in the Santa Fe area. | 505/852–4265.

JULY: *Santa Fe Rodeo.* Cowboys and cowgirls from all over the region compete at this well-attended event on the Rodeo Grounds. | 505/471–4300 or 505/473–5885.

JULY: *Spanish Market.* Spanish Colonial–inspired crafts by local artisans are displayed along the Plaza in Santa Fe. | 505/983–4038.

JULY–AUG.: *Santa Fe Chamber Music Festival.* Visiting musicians play chamber music nightly, in the St. Francis Auditorium. | 505/983–2075.

JULY–AUG.: *Santa Fe Opera.* One of America's outstanding opera companies is 7 mi north of Santa Fe. | 505/986–5955 or 505/986–5900.

AUG.: *Fiesta at Santo Domingo Pueblo.* The largest and best known of the Rio Grande Pueblo fiestas is at Santo Domingo Pueblo. | 505/465–2214.

AUG.: *Indian Market.* Tribes from all over the United States are featured in this Native American arts-and-crafts market on the Plaza, the largest such gathering in the world. | 505/983–5220.

AUG.: *Invitational Antique Indian Art Show.* This show of pre-1935 Native American arts and crafts at the Sweeney Center draws visitors from all over America and the world. | 505/984–6760 or 800/777–2489.

SEPT.: *Santa Fe Fiesta.* This event on the Plaza, an ancient folk festival dating back to 1712, celebrates the reconquest of Santa Fe by the Spanish, featuring arts and crafts, street dancing, and food. | 505/984–6760 or 800/777–2489.

SEPT.–MAY: *Santa Fe Pro Musica.* Chamber orchestra and chamber ensemble performs classical and contemporary music. | 505/988–4640.

DEC.: *Christmas Eve Celebrations.* Offering dancing and a *farolito* (little glowing lanterns) display, this celebration takes place in the Santa Fe Plaza as well as some surrounding pueblos. | 505/984–6760 or 800/777–2489.

WALKING TOUR

Downtown Santa Fe Walking Tour (approximately 5 hours)

This tour will take you to the major points of interest in the Plaza section of Santa Fe. It's best done any day but Monday, when the Museum of Fine Arts and the Palace of the Governors are both closed. Given the length, it's best to begin in the morning.

A good place to start your walking tour of Santa Fe is the **Museum of Fine Arts,** located on East Palace Avenue between Lincoln and Sheridan streets. This museum features the works of many of the famous artists who frequented Santa Fe and Taos in the early part of the 20th century. Across Lincoln Street your next stop will be the ancient **Palace of the Governors,** on Palace Avenue, on the north side of the town Plaza. In addition to containing a museum that houses more than 17,000 artifacts, the complex features a wonderful book and gift shop and the famous Press of the Palace of the Governors, where printing is still done on ancient letter presses. Leaving the Palace via its gift and bookstore on Washington Street, proceed east on Palace Avenue, cross Palace at Cathedral Place, and visit the **Institute of American Indian Arts Museum,** which features a wide variety of contemporary arts and crafts gathered from all over the country. Just across Cathedral Place is **Saint Francis Cathedral.** Completed in 1884, the stately church, which took 15 years to complete, has stained-glass windows imported from France. Be sure to visit the sanctuary, which displays a serene European beauty. By the time you've seen everything at these four sites, you should be hungry and about ready to eat lunch.

After lunch, tour the lobby of the world-famous **La Fonda Hotel,** on the southeast corner of the Plaza on East San Francisco Street. There has been a hotel on this spot almost from the time of the founding of Santa Fe in the early 17th century, though this building is not the original. After seeing the La Fonda, visit the jewelry stores, art galleries, and other unique shops that occupy both sides of East and West San Francisco Street and around the Plaza. From La Fonda, walk south on Washington Street one block to East Water Street and turn left. Follow East Water a block to its intersection with the Old Santa Fe Trail. Head south on Old Santa Fe Trail to the **Loretto Chapel.** Inside the chapel, view the famous freestanding staircase. Continue south on the Santa Fe Trail across Alameda Street, the tiny Santa Fe River, and East De Vargas Street, and you come to the oldest church in Santa Fe, the **San Miguel Mission,** dating from 1610. After leaving San Miguel Mission, stroll the few yards south on the Old Santa Fe Trail until you see the **State Capitol** on your right, at the intersection with Paseo de Peralta.

From the Capitol, if you have energy left for shopping, retrace your steps back along the Santa Fe Trail to its intersection with East De Vargas Street at the San Miguel Mission. Turn right into East De Vargas and proceed east until it turns into Canyon Road, on the other side of Paseo de Peralta. Visit the shops, art galleries, and other sites along both sides of Canyon Road.

Dining

INEXPENSIVE

Bert's Burger Bowl. American/Casual. Since the 1950s this tiny hamburger shop has been churning them out. Try the No. 6 (green chile with cheese). You can also get excellent pressure-cooked chicken, carne adovada, crispy fries, and old-fashioned shakes. There are tables outside and a few chairs indoors. | 235 N. Guadalupe St. | 505/982–0215 | $2–$5 | No credit cards.

Blue Corn Cafe. Mexican. This second-floor eatery in the heart of historic downtown may very well be the best restaurant for the money in Santa Fe. Try the tortilla burger or Portobello fajitas. Kids' menu. | 133 Water St. | 505/984–1800 | $7–$13 | AE, D, DC, MC, V.

The Burrito Company. Mexican. This counter-service restaurant is just off the Plaza. Try any of the hand-held burritos. Kids' menu. | 111 Washington Ave. | 505/982–4453 | $4–$8 | No credit cards.

Dave's Not Here. American/Casual. Dave may not be here at this restaurant west of St. Francis Drive, but you will find some of Santa Fe's best burgers, served with heaps of onions, mushrooms, avocado, or cheese. Or try the super made-from-scratch chiles rellenos. For dessert try the slab of deep chocolate cake. | 1115 Hickox St. | 505/983–7060 | Closed Sun. | $6–$7 | No credit cards.

El Comedor. Mexican. On the road connecting Interstate 25 with historic downtown, this place is known for its blue corn enchiladas. Open-air dining on a patio with a kiva fireplace. Kids' menu. Beer and wine only. | 727 Cerrillos Rd. | 505/989–7575 | $6–$12 | AE, D, DC, MC, V.

Garduño's. Mexican. A plant-filled outdoor patio overlooks downtown Santa Fe and the Plaza at this popular second-floor restaurant serving basic dishes like enchiladas, fajitas, and burritos. Brightly painted booths, colorful tiles, blankets, and pottery, contribute to a festive atmosphere. Entertainment weekends. Kids' menu. | 130 Lincoln Ave. | 505/983–9797 | www.gardunosrestaurant.com/Santa_fe/index.html | $7–$14 | AE, D, DC, MC, V.

La Choza. Southwestern. Blue corn enchiladas and *carne adobada* (marinated pork or chicken) are popular at this restaurant. Enjoy your meal indoors or on one of the two outdoor patios. | 905 Alarid | 505/982–0909 | Closed Sun. | $7–$9 | AE, D, MC, V.

Little Anita's. Mexican. Although not much to look at, this small restaurant on Santa Fe's main hotel and fast food strip serves homemade, authentic Mexican food for great prices. Try the fresh guacamole and flautas, or a large serving of sizzling fajitas. Kids' menu. Beer and wine only. | 2811 Cerrillos Rd. | 505/473–4505 | $6–$12 | AE, D, MC, V.

★ **Plaza Café.** American/Casual. At this diner, the oldest operating restaurant in Santa Fe, in business since 1918, walls are hung with vintage photos, and an eclectic American diner menu is offered—everything from spicy pasta to blue corn enchiladas to New Mexico meat loaf. Kids' menu. Beer and wine only. | 54 Lincoln Ave. | 505/982–1664 | Reservations not accepted | $6–$13 | AE, D, MC, V.

The Shed. Southwestern. A quaint, intimate restaurant in the oldest part of town (the adobe building itself dates to 1692). Known for green-chile chicken enchiladas and *pollo adobo,* a chicken and chile stew. Open-air dining on a small, colonial-style courtyard with trees and plants. No smoking. | 113½ E. Palace Ave. | 505/982–9030 | Closed Sun. No dinner Mon., Tues. | $7–$14 | AE, D, DC, MC, V.

Tomasita's. Southwestern. This casual, family-friendly restaurant near the train station is hugely popular and accepts no reservations, so even at odd hours you might still wait. Try the chiles rellenos or burritos, but be warned: this traditional New Mexican food is hot. Kids' menu. | 500 S. Guadalupe | 505/983–5721 | Reservations not accepted | Closed Sun. | $5–$11 | MC, V.

Whistling Moon Café. Mediterranean. The menu at this cozy and friendly café includes Greek- and Middle Eastern–inspired favorites such as cumin-dusted french fries, Greek salad, pasta calamari, and Greek honey cheesecake. Beer and wine only. | 402 N. Guadalupe St. | 505/983–3093 | Reservations essential for 6 or more | $7–$12 | D, DC, MC, V.

MODERATE

Andiamo! Italian. This intimate restaurant serves Northern Italian cuisine made from the freshest ingredients available. Try crispy polenta with rosemary and Gorgonzola sauce, any pizza, or linguine putanesca with grilled tuna. Open-air dining. Beer and wine only. No smoking. | 322 Garfield | 505/995–9595 | No lunch | $11–$18 | AE, D, MC, V.

Celebrations. Contemporary. You'll find American bistro dishes like roasted rack of lamb with braised leeks and mashed potatoes, or beef tenderloin with a cabernet sauce at this popular restaurant with a plant-filled patio in back. Sun. brunch. | 613 Canyon Rd. | 505/989–8904 | $8–$18 | D, MC, V.

Chow's Contemporary Chinese Food. Chinese. A simple place with cheerful service, the food here stands out. Try the dragon sesame chicken or the green beans with chicken, beef, or shrimp. Beer and wine only. | 720 St. Michaels Dr. | 505/471–7120 | Closed Sun. | $3–$16 | MC, V.

Corn Dance Cafe. Contemporary. The menu at this restaurant in the Hotel Santa Fe marries contemporary cooking techniques to traditional Native American ingredients, such as buffalo. Try the little big pie, toasted Indian bread with your choice of shrimp, buffalo, or goat cheese; other specialties include penne with quail, and an American bison tenderloin. An open-air enclosed patio with plants and umbrella-clad tables is perfect for summer dining. No smoking. | 1501 Paseo de Peralta | 505/982–1200 | Closed Sun.–Mon. | $7–$22 | AE, D, DC, MC, V.

Cowgirl Hall of Fame. Southwestern. This loud, fun place serves Texas-style brisket and barbecue and good New Mexican fare, including tasty chiles rellenos, grilled-salmon soft tacos, and butternut-squash casserole. In summer you can dine on tree-shaded patios and kids can eat in the Corral, a special area with its own menu. Entertainment nightly. | 319 S. Guadalupe St. | 505/982–2565 | $10–$16 | AE, D, MC, V.

Coyote Cafe Rooftop Cantina. Latin American. In summer, locals love to gather at the Coyote Cafe's Rooftop Cantina, where lively and delicious Cuban and Mexican dishes are offered for much less starstruck prices. | 132 W. Water St. (upstairs) | 505/983–1615 | $10–$15 | AE, D, DC, MC, V.

Gabriel's. Southwestern. Try the margaritas and guacamole, which is made at your table, at this pleasant restaurant 11 mi northwest of Santa Fe. From the patio, you have great views of the Sangre de Cristo Mountains. Kids' menu. | U.S. 285 | 505/455–7000 | $7–$16 | AE, D, DC, MC, V.

Grant Corner Inn. Continental. The antique-filled dining room in this 19th-century mansion, now serving as an inn, offers well-prepared breakfasts in an elegant setting. A rotating menu offers a choice between savory and sweet, often including choices like huevos rancheros, cinnamon raisin French toast, and omelets. A private outdoor patio is surrounded by willow trees and flowers. Guitarist Sun. | 122 Grant Ave. | 505/983–6678 | No lunch or dinner. Sunday brunch | $9–$16 | AE, MC, V.

Il Piatto. Italian. This restaurant, from the owners of Bistro 315, is decorated with paintings by regional artists. Known for creative pasta dishes, such as their signature dish, pumpkin ravioli with brown sage butter. | 95 W. Marcy | 505/984–1091 | $7–$15 | AE, MC, V.

India Palace. Indian. The deep pink interior of this elegant Indian restaurant is a lovely setting for such favorites as tender tandoori chicken and superb curried seafood; vegetarian dishes are also served. Dine on the patio, which has a fountain. Lunch buffet. Beer and wine only. | 227 Don Gaspar | 505/986–5859 | $7–$25 | AE, D, DC, MC, V.

Los Mayas. Latin. This restaurant, which opened in a nondescript building 1998, is a casual, cozy space with a patio for very large parties. The menu offers a taste of the Americas; try the enchilada banana, a baked plantain served with *mole* (a sweet and savory sauce of blended chiles, nuts, and chocolate). Entertainment nightly. | 409 W. Water St. | 505/986–9930 | $11–$16 | AE, D, MC, V.

Mañana Restaurant and Bar. Southwestern Continental. This tasteful restaurant off the Plaza caters mostly to tourists and offers a wide variety of steaks, salads, and seafood dishes. A shaded patio in back is quiet and prive. Pianist nightly. Kids' menu. | 234 Don Gaspar Ave. | 505/982–4333 | $7–$20 | AE, D, DC, MC, V.

Maria's New Mexican Kitchen. Southwestern. The dining room here is hung with original art, but diners arrive to eat basic New Mexican favorites like chiles rellenos, enchiladas, and carne adovada. The margaritas are great, and the bar pours 80 different kinds of tequila. Open-air dining on patio. Kids' menu. | 555 W. Cordova Rd. | 505/983–7929 | $7–$17 | AE, D, DC, MC, V.

Old Mexico Grill. Mexican. In a shopping center with delightfully ample parking, sample serious Mexican cuisine, such as stuffed chicken breast filled with cheese, tomatoes, and chiles, or *arracheras* (the traditional name of fajitas). | 2434 Cerrillos Rd. | 505/473–0338 | $10–$18 | D, MC, V.

Osteria D'Assisi. Italian. This cozy Italian restaurant with wood and tile floors and stucco walls offers personal service and great food for reasonable prices. Try the ravioli with wild mushrooms in cream sauce, ricotta- and spinach-stuffed eggplant, or veal scallopine. Open-air dining on a terrace with trees. Beer and wine only. No smoking. | 58 S. Federal Plaza | 505/986–5858 | Closed Sun. | $6–$16 | AE, D, DC, MC, V.

Paul's. Contemporary. Wooden lizards and snakes roam these peach-painted walls, but locals keep coming back for the serious American food at reasonable prices. Try the baked salmon with sorrel. Beer and wine only. No smoking. | 72 W. Marcy St. | 505/982–8738 | $6–$20 | AE, D, DC, MC, V.

Pranzo Italian Grill. Italian. This rail-yard district mainstay is known for northern Italian pastas with a touch of cream. Also try the osso buco. If the weather is nice, you can dine on a semi-covered terrace with a view of Santa Fe spread out below. | 540 Montezuma Ave. | 505/984–2645 | No lunch Sun. | $6–$20 | AE, D, DC, MC, V.

Zia Diner. American. This upscale diner in the rail-yard district offers a menu that keeps everyone well covered. Try one of their weeknight blue-plate specials, like Friday night's Pescado Vera Cruz, or just enjoy a thick slice of strawberry-rhubarb pie or an appetizer. Service is fast and friendly, and the food is fresh and more imaginative that most diner fare. Patio dining is also available. | 326 S. Guadalupe St., 87501 | 505/988–7008 | fax 505/820–7677 | $9–$19 | AE, MC, V.

EXPENSIVE

Bistro 315. Contemporary. This popular, sophisticated restaurant prepares updated bistro fare with organic ingredients and is very popular among locals. Try the steak frites or country pâté. At sunset the patio offers great views. Beer and wine only. | 315 Old Santa Fe Trail | 505/986–9190 | $17–$26 | AE, MC, V.

★ **Cafe Pasqual's.** Southwestern. This small restaurant serves up regional and Latin American specialties such as huevos Motuleños (black beans and eggs over a blue corn tortilla with tomatillo sauce and goat cheese) and chile-rubbed, pan-roasted salmon. Breakfast is always popular here. Its murals are by Oaxacan artist Leo Uigildo-Martinez. Sunday brunch.

Beer and wine only. No smoking. | 121 Don Gaspar | 505/983–9340 | Breakfast also available | $15–$26 | AE, MC, V.

El Farol. Spanish. Order the classic paella, one of the 20 tapas—from tiny fried squid to *croquetas*, and a pitcher of sangria to make the meal complete. Dine indoors or on the outdoor patio. Entertainment nightly. | 808 Canyon Dr. | 505/983–9912 | $16–$26 | AE, D, DC, MC, V.

El Nido. American. This restaurant, housed in a 1920s-vintage adobe structure in Tesuque, 6 mi from Santa Fe, serves up choice aged beef, fresh seafood, and local favorites like chunky green-chile stew. | Bishops Lodge Rd., Tesuque | 505/988–4340 | Closed Mon. No lunch | $14–$25 | AE, MC, V.

Julian's. Italian. A dark, intimate restaurant that is considered one of the most romantic in Santa Fe. Try *pollo in agro dolce con cipollini* or sautéed shrimp and cheese. Open-air dining on a small, secluded patio. | 221 Shelby St. | 505/988–2355 | No lunch | $14–$27 | AE, D, DC, MC, V.

Ore House. Southwestern. With a menu featuring such staples as blackened prime rib and salmon with spinach pecan pesto, this wildly popular restaurant overlooking the Plaza is always mobbed. Margaritas are anything but ordinary. Kids' menu. | 50 Lincoln Ave. | 505/983–8687 | $16–$28 | AE, MC, V.

Palace. Continental. This Victorian saloon located just off the Plaza draws an older crowd who appreciates time-honored favorites such as Caesar salad, osso buco, and crab cakes with aurore sauce. There's a beautiful garden patio. Pianist. | 142 W. Palace Ave. | 505/982–9891 | No lunch Sun. | $15–$25 | AE, D, DC, MC, V.

Pink Adobe. Eclectic. This rosy-hue building dates from the early 1700s. With a menu encompassing New Orleans Creole, Continental, and New Mexican dishes, the Pink Adobe is known for such specialities as steak Dunnigan (smothered in green chiles and mushrooms) and shrimp Louisianne. You can warm yourself at the hearth in winter. Entertainment Tuesday–Thursday, Saturday. | 406 Old Santa Fe Trail | 505/983–7712 | Reservations essential | No lunch weekends | $11–$23 | AE, D, DC, MC, V.

Piñon Grill. Continental. This clubby steak house in the Hilton of Santa Fe offers consistently well-prepared food, such as potato-encrusted sea bass and green chile-stuffed filet mignon, in an elegant setting. Kids' menu. | 100 Sandoval St. | 505/986–6400 | No lunch | $18–$28 | AE, D, DC, MC, V.

Ristra. Contemporary. In this minimalist space decorated with Navajo blankets and pueblo pottery, continental cuisine gets a touch of the Southwest in such dishes as mussels in chipotle and mint broth, rack of lamb with creamed garlic potatoes, and a perfectly grilled salmon. The wine list is commendable. Open-air dining. Beer and wine only. | 548 Agua Fria | 505/982–8608 | No lunch | $17–$26 | AE, MC, V.

SantaCafé. American. In the historic Padre Gallegos House, this is one of Santa Fe's finest spots to sample southwestern fusion cuisine with Asian and European touches. Try shrimp and spinach dumplings with tahini sauce or shiitake mushroom and cactus spring rolls. Seasonal ingredients are emphasized. Open-air dining on a patio. | 231 Washington Ave. | 505/984–1788 | $10–$24 | AE, D, MC, V.

Shohko-Cafe. Japanese. This small restaurant off the Plaza offers authentic Japanese dishes and the largest sushi bar in Santa Fe. Known for tempura, sushi, and seafood. Beer and wine only. | 321 Johnson St. | 505/983–7288 | $9–$25 | AE, D, MC, V.

Steaksmith at El Gancho. Steak. This restaurant at the El Gancho Tennis Club, about 4 mi south of the Plaza, serves seafood as well as steaks. Specialties of the house include broiled salmon, sirloin steak teriyaki, beef kebabs, and free-range chicken enchiladas. | Old Las Vegas Hwy. | 505/988–3333 | No lunch | $10–$28 | AE, D, DC, MC, V.

VERY EXPENSIVE

The Anasazi. Southwestern. Stone walls, a beamed ceiling, artwork, and antiques set the scene at this restaurant in the Inn of the Anasazi for innovative takes on local and regional cuisine. Try tortilla soup, flat bread with fire-roasted sweet peppers, or the cinnamon-chile filet mignon chop. Elegant but not dressy. Kids' menu. Sunday brunch. | 113 Washington Ave. | 505/988–3236 | $17–$33 | AE, D, DC, MC, V.

Coyote Cafe. Southwestern. Here Southwest meets Hollywood, with a superb, inventive menu offered in a boldly designed room full of calfskin-covered chairs and a zoo of wooden animals. Try the "Cowboy" rib eye dusted with red chile or ravioli filled with boar sausage and goat cheese. The Rooftop Cantina offers a separate menu of lively Cuban and Mexican dishes for much less money. | 132 W. Water St. | 505/983–1615 | $43 prix–fixe | AE, D, DC, MC, V.

★ **Geronimo.** Contemporary. The eclectic fare ranges from grilled Thai prawns with guava banana catsup, to mesquite-grilled elk tenderloin with risotto. In a Territorial-style hacienda dating from the mid-18th century. Open-air dining in the front portal. | 724 Canyon Rd. | 505/982–1500 | No lunch Mon. | $26–$40 | AE, MC, V.

La Casa Sena. Southwestern. This restaurant in a Territorial-style, early-19th-century adobe offers up a menu of rich and beautifully presented fare. The specialty of the house is *trucha en terra-cotta* (fresh trout wrapped in corn husks and baked in clay). Open-air dining on a patio with a fountain, plants, trees, and flowers. | 125 E. Palace Ave. | 505/988–9232 | $20–$30 | AE, D, DC, MC, V | Reservations essential.

The Old House. Contemporary. This intimate restaurant in the Eldorado Hotel offers an ever-changing menu, but the cuisine often has Asian-French touches, evident in dishes such as the cider and sun-dried tomato-glazed pork tenderloin and the cashew- and sesame-crusted tuna tacos. | 309 W. San Francisco St. | 505/988–4455 | No lunch | $21–$30 | AE, D, DC, MC, V.

Vanessie of Santa Fe. American. In a large, airy adobe building next to the Water Street Inn, this establishment also has a lounge. The simple menu focuses on high-quality cuts of meat, fresh seafood, and very simple side dishes. Open-air dining on a covered patio. Pianist nightly. | 434 W. San Francisco St.) | 505/982–9966 | No lunch | $13–$43 | AE, D, DC, MC, V.

SANTA FE LIVE

If you are a lover of music and the performing arts, Santa Fe is your kind of place. Sometimes affectionately called the Salzburg of the Southwest, New Mexico's capital and second-largest city offers a variety of cultural events that will satisfy the most discriminating taste. The Santa Fe Opera consistently mixes old favorites with works not as well known. Recently the Opera inaugurated a sound system that emits a simultaneous translation of each opera performance from a speaker mounted on the seat in front of you. Another popular venue, the Santa Fe Chamber Music Festival, performs from mid-July until mid-August and features music from South America, Spain, and Mexico. The Santa Fe Concert Association has brought internationally acclaimed artists to the city for 62 years, and future events will feature pianist Radu Lupu, Chamber Orchestra Kremlin, and the Eroica Trio. Shakespeare in Santa Fe offers outdoor summertime performances of the Bard's best plays with professional and local actors. If you like flamenco dancing, try the Maria Benitez Teatro Flamenco, an internationally known group that has been dazzling Santa Feans for more than 30 years. Your chief complaint about all of these cultural events, plus many others, will be that you don't have time to experience all of them.

© Artville

Lodging

INEXPENSIVE

Best Western Lamplighter. This motel adjacent to the College of Santa Fe is 3 mi from the Plaza, about halfway between downtown and Interstate 25. Restaurant, picnic area. Some kitchenettes, refrigerators, cable TV, some in-room VCRs. Pool. Hot tub. Laundry facilities. Business services. | 2405 Cerrillos Rd. | 505/471–8000 | fax 505/471–1397 | www.bestwestern.com | 80 rooms | $72–$95 | AE, D, DC, MC, V.

Best Western Santa Fe. The majority of regular rooms are fairly small at this chain motel built in 1990, but the more expensive doubles and all suites are larger; some have balconies. The motel is a 15-minute drive from the Plaza. Complimentary Continental breakfast. Some refrigerators, cable TV. Pool. Hot tub. Laundry facilities. Business services. Some pets allowed. | 3650 Cerrillos Rd. | 505/438–3822 | fax 505/438–3795 | 97 rooms | $45–$145 | AE, D, DC, MC, V.

El Paradero. An 1820 Spanish adobe in downtown Santa Fe with details from 1880 and 1912 remodelings. There are skylights, fireplaces, and many antiques, and some rooms have balconies. Complimentary breakfast. Some kitchenettes, cable TV in some rooms, no TV in some rooms, TV in common area. Library. Pets allowed (fee). No kids under 4. | 220 W. Manhattan | 505/988–1177 | www.elparadero.com | 12 rooms, 2 suites | $75–$140, $125–$140 suites | AE, MC, V.

Howard Johnson Express Inn Santa Fe. A moderately priced motel 5 mi from the airport and 1 mi north of Interstate 25. Complimentary Continental breakfast. Cable TV. Business services. | 4044 Cerrillos Rd. | 505/438–8950 | fax 505/471–9129 | www.hojo.com | 47 rooms | $54–$120 | AE, D, DC, MC, V.

La Quinta Inn Santa Fe. Comfortable, basic three-story hotel, 3 mi from Interstate 25. Complimentary Continental breakfast. In-room data ports, some refrigerators, cable TV. Pool. Laundry service. Pets allowed. | 4298 Cerrillos Rd./Business Loop I–25 | 505/471–1142 | fax 505/438–7219 | 130 rooms | $60–$110 | AE, D, DC, MC, V.

Los Pinos Guest Ranch. At this complex 45 mi northeast of Santa Fe, you stay in one of four aspen log cabins, each with a front porch, a private bath, a wood-burning stove, and plenty of warm blankets. At this ranch at 8,500 ft, you don't have to worry about pesky insects. On the property are hiking and horseback trails, and plenty of fishing and birdwatching. Dining room. No room phones, no TV in cabins. Library. | Hwy. 63, Glorieta | 505/757–6213 or 505/757–6679 | 4 cabins | $100 per person per night (2–night minimum stay) | Closed Labor Day–May | AP | No credit cards.

Luxury Inn. This small, two-story stucco motel 3 mi north of Interstate 25 offers basic hotel rooms at reasonable prices. Complimentary Continental breakfast. Microwaves, refrigerators, cable TV. Pool. Hot tub, sauna. | 3752 Cerrillos Rd. | 505/473–0567 or 800/647–1346 | fax 505/471–9139 | luxuryinn@travelbase.com | 51 rooms | $35–$90 | AE, D, DC, MC, V.

Motel 6 Santa Fe North. This well-maintained budget motel is 1½ mi from the Villa Linda Mall. Cable TV. Pool. Some pets allowed. | 3007 Cerrillos Rd. | 505/473–1380 or 800/466–8356 | fax 505/473–7784 | www.motel6.com | 104 rooms | $42–$54 | AE, D, MC, V.

Quality Inn. This is a convenient, economical choice 4 mi from Interstate 25. Some refrigerators, cable TV. Pool. Tennis courts. Playground. Laundry facilities, laundry service. Business services, airport shuttle. Some pets allowed. | 3011 Cerrillos Rd. | 505/471–1211 | fax 505/438–9535 | www.qualityinn.com | 99 rooms | $55–$105 | AE, D, DC, MC, V.

Ramada Limited Santa Fe. This hotel is 4 mi from the Plaza. Complimentary Continental breakfast. Cable TV. Indoor pool. Hot tub, sauna. No pets allowed. | 3625 Cerrillos Rd. | 505/474–3900 | fax 505/474–4440 | www.ramada.com | 77 rooms | $79–$89 | AE, D, DC, MC, V.

Santa Fe Budget Inn. On the southern edge of the rail-yard district, six blocks from the Plaza, this motel offers basic, no-frills rooms. 2 restaurants, complimentary breakfast. Cable TV.

Pool. | 725 Cerrillo Rd. | 505/982–595 or 800/288–7600 | fax 505/984–8879 | www.santafee-budgetinn.com | 160 rooms | $54–$82 | AE, DC, MC, V.

Santa Fe Motel and Inn. Five blocks from the Plaza, this motor hotel is an unusually successful upgrade of a standard motel. Some rooms have fireplaces, and there are an outdoor deck and patio. Complimentary Continental breakfast. Some kitchenettes, some microwaves, some refrigerators, cable TV, some in-room VCRs. Business services. | 510 Cerrillos Rd., 87501 | 505/982–1039 or 800/999–1039 | fax 505/986–1275 | www.santafemotelinn.com | 13 rooms, 8 casitas | $89–$179 | AE, D, DC, MC, V.

Silver Saddle Motel. This kitschy 1950s motel on Cerrillos Road offers cheap, no-frills rooms. It's right next door to the Mexican-style market, Jackalope, which has a café. Cable TV. | 2810 Cerrillos Rd. | 505/471–7663 | fax 505/471–1066 | www.motelsantafe.com | 27 rooms | $40–$59 | DC, MC, V.

Stage Coach Inn. This small, basic Santa Fe-style adobe motel offers quiet rooms decorated in southwestern pastels and larger than average bathrooms with tile floors. The motel has a free shuttle to the Plaza, only 10 minutes away, so this is a good choice if you're on a budget. Picnic area. Cable TV. | 3360 Cerrillos Rd. | 505/471–0707 | fax 505/471–0707 | 14 rooms | $89–$150 | AE, MC, V.

Steve's Santa Fe Inn. This hotel is 4 mi from the Plaza. Cable TV. Pool. Laundry service. Business services. Pets allowed. | 2907 Cerrillos Rd. | 505/471–3000 | fax 505/424–7561 | 265 rooms | $40–$90 | AE, D, DC, MC, V.

MODERATE

Adobe Abode. Rooms in the B&B near the Georgia O'Keeffe Museum are decorated with objects the owner has gathered from all over the world. Some rooms have fireplaces and/or private patios. Complimentary breakfast. Cable TV. | 202 Chapelle St. | 505/983–3133 | fax 505/424–3027 | www.adobeabode.com | 6 rooms (3 with shower only) | $125–$165 | D, MC, V.

Alexander's Inn. This B&B is an antiques-furnished, 1903 Craftsman-style house with a backyard garden, within walking distance of the Plaza. The inn also encompasses a seven-room adobe hacienda three blocks away and several cottages in the surrounding blocks. Some rooms have fireplaces. Complimentary Continental breakfast. No smoking, cable TV, no TV in some rooms. Hot tub. Business services. Some pets allowed. | 529 E. Palace Ave. | 505/986–1431 or 888/321–5123 | fax 505/982–8572 | www.collectorsguide.com/alexandinn | 18 rooms in 2 buildings, 7 cottages | $80–$175 | D, MC, V.

Courtyard Santa Fe. This hotel has a beautifully appointed lobby and it's 2 mi from the Villa Linda Mall. Restaurant, bar. In-room data ports, some microwaves, refrigerators, cable TV. Pool. Hot tub. Gym. Laundry facilities. Business services, airport shuttle. | 3347 Cerrillos Rd. | 505/473–2800 | fax 505/473–4905 | courtyard.com/safcy | 181 rooms, 32 suites | $69–$149, $99–$179 suites | AE, D, DC, MC, V.

Dancing Ground of the Sun. Most rooms in this downtown 1930s adobe have motifs in keeping with the heritage of the local pueblos. The casitas have full kitchens. Complimentary Continental breakfast. Some kitchenettes, cable TV. Business services. No smoking. | 711 Paseo de Peralta | 505/986–9797 or 800/645–5673 | fax 505/986–8082 | www.dancingground.com | 5 rooms, 5 casitas, 2 studios | $95–$165, $165–$175 casitas, $105–$135 studios | MC, V.

Dunshee's. A mile from the Plaza, on *Acequia Madres* (Mother Ditch), which runs parallel to Canyon Road, this small B&B offers only two accommodations. The suite is in the restored adobe home of artist Susan Dunshee, the proprietor; the adobe casita is good for families. Both have fireplaces and are furnished with antiques. Complimentary Continental breakfast. Refrigerators, cable TV, room phones. Some pets allowed. No smoking. | 986 Acequia Madres | 505/982–0988 | www.bbhost.com/dunshee | 1 suite, 1 casita | $125 suite, $135 casita | MC, V.

El Farolito B and B Inn. A quaint B&B consisting of several adobe casitas, all with private entrances, arranged in a compound downtown, with fireplaces in all rooms. Complimentary Continental breakfast. Cable TV. | 514 Galisteo St. | 505/988–1631 or 888/634–8782 | fax 505/988–4589 | www.farolito.com | 8 rooms | $110–$180 | AE, D, MC, V.

El Rey Inn. This is a 1930s-style white stucco inn features Oriental rugs and vigas in the lobby. Some rooms have fireplaces. Picnic area, complimentary Continental breakfast. Some kitchenettes, cable TV. Pool. Hot tub, sauna. Playground. Laundry facilities. Business services. | 1862 Cerrillos Rd. | 505/982–1931 | fax 505/989–9249 | 86 rooms | $60–$185 | AE, D, DC, MC, V.

Galisteo Inn. An 18th-century hacienda on 8 acres, 23 mi south of Santa Fe, this quiet retreat has thick adobe walls and lovely views. Some rooms have fireplaces and sitting areas. Restaurant, complimentary breakfast. No air-conditioning, no room phones, no TV in some rooms. Pool. Hot tub, massage, sauna. Hiking, bicycles. Business services. No kids under 6. | 9 La Vega, Galisteo | 505/466–4000 | fax 505/466–4008 | www.galisteoinn.com | 12 rooms (4 with shared bath) | $80–$200 | Closed Jan. | D, MC, V.

Garrett's Desert Inn. This two-story hotel built in the 1950s is just two blocks from the Plaza. Restaurant, bar, room service. Cable TV. Pool. Business services. | 311 Old Santa Fe Trail | 505/982–1851 or 800/888–2145 | fax 505/989–1647 | www.bolack.com/lodging/nm/garretts.htm | 82 rooms | $74–$120 | AE, D, MC, V.

Grant Corner Inn. This colonial-style inn with a porch and gazebo is in downtown Santa Fe, with two rooms in a nearby hacienda. Complimentary breakfast, room service. Cable TV. Massage. Business services. No kids under 8. No smoking. | 122 Grant Ave. | 505/983–6678 | fax 505/983–1526 | 10 rooms | $125–$200 | AE, MC, V.

Guadalupe Inn. This attractive inn is in the historic Railroad District. No two rooms are alike, and some have balconies. Picnic area, complimentary breakfast. Some in-room hot tubs, cable TV. Business services. No smoking. | 604 Agua Fria St. | 505/989–7422 | fax 505/989–7422 | www.guadalupeinn.com | $135–$185 | AE, D, MC, V.

Holiday Inn. This hotel is 5 mi from the Plaza. There's a four-story Holidome atrium. Restaurant, bar, room service. In-room data ports, some refrigerators, cable TV. Indoor-outdoor pool. Hot tub, sauna. Gym. Business services, airport shuttle. Some pets allowed. | 4048 Cerrillos Rd. | 505/473–4646 | fax 505/473–2186 | www.holiday-inn.com | 130 rooms | $89–$149 | AE, D, DC, MC, V.

Inn on the Paseo. This appealing inn a few blocks from the Plaza is decorated with quilts handmade by the owner. Rooms are average size, with southwestern furnishings. There is also a sundeck. Complimentary breakfast. Cable TV. Business services. No smoking. | 630 Paseo de Peralto | 505/984–8200 or 800/457–9045 | fax 505/989–3979 | www.innonthepaseo.com | $85–$175 | MC, V.

La Tienda Inn. Rooms are done in antiques and custom-made southwestern-style furniture. 11 rooms in 2 century-old houses and a restored adobe building from the 1920s. Just four blocks from the Plaza. Complimentary Continental breakfast. Air-conditioning in most rooms, some in-room data ports, some refrigerators, cable TV. No smoking. | 445–447 and 511 W. San Francisco St. | 505/989–8259 or 800/889–7611 | fax 505/820–6931 | www.latiendabb.com | 7 rooms | $90–$160 | MC, V.

Madeleine Inn. Formerly the Preston House, this late-Victorian shingle-style mansion is four blocks east of the Plaza and filled with period antiques; there are fireplaces in some rooms. Complimentary Continental breakfast. No air-conditioning in some rooms. Business services. Some pets allowed. No smoking. | 106 Faithway St. | 505/982–3465 or 888/321–5123 | fax 505/982–8572 | 6 rooms, 2 cottages | $70–$165 | D, MC, V.

Pueblo Bonito Bed & Breakfast Inn. Rooms in this adobe estate, which dates from 1873, are furnished with handmade and hand-painted furnishings and southwestern art. All have fireplaces and many have full kitchens. It's a five-minute walk from the Plaza. Complimentary Continental breakfast. Some kitchenettes, cable TV. Hot tub. | 138 W. Manhattan | 505/984–8001 or 800/461–4599 | fax 505/984–3155 | www.pueblobonitoinn.com | 24 rooms, 7 suites | $70–$150 | AE, D, MC, V.

Residence Inn by Marriott. This all-suite hotel 1½ mi from the Plaza has fantastic mountain views. All rooms have full kitchens. Picnic area, complimentary Continental breakfast. In-room data ports, kitchenettes, refrigerators, cable TV. Pool. Hot tub. Laundry facilities, laundry service. Business services, airport shuttle. Some pets allowed (fee). | 1698 Galisteo St. | 505/988–7300 | fax 505/988–3243 | www.marriott.com | 120 suites | $169–$209 suites | AE, D, DC, MC, V.

Spencer House. This 1920s adobe, four blocks from the Plaza and around the corner from the Georgia O'Keeffe Museum, is furnished with English and American Colonial antiques. Bathrooms are spacious; some rooms have fireplaces. Complimentary breakfast. Some in-room Jacuzzis, cable TV. No kids under 12. | 222 McKenzie | 505/988–3024 or 800/647–0530 | fax 505/984–9862 | www.spencerhse-santafe.com | 6 rooms | $99–$175 | AE, MC, V.

Territorial Inn. This redbrick inn two blocks from the Plaza is on a busy street but set back. Rooms have Victorian period decor and some have fireplaces. Complimentary Continental breakfast. Cable TV. Hot tub. No kids under 12. Business services. | 215 Washington Ave. | 505/989–7737 or 800/745–9910 | fax 505/986–9212 | www.territorialinn.com | 19 rooms (2 with shared bath, 1 with shower only) | $85–$170 | AE, D, DC, MC, V.

EXPENSIVE

Dos Casas Viejas. This hotel is in two Civil War–era buildings, enclosed by an adobe wall. Rooms have red tile floors, and you can warm yourself in front of a kiva-style fireplace. Complimentary Continental breakfast. Refrigerators, cable TV. Pool. Spa. Business services. No smoking. | 610 Agua Fria St. | 505/983–1636 | fax 505/983–1749 | www.doscasasviejas.com | 8 casitas | $195–$295 | MC, V.

Hilton of Santa Fe. This three-story hotel is two blocks from the Plaza, occupying the grounds of the Ortiz family estate. Rooms are large and furnished with southwestern-style furnishings. Restaurants (*see* Piñon Grill), bar, room service. In-room data ports, cable TV, some in-room VCRs (and movies). Pool. Hot tub. Gym. Business services. | 100 Sandoval St. | 505/988–2811 | fax 505/986–6439 | www.hiltonofsantafe.com | 158 rooms, 3 suites, 3 casitas | $189–$289, $400–$650 suites and casitas | AE, D, DC, MC, V.

Hotel Plaza Real. Large rooms surround a brick-floor courtyard and are decorated with southwestern-style furnishings. Most have patios or balconies and fireplaces. In summer, there is an outdoor fajita grill on the common patio, and a light breakfast is served year-round for an additional fee. Bar. In-room data ports, cable TV. | 125 Washington Ave., 87501 | 505/988–4900 or 800/537–8483 | fax 505/983–9322 | 56 rooms | $199–$299 | AE, D, DC, MC, V.

Hotel St. Francis. This three-story hotel, which dates from 1920, is one block south of the Plaza. Rooms have brass beds, antique furnishings, and high ceilings. Afternoon tea in the lobby is a tradition. Restaurant, bar, room service. In-room data ports, refrigerators, cable TV. Business services. | 210 Don Gaspar Ave. | 505/983–5700 or 800/529–5700 | fax 505/989–7690 | hst@ix.netcom.com | 83 rooms | $98–$353 | AE, D, DC, MC, V.

★ **Hotel Santa Fe.** Run by the Indians of Picuris Pueblo, this three-story downtown hotel (about a 10-minute walk from the Plaza) is furnished with locally made furnishings and pueblo paintings, many by Gerald Nailor. Regular rooms are fairly small. Restaurant, bar (with entertainment). Minibars, cable TV. Pool. Hot tub. Laundry facilities, laundry service. Business services, airport shuttle. | 1501 Paseo de Peralta | 505/982–1200 or 800/825–9876 | fax 505/984–2211 | www.hotelsantafe.com | 40 rooms, 89 suites | $149–$219 | AE, D, DC, MC, V.

Inn of the Turquoise Bear. The former home of poet Witter Bynner, this 19th-century adobe offers simply furnished rooms that may have been slept in by D. H. Lawrence or Robert Oppenheimer. The terraced flower gardens offer a nice place to relax. Complimentary Continental breakfast. Cable TV. Library. Laundry facilities. Some pets allowed. No smoking. | 342 E. Buena Vista, 87501 | 505/983–0798 or 800/396–4104 | fax 505/988–4225 | www.turquoisebear.com | 8 rooms, 2 suites | $95–$195, $175–$195 suites | D, MC, V.

Radisson Santa Fe. This hotel north of Santa Fe, 7 mi from the Opera House, offers large rooms and suites done up in southwestern style. Restaurant, bar (with entertainment), room service. Cable TV. Pool. Business services. | 750 N. St. Francis Dr. | 505/992–5800 | fax 505/992–5865 | www.radisson.com | 163 rooms, 7 condos | $159–$439 rooms, $209 1–bedroom condo, $249 2–bedroom condo | AE, D, DC, MC, V.

★ **Rancho Encantado.** Celebrities from Robert Redford to the Dalai Lama have stayed at this resort on 168 acres, 8 mi north of Santa Fe, with views of the Jemez Mountains. Under new management, it is expected to reopen in Fall 2001 after a major renovation and expansion. | Hwy. 592, near Tesuque | 505/982–3537 or 800/722–9339 | fax 505/983–8269 | www.ranchoencantandosantafe.com.

★ **Water Street Inn.** This adobe four blocks from the Plaza offers southwestern-style rooms furnished with antiques, some with fireplaces. There's an afternoon wine hour. Complimentary Continental breakfast. In-room data ports, cable TV, in-room VCRs (and movies). Hot tub. Business services. No smoking. | 427 W. Water St. | 505/984–1193 or 800/646–6752 | fax 505/984–6235 | www.waterstreetinn.com | 12 rooms | $100–$247 | AE, D, MC, V.

VERY EXPENSIVE

Bishop's Lodge. This resort, which was formerly the country retreat of Santa Fe's first archbishop, Jean Baptiste Lamy, is 2½ mi (a five-minute drive) north of the Plaza but feels far removed. Accommodations are in one- and three-story lodges. This place tends to draw families. Restaurant, bar, room service. In-room data ports, some refrigerators, cable TV, some in-room VCRs. Pool, pond. Hot tub. Tennis. Gym, hiking, horseback riding, fishing. Children's programs (ages 4–12), playground. Business services. | Bishop's Lodge Rd. | 505/983–6377 or 800/732–2240 | fax 505/989–8739 | www.bishopslodge.com | 88 rooms in 11 lodges | $300–$450 | AE, D, DC, MC, V.

Hotel Loretto. This four-story hotel two blocks from the Plaza is modeled after the Taos Pueblo and built in 1975. The Loretto Chapel is next door Restaurant, bar, room service. Refrigerators, cable TV, some in-room VCRs. Pool. Barbershop, beauty salon, massage. Shops. Business services. | 211 Old Santa Fe Trail | 505/988–5531 | fax 505/984–7988 | www.noblehousehotels.com | 135 rooms, 5 suites | $239–$289 rooms, $500–$1500 suites | AE, D, DC, MC, V.

★ **Inn of the Anasazi.** This boutique hotel one-half block off the Plaza was built in 1991, and though small has a feeling of grandeur and excellent service. Its restaurant is also one of the finest in Santa Fe. Restaurant (see The Anasazi). In-room safes, minibars, cable TV, in-room VCRs (and movies). Massage. Gym. Business services. Some pets allowed (fee). | 113 Washington Ave. | 505/988–3030 or 800/688–8100 | fax 505/988–3277 | www.innoftheanasazi.com | 59 rooms | $199–$429 | AE, D, DC, MC, V.

Inn of the Governors. A luxurious hotel two blocks from the Plaza. Rooms are southwestern style; deluxe rooms have balconies and fireplaces. Restaurant (see Mañana Restaurant and Bar), bar (with entertainment), room service. In-room data ports, some minibars, cable TV. Pool. Business services. | 101 W. Alameda | 505/982–4333 or 800/234–4534 | fax 505/989–9149 | www.inn-gov.com | 100 rooms | $179–$355 | AE, D, DC, MC, V.

Inn on the Alameda. Some rooms in this inn, two blocks from the Plaza on the Santa Fe River, have kiva fireplaces and a balcony or other outdoor space. Bar, complimentary Continental breakfast. In-room data ports, cable TV, some in-room VCRs. Hot tub, massage. Gym. Library. Business services. Pets allowed (fee). | 303 E. Alameda | 505/984–2121 or 800/289–2122 | fax 505/986–8325 | www.inn-alameda.com | 69 rooms | $147–$334 | AE, D, DC, MC, V.

La Fonda. Tradition has it that there has been a hostelry of some kind on the southeast corner of Santa Fe's Plaza since the early days of Spanish domination. The current building, built in the 1920s, is a Pueblo Revival building offers rooms with hand-decorated furnishings, some with fireplaces. Restaurant, room service. In-room safes, cable TV. Pool. 2 indoor hot tubs, massage. Shops. Laundry service. Parking (fee). | 100 E. San Francisco St. | 505/982–5511 or 800/523–5002 | fax 505/988–2952 | www.lafondasantafe.com | 145 rooms, 22 suites | $199–$249, $299–$500 suites | AE, D, DC, MC, V.

La Posada de Santa Fe Resort and Spa. Two blocks from the Plaza, this resort has southwestern-style rooms, some with fireplaces, some with outdoor patios. The main building was once a Victorian mansion; additions are in the Santa Fe pueblo style. Restaurant, bar, room service. Cable TV. Pool. Beauty salon, hot tub, sauna, spa. Business services. | 330 E. Palace Ave. | 505/986–0000 or 800/727–5276 | fax 505/982–6850 | www.laposadadesantafe.com | 159 rooms | $199–$499 | AE, D, DC, MC, V.

Santero Resort-Villas de Santa Fe. At this all-suite hotel, the 1-bedroom suites come in varying sizes, all decorated with Native American Indian art. All have full kitchens; some have fireplaces. Picnic area, complimentary Continental breakfast. In-room data ports, kitchenettes, microwaves, cable TV, in-room VCRs. Pool. Hot tub. Gym. Laundry facilities. Business services. | 400 Griffin St. | 505/988–3000 | fax 505/988–4700 | www.villasdesantafe.com | 105 suites | $179–$340 | AE, D, DC, MC, V.

SANTA ROSA

MAP 9, G5

(Nearby town also listed: Tucumcari)

Along I–40, 120 mi east of Albuquerque, Santa Rosa is a small town of about 3,000 on historic Route 66. Established in 1865 as a Santa Fe Railroad depot, the area was once home to the Anasazi culture, and served as one of Billy the Kid's many stomping grounds. Today, Santa Rosa is a stopping-off place for tourists and a gateway to various outdoor attractions that surround the area. Some of the most notable include several lakes offering outstanding boating, fishing, and nature-watching opportunities. A unique nearby 81-ft-deep artesian spring called the Blue Hole provides excellent year-round scuba diving. The village of Puerto de Luna, ten miles south of Santa Rosa, is one of the oldest communities in the area, and many of the old buildings are preserved from the late 1800s and early 1900s.

Information: **Santa Rosa Chamber of Commerce** | 486 Parker Ave., Santa Rosa, 88435 | 800/450–7084 or 505/472–3763 | www.santarosanm.com.

Attractions

Blue Hole. Appropriately enough, this 81-ft-deep, crystal clear artesian spring a mile east of Santa Rosa is also sometimes called "Nature's Jewel." The deep pool produces 3,000 gallons of fresh water per minute at a constant temperature of 67°. It's a popular scuba-diving site (you must be certified). | La Pradira La., east of downtown | 505/472–3763 or 800/450–7084 | Free | Daily dawn to dusk.

Fort Sumner. This small farming and ranching town of 1,300, some 42 mi south of Santa Rosa, is mostly known as the burial site of Billy the Kid. Nearby is the original fort, which is now a state historic site. | U.S. 84 | 505/355–7705 Fort Sumner/DeBaca Co. Chamber of Commerce | fax 505/355–2850.

Billy the Kid Museum. Most everyone already knows that Sheriff Pat Garrett shot and killed Billy the Kid at Pete Maxwell's house in Fort Sumner, 44 mi southeast of Santa Rosa. This private museum keeps the myth and legend alive. | 1601 E. Sumner Ave. | 505/355–2380 | $4 | Mon.–Sat. 8:30–5, Sun. 11–5.

Fort Sumner State Monument. Before Fort Sumner became famous as the place where Billy the Kid met his maker, the community had attained a degree of notoriety as the disastrous depository for 12,000 Navajo and Apache Indians rounded up in the mid-1860s by Kit Carson. This monument about 7 mi southeast of the town of Fort Sumner tells the story. | Billy the Kid Rd. (Hwy. 212) | 505/355–2573 | $1 | Daily 8:30–5.

Old Fort Sumner Museum. This small museum ¼ mi east of Fort Sumner State Monument has displays on the fort itself and on Billy the Kid. The museum is located adjacent to Billy the Kid's gravesite. | Billy the Kid Rd. | 505/355–2942 | $3 | Sept.–May, 8:30–4; Jun.–Aug. 8:30–5.

Sumner Lake State Park. The lake 10 mi north of Fort Sumner is stocked with a wide variety of fish and offers waterskiing, boating, and camping. Go 10 mi north of Fort Sumner on U.S. 84, then 5 mi west on Hwy. 203. | U.S. 84 | 505/355–2541 | $4 per vehicle; $8–$14 for overnight camping | Daily.

Janes-Wallace Memorial Park. The spring-fed, man-made lake behind the dam 1 mi south of Santa Rosa features some of the best catfish, trout, and bass fishing around. | 3rd St. | 505/472–3763 or 800/450–7084 | Free | Daily.

Park Lake. Park Lake offers a wide variety of free recreational activities, including swimming, tennis, basketball, and softball. | Park Lake Dr. | 505/472–3763 or 800/450–7084 | Free | Daily.

Puerta de Luna. Legend has it that Coronado built the first bridge over the Pecos River near this point 10 mi south of Santa Rosa. The town was first established in 1862 and served as the county seat of Guadalupe County for years. | Hwy. 91 | 505/472–3763 | Daily.

Grzelachowski Territorial House. This house was a mercantile establishment in the 19th century; its owner fought in the Battle of Glorieta Pass. Although the house is located behind a private residence, visitors may drive up to the site and view it on their own. | S. Hwy 91, MM 10 | 505/472–5320 | Free | Daily 10–5.

Guadalupe County Courthouse. Built in the mid-1800s when the surrounding territory was still wild and woolly, this symbol of law and order held sway over an 1,800-square-mi area. | 4th St. | 505/472–3763 or 800/450–7084 | Free | Weekdays 8–5.

Rock Lake Rearing Station. State-run fish hatchery for walleye pike (seasonally) and rainbow trout 2 mi south of Santa Rosa, off Interstate 40. Go 2 mi down River Road; the hatchery is at the end of the road. | River Rd. | 505/472–3690 | Free | Daily 8–5.

Santa Rosa Lake and State Park. This man-made lake 9 mi north of Santa Rosa is a prime fishing spot. There's an Army Corps of Engineers visitor center that documents the dam and local history surrounding it. You can also hike, sail or do other boating, camp, and picnic around the lake. | Hwy. 91, 9 mi north of Santa Rosa | 505/472–3115 | www.emnrd.state.nm.us/nmparks | $4 per vehicle | Daily.

ON THE CALENDAR

MAY: *Santa Rosa Day Celebration.* a Memorial Day carnival, softball, dancing, and sports events at Park Lake. | 505/472–3763 or 800/450–7084.

JUNE: *Old Fort Days.* A staged bank robbery, barbecue, rodeo, and parade are just a few of the events highlighted at the Old Fort Days at the De Baca County Fairgrounds in Ft. Sumner. | 505/355–2380.

JULY: *Señora del Refugio Fiesta.* A mass begins this day of festivities that includes food, entertainment, and a dance in Puerta de Luna. | 505/472–3763 or 800/450–7084.

Dining

Mateo's Restaurant Mexican. The popular choices are the combination platter, which includes an enchilada, a taco, a tamale, a chile relleno, rice, beans, and a sopaipilla, and the enchilada platter that has chicken, beef, and cheese enchiladas. Kids' menu. | 500 Coronado W | 505/472–5720 | $5–$12 | AE, MC, V.

Lodging

Best Western Adobe Inn. This two-story motel offering larger-than-average-size rooms is built around a courtyard containing a large outdoor pool. Restaurant, complimentary

Continental breakfast. In-room data ports, cable TV. Pool. Business services. Pets allowed. | 1501 Will Rogers Dr. (I-40, exit 275) | 505/472-3446 or 800/528-1234 | fax 505/472-5759 | www.bestwestern.com | 58 rooms | $38-$65 | AE, D, DC, MC, V.

Holiday Inn Express. This hotel has interior hallways and nice rooms. Cable TV. Pool. Hot tub, sauna. Laundry facilities. Business services. Pets allowed. | 3202 Will Rogers Dr. | 505/472-5411 or 800/465-4329 | fax 505/472-3537 | www.hiexpress.com | 100 rooms | $30-$70 | AE, D, DC, MC, V.

Ramada Limited Hotel. This is a two-story motel in the heart of Santa Rosa. The suites have microwaves and refrigerators. The indoor pool is a great place to relax. Complimentary Continental breakfast. Some microwaves, some refrigerators, cable TV. Pool. Hot tub. Gym. Laundry facilities. Free parking. Pets allowed (fee). | 1701 Will Rogers Dr. | 505/472-4800 or 800/272-6232 | fax 505/472-4809 | www.ramada.com | 60 rooms | $75 | AE, D, MC, V.

SILVER CITY

MAP 9, B8

(Nearby towns also listed: Deming, Lordsburg)

Silver City, with a current population of about 11,000, was founded in 1870 as a rough and tough mining camp soon after silver was discovered in this area of what is now southwestern New Mexico. While other similar towns flourished, flickered, and then died, Silver City managed to become the area's most populous city, a county seat, and a regional trade center, helped along by the arrival of the railroad in 1881. When the silver played out, nearby copper mines became the mainstay of the town's economy, and remain so today.

Because the town fathers had the foresight to prohibit wood-frame buildings because of the risk of fire, much of the town's historic downtown area has survived. Flat-roofed brick and adobe Victorian buildings line most streets in the older parts of town. The town's popular claim to fame is as the adolescent home of young Henry McCarty, who is perhaps better known as Billy the Kid; he once waited tables in the Star Hotel, and his mother is buried in the local graveyard.

The Gila National Forest, which surrounds the town, was the nation's first designated wilderness area, so proclaimed in 1924. As a result of its protection, the Gila Wilderness is home to a large variety of otherwise rare, and in some cases endangered, wildlife. Today, in addition to nature-watching, the Gila National Forest offers hiking, camping, and fishing.

Information: Silver City/Grant County Chamber of Commerce | 201 N. Hudson St., Silver City, 88061 | 800/548-9378 or 505/538-3785 | www.silvercity.org.

Attractions

City of Rocks State Park. About 30 mi southeast of Silver City, off U.S. 180, in the town of Faywood, you'll find this aptly named park. Boulders—some house size—that were formed when ash spewed from an ancient volcano seem to rise out of the prairie. The bizarre "city," which might appear to have streets and alleyways, has campsites and picnic tables among the boulders. The main activity is hiking among the boulders, but you'll also find a cactus garden and a visitor center. | U.S. 61, Faywood | 505/536-2800 | www.emnrd.state.nm.us/nmparks | $4 per vehicle; $10-$14 overnight camping | Daily 7 AM-9 PM (park gate), 10-4 (visitor center).

Gila National Forest. The huge Gila National Forest surrounds Silver City on all sides except the southeast. Call headquarters for details of camping sites, hiking trails, and other attractions. | 3005 Camino del Bosque | 505/388-8201 | www.fs.fed.us/r3/gila | Free | Daily.

The Catwalk. This steep trail crosses a suspension bridge spanning the 250-ft deep White Water Canyon off U.S. 180 about 65 mi north of Silver City. | Hwy. 174, Glenwood | 505/539–2481 | $3 | Daily 6 AM–10 PM.

Gila Cliff Dwellings National Monument. These 13th-century cliff dwellings 44 mi north of Silver City were built by the Mogollon culture between 1282–1287. The visitor center contains a small museum and a bookstore. The 42 rock-walled rooms, accessible by a fairly steep 1-mi loop trail, are well preserved, looking pretty much the way they looked 700 years ago. | Hwy. 15 | 505/536–9461 | www.nps.gov/gicl | $3 | Memorial Day–Labor Day, daily 8–6 (monument), 8–5 (visitor center); Labor Day–Memorial Day, daily 9–4 (monument), 8–4:30 (visitor center).

Mogollon. Early in the 20th century, mines around the town of Mogollon accounted for 40% of New Mexico's gold and silver production. As the valuable ore played out, residents left for greener pastures, and Mogollon, 75 mi northwest of Silver City, became a ghost town. Today you can see several of the old deserted hotels and saloons that once lined the town's streets, and visualize what it might have been like during the village's heyday. (Note that Route 159 is closed November–April, east of the ghost town.) | Hwy. 159 | 505/539–2481 | Free | Daily.

Chino Mine Company. Originally mined by Native Americans, then by the Spaniards when the area was part of their territory, the Chino copper mine was in use long before it became an open pit in 1911. The massive 1,900-ft deep, 1½ mi-wide pit is now operated as a partnership between the Phelps-Dodge Corporation and the Heisei Mineral Company. You can view the copper mine from an overlook on Hwy. 356 where the town of Santa Rita used to be, about 15 mi southeast of Silver City, or take a three-hour tour of the mine, smelter, and concentrator, which originates in the town of Hurley (20 mi southeast of Silver City). | Overpass Hwy. 356 | 505/537–3381 | Free | Overlook daily dawn to dusk; tours weekdays 9 AM by appointment only.

Royal Scepter Gems and Minerals. This store has its own mineral museum that exhibits minerals from around the world and also features those found locally. See examples of minerals from each continent and some of the tools used to mine the minerals. You can purchase gifts, jewelry, petrified wood, fossils, and lapidary supplies. | 1805 Little Walnut Rd. | 505/538–9001 | www.zianet.com/royal-scepter | Free | Mon.–Sat. 9–5.

Silver City Museum. Indian artifacts, mining exhibits, and regional history displays make up the majority of this museum, which is housed in the Ailman House, built in 1881. You can also buy self-guided walking tour maps of Silver City's historic areas at the museum gift shop. | 312 W. Broadway | 505/538–5921 | Free | Tues.–Sun. 9–4:30.

Western New Mexico University Museum. This museum displays the largest collection of Mimbres pottery in the country. It also exhibits Hispanic folk art and has displays documenting the natural history of the region. It's on the campus of Western New Mexico University. | 1000 W. College Ave. (10th St. at top of hill, off West St.) | 505/538–6386 | Free | Weekdays 9–4:30, weekends 10–4; closed all university holidays.

ON THE CALENDAR

JULY–AUG.: *Hummingbird Festival.* This event has daily lectures, bird viewings, bird-banding, slide presentations, and over 4,000 hummingbirds. Held at the Grey Feathers Lodge. | 505/536–3206.

Dining

Adobe Springs Café. American. Greenery and paintings add a touch of class to this adobe-style establishment in the Piñon Shopping Plaza. Pastas, steaks, and southwestern entrées such as blue-corn enchiladas are among the specialties. This is a popular place for business lunches and leisurely evening dining. | 1617 Silver Heights Blvd. | 505/538–3665 | $6–$13 | AE, MC, V.

A.I.R. Coffee Company. Café. A.I.R. stands for Artist-In-Residence, which is exactly what the owner is. This ice-cream and coffee shop (coffee is roasted in-house) is a place where folks gather for long chats. Relax on a plump sofa or enjoy the mountain breezes out on the rear patio. Specialties are mochas and cappuccinos, along with hot chocolates, truffles, and toffees. Waffle cones, gourmet ice cream, and frozen yogurt are also served. | 112 W. Yankie St. | 505/388–5952 | Breakfast also available. No dinner | $2–$5 | No credit cards.

Buckhorn Saloon and Opera House. American/Casual. This genuine 1800s saloon in Pinos Altos, 6 mi north of Silver City, offers up steaks and other hearty fare like fried shrimp and hamburgers. The bar opens at 3 PM. The adjoining opera house stages melodramas on Friday and Saturday nights. Entertainment nightly except Tuesday. | 32 Main St., Pinos Altos | 505/538–9911 | Closed Sun. No lunch | $7–$35 | MC, V.

Diane's Bakery and Café. Café. This popular spot in the historic downtown district of Silver City offers fabulous sandwiches on home-baked bread. All baked goods are light and exceptionally tasty, prepared by the in-house pastry chef. A rotating dinner menu includes house specialties like duck, rack of lamb, shrimp scampi, and fresh fish dishes. Beer and wine only. | 510 N. Bullard St. | 505/538–8722 | Closed Mon. | $8–$20 | AE, D, MC, V.

Jalisco Café. Mexican. This restaurant is noted for dishes such as enchiladas and chiles rellenos based on old family recipes. Mexican tchotchkes help brighten the restaurant, which also exhibits colorful paintings of Mexican marketplaces by a local artist. | 103 S. Bullard St. | 505/388–2060 | Closed Sun. | $6–$10 | D, MC, V.

Vicki's Eatery. American/Casual. A hint of Germany can be detected in this delicatessen restaurant, which sells sausages, imported cheese, and homemade soups and sandwiches, not to mention beguiling, rich chocolate brownies. Dinner menus vary, but can feature pork tenderloin cordon bleu, seafood ravioli marinara, as well as vegetarian and German dishes. In summer, you can eat on an outdoor patio. | 107 W. Yankie St., 88061 | 505/388–5430 | Closed Sun. No dinner Mon. | $9–$15 | AE, D, MC, V.

Lodging

Carter House Bed & Breakfast Inn. This B&B in a 1906 home has soaring ceilings and antique woodwork and is furnished with sturdy, comfortable antique and contemporary pieces. It's next door to the historic Grant County Courthouse. A 22-bed youth hostel is operated, quietly and separately, in the downstairs portion of the building. Complimentary breakfast. No room phones, no TV, TV in common area. No smoking. | 101 N. Cooper St. | 505/388–5485 | 4 rooms (1 with shower only), 1 suite | $62–$80, $80 suite | AE, MC, V.

Comfort Inn. This two-story motel is 8 mi from Gila National Forest. It offers basic rooms. Contemporary Continental breakfast. In-room data ports, some in-room hot tubs, cable TV. Pool. Hot tub. | 1060 E. U.S. Hwy. 180 | 505/534–1883 or 800/228–5150 | fax 505/534–0778 | www.comfortinn.com | 52 rooms | $65–$150 | AE, D, DC, MC, V.

Copper Manor. This 1970s motel is centrally located, with simple rooms. The ones in the back, away from the street, are quieter. Restaurant, room service. Some refrigerators, cable TV. Pool. Hot tub. Business services. | 710 Silver Heights Blvd. (U.S. 80) | 505/538–5392 or 800/853–2996 | fax 505/538–5830 | 68 rooms | $42–$52 | AE, D, DC, MC, V.

★ **The Cottages.** These suites and detached cottages along the Continental Divide are on an 80-acre estate that has access to trails, a forest, and natural wildlife. The cottages have wood-burning fireplaces, and the full kitchens are supplied with cooking utensils and staples such as eggs, milk, fresh fruit, snacks, and frozen lunch and dinner items. The suites are spacious and cozy. Complimentary Continental breakfast (for guests in suites). Kitchenettes, microwaves, refrigerators, in-room VCRs. Hiking. No smoking. | 2037 Cottage San Rd. | 505/388–3000 or 800/938–3001 | www.silvercitycottages.com | 2 suites, 3 cottages | $119–$159 | AE, D, MC, V.

Drifter Motel and Pancake House. This motel is centrally located and and offers basic rooms. The pancake house adjacent is a popular breakfast spot. Restaurant, bar. No air-conditioning, cable TV. Indoor-outdoor pool. Hot tub. Business services. | Silver Heights Blvd. (U.S. 180 E) | 505/538–2916 or 800/853–2916 | fax 505/538–5703 | 69 rooms | $40–$49 | AE, D, DC, MC, V.

Econo Lodge Silver City This three-story chain motel is on a mesa overlooking Silver City and has a fountain courtyard. Some of the spacious rooms have spectacular views of town. Complimentary Continental breakfast. In-room data ports, some microwaves, some refrigerators, cable TV. Pool. Hot tub. Gym. Laundry facilities, laundry service. Pets allowed. | 1120 E. Hwy. 180 | 505/534–1111 or 800/553–2666 (central reservations) | fax 505/534–2222 | www.econolodge.com/hotel/nm014 | 62 rooms | $54–$61 | AE, D, DC, MC, V.

Holiday Motor Hotel. Many rooms at this two-story motel have views of the attractively landscaped lawn. Restaurant, room service. Cable TV. Pool. Business services, airport shuttle. Pets allowed. | 3420 Hwy. 180 E | 505/538–3711 or 800/828–8291 | www.holidayhotel.com | 79 rooms | $42–$48 | AE, D, DC, MC, V.

Palace Hotel. This Victorian-era hotel in downtown Silver City originally opened in 1882. Rooms have either western or Victorian decor and handmade quilts. Complimentary Continental breakfast. Some refrigerators, cable TV. | 106 W. Broadway | 505/388–1811 | fax 505/388–1811 | www.zianet.com/palacehotel | 20 rooms (6 with shower only) | $32–$53 | AE, D, DC, MC, V.

Super 8. This two-story motel is surrounded by juniper trees and piñons. Most rooms have double beds; five business minisuites have recliners, refrigerators, data ports, and coffeemakers. Complimentary Continental breakfast. In-room data ports, some refrigerators, cable TV, some in-room VCRs. Pets allowed (fee). | 1040 E. U.S. 180 | 505/388–1983 or 800/800–8000 | fax 505/388–1983 | www.super8.com | 69 rooms | $39–$52 | AE, D, DC, MC, V.

SOCORRO

MAP 9, D6

(Nearby town also listed: Truth or Consequences)

This small town of around 7,000 can trace its roots back to the earliest Spanish explorations of what is now New Mexico. The permanent settlement here was established in 1598 by Juan de Oñate, though the first settlement was almost completely destroyed during the Pueblo Revolt of 1680. It was reestablished in 1816, and that's the modern town you see today.

The town's main business is the well-regarded New Mexico Institute of Mining and Technology. But Cibola National Forest and the fantastic Bosque del Apache National Wildlife Refuge beckon to the residents. The entrance to the White Sands Missile Range is near Socorro, and it's through this gate that you get the most direct route to the Trinity Site, open only twice each year (*see* Las Cruces).

Information: Socorro County Chamber of Commerce | Box 743, Socorro, 87801 | 505/835–0424 | www.socorro-nm.com.

Attractions

Bosque del Apache National Wildlife Refuge. If you are visiting this wildlife haven at the right time, you can see tens of thousands of snow geese and sandhill cranes fly overhead on their way from or to their nesting grounds far to the north. It's 18 mi south of Socorro. | 1001 Hwy. 1 | 505/835–1828 | southwest.fws.gov/refuges/newmex/bosque.html | $3 per vehicle | Daily dawn to dusk.

New Mexico Institute of Mining and Technology. This mining sciences institute is also famous for other science and engineering curricula. | 801 Leroy Pl. | 800/428–8324 | www.nmt.edu | Free | Weekdays 9–5.

New Mexico Bureau of Mines and Mineral Resources Mineralogical Museum. On the campus of the New Mexico Institute of Mining and Technology, this museum's collection of mineral samples highlights various mining districts around the state. | In the Workman Addition, Canyon Rd. and Olive La. | 505/835–5140 | www.nmt.edu | Free | Weekdays 8–5, weekends 10–3; closed weekends during academic holidays.

New Mexico Tech Golf Course. Considered one of the most challenging golf courses in New Mexico, this 18-hole championship course on the campus of the New Mexico Institute of Mining and Technology is also considered one of the top public golf courses in the entire country. | Canyon Rd. | 505/835–5335 | www.nmt.edu | Mon. noon–dusk, Tues.–Fri. 7:30–dusk, weekends 6:30–dusk.

National Radio Astronomy Observatory. This site 50 mi west of Socorro features the world's largest assemblage of radio telescopes. | Hwy. 60 | 505/835–7302 | www.nrao.edu | Free | Daily 8:30 AM–dusk.

San Miguel Mission. This Spanish mission church, now restored, was active from 1615 to 1628, although the back wall dates from 1598. | 403 El Camino Real | 505/835–2891 | Free | Weekdays 7–7.

ON THE CALENDAR

APR. AND OCT.: *Trinity Site Tour.* Twice a year, on the first Saturday of the month, you can visit the site of the first atomic bomb explosion. *See* Las Cruces for more information. | 505/437–6120 or 800/826–0294.

JUNE: *Conrad Hilton Open Golf Tournament.* Golfers come from all over the country for this tournament at the New Mexico Tech Golf Course, named after the elder Conrad Hilton, who hailed from Socorro. | 505/835–0424.

SEPT: *Enchanted Skies Star Party.* This astronomical event is held beneath the cloak of darkness at New Mexico Tech. | 505/835–0424.

SEPT.: *Socorro County Fair and Rodeo.* Arts and crafts, livestock, a rodeo, and good food signal this annual fair at Socorro County Fair Grounds. | 505/835–0424.

NOV.: *Festival of the Crane.* This event at the Bosque del Apache National Wildlife Refuge celebrates the arrival of more than 100,000 sandhill cranes, snow geese, and other migratory birds from the far north. | 505/835–0424.

Dining

El Sombrero. Southwestern. This is a favorite of locals, embellished with a garden room and fountain. Known for New Mexico–style enchiladas, tortillas, fajitas. Beer and wine only. | 210 Mesquite NE | 505/835–3945 | $4–$11 | AE, D, DC, MC, V.

Martha's Black Dog Coffeehouse. Café. The signature vegetarian green corn tamales can't be missed. The meat loaf and the salads are very popular as well. Homemade desserts like cheesecake and rich chocolate cake are very popular. Art exhibits decorate the walls. Evening closing hours can vary, so call ahead if it is after 6. | 110 Manzanares St. | 505/838–0311 | $2–$10 | AE, D, MC, V.

Val Verde Steak House. Steak. In the Val Verde Hotel, this restaurant has an old oak-and-brass cooler and mural landscapes that were painted by a patron who was working off his bar tab. The popular items are the steaks, especially the fillet, the seafood, and the tequila piñon chicken breast. | 203 Manzanares St. | 505/835–3380 | $10–$18 | AE, D, DC, MC, V.

Lodging

Best Inn. This two-story chain motel is near Socorro's main street, 1 mi from New Mexico Tech. Restaurant, complimentary Continental breakfast. Microwaves, refrigerators, cable TV. Pool. Some pets allowed. | 507 N. California St. | 505/835–0230 | fax 505/835–1993 | www.bestinn.com | 41 rooms | $35–$55 | AE, D, DC, MC, V.

Econo Lodge. This motel has spacious rooms. All have a king- or a queen-size bed. Complimentary Continental breakfast. In-room data ports, microwaves, refrigerators, cable TV. Pool. Hot tub, sauna. Gym. Laundry facilities. Pets allowed. | 713 N. California | 505/835–1500 | www.econolodge.com | 64 rooms | $46–$58 | AE, D, DC, MC, V.

Holiday Inn Express. These rooms and suites are ample, quiet, and well maintained. The rooms have coffeemakers and a phone in the bathroom. The nice pool, hot tub, and other amenities set this specific property apart from the other chains in town. Complimentary Continental breakfast. In-room data ports, microwaves, refrigerators, cable TV, some in-room VCRs. Pool. Hot tub. Gym. Laundry service. Business services. Pets allowed (fee). | 1100 California NE | 505/838–0556 or 888/526–4657 | fax 505/838–0598 | www.hiexpress.com | 80 rooms | $79–$109 | AE, D, DC, MC, V.

San Miguel Inn. This small, basic motel is located less than a mile from the New Mexico Tech campus. Complimentary Continental breakfast. Some microwaves, some refrigerators, cable TV. Pool. Laundry facilities. Business services. | 916 California St. NE | 505/835–0211 or 800/548–7938 | fax 505/838–1516 | 40 rooms | $39–$46 | AE, D, DC, MC, V.

Super 8. This two-story motel built in 1989 is just off the highway. Some refrigerators, cable TV. Pool. Hot tub. Laundry facilities. Business services. | 1121 Frontage Rd. NW | 505/835–4626 | fax 505/835–3988 | 73 rooms, 15 suites | $50–85, $90–$110 suites | AE, D, DC, MC, V.

TAOS

MAP 9, F3

(Nearby towns also listed: Angel Fire, Chimayó, Española)

With a population of about 6,500, Taos is hardly the small backwater one might expect from memories of TV's Marshall Sam McCloud. On a rolling mesa at the base of the Sangre de Cristo Mountains, it is actually more like three towns. The first is the low-key business district of art galleries, restaurants, and shops that recalls the Santa Fe of a few decades ago. The second area, 3 mi north of the commercial center, is Taos Pueblo, home to Tiwa-speaking Indians, and also a UNESCO World Heritage Site. Life in the Pueblo predates the arrival of the Spanish in the Americas by centuries. The third Taos, 4 mi south of town, is Ranchos de Taos, a farming and ranching community settled by the Spanish, perhaps best known for the San Francisco de Asís Church.

What usually comes to mind for art-lovers is the Taos of the 1920s and 1950s, when such artists and literary figures as Georgia O'Keeffe, Ansel Adams, and D. H. Lawrence were drawn here by the haunting landscapes and clean mountain air, and the gallery-owners who followed them and made Taos more of a destination. The Taos Society of Artists, established in 1915, which included Joseph Henry Sharp, Ernest Leonard Blumenstein, and Bert Geer Phillips, left a great artistic legacy of paintings, which can be viewed in the museums of both Taos and Santa Fe. They were perhaps kept here by the hospitality of Mabel Dodge Luhan, who arrived in 1917. She persuaded D. H. Lawrence of the beauty of Taos and wrote *The Plumed Serpent* here, among other works.

In the early part of the century, living conditions were spartan, with no running water, electricity, or even indoor plumbing. Though Taos is resolutely rustic, the city is not the haven it once was. Traffic on the dusty (or muddy) streets can be heavy in the peak summer and winter seasons. There's definitely a laid-back attitude here. But visitors will appreciate the wealth of museums, galleries, and quaint B&Bs, not to mention good nearby ski slopes. Not really a resort town in the usual sense of the term, Taos is a real place where people live but where they also like to go, and that gives it richness most resorts lack.

Information: **Taos County Chamber of Commerce** | Drawer I, Taos, 87571 | 800/732–8267 or 505/758–3873 | www.taoschamber.org.

NEIGHBORHOODS

Downtown Taos. Taos is a small and quaint place; more than four centuries after it was laid out, Taos Plaza remains the center of commercial life in Taos and in the downtown area. Bent Street, where New Mexico's first American governor lived and died, is the town's upscale shopping street.

Rancho de Taos. The first Spanish settlers were farmers who faced raids by non–Pueblo Indians like the Comanches. Rancho de Taos, which grew up into a real town around the original Martinez hacienda, is about 3 mi south of downtown.

Taos Pueblo. Two miles north of downtown is the place where the original Taos residents lived and still live.

Taos Ski Valley. There are five ski resorts within a 90-mi drive of Taos. The Taos Ski Valley lies about 30 mi northeast of town, and it's the closest of the resorts. Several B&Bs are out this way, as are some restaurants that are worth driving out to.

TRANSPORTATION

Airports: Albuquerque International Sunport (505/842–4366) is over two hours' drive and is served by most major airlines.

Airport Transfers: Pride of Taos (505/758–8340) runs daily shuttle service to Albuquerque International Sunport and between Taos and Santa Fe.

Driving and Parking: The downtown area around the Plaza is a small one and is easily navigable on foot. Most of the galleries, restaurants, stores, and boutiques are near the Plaza. The main street through town is Paseo del Pueblo. You'll need a car if you want to go to Rancho de Taos, the pueblo, or the Taos Ski Valley. In summer, traffic in this dusty town can be maddeningly heavy and parking difficult. But there are many metered and unmetered lots all over town, plus parking on the street is allowed.

Attractions

ART AND ARCHITECTURE

Fechin Institute. This adobe house, which was built between 1927 and 1933 by artist Nicolai Fechin (who died in 1955), is a showcase of daring colorful portraits and landscapes. The house, listed in the National Register of Historic Places, and the Fechin Institute offer exhibits on the artist and his work. | 227 Paseo del Pueblo Norte | 505/758–1710 | $4 (or included in the 1-year $20 Museum Combination Ticket) | Wed.–Sun. 10–2.

Historic Ledoux Street. This one block is filled with museums, stores, galleries, and residences in some of the restored homes and studios of artists who once inhabited Taos. The distinctive adobe architectures add to the pleasant stroll down a street full of the city's culture and heritage. | Ledoux St. | 505/758–3873 or 800/732–8267 | www.aart.com/aart/ledoux.html | Free | Daily.

BEACHES, PARKS, AND NATURAL SIGHTS

Carson National Forest. Altitudes in this large forest preserve average nearly 7,700 ft. The forest, which surrounds Taos and spans almost 1.5 million acres across northern New Mexico contains over 50 recreation sites, including lakes, the Wheeler Peak Wilderness Area, and Pecos Wilderness Area. There are myriad opportunities for hiking, biking, fishing, skiing, horseback riding, boating, and wildflower viewing. | Headquarters: 208 Cruz Alta Rd. | 505/758–6200 | www.fs.fed.us | Free | Headquarters weekdays 8–4:30.

Kit Carson Memorial Park. You'll find the graves of both Kit Carson and Mabel Dodge Luhan, of the automobile Dodges who was an early patron of the Taos art colony, in this picturesque 20-acre park in downtown Taos, which also has tennis courts, picnicking facilities, and a playground. | Paseo del Pueblo Norte, at Civic Plaza Dr. | 505/758–8234 | Free | Memorial Day–Labor Day, daily 8–8; Labor Day–Memorial Day, 8–5.

Orilla Verde Recreation Area. You can hike, fish, camp, and picnic at this area 16 mi south of Taos along the banks of the Rio Grande; it was formerly known as Rio Grande Gorge State Park. There's a stunning view of the Rio Grande as it belches forth from the canyon lands.

The staging area for the region's popular white-water rafting trips is nearby. | Visitor Center: Hwy. 570 and Hwy. 68, Pilar | 505/758–8851 | $3 per vehicle | Daily.

Sipapu Ski and Summer Resort. This was northern New Mexico's first ski area, and today it is one of the state's most affordable ski areas. Summer attractions include excellent fishing in the Rio Pueblo, family facilities, and a delightful disc (Frisbee) golf course with resident golf pro. It's 25 mi southeast of Taos and 3 mi west of Tres Ritos. | Hwy. 518, Vadito | 800/587–2240 or 505/587–2240 | www.sipapunm.com | Daily, Dec.–late Mar. for skiing.

Taos Ski Valley. This ski resort 18 mi northeast of Taos is included in many top-10 ski resort lists in the United States and Canada. It has a world-class ski school and a wide variety of runs. You'll find 72 runs, but there is no snowboarding. | Taos Ski Valley Rd./County Rd. 150 | 505/776–2291 or 800/776–1111 (accommodations) | www.skitaos.org | Late Nov.–early Apr.

Wild Rivers Recreation Area. At the confluence of the Rio Grande and Red rivers near Questa, 35 mi north of Taos, you'll find a visitor center, picnic area, and campground with parking, drinking water, and rest rooms. These sections of the rivers are also popular white-water rafting destinations; Taos is the center for white-water rafting trips in north-central New Mexico. | Hwy. 522/Hwy. 378 | 505/758–8851 | www.nm.blm.gov | $3 per vehicle | Visitor center: Memorial Day–Labor Day, daily 10–4; area: daily 6 AM–10 PM.

CULTURE, EDUCATION, AND HISTORY

D. H. Lawrence Ranch and Memorial. Taos drew writers as well as artists, and the author of *Lady Chatterley's Lover* was one of the first to come here, at the invitation of Mabel Dodge Luhan, who provided for him at the Kiowa Ranch. The ranch where he lived for almost two years, 15 mi north of Taos, is now an education and conference center and has been named after him. The house, owned by the University of New Mexico, is not open to the public, but you can visit the memorial where Lawrence's ashes were scattered and where his wife Frieda is buried. | Hwy. 522, San Cristobal | 505/776–2245 | Free | Daily 8:30–5.

E. L. Blumenschein Home and Museum. In fall 1898, artists Ernest Blumenschein and Bert Phillips broke a wagon wheel on the outskirts of Taos on their way west. Infatuated with the village, they never left. Blumenschein's adobe-style home today is just as it was when he painted some of his most noted works there. It's a good introduction to the history of the Taos art scene, and you can see some of Blumenschein's paintings here. | 222 Ledoux St. | 505/758–0505 | www.taosmuseums.org | $5 (or included in the 1-year $20 Museum Combination Ticket) | Memorial Day–Labor Day, daily 9–5; Labor Day–Memorial Day, daily 11–4.

Firehouse Collection. This functioning volunteer firehouse has a collection of more than 100 works by well-known Taos artists like Joseph Sharp, Ernest L. Blumenschein, and Bert Phillips. The exhibit space is adjacent to the station house, where five fire engines remain at the ready and an antique fire engine is on display. | 323 Camino de la Placita | 505/758–3386 | www.town.taos.nm.us/tvfd/index.html | Free | Weekdays 9–4:30.

La Hacienda de los Martinez. This beautifully restored Spanish hacienda 2 mi west of the Town Plaza, in Rancho de Taos, shows what life in New Mexico in 1800 was like. Occasional demonstrations of country arts and crafts are offered. | 708 Ranchitos Rd., off Hwy. 240 | 505/758–1000 | www.taosmuseums.org | $5 (or included in the 1-year $20 Museum Combination Ticket) | Memorial Day–Labor Day, daily 9–5; Labor Day–Memorial Day, daily 10–4.

Taos Plaza. At the heart of the Taos downtown area, the Plaza is one of the oldest parts of the city. The covered gazebo here was donated by Mabel Dodge Luhan. On the Plaza's southeastern side is the Hotel La Fonda de Taos, a historic hotel. By a special act of Congress, the U.S. flag flies 24 hours a day here in honor of Kit Carson's stand against the Confederacy during the Civil War. | Don Fernando Rd. | No phone | Free | Daily.

★ **Taos Pueblo.** Much-photographed Taos Pueblo, 2½ mi north of Taos, was built as many as 1,000 years ago. There are two main buildings, Hlauuma and Hlaukwima, divided by a tiny stream. The Tiwa-speaking inhabitants provide an idyllic look at Pueblo Indian life centuries ago. Craftspeople work out of their homes, and handicrafts are authentic. Taos, as well as other pueblos in the region, observes many religious ceremonies throughout the year. A reminder: cameras are not allowed at these ceremonies, but they may be used (with a hefty fee) when you are just touring the Pueblo. The Pueblo Church of San Geronimo dates to 1850. Go right off Paseo del Pueblo Norte just past the Best Western Kachina Lodge. | 505/758–9593 or 505/758–1028 | taosvacationguide.com/history/pueblo.html | $8, still camera fee $10, video camera fee $20 | Daily 8–5; closed during certain ceremonies and funerals.

MUSEUMS

El Rincon Museum. This small private museum and gift shop, next door to La Doña Luz Inn and Historic Bed and Breakfast, exhibits Native American and Spanish Colonial artifacts as well as Kit Carson's leather pants. Some of the other items on display include a holy water cup from the San Miguel Church dating to 1610, Plains Indians buckskin items, and various Native American church artifacts. | 114 Kit Carson Rd. | 505/758–9188 | Free | Daily 10–5.

Governor Bent Home and Museum. Newly appointed New Mexico governor Charles Bent was killed by an unruly mob of Mexicans protesting the U.S. annexation of New Mexico in this house one block north of Town Plaza during the Taos Revolt of January 1847. See the hole in the wall through which Bent's frantic wife and children tried to escape. | 117A Bent St. | 505/758–2376 | $2 | Daily 10–5.

Harwood Foundation Museum. Operated by the University of New Mexico since 1936, this is the second-oldest museum in the state, exhibiting paintings, crafts, and photographs by area artists, including some by members of the famous Taos artists' colony. A major expansion in 1997 includes a gallery of works by Agnes Martin. | 238 Ledoux St. | 505/758–9826 | www.taosmuseums.org | $5 (or included in the 1-year $20 Museum Combination Ticket) | Tues.–Sat. 10–5, Sun. noon–5.

Kit Carson Home and Museum. Between the times he accompanied Fremont on his explorations of the American West, mountain man Kit Carson lived here with his New Mexican wife, Josefa Jaramillo. Exhibits include 19th-century lifestyle artifacts and a nice herb and flower garden. The bookstore is well stocked with regional titles. | Kit Carson Rd. at U.S. 64 | 505/758–4741 | $5 (or included in the 1-year $20 Museum Combination Ticket) | Daily 9–5.

Millicent Rogers Museum. This museum 4 mi north of Taos displays a dazzling collection of silver and turquoise jewelry, as well as an outstanding selection of traditional and contemporary Native American arts and crafts from northern New Mexico. Pottery by the late Maria Martinez is a special feature. | 1504 Millicent Rogers Rd. (Hwy. 522) | 505/758–2462 | www.millicentrogers.org | $6 (or included in the 1-year $20 Museum Combination Ticket) | Daily 10–5 (closed Mon. Nov.–Mar.).

Ridhwan Sculpture Garden. Next door to the Mabel Dodge Luhan House is this excellent private park that displays the work of notable nationally known sculptors. It is open to the public during the business hours of the Lumina Gallery, and the pieces on display are for sale. | 239 Morada La. | 505/758–7282 | www.luminagallery.com | Free | Daily 10–5:30; Jun.–Sept. weekends 10–6.

Stables Art Center. Once an actual stable, this is also the house where the Taos Artists' Association began showing its members' work. The building was purchased by the Association in 1952, and it is now the organization's visual arts gallery. | 133 Paseo del Pueblo Norte | 505/758–2036 | Free | Daily 10–5.

Van Vechten-Lineberry Taos Art Museum. This private museum shows the works of Duane Van Vechten, the wife of Edwin C. Lineberry, as well as those of more than 50 other Taos artists. | 501 Paseo Del Pueblo Norte | 505/758–2690 | www.vvltam.org | $6 (or included in the 1-year $20 Museum Combination Ticket) | Wed.–Fri. 11–4, weekends 1:30–4.

RELIGION AND SPIRITUALITY

Our Lady of Guadalupe Church. This adobe chapel was built in the 1960s. A large portrait of its patron saint, as well as various stained glass windows portraying her, adorn the walls inside. | 404 San Felipe St. NW | 505/758–9208 | Free | Weekdays 8–2.

San Francisco de Asís Church. This Spanish Mission-style church dates to the 18th century, but it was not restored until 1979. It is most famous for the resident painting *Shadow of the Cross*, by Henri Ault, on which each evening the shadow of a cross appears over Christ's shoulder. The phenomenon is unexplained. | Hwy. 68, 500 yards south of Hwy. 518, Rancho de Taos | 505/758–2754 | $2 | Mon.–Sat. 9–4; masses on Sun. at 7, 9, and 11:30.

SHOPPING

Blue Rain Gallery. This gallery carries some of the finest examples of pueblo pottery and Hopi katsina dolls to be found anywhere, as well as Indian-made jewelry and art. Prices range from several hundred dollars to several thousand. | 117 S. Plaza | 505/751–0066 | www.blueraingallery.com | Free | Mon.–Sat. Closed Sun.

Casa Cristal Pottery. This store 2½ mi north of the Plaza has a wide selection of stoneware, clay pots, Native American jewelry and ironwood carvings, and other crafts. | 1306 N. Hwy. 522 | 505/758–1530 | Free | Daily.

El Rincón. This dark, cluttered 19th-century adobe building has Native American items of all kinds, as well as Hispanic and Anglo Wild West artifacts. | 114 E. Kit Carson Rd. | 505/758–9188 | www.ladonaluz.com | Free | Daily.

La Tierra Gallery. This gallery features fossils and minerals for the serious collector, some of which have been crafted into jewelry or graceful carvings. | 124-G Bent St. | 505/758–0101 | Free.

Lumina Gallery. This gallery exhibits paintings solely by artists who have lived in New Mexico at least 20 years, including Joe Waldrun and Chuck Henningsen. It's housed in the former adobe home of Victor Higgins, one of the original members of the Taos Society of Artists. The sculpture garden in the back is worth lingering in. | 239 Morada La. | 505/758–7282 or 800/790–0101 | Free | Daily.

Michael McCormick Gallery. This gallery displays and sells works by such artists as Miguel Martinez, J. D. Challenger, and Margaret Nes. | 106C Paseo del Pueblo Norte | 505/758–1372 | www.mccormickgallery.com | Free | Daily.

New Directions Gallery. This gallery displays works by contemporary Taos artists, including Larry Bell, Ted Egri, and Maye Torres. | 107-B N. Plaza | 505/758–2771 or 800/658–6903 | tbs@newmex.com | Free | Daily.

Taos Book Shop. The oldest bookstore in New Mexico, founded in 1947, specializes in out-of-print and other books on the Southwest and Western Americana. | 122D Kit Carson Rd. | 505/758–3733 | Free.

SIGHTSEEING TOURS/TOUR COMPANIES

Historic Taos Trolley Tours. This company conducts two- to three-hour narrated tours of Taos during the busiest tourist season. | Taos Visitor Center: 1139 Paseo del Pueblo Sur | 505/751–0366 | www.taostrolleytours.com | $25 | May–Oct. daily (tours at 10:30 AM and 2 PM).

Native Sons Adventures. Organizes biking, hiking, rafting, snowmobiling, and horseback tours. | 715 Paseo del Pueblo Sur | 505/758–9342 or 800/753–7559 | $35–$108 | Daily, by reservation only.

Taos Indian Horse Ranch. This company conducts two-hour trail rides as well as horse-drawn sleigh rides in winter through the Taos Pueblo backcountry. Escorted horseback rides go through Native American lands mostly and are conducted by reservation only. | 1 Miller Rd., Taos Pueblo | 505/758–3212 or 800/659–3210 | hoofbeats@laplaza.org | $35–$135 | Daily, by reservation only.

OTHER POINTS OF INTEREST

Rio Grande Gorge Bridge. A spectacular view greets you as you walk across this bridge 11 mi northwest of Taos high above the Rio Grande. But hold on to your hat—the wind is strong. | U.S. 64, 11 mi northwest of Taos | No phone | Free | Daily.

ON THE CALENDAR

JAN.: *New Year's Celebration.* A celebration of food and dance brings in the New Year at Taos Pueblo. | 505/758–9593.

APR.: *Taos Talking Picture Festival.* A four-day festival featuring films by independent filmmakers. | 505/751–0637.

MAY: *Spring Arts Festival.* Area artisans offer their contemporary fine-art and arts-and-crafts products for sale. | 505/758–3873 or 800/732–8267.

JUNE–JULY: *Taos Rodeo.* A PRCA-sanctioned event brings competing cowboys and cowgirls from all over the region to the Taos Rodeo Grounds. | 505/758–3873 or 800/732–8267.

JUNE–AUG.: *Taos School of Music Chamber Music Festival.* This festival features presentations of chamber music at Southern Methodist University-Fort Burgwin and the Hotel St. Bernard. | 505/776–2388.

JULY: *Annual Powwow.* Many tribes from all over the United States, Mexico, and Canada gather at this large festival at Taos Pueblo. | 505/758–7762.

JULY: *Fiestas de Santiago y Santa Ana.* This event features a parade, arts-and-crafts exhibits, and good food in Taos Plaza. | 505/758–3873 or 800/732–8267.

JULY: *Taos Indian/Spanish Market.* Sales of handcrafted items in Kit Carson Memorial Park are made by local artisans from Taos Pueblo. | 800/732–8267.

AUG.: *Taos County Fair.* An annual event featuring livestock, agricultural exhibits, food, and entertainment. | 800/732–8267.

SEPT.: *San Geronimo Eve Sundown Dance.* Men's dances, a trade fair, a feast day, and intertribal dancing are showcased at this event at Taos Pueblo. | 505/758–9593.

SEPT.–OCT.: *Taos Arts Festival.* There are arts and crafts, music, and plays at this festival. | 505/758–3873 or 800/732–8267.

OCT.: *Taos Mountain Balloon Rally.* This balloon festival is limited to 60 invitational balloons, with takeoff in Wiemer Field. | 800/732–8267.

DEC.: *Taos Pueblo Deer or Matachines Dance.* This traditional dance features clowns and a bonfire procession in Taos Pueblo. | 505/758–9593 or 800/732–8267.

DEC.: *Yuletide in Taos.* Christmastime in Taos features a Christmas parade, fireworks, art exhibits, a craft fair, dancing, and food. | 505/758–3873 or 800/732–8267.

WALKING TOUR

Downtown Taos Walking Tour (4 or 5 hours)

A walk around the heart of downtown Taos can be done in half a day, but allow an entire day if you want to make the stroll leisurely, stopping for a lengthy lunch, exploring museums, browsing in some of the galleries and shops. This walk is probably best done on a Wednesday, Thursday, or Friday since the Fechin Institute is closed Mondays and Tuesdays, and many Taos museums are closed weekends. You might want to consider buying a combination ticket from the Taos Museum Organization that includes admission for up to one full year (transferable) to the seven major museums in Taos.

The focal point of Taos, as it is with most small New Mexican towns, is the **Plaza,** and from there the walking tour begins. Because local citizens defended Taos from Confederate invasion during the Civil War, the Plaza is allowed to fly "Old Glory" day and night, by special order of Congress (it normally must be brought down by sunset). The gazebo is the gift of the famed Taos resident and automobile fortune heiress Mabel Dodge Luhan, and the nearby monument commemorates local World War II veterans who died during the Bataan Death March.

Across the street on the south side of the Plaza is the **La Fonda Hotel,** where you will find a selection of the famous D. H. Lawrence paintings. These works were so erotic in nature that they were banned in London when they went on tour early in the 20th century, but you can view them for a small fee. On the opposite (north) side of the Plaza is the **Old County Court building.** Inside and upstairs, in one of the old courtrooms, is a fine series of wall paintings done by WPA artists during the Great Depression. The Plaza is surrounded by restaurants and jewelry, antique, art, clothing, and specialty shops, where you can spend several hours browsing.

When you're finished with the Plaza, walk to its northeast corner and proceed up the street to the intersection of Kit Carson Road and U.S. 64, also known as Paseo del Pueblo Norte. Cross Paseo and follow Kit Carson Avenue to the **Kit Carson House** on the left. This was the mountain man's home while he lived in Taos, and today it preserves some of the artifacts associated with his life. The house includes a good bookstore, if you are interested in the history of the area. Kit Carson Avenue is lined with art galleries, so plan to spend some time in these, observing the style and coloration of Taos-inspired paintings. Also located on this street, opposite the Kit Carson House, is the renowned **Taos Book Shop,** a wonderfully stocked store with a rare and out-of-print section featuring the works of D. H. Lawrence, Mabel Dodge Luhan, Willa Cather, and other writers associated with Taos.

Returning to Paseo del Pueblo Norte, turn right (north) and proceed to its intersection with Bent Street (one block). Cross over and go down Bent Street to **Governor Charles Bent's residence,** which today is a museum. This is the house in which the governor was murdered in January 1847 by a large group of dissident Mexicans and Taos Indians, still brooding over the recent occupation of New Mexico by the American army. Bent Street also has a number of arts-and-crafts galleries that are well worth exploring. Across Bent Street is a small shopping mall, dominated by the John Dunn house, now the **Moby Dickens Book Shop.** Following the mall will bring you back to the Plaza, or if you wish, you can retrace your steps back to Paseo del Pueblo Norte, turn left, and proceed until you arrive at **Kit Carson Park** on your right. Old Kit and his wife, Josefa, are buried here, as well as Mabel Dodge Luhan. Nearby is a **monument dedicated to Padre Martinez,** one of the most influential churchmen ever to hail from this region. When you leave the park, turn right, and follow Paseo del Pueblo Norte a short distance to the **Fechin Institute,** the onetime home of Taos artist Nicolai Fechin. The home is furnished with Fechin's own Russian wood carvings and is well worth the visit. Return now to the Plaza, via Paseo del Pueblo Norte, and exit its northwestern corner across Camino de la Placita to **Our Lady of Guadalupe Church,** located on the right on Don Fernando Street. Notice the fine carved stations of the cross, crafted by the eminent *santero* Pedro Chavez. Return to Camino de la Placita and follow it south for a couple of short blocks until Ledoux Street meets it from the west. Walk down Ledoux and visit the **Blumenschein Home and Museum** on your left. This was the home of early Taos artist Ernest Blumenschein, and is decorated with his original art and a fine selection of European antiques. Just down Ledoux Street is the **Harwood Foundation Museum** of the University of New Mexico. Many contemporary Taos artists are represented here, and the museum also has on display a fine collection of 19th-century *retablos*, which are religious paintings on wood. If you still have the energy, you'll probably have no difficulty finding some shops and eateries that you missed earlier.

Dining

INEXPENSIVE

Abe's Cantina y Cocina. Mexican. Enjoy a breakfast burrito, rolled tacos, or homemade tamales at this inexpensive restaurant that is primarily takeout. It has small tables and a bar that does not serve food. You never know when the place may be closed for golf outings. | Taos Ski Valley Rd. (County Rd. 150) | 505/776–8516 | Closed Sun. | $3–$5 | MC, V.

The Alley Cantina. American/Casual. Tradition has called the Alley Cantina's edifice the oldest house in Taos; it has an atrium and fireplaces. Known for pizza, sandwiches. Open-air dining on a plant-filled patio. Kids' menu. | 121 Teresino La. | 505/758-2121 | No lunch Dec.–mid-May | $5–$9 | AE, D, DC, MC, V.

Bravo! Eclectic. This restaurant, in a gourmet grocery and wine shop, has a nice selection of delicacies, though it's a little short on atmosphere. Try the calamari, egg rolls, escargot, or the salmon quesadillas. Diverse wine and beer list. Kids' menu. | 1353A Paseo del Pueblo Sur | 505/758-8100 | Closed Sun. | $6–$15 | MC, V.

Eske's Brew Pub. American. The popular dishes at this casual spot include fried chicken, green chile stew, and Mediterranean salad. The microbrewery downstairs produces a range of beers from dark stouts to light ales. Live music on weekends. | 106 des Georges La. | 505/758-1517 | $5–$12 | MC, V.

Fred's Place. Southwestern. Quirky decorations—the carved crucifixes and *santos,* the ceiling mural of hell—and a hip reputation keep folks lined up to get in. The wait can be extensive, but once you are seated the popular items such as the carne adovada and the blue-corn enchiladas will have made it worthwhile. | 332 Paseo del Pueblo Sur | 505/758-0514 | Reservations not accepted | Closed Sun. No lunch | $5–$13 | MC, V.

JJ's Bagels. Café. In a storefront, away from the tourist hub, this cyber-café bakes bagels and serves soups, salads, sandwiches, and pastries. Surf the Net, enjoy a fresh bagel and cream cheese, or have dessert. | 710 Paseo del Pueblo Sur | 505/758-0045 | Breakfast also available. No dinner | $1–$6 | MC, V.

Michael's Kitchen and Bakery. American. This casual homey restaurant with exposed viga ceilings and filled with antiques is three blocks north of the Plaza. It's known for hamburgers, enchiladas, and stuffed sopaipillas. Kids' menu. | 505/758-4178 | Breakfast also available; closed Nov. | $6–$11 | AE, D, MC, V.

Orlando's. Southwestern. This family-run restaurant frequented by locals features chicken enchiladas, blue-corn enchiladas, and shrimp burritos. The intimate dining room is casual, and it does a sizable take-out business. Off of Paseo del Pueblo Norte. | 114 Don Juan Valdez La. | 505/751-1450 | Closed Sun. | $6–$8 | No credit cards.

Taos Cow. Café. This is the world headquarters for the ice cream featured in area health-food stores; it's made from growth-hormone-free milk. The three dozen flavors include Cherry Ristra, Piñon Caramel, Vanilla, and an assortment of luxurious chocolates. Deli sandwiches, coffee, and juices are also served. | Taos Ski Valley Rd. (County Rd. 150) | 505/776-5640 | Breakfast also available; no dinner | $3–$8 | MC, V.

Taos Wrappers. Delicatessen. These healthful alternatives to sandwiches are flavored tortillas filled with ingredients like pesto chicken, roasted veggies, and curried tuna. Soups, salads, and desserts are also served. There are a few tables for those who wish to eat in. | 616 Paseo del Pueblo Sur | 505/751-9727 | Closed weekends | $3–$7 | No credit cards.

MODERATE

Apple Tree. Contemporary. Some say this is the best restaurant in Taos. You'll enjoy indoor eating surrounded by original art, or dine outdoors in a courtyard, where you can watch the sparrows come to beg crumbs. Try the grilled lamb or chicken fajitas. It's one block north of the Plaza and a block south of the convention center. Sunday brunch. Beer and wine only. | 123 Bent St. | 505/758-1900 | $8–$20 | AE, D, DC, MC, V.

Bent Street Deli and Café. American/Casual. This upscale deli is just across Bent Street from Governor Bent's house. A partially outdoor, café-style restaurant with plenty of light and flowers, it features 18 different kinds of deli sandwiches, as well as great salads, homemade breads, and super shrimp and beef dishes. | 120 Bent St. | 505/758-5787 | $10–$16 | MC, V.

Byzantium. Eclectic. This intimate restaurant in an adobe structure on Ledoux Street has made-to-order specialties from all over the globe, such as Wu Tang chicken, baba ghanoush, grilled polenta, or a green lip mussel hot pot. Known for good service and personal attention. | Ledoux St. and La Placita | 505/751–0805 | Closed Tues., Wed. No lunch | $7–$18 | AE, MC, V.

Casa de Valdez. Southwestern. Enjoy specialties such as hickory-smoked barbecues, charcoal-grilled steaks, and regional New Mexican cuisine in a large A-frame building with wood-panel walls and beam ceilings. | 1401 Paseo del Pueblo Sur | 505/758–8777 | Closed Wed. | $9–$20 | AE, D, MC, V.

Jaquelina's. Southwestern. At this upscale restaurant known for its knowledgeable servers, try the grilled salmon with tomatillo salsa, or the barbecued shrimp with *poblano* corn salsa (poblano is a dark green chile ranging from mild to fiery). | 1541 Paseo del Pueblo Sur | 505/751–0399 | Closed Mon. No lunch | $8–$13 | MC, V.

Momentitos de la Vida. Contemporary. Enjoy fine dining in summer on the enclosed outdoor terrace with a bar facing an orchard. The elegant interior is the perfect setting in which to enjoy the daily risotto special or grilled Colorado lamb chop. Desserts include raspberry pie and chocolate creations. Commendable wine list. Live jazz at the piano bar. Sunday brunch. | Taos Ski Valley Rd. (County Rd. 150) | 505/776–3333 | Reservations essential | Closed Mon. No lunch | $17–$18 | AE, MC, V.

Ogelvie's Bar and Grill. American. On the second floor of an adobe building on the Plaza, this is a good people-watching spot. The most straightforward dishes, including Angus beef, grilled Rocky Mountain trout, and meat or cheese enchiladas, rarely disappoint. Open-air dining on a patio overlooking the Plaza. Kids' menu. | 103 Suite I | 505/758–8866 | $6–$20 | AE, MC, V.

Roberto's Restaurant. Southwestern. The New Mexican dishes here are created from family recipes that have been handed down through the generations. Enjoy the ever popular chiles rellenos and tacos in one of the three intimate dining rooms that are filled with family antiques. | 122B E. Kit Carson Rd. | 505/758–2434 | Closed Tues. No lunch | $10–$15 | AE, D, MC, V.

EXPENSIVE

Joseph's Table. Contemporary. The subtle lighting sets a romantic stage for the most popular spot in Rancho de Taos. Some of the specialties include pepper steak with garlic mashed potatoes, risotto cake with Parmigiano, and prosciutto in a Portobello mushroom syrup. The ornate desserts are a great finish to the meal. | 4167 Paseo del Pueblo Sur, Ranchos de Taos | 505/751–4512 | Closed Mon., Tues. No lunch | $15–$24 | AE, D, DC, MC, V.

Lambert's of Taos. Contemporary. This restaurant 2½ blocks south of the Plaza is known for crab cakes and pepper-crusted lamb. Desserts, such as the chocolate mousse and homemade ice-creams and sorbets, are also highly praised, as is the wine list, especially the selection of fine California varietals. Kids' menu. | 309 Paseo del Pueblo Sur | 505/758–1009 | No lunch | $13–$25 | AE, MC, V.

Stakeout at Outlaw Hill. Continental. This old adobe house is nestled in the Sangre de Cristo Mountains 8½ mi south of Taos in Rancho de Taos. Known for steak, prime rib, seafood, shrimp scampi, and daily pasta specials. Open-air dining on a patio with views of the gorge. Entertainment weekends. Kids' menu. | 101 Stakeout Dr. | 505/758–2042 | www.stakeoutrestaurant.com | No lunch | $12–$26 | AE, D, DC, MC, V.

Tim's Chile Connection. Southwestern. At this place 5 mi north of the Plaza, past the turnoff for the Taos Ski Valley, you can warm yourself at the hearth in winter. Known for barbecue ribs, tres leches (three milk) cake, and molé. Open-air dining on a patio overlooking the expansive lawn. Entertainment. Kids' menu. | 1 Ski Valley Rd. (County Rd. 150) | 505/776–8787 | $5–$25 | AE, MC, V.

★ **Trading Post Café.** Contemporary. The imaginative menu offers appetizers such as marinated salmon gravlax and paella. The pasta portions are generous and flavorful. For dessert try the homemade raspberry sorbet or the flan. Coming from the north, take the left turn onto Highway 518 (Talpa Road) just before the restaurant to reach the more ample parking lot. Be careful not to walk over the neighbor's yard; to reach the entrance walk back along Talpa Road. | 4178 Paseo del Pueblo Sur, Ranchos de Taos | 505/758–5089 | Closed Sun. | $7–$28 | D, DC, MC, V.

Villa Fontana. Italian. Dining here is like stepping into a sophisticated Italian country inn. Notable dishes include the osso buco and the ravioli with porcini mushrooms. The gleaming hardwood tables and starched linens add to the elegance. It's 5 mi north of Taos Plaza. | 71 Hwy. 522, Arroyo Hondo | 505/758–5800 | Closed Sun., Mon. No lunch | $16–$24 | AE, D, DC, MC, V.

Lodging

INEXPENSIVE

Best Western Kenicha Lodge de Taos. In a pueblo-style adobe, the large rooms are actually separate casitas and are positioned around the "Dance Circle," where a troupe from Taos Pueblo perform nightly ritual dances from May through October. The handmade and hand-painted furnishings are wonderful accents. Kids under 12 stay free. 2 restaurants, 1 bar, complimentary Continental breakfast. In-room data ports, some microwaves, some refrigerators, cable TV. Pool. Hot tub, beauty salon. Shops. Laundry facilities. Business services. No pets. | 413 N. Pueblo Rd. | 505/758–2275 or 800/522–4462 | fax 505/758–9207 | www.kachinalodge.com | 118 rooms | $69–$89 | AE, D, DC, MC, V.

Brooks Street Inn. This adobe B&B is three blocks north of the Plaza. An elaborately carved korbel arch leads into a walled garden. Fresh flowers and original artworks grace the rooms. Complimentary breakfast. No air-conditioning, no room phones. No kids under 10. No smoking. | 119 Brooks St. | 505/758–1489 | www.brooksstreetinn.com | 6 rooms | $80–$110 | AE, D, MC, V.

Casa Europa. This adobe inn with viga ceilings is set on 6 acres. The rooms are furnished with European antiques as well as a few southwestern pieces. Picnic area, complimentary breakfast. No air-conditioning, cable TV, no TV, TV in common area. Hot tub, sauna. | 840 Upper Ranchitos Rd. | 505/758–9798 or 888/758–9798 | www.travelbase.com/destinations/taos/casa-europa | 7 rooms | $65–$135 | MC, V.

Comfort Suites. The southwestern lobby has a great adobe fireplace. Each suite contains a living room with a sofa bed, a bedroom with a king- or queen-size bed, and a television in both living and sleeping area. Complimentary Continental breakfast. In-room data ports, microwaves, refrigerators, cable TV. Pool. Outdoor hot tub. Laundry service. Business services. No pets. | 1500 Paseo del Pueblo Sur | 505/751–1555 or 888/751–1555 | www.taosweb.com/taoshotels/comfortsuites | 60 suites | $69–$149 | AE, D, DC, MC, V.

Dreamcatcher. Some rooms at this moderately priced bed-and-breakfast have kiva fireplaces. Picnic area, complimentary breakfast. No air-conditioning, no room phones. Hot tub. Library. | 416 La Lomita Rd. | 505/758–0613 | fax 505/751–0115 | www.dreambb.com | 7 rooms | $84–$119 | AE, D, MC, V.

Holiday Inn Don Fernando de Taos. There are fireplaces in some rooms in the pueblo-style hotel. Rooms are furnished with hand-carved New Mexican furnishings. A free shuttle takes guests to the town center. Restaurant, bar, room service. Cable TV, some in-room VCRs. Indoor-outdoor pool. Hot tub. Tennis. Business services, airport shuttle. Pets allowed. | 1005 Paseo del Pueblo Sur | 505/758–4444 | fax 505/758–0055 | www.taosweb.com/holidayinn | 124 rooms | $65–$149 | AE, D, DC, MC, V.

Hotel La Fonda de Taos. On Taos Plaza, this adobe hotel has many antiques and a collection of erotic paintings by D. H. Lawrence (which can be viewed for a small fee). Just steps away from the town's shops, galleries, and restaurants. The rooms are comfortable and clean. No TV in some rooms, TV in common area. No smoking. | 108 S. Plaza | 505/758–2211 or 800/833–2211 | fax 505/758–8508 | www.silverhawk.com/taos/lafonda.html | 24 rooms | $50–$110 | AE, MC, V.

La Doña Luz Inn and Historic Bed & Breakfast. Spanish colonial furnishings, custom wood-work, elaborate carvings, and Native American artifacts and pottery add elegant and distinct touches to this 1802 hacienda-style inn. Many rooms have fireplaces and private hot tubs; ask about the guest room with the 100-mi view—its deck is the highest point in Taos. Right on the Plaza, this place is special without being horribly expensive. Picnic area, complimentary Continental breakfast. Some microwaves, cable TV, in-room VCRs (and movies), no room phones. Business services. Pets allowed (fee). | 114 Kit Carson St. | 505/758–4874 or 800/758–9187 | fax 505/758–4541 | www.ladonaluz.com. | 15 rooms | $59–$199 | AE, D, MC, V.

La Posada de Taos. A 1906 adobe building with a traditional central court two blocks from the Plaza. All rooms but one have kiva fireplaces. Complimentary breakfast. No TV, TV in common area. | 309 Juanita La. | 505/758–8164 or 800/645–4803 | fax 505/751–4696 | 6 rooms (3 with shower only) | $85–$145 | AE, MC, V.

Little Tree Bed and Breakfast. This old adobe hacienda 10 mi from the Plaza, halfway between Taos and Taos Ski Valley, has great views and a tranquil location. Some rooms have fireplaces, and all have queen-size beds. Complimentary Continental breakfast, some in-roof VCRs, no TV in some rooms. | 226 Hond-Seco | 505/776–8467 | 4 rooms | $85–$105 | AE, D, DC, MC, V.

Old Taos Guesthouse. Once an adobe hacienda, this B&B is on 7½ acres of land. All rooms have private entrances, private baths, and either a king, queen, or twin bed. Some rooms have skylights or fireplaces. Hand-carved doors and furniture, 80-mi views from the outdoor hot tub, and western antiques make this place unique. Complimentary Continental breakfast. Some kitchenettes, no room phones, no TV, TV in common area. Hot tub. No smoking. | 1028 Witt Rd. | 505/758–5448 or 800/758–5448 | fax 505/758–5448 | www.oldtaos.com | 9 rooms | $70–$125 | MC, V.

Orinda B and B. This B&B is housed in a very private 50-year-old adobe amid beautiful landscaping, a 15-minute walk from Taos Plaza, with great views of the nearby mountains. Two rooms share a common sitting area. Complimentary breakfast. No smoking. | 461 Valverde St., on Valverde Park | 505/758–8581 or 800/847–1837 | fax 505/751–4895 | 5 rooms | $90–$145 | AE, D, MC, V.

Quality Inn. This motel is on busy Route 68, 2 mi south of the Plaza. Restaurant, bar, picnic area, room service. In-room data ports, some microwaves, refrigerators, cable TV, some in-room VCRs. Pool. Business services. Pets allowed (fee). | 1043 Camino del Pueblo Sur | 505/758–2200 or 800/845–0648 | fax 505/758–9009 | www.qualityinntaos.com | 99 rooms | $55–$175 | AE, D, DC, MC, V.

Rancho Ramada Inn de Taos. This cozy hotel is not quite so cookie-cutter as you might expect, and some rooms have fireplaces. Restaurant, bar. Cable TV. Pool. Hot tub. Business services. | 615 Paseo del Pueblo Sur (Hwy. 68) | 505/758–2900 | fax 505/758–1662 | 124 rooms | $79–$120 | AE, D, DC, MC, V.

Sagebrush Inn. Many rooms in this 1929 pueblo-style adobe 3 mi south of the Plaza have fireplaces. Rooms are furnished with Native American crafts and southwestern antiques. Georgia O'Keeffe once lived in one of the third-floor rooms. Restaurant, bar (with entertainment), complimentary breakfast. Some refrigerators, cable TV. Pool. Hot tub. Business services. Pets allowed. | 1508 Paseo del Pueblo Sur | 505/758–2254 or 800/428–3626 | fax 505/758–5077 | www.sagebrushinn.com | 100 rooms | $65–$140 | AE, D, DC, MC, V.

Sun God Lodge. This adobe motel is on the main highway, 1½ mi from Taos Plaza. The well-priced rooms overlook a courtyard. There are several suites that have fireplaces and kitchenettes. Picnic area. Some in-room data ports, some kitchenettes, some microwaves, some refrigerators, cable TV, some in-room VCRs. Hot tub. Laundry facilities. Pets allowed (fee). | 919 Paseo del Pueblo Sur | 505/758–3162 or 800/821–2437 | fax 505/758–1716 | www.sungodlodge.com | 55 rooms | $55–$139 | AE, D, DC, MC, V.

MODERATE

Adobe and Pines B and B. This B&B 3 mi south of the Plaza has uniquely decorated rooms that feature fireplaces and sunken baths. Guests can enjoy a gourmet breakfast and a great view of Taos Mountain or the beautifully landscaped grounds. | Hwy. 68, Rancho de Taos | 505/751–0947 or 800/723–8267 | fax 505/758–8423 | www.newmex.com/apbandb | 8 rooms | $95–$185 | AE, D, DC, MC, V.

American Artists Gallery House. An unusual hotel with an art display and a quiet, secluded location. Complimentary breakfast. TVs in some rooms. No kids under 8. Some pets allowed. | 132 Frontier La. | 505/758–4446 or 800/532–2041 | fax 505/758–0497 | taoswebb.com/hotel/artistshouse | 10 rooms (5 with shower only) | $75–$150 | AE, MC, V.

Casa Benavides Bed & Breakfast Inn. This bed-and-breakfast one block from the Plaza combines the charm of an old Taos adobe with modern luxuries. Rooms are furnished with antiques and original art works, and there is a lovely courtyard in the main building. Many rooms have fireplaces and even skylights. Complimentary breakfast. Some kitchenettes, some refrigerators, cable TV, some in-room VCRs (and videos), some room phones, no TV in some rooms. 2 hot tubs. | 137 Kit Carson Rd. | 505/758–1772 or 800/552–1772 | fax 505/758–5738 | www.taosnet.com/casabena | 33 rooms | $80–$195 | AE, D, MC, V.

Cottonwood Inn. Six miles north of Taos, this inn built in 1947 was once the residence of flamboyant local artist Wolfgang Pogzeba and was decorated by him as a pueblo-style adobe. Rooms have excellent views and many have fireplaces. Picnic area, complimentary breakfast. No air-conditioning, some microwaves, some refrigerators, some in-room hot tubs, no room phones, TV in common area. Outdoor hot tub, sauna. Business services. | 2 Hwy. 230, El Prado | 505/776–5826 or 800/324–7120 | fax 505/776–1141 | www.taos-cottonwood.com | 7 rooms (1 with shower only) | $95–$175 | AE, D, MC, V.

El Pueblo Lodge and Condominiums. This property is on 3½ acres north of town, near Kit Carson Park. Rooms are offered in a 1950s-style motel around a courtyard, in a newer two-story building dating from 1972, and an even newer building, which has the nicest rooms. Condominium units are also available and are good for families; these can be rented by the unit or by the individual room. Some rooms have fireplaces. Complimentary Continental breakfast. In-room data ports, some kitchenettes, microwaves, refrigerators, cable TV. Pool. Hot tub. Pets allowed (fee). | 412 Paseo del Pueblo Norte | 505/758–8700 or 800/433–9612 | fax 505/758–7321 | www.taoswebb.com/hotel/elpueblo | 60 rooms | $70–$165 rooms, $115–$248 condos | AE, D, MC, V.

★ **Hacienda del Sol.** This pueblo-style house belonged to Mabel Dodge Luhan. Most rooms have kiva-style fireplaces and southwestern, handcrafted furnishings and original artwork. Check out the jet-black bathroom of the Los Amantes Room. This has been named one of the most romantic places to stay in Taos. Picnic area, complimentary breakfast. No air-conditioning, refrigerators, no TV, TV in common area. Business services. No smoking. | 109 Mabel Dodge La. | 505/758–0287 | fax 505/751–0319 | www.taoshaciendadelsol.com | 11 rooms (2 with shower only), 2 suites | $75–$225 rooms, $135–$175 suites | MC, V.

Mabel Dodge Luhan House. This lodging was the former home of Mabel Dodge and her husband, Tony Luhan. Hundreds of famous people have stayed here including D. H. Lawrence, Paul Strand, Ansel Adams, and Georgia O'Keeffe. The house is in the National Register of Historic Places and has antiques, fireplaces, and hardwood floors, but pretty basic amenities. The historic gate house is perfect for groups or families, and includes a full kitchen. Complimentary breakfast. | 240 Morada La. | 505/751–9686 or 800/846–2235 | fax 505/737–0365 | 17 rooms (2 with shared bath), 1 gate house | $85–$160 rooms, $200 gatehouse (for four) | MC, V.

Quail Ridge Inn Resort. This large resort is well situated between Taos Ski Valley and Taos. It consists mostly of one- and two-story modern adobe bungalows. Some suites have kitchens and fireplaces. Restaurant, bar. No air-conditioning, some kitchenettes, microwaves, refrigerators, cable TV, in-room VCRs. Pool. Hot tub, massage. Tennis. Gym. Children's programs (ages 5–15) in summer. Business services. | 8 Taos Ski Valley Rd. | 505/776–2211 or 800/

624–4448 | fax 505/776–2949 | www.quailridgeinn.com | 50 rooms, 60 suites | $60–$140, $170–$300 suites | AE, D, DC, MC, V.

EXPENSIVE

Inn at Snakedance. Fashioned after the classic European Alpine lodges, the inn is 19 mi from Taos in the Taos Ski Valley. The dining room's high ceilings have 100-year-old beams. The library and the fireplace are spots to relax and enjoy an after-ski coffee. The rooms, some with fireplaces, have king- or queen-size beds and a bath with separate vanity. Restaurant. Minibars, refrigerators, cable TV. Hot tub, massage, sauna. Gym. Library. Laundry facilities. Free parking. No smoking. | 110 Sutton Pl | 505/776–2277 or 800/322–9815 | fax 505/776–1410 | www.taosweb.com/snakedance | 60 rooms | $75–$270 | AE, D, DC, MC, V.

★ **Inn on La Loma Plaza.** A genuine adobe hacienda with fireplaces and a terrace, this building is in the National Register of Historic Places, 2½ blocks from the Plaza. With expansive gardens and spectacular mountain views. Complimentary breakfast. Cable TV. Pool. Hot tub. | 315 Ranchitos | 505/758–1717 or 800/530–3040 | fax 505/751–0155 | 5 rooms, 2 suites | $80–$195, $145–$440 suites | AE, D, MC, V.

Salsa del Salto Bed and Breakfast. At this luxurious B&B 10 mi north of Taos you can opt to look out over the Sangre de Cristo Mountains or the Taos Mesa. Some rooms have fireplaces. Picnic area, complimentary breakfast. No air-conditioning, some in-room hot tubs, some in-room VCRs, no room phones, no TV in some rooms, TV in common area. Pool. Hot tub. Tennis. No kids under 6. No smoking. | 505/776–2422 or 800/530–3097 | fax 505/776–5734 | www.bandbtaos.com | 10 rooms | $85–$160 | AE, MC, V.

San Geronimo Lodge. Just off Kit Carson Road, this 1925 lodge, which sits on 2½ acres, has great views of the Sangre de Cristo Mountains and attractive grounds. Many rooms have fireplaces. Complimentary breakfast. Cable TV. Pool. Hot tub. | 1101 Witt Rd. | 505/751–3776 or 800/894–4119 | fax 505/751–1493 | sgl@newmex.com | 18 rooms | $95–$150 | AE, D, DC, MC, V.

Taos Inn. Some rooms at this historic inn are quite small, others are luxuriously large. All are decorated with Mexican bedspreads and have Mexican-tile baths; some have fireplaces. Restaurant, bar (with entertainment). No air-conditioning in some rooms, cable TV. Pool. Hot tub. Business services. | 125 Paseo del Pueblo Norte | 505/758–2233 or 800/826–7466 | fax 505/758–5776 | taosinn@taos.newmex.com | www.taosinn.com | 36 rooms in 3 buildings | $85–$225 | AE, D, DC, MC, V.

Willows Inn. Beautiful landscaped gardens with fountains add grace to this majestic, two-story adobe that once was home to Taos artist E. Marin Hennings. Extra touches include in-room CD players and kiva fireplaces. Complimentary breakfast. | 412 Kit Carson Rd. | 505/758–2558 or 800/525–8267 | fax 505/758–5445 | 5 rooms | $100–$150 | AE, D, MC, V.

VERY EXPENSIVE

Adobe and Stars Inn. This impressive B&B offers spacious rooms, all with fireplaces, hot tubs or double showers, ceiling fans, and beamed ceilings. Large windows and decks enhance views of the surrounding Sangre de Cristo Mountains. Courtyard rooms have private entrances. Complimentary breakfast. No air-conditioning, in-room VCRs (and movies), TV in common area. Some pets allowed. No smoking. | 584 Hwy. 150 | 505/776–2776 or 800/211–7076 | fax 505/776–2872 | www.taosnet.com/stars | 7 rooms (3 with shower only) | $115–$180 | AE, D, MC, V.

Alma del Monte. This B&B has mountain views and is midway between the Plaza and the slopes of Taos Ski Valley. The luxurious rooms have Saltillo-tile floors, a vanity, a fireplace, a sitting area, and large bathrooms. Three of the rooms have private gardens. Afternoon refreshments are served daily. Complimentary breakfast. In-room hot tubs, no TV. | 372 Hondo Seco Rd. | 505/776–2721 or 800/273–7203 | fax 505/776–8888 | www.newmex.com/spirit | 5 rooms | $150–$250 | AE, MC, V.

Austing Haus. This large timber-frame building (the largest in the United States) is surrounded by national forest land, about 18 mi northeast of Taos. Especially popular with skiers due to its proximity to the Taos Ski Valley (1½ mi), but cheaper rates keep it popular in summer too. Dining room, complimentary Continental breakfast. No air-conditioning, cable TV. Hot tubs. Laundry facilities. Business services. Pets allowed. | 1282 Hwy. 150/Taos Ski Valley Rd. | 505/776–2649 or 800/748–2932 | fax 505/776–8751 | taoswebb.com/hotel/austinghaus | 24 rooms in 3 buildings | $120–$180 | Closed mid-Apr.–mid-May | AE, DC, MC, V.

Casa de las Chimeneas. The inn's most notable feature is a large formal garden with fountains surrounded by adobe walls, a restful place for guests year-round. Common areas feature regional art; all rooms have private entrances, kiva fireplaces, French doors, traditional ceiling beams, and hand-carved furniture. Complimentary breakfast. No air-conditioning, refrigerators, cable TV. Massage. Gym. Library. No smoking. | 405 Cordoba La. | 505/758–4777 | fax 505/758–3976 | www.visittaos.com | 6 rooms, 2 suites | $160–$290, $325–$575 suites | AE, D, DC, MC, V.

Casa Grande Guest Ranch. View the majestic Sangre de Cristo Mountains from this 40-acre ranch between Taos and Taos Ski Valley. There is a patio, garden, and fireplaces in the common area. Two- and three-night special horseback-riding packages are offered that include pack trips to an 8,000-acre ranch. Complimentary breakfast. Hot tub. Gym, horseback riding. No kids under 18. | 75 Luis O. Torres Rd. | 505/776–1303 or 888/236–1303 | fax 505/776–2177 | www.taosguestranch.com | 3 rooms | $125–$195 | AE, MC, V.

Fechin Inn. Located next door to the former home of Taos artist Nicolai Fechin, this luxury hotel built in 1996 is dominated by a handsome two-story lobby; the large rooms are decorated in southwestern style. Guests have free admission to the Fechin Institute, next door. Hot tub. Health club. Library. Business services. Pets allowed. | 227 Paseo del Pueblo Norte | 505/751–1000 or 800/811–2933 | fax 505/751–7338 | www.fechin-inn.com | 84 rooms | $109–$319 | AE, D, DC, MC, V.

★ **Touchstone B&B.** This historic adobe estate along the edge of Taos Pueblo is secluded. Some rooms, which are furnished with antiques and original art, have fireplaces and hot tubs. Complimentary breakfast. No air-conditioning, cable TV, in-room VCRs (and movies). Gym. Business services. No smoking. | 110 Mabel Dodge La. | /758–0192 | fax 505/758–3498 | taoswebb.com/nmusa/touchstone | 8 rooms | $105–$250 | AE, MC, V.

TRUTH OR CONSEQUENCES

MAP 9, D8

(Nearby town also listed: Socorro)

When Ralph Edwards, the host of the *Truth or Consequences* radio show of the late 1940s, offered to broadcast his show live from any town in the country that would change its name to that of his program, the Hot Springs, New Mexico, Chamber of Commerce took him up on the deal. Edwards arrived on April 1, 1950, and Truth or Consequences became the state's newest town. A Ralph Edwards Truth or Consequences Fiesta is still held annually in the town.

Truth or Consequences is near the center of Sierra County and is convenient to Elephant Butte Lake, which offers outstanding water sports and fishing, as well as the Gila and Cibola national forests, where hiking, backpacking, fishing, and other wilderness pastimes can be pursued. The Geronimo Springs Museum is a good place to get your bearings on what to see in this diverse region.

Information: Truth or Consequences/Sierra County Chamber of Commerce | Drawer 31, Truth or Consequences, 87901 | 800/831–9487 or 505/894–3536 | village.global-drum.com/sierra_newmexico.

Attractions

Caballo Lake State Park. This state park 18 mi south of Truth or Consequences offers swimming, fishing, boating, windsurfing, and other water sports. | Off I–25 | 505/743–3942 | www.emnrd.state.nm.us | $4 per vehicle | Daily.

Callahan's Auto Museum. This museum, dedicated to vintage cars, has over 1,000 toy vehicles, old gas pumps, old service-station signs, vintage auto parts, and antique vehicles such as a 1936 Pierce Arrow Limousine and a 1960 Ford Thunderbird. | 410 Cedar St. | 505/894–6900 | www.village.globaldrum.com/sierra_newmexico/auto.htm | $3 | Mon.–Sat. 10–4.

Elephant Butte Lake State Park. A 1916 dam across the Rio Grande formed this lake 15 mi north of Truth or Consequences. It reaches behind the dam for more than 40 mi and encompasses some 36,000 surface acres of water and 200 mi of shoreline. The lake and surrounding countryside became a New Mexico state park in 1965 and today is the most popular unit in the system. You can fish, boat, picnic, water-ski, hike, or just relax at this top-of-the-line facility. | Hwy. 51, 15 mi north of Truth or Consequences | 505/744–5421 | www.emnrd.state.nm.us | $4 per vehicle | Daily.

Geronimo Springs Museum. This large museum exhibits the history of Sierra County and the surrounding region, from prehistoric times to the present. The Ralph Edwards Room tells the story of how the town became Truth or Consequences. | 211 Main St. | 505/894–6600 | $2 | Mon.–Sat. 9–5.

ON THE CALENDAR

APR.: *Elephant Butte Balloon Regatta.* This balloon-baton-boat rally is a visual delight. Over 50 pilots touch down on Elephant Butte Lake in their hot-air balloons to pass a baton to a boat that then takes it to the race's final destination. | 505/744–4708.

Dining

Hodges Corner Restaurant American/Casual. This is a good place to have a meal after a day of boating and fishing at Elephant Butte Lake. Enjoy the barbecued pork ribs, cube steaks, and deep-fried fish. The portions are generous. | 915 NM 195, Elephant Butte | 505/744–5626 | $7–$15 | AE, D, MC, V.

Los Arcos Steak House. Steak. Steaks and seafood are served up in a hacienda-like building that features a lovely garden. Open grill. Salad bar. | 1400 N. Date St. | 505/894–6200 | No lunch | $6–$39 | AE, D, DC, MC, V.

Town Talk Café. American/Casual. The locals really do come here to catch up on the latest gossip. Try the deep-fried catfish or the red or green chile burrito. | 426 Broadway | 505/894–3119 | $4–$6 | No credit cards.

Lodging

Ace Lodge. This small, quiet, and economical motel is in the heart of town. Restaurant, bar, picnic area. Cable TV. Pool. Playground. Airport shuttle. Some pets allowed. | 1302 N. Date St. (I–25 Business) | 505/894–2151 | 38 rooms | $33–$70 | AE, DC, MC, V.

Best Western Hot Springs Inn. A modern, clean facility convenient for when you're passing through. Cable TV. Pool. Business services. | 2270 N. Date St. | 505/894–6665 | fax 505/894–6665 | 40 rooms | $55—$60 | AE, D, DC, MC, V.

Charles Motel and Bath House. Built in the 1940s, this hotel and spa was created as a place for relaxation. The apartment-style rooms are peaceful, and to help you center yourself, some rooms do not have phones for needless intrusions. This is a place to recuperate from the stress of life. Enjoy the massage therapy, reflexology, holistic healing, and wraps. Kitchenettes, refrigerators, cable TV, some room phones. Hot tub, massage, sauna, spa. Gym. Pets allowed. | 601 Broadway | 505/894–7154 or 800/317–4518 | www.globaldrum.com/sierra_newmexico/spa | 20 rooms | $35–$45 | AE, D, MC, V.

TRUTH OR
CONSEQUENCES

INTRO
ATTRACTIONS
DINING
LODGING

Dam Site Recreation Area. At the Elephant Butte Dam, these one- to four-bedroom cabins 5 mi east of town have lake views. Some of the cabins have kitchenettes, but none have phones or TVs. The combination bar/restaurant serves steak, seafood, and sandwiches. Restaurant, bar. Some kitchenettes, some refrigerators, no room phones, no TV. | 77B Engle Star Rte | 505/894–2073 | 16 cabins | $60–$140 | AE, D, MC, V.

Quality Inn. This well-situated hotel 5 mi north of Truth or Consequences overlooks the lovely Elephant Butte Lake. Restaurant, bar, picnic area, room service. Cable TV. Pool, lake. Tennis court. Playground. Business services. Pets allowed. | Hwy. 195 at Warm Springs | 505/744–5431 | fax 505/744–5044 | 48 rooms | $69–$90 | AE, D, DC, MC, V.

TUCUMCARI

MAP 9, H4

(Nearby towns also listed: Las Vegas, Santa Rosa)

Tucumcari sits astride historic Route 66, and as you drive through the town you are reminded of a 1950s movie. The community had its beginnings in the early 1900s, when the railroad was routed nearby, and before long eight trains were stopping daily. Today Tucumcari is the easternmost travel-services center in the state along Interstate 40, and provides visitors with a wealth of recreational and cultural attractions, including an array of outdoor activities on nearby Conchas and Ute lakes, nature-watching along the Canadian River, and delving into the prehistoric past at the Mesalands Dinosaur Museum. There are many chain motels in the area, as well as a variety of restaurants.

Information: **Tucumcari/Quay County Chamber of Commerce** | Drawer E, Tucumcari, 88401 | 505/461–1694 | www.tucumcarinm.com.

Attractions
Conchas Lake State Park. The fishing at this 9,600-acre lake, 34 mi from Tucumcari, is great—go for bass, catfish, walleye pike, and crappie. Rental boats available. | NM 104 | 505/868–2270 | www.emnrd.state.nm.us | $4 per vehicle | Daily.

Mesalands Dinosaur Museum. This museum has a large hands-on collection of prehistoric skeletons, fossils, and creatures. Also has the world's only Torvosaurus skeleton (a 30-ft-long carnivore that is a close relative to T-Rex) on exhibit. | 1st and Laughlin Sts. | 505/461–DINO | www.mesatc.cc.nm.us/adminserv/admindino2.htm | $5 | Tues.–Sat. noon–8.

Tucumcari Historical Museum. Legends come alive in this two-story, redbrick, Victorian building via thousands of artifacts depicting life in Indian days and among the region's first pioneers. There are also a genuine nickelodeon and a moonshine still. | 416 S. Adams St. | 505/461–4201 | $3 | June–Aug., Mon.–Sat. 9–6; Sept.–May, Tues.–Sat. 9–5.

Ute Lake State Park. Outstanding marina facilities as well as campsites and rental boats are available at this lake, 22 mi northeast of Tucumcari. The fishing is good for walleye pike, and there's waterskiing and swimming. | U.S. 54, Logan | 505/487–2284 | www.emnrd.state.nm.us | $4 per vehicle | Daily.

ON THE CALENDAR
JULY: *Route 66 Diamond Jubilee Celebration.* This event is held in conjunction with the Quay County Fair at the Quay County Fairgrounds. | 505/461–1694.
OCT.: *Tucumcari Rotary Club Air Show.* This event at the Tucumcari Municipal Airport features jet teams doing aerial acrobatics. | 505/461–1200.

Dining

Del's Restaurant. Mexican. This restaurant is popular with the locals. Specialties include steak or chicken fajitas, and juicy rib-eye steaks. In the heart of town. | 1202 E. Tucumcari Blvd. | 505/461–1740 | Closed Sun. | $6–$15 | MC, V.

K-Bob's Restaurant. Steak. This busy chain steak house has a varied menu, with an emphasis on meat. You can dine on steaks, shrimp, chicken, sandwiches, burgers, and salads. Next door to the Best Western Discovery Inn. | 215 E. Estrella | 505/461–0002 | $5–$13 | AE, D, MC, V.

La Cita Restaurant. Mexican. This friendly restaurant is underneath a big sombrero and was built in the 1950s on historic Route 66. The green-chile chicken enchiladas and the chicken or beef fajitas are very popular. | 812 S. 1st St. | 505/461–0949 | $7–$10 | AE, D, MC, V.

Martin's Ice Cream Shop and Catering. American/Casual. This ice-cream shop has more than just ice cream. The specialties include the "Famous 66 Burger" with cheese, green chile, and all the trimmings, and the Tucumcari taco salad. | 1920 E. Tucumcari Blvd. | 505/461–2200 | Closed Mon. | $2–$6 | No credit cards.

Pow Wow Restaurant & Lounge. American/Casual. This restaurant is in the Best Western Pow Wow Inn. You can enjoy a hamburger, the steak *tampico* (center-cut filet mignon with tomatoes, onions, jalapeno peppers, and spices in a white wine sauce), or the combination platter that has a beef rolled enchilada, a chicken taco, a tamale, salsa, and chips. Entertainment weekends. | 801 Tucumcari Blvd. | 505/461–2587 | $7–$17 | AE, D, MC, V.

Lodging

Best Western Discovery Inn. This motel is Mission-style outside, but basic motel-style inside. It has reliable basic amenities, and it's just off Interstate 40. Restaurant. In-room data ports, some refrigerators, cable TV, some in-room VCRs (and movies). Pool. Hot tub. Gym. Laundry facilities. Business services, airport shuttle. | 200 E. Estrella St. | 505/461–4884 | fax 505/461–2463 | www.bestwestern.com | 107 rooms | $50–$70 | AE, D, DC, MC, V.

Budget Host Royal Palacio. This affordable small motel is on historic Route 66. Picnic area. Cable TV. Laundry facilities. Pets allowed. | 1620 E. Tucumcari Blvd. | 505/461–1212 | www.budgethost.com | 24 rooms | $20–$30 | AE, D, MC, V.

Comfort Inn. This modern two-story motel has mountain views, and it's right on historic Route 66. Complimentary Continental breakfast. Cable TV. Pool. Pets allowed. | 2800 E. Tucumcari Blvd. | 505/461–4094 or 800/228–5160 | fax 505/461–4099 | www.comfortinn.com | 59 rooms | $54–$66 | AE, D, DC, MC, V.

Days Inn–Tucumcari. This motel is 1 mi from the business district. The rooms are clean, quiet, and comfortable. The rates are reasonable. Complimentary Continental breakfast. Cable TV. Pets allowed. | 2623 S. 1st St. | 505/461–3158 or 800/544–8313 | fax 505/461–4871 | www.daysinn.com | 40 rooms | $45–$66 | AE, D, DC, MC, V.

Dream Catcher B&B. This mansion built in the 1900s has one suite with a queen bed and a private bath, four rooms that share a bath, and a third-floor sleeping dorm with three full beds and three twin beds, all of which share one bath. There's a large veranda for sipping tea and relaxing. Antiques fill the home, and it's your only nonchain choice in town. Picnic area, complimentary Continental breakfast. Some refrigerators, no room phones, no TV in some rooms, TV in common area. Library. Laundry facilities. Free parking. Pets allowed (fee). | 307 E. High St. | 505/461–2423 | 5 rooms (4 with shared bath), 1 dorm-style room (with shared bath) | $65 | MC, V.

Econo Lodge. This small and affordable motel is on historic Route 66. Cable TV. Business services. Pets allowed. | 3400 E. Tucumcari Blvd. | 505/461–4194 | fax 505/461–4911 | www.econolodge.com | 41 rooms | $40–$76 | AE, D, DC, MC, V.

Holiday Inn. This nice motor hotel is especially suited for the business traveler, with generous work desks and a place to hook up a laptop. Restaurant, bar, room service. In-room data ports, cable TV. Pool. Hot tub. Playground. Laundry facilities. Business services. Pets allowed. | 3716 E. Tucumcari Blvd. | 505/461–3780 or 800/335–3780 | fax 505/461–3931 | www.holiday-inn.com | 100 rooms | $45–$79 | AE, D, DC, MC, V.

Microtel Inn. This motel is right off of Interstate 40. The rooms are comfortable and relatively spacious, basic accommodations that are centrally located. Complimentary Continental breakfast. In-room data ports, cable TV. Pool, hot tub. Pet allowed. | 2420 S. 1st St. | 505/461–0600 | 53 rooms | $50–$65 | AE, D, DC, MC, V.

Rodeway Inn West. This motel on historic Route 66 is in Tucumcari's main business district, on the west side of town. Complimentary Continental breakfast. Cable TV. Pool. Pets allowed (fee). | 1302 W. Tucumcari Blvd. | 505/461–3140 | fax 505/461–2729 | 61 rooms | $33 | AE, DC, MC, V.

Super 8. This budget motel is on historic Route 66; the year-round pool is a boon for traveling families. Cable TV. Pool. Laundry facilities. Business services. | 4001 E. Tucumcari Blvd. | 505/461–4444 | fax 505/461–4320 | www.super8.com | 64 rooms, 13 suites | $37–$53, $46–$56 suites | AE, D, DC, MC, V.

ZUÑI PUEBLO

MAP 9, B5

(Nearby towns also listed: Gallup, Grants)

Zuñi Pueblo was first viewed by Europeans in 1539, when a Spanish priest named Fray Marcos de Niza visited there and described the town as "larger than the city of Mexico." De Niza's wonderful tales of untold riches in the area brought Coronado to the place the following year. Finding no gold, the conquistador attacked the pueblo, which they called Hawikul, and sacked the village, but not before being wounded himself.

It is said that no village in North America has more skilled craftsmen than Zuñi Pueblo. Accordingly, there is a high concentration of arts, crafts, and curio shops in the immediate area, highlighting local artisans' wonderful silver and turquoise jewelry, exquisite pottery, and fine furniture. The pueblo is 73 mi southwest of Grants and 34 mi south of Gallup.

Information: **Zuñi Pueblo** | Hwy. 53 | 505/782–4481.

Attractions
A:shiwi A:wan Museum and Heritage Center This museum celebrates Zuñi history and culture, and was built in harmony with traditional and environmental values of the Zuñi people. Its mission is to be a learning museum; food preparation classes, storytelling, and other activities take place here in addition to changing exhibits. Be sure to see the *Emergence and Migration* mural, as well as the artifacts, baskets, and pottery on display. | 1222 NM 53 | 505/782–4403 | Free | Weekdays 9–5:30.

ON THE CALENDAR
AUG.: *Zuñi Tribal Fair and Rodeo.* This four-day festival at the Zuñi Fairgrounds has a carnival, a rodeo, food vendors, children's activities, and nightly dance performances. | 505/782–4481.

Dining
Route 53 Café. American/Casual. Enjoy a burger, a sandwich, soup, or salad at this casual restaurant that is frequented by locals and tourists alike. | 1169 Hwy. 53 | 505/782–4404 | $2–$7 | AE, MC.

Lodging

The Inn at Halona. This B&B is in a three-story pueblo-style building that has an outdoor patio. The inn's lounge area has a TV, gas fireplace, fax machine, and a single data port. The comfortable rooms are decorated with Zuñi and southwestern art; some have views, ceiling fans, and king-size beds. Complimentary breakfast. Some in-room VCRs, no TV in some rooms, TV in common area. Laundry facilities. No pets. | 23 B Pia Mesa Rd. | 505/782–4547 or 800/752–3271 | fax 505/782–2155 | www.halona.com | 8 rooms (5 with shared baths) | $79–$110 | MC, V.

ZUÑI PUEBLO

INTRO
ATTRACTIONS
DINING
LODGING

Index

Notes

Notes

Notes

Notes

Notes

Notes

Notes

Notes

Notes

TALK TO US

Fill out this quick survey and receive a free *Fodor's How to Pack* (while supplies last)

1 Which Road Guide did you purchase?
(Check all that apply.)
❐ AL/AR/LA/MS/TN   ❐ IL/IA/MO/WI
❐ AZ/CO/NM   ❐ IN/KY/MI/OH/WV
❐ CA   ❐ KS/OK/TX
❐ CT/MA/RI   ❐ ME/NH/VT
❐ DE/DC/MD/PA/VA   ❐ MN/NE/ND/SD
❐ FL   ❐ NJ/NY
❐ GA/NC/SC   ❐ OR/WA
❐ ID/MT/NV/UT/WY

2 How did you learn about the Road Guides?
❐ TV ad
❐ Radio ad
❐ Newspaper or magazine ad
❐ Newspaper or magazine article
❐ TV or radio feature
❐ Bookstore display/clerk recommendation
❐ Recommended by family/friend
❐ Other:_____

3 Did you use other guides for your trip?
❐ AAA   ❐ Insiders' Guide
❐ Compass American Guide   ❐ Mobil
❐ Fodor's   ❐ Moon Handbook
❐ Frommer's   ❐ Other:_____

4 Did you use any of the following for planning?
❐ Tourism offices   ❐ Internet   ❐ Travel agent

5 Did you buy a Road Guide for (check one):
❐ Leisure trip
❐ Business trip
❐ Mix of business and leisure

6 Where did you buy your Road Guide?
❐ Bookstore
❐ Other store
❐ On-line
❐ Borrowed from a friend
❐ Borrowed from a library
❐ Other:_____

7 Why did you buy a Road Guide? (Check all that apply.)
❐ Number of cities/towns listed
❐ Comprehensive coverage
❐ Number of lodgings   ❐ Driving tours
❐ Number of restaurants ❐ Maps
❐ Number of attractions ❐ Fodor's brand name
❐ Other:_____

8 Did you use this guide primarily:
❐ For pretrip planning   ❐ While traveling
❐ For planning and while traveling

9 What was the duration of your trip?
❐ 2-3 days   ❐ 11 or more days
❐ 4-6 days   ❐ Taking more than 1 trip
❐ 7-10 days

10 Did you use the guide to select
❐ Hotels   ❐ Restaurants

11 Did you stay primarily in a
❐ Hotel   ❐ Hostel
❐ Motel   ❐ Campground
❐ Resort   ❐ Dude ranch
❐ Bed-and-breakfast ❐ With family or friends
❐ RV/camper   ❐ Other:_____

12 What sights and activities did you most enjoy?
❐ Historical sights   ❐ Shopping
❐ Sports   ❐ Theaters
❐ National parks   ❐ Museums
❐ State parks   ❐ Major cities
❐ Attractions off the beaten path

13 How much did you spend per adult for this trip?
❐ Less than $500   ❐ $751-$1,000
❐ $501-$750   ❐ More than $1,000

14 How many traveled in your party?
___ Adults   ___ Children   ___ Pets

15 Did you
❐ Fly to destination   ❐ Rent a van or RV
❐ Drive your own vehicle   ❐ Take a train
❐ Rent a car   ❐ Take a bus

16 How many miles did you travel round-trip?
❐ Less than 100   ❐ 501-750
❐ 101-300   ❐ 751-1,000
❐ 301-500   ❐ More than 1,000

17 What items did you take on your vacation?
❐ Traveler's checks   ❐ Digital camera
❐ Credit card   ❐ Cell phone
❐ Gasoline card   ❐ Computer
❐ Phone card   ❐ PDA
❐ Camera   ❐ Other

18 Would you use Fodor's Road Guides again?
❐ Yes   ❐ No

19 How would you like to see Road Guides changed?

☐ More ☐ Less Dining
☐ More ☐ Less Lodging
☐ More ☐ Less Sports
☐ More ☐ Less Activities
☐ More ☐ Less Attractions
☐ More ☐ Less Shopping
☐ More ☐ Less Driving tours
☐ More ☐ Less Maps
☐ More ☐ Less Historical information
☐ Other:_____

20 Tell us about yourself.

☐ Male   ☐ Female

Age:
☐ 18-24   ☐ 35-44   ☐ 55-64
☐ 25-34   ☐ 45-54   ☐ Over 65

Income:
☐ Less than $25,000   ☐ $50,001-$75,000
☐ $25,001-$50,000   ☐ More than $75,000

Name:_____ E-mail: _____

Address:_____ City: _____ State: _____ Zip: _____

Fodor's Travel Publications
Attn: Road Guide Survey
280 Park Avenue
New York, NY 10017

Atlas

ON

MONTANA

IDAHO

WYOMING

DA

UTAH

COLORADO

ARIZONA

NEW MEXICO

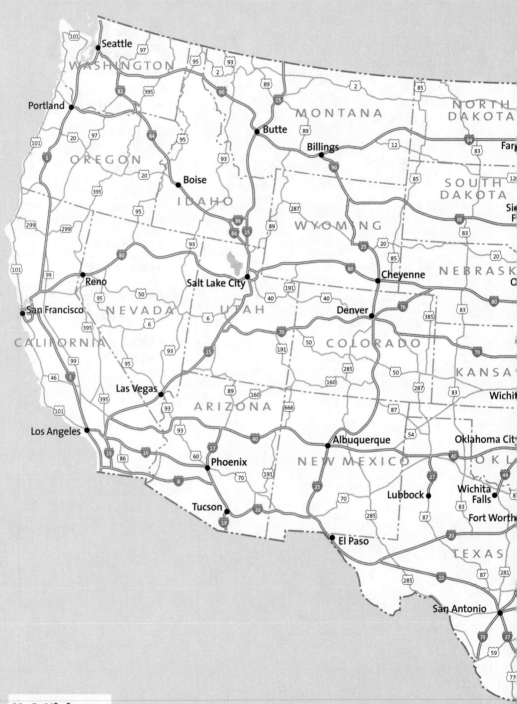

U. S. Highways

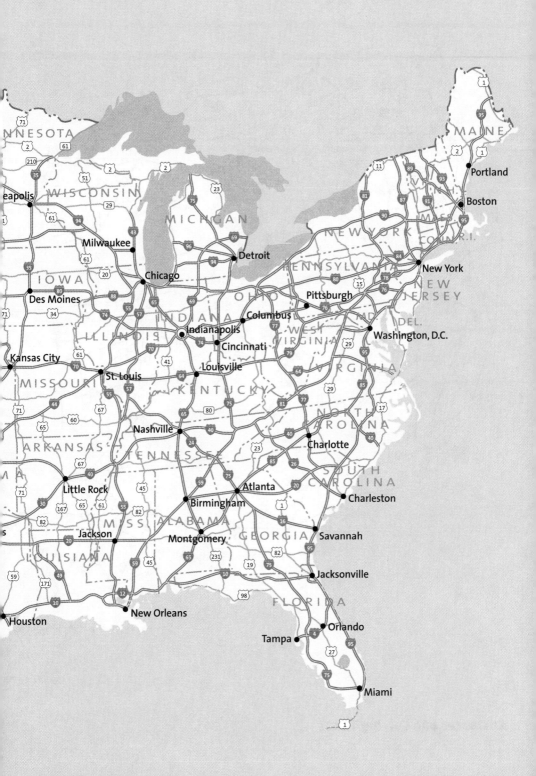

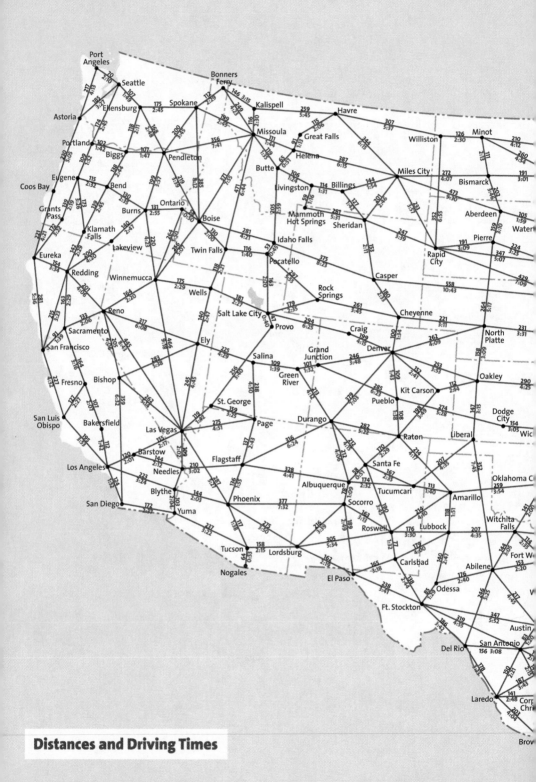

Distances and Driving Times

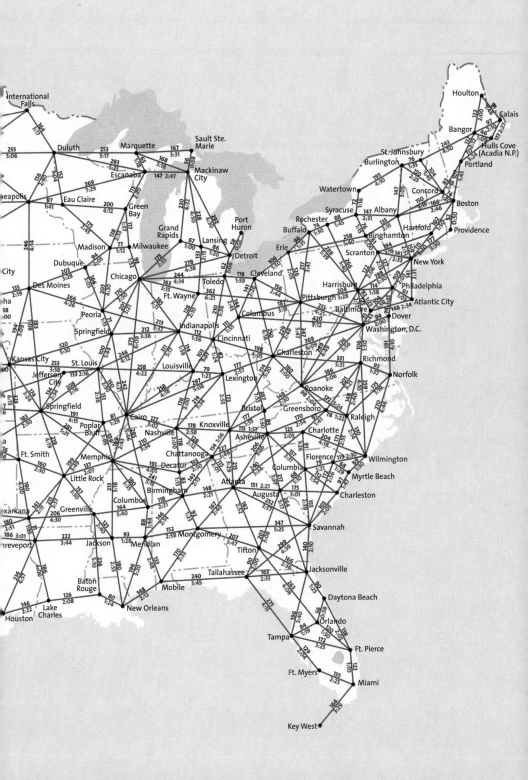

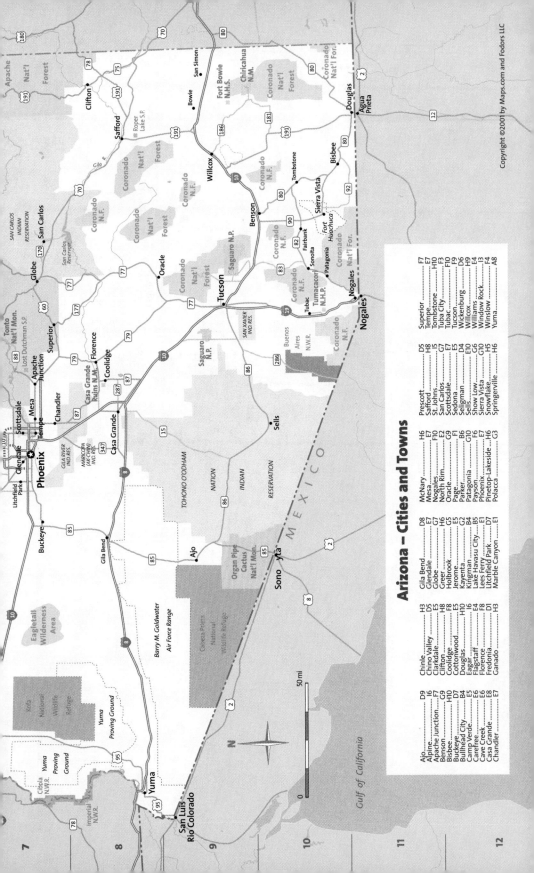

Arizona – Cities and Towns

Copyright ©2001 by Maps.com and Fodors LLC

Ajo	D9
Alpine	I6
Apache Junction	F7
Benson	G9
Bisbee	H10
Buckeye	D7
Bullhead City	B4
Camp Verde	E5
Carefree	E6
Cave Creek	E6
Casa Grande	E8
Chandler	E7

Chinle	H3
Chino Valley	D5
Clarkdale	E5
Clifton	H8
Coolidge	E8
Cottonwood	E5
Douglas	H10
Eagar	I6
Flagstaff	E5
Fredonia	D1
Ganado	H3

Gila Bend	D8
Globe	E7
Greer	F10
Holbrook	G5
Jerome	E5
Kayenta	F1
Kingman	C2
Lake Havasu City	B4
Lees Ferry	E1
Litchfield Park	D7
Marble Canyon	H3

McNary	H6
Mesa	E7
Nogales	F10
North Rim	E2
Oracle	G9
Page	E2
Parker	B6
Patagonia	G10
Payson	F6
Phoenix	E7
Pinetop-Lakeside	H6
Polacca	G3

Prescott	D5
Safford	H8
St. Johns	J5
San Carlos	G7
Scottsdale	E7
Sedona	E5
Seligman	D4
Show Low	G6
Sierra Vista	G10
Snowflake	H5
Springerville	G3

Superior	F7
Tempe	E7
Tombstone	H10
Tuba City	F3
Tubac	F10
Tucson	F9
Wickenburg	D6
Willcox	H9
Williams	E4
Window Rock	J3
Winslow	F4
Yuma	A8

50 mi

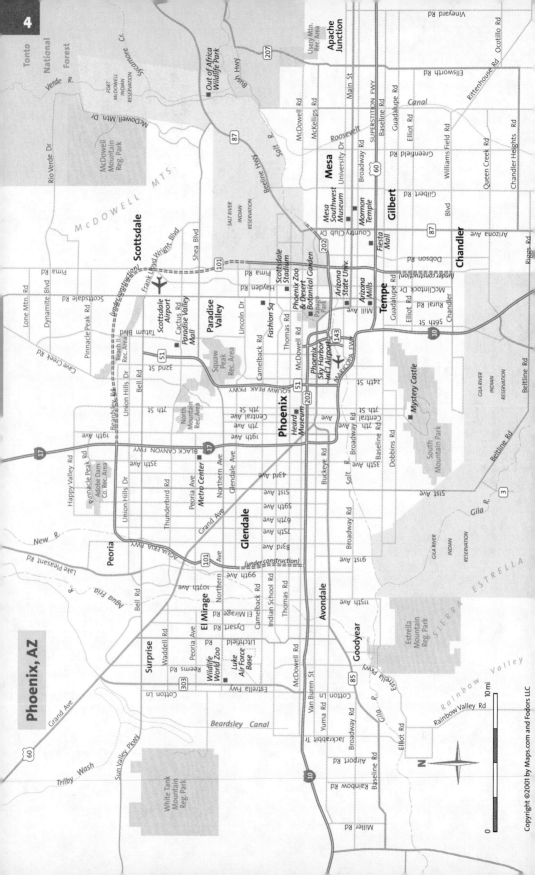

Saguaro National Park (West)

Tucson

South Tucson

Davis-Monthan Air Force Base

Davis-Monthan Air Force Base

Tucson Mountain Park

Tucson Int'l Airport

Points of interest / Labels:

Melpomene Way
Fort Lowell Rd
Tanque Lp Verde Rd
Snyder Rd
Houghton Rd
Catalina Hwy
Broadway Blvd
Old Spanish Trail
Pantano Wash
Houghton Rd
Bear Canyon Rd
Speedway Blvd
Camino Seco
Harrison Rd
Irvington Rd
Valencia Rd
22nd St
Sabino Canyon Rd
Escalante Rd
Lincoln Reg. Park
Sunrise Dr
River Rd
Tanque Verde
Morris K. Udall Reg. Park
Pantano Rd
Kolb Rd
Fort Lowell Park
Golf Links Rd
Wilmot Rd
Pima Air & Space Mus.
Thomas Jay Reg. Park
Craycroft Rd
Craycroft Rd
Los Reales Rd
Ft. Lowell Hist. Site Rd & Mus.
Swan Rd
Swan Rd
Grant
Tucson Botanical Gardens
Alvernon Way
Valencia Rd
Fort Lowell Rd
Country Club Rd
Reid Park
Reid Park Zoo
Alvernon Way
Palo Verde Rd
Aviation Pkwy
River Rd
Campbell Ave
Univ. of Arizona
Broadway Blvd
22nd St
10
10
Prince Rd
Arizona State Mus.
Park Ave
Tucson Blvd
S. Campbell Ave
1st Ave
Stone Ave
Convention Center
S. Park Ave
77
La Canada Dr
Wetmore Rd
77
S 6th Ave
S 12th Ave
Tucson Rodeo Grounds
19
Nogales Hwy
La Cholla Blvd
Silverbell Rd
19
Santa Cruz R.
Sentinel Peak Park
W. Br. Santa Cruz R.
Mission Rd
Christopher Columbus Reg. Park
10
El Camino del Cerro
Ironwood Hill Dr
Anklam Rd
22nd St
John F Kennedy Park
Irvington Rd
Valencia Rd
W. Sunset Rd
Camino de Oeste Dr
Speedway Blvd
Ajo Way
Joseph Ave
International Wildlife Mus.
Gates Pass Rd
86
N
Kinney Rd
Bopp Rd
Camino Verde

0   3 mi

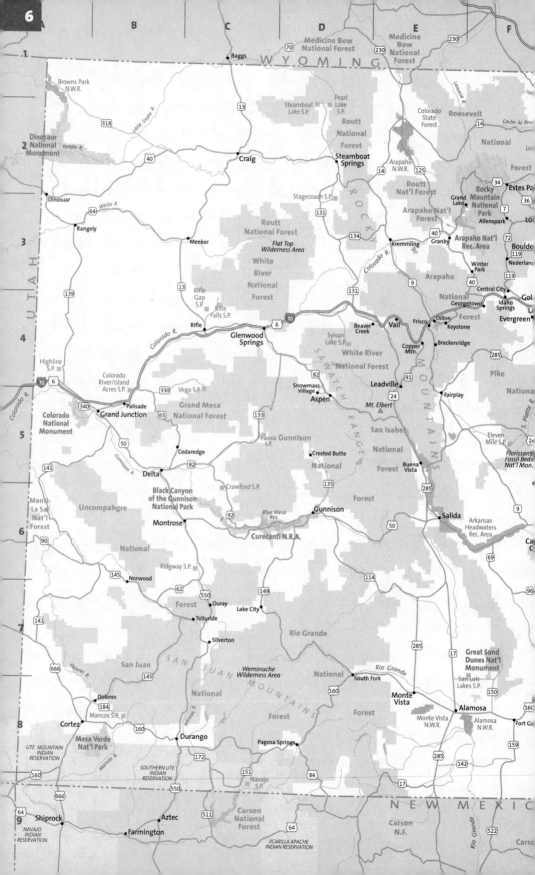

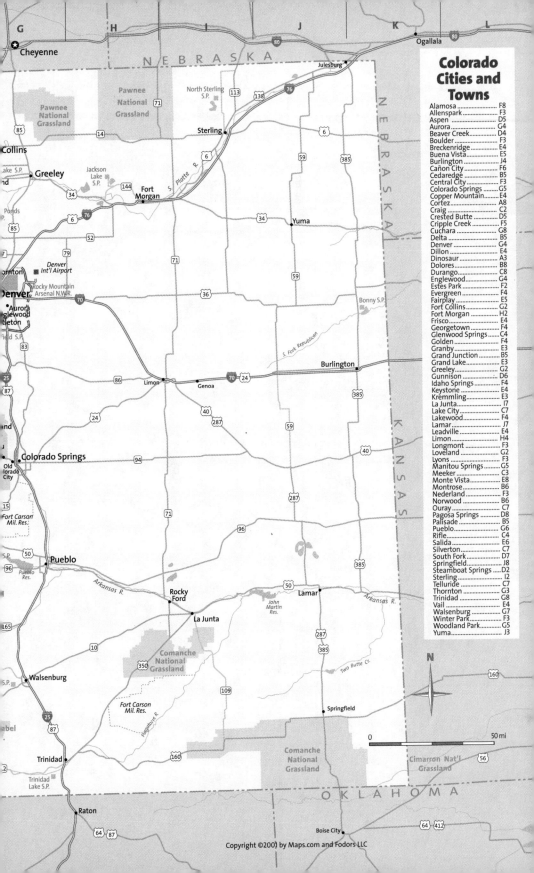

Colorado Cities and Towns

Denver, CO

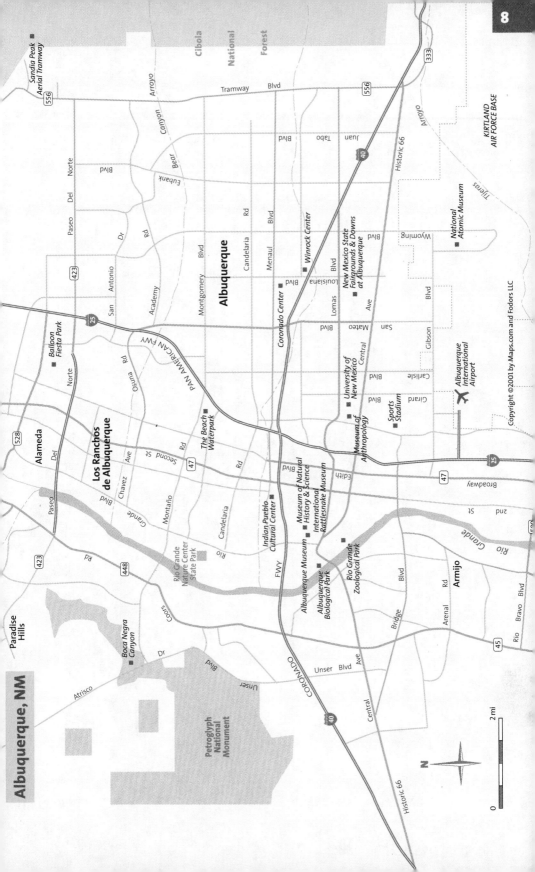

Albuquerque, NM

CIBOLA   National   Forest

■ Sandia Peak
Aerial Tramway

556

556

Tramway   Blvd

333

KIRTLAND
AIR FORCE BASE

Arroyo

Canyon

Arroyo

Bear

Paseo   Del   Norte   Blvd

Eubank   Blvd

Juan   Tabo   Blvd

40

Historic 66

Tijeras

Arroyo

423

Dr

Rd

San   Antonio

Academy

Rd

Blvd

Montgomery   Blvd

Candelaria   Rd

Menaul   Blvd

Albuquerque

■ Winrock Center

Louisiana   Blvd

■ National
Atomic Museum

Wyoming   Blvd

25

Norte

Blvd

Osuna   Rd

PAN AMERICAN FWY

Balloon
Fiesta Park ■

Coronado Center ■

Lomas   Blvd

Mateo   Blvd

San

Gibson   Blvd

Copyright ©2001 by Maps.com and Fodors LLC

528

Alameda

Paseo   Del   Norte   Blvd

Los Ranchos
de Albuquerque

Second St

Rio   Grande   Blvd

Chavez   Ave

Rd

47

The Beach
Waterpark ■

Montaño   Rd

Candelaria   Rd

Rio   Rd

University of
New Mexico

Central   Ave

Carlisle   Blvd

Girard   Blvd

Museum of
Anthropology ■

Sports
Stadium

✈ Albuquerque
International
Airport

25

47

Broadway

Edith   Blvd

423

Rd

448

Coors   Blvd

Rio   Grande   Nature   Center   State   Park ■

FWY

Indian Pueblo
Cultural Center ■

Museum of Natural
History & Science ■

Albuquerque Museum ■

International
Rattlesnake Museum ■

Albuquerque
Biological Park ■

Rio Grande
Zoological Park ■

Rio   Grande

2nd   St

Blvd

Armijo

Bridge   Blvd

Arenal   Rd

Rio   Bravo   Blvd

45

Paradise
Hills

Boca Negra
Canyon ■

Coors   Dr

Blvd   Unser

Petroglyph
National
Monument

Atrisco

Unser   Blvd   Ave

CORONADO   FWY

40

Central   Ave

Historic 66

N

0   2 mi

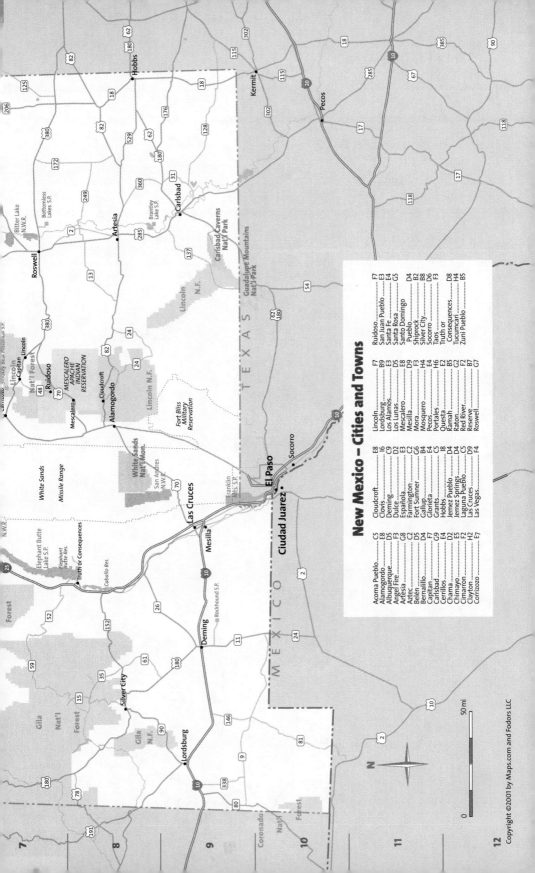

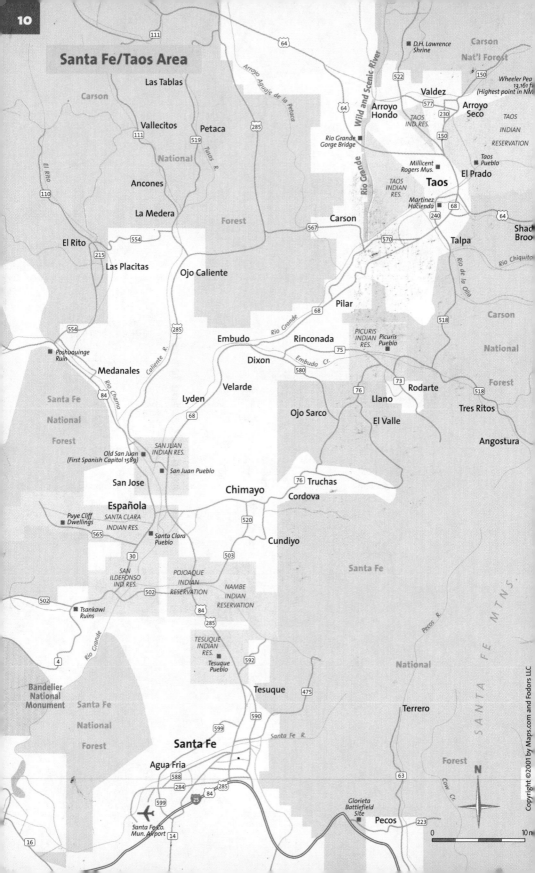

Santa Fe/Taos Area

111

64

Carson Nat'l Forest

D.H. Lawrence Shrine

Carson

522

150

Wheeler Pea 13,161 ft (Highest point in NM)

Las Tablas

Arroyo Aguaje de la Petaca

Valdez

Vallecitos

Petaca

111

519

Tusas R.

285

64

Arroyo Hondo

577

230

150

Arroyo Seco

TAOS IND. RES.

TAOS INDIAN RESERVATION

Taos Pueblo

National

Ancones

Rio Grande Gorge Bridge

Millicent Rogers Mus.

El Rito

110

La Medera

Forest

TAOS INDIAN RES.

Taos

El Prado

Martinez Hacienda

68

El Rito

554

Carson

567

240

64

Las Placitas

215

Ojo Caliente

570

Talpa

Shad Broo

Rio Chiquito

Rio de la Olla

554

285

Caliente R.

Pilar

68

518

Carson

Poshuouinge Ruin

Medanales

Rio Chama

84

Embudo

Rio Grande

Rinconada

75

PICURIS INDIAN RES.

Picuris Pueblo

National

Dixon

Embudo Cr.

580

73

Rodarte

Forest

Lyden

Velarde

76

Llano

518

68

Ojo Sarco

El Valle

Tres Ritos

Santa Fe

National

SAN JUAN INDIAN RES.

Angostura

Forest

Old San Juan (First Spanish Capitol 1589)

San Juan Pueblo

San Jose

Chimayo

76

Truchas

Española

Cordova

Puye Cliff Dwellings

SANTA CLARA INDIAN RES.

520

565

Santa Clara Pueblo

Cundiyo

Santa Fe

30

503

SAN ILDEFONSO IND. RES.

POJOAQUE INDIAN RESERVATION

502

502

NAMBE INDIAN RESERVATION

Tsankawi Ruins

84

285

Bandelier National Monument

4

Pecos R.

SANTA FE MTNS.

TESUQUE INDIAN RES.

Tesuque Pueblo

592

National

Rio Grande

Santa Fe

National

Forest

475

Tesuque

Terrero

590

599

Santa Fe R.

Santa Fe

63

Agua Fria

588

N

284

25

84

285

599

Glorieta Battlefield Site

Forest

16

Santa Fe Co. Mun. Airport

14

Pecos

223

0   10 m